A HANDBOOK OF

Clinical Scoring Systems for Thematic Apperceptive Techniques

Series in Personality and Clinical Psychology
Irving B. Weiner, Editor

Bornstein/Masling (Eds.) • *Scoring the Rorschach: Seven Validated Systems*
Calhoun/Tedeschi • *Facilitating Posttraumatic Growth: A Clinician's Guide*
Dana (Ed.) • *Handbook of Cross-Cultural and Multicultural Personality Assessment*
Eisen/Quas/Goodman (Eds.) • *Memory and Suggestibility in the Forensic Interview*
Exner (Ed.) • *Issues and Methods in Rorschach Research*
Frederick/McNeal • *Inner Strengths: Contemporary Psychotherapy and Hypnosis for Ego-Strengthening*
Gacono (Ed.) • *The Clinical and Forensic Assessment of Psychopathy: A Practitioner's Guide*
Gacono/Meloy • *The Rorschach Assessment of Aggressive and Psychopathic Personalities*
Ganellen • *Integrating the Rorschach and the MMPI-2 in Personality Assessment*
Goodman/Rudorfer/Maser (Eds.) • *Obsessive-Compulsive Disorder: Contemporary Issues in Treatment*
Hall/Bernieri (Eds.) • *Interpersonal Sensitivity: Theory and Measurement*
Handler/Hilsenroth (Eds.) • *Teaching and Learning Personality Assessment*
Huprich (Ed.) • *Rorschach Assessment of the Personality Disorders*
Hy/Loevinger • *Measuring Ego Development, Second Edition*
Jenkins (Ed.) • *A Handbook of Clinical Scoring Systems for Thematic Apperceptive Techniques*
Kelly • *The Assessment of Object Relations Phenomena in Adolescents: TAT and Rorschach Measures*
Kelly • *The Psychological Assessment of Abused and Traumatized Children*
Kohnstamm/Halverson/Mervielde/Havill (Eds.) • *Parental Descriptions of Child Personality: Developmental Antecedents of the Big Five?*
Loevinger (Ed.) • *Technical Foundations for Measuring Ego Development: The Washington University Sentence Completion Test*
McCallum/Piper (Eds.) • *Psychological Mindedness: A Contemporary Understanding*
Meloy/Acklin/Gacono/Murray/Peterson (Eds.) • *Contemporary Rorschach Interpretation*
Needleman • *Cognitive Case Conceptualization: A Guidebook for Practitioners*
Nielsen/Johnson/Albert Ellis Institute • *Counseling and Psychotherapy With Religious Persons: A Rational Emotive Behavior Therapy Approach*
Nolen-Hoeksema/Larson • *Coping With Loss*
Rosowsky/Abrams/Zwieg (Eds.) • *Personality Disorders in Elderly: Emerging Issues in Diagnosis and Treatment*
Sarason/Pierce/Sarason (Eds.) • *Cognitive Interface: Theories, Methods, and Findings*
Silverstein • *Self Psychology and Diagnostic Assessment: Identifying Selfobject Functions Through Psychological Testing*
Taylor (Ed.) • *Anxiety Sensitivity: Theory, Research, and Treatment of the Fear of Anxiety*
Tedeschi/Park/Calhoun (Eds.) • *Posttraumatic Growth: Positive Changes in the Aftermath of Crisis*
Van Hasselt/Hersen (Eds.) • *Handbook of Psychological Treatment Protocols for Children and Adolescents*
Weiner • *Principles of Rorschach Interpretation*
Wong/Fry (Eds.) • *The Human Quest for Meaning: A Handbook of Psychological Research and Clinical Applications*
Zillmer/Harrower/ Ritzler/Archer • *The Quest for the Nazi Personality: A Psychological Investigation of Nazi War Criminals*

A HANDBOOK OF Clinical Scoring Systems for Thematic Apperceptive Techniques

EDITED BY

SHARON RAE JENKINS

University of North Texas

Denton, Texas

LEA Lawrence Erlbaum Associates

Taylor & Francis Group

New York London

Lawrence Erlbaum Associates
Taylor & Francis Group
270 Madison Avenue
New York, NY 10016

Lawrence Erlbaum Associates
Taylor & Francis Group
2 Park Square
Milton Park, Abingdon
Oxon OX14 4RN

Lawrence Erlbaum Associates is an imprint of Taylor & Francis Group, an Informa business

Printed in the United States of America on acid-free paper
10 9 8 7 6 5 4 3 2 1

International Standard Book Number-13: 978-0-8058-4373-6 (Hardcover)

Library of Congress Cataloging-in-Publication Data

A handbook of clinical scoring systems for thematic apperceptive techniques / editor, Sharon Rae Jenkins.
p. cm. -- (Personality and clinical psychology)
Includes bibliographical references and indexes.
ISBN-13: 978-0-8058-4373-6 (alk. paper) 1. Thematic Apperception Test. I. Jenkins, Sharon Rae.

BF698.8.T5H36 2007
155.2'844--dc22 2007025351

Visit the Taylor & Francis Web site at
http://www.taylorandfrancis.com

and the LEA and Routledge Web site at
http://www.routledge.com

CONTENTS

PREFACE

Sharon Rae Jenkins

> The story—from *Rumplestiltskin* to *War and Peace*—is one of the basic tools invented by the human mind, for the purpose of gaining understanding. There have been great societies that did not use the wheel, but there have been no societies that did not tell stories.
>
> **Ursula K. LeGuin, 1979**

When I am having difficulty understanding a therapy client's problem, I usually want to ask for examples of the problem. Sometimes this works, but more often, the client's response is hesitant and fragmented. A small change in wording is invariably helpful: "Tell me a story about a time when that happened." What follows usually flows into a clear illustration of the problem and its context, antecedents, and sequelae. Omissions can be important, too. Taping the session would allow for post hoc analysis of the response using relevant scoring systems from this book.

As a field, psychology has been struggling for over half a century to integrate science and practice. As a culture, one challenge for American society from the beginning has been to integrate into a functioning social system peoples having very different nationalities, ethnic habits, and personal histories. Our technology-driven lives only increase in complexity, with resulting tensions toward social fragmentation straining all our integrative functions.

Storytelling is a quintessentially integrative function, as shown by studies of narrative memory. Stories bring people, ideas, and feelings together around campfires and research groups. Folktales build cultures; bedtime stories raise children. Stories show what people and their societies value and wish to communicate. Understanding stories helps us understand these things, which makes them useful for clinical work with clients who have trouble understanding themselves. This use of stories has a 70-year history.

The tensions in that history are in part the tensions between science and practice. The skilled clinician accrues a repertoire of analytic approaches over a lifetime of experience—but where is the objective evidence of reliability and validity? The researcher demonstrates associations between features of stories and people's career choices and long-term health outcomes—but how is this relevant for an individual client? How can we make generalizations about individuality?

A fundamental hypothesis behind this book is that structured scoring systems for thematic apperceptive techniques (TATs) are one way to bridge the scientist–practitioner gap by enabling scientifically sound, efficient, and clinically informative examination of clients' stories to answer focused clinical questions relevant to diagnosis, estimation of prognosis, and effective treatment planning. Testing this hypothesis requires a body of research using specific systems for clinically appropriate purposes. Such research has been difficult because the scoring manuals and practice stories necessary for both clinical and research use have not been available widely, if at all. This collection of scoring manuals makes available a selection of promising ones, and the summary chapters for each explain their best uses, evidence for validity and reliability, and priorities for future research.

This book should be in the library of every faculty member and clinical supervisor who is responsible for teaching courses in psychological assessment or supervising assessment students in clinical, counseling, school, or forensic psychology, whether in academic or practice settings, practicum sites, or internships. It may also be useful as an assessment course text. In chapter 2, procedures for learning how to score will be especially useful for that purpose, as its pedagogical principles generalize to data from other less structured assessment techniques. Practicing assessment psychologists will find the book a handy reference resource, given its coverage of common clinical problems. Researchers in these areas who are interested in storytelling techniques, especially thesis and dissertation students, will find it useful for identifying interesting research problems and choosing variables, as well as for training scorers. They may also turn to chapter 3 for broader suggestions for future research.

Any movement from general to specific, or vice versa, involves a leap of inference. The traditional clinical approach to story analysis has involved large leaps of inference—albeit highly educated—using abstract theoretical constructs and frameworks to structure the assessor's understanding of the stories and thus of the particular client. This approach allows for a highly detailed and individualized understanding of the person, but might make it difficult to see the client's commonalities with others. Yet if no generalizations can be made, how can we know whether what helped the last client might help this one?

Structured scoring systems minimize leaps of inference by providing the assessor with detailed, specific descriptions of what to look for in each story: words, phrases, images, structural features, degrees of intensity. These *scoring category criteria* indicate what to do if the material described is found: assign a point or a scale rating, or make some other decision. One requirement of these descriptions is that they be sufficiently clear and detailed that most appropriately trained people, given the same rules for observation, will usually see the same thing in the same place. This requirement of *interscorer reliability* meets the scientific criterion for objectivity, that is, agreement on whether or not the phenomenon to be identified has in fact been observed.

Academic psychology has had a 55-year history of such scoring systems for personality variables, most notably the human motivation scoring systems pioneered by David C. McClelland, John W. Atkinson, David G. Winter, and their colleagues, as discussed in more detail in chapter 1. The fact that there is a parallel 55-year history in clinical psychology is less well known, in part because the lengthy and detailed materials for using these systems have rarely been published. Phebe Cramer's 1991 book, *The development of defense mechanisms* (Springer-Verlag), is a notable exception. For my Faculty Development Leave from the University of North Texas, I set out to locate interesting systems for which there was both some evidence of interscorer reliability and some evidence for validity of a clinically useful nature, as described in more detail in chapter 1. Unfortunately, from the start my search was limited by my lack of adequate competence in languages other than English, which forced the omission of Vica Shentoub's highly recommended 1990 *Manuel d'utilisation du TAT* (Dunod).

Not only were there many more systems with publication records than I had guessed, but also there were so many that I had to set priorities for choosing among similar systems! Of the 37 clinically interesting systems that were initially identified and ultimately not included, 14 were dropped for lack of at least one solid published clinical validational study or evidence of one in progress, and seven did not report evidence of interscorer reliability. In some cases, more recent systems known to me had incorporated older ones, making pursuit of the latter unnecessary; seven were redundant with and superseded by a system that met more criteria better.

The next challenge was to find the originator and to explore the possibility of chapter authorship. In that, too, I was surprisingly successful, given the ages of some of the earlier authors. Melvin Feffer was pleased and flattered to hear from me in his retirement, he said, and he gave permission for me to revise and elaborate on the manual that he had thoughtfully archived at the Library of Congress American Documentation Institute. Sadly, he died before seeing the final product. Sidney Ornduff was in a somewhat similar situation with Reuben Fine, whose manual she obtained before his death and developed for the studies described in her contribution herein. The authors who present their work here are to be commended for rooting through files that were not always ready at hand, and that in some cases might have required Stygian labors for their retrieval from basement boxes of dissertations long past.

Of the nine systems that were pursued but are not included here, two authors could not be located or did not respond to communications. Four authors declined to have their systems included. Only three systems were lost due to the tidy habits of retired authors who had discarded their materials.

The systems included here are organized into four sections, presented in roughly chronological order of their first appearance in publication, as are the systems within each:

Perceptual-Cognitive: Edith Weisskopf, Richard Dana, Melvin Feffer, George Ronan and Margaret Gibbs, Barry Ritzler

Psychodynamic: Reuben Fine, Robert Holt, Bertram Karon, Steven Huprich, Frank Summers, David Harder and Deborah Greenwald

Social-Emotional: Margaret Singer and Lyman Wynne; Antoinette Thomas; Giuseppe Costantino and Robert Malgady; Hedwig Teglasi, Constance Locraft, and Kelly Felgenhauer; David Joubert; Michelle Hoy-Watkins and Valata Jenkins-Monroe

Needs and Concerns Focused: Louis Chandler, David Ephraim

Each system is discussed in more detail toward the end of chapter 1.

Although Weisskopf died some years ago, Max Prola had preserved a version of her scoring manual as an appendix to his dissertation. With the much appreciated help of Clifford Swenson and Chris Smith at Purdue University, I subsequently located her original manual and practice stories in the collection of her papers at the State University of West Georgia. I thank Myron House and Laura Henry at the University of West Georgia's Special Collections for their assistance during a pleasant but busy afternoon in their archives.

For my personal history with TATs, I thank Richard Teevan, who chaired my undergraduate honors thesis at Bucknell University on achievement motivation and fear of failure in groups. When I was ready to find a graduate school, Jacqueline Fleming welcomed my interest in Matina Horner's research on fear of success, taught me the scoring system, and invited me to their research group. There I met Abigail Stewart, who coincidentally came to Boston University to teach in the same week that I arrived there as a student in the new personality program. She taught me her scoring systems and supervised my dissertation using human motivation variables and her own Self-Definition/Social Definition system. Much of chapter 2 grew directly from my experiences of learning to score through individual study with Fleming and in Stewart's scoring groups.

When Carol Huffine recruited me to teach research methods courses at the California School of Professional Psychology, Berkeley/Alameda (CSPP-B/A), I was quite surprised to learn how differently my clinical psychology doctoral students approached TAT stories. It was disorienting not to have the focus of a structured scoring system's organizing principles for looking at a story. And they saw things that they said were obvious, but I could not see them! Sometimes I was not alone in that, either—so much for interscorer reliability, which did not seem to bother them as much as it did me. That was my introduction to the clinical uses of TATs, which was sufficiently provocative to interest me in learning more by taking a postdoctoral clinical certificate at CSPP-B/A, where I subsequently studied assessment with Gerald Michaels, Jacqueline Singer, David Stein, and Susan Fair.

Most of my clinical training with TATs has come from books by Magda Arnold, Leo Bellak, Phebe Cramer, William Henry, and Silvan Tomkins, with my clinical faculty and supervisors helping with the integrative functions of weaving the resulting observations into the rest of the data from the classical full battery assessment. I came to appreciate those authors' depth of insight, while also wondering, on internship working with Kevin Riley, where they could possibly find the time to take this approach with all of their clients. Clearly, the haste of modern life would not make this easy. Arguably, one advantage of structured scoring systems is that they enable well-focused information gathering with relatively less time and cogitation.

Several senior clinician scientists have been generous with their time and encouragement for this project. Phebe Cramer's 1996 book, *Storytelling, narrative, and the Thematic Apperception Test* (Guilford), was among my first sources of systems to pursue. Her willingness to spend time with me to offer suggestions about avenues to search and people to contact was essential to my rapid progress. Richard Dana became enthusiastic quickly, offering advice whenever I asked and sometimes before I was aware of needing it. His ambitions for the book inspired me. I thank Hedwig Teglasi for her 1993 book, *Clinical use of story telling* (Allyn & Bacon), another major reference source, and for her professional contributions to making TATs accessible to clinicians working with children, for our conversations, and for her enthusiasm for the work.

I am much indebted to Charles P. Smith for the careful structuring of his 1992 volume, *Motivation and personality: A handbook of thematic content analysis* (Cambridge University Press), which was the first inspiration for this project. Examining it closely shaped my thinking about how to organize this book and what features likely would help readers. His suggestions at an early stage proved strategically useful.

Virginia Demos and Chris Fowler lent their sensitive ears and inquiring minds to the early stages of my ideas for the project and its later development. Bonnie Strickland alerted me to articles of likely interest, and she and Marjorie Nott shared their home for workspace during my leave time. Bob Holt and Bert Karon were always ready to engage with the progress of the work. Irving Weiner and Drew Westen furnished stimulating ideas in writing, presentations, and conversations.

Important boosts in the search process came from Amanda Phillips, Gladys Croom, Stephanie Dudek, Clifford Swenson, Sandra Russ, Jack Gerber's Rorschach Discussion List, the Projectives Discussion List, Robert Garlan, Norm Abeles, Lee Zimmerman, and David B. Baker, director of the Archives of the History of American Psychology at the University of Akron. The assistance and hospitality of the library staff at the University of Massachusetts at Amherst's W.E.B. DuBois Library was invaluable to this guest user. The availability on their shelves of their entire collection facilitated the necessary hand search of tables of contents of the three major journals that published structured scoring systems in my pursuit of the many systems that evaded electronic indexing. My literature searches there formed the backbone of this volume.

The staff of the University of North Texas Interlibrary Loan merits special mention for handling the incoming stream of dissertations that might contain usable scoring systems. Among our Psychology Department staff, Lee Ward provided crucial support by decoding my edits, anticipating what I should have said, and formatting references with her expertise using American Psychological Association style; Phyllis Dever and Stacy Suits solved problems that, thanks to their timely intervention, never came to my attention.

Among my students, I thank Lauren Dobbs, Melissa Leeper, Luis E. Perez, Rachel White, and Derrick Carter for trusting me to guide their honors theses into potentially Herculean labors. Numerous scorers contributed suggestions and examples for the development of Ephraim's Psychocultural System, Feffer's Interpersonal Decentering, Huprich's Oral Dependency, Thomas's Affective Scale, and Weisskopf's Transcendence Index, as those authors have acknowledged. I appreciated their comments, additions, and elaborations as they pilot tested the appendix for chapter 2 on learning scoring. Diana Brown and Lizzie Woodruff were helpful in so many ways that I am sure I have not recalled them all, because they recognize how helpful unobtrusiveness can be.

At Routledge, I thank Susan Milmoe, my original editor, for her encouragement and support; Steve Rutter, her successor, for his patience with my creative approach; Nicole Buchmann, for her rapid responses at crunch time, also a time of transition for the organization; George Zimmar, Mimi Williams, Robert Sims, and the production staff at Taylor and Francis for seeing it through the final process; and Larry Erlbaum for his congenial hosting of the social hours at the Society for Personality Assessment meetings that helped me network to locate systems.

Finally, I thank Kwame Azalius Ross for the concept of *accountability to the work.*

Sharon Rae Jenkins

I

SECTION

General Principles

1

CHAPTER

Introduction

Why "Score" TATs, Anyway?

Sharon Rae Jenkins

Introduction

The Thematic Apperception Test—"the TAT" (Murray, 1943)—has a long, honorable, and well-argued 65-year history in psychological research and clinical assessment. In a recent surge of activity, several books have taken stock of that history (Douglas, 1993; Gieser & Stein, 1999; Robinson, 1992) or have reviewed important research and clinical applications (e.g., Aronow, Weiss, & Reznikoff, 2001; Costantino, Malgady, & Rogler, 2002; Cramer, 1991, 1996, 2006; Dana, 2005; Costantino, Dana, & Malgady, 2007; Kelly, 1996, 1997; Smith, 1992a; Teglasi, 1993, 2001). In response to the historical and cultural specificity of the original pictures, new picture sets have been developed, each with its own scoring system, four of which are described in this book. As there is only one "the TAT"—Henry Murray's (1943) set of published picture stimuli—all of these and the associated scoring systems are here referenced collectively as thematic apperceptive techniques (TATs).

Clinical and counseling psychologists have long known the usefulness of TAT story protocols for those insights into how a client sees the world that can be gained through systematic idiographic interpretation (Aron, 1949; Arnold, 1962; Bellak, 1954; Henry, 1956; Shneidman, 1951; Stein, 1981; Tomkins, 1947). Academic researchers have made heavy use of similar stories with objective, structured scoring systems to measure human motivation and other personality characteristics (e.g., Atkinson, 1981; McAdams, 1980, 1985; McClelland, 1965, 1975, 1985a, 1985b, 1989; Smith, 1992a; Stewart, 1992; Winter, 1973). Unfortunately, clinicians and academic researchers seldom discuss these common interests, leaving a gap between the wide clinical application of TATs and the scientific evidence for their validity. Despite early attempts at integrating these views (e.g., Dana,

1955a, 1959; Holt, 1978; Murstein, 1972; Zubin, Eron, & Schumer, 1965), further developments in clinical research historically have been slow. In academic psychology, Smith (1992a) collected empirically supported scoring systems for 14 of the most widely used narrative-based research measures of motivation and personality. Each is represented by a research summary, a detailed scoring manual, and practice stories with expert scoring that are designed to make a system self-teaching. There are also several integrative chapters on historical, conceptual, and methodological issues. That volume was the original model and inspiration for this one.

This book brings together the best available clinical scoring systems for TATs, presented in research summaries along with detailed scoring manuals and practice stories. Chapter 2 concerns how to learn and teach these systems. It is designed to enable clinicians, researchers, faculty, and supervisors to apply these systems efficiently and accurately. Chapter 3, on future directions, discusses needed clinical applications and research programs to encourage further research contributions. Like Smith (1992a), this one is essentially a user's manual designed for professional self-teaching, training research teams, and classroom instruction.

Why Structured Scoring Systems?

The strengths of structured scoring systems lie in their flexibility, efficiency, generalizability, consistency, and objectivity. The strength of flexibility is that, like the Rorschach Ink Blots and unlike structured self-report scales, TATs are essentially data-gathering techniques that entail a two-step process. First, storytellers are shown a series of pictures and are asked to tell a story about each one, under standardized conditions (or in specified experimental situations). Second, and separately, useful information is gleaned from the resulting protocols. Structured self-report measures depend on conceptualization of the construct for the proper wording of items, which might not generalize across conceptualizations, theories, or cultures. In contrast, any theoretical perspective or data-analysis approach can be used with TATs once the stories have been gathered; the data are transparent to purpose. It is this second step that is evaluated for psychometric validity and reliability, as those terms are meaningless for narrative data. Anastasi (1988, p. 23) defined a psychological test as "an objective and standardized measure of a sample of behavior." For structured self-reports, the measure is the sample, but for TATs, the objective and standardized measure is quite separate from the sample.

Unlike the Rorschach, which has a standard set of 10 card stimuli, the first step also allows flexibility for TATs, as a set of stimuli must be chosen. Although these are typically pictures, sentence cues have been used effectively in research (Jenkins, 1987, 1994; Smith, Feld, & Franz, 1992) and hold promise for clinical use with visually impaired persons. For some standard picture sets, the choice of stimuli and their order are fixed (see chapters 12, 29, 32, and 33 in this volume). For others such as the Murray TAT, some clinicians prefer to choose the pictures that seem most relevant to each client's situation, in order to sample the client's responses to similar nontest circumstances that hopefully will generalize to that specific life situation. This line of thinking—*generalizing to specific circumstances*—is unfamiliar, even alien, to most researchers.

TAT data gathering permits flexible applications, but this strength must be balanced by efficiency. In fact, arguably it is the efficiency of structured scoring systems that makes the flexibility of TATs a strength. Like the Rorschach, TAT story protocols provide a literal embarrassment of richness that is daunting for students and can be exhausting for the expert. Hopefully the present volume will help to make the process more efficient than it was when Fosberg (1949) proposed a minimum one-year academic course in projective testing alone (to be supplemented by continuing education workshops), with three years of course work ideally recommended as adequate preparation for clinical assessment. Manualized structured scoring approaches permit efficient analysis of these useful data sources by giving systematic decision rules for identifying features of stories that are linked to specific theoretical constructs or characteristics of the storyteller. Even a novice clinical assessment student may be able to use TAT data to answer specific referral questions if an appropriate scoring system is available and the student has attained the interscorer reliability standard (facilitated perhaps by chapter 2 in this volume). This efficiency allows for better focused psychological services to more clients at lower cost.

This more structured and efficient approach to TATs makes possible the systematic study of clinically important processes, as valid story data can be gathered either by traditional individual clinical assessment or via group administration, and by non-clinicians (Smith et al., 1992). Pretenure faculty need not be discouraged from undertaking research programs using TATs, because student assistants can be trained to score large numbers of stories reliably (see chapter 2), thus enabling more rapid data analysis and publication. Furthermore, once the data are in hand, several scoring systems can be applied for different publications, provided only that the theoretically relevant correlate variable data have been gathered. This feature permits graduate students to join forces for economical cooperative data gathering, with each one scoring the TAT stories using a different system.

This efficiency is not costly to the data, either. Unlike manualized psychotherapy approaches, scoring manuals for assessment data are not intrusive. They do not change the data that have been gathered, they only assist focused and strategic data analysis to answer specific referral questions. New questions can be answered long after the data have been gathered by simply applying another scoring system. The only limit to the number of scores that can be extracted is the number of scoring systems currently available and the time available for using them. The only cost comes from the investment in learning what to look for in stories; that process is transparent to the storyteller.

Generalizability to storytellers' lives is an important strength of TAT data, regardless of the analytic approach. Emerging basic psychological and cross-cultural research on narrative processes suggests that storytelling may be one crucial link between the individual's intrapsychic functioning and the construction of a life in a society (e.g., De Vos & De Vos, 2004; LeVine, Strangman, & Unterberger, 1966; McAdams, 1997; McClelland, 1961; Veroff & Feld, 1970). How a person tells a story reflects a host of mediating processes that connect perceptions, thoughts, and feelings to actions, knitting together the psychological context and behavior in vivo.

Just how this works is not precisely clear as yet, but there is evidence (in this book and others cited previously) that these processes and the stories that illustrate them provide useful data that are quite different from the data yielded by most other forms of clinical assessment. If we consider stories to represent samples of the storyteller's imaginative thought and inner experiences about situations similar to those in the pictures (McClelland, 1980), then it is only a small step of modest inference to assume that what the client says in the story resembles what the client might think or feel in similar real-life situations.

It is crucial to note—and is historically overlooked—that *these experience samples might generalize well to **thoughts** in real life, but this does not mean that they will necessarily predict well* *to* ***actions*** *in real life*! There are a host of reasons why people do not do everything that they are capable of thinking or saying. In fact, one noted weakness of structured self-reports is that people do not always do what they say they do, or will do (Mischel, 1968). Structured scoring systems improve generalizability by enabling the scorer to identify and classify specific features of stories that can be connected to parallel inner experiences—and *perhaps* overt actions—in vivo. This parallelism can be tested directly using collaborative assessment models (Fischer, 1994) or therapeutic assessment interventions (Finn, 2007; Finn & Tonsager, 1992, 1997).

The consistency of analysis gained from structured TAT scoring, like its efficiency, is a unique benefit (over and above the richness of the unscored stories) that further amplifies the usefulness of the data. The consistent interpretation of story data begins with stable and precise application of the system's scoring rules, as evaluated by calculating interscorer agreement or intrascorer agreement over time. Once the system has been learned, it can be applied to the same stories—or to different ones—by the same or different scorers, the same way now and next year. This consistency is attained by having a standard frame of reference for understanding stories so as to generalize the same observations across different storytellers, which makes systematic research, as well as systematic clinical use, possible.

The consistency of structured scoring systems enables two particularly helpful applications. First, admittedly at this writing some way in the future, the use of several scoring systems in combination can provide a consistent frame of reference for idiographic interpretation, much as the Rorschach Comprehensive System is now used. Second, this frame of reference might serve as a platform for comparison of clients' scores with the clinician's database of local norms and with existing research literature using samples from similar populations. Third, it enables evaluation of change over time in the individual client on the constructs of interest.

Consistency does not enforce uniformity, though. In-depth idiographic content analysis is not ruled out by structured scoring. It can be used along with specific scoring systems and can be enriched thereby. For example, suppose that a client has told three stories about achievement concerns (identified by the Psychocultural System) that involve characters in parent–child roles and negative affect (scored with the Affective Scale). The clinician might examine the specific nature of the concern and its apparent function in the relationship that produces negative affect, and in whom, for more precise discussion with the client.

Finally, although flexibility, efficiency, generalizability, and consistency are helpful in both clinical and research work, structured scoring systems allow for the objectivity that is the sine qua non of science in our field. This objectivity is exemplified first by the attainment of interscorer reliability between different observers applying the same scoring rules. Only individual scoring systems, not "the TAT," can be evaluated for validity and reliability, making scientific evaluation of TAT data possible. The phrase *validity of the TAT* is meaningless, because validity is specific not to the pictures, but to the set of scores derived from the population, purpose, and circumstances involved in any given data collection, as discussed in this chapter. Furthermore, for TATs validity is specific to the method of obtaining scores from stories. (Curiously, it is conventional to call *objective* the structured self-report items commonly used in social and personality psychology to elicit respondents' subjective perceptions and attitudes toward themselves and the world. The content of these items is certainly not objective in any meaningful way, as the experiences reported cannot be independently verified apart from the respondents' introspection.)

Why This Book, This Way?

Numerous clinical scoring systems for TATs have been published in the last half century, but few have been available for use beyond the laboratories of the originators and their students. For reasons of length, journal articles typically include no more than a brief description of the scoring categories, which is not adequate for either clinicians or researchers to attain interscorer reliability. Many clinically useful systems are sufficiently complex and subtle to require for training a detailed scoring manual with several sets of stories to be scored for practice, along with expert scores and commentary on the more difficult ones. Working with these materials allows others—who may differ in theoretical orientation, clinical specialty, level of experience, institutional context, client population, and personality style—to replicate the scoring decision process accurately. Because such materials are rarely circulated widely, few of these systems have accumulated the amount of published empirical support that we would ideally like to see for clinical practice.

Furthermore, the more subtle the theoretical constructs, the more complex the system, and the higher its information yield, the more training material (and for some, such as the Adult Attachment Projective [AAP], supervised practice) is needed. A full range of examples and practice scoring materials helps the interested user learn the scoring procedures and contingencies of scoring decisions. A detailed, specific scoring manual provides the learner with the rule system for decision making that constitutes the *statutory law* that minimizes the leaps of inference that the scorer makes in the process of scoring decisions. The process of working through the practice scoring materials corresponds to the study of the *case law*, by which the scorer learns how to reason deductively from the rule system to its application across a range of specific instances. These instructive examples show the application of statutory principles and help the learner to make the occasional unavoidable inferences by internalizing a reasoning process similar to that used by the expert scorer. The use of a scoring group for establishing and maintaining interscorer reliability parallels other learning processes relying on the case-study method (Stenzel & Feeney, 1970), and is discussed in chapter 2.

The goals of this book are (1) to raise awareness about the availability and usefulness of TAT scoring systems for research, training, and clinical practice; (2) to provide the materials needed for learning and using the most useful available clinical systems; and (3) to facilitate their use by making independent learning and systematic research easier. The systems gathered here have the most extensive supportive research evidence among those for which the original authors or interested successors could be located, had preserved the needed materials, and were willing to contribute same to this volume. These systems and their training materials are presented for clinical use as well as to facilitate the development of the needed research literature. If this book does its job, it will enable such a wealth of research as to make itself outdated rapidly.

Each system is represented by a chapter that describes the system within its conceptual framework, summarizes the available research evidence, and suggests an agenda for future research that is designed to inspire graduate students and other researchers. Scoring manuals for most of the systems—those that are not proprietary to publishers and can be self-taught feasibly—are also included. Some have numerous practice stories with expert scoring, others only a few, depending on their availability.

The following sections set this work in its historical, cultural, and disciplinary context, first recounting a brief (and necessarily too general) history of structured scoring systems; second, reviewing the challenges that developed with the scientist–practitioner gap; third, considering from a clinician's viewpoint the scientific status of the methods historically called *projective*; and, finally, reviewing the plan of the book and introducing the systems that follow.

☐ What Led Up to It, and What Will Happen Next?

"Projective" Assessment and TAT Interpretations: A Brief History

TATs have been called an ambiguous stimulus on which practitioners and scientists of all persuasions have projected their own assumptions, views, and preferences for how science or practice should be done. In the early years of TATs, psychological science and practice were better integrated than they are at present, and a variety of theoretical and methodological approaches were used for story interpretation. Holt's (1950) publication of Charles E. Thompson's 377-item bibliography on the TAT contains 80 that Holt identified as "principal references"—many including or reviewing research—and 82 research and methodological studies, along with 28 published case studies.

The "Projective Hypothesis" and Assumptions About Consciousness

Historically, the clinical use of TATs has been supported by Frank's (1939) "projective hypothesis". Consistent with the psychoanalytic conceptualization of psychological functioning, this hypothesis presented stories as reflecting the internalization (i.e., "taking in", or introjection) of early experiences that are then externalized (i.e., "projected") onto situations that evoke the original learning experience. As usually presented in undergraduate psychology textbooks, this projection process, and often the original learning situation itself, is presumptively unconscious, theoretically due to defensive repression of traumatic memories that arouse extreme, intolerable anxiety and other uncomfortable affects.

One unfortunate corollary of the theoretically unacceptable impulses and unconscious processes involved in the projective hypothesis is that then by definition, in assessment and psychotherapy the interpreter–analyst is presumably better able to understand the client than is the client. This might best be illustrated by Murray's (1943, p. 1) unfortunate choice of words in the TAT manual:

> Special value resides in [the TAT's] power to expose the underlying inhibited tendencies which the subject, or patient, is not willing to admit, or can not admit because he is unconscious of them.... As a rule the subject leaves the test happily unaware that he has presented the psychologist with what amounts to an X-Ray picture of his inner self.

Revolt by female clients against this one-down, almost Machiavellian attitude among mental health professionals and the increased popularity in the 1970s and 1980s of feminist therapists, who prioritized empowering the client, may have contributed to the subsequently decreased popularity of assessment techniques that appeared to depend on the projective hypothesis, as also happened with psychoanalysis, in part for similar reasons.

Rigor and Scoring Systems

To Murray's credit, however, although he resisted systematic scoring of the sort presented here (Gieser & Stein, 1999), he also emphasized the importance of rigorous training and discipline for the interpreter:

> Even an old hand at the game must rely on the same process—empathic intuition first and last, disentangled as far as possible from personal elements. No true scientist will scorn the use of a function which when properly disciplined is capable of yielding precise and pertinent information. Of course intuition alone is highly unreliable; what is required is a rigorously trained *critical intuition*.... TAT stories offer boundless opportunities for the projection of one's own complexes or one's pet theories, and the amateur psychoanalyst who is disrespectful of solid facts is only too apt to make a fool of himself if, in interpreting the TAT, he gives free rein to his imagination. The future of the TAT hangs on the possibility of perfecting the interpreter ... more than it does on perfecting the material. (Murray, 1943, p. 6. italics in original)

According to Piotrowski (1950), interpreters of "projective" tests quickly broadened that concept in their reading of data to include conscious, acceptable impulses and realistic, healthy adaptations as well (Bellak, 1954, p. 2). Indeed, Frank's (1939) original description emphasized the meaning that storytellers give to the test stimuli, as well as their subsequent actions and emotions, as expressions of personality paralleling their typical responses in social situations. Contrary to the usual undergraduate textbook depiction of idiosyncratic TAT interpretation (Mihura & Alperin, 2000), a half century ago Piotrowski was moving to formalize Murray's trained intuition, calling for "a dictionary and rules which would enable us to translate the test data into habitual modes of behavior in interpersonal relationships" (p. 102).

Within a decade, papers presenting systematic objective (Dana, 1959) scoring systems were being published. These included both research-focused (Aron, 1949; Weisskopf, 1950) and clinically oriented systems (e.g., Cox & Sargent, 1950; Eron, 1950; Holt, 1956; Libo, 1956, 1957; Shorr, 1948) and the first empirically derived content analysis research measures of human motives by McClelland and Atkinson (e.g., Atkinson, 1958; McClelland, Atkinson, Clark, & Lowell, 1953; McClelland, Clark, Roby, & Atkinson, 1949). Although individuals may have specialized in either academic or clinical work, familiarity with both uses of TATs, and mutual respect among these communities, seemed more the rule in those early years than at present.

What made these systems objective was not only the existence of documented decision rules for quantifying text material that minimized the level of inference exercised by the scorer, but also their simplicity, clarity, and concreteness under the logical positivist insistence on establishing the objectivity of observations by confirmation of hypotheses (e.g., Carnap, 1936, 1937). Confirmability required that anyone who applied correctly the rules required to make an observation should see the same phenomenon. Clear and concrete decision rules facilitated consistent scoring decisions by making the relevant material easier to identify in the stories despite differences in training, personality, and preferred theory among scorers.

Theory-based interpretation of TATs and other less structured measures demanded higher level inferences to deduce the meaning of the data from the principles of theory. Theory was needed to specify the conceptual structure to be imposed on the data to evaluate each theoretical construct. Unfortunately, not everyone made the same deductions the same way from the same rules, even when they used the same theory, resulting in rather more variable interpretation that relied on the interpreter's understanding and application of theory. The master interpreters previously cited built their careers on their ability to connect intricate theoretical filigree to their patients' labyrinthine problems using the stories as a conduit for images and intuitions. Learning to do this well was generally a lifelong enterprise.

In the fertile period for scoring system development from 1950 to about 1980, authors defined their goals diversely. Some attempted comprehensive catalogs of all relevant features of story narratives that were exhaustive of the data, and quite likely the interpreter (Aron, 1949; Bellak, 1954; Fine, 1955; Friedman, 1957; Haworth, 1963, 1966; Shatin, 1953, 1955; Weisskopf, 1950). Others identified important aspects of personality that they expected would be captured in most stories (Dana, 1959; Eron, 1950). Several selected quite specific theoretical constructs that should be evident in both TATs and Rorschach protocols or other less structured measures, and developed scoring systems for both kinds of data (Harder, 1979; Holt, 1956; Masling, Rabie, & Blondheim, 1967; Singer & Wynne, 1966). Weisskopf's (1950) and Murstein's (1972) goal was to identify the specific characteristics of picture stimuli that encouraged richer, more informative stories for clinical use. Arnold (1962) developed a method for extracting the essence, or import, of each story for interpretation and then studying the sequence of imports across the series of stories. These different approaches rested on a variety of assumptions about the nature of story data as a representation of something about the person and as a tool for identifying problems and predicting behavior.

The Scientist–Practitioner Gap

Although there had always been partisan arguments, between 1970 and the present the early integration and mutual respect among clinical scientists and practitioners in psychology as a field deteriorated steadily. Fewer clinicians using TATs concerned themselves with research evidence; some of the master interpreters were actively hostile to the emerging structured scoring systems. Researchers and textbook writers began dismissing the less structured measures out of hand rather than contributing to building the necessary technical scaffolding. Among academic TAT researchers, psychometric questions were too often handled dismissively in favor of getting on to the interesting substantive questions, to the frustration of one writer in that tradition (Fleming, 1982).

Nevertheless, studies using human motivation scoring systems flourished following the publication of the first collection of research articles and scoring manuals for the big three motives—need for Achievement (*n* Ach), need for Affiliation (*n* Aff), and need for Power (*n* Pow; Atkinson, 1958), the precursor of the one by Smith (1992a). McClelland and Winter's (1969) major cross-cultural longitudinal study of business executives in India followed, as did studies using survey research methods (Veroff & Feld, 1970) and Winter's (1973) revision of the need for Power system (McClelland, 1975). Although these systems were originally empirically derived and atheoretical, accumulating findings led to the development of theory (Atkinson, 1981; Atkinson & Birch, 1970; McClelland, 1961, 1981, 1985a, 1989; Winter, 1973; Winter, John, Stewart, Klohnen, & Duncan, 1998), a psychometric literature (e.g., Lundy, 1985, 1988; McClelland, 1980; Smith, 1992b; Winter & Stewart, 1977), applications in business (Litwin & Stringer, 1968) and clinical psychology (Cutter, Boyatzis, & Clancy, 1977; McClelland, 1977; McClelland, Davis, Kalin, & Wanner, 1972), and computer models of theoretically expected patterns of storytelling (Atkinson, Bongort, & Price, 1977; Reuman, 1982).

Surprisingly, this literature is often unknown to present-day clinicians and to researchers in other traditions, one of many puzzles in the history of this interesting method. This track record has typically gone unreferenced in clinical assessment texts and review articles. The present isolation of the clinical practitioner from the academic scientist communities regarding TATs has discouraged the growth of the kind of coherent research literature that clinical researchers have produced to support the Rorschach Comprehensive System over the past 30 years. Acknowledgement of the human motivation paradigm's relevance for clinical approaches to TATs is relatively recent but growing, as evidenced by the coverage of this literature in recent books (e.g., Cramer, 1996; Ganellen, 1996; Meyer, 2004; Teglasi, 1993) and journal articles reaching an audience of clinical psychologists (e.g., Blankenship et al., 2006; Pang & Schultheiss, 2005; Schultheiss & Brunstein, 2001).

The increasing cultural alienation between psychological scientists and practitioners just described has been a major social-structural barrier to the understanding and effective use of TATs. Research-oriented and clinically oriented psychologists appear to sort themselves out as early as graduate school (Weisskopf-Joelson, 1955), and communication between them thereafter is sparse (Zachar and Leong, 2000), so that their frames of reference diverge as they gain experience with contrasting tasks and data. One result is a lack of consensus on the best way to understand and use TATs that satisfies the requirements of both research and clinical work. The cultures of academic science and clinical practice are sustained by differences between both the functions of culture members in their daily work lives and the institutional structures that shape those functions. These structural and functional differences in turn support quite different value systems for what makes a measure a good one.

Challenges From Classical Test Theory

Differences of purpose, incompatible frames of reference, and resulting failures of communication have contributed to a narrowing of perspectives and hardening of positions on both sides of the gap, further restricting the knowledge bases in both communities about the best uses of TATs and similar measures. In their struggle for hegemony in the literature, proponents of each perspective have increasingly in the past two decades adopted a dismissive stance toward each other's goals and the tools used to attain them. As clinical researchers began to import into personality assessment the psychometric procedures of classical test theory designed for structured cognitive ability tests, misapplication of these tools to less structured measures generated hostile reviews based on classical test theory (e.g., Entwisle, 1972; Klinger, 1966) that centered on TAT scores' generally lower internal consistency reliability (across stories) and test–retest stability.

The historical evolution of the concept of reliability is a curiosity of our field beyond the scope of this book. However, understanding it is important for TATs because it has so often been a locus of criticism and contention. A too-brief review of this history reveals that the concept of reliability evolved in an effort to identify the sources of inconsistency in scores on structured ability tests. This inconsistency was attributed to random error, that is, fluctuation in scores (error of measurement) when the same person took the same test on repeated occasions, or when some items on the test did not correlate highly with the rest. In the case of TATs, which are less pervasive in American culture than are standardized cognitive ability tests, consistency across repeated administrations is of less practical interest and importance as a source of measurement error than is consistency across scorers, that is, interscorer reliability.

Some of the assumptions underlying the concept of reliability are peculiar to structured ability tests. The first is that the abstract entity called an *ability* is an unchanging aspect of the person, constant over time and situations. The second is that whenever the person's score differs from this "true score", this mistake in the test's estimation of that ability reflects flaws in the test and not real changes in the person. This rules out a considerable amount of individuality in how people approach tests, not only habitually but also due to day-to-day fluctuations in motivation and priority setting.

Structured ability tests use a response format that structures examinees' tasks by imposing strict constraints on the examinee's behavior. One reason for this is to reduce random error, that is, to bring the test scores into conformity with these theoretical assumptions by ruling out nontest influences on scores. Considering that a test samples behavior in order to generalize to theoretically similar nontest behavior (Anastasi, 1988), scores on these and similar highly structured tests generalize well to situations that impose similar constraints (McClelland, 1980).

The concepts of test–retest and internal consistency reliability might generalize well from ability tests to highly structured personality tests that involve stable traits and impose similar constraints on the test taker. However, the assumptions underlying these concepts simply *do not fit either the kinds of behavior sampled by less structured methods such as TATs, or the range of nontest behavior to which they are designed to generalize*. Indeed, one problem of more structured measures is that they do not predict so well to the less constrained behaviors of most interest to most people, such as mental health, career choices, and success in life (McClelland, 1980; Mischel, 1968). But why would this be a surprise, given that statisticians know that restricting the range of a variable makes it mathematically less likely to correlate with other variables, all else equal? If restricted-range variables relate less well to other variables, *why would restricted-range samples of behavior relate well to nontest, less restricted behavior*?

This is especially not surprising, given that some of the restrictions imposed to sample behavior "reliably" create problems of their own. Different test takers respond to those constraints differently, but predictably—that is, they are consistent in giving patterns of answers that may have nothing to do with the construct being measured and everything to do with the shape of the constraint imposed by the test. These patterns include response sets that are specific to the design of item response formats (Block, 1965; Schwarz, 1999), personality variables such as social desirability and need for approval that relate to the content of items (Crowne & Marlowe, 1960), and response styles of other sorts (Meyer, 1999). This kind of measurement error is systematic—constant over time and situations, like an ability or personality trait—and is *indistinguishable from the construct being measured* without complex data analysis techniques such as structural equation modeling, which clinicians rarely use with their clients.

The structure and assumptions underlying most clinical TAT scoring systems do not fit the requirements for evaluating internal consistency reliability that are described by Streiner (2003). Neither do the theoretical properties of human motive scoring systems, in particular (Atkinson, 1981; McClelland, 1980; Smith, 1992b). However, appropriate scientific evaluation of our tools remains important for both good practice and good science. How might this best be done?

Strengths of Integrating Science and Practice

First, it is important to recognize that a true integration of science and practice requires adaptation on both sides, including learning each others' languages, and change is not easier for clinicians and researchers than for clients. The main difficulty of these historical oppositions is that they have obscured the potential value of a more balanced approach that treats each data source within a framework that specifies its contribution to a comprehensive view of the client. The beginnings of such a framework can be glimpsed in recent work that clarifies the individual and combined contributions of the Rorschach Comprehensive System and the Minnesota Multiphasic Personality Inventory-2 (MMPI-2) in psychological assessment (Ganellen, 1996; Meyer, 1999; Meyer, Riethmiller, Brooks, Benoit, & Handler, 2000). One important dimension of the framework involves appraising the sources of systematic measurement error variance, such as format-specific response sets and related biases (Block, 1965; Schwarz, 1999), and irrelevant personality variance (e.g., social desirability, defensiveness, and other self-presentation biases).

How these combine for the individual client is important in interpretation when the client's Rorschach and MMPI-2 findings suggest contrasting conclusions (Ganellen, 1996; Meyer, 1999; Meyer et al., 2000). Meyer showed that convergent validity is higher when examinees have similar response styles on both kinds of measures (i.e., either open on both or guarded on both) than when they respond differently to the different methods. The same is likely true for TATs. Hopefully the multidimensional framework that is beyond the scope of this book not only can provide for the incorporation of other measures into both the larger conceptual picture and a comprehensive treatment planning strategy, but also can inspire the development of new measures in areas that are currently underpopulated.

TATs, like the Rorschach, may be especially suitable for an integrated scientist–practitioner approach because of the combined richness of their data and flexibility for various rigorous interpretive strategies. Commitment to such an approach eventually compels innovative and appropriate answers to psychometric questions like those described already. By first gathering a sample of client data, then subjecting it to careful objective scoring consistent with theory and validational studies, users of these techniques may attain both the rich detail that clinicians find most useful and the rigor that scientists require. Unfortunately, scant institutional support has been available for creating scoring systems, and there are continuing widespread failures of textbooks and journal review processes to distinguish between psychometric criteria appropriate for more structured measurement approaches and those suitable for less structured measures. As a result, there remain risks of both clinical misapplication and scientific misevaluation.

An integrated scientist–practitioner perspective necessarily must bring together the quite different strengths of story protocol material in both its research and clinical uses. Clinicians of various theoretical persuasions appreciate the richness and depth that a story protocol contributes to our understanding of a client's social world (Schorr, 1993). Compared with self-report measures like personality inventories and symptom scales, it is more difficult for the storyteller to manipulate the data because there is literally no right answer or wrong story. A fortunate advantage of narrative protocols for research purposes is that data gathered under one research plan can be scored long after the fact from a range of quite different perspectives, an activity that I hope this book will encourage.

But when it comes to the process of developing and validating a measure, TAT scoring systems, like Rorschach Comprehensive System scores, are still confronted with a monolithic psychometric frame of reference that defines the established normal science paradigm (Kuhn, 1962) designed for more structured cognitive ability measures. The rules derived from this vantage point historically have been misapplied to less structured measures, which are best used for constructs having different theoretical properties, sources of error variance, and fields of generalization than do the more structured ability measures. In the wake of recent attacks on the Rorschach Comprehensive System, it is clear that the scientific issues involved are broader than TATs. Thus, these issues require discussion elsewhere both as general principles for evaluating less structured measurement methods and as technical specifications unique to story protocols. A more appropriate frame of reference is needed that integrates clinical richness with scientific precision. The following section builds a case for what that frame of reference should look like.

☐ Toward Scientific Practice with TATs

As is clear from Murray's (1943) emphasis on the "true scientist" as previously cited and from the volumes of research since then, scientific practice has been a major rationale behind the use of TATs from the beginning. The need for scientific evidence is more urgent now. Parity of mental health services in relation to medical services is by no means secure in either public or private arenas, and both have become political footballs in recent elections. As decreased funding for mental health produces pressure for the deskilling of psychological services to masters-level practice, the more specialized and potentially cost-effective assessment tools of doctoral-level psychologists become less and less available to the general public, lowering the visibility of our practice to society and to third-party payers in a self-fulfilling prophecy. This is a greater hazard for less structured measures than for others because they are relatively time-intensive and individualized. The efficiency in training, research, and practice gained by structured scoring systems is essential to the effective use of TATs in managed-care environments, and improved empirical support for the use and interpretation of all assessment techniques is increasingly seen as important for ethical practice.

Stories and Science

One major cost to our functioning as a field of the gap between science and clinical practice is that *scientific evaluation of our measures rarely resembles the ways in which those measures are best used in clinical practice*. Psychological research proceeds normatively, but clinicians make decisions ipsatively. The prediction of the average behavior of groups on single variables is of little use to clinicians compared with the precise description of multiple interacting influences in dynamic tension within the individual. Clients' actions in the midst of their lives are influenced more by the external and internal contexts of those actions than they are by comparisons with normative samples. Pictures and the internal narratives that they stimulate may be key to the development of the kind of person–situation interactional psychology proposed in the 1970s and 1980s (e.g., Endler and Magnusson, 1976; Magnusson, 1988), whether one conceptualizes the assessment process as the activation of internal object representations or as an analog behavioral observation.

Against the conventions of tests-and-measurement textbooks, the outline given to authors for this volume asked them to present the evidence for their system's validity first, then to discuss its generalizability across populations, and finally its reliability. The priority of position given to reliability over validity in the chapter order of most textbooks is bewildering, given that so many of the classical psychometricians said clearly that validity was the far more important characteristic for evaluating a measure (e.g., Anastasi, 1988). The view that follows integrates the perspective of academic scientists who study TATs with that of clinicians who use them to understand and help their clients. Hopefully, what emerges will enrich the tactics available to those in both roles.

Validity Considerations for TATs

The validity of a measure is nearly a misnomer, as validity is a property of the interpretation of a set of scores obtained from a specific sample of people gathered for a particular purpose under certain circumstances (Anastasi, 1988; Cureton, 1951; Shneidman, 1959). Thus, all clinicians share responsibility for determining the kind and degree of validity that each measure has for their clients. Content validity, however, is indeed a property of TAT scoring systems, not of the set of scores. A distinct advantage of content validity for TATs is that what appears in the stories is a literal sample of imaginative thought (McClelland, 1980), not a sign or a symbol—though these can be inferred from stories as from other human products. These samples can be understood by the clinician as representing special instances of the abstraction described in the scoring categories, and yet understood by the client as concrete examples of a personal recurring and problematic action pattern. Stories have face validity, once told and scored, even though the storytelling task imposes none when the client first confronts it.

Construct validity indicates in addition that the properties of the set of scores are consistent with the theoretical properties and nomological network of the construct being measured (Cronbach & Meehl, 1955). That is, if the construct is theoretically stable, such as an intellectual ability or personality trait, the scores should have high test–retest reliability, even over quite long intervals. Scores for measures of unstable constructs such as mood or state anxiety should not be so stable; high test–retest reliability for those scores (i.e., consistent scores for inconsistent constructs) is evidence that the measure is invalid. Scores for situation-specific constructs such as test anxiety or state-dependent memory should only be consistent when the person is in the specified situations and should not generalize to other situations, by definition (Anastasi, 1988).

McClelland (1980, 1981) and McClelland, Koestner, and Weinberger (1989) extended this reasoning about congruence between the measurement method, the construct, and the criterion behavior to be predicted to demonstrate construct validity. His studies emphasized the structural similarity between the measurement situation and the person's population of life situations to which generalization from the behavior sample—in this case, imaginative thought—is desired. Specifically, these studies showed that structured self-report measures tend to predict scores on other structured self-reports, whereas scores from less structured non-self-report measures (TAT stories) predict better to less structured situations, such as people's daily life activities and long-term outcomes.

In part, McClelland argued, this was due to the theoretical properties of the constructs being measured—stable cognitive schemas, attitudes, and abilities versus situationally activated motives—but an additional issue was the sources of error variance typical of each measurement method. That is, self-report measures are notoriously subject to social desirability and other systematic biases due to self-presentation and social comparison processes. They are also vulnerable to format-specific response biases coming from the response options that examinees are given (Block, 1965; Schwarz, 1999). These forms of systematic measurement error tend to be stable and to cause items and measures to intercorrelate cross-sectionally and over time even when the constructs that they measure are unrelated (Campbell & Fiske, 1959). Those tendencies increase reliability, but at the expense of lowering validity.

In contrast, TAT scores for motives, theoretically and empirically being more situationally influenced, tend to differ across situations (yielding lower internal consistency reliability among stories) and over time (showing low test–retest reliability to the extent that major events and changes in people's lives might influence their actual motives, as shown by Jenkins, 1987, 1994). Furthermore, storytellers tend to see their task as a demonstration of creativity, so they tend to avoid telling similar stories if they can (Lundy, 1985; Tomkins, 1947; Winter & Stewart, 1977). Nevertheless, these scores correlate well with the kinds of situations people choose to be in and what they do when there, even in longitudinal studies over more than a decade (Jenkins, 1987, 1994; McClelland, 1965, 1980, 1985b; Stewart, 1980), showing high predictive validity despite low reliability.

Because the lesser structure of TATs allows more variability in behavior generally, when compared with structured self-reports, one common source of systematic measurement method error variance that might dilute the validity of scores is simple response productivity: story length, which must be evaluated and perhaps controlled statistically (McClelland, 1980). Another might be story richness, as represented by Edith Weisskopf's Transcendence Index (TI) herein, which is conceptually comparable to Lambda in the Rorschach Comprehensive System. For some scoring systems, telling longer, richer stories is likely to gain higher scores; storytellers who give shorter, more literally descriptive responses are likely to score lower. But in contrast to the measurement error common in structured self-reports, story length and richness might vary across stories and over time, to the extent that storytellers find some pictures more engaging than others, are more energized or fatigued at different times, or are otherwise affected by changes in their internal state. To the extent that this happens, unsystematically, what we would otherwise think of as systematic method error *becomes random error,* changing independently of the construct of interest. As such, it is likely to lower both internal consistency reliability and test–retest reliability, even when the construct being measured is relatively stable. However, this random error is cancelled out when per-story scores are aggregated into a summary score.

Local norms are often the best for valid clinical interpretation (Anastasi, 1988), as these will capture both ethnic and regional variations in idiomatic meanings, which are especially evident in orally given narrative data. For TATs, these norms should include not only scores, but also annotations to scoring manuals that indicate how common idioms were classified and other difficult scoring decisions were made, in order to ensure consistency of those decisions across clients and over time (see chapter 2). The ubiquity of computer use for practice management is a considerable asset for such record keeping, as it allows clinicians to maintain easily complete databases of their assessment scores from their clientele as local clinical scientists (Stricker, 2006).

Situation Specificity of TATs

A major strength of TATs that has been obscured by the often inappropriate psychometric emphasis on internal consistency and test–retest reliability is their usefulness for appraising the situation specificity of storytellers' social perceptions and responses. Presenting a series of pictured situations to a storyteller is a way of *sampling objectively and systematically,* in a context standardized by administration instructions, from among the storyteller's imaginative repertoire of possible social scenarios. To the extent that the pictures differ, the stories and scores should differ. After all, storytellers understand their task as one of telling a *different* story about each picture. To the extent that they do so, the assessment yields a broader sample of behavior that should generalize to more of the storyteller's various life contexts.

If the assessment clinician or researcher seeks more information about certain kinds of situations to answer a specific referral question or to test a specific hypothesis, then more pictures that sample that class of situations can be used. For example, pictures that might plausibly be a romantic couple sample the storyteller's perceptions, ideation, and affect relevant to romantic situations; pictures of cross-generational dyads sample implicit experiences of parent–child relationships (see chapter 27 in this volume). Survey researchers often use this principle, called a stratified sampling procedure, to oversample particular population groups for certain purposes. Just as survey researchers might be interested in comparing subpopulations of people, clinicians might be interested in comparing storytellers' responses to different populations of situations (as done explicitly by Thomas's Affective Scale in chapter 27 in this volume), as well as in their more trait-like average responses across all situations. This information can be obtained easily by aggregating (i.e., adding or averaging) scores across all pictures to generalize to average (trait-like) behavior (e.g., "dangerousness") or by aggregating only the scores from one kind of picture to generalize to only that class of situations (e.g., probability of thoughts related to violent childhood abuse, or to street fights).

Given that the set of pictures used for an assessment can be seen as a tool for systematic sampling of the storyteller's range of life circumstances, how should that process be structured? What dimensions are most important? For general-purpose, comprehensive clinical assessment, three dimensions seem salient and generalizable across cultures as a sociological framework for organizing the human life course: social roles, as defined by age-gender combinations (Neugarten & Gutmann, 1958); activity context, as defined by characters' focusing on people or on impersonal tasks; and emotional tone, as defined by the facial expressions and postures of the characters. Classification by these or other dimensions allows for comparing the storyteller's responses to different kinds of situations, as well as comparisons across individuals and studies.

Population Generalizability

One important aspect of any psychological frame of reference is its cross-population generalizability. Recognizing the importance of validity generalization across populations, this issue is discussed in each scoring system's summary chapter in this volume. Individual psychosocial functioning, if adaptive, is shaped by its sociocultural context, and one culture's healthy adaptation might be another's insanity. In a rapidly shrinking world, generalizable measurement techniques are increasingly desirable, but the challenges of linguistic and cultural translation and cross-cultural norming are just beginning to be appreciated fully (Dana, 1993, 1998, 2005; Helms, 1992).

Clinical TATs in the United States have a 50-year history of accumulated cross-cultural knowledge via such authors as Richard Dana, George De Vos, David Ephraim, and William Henry. The need for racially and culturally specific stimuli was recognized early on, as described by Michelle Hoy-Watkins and Valata Jenkins-Monroe in this volume's chapter 33. Although debates continue about the culture-specific details of picture cues and identification with one main character in the story, and about the influence of cultural differences in values, beliefs, and symbols, it remains that nearly all cultures use storytelling to socialize their children (Howard, 1991), whereas few cultures use Likert scales or multiple-choice questions in that capacity. Thus, what TATs require participants to do is likely to be familiar, even enjoyable, to them, in contrast to most of our multiscale personality inventories. Although cross-cultural generalizability of results is a property of the specific picture cues and interpretive system used, few individuals in most cultures will have difficulty with the basic data-gathering task of telling a story about people in pictures.

Reliability

Many of the classical psychometricians observed that less structured personality measures are clinically valuable, but that classical test theory is not appropriate for appraising their validity or reliability (e.g., Anastasi, 1988; Guilford, 1954; Harrison & Rotter, 1945). They framed clearly two basic assumptions underlying all psychological measures that, if taken seriously for TATs, serve as an adequate response to the misapplications noted in the literature.

1. The ways in which the validity and reliability of measures are evaluated must be consistent with the theoretical properties of the constructs measured by the scoring system (e.g., measures of transient states such as mood should not show stability across situations and over time; wide-band constructs with fewer redundant items will have lower internal consistency reliability).

2. In contrast to the priority implied by the order of chapters in most measurement textbooks—including Anastasi (1988)—validity should take precedence over reliability (Anastasi, 1988; Guilford, 1946; Gulliksen, 1950; Karon, 1966, 1981; Thorndike, 1985).

McClelland (1980) added a third: The ways in which the validity and reliability of measures are evaluated must consider the measure's sources of error variance, both stable and unstable, and whether the criterion correlate variables share the same sources of systematic measurement method error variance.

Psychometric work on TATs not only requires bridging the scientist–practitioner gap; on the academic side it exists *in* the gap, as some academic personality researchers have never fully accepted even the human motivation paradigm. One challenge on this side is that the human motivation tradition's use of story data makes it appear "too clinical", and therefore scientifically suspect to those who equate science with structure. The use of formal scoring systems has not been well understood, in part due to its omission from or misrepresentation in measurement texts. For example, although Anastasi (1988) speaks well of both Exner's (1978, 1986) then-emerging Rorschach Comprehensive System and McClelland (1985a) and Atkinson's (1958, 1981) work on need for Achievement as promising scientific developments, this brief acknowledgement is a belated exception to its context in the book, a general damnation of projective techniques. Thus, her positive, albeit cautious, view of these systems is apparently often overlooked.

There have been occasional attempts at rapprochement, however, with efforts on both sides of the growing scientist–practitioner gap to hear and address the assumptions of the other's frame of reference and to develop new constructs and language reflecting that conceptual adaptation. On the more clinical side—but writing for research audiences as well—Karon (1966, 1981) distinguished the kinds of validity and reliability important for projective measures, as did McClelland (1980) for the research use of human motivation scoring systems.

To make the methodological differences and their implications more salient, McClelland has repeatedly offered concise labels for these paradigms that draw attention to the methodological reasons for the low correlations between story-based measures of motives and structured self-report measures of similar-sounding constructs. He first called these approaches *operant* and *respondent*, respectively, in part to recast in behavioral terms the theoretical assumptions attending the projective hypothesis (McClelland, 1980). Then he presented findings contrasting his measure of the achievement *motive* with measures of achievement *values* such as the Edwards Personal Preference Schedule (McClelland, 1985a) and did the same for affiliation (McClelland, 1989). Finally, McClelland et al.'s (1989) empirical illustration of the different properties of *implicit* (i.e., measured in stories) and *explicit* or *self-attributed* (i.e., structured self-report) motives seems to have recruited the attention of the academic science community (e.g., Baumann, Kaschel, & Kuhl, 2005; Brunstein & Maier, 2005; Schultheiss & Brunstein, 1999, 2001; Schultheiss et al., 2005; Spangler, 1992; Woike, 1995; Woike, Lavezzary, & Barsky, 2001) and a smaller but well-respected group of clinical researchers (e.g., Bornstein, 1998).

Returning to the goals of the original psychometricians, the purpose of appraising reliability is to identify the amount of error variance in a measure's scores. But classical test theory considers only random error, and does not evaluate systematic measurement method error variance (Campbell, 1996), so it gives only a partial picture, even for the purpose for which it was originally developed. Because they impose less restriction on the range of the storyteller's responses, TATs and other less structured measures may have less built-in stable measurement error than do more structured measures of traits and abilities. Thus, they may be more sensitive to changes in the person across time and situations, and consequently can be especially useful for measuring less stable constructs such as mood, as well as other kinds of situation-specific responses such as motives and interpersonal scenarios. As already described, TATs in particular can be used flexibly to sample a broad or narrow range of situations represented in the stimuli used to generate stories, so that the results might better generalize to a broad or narrow range of situations in the storyteller's life.

This does not mean that reliability is unimportant in evaluating TATs. The most crucial source of random error threatening all less structured measures is inconsistency in scoring. Attaining and maintaining interscorer reliability is thus a central issue in evaluating TAT scoring systems, important enough to merit its own chapter in this book (see chapter 2).

This does not mean that other forms of reliability are unattainable for TATs, given that the construct measured is narrow-band, theoretically stable, and trait-like (i.e., consistent across situations), or that the sample of stories is large enough, due to the influence of number of items on the calculation of Cronbach's alpha (Streiner, 2003). Dana's (1959) three scales presented in chapter 7 measure narrow-band, trait-like perceptual constructs, and these show high internal consistency reliability with only five stories. By careful matching of theoretically appropriate constructs and methods with precisely chosen psychometric challenges, Hibbard, Mitchell, and Porcerelli (2001) produced a landmark paper on TAT internal consistency reliability, showing that samples as large as 10 stories show high internal consistency reliability for the much more complex, wider-band Social Cognition and Object Relations Scales (SCORS; Westen, Lohr, Silk, Gold, & Kerber, 1990), whereas smaller samples do not.

A different approach to increasing the number of items is to obtain more "items" from the same number of stories. Using a computerized administration technique for which students typed their own stories, Blankenship and Zoota (1998) increased the internal consistency reliability for need for Power, and Blankenship et al. (2006) for need for Achievement, by separating the traditional four aspects of a story requested in the administration instructions (tersely: what is happening, what led up to it, what are people thinking and feeling, how will it come out) into separate questions, each with its own paragraph. Thus, five "stories" yielded 20 "items". However, this approach is generally inappropriate for clinical use because it tends to disrupt the narrative coherence needed for clinical purposes and for some other scoring systems. The better response to the classical test theory challenge of internal consistency reliability for clinical scoring systems is to gather a large enough sample of stories, 10 apparently being a reasonable minimum for a broad-based assessment. As discussed previously, though, the minimum number of stories needed may depend on the kinds of situations in the client's life to which generalization is wanted, and the number of stimuli needed to give an adequate sampling of those situations for the purpose at hand.

More recent responses to the reliability challenge have bypassed classical test theory in favor of item response theory (IRT; Tuerlinckx, DeBoeck, & Lens, 2002) and the Rasch model (Blankenship et al., 2006). These studies have applied these forms of item analysis toward the goal of identifying and selecting pictures that evoke, or pull for, more need for Achievement imagery than other pictures as a way of reducing variability of scores between pictures. They are valuable for having demonstrated solutions-in-principle to the internal consistency reliability problem for TATs by increasing the structure of the stimulus situations in the pictures. It is unclear whether these solutions will apply to other scoring systems, as IRT and the Rasch model both were designed for ability-like constructs that are presumed stable over time and situations rather than being transient states or situation-specific responses. Furthermore, for clinical purposes it is usually desirable to choose pictures of different kinds of situations and people, rather than a more structurally homogeneous set, in order to generalize the findings to a wider variety of the client's life circumstances.

□ Meeting the Challenges: Goals of the Book

This book was written for both clinical practice and academic research communities. It is designed to make the most useful available clinical scoring systems accessible to potential users, providing scientifically and clinically promising tools for the improved use of TATs.

Plan of the Book

Chapter 2 presents a strategy for learning to score structured scoring systems that is suitable both for individuals who are using a manual for self-teaching and for supervised research teams. This chapter grew from my work with undergraduate scorers that in our lab has enabled them to attain and maintain high interscorer reliability standards even with quite complex systems. The Appendix to that chapter is designed as a handout for scorer trainees; the bulk of the chapter is directed to the supervisor. It covers a detailed description of the learning process and its challenges, along with suggestions for using the group's dynamics to improve the accuracy and efficiency of the learner's developing competence with scoring. Chapter 3 extends the contents of the present volume toward the future, supplementing the research recommendations offered by authors for their specific systems and noting existing systems not included here that merit further study. It proposes more general avenues for conceptual and methodological developments, discussing the kinds of research and clinical problems for which TATs are most useful. Students and early-career researchers hopefully will find there some helpful inspiration, ideas, and strategies for theses and dissertations using these methods.

The remaining chapters present the research summaries and scoring manuals. An overview chapter describes each system, covering its conceptual framework; theoretical, clinical, or empirical basis and assumptions; scoring categories; research evidence; an optional illustrative case; and suggestions for future research that are meant to inspire theses and dissertations. Most are followed by a detailed scoring manual. Many of these include stories that readers can score for practice, along with expert scoring so that readers can check their scoring accuracy.

Systems Represented Here

Few of the systems represented here were located by electronic search, as the indexing keywords used were either too general or too specific, and searchable abstracts appeared only in the mid 1970s. I began with those references cited by Cramer (1991, 1996), Teglasi (1993), and Zubin, Eron, and Schumer (1965) that had promising titles. Early consultation with Phebe Cramer and with Richard Dana was also helpful in locating both specific systems and promising search strategies. When it became clear that the most likely journal sources were the *Journal of Personality Assessment* and its ancestors, the *Journal of Clinical Psychology*, and the *Journal of Consulting and Clinical Psychology*, I spent much of my faculty development leave during 2000–2001 in the stacks of the W.E.B. Dubois Library at the University of Massachusetts at Amherst hand searching the tables of contents for these journals—and occasionally others—back to 1945, looking for suggestive titles and review articles. Stricker and Healy's (1990) and Vane's (1981) reviews were notably helpful. A few other useful leads came from colleagues, conference presentations, and Internet discussion lists.

My criteria for pursuing a system further included (1) evidence of the existence of an adequate scoring manual, typically a citation to same in the article or presentation; (2) evidence of interscorer reliability; (3) empirical evidence for validity or clinical utility in samples with probable generalizability; (4) importance, promise, and clarity of the theoretical constructs measured; (5) feasibility of learning to score largely through self-teaching with the manual (i.e., not dependent on extensive knowledge of a particular theory); and (6) recommendation by a colleague. Not all systems met all criteria. Unfortunately, it was necessary to omit systems not in English, which eliminated Shentoub's (1990) highly recommended system.

The systems are organized in the table of contents loosely according to theoretical orientation, with these in a rough historical sequence, the earliest publication first. Similarly, they are ordered chronologically within groups. In the section that follows, they are described in historical order of publication, without subgrouping. Table 1.1 summarizes in crude categories each manual's theoretical foundation, how the scores are derived (which is useful for conceptualizing the distributions of scores and their statistical properties, and

TABLE 1.1 Concise Guide to the Scoring Manuals

System	Theoretical Foundation	Nature of Scores	Main Validity Type	Best Referral Question(s): Diagnosis	Prognosis	Treatment Planning	General Social	Close Relationships
Perceptual-Cognitive								
Transcendence Index	Eclectic	Content Analysis	Content			☑		
Objective TAT Scoring	Eclectic	Content Analysis	Criterion	☑	☑			
Interpersonal Decentering	Piaget	Two-step	Content Criterion			☑	☑	☑
Personal Problem Solving	Cognitive behavioral	Rating	Content Criterion		☑	☑		
Picture Projection Test 1	Eclectic	Mixed	Criterion	☑	☑	☑		
Psychodynamic								
Fine's Scoring Scheme	Psycho-dynamic	Mixed	Content Criterion		☑	☑	☑	☑
Primary Process	Psycho-dynamic	Mixed	Content Construct[2]	☑				
Pathogenesis	Psycho-dynamic	Two-step	Content Construct			☑	☑	☑
Oral Dependency	Psycho-dynamic	Content Analysis	Content Construct[2]	☑	☑	☑	☑	☑
Symbiosis	Psycho-dynamic	Two-step	Content Criterion	☑	☑	☑	☑	☑

Ambitious-Narcissistic Character Style	Psychodynamic	Two-step	Content Construct[2]	✓		✓	✓	✓
Social-Emotional								
Affective Scale	Interpersonal	Two-step	Content Criterion		✓	✓	✓	✓
Empathy	Schema	Rating	Content Criterion		✓	✓	✓	✓
Contemporized Themes Concerning Blacks[1]	Africentric	Rating	Content		✓	✓	✓	
Needs-Concerns Focused								
Need-Threat Analysis	Murray	Content Analysis	Content		✓	✓	✓	
Psychocultural Scoring	Anthropology, Motivation	Two-step	Content		✓	✓	✓	

[1] Has its own picture set.

[2] Rorschach scoring manual also published.

Note. Nature of scores = Content analysis (identified content scored present-absent), Rating (global ratings of entire story), Two-step (first identify content if present, then score or rate it), or Mixed (some combination of these for different scores). Main validity type = Content (congruence of category descriptions with construct and/or behavior represented), Criterion (scores differed between theoretically relevant groups or correlated with other theoretically relevant measures), or Construct (Criterion, plus scores converged with measures of the same construct using other measurement methods). Diagnosis = Utility for identifying one or more Axis I or II diagnostic criteria; none are comprehensive. Prognosis = Utility for estimating prognosis under different situational conditions. Treatment planning = Utility for suggesting likely response to various treatment alternatives and interventions. General Social, Close Relationships = Utility for identifying client's strengths and weaknesses in general social interaction and close relationships, respectively.

the types of validity evidence that are available thus far. The likely utility of each system for addressing different aspects of referral questions is also indicated crudely. This classification is impressionistic and not necessarily well supported by current validity evidence, except in the case of diagnosis; a check in that column indicates that at least one validational study differentiated clinical groups significantly or showed convergence with other clinically validated scales as expected. For the other four referral question categories, classification is based on the content or criterion validity of the measure and the likely utility of that information for estimating prognosis under different situational conditions, suggesting likely response to various treatment alternatives and interventions, or identifying client's strengths and weaknesses in general social interaction and in close relationships, respectively.

The first reasonably detailed published scoring manual found to include interscorer reliability data is Weisskopf's Transcendence Index. It was not designed for scoring stories, but rather for identifying ways in which people who are asked simply to describe a picture "transcend the stimulus" spontaneously, for example, by attributing thoughts, feelings, abilities, and physiological characteristics to the characters; by going beyond the picture in time or space; by specifying social relations such as kinship, occupational roles, or possession; or by making editorial comments such as imperatives, evaluation, or noting the atmosphere or symbolism of the picture. Weisskopf's primary use of the system was to compare the usefulness of different stimuli and administration conditions for eliciting more transcendent descriptions, and thus presumably richer, more informative stories for clinical application.

One long-standing question about the validity of TAT data has been, "What constitutes an adequate story for interpretation?" Although even very brief stories can sometimes be clinically useful, more often they are not, and it is scientifically silly to say only that short stories are invalid unless something valid is obvious. Regarding the storytelling process as a process of thought sampling highlights this question, parallel to population sampling in survey research, because the validity of data rests in part on the validity of the sampling process. Stories with little transcendence do not provide a trustworthy sample of thoughts for interpretation beyond the observation of apparent constriction in responding.

I think that the TI is a good candidate for a TAT validity index comparable to Lambda in the Rorschach Comprehensive System. A person who does not give much more than a literal description when asked to tell a story about a picture is simply not giving enough information—regardless of the reason—for the stories to be useful for more than individualized appraisal. If so, then eliminating uninformative stories, or correcting for TI scores along with story length, in research may well improve the quality of our results. Although the various scoring categories have not been studied individually, their face validity for the most common content domains of transcendence makes them worthy of study for their potential generalizability to clients' repetitive patterns of social behavior—and deficits thereof.

Fine's Scoring Scheme measures the manifest content of the story characters' feelings and outcomes, scored as either present or absent in the story, and of interpersonal dyads, scored as to whether the latter are moving toward, away from, or against one another. These classifications are quite detailed, with 36 subcategories for feelings and outcomes, and with 16 dyad types that include distinctions between initiating members of asymmetric dyads (e.g., separating mother's movement with respect to child from child's movement with respect to mother). The comprehensiveness of this system should make it useful for a variety of purposes, and the concrete nature of the categories should make it easy to score.

The Primary Process System scores content that meets criteria for this classical Freudian construct by reflecting attention to libidinal or aggressive themes, and also scores formal aspects of stories that suggest defenses against or control of these contents. Manifest content is identified and scored in the story, and in some cases is then given an additional score for severity. Although high scores might indicate psychopathology—especially if uncontrolled—adaptive regression in the service of the ego (ARISE) might also yield notable scores. This is one of several systems developed during an era in which it was common to create in the same article parallel scoring systems for the same construct using two or more measurement methods so as to have validational associations with a parallel system scored from other less structured data—in this case Rorschach Ink Blot protocols. Like the Oral Dependency Scale, the Rorschach version of Primary Process has more extensive research support, but there is also some evidence of TAT validity.

Dana's Objective TAT Scoring System was designed to capture aspects of "the psychological relatedness of person and environment," specifically the storyteller's approach to the assessment situation (i.e., following directions to include specific information in stories), the similarity of responses to those of nonpatient samples, and the rarity of responses that are more common among patients. In contrast to some of the more intricate, exhaustive, and multifaceted systems of the time, such as Reuben Fine's and Robert Holt's, Dana's was designed to be of broad theoretical and practical importance, but to minimize inference so as to be simple enough to be scored by a clerk. These three scales discriminated between contemporaneously defined "normal", neurotic, and psychotic persons. Like Weisskopf's TI, Dana's system has been used in numerous unpublished dissertations that were necessarily beyond the scope of the present review, but that might be informative if pursued.

Singer and Wynne's Communication Deviance (CD) System is based on clinical observations of families in which CD in parents' stories has been related to the later development of schizophrenia spectrum disorders in their children. Rather than identifying content as do most other systems, CD captures the structure of communication and problems of integration in language. These include closure problems, disruptive behavior, peculiar perceptions and verbalizations, and other formal characteristics. This system has produced a relatively large number of publications among the systems herein. These are primarily from large-scale family studies, mostly from the University of California–Los Angeles (UCLA) Family High Risk Project. Benjamin Chapman's very thorough review of this literature in the present chapter 26 traces the system's history from the original 1966 publication, based on National Institute of Mental Health (NIMH) family studies that included both TAT and Rorschach manuals, to its use in the UCLA studies. The use of Singer and Wynne's evolving theory about the role of parental communication in the development of schizophrenia, plus the availability of clinical and research observations of the NIMH families, makes this system both theoretically and empirically derived. Supportive findings have come from Spanish-speaking and Norwegian samples as well as from studies primarily of Anglo Americans.

The authors of the current highly developed scoring manual declined permission to publish it here. Although no reason was given, one plausible rationale might be the possible sensitivity of its implications for parental functioning in the event of child custody litigation. The original manual is presented in Singer and Wynne's 1966 publication along with its Rorschach counterpart, but it lacks the specificity of the one that has accrued the most empirical support.

Pathogenesis is based on clinical observations of the unconscious defenses that may be activated within different relationships. The content-valid whole-story score involves first locating instances in which a dominant and a dependent character are interacting in a situation in which their needs might conflict. Each such instance is then scored as to whether or not the dominant character takes the other's needs into account, the latter being the pathogenic response. Despite the theoretical emphasis on the unconscious, the content of the thought sample clearly depicts behavior that, if acted out, could well have the consequences that have been supported by research. Although it originated with studies of families having a child with schizophrenia, research has shown its validity for parents who abused their children, parents having a child who has become delinquent, and for distinguishing therapists who are or are not helpful. Like CD, its closest relative here (but very different in what is scored), and like Symbiosis, the Affective Scale, Interpersonal Decentering, and parts of Fine's Scoring Scheme, Pathogenesis is highly interpersonal and arguably has its best use in the study of dyads.

The TAT Oral Dependency Scale identifies content associated with this Freudian construct and is quite simple to score. Some categories involve only recognition of relevant words or phrases (e.g., parental figures; help; helplessness, loneliness, or depression; food- and mouth-related references; belief in luck or magic), and others need only minimal inferences (e.g., passive dependency, overly optimistic endings). The Rorschach version (Bornstein, 1996) has received considerable research support, but the TAT system has had much less published research attention. Like hostility and aggression, dependency is not socially desirable in mainstream American culture, and more literal representation in stories might have complex associations with overt behavior. Future studies using this system should examine the relative usefulness of the scoring categories separately until it is clear which yield the best data for which populations. The success of the Rorschach system, and the usefulness of manifest story content as a representation that likely generalizes to clients' real lives in individualized interpretation, make this system worth further study and development.

Melvin Feffer's Interpersonal Decentering is simple in structure but requires making careful distinctions. Scoring this two-step system involves first isolating instances of interaction between story characters, and then rating the cognitive complexity of each as undifferentiated, sequentially coordinated (i.e., action–reaction statements without internalized states, at three levels of complexity), or simultaneously coordinated (i.e., reflecting a character's internal awareness of another, at five levels of complexity). In the original study, it was validated against Feffer's better-known Role-Taking Task, as described in chapter 8. It provides a content-valid sample of how the storyteller conceptualizes relationships; the most typical score calculation method represents the balance between action–reaction and internalized interactions.

The Psychocultural System identifies the substantive content with which cultures and individuals are most likely to be preoccupied. Although some of its categories imply the pursuit of goals (e.g., Achievement, Affiliation, Esteem, Mastery, Power), others imply ongoing engagement in social processes (e.g., Competition, Harmony, Nurturance, Responsibility, Solidarity). It is perhaps the most thorough and exhaustive extant representation of storytellers' concerns and preoccupations among all those that have been designed to measure one or more of Murray's (1938) needs and presses. However, this system is more cosmopolitan in that it was created by psychological anthropologist George De Vos for cross-cultural studies, and thus includes more categories that would concern members of collectivist cultures. Some of the categories appear to parallel the human motivation systems for needs for Achievement (McClelland et al., 1953; McClelland & Koestner, 1992), Affiliation (Heyns, Veroff, & Atkinson, 1958; Koestner & McClelland, 1992), and Power (Winter, 1973, 1992). However, the Psychocultural System scores only the presence of imagery, and not the subcategories reflecting an imagined sequence of goal pursuit that characterize the human motive systems. One beneficial connection to theory is that David Ephraim organizes these concerns along the two major axes of agency and communion, also called dominance–submission and love/affiliation–hate/separation, that have become prominent higher-order factors for interpersonal relationships in recent decades (e.g., Alden, Wiggins, & Pincus, 1990; Benjamin, 1993; Leary, 1957).

The Symbiosis System appraises the kind and degree of self-other differentiation problems between story characters, because a deficient awareness of people as distinct individuals is important in several character pathologies. Symbiotic attachment is scored by first locating representations of dyads, as for Fine's scoring scheme, and then scoring the presence or absence of each form of symbiosis according to the direction of attachment. Thus, problems of psychological merger, intrusiveness, negative reactions to separation, jealous reactions, dependency, and attempts to control the other can be seen as diffused among relationship types or localized in just one. The validational family studies have shown that symbiosis scores differentiate among patients, and also in parallel, among parents of patients.

The Ambitious–Narcissistic Style Scale identifies indicators of this character style using five theory-based content-valid categories: Intrusiveness/Thrusting, Exhibitionistic/Voyeuristic, Urethral Excitation, Mastery/Competence/Power, and Self-Potency. Each, if present in the story, is then rated at one of three intensity levels. Oedipal and autonomy concerns are also rated, primarily to assist in differentiating these from the other categories. Most of the extant theory and research is on men, though there is a little evidence for women. The single published study is especially strong, showing both convergent validity with parallel scores from Rorschach and early memories protocols and criterion discrimination between men judged by clinical raters as having or not having this style.

The Affective Scale requires first identifying the role relationships in a story and then rating each on a four-point scale of positive versus negative affect. It developed in a classical fashion from clinical observations that led to qualitative data gathering, which in turn was formalized into a content-analysis scoring system. Its simplicity comes from its reliance on formally defined role relationships among story characters, the central assumption being that perceptions of relationships among story characters are drawn from—and thus generalize to—the role relationships in the storyteller's life. Thus, married partners' depictions of married story characters represent their own implicit definitions of marital roles, including the assumptions, attitudes, and actions that they expect from each other and from others toward their spouse and their couplehood. The validational study showed that couples whose spouse representations were more positive than their representations of parents had better dyadic adjustment than did couples whose parent representations were rated more positively than their spousal dyads. However, Thomas wisely provided for the generalization of her approach to a variety of relationships that might be of concern to different populations. There is no obvious reason why it should not be applicable to members of cultures that operate under differently structured kinship systems.

The Tell-Me-A-Story (TEMAS), designed for children and adolescents, is a particularly important innovation for its picture set, which not only reflects people with racial minority features in culturally familiar urban settings but also includes a nonminority version. The design of both the pictures and the scoring system is well grounded in the research history of other TATs regarding use of color and moderate to low levels of ambiguity compared with the Murray TAT. The setting, postures, and facial expressions of the characters suggest problems to be solved, sometimes with alternative courses of action suggested. The theory-grounded scoring system was designed to capture personality functions drawn from ego psychology, along with a host of descriptive indicators for clinical use. An up-to-date review of TEMAS literature appears in Costantino, Dana, and

Malgady (2007). The published picture set and the manual are available from Western Psychological Services.

The Need–Threat Analysis for the Children's Apperception Test (CAT) identifies the major sources of stress perceived by children, which typically revolve around getting needs met or the threat posed by deprivation. Five content-valid need–threat binaries are scored present or absent in each story: Independence–Domination; Affiliation–Rejection; Security–Insecurity; Achievement–Failure; and Aggression–Punishment. A sixth category for "other" may be added. A computerized content analysis dictionary has been developed to assist interscorer reliability, but the story context must be considered to validate each score. Because of the emphasis on content validity to inform treatment interventions, the major research presents frequency norms for each of the 10 CAT cards. There is scant evidence of gender or age differences in scores. This system seems likely to be valid for adults and for application to stories elicited by other picture stimuli as well.

The Personal Problem-Solving Scale-Revised uses global rating scales for structural features of stories to provide a comprehensive picture of each story as presenting a problem to be solved (implicit in the plot) and one or more solutions. The subscales of the Story Design category indicate the structural aspects of problem appraisal, those of Story Orientation describe approaches to problem solving, the number of solutions is simply counted, and the components of Story Resolution identify different aspects of success. This cognitive behavioral framework is explicitly a content-valid translation to story data of several self-report problem-solving scales that have yielded few significant findings, exemplifying the gaps among what people say, what they think, and what they actually do. The system is very efficient; the several supportive studies thus far have used only three stories.

The Adult Attachment Projective (AAP) is a new and promising method that, like the TEMAS, the Contemporized Themes Concerning Blacks, and the Picture Projection Test, uses new stimuli developed to sample construct-relevant experience, in this case involving interpersonal attachment. The eight AAP stimuli are simple black line drawings, given in a fixed sequence, representing increasingly stressful situations that evoke attachment concerns for most people. The resulting scores include classification of the storyteller as Secure-Autonomous, Dismissing, Preoccupied, or Unresolved. Supportive findings have included native speakers of French and German, and several studies based in other cultures are in progress. The scoring system is well grounded in attachment theory, and requires considerable in-person training and certification for attainment of interrater reliability; thus, no manual is included in this volume. Interested readers should contact Dr. Carol George at Mills College (george@mills.edu) for information about scheduled scoring workshops.

The Empathy System has only three rating scales that are applied globally to all stories, but like those of Westen et al.'s (1990) SCORS, the distinctions between levels must be made precisely and are facilitated by sophistication with theory. The four levels of Perceptual Integration identify the accuracy of the storyteller's perception of emotional tensions shown in the picture and the congruence between the latter and the story. The four levels of Affect Source distinguish increasing sophistication of coordination between internal and external sources of affect for story characters. The five levels of Mutuality of Autonomy capture the differentiation of individual characters' internal worlds and the coordination among different characters, consistent with their internalized values and concern for others. It is well grounded in developmental theory and in the authors' theoretical analysis and integration of the research literature on prosocial behavior more broadly. The authors have built on and adapted features of several previous scoring systems, including one for Rorschach Ink Blots protocols (Urist's 1977 Mutuality of Autonomy), strengthening the carefully explained scoring categories. The few studies to date are nevertheless very strong, with the major validational study relating Empathy scores to teachers' ratings of children's empathic behavior.

The Contemporized Themes Concerning Blacks Test (C-TCB) is a revision of Robert Williams's (1972) Themes Concerning Blacks Test. It consists of a set of 27 chromatic cards representing contemporary African American daily life and a scoring system grounded in Africentric theory. The content-valid categories consist of eight personality traits rated globally on five-point Likert scales and nine affective states rated globally on four-point Likert scales for all stories. The situational themes include parenting and family experiences, racism, media portrayal of African Americans, substance abuse, and HIV/AIDS. The personality traits include interpersonal, family, and group concerns; goal setting and motivation; self-concept and identity, autonomy, and Black pride. A careful analysis by a panel of raters evaluated the content validity of the card pulls for their intended themes and the personality traits and affective states attributed to each. Frequency norms for 100 participants are given herein.

The Picture Projection Test (PPT) is a revision of a scoring system that has been used with different sets of picture stimuli, culminating in a new set of chromatic paintings that can be computer-administered, potentially over the Internet. The scoring categories were developed to parallel conceptually those of the Rorschach Comprehensive System (Exner, 2003). The findings reported here are especially exciting in that they show surprising consistency between TAT/PPT and Rorschach measures of form, affect modulation, and various forms of experienced distress. That the effect sizes of this consistency are modest reflects the considerably different characteristics of the stimuli and the task involved, namely perception with minimal ideation for the Rorschach compared with construction of a narrative for the TAT. Interestingly, the pattern of correlations with Rorschach scores for PPT scores obtained from stories told to TAT pictures is remarkably similar to that from stories to his new PPT pictures. This suggests that the underlying constructs are remarkably robust when aggregated across 8 to 10 stories, even when different pictures were used by different examiners—as was the case for the archival TAT stories.

What's Not Here

The two most obvious absences from the array of the best available clinical scoring systems for TATs are the two that have received the most research attention since 1990: Cramer's Defense Mechanism Manual (DMM) and Westen et al.'s (1990) SCORS. Cramer's system describes three major defense mechanisms—Denial, Projection, and Identification—as exemplars of successively more mature defensive processes. She published her scoring manual, along with an extensive literature review and theoretical integration, in Cramer (1991). Cramer (1996) updated her accumulated research findings again in the context of narrative interpretation more broadly conceived, including chapters on other scoring systems. Cramer (2006) included important extensions of theory and application as well. Her key empirical publications (Cramer, 2005; Cramer & Blatt, 1990, 1993; Cramer, Blatt, & Ford, 1988) merit careful attention for their integration of theory and data analysis. She has now made the DMM available on the Web at http://www.williams.edu/Psychology/Faculty/Cramer/cramer.html (select "Defense Mechanism Manual").

Unlike most of the systems collected here, Westen et al.'s (1990) SCORS was developed empirically—though guided by psychodynamic theory—by comparing patients in three diagnostic groups. The SCORS identifies differences in the stories told by patients diagnosed with borderline personality disorder and those told by patients having depression or schizophrenia-spectrum diagnoses. The SCORS too has generated a quantity of significant results. Many of these papers, along with the SCORS manual, are available on Westen's Web site at http://www.psychsystems.net/lab/.

Finally, given the importance of violence, aggression, and hostility among patients and forensic populations, the absence of a system covering this area is notable. However, though often researched, few studies of aggression represented in TAT stories have shown consistent findings from any scoring system beyond an initial study (as discussed by Ritzler in chapter 12 in this volume); thus, none is included in the present volume. Rorschach research on aggression has found that more overtly aggressive responses that include human movement (AG) are less related to socially unacceptable aggression than is more subtle and symbolic representation of aggression via simple aggressive content (e.g., guns, wolf teeth; Meloy & Gacono, 1993). It may be that overtly aggressive content in TAT stories is so transparently undesirable in so many social circumstances that its presence is a better clue to an oppositional response style or a failure of self-censoring control (e.g., Holt's Primary Process in chapter 16 in this volume) than to likelihood of aggressive behavior. In any case, Hafner and Kaplan's (1960) scale has been included in Ritzler's PPT, permitting study of its vicissitudes in the context of other personality and situational variables.

Looking Ahead: An Integrated Approach

TATs begin with perceptually sensible stimuli (pictures of people in situations) and ask the storyteller to make sense of human social interaction. Structured scoring systems define some dimensions that might characterize such interaction. These might reflect what the client's dilemma is, especially if the client sees the task as to make up a story about the presenting problem. But arguably the most useful information for the clinician concerns what it is that makes this a dilemma for the client.

The systems presented here lay out the psychological context of the client's problem: what the client cares about (Need–Threat, Psychocultural), who is involved and whether they are supportive (AAP, Affective Scale, Fine's Scoring Scheme, Pathogenesis), the client's empathy for (Empathy) and depth of insight into those others and their relationship (Interpersonal Decentering) as compared with constriction (TI), the clarity of the client's communication (CD), the accuracy (or at least conventionality) of the client's social perceptions and responses (Dana's Perceptual Range and Perceptual Personalization, PPT, Primary Process), the client's responsiveness to the social environment's reasonable demands (Dana's Perceptual Organization, AAP, PPT) and ability to problem solve about those (Personal Problem-Solving System–Revised, Contemporized Themes Concerning Blacks Test, TEMAS), the client's dependency versus independent functioning (AAP, Fine's Scoring Scheme, Oral Dependency, Symbiosis), the client's emotional experiences and ability to modulate these (Contemporized Themes Concerning Blacks Test, Fine's Scoring Scheme, PPT), and the client's characterological strengths and problems (Ambitious-Narcissism, Contemporized Themes Concerning Blacks Test, Need–Threat, Symbiosis, TEMAS). If the client cannot see the big picture, the well-informed assessor might be able to piece it together using the mosaic thus created.

An array of these more systematic approaches should not replace individualized idiographic interpretation using narrative analysis any more than the medical student's review of systems will replace the seasoned physician's immediate recognition of a specific constellation of symptoms, or than either should replace magnetic resonance imaging (MRI). Each view is an essential backdrop to the next more resource-intensive and expensive step, and each provides its own unique information yield without which the diagnosis may be missed and the prescribed regimen inappropriate for the patient's needs. None can be replaced with either guesswork or the more wasteful practice of providing cheap and possibly misdirected treatment in lieu of a clear and solid picture of the client's problem. The information yield of structured scoring systems such as those presented here may make it easier for each generation of novices to acquire rapidly and more easily an introductory level of competence in focused topic areas. All clients, regardless of payment method, deserve treatment that is guided by appropriate assessment to be efficient, problem focused, and effective.

□ References

Alden, L. E., Wiggins, J. S., & Pincus, A. L. (1990). Construction of circumplex scales for the Inventory of Interpersonal Problems. *Journal of Personality Assessment, 55*, 521–536.

Anastasi, A. (1988). *Psychological testing* (6th ed.). Upper Saddle River, NJ: Prentice Hall.

Aron, B. (1949). *A manual for analysis of the Thematic Apperception Test, a method and technique for personality research*. Berkeley, CA: Willis E. Berg.

Arnold, M. B. (1962). *Story sequence analysis: A new method of measuring motivation and predicting achievement.* New York: Columbia University Press.

Aronow, E., Weiss, K. A., & Reznikoff, M. (2001). *A practical guide to the Thematic Apperception Test: The TAT in clinical practice*. Philadelphia: Brunner-Routledge.

Atkinson, J. W. (1958) (Ed.). *Motives in fantasy, action, and society: A method of assessment and study.* Princeton, NJ: Van Nostrand.

Atkinson, J. W. (1981). Studying personality in the context of an advanced motivational psychology. *American Psychologist, 36*, 117–128.

Atkinson, J. W., & Birch, D. (1970). *The dynamics of action*. New York: John Wiley and Sons.

Atkinson, J. W., Bongort, K., & Price, L. H. (1977). Explorations using computer simulation to comprehend thematic apperceptive measurement of motivation. *Motivation and Emotion, 1*, 1–27.

Baumann, N., Kaschel, R., & Kuhl, J. (2005). Striving for unwanted goals: Stress-dependent discrepancies between explicit and implicit achievement motives, reduce subjective well-being and increase psychosomatic symptoms. *Journal of Personality and Social Psychology, 89*(5), 781–799.

Bellak, L. (1954). *The Thematic Apperception Test and the Children's Apperception Test in clinical use.* New York: Grune and Stratton.

Bellak, L. (1993). *The Thematic Apperception Test, the Children's Apperception Test, and the Senior Apperception Technique in clinical use* (5th ed.). Boston: Allyn and Bacon.

Benjamin, L. S. (1993). *Interpersonal diagnosis and treatment of personality disorders.* New York: Guilford Press.

Blankenship, V., Vega, C. M., Ramos, E., Romero, K., Warren, K., Keenan, et al. (2006). Using the multifaceted Rasch model to improve the TAT/PSE measure of need for achievement. *Journal of Personality Assessment, 86*(1), 100–114.

Blankenship, V., and Zoota, A. (1998). Comparing power imagery in TATs written by hand or on the computer. *Behavior Research Methods, Instruments, and Computers, 30*(3), 441–448.

Block, J. (1965). *The challenge of response sets: Unconfounding meaning, acquiescence, and social desirability in the MMPI.* New York: Appleton-Century-Crofts.

Bornstein, R. F. (1996). Construct validity of the Rorschach Oral Dependency Scale: 1967–1995. *Psychological Assessment, 8,* 200–205.

Bornstein, R. F. (1998). Implicit and self-attributed dependency strivings: Differential relationships to laboratory and field measures of help seeking. *Journal of Personality and Social Psychology, 75*(3), 778–787.

Brunstein, J. C., & Maier, G. W. (2005). Implicit and self-attributed motives to achieve: Two separate but interacting needs. *Journal of Personality and Social Psychology, 89*(2), 205–222.

Campbell, D. T. (1996). Unresolved issues in measurement validity: An autobiographical overview. *Psychological Assessment, 8*(4), 363–368.

Campbell, D. T., & Fiske, D. W. (1959). Convergent and discriminant validation by the multitrait-multimethod matrix. *Psychological Bulletin, 56*(2), 81–105.

Carnap, R. (1936). Testability and meaning. *Philosophy of Science, 3,* 420–471.

Carnap, R. (1937). Testability and meaning—Continued. *Philosophy of Science, 4,* 1–40.

Costantino, G., Dana, R. H., & Malgady, R. (2007). *TEMAS (Tell-Me-A-Story) assessment in multicultural societies.* Mahwah, NJ: Lawrence Erlbaum.

Costantino, G., Malgady, R., & Rogler, L. H. (2002). *TEMAS (Tell-Me-A-Story) manual.* Los Angeles: Western Psychological Services.

Cox, B., & Sargent, H. (1950). TAT responses of emotionally disturbed and emotionally stable children: Clinical judgment versus normative data. *Journal of Projective Techniques, 14,* 60–74.

Cramer, P. (1991). *The development of defense mechanisms: Theory, research and assessment.* New York: Springer-Verlag.

Cramer, P. (1996). *Storytelling, narrative, and the Thematic Apperception Test.* New York: Guilford Press.

Cramer, P. (2005). Another "lens" for understanding therapeutic change: The interaction of IQ with defense mechanisms. In J. S. Auerbach, K. N. Levy, and C. E. Schaffer (Eds.), *Relatedness, self-definition and mental representation: Essays in honor of Sidney J. Blatt* (pp. 120–133). New York: Routledge.

Cramer, P. (2006). *Protecting the self: Defense mechanisms in action.* New York: Guilford Press.

Cramer, P., & Blatt, S. J. (1990). Use of the TAT to measure change in defense mechanisms following intensive psychotherapy. *Journal of Personality Assessment, 54,* 236–251.

Cramer, P., & Blatt, S. J. (1993). Change in defense mechanisms following intensive treatment, as related to personality organization and gender. In W. Ehlers, U. Hentschel, G. Smith, and J. G. Draguns (Eds.), *The concept of defense mechanisms in contemporary psychology* (pp. 310–320). New York: Springer-Verlag.

Cramer, P., Blatt, S. J., & Ford, R. Q. (1988). Defense mechanisms in the anaclitic and introjective personality configuration. *Journal of Consulting and Clinical Psychology, 56,* 610–616.

Cronbach, L. J., & Meehl, P. E. (1955). Construct validity in psychological tests. *Psychological Bulletin, 52,* 281–302.

Crowne, D. P., & Marlowe, D. (1960). A new scale of social desirability independent of psychopathology. *Journal of Consulting Psychology, 24,* 349–354.

Cureton, E. E. (1951). Validity. In E. F. Lindquist (Ed.), *Educational measurement* (pp. 621–694). Washington DC: American Council on Education.

Cutter, H. S., Boyatzis, R. E., & Clancy, D. D. (1977). Effectiveness of power motivation training in rehabilitating alcoholics. *Journal of Studies on Alcohol, 38,* 131–141.

Dana, R. H. (1955a). Clinical diagnosis and objective TAT scoring. *Journal of Abnormal and Social Psychology, 50*(1), 19–24.

Dana, R. H. (1955b). The objectification of projective techniques: Rationale. *Psychological Reports, 1,* 93–102.

Dana, R. H. (1959). A proposal for the objective scoring of the TAT. *Perceptual and Motor Skills, 9,* 27–43.

Dana, R. H. (1993). *Multicultural assessment perspectives for professional psychology.* Needham Heights, MA: Allyn and Bacon.

Dana, R. H. (1998). *Understanding cultural identity in intervention and assessment.* Thousand Oaks, CA: Sage Publications.

Dana, R. H. (2005). *Multicultural assessment: Principles, applications, and examples.* Mahwah, NJ: Lawrence Erlbaum.

De Vos, G. A., & De Vos, E. S. (2004). *Basic dimensions in conscious thought: The self and socialization of human concerns.* Lanham, MD: Rowman and Littlefield.

Douglas, C. (1993). *Translate this darkness: The life of Christiana Morgan.* New York: Simon and Schuster.

Endler, N. S., & Magnusson, D. (1976). Toward an interactional psychology of personality. *Psychological Bulletin, 83,* 956–974.

Entwisle, D. R. (1972). To dispel fantasies about fantasy-based measures of achievement motivation. *Psychological Bulletin, 77*(6), 377–391.

Eron, L. D. (1950). A normative study of the Thematic Apperception Test. *Psychological Monographs, 64*(9), Whole No. 315.

Exner, J. E., Jr. (1978). *The Rorschach: A comprehensive system, Vol. 2: Current research and advanced interpretation.* Oxford: John Wiley and Sons.

Exner, J. E., Jr. (1986). *The Rorschach: A comprehensive system, Vol. 1: Basic foundations* (2nd ed.). New York: John Wiley and Sons.

Exner, J. E., Jr. (2003). *The Rorschach: A comprehensive system, Vol. 1: Basic foundations* (4th ed.). Hoboken, NJ: John Wiley & Sons, Inc.

Fabrick, J. M. (2000). *The Thematic Apperception Test: The relationship between scored fantasy aggression and aggressive behavior.* Unpublished master's thesis, University of North Texas.

Fine, R. (1955). A scoring scheme for the TAT and other verbal projective techniques. *Journal of Projective Techniques, 19,* 306–316.

Finn, S. E. (2007). *In our clients' shoes: Theory and techniques of therapeutic assessment.* Mahwah, NJ: Erlbaum.

Finn, S. E., & Tonsager, M. E. (1992). Therapeutic effects of providing MMPI-2 test feedback to college students awaiting therapy. *Psychological Assessment, 4,* 278–287.

Finn, S. E., & Tonsager, M. E. (1997). Information-gathering and therapeutic models of assessment: Complementary paradigms. *Psychological Assessment, 9*(4), 374–385.

Fischer, C. T. (1994). *Individualizing psychological assessment.* Hillsdale, NJ: Lawrence Erlbaum.

Fleming, J. (1982). Projective and psychometric approaches to measurement: The case of fear of success. In A. J. Stewart (Ed.), *Motivation and society* (pp. 63–96). San Francisco: Jossey-Bass.

Fosberg, I. A. (1949). On teaching projective techniques in an academic setting. *Journal of Clinical Psychology, 5,* 409–414.

Frank, L. K. (1939). Projective methods for the study of personality. *Journal of Psychology: Interdisciplinary and Applied, 8,* 389–413.

Friedman, I. (1957). Objectifying the subjective: A methodological approach to the TAT. *Journal of Projective Techniques, 21,* 243–247.

Ganellen, R. J. (1996). *Integrating the Rorschach and the MMPI-2 in personality assessment.* Mahwah, NJ: Lawrence Erlbaum Associates.

Gieser, L., & Stein, M. I. (1999). *Evocative images: The Thematic Apperception Test and the art of projection.* Washington, DC: American Psychological Association.

Guilford, J. P. (1946). New standards for test evaluation. *Educational and Clinical Management, 6,* 427–438.

Guilford, J. P. (1954). *Psychometric methods.* New York: McGraw-Hill.

Gulliksen, H. (1950). *Theory of mental tests.* New York: Wiley.

Hafner, A. J., & Kaplan, A. M. (1960). Hostility content analysis of the Rorschach and TAT. *Journal of Projective Techniques, 24,* 137–143.

Harder, D. W. (1979). The assessment of ambitious-narcissistic character style with three projective tests: The Early Memories, TAT, and Rorschach. *Journal of Personality Assessment, 43*(1), 23–32.

Harrison, R., & Rotter, J. B. (1945). A note on the reliability of the Thematic Apperception Test. *Journal of Abnormal and Social Psychology, 40,* 97–99.

Haworth, M. R. (1963). A schedule for the analysis of CAT responses. *Journal of Projective Techniques and Personality Assessment, 27,* 181–184.

Haworth, M. R. (1966). *The CAT: Facts about fantasy.* Oxford, England: Grune and Stratton, Inc.

Helms, J. E. (1992). Why is there no study of cultural equivalence in standardized cognitive ability testing. *American Psychologist, 47*(9), 1083–1101.

Henry, W. E. (1956). *The analysis of fantasy: The thematic apperception technique in the study of personality.* New York: Wiley.

Heyns, R. W., Veroff, J., & Atkinson, J. W. (1958) A scoring manual for the affiliation motive. In J. W. Atkinson (Ed.), *Motives in fantasy, action, and society* (pp. 205–218). Princeton, N.J.: Van Nostrand.

Hibbard, S., Mitchell, D., & Porcerelli, J. (2001). Internal consistency of the object relations and social cognition scales for the Thematic Apperception Test. *Journal of Personality Assessment, 77*(3), 408–419.

Holt, R. R. (1956). Gauging primary and secondary processes in Rorschach responses. *Journal of Projective Techniques, 20,* 14–25.

Holt, R. R. (1978). *Methods in clinical psychology.* New York: Plenum Press.

Holt, R. R., & Thompson, C. E. (1950). Bibliography for the TAT. *Journal of Projective Techniques, 14,* 80–100.

Howard, G. S. (1991). Culture tales: A narrative approach to thinking, cross-cultural psychology, and psychotherapy. *American Psychologist, 46,* 187–197.

Jenkins, S. R. (1987). Need for achievement and women's careers over 14 years: Evidence for occupational structure effects. *Journal of Personality and Social Psychology, 53*(5), 922–932.

Jenkins, S. R. (1994). Need for power and women's careers over 14 years: Structural power, job satisfaction, and motive change. *Journal of Personality and Social Psychology, 66,* 155–165.

Jenkins, S. R. (1996). Self-definition in thought, action, and life path choices. *Personality and Social Psychology Bulletin, 22,* 99–111.

Karon, B. P. (1966). Reliability: Paradigm or paradox, with especial reference to personality tests. *Journal of Projective Techniques and Personality Assessment, 30,* 223–227.

Karon, B. P. (1981). The Thematic Apperception Test (TAT). In A. I. Rabin (Ed.), *Assessment with projective techniques: A concise introduction* (pp. 85–120). New York: Springer.

Kelly, F. D. (1996). *Object relations assessment in younger children: Rorschach and TAT measures.* Springfield, IL: Charles C. Thomas.

Kelly, F. D. (1997). *The assessment of object relations phenomena in adolescents: TAT and Rorschach measures.* Mahwah, NJ: Lawrence Erlbaum.

Klinger, E. (1966). Fantasy need achievement as a motivational construct. *Psychological Bulletin, 66*(4), 291–308.

Koestner, R., & McClelland, D. C. (1992). The affiliation motive. In C. P. Smith (Ed.), *Motivation and personality: Handbook of thematic content analysis* (pp. 205–210). New York: Cambridge University Press.

Kuhn, T. S. (1962). *The structure of scientific revolutions.* Chicago: University of Chicago Press.

Leary, T. F. (1957). *Interpersonal diagnosis of personality.* New York: Ronald Press.

LeVine, R. A., Strangman, E., & Unterberger, L. (1966). *Dreams and deeds: Achievement motivation in Nigeria.* Chicago: University of Chicago Press.

Libo, L. M. (1956). *Picture impressions: A projective technique for investigating the patient–therapist relationship.* Baltimore: University of Maryland Medical School, Dept. of Psychiatry Publication Series.

Libo, L. M. (1957). The projective expression of patient–therapist attraction. *Journal of Clinical Psychology, 13,* 33–36.

Litwin, G. H., & Stringer, R. A., Jr. (1968). *Motivation and organizational climate.* Boston: Division of Research, Graduate School of Business Administration, Harvard University.

Lundy, A. L. (1985). The reliability of the Thematic Apperception Test. *Journal of Personality Assessment, 49,* 141–145.

Lundy, A. L. (1988). Instructional set and Thematic Apperception Test validity. *Journal of Personality Assessment, 52,* 309–320.

Magnusson, D. (1988). *Individual development from an interactional perspective: A longitudinal study.* Hillsdale, NJ: Lawrence Erlbaum Associates.

Masling, J., Rabie, L., & Blondheim, S. H. (1967). Obesity, level of aspiration and Rorschach and TAT measures of oral dependence. *Journal of Consulting Psychology, 31,* 233–239.

McAdams, D. P. (1980). A thematic coding system for the intimacy motive. *Journal of Research in Personality, 14*(4), 413–432.

McAdams, D. P. (1985). *Power, intimacy, and the life story: Personological inquiries into identity.* Homewood, IL: Dorsey.

McAdams, D. P. (1997). *The stories we live by: Personal myths and the making of the self.* New York: Guilford Press.

McClelland, D. C. (1961). *The achieving society.* Princeton, NJ: Van Nostrand.

McClelland, D. C. (1965). N Achievement and entrepreneurship: A longitudinal study. *Journal of Personality and Social Psychology, 1,* 389–392.

McClelland, D. C. (1975). *Power: The inner experience.* New York: Irvington Press.

McClelland, D. C. (1977). The impact of power motivation training on alcoholics. *Journal of Studies on Alcohol, 38,* 142–144.

McClelland, D. C. (1980). Motive dispositions: The merits of operant and respondent measures. In L. Wheeler (Ed.), *Review of personality and social psychology* (Vol. 1) (pp. 10–41). Beverly Hills, CA: Sage Publications.

McClelland, D. C. (1981). Is personality consistent? In A. I. Rabin, J. Aronoff, A. M. Barclay, & R. A. Zucker (Eds.), *Further explorations in personality* (pp. 87–113). New York: Wiley.

McClelland, D. C. (1985a). *Human motivation.* Glenview, IL: Scott, Foresman.

McClelland, D. C. (1985b). How motives, skills, and values determine what people do. *American Psychologist, 40,* 812–825.

McClelland, D. C. (1989). Motivational factors in health and disease. *American Psychologist, 44,* 675–683.

McClelland, D. C., Atkinson, J. W., Clark, R. A., & Lowell, E. L., (1953). *The achievement motive.* Cambridge, MA: Appleton-Century-Crofts.

McClelland, D. C., Clark, R. A., Roby, T. B., & Atkinson, J. W. (1949). The projective expression of needs. IV. The effect of the need for achievement on thematic apperception. *Journal of Experimental Psychology, 39*(2), 242–255.

McClelland, D. C., Davis, W. N., Kalin, R., & Wanner, E. (1972). *The drinking man: Alcohol and human motivation.* New York: Free Press.

McClelland, D. C., & Koestner, R. (1992). The achievement motive. In C.P. Smith (Ed.), *Motivation and personality: Handbook of thematic content analysis* (pp. 143–152). New York: Cambridge University Press.

McClelland, D. C., Koestner, R., & Weinberger, J. (1989). How do self-attributed and implicit motives differ? *Psychological Review, 96,* 690–702.

McClelland, D. C., & Winter, D. G. (1969). *Motivating economic achievement.* New York: Free Press.

Meloy, J., and Gacono, C. (1993). The aggression response and the Rorschach. *Journal of Clinical Psychology, 48,* 104–113.

Meyer, G. J. (1999). The convergent validity of MMPI and Rorschach Scales: An extension using profile scores to define response and character styles on both methods and a reexamination of simple Rorschach response frequency. *Journal of Personality Assessment,* 72, 1–35.

Meyer, G. J. (2004). The reliability and validity of the Rorschach and Thematic Apperception Test (TAT) compared to other psychological and medical procedures: An analysis of systematically gathered evidence. In M. J. Hilsenroth, D. L. Segal, & M. Hersen (Eds.), *Comprehensive handbook of psychological assessment* (Vol. 2) (pp. 315–342). Hoboken, NJ: John Wiley and Sons.

Meyer, G. J., Riethmiller, R. J., Brooks, R. D., Benoit, W. A., & Handler, L. (2000). A replication of Rorschach and MMPI-2 convergent validity. *Journal of Personality Assessment, 74*(2), 175–215.

Mihura, J. L., & Alperin, R. (2000, March). *What are introductory psychology textbooks telling students about the Rorschach?* Paper presented at the annual meeting of the Society for Personality Assessment, Albuquerque, NM.

Mischel, W. (1968). *Personality and assessment.* New York: Wiley.

Murray, H. A. (1938). *Explorations in personality.* New York: Oxford University Press.

Murray, H. A. (1943). *Thematic Apperception Test manual.* Cambridge, MA: Harvard University Press.

Murstein, B. I. (1972). Normative written TAT responses for a college sample. *Journal of Personality Assessment, 36*(2), 109–147.

Neugarten, B. L., & Gutmann, D. L. (1958). Age-sex roles and personality in middle age: A thematic apperception study. *Psychological Monographs, 72*(17, Whole No. 470).

Pang, J. S., & Schultheiss, O. C. (2005). Assessing implicit motives in U.S. college students: Effects of picture type and position, gender and ethnicity, and cross-cultural comparisons. *Journal of Personality Assessment, 85,* 280–294.

Piotrowski, Z. A. (1950). A new evaluation of the Thematic Apperception Test. *Psychoanalytic Review, 37*(2), 101–127.

Reuman, D. A. (1982). Ipsative behavioral variability and the quality of thematic apperceptive measurement of the achievement motive. *Journal of Personality and Social Psychology, 43*(5), 1098–1110.

Robinson, F. G. (1992). *Love's story told: A life of Henry A. Murray.* Cambridge, MA: Harvard University Press.

Schorr, A. (1993). Projective testing in behavior therapy. *European Journal of Psychological Assessment, 9*(3), 213–221.

Schultheiss, O. C., & Brunstein, J. C. (1999). Goal imagery: Bridging the gap between implicit motives and explicit goals. *Journal of Personality, 67,* 1–38.

Schultheiss, O. C., & Brunstein, J. C. (2001). Assessment of implicit motives with a research version of the TAT: Picture profiles, gender differences, and relations to other personality measures. *Journal of Personality Assessment, 77,* 71–86.

Schultheiss, O. C., Wirth, M. M., Torges, C. M., Pang, J. S., Villacorta, M. A., & Welsh, K. M. (2005). Effects of implicit power motivation on men's and women's implicit learning and testosterone changes after social victory or defeat. *Journal of Personality and Social Psychology, 88,* 174–188.

Schwarz, N. (1999). Self reports: How the questions shape the answers. *American Psychologist, 54*(2), 93–105.

Shatin, L. (1953). Rorschach adjustment and the Thematic Apperception Test. *Journal of Projective Techniques, 17,* 92–101.

Shatin, L. (1955). Relationships between the Rorschach Test and the Thematic Apperception Test. *Journal of Projective Techniques, 19,* 317–331.

Shentoub, V. (1990). *Manuel d'utilisation du TAT.* Paris: Dunod.

Shneidman, E. S. (1951). *Thematic test analysis.* New York: Grune and Stratton.

Shneidman, E. S. (1959). Symposium: Current aspects of the problem of validity: Suggestions for the delineation of validation studies. *Journal of Projective Techniques, 23,* 259–262.

Shorr, J. E. (1948). A proposed system for scoring the TAT. *Journal of Clinical Psychology, 4,* 189–194.

Singer, M. T., & Wynne, L. C. (1966). Principles for scoring communication defects and deviances in parents of schizophrenics: Rorschach and TAT scoring manuals. *Psychiatry, 29,* 260–288.

Smith, C. P. (Ed.). (1992a). *Motivation and personality: Handbook of thematic content analysis.* New York: Cambridge University Press.

Smith, C. P. (1992b). Reliability issues. In C. P. Smith (Ed.), *Motivation and personality: Handbook of thematic content analysis* (pp. 126–139). New York: Cambridge University Press.

Smith, C. P., Feld, S. C., & Franz, C. E. (1992). Methodological considerations: Steps in research employing content analysis systems. In C. P. Smith (Ed.), *Motivation and personality: Handbook of thematic content analysis* (pp. 515–536). New York: Cambridge University Press.

Spangler, W. D. (1992). Validity of questionnaire and TAT measures of need for achievement: Two meta-analyses. *Psychological Bulletin, 112,* 140–154.

Stein, M. L. (1981). *The Thematic Apperception Test* (2nd ed). Springfield, IL: Charles C. Thomas Publisher.

Stenzel, A. K., & Feeney, H. M. (1970). *Learning by the case method: Practical approaches for community leaders*. New York: Seabury Press.

Stewart, A. J. (1980). Personality and situation in the prediction of women's life patterns. *Psychology of Women Quarterly, 5,* 195–106.

Stewart, A. J. (1978). A longitudinal study of coping styles in self-defining and socially defined women. *Journal of Consulting and Clinical Psychology, 46,* 1079–1084.

Stewart, A. J. (1980). Personality and situation in the prediction of women's life patterns. *Psychology of Women Quarterly, 5,* 195–206.

Stewart, A. J. (1992). Self-definition and social definition: Personal styles reflected in narrative style. In C. P. Smith (Ed.), *Motivation and personality: Handbook of thematic content analysis* (pp. 481–488). New York: Cambridge University Press.

Stewart, A. J., & Winter, D. G. (1974). Self-definition and social definition in women. *Journal of Personality, 42,* 238–259.

Stone, H. (1956). The TAT aggressive content scale. *Journal of Projective Techniques, 20,* 445–452.

Streiner, D. L. (2003). Starting at the beginning: An introduction to coefficient alpha and internal consistency. *Journal of Personality Assessment, 80*(1), 99–103.

Stricker, G. (2006). The local clinical scientist, evidence-based practice, and personality assessment. *Journal of Personality Assessment, 86*(1), 4–9.

Stricker, G., & Healey, B. J. (1990). Projective assessment of object relations: A review of the empirical literature. *Psychological Assessment,* 2(3), 219–230.

Teglasi, H. (1993). *Clinical use of story telling: Emphasizing the T.A.T. with children and adolescents.* Needham Heights, MA: Allyn and Bacon.

Teglasi, H. (2001). *Essentials of TAT and other storytelling techniques assessment.* New York: John Wiley and Sons.

Thorndike, R. L. (1985). Reliability. *Journal of Counseling and Development, 63,* 528–530.

Tomkins, S. (1947). *The Thematic Apperception Test: The theory and technique of interpretation.* New York: Grune and Stratton.

Tuerlinckx, F., DeBoeck, P., & Lens, W. (2002). Measuring needs with the Thematic Apperception Test: A psychometric study. *Journal of Personality and Social Psychology, 82,* 448–461.

Urist, J. (1977). The Rorschach Test and the assessment of object relations. *Journal of Personality Assessment, 41*(1), 3–9.

Vane, J. R. (1981). The Thematic Apperception Test: A review. *Clinical Psychology Review, 1,* 319–336.

Veroff, J., & Feld, S. C (1970). *Marriage and work in America: A study of motives and roles.* New York: Van Nostrand-Reinhold.

Weisskopf, E. A. (1950). A transcendence index as a proposed measure in the TAT. *Journal of Psychology, 29,* 379–390.

Weisskopf-Joelson, E. (1955). Some speculations concerning the selection of clinical psychologists. *Journal of Abnormal and Social Psychology, 51,* 697–699.

Westen, D., Lohr, N., Silk, K. R., Gold, L., & Kerber, K. (1990). Object relations and social cognition in borderlines, major depressives, and normals: A Thematic Apperception Test analysis. *Psychological Assessment, 2*(4), 355–364.

Williams, R. L. (1972). *Themes Concerning Blacks Test and manual.* Saint Louis, Missouri: R. L. Williams & Associates.

Winter, D. G. (1973). *The power motive.* New York: Free Press.

Winter, D. G. (1987). Leader appeal, leader performance, and motive profiles of leaders and followers: A study of American presidents and elections. *Journal of Personality and Social Psychology, 52,* 196–202.

Winter, D. G. (1991). Measuring personality at a distance: Development of an integrated system for scoring motives in running text. In A. J. Stewart, J. M. Healy, Jr., & D. J. Ozer (Eds.), *Perspectives in Personality: Approaches to understanding lives* (Part B, pp. 59–89). London: Jessica Kingsly Publishers.

Winter, D. G. (1992). Power motivation revisited. In C. P. Smith (Ed.), *Motivation and personality: Handbook of thematic content analysis* (pp. 301–310). New York: Cambridge University Press.

Winter, D. G., John, O. P., Stewart, A. J., Klohnen, E. C., & Duncan, L. E. (1998). Traits and motives: Toward an integration of two traditions in personality research. *Psychological Review, 105*(2), 230–250.

Winter, D. G., & Stewart, A. J. (1977). Power motive reliability as a function of retest instructions. *Journal of Consulting and Clinical Psychology, 45,* 436–440.

Woike, B. A. (1995). Most-memorable experiences: Evidence for a link between implicit and explicit motives and social cognitive processes in everyday life. *Journal of Personality and Social Psychology, 68,* 1081–1091.

Woike, B. A., Lavezzary, E., & Barsky, J. (2001). The influence of implicit motives on memory processes. *Journal of Personality and Social Psychology, 81,* 935–945.

Zachar, P., & Leong, F. T. L. (2000). A 10-year longitudinal study of scientist and practitioner interests in psychology: Assessing the Boulder Model. *Professional Psychology: Research and Practice, 31,* 575–580.

Zubin, J., Eron, L. D., & Schumer. F. (1965). *An experimental approach to projective techniques.* New York: Wiley.

2

CHAPTER

Teaching How to Learn Reliable Scoring

Sharon Rae Jenkins

☐ Introduction

Accurate, efficient, even enjoyable scoring is key to both scientific clinical use of thematic apperceptive techniques (TATs) and the rapid production of research using structured scoring systems. Successful teaching and learning of low-inference structured scoring systems provides more systematic structure for the learning process than does teaching idiographically organized clinical TAT interpretation; these differ dramatically. Perhaps the best argument for structured systems is that they make learning good idiographic interpretation possible in less than 10 years. There will never be a substitute for 10 years' experience, but structured systems give the clinician some skills to use productively meanwhile.

Academic faculty approach teaching quite differently from clinicians. The former provide more systematic structure for information and processes, whereas the latter tend to see structure as an imposition on the client's preexisting structure (which for novice clinicians it sometimes is). For these systems, a less structured teaching strategy is inefficient at best and frustrating to the scorer at worst. Good teaching, like good parenting, arguably requires reliable structure and seriousness of purpose at the outset, with a gradual lessening of external controls as structure and process become internalized.

The manuals in this book provide a structure and materials for self-teaching, and the Appendix to this chapter gives directions to the scorer for using them. The teaching process can best be described as teaching how to learn reliable scoring, more a matter of supervision and guidance in the concept formation process than of pedagogy. This chapter presents some guidelines for supervision of those working with these materials so as to develop scoring expertise rapidly and accurately.

This chapter is designed to help both the individual learning alone and the supervisor of trainees (the latter may be experienced professionals or undergraduate students—or nonstudents). The former may turn at the end of the next section directly to the Appendix, and then review the remainder of this chapter as needed for clarification. The Appendix is directed to the trainee to guide self-teaching, and is designed to stand alone or to supplement a supervisor's guidance. Most of the rest of this chapter is directed to the supervisor.

Orientation to the Scoring Process

Objective observation, meaning that two individuals following the same observation rules under the same conditions will note the same phenomenon, is a central rule of empirical psychological science (e.g., Carnap, 1936). The scoring manuals in this volume provide a variety of such rule systems that have shown adequate objectivity in previous research. However, the application of these rules by research teams in other laboratories might reveal unarticulated theoretical assumptions and unexpected effects of cultural differences. Training scorers to apply manuals accurately and to follow them consistently thus involves not only learning the manual as given, but also attending to any needed local cultural adaptations (Hwang, 2006; Jenkins, 2000). This labor-intensive process has historically been an impediment to research with both TATs and the Rorschach systems.

This chapter is designed to reduce that impediment by describing the group learning process used in my lab with several of the systems in this book (Dobbs, Leeper, & Jenkins, 2004; Jenkins, Dobbs, & Leeper, 2004, 2005; White, McFarland, Londenberg, Chlipala, & Jenkins, 2004). Just as these structured scoring systems make the interpretation of stories more focused and efficient for specific purposes, so also the group learning process herein described can expedite scoring while also improving accuracy and reducing scorer attrition.

Considering scorer training as a developmental process with three phases allows for the differing needs of scorers at each phase. A more structured first phase facilitates rapid learning of the system's structure and content and establishes group norms for the scoring process. In the second phase, shifting the responsibility for structure to the group builds scorer competence and confidence while also supporting convergence on a shared cognitive strategy. In the third phase, supporting increased autonomy with continued objectivity as the internalization process is completed minimizes scorer drift and makes the scoring process more efficient and faster. Allowing a minimal level of error by omission ensures that scoring will be conservative, reduces false positives, and improves specificity. It also reduces scorer boredom, burnout, and attrition from the project.

Learning a scoring system is best done with an intensive period of work in which the trainee first studies the manual closely, and then reads and scores a number of stories systematically, looking for specific features that are identified by the manual. These features are described by the manual's scoring categories in terms of the words, phrases, images, or other patterns in the story that are to be given a score. The score might be a simple notation of presence or absence of the feature, or might involve rating the feature—or the whole story—on an ordinal scale representing the degree or intensity of the feature. Quite complex and subtle characteristics of stories can be scored in this way, provided that the description in the manual is sufficiently clear and specific.

For individuals learning on their own, a partner is extremely helpful at some point in the process, first as a sounding board for alternative understandings of a category or scoring dilemma. Second, in order to report interscorer reliability on the new data, a second scorer (and perhaps a third) will be needed. Third, having two learners who can confer to develop any scoring conventions that may be necessary is more likely to result in reliable scoring, that is, scoring with which scorers trained in other situations would agree. For most of the systems in this volume, scoring partners need not be psychologists; the Appendix was developed for undergraduates.

The following sections present my approach to supervising the learning process, which is heavily indebted to my graduate education in TAT scoring with Jacqueline Fleming and Abigail Stewart, and which comes from the methodological paradigm described in more detail by Smith, Feld, and Franz (1992). For readability, I have omitted numerous well-deserved personal communication citations to Fleming and Stewart, and others to the Smith, Feld, and Franz chapter, which my training predated.

The Appendix summarizes what I have said to my student scorer groups for the past several years, and consists of edited transcripts of my instructions to a recent scoring group that I conducted. Lately, I have been able to hand students the Appendix and a manual with only a polite preamble, and they have been able to proceed rapidly into our scoring groups with little further active direction from me; however, as described in the phase 3 section of this chapter, ongoing monitoring of interscorer reliability is important. The Appendix is designed to be copied and given to scorer trainees, along with a copy of the scoring manual to be studied for the next meeting.

Components of effective supervised learning include (1) proper selection and preparation of trainees; (2) clear initial orientation that begins with more structure, teaches problem solving, increases the scorer's self-awareness and self-observation, and prepares the scorer for eventual authority over the results; (3) a priori stress innoculation that prepares the trainee for the challenging aspects of the learning process; and (4) for group supervision, good use of the scorer group's process dynamics during training. The next section focuses on undergraduate scorers but applies equally—though with fewer caveats—to graduate students.

Selection and Preparation of Undergraduate Scorer Trainees

In my experience, bright, ambitious undergraduates can become reliable scorers of surprisingly complex systems if taught properly. I prefer to supervise scorers in groups of four to eight—a minimum of two two-person teams, perhaps with an alternate in case of attrition. This is large enough to lighten the load of scoring a large data set and to encourage supportive friendships among the kinds of students who are typically attracted to and selected for this work. It is also large enough to dilute somewhat the possible personality conflicts that may arise with the intensity of collaborative work, and to include a variety of individual perspectives that can cancel each other out in the scoring process and thus reduce scorer drift.

In regular group meetings, individuals often benefit from hearing the reasoning behind others' scoring decisions. A larger sample of individual idiosyncrasies makes it more likely that at least one person will share or understand the idiosyncrasies of the system's author. However, to avoid compounding confusion, it is important that individuals learn not to be wedded to their own unique views if articulating these is distracting the group from the goal of developing a common understanding of the system.

I find that the best undergraduate scorers are bright psychology majors recruited from methods and measurement courses who enjoy learning new things and are verbally astute, motivated to learn about research, bound for graduate school, and needing letters of reference from faculty. The latter extrinsic reasons may be their initial motives for volunteering; the first two are my major selection criteria.

All other things remotely equal, I choose a student who is curious and intrinsically motivated by enjoyment of learning over a student who articulates graduate school ambitions but who cares more about grades or about pleasing me than about exploring ideas for their own sake. My preferred students can use the group process readily to improve their scoring skills and to sustain their reliability. However, they may be more vulnerable than the externally motivated to discouragement and disappointment in themselves during the stressful parts of learning described below. It may be harder for them than for others to manage the initial failure experiences and the later resurgences of same that are involved in the trial-and-error part of the learning process.

In my experience, these undergraduates have some advantages over graduate students as TAT scorers for systems not requiring advanced clinical skills or knowledge of theory; however, the best of them can handle even quite sophisticated systems (see Feffer's Interpersonal Decentering in chapters 8 and 9 of this volume). Those who are essentially pregraduate students are just as bright and curious, but are less overloaded, anxious, and preoccupied than current graduate students—indeed less than they themselves will be in that role eventually. Furthermore, they are probably intellectually underemployed by their undergraduate coursework. Learning to score offers a cure for their boredom by presenting an engaging and challenging task at which they can self-observe their own growing verbal competence. At this earlier stage of their education, they may be a little more concrete, and thus less prone to make abstract inferences that decrease interscorer agreement, compared with graduate students.

Bright undergraduates, and some graduate students, who otherwise make good scorers have corresponding weaknesses that must be managed in teaching them. First, some of the brightest and most creative have largely evaded the education process by virtue of their preexisting verbal skills, and may even have developed a certain contempt for mass higher education, perhaps an artifact of its increasing dependence on large classes and depersonalized multiple-choice testing. Although capable, some are unaccustomed to focusing their considerable resources in a sustained fashion. Proper scorer supervision can give them the necessary discipline and break them of undesirable habits, preparing them for graduate school in attitude as well as in verbal sophistication.

Second, once they recognize a challenge, in rising to it such students may mobilize resources of creativity that decrease interscorer agreement if not controlled. Third, some—most often women—lack insight into their strengths, and their low self-confidence reduces their conviction in mounting a persuasive argument in favor of their scoring decisions, even when their reasoning is sound. They may also tend to obsess.

Supervising scorers in groups helps to control these specific problems, builds character, teaches discipline, and develops academic skills that will serve them well in graduate school. These latter include skill and persistence in mounting a persuasive evidence-based argument and explicating a self-critical insight. This process also increases and maintains their motivation to learn and execute competent scoring. As discussed in a later section, these potential problems are addressed directly in the Appendix and in the brief lecture portions of my first and second group sessions, and indirectly throughout the process by jokes and teasing as well as by the way I structure the process.

Depending on the needs of a particular group, I might also say to reassure anxious strivers and to defuse potential competitiveness, "You are working with the best and brightest of the psychology majors at this university, who are in turn often the brighter undergraduates. Our situation here may be unfamiliar to you; very bright people may be used to being the smartest in any group, and may assume that this is expected of them. Now you are with others, some of whom may be like you in this way, and you may understand that about each other. One reason I chose you all was so that you could learn from each other about your differences and similarities. I will be interested to see what you learn from this about how to work with others who are at your level in some ways. Watch, notice, and learn from what they do. This will be good preparation for graduate school and your future career as a psychologist." One serendipitous benefit of learning to score for graduate students who hope for academic careers is that it enhances one's capacity to focus on picayune detail, arguably a beneficial skill for faculty life.

Use of this group process has important secondary benefits for faculty whose students will be scoring. My scorers are invited to participate in weekly undergraduate research team meetings as one benefit of their labors. These meetings serve a variety of informal training purposes that incorporate both their own proffered agendas (e.g., information about graduate study, how to choose a graduate school, how to write an honors thesis) and mine (e.g., training in literature review writing, statistical analysis, and preparation of presentations and publications). Experienced scorers are thus well prepared to use the scored data for honors theses and unusually advanced professional offerings, to the benefit of all concerned and the field as a whole.

☐ The First Phase of Learning

There are three general phases of learning to score: (1) initial work with the manual and practice stories, which teaches the basics of the system, and in group supervision establishes processes for arriving at a common understanding within the group; (2) the move beyond the expert-scored learning materials, which for groups teaches reliance on the collective agreement process for individual scoring decisions; and (3) the move to stories told to different stimuli or by different participant populations, which teaches generalization of this process from familiar material and scoring decisions to new material. Although I give trainees the entire Appendix at the beginning, I pace them through their reading at the points where their experience prepares them to understand what is said. That is, I suggest that they read only the "General Orientation" section at phase 1, then "Tips for Sessions 3–4" before those sessions, phase 2 when the manual's practice stories are exhausted, and phase 3 when the first collaborative story set is completed.

A good scoring group is a better decision maker than any of its members because their individualities will average out with discussion, which likely makes for better interscorer reliability and more generalizable scores. At the initial phase, scorers learn to rely on the manual and expert scoring as absolute authority. As they develop a consensual decision-making process that reinforces close adherence to the scoring manual and expert scoring, group members can internalize that reasoning and can apply it to new material with minimal inference. At the second and third phases, once they have achieved documented reliability, they will move beyond these materials to generalize these principles, recognizing and making decisions from the authority of their own expertise.

Initial Orientation and Instructions

The first phase of learning has three parts: (1) studying the manual; (2) scoring the practice stories; and (3) beginning to develop self-awareness about personal idiosyncrasies that might affect their scoring. These phases and skills probably apply to nearly all content analysis systems—broadly conceived—and can be adapted readily for scoring of similar narrative material such as the Rorschach Comprehensive System (Exner, 2003).

My initial and subsequent structured presentations to trainees about the scoring process define the scoring process and its challenges so as to convey my confidence in their competence, my expectations for their performance, and support for the stresses inherent in the learning process. The first step is to orient them as a group to the process of scoring and its challenges. The essence of this lecture, provided in the first "General Orientation" section of the Appendix, is (1) a general orientation to the scoring process; (2) how to study and learn the manual; (3) how to use the practice scoring materials and expert scoring; and (4) a brief overview of expected stressors. The second (and sometimes third) session is usually spent addressing their questions about the process. In the third or fourth session, we cover "Tips for Sessions 3–4" in the Appendix, which includes (5) how to recognize and manage implicit inferences and (6) how to develop personal scoring notes to complement the manual.

Although the overt purpose of the first lecture is to tell them what to do and how to do it, several less obvious functions are served: (1) to teach them to depend on and internalize the scoring manual and expert scoring of the practice stories as the final authority in scoring decisions; (2) to encourage and support self-critique of their own scoring errors as an important part of the self-teaching process; (3) to prepare them to develop as a group a positive, cooperative working climate that encourages active learning and mutual respect; (4) to defuse some of the potential competitiveness that may develop in students who are accustomed to being the best in any class that they take, and for whom anything less is experienced as a demoralizing failure; and (5) to prepare them for constructive handling of the expected disagreements on scoring decisions that will arise in the learning process.

First Session: General Orientation

When I meet with scorers for the first time, I begin by describing the scoring process as a process of concept formation, the ability to recognize familiar patterns in new material. The learning process is the acquisition of that familiarity to the point where recognition requires little thought, like being able to tell an apple from an orange. I give them each a copy of the Appendix, asking them to read the first sections through "Learning the Manual" and to do what it says for our next meeting, that is, to study the manual thoroughly, making notes as described in the Appendix, and then to score the first 5 to 20 stories, as appropriate to the complexity of the system.

The simpler systems have fewer categories and require primarily recognition of concrete semantic category memberships signaled by a few specific words, such as portions of Steven Huprich's Oral Dependency, or Antoinette Thomas's Affective Scale. A distinction of language here: The Thomas system is a two-step system requiring a first reading to locate scorable material—role relationships—and a second reading to assign a value—affective valence. The phrase *scoring category* does not quite apply to such ordinal scales, as they are scored as alternatives rather than as presence–absence as are most of the others. Some of Barry Ritzler's Picture Projection Test categories are also scored as ordinal scales. More complex systems such as David Ephraim's Psychocultural System, Reuben Fine's Scoring Scheme, Michelle Hoy's Contemporized

Themes Concerning Blacks Test, or Edith Weisskopf's Transcendence Index (all herein) have many categories requiring subtle distinctions. For these, scorers might benefit from learning a handful of categories well before moving on to others.

For most novice scorers, it is easier to grasp the scoring process if on the first day they start by scoring just one or two categories for the first five stories to be scored, review the expert scores for those categories, then score the next one or two categories for the same stories, and so forth. For the simpler systems, they might be able to manage all the categories for 10–20 stories, given 2 or 3 days to do it along with studying the manual. For the most complex systems, I might ask them to score just four or five categories for the first meeting, perhaps for the first week, for only five stories the first session, with graded increases thereafter paced to their comfort level. Those who have scored other systems or other kinds of content analysis will probably find learning these systems to be less challenging and might start with more categories simultaneously.

When they have a sense of the process and the categories, they will be ready to score all categories in each story. However, the most complex systems can be very demanding on the scorer's attention and concentration. For the sake of both efficiency and accuracy with these systems, I would consider first determining the number of variables that scorers seem able to hold in attentional focus simultaneously without strain. Then I might have them score the entire story set—even the entire data set—for just those categories. The remaining categories could be scored by the same scorers on a second pass through the data, or by a second team.

As I structure the group's work process and define the number of stories to be scored for each meeting, I keep in mind the research on human motivation and performance. Need for Achievement (*n* Ach), which likely improves scoring accuracy, is best aroused and maintained by working independently with control over outcomes on tasks that are moderately difficult (challenging), neither too easy (boring) nor too difficult (anxiety arousing or frustrating) and by providing rapid feedback as to task success (McClelland & Koestner, 1992). TAT scoring is thus an excellent activity for arousing and maintaining *n* Ach As the scoring process becomes familiar and easier and threatens to become boring for the experienced scorer, I find that *n* Ach can be maintained by engaging scorers in increasingly difficult tasks so as to pace the level of challenge along with their improved abilities. Such tasks related to scoring include helping them to make more precise verbal distinctions by benchmarking, encouraging them toward increased self-insight and self-awareness, and eventually suggesting that they balance more obsessive distinction making with a more rapid scoring pace, all of which are discussed in following sections.

Second Session: Scorer Group's Problem Solving

This section describes instruction that is best delivered in the second session after the first few stories have been scored. Now you have a chance to shape the group discussion process by example. Your routine questions and prompts in response to the scorers' questions are important examples of the questions that scorers should learn to ask themselves when confronting difficult decisions. Asking this sequence of questions in response to questions about particular scoring decisions models the decision-making process of scoring. It also conveys implicitly your expectation that scorers will have made good-faith efforts to problem solve about their own errors. These questions are as follows:

1. "Let's look at the manual. How far did it take you with this story, and where did you get stuck? What fits, and what doesn't? What words or phrases make it fit, and what makes you uncertain?"

2. "What examples in the manual come closest to the part that gives you trouble? How closely did they fit, and how did they not fit?"

3. "Who [in the group] got this one right? How did you see it? What did you notice that told you it should [not] score?"

4. [To the one who got it wrong:] "Can you make sense of it that way [as in 3]? What note can you add to your manual to help you get it right next time?"

Although this process might seem overly concrete to those accustomed to more idiographic and theory-based interpretation, it allows for the precise rendering of even subtleties such as "emotional tone". The point is to achieve a sufficient tally of specific material, not a thorough, complete, and broad-based interpretation. This approach is also quite effective for working with undergraduates who have been educated recently in states that have emphasized mass standardized educational testing that requires memorized facts as a criterion for high school graduation.

Scorers' responses to these questions make their reasoning processes available for group discussion, which should consist largely of comparisons among scorers' rationales rather than a leader's reiteration of the manual. At this phase, the best rationale is the one most consistent with the manual and in agreement with the expert scoring. As scorers learn to recognize and articulate the features that distinguish this best rationale, they are preparing to move to new material having no expert score.

At the end of the second session, I first ask trainees for feedback about how this process has been working for them. Then I ask how many stories they feel they can score by our next meeting, and we set as a goal the lowest common denominator. Then I say, "What we've accomplished today is to look at the reasoning process that goes between the manual and the expert scoring. Now, after you've finished scoring the first five of the stories for our next meeting, look at the expert scoring and then correct your own scoring. Then score the next five and correct those, and so on. Try to finish [the goal number]. When you're done, look over your errors and see if you can see patterns in them. Then try to go through today's reasoning process yourself and see how far you can get with it. Try to figure out your errors and where you went wrong. What was the expert probably noticing that you missed, or what might have been missing in a response that you scored and the expert didn't? Then in our meeting we'll focus on just those errors where you can't figure out what was wrong." This is the group's routine process until all of the practice stories have been scored, checked, and discussed.

Increasing Self-Observation and Self-Awareness

The first step of increased insight is for scorers to learn to observe their own internal processes as they score, in order to recount and correct their scoring rationales as they learn the system. Such self-observation can be encouraged by questions such as #4 in the previous section that ask for explicit self-correction, and by an emphasis on elaborating on their manual notes to document their decisions. Such documentation should be part of the permanent file for the project. In session 3 or 4, most scorers will be ready to read the Appendix section on "Tips for Sessions 3–4," which is designed to increase self-awareness.

Especially early in the learning process, it is helpful to emphasize *improvement* and *insight into one's individuality* as the criteria for progress in learning rather than *being right* the first time. Accurate self-critique (e.g., "I know I tend to overscore this category because certain stories to this picture remind me of how my family expressed closeness") should be rewarded as an indicator of increasingly sophisticated self–other individuation in forming scoring judgments.

The Scorer Group's Process Dynamics

Once the manual has been learned, application to new data is a social process. When scorers are working as a group, developing a systematic work process will not only improve interscorer reliability, but also keep scorers motivated for productivity. The group's emotional climate can be created and mobilized to facilitate learning and to minimize interpersonal conflicts. An enjoyable group process acts as a secondary incentive for participation by students who rarely can be paid for their work, reducing scorer attrition.

But more important for effective scoring is the development of a collective decision-making process in which individual scorers' personal idiosyncrasies can cancel out as they learn about how their own individuality is reflected in their scoring decisions. It is helpful to have scorers who are aware of the local cultures of the storytellers, because the general principles of the manual might translate accurately into somewhat different words, depending on language and local cultural meanings. For example, in scoring *n* Ach, what counts as a *traditional achievement goal* may differ cross-culturally, and is to be scored consistent with the storyteller's culture.

In the process of splitting fine verbal hairs, my teams sometimes discuss the meanings of particular words in scorers' own families and regional cultures. Some scoring differences arise from personal meanings within scorers' verbal associative networks that come from their own or family members' histories of involvement with particular occupational or leisure-time activities, regional or ethnic cultures, religious traditions, atypical family values, and other sources of individuality that make life interesting and scoring agreements complex (see "Making Your Personal Manual" in the Appendix).

A properly developed group process can help students develop insights into the sources of their individuality that will make them better scorers as they learn to distinguish their personal from more general cultural meanings. (This should also make them better candidates for careers in clinical and counseling psychology.) A *properly developed process* is defined by the group serving this purpose effectively while arousing minimal defensiveness and other undesirable reactions in its members.

At this point, I teach them to use as their frame of reference *what the group would likely agree on* rather than their own individuality as the basis for difficult decisions. To accomplish this, it is necessary to establish from the beginning a group process that reinforces their recognition of each other's valid arguments based on the manual and expert scoring, and that reduces their competitive investment in "being right"—and possible shame at "being wrong"—in their initial decision.

☐ The Second Phase: New Data

The goal of phase 2 is for each scorer to establish and maintain interscorer reliability with the other scorers on previously unscored data, scoring independently without discussion. This requires using a minimal-inference reasoning process to generalize from examples in the manual and practice stories to cover instances not included in either. When the group has converged on sound reasoning processes using the manual and has finished scoring the available practice stories, the group is ready to move beyond the manual's expert scoring to previously unscored data. At this point, I move the whole group to a set of stories told to the same picture, preferably a picture that is well represented in the manual and expert scoring.

(In my lab, stories are organized, typed, and scored by picture to facilitate consistent and efficient scoring. This practice minimizes possible bias among stories told by the same storyteller. For consistent reliability, clinicians should score each of the client's responses independently of all others rather than making some scoring judgments based on scores of other responses. Some clinicians are in the habit of using a client's scores on other stories to shape questionable or unclear scoring decisions in favor of similarity to scores on other stories, violating the rule that stories should be scored independently.)

For some manuals having few practice stories, this move will be precipitated earlier by the exhaustion of those stories. In such cases, the "Tips for Sessions 3–4" section of the Appendix can be assigned at Session 2 and the "Moving to Phase 2" section along with the new story set. More time and discussion might then be needed at phase 2 to establish the necessary consistent distinctions and to elaborate the manual appropriately for the less familiar stories. Good documentation of these elaborations will be especially important in these cases to guide future researchers, and its availability should be noted in publications, as discussed in the section on "Finishing Up."

Phase 2 prepares the scorers to make decisions as a group and to see the group as the authority, in the absence of an external expert. When this learning process has consolidated in phase 3, pairs of students may each work on batches of stories told to different pictures. A *batch* is defined by the group or pair as a reasonable number of stories to finish scoring by the next meeting, the size of which will vary with story length and system difficulty. Because the first batch of stories for any new picture or population will typically generate more disagreements, and thus more discussion, while scorers orient to the new material, I typically start with half the usual number of stories that I would expect to finish were they familiar.

Orientation to Phase 2

The general orientation to phase 2 embeds additional self-esteem stress innoculation in my explanation of the changes in group process. Helpful process changes in the move to new stories are (1) establishing turn taking within the group when reviewing and recording their scoring decisions, and when summarizing the day's work, to equalize their engagement with the process, decision-making power, and the workload, which often results in (2) increasing their reliance on the group's common frame of reference for rationales to support their inferences; and (3) teaching them to formalize the rationale for recurrent picture-specific or population-specific inferences as conventions (e.g., benchmarks) for scoring. You will probably want to decide in advance how you will centralize the recording of individual and consensus scores for the calculation of interscorer reliability and for later data analysis. Each scorer should record the consensus scores for reference in later scoring decisions.

Turn Taking and Reliance on the Group

Whereas in phase 1 discussion was organized by scorers' questions about understanding the manual and its examples, in phase 2 it proceeds systematically through each of the stories that has been scored. The first step of each meeting is to review the scoring for each story in order, by each scorer in turn presenting her or his scores and the others identifying their agreement or disagreement. This turn-taking process sets important process precedents in that it positions each scorer to take responsibility for having an opinion worth considering seriously, and minimizes a tendency to rely on one as a putative expert, which might result in incomplete processing of story information and scoring criteria. Scorer Erin Cobb (personal communication, July 15, 2005) noted that "consistent acquiescence to [an expert partner's] rationales leaves one feeling like a puny pushover. It's pretty easy for me to just nod my head when [given an explanation].... For first-timers, it should be priority to vocalize why you thought something was the way it was. If not, you end up just nodding your head."

A variation on the sequence of questions in phase 1 provides the structure for discussing and reconciling discrepancies in scoring as each occurs. Because scoring should be conservative, the burden of proof is on the ones who scored the category present—or highest, for ordinal scales, unless stated otherwise in the manual—so this scorer addresses the following sets of questions:

1. "Why did you score it [that way/so high]? What did you see in the story that makes it scorable that way? Where in the manual does it describe that as something that would score? How does this meet those criteria? Where does it say that in the story?"

2. "What examples or practice stories are most like that one? How were they scored?" (When the scorer has thus made the case, those who didn't score it [so highly] respond to the third set of questions.)

3. "How did you see it? Did you consider scoring it [that highly]? What told you not to score it?"

Addressing these questions thoroughly at first, and then in more abbreviated form as scorers learn the routine, sets a second important process precedent, establishing the structure of a thorough survey of relevant information when reconciling discrepancies. This serves further to reinforce the importance of considering all opinions, even if one scorer is clearly more accurate than the others and even in those cases for which the non-scorers readily admit having overlooked an obvious piece of evidence. You might then reassure them that anyone can have a moment of oversight and that this is a routine part of learning how to focus their attention in this new way. This gives scorers the opportunity to share their tactics for attention management.

As the group engages in these discussions, they reinforce each other's learning of the manual, identify and learn to manage their individual differences in language use, and build functional working relationships. In the process, they develop a consensual reasoning process and a common frame of reference for applying the manual to storytellers from the cultures represented in the data. It is especially helpful, of course—and in some cases essential—for the major cultural groups represented in the data to be represented likewise in the scorer group. If the scorers have opportunities to discuss their own cultural backgrounds among themselves, it might be easier for them to notice when a particular scoring discrepancy might be rooted in culture-specific experience or use of language.

Using Conventions to Increase Interscorer Reliability

Later in phase 2, when they have become accustomed to the process of reconciling discrepancies, I introduce scorers to the concepts of *interscorer reliability* and *scoring conventions* (see the Appendix section on "Some Common Conventions and Strategies"). There is little on the former in this chapter or the Appendix because the appropriate way of calculating reliability is specific to the mathematical properties and underlying assumptions of each system. Also neglected here are the specific means of computerizing the data, as this process will probably differ among labs; indeed, in my lab, it differs among scoring teams based on individual scorers' computer skills and interests. I do give scorers an oral explanation of the principles and practice of interscorer reliability determination that is appropriate to their system, and, when feasible, I show them a scatterplot of two scorers' scores along with the reliability coefficient for the plot.

New picture stimuli may require finer distinctions on one or more dimensions that are different from the stimuli used for the practice materials, and storytellers from differing populations may respond quite differently to some aspects of the pictures. Thus, each new picture or population might require scorers to agree on certain specific scoring conventions for that situation to produce consistent scoring decisions.

Scorers who have attained consistent reliability with the original practice materials have typically internalized the decision-making process well enough to develop picture-specific scoring conventions that produce consistent local applications of the general rules of the system. If the practice stories are too few to establish reliability, the development of conventions may not be so confident, but remains necessary, as is careful documentation of those decisions and benchmarks. These conventions might, for example, identify specific frequently occurring words, phrases, or images that might be clear in the scoring manual but take on ambiguous meanings in application. These might be loci of disagreements between the scorers in the first set of previously unscored stories and at the beginning of each story set told to an unfamiliar picture.

Benchmarking

In such cases, after the scorers have conferred about their disagreements using the three sets of questions listed in the previous section and have identified several similarly problematic responses, the group of responses should be reviewed together along with the relevant scoring rules. To make a general decision about these cases, it is often helpful to try to put them in some order or in clusters according to one or more relevant similarities and differences. Then it should be possible to decide on one or more cut-points or decision rules that seem most faithful to the manual. Where to draw the line may be somewhat arbitrary. The important thing is to be consistent about where the line is. This process often generates a list of words and phrases that are to be scored and another list that will not score, as described in the Appendix under "Benchmarking." Working with these lists makes scoring both faster and more accurate.

An example of such a specific convention taken from Rorschach Comprehensive System scoring (Exner, 2003) is the use of *talking* as a benchmark for distinguishing active from passive human movement. Arbitrarily, *talking* is scored passive, as is anything more passive than that (e.g., *whispering*); verbs that are more active than *talking* (e.g., *shouting* or even *talking loudly*) are scored as active. Similarly, TAT scorers might review the specific words and phrases often used for a picture in a data set and agree on such benchmarks.

Calculating and Monitoring Interscorer Reliability

In scoring for research purposes, it is necessary to determine and report interscorer reliability for the stories told to each picture separately. This is because for each system and storyteller population, certain pictures are likely to elicit stories that call for difficult decisions regarding one or more categories because of the imagery in the picture. For example, in some populations, Card 1 (boy with violin) elicits many stories about the boy preferring to play with friends rather than practice the violin. Whether or not those stories are scorable for need for Affiliation (*n* Aff; Heyns, Veroff, & Atkinson, 1992) hinges in part on whether *playing with friends* is depicted as motivated by a wish to approach companionship or friendship, or instead to avoid the violin. In such cases, initial interscorer reliability might be low until the problematic cases have been identified and the scoring dilemma articulated and resolved—the purpose of developing conventions.

I typically begin monitoring interscorer reliability with the last 30–50 stories of the story set scored at phase 2, provided that at least 20–30 stories have already been scored and conventions developed. Discussion of the statistical evaluation of interscorer reliability is beyond the scope of this chapter because it is specific to the number of scorers being compared, scalar properties of the scores (nominal/categorical, such as presence–absence content analysis; ordinal, such as ranks and rating scales; interval, such as frequency counts; or ratio, which are generally rare for these scores as a score of 0 usually does not represent a complete absence of the underlying characteristic, only its low representation in the story sample) and the assumptions about the underlying construct (e.g., a simple behavior count; a continuum of personality dispositions divided for convenience into a crude integer scale). The reader should consult appropriate statistical resources, which might include the editorial preferences of journals that are being considered as publication outlets. In our lab, we usually use category agreement (Smith et al., 1992) to monitor agreement on presence of presence–absence categories in each story, and either Spearman's rho or intraclass correlation for summary scores.

Most of the scoring manuals presented here include appropriate interscorer reliability calculations for their systems. Some of the older ones are exceptions in that they use percentage agreement, and it might not be clear whether this is calculated only on presence or on both presence and absence of a category. The latter approach might be inflated by agreement on absence, which results in overestimation of scoring accuracy for infrequent categories (Smith et al., 1992).

If all scorers' interscorer reliability with their consensus scores is at or above the minimum needed for publication, the group is ready to move to phase 3. If not, the group scores another set of stories together in the same way, with interscorer reliability calculated similarly at the end. For a difficult system, challenging stories, or a small sample study, all stories might be scored this way and average reliability with consensus scores reported.

Additional Stress Innoculation

In conjunction with beginning to monitor interscorer reliability—which might induce anxiety or competitive feelings—I continue to talk about the stresses of the learning process. Now I emphasize the challenges presented by the process of articulating and defending one's position for individuals who care about getting things right and not making mistakes (see the Appendix, "Moving to Phase 2"). I emphasize that mistakes are inherent in the learning process and that the point is to learn from them by returning to the manual and studying it carefully to understand why the wrong decision was made and to correct one's thinking. I provide stress innoculation by warning them that these necessary mistakes can be discouraging, especially when they are repeated, and that most people will repeat some.

☐ The Third Phase: Working in Pairs

This phase begins when the group members have attained consistent reliability with each other and their consensus scores—or else have been eased out of the group into an alternative aspect of the research project. The goal in phase 3 is to increase efficiency and speed of scoring without loss of accuracy. For the sake of moving through a large data set, the group may be divided into pairs that score different sets of stories and that confer only with each other to finalize scores. The now familiar aspects of group process that will generalize to work in pairs include turn taking in reviewing scores, and self-critique in consultation now with the pair partner to resolve discrepancies.

At this phase, scorers are typically well practiced in the discrepancy resolution process and can carry out this work in the absence of a supervisor, needing assistance only in the determination of a very few decisions. However, supervision is helpful for the first several pair meetings as they become accustomed to the new data and consolidate their work process, and again as they begin each new story set. The new supervision task at this phase is to begin calculating interscorer reliability between the pairs and with their consensus scores on a regular basis as each story set is finished. As there is no majority when pairs disagree, discrepancy resolution might be a little more complex and depends for its success on the skills and self-confidence developed in the group.

The central data quality issue at this phase is to minimize scoring drift, which is the tendency of individual scorers to become less reliable over time due to regression toward their different individual means. It is helpful for this issue to take care in forming pairs. Whenever possible (i.e., not precluded by scheduling conflicts), I pair scorers who are about equally reliable but not necessarily with each other. That is, I pair scorers who agree *less* within the larger group, preferably who tend toward opposite biases when they disagree, rather than those who score most similarly. This reduces pair-wise scoring drift. It is helpful if they seem to get along well, but more important for data quality that they be equally assertive. Having compatible schedules and other logistical matters should be lesser considerations if these are not absolutely prohibitive.

Orientation to Phase 3

When I orient scorers to phase 3, I typically explain the rationale behind my pairings as given in the previous section, to reinforce their understanding of the importance of thorough discussion and resolution of their differences. I remind them to continue using the group's decision-making process, not only each other, as their frame of reference for interscorer reliability, and to identify and document additional picture- or population-specific conventions that may be needed for stories obtained from new stimuli. When they have completed the first batch or two of stories and have settled their initial conventions, we discuss increasing the pace of scoring and how to reduce infinite regress into interminable analyses. When they will be entering their own data, we discuss any necessary logistics.

Moving Right Along

As their expertise and their capacity for discriminating among fine shades of meaning increase, some scorers may tend to bog down in perseveration over details that are smaller than the storyteller could detect. This is more likely to exhaust the scorer than to improve the accuracy of scoring. It may also generate interminable arguments between scorers about trivial distinctions. These likely will not increase the accuracy of scores but will waste time and risk making the scoring process so tedious and aversive as to reduce accuracy. I prefer to rely on the presence of another scorer to catch possible oversights, and I maintain *n* Ach arousal by suggesting increased speed as a positive value for high performance. I so indicate to the scorers as described in the Appendix. At this stage, as each pair becomes able to sustain acceptable levels of interscorer reliability, I find it helpful to ask them to monitor their scoring pace and try to increase it.

Picking Up the Pace

Suggesting attention to speed can be used to draw further attention to scorers' self-monitoring processes. I invite them to test their growing observational skills by scoring several stories faster than usual, and then going back and reviewing them more slowly to see whether they would change any of their scores. This tactic can be quite effective for systems and categories that rely heavily on visual scanning for literal recognition of keywords and synonyms that might not occur in every story or are even more rare.[1] Accuracy of scoring for these kinds of categories often suffers as much from scorer boredom and inattention as from lack of diligence. However, it should be used with caution for categories that require identification of more complex patterns and those for which each story receives at least one score. For this reason, there is no section in the Appendix on this topic; the supervisor should appraise the capabilities of the scorers in relation to the demands of the system and should address this topic orally as needed.

Avoiding Hypotheticals

Although it may be helpful at earlier stages to discuss scoring decisions in terms of hypotheticals (i.e., what words, if added, changed, or removed would make a response scorable or not), as the distinctions involved become finer this can become tedious and interminable. At that point hypotheticals should be discouraged in favor of responses that have actually occurred. Although there might be some small gain in refinement at that point, the cost to smooth and efficient group functioning outweighs this benefit. At this point, I might say, "Let's let that one go. There will always be one or two responses where even excellent scorers disagree because the story is just not clear. If it hasn't come up before this point, it's really not likely to come up again often enough to make discussing it worthwhile. Let's save our energy and move on."

After a Break

I typically caution scorers not to score when they are too tired or stressed to concentrate effectively, such as during exam week. When a scorer has not scored for a couple of weeks, especially over vacation breaks, a refresher review of the manual is needed, along with rescoring the practice stories and checking against the expert scores. As described in the final Appendix section, it is also helpful to rescore and calculate *intra*scorer reliability for a previously scored story set before beginning a new one. This will be most effective if the former set is somewhat similar to the new one.

Finishing Up

Monitoring and Reporting Accurate Scoring

For TAT scoring systems, good interrater reliability is the primary indicator of score adequacy for research purposes—necessary but not sufficient. Interscorer reliability should be computed and reported separately for stories to each separate stimulus in the data set and for each individual category, perhaps as a range. That for scorers should be tracked to identify any retraining needed, but need not be reported unless requested by a journal. I typically calculate reliability on the last 30–50 stories of each set, after the initial development of conventions, more for systems having rarer presence–absence categories, because a low base rate will lower interscorer reliability, all else equal. Adequate interrater reliability reported for other studies indicates only that it is *possible* to score the system reliably. But as the scores are a product of the stimuli, the stories, the manual, the scorers, and the latter's state of mind as well as expertise, there is no "interrater reliability of the system" beyond its application in a particular study, any more than there is a "the TAT" above and beyond the Murray (1943) picture set.

The interrater reliability calculation indicates only that *these* scorers, working independently, were able to apply the manual to *these* stories consistently so as to arrive at the same conclusions for most of the decisions involved. Inadequate interrater reliability for a study typically indicates slippage in any one or more of these four areas, or a mismatch between them. This could be due to a lack of clarity and specificity in the manual; gaps in the preparation or diligence of the scorers; cultural differences among the manual developer, the storytellers, and the scorers; or some combination of these.

Documentation of Scoring Decisions and Archiving of Revised Manuals

Because of this central role of scoring, and because of the wide variability of stories told by clinical populations—in contrast to the college students so often studied in the human motivation research tradition—questions and dilemmas that arise in the scoring process should be documented and archived as part of a revised manual that is considered part of the data set. This should be made available to other researchers on request for the benefit of consistent application across laboratories, and this availability should be noted in reports. In the event that outside examination of the data becomes desirable, for example by researchers wishing to conduct additional analyses as provided by the American Psychological Association's Ethical Principles and Guidelines, the scoring documentation should be part of the information given.

As a scoring system matures and the scoring rules become more explicit and less ambiguous, less inference is needed in applying the rules to most responses, and the expert scoring in the revised manual appears more consistent to the novice. These refinements are the product of teaching the system to additional scorers and of elaborating the scoring rule descriptions to anticipate and address frequently asked questions. As such, the revised manual becomes a valuable scientific contribution in its own right, quite apart from any substantive findings from its scores.

The essential material to be archived is what would allow other well-prepared scorers to attain reliability with the original scorers for the stories in question. Typically this would include the notes on scoring conventions and benchmarks made by scorers for each picture that were used as scoring guides for the data set. Scorers' personal manual notes on their own unique scoring challenges are not so relevant and need not be included. However, if more than one scorer finds a clarifying note useful for the same data set, it may be that this note belongs in the more general consensual scoring notes.

The chief decision for manual archiving is documentation accessibility. One option for such materials is the archiving service of the Library of Congress; another is the Education Resources Information Center (ERIC). For manuals having historical value, the Library of the History of American Psychology at the University of Akron might appreciate a copy. For dissertations and theses, manuals should be added as appendices. Most of these are now available to university libraries through interlibrary loan.

☐ References

Carnap, R. (1936). Testability and meaning. *Philosophy of Science, 3,* 420–471.

Dobbs, L., Leeper, M., & Jenkins, S. R. (2004, July). Feffer's interpersonal decentering TAT scoring system and close relationships. Poster presented at the 112th annual convention of the American Psychological Association, Honolulu, HI.

Exner, J. E., Jr. (2003). *The Rorschach: A comprehensive system* (4th ed.). Hoboken, NJ: John Wiley and Sons, Inc.

Heyns, R. W., Veroff, J., & Atkinson, J. W. (1958). A scoring manual for the affiliation motive. In J. W. Atkinson (Ed.), *Motives in fantasy, action and society* (pp. 205–218). Princeton, NJ: Van Nostrand. Reprinted with notes in C. P. Smith (Ed.), *Motivation and personality: Handbook of thematic content analysis* (pp. 211–223). New York: Cambridge University Press.

Jenkins, S. R. (2000). Toward theory development and measure evolution for studying women's relationships and HIV infection. *Sex Roles, 42*, 751–780.

Hwang, W. (2006). The Psychotherapy Adaptation and Modification Framework: Application to Asian Americans. *American Psychologist, 61*, 702–715.

Jenkins, S. R., Dobbs, L., & Leeper, M. (2004, March). Melvin Feffer's Decentering scoring system. Paper presented at the annual meeting of the Society for Personality Assessment, Miami, FL.

Jenkins, S. R., Dobbs, L., & Leeper, M. (2005, March). Feffer's interpersonal decentering TAT scoring system and relationship violence in a clinical sample. Paper presented at the annual meeting of the Society for Personality Assessment, Chicago, IL.

McClelland, D. C., & Koestner, R. (1992). The achievement motive. In C. P. Smith (Ed.), *Motivation and personality: Handbook of thematic content analysis* (pp. 143–152). New York: Cambridge University Press.

Murray, H. A. (1943). *Thematic Apperception Test*. Cambridge, MA: Harvard University.

Osgood, C. E., Suci, G. J., & Tannenbaum, P. H. (1957). *The measurement of meaning*. Urbana: University of Illinois Press.

Smith, C. P., Feld, S. C., & Franz, C. E. (1992). Methodological considerations: Steps in research employing content analysis systems. In C. P. Smith (Ed.), *Motivation and personality: Handbook of thematic content analysis* (pp. 515–536). New York: Cambridge University Press.

White, R., McFarland, M., Londenberg, L., Chlipala, L., & Jenkins, S. R. (2004, August). TAT interpersonal affect and relational functioning. Paper presented at the 112th annual convention of the American Psychological Association, Honolulu, HI.

Notes

[1] Although these systems are for the most part too complex and context dependent to be fully scorable by computer, some categories that have a limited number of keywords might have their scoring facilitated by Nudist or a similar thesaurus-type software package. This could reduce errors of omission by allowing scorers to locate the relevant keywords efficiently and then to make a separate context-based judgment for each. This has not been tested in my lab, however.

I thank the scorers whose initial efforts to learn the systems in this book taught me what they needed to know: Meryl Bazaman, Diana Brown, Diane Brüger, Summer Dae Burkman, Kirstine R. Carter, Linda Chlipala, Joni DeGrado, Lauren Dobbs, Michele Elefante, Graciela Fraga, Andrea Haag, Tamara Hale, Melissa Leeper, Lindsay Londenberg, Mike McFarland, Ashley Nicklas, Cara Santa Maria, Luis Perez, Enedelia Sauceda, Rachel White, and Lizzie Woodruff.

Appendix: To the Scorer

You have been invited to learn this scoring skill because you are bright, competent, and probably underused by your education to this point. You deserve a challenge that will increase your abilities. In this process, you will learn to argue your case, but also to be flexible, and to respect the different strengths that your colleagues may bring to the table. You might be used to being "right"—or feeling like you should be—nearly all of the time;

now you will learn to collaborate with colleagues who have different opinions and to put your arguments together to come up with the best answer.

There are three general phases of learning to score. The first phase involves learning the manual and getting used to the scoring process. For that phase, read the "General Orientation" section, and have a couple of scoring sessions as that section describes. Then when you have had a little scoring experience, read "Tips for Sessions 3–4" before those sessions. Read "Moving to Phase 2" when the manual's practice stories are exhausted and "Phase 3" when you have attained interscorer reliability (if you are working with a group) or when you feel comfortable with phase 2 (if you are working individually).

☐ General Orientation

Scoring TAT stories involves reading each story and deciding whether or not it meets the criteria described in the scoring manual for each of the scoring categories of the system. That is, does the story include the content described by the category or the rating scale, or is the story told in the way described by the category? During this first phase of the learning process, you will study and memorize your scoring manual. Then each day you will score some stories, compare your scores with the correct expert scoring, and try to figure out where you went wrong when you disagreed with the expert scoring.

Please plan to score for half an hour to an hour nearly every day, especially while you are learning, but not more. Distributed practice is more efficient and less exhausting for this than massed practice. Pick a time each day when your head is usually clear and you are not too stressed or tired to focus, and set that aside as your scoring time. You might have to try some different times until you find one that works in terms of your energy level and mental attitude.

This Appendix and your manual are designed for self-teaching, but it is easier to learn and stay reliable if you work with a group. It also helps to start out with a more intense period of immersion while you are learning the manual and getting used to the process. In your group meetings, you will review your scoring together each day or two for the next week or two, looking at how close your scoring is to the expert's, and whether there are any patterns in where you are going wrong. You will also discuss any aspects of this process that might be challenging. This may include parts of the manual or expert scores that you find hard to understand, or particular categories that may be hard for you to get right. This discussion is likely to be helpful in cases where several of you are making similar errors; one of you may have an insight about how you went wrong in your scoring decisions and can explain it to the others.

The process of learning to score TATs is partly cognitive and partly emotional. The cognitive part involves your learning to discipline your attention so that you do not miss things that you should score, and to split verbal hairs accurately. That is, you will develop a sophisticated eye for fine distinctions of meaning between words that score and words that do not, which you may now see as almost synonyms. Gradually, as you learn the system, what begins as a laborious decision-making process will become a recognition process. You will become so familiar with the scoring criteria that you might say, like one scorer I taught, "I know I'm getting it because most of the time I can just see it; I don't have to think about it. It just gets my attention." At this point, you may find yourself automatically scoring incidental print such as billboards, cereal boxes, and your textbooks.

It is helpful to know about the emotional part of scoring to prepare you for the stresses of the process. You are bright and competent, or you would not have been invited to score. But the process can be stressful too, and some stress innoculation is useful. The process of reconciling disagreements can be hard on the self-esteem, but we will come back to that later.

The cognitive part of learning to score involves reading and understanding the scoring manual that you are working with. When you go home tonight, study your manual using the strategy described in the next section. Then score a few practice stories; you will discuss those in your next meeting.

Now, turn to the section of your manual that describes the scoring categories of the system. This section tells you what it is that you are looking for in the story and what to do when you think you see it. There are also examples illustrating the rules and the decision process. Applying these rules is a process of making generalizations to new stories from the abstract rules and the particular examples given in the manual, and deciding whether each new story fits that rule or resembles an example closely enough to be scored. As you are learning and applying each rule, you will be thinking of all the different ways that scorable material might appear.

These decision-making rules can be thought of as *statutory law,* like the laws passed by Congress and state legislatures. When you read stories, you are sifting through the text looking for evidence of something to score—that is, words and phrases that fit the rules given. This is the same process that lawyers and judges use when applying statutory laws to particular cases. The historical record of the decisions they make is called *case law;* each new case is argued based on both statutory law and the accumulated precedents of case law. Studying the statutory law alone is not enough, because storytellers have many different styles and thus different ways of expressing the characteristics that the scoring system is designed to identify.

Each picture has common things people say that will often be scorable. As you learn the scoring system, you learn to recognize these things, and they become familiar to you. Then you consult the manual for your specific rules and run the word or phrase that looked familiar through the rule system to see if it meets the criteria for scoring. As you get more experienced at that process and with the stories people often tell about a picture, you will find it easier to recognize what you are looking for. The patterns will become repetitive, and scoring will often feel like a reflex. Although it will be slow to start with, you will find that you score more quickly as you go along.

And at times you will be wrong a lot, which brings up the emotional side. Everybody who has done this has gone through periods of being wrong a lot. It builds character. Not only that, but if you have been getting through school writing papers the night before they are due and still getting A's because you are so smart, you will benefit from some humility.

When you finish scoring the practice stories in the manual, you will be starting on a new set of stories from a different sample of storytellers than the ones who told the stories in the manual. There will not be expert scoring for those, so your group will have to become the experts. Then you will determine reliability by comparing your scores within the group. In doing that, you will be explaining your scoring decisions to each other, referring to the statutory law in the manual and also to the case law of your notes about the scoring examples and previously scored stories that resemble the one you are discussing. So when you find that a particular decision is difficult for you, make a note about the evidence for and against scoring it each way. That will help you learn the manual and will also be important as a record of your group's decision processes for future scorers to use.

Learning the Manual

For your next meeting, take home the scoring manual and study it, and then score the first batch of stories. This kind of studying is a more complex and thorough process than most people are used to. Memorizing the manual is only the beginning. You must embed the category descriptions into your own cognitive structure so that you can articulate them for yourself in your own terms and can execute consistently and accurately the decision process they describe.

Begin by outlining the manual—memorizing as you go—so that you can have the list of categories and brief scoring criteria in front of you as you score. Leave extra spaces so you can make notes on each section and bring a copy to each scoring meeting. As you discuss each story, you can add notes on how it is scored, if you missed something or had questions.

Scoring the Practice Stories

When you have finished outlining the manual, locate the practice story section and bookmark it, and then locate the expert scoring for the first story, bookmark it, and hide the expert scores for the second story. Then read through the first story with the first scoring categories or decision tasks at hand, and look for evidence that the story might merit a score. At first you may need to go through the story sentence by sentence while you try to keep the scoring category details in mind. If you see something that looks plausibly scorable; then go through the scoring criteria systematically to make sure it fits in all ways.

When you have decided whether you see it or not and how to score it, compare your score with the expert scoring. Then turn back to the second story and do the same thing, hiding the expert scores for the third story, and so on for the first five stories. If your manual has so many categories or complex decisions that it is hard to keep them all in your head together, you might want to do a smaller number for the first five stories until you have some idea how the process works and you feel clear about them. Then go back and do the same for the rest. If you are feeling confident after five stories, you might wish to continue scoring with a few more in the same reading.

Make notes on your copy of the stories as to what fits and why—for example, by underlining the word or phrase that seems to capture what you're looking for—or make a note in the margin. You will be finished scoring the story when you have decided for each category whether you see or do not see enough, or any, evidence that it meets the criteria for scoring in a particular category. Then compare your scoring with the expert scoring, and see whether you agreed with the expert or not. In scoring your stories, always work by yourself, and do not discuss with others until you have made your scoring decisions.

At each meeting, the group will go over the stories that you scored and will discuss how to understand what the manual says to do so that you make the same decisions as the expert. There may indeed be parts of the manual that are unclear or not very specific about how to score a particular story, but we figure the expert is always right, so the question is how to understand and apply the rules consistently to each story. There will sometimes be borderline cases in which particular word choices make a decision difficult. However, the expert scoring is always right, and your job is to reason from the scoring manual to the expert's decision, using the latter to understand how the manual should be applied: what fits the rules, which kinds of expressions are strong enough and which are too weak, and where to draw the line.

Thus, learning a system is partly a memorization task (i.e., learning the category definitions and their boundaries) and partly a generalization task (i.e., learning how to apply the decision-making process consistently to different kinds of stories). You will be scoring each story by applying the statutory law of the manual, plus the case law reflected in the examples and in your previously scored practice stories (when you have some), to each scoring decision. You should add to your notes in your manual the reasoning behind each difficult decision so that you have a record of your own case law and your own precedents.

Attitude

Even for established professionals, self-teaching presents its own unique challenges involving the right mental attitude. Those who wish to learn to use these systems will benefit from approaching the manual with a receptive, noncritical attitude during the learning process. You are learning how someone else defined these concepts, which might differ slightly from the meaning that they have for you. Accepting the manual's rules for scoring as the Voice of Authority is essential until internalization has occurred. Some basic principles should be kept in mind or on a large wall poster above the scorer's work area:

(1) The manual is always right but sometimes needs clarification, so you must provide it for yourself by diligent study of the literal words and phrases given, and of the expert scoring, so as to make appropriate generalizations to new material.

(2) The unfortunate reality: Sometimes the expert is inconsistent or obscure. This makes (1) more difficult but no less true.

(3) The moral of the story: Diligent persistence pays off.

☐ Tips for Sessions 3–4

As you begin to understand the scoring process, you will likely find that it is useful to be able to observe your own thoughts, feelings, and decision-making processes and to reflect on them. This is a particularly helpful skill to have if you want to go into clinical or counseling fields. You might begin by watching your own developing attentional process. For some systems and categories, noticing key words is important, but do you more often miss those that appear at the ends of lines? How can you solve that visual scanning problem? For some systems and scorers, visualization of the story might be good, but for others it might be a trap.

Do Not Score Your Head Movie

These are low inference scoring systems, which means that you have to score concretely rather than abstractly. That is, you should think in terms of being able to underline specific words and phrases that meet the scoring criteria and serve as evidence that the story should be scored. You must be sure that the scoring criteria are met by what the storyteller actually says in the story, not by what you imagine while you are reading. We say, "Score the words on the paper; do not score the movie you get in your head when you read the story." If you are inclined to visualize as you are reading, you may tend to score what you see in your mind's eye so that you are no longer scoring the storyteller's words. Accuracy of scoring depends on scoring only what the person actually says as opposed to what you think they mean.

One of the challenges of learning to score is learning not to use your imagination in this otherwise helpful way that has helped you to get this far in your life. Folks who are bright and verbal can often find creative reasons to score things that are not so obvious to others. One challenge, then, becomes knowing when to quit. The two golden rules of scoring are, "When unsure, score like everyone else (especially the expert) would," and "When in doubt, don't (score)." Consider that a story is written as a brief snapshot, or maybe a video, out of the characters' lives. Score only what occurs within the framework that the author gives.

Making Your Personal Manual

The fine line to walk is between making too many inferences (i.e., making leaps from the story on paper to your visualization of the action and your assumptions about what you would do if you were the character) and taking the manual too literally, making no inferences at all. The problem with the first is that we are all different people, and we may visualize the story action and infer the character's motivations differently because of the personal meaning of the story for each of us; this is bad for interscorer agreement. But if we make no inferences at all, it becomes impossible to make generalizations to new stories told about new pictures with different wording.

One purpose of the scoring group is for scorers to develop skills as a group in learning to walk that fine line and in helping each other control your creativity and individuality so that you all apply the rules in the same way. Because we mostly grow up in different families, each of us has particular ways of understanding certain words, phrases, or social conventions that may come to light in the process of discussing the assumptions behind our scoring decisions. For the purpose of improving your scoring reliability, each of you may have specific points on which you need to make personalized notes in your manuals about the meaning of certain things for you as they are to be applied in scoring. We can think of this as a *personal scoring manual* that elaborates on the author's manual. These personal manual notes may be a little different for everyone, because they mediate between our own individual cognitive structures, the author's meaning, and the general wisdom of the group, for the sake of improving interscorer reliability.

☐ Moving to Phase 2

Now you are ready to become experts yourselves, as you move to new stories that do not have expert scoring. At first you will all be scoring the same stories; later you will be working in pairs. For your next meeting, score the first batch. When you meet, you will compare scores to identify agreements, and then you will discuss and reconcile discrepancies in scoring.

Reconciling Discrepant Scores

Because you will not have expert scoring to compare with anymore, now you will be developing the expert scoring by consensus among the group. When scorers differ, you will explain why you scored the story as you did, and the other scorers will explain why they scored as they did. Your leader will referee the discussion and will help you to put together the two sets of reasoning about why the response should be scored in a particular way to come to the best decision. Keep track of your original score—do not "correct" it—and record the consensus score with a note.

Sometimes the process of reconciling discrepancies will be a simple matter of having overlooked something that is obvious once someone else has pointed it out. This is how you learn to be more careful. Other times you will have considered a score but decided against it for a reason that you can explain. Then it is up to the one who scored it to persuade you that the scoring criteria are met. At still other times, you will not have considered that score and it is not at all obvious, in which case the other scorer will have to make a very persuasive argument before you agree. If you are the one who scored it, it is up to you to make a persuasive case, putting together the manual rules, the expert scoring, and your notes on previous decisions. If you did not score it, it is your job to resist until the other person's argument and evidence from the story persuade you. Remember, this is not an exercise in either creativity or compliance; follow the rules, do not work too hard, and try to score only what would be obvious to most people in the group.

If you are a person who is not used to making mistakes, this part might be painful. As the scoring process involves working in groups and then in pairs, you will be comparing your scores with those of others. Now that you are beyond the stories that the expert has scored and you are working together to become the experts, a certain amount of contentiousness might arise, along with a certain investment in being right. Be warned in advance that probably you will not win more than half of those battles, but doing well at scoring is not about that. Doing well at scoring is being able to explain why you made the judgment that you made, which should improve your ability to stand up for your ideas.

Be aware that most people do not improve continuously at a steady rate. Often the first wave of confidence after a much improved batch of scoring is followed by a discouragingly worse one. Error patterns also change, with a period of overscoring followed by one of underscoring, or vice versa. Try to be patient.

There will be three kinds of outcomes of these discussions. First, when you have been able to make a clear decision, the rationale for decision making will be clearer to everyone, and you will add that rationale to your scoring manual. That rationale might be specific to that picture but also might generalize to other pictures. The addition to your manual will help you make that decision the same way again when it comes up next.

The second helpful outcome will be that both scorers will be more accurate with that decision next time, having an explicit reason for scoring, which may involve refining your scoring rationale a little bit. That is a normal part of the learning process. The third product will be a scored story, for which the scores can be trusted because both scorers agreed that the scoring criteria were present and felt confident enough in their score that they could persuade someone else. Be sure to record your consensus score with an explanation, and keep your original score unchanged, so that you know where you started from.

So the three products are an elaborated scoring manual for yourself that helps you to manage your individuality and creativity so as to score reliably; useful learning for you; and scored data that can be used for research. Your learning includes how to make fine distinctions about words and about a particular TAT scoring system. Through the process of learning this, you will likely also gain more ego strength, more humility, and some group collaboration skills that will help you in graduate school.

Some Common Conventions and Strategies

In scoring, a *convention* is a guideline adopted by a group of people to establish agreement in matters for which several options are about equally good and there is a need to settle, somewhat arbitrarily, on one of them. Conventions serve to establish agreement about scoring questions involving fine distinctions that come up relatively often, usually due to ambiguity or not enough information in the story. Like social conventions, scoring conventions are rules for handling minor decisions that might reflect chance fluctuations in a person's word choices rather than important aspects of personality, but for which a line must be drawn to define an essentially arbitrary distinction between very similar words and phrases as to which should be scored and which not. For example, because each picture prompts stories with typical themes that appear often, sometimes fine distinctions must be made about these frequent themes to distinguish between stories that are merely recounting the picture and those that go beyond the picture far enough to be interpreted as representing the person's internal world rather than only the picture.

General conventions that improve interscorer reliability include scoring conservatively—that is, scoring only confident decisions that have clear evidence, not merely possible or plausible inferences. Conventions that facilitate learning include learning to be concrete and specific, which is difficult for some intelligent and creative people. A second kind of convention is called a *benchmark.*

Benchmarking

Sometimes a scoring dilemma recurs for a particular story set because people tell similar stories about the same picture. Then it becomes helpful to review several stories together and to make a clear decision that will cover all of them and that can be applied consistently to the rest of the story set. Reading the manual and its examples, and the expert scoring of the practice stories, we can look for pivotal words indicating the strength of the statement being scored that fall on either side of a cut-point. These words can be called *benchmarks.*

A venerable line of research on the semantic mapping of language factor analyzed the structure of English vocabulary (Osgood, Suci, & Tannenbaum, 1957) and found three main dimensions that underlie and can be used to rate all words: evaluation (good–bad), potency (strong–weak), and activity (active–passive). If we had to, we could look up the ratings of the words in question on these dimensions. However, that is a lot of work, and most good scorers can probably make reasonably accurate judgments that also take into account the context of the word's use, which the factor scores do not include. And usually all we need is one clearly defined point—the cut-point or benchmark—that separates what scores in a category from what does not.

For example, we can think of a set of emotion words as ranked on a continuum with terror, horror, fear, dread, apprehension, concern, and the like at one end and ecstasy, joy, happiness, pleasure, comfort, safety, and the like at the other end, with indifference in the middle. Scoring on that dimension then means making a decision about what is strong enough to score and what is not. If the manual says to score *positive emotion words* and *negative emotion words,* then everything between ecstasy and comfort would probably score as positive, and everything between terror and apprehension would likely score as negative. But if there is an ordinal scale that ranks words as strongly positive, somewhat positive, somewhat negative, and strongly negative, then it is necessary to decide where to divide the numbers on the rating scale. Fear seems pretty strong, but how about dread? Is happiness strong, or only somewhat positive? Different scoring systems might define these benchmarks differently. In your manual notes, you will be gathering lists of what scores and what does not; then each new word should be scored in terms of whether it is more like the first list or the second list in terms of the degree of the dimension to be scored.

Precedence

In some systems, it is important to decide which scoring category of several mutually exclusive alternatives should take precedence. Three useful ways of doing this come from survey research: priority, intensity, and frequency. That is, respondents can indicate relative importance by mentioning something first, by mentioning it more often (e.g., saying two or more things that score in the same category), or by using stronger language (or saying, "Really, the most important is ..."). In the context of how a story is typically organized, mentioning something first may be dictated by its chronology in the action rather than its importance, and mentioning something more often is likely to be influenced by verbosity, creating a bias related to story length. Thus, we often fall back on the strength or intensity of the words chosen, using benchmarking to indicate priority. However, in some systems, considering multiple mentions is a permissible and useful tactic.

Strategic Guessing

Scorer Erin Cobb (personal communication, July 15, 2005) found it helpful to begin with initial guesses about alternative categories that might apply in a particular situation. For each, she reviewed the criteria for scoring each category, tallying one point for each criterion that matched something in the story. This would include each similar example in either the manual or the practice stories. Then she added up the points and scored the one with the most points. This approach is not appropriate for all categories, as they may differ in the number of criteria involved; however, it should work for examples and practice stories. She noted that this approach reinforced her learning of the category criteria and her ability to make distinctions among them.

Alternative Understandings

One useful exercise when you are pondering a score about an ambiguous phrase and trying to decide how much of an inference is legitimate to make is to think of alternative understandings of what the storyteller might mean as a way of benchmarking your inferences. Look at the unambiguous words and phrases that come closest to the one you are trying to score that you would use as examples in arguing on one side or other. Then ask yourself what other explanations for these words and phrases might there be in the context of *this* story that would not score. For example, the phrase *defending one's honor* (not otherwise clarified) might be a matter of professional ethics of a financial nature, personal morality in the eyes of God, or sexual chastity so as not to dishonor one's family, depending on the context in the story and the cultural frame of reference of the storyteller. Each of these might score differently in different systems, so it would be important to decide which meaning was closest to the storyteller's frame of reference.

☐ Moving to Phase 3

Orientation to Phase 3

Moving on to your next set of stories, you will now be working in pairs. For your next meeting, each pair will score the first batch of the new set of stories, and then will meet and compare your scores as you did with the group. Take turns giving your scores the same way. Record each of your scores in the master file, with your agreements in the consensus score section. See how many of your disagreements you can reconcile, and record those under consensus too. Then bring your unreconciled disagreements, and any other questions that come up, to the next group meeting.

Typically, when you shift to a new picture, things change. Themes that came up in the familiar picture do not come up anymore, and new ones emerge that are phrased differently. Similar thoughts and feelings may be expressed differently, so new conventions might be needed to cover the different words and phrases that people often use. You might need a new set of benchmarks so that you can decide how strong or weak something is. In addition to improving accuracy and reliability, conventions can be used to simplify tedious arguments about scoring decisions that matter little in the final score.

Moving Right Along

As you become familiar with the system, the manual, and the scoring process, you will find that you can score more rapidly without increasing your error rate. Clinical psychologists learn a skill for attention management called *evenly hovering attention.* As applied to scoring, this means not necessarily focusing on each word separately but moving rapidly over a stream of them in a smooth continuous process of observation. It is still necessary to read the story carefully, but—having turned off your head movie!—scorable material will begin to jump out into the net of your waiting attention. The absence of scorable material will be easy to detect because nothing jumps out, reducing the rereading of stories without it.

Shifting to each new story set means scoring more slowly for a while as new benchmarks and conventions are established, but then you will gradually pick up speed again. Score as rapidly as you comfortably can while maintaining agreement with your teammate. Continue to score independently; that is, score all the assigned stories before discussing them with anyone else.

By now you are now all experienced scorers, with highly developed verbal skills that allow you to split the hairs of this scoring system very finely. As you go through the benchmarking process and the convention development process, part of the reason to have these is to impose cloture (cut off debate) on potentially interminable analyses of small differences of word choice that are likely due to psychological error variance or irrelevant aspects of the storyteller's personality. Conventions and benchmarks are one way of decreasing the cost–benefit ratio of long interscorer debates, and they will solve many problems, but not all.

As with medical lab tests and umpires' calls, there will always be a handful of responses that are indeterminate, about which even expert scorers will disagree and about which exhaustive debate only recycles unconvincing arguments. There is a point at which the distinctions become so small that they likely do not contribute much to predicting what the person will do in real life. So if a discussion of a particular scoring decision takes longer than five minutes, it is time to stop and to agree that reasonable expert scorers may disagree. When the manual, the expert scoring of the practice stories, the conventions and benchmarks and previously scored stories, and consultation with other scorers do not yield a clear decision, the final scoring convention is, "When in doubt, don't." That is, if one scorer cannot persuade the other after five minutes, do not score it; it is not strong enough. The aim is not always to be "right"; you are probably both half right. Some distinctions are too fine to matter; now agree on a common denominator by being conservative in your scoring. This makes the scoring process move along more rapidly and smoothly and improves interscorer reliability.

After a Break

Like riding a bicycle, scoring is a skill that will stay with you, but when you have not been doing it for a while, you lose condition and need to get back in shape before you can do it as well as you used to. So after a period of a week or a month without scoring, you should go back and study the manual and your notes thoroughly again. You might be surprised what you have forgotten. The categories that were not very frequent in the last story set that you scored will probably be especially weak.

Then rescore the practice stories and compare them with the expert scoring again, also. Finally, go back to the last set that you scored, or the one with the picture most like the one you will be scoring next, and rescore 20–30 of those stories. If your interscorer reliability with your previous scores for those is good, then you are ready to resume. If not, continue to practice on previously scored stories, and discuss your challenges with your supervisor or another scorer. That should do the trick.

3

CHAPTER

Future Directions for Thematic Apperceptive Techniques

Sharon Rae Jenkins

Introduction

The bounty of divergent perspectives represented by the scoring systems in this volume invites a wealth of future research. It remains in this chapter to offer some priorities for the likely most important and fruitful pursuits. The authors in this volume have each included in their summary chapters a section on future research needed. However, there are some larger questions that, if explored, might make notable contributions to the literature by improving the clinical utility and scientific precision of most of these systems.

For parsimony's sake, I propose a set of assumptions that I hope will facilitate discussion, if not consensus, on these questions across members of different theoretical and methodological communities:

(1) Picture stimuli sample the storyteller's imagined interpersonal scenarios in hypothetical situations.

(2) These scenarios reflect the storyteller's experiences, direct or vicarious, of role relationships, plausible activities and motivations of characters in those roles, and prevailing affects in situations like the one pictured.

(3) The experiences related in the scenarios generalize to similar internal experiences—*not necessarily similar actions*—in similar situations in the storyteller's life.

(4) These similarities can be at high and unobvious levels of abstraction, as well as at lower levels of more concrete and literal representations.

(5) The relations between inner experience and overt action—and thus the predictive power of single scores on *any* measure—become more complex and less direct as a healthy person matures.

(6) Therefore, one general high priority for thematic apperceptive technique (TAT) research resides in studying the gap between inner experience and overt action, for example, by including demographic variables, other personality characteristics, and life circumstance influences as controls, moderators, and mediating variables.

(7) Therefore, one efficient strategy for such research involves multivariate studies using combinations of TAT scoring systems.

Careful conceptualization of how different aspects of inner and outer social experiences combine in the storyteller's situation might forestall a host of negative findings using single systems and overly simplistic predictive models. We now have the technology to handle complex decision trees and multivariate hypotheses, and we should be applying it to these larger questions.

The larger questions begin with how best to strengthen the empirical foundations of the clinical systems presently available. Can any general statements be made about the best directions and caveats for establishing their validity, generalizability, and reliability? Then, what other scoring approaches should be tried for clinical use? What do we most need to know about these systems' utility for the tasks of clinical practice assessment: establishing the diagnosis, estimating prognosis under varying circumstances, and treatment planning? How about studying the treatment process? What general methodological refinements should be considered? In particular, what about the need for more sets of pictures for both general and specific purposes? The effects of different picture characteristics on criterion-related validity merit attention and likely vary across systems. Finally, studies that combine two or more systems as complementary tools for the same purpose would give a more integrated picture of how story narratives might reflect storytellers' typical social functioning.

□ General Agenda for Present Systems

The systems in this book were chosen for their promise; only a few—Communication Deviance, Objective Scoring, Transcendence Index (TI)—have yet accrued a substantial validational literature. For most, it will be easy to contribute to the basic research foundation because so much remains to be done. In some cases, conceptual replications of the initial validational studies would be useful, though for some systems this might be challenging for legitimate reasons of cultural change, as discussed in a later section. For nearly all, the content validity of their scoring categories is clear and consistent with theory, but additional aspects of validity need supporting evidence. The range of validity generalization across population—by age, gender, and educational level as well as by ethnicity and culture—is a high priority for all. Any questions of interscorer reliability in relation to the theoretical properties of the construct and the developmental stage of the scoring manual should be addressed. Examination of test–retest stability and cross-situational consistency versus situational specificity can provide clarity about the match between the measure's properties and the theoretical properties of the construct.

Validity Studies

The specific validity studies needed vary across systems and are best addressed in each summary chapter. Some general strategies and caveats applying to most systems are given here. These involve identifying the minimal valid story, choosing appropriate criterion variables, improving our understanding of the structure and properties of the construct as measured in the population of interest, and addressing challenges in revalidating or rederiving measures under conditions of social change.

The question of the minimal valid story concerns the validity of the data sample (i.e., stories) rather than of the scoring system used, though systems likely differ in this area. How much information is enough to make a confident statement about the storyteller's response to the pictured situation? This could be framed as the number of items (i.e., stories) or as the average size of each one (i.e., story length). Empirical studies of the Rorschach Comprehensive System (Exner, 2003) established a minimal protocol length of 14 responses, or items, for validity; few of the present TAT systems have comparable empirical evidence.

Story length has received much less attention in the clinical literature than in the academic studies, especially at the level of the individual story. The major concern has been evaluating the degree to which simply telling longer stories gets higher scores, rather than establishing a cutoff point for protocol validity. Dana (1959) examined and found correlations for his variables with number of words in the whole protocol, and research in the human motivation tradition routinely appraises and corrects scores for correlations with protocol length (Smith, Feld, & Franz, 1992).

In addition to that evaluation of possible measurement method error variance from response productivity, validity studies should routinely report exploratory analyses of the effects on validity coefficients of retaining or eliminating both short stories (say, arbitrarily, fewer than 25–50 words, depending on the complexity of the scoring system) and short protocols (arbitrarily, an average of 25–100 words per story). In chapters 12 and 13 in this volume on Barry Ritzler's Picture Projection Test (PPT), he reported stronger hypothesized validity coefficients relating PPT and Rorschach variables in a subsample consisting of those participants having "open" protocols (Rorschach Lambda less than 1.00; PPT stories averaging more than 50 words in length) than for the sample as a whole. Many of the less central, unhypothesized, but theoretically reasonable associations also increased, especially those involving PPT Affect Suppression and the Rorschach Comprehensive System Depression Index and Texture scores. Graphic data analysis techniques such as scatterplots of TAT scores against story length, and comparing plots of criterion variables against scores corrected and uncorrected for story length, might reveal important nonlinear effects. Over time, cumulation of findings might indicate appropriate minimal story cutoffs for each system.

The question of story richness versus impoverishment, or the degree to which a story goes beyond merely describing the picture, as a measure of story validity has been little noted since Weisskopf's (1950) publication of her TI (see chapters 4 and 5 in this volume), but that system should be explored as a possible counterpart to Lambda in the Rorschach Comprehensive System (Exner, 2003). Like Lambda, TI scores might reflect character style, a defensive response set, or neurological deficit, any of which might render questionable the usefulness of stories for some scoring systems.

Careful criterion variable selection links TAT scores to clinical practice. The best appraisal of a TAT system's validity for clinical practice, beyond content validity, involves choosing criterion variables that theoretically should be related to its scores within an appropriate population for a particular purpose under the right circumstances, and looking at the association between the system's scores and the criterion variables. The most effective tests of such associations will involve, first, variables that are similar in frequency distribution and other properties described in any introductory statistics or measurement textbook. That is a given for any data analysis.

But second, TAT scores and the criterion variables should measure constructs that have similar structure and properties. TAT scores provide structured ways of looking at less structured data, and they correlate most highly with criterion variables that similarly provide structure for less structured behavior, such as experience sampling measures (McAdams & Constantian, 1983) and long-term career outcomes (McClelland, 1965, 1980, 1985a, 1985b). Regarding the properties of constructs, TAT scores for constructs that are theoretically trait-like should be compared with criterion variables that are likewise cross-situationally consistent (McClelland, 1981). Situation-specific constructs chosen to shed light on localized client problems should be measured using at least several pictures that evoke, or "pull for", that specific situation (Blankenship et al., 2006; Tuerlinckx, DeBoeck, & Lens, 2002). Scoring systems for constructs that represent transient states or situation-specific responses might be studied with repeated-measures designs that compare scores from the same individuals studied under different administration conditions and instructional sets. Rather than overgeneralizing the results of such studies beyond particular systems to "the TAT," they should be understood as unique to each individual scoring system until proven otherwise.

Now to the caveats for validity studies. Correlating TAT scores with similarly named constructs measured by structured self-report scales is rarely successful or useful as a validational strategy (Bornstein, 1998; McClelland, 1980, 1985a, 1985b; McClelland, Koestner, & Weinberger, 1989; Spangler, 1992; Winter, John, Stewart, Klohnen, & Duncan, 1998). As noted in chapter 1, construct names can be misleading, obscuring differences in theoretical origins and basic assumptions. Contrasting sources of systematic measurement error can also produce modest statistical associations and contrasting patterns of correlates (McClelland, Koestner, & Weinberger, 1989).

The effects of historical cultural change on validity studies should not be overlooked. Those who might wish to replicate a previous validational study to rederive or revalidate a system should consider carefully the ways in which the original studies for the older measures might not be reproducible with the necessary precision. What cultural changes might have taken place that might affect the findings? If the roles and opportunities available to a class of individuals have changed dramatically, the pattern of correlates for personality variables might change as well (Jenkins, 1987, 1996). If diagnostic categories are involved, some of these have changed considerably since the advent of the first psychiatric Diagnostic and Statistical Manuals (DSMs). For example, Dana's Objective System (1959; see also chapters 6 and 7 in this volume) differentiated psychotic, neurotic, and normal groups. More precise distinctions among criterion groups would be both advisable and available with present-day DSM diagnoses, but the pattern of correlates for TAT scores might change.

For another case, Masling, Rabie, and Blondheim's (1967) original derivation study for the Oral Dependency measures used obese and nonobese patients in Israel, as described in Steven Huprich's summary chapter in this volume (chapter 20). To what extent might the causes of obesity in present-day American culture differ from those of the original project? Pervasive public health messages currently suggest that obesity is virtually epidemic in the United States; these implicate modern diets (e.g., starchy school lunches;

overconsumption of candy, sugar-filled drinks, and saturated fatty snacks; oversized restaurant meals) and chronically sedentary lifestyles. Few if any of these were operative in Israeli culture in 1967. Currently these cultural habits likely play a considerable role in obesity. Although oral dependency cannot be ruled out as an influence on who takes up these habits, there are also strong situational effects due to institutional factors that make fattening foods more available than healthy foods and sedentary office jobs more common than formerly. These other effects should then be measured and statistically controlled if the Oral Dependency scoring system is to be revalidated. It might be simpler just to choose criterion variables that might be more suitable to present-day American culture, as Huprich did.

Generalizability Studies

Each of the systems here was developed with a particular examinee population in mind, and the available research may or may not have been conducted exclusively on that population. Wide generalizability is not necessary for a system to be useful; narrowly targeted systems may fill unique niches in our assessment toolbox where nothing else will do. However, within or outside that niche, these questions should be addressed and answered by systematic studies: Are findings equally useful for examinees of all ages? All educational levels? Across languages? Across cultural backgrounds, including institutional and regional culture as well as ethnic, religious, and national cultures (Helms, 1992)? What does the theoretical foundation of the system lead us to expect? The face validity of the scoring categories? The literature?

Adequate information about population generalizability and its limitations may require innovation in our journals to encourage the publication of brief reports of null results *for all measures*. Without well-documented records in accountable reporting venues, measures are subject to gossip-like whispering campaigns that globalize the findings into a generalized failure of "the TAT" (e.g., "We used it and didn't get anything"). Instead, a scientific attitude encourages specification of the conditions under which null findings were obtained and closer scrutiny of the methods used. Effective use of TAT measures requires thoughtful, theory-guided picture selection, carefully standardized administration, and reliable scoring, and failure of any one of these might yield invalid data (Lundy, 1985, 1988). Such reports are necessary to isolate the possible sources of null results in terms of the population assessed, the data gathered, the scoring system, statistical artifacts such as restriction of range or marginal interscorer reliability, and other data features discussed by Wilkinson et al. (1999). This useful information should be recognized with publication credit as well as to make the information available to future researchers.

Reliability

As noted in chapter 1, the major potential source of random error for TATs is low interscorer reliability. As described in chapter 2, appropriate scorer training and documentation of scoring conventions for data sets are important to secure scientific quality control. The relevance of internal consistency and test–retest forms of reliability for TATs is often questionable (1) because the nature of the storytelling task encourages storytellers to tell differing stories; (2) because the number of stories gathered is usually relatively small compared with structured self-report scale items, which reduces reliability (Streiner, 2003); and (3) because the properties of the constructs being measured often include a more transient state or situational component, even when they are theoretically cross-situationally consistent traits (Atkinson, 1981; McClelland, 1980; Smith, 1992a; Smith et al., 1992).

However, recent studies that increase the number of "items"(Blankenship et al., 2006; Blankenship & Zoota, 1998; Hibbard et al., 2001), evaluate trait-like constructs (Hibbard et al., 2001), or that make the items (i.e., pictures) more homogeneous to pull for a single construct (Blankenship et al., 2006; Tuerlinckx et al., 2002) have found internal consistency reliabilities comparable to structured self-report measures of similar length and construct properties. In an older study, Dana's (1959) Objective Scoring variables—Perceptual Organization, Perceptual Range, and Perceptual Personalization—showed high internal consistency reliability with only five cards for these theoretically trait-like narrow-band variables, with no notable loss of validity in discrimination between the criterion groups. Hibbard, Mitchell, and Porcerelli (2001) found that 10 TAT stories yielded good internal consistency for the Social Cognition and Object Relations Scale (SCORS; Westen, Lohr, Silk, Gold, & Kerber, 1990). These scales are somewhat wider band, more ideational-emotional-social, and perhaps a bit more influenced by situational differences than are Dana's more perceptual variables.

These studies represent important demonstrations that the internal consistency reliabilities of TATs are much affected by the structural differences between TATs and the ability measures for which the idea of reliability was originally created (as noted in chapter 1 in this volume). Structuring the TAT data to be more like that from ability measures increases internal consistency reliabilities. Hopefully these results will settle questions about the reliability of "the TAT." It is unclear whether these tactics will generalize to other scoring systems, or, more importantly, whether any gain in validity comes along.

Use of tactics that change the structure of the stories comes at a cost, however, especially for clinical applications and for scoring of archival TATs by new systems. Both of these benefit from having a larger sample of more heterogeneous pictures that elicits stories representing responses to a wider variety of the client's life situations. It is this breadth that supports arguments for validity generalization from stories to clients' lives, so narrowing the topics evoked by the picture sample also narrows the range of generalizability for the resulting scores. Further, what makes a sample of pictures more evocative of one construct is likely to make them less evocative of other quite different constructs, narrowing the range of constructs for which the stories yield adequate response frequencies.

Similarly, Blankenship et al.'s (2006) and Blankenship and Zoota's (1998) tactic of separating stories into paragraphs directed by the usual standard probes is an ingenious solution to the problem of "participant burden" that would be induced by asking a sample of uninvested student volunteers to write 20 stories. This indeed solved the technical problem of reliability, although it required some alterations in the need for Power (*n* Pow) scoring system. For clinical purposes, though, because it imposes stronger constraints on the storyteller's narrative, this data-gathering technique would make the stories useless—or the scores misleading—for scoring systems that evaluate spontaneously emergent narrative structure. These include at least the Adult Attachment Projective (AAP), Richard Dana's Objective Scoring, Interpersonal Decentering, and the TI; all are sensitive to the breakup of narrative continuity and a stronger probe structure. The negative impact of the changed structure on scores for the other systems here is less obvious, but would require careful evaluation.

☐ Clinical Research Needed

A major effort is needed to provide empirical support for the three classic tasks of clinical assessment—contributing to diagnosis, evaluating prognosis contingencies, and informing treatment planning—and for the emerging area of collaborative (Fischer, 1994) and therapeutic (Finn, 2007; Finn & Tonsager, 1992, 1997) assessment. The magnitude of the effort needed goes well beyond TAT assessment and the scope of this book. Still, a focused appraisal of these systems is a worthy goal for future research.

Clinical Utility for Diagnosis

Although helpful for identifying contributing risk factors in some cases, TATs are generally not instruments of choice for determining DSM Axis I diagnoses. TATs may show evidence of clients' meeting diagnostic criteria for some kinds of thought disorder such as social delusions, for which Ritzler's PPT form quality scores might be useful, or of more primitive problems via Robert Holt's TAT primary process for psychotic disorders (chapters 16 and 17), but the Rorschach is probably a more sensitive indicator of most forms. For depressive disorders, Ritzler's PPT emotional stress variables might be useful in establishing criteria related to negative mood among individuals who are reluctant to self-report these, but linkages between emotion scores and idiographically interpreted story content are probably more useful for prognosis and treatment planning. The AAP in this volume shows promise for identifying and describing attachment disorders. Dana's Objective Scoring in this volume shows validity for global appraisal of disorder severity, discriminating nonpatient, neurotic, and psychotic storytellers using much older diagnostic criteria than those used at present.

TATs' best use for diagnostic purposes is probably for the Axis II personality disorders. These would include David Harder and Deborah Greenwald's Ambitious-Narcissism system in this volume (chapters 24 and 25) for narcissistic personality disorder or features thereof; TAT Oral Dependency for dependent personality disorder or features (chapters 20 & 21); Summers's Symbiosis in chapters 22 and 23 for borderline personality disorder and other disorders involving poor identity differentiation; or Westen et al.'s (1990) SCORS, which was developed to discriminate individuals diagnosed with borderline personality disorder from those with other disorders.

Research designs to test criterion validity hypotheses relating scoring systems to diagnoses would typically be cross-sectional, and might involve historical data and other sources of diagnostic information. One especially useful strategy for the development of new scoring systems for diagnostic purposes is empirical criterion keying (Anastasi & Urbina, 1997, pp. 350–351) or empirical derivation, the process used to develop the original Minnesota Multiphasic Personality Inventory (MMPI), the Oral Dependency system in this volume, and Westen's SCORS, as well as some of the academic TAT scoring systems (McAdams, 1980; Stewart, 1992; Stewart & Winter, 1974; Winter, 1973, 1992a; Winter & Barenbaum, 1985). This strategy requires two or more clearly defined *gold standard* criterion groups, such as pure diagnostic groups (without comorbidities) that do not differ on other potentially confounding variables such as demographic characteristics. Stories told to the same stimuli by the two groups are compared to identify unique features that are relatively common in one group and rare in the other. Scoring category descriptions are then written to describe these differences as precisely as is feasible (perhaps using strategies in Boyatzis, 1998). As a check against differences that might appear by chance, the resulting categories should be cross-validated on a new sample of similar groups, as described by Anastasi and Urbina (1997, pp. 194–196).

Clinical Utility for Estimation of Prognosis

Not only might these scoring systems support diagnosis by giving evidence for diagnostic criteria, they also locate the criteria in a social context that might parallel the storyteller's life experience. Does the problem appear localized to a particular kind of situation, or is it cross-situationally pervasive? In what story situations is the storyteller's disorder most prominent or most disruptive? What seems to be the most important aspect of those circumstances: the role relationships of the people involved, the activity that the client says they are involved in, the thoughts or feelings that prevail, or some other aspect?

Read idiographically for consistent patterns of scores across types of stories, this information may be helpful in suggesting prognosis and in forming the treatment plan. What social role relationships are involved in the storyteller's more positive stories compared with the more negative ones, and does this suggest an easier therapeutic alliance with an older or younger therapist of a particular gender? Under what stimulus conditions—and with what scores on which systems—do the characters do well compared with other conditions? In what ways, if any, might these conditions mirror the conditions in some aspect of the storyteller's problematic life, either material or mental? Thus, what situations might make the client more likely to benefit, or more vulnerable to collapse or relapse of the sort identified by the system? Which should the client learn to avoid because they evoke malevolent object representations that the client is currently unable to manage? What are the key features of the client's subjective situation to mimic for exposure therapy with response prevention? In what circumstances might the client more confidently pursue the treatment goals?

The usefulness of TATs for prognostication comes from the fact that each story can be read with content validity as a representation of a particular social context; the series of stories covers a range of same. Here, the variability among stories that is a challenge for internal consistency reliability takes on a positive value. This use of TATs can give hints about the life conditions under which the client might do better or deteriorate, and the context of the story might give hints as to why, which can be explored with the client in therapy.

The challenge for research testing hypotheses about prognosis is of course that longitudinal or time-series case-study designs are typically necessary. However, such designs are within the capability of practice research groups, university training clinics, internship sites, and some individual clinicians, if their clients consent and if appropriate ethical guidelines for research are followed. A double-blind prospective design would likely be beyond the reach of most clinicians who use the initial TAT scores as a guide to their own treatment plans. However, the stories gathered early in treatment perhaps could be rescored retrospectively for other systems not used by the clinician at the time, thus avoiding biases particular to those systems.

Clinical Utility for Treatment Planning

The role of TAT scores in treatment planning depends on whether the scores are related to the diagnosis that is the focus of treatment, or whether they represent ancillary personality information that was gathered to suggest prognosis or treatment response, such as the likely developmental trajectory of a therapeutic alliance. TATs give unique information not only about the storyteller's psychological strengths and weaknesses but also about the situations in which those might be most beneficial or problematic. There is evidence that treatments are more effective if they build on clients' strengths rather than depending on their weaknesses. For example, Blatt and Felsen's (1993) patients with cognitive strengths did better in cognitive behavioral therapy, whereas those with social strengths did better in interpersonal therapy.

Information about the conditions under which story characters do well—as defined by the relevant scoring system—suggests the conditions that might be most comfortable and familiar to the storyteller in psychotherapy. These are not necessarily the most therapeutically helpful conditions for the long run (if one is needed), but if there is evidence that the client might have difficulty forming a psychotherapy alliance, the creation of these conditions—to the extent feasible—might facilitate the initial bonding process.

If TAT scores are related to the diagnosis being treated, they might be useful for evaluating treatment progress in a pretest–posttest repeated measures research design. This relation might reflect either the presence of a problem, such as Primary Process (chapters 16 and 17) or Ambitious Narcissism (chapters 24 & 25), or the attainment of a treatment goal, such as an increase of Personal Problem-Solving ability (see chapters 10 and 11 in this volume), Empathy (chapters 30 & 31 in this volume), or Decentering (chapters 8 and 9 in this volume), or the maturation of defenses (DMM; Cramer, 2006). In such cases, successive administrations should include an instruction either to try to tell the same stories again, or to make explicit that it does not matter whether the stories are the same or different. Resolving this ambiguous implicit assumption for storytellers yields better data (Lundy, 1985; Smith et al., 1992; Winter & Stewart, 1977).

Uses in Therapy Process

Additional studies of key clinical processes are needed. To what extent do characteristic patterns of interaction in stories resemble the storyteller's patterns of interaction in psychotherapy? The formation of an appropriate therapeutic alliance contributes significantly to outcome in both brief and long-term psychotherapy. TATs may be particularly useful for studies of psychotherapy processes because TAT stimuli elicit internal representations of interpersonal interactions, which may shed light on how a therapeutic alliance develops as well as on the client's interpersonal presenting problems. Process-oriented measures such as Communication Deviance (chapter 26 in this volume), Interpersonal Decentering (chapters 8 & 9 in this volume), Pathogenesis (chapters 18 & 19 in this volume), Personal Problem-Solving (chapters 10 & 11 in this volume), and portions of Fine's Scoring Scheme (chapters 14 & 15) might be useful in this regard.

Brief interpersonal approaches to psychotherapy (e.g., Levenson, 1995; Luborsky & Crits-Christoph, 1990; Strupp & Binder, 1984) share a focus on identifying the client's central relationship difficulty in the form of a schematic outline called a cyclical maladaptive pattern (CMP; Levenson, 1995) or core conflictual relationship theme (CCRT; Luborsky & Crits-Christoph, 1990). These models assume that the client's interpersonal scenario is reflected similarly in the client's interpersonal behavior both with the therapist and in outside relationships. Probably at least some of the client's TAT stories reflect important aspects of the same scenario. Other aspects might reflect the client's theory of mind, or why the client thinks other people do what they do. People often respond to what they believe are others' intentions, in addition to their own attitudes, beliefs, personality characteristics, and actions.

Scoring system categories might be useful for therapists to shape the focus of brief dynamic and narrative psychotherapy approaches that help clients rewrite their life stories (Lieblich, McAdams, & Josselson, 2004; White & Epston, 1991). Clients might be shown the scoring category description fitting their problematic storytelling pattern and asked to rewrite their stories to fit the scoring categories associated with more adaptive relationship patterns. In theory, "rewriting the story" should help to reshape both the client's internal interpersonal scenario and the problematic interpersonal behavior pattern. This approach exemplifies working with the client's material and giving the client control. However, using stories as *fictional* analog behavioral self-observations might be less threatening and difficult for some clients than a more realistic context would be, and so might avoid the arousal of defenses.

Some useful interventions might combine the brief interpersonal and narrative therapy approaches (i.e., identifying and helping clients to rewrite their stories) with the collaborative and therapeutic assessment intervention strategy (i.e., inviting clients to examine and interpret their own data as a way of understanding and changing maladaptive patterns). Perhaps the best example in practice is Fischer's (1994) approach to collaborative assessment feedback, in which some of the client's responses in the assessment session are reflected back to the client as examples of the conclusions in the report. This way of making the output of the assessment process visible is an excellent example of demystification by information.

☐ Methodological Refinements Needed

A full treatment of research methods and methodological considerations for TATs is beyond the scope of this book. Interested readers should consult Smith (1992a), Smith et al. (1992), Veroff (1992), Winter (1992b), and perhaps others in Smith's (1992b) collection. Some of the most pressing issues are summarized here.

Data Collection

Without question, as Ritzler argues in chapter 12 of this volume, new picture sets are needed that are contemporary in design and content, and are suitable for a broad range of clinical purposes. Some might be tailored to the measurement of specific constructs (e.g., the AAP and PPT in this volume), others to particular cultural groups as well (e.g., the Contemporized Themes Concerning Blacks and the Tell Me A Story [TEMAS] in this volume; see also the Gerontological Apperception Test in Hayslip, Francis, Radika, Lambert, Panek, & Bosmajian, 2002). More important, however, is to open communication among clinical practitioners and researchers about strategic planning when it comes to the design of picture sets. What are the desirable features of a good picture? A good set? What kinds of pretesting are most useful in designing a set? Is it possible to develop a common language and goals for answering these questions?

Most clinical assessments would benefit from having available a large enough sample of diverse pictures to allow for oversampling of particular content areas. Murray's

(1943) set is not balanced in this way; there are many pictures of individuals or same-gender groups that are seldom used either clinically or in research (Keiser & Prather, 1990). Few Murray pictures suggest work situations, and as noted by Ritzler in chapter 12 of this volume, the emotional tone ranges from neutral to gloomy. There should be a balanced selection of genders, ages, and gender-age combinations among the characters; more situations depicted that show people engaged with impersonal tasks; and a wider emotional range.

A second area that needs careful thinking involves the situational specificity of stimuli, especially pictures. This strength has been virtually untapped in research, though widely used by clinicians. A few studies have used pictures of a narrow range of situations for the purpose of predicting behavior in a specific circumstance (e.g., Libo, 1956, 1957, 1969) or to pull for particular constructs (Blankenship et al., 2006). Too many of these in one set might be ineffective for most clinical purposes given the typical alternating pattern seen in stories (Arnold, 1962; Atkinson, 1981; Reuman, 1982), or if the tactic is obvious to the storyteller.

A better approach would be to create a large enough selection of stimuli to allow for sampling a variety of situation types within the 9–10 pictures that are recommended for clinical or clinical research purposes (Hibbard et al., 2001, cf. Smith et al., 1992), while also allowing for oversampling the one or two areas of interest to which the client's problem might be localized. The scores for similar pictures can be used as a subscale, and predictions obtained from that subscale can be compared to the scores from the remaining pictures. Thus, subscales can be defined either by the features of the picture, by the content of the story, as done with Thomas's Affective Scale (chapters 27 & 28), or by the life circumstances to which generalization of the findings is wanted.

Data Analysis

Data analysis is the pivotal link between stories and results from structured scoring systems and is perhaps the least comfortable for clinicians. But failures of conceptualization at this stage have brought down more than one worthy project. This section addresses subscale creation and error variance. This chapter and chapter 1 present arguments for the possible usefulness of subscales that aggregate the scores from similar pictures to represent clients' likely responses to the type of situation involved.

One question for clinical data analysis then is when subscales are being formed, which is more important, the stimulus or the story? If the storyteller's plot discusses siblings in response to a picture designated as a romantic couple, what then? The research answer to this empirical question about subscale creation depends on which classification of the story, by stimulus (picture type) or by response (e.g., the Symbiosis System's dyad type; the roles and valences in Thomas's Affective Scale), is more consistent with theory or produces the stronger validity coefficient in an atheoretical study. Does the criterion score assess a social structural variable or a subjective perception? The best answer might differ across systems and correlates. For the clinical answer, the clinician might look to see how many romantic stories had already been told and also check the Rorschach space score; was the storyteller being creative or oppositional?

The question of error variance is worth raising because it represents a source of inaccuracy in scores that might be controlled or avoided. Why do scores differ, other than actual differences on the construct being measured? High on the priority list for the advancement of research on TAT data-gathering methods in general, as well as for each specific scoring system, is a better understanding of what each score represents.

Hopefully most individual differences in scores are due to differences between storytellers on the construct of interest. However, some part of that difference might be due to systematic measurement error (e.g., response style, verbal fluency) or to random error, which is not traceable to a specific systematic source. Probably there are some general sources of measurement error such as verbal fluency (McClelland, 1980; Smith et al., 1992), and response constriction versus dilation (Shatin, 1958; see also chapters 4 & 5 in this volume) that can be controlled statistically, as described by Smith et al. (1992). Random error is best minimized by careful attention to correct and consistent administration so that stories are gathered under standardized conditions for all storytellers, especially regarding instructional set (Lundy, 1988). In the event of doubt about variations in administration, it might be better to eliminate from a research data set those protocols for stories told under nonstandard conditions, as they might yield scores that are outliers on some systems.

It appears that TATs have no obvious social desirability response set as exists for self-report methods, but the question of a general positive–negative affectivity dimension is open for empirical test. It is possible that under some conditions for some systems, examinees may suppress certain kinds of stories and thus may lower their scores on variables involving more unpleasant or obviously threatening imagery. Such efforts at data manipulation may have differing impacts—or no impact—on scores from different systems. Evaluating this issue is an important validational step for TAT systems.

In general, we need a comprehensive, theory-informed picture of what sorts of further validity indices might be needed and for which systems, in which populations, for what purposes, in which circumstances. These may include an extension of the use of moderator variables proposed by Dana (1993, 1998, 2005) for work in evaluating the cross-cultural validity of assessment methods. This tactic can be applied broadly to check the validity generalization of scores to a variety of populations within the same culture as well.

☐ Developing Further Systems

Recovering More of the Clinical Past, Developing the Future

Much interesting work has not been included here, as noted in chapter 1. In particular, my searches located several dissertations that began work on promising systems but remained unpublished. Undoubtedly there are more. The original documents are usually available through university libraries, and some might include adequate scoring manuals as appendices. (Max Prola's inclusion of his adapted version of Weisskopf's TI scoring manual in his dissertation's appendix gave me a version I could use until I located the original in the collection of Weisskopf's papers.) Some additional background information, perhaps even data usable for training purposes, might be available from the original researchers or their former academic institutions, or from the American Documentation Institute at the Library of Congress. That is where I—or rather, Myron Chace in his careful sleuthing—located Melvin Feffer's scoring system, thanks to the latter's footnote in Feffer and Jahelka (1968). Enterprising graduate students, especially those with an interest in the field's history, should continue to locate, retrieve, evaluate, use, adapt, and refine these scoring systems.

Arnold's (1962) Story Sequence Analysis System would be a good example of a system too complex to include in this volume, but it merits further development. Arnold's method has more in common with a grounded theory approach to open-ended data than with formal or content-analytic approaches. Thus, it captures better the individuality of the storyteller than do the other systems in this book, at some cost to the precision of systematic interindividual comparison. Recent advances in thematic analysis (e.g., Boyatzis, 1998) and narrative analysis (e.g., Josselson, Lieblich, & McAdams, 2003; Lieblich et al., 2004) might enable the refinement of Arnold's system to allow such comparisons. For example, Arnold provided in her scoring manual for evaluation of stories along a gross positive–negative dimension for characters' motivations. It seems likely that this dimension might underlie several of the scoring systems in this book.

The more interesting and unique aspect of her system, however, is the analysis of the sequence of imports across the stories in the protocol, viewing these as a series of scenes in a larger play with its own structure, interconnecting themes, and resolution. Here, as with Atkinson's (1981) and Reuman's (1982) work on the sequencing of motivation themes in successive stories, is a bigger picture than other approaches give, one that is more challenging to quantify—and probably nonlinear—but potentially fruitful for both clinical and research purposes. For example, the degree to which successive themes connect might reflect a broader openness or dilation versus defensive constriction, as well as integration versus compartmentalization of the client's experience, in ways quite different from Weisskopf's (1950) TI, which applies only to individual stories.

Repurposing the Past: Clinical Applications of Academic Systems

The gap between experience and action mentioned in assumptions (5) and (6) at the beginning of this chapter can have both mental and physical health consequences. Structured self-report measures cannot bridge this gap effectively (Shedler, Mayman, & Manis, 1993). Inhibition of action might play a role in the association between stress and mood (Langens & Stucke, 2005). Some of the most interesting TAT studies in the late David McClelland's career are those linking measures of need for Power (*n* Pow), combined with need for Affiliation (*n* Aff), inhibition of action, and other variables, to health outcomes such as short-term immune functioning and longer-term hypertension and cardiovascular disorders (reviewed in McClelland, 1979, 1985a, 1989; McClelland, Davidson, & Saron, 1985). Although McClelland, not being a clinician himself, repeatedly insisted that motive measures were not designed for clinical use, and the existing literature includes few if any studies of clinical populations, these findings are certainly clinically relevant. It seems time to launch exploratory efforts in this direction using individual clinical administration and the larger picture sets that would allow for generalization to a wide variety of life circumstances.

Another excellent application is McKay's (1991, 1992) Affiliative Trust–Mistrust System for isolating thought patterns associated with immunocompetence decrements under conditions of positive affiliative arousal. The use of object relations theory to shape the scoring categories of this system stands as a model for clinical health research in this area that calls for follow-up by interdisciplinary teams including physiological and clinical psychologists. Astute theory development will be important for identifying the processes to study, the points at which measurement should best occur, and what (possibly nonlinear) form the expected associations might take.

Some of the other personality measures included in Smith (1992a) merit research exploration for possible clinical use. Indeed, two studies have found that people higher in the intimacy motive show evidence of better adjustment than those with lower scores (McAdams & Bryant, 1987; McAdams & Vaillant, 1982). Abigail Stewart's measure of self-definition and social definition provides a view of how a client might navigate stressful situations—especially situations involving social pressure and differences from social conventions (Jenkins, 1996; Stewart, 1978, 1992; Stewart & Winter, 1974).

New Uses for Non-TAT Scoring Systems

Another advantage of less structured techniques is that some scoring systems are robust across data collection methods, supporting the conceptualization of these measures as tapping a person's habitual thought patterns and ways of organizing and interpreting situations, which generalize across these different methods of sampling them. McClelland (1961) scored folk tales and children's stories for motives; Winter (1987, 1991) scored presidential inaugural addresses; and LeVine, Strangman, and Unterberger (1966) scored recalled dreams. De Vos has applied his psychocultural scoring system similarly to a variety of ethnographic data such as folklore and ritual as well as literature and dreams (Ephraim, 2000).

This broad utility goes both ways. Several researchers, often graduate students (see Kuhn, 1962) have applied to TAT stories theory-grounded systems developed for other material. Sutton and Swenson (1983) scored TAT stories according to Loevinger's (1970) ego development scoring system originally designed for a standard sentence completion task. Kalliopuska (1982) used Urist's (1977) Mutuality of Autonomy (MOA) Scoring System, originated for the Rorschach, and found associations consistent with interpretation of MOA scores as measuring empathy. Black, Jenkins, Evans, and Shafenberg-Murry (2003) adapted for TAT scoring Benjamin's (1993) Structural Analysis of Social Behavior method for scoring interview data and found these scores related to MOA scores from Rorschach protocols.

In summary, for those not wishing to initiate new scoring systems, as described in previous sections, there are numerous systems in varying stages of empirical development that merit further work. Some of these come from clinical contexts and need more validity evidence, and perhaps more detailed manuals, to improve interscorer reliability. Others are from academic research settings and have well-supported validity for their current uses but need testing for applicability to clinical purposes. Additional options include translation to TATs of scoring systems developed for other narrative material. All these options could be tested more readily by increased sharing of data among researchers and clinicians.

Given the labor and expense of gathering and archiving TAT data, far-sighted researchers might gather such data for the initial purpose of evaluating one system, and then make the protocols available to those working with other systems for similar application. Maintaining an archive of such data sets would be a worthy enterprise for a research institute somewhere, facilitating the economical evaluation of scoring systems early in their development sequence. Such an archive already exists and has a large collection of data sets including TAT stories that have been scored for human motives and could be scored for other systems. That archive is the Henry A. Murray Research Archive at the Harvard–MIT Data Center. Further information is available on its Web site at http://www.murray.harvard.edu/mra/index.jsp. According to its site, "The Henry A. Murray Research Archive holds a significant collection of social science data for use in the study of human development in the context of social change. The Archive provides access to both quantitative data and qualitative data (case histories, open-ended interviews, and audio- and video-tapes)" for use by qualified researchers.

Science–Practice Gap, Reprise: Changes Needed in Research Process

Research must lead practice when it comes to systematizing and validating new scoring systems using controlled criterion groups, experimental designs, and quantitative methods. But clinical practice must lead research when it comes to defining problems that need solution, developing theory that can guide the scoring system development process, and defining criterion groups and variables for the development of those systems. Idiographic and qualitative methods are more useful in formulating questions and theory for scoring system development than are more structured and quantified measures. The lack of respect that systematic qualitative research methods have received in graduate training in clinical psychology in the last quarter century has been a major hindrance to both theory development and scoring system validation where TATs are concerned. Obviously, the best approach is Boulder model scientist–practitioner training!

The appropriateness of participant samples for particular research questions also is important to address. College student samples may be appropriate for obtaining psychometric and validity data in the middle phases of measure development when large samples are needed—assuming (a large, quite likely erroneous, but frequent assumption) that such samples include an adequate range of variation in the clinical features of interest. However, for the earliest phases of scoring category definition and refinement, and for the later stages of validation, samples of clients or therapists may be a requisite, depending on the nature of the measure and its theoretical foundation.

Finally, clinicians must educate researchers about improvements needed in areas that are usually considered the purview of researchers, but that are currently less productive for clinical practice than they might be—and researchers must listen. For example, journal reviewers need guidelines for making judgments that balance the clinical relevance of manuscripts against the degree of rigor possible given a new measure's state of development. These guidelines are especially important for the less structured methods because of their greater sensitivity to administration conditions generally, and for TATs in particular because of the stimulus sampling and other technical issues described in chapter 1.

Attention to research findings and their application to practice is increasingly important for clinicians, but unless those findings are externally valid (Sue, 1999), clinically workable, and presented comprehensibly to clinicians, researchers' efforts may not get the attention that they would merit otherwise. Active collaboration with practicing assessment clinicians can help to enrich psychological scientists' grasp of how a TAT system's validity can best be evaluated, as recommended by Westen (2002) for the development of empirically supported treatment manuals. Furthermore, such collaboration can encourage open-minded clinicians to have a broader grasp of what is possible in research, and perhaps to join one of the growing practice research networks.

Some of the very most pressing clinical research needs are those that historically have been caught in the scientist–practitioner gap. The continued viability of both assessment research and scientific professional practice depend on our closing this gap as quickly and solidly as possible. The reward of undertaking work in any part of the above enterprise is participating in the lively process of real clinical science, laboring in the woodshed, planting the vineyard, tracing the phenotypes of crop after crop to improve the breed. There is productive labor aplenty for everyone, from senior clinicians and researchers to undergraduate research assistants, from carrying water and planting the seeds to grafting and harvesting and pruning the unproductive. The final recommendation from this chapter is to continue the mapping of the landscape, with comments on the quality, unique characteristics, and depth of the soil in each area of the field so that those to come may find the most fertile spot for their particular labors.

These worthy activities toward the development and refinement of structured scoring systems may serve as a general foundation for clinical assessment practice. However, they should not threaten the established clinical wisdom of the seasoned practitioner, who may come to quite similar conclusions by a more implicit route. The wise assessor will not ignore these tools, but rather will build on and modify them to improve their fit to particular presenting problems, client populations, diagnostic groups, treatment programs, and institutional needs. Such systems may facilitate teaching and learning, make practice more efficient, and contribute to theory development, but they are merely a means to an end. The experience of the highly trained and sensitive psychologist integrating these systems with other test and nontest data is ultimately the best assessment technique.

☐ References

Anastasi, A., & Urbina, S. (1997). *Psychological testing* (7th ed.). Upper Saddle River, NJ: Prentice-Hall.

Arnold, M. B. (1962). *Story sequence analysis: A new method of measuring motivation and predicting achievement.* New York: Columbia University Press.

Atkinson, J. W. (1981). Studying personality in the context of an advanced motivational psychology. *American Psychologist, 36,* 117–128.

Benjamin, L. S. (1993). *Interpersonal diagnosis and treatment of personality disorders.* New York: Guilford Press.

Black, L., Jenkins, S. R., Evans, A. P., & Shafenberg-Murry, S. (2003, August). *SASB scoring applied to the TAT: Assessing object relations.* Paper presented at the 111th annual convention of the American Psychological Association, Toronto, Ontario, Canada.

Blankenship, V., Vega, C. M., Ramos, E., Romero, K., Warren, K., Keenan, K., et al. (2006). Using the multifaceted Rasch model to improve the TAT/PSE measure of need for achievement. *Journal of Personality Assessment, 86*(1), 100–114.

Blankenship, V., & Zoota, A. (1998). Comparing power imagery in TATs written by hand or on the computer. *Behavior Research Methods, Instruments, & Computers, 30*(3), 441–448.

Blatt, S. J., & Felsen, I. (1993). Different kinds of folks may need different kinds of strokes: The effect of patients' characteristics on therapeutic process and outcome. *Psychotherapy Research, 3,* 245–259.

Bornstein, R. F. (1998). Implicit and self-attributed dependency strivings: Differential relationships to laboratory and field measures of help seeking. *Journal of Personality and Social Psychology, 75*(3), 778–787.

Boyatzis, R. E. (1998). *Transforming qualitative information: Thematic analysis and code development.* Thousand Oaks, CA: Sage.

Dana, R. H. (1959). A proposal for the objective scoring of the TAT. *Perceptual and Motor Skills, 9,* 27–43.

Dana, R. H. (1993). *Multicultural assessment perspectives for professional psychology.* Needham Heights, MA: Allyn & Bacon.

Dana, R. H. (1998). *Understanding cultural identity in intervention and assessment.* Thousand Oaks, CA: Sage Publications.

Dana, R. H. (2005). *Multicultural assessment: Principles, applications, and examples.* Mahwah, NJ: Lawrence Erlbaum.

Ephraim, D. (2000). Psychocultural approach to TAT scoring and interpretation. In R. H. Dana (Ed.), *Handbook of cross-cultural and multicultural personality assessment* (pp. 427–445) Hillsdale, NJ: Erlbaum.

Exner, J. E., Jr. (2003). *The Rorschach: A comprehensive system* (4th ed.). Hoboken, NJ: John Wiley & Sons, Inc.

Feffer, M., & Jahelka, M. (1968). Implications of the decentering concept for the structuring of projective content. *Journal of Consulting and Clinical Psychology, 32*(4), 434–441.

Finn, S. E. (2007). *In our clients' shoes: Theory and techniques of therapeutic assessment.* Mahwah, NJ: Erlbaum.

Finn, S. E., & Tonsager, M. E. (1992). Therapeutic effects of providing MMPI-2 test feedback to college students awaiting therapy. *Psychological Assessment, 4,* 278–287.

Finn, S. E., & Tonsager, M. E. (1997). Information-gathering and therapeutic models of assessment: Complementary paradigms. *Psychological Assessment, 9,* 374–385.

Fischer, C. T. (1994). *Individualizing psychological assessment.* Hillsdale, NJ: Lawrence Erlbaum.

Hayslip, B. Jr., Francis, J., Radika, L. M., Lambert, P., Panek, P. E., & Bosmajian, L. (2002). The development of a scoring system for the Gerontological Apperception Test. *Journal of Clinical Psychology, 58,* 471–478.

Helms, J. E. (1992). Why is there no study of cultural equivalence in standardized cognitive ability testing. *American Psychologist, 47*(9), 1083–1101.

Hibbard, S., Mitchell, D., & Porcerelli, J. (2001). Internal consistency of the object relations and social cognition scales for the Thematic Apperception Test. *Journal of Personality Assessment, 77*(3), 408–419.

Jenkins, S. R. (1987). Need for achievement and women's careers over 14 years: Evidence for occupational structure effects. *Journal of Personality and Social Psychology, 53*(5), 922–932.

Jenkins, S. R. (1996). Self-definition in thought, action, and life path choices. *Personality and Social Psychology Bulletin, 22,* 99–111.

Kalliopuska, M. (1982). Empathy measured by Rorschach and TAT. *British Journal of Projective Psychology & Personality Study, 27*(2), 5–11.

Josselson, R., Lieblich, A., & McAdams, D. P. (2003). (Eds.). *Up close and personal: The teaching and learning of narrative research.* Washington, DC: American Psychological Association.

Katz, H. E., Russ, S. W., & Overholzer, J. C. (1993). Sex differences, sex roles, and projection on the TAT: Matching stimulus to examinee gender. *Journal of Personality Assessment, 60,* 186–191.

Keiser, R. E., & Prather, E. N. (1990). What is the TAT? A review of ten years of research. *Journal of Personality Assessment, 55,* 800–803.

Kuhn, T. S. (1962). *The structure of scientific revolutions.* Chicago: University of Chicago Press.

Langens, T. A., & Stucke, T. S. (2005). Stress and mood: The moderating role of activity inhibition. *Journal of Personality, 73*(1), 47–78.

Levenson, H. (1995). *Time-limited dynamic psychotherapy: A guide to clinical practice.* New York: BasicBooks.

LeVine, R. A., Strangman, E., & Unterberger, L. (1966). *Dreams and deeds: Achievement motivation in Nigeria.* Chicago: University of Chicago Press.

Libo, L. M. (1956). *Picture impressions: A projective technique for investigating the patient–therapist relationship.* Baltimore: University of Maryland Medical School, Department of Psychiatry Publication Series.

Libo, L. M. (1957). The projective expression of patient–therapist attraction. *Journal of Clinical Psychology, 13,* 33–36.

Libo, L. M. (1969). *The Picture Impressions Test.* Consulting Psychologists Press.

Lieblich, A., McAdams, D. P., & Josselson, R. (2004). (Eds.). *Healing plots: The narrative basis of psychotherapy*. Washington, DC: American Psychological Association.

Loevinger, J. (1970). *Measuring ego development*. San Francisco, Jossey-Bass.

Luborsky, L., & Crits-Christoph, P. (1990). *Understanding transference: The CCRT method*. New York: Basic Books.

Lundy, A. L. (1985). The reliability of the Thematic Apperception Test. *Journal of Personality Assessment, 49,* 141–145.

Lundy, A. L. (1988). Instructional set and Thematic Apperception Test validity. *Journal of Personality Assessment, 52,* 309–320.

Masling, J., Rabie, L., & Blondheim, S. H. (1967). Obesity, level of aspiration and Rorschach and TAT measures of oral dependence. *Journal of Consulting Psychology, 31,* 233–239.

McAdams, D. P. (1980). A thematic coding system for the intimacy motive. *Journal of Research in Personality, 14,* 413–432.

McAdams, D. P., & Bryant, F. B. (1987). Intimacy motivation and subjective mental health in a nationwide sample. *Journal of Personality, 55,* 395–413.

McAdams, D. P., & Vaillant, G. E. (1982). Intimacy motivation and psychosocial adjustment: A longitudinal study. *Journal of Personality Assessment, 46,* 586–593.

McClelland, D. C. (1961). *The achieving society*. Princeton, NJ: Van Nostrand.

McClelland, D. C. (1979). Inhibited power motivation and high blood pressure in men. *Journal of Abnormal Psychology, 88,* 182–190.

McClelland, D. C. (1980). Motive dispositions: The merits of operant and respondent measures. In L. Wheeler (Ed.), *Review of personality and social psychology* (Vol. 1). Beverly Hills, CA: Sage Publications.

McClelland, D. C. (1981). Is personality consistent? In A. I. Rabin, J. Aronoff, A. M. Barclay, & R. A. Zucker (Eds.), *Further explorations in personality* (pp. 87–113). New York: Wiley.

McClelland, D. C. (1985a). *Human motivation*. Glenview, IL: Scott, Foresman.

McClelland, D. C. (1985b). How motives, skills, and values determine what people do. *American Psychologist, 40,* 812–825.

McClelland, D. C. (1989). Motivational factors in health and disease. *American Psychologist, 44,* 675–683.

McClelland, D. C., Davidson, R. J., & Saron, C. (1985). Stressed power motivation, sympathetic activation, immune function, and illness. *Advances, 2,* 42–52.

McClelland, D. C., Koestner, R., & Weinberger, J. (1989). How do self-attributed and implicit motives differ? *Psychological Review, 96,* 690–702.

McKay, J. R. (1991). Assessing aspects of object relations associated with immune function: Development of the Affiliative Trust–Mistrust coding system. *Psychological Assessment, 3,* 541–547.

McKay, J. R. (1992). Affiliative Trust–Mistrust. In C. P. Smith (Ed.), *Motivation and personality: Handbook of thematic content analysis* (pp. 254–265). New York: Cambridge University Press.

Murray, H. A. (1943). *Thematic Apperception Test manual*. Cambridge, MA: Harvard University Press.

Reuman, D. A. (1982). Ipsative behavioral variability and the quality of thematic apperceptive measurement of the achievement motive. *Journal of Personality and Social Psychology, 43*(5), 1098–1110.

Shatin, L. (1958). The constriction–dilation dimension in Rorschach and TAT. *Journal of Clinical Psychology, 14,* 150–155.

Shedler, J., Mayman, M., & Manis, M. (1993). The illusion of mental health. *American Psychologist, 48,* 1117–1131.

Smith, C. P. (1992a). Reliability issues. In C. P. Smith (Ed.), *Motivation and personality: Handbook of thematic content analysis* (pp. 126–139). New York: Cambridge University Press.

Smith, C. P. (Ed.) (1992b). *Motivation and personality: Handbook of thematic content analysis*. New York: Cambridge University Press.

Smith, C. P., Feld, S. C., & Franz, C. E. (1992). Methodological considerations: Steps in research employing content analysis systems. In C. P. Smith (Ed.), *Motivation and personality: Handbook of thematic content analysis* (pp. 515–536). New York: Cambridge University Press.

Spangler, W. D. (1992). Validity of questionnaire and TAT measures of need for achievement: Two meta-analyses. *Psychological Bulletin, 112,* 140–154.

Stewart, A. J. (1978). A longitudinal study of coping styles in self-defining and socially defined women. *Journal of Consulting and Clinical Psychology, 46,* 1079–1084.

Stewart, A. J. (1992). Self-definition and social definition: Personal styles reflected in narrative style. In C. P. Smith (Ed.), *Motivation and personality: Handbook of thematic content analysis* (pp. 481–488). New York: Cambridge University Press.

Stewart, A. J., & Winter, D. G. (1974). Self-definition and social definition in women. *Journal of Personality, 42,* 238–259.

Streiner, D. L. (2003) Starting at the beginning: An introduction to coefficient alpha and internal consistency. *Journal of Personality Assessment,* 80(1), 99–103.

Strupp, H. H., & Binder, J. L. (1984). *Psychotherapy in a new key: A guide to time-limited dynamic psychotherapy.* New York: Basic Books.

Sue, S. (1999). Science, ethnicity, and bias: Where have we gone wrong? *American Psychologist, 54,* 1070–1077.

Sutton, P. M., & Swensen, C. H. (1983). The reliability and concurrent validity of alternative methods for assessing ego development. *Journal of Personality Assessment, 47*(5), 468–475.

Tuerlinckx, F., DeBoeck, P., & Lens, W. (2002). Measuring needs with the Thematic Apperception Test: A psychometric study. *Journal of Personality and Social Psychology, 82,* 448–461.

Urist, J. (1977). The Rorschach Test and the assessment of object relations. *Journal of Personality Assessment, 41*(1), 3–9.

Veroff, J. (1992). Thematic apperceptive methods in survey research. In C. P. Smith (Ed.), *Motivation and personality: Handbook of thematic content analysis* (pp. 100–109). New York: Cambridge University Press.

Weisskopf, E. A. (1950). A transcendence index as a proposed measure in the TAT. *Journal of Psychology, 29,* 379–390.

Westen, D. (2002). Manualizing manual development. *Clinical Psychology: Science and Practice, 9,* 416–418.

Westen, D., Lohr, N., Silk, K. R., Gold, L., & Kerber, K. (1990). Object relations and social cognition in borderlines, major depressives, and normals: A Thematic Apperception Test analysis. *Psychological Assessment, 2,* 355–364.

White, M., & Epston, D. (1991). *Narrative means to therapeutic ends.* New York: Norton.

Wilkinson, L., & the Task Force on Statistical Inference (1999). Statistical methods in psychology journals: Guidelines and explanations. *American Psychologist, 54*(8), 594–604.

Winter, D. G. (1973). *The power motive.* New York: Free Press.

Winter, D. G. (1987). Leader appeal, leader performance, and motive profiles of leaders and followers: A study of American presidents and elections. *Journal of Personality and Social Psychology, 52,* 196–202.

Winter, D. G. (1991). Measuring personality at a distance: Development of an integrated system for scoring motives in running text. In A. J. Stewart, J. M. Healy, Jr., & D. J. Ozer (Eds.), *Perspectives in Personality: Approaches to understanding lives* (Part B, pp. 59–89). London: Jessica Kingsly Publishers.

Winter, D. G. (1992a). Responsibility. In C. P. Smith (Ed.), *Motivation and personality: Handbook of thematic content analysis* (pp. 500–505). New York: Cambridge University Press.

Winter, D. G. (1992b). Content analysis of archival materials, personal documents, and everyday verbal productions. In C. P. Smith (Ed.), *Motivation and personality: Handbook of thematic content analysis* (pp. 110–125). New York: Cambridge University Press.

Winter, D. G., & Barenbaum, N. B. (1985). Responsibility and the power motive in women and men. *Journal of Personality, 53,* 335–355.

Winter, D. G., John, O. P., Stewart, A. J., Klohnen, E. C., & Duncan, L. E. (1998). Traits and motives: Toward an integration of two traditions in personality research. *Psychological Review, 105*(2), 230–250.

Winter, D. G., & Stewart, A. J. (1977). Power motive reliability as a function of retest instructions. *Journal of Consulting and Clinical Psychology, 45,* 436–440.

II

SECTION

Perceptual-Cognitive Systems

4

CHAPTER

Edith Weisskopf's Transcendence Index

Benjamin P. Chapman

Abstract

Weisskopf's (1950) Transcendence Index (TI) was developed as a general measure of the amount of projection present in a thematic apperceptive technique (TAT) narrative when respondents were asked simply to describe a picture. The TI is calculated by scoring the number of ways that a narrative exceeds pure description of the stimuli present in the picture and by using several different scoring categories. Because the TI is an inherently face-valid measure of projection, it has been employed as a standard criterion measure of projection or fantasy in studies examining, for instance, the degree to which similarity between projective stimuli and respondents influences projection. Reports indicate that it can be scored reliably, and, although most studies have used it with children and college students, it is not inherently limited to such populations. Little work has employed the TI in recent decades, and future research might productively investigate the degree to which transcendence is a stable person variable or a state that is dependent on the testing situation or other variables. Research also might assess the degree to which the TI converges with and discriminates between other measures of constriction–dilation on projective tasks and measures of defensiveness on self-report personality inventories.

Description of the System

Conceptual Framework

Weisskopf (1950) originally developed the TI as a general measure of the amount of projection present in a TAT protocol. Her goal was to find a way to distinguish projected material from descriptive material and to quantify projection. Such an index, in her view, would accomplish two things. First, it would provide an indication of the clinically useful material in a protocol. Second, it would suggest which cards in the TAT were more apt to elicit projection. The first indicator is essentially an individual difference variable, and the second is a variable that could be clinically manipulated by selecting cards to facilitate maximum production of projective material with psychodiagnostic value.

Weisskopf (1950) noted that because the TAT contains real-life scenes, some examinees are drawn simply to describe a picture without elaborating or creating a narrative structure that goes beyond what is present in the card. Such sparse descriptions impede the usefulness of TAT responses more so than, for instance, purely descriptive responses impeded Rorschach usefulness. In the TAT, material produced beyond or added to what is already present in cards forms the basis of clinical personality inference. In contrast, because the Rorschach entails stimuli inherently more ambiguous, projection occurs in what and how ink blots are perceived rather than what is added to them.[1]

Weisskopf (1950, p. 379) proposed that projection could be quantified as the simple number of "comments about [the] picture which go beyond pure description." The resulting TI is thus a number that can be compared across individuals, across cards, or across different sorts of apperceptive techniques. Although the TI spurred research on projectives throughout the 1950s, and then again in the early 1970s, it unfortunately never generated the empirical critical mass of, say, the Rorschach Comprehensive System (e.g., Exner, 2003). One reason for the lack of a standard progression of research from scale development to criterion and convergent validation appears to be the face validity of the TI. By definition, elements of the narrative that go beyond objective stimulus elements must involve some degree of projection. Thus, subsequent research used it as a gold standard criterion for projection, imagination, or general fantasy (e.g., Singer, Wilensky, & McCraven, 1956; Prola, 1970), in which the amount of projected material was of interest in addition to specific content categories. For the present purposes, no distinction will be made between the term *projection* and fantasized or imagined elements that are verbalized in response to a projective stimulus.

Contemporaneous with 1950s research on the TI, Shatin (1958) explored a similar set of dimensions involving constriction–dilation in both the Rorschach and TAT. Shatin defined Rorschach constriction in terms of classic variables such as F% and card rejections (higher values indicating greater constriction), as well as movement plus summed color responses and response total (higher values indicating greater dilation). TAT constriction was defined by variables such as word count and strength of interpersonal relationships (higher scores indicating greater dilation) and number of card rejections and very popular stories (higher scores indicating greater constriction). Shatin found that the majority of TAT and Rorschach constriction–dilation variables were associated in the expected direction.

Later, slightly after the early 1970s research on the TI, Selmon, Holzwarth, Lewis, and Sitko (1976) developed a related pair of TAT scales. The first, Associative Elaboration, measured the extent to which respondents provided story elements beyond mere description, and the second, Integration, assessed the degree to which plot elements in a TAT story were coherent. The Associative Elaboration scale, which they acknowledged was similar to Weisskopf's (1950) work, appears conceptually identical, but scoring is not detailed and it has no separate categories. The authors could not be located to obtain further information. Good interrater reliability was achieved for the scale on the TATs in a sample of children in a psychiatric facility (e.g., average *r* across three raters of .91), but Selmon et al. abandoned the Integration scale because interrater reliabilities were lower (*r*s of .62–.72) and because it correlated .81 with the Associative Elaboration scale. Later, in a sample of schoolchildren using CAT, Schroth (1977) obtained sufficient interrater reliabilities for the integration scale (*r*s between three judges of .80–.84) and a somewhat lower correlation with associative elaboration (r = .71). Both Selmon et al. and Schroth found no correlation between either scale and IQ, and Selmon et al. found cross-sectional age increases in associative elaboration from ages 9 to 11 and then a leveling off from 11 to 15, whereas Schroth et al. found no cross-sectional age increases between 6 and 8 but then increases from ages 8 to 10. Such evidence might be considered consistent with possible developmental changes in the use of fantasy.

Although constriction–dilation variables and the Associative Elaboration scale may measure something similar to the TI, one appeal of the TI is the existence of multiple scoring categories originating in Weisskopf's (1950) work and later developed by Prola (1970). These categories, though they lack individual research on interrater reliability and predictive validity, nonetheless form a rich conceptual framework with which to view projective responses. We now turn to the scoring categories.

Scoring Categories

Weisskopf (1950) originally included 11 separate scoring categories and then later added four more (Weisskopf, undated). Prola also divided the 15 categories into movement-based (MT) and nonmovement (NMT) transcendence and offered some more specific instructions for scoring, as well as scoring examples (see Prola, 1970, Appendix A). It is important to note, however, that the majority of published research occurred prior to Prola's work and used Weisskopf's 11 original categories. Subsequent work (Custy, 1994; Ottenstein, 1983; Taggart-Thompson, 1980) also used the Weisskopf categories, and the movement–nonmovement distinction has not been retained, as it received little support in Prola's (1970) dissertation.

The complete complement of scoring categories from Weisskopf (1950, n.d.) are described below. Although the distinction was not useful in Prola's (1970) research, the first 10 categories are NMT, and the last 5 categories are MT. NMT and MT were correlated .80, and, unsurprisingly, failed to change differentially as a result of Prola's experimental manipulation (see below). Finally, in all work except Prola's (1970) effort to distinguish between MT and NMT, researchers have simply computed a total TI score by summing the incidences of each category over the cards administered. Sometimes this overall total has been augmented by single card totals, which are obtained by summing the incidence of all scores for that card. Detailed descriptions of the categories can be found in the scoring manual chapter of this volume and are briefly presented in Table 4.1.

□ Research Evidence

Validity

Research has tended to use the TI as content-valid prima facie evidence of projection or fantasy rather than viewing it as a tentative index that must be validated against existing, similar measures or other criteria of projection or fantasy. This is understandable, given the TI's face validity: Anything attributed to a card that is not directly obvious from the

TABLE 4.1 Scoring Categories

Category	Description
Relationship[a]	Typically kinship
Evaluation[a]	An aesthetic or moral evaluation
Atmosphere[a]	Characterization in terms of emotional response
Symbolism[a]	Ascription of symbolic meaning
Emphasis[a]	Singling out a specific part of the picture
Physiological Condition	Attribution or inference of a physiological characteristic
Possession	Implication of ownership
Occupation	Attribution of occupation
Quantification	Numerical statements about some element of the picture
Spatial Transcendence[a]	Events or objects outside the picture
Speech Content[a]	Attribution of specific statements to figures
Temporal Transcendence[a]	Inclusion of prior or subsequent events
Intraception[a]	Ascription of emotions, desires, thoughts, or movements
Imperative[a]	*Should, must,* or *supposed to* descriptions
Ability	Statements that a figure in the picture is capable of doing something

[a] Original Weisskopf category.

card must logically be a projection of some sort. This assumption appears to have been accepted readily during the 1950s, and the TI was immediately adopted as a dependent variable in projective research rather than pursued as something to be scrutinized psychometrically in and of itself.

Despite this, the validity of the TI can be inferred to some extent from the body of studies which used it, which are summarized in Table 4.2. Work using the TI has involved four main thrusts. First, researchers attempted to draw some distinctions between early, everyday series cards or later fantastic series cards (Murray, 1943) as eliciting greater projection. Second, differences in projection elicited by human or animal figures in the CAT have been investigated with the TI. Third, researchers attempted to determine whether stimuli closely resembling a subject would elicit more projection than dissimilar stimuli. A fourth group of studies has borne more directly on the validity of the TI itself by examining, for instance, whether it varies as a function of word count (e.g., Prola, 1972b). Work after 1972 has been quite sparse, but ongoing research at the University of North Texas (Jenkins, Brown, Perez, & Allen, in progress) is examining the TI's convergence with other measures of constriction and dilation on the Rorschach.

With respect to the first area, Weisskopf's (1950) initial study was designed to test whether one series of cards or certain individual cards would evoke more projection than others. Additionally, Weisskopf examined whether subjects projected more onto characters of the same gender. These questions arose from the claims forwarded by Murray (1943)—namely, that (1) differential amounts of projection would occur between

TABLE 4.2 Studies Employing Weisskopf's (1950) Transcendence Index

Study	Finding
Weisskopf (1950)	Men and women do not project more onto same-sex hero cards; women having higher TIs than men; early (everyday series) cards evoke more projection than later (fantasy series) cards; parent–child and heterosexual relationship cards evoke more projection than other cards.
Kenny (1953)	TAT TI correlates .64 with revelation of personality through Q-sort task.
Weisskopf-Joelson and Lynn (1953)	Incompletely contoured (i.e., partially outlined) CAT cards elicit greater transcendence than standard cards among fourth-grade children.
Weisskopf-Joelson and Money (1954)	No differences in TI between standard TAT cards and those in which photograph of examinee's face was placed on card over central figure's face.
Kenny (1954)	TAT cards from fantasy series do not elicit higher TI than cards from first series.
Singer, Wilensky, and McCraven (1959)	TI loads on a factor with motor inhibition, planning ability, and fantasy.
Gurel and Ullman (1958)	TI correlates .85 with number of emotional words in story, but emotional words also included in TI scores.
Lindzey and Silverman (1959)	Word count and TI scores correlate .76 in group administration with "tell a story" instructions.
Weisskopf-Joelson and Foster (1962)	No differences in TI between human or animal, chromatic, or achromatic CAT cards.
Prola (1970)	TI is uncorrelated with a self-report measure of fantasy, unaffected by experimental manipulation of motor inhibition.
Prola (1972b)	Significantly more transcendent comments in second half of TAT responses.
Neuringer and Livesay (1970)	No differences in TI between human and animal CAT cards.
Weisskopf-Joelson and Wexner (1970)	TI is higher in male subjects presented with stimuli relevant to men than with stimuli relevant to women, but no evidence men projected more onto cards with male figures or women onto cards with female figures.
Weisskopf-Joelson, Zimmerman, and McDaniel (1970)	No differences in TI on Make-a-Picture-Story test figures rated as highly similar or highly dissimilar to subjects.

(*Continued*)

TABLE 4.2 Studies Employing Weisskopf's (1950) Transcendence Index (Continued)

Study	Finding
Taggart Thompson (1980)	Picture Story Test and School Apperception Method elicit more projection than TAT.
Ottenstein (1983)	TI is unrelated to number of imaginative transformations in play of 5- or 7-year-olds.
Imanus, Keinonen, and Vanhamäki (1992)	Physically handicapped children produce higher TIs than nonhandicapped children.

the first mundane part of the card series and the latter fairy tale sequence containing more ambiguous or bizarre scenes; and (2) male test takers would project more onto male figures in the BM (boy-male) cards and female test takers would project more onto female heroes in the GF (girl-female) cards rather than respondents projecting more onto opposite gender heroes.

In a sample of 66 college students (36 male) asked to provide written descriptions of all pictures in the series, the fairy tale cards actually elicited less transcendence than the mundane or everyday series. Within the everyday series, cards involving multiple characters (e.g., parent–child and man–woman cards: 2, 6BM, 7BM, 7GF, 4, 6GF, 10, 13MF) produced more transcendence than a group of remaining cards involving human figures. Cards 6BM (old woman and young man), 4 (couple with half-dressed girl), 7BM (old and young men), 7GF (woman and girl with doll), and 2 (farm scene) elicited the highest numbers of transcendent comments, and 12M (man lying on couch, one bending over him), 17GF (woman standing on a bridge), 13G (girl ascending stairs), 20 (man standing under streetlamp), and 9BM (four men lying in grass) evoked the lowest number. Weisskopf (1950) also discovered that men and women did not produce more transcendent comments about characters matched to their gender but that women did produce significantly higher transcendence scores for the entire card set, noting, consonant with gender perceptions of the time: "... These differences correspond to the popular stereotype of women tending to observe less objectively and to project their own emotions into the external world" (p. 388). Later research replicated these results in broad strokes: Kenny (1954) found no differences between the everyday and fantastic series on the TI, and Weisskopf-Joelson and Wexner (1970) found that men did not project more onto cards with male figures and that women did not project more onto cards with female figures than figures opposite in gender to the respondent.

The second group of studies implementing the TI has involved the CAT. Weisskopf-Joelson and Lynn (1953) manipulated the ambiguity of CAT cards by creating an alternate set with incompletely traced contours. These pictures were administered to 50 fourth-grade (nine-year-old) children, and two weeks later, intact versions of the same CAT cards were administered. Although specific statistics were not reported, subjects produced significantly lower TIs in response to the initial, unaltered cards, suggesting that stimulus ambiguity contributes to projection. The authors dismissed the likelihood that repeated measurement accounted for the difference, on the basis of an unpublished earlier study by Weisskopf suggesting that repetition did not affect the TI for incomplete pictures.

In another study with a creative design, Weisskopf-Joelson and Foster (1962) used the TI to examine whether animal cards or human cards elicit more projection in

40 kindergarteners. The features of four CAT cards were manipulated so that the characters were (1) either animal or human and so that (2) the card was either chromatic or achromatic. Thus, there were four versions of each of the four cards used (i.e., animal-chromatic, animal-achromatic, human-chromatic, human-achromatic for each card), for a total of 16 possible cards. The 40 children were each administered one card from each animal/human-chromatic/achromatic combination, determined on the basis of a Latin Square. T-tests revealed no differences in projection between animal or human, or chromatic or achromatic cards, and a subsequent insignificant omnibus F-test indicated no interaction between the two experimental conditions. When Weisskopf-Joelson and Foster split the sample into the 11 children with highest and lowest transcendence scores, they still failed to find significant differences, although they noted a trend for children with high TIs tended to make more transcendent comments on chromatic cards.

Earlier, Neuringer, and Livsay (1959) had obtained a similar null result with the CAT in a series of 30 fourth-grade children. However, in another comparative study, Taggart Thompson (1980) found that the TAT yielded lower TIs than the Picture Story Test (Symonds, 1948) or the School Apperception Method (Solomon & Starr, 1968). With respect to the TAT specifically, Taggart Thompson reviewed literature suggesting that the psychological and social themes of foremost concern during the 1970s deviated somewhat from those of the 1930s, during which the TAT was constructed. Her review suggested that the top five such themes at the time were achievement, authority, family, health, and getting along with others. She then grouped TAT cards according to the contemporary theme they appeared most associated with. Within the TAT, the getting along theme elicited significantly less transcendence than achievement, family, authority, or health themes. The implication of these results for the validity of the TI itself is, at best, ambiguous.

A somewhat related line of research involved the notion that stimuli similar to the subject would elicit greater projection than stimuli dissimilar to the subject. Two studies roundly refuted this, however. In the first, Weisskopf-Joelson & Money (1953) designed an ingenious experiment in which 10 subjects were administered two sets of cards. One set contained no alterations to the figures, but in the second set, the face of the central figure in the card was replaced with a photographic reproduction of the subject's face. TIs did not differ significantly between these two conditions, however. Later, Weisskopf-Joelson, Zimmerman, and McDaniel (1970) had subjects rate 20 figures on the Make-a-Picture-Story Test for degree of similarity to themselves. Then, subjects were asked to describe the three figures most like themselves and the three most unlike themselves, and TIs were calculated for these descriptions. Again, no difference emerged, corroborating the notion that degree of subject-stimulus similarity has no impact on amount of projection.

In a somewhat related study, Custy (1994) examined the extent to which empathy—operationalized through imitation of facial expression—produced more inferential statements (i.e., transcendent statements) about a target. Custy asked subjects to imitate the facial expressions of a target individual shown on a 30-second video tape (the target). The target was speaking, but no sound accompanied the video. Custy then asked subjects to describe the video and examined the TIs of narratives. His interest was whether subjects would provide more transcendent statements when imitating certain facial expressions (e.g., happy, sad, mad) and whether the degree of matching in facial expression between subject and target would correlate with greater transcendence. Although subjects imitating facial expressions provided no higher TIs than those not instructed to imitate the expressions, the degree of matching between imitated facial expressions and those of the target correlated highly with TI (r = .47), in terms of Cohen's (1992) effect size guidelines. Furthermore, subjects who imitated happy expressions produced more transcendent statements than those imitating sad or angry expressions. TI scores also correlated .55 with independent raters' judgments of the degree of psychological distance, or abstraction, characterizing subjects' responses (i.e., greater distance analogous to greater transcendence). These results are interesting in that, within the framework of Custy's operationalization of empathy as imitative expression, they suggest that empathy may involve some degree of projection by the empathizer onto the empathizee.

As is evident from such studies, the validity of the TI itself as a measure of projection has not been a direct focus in most research. A few studies, however, examined this issue somewhat more closely. In the first, Kenny (1953) correlated the TI with a Q-sort task that tapped the degree to which individuals revealed important elements of their personality and obtained an *r* of .64. A later study (Gurel & Ullman, 1958) attempted to address a similar issue by correlating TI with the number of emotional words emerging from a protocol, but, since the TI itself included emotional words, the obtained correlation of .84 suffers from some degree of criterion contamination. In another effort, Singer et al. (1956) found that the TI loaded on a factor with measures of motor inhibition, planning ability, and fantasy; they interpreted the factor as a measure of introspective tendency or imagination.

In contrast, Prola's (1970) work found that the TI did not change as a result of an experimental manipulation that, he theorized, should induce more fantasy. In a randomized between subjects design, Prola experimentally induced motor inhibition—which involved strapping subjects to a chair for 15 minutes prior to administration of the TAT—in one group and examined whether this would result in increased fantasy, measured by the TI, compared with a control group. Both Jerome Singer and Jacob Cohen were on Prola's dissertation committee, and the latter's presence is evident in Prola's use of a fairly rigorous set of regression analyses that probably mitigated chances of finding a difference between the treatment and control groups.

Cohen's preference for multiple regression rather than analysis of variance (ANOVA)-based analyses of experimental data is well known (see Cohen, Cohen, West, & Aiken, 2003) and involves contrast coding the experimental conditions. Prola (1970), however, entered several covariates in a hierarchical regression prior to the experimental treatment term, including pretest MT, NMT, and total TI scores, as well as word count, as first-block covariates. These TI variables correlated with their posttest counterparts in the .6–.7 range and naturally accounted for the lion's share of variance in posttest TI scores, leaving little criterion variance uniquely predicted by the experimental condition block. It is important to note that the same results would have been obtained if he had simply used an analysis of covariance (ANCOVA) with the same covariates, so the issue is not one of ANOVA-based versus regression analyses but of methodological rigor represented by partialing out variance due to pretest TI scores.

An exploratory analysis by Prola (1970) bearing more directly on the convergent validity of the TI revealed no association between transcendence scores and a daydreaming factor in the self-report Imaginal Processes Inventory. Some support for the motor inhibition-fantasy hypothesis, however, comes from the more recent findings of Ihanus, Keinonen, and Vanhamäki (1992). These authors found that the TIs of handicapped, physically limited children were significantly higher than those of nonhandicapped children. Finally, more recently, Ottenstein (1983) found no correlation between TI scores and the number of transformations observed in the play of 5- and 7-years-olds. Transformations were operationalized as pretending to be something or someone else (e.g., an animal, machine) or taking on or assigning roles in play. Thus, transformations were themselves a measure of imagination or fantasy.

The extent to which such results speak to the validity of the TI as a measure of fantasy or imagination is difficult to discern, but three issues appear germane. First, null results following the drastic motor inhibition in Prola's (1970) initial work may simply reflect less projection as a function of irritation, fear, or perplexity and may have little bearing on the TI's validity itself. Second, with respect to Prola's null correlation between the TI and self-reported fantasy, an obvious possibility is that fantasy or imagination manifests in many different varieties that may be unrelated. For instance, there would appear to be no necessary connection between general daydreaming, which likely occurs sporadically, privately, and without external prompting, and projection, delivered implicitly on cue, in a discreet situation, as a response to a projective task. Third, from a measurement perspective, Prola's (1970) and Ottenstein's (1983) insignificant correlations may have been attenuated by lack of shared method variance, range restriction, or unreliability in one or both instruments. In particular, circling Likert-scale responses to a series of statements about one's tendency to daydream is a qualitatively different mode of response than verbal narrative solicited by an examiner wielding pictures, a legal pad, and a pen. Thus, it is difficult to draw any meaningful conclusions about the TI's validity from this set of results.

A final issue that has arisen with respect to the validity of the TI is the degree to which it is simply an epiphenomenon of verbal productivity. In a protocol crowded with verbiage, one would naturally expect to see more transcendent comments. Lindzey and Silverman (1959), for instance, reported that number of words in TAT stories correlated .84 with TI scores. Prola (1970) reported a similar *r* of .76 and later argued that although such a correlation was understandable when subjects were given traditional instructions to tell a story about a picture, an association of that magnitude was more problematic in situations where subjects were asked only to describe the situation (Prola 1972b). He developed a theoretical response model to explain transcendence, positing that subjects initially offer pure description, but, as the describable stimulus elements of the picture are exhausted and the subject feels further verbal productivity pressure, transcendent comments become more frequent. He tested this hypothesis by examining the number of transcendent comments in the first and second halves of protocols and found significantly more transcendent comments in the second half. These results provide some support for his response model. However, the issue would seem to be one of individual differences in verbal productivity, and his analysis speaks only to mean differences on the TI in a single group at two time points. Regardless, a link between productivity and transcendence seems unsurprising because transcendence is impossible without verbiage. Therefore, the implications of Prola's response model and the probable link between verbal productivity and transcendence constitute, if anything, evidence for the validity of the TI as a measure of projection.

Generalizability

By logic, the TI generalizes to any use of projective techniques where verbal response is called for. As noted before, the TI has been used with other projective tests, such as the CAT (Weisskopf-Joelson & Foster, 1962) and even with narratives provided in response to viewing a silent film (Custy, 1994). Because it is a general measure of projection, transcendence is not logically confined to the TAT, although one fundamental requirement would be a projective stimulus with intelligible, everyday details that can be either described or transcended. Clearly, the aforementioned scoring categories could not be used sensibly with projective stimuli that have no characters or distinct scenes, such as Rorschach or Holtzman ink blots.

Similarly, there are few restrictions on the population with which the TI might be used. Most research has used either children (e.g., Taggart Thompson, 1980; Weisskopf-Joelson & Foster, 1962) or college students (e.g., Prola, 1970, 1972b; Weisskopf, 1950). However, because the TI is a general index designed to provide a baseline quantification of the amount of projection inherent in a narrative, any individual capable of understanding projective administration instructions and rendering a verbal response could produce transcendent material. One area where circumspection would appear necessary, however, would be in the protocols of subjects who are not fluent English speakers. In such cases, a respondent's ability to transcend the stimulus clearly would be limited by vocabulary and syntactical issues. Because of such things, scoring reliability would likely be lower as well. Let us turn now to existing reliability evidence, however, which has been quite good.

Reliability

In the initial 1950 study, Weisskopf noted that "decisions about units of transcendence and other similar problems were made according to an extensive set of scoring standards" (p. 384) but made no other mention of the reliability of TI scoring categories other than a footnote stating that a study of interrater reliability was in progress at the time. Although it is not clear that a separate study strictly on interrater reliability was ever published, Weisskopf-Joelson and Dunlevy (1952) rescored a set of protocols after 1 year and obtained a stability coefficient of .95 with respect to total scores. Weisskopf-Joelson and Lynn (1953), after an interval not specified, also obtained a high stability coefficient (.98).

Agreement between scorers has typically involved product moment correlations between sets of scores, or occasionally involved kappas or intraclass correlations between total scores. Table 4.3 is an updated summary of reliability reports, after Prola (1972a). As can be seen, interrater reliability is typically quite good. One difficulty is that these reliabilities pertain to the overall TI, and there are no data on the interrater reliability of discreet scoring categories. By inference, however, agreement on specific categories must be reasonably good since the TI is simply a sum of category scores. Regarding the TI's unidimensionality, Prola's (1970) Cronbach's alpha internal consistency estimates for total transcendence scores derived from summing categories across stories were .90 and .95, suggesting that total TI is a homogenous construct.

Another thing to note with respect to administration and research is that no particular set of TAT cards has been uniformly employed and that researchers have at times administered the cards with standard TAT instructions, specifically requesting a story (e.g., Gurel & Ullman, 1958), while at other times, such as in Weisskopf's introductory study, cards were administered with the instruction simply to describe the card (e.g., Weisskopf-Joelson & Dunlevy, 1952). However, in most studies (e.g., Ottenstein, 1983; Taggart-Thompson, 1980), standard instructions appear to have been used because the focus of the study has not been the psychometrics of TI itself. Furthermore, protocols at times appear to have been written by examinees (Weisskopf, 1950) and at other times to have been recorded and transcribed later (Weisskopf-Joelson & Foster, 1962).

Finally, the degree of training or education necessary to obtain adequate scoring appears quite reasonable. For instance, in a pilot study Custy (1994) trained 3 raters over a series of 25 responses and obtained an intraclass *r* of .91 for total TI scores. Raters have

TABLE 4.3 Reliability Reports of the Transcendence Index

Study	Type of Reliability	Coefficient
Beller and Haralson (1951)	Interrater *r*	.86
	1-year test–retest	.95
Weisskopf-Joelson and Dunlevy (1952)	Rescoring after 1 year	.95
Weisskopf-Joelson and Lynn (1953)	Average interrater *rs among* three judges	.73–.96
	Rescoring after unspecified time	.98
Herman (1957)	Interrater *r*	.80
Gurel and Ullman (1958)	Rescoring after 1 to 2 months	.98
Laskowitz (1959)	Average interrater *r* among three judges	.81
Neuringer and Livesay (1970)	Interrater *r*	.78
Prola (1970)	Interrater *r*	.96
	Coefficient alphas, two response sets	.90 and .95
Taggart Thompson (1980)	Interrater *r*	.86
Ottenstein (1983)	Kappa	.80
Custy (1994)	Average interrater *r*, three judges	.90
	Intraclass correlation	.97

Adapted from Prola (1972) with permission.
Notes: Reliabilities for all are total TI scores calculated by summing Weisskopf's (1950) 11 categories. Prola (1970) added his occupation category.

typically been advanced graduate students (e.g., Taggart-Thompson, 1980), or graduate student–psychologist pairs (e.g., Ottenstein, 1983). However, advanced undergraduates have attained satisfactory agreement (Jenkins et al., in progress). The general level of training in psychology necessary to achieve reliability appears by no means prohibitive, though prior familiarity with open ended narrative scoring may be helpful.

□ Future Research Needed

One thing noteworthy in Weisskopf's (1950) original work was that she looked for significant mean differences across cards, card types (e.g., fantasy vs. everyday series), and genders (as well as interactions among these variables). Although experimental or person by environment designs may ascertain the impact of various types of projective test administration, basic issues of construct validation and predictive validity remain to be resolved.

For instance, projection can be conceptualized as a transient, state-like variable fluctuating with degree of comfort in a testing situation, mood, or sense of threat or a trait-like variable closely tied to characteristic defensive processes. With respect to the first issue, Beller and Harrelson (1951) found a 1-year test–retest reliability of .95.

This is exceptionally high, and it would seem important to replicate such a stability estimate. If other stability coefficients of a similar magnitude are obtained, one might infer that transcendence is relatively trait like for almost everyone. However, test–retest correlations render only an assessment of the rank-order stability of interindividual differences within a sample, and, as with all methods that involve averaging across individuals, important intraindividual change may be obscured. Therefore, if future research produces lower stability coefficients, it would be worthwhile to discriminate between individuals for whom transcendence remains relative stable (trait like) and those for whom it may fluctuate according to situational demands or in association with other important personality characteristics. Such knowledge would be useful for clinicians because it would help discern initially state-defensive subjects who might eventually produce more usable TAT narratives—after rapport and trust had been built—from those who will always tend toward simple description due to ingrained defensiveness or characteristic concreteness.

Most important, however, future research should strive to validate the TI as a measure of projection by comparing it to known measures of constriction or defensiveness, such as Rorschach lambda or number of responses. Moderate correlations with such indices would indicate some degree of convergence between the TI and other measures designed to tap a similar process of self-exposure, task engagement, and openness. In addition to examining correlations between other projective indices of constriction–dilation, researchers may wish to ascertain TI correlations with self-report validity indices measuring defensiveness. Heteromethod correlations, although they are likely to be lower, will help to demonstrate that the monomethod convergence with constriction–dilation variables on other projectives is not simply a function of common method variance. For instance, one might examine correlations between the TI and the Minnesota Multiphasic Personality Inventory (MMPI) K or between TI and the Millon Clinical Multiaxial Inventory (MCMI) Disclosure. Finally, simulation studies, in which one group of subjects is instructed to respond in a guarded way, another in an unguarded way, may also speak usefully to the validity issue. In the end, the TI is a useful construct in projective testing that would benefit from renewed investigation and use.

□ Notes

[1] It is important to note that the modern Rorschach Comprehensive System (Exner, 1993) also encompasses embellishments or responses that go beyond what is present in stimulus features.

□ References

Beller, E. K., & Haralson, E. J. (1951). *A study in the reliability of the Transcendence Index.* Unpublished master's thesis, Indiana University.

Cohen, J. (1992). A power primer. *Psychological Bulletin,* 112, 155–159.

Cohen, J., Cohen, P., West, S. G., & Aiken, L. (2003). *Applied multiple regression/correlation analysis for the behavioral sciences* (3rd ed.). Mahwah, NJ: Lawrence Erlbaum.

Custy, J. E., III (1994). *Facial kinesthetic empathizing as a process of forming inferences during personal interactions.* Unpublished doctoral dissertation, University of Michigan.

Exner, J. E. (2003). *The Rorschach: A Comprehensive System, Volume 1* (4th edition). New York: Wiley Interscience.

Gurel, L., & Ullman, L.P. (1958). Quantitative differences in response to TAT cards: The relationship between transcendence scores and the number of emotional words. *Journal of Projective Techniques, 22,* 399–401.

Herman, J. L. (1957). *Ideational and motor correlates of the Rorschach experience type.* Unpublished doctoral disseration, New York University.

Ihanus, J., Keinone, M., & Vanhamäki, S. (1992). Rorshach movement responses and the TAT Transcendence Index in physically handicapped children. *Perceptual and Motor Skills, 74,* 1115–1119.

Jenkins, S. R., Perez, L., McConduit, J., Dato, D., Brown, D. R., & Allen, K. (in progress). *Unpublished analyses.* University of North Texas, Denton.

Kenny, D.T. (1954). Transcendence indices, extent of personality factors in fantasy responses, and the ambiguity of TAT cards. *Journal of Consulting Psychology, 18,* 345–348.

Laskowitz, D. (1959). *The effect of varied degrees of pictorial ambiguity on fantasy evocation.* Unpublished doctoral dissertation, New York University.

Lindzey, G., & Silverman, M. (1959). Thematic Apperception Test: Techniques of group administration, sex differences, and the role of verbal productivity. *Journal of Personality, 27,* 311–323.

Murray, H. A. (1943). *Thematic Apperception Manual.* Cambridge, MA: Harvard University Printing Office.

Neuringer, C., & Livesay, R. C. (1970). Projective fantasy on the CAT and CAT-H. *Journal of Projective Techniques and Personality Assessment, 34,* 487–491.

Ottenstein, R. J. (1983). *Symbolic play and imaginative predisposition: A study of their relationship and the impact of cognitive development and gender.* Unpublished doctoral dissertation, The Catholic University of America.

Prola, M. (1970). *A re-evaluation of the motor inhibition-fantasy hypothesis.* Unpublished doctoral dissertation, New York University.

Prola, M. (1972a). A review of the Transcendence Index. *Journal of Personality Assessment, 36,* 8–12.

Prola, M. (1972b). Verbal productivity and transcendence. *Journal of Personality Assessment, 36,* 445–446.

Schroth, M. (1977). The use of Associative Elaboration and Integration scales for evaluating CAT protocols. *Journal of Psychology, 97,* 29–35.

Selmon, A. G., Holzwarth, E. J., Lewis, J., & Sitko, M. (1976). Associative Elaboration and Integration scales for evaluating TAT protocols. *Journal of Personality Assessment, 40,* 365–369.

Shatin, L. (1958). The constriction–dilation dimension in Rorschach and TAT. *Journal of Clinical Psychology, 17,* 151–154.

Singer, J. L., Wilensky, H., & McCraven, V. (1959). Delaying capacity, fantasy, and planning ability: A factorial study of some basic ego functions. *Journal of Consulting Psychology, 20,* 375–383.

Solomon, I. L., & Starr, B. D. (1968). *School Apperception Method.* New York: Springer Publishing Co.

Symonds, P. M. (1948). *Symonds Picture-Story Test.* New York: Columbia University Press.

Taggart Thompson, B. (1980). *A comparison of three apperception tests with adolescents using selected themes.* Unpublished doctoral dissertation, Saint Louis University.

Weisskopf, E. A. (1950). A Transcendence Index as a proposed measure in the TAT. *Journal of Psychology, 29,* 379–390.

Weisskopf, E. A. (n.d.). *Scoring standards for transcendence indices.* Mimeographed.

Weisskopf-Joelson, E., & Dunlevy, G. P. (1952). Body similarity between subject and central figure in the TAT as an influence on projection. *Journal of Abnormal and Social Psychology, 47,* 441–445.

Weisskopf-Joelson, E., & Foster, H. C. (1962). An experimental study of stimulus variation upon projection. *Journal of Projective Techniques, 26,* 366–370.

Weisskopf-Joelson, E., & Lynn, D. B. (1953). The effect on variations in ambiguity on the projection in the Children's Apperception Test. *Journal of Consulting Psychology, 17,* 67–70.

Weisskopf-Joelson, E., & Money, L. (1953). Facial similarity between subject and central figure in the TAT as an influence on projection. *Journal of Abnormal and Social Psychology, 48,* 341–344.

Weisskopf-Joelson, E., & Wexner, L. B. (1970). Projection as a function of situational and figural similarity. *Journal of Projective Techniques and Personality Assessment, 34,* 397–400.

Weisskopf-Joelson, E., Zimmerman, J., & McDaniel, M. (1970). Similarity between subject and stimulus as an influence on projection. *Journal of Projective Techniques & Personality Assessment, 34,* 328–331.

5

CHAPTER

Scoring Manual for Edith Weisskopf's Transcendence Index

Edith Weisskopf, Max Prola, Luis E. Perez, and Sharon Rae Jenkins

Introduction

The Transcendence Index (TI; Weisskopf, 1950) is a content analysis system that was developed originally to provide empirical support for the design and selection of picture stimuli for storytelling techniques. Weisskopf conceptualized and quantified the variety of ways that people who were asked simply to describe a picture went beyond, or transcended, the stimulus by adding projective material. Thus, the TI was not conceptualized as a measure of personality per se; in undated lecture notes, Weisskopf equated projection to "the process by which personality structure affects behavior."

However, the TI's conceptual resemblance to the Rorschach Comprehensive System (Exner, 2003) Lambda score as a personality variable invites convergent validity studies of constriction–dilation as an index of response style that bears on protocol validity. TI might be especially useful for appraising protocols given by psychiatrically impaired populations, as some individuals have difficulty mustering a complete story even under storytelling instructions, whereas others tell longer stories showing perseveration or poverty of content, and still others relate short stories that depart considerably from the stimulus. This would produce lower TI scores in the former two cases and higher in the latter relative to story length, reducing the correlation between these variables. The third response style might yield high TI scores and useful personality information despite its brevity.

Previous studies reviewed by Benjamin Chapman (chapter 4, this volume) have used both Weisskopf's (1950) original administration instructions to "describe the pictures" and the storytelling instructions used for other thematic apperceptive techniques (TATs).

In the former case, the scores of interest were typically the relative transcendence scores of the various stimuli. Some studies of stories have compared stimuli similarly; others have used only the total score across the entire protocol, but none have distinguished among the specific content categories. However, the thoroughness of the system's classification of nondescriptive material invites examination of the separate categories in relation to other measures and to overt behavior.

☐ Administration

Format

The original administration instructions are not detailed in Weisskopf (1950): "The subjects were instructed to describe the *TAT* pictures" (p. 382, italics in original). Subsequent research reviewed by Chapman (chapter 4, this volume) used this and a variety of storytelling instructions, as well as a range of response options (e.g., handwritten by participants, audio recording with later transcription). The salient issue for these choices is that they be congruent with the purpose of the research, the preferred interpretation of the scores, and the capabilities of the examinees. In this manual, *story* designates protocols elicited under any instructional set.

One qualification about scoring stories elicited under storytelling instructions is that *no inquiry should be used.* The point of the system is to see how much nondescriptive material the examinee gives *spontaneously without prompting.* If stories gathered for other purposes are being scored, and queries are noted in the protocol, responses that occur after the examiner's first question or comment *of any kind* should be ignored.

Stimuli

As noted in Chapman's review chapter in this volume, a variety of stimuli has been used, which is appropriate to the original purpose of the system, the evaluation of stimuli. There is no obvious reason related to the TI for restriction on the nature of stimuli, provided that the resulting score interpretation is consistent with the task and instructions given to participants.

☐ Scoring Process

The scorer's task is to read the story and to identify words and phrases that go beyond a literal description of the picture. The scorer should be sufficiently familiar with the picture to be able to discriminate between true additions to the scene and plausible misperceptions of an object or person that is clearly present in the picture. When additions and other transcendent elements have been identified, each is then classified according to the scoring categories described in the next section.

There are three general rules for scoring the Transcendence Index. The first states that if alternative or multiple descriptions are given, both are scored, unless the descriptions repeat the same exact word or phrase (see the second rule). For example, in the sentence, "He is trying to console his mother who seems to be worried about his leaving, or maybe sad about something," there are five scorable elements. *He is trying to console, mother, worried, about his leaving,* and *sad* all score under different categories: Intraception, Relationship, Intraception, Intraception-Content, and Intraception, respectively.

The second rule is that if a transcendent comment is repeated, it is scored only once if exactly the same scorable words are used. That is, modifiers may be added or removed, word order changed, and so forth, but if these do not change the scoring, the repetition should not be scored in addition to the previous instance. Different forms of the same verb or noun are not considered different words. For example if the participant says, "He thinks" and later says, "He is thinking" the second statement is not scored, unless what he is thinking about is different—which would result in two separate scores for Intraception-Content.

The final rule is that when the same word, phrase, or simple sentence could be scored under more than one category, score the one not yet scored or scored the least often in the story. In the case that all applicable scoring categories have been scored elsewhere in the story and Intraception-Content is one of the options, score the comment as Intraception-Content. This will yield the highest transcendence score, as well as give a more precise measure of the storyteller's tendency to transcend.

In Weisskopf's (1950) original system, no stringent standards were given concerning differentiations among the specific transcendence categories. When the total transcendence score is the focus, it makes no difference which category yields the score for a given element because the different kinds of transcendence are not of interest. The present manual has sharpened these distinctions for those wishing to use the categories separately. Additional decision rules for this purpose are given following the scoring category criteria.

The scorer must read each story and underline all transcendent comments according to the rules given, noting the category abbreviation in the margin. In addition, Movement Transcendence (MT) may be differentiated from Nonmovement Transcendence (NMT), an exploratory scoring developed by Prola (1970), which is applicable to material scored in categories 10 through 16. If movement is specified, bracket the comment in addition to underlining it, and add MT to the abbreviation in the margin.

Throughout, negative statements should be scored in the same manner as affirmative statements—that is, "He is not afraid" is scored the same as "He is afraid," and "She is not his mother" the same as "She is his mother."

Scoring Category Criteria

Relationship (REL)

Relationship refers to the characterization of figures as related to other figures shown in the same picture, not transcendent figures. A relationship needs a social role term. The great majority refers to kinship, but others, such as friend, boss, suitor, and fiancé, are also included. Examples of REL are "She is the mother" or "He is the father." Note, however, that sequiturs should not be scored separately in addition; that is, score each dyad only once per story rather than each role involved. For example, in the description, "She is his mother. The son is standing behind her" only one score is given for relationship, not two. A relationship to a figure not in the picture should not be scored; both figures must be in the picture. However, the figure not in the picture would likely be scored as Spatial or Temporal Transcendence.

Evaluation (EVA)

Evaluation refers to the storyteller's characterization of figures or objects in the picture, or the picture itself, by an evaluative statement, either aesthetic (e.g., beautiful, ugly), moral (e.g., bad, good, morally superior or not), or artistic (e.g., characteristics of the scene depicted, including references to similar features elsewhere). These statements must be given within the present picture context (i.e., the present time period, regardless of tense used), for example, "... In the background is what I call a vile picture...."

Comments about the historical era of the picture (e.g., "old-fashioned") or from which the clothing, hairstyles, makeup, and so forth are derived are considered artistic evaluation, as is description of the picture as being derived from a novel, play, movie, or television program. Similarly included are descriptions of a figure in the picture as resembling some well-known person, such as an actor or political figure, and references to having seen a similar picture before, as in a psychology textbook. Indecision or ambivalence about the gender, race, or other physical features of a figure is also scored as EVA, even if the indecision is eventually resolved.

Personalized editorial comments that a figure or object in a picture, or the picture as a whole, remind the storyteller of a person, place, object, or event in his or her own life are only given one score (if any), regardless of the length of the statement. Content within these self-referential statements that does not refer to the picture is not scored.

If the evaluation is made of more than one person or object simultaneously (e.g., "They are ugly"), only one score is given. However, if the persons or objects are mentioned separately (e.g., "The old woman and the young girl are ugly"), each receives a score. This category and Intraception are the only two categories where this rule applies.

Statements about visible facial expressions, such as facially expressed emotions, cannot be EVA, because EVA is in the eye of the beholder. These will typically qualify as Atmosphere if they are transcendent at all, or as Intraception if internal experience of emotions is described. However, such expressions may be subject to scorable editorial EVA: "She has a pretty smile."

Atmosphere (ATM)

Atmosphere includes (a) the characterization of the whole or part of a picture in terms of the internal response that the setting elicits in the storyteller or character, and (b) giving a specific appellation to the setting that tends to elicit distinctive social and emotional responses, such as *courtroom, jungle,* or *dining room.* Examples of ATM are "This scene looks calm and peaceful," "This picture is uncanny," and "He is in his classroom staring at his violin" (to card 1). These statements must be given within the present context for the picture (i.e., the time period given in the picture, regardless of tense used).

Category (a) includes editorial comments about the intentions of the artist to elicit a particular response, comments about the picture being unreal or surrealistic, and statements of an inability to discern the facial expression or emotions of a figure. Category (b) is not scored when the setting is clearly given in the picture, such as the farm in card 2, the graveyard in card 15, or the bedroom in card 13MF. Comments about the physical aspects of the picture, such as *fuzzy, grainy, a rubbed effect, a painting,* or *a sketch,* are not scored if they are limited to the visible features of the image, as they are not transcendent; neither is the season of the year in an outdoor picture, unless emotionally toned words are present—for example, "This feels like spring."

Symbolism (*SYM*)

Symbolism refers to the conscious and explicitly verbalized ascription of a symbolic or metaphorical meaning to the picture—for example, "She has opened the door to the future," "This is climbing the ladder of success," or "dying to succeed."

Emphasis (*EMP*)

Emphasis refers to the singling out or stressing of a part of the picture, such as, "The most important part of this picture is ..."

Physiological Condition (*PHY*)

Physiological Condition refers to statements attributing to a figure in a picture physical states that cannot be represented pictorially in an unambiguous manner. "He is asleep," "She is dead," "He has a weak heart," or "He is sick" are examples. However, in card 2, the pregnancy of the woman who is leaning against the tree is evident enough that it should not be scored as transcendent.

Possession (*POS*)

Possession refers to comments that an individual owns an object in the picture—for example, "The violin belongs to him," "These are his books," or "The land belongs to the mother." Statements of this kind, however, are not scored if the object is a piece of clothing that is worn or carried by the figure. Statements such as, "The violin was given to him" are also scored as POS. Relationships are not scored (*her mother* is scored only for REL).

Occupation (*OCC*)

Occupation refers to the assignment of an occupation to a figure in the picture, such as *doctor, lawyer, farmer.* For example, the statement, "The doctor stood over him" is scored. Here also, sequiturs are not scored: "A doctor and his patient" or "A lawyer and her client" each receives only one score.

Quantification (*QUA*)

Quantification refers to numerical statements about the specific time of day, dates, ages, heights, and so forth—"He is 20 years old," for example. Such statements are scored only if they are exact and not approximations. "She is about 20" does not receive a score.

Speech Content (*SPC*)

Speech Content refers to verbal statements attributed to figures in the pictures. The speech need not be made during the present moment of the picture, as long as the speaker is in the picture. It is scored only if the specific content of the conversation is given, as though in a cartoon speech balloon, or if the verb used gives an indication of the content of the speech: "She is pleading," "He is consoling," or "He is arguing."—for example, "He demands an explanation as to where the money ... had gone," "The mother is telling the girl to get an education," "She is pleading for her life," or "I imagine the lady is attempting to explain the infant's entrance into this world to the little girl...." In the previous example, the portion consisting of *the infant's entrance into this world* technically qualifies as Intraception, but do not score the actual content of the speech under another transcendence category in addition to SPC. This category does not include statements such as, "She is saying something" or "He is speaking to her" if no content is given. These statements might not be transcendent if consistent with the picture. An example of Speech Content with Movement (SPC-MT) is, "She told him to mow the lawn."

Spatial Transcendence (SPA)

Spatial Transcendence refers to the inclusion of events, persons, or objects that are outside the field of vision represented within the picture's present context (i.e., the present time period, regardless of tense used). To score this category correctly it is important for the scorer to be familiar with the TAT card. The statement, "Other children are playing outside," which is so frequently made as a response to card 1, is an illustration of this category, and also of Movement (SPA-MT). *Rural area* refers to something outside the field of vision depicted in the picture—even for card 2—and is scored as SPA. *Somebody* is scored SPA when it refers to someone not visible in the picture.

Temporal Transcendence (TEM)

Temporal Transcendence refers to the inclusion of events that occur prior to or after the event shown in the picture, such as, "He will begin his lessons soon" or "His mother had just left the room." The latter is also scored for Movement (TEM-MT), whereas the former is too abstract and need not involve physical action. Although the traditional instructions given with TATs (i.e., "Tell what has happened before ... and how it will come out") call for such transcendence, the inclusion of past or future events represents additions to what the instructions require when the examinee is asked only to describe the picture.

Intraception (INT)

Intraception refers to the ascribing of emotions, desires, thoughts, fantasies, actions, movements, and other subjective experiences to the figures in the picture within the present time context: "The person is pleased," "He is worrying," "He is consoling her," or "She is coming through the door," for example (the latter also scored for Movement [INT-MT]). Simple statements that meet this criterion are given one score: "She is trying to," "He is wanting to," "He is daydreaming," "He is thinking," or "She is running" (the latter INT-MT).

If more than one person is listed separately in an INT (e.g., "They are thinking"), only one score is given. However, if the persons are mentioned separately (e.g., "The old woman and the young girl are thinking"), one score is given for each person. This category and EVA are the only two categories where this applies.

Phrases like *pleased* and *happy* are scored as nonmovement INT. Phrases like *attempting to go on it* and *coming through the door* attribute physical action to the figure and are scored as INT with Movement (INT-MT). Further details about this discrimination are included in the section on Movement Transcendence.

Intraception Content (INT-C)

Intraception Content is scored when the specific content of the emotions, feelings, thoughts, or movement that have been scored as INT is given. That is, INT-C is the object of INT verbs: "The woman is thinking about the man," "He is daydreaming about his girlfriend," "She is looking for apples," or "He thinks, 'I'd like to play baseball'" (the latter two are scored as Movement [INT-C-MT]). The content of the INT should be scored only if it is specific—do not score *something* or *somebody*—and is in itself transcendent. In the previous example, if the girlfriend is not in the picture, a score is given for content of INT, and if the girlfriend is in the picture, no score is given for content of INT. However, if the daydreamer is not a figure in the picture, SPA should be scored rather than either INT or the transcendent content, since INT refers to ascribing, for example, emotions, thoughts, and movement to figures in the picture. As is the case for SPC, the entire content statement is treated as a single unit, and no additional scores are given within that unit.

Imperative (IMP)

Imperative refers to comments that a person in the picture *should, must, will, is supposed to,* or is otherwise compelled to act, feel, or think in a certain manner. Imperative comments are phrased in the voice of the narrator, not another character. Examples include, "He shouldn't talk to his mother like that," "His parents are forcing him," "The young man should feel kindly toward his father," or "This boy is supposed to play the violin," which is a frequent response to card 1. An example of IMP with Movement (IMP-MT) is, "He forced her into the room."

Ability (ABL)

Ability refers to statements that a figure in the picture can, cannot, or is able to do something. For example, "The girl is able to continue her studies," or "The boy can't play the violin." An example of ABL with Movement (ABL-MT) is, "He can pluck the strings faster than any other child in his class."

Movement Transcendence

Movement Transcendence (MT) is scored as a supplement to scores in categories 10–16 when the activity scored under that category involves physical action or gross motor movement. The number of instances of Movement is tallied as a separate score and is not added to the total transcendence score. Prola (1970) added this score to Weisskopf's (1950) original manual as a means to test the hypothesis that inhibition of the participant's motor movement by physical restraint would result in greater attribution of physical action to the characters in stories. Examples have been provided under the previous category descriptions.

The most frequent discrimination to be made in scoring MT is between action and other more abstract or passive uses of the same verbs, such as orientation. Only the former should be scored as Movement. The distinction can be made by considering the verb *to look,* which is often used figuratively, metaphorically, or positionally. For example, "She is looking out over the valley," and "He is looking at the violin" describe the physical orientation of the character and imply activity but do not denote action. (In fact, the latter statement about card 1 is not transcendent.) However, "He is looking the horse over," "She is looking to stop him," and "He is looking for his shoes" all indicate physical action. "He is looking for a way out" is ambiguous; it should be scored as Movement if the search is for a physical path but not if it describes a cognitive evasion. Such differentiations must come from the story context.

Although this category resembles in some ways the Human Movement score of the Rorschach Comprehensive System (Exner, 2003), it differs in that (1) typical picture stimuli unambiguously depict humans who are engaged in some form of activity, and (2) internal states and states of passive tension that could be scored as Rorschach Human Movement are not so scored here. Picture stimuli used for storytelling often show people in states of postural or gestural tension that are strongly suggestive of gross motor movement; descriptions of this activity are nontranscendent and thus are not scorable for any category. However, when that postural tension is integrated into a movement process, it should be scored. Thus, "He is throwing something" would be scored as INT-MT, whereas "His arm is raised" would not. Neither "She is leaning against the tree" nor "She is resting" would be scored as INT-MT. "She is going to school" would not be scored, nor would "She is waiting for the bus," but "She is walking to school" and "She is catching the bus" qualify as gross motor movement and should be scored as INT-MT.

Nontranscendent Remarks

The following types of responses, which occur with some frequency, should not be scored as transcendence: comments about the physical aspects of the picture (e.g., *fuzzy, grainy, a rubbed effect, a painting, a sketch*); statements about the physical size or weight of a figure (unless there is no objective basis in the picture for making such a judgment); the season of the year in an outdoor picture; and references to having seen the exact same picture before, as in a psychology textbook, for example. Note the difference between this exact reference and EVA. Do not score names.

Discriminating Among Scoring Categories

The present manual makes finer distinctions among categories than those available in Weisskopf's (1950, n.d. a, n.d. b) original materials in order to reduce the ambiguity of scoring. For example, people and events that are removed from the picture in both space and time could be scored originally as either Temporal or Spatial—these have been assigned somewhat arbitrarity to TEM. However, some of these categories address topics of clinical interest, such as the tendency to introduce new characters not shown in the picture or to move the story through time, which have small research literatures (e.g., Barndt & Johnson, 1955; Epley & Ricks, 1963; Rosen & Neugarten, 1960; Rousseau, Fort, & Corin, 2002; Squyres & Craddick, 1982). Some users may wish to prioritize the scoring of categories that are more central to the user's purpose when the story material meets the criteria for two or more categories equally well. The category specifications given here may be modified accordingly. The list of categories given in Table 5.1 is in priority order as used in the latter two authors' studies at the University of North Texas. Scores appearing earlier in each list are scored in preference to those that appear later, in those cases for which both apply.

TABLE 5.1 Transcendence Index Scoring Categories Classified By Location in Time and Space

	In the Picture	Out of the Picture
Present Time	REL INT SPC IMP ABL ATM EVA PHY OCC SYM POS QUA EMP	SPA SYM QUA EMP
Past, Future, or Other Time	REL TEM SPC IMP ABL ATM EVA PHY OCC SYM POS QUA EMP	TEM SYM QUA EMP

Note: Categories are listed in order of scoring priority for ambiguous cases.

Calculating Scores

All categories are scored 1 for each instance in the story and 0 if not present in the story. The total score for each category is the number of instances scored for each story, summed across stories to make totals for each category. Alternatively or in parallel, the total transcendence score for each story can be summed across categories within the story. The total transcendence score for each storyteller may be summed across either of these, as they should be equal. Then record the total number of bracketed statements as MT.

☐ Examples of Scoring

Six Examples of Picture Descriptions (Weisskopf, n.d. b)

Card numbers refer to the Murray (1943) TAT.

 INT/INT-C INT/INT-C	Card 8BM In this picture I see a young man of about 14 years, who is looking into his future through his mind. In other words his ambition in life must be to be a great surgeon.

Scores: INT=2, INT-C=2; TI=4

 TEM/INT REL/INT/INT-C	Card 6BM In this picture I see a fellow on leave from the service who is about to return back to his station. He is trying to console his mother who seems to be worried about his leaving.

Scores: REL=1, TEM=1, INT=2, INT-C=1; TI=5

EVA TEM-MT INT-MT/INT-C	Card 12BG In this picture I see a beautiful summer day. The deserted boat is an indication that a couple of boys [were out boating] and after a while [decided to go] into the water for a swim.

Scores: EVA=1, TEM-MT=1, INT-MT=1, INT-C=1; MT=2, TI=4

EVA SPA/TEM EVA INT/INT-C/OCC	Card 8GF In this picture I see a beautiful woman who is posing for some artist. She looks like she put in a hard day's work and doesn't seem to have very fine clothes. Apparently the artist whom she is posing for wants a portrait of a washwoman or a housewife.

Scores: EVA=2, SPA=1, TEM=1, INT=1, INT-C=1, OCC=1; TI=7

 EVA/EVA SPC	Card 4 This picture shows two persons—a young and very handsome man and a young and very beautiful woman. The woman is dressed in white and is a brunette. She has her left hand on his right shoulder and he seems to be turning away from her while she seems to be pleading with him. In the background can be seen part of a curtained window and a picture of a "pin-up" girl.

Scores: EVA=2, SPC=1; TI=3

 INT EVA	Card 12F This picture shows two women—one very old and one mid-aged. The younger of the two seems concerned about something. She has dark short hair. The older had an odd smile on her face with her hand up to her mouth. Her face is very wrinkled. Her hair is white. It seems that she has a dark shawl on her head.

Scores: EVA=1, INT=1; TI=2

One Scoring Example (Prola, 1970)

	Card 5 I see a picture of a woman looking into a room. It appears
ATM/INT/SPA	to be a living room, and she may be observing somebody, but she
INT/INT	doesn't appear to be pleased or happy about it. Or, she may be just
INT-MT/INT/EVA	[coming through the door] and wondering. It's an old-fashioned
	room with a vase of flowers, a lamp, and a drop-leaf table. Some
	pictures on the wall.

Scores: ATM=1, INT=4, INT-MT=1, SPA=1, EVA=1; MT=1, TI=8

Three Examples of Stories

IMP/	Card 1 Card He's probably supposed to be studying or practicing on
POS/INT/INT-C	his violin. He's not too enthused about it. It's probably something
SPA/TEM-MT/	his parents or a parent [told him to take up and learn to play]. I
TEM-MT/TEM-MT	think eventually he [will pick it up] and [start practicing it]. He just
IMP	has to find a way to get motivated about it. I think if he had a choice he
TEM	would have picked another instrument to play—something he likes.

Scores: IMP=2, POS=1, INT=1, INT-C=1, SPA=1, TEM=1, TEM-MT=2;
MT=2, TI=9

OCC/REL/TEM	Card 2 There's a farmer and his wife and they have been married
	for some time living out on a farm undisturbed, and one day
SPA-MT/SPA-MT*	the farmer [goes into town to buy some fertilizer] and [meets
INT/INT-C/INT	up with a] school girl who finds him attractive and he seems to
INT-C/TEM	like the attention he's not used to getting, so they have an affair,
	but in the meantime his wife at home, who's preg . . . becomes
INT/INT-C/INT/	pregnant, so the end . . . she loves him and she's attracted to him,
INT-C	I'm talking about the other woman, the other woman loves him,
SPC/IMP	but he tells her that it's just infatuation and she'll have to get over
TEM	it because now he's got a family, he will have a family.

*Although the school girl is in the picture, the event of their meeting is not. Their later affair takes place over time. The wife's pregnancy is apparent in card 2.

Scores: OCC=1, REL=1, TEM=3, SPA-MT=2, INT=4, INT-C=4, IMP=1, SPC=1;
MT=2, TI=17

ABL-MT	Card 1 His name is Mark and Mark is [having problems playing] the
SPA/INT/INT-C	violin like his teacher can and he wants to be like his teacher.
TEM-MT/QUA	He's [been playing the violin] for 2 years and he [can't seem to
ABL-MT/TEM	play like his teacher] does. So one day he talked to his teacher
TEM	and his teacher told him that he's been playing the violin for
QUA*/TEM	25 years and that it takes a lot of practice so all Mark can do
ABL-MT	is keep practicing so he can learn to play just like his teacher.

INT/INT-C QUA TEM-MT/TEM-MT	So Mark made a commitment to himself that every day after school he's going to spend 2 hours studying. So 25 years later, [Mark is teaching] music class and [he's playing like his teacher played].

*"He's been playing the violin" was previously scored, so no Movement. Teacher is SPA, so no SPC.

Scores: ABL-MT=3, SPA=1, INT=2, INT-C=2, TEM=2, TEM-MT=4, QUA=3; MT=7, TI=17

References

Barndt, R. J., & Johnson, D. M. (1955). Time orientation in delinquents. *Journal of Abnormal Psychology, 51,* 343–345.

Epley, D., & Ricks, D. R. (1963). Foresight and hindsight in the TAT. *Journal of Projective Techniques, 27,* 51–59.

Exner, J. E. (2003). *The Rorschach: A comprehensive system, Volume 1* (4th ed.). New York: Wiley Interscience.

Murray, H. A. (1943). Thematic Apperception Test. Cambridge, MA: Harvard University Press.

Prola, M. (1970). *A re-evaluation of the motor inhibition-fantasy hypothesis*. Unpublished doctoral dissertation, New York University.

Rosen, J. L., & Neugarten, B. L. (1960). Ego functions in the middle and later years: A thematic apperception study of normal adults. *Journal of Gerontology, 15,* 62–67.

Rousseau, C., Fort, G. G. Du, & Corin, E. (2002). Time perspective in children living in a situation of armed conflict. In F. J. C. Azima & N. Grizenko, *Immigrant and refugee children and their families: Clinical, research, and training issues* (pp. 113–132). Madison, CT: International Universities Press.

Squyres, E. M., & Craddick, R. A. (1982). A measure of time perspective with the TAT and some issues of reliability. *Journal of Personality Assessment, 46*(3), 257–259.

Weisskopf, E. A. (1950). A transcendence index as a proposed measure in the TAT. *Journal of Psychology, 29,* 379–390.

Weisskopf-Joelson, E. A. (n.d. a). *Scoring standards for Transcendence Indices.* Mimeographed.

Weisskopf-Joelson, E. A. (n.d. b). *Transcendence Indices: Scoring samples.* Mimeographed.

Note

The surviving authors thank Myron House and Laura Henry at the University of West Georgia's Ingram Library Special Collections for their assistance in retrieving materials essential for this chapter. We appreciate the perseverance of Daria Dato, Sheena McIntire, Jonathan McConduit, and Adrienne N. Ortega in pilot testing this manual. Communication about this system can be sent to jenkinss@unt.edu. For more recent information about this and other scoring systems, visit http://www.psyc.unt.edu/~jenkinss/.

6

CHAPTER

Richard Dana's Objective TAT Scoring System

Cara L. Santa Maria

Abstract

Richard Dana's Objective Thematic Apperception Test (TAT) Scoring System was developed in an effort to create a simple approach to projective testing that is both economical and facilitative in the clinical setting. Three scoring categories—Perceptual Organization, Perceptual Range, and Perceptual Personalization—are used to identify participants' varying degrees of mental illness. Dana's system can be scored with high interrater reliability by a psychologically naive clerk. Using five different TAT cards for men and for women, Dana has shown good criterion-related validity and cross-validation, correctly placing individuals into clinical groups (i.e., normal, neurotic, and psychotic) a large percentage of the time. Dana's system also has utility in the domain of personality research; both applications continue to be relevant today.

Description of System

Conceptual Framework

Dana (1954) argued for the necessity of an empirical measure of the orientation aspect of personality theory. Dana's operational definition of *personality orientation* represents relative resistance to the test-taking environment, reflected by the stimulus cards themselves as well as explicit directions given. In response to research marginalizing the diagnostic efficacy of objective TAT approaches, Dana (1955a) introduced a new low-inference scoring system that was designed to differentiate among normal, neurotic, and psychotic groups.

Dana was especially interested in devising a clear, objective system that could be scored easily by a clerk. The rationale for this system was based on three aspects of test behavior thought to comprise a basic developmental foundation for an objective scoring system:

> (1) approach to the situation (reflected, for example, in the manner standard directions are followed); (2) normality of responses (abstractions of structural and content material included by specified percentages of "normal" *Ss* [subjects]); (3) rarity of responses (those infrequent responses in a "normal" population which appear with significantly higher frequency in psychopathological conditions. (Dana, 1955b, p. 95)

These three domains of test behavior were translated into Dana's TAT scoring categories of Perceptual Organization (PO), Perceptual Range (PR), and Perceptual personalization (PP). Dana (1955b) described the assumptions underlying these domains. He indicated that in a controlled environment, any given behavior sample theoretically could reveal all relevant personality information. It was also assumed that samples of behavior could be examined according to the way that the person incorporates environmental cues into the behavior in question. Finally, Dana asserted that "syndromes of personality characteristics" could be indicated according to the degree of incorporation of the aforementioned environmental cues (p. 96). Derived from said assumption that such behavior samples could be appropriately analyzed based on the participant's personality orientation, these three domains make up the theoretical framework underlying Dana's objective TAT system.

Scoring Categories

Table 6.1 includes a brief discussion of the following three scoring categories and their associated components.

Perceptual Organization

The participant's ability to follow standard instructions is the construct measured in Dana's PO score. This category appraises the participant's productions in response to the direction to "tell a story," including the seven components in Table 6.1: card description, present behavior, past events, future events, feelings, thoughts, and outcome. Each of these seven divisions is based on how closely participants follow test directions. The PO category is scored by giving a plus (+) or minus (–) for presence or absence of the seven category components for each card (Dana, 1955a; see also Dana, 1959a, for a detailed discussion of each of the seven scoring divisions included in the PO score). Dana (1960a) indicated that this scoring category could be used with any of the TAT cards, not solely the ones selected for use in his system, because it is independent of the particular stimulus value of the individual card.

Of Dana's three well-established scoring categories, the PO score has been most widely studied, possibly because of its broader applicability. Dana (1960a) reported that PO is the maximally discriminating category, successfully identifying 88% of normal, 72% of neurotic, and 88% of psychotic individuals. Furthermore, the PO score has been explored beyond its clinical applications. Dana (1959b) examined the PO stimulus value of the TAT cards, as

TABLE 6.1 Dana's Objective TAT Scoring Categories

Perceptual Organization[a]	
Components	**Description**
Card Description	Physical description of two or more things or persons actually present in the picture. This may occur anywhere in the story.
Present Behavior	Any activity or behavior that occurs in the present or is in the process of occurring within the picture.
Past Events	Things, events, or situations that have taken place in the story. These may be in the immediate or the remote past and must be specified and definite.
Future Events	Things, events, or situations that will take place or do take place in the future. These may be in the immediate or remote future.
Feeling	Any expression of feeling or emotion on the part of the characters present in the story. This includes affect.
Thought	Any expression of thought, memory, dream, or allied mental state present in the story. This includes decision, belief, rationalization, knowing, praying, and figuring.
Outcome	The inclusion of a specific statement that indicates the ending, denouement, finale, or conclusion of the story. This may consist in behavior, feeling, thought, or even, rarely, be present by implication of future events.

Perceptual Range Stimulus Properties[b]		
Card	**Male**	**Female**
2	(a) Family: young girl, woman (activity specified), adult male (b) Fields or farm (c) Books or school	(a) Family: young girl (activity specified), woman, adult male (b) Fields or farm (c) Books or school
3	(d) Figure (sex and age specified) (e) Emotions noted (f) Activity specified	(d) Female (e) Emotions noted; activity specified. (f) Story: death, murder, illness, frustration.
4	(g) Male (emotions noted; activity specified) (h) Female (activity specified) (i) Conflict or cooperation	(g) Male (emotions noted; activity specified) (h) Female (activity specified) (i) Conflict or cooperation
6	(j) Male (emotions noted; activity specified) (k) Female (emotions noted) (l) Personality referent	(j) Male (activity indicated) (k) Female (emotions noted) (l) Relationship indicated
7	(m) Older male (activity specified; relationship specified) (n) Male (emotions noted) (o) Personality referent	(m) Adult female (activity specified; emotions noted) (n) Child, female (emotions noted) (o) Relationship specified

(*Continued*)

TABLE 6.1 Dana's Objective TAT Scoring Categories (Continued)

Perceptual Personalization[c]	
Component	**Examples**
Questions	"Is that a boy or a girl?" "What's that supposed to be?"
Adequacy of Performance	"I can't figure that one out."
Qualifications	"Wait a minute ..." "It's not really that at all."
Picture Criticisms	"This picture is silly." "There is no point to this at all."
Parenthetical Comments	"That's about all on that." "There is not much connected with it."
Adventitious Descriptive Comments	Any remarks just thrown in without apparent connection to the rest of the story. These remarks often pertain to physical description of the picture or the people in it.
Vagueness and Evasion	"or ... or" "either ... or" "more or less" "or something" "... whatever it is"
Personal Reference	Any reference to "I." Any inclusion of personal information that is identified as such by the participant.

Adapted with permission from Dana (1959a).

[a] Scored on the scoring protocol as a plus (+) for each of the seven components included and minus (-) for each of the seven components excluded in the story.

[b] Scored on the scoring protocol as a plus (+) for those criteria present and minus (-) for those omitted from the story.

[c] On the scoring protocol, one point is given for each "out of place" word or phrase included in the story that qualifies as a PP response.

reflected by number, order, and frequency of PO components. With regard to personality research, a later article attempted to answer the question, "For what personality variables may the scoring category, Perceptual Organization (PO), be used" (Dana, 1960b, p. 154)?

Perceptual Range (PR)

The PR scoring category is designed to sample what is most commonly included in a typical TAT story. During development of this category, empirical evidence was used to establish criteria as to what a sample of male participants defined as *normal* 90% of the time (Dana, 1955a). Three separate stimulus properties were chosen for each of five cards based on this inclusion principle. In this study, cards 2, 3BM, 4, 6BM, and 7BM of the 1943 TAT series were used in an effort to depict typical life situations that a man may experience: a man alone, a man and a woman, a father and son, a mother and son, and a family group. These cards were administered to 50 normal, 50 neurotic, and 50 psychotic males, and the results were cross-validated (Dana, 1956a). New stimulus properties were then described for the female population during validation of Dana's (1960a) Objective System on a sample of women. An analogous set—including cards 2, 3GF, 4, 6GF, and 7GF—was chosen to

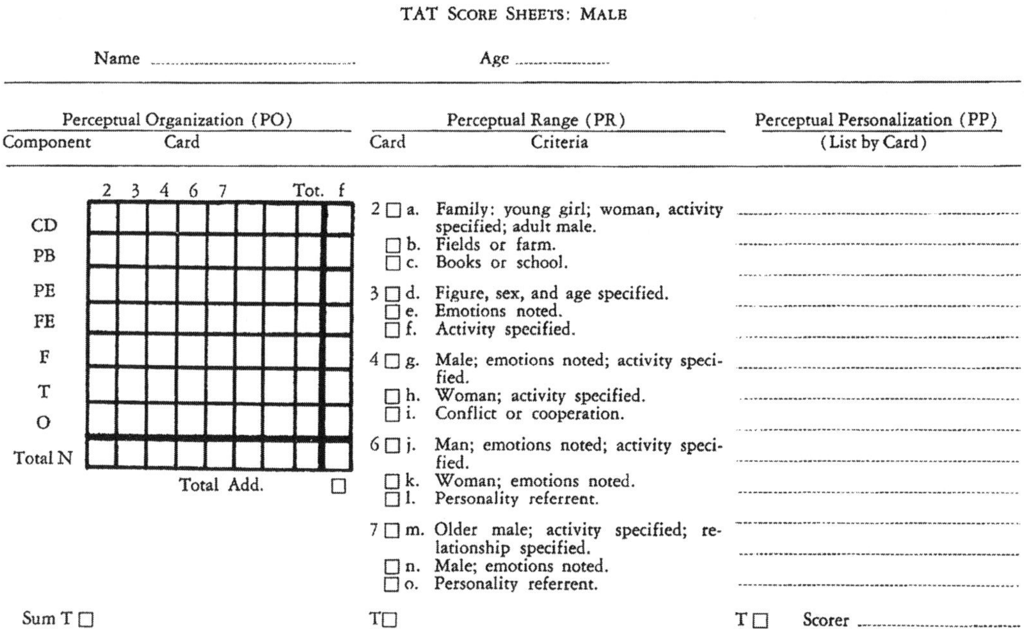

TAT SCORE SHEETS: MALE

Name .... Age ....

Perceptual Organization (PO)		Perceptual Range (PR)		Perceptual Personalization (PP)
Component	Card	Card	Criteria	(List by Card)

PO grid — Card columns: 2, 3, 4, 6, 7, Tot. f; Component rows: CD, PB, PE, FE, F, T, O, Total N. Total Add. ☐

2 ☐ a. Family: young girl; woman, activity specified; adult male.
☐ b. Fields or farm.
☐ c. Books or school.

3 ☐ d. Figure, sex, and age specified.
☐ e. Emotions noted.
☐ f. Activity specified.

4 ☐ g. Male; emotions noted; activity specified.
☐ h. Woman; activity specified.
☐ i. Conflict or cooperation.

6 ☐ j. Man; emotions noted; activity specified.
☐ k. Woman; emotions noted.
☐ l. Personality referrent.

7 ☐ m. Older male; activity specified; relationship specified.
☐ n. Male; emotions noted.
☐ o. Personality referrent.

Sum T ☐ T☐ T☐ Scorer ....

FIGURE 6.1 Dana's original scoring sheet for male participants includes the PO, PR, and PP scoring categories for each of five specific TAT cards. Reproduced From Dana (1959a) With Permission by the author.

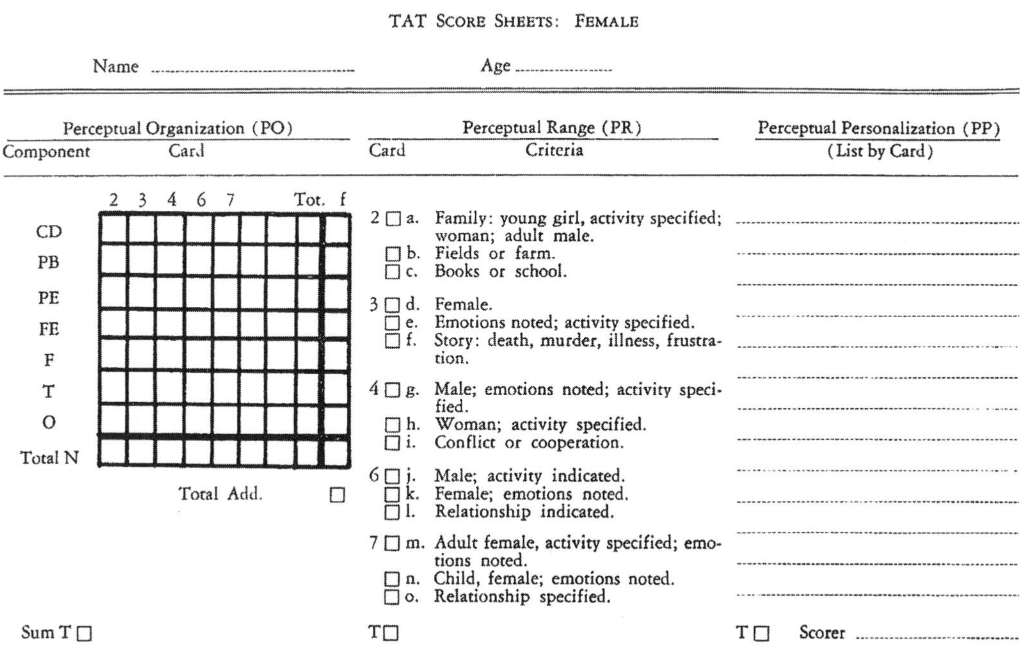

TAT SCORE SHEETS: FEMALE

Name .... Age ....

Perceptual Organization (PO)		Perceptual Range (PR)		Perceptual Personalization (PP)
Component	Card	Card	Criteria	(List by Card)

PO grid — Card columns: 2, 3, 4, 6, 7, Tot. f; Component rows: CD, PB, PE, FE, F, T, O, Total N. Total Add. ☐

2 ☐ a. Family: young girl, activity specified; woman; adult male.
☐ b. Fields or farm.
☐ c. Books or school.

3 ☐ d. Female.
☐ e. Emotions noted; activity specified.
☐ f. Story: death, murder, illness, frustration.

4 ☐ g. Male; emotions noted; activity specified.
☐ h. Woman; activity specified.
☐ i. Conflict or cooperation.

6 ☐ j. Male; activity indicated.
☐ k. Female; emotions noted.
☐ l. Relationship indicated.

7 ☐ m. Adult female, activity specified; emotions noted.
☐ n. Child, female; emotions noted.
☐ o. Relationship specified.

Sum T ☐ T☐ T☐ Scorer ....

FIGURE 6.2 Dana's original scoring sheet for female participants follows homologous structure to that for men, although the cards used and PR criteria chosen vary slightly. Reproduced from Dana (1959a) with permission by the author.

represent situations that a woman typically experiences. In the PR scoring category, for each gender, one point is scored for a mention of each of the 15 stimulus properties listed on the scoring sheet (see Figure 6.1 and 6.2). Dana (1959a) included a detailed explanation of the stimulus properties observed for each TAT card.

Perceptual Personalization (PP)

Deviations from normal response patterns are identified by the PP score. Such spontaneous response productions are seen as being highly incongruent, tangential, or irrelevant given the PP stimulus card in question. Comments that are scorable in the PP category can be neither stimulus reproductions (e.g., story descriptions) nor additions to the stimulus (e.g., story elaborations). Dana (1959b, p. 30) referred to such deviations as "... things labeled performance adequacy, comments, parenthetical remarks, qualifications, picture criticisms, adventitious descriptions, vagueness, evasion, or direct personal reference." Such responses may include either highly unusual response patterns that fall into one of the aforementioned categories or outright nonstory remarks. One point is given for each word, phrase, or question concerning the participant's feelings about his or her performance, the picture, and himself or herself (as indicated by the scoring protocol).

Additional Categories

Dana's earliest attempts at an objective system for scoring TAT stories were lengthier than later versions, when his method was better established. Initially, two additional categories were developed: perceptual keenness (PK) and perceptual energy (PE). These domains were intended to quantify the participants' inclusions of details regarding actual objects present in the stimulus picture and elaborations of objects not directly observed, respectively. Dana (1955a) found that scoring category PK did not differentiate significantly between groups, whereas scoring category PE differentiated significantly between only normal and clinical groups—as opposed to distinguishing individuals with neuroses from those with psychoses. Later employment of Dana's objective TAT system omitted these two scoring categories, so they will not be discussed further.

☐ Research Evidence

Validity

Dana's validation attempts primarily focused on the accuracy of differentiation between groups with and without psychopathology and, further, between neurotic and psychotic individuals. Early methods called solely for tests of such criterion-related validity, whereas a more specific approach toward predictive validation was later developed (see Dana, 1955a, 1955b for examples of each validation approach). A comprehensive review of the literature reveals few additional congruent, convergent, and cross-validation attempts.

Criterion-Related Validity

Diagnostic efficacy of Dana's Objective TAT Scoring System was first investigated by questioning whether or not the three scoring categories used—PO, PR, and PP—did, in fact, differentiate among normal, neurotic, and psychotic groups. Since these scores often failed to fulfill the assumptions underlying analysis of variance-based tests of significance, an approach delineated by Cronbach (1949) was used. A nonparametric median test yielded scores that were then rank ordered. Obtained medians for each group of interest were then used to compare the groups of interest: normal–neurotic, normal–psychotic, and neurotic–psychotic participants. Chi-square analyses revealed significant differences between groups (Dana, 1955a, 1960a).

In the first study, Dana (1955a) found that each of the three scoring categories differentiated significantly between groups. A later study (Dana, 1960a) revealed, however, that only the PO and PR scores differentiated significantly between all three groups. Here, the PP score failed to show a significant difference between the neurotic and psychotic groups; this result is seen consistently throughout the literature (Dana 1956a, 1959a).

Dana's (1955b, p. 99) rationale held that "prediction [of current behavior or responses to treatment] is currently the most powerful validating method which can be used with projective techniques." The accuracy with which Dana's Objective TAT System could differentiate among normal, neurotic, and psychotic persons was, in essence, the central question regarding its efficacy. Later approaches to this more specific validation were concerned with detection of category membership of unclassified persons based on the percentage of already classified assessees having similar scores (as is discussed following).

Dana (1956a) used his established nonparametric median and chi-square analyses; he then combined these scores with a prediction measure that was obtained by comparing the established score medians reported in his first study. New normal–neurotic, normal–psychotic, and neurotic–psychotic medians were thus established as criterion measures (and cutoff scores) defined as being maximally discriminatory (i.e., between 98% of normal, 81% of neurotic, and 84% of psychotic individuals). This validation measure is discussed in detail in Dana (1957). This cross-validation approach further supported Dana's suggestion that PO and PR scores were effective discriminators of neurotic and psychotic pathologies, whereas PP also identified psychopathology effectively but not the differentiating features of such illnesses.

Additional validation attempts discussed in greater detail the rationale for a more sophisticated analysis beyond the nonparametric median plus chi-square method. Dana (1959a, p. 36) wrote, "The statistical fact of significant differences between diagnostic groups does not indicate the predictive efficiency of a scoring system." Therefore, the newly developed cutoff scores using normal–neurotic, normal–psychotic, and neurotic–psychotic median criteria became the standard validation approach (Dana, 1957, 1959a).

Additional Validation Approaches

Less relevant to the clinical aspect of Dana's system were some of his later investigations into additional applications of its features, although they do warrant a brief discussion. For example, Dana and Mueller (1961) discussed the congruent validation of the PO TAT score using the following Minnesota Multiphasic Personality Inventory (MMPI) scales: anxiety, control, hostility, and social introversion–extroversion. *Congruent validation* here refers to the extent to which PO components are related to personality characteristics. Preliminary evidence was found supporting a relationship between several PO component scores and MMPI personality variables. These include a significant relationship obtained for high future events (PO) and total PO with low social introversion–extroversion (MMPI), high feeling and thought (PO) with high control (MMPI), and low outcome (PO) with high control (MMPI). Dana and Mueller explained that the relationship between several

PO components and MMPI scales of social introversion–extroversion and control related to the total PO score acting as a broad measure of psychological adjustment. However, he wrote, "Due to the small number of significant relationships cross-validation is mandatory" (p. 156).

A later investigation into the convergent validity of TAT and Rorschach ego strength was also undertaken (Dana & Cunningham, 1983). Although no convergent validity was found between the Rorschach and TAT, significant intercorrelations were observed for Dana's PO and PR scores ($p < .0001$).

The following paragraph, authored by Dana, is included per his request: Nawas (1961) called PO, PR, and PP an Ego Sufficiency Scale (ESS) for evaluating efficiency of ego functioning but later omitted PP because it "applies essentially to severely disturbed individuals and contributes very little to improving the efficiency of the scale" (Nawas, 1965, p. 457). These scores were employed in Nawas's (1961) dissertation and in master's theses by two colleagues, David Pearson and David Miller at the University of Chicago. These studies all replicated and confirmed Dana's original interjudge and intrajudge reliability data (e.g., Nawas 1965, 1971). In addition, ESS was successfully validated against different levels of functioning provided by interviewer ratings on Cartwright's Adjustment Scale (1954), Dymond's Mental Health Scale (1954), and a Complexity Scale adapted by Nawas (1965) from the Role Repertory Construct Test (Kelly, 1955). Nawas (1965) described the relevance of his findings for PO and PR per se as well as to ESS validation by ratings of different functioning levels as a contribution to clarification of the relationship between overt behavior and projective material, an enduring but muddled issue of theoretical and practical significance (see Carr, 1960).[1]

Generalizability

Although Dana's papers did not comment explicitly on the generalizability of his findings, some assumptions will be offered. For example, the scoring protocol appears to be highly generalizable with regard to economy and consistency. Dana's Objective System was intended to be scored by clerks who were untrained and naive with regard to psychological science. In addition to reducing the amount of time, effort, and money involved in scoring endeavors, such an approach greatly reduces the potential for differing opinions based on the theoretical orientations and psychological inferences often made by professionals (Dana, 1955b).

Dana's initial studies involved Caucasian male participants, either normal college students, neurotic, or psychotic individuals with histories of inpatient hospitalization and prior diagnoses of neurosis and schizophrenia, respectively. A later study (Dana, 1960a) investigated the system's diagnostic efficacy among a sample of women. Although different cards were chosen to depict basic situations a woman typically experiences in her lifetime (cards 2, 3GF, 4, 6GF, and 7GF), similar diagnostic criteria were used. In this study, though, *neurotics* were defined as individuals having received outpatient treatment. Results obtained were nearly identical to those found among male participants; therefore, generalizability of results is extended to both genders.

The influences of length of TAT responses and IQ scores were investigated as well in an effort to reduce error variance and further qualify generalizability of the system. Although Dana held that response length did not appreciably affect the scoring categories' discriminatory ability, he offered a less convincing argument regarding the effect of IQ score differences. Dana (1960a, p. 162, italics in original) stated, "... I.Q. scores and these

TAT scoring categories are not related *per se*.... Those neurotics with higher I.Q. scores tend to ... obtain better TAT scores." Thus, efficacy may have been limited when testing neurotic individuals of high intelligence. No mention was made regarding applicability of the system with regard to culturally and ethnically diverse individuals or age differences.

Generalizability of the scoring protocol to other TAT cards and projective approaches can also be inferred from the literature. Dana (1959b) asserted that since all TAT cards had equivalent stimulus features for his intents and purposes, it did not necessarily matter which cards were used—at least when working with the PO score. As long as precisely five cards were offered, PO components were not seen to vary significantly. Thus, with Dana's most extensively employed scoring category, usefulness is further increased by reducing rigid administration limitations.

Reliability

As mentioned previously, one of the most facilitative aspects of Dana's Objective System is its ease and utility of scoring. In an effort to reduce restrictions imposed by cumbersome and complex scoring procedures, his method is designed to be scored by a clerk. Such psychologically naive individuals can be trained easily to collect data that is then clinically interpreted by a trained professional. Dana (1959a, p. 28) stressed, "The use of objective scoring does not imply abandonment of content analysis but is merely a formal aid to this process." Dana (1955b) reported that with increased scoring direction clarification, both clerks and psychologists obtained 76% to 94% agreement.

An in-depth discussion is offered in Dana (1955b) regarding appropriate reliability measures for use with projective tests. Overall, he concluded that "scorer reliability ... may be the only critical reliability data that objective scoring systems should provide" and that "only percentage of agreement makes no assumptions and provides figures which can be interpreted easily" (p. 97). Test–retest reliability depends on the temporal stability of the psychological function being measured. Therefore, interrater reliability was the only form discussed throughout Dana's research. This scorer reliability was broken down into two subtypes: scoring category reliability and reliability of the items composing the categories.

Interrater (i.e., scoring category) reliability was good in Dana's studies, ranging from 81% to 94% for the PO category, 75% to 91% for the PR category, 68 to 86% for the PP category, and 82% to 91% overall. See Table 6.2 for a breakdown of scoring category reliabilities spanning five studies across five years. Reliability of the items composing the categories was found only for PO and PR scores, since these contained items that were defined prior to screening. Percentage of agreement for the PO score ranged from 75% to 100%. More variability was seen in the PR score, ranging from 47% to 100%. For further detail of these reliabilities, see Dana (1955a, 1956a, 1957, 1959a, 1960a).

☐ Future Research Needed

Most of Dana's recommendations for further research, dating back to 1956, centered on validation attempts at producing descriptive personality data (in concert with passive categorical, clinical distinction). Later discussions indicated a need for correlational attempts

TABLE 6.2 Scoring Category Reliabilities

Scoring Category	Dana (1955a)	Dana (1956a)	Dana (1957)		Dana (1959a)	Dana (1960a)
			M[a]	F[a]		
Perceptual Organization	81–88	93	93	94	88–94	94
Perceptual Range	75–86	90	89	91	86–91	91
Perceptual Personalization	68–86	75	75	76	75–86	76
Overall	82	89	89	91	n/a	91

Note: All numbers in percent.
[a] Male (M) and female (F) participants.

to isolate personality characteristics related to the PO score, in particular. A preliminary investigation into this relationship yielded less than promising results (Dana, 1960b); however, resulting hypotheses have yet to be thoroughly examined. See also Dana (1961) for a discussion of the PO score in the context of MMPI personality features.

Early studies (e.g., Dana, 1955a) discussed a need for future research into scoring system improvements. Although systematic developments can be observed throughout the literature, some such efforts are still necessary—for example, the use of updated diagnostic criteria and nomenclature for the clinically neurotic population. Additionally, applicability to varied clinical populations could be explored. Dana's scoring system may also be extended to projective measures other than the TAT in future applications, following a parallel structure.

Dana's Objective System has been loosely employed in later studies, with different purposes than are reflected by his previous work. For example, as mentioned previously, an investigation into ego strength measures was undertaken using the TAT and MMPI (Dana & Cunningham, 1983). This study calls for further conceptual identification of ego strength, as well as convergent validity assessment. Dana's Objective TAT Scoring System has been cited repeatedly and applied to a variety of settings, both in the clinical and personality research domains. With some minor adjustments and modern cross-validation approaches, it appears as though this system continues to be valuable.

The following closing statement, written by Dana, is included per his request: In addition, this system resulted in a popular perennial laboratory exercise (Brookings, 1995) in which students write and score five of their own TAT stories to cards recommended by Dana (1956b). Measurement-oriented students are impressed by the psychometric properties, whereas clinically oriented students criticize the loss of story content relevant to the inner workings of the psyche. This exercise permits discussion of strengths and weaknesses of objective approaches to scoring projective methods relative to traditional content-based systems. This exercise also is consistent with subsequent evaluations of objective TAT scores including this system (Dana, 1968, 1972, 1977):

The TAT began as an instrument to gather personality data in the service of personality theory. It was adopted by assessors with other theoretical biases and a consensual model of clinical inference. A research history tried in vain to force the TAT into psychometric test strictures. Personality assessors are now in the position of having instruments like the TAT that are unusable as psychometric personality tests. Similarly, the model of clinical inference that undergirded the interpretive use of these assessment devices has proven faulty. The long history of TAT research, especially on needs, has proven unassimilable into clinical practice. Thus, the TAT now has the status of an instrument for personality study and not a test per se. (Dana, 1977, p. 141)[2]

References

Brookings, J. B. (1995). "Objective" scoring of projective tests: A laboratory exercise using the Thematic Apperception Test (TAT). *Measurement Forum, 1,* 2–3.

Carr, A. C. (Ed.) (1960). *The prediction of overt behavior through the use of projective techniques.* Springfield, IL: C. C. Thomas.

Cartwright, D. R. (1954). Adjustment changes over therapy from TAT ratings. In C. R. Rogers & E. D. Cartwright (Eds.), *Psychotherapy and personality change.* Chicago: University of Chicago Press.

Cronbach, L. (1949). Statistical methods applied to Rorschach scores: A review. *Psychological Bulletin, 46,* 393–429.

Dana, R. H. (1954). Personality orientation: An organizational focus for current research. *Journal of Psychology, 37,* 139–150.

Dana, R. H. (1955a). Clinical diagnosis and objective TAT scoring. *Journal of Abnormal and Social Psychology, 50*(1), 19–24.

Dana, R. H. (1955b). The objectification of projective techniques: Rationale. *Psychological Reports, 1,* 93–102.

Dana, R. H. (1956a). Cross-validation of objective TAT scoring. *Journal of Counseling Psychology, 20*(1), 33–36.

Dana, R. H. (1956b). Selection of abbreviated TAT sets. *Journal of Clinical Psychology, 12,* 36–40.

Dana, R. H. (1957). Norms for three aspects of TAT behavior. *Journal of General Psychology, 57,* 83–89.

Dana, R. H. (1959a). Proposal for objective scoring of the TAT. *Perceptual and Motor Skills, 9,* 27–43.

Dana, R. H. (1959b). The perceptual organization TAT score: Number, order, and frequency of components. *Journal of Projective Techniques, 23*(3), 307–310.

Dana, R. H. (1960a). An application of objective TAT scoring. *Journal of Projective Techniques, 20,* 159–163.

Dana, R. H. (1960b). Objective TAT scores and personality characteristics: Perceptual organization (PO). *Perceptual and Motor Skills, 10,* 154.

Dana, R. H. (1968). Thematic techniques and clinical practice. *Journal of Projective Techniques and Personality Assessment, 32,* 204–214.

Dana, R. H. (1972). Thematic Apperception Test. In O. Buros (Ed.), *7th Mental Measurements Yearbook* (pp. 457–460). Highland Park, NJ: Gryphon.

Dana, R. H. (1977). Thematic Apperception Test. In, B. B. Wolman (Ed.), *International Encyclopedia of Psychiatry, Psychology, Psychoanalysis, and Neurology* (pp. 140–142). New York: Human Sciences Press.

Dana, R. H., & Cunningham, K. M. (1983). Convergent validity of Rorschach and Thematic Apperception Test ego strength measures. *Perceptual and Motor Skills, 57,* 1101–1102.

Dana, R. H., & Mueller, D. J. (1961). Congruent validation of a TAT score: Perceptual organization. *Journal of Psychological Studies, 12*(4), 150–156.

Dymond, R. (1954). Adjustment changes over therapy from TAT ratings. In C. R. Rogers & R. Dymond (Eds.), *Psychotherapy and personality change.* Chicago: University of Chicago Press.

Kelly, G. A. (1955). *The psychology of personal constructs.* New York: Norton.

Nawas, M. M. (1961). *From adolescence to adulthood through the TAT.* Unpublished doctoral dissertation, University of Chicago.

Nawas, M. M. (1965). Objective scoring of the TAT: Further validation. *Journal of Projective Techniques and Personality Assessment, 29,* 456–460.

Nawas, M. M. (1971). Change in efficiency of ego functioning and complexity from adolescence to young adulthood. *Developmental Psychology, 4*(3), 412–415.

Vane, J. R. (1981). The Thematic Apperception Test: A review. *Clinical Psychology Review, 1,* 319–336.

Note

I would like to acknowledge Richard H. Dana for his lifelong dedication to this system, as well as all of his help in research and execution of this text.

7

CHAPTER

Manual for Objective TAT Scoring

Richard H. Dana[1]

Introduction

This manual presents a concise but abbreviated statement of *one* objective Thematic Apperception Test (TAT) scoring system and its predictive efficiency. It is designed to facilitate application of this approach to TAT scoring. Although the rationale on which this method is predicated derives from certain specific assumptions regarding personality, the clinical use of these categories does not demand any *particular* theoretical persuasion. The author recognizes two kinds of validity germane to projective instruments: (1) validity$_1$, prediction of clinical diagnosis; and (2) validity$_2$, prediction of personality characteristics. This manual deals only with validity$_1$. As the material contained herein is still largely in tentative form, the author welcomes suggestions, ammendations, elaborations, criticism. This manual owes its existence to many individuals who helped collect the data, score the protocols, apply statistical techniques, and type the various manuscripts. Their combined efforts have made this manual possible.

Clinical use of the TAT has been largely restricted to content analysis by the plethora of cumbersome scoring systems currently available. That scoring systems should be simple, objective, employ stimulus properties of the TAT cards, and be related to personality theory is becoming empirically evident. That TAT scoring can be a clerical procedure and interpretation a clinical skill is congruent with the new look in projective testing. The use of objective scoring does not imply abandonment of content analysis but is merely a formal aid to this process. Discussion of the approach to personality theory that antedated the rationale for TAT scoring is not appropriate here (Dana, 1954). However, there are at least three aspects of test behavior to be considered in devising objective scoring systems (Dana, 1955a): (1) approach to the situation (reflected, for example, in the manner standard test directions are followed); (2) normality of responses (abstractions of structural and content material included by specified percentages of normal *Ss*); and (3) rarity of responses (infrequent responses in a normal population that appear with significantly higher frequency in psychopathological conditions). These three aspects of test behavior have been objectified as Perceptual Organization (PO), Perceptual Range (PR), and Perceptual Personalization (PP), respectively.

Administration

The instructions given to the assessee are approximately as follows: "Please tell a story describing the card, telling what the people are doing, what they have done in the past, and what they may do in the future. Say something about the feelings and thoughts of the characters, and then give an outcome." The important feature here is that the instructions specify discrete parts so that the scoring of the stories can examine their conformity with a standardized set of directions (Dana, 1982).

Stimuli

Five TAT cards were selected to compose the basic life situations: cards 2, 3BM, 4, 6BM, and 7BM for boys and men; and cards 2, 3GF, 4, 6GF, and 7GF for girls and women. The use of short-form TAT sets has been experimentally evaluated by comparing PO scores for short-form sets with the total set of cards (Dana, 1956a). The inclusion of particular cards was found to be less important than the actual number of cards selected. TAT sets of as few as five cards, when scored for PO, provide data that is roughly equivalent to that from the entire series. PO scores from the short-form set for women correlated .91 with scores from the entire set.

☐ Scoring Process

Scoring Category Criteria

Perceptual Organization (PO)

This category reflects the *S*'s ability to follow the standard directions to tell a story. Seven possible components are included: (1) card description (CD); (2) present behavior (PB); (3) past events (PE); (4) future events (FE); (5) feeling (F); (6) thought (T); and (7) outcome (O). You are scoring to see how closely the subject followed the original test directions. Score sheets are provided (Figures 7.1, 7.2), which are used to record PO, PR, and PP.

TAT SCORE SHEETS: FEMALE

Name ______________ Age ________

Perceptual Organization (PO)

Component	2	3	4	6	7			Tot.	f
CD									
PB									
PE									
FE									
F									
T									
O									
Total N									

Total Add. ☐

Sum T ☐

Perceptual Range (PR)

Card		Criteria
2	☐ a.	Family: young girl, activity specified; woman; adult male.
	☐ b.	Fields or farm.
	☐ c.	Books or school.
3	☐ d.	Female.
	☐ e.	Emotions noted; activity specified.
	☐ f.	Story: death, murder, illness, frustration.
4	☐ g.	Male; emotions noted; activity specified.
	☐ h.	Woman; activity specified.
	☐ i.	Conflict or cooperation.
6	☐ j.	Male; activity indicated.
	☐ k.	Female; emotions noted.
	☐ l.	Relationship indicated.
7	☐ m.	Adult female, activity specified; emotions noted.
	☐ n.	Child, female; emotions noted.
	☐ o.	Relationship specified.

T ☐

Perceptual Personalization (PP)

(List by Card)

T ☐ Scorer ______________

FIGURE 7.1 Dana's original scoring sheet for male participants includes the PO, PR, and PP scoring categories for each of five specific TAT cards. Reproduced from Dana (1959a) with permission by the author.

TAT SCORE SHEETS: MALE

Name ______________________ Age __________

Perceptual Organization (PO)

Component	2	3	4	6	7			Tot.	f
CD									
PB									
PE									
FE									
F									
T									
O									
Total N									

Total Add. ☐

Sum T ☐

Perceptual Range (PR)

Card	Criteria	Perceptual Personalization (PP) (List by Card)
2 ☐ a.	Family: young girl; woman, activity specified; adult male.	________
☐ b.	Fields or farm.	________
☐ c.	Books or school.	________
3 ☐ d.	Figure, sex, and age specified.	________
☐ e.	Emotions noted.	________
☐ f.	Activity specified.	________
4 ☐ g.	Male; emotions noted; activity specified.	________
☐ h.	Woman; activity specified.	________
☐ i.	Conflict or cooperation.	________
6 ☐ j.	Man; emotions noted; activity specified.	________
☐ k.	Woman; emotions noted.	________
☐ l.	Personality referrent.	________
7 ☐ m.	Older male; activity specified; relationship specified.	________
☐ n.	Male; emotions noted.	________
☐ o.	Personality referrent.	________
T☐		T ☐ Scorer ________

FIGURE 7.2 Dana's original scoring sheet for female participants follows homologous structure to that for men, although the cards used and PR criteria chosen vary slightly. Reproduced from Dana (1959a) with permission by the author.

The score sheet contains a list of the seven components (abbreviated as CD, PB, PE, FE, F, T, and O, respectively), and spaces to record presence or absence of each component for each card used. Columns have been labeled for cards 2, 3, 4, 6, and 7, and space is left for any other cards that may have been administered. Each PO component present in the story is scored by placing a plus (+) in the appropriate space on the score sheet. A minus (–) is scored for components not included. No score is given for frequency of appearance on each card.

Any of these components that appear after the first question by the examiner (additional scores) should be entered on the sheet and the entry circled.

All stories given by the subject may be scored. The total PO score is the sum of scores to the five stories from cards 2, 3, 4, 6, and 7. Note that space is provided for tallying frequency (f) of components for all cards. Circled PO components *should not* be added in obtaining the total PO score. Enter the total score in the box labeled *T*; enter the total additional scores in the box labeled *T add.*

(1) *Card description* (CD). Physical description of two or more things or persons actually present in the picture. It may be a listing such as, "This is a man, a woman, a tree, etc." It may serve to introduce the story: "The boy is on the floor" or "The woman who is by the tree is ..." In these cases there is never any action—merely description. If the word *picture* is used, then only one person or thing need follow, for example, "This is a picture of a boy." CD may occur anywhere in the story.

(2) *Present behavior* (PB). Any activity or behavior that occurs in the present or is in the process of occurring within the picture. For example (card 2), "The man is plowing the field." Activity that occurs outside of the frame of reference of the picture is scored PE or FE.

(3) *Past events* (PE). Things, events, or situations that have taken place in the past—that is, before the time of the scene pictured on the card and described in the story. These may be in the immediate or the remote past and must be specified and definite things, events, or situations.

(4) *Future events* (FE). Things, events, or situations that will take place or do take place in the future—that is, after the time of the scene pictured on the card and described in the story. These may be in the immediate or remote future and must be specified and definite things, events, or situations.

(5) *Feeling* (F). Any expression of feeling or emotion on the part of the characters present in the story. This includes affect (e.g., sad, mad, in love) and desire (e.g., wishing and wanting) but not *need*.

(6) *Thought* (T). Any expression of thought, memory, dream, or allied mental state present in the story. This includes decision, belief, realization, knowing, praying, and figuring.

(7) *Outcome* (O). The inclusion of a specific statement that indicates the ending, denouement, finale, or conclusion of the story. This may consist in behavior, feeling, or thought or even, rarely, be present by implication in future events. If this does occur, both outcome and future events are scored. Usually appears at or near the end of the story (i.e. the last sentence or phrase).

Perceptual Range (PR)

Empirical evidence has been used to establish criteria as to content that a group of "normal" *S*s will include in their TAT stories a given percentage of the time (Fleming, 1946). Three separate stimulus properties were chosen for each card on the basis of inclusion by approximately 90% or more of this "normal" group. You are scoring to see how closely the subject adheres to norms for various aspects of the stories. The 15 stimulus properties for men are as follows:

(1) Card 2 (a) family: young girl, woman, activity specified; man; (b) fields or farm; (c) books or school

(2) Card 3 (d) figure, sex and age specified; (e) emotions noted; (f) activity specified

(3) Card 4 (g) man; emotions noted, activity specified; (h) woman; activity specified; (i) conflict or cooperation

(4) Card 6 (j) man; emotions noted, activity specified; (k) woman; emotions noted; (l) personality referrent

(5) Card 7 (m) older man, activity specified, relationship specified; (n) man, emotions noted; (o) personality referrent

The 15 stimulus properties for women are as follows:

(1) Card 2 (a) family: young girl, activity specified; woman; man; (b) fields or farm; (c) books or school

(2) Card 3 (d) woman; (e) emotions noted; activity specified; (f) story: death, murder, illness, frustration

(3) Card 4 (g) man; emotions noted; activity specified; (h) woman; activity specified; (i) conflict or cooperation

(4) Card 6 (j) man, activity indicated; (k) woman, emotions noted; (l) relationship indicated

(5) Card 7 (m) woman, activity specified, emotions noted; (n) girl, emotions noted; (o) relationship specified

You have been provided with criteria lists on a score sheet (M or F; Figures 7.1, 7.2). All items included in each criterion must be mentioned for a score to be earned. No score is given for indefinite or ambiguous statements. For example, in card 2 (men), if the family, the young girl, the woman, and the man are mentioned, no score is given because the activity of the woman is not specified.

Read each story once, and then go back and look for each particular item in each criterion; finally, check off complete criteria on the score sheet—plus (+) for those present and minus (–) for those not included in the story. To obtain the total PR score, add the plus scores obtained for each story, and enter in the box labeled *T.*

Perceptual Personalization (PP)

Some expressions, words, and phrases used in the story are incongruous and have no obvious reference to the story that *S* is trying to relate. These inclusions are clearly neither stimulus reproductions nor additions to the stimulus. PPs are deviations from the relatively consistent, organized, coherent protocol-product, the TAT story. These deviations, to be scored, must be extreme. They may refer to things labeled performance adequacy, comments, parenthetical remarks, qualifications, picture criticisms, adventitious descriptions, vagueness, evasion, or direct personal reference.

As you read each story, you will note that certain words and phrases do not seem to belong with the rest of the story. They do not add anything to the ideas and events in the story. These words and phrases include all questions and remarks concerning the way the subject feels about his or her performance, the picture, and himself or herself. They may refer to things that have been called *adequacy of performance, qualification, picture criticisms, vagueness and evasion,* and *personal reference.*

Examples of these "out-of-place" words and phrases follow:

- *Questions*: "Is that a boy or a girl?" "What's that supposed to be?"
- *Adequacy of performance*: "I can't figure that one out."
- *Qualifications*: "Wait a minute ...." "It's not really that at all."
- *Picture criticism*: "This picture is silly." "There is no point to this at all."
- *Parenthetical comments*: "That's about all on that." "There is not much connected with it."
- *Adventitious descriptive comments*: Any remarks just thrown in without apparent connection to the rest of the story. These remarks often pertain to physical description of the picture or the people in it.
- *Vagueness and evasion*: "or ... or," "either ... or," "more or less," "or something," ".... whatever it is."
- *Personal reference*: Any reference to "I"; any inclusion of personal information that is identified as such by the subject.

List the words and phrases by number for each card scored on the appropriate score sheet (M or F). List each word or phrase to be scored separately. One point is given for each word or phrase listed. The PP score is the total number of points for all cards scored. Enter the total PP score in the box labeled *T.*

□ Discussion

This manual presents TAT scoring categories that may be reliably scored by naive scorers and that provide correct prediction of a significant percentage of three diagnostic groups. However, the information actually obtained by this scoring system goes considerably beyond prediction of clinical diagnosis. The scores of an *S* are believed to represent *degree of psychiatric illness*. Thus, any expectation of 100% distinction among groups would not be supported.

Mental illness, as tapped by this system, consists in deviations from normative TAT behavior and represents changes in subjective, internalized meaning systems called *reality*. Certain concomitants of mental illness are emphasized by this system: (1) awareness of reality is diminished; (2) experience can be organized with difficulty, if at all; and (3) the desire to give an acceptable account of oneself diminishes. These appear as attributes of a loss of psychic energy necessary for optimal individual function.

The manual can be considered an enterprise preliminary to the major responsibility of any projective technique, that is, validity$_2$.

□ References

Dana, R. H. (1949). *The Thematic Apperception Test applied to an experiment in perception and personality.* Unpublished bachelor's thesis, Princeton University.

Dana, R. H. (1953). *The diagnostic efficacy of a theoretically derived objective scoring system for the Thematic Apperception Test.* Unpublished doctoral thesis, University of Illinois.

Dana, R. H. (1954). Personality orientation: An organizational focus for current research. *Journal of Psychology, 37,* 139–150.

Dana, R. H. (1955a). The objectification of projective techniques: Rationale. *Psychological Reports, 1,* 93–102.

Dana, R. H. (1955b). Clinical diagnosis and objective TAT scoring. *Journal of Abnormal and Social Psychology, 50,* 19–25.

Dana, R. H. (1955c). Rorschach scorer reliability. *Journal of Clinical Psychology, 11,* 401–403.

Dana, R. H. (1956a). Selection of abbreviated TAT sets. *Journal of Clinical Psychology, 12,* 36–40.

Dana, R. H. (1956b). Cross-validation of objective TAT scoring. *Journal of Consulting Psychology, 20,* 33–36.

Dana, R. H. (1956c). An application of objective TAT scoring. *Journal of Projective Techniques, 20,* 159–163.

Dana, R. H. (1957). Norms for three aspects of TAT behavior. *Journal of General Psychology, 57,* 83–89.

Fleming, E. (1946). *A descriptive analysis of responses in the Thematic Apperception Test.* Unpublished master's thesis, University of Pittsburgh.

[1]*The research in this chapter was carried out in connection with an investigation supported in part by a research grant from the National Institute of Mental Health, of the National Institutes of Health, Public Health Service. This chapter is an edited version of Dana's original scoring manual, restructured to resemble the format of the other scoring manual chapters.*

□ Appendix

The *S*s on whom this manual is based were from validation and cross-validation samples (Dana, 1955b, 1956b, 1956c, 1957). The validation sample contained 300 *S*s—150 men and 150 women—with 100 normals, 100 neurotics, 100 psychotics. The cross-validation sample contained 90 men, 30 normals, 30 neurotics, 30 psychotics. The normal men *S*s were college students with no history of psychiatric illness; the normal women were student nurses with Minnesota Multiphasic Personality Inventory (MMPI) T scores all below 70. The neurotic and psychotic men were chosen in terms of previously determined criteria: (1) hospitalized; (2) diagnostic agreement between psychiatrist and psychologist;

TABLE 7.1 Product–Moment Correlations of PO Scores for Each Card With PO Score for All Cards (67 Normal Women)

Card	*r*
1	.72
2	.68
3	.76
4	.69
5	.73
6	.64
7	.74
8	.74
9	.75
10	.77
11	.70
12	.70
13	.72
14	.78
15	.71
16	.60
17	.63
18	.63
19	.65
20	.64

Note: Mean *r* .70 (*z* transformation).

TABLE 7.2 Product–Moment Intercorrelations Between PO Scores on Five Cards (67 Normal Women)

Card	3	4	6	7
2	.62	.40	.50	.53
3		.61	.57	.58
4			.58	.57
5				.60

Note: All figures are significant at < .01 level of confidence.

TABLE 7.3 Product–Moment Intercorrelations of Categories PO, PR, PP for Three Groups of Men

Category	PR	PP
PO		
Group:		
Normal	.25	–.40**
Neurotic	.43**	–.32*
Psychotic	.53**	–.40**
PR		
Group:		
Normal		–.18
Neurotic		.01
Psychotic		–.34*

Notes: *Significant at the .05 level of confidence. **Significant at the .01 level of confidence.

(3) independent diagnostic formulations; and (4) diagnosis: neurosis or schizophrenia. The neurotic and psychotic women were chosen in terms of these same criteria with one exception: Outpatient clinic neurotics were used. The men in the cross-validation sample were chosen in terms of these same criteria with one exception: Outpatient clinic neurotics were used. All *S*s were between the ages of 20 and 40, with IQ scores of average or better.

Table 7.1 presents correlations of PO scores for each card with the scores for the entire set with Z transformations to provide a mean correlation.

Table 7.2 presents the product–moment intercorrelations of PO scores for normal women. These data indicate that the stimulus values of the selected TAT cards (in terms of *N* of PO items) are approximately equivalent.

Table 7.3 summarizes the product–moment intercorrelations of scoring categories PO, PR, and PP, for three diagnostic groups of men (Dana, 1953). Significant relationships obtain among all three categories. PO and PP are inversely related such that high scores on PO tend to occur with low scores on PP. To a considerably lesser degree PR and PP are also inversely related. These figures raise the question of overlap between PO and PR especially and to a lesser extent between PO and PP. Further research must explore the significance of these interrelationships. The assumptions concerning personality that led to this TAT manual are thoroughly congruent with such associations among scoring categories.

☐ Reliability

Two kinds of scorer reliability were used (Dana, 1955a, 1955c): (1) scoring category reliability; and (2) reliability of the items composing the categories. Scorer reliability was determined by means of percent of agreement. Both kinds of scorer reliability were calculated for all three groups, with various scorers, psychologists, and clerks. From the male validation sample 75 stories, 25 from each group, were randomly drawn, coded, and scored for reliability. The same process was used for 150 stories from the female sample and for 75 stories from the male cross-validation sample. In all the reliability

TABLE 7.4 Scoring Category Reliability (Percentage of Agreement) for Male Validation, Male Cross-Validation (C), and Female Validation Samples

Sample	Category		
	PO	PR	PP
Men	88	86	86
Men (C)	93	89	75
Women	94	91	76

tables the figures reported for the male validation sample represent the average percent of agreement for three scorers; the figures for the male cross-validation sample and the women represent the percentage of agreement for two scorers.

Table 7.4 summarizes the percentage of agreement figures for scoring category reliability. The highest figures obtained for the male validation sample are reported. The reliability for PO ranges from 88% to 94% of agreement, PR from 86% to 91%, and PP from 75% to 86%. The increase in reliability for the women's and men's cross-validation samples is attributable to (1) additional practice in scoring and (2) formalization of scoring criteria on an easily used score sheet. It should be noted that although the PR criteria differ for men and women that the reliability of scoring is almost identical. The reliability of scoring separate PO and PR items is presented in Tables 7.5 and 7.6. The mean reliability figures (scoring category reliability) differ in some instances for the male sample from those reported in Table 7.4 because the component entries are themselves mean agreements of three scorers. No consistent or large differences appear between men and women, and there were no significant differences in scoring the three diagnostic groups. Thus, the reliability figures for each diagnostic group are omitted. The reliability of scoring separate PO items (on all samples) ranged from 89% to 97% of agreement and PR from 60% to 100% of agreement.

TABLE 7.5 PO Item Reliability (Percentage of Agreement) for Male Validation, Male Cross-Validation (C), and Female Validation Samples

	Sample		
Item	Men	Men (C)	Women
Card Description	91	91	91
Present Behavior	89	91	94
Past Events	90	91	94
Future Events	89	97	93
Feeling	89	90	95
Thought	81	89	96
Outcome	92	99	96
Mean	89	93	94

TABLE 7.6 PR Item Reliability (Percentage of Agreement) for Male Validation, Male Cross-Validation (C), and Female Validation Samples

	Sample		
Item	Men	Men (C)	Women
1	69	93	87
2	86	93	100
3	100	100	87
4	93	100	100
5	86	87	93
6	71	87	83
7	82	87	93
8	95	87	93
9	93	80	90
10	60	93	93
11	82	80	87
12	62	87	87
13	84	80	80
14	69	87	97
15	69	93	100
Mean	80	89	91

☐ Validity

Table 7.8 presents the means, ranges, and standard deviations for each category from all diagnostic groups on all samples. Validity was estimated by a nonparametric, median, chi-square analysis (Tables 7.9, 7.10, and 7.11). The statistical fact of significant differences between diagnostic groups does not indicate the predictive efficiency of a scoring system. For this reason prediction scores were developed by using as criteria (cutoff scores) the normal–neurotic and neurotic–psychotic medians for each sample (Table 7.12). The relatively

Table 7.7 PP Category Reliability (Percentage of Agreement) by Gender and Diagnostic Group

	Group		
Gender	Normal	Neurotic	Psychotic
Men	88	84	76
Men (C)	82	73	74
Women	78	77	76

TABLE 7.8 Means, Standard Deviations (SD), and Ranges for Male (M), Male Cross-Validation (C), and Female (F) Validation Samples of Normal, Neurotic, and Psychotic Groups on Each Scoring Category

	Mean			SD			Range		
Category	M	C	F	M	C	F	M	C	F
PO									
Group									
Normal	26.6	26.5	27.5	3.7	2.6	3.9	19–32	22–31	16–35
Neurotic	20.8	18.5	18.5	4.2	3.2	4.3	12–29	11–24	10–25
Psychotic	13.2	10.8	8.5	4.1	2.9	2.9	6–24	6–21	5–18
PR									
Group									
Normal	12.1	13.4	14.2	1.8	1.3	1.0	8–15	11–15	11–15
Neurotic	9.8	8.8	9.7	2.2	1.5	1.7	4–15	5–11	5–12
Psychotic	4.9	5.2	5.4	5.8	1.6	1.9	0–12	1–9	1–11
PP									
Group									
Normal	1.0	.3	.2	.5	1.3	1.1	0–6	0–6	0–13
Neurotic	5.9	3.8	6.1	2.7	4.3	6.0	0–17	0–29	0–30
Psychotic	12.1	5.0	8.5	9.1	6.0	6.6	1–43	0–40	0–29

small differences between men and women permit use of combined medians obtained from the total sample rather than separate cutoff scores for each gender. These combined medians (rounded for convenient clinical application) are 23 and 15 for PO, 11 and 7 for PR, and 2 and 6 for PP. PO and PR scores above the normal–neurotic medians were given 0, scores between the normal–neurotic and neurotic–psychotic medians were given 1, and scores below the neurotic–psychotic medians were given 2. PP scores below the normal–neurotic median were given 0, scores between the normal–neurotic median and the neurotic–psychotic median were given 1, and scores above the neurotic–psychotic median were given 2. Table 7.13 presents the percentages of men (validation plus cross-validation samples) and women, in each diagnostic group receiving scores of 0, 1, or 2. This table can be used directly to evaluate the probability that a particular scored TAT record, when translated into prediction scores, will fall into the normal, neurotic, or psychotic group. This table constitutes preliminary norms for these three TAT scoring categories.

Past TAT research (Dana, 1949) has indicated that length (i.e., number of words) may be related to objective scoring. The question of whether the median test differences were a result of length was raised in the male validation study. That is, would the groups have been alike in PO scores had their protocols been of equivalent length? The assumptions necessary for covariance adjustments are not satisfied, so a crude test that provides a correction for regression and takes trend into account was used. A graphical procedure was employed analogous to the median test except that a kind of average regression line or sliding dividing line was used in lieu of the median. Regression lines were plotted for the three groups for PO on length; a line of split (sliding dividing line) was made for each

TABLE 7.9 Summary of Median Test Results on PO, PR, PP Scores of Male Validation Sample, Combined Average

Category	Combined Median	Above Median	X^2	P
PO				
Group:				
Normal	24.50	37.0	23.0	<.001
Neurotic		13.0		
Normal	20.25	46.5	73.9	<.001
Psychotic		3.5		
Neurotic	16.94	40.8	39.9	<.001
Psychotic		9.2		
PR				
Group:				
Normal	11.19	35.5	17.6	<.001
Neurotic		14.5		
Normal	8.90	46.8	76.0	<.001
Psychotic		3.2		
Neurotic	7.68	42.7	50.1	<.001
Psychotic		7.3		
PP				
Group:				
Normal	1.90	12.6	24.6	<.001
Neurotic		37.4		
Normal	2.83	7.7	47.9	<.001
Psychotic		42.3		
Neurotic	7.37	17.9	8.1	<.01
Psychotic		32.1		

pair of groups; the number of cases above and below was counted; and chi-square was applied. No appreciable differences in PO were found. A less rigorous method would be to plot PO against length for the total sample, to draw a line fitting the medians of the columns, and to compare by chi-square the proportions of the cases in each group falling above the line of medians.

Product–moment correlations were calculated between scoring categories and length for the male and female samples (Table 7.14). The magnitude of the PO–length correlations for the two genders do not differ to any great extent. The marked similarity of the respective distributions indicates that the influence of length on median test differences for the women is not important. Some PR–length and PP–length correlations are significant for the women. However, neither correlation for the normal group approaches significance. This suggests that length does not influence the scoring categories per se but

TABLE 7.10 Summary of Median Test Results on PO, PR, and PP Scores of Female Validation Sample

Category	Combined Median	Above Median	X^2	P
PO				
Group:				
Normal	22.50	43.5	47.7	<.001
Neurotic		9.0		
Normal	16.50	49.5	94.1	<.001
Psychotic		1.0		
Neurotic	12.10	44.7	59.3	<.001
Psychotic		6.2		
PR				
Group:				
Normal	11.90	48.2	49.5	<.001
Neurotic		14.1		
Normal	10.84	50.0	96.1	<.001
Psychotic		1.0		
Neurotic	7.68	44.3	33.9	<.001
Psychotic		15.8		
PP				
Group:				
Normal	1.50	6.5	62.6	<.001
Neurotic		46.0		
Normal	1.30	7.1	58.8	<.001
Psychotic		45.4		
Neurotic	6.84	23.8	1.3	—
Psychotic		29.5		

may be related to psychopathology. Again the magnitude of the obtained correlations in comparison with the magnitude of the chi-square differences between groups provides evidence against any appreciable constant effect on either PR or PP prediction scores.

Although consensus of experts has not considered intelligence to be related to TAT scores, product–moment correlations were calculated between scoring categories and intelligence as estimated by Wechsler-Bellevue, Form I, IQ scores (Table 7.15). The correlations between PO and PR scores and intelligence scores for neurotics were significant at $< .05$ and $> .05$ levels of confidence, respectively. None of the correlations for the normal or psychotic groups were significant. It is suggested that IQ scores and these TAT scoring

TABLE 7.11 Summary of Median Test Results on PO, PR, and PP Scores of Male Cross-Validation Sample

Category	Combined Median	Above Median	X^2	P
PO				
Group:				
Normal	23.00	29.0	52.3	<.001
Neurotic		1.0		
Normal	21.50	30.0	58.0	<.001
Psychotic		.5		
Neurotic	14.00	28.0	45.1	<.001
Psychotic		2.0		
PR				
Group:				
Normal	11.07	29.8	58.0	<.001
Neurotic		.3		
Normal	9.50	30.0	56.1	<.001
Psychotic		1.0		
Neurotic	7.00	29.0	39.7	<.001
Psychotic		4.8		
PP				
Group:				
Normal	1.95	8.2	24.6	<.001
Neurotic		27.1		
Normal	2.60	6.2	30.4	<.001
Psychotic		27.4		
Neurotic	4.33	15.0	.6	—
Psychotic		18.0		

categories are not related per se but that those neurotics with higher intelligence tend to be more in contact and thus obtain better TAT scores.

□ T Scores

Several problems are involved in use of Table 7.13 as preliminary norms for these TAT scoring categories. The complexity of the clerical process, the absence of uniform procedure, and the use of unequal score units make mandatory a more communicable method

TABLE 7.12 Normal–Neurotic and Neurotic–Psychotic Medians for Male Validation, Male Cross-Validation (C), Female Validation, Total Male, and Total Male and Female Samples for TAT Scoring Categories PO, PR, and PP

	Median	
Category	Normal–Neurotic	Neurotic–Psychotic
PO		
Sample		
Men	24.5	16.9
Men (C)	23.0	14.0
Women	22.5	12.1
Total Men	23.8	16.3
Total Men and Women	23.4	14.7
PR		
Sample		
Men	11.2	7.7
Men (C)	11.1	7.0
Women	11.9	7.7
Total Men	11.1	7.3
Total Men and Women	11.4	7.5
PP		
Sample		
Men	1.9	7.4
Men (C)	1.9	4.3
Women	1.5	6.8
Total Men	1.9	6.2
Total Men and Women	1.8	6.4

of presenting normative data. For these reasons conversion to T-score equivalents was undertaken.

T scores assume a standard group of *S*s. Although the total number of *S*s remains relatively small ($N = 390$) and may not be representative of normal or clinical populations over a broad range of situations, the advantages of T scores are recognized. Primarily, however, the opportunity for maximizing differences between groups by use of combined scores was obtained. Thus, these scores when normalized become units common to psychological measurement and their meaning is enhanced.

Table 7.16 presents the T-score equivalents for each TAT scoring category. Table 7.17 contains T-score percentages of normal, neurotic, and psychotic samples for each scoring category. It should be noted that Tables 7.13 and 7.17 present highly similar percentage figures, differing only as a function of choice of cutoff points. However, when T scores are added to provide the combinations for PO and PR, PO and PP, PR and PP, and PO, PR, PP, striking differences occur in the predictive efficiency of the scoring categories. Tables 7.18,

TABLE 7.13 Percentage of Ss in Each Group Receiving Scores of 0, 1, or 2 on Each Category

	Category		
Group	PO	PR	PP
Normal			
Score			
0	82	84	87
1	18	16	12
2	0	0	1
Neurotic			
Score			
0	17	14	26
1	68	81	40
2	15	5	34
Psychotic			
Score			
0	1	1	13
1	16	29	42
2	83	70	45

TABLE 7.14 Product–Moment Correlations Between Categories PO, PR, and PP and Length for Two Samples, Men and Women, Each of Three Groups, 50 *S*s in Each Group

	Category		
Length	PO	PR	PP
Men			
Group			
Normal	.23	.15	.16
Neurotic	.52**	.12	.11
Psychotic	.30*	–.02	.21
Women			
Group			
Normal	.55**	.10	–.00
Neurotic	.34*	.50**	.40**
Psychotic	.42**	.20	.39**

Note: *Significant at the .05 level of confidence. **Significant at the .01 level of confidence.

TABLE 7.15 Product–Moment Correlations Between Categories PO, PR, and PP and Intelligence Test Scores for Three Groups of Women

	Category		
Intelligence	PO	PR	PP
Group			
Normal (N = 50)	.02	–.04	.06
Neurotic (N = 34)	.34*	.31	.05
Psychotic (N = 40)	.22	.23	.00

Note: *Significant at the .05 level of confidence.

7.19, 7.20, and 7.21 provide this information. When PO and PR T scores are combined (Table 7.18), 79% of normal *S*s fall between scores of 112 and 145, 88% of neurotic *S*s fall between 80 and 111, and 83% of psychotic *S*s fall between 49 and 88. Combinations of PO and PP (Table 7.19) and PR and PP (Table 7.20) do not provide any increments to

TABLE 7.16 T Scores for Categories PO, PR, and PP

	Category		
T Score	PO	PR	PP
78	35–37		
72	32–34		
67		15	
65	29–31		
62		14	
59	26–28		
58		13	0–2
56		12	
55	23–25		
53		11	
52	20–22		
51		10	
50			3–5
49	17–19	9	
47		8	
46	14–16		

(Continued)

TABLE 7.16 T Scores for Categories PO, PR, and PP (Continued)

	Category		
T Score	PO	PR	PP
45		7	6–8
43	11–13	6	
42	9–11		
40		5	
39			12–14
38	8–10		
37		4	15–17
35			18–20
33		3	
32	5–7		21–23
30		2	24–26
28			27–29
26		1	30–35
25			36–38
24			39–41
19		0	42–44

TABLE 7.17 T Score Percentages of Normal, Neurotic, and Psychotic *Ss* for Each Scoring Category

	Normal			Neurotic			Psychotic		
T Score	PO	PR	PP	PO	PR	PP	PO	PR	PP
55–78	88	84	87	24	14	25	2	1	13
46–54	12	16	8	65	71	22	18	12	23
19–45	0	0	5	11	15	53	80	87	64

TABLE 7.18 T Score Percentages of Normal, Neurotic, and Psychotic *Ss* for Scoring Categories PO and PR Combined

T Score	Normal	Neurotic	Psychotic
112–145	79	6	0
89–111	21	88	17
49–88	0	6	83

TABLE 7.19 T Score Percentages of Normal, Neurotic, and Psychotic *S*s for Scoring Categories PO and PP Combined

T Score	Normal	Neurotic	Psychotic
109–136	92	18	2
89–108	8	62	27
49–88	0	20	71

TABLE 7.20 T Score Percentages of Normal, Neurotic, and Psychotic *S*s for Scoring Categories PR and PP Combined

T Score	Normal	Neurotic	Psychotic
108–125	92	14	1
91–107	8	65	23
38–90	0	21	76

TABLE 7.21 T Score Percentages of Normal, Neurotic, and Psychotic *S*s for Scoring Categories PO, PR, and PP Combined

T Score	Normal	Neurotic	Psychotic
166–203	88	9	1
134–165	12	81	20
70–133	0	10	79

prediction. When all three scoring categories are combined (Table 7.21), 88% of normal *S*s obtain combined T scores of 166 to 203, 81% of neurotic *S*s obtain scores between 134 and 165, and 79% of psychotic *S*s obtain scores between 70 and 133.

It is suggested that scores from each category be transformed into T-score equivalents (Table 7.16), these T scores added, and Table 7.21 be used directly to evaluate the probability of accurate diagnostic placement of a given individual *S*.

8

CHAPTER

Melvin Feffer's Interpersonal Decentering

Melissa Leeper, Lauren Dobbs, and Sharon Rae Jenkins

Abstract

Feffer's (1959) theory of interpersonal decentering stems from Piaget's (1972) theory of decentering as an aspect of operational thought. This ability to consider simultaneously more than one feature of a situation is seen by Piaget in a primarily impersonal realm involving perspective taking, the ability to see the same situation from more than one point of view. Feffer (1959) applied it to interpersonal interactions as role taking, the capacity to coordinate complementary roles in a social situation. The Interpersonal Decentering System assigns a lower score for action–reaction statements describing an interaction, because the character corrects his or her behavior in response to another's action instead of anticipating the intended behavior. This is representative of the more primitive preoperational sequential thinking. Anticipating another's behavior, which requires internalization, represents a higher level of decentering because it shows operational simultaneous thought. The ability to differentiate the characters while simultaneously maintaining a relationship between them indicates a high level of decentering ability in the Interpersonal Decentering categories. As a mature social cognition, higher levels of decentering represent an advance over more concrete social perception. Thus, interpersonal decentering is theorized to play a considerable role in the exchange of ideas among people and in the development and maintenance of familial, friend, romantic, and business relationships.

Description of System

Conceptual Framework

The egocentrism characteristic of early stages of childhood appears in social interaction as an inability to consider simultaneously one's own feelings and thoughts and those of another person. Young children focus sequentially and exclusively either on themselves or on the other.

As children mature, a capacity for multidimensional thought emerges, allowing them to assess social situations more accurately by thinking not only about their own internal state but also about the states of those around them before acting. They are then able to refocus, or to *decenter* in Piaget's (1972) terms, to distinguish their own and the other's thoughts and feelings.

Piaget's (1972) concept of decentering captures this refocusing of attention as one aspect of the capacity for abstract thought that he related to the principles of conservation. In earlier stages of development, children may focus only on immediate sensory perceptions of, for example, either height or width when comparing two volumes differing in shape. At later stages of development, children can create an abstract mental representation of the objects, and thus consider the height and width simultaneously in judging which has greater volume. As development advances, preoperational thinking changes from shifting focus sequentially among various aspects of the physical world to mature decentering ability, which requires balancing and integrating simultaneously various aspects of an internalized representation of the world.

Most of Piaget's work concerned impersonal aspects of cognitive development. Feffer (1959) expanded the concept of decentering to apply it to the developmental, cognitive processing of social thought. With increasing maturity of decentering, children can comprehend their physical environment more accurately. Through interpersonal decentering people can more accurately understand various aspects of a social situation and adapt their behavior accordingly (Feffer, 1967). An individual functioning at a high level of interpersonal decentering will be able to view her or his planned behavior from the point of view of another person who may be affected by the action. The individual can then modify the planned behavior considering the other's point of view and her or his own view at the same time.

Interpersonal conservation, as Feffer (1959) defined it, involves two complementary roles, such as talker–listener or leader–follower. The more primitive form of interpersonal conservation, sequential decentering, involves a series of alternating stimulus–response exchanges in which each subject in turn acts as a stimulus to the other's response. Feffer adopted Asch's (1952) definition of simultaneous decentering as one person anticipating another's actions while considering at the same time his or her own actions. Thus, each person's action interpenetrates and regulates the other's action or response.

The first measure of interpersonal decentering developed by Feffer was the Role-Taking Task (RTT). To use the RTT, the researcher asks the participant to tell the initial story, a standard thematic apperceptive technique (TAT)-type story about an ambiguous picture. Then the participant is asked to tell the story again from each character's individual point of view (Lowenherz & Feffer, 1969). The data analysis involves comparing these successive stories and appraising two aspects of decentering activity, abstractness of the descriptions of actors, and consistency of content when describing different actors (Feffer, 1959).

Several empirical studies were conducted using the RTT measure (Buxer, 1974; Feffer, 1959; Feffer & Jahelka, 1968; Lowenherz & Feffer, 1969; Olshansky, 1971; Ward, 1975). Using this method, interpersonal decentering was shown to be significantly related to developmental indices scored from Rorschach protocols for White males of mean age 36 (Feffer, 1959). Lowenherz and Feffer (1969) found that female college students showed more difficulty coordinating perspectives when the characters they were describing were given attributes that the individual perceived as undesirable. In Buxer's (1974) study, the comparison groups of either self-indulgent or self-depriving psychiatric patients both showed more difficulty coordinating roles when taking the ego–alien role perspective.

Olshansky (1971) and Ward (1975) used the RTT to evaluate decentering ability and measured role taking by assigning scores of no role taking (NR), simple role taking (SR), or role taking (RT), with each of these categories breaking role taking down into three more levels. Olshansky (1971) and Ward (1975) both examined participant's sequential decentering when exposed to defensively isolated situations. The term *defensively isolated,* also known as *disjunctive,* refers to reciprocal statements. Olshansky (1971) required participants to create one story based on conjunctive role content and another story on disjunctive role content. Ward (1975) documented participants' delusions and then examined their ability to take the perspective of other participants' delusions. Olshansky (1971) and Ward (1975) found that participants showed greater sequential decentering when exposed to disjunctive role-reciprocal statements than when exposed to conjunctive role-reciprocal statements.

A significant study by Feffer and Jahelka (1968) examined the suggestion that performance on the RTT may be entirely dependent on the decentering evident in the individual's initial TAT story. They used a scoring system for the initial story (Feffer, 1966) with nine levels of increasing sophistication of decentering, which captures the structure of sequential and simultaneous decentering and which has been elaborated into the manual in this volume.

Similarly to the RTT scoring, the nine levels of Feffer and Jahelka's (1968) TAT Interpersonal Decentering System took into consideration the level of actor description and the extent of role taking. Instead of assessing coordination between parallel versions of a story, the TAT scoring system measures decentering according to the maturity of the relationships seen in the single initial story (Feffer & Jahelka, 1968). In the first phase of this study, the participants completed the normal RTT procedure. Analysis of these data showed a significant association between the initial story's TAT score and the RTT score. In the second phase, the initial story was completed, scored, and typed. The next week participants returned to complete the RTT with their own initial story and the stories of two other participants. These data revealed that initial story performance and RTT performance were both more closely related to the decentering level of the participant than to the decentering level of the author of the initial story used in the role-taking task. This study shows that the initial TAT story alone could be as accurate a measure of interpersonal decentering as the RTT had been.

Scoring Categories

Interpersonal Decentering scores are derived from TAT stories using the scoring manual originally developed by Melvin Feffer (1966) and elaborated in this volume. Stories are first divided into social interaction units. An interaction unit must involve at least two characters, either two or more present in the scene or one character internalizing another. A series of actions or thoughts remain one unit if there is no change in the place, characters present, or significant change in time. Each unit receives a separate Decentering score.

Action–reaction statements represent the more primitive sequential decentering and are given lower scores because the character's behavior changes after the fact of the other's action instead of anticipating the other's behavior. Anticipating another character's behavior is considered to represent internalization, a higher level of simultaneous decentering because it shows the writer has the capability to think in more abstract, less egocentric, multidimensional terms. The ability to differentiate the characters while simultaneously maintaining a relationship that integrates their interactions abstractly displays a high level of decentering ability according to the TAT decentering categories.

TABLE 8.1 Scoring Categories for Interpersonal Decentering

Category	Name	Example
1	Undifferentiated relationship	"They like sports."
2	Nonreactive directional relationship	"She gives him food."
3	Reactive directional relationship	"She gives him food which he appreciates."
4	Interactive directional relationship	"She gives him food that he likes. She is glad."
5	Internalized other, simple representation	"He plans on telling her later."
6	Internalized other, surface characteristics	"He plans on telling her how she looks."
7	Internalized other, internalized state	"He plans on telling her when she feels better."
8	Internalized others	"He plans on telling her that Bill likes her."
9	Internalized self-other	"He felt he was wrong in telling her that."

Note: Scored once for each interaction segment (same characters, same time and place) in the story.

Scores are arranged on a scale of 1–9, with 1 representing the lowest level of Decentering and 9 representing the most advanced level. A score of 1 represents an undifferentiated relationship (i.e., no decentering) in which both characters are involved in the same activity (e.g., "They went to see the game."). The next highest categories involve differentiated characters but only sequential decentering. For example, a score of 2 involves a shift of focus with no stated or implied effect of the action of the acting character on the receiving character (e.g., "She told him about the rain."). If the character reacts, this indicates a second shift in focus, which would receive a score of 3. If this reaction then elicits a reaction from the original character, this would be a third shift, which would increase that interaction unit's score to 4 (see Table 8.1).

The higher levels of Interpersonal Decentering (5–9) involve one character or group internalizing the attributes of another character. In general, the latter character is represented as the object of the main character's thoughts or feelings. In increasing levels of decentering, the object character is represented as the simple object of the main character's internalized state (score of 5); an object elaborated by external attributes or behaviors (score of 6); or elaborated by his or her own internalized state (score of 7). A score of 8 indicates that the main character is internalizing two other characters, in which one of them is the object of the internalized state of the other. In the highest level of Decentering (score of 9), the object of the internalized state is the self in an interactive relationship with another (e.g., "He is thinking about playing outside with his friends," *playing* is an interactive relationship).

The mean Decentering score is the average score across all interaction units for each story. The final score for each participant is the average (or sum, for Carberry, 1982) across all stories. However, other scoring approaches may be tried (e.g., Dobbs,

Leeper, & Jenkins, 2004). Each of the several most obvious ways of deriving a summary score makes different assumptions about storytelling and about the construct of decentering. If decentering is conceptualized as a skill or ability such as Piaget's (1972) conservation, then in a less structured spontaneous task such as story-telling, perhaps the best measure is the single highest score across all stories. If it is seen as a personality trait that should be consistent across all aspects of all situations, then as in past studies, scores should be averaged across all interaction units within each story (total story score divided by number of interaction units) and then averaged across stories. If it is something that might emerge sporadically, not uniformly, in normal interaction, then the highest score for each story should be averaged across all stories, effectively ignoring lower-level back-and-forth sequential interactions if even one simultaneous, internalized interaction is present. If it is situation-specific—that is, there is more variability in scores between pictures within assessees than between assessees for the same picture—then some more complex means of score derivation is needed.

☐ Research Evidence

Validity

The scoring categories of the Interpersonal Decentering System show a high level of content validity, as they correspond quite literally to both sequential and simultaneous cognitive processing and, within the latter, to increasingly complex object representation and levels of internalization. Considering stories as samples of imaginative thought, they could be said to sample the storyteller's implicit theory of mind. Given that the task of the storyteller is to make sense of the picture, and explicitly to discuss the characters' thoughts and feelings, the failure to attain any scores in categories 5–9 suggests that if the teller has developed a theory of mind, it is not used often to understand other people's actions.

Since the Feffer and Jahelka (1968) study that established the nine-level scoring system, only three empirical studies have used the TAT Interpersonal Decentering System (Carberry, 1982; Dobbs et al., 2004; Strober, 1979). The former and latter were designed for clinical exploration rather than for further validating the scoring system. Strober (1979) found that adolescents with schizophrenia, when compared with the control group of adolescents in the same psychiatric setting, showed significantly lower levels of Interpersonal Decentering. Carberry (1982) examined how well Interpersonal Decentering scores predicted social skills and treatment status of children at high risk of psychosis. She did not find any of the relationships she had anticipated to be significant. In an exploratory analysis, however, she found a significant correlation between Interpersonal Decentering at time 1 and social interaction as assessed by a teacher at time 2 when controlling for the number of siblings in the study (i.e., the scores for each group of siblings were averaged to create sibship-average scores); however, this relationship was not found for individual participants' uncontrolled scores.

More recently, Dobbs et al. (2004) studied the associations of Interpersonal Decentering with social network involvement, having a confidant, and scores on the Inventory of Interpersonal Problems for a sample of college students. Those higher in Decentering were modestly more engaged with their social networks, and men were more likely to have a confidant. Higher Decenterers reported more problems in the area of subassertiveness, and those who Decentered less endorsed more difficulties with being too domineering.

Generalizability

Compared with many other constructs in psychology, there is relatively little research on the topic of interpersonal decentering. From these few studies, however, we see patterns indicating that (1) the RTT and TAT scoring method measure a common variable of interpersonal decentering; (2) participants have more difficulty decentering when writing about characters with attributes opposing those the individual identifies with (this is particularly difficult for psychiatric patients); and (3) this measure does show some concurrence with other developmental constructs and may be related to schizophrenia in adolescents.

Participant samples have emphasized both college students and clinic clients, primarily Anglo American. Samples emphasizing individuals of other cultural backgrounds should consider the role of storytelling in their cultures, and specifically the rules of courtesy regarding the discussion of other people's internal states, both in general and in a storytelling context.

Reliability

Feffer and Jahelka (1968, p. 436) reported that Jahelka had attained interscorer reliability of *rho* = .71 with "another person trained in the use of the scoring system." Strober's (1979) interscorer reliability correlation indicated satisfactory agreement on 20 stories between the author and a research assistant ($r = .78$). The reliability between the author and a clinical graduate student for a random sample of 20 stories in Carberry's study (1982) was adequate ($r = .85$).

For the research by Dobbs et al. (2004), all stories were scored by one of the present first and second authors working independently (Dobbs, 2003; Leeper, 2004), and discrepancies were resolved by discussion and consensus. These senior undergraduate honors students required approximately 3 hours of training and 10 hours of practice before interscorer reliability between them was adequate. These two then trained three other assistants—one undergraduate and two postbachelors—whose comments and questions were valuable for refining the manual.[1]

To check reliability, 30 stories were scored independently by the two expert coders. The reliability for the mean scores was adequate (*rho* = .79), and higher reliabilities were found for total scores (*rho* = .89) and for number of interaction units (*rho* = .84). These reliabilities were attained using Feffer's original scoring manual; higher reliabilities should be expected using the elaborated manual produced by that study (Feffer, Leeper, Dobbs, & Jenkins, this volume). Another scoring team has achieved reliabilities consistently above .90 with this manual.[2]

□ Future Research Needed

Due to the limited amount of previous research, much construct validity work remains to be done. Other measures could be used to establish construct validity for interpersonal decentering through convergent and discriminant validity. For example, considering decentering as an adaptive social skill, scores might be expected to correlate positively with scores on the Wechsler Adult Intelligence Scale (WAIS) Comprehension and Picture Arrangement subtests, and perhaps aspects of emotional intelligence (Boyatzis, Goleman, & Rhee, 2000). To build theory, studies are needed to clarify the nature of the construct as measured by this scoring system. Is it an ability or capacity—as Piaget (1972) indicated—or a spontaneously exercised performance? A personality trait—as implied by the usual calculation of average scores across all interactions? To what extent might it be an adaptive response to certain kinds of situations for most people, in contrast to other kinds of situations, making it a situation-specific trait (Anastasi, 1988)?

Research with children and adolescents should explore in nonclinical samples whether Interpersonal Decentering scores increase in parallel with other aspects of Piagetian cognitive development and with the development of a theory of mind. Future studies of Interpersonal Decentering could relate it to measures of social competence, especially social insight and empathy. Decentering capacity might be a cognitive prerequisite for the development of the latter two.

Studies of clinical samples across the age spectrum might compare patients with disorders that could be characterized as overly decentered (e.g., social phobias, dependent personality disorder, and perhaps internalizing disorders such as depression) with those having diagnoses in the antisocial or asocial (e.g., schizoid, avoidant personality disorder, and perhaps externalizing disorders such as conduct disorder) spectra. If Decentering scores are found to increase following psychoeducational groups or interpersonal forms of psychotherapy compared with preintervention, this measure might be useful as a program evaluation tool and an indicator of which patients may benefit most. Teaching the scoring system to patients might help them learn to evaluate their own maladaptive social cognitions.

☐ References

Anastasi, A. (1988). *Psychological testing* (6th ed.). Upper Saddle River, NJ: Prentice Hall.

Asch, S. (1952). *Social psychology.* New York: Prentice Hall.

Boyatzis, R. E. (1998). *Transforming qualitative information: Thematic analysis and code development.* Thousand Oaks, CA: Sage.

Buxer, C. G. (1974). *Symptomatic behavior as an expression isolation between role schemata.* Unpublished doctoral dissertation, Yeshiva University.

Carberry, A. T. (1982). *Interpersonal decentering, social interaction, and treatment status in children at risk for psychosis.* Unpublished doctoral dissertation, Saint Louis University.

Dobbs, L. (2003). *Interpersonal decentering and mutuality in close relationships.* Unpublished senior honors thesis, University of North Texas, Denton.

Dobbs, L., Leeper, M., & Jenkins, S. R. (2004, July). *Feffer's Interpersonal Decentering TAT scoring system and close relationships.* Poster presented at the 112th annual convention of the American Psychological Association, Honolulu, HI.

Feffer, M. H. (1959). The cognitive implications of role-taking behavior. *Journal of Personality, 27,* 152–158.

Feffer, M. H. (1966). *Initial story (TAT) scoring categories.* Washington, DC: Library of Congress. American Documentation Institute 10032.

Feffer, M. (1967). Symptom expression as a form of primitive decentering. *Psychological Review, 74*(1), 16–28.

Feffer, M., & Gourevitch, V. (1960). Cognitive aspects of role taking in children. *Journal of Personality, 28,* 383–396.

Feffer, M. H., & Jahelka, M. (1968). Implications of the decentering concept for the structuring of projective content. *Journal of Consulting and Clinical Psychology, 32*(4), 434–441.

Leeper, M. (2003). Interpersonal decentering and interpersonal problems. Unpublished senior honors thesis, University of North Texas, Denton, TX.

Lowenherz, L., & Feffer, M. H. (1969). Cognitive level as a function of defensive isolation. *Journal of Abnormal Psychology, 74*(3), 352–357.

Olshansky, P. M. (1971). *Cognitive parallels RE self-structure.* Unpublished doctoral dissertation, Yeshiva University.

Piaget, J. (1950). *The psychology of intelligence.* New York: Harcourt Brace.

Strober, M. (1979). The structuring of interpersonal relations in schizophrenic adolescents: A decentering analysis of Thematic Apperception Test stories. *Journal of Abnormal Child Psychology, 7*(3), 309–316.

Ward, C. A. (1975). *Delusions as a form of primitive decentering.* Unpublished doctoral dissertation, Yeshiva University.

Notes

1. We thank Michele Elefante, Andrea Haag, and Michael McFarland for their assistance with this study.
2. We thank Summer Burkman and Luis Perez for their work on this scoring.

9

CHAPTER

Scoring Manual for Feffer's Interpersonal Decentering

Melvin Feffer, Melissa Leeper, Lauren Dobbs, Sharon Rae Jenkins, and Luis E. Perez

Introduction

According to Feffer's (1959) theory, interpersonal decentering is an aspect of operational thinking that involves an ability to be aware of, respond to, and anticipate another person's ideas, thoughts, feelings, or actions. In stories, it is represented by two main levels of interaction: (1) preinternalization, representing preoperational one-dimensional and sequential thinking (scores 1–4), in which characters act and react with each other; and (2) internalization, reflecting operational multidimensional and simultaneous thinking (scores 5–9). In these latter levels, characters first conceptualize others, who might not be present, via internal representation, independently of overt action (scores 5–6) and then may envision other characters as having their own internalized states (scores 7–9). The scoring process involves first identifying and isolating instances of interaction between story characters—which may occur in the imagination of one—and then assigning a decentering category score that represents one of the nine levels.

Administration

Format

Studies have produced significant results using both individual clinical administration and group administration with storytellers handwriting their own stories. Feffer and Jahelka (1968) used group administration with a screen-projected picture and handwritten stories for a college student sample. In Strober's study (1979), the Thematic Apperception Test (TAT) was administered individually by a clinician during the adolescent patients' first two weeks of hospitalization. In studies now in progress at the University of North Texas, graduate student clinicians administered the TAT individually to psychology clinic clients using standard clinical instructions. One study of college students used a group administration with projected pictures and handwritten stories. In scoring these stories, the second and third authors noted no obvious differences in the scoring process for these samples. However, if the examiner uses probe questions to prompt for specific story aspects, material given after the first probe probably should not be scored. Decentering scores should come from the spontaneously told story in the way that the examinee organizes it. The usual probes for characters' thoughts and feelings are likely to elicit internalization responses that would not have been given otherwise.

Stimuli

A variety of card stimuli have been used. Feffer and Jahelka (1968, p. 435) used only one picture, which was "a barroom quarrel between a male and female," possibly card 4. Strober (1979) used Murray's (1943) cards 2, 6BM, and 7BM, which were chosen as most likely to elicit interpersonal content. For Carberry's dissertation (1982), cards 2, 7GF, and 8BM were used because each contains more than one human figure. Studies at the University of North Texas have used cards 1, 2, 3BM, 4, 10, and 13MF.

Although pictures with two or more figures are likely to elicit more interaction units—and thus more decentering scores—than are pictures of one person, it is not clear that scores from the latter pictures are any less valid. In the University of North Texas studies, pictures of one person tended to elicit more stories involving internalized others, with the single character thinking about or recalling someone not present. In fact, in the college student study, card 1 (boy with violin) had the highest decentering mean score (4.5), whereas card 10 (two people embracing) had the lowest (3.0; Dobbs, 2003). Likely due to its strong pull for intimacy themes, the latter card drew many dedifferentiated stories in which the characters shared a common experience, and such interactions receive the lowest score (1).

As yet there is no evidence or rationale suggesting that stories elicited using other stimuli (e.g., sentence cues, music) would be any less valid than stories elicited with pictures. Nonstory narratives are probably less likely to encourage the depiction of the interaction units needed for scoring. However, story-like narratives (e.g., folk tales, autobiographies) might yield scorable interaction units, the validity of which is an empirical question.

☐ Scoring Process

First, the scorer identifies the interaction units in the story, separating them by putting each of the units inside brackets or parentheses. Then each interaction unit is assigned a decentering category score, which is noted in the margin, as shown in Table 9.1.

TABLE 9.1 Two Examples of Decentering Scoring

Score	
9	**Card 2: [There's a young woman who has a crush on the farmer guy—the guy who's working. *She pretends not to notice him.* She's well educated because she has books and *pretends not to be in love with him,* but she is.]**
1	**[*They had a secret affair* in the past where they met in the barn or house and *had a romantic encounter.*]**
6	**[The other woman is the *mother and doesn't approve that they're in love* and has to watch very closely because *she might suspect that they're in love,* and she doesn't approve.]**
2	**[And eventually they'll run away together, and *she'll admit her love for him* and they will be happy.]**
Highest score = 9 ***Interaction Units = 4 Average = 18/4 = 4.5***	
5	**Card 2. [This lady decided to go off to college and *leave her family.*]**
9	**[Then she finds out that her mother is pregnant and she can't decide on whether to go to college or not because *she thinks she needs to stay and help her mother* on the farm.]**
2	**[*Her mother reassures her* that everything will be okay on the farm.] So she ends up going to college and becoming a teacher. Right now she's feeling confused about her obligations.**
Highest score = 9 ***Interaction Units = 3 Average = 16/3 = 5.33***	

Note: Interaction units are demarcated by brackets indicating changes in time, place, or persons. Italicized text indicates the phrase within each interaction unit that determines its decentering score. The first story is unusually repetitive; each of the first three interaction units has two repetitions of the same scorable material, which does not change its score due to the way that the interaction units are divided.

Scoring Category Criteria

Interaction Units

Interaction units involve two or more characters who are interacting in the same time and place. It is considered the same interaction if there is no change in characters present, time, or place. When unsure about the divisions between interaction units, leave them as larger units. Generally, only separate the units if the time, place, or characters changes. A change in which character is the main focus does not signal a change in interaction as long as the same characters are maintained (i.e., no new characters). Note that throughout this chapter, examples and stories are rendered verbatim, including the errors of grammar and punctuation that may induce ambiguity and make accurate scoring a challenge at times!

> Change of characters: [She will become a doctor and support her family] (2) and [they will be happy for ever.] (1) (*She* and *they* are separate, as they can happen independently.)

No change in character: [The young lady is in love w/ the man, and visa-versa.] (3)

No change in the situation: [I just want to spend more time with him. I want to talk to him, feel his eyes on me as I pretend to look away.] (9)

Change of characters: [They tried many specialists] (4), but [none could find the source of her ailment.] (2)

In the last example, there is a change in characters at the *but,* which signals a new interaction. The characters in the first interaction are *they,* referring to the husband and wife, and *specialists.* The characters in the second interaction are *none,* in reference to the specialists mentioned previously, and *her.* In this example, the phrase *tried many* indicates a multifaceted interaction between the couple and the efforts of several doctors. Similarly, when one act causes two different characters to react independently, the reactions are coded as two separate interactions:

[When they came back home she decided to tell her mom and dad. Sara's dad was happy for them] (3), but [her mom disapproved.] (3)

A change of activity that represents an evolution over time does not signal a new interaction, unless accompanied by a change in time, place, or character:

[They grew up together. They were the best of friends and had planned on running away together when they were older.] (1) (Note that the planning process occurs during the growing up.)

If one interaction shows the general situation and another is a specific example of the general statement, it is considered part of the same interaction. However, if it is a slight variation in content it is scored separately:

[The man lying in bed is perturbed because of his mother's fussing. The mother is bringing his food in on a tray.] (3) (The second sentence elaborates on the mother's fussing and is not a separate instance of social interaction.)

[Mary's mother will start to suspect that Matt and Mary feel something for each other by the way they act. One day she walks in on Mary and Matt having sex.] (7) (Having sex is an elaboration of *the way they act.*)

When two different interactions are connected by conjunctions such as *because, so,* or *when,* score only the highest interaction. The second interaction is considered an elaboration of the first:

[Her parents forbid her to see him (~~2~~) because they don't consider him to be in the higher class of society.] (6)

However, if the two interactions are separated by conjunctions such as but, and, or, etc., such that they can be seen as independent of each other or as alternatives, score each separately. Alternative interactions often cannot exist simultaneously:

[They live on a farm] (1), and [they raise chickens.] (1)

[She think she too young] (6), or maybe [she didn't like the boy.] (5)

Although the verb *to watch* implies a more directive and purposeful interaction with another than does the verb *to see,* a character merely acknowledging the presence of another is the minimal condition to score an interaction.

[As she walked home from school, the girl saw the handsome young man working hard in the fields.] (2)

[As she walked home from school, the girl stopped to watch the handsome young man working hard in the fields.] (2)

In the first example, the girl could have kept walking completely oblivious to her surroundings and to others around her. But since she decentered from herself long enough to notice another person, this scores as a directed action. In the second example, the girl is again decentering from herself enough to notice another person. Although she may be more purposeful in this observation, the motive for the interaction is not of concern here, and there is no evidence that she is internalizing the young man, which would justify a higher score.

When a character is involved in a dream, fantasy, or memory, this is still the character's current reality. He or she is not concerned with real physical time or space, so the dream state is scored with the same rules as for physical reality. However, changes in time, place, and person within this state all signal new interactions, just as they would in physical reality.

Interactions that are personalized or self-referential are not scored. This decision was made based on the assumption that this loss of distance from the card is an indication that the storyteller has difficulty decentering from self:

"This is Bob and myself and we're gonna go to a ballgame." (no interaction)

"She's scared of you." (no interaction)

"He killed you cause this was you." (no interaction)

Decentering Category Scores

Each interaction unit receives one and only one decentering category score. Some of the categories include content that could be coded into a lower category, but the highest possible category for the whole unit is the one to be scored. For example, category 4 will always include a 2 and 3. When in doubt, the unit should be given the highest score for which there is solid, explicit support.

There are nine decentering categories, which are currently conceptualized as forming an ordinal scale because the change at category 5 to the requirement of an internalized other, and the increased complexity of successive categories thereafter, might signal unequal intervals at different levels of cognitive development.

(1) *Undifferentiated relationship*: Both characters involved in the relationship are described as (a) alike in some way, or (b) being engaged in similar activity. These statements describe the characters as engaged in the same relationship. It is not directional, nor are the characters differentiated from one another.

They both like sports.

The son came with him.

They were talking with each other.

His parents are very proud.

They can enjoy each other and everything they do is mutual.

The girl and woman live all alone.

They are married.

They are husband and wife.

They will get married.

(2) *Nonreactive directional relationship*: The characters in the relationship are differentiated; the activity of one character directed toward the other evokes no reaction from the other. These interactions are directional and allow the other character to have a different opinion or action. Although directional, they do not state what the other character will do or feel in response (nonreactive).

His mother and father bought him a violin.

He is waiting for her.

He ain't telling them nothing. (withholding information is considered a directed action)

She meets this man.

She's going to marry him.

His son accidentally shot him. (motivation issue ignored)

He's going to end up having to stay at home and support his family. (future tense okay)

The doctors are taking the bullet out of him.

The grandmother kept talking to him but it didn't do no good.

Love is an abstract concept; one can see the behavioral manifestations (directed actions) of the emotion, such as facial expression, interpersonal behaviors, eye contact, and vocal affect, but the concept itself remains abstract, and thus difficult to score. For scoring purposes, love is considered an action rather than an internalization.

[They love each other.] (1)

[He loves her.] (2)

In the first example, *they* is a grouped pronoun that serves to deindividuate the characters. *They* are not distinguished from one another. In contrast, the subject of the second example is the pronoun *he*. This implies a unidirectional interaction. The author provides the characters with the ability to be individuals with different emotions and/or different types of love.

(3) *Reactive directional relationship*: The characters in the relationship are differentiated; the activity of one character directed toward the other evokes a reaction from the other which (a) is not explicitly directed back to the initiator or (b) is explicitly directed back to the initiator but does not evoke a counter reaction.

He would always ask his grandpa if he could play, but his grandpa said no, that it was very fragile.

Then one day the lady found out and told the police and they put him in jail.

By the end of the day she has made 3 new girlfriends. (The minimum interaction implied in *making friends* would be an action and a reaction; thus, this statement can be coded as a 3.)

The mother is reading her a story but she isn't listening at all. (scorable despite negative reaction because it shows that the child telling the story can conceptualize the possibility of a listening response)

(4) *Interactive directional relationship*: The activity of one character directed toward the other evokes a reaction from the other, which in turn has an effect on the initiator. The two characters may continue to interact back and forth over a period of time, and this is still scored as one interaction as long as it remains continuous and between the same characters. Changes in time, place, or characters require scoring as a separate interaction.

"Auntie, I don't want to practice my violin." "Well, sonny, if you want to be that great concert violinist then you must practice." "You're right; I will practice every day."

His mother is bringing him food, which he gives back to her. She is unhappy.

She runs to him and spills her heart; to her surprise John had felt the same.

(5) *Internalized other, simple representation*: One character is represented as an object of another's feelings, thoughts, intentions, or conjectures. The former character may or may not be physically in the presence of the latter, but is represented as the simple object of such an internalized state. The internalized character is only the target of the other character's needs and actions. The target person is featureless.

The boy wants to be like his father.

She thought she loved her mother.

He decided to listen to him from now on.

He was thinking about killing his father. (No internal response to cognition, so not a 9; he is not imagining *himself* killing his father; he is shooting at a target.)

The boy is sad because he has no mother. (Although the mother in question does not exist, an internal representation of *a mother* does and is scored.)

She's thinking about having a baby. (The baby does not yet exist, but the internal representation does.)

(6) *Internalized other, surface characteristics*: One character is represented as an object of another's feelings, thoughts, intentions, or conjectures. The object character is elaborated in terms of such external attributes as location, action, or descriptive qualities, superficial features that affect the main character's response, characteristics that intrude on the main character.

He remembers the nagging of his parents.

She thought her mother loved her.

She was ashamed of his being drunk.

Then he realized that if he closed his eyes and listened really hard, he could hear his grandpa playing. This enabled Tommy to imitate the music.

She's feeling sad because the baby died.

At this boy's house, they're always fussing and arguing, and he's tired of it.

She buried him in the backyard late at night, and no one ever knew. (*No one* is a *generalized other* represented internally, and that character's not knowing is a scorable attribute.)

(7) *Internalized other, internalized state*: One character is represented as an object of another's feelings, thoughts, intentions, or conjectures. The object character is also

represented as having an internalized state. The main character perceives that the other person has feelings and other internalized states, too, that may be independent of the main character.

She wanted his opinion.

He wasn't interested in the violin but his dad thought he was.

He wants to make his mom and dad proud at the performance on Friday evening.

Dorothy's family will support her in what ever she chooses to do.

He's wondering if they're thinking about him.

(8) *Internalized others*: The object of the internalized state is two other characters in relation to each other. The relationship between these two other characters is such that one is the object of the internalized state of the other.

Mary believed that her husband really understood what her mom was thinking.

He feels that she is wrong in believing that Bill is a mean person.

John felt that Mr. White was the wrong person to be judging Kevin's actions.

The last thing she wants is for her daughter to be so obsessed with a man that isn't their rank in society.

(9) *Internalized self-other*: The object of the internalized state is the self in an interactive relationship with another. The main character is contemplating her or his own feelings or other internal state or actions in relation to another character.

The boy thinks that if he doesn't do well at the performance he will disappoint his parents.

He's trying to decide whether he should keep going because his father wants him to.

He's thinking about being out with his friends. ([*Himself*] *being out with his friends* is a collective action that includes him.)

He thinking if his father will get him one and when his father get him one he might tear it up.

He's feeling proud because he didn't kill his best friend.

She felt like she could succeed without her mother.

She's wishing she could help these people.

He finally decides it isn't worth taking the gun and the chance of somebody getting hurt.

He feels responsible to her because she took care of him when he was young.

She felt she was doing it for the girl's own good.

Additional Scoring Conventions

When a character internalizes herself or himself, it does not count as an interaction:

> "She is determined to make a better life for herself." (No interaction; although she is internalizing herself, there is no other, no one to interact with, resulting in an egocentric statement that does not score.)

First-person stories can be scored if that person does not interact with the characters in the story, but shows internalization, as in the role of a narrator. It is not considered a loss of distance if the writer uses first person from the perspective of a character in or relating to the picture.

> [I have so much studying to do, but my family needs help with the farm.] (7)

> [For as long as I can remember my parents have forced me to do things.] (9)

Statements that imply an interaction but that do not articulate an other (i.e., "invisible actor" statements) are not scored. These are often in the passive voice:

> "The boy was told to practice all night." (no interaction)

However, if an internalized character is nonspecific (e.g., nobody, somebody, anybody) and it appears that the main character is imagining an other who could fill this role, this nonspecific "generalized other" is considered internalized:

> [The boy is sad because he has no mother.] (5)

However, if the nonspecific character's physical presence is implied, there is no internalization.

> [She looks around to see if anyone notices her misplacement.] (2)

Mythical, imaginary, noncorporeal, and spiritual characters are coded if they interact as a human would. References to religious figures, such as gods, can be complex in this regard, as it may be unclear when a character "prays to God" whether the praying or some divine response should both be scored. The praying is a form of internalization, but the response may only be scored if it is within the context of human capability.

> [He wishes a fairy would come down and fix his violin.] (6)

"She's in deep thought over something she read in the books she holds, and those thoughts are depicted with the presence of the human figure at the right of the picture." (no interaction)

Animals, abstract concepts, and inanimate objects are not scored.

"She is fed up with society." (not scored because she is reacting to the concept of society—rules and constraints—rather than to a group of individuals who make up a society)

Characters who are dead are not capable of interacting, so any dialogue or internalizations by another character are not scored. This same principle is applied to dolls, animals, and other inanimate objects. The exception to this rule is when the character is remembering past interaction, is fantasizing, or is having a psychotic break, and "brings him or her [back] to life".

[She remembered her grandmother's singing.] (6) (Her grandmother had died.)

[The doll sprang to life and began dancing with the girl.] (1)

[The police phoned to tell her that her husband had been in a bad car accident and was instantly killed. She couldn't accept it; she knew that he would walk through that door any moment, hug her and tell her it was all a mistake.] (9)

If the object of the main verb is not a person and has a modifying clause that implies an interaction, it is coded as an interaction.

[Johnny is sad because he was playing with his violin that his father gave him before he left for the war.] (2)

With certain interactions there is an implied response or series of responses. These often involve idiomatic expressions. Some words that almost always imply a forced reaction or series of interactions are demanding, forcing, making, and teaching. The unit is scored for the minimum amount of interaction implied by the content.

[She talks him out of it.] (3) (Minimum interaction is that she talks and he responds by being talked out of it.)

Statements of tentativeness, motivation, and tense should be ignored. This includes cases of an internalized desire involving someone else's internalized state; the motives of the person who is internalizing the other are not considered when scoring an interaction unit.

[She *probably* be lookin' at the doctor.] (2)

[His son *accidentally* shot him.] (2)

[Her mother wants her to follow her dream *because she couldn't do so herself.*] (7)

In this last example, the mother has a specific reason for what she wishes her daughter to do; however, this motive is not taken into consideration in scoring the interaction. It does not serve as an elaboration to the internalized character and is therefore ignored. The dream is the daughter's internalized state.

Negative reactions are acceptable because they show that the storyteller has the ability to conceptualize the possibility of positive response. Reactions can include actions on others or simply emotional reactions.

> [The mother is reading her a story but she isn't listening at all.] (3)

> [The man wanted half the money and she said she did not have it, so the man killed her husband.] (4)

> [His mother is bringing him food which he gives back to her. She is unhappy.] (4)

If a character is dreaming about another, that person is internalized. Dying or widowing is not an interaction unless the character perceives it as an interaction, such as being "left".

> [But her mom, still resenting her husband for "leaving" her,] (6) [would not allow an educated woman to conspire with a male laborer.] (6) (It was made clear earlier in the story that her husband died.)

Calculating Scores

In previous studies using this scoring method (Carberry, 1982; Feffer & Jahelka, 1968; Strober, 1979), researchers averaged all category scores within a story. Strober used the mean of the within-story averages, and Carberry added them, to create a composite score for each participant. The University of North Texas studies are exploring the relative predictive power of two other ways of calculating summary scores: the highest score for any story, and the average of the highest score for each story.

Taking the set of stories as a sample of the storyteller's imagined responses that people might have to different social contexts, it seems logical that these methods represent different ways that imaginal decentering might occur in the storyteller's real life. We have noted that the previously used average of within-story average scores tends to be lowered by action-packed stories that have many back-and-forth interactions, even if there is also one much higher score. This composite average seems to represent the storyteller's tendency to sustain a high level of decentering—and to omit lower-level sequences—both within and across stories, suggesting a more reflective, perhaps internalizing personality, in contrast to operating typically at a lower action-oriented and concrete level, suggesting a less reflective, perhaps externalizing personality.

In contrast, the highest-score-only approach would estimate the person's likely highest level of decentering across a sample of real-life situations of about the same size and variety as the sample of pictures. This approach to aggregation of scores emphasizes the storyteller's ability to imagine and to rise to an occasion that calls for decentering, regardless of whether this is a habitual way of interacting. Conceptually, this would be a situation-specific trait (Anastasi, 1988). The average-of-highest calculation approach represents a compromise that aggregates across stories the person's highest level of decentering within any single story. This method captures the generalizability of the storyteller's habitually exercised decentering capacity across a range of situations without being lowered by the presence of action-oriented low-scoring interactions.

Similarly, the standard deviations of scores within and across stories might estimate the degree of variability in the storyteller's tendency to decenter within and across contexts. Individual differences in this variability might explain individual differences in cross-situational consistency—for example, why one person might act and be seen quite differently when with coworkers compared with family members, whereas another might be consistent. We have not yet explored this option.

☐ Practice Scoring

Practice Stories Set 1

(1) His name is Mark and Mark is having problems playing the violin like his teacher can and he wants to be like his teacher. He's been playing the violin for 2 years and he can't seem to play like his teacher does. So one day he talked to his teacher and his teacher told him that he's been playing the violin for 25 years and that it takes a lot of practice so all Mark can do is keep practicing so he can learn to play just like his teacher. So Mark made a commitment to himself that every day after school he's going to spend 2 hours studying. So 25 years later, Mark is teaching music class and he's playing like his teacher played. – 165.1

(2) The little boy has been given the violin as a present. He's staring at it, thinking, "I wanted a car." It came from his grandfather, and he's going to have to take lessons because he wants to please his grandfather. But he really wanted a toy car. –105.1

(3) He's a little boy contemplating over the violin on whether he wants to really learn how to play it or not. He's frustrated. It's a part of him, the violin, the whole music. But he's young and doesn't know how he feels about it. He's going to set it aside and leave it there for a few years until he's ready to play it. – 102.1

(4) Looks like the couple has just maybe gotten into an argument. He's trying to walk away from her. She's not letting him. She's trying to keep him back. The reason being is so they can talk out their problems. After a little while, he calms down and they talk. –112.4

(5) Somebody gave this boy a violin, and now he's looking at it and thinking that he's going to have to get violin lessons. He's feeling probably not too happy about it, and then he'll probably have to take violin lessons because his parents will make him. – 183.1

(6) Well, that guy, he—that's his lover in the bed and he's not married, neither is she, but she was seeing somebody else, so he strangles her. And he's all upset cause he got into a rage and didn't know what he did and he just realized he killed her. He's upset cause he knows he's gonna miss her—he didn't mean to kill her. He's miserable cause he was in love with her and he just killed the person he loves. Right now he's mourning, but pretty soon he starts thinking about the police and stuff. So he hides her body and then goes on about his life with this hanging over his head. – 134.13MF

(7) This looks like Scarlett O'Hara and Rhett Butler and he's going off to war and she's saying, Don't leave. He's going to defend his country and she knows he's going no matter what she says. – 129.4

(8) Looks like her parents are out working in the field and she's going off to school like they're just standing there waiting for her to go in to do her work inside.... They all seems a little cool toward each other.... She ends up leaving home not feeling she was really loved as some kids. – 135.2

(9) Okay, this man, let me think about this for a second... this is kind of confusing... when, okay, best story I have for it, that he's bored at home and seeks attention from outside his wife. So he goes to the, down to the whore house and uhm, like, maybe talks to the lady, talks to the ladies and starts to realize that this isn't for him so decides he needs to get out of there and improve his marriage, but while he's leaving, one of the ladies tries to stop him and talk him into staying but he is determined to leave. – 117.4

(10) There's a man that looks really shameful. He looks sensitive. The woman is in bed. I don't know if he exploited her or what, possibly, or whether she exploited herself. He is getting up and leaving. I don't think she really cares. – 102.13MF

(11) There's a farmer and his wife and they have been married for some time living out on a farm undisturbed, and one day the farmer goes into town to buy some fertilizer and meets up with a school girl who finds him attractive and he seems to like the attention he's not used to getting, so they have an affair, but in the meantime his wife at home, who's preg ... becomes pregnant, so the end... She loves him, and she's attracted to him, I'm talking about the other women, the other woman loves him, but he tells her that it's just infatuation and she'll have to get over it because now he's got a family, he will have a family. –117.2

(12) Like a country family with the daughter coming home from school seeing her dad out working in the fields her mom's just watching over him and the daughter's just thinking if she wants to be just like her mom when she grows up or if she wants to push harder and stay in school and do more. And it ends up that she does and her parents stay on the farm and she goes to school and goes and makes something of herself. – 125.2

(13) This is a pitiful picture. I don't know her name, but her brother used to beat her all the time. She is now feeling horribly sick because she shot him and killed him. She's now leaning on the bed in despair because she can't believe she killed her brother. She's trying to decide if she should kill herself or not, what would be the right thing to do. I'm not sure how it ends.... – 106.3BM

(14) This girl is extremely upset about something. She is huddled against her bed crying. I don't know what she is upset about. Well, she has some scissors beside her—maybe she was making something special to wear to a special event and she was going with someone special. Then she found out that she's not going to get to go—she was really counting on going with this special person—now not only is she not getting to go, but she will never see the person again. I don't know why she won't, maybe he runs away with another woman. – 159.3BM

(15) This woman is in big trouble. You can tell by how the arm is and how drab her clothes are that she's in some sort of secured court and it looks like the guards came to check on her and she did something to hurt the guards and there's some kind of object by her feet that looks like a gun and she's thinking how foolish it was what she did. She's hard to read right she's all—held up. She's not happy with herself physically. – 187.3BM

(16) Rosaline and Randall met at a social gathering on an early fall evening. Rosaline thought that she liked the man very much, and he seemed to like her too. They talked easily with one another and decided to go out again soon. They did and Rosaline thought that she was falling in love with the man. He seemed to love her too. Their relationship became more serious and she decided that she would giver her whole self to him one evening after a very nice time that they had out. The next morning after Randall was dressed he told her that he didn't want to see her anymore and it devastated her. As much as she cared for him and thought that she loved him, she told him that she didn't want to see him anymore. They both went their own ways but Rosaline never forgot Randall. – 155.13MF

(17) This is a man that's an alcoholic and his family, his wife is reaching out to him, trying to get him to realize that he needs help. He is in denial and turning away from her. She is saying let me help you. So he realizes he has got a problem. (pauses) Well, looks like it could have been a little "spicier" because that looks like a nude female in the background. –103.4

(18) This lady, she got raped and the husband came home and found her lying naked on the bed with the wounds to her stomach, laying dead. He's gonna call the police. Thinking, how did it happen, who did this. A lot of thoughts going through his head. He's really sad and worried. He can't do anything about it now because she's already bleeding. He's angry and hurt. – 113.13MF

(19) It's been a long time since she's seen her husband and he's going back to a job, but he's staying over with her tonight and he's away a lot and he really misses her and now they're together and that's all. – 113.4

Expert Scoring Set 1

Interaction units are demarcated by brackets indicating changes in time, place, or persons. For some ambiguous cases, italicized text indicates the phrase(s) within each interaction unit that determines its decentering score. Unmarked text does not contain interactions and so receives no score. Expert scorer's comments are sometimes included in parentheses.

(1) His name is Mark and Mark is having problems [playing the violin like his teacher can and he wants to be like his teacher. He's been playing the violin for 2 years and he can't seem to play like his teacher does.] (6) (The boy wants to be like, and thus has internalized, his teacher, who is defined by the physical action of playing the violin; the second sentence has the same scorable content as the first.) [So one day he talked to his teacher and his teacher told him that he's been playing the violin for 25 years and that it takes a lot of practice so all Mark can do is keep practicing so he can learn

to play just like his teacher. So Mark made a commitment to himself that every day after school he's going to spend 2 hours studying.] (4) (Mark "talked" to the teacher; the teacher responds by telling him about his practice, Mark reacts by making the commitment.) So 25 years later, Mark is teaching music class, and [he's playing like his teacher played.] (1) (The characters are engaged in the same activity.) – 165.1

(2) The little boy has been given the violin as a present. He's staring at it, thinking, "I wanted a car." It came from his grandfather, and [he's going to have to take lessons because he wants to please his grandfather.] (7) (The word *wants* implies that the boy is internalizing the grandfather; pleasure is an internal state.) But he really wanted a toy car. – 105.1

(3) He's a little boy contemplating over the violin on whether he wants to really learn how to play it or not. He's frustrated. It's a part of him, the violin, the whole music. But he's young and doesn't know how he feels about it. He's going to set it aside and leave it there for a few years until he's ready to play it. (no interaction units, no score) – 102.1

(4) [Looks like the couple has just maybe gotten into an argument. He's trying to walk away from her. She's not letting him. She's trying to keep him back. The reason being is so they can talk out their problems.] (3) (First sentence is general statement elaborated by the sentences that follow; his *trying to walk away* is considered a directed action because of her reaction of *not letting him.)* [After a little while, he calms down and they talk.] (1) (They are engaged in the same activity of talking.) –112.4

(5) [Somebody gave this boy a violin, and now he's looking at it and thinking that he's going to have to get violin lessons.] (3) (*Somebody* is treated as a character; the boy reacts to the somebody's action.) He's feeling probably not too happy about it, and [then he'll probably have to take violin lessons because his parents will make him.] (3) (*Making* him take lessons implies a minimum interaction of the parents telling the boy what to do and the boy doing it.) – 183.1

(6) Well, that guy, he—that's his lover in the bed and he's not married, neither is she, but [she was seeing somebody else, so he strangles her.] (3) And he's all upset cause he got into a rage and [didn't know what he did and *he just realized he killed her.* He's upset cause he knows he's gonna miss her—he didn't mean to kill her. He's miserable cause he was in love with her and he just killed the person he loves. Right now he's mourning,] (5) (No interactive relationship; she is not elaborated.) but [pretty soon he starts thinking about the police and stuff.] (5) So he hides her body and then goes on about his life with this hanging over his head. – 134.13MF

(7) This looks like Scarlett O'Hara and Rhett Butler and he's going off to war and [she's saying, don't leave. He's going to defend his country and *she knows he's going no matter what she says.*] (9) (She has imagined the possibilities of an interaction of saying something and him leaving anyway.) – 129.4

(8) Looks like [her parents are out working in the field] (1) and she's going off to school like [they're just standing there *waiting for her* to go in to do her work inside.... They all seems a little cool toward each other.] (2) ... [She ends up leaving home not feeling she was really loved as some kids.] (6) (She compares herself with the kids who were really loved.) – 135.2

(9) Okay, this man, let me think about this for a second... this is kind of confusing... when, okay, best story I have for it, that he's bored at home and [seeks attention from outside his wife.] (2) (Implies the author is also capable of conceptualizing the opposite) [So he goes to the, down to the whore house and uhm, like, maybe talks to the lady, talks to the ladies and starts to realize that this isn't for him so decides he needs to get out of there and improve his marriage, but while he's leaving, one of the ladies tries to stop him and talk him into staying but he is determined to leave.] (4) – 117.4

(10) There's a man that looks really shameful. He looks sensitive. The woman is in bed. I don't know if [he exploited her] (2) or what, possibly, or whether she exploited herself. [He is getting up and leaving. I don't think she really cares.] (3) (The fact that she may or may not care suggests that leaving in this case is an action directed toward her.) – 102.13MF

(11) [There's a farmer and his wife and they have been married for some time living out on a farm undisturbed,] (1) (two characters engaged in the same activity) and [one day the farmer goes into town to buy some fertilizer and *meets up with a school girl who finds him attractive* and *he seems to like the attention* he's not used to getting, so *they have an affair,*] (4) but in the meantime his wife at home, who's preg ... becomes pregnant, so the end ... [*she loves him* and she's attracted to him, I'm talking about the other women, the other woman loves him, but *he tells her* that it's just infatuation and she'll have to get over it because now he's got a family, he will have a family.] (3) –117.2

(12) Like a country family with [the daughter coming home from school seeing her dad out working in the fields] (2) [her mom's just watching over him] (2) (Separated due to jump in main character) and [the daughter's just thinking if she wants to be just like her mom when she grows up or if she wants to push harder and stay in school and do more.] (5) And it ends up that she does and [her parents stay on the farm] (1) and she goes to school and goes and makes something of herself. – 125.2

(13) This is a pitiful picture. I don't know her name, but [her brother used to beat her all the time.] (2) [She is now feeling horribly sick because she shot him and killed him. She's now leaning on the bed in despair because *she can't believe she killed her brother.*] (9) (reacting to her directed action on another, separated from first interaction unit by time—past then present) She's trying to decide if she should kill herself or not, what would be the right thing to do. I'm not sure how it ends.... – 106.3BM

(14) This girl is extremely upset about something. She is huddled against her bed crying. I don't know what she is upset about. Well, she has some scissors beside her—maybe she was making something special to wear to a special event and [she was *going with* someone special. Then she found out that she's not going to get to go—she was really counting on *going with* this special person] (1) (all in the recent past)—now not only is she not getting to go, but [she will never see the person again.] (2) I don't know why she won't, maybe [he runs away with another woman.] (1) – 159.3BM

(15) This woman is in big trouble. You can tell by how the arm is and how drab her clothes are that she's in some sort of secured court and it looks like [the guards came to check on her and she did something to hurt the guards, and there's some kind

of object by her feet that looks like a gun and *she's thinking how foolish it was what she did*.] (9) She's hard to read right; she's all—held up. She's not happy with herself physically. – 187.3BM

(16) [Rosaline and Randall met at a social gathering on an early fall evening. Rosaline *thought that she liked the man very much*, and he seemed to like her too. They talked easily with one another and decided to go out again soon.] (5) [They did and Rosaline *thought that she was falling in love with the man*. He seemed to love her too. Their relationship became more serious] (5) and [she decided that she would giver her whole self to him one evening after a very nice time that they had out.] (9) (She is thinking about future interaction, separated from last interaction unit by time—general long time period versus one evening) [The next morning after Randall was dressed he told her that *he didn't want to see her anymore* and it devastated her. As much as *she cared for him* and *thought that she loved him*, she told him that *she didn't want to see him* anymore.] (5) [They both went their own ways but Rosaline *never forgot* Randall.] (5) – 155.13MF

(17) [This is a man that's an alcoholic and his family, his wife is reaching out to him, *trying to get him to realize that he needs help*. He is in denial and turning away from her. She is saying let me help you. So he realizes he has got a problem.] (7) (pauses) Well, looks like it could have been a little "spicier" because that looks like a nude female in the background. – 103.4

(18) This lady, she got raped and the husband came home and found her lying naked on the bed with the wounds to her stomach, laying dead. (not scored because she is dead and not internalized) [He's gonna call the police.] (2) [Thinking how did it happen, *who did this*.] (6) A lot of thoughts going through his head. He's really sad and worried. He can't do anything about it now because she's already bleeding. He's angry and hurt. – 113.13MF

(19) [It's been a long time since *she's seen her husband* and he's going back to a job,] (2) but [he's staying over with her tonight] (1) and [he's away a lot and *he really misses her*] (5) and [now they're together and that's all.] (1) – 113.4

Practice Stories Set 2

(1) This is a story about a man who was called to do something he might have been called into the service or he might be called to do something dangerous, he might be a forest ranger or something. This woman is his wife and she really cares for him and doesn't want him to leave before she insists that he be careful. She wants to make sure that he knows she loves him. He doesn't have time for that right now, he has a much higher calling. I feel this has been the most dangerous situation they've ever been in. I think her fears will be realized. This was their last time together. – 161.4

(2) She feels despair, loneliness. I mean real lonely. Crying, thinking gonna kill themselves with a straight edge razor. Reason she's gonna kill herself is because (pause) Reason she's gonna kill herself is ... someone raped her and she feels ashamed. Don't

fell like can face life again. As thoughts race through head she prays to God to help her. God helps her. Decides it's not so bad after all and get psychiatric help. Things not so bad after all. – 118.3BM

(3) This looks like an old movie. It looks like they may have had a fight because he looks kinda angry and, well, yeah OK, and he wants he's sick of it and he wants to leave and she is telling him to stay and calm down or something like that. And after well like I said they just had a fight because he looks angry. She is trying to tell him to calm down and relax and everything and then they talk. And he's not so mad and she's not mad and they talk and they settle whatever happened, I guess, she looks pretty calm. – 171.4

(4) Wow, looks kind of like Greece or some agrarian family—pastoral family I mean. Looks like a girl going away to school for the day with her mom and brother. Her mom is upset, her brother is just working in the field. Probably they're upset that she gets to go to school and they have to stay and work. She seems to be a little concerned about her brother and mother at the same time, she's glad she's going to school. She's probably thinking she'll be able to make a better life for herself than her brother and her mom have done. Her mom seems to be stubborn about something and seems like there's something the family forgot about that's unresolved. Her brother seems less upset the mother. He seems more glad that she's getting ... The mother seems to be kind of hurt that the daughter is going away. She's proud of her life and thinks the pastoral life is the best way—she's upset that her daughter rejects that kind of life. Brother seems to be on his sister's side but doesn't know how to take up for her, doesn't know what to say. She, girl is worried about family, at same time wonders what will go on at school. She knows she's got the strength and intelligence to compete. She goes on to school, gets an education and achieves everything she wants to achieve, but decides to stay on the farm. – 136.2

(5) The man has just killed somebody with a gun, lying on the floor. He did not want to but was forced to by someone in control of his life. If he did not kill for the one controlling his life his family would suffer or die. After realizing his no-win situation he sends his family away, kills the one controlling his life and dies in the process. – 192.3BM

(6) As John entered the driveway he saw Bill leave through the back door. He noticed that Bill had been coming to see his daughter every day this week. John did not like Bill because Bill was unemployed and could not provide a decent life for his daughter. John stormed into the house. With anger he searched the house for his daughter. She was in her bedroom playing with the cat. As John entered the living room he said, "I don't want him back in this house. I am going to find him and warn him that if he ever returns (crying) I will kill him." As he turned to leave Peggy, his wife, took hold of him and said, "leave them alone. They are children and I want them to be happy. Bill is doing nothing wrong and he loves our daughter. Give him time to prove that he can take care of our little girl." John turned back and agreed with his wife. He said, "I'll give him time, but that time will end the day my daughter graduates." He then asked, "What's for dinner? I'm hungry." His wife said, "You go get washed up, and I'll have dinner on the table. We're having meatloaf, green beans, and okra. For dessert your daughter made a German chocolate cake." – 164.4

(7) He's got some kind of—he's real determined to do something. He's got this friend or female friend, not the one in the picture, his friend is in trouble and he wants to help her. The woman in the picture is trying to talk sense into him. Her sense isn't that—her motives aren't for anybody but her self to talk sense into him—to go help his friend. The guy does like the girl in the picture—He thinks he loves her, but in reality he actually loves his friend but doesn't know it yet. He's in the process of finding out. In the end he leaves her, goes to help his friend, and that's it. But it takes a real long time to realize it. – 134.4

(8) This is a little boy who's having to take fiddle lessons and he doesn't want to. He looks like he's, someone's making him take these lessons and he's laid it down and he's thinking why do I have to take these lessons and he's feeling very frustrated. And he's thinking of a way to tell his mom, or whoever's making him take these lessons, why he doesn't want to do this. – 110.1

(9) A woman and an old guy had a son and a daughter. Hans and Corrine. Hans had to work their farm every day. And the land was fertile, but Olga's father was dead so that the work was still very hard. As hard as it would have been if they'd had a much worse plot of land. And Hans didn't resent this. In a way he enjoyed the work more when it was harder. He often wondered if he would ... if he would be able to find anything to do if there weren't the constant burden of plowing and reaping and planting. Olga wanted Corrine, on the other hand to go to school and to learn refined ideas and manners. And to pick up that almost magical essence which allows a poor girl from a mean background to be accepted by her social betters. Corrine doesn't like leaving the farm, leaving the work to others but somehow she can't find any compelling reason or any way to defeat her mother's will. And so she does what she's expected to do things that maybe if her mother would simply die young then she could leave her boarding school and take over the farm. Olga was unaware of these conflicts within her daughter. Her mind doesn't wander past the beginning of next season. – 132.2

(10) This is a big, thing oh, now that I have the violin, I would like to know how to play violin and I don't know. Who can teach me that. Now that I have the violin I don't know what to do. I would like to find someone that can teach me how to play it. So I can tell my feelings and I will be able to go to orchestra to feel good and show the people that I can play my violin. Now that I look at the violin, it has 6 strings and I like this, how it's made, this looks like fine, good. And I would like to know why, how it sounds, when I learn to play, when I would learn how to play. – 200.1

(11) Um, this man is a bachelor, and there's been a real sick practical joker at his office lately. So when he went home today the young male looked around to make sure the practical joker didn't get into his apartment and he doesn't notice anything out of the ordinary and he thinks well maybe the practical joker left me alone today and he feels kinda glad about that until he goes into his bedroom to change his clothes and he happens to glance at the bed and he's horrified at what he sees and he feels really angry at the practical joker for thinking it was funny to put this mannequin in his bed. He thinks tomorrow I'm really gonna punch that practical joker in the nose for this," so he walks out into the hallway, he opens the cupboard and takes out an old, old, really old blanket that was stuck way in the back, comes back in, wraps the mannequin up in it and puts it on the the, oh what do you call those, um he

puts the mannequin and leans it up against the wall so he can carry it to work with him in the morning. He decides that this time he's going to get play a little practical joke of his own on the practical joker. He's gonna, he says to himself first I'm gonna put some knockout drops in the practical joker's drink and then we'll just see how he feels when he wakes up with this thing sitting in his lap then he kinda grins to himself my best friend Bernie at the office has been wanting me to get back at this practical joker for a long time now so I can't wait to see the look on Bernie's face when I tell him what I'm gonna do to that practical joker tomorrow. Then he just smiles to himself and goes mainly about his business for the rest of the day knowing that this time he's got the upper hand in that practical joke. –109.13MF

Expert Scoring Set 2

(1) This is a story about a man who was called to do something he might have been called into the service or he might be called to do something dangerous, he might be a forest ranger or something. This woman is his wife and [she really cares for him and doesn't want him to leave before she insists that be careful. *She wants to make sure that he knows she loves him.*] (9) He doesn't have time for that right now, he has a much higher calling. [I feel this has been *the most dangerous situation they've ever been in*. I think her fears will be realized. *This was their last time together.*] (1) – 161.4

(2) She feels despair, loneliness. I mean real lonely. Crying, thinking gonna kill themselves with a straight edge razor. Reason she's gonna kill herself is because (pause) Reason she's gonna kill herself is ... [someone raped her and she feels ashamed.] (3) Don't fell like can face life again. [As thoughts race through head she prays to God to help her. God helps her.] (6) (way of relating to God is internalized; God is elaborated by action of helping. This interaction incited considerable discussion among the scoring team because the nature of the action that God takes is vague in the story. It is not clear whether the help given by God is something a human could do or whether it is having God internalized as helpful that helps her. When scoring an ambiguous action, always exercise caution and take the lower score. If the help of God had been described as within human capability, such as comforting her, this interaction may have warranted a score of 9, with both *God* and *she* being internalized and the *help* being descriptive of their interactive relationship. For clinical purposes, more information about the client's spirituality would be needed to clarify whether God is seen as corporeal or noncorporeal. The latter is the default option for divine entities.) Decides it's not so bad after all and get psychiatric help. Things not so bad after all. – 118.3BM

(3) This looks like an old movie. [It looks like they may have had a fight because he looks kinda angry and, well, yeah OK, and he wants he's sick of it and he wants to leave and *she is telling him to stay and calm down* or something like that. And after well like I said they just had a fight because he looks angry. She is trying to tell him to calm down and relax and everything and then *they talk*. And *he's not so mad and she's not mad* and they talk and they settle whatever happened, I guess, she looks pretty calm.] (4) – 171.4

(4) Wow, looks kind of like Greece or [some agrarian family—pastoral family I mean. Looks like a girl going away to school for the day with her mom and brother.] (1) Her mom is upset, her brother is just working in the field. Probably [they're upset that she gets to go to school and they have to stay and work.] (6) [She seems to be a little concerned about her brother and mother at the same time, she's glad she's going to school. She's probably thinking she'll be able to make a better life for herself than her brother and her mom have done.] (6) Her mom seems to be stubborn about something and [seems like there's something *the family forgot* about that's unresolved.] (1) Her brother seems less upset the mother. [He seems more glad that she's getting ...] (5) [The mother seems to be kind of hurt that the daughter is going away. She's proud of her life and thinks the pastoral life is the best way—*she's upset that her daughter rejects that kind of life*.] (6) [Brother seems to be on his sister's side but doesn't know how to take up for her—doesn't know what to say.] (5) [She, girl is *worried about family*,] (5) at same time wonders what will go on at school. She knows she's got the strength and intelligence to compete. She goes on to school, gets an education and achieves everything she wants to achieve, but decides to stay on the farm. – 136.2

(5) [The man has just killed somebody with a gun, lying on the floor.] (2) [He did not want to but was forced to by someone in control of his life.] (3) (change of characters) [If he did not kill for the one controlling his life *his family would suffer or die*. After *realizing his no-win situation* he sends his family away, kills the one controlling his life and dies in the process.] (6) – 192.3BM

(6) [As John entered the driveway he saw Bill leave through the back door.] (2) [He noticed that Bill had been coming to see his daughter every day this week. *John did not like Bill because Bill was unemployed* and could not provide a decent life for his daughter.] (6) (This is about Bill's ability; Bill does not internalize her.) John stormed into the house. [With anger he searched the house for his daughter. She was in her bedroom playing with the cat. As John entered the living room he said, "I don't want him back in this house. I am going to find him and warn him that if he ever returns (crying) I will kill him."] (6) [As he turned to leave *Peggy, his wife, took hold of him* and said, "*leave them alone. They are children and I want them to be happy.* Bill is doing nothing wrong and he loves our daughter. Give him time to prove that he can take care of our little girl." John turned back and agreed with his wife. He said, "I'll give him time, but that time will end the day my daughter graduates." He then asked, "What's for dinner? I'm hungry." His wife said, "You go get washed up, and I'll have dinner on the table. We're having meatloaf, green beans, and okra. For dessert your daughter made a German chocolate cake."] (9) – 164.4

(7) He's got some kind of—he's real determined to do something. [He's got this friend or female friend, not the one in the picture, his friend is in trouble and *he wants to help her*.] (5) [The woman in the picture is *trying to talk sense into him*. Her sense isn't that—her motives aren't for anybody but her self to talk sense into him—to go help his friend.] (7) [The guy does like the girl in the picture—he thinks he loves her,] (5) but [in reality he actually loves his friend but doesn't know it yet. He's in the process of finding out.] (5) [In the end he leaves her, goes to help his friend,] (2) and that's it. But it takes a real long time to realize it. – 134.4

(8) This is a little boy who's having to take fiddle lessons and he doesn't want to. He looks like he's, [someone's making him take these lessons] (3) (Making him implies action of another and reaction by the subject.) and he's laid it down and he's thinking why do I have to take these lessons and he's feeling very frustrated. And [he's thinking of a way to tell *his mom*, or *whoever's making him take these lessons*, why he doesn't want to do this.] (5 and 6) (This unit is actually two in one and received two separate scores. *His mom* and *whoever's making him take these lessons* could be the same person, or they could be two distinct characters. The use of *or* in this situation was the deciding factor; they are considered two distinct possibilities that cannot exist simultaneously. The boy is thinking of either, not both.) – 110.1

(9) [A woman and an old guy had a son and a daughter.] (1) Hans and Corrine. Hans had to work their farm every day. And the land was fertile, but Olga's father was dead so that the work was still very hard. [As hard as it would have been if they'd had a much worse plot of land.] (1) And Hans didn't resent this. In a way he enjoyed the work more when it was harder. He often wondered if he would ... if he would be able to find anything to do if there weren't the constant burden of plowing and reaping and planting. [Olga wanted Corrine, on the other hand to go to school and to *learn refined ideas and manners*. And to pick up that almost magical essence which allows a poor girl from a mean background to be accepted by her *social betters*.] (7) (The part about the *social better* is too far removed for them to be considered internalized; the mother is internalizing the "essence" rather than the characters.) [Corrine doesn't like leaving the farm, leaving the work to others] (6) but [somehow *she can't find* any compelling reason or *any way to defeat her mother's will*. And so she does what she's expected to do things that maybe if her mother would simply die young then she could leave her boarding school and take over the farm.] (7) [Olga was unaware of these conflicts within her daughter.] (7) Her mind doesn't wander past the beginning of next season. – 132.2

(10) This is a big, thing oh, now that I have the violin, I would like to know how to play violin and I don't know. [Who can teach me that. Now that I have the violin I don't know what to do. I would like to find someone that can teach me how to play it.] (9) (The character is imagining someone who could teach him to play; teaching implies a series of interactions.) [So I can tell my feelings and I will be able to go to orchestra to feel good and show the people that I can play my violin.] (5) (The character is imagining acting on specific but featureless *people*.) Now that I look at the violin, it has 6 strings and I like this, how it's made, this looks like fine, good. And I would like to know why, how it sounds, when I learn to play, when I would learn how to play. – 200.1

(11) Um, this man is a bachelor, and there's been a real sick practical joker at his office lately. So when he went home today the young male looked around to make sure the practical joker didn't get into his apartment and he doesn't notice anything out of the ordinary, and [he thinks well, maybe the practical joker left me alone today and he feels kinda glad about that] (9) until he goes into his bedroom to change his clothes and he happens to glance at the bed and he's horrified at what he sees and [he feels really angry at the practical joker for thinking it was funny to put this

mannequin in his bed.] (7) [He thinks tomorrow I'm really gonna punch that practical joker in the nose for this," so he walks out into the hallway, he opens the cupboard and takes out an old, old, really old blanket that was stuck way in the back, comes back in, wraps the mannequin up in it and puts it on the the, oh what do you call those, um he puts the mannequin and leans it up against the wall so he can carry it to work with him in the morning. He decides that this time he's going to get play a little practical joke of his own on the practical joker. He's gonna, he says to himself first I'm gonna put some knockout drops in the practical joker's drink and *then we'll just see how he feels when he wakes up with this thing sitting in his lap* then he kinda grins to himself] (9) [my best friend *Bernie* at the office *has been wanting me to get back at this practical joker* for a long time now, so I can't wait to see the look on Bernie's face when I tell him what I'm gonna do to that practical joker tomorrow.] (7) Then he just smiles to himself and goes mainly about his business for the rest of the day knowing that this time he's got the upper hand in that practical joke. –109.13MF

☐ References

Anastasi, A. (1988). *Psychological testing* (6th ed.). Upper Saddle River, NJ: Prentice Hall.

Dobbs, L. (2003). *Interpersonal decentering and mutuality in close relationships.* Unpublished senior honors thesis, University of North Texas.

Carberry, A. T. (1982). *Interpersonal decentering, social interaction, and treatment status in children at risk for psychosis.* Unpublished doctoral dissertation, Saint Louis University.

Feffer, M. H., & Jahelka, M. (1968). Implications of the decentering concept for the structuring of projective content. *Journal of Consulting and Clinical Psychology, 32*(4), 434–431.

Strober, M. (1979). The structuring of interpersonal relations in schizophrenic adolescents: A decentering analysis of Thematic Apperception Test stories. *Journal of Abnormal Child Psychology, 7*(3), 309–316.

☐ Notes:

We thank Summer Burkman, Michele Elefante, Andrea Haag, Michael McFarland, and Luis Perez for their comments, questions, and scoring notes that helped us to improve this manual and its practice scoring sets. We thank Dr. Ann Carberry for allowing us to include some of the examples of scoring from her dissertation.

10

CHAPTER

Personal Problem-Solving System—Revised

George F. Ronan, Margaret S. Gibbs, Laura E. Dreer, and Jennifer A. Lombardo

Abstract

The Personal Problem-Solving System-Revised (PPSS-R) uses Thematic Apperception Test (TAT) responses to assess how people are likely to resolve personal problems. Responses are scored across four broad cate gories: story design, story orientation, story solution, and story resolution. The PPSS-R provides a convenient way for clinicians to look at problem solving and social functioning in their clients. In addition, the PPSS-R provides a method for researchers to employ when assessing personal problem-solving performance using a measure that is largely independent of social desirability effects. We reviewed a number of reliability and validity studies and provided detailed scoring instructions.

Description of the Personal Problem-Solving System—Revised (PPSS-R)

Conceptual Framework

The use of stories to convey thoughts, feelings, and behavior has an ancient and widespread history. For instance, folktales, such as Aesop's fables, and Bible stories were designed to be instructive. Although current-day use of stories is rooted in many other theories (e.g., construct theory) (Viney, 1996), the recent surge in popularity has been attributed to developments stemming from work with the native peoples of New Zealand (see Monk, Winslade, Crocket, & Epston, 1997) and Australia (White & Epston, 1990). Expert clinicians within many different cultural groups suggest that an approach using stories or metaphors can be more useful than direct methods (e.g., LaFramboise & Rowe, 1983; Shon & Ya, 1982).

The PPSS-R uses stories generated to TAT cards to assess how people identify, conceptualize, and resolve personal problems. A basic tenet of problem-solving formulations of mental health is that personal problem-solving skills are inversely related to psychological distress (D'Zurilla, 1988). That is, people who are able to resolve personal problems are likely to demonstrate positive mental health. There also has been a growing interest in personal problem-solving formulations of psychopathology (e.g., Bellack, Sayers, Mueser, & Bennett, 1994; Cantor & Harlow, 1994; Clum & Febbraro, 1994; D'Zurilla, 1988; Nezu, Nezu, & Perri, 1989; Platt & Husband, 1993). Dobson and Block (1988) noted that problem-solving therapies represent one of the three main types of cognitive-behavioral approaches. Though the idea of using a projective test to measure personal problem solving is not new (see Sobel, 1981), this is the first easily implemented, theoretically sound, and empirically supported system that employs narratives to assess personal problem-solving skills.

The relationship between problem-solving deficits and psychopathology has been studied from a variety of perspectives. For example, psychoanalytically oriented theorists have recommended problem-solving techniques during dynamically oriented treatment (e.g., Garner, 1970; Sifneos, 1969). Most of the accumulated empirical evidence about problem solving, however, derives from the cognitive-behavior a framework. Initial investigations of problem-solving deficits associated with psychopathology employed noninterpersonal, anagram-type tasks (cf. Hiroto & Seligman, 1975; Miller & Seligman, 1975). Some researchers found deficits associated with specific diagnostic categories (Willis & Blaney, 1978), whereas others failed to find deficits (Sacco & Hokanson, 1978). The equivocal findings may well have been a consequence of generalization difficulties: anagram performance may not generalize to solving real-life problems. Subsequent research focused on social, personal, or interpersonal problem-solving skills. An often used model of personal problem solving was developed by Spivack, Platt, and Shure (1976). Their model, cognitive developmental in nature, proposes that personal problem-solving skills develop because of maturation and experience with significant others. The component skills include the ability to identify accurately problem situations, the capacity to generate alternative solutions to a problem situation, the ability to generate a step-by-step plan for problem resolution, and the ability to understand one's own motives as well as the motives of others.

The Means-Ends Problem Solving (MEPS) task is most frequently used to assess differences between psychiatric and nonpsychiatric samples (Spivack & Platt, 1975). The MEPS provides individuals with the beginning and ending to 10 different problem situations. Participants fill in the middle or provide the means used to arrive at the given solution. For a variety of reasons, the MEPS has not enjoyed widespread clinical use (for reviews see Butler & Meichenbaum, 1981; D'Zurilla & Nezu, 1982).

D'Zurilla and Goldfried (1971) developed a social problem-solving model from a behavioral perspective. Component skills included maintaining a productive mind-set when approaching problems, defining problems, generating strategies for resolving problems, selecting the best alternative, and contrasting expected and observed outcomes. Although several studies have evaluated the relationship between the components of this model and psychopathology, the performance-based measures employed are not appropriate for most clinical populations (e.g., D'Zurilla & Nezu, 1980; Nezu & D'Zurilla, 1981). D'Zurilla and Nezu (1990), however, developed a self-report measure based on this model—the Social Problem-Solving Inventory (SPSI)—which contains 70 items arranged in a Likert-type format. The SPSI is thus a retrospective self-report measure, whereas the PPSS-R is a concurrent performance-based measure. D'Zurilla and Maydeau-Olivares (1995) and Maydeau-Olivares and D'Zurilla (1996) provide reviews of the SPSI and similar measures.

Employing a slightly different approach, Heppner (1978) reviewed the problem-solving literature and developed a five-component model similar to the previously described D'Zurilla and Goldfried (1971) model. Heppner and Peterson (1982) generated a series of self-statements reflecting these five components, and college students rated their agreement with each statement. Factor analysis revealed three underlying components which they labeled as approach–avoidance style, problem-solving confidence, and perceived control. The resulting 32-item inventory—the Problem-Solving Inventory (PSI)—is used in a wide variety of studies to evaluate individual differences in personal problem solving (Heppner, 1988; Heppner & Anderson, 1985; Heppner, Hibel, Neal, Weinstein, & Rabinowitz, 1982; Heppner, Reeder, & Larson, 1983). Similar to the SPSI, the PSI is a retrospective self-report measure and research has often found no relationship between self-report and performance-based measures of personal problem solving (Heppner & Peterson, 1982; Ronan, Colavito, & Hammontree, 1993). These models served as the basis for developing PPSS-R elements. Although the PPSS-R was designed primarily for clinicians and researchers working within a cognitive-behavioral framework, clinicians from a wide range of orientations have found the system useful.

Scoring Categories

The PPSS-R conceptualizes the TAT cards as depicting social and personal situations to which the subject responds. Traditional TAT criteria relevant to personal problem solving were also considered (e.g., identification of the main character; retrospective versus prospective focus). Elements were developed using both theoretical and empirical approaches. Twelve of the elements use a five-point rating format, whereas the remaining element requires counting the number of story solutions. The 13 scoring criteria are organized into four broad categories: story design, story orientation, story solution, and story resolution. Scoring components, elements, and a brief theoretical and empirical justification for inclusion are presented in Table 10.1. The link between social problem-solving skills and each of the component scores is detailed following.

Story Design

This component is similar to the process of problem formulation (D'Zurilla & Nezu, 1982). Story design assesses worldviews and cognitive functioning through an evaluation of the respondent's use of time, causal ascriptions, distorted beliefs, and integrative thinking. It is necessary to see the connection among past, present, and future if one is to achieve an adequate formulation of a problem and its solution. A number of authors (Dana, 1955; Epley & Ricks, 1963; Johnson, 1994) have found that time span in a story relates to better academic performance and more interpersonal involvement. Within a psychodynamic model, time span is part of the concept of delay of gratification, a key element of ego strength (Freud, 1946). Within a cognitive behavioral model, Mischel (1977) demonstrated the mechanisms used by children to delay their responses to obtain a larger reward. A client who gives to card 2 a description of a moment in time, "The man is plowing his field, the woman in front is dreaming, etc." is probably not understanding and coping with the world as well as someone who creates a story about past experiences on the farm and plans for the future.

TABLE 10.1 Facets Associated With Each Component

Component	Scored Elements
Story Design	*Does the story problem contain a past, present, and future?* A variety of labels have described the inclusion of past, present, and future in TAT responses—for example, perceptual organization (Dana, 1955); maintaining instructional set (Johnson, 1994). The inclusion of a past, present, and future correlates with a number of indicators of achievement and successful interpersonal adjustment (Dana, 1955; Johnson, 1994). Inclusion of a long-term future is also related to planning ability (Epley & Ricks, 1963). It is necessary to see the connection among past, present, and future if one is to achieve an adequate formulation of a problem and its solution. *Indicate the cause of the story problem or trouble.* Causal explanations for events have been reliably evaluated using TAT responses (Peterson & Ulrey, 1994). Research suggests that causal ascription can interact with problem-solving skill to produce outcomes (e.g., Nezu, Kalmar, Ronan, & Clavijo, 1986). *Rate the level of distorted beliefs, appraisals, and assumptions about the story problem.* Research suggests that distorted beliefs, appraisals, and assumptions are associated with less effective problem-solving skills (e.g., Dugas, Letarte, Rheaume, & Freeston, 1995; Heppner, Hibel, Neal, Weinstein, & Rabinowitz, 1982). *Rate how well the story problem is integrated and detailed.* An integrated and detailed approach toward a problem is more likely to be successful. Some TAT scoring systems have stressed integrative complexity (Suedefeld, Tetlock, & Streufert, 1992) or the complex understanding of social causation (Westen, Lohr, Silk, Kerber, & Goodrich, 1985). Other scoring systems have focused on the ability to develop and maintain a shared focus of attention with the examiner (Singer & Wynne, 1966).
Story Orientation	*How positively motivating is the situation?* There is considerable empirical support for using the TAT to assess levels of motivation (e.g., Atkinson, 1992; Shapiro, Gilborn, & Grolnic, 1991; Spangler, 1992). Appraising problems as a challenge and positively motivating is associated with effective problem resolution (e.g., Lazarus & Folkman, 1984). *How likely is it that there will be an attempt to exert personal control over the problem?* Perceptions of personal control contribute to effective problem solving (e.g., Heppner & Anderson, 1985; Heppner, Reeder, and Larson, 1983). *How much confidence is demonstrated for dealing with the problem?* Problem-solving confidence has been related to effective problem solving (e.g., Heppner & Anderson, 1985; Heppner et al., 1982).

(*Continued*)

TABLE 10.1 Facets Associated With Each Component (Continued)

Component	Scored Elements
	Rate the level of emotional distress. Emotional distress can interfere with performance on complex tasks in general (e.g., Yerkes & Dodson, 1908) and problem solving in particular (Lewinsohn & Mano, 1993; Nezu, 1987; Ronan, Gibbs, Nezu, & Bernstein, 1985). Several traditional TAT scoring systems also assess levels of emotional distress (e.g., Veroff, 1992) or negative feelings (Fine, 1955; Pistole & Ornduff, 1994). Higher scores are indicative of lower levels of emotional distress.
Story Solutions	*Record the number of overt and covert story solutions.* Generating more than one story resolution on the TAT traditionally has been labeled obsessive doubting (Schafer, 1948); however, the meaning of the generation of alternatives must be considered from the logical perspective of the story (Husain, Rossel, & Merceron, 1988). PPSS-R instructions orient the subject to problem solving, and the number of story solutions generated covaries with optimal story resolution and is related to the concept of *brainstorming* (Osborne, 1963). This is similar to both means–end thinking and the generation of alternative solution components of traditional problem-solving models (D'Zurilla & Nezu, 1980; Platt & Spivack, 1972; Nezu & Ronan, 1987). Similar to Lazarus & Folkman (1984), story solutions can be categorized as overt (i.e., observable) or covert (i.e., within-subject) solutions.
Story Resolution	*Rate the degree to which the story solutions minimize personal distress.* The minimization of perceived risk is an important factor in decision making (e.g., Sitkin & Weingart, 1995). This element is also similar to traditional scoring system variables such as the emotional tone of the outcome (Ritzler, Sharkey, and Chudy, 1980). *Rate the degree to which the positive consequences for the main character outweigh the negative consequences* This element reflects the positive outcome included in many scoring systems (e.g., McClelland, Atkinson, Clark, & Lowell, 1958; Eron, 1965). Effective story resolutions have a more optimal cost–benefit ratio (e.g., Goddard & McFall, 1992). *Rate the degree to which story solutions address both short and long-term goals.* Both short- and long-term consequences should be considered when resolving personal problems (e.g., Nezu & D'Zurilla, 1981). Epley and Ricks (1963) found that TAT stories with a longer-range future reflected higher levels of achievement and adaptation. *Rate the degree to which the concerns are ameliorated.* This element requires an overall determination about the attainment of problem-solving goals. This question taps the overall level of success in resolving the problem.

Time span is also a key value orientation that differentiates cultures (Kluckhohn, 1951). Western cultures, especially the American culture, are future oriented, and people work to achieve for the future. Other cultures focus on living in the moment (e.g., Latino, American Indian) or revere their pasts (e.g., Asian). A decision that the Latino story of present time represents less psychological strength may reflect Western biases about psychological functioning (e.g., Katz, 1985). As clinicians, we need to be alert to unfamiliar ways to cope with the problems of living. The development of local-culture norms would facilitate the clinician in adopting a suitable frame of reference.

Scoring the cause of the problem also has important links to clinical theory, and identifying a cause for a problem can make it easier to solve. The scoring category *cause of the problem* also has important links to clinical theory. Psychodynamic therapists talk about the balance between superego and ego functions and the importance of being able to be self-critical without being self-punitive (Hartmann & Loewenstein, 1962). Perls (1970) discussed *response-ability:* the notion that people must acknowledge their contribution to their problems to be able to act. As in other dynamic theories, responsibility did not involve self-blame. Perls focused instead on the role of self-awareness. The cognitive behavioral model has been identified as helpful partly because it separates responsibility for causing a problem from responsibility for curing it; it shows individuals are empowered to change their problems without having to feel guilty about having caused them (Brickman, Rabinowitz, Karuza, Coates, Cohn, & Kidder, 1983). This model still, then, shows recognition of the need to avoid destructive self-blame while taking action to resolve problems. Regardless of theoretical orientation, clinicians would want to attend to a card 1 story involving a boy too dumb to learn the violin, although their modes of handling such self-criticism may differ.

Distorted beliefs are so clearly clinically important that few comments are needed. Most interpreters of the TAT (e.g., Shneidman, 1951; Semeonoff, 1976) have included distorted beliefs in the story as an important element in diagnosing dysfunction and thought disorder. Both cognitive behaviorists (e.g., Ellis, 1962) and psychodynamicists (e.g., Jacobson, 1964) believe that the client's distorted thinking is an important element in understanding the psychopathology and determining the course of treatment. The PPSS-R can be valuable in providing a framework for the clinician to gauge the extent of distortions.

The manner in which the story is detailed and integrated has clear ties to Kelly's (1955) Personal Construct Theory, which is enjoying new popularity because of its association with narrative therapy (e.g., Viney, 1996). Kelly postulated that people develop constructs with which to predict and control their environment and that these are more effective to the extent that they are appropriately integrated and detailed. Cognitive complexity became a key concept linked to predictive ability (Neimeyer, 1993). Loevinger and Wessler (1970) incorporated this cognitive complexity model within their ego development scoring system for sentence completions. This one element on the PPSS-R can alert the clinician to the client's cognitive coping abilities. A client who is able to integrate all three card 2 characters into a story is better able to understand and deal with interpersonal relationships than a client who simply describes a girl walking by a farm.

Story Orientation

This component parallels the general orientation component of traditional personal problem-solving models (e.g., D'Zurilla & Nezu, 1982; Heppner, 1978, 1988). It is important for clinicians to assess health, as well as dysfunction, in their clients, and this component provides that opportunity. The story orientation component assesses level of positive motivation, personal control, confidence, and emotional distress. Conceptualizing problems as a challenge and as positively motivating is related to the openness to experience concept from the NEO Five-Factor Inventory (Costa & McCrae, 1992). Within the Rogerian (1969) model, individuals who view problems as new opportunities tend to live more existentially and are more fully functioning.

Every clinical model from Freud (1946) to Foa (Riggs & Foa, 1993) has talked about personal control as an important component of human functioning. Clients whose story characters exhibit more ability to confront problems show they have an understanding of how to tackle problems. The perception of being able to exert control over problematic situations has been associated with positive mental health. For instance, Rotter (1946) noted that interpreting a TAT story entails looking for the wish or need—or problem, within our model—as well as the manner in which it is addressed. If the individual expects reinforcement for acting on wishes, then it is more likely that the person will actually act to attain those goals. To use Rotter's terms, an internal locus of control stems from experience wherein one's behavior was reinforced. Although locus of control can be specific to particular needs or domains (e.g., health locus of control), soliciting responses to a variety of TAT cards can assess the degree to which locus of control generalizes across situations. Similarly, problem-solving confidence is a domain-specific aspect of general self-confidence. Moreover, problem-solving confidence is related to optimism, which Schier and Carver (1992) correlated with many aspects of physical and psychological well-being.

There is hardly any need to support the importance of emotional distress as a useful scoring category. Even the strictest behaviorist assesses emotional distress, both for the potential risk to the client and for the positive motivating aspects of distress. The use of this scale allows clinicians to gauge the extent of the distress present.

Story Solutions

The number of story solutions generated covaries with optimal story resolution and stems from the concept of *brainstorming* (Osborne, 1963). This is similar to both means–end thinking and the generation of alternative solution components of traditional problem-solving models (D'Zurilla & Nezu, 1980; Nezu & Ronan, 1987; Platt & Spivack, 1972). The generation of problem solutions is an important aspect of therapy that is often taught to clients. Scoring the number of solutions is perhaps best tied to a concept of impulsivity versus thoughtfulness. That is, the individuals who generate only one solution and act on it are often more impulsive than individuals who generate several solutions and choose the one likely to have the best outcome. Of course the type of solution generated is important: Clients who think before responding may generate several responses and produce only the best one as part of the story.

Story Resolution

This component is based on a utility model of decision making (Janis & Mann, 1977). Several studies have noted the positive impact of adopting a systematic decision-making strategy (e.g., Nezu & D'Zurilla, 1979; Nezu & Ronan, 1987). Elements in this component stem from the model proposed by D'Zurilla & Nezu (1982) and assess the degree to which positive aspects of the story resolution outweigh the negative, the likelihood of maximizing both short and long-term goals, and the time and energy required to bring about problem resolution. Research suggests that the minimization of perceived risk is an important factor in decision making (e.g., Sitkin & Weingart, 1995). This element is also similar to traditional scoring system variables such as emotional tone of the outcome (Ritzler, Sharkey, and Chudy, 1980).

The outcome of the story is a measure of effectiveness. In addition to providing an indication of actual effectiveness, it is a measure of the client's perception of effectiveness, which is important in its own right. The client may generate many apparently effective problem solutions, but if she or he has no expectation that acting on these solutions will bring reinforcement, then the client, in Rotter's (1946) model, is not likely to address the problem. This component assesses whether the solutions minimize personal distress, optimize the positive consequences, address both short and long-term goals, and effectively resolve the problem. The PPSS-R acknowledges the importance of both internal and behavioral change. Client perceptions about whether an action will lessen their personal distress may be an indicator of motivation for change.

Cognitively complex clients, as previously discussed, see several possible consequences of an action, so the inclusion of negative consequences need not mean an ineffective solution or that the person is unlikely to act. Positive consequences must outweigh the negative ones, however, for an effective and reinforcing solution. As with time span of the story, it is important to ascertain if the story solutions address short-term goals, long-term goals, or both. Again, from an ego psychological point of view, coping strength and delay of gratification are related to the ability to hold off immediate rewards in favor of more long-term ones. Individuals who are more impulsive are probably the ones who are more concerned with short-term outcomes. Determining whether the respondent believes the problem is ameliorated provides the best single indicator of effectiveness and expectancy of reinforcement.

☐ Research Evidence

As with most narrative scoring systems, decisions are made regarding the unit of analysis for calculating reliability and validity estimates. Should analyses be per card or aggregated across cards? Should analysis be conducted at the level of elements, components, or the total score? In an effort to present these data in a user-friendly format, we present reliability and validity estimates using aggregate and total scores because these mimic the level of analysis most likely to be used in research and applied settings.

Validity

Validity, the degree to which a test measures what it purports to measure, is often separated into content, criterion, outcome, and construct validity, as well as generalizability. Data presenting each of these domains are considered in turn.

Content Validity

Content validity can be based on face validity, sampling validity, or both (Allen & Yen, 1979). PPSS-R elements were developed using sampling validity. Theoretical and empirical models of personal problem solving were perused and elements were developed to capture significant aspects of this literature. Traditional TAT scoring criteria were also evaluated and relevant elements were integrated into a problem-solving framework. Preliminary work completed by scoring TAT responses was helpful in developing and selecting elements that tapped traditional scoring systems (Gibbs, Ronan, Nezu, Carideo, & Grossman, 1985). Additional review and refinement resulted in 21 elements, and scoring criteria were developed to tap relevant problem-solving domains. Initial PPSS elements were organized into four categories: design of the story (five elements); general orientation of the story (seven elements); generation of story solutions (two elements); and story resolution (eight elements). These 21 elements were further reduced based on an analysis of the internal consistency associated with each component, as well as the ease with which raters could score individual elements. Table 10.1 lists the 13 elements contained in the PPSS-R and a brief justification for each element.

Concurrent Validity

Data comparing performance on the PPSS-R with performance on problem-solving measures or comparisons across samples are presented following. Ronan et al. (1993) correlated performance on the PPSS-R with performance on the MEPS (Spivack & Platt, 1975). As discussed earlier, the MEPS is a performance-based measure of interpersonal problem solving that provides the beginning and ending of vignettes; participants fill in the means for connecting the beginning and ending. Eighty-seven undergraduate students responded to three TAT cards (cards 1, 2, and 4), as well as three MEPS vignettes. As expected, the PPSS-R score correlated with the number of relevant means generated ($r = .46$) and supported the concurrent relationship between the PPSS-R and the most frequently used performance-based measure of interpersonal problem solving. The SPSI (D'Zurilla & Nezu, 1990) was also administered and found to be unrelated either to the PPSS-R ($r = .17$) or the MEPS procedure ($r = .18$). Although the exact reason for the lack of a relationship between self-report and performance-based measures of problem solving is unknown, others have failed to find a correlation between self-report and performance-based measures of problem solving (Heppner & Peterson, 1982; Metcalfe, 1986; Nisbett & Wilson, 1977; Ronan, Nezu, & Gibbs, 1984).

Ronan et al. (1996) evaluated the known groups' validity of the PPSS-R. Study 1 compared the rating of personal problem-solving effectiveness, as measured by the PPSS-R, with clinician's ratings. The mental health records of 46 clients treated at a psychology department training clinic provided the data for this study. References to the psychological test data were removed from these records, and two clinicians rated the remaining documentation (e.g., intake, treatment summaries, progress notes) for effectiveness of problem solving using a seven-item scale. Verbatim responses to TAT cards 1, 2, and 4 were scored by two different doctoral students. Clinician ratings were divided at the mean; the group differences correlated significantly with PPSS-R scores, even after controlling for the potential confounds of education, Wechsler Adult Intelligence Scale-Revised (WAIS-R) IQ scores (Wechsler, 1981), and the number of words used in responding to the TAT. That is, scores for the two groups differed significantly on two of the three TAT cards, as well as on the total PPSS-R score. In addition, scores on two of the four aggregated component scores differed significantly.

These findings were obtained in spite of the lack of variability in clinician-rated problem solving. Clinicians rated problem-solving skills using a seven-item scale that was arranged in a six-point Likert-type format. The average score on this scale was theoretically about 24; however, participants in the above-average group only obtained a mean rating of 22. All participants were receiving psychological services, and the lack of variability in clinician ratings may have reflected a real lack of variability in client problem-solving skills. PPSS-R scores were low for the above-average group. A second study addressed this concern by comparing a chronic-psychiatric sample with a community-based sample.

Study 2 compared the performance of 47 long-term patients in a community mental health center with 47 people living in the same rural community. Participants completed a Life History Questionnaire, the Symptom Checklist 90-R (Derogatis, 1983), and the Problem Experiences Checklist (Silverton, 1991) and responded to TAT cards 1, 2, and 4. The psychiatric sample obtained lower scores on the total PPSS-R score and subscale scores than did the nonpsychiatric sample. The psychiatric sample also endorsed a greater number of problems than did the nonpsychiatric sample. Discriminate function analysis revealed that 72% of the sample was correctly classified as psychiatric or nonpsychiatric using the PPSS-R score. Because of differences in age, education, Problem Experiences Checklist scores, and Symptom Checklist 90-R scores, a hierarchical discriminate functions analysis was next used to control for these variables. Total PPSS-R scores were entered after age, education, Problem Experiences Checklist scores, and Symptom Checklist 90-R scores. PPSS-R scores still predicted group membership, and the overall model resulted in the correct classification of 92% of the cases.

Reece (2001) compared the PPSS-R performance of 22 psychiatric patients enrolled in a partial hospitalization program with the performance of 22 community residents. Participants in each group were similar in age (39 vs. 38 years of age) and had completed a similar level of education (14 years of formal schooling). Participants completed a variety of measures, including the Social Problem Solving Inventory-Revised (SPSI-R), and responded to TAT cards 1, 2, and 4. TAT responses were scored using the PPSS-R and significant differences emerged for the total score and the four subscale scores. The correlation between the SPSI-R (Short Form) and the total PPSS-R score was calculated using the 44 participants and reached significance (r = .79). After controlling for the influence of SPSI-R (Short Form) scores, the PPSS-R total scores increased the number of cases correctly classified by 10%.

Predictive Validity

Miller (2002) assessed the ability of the PPSS-R scores to predict rehospitalization for 201 rural psychiatric inpatients. Patients were administered three TAT cards (cards 1, 2, and 4) prior to discharge from the psychiatric hospital. Patients were contacted at three and six months postdischarge to determine whether they had been rehospitalized. PPSS-R scores predicted a significant amount of the variance associated with rehospitalization at three months postdischarge even after controlling for factors related to age, symptom severity, discharge environment, and compliance with follow-up treatments. PPSS-R scores were not a significant predictor of rehospitalization at six months after controlling for age, symptom severity, discharge environment, and compliance with follow-up treatments.

Outcome Validity

Two studies by Ronan, Date, and Weisbrod (1995) showed that training in social problem solving increased PPSS-R scores. Study 1 provided undergraduate students with either detailed (n = 29) or minimal (n = 30) training in the generation of alternatives component of the D'Zurilla and Goldfried (1971) social problem-solving model. Participants in the minimal-training control group were instructed to think up as many alternative solutions as possible and were given concrete examples using interpersonal problems. Participants in the detailed training condition were trained in how to generate a large number of alternative problem solutions and how to defer judgment about the effectiveness of generated solutions. These participants were also provided with specific, concrete examples using interpersonal problems. Participants who received detailed training obtained higher scores on the generation of alternatives subscale of the SPSI) D'Zurilla & Nezu, 1990), indicating that the training was understood. The goal was to evaluate whether the effects of training would spontaneously generalize to PPSS-R scores, and participants subsequently responded to TAT cards 1, 2, and 4. Between-group differences emerged for the total PPSS-R score and three of the component scores. As expected, the largest differences were obtained on the story solutions score: The mean score for subjects who received detailed training was two and a half standard deviations above the mean score for subjects who received minimal training.

Study 2 evaluated the influence of training participants in the decision-making component of the D'Zurilla and Goldfried (1971) model of social problem solving. In the study, 29 female and 15 male college students received either minimal (n = 22) or detailed (n = 22) training. Participants in the minimal-training control group were instructed to use a systematic approach to making decisions and were given concrete examples using specific interpersonal problems. Participants who received detailed training were instructed in a utility model of decision making. They were taught to maximize both long- and short-term goals while considering the likely impact that a given solution would have on family, friends, and their own value system. These participants were also provided with specific, concrete examples. Those who received detailed training obtained higher scores on the decision-making subscale of the SPSI (D'Zurilla & Nezu, 1990), suggesting that the training was understood. Between-group differences emerged for the total PPSS-R score and the four aggregate component scores, with those who received detailed training receiving the higher scores.

Ronan (2002) developed a self-control training protocol based on a social problem-solving analysis of difficulties faced by inmates on release from prison. TAT cards 1, 2, and 4 were administered pre- and posttreatment to inmates to assess treatment related changes in changes in personal problem-solving skills. Significant differences emerged between pre- and posttreatment administrations (Eta^2 = .65). PPSS scores were sensitive to changes in treatment-related changes in problem-solving skills.

Construct Validity

Mitchell (1998) explored the relationship between PPSS responses and various Rorschach indices using protocols collected from 85 patients. Some minimum support emerged: (1) The PPSS variable number of story solutions was related to the Rorschach variable R with lambda ($r = .44$, $p < .001$); and (2) the story design element rating level of distorted beliefs, appraisal, and assumptions related to the Rorschach variables *SCZI* ($r = -.18$, $p = .02$) and X – % ($r = -.17$, $p = .03$).

Some preliminary investigations have explored the relationship between performance on the PPSS-R and underlying neuropsychological constructs. For instance, Rath, Hennessy, and Keitel (2000) coded the TAT responses of 45 traumatic brain injury (TBI) patients and 15 non-brain-injured comparison participants using the PPSS-R. TBI patients obtained significantly lower scores than the non-brain-injured comparison group ($d = .52$). Ziegler (2002) found a relationship ($r = .42$) between the performance of college students on the PPSS-R and the degree of preservation measured using the Revised Strategies Application Test (Levine, Dawson, Schwartz, Boutet, & Studd, 2000).

One tenet of the personal problem-solving model is that problem-solving skills moderate the influence of stress on psychiatric symptoms (Clum & Febbraro, 1994; D'Zurilla & Sheedy, 1991; Goodman, Gravitt, & Kaslow, 1995; Marks, Williams, & Claridge, 1992; Nezu, 1987). This has been found using both cross-sectional (Nezu & Ronan, 1985) and prospective designs (Nezu & Ronan, 1988). In the study, 79 undergraduate students completed a measure of negative life events, the Life Experiences Survey (Sarason, Johnson, & Siegal, 1978), and the Beck Depression Inventory (Beck, Ward, Mendelsohn, Moch, & Erbaugh, 1961), and responded to TAT cards 1, 2, and 4. Responses to the TAT cards were scored using the PPSS-R. The interaction between negative life events and the total PPSS-R score accounted for a significant proportion of the variance ($R^2 = .18$). Participants reporting high levels of negative life events, who also obtained low PPSS-R scores, endorsed the most depressive symptoms. A second group of 79 undergraduate students completed the Life Experiences Survey (Sarason et al., 1978) and the state version of the State-Trait Anxiety Inventory (Spielberger, 1983) and responded to TAT cards 7, 10, and 13. Responses to the TAT cards were scored using the PPSS-R. The interaction between negative life experiences and PPSS-R scores accounted for a significant proportion of the variance ($R^2 = .14$). Participants reporting high levels of negative life events, who also obtained low PPSS-R scores, endorsed the highest level of anxiety symptoms on the State-Trait Anxiety Inventory. Both studies are congruent with those using different measures of personal problem solving (e.g., Clum & Febbraro, 1984; D'Zurilla & Sheedy, 1991; Goodman, Gravitt, & Kaslow, 1995; Nezu & Ronan, 1988) and suggest that the PPSS-R scores interact with psychosocial stressors to predict negative affective states.

Several researchers have found that social problem-solving skills differentiate between college students who do and do not engage in heavy episodic drinking. Dreer (2002) used PPSS-R scored responses to five alcohol-related vignettes to predict subsequent alcohol consumption during a two-week period. The goal was to determine whether self-report or performance-based measured of social problem solving would be most predictive. PPSS-R scored scenarios predicted a significant and unique portion of variance ($R^2 = .17$) beyond that accounted for by demographic and self-reported problem-solving skills.

Ronan, Jaffa, Dollard, & Forsche (2000) used the PPSS-R to code the personal problem-solving skills evinced in the inaugural addressees of the six highest- and six lowest-ranked presidents of the United States (Ridings & McIver, 1997). PPSS-R component and total scores reliably predicted group membership. Indeed, all of the lowest-ranked presidents except Richard Nixon obtained PPSS-R scores significantly below those of the highest-ranked presidents. The results maintained themselves even after controlling for the epoch within which the president served.

TABLE 10.2 Means and Standard Deviation for Nine Samples

Samples Using Cards 1, 2, and 4		SD	SO	SS	SR	Total
Undergraduate Students (n = 172)	M	5.22	5.25	4.13	3.46	18.06
Age: 20; Education: 14 years; Female: 54%	SD	1.65	1.71	1.88	2.02	5.68
Rural Community Residents (n = 47)	M	5.47	4.02	4.8	3.05	17.35
Age: 27; Education: 13 years; Female: 70%	SD	1.45	1.95	12.72	1.14	7.00
Urban Community Residents (n = 22)	M	4.94	3.41	4.22	3.35	15.93
Age: 38; Education: 14 years; Female: 84%	SD	1.99	1.70	1.48	2.02	6.18
Psychology Clinic Clients (n = 46)	M	4.52	3.77	3.21	2.88	14.29
Age: 19; Education: 13; years; Female: 57%	SD	3.77	1.89	1.34	2.14	5.96
County Jail Inmates (n = 34)	M	2.61	2.44	3.56	2.59	11.20
Age: 28; Education: 12 years; Female: 17%	SD	1.77	1.72	2.10	1.96	6.57
CMHC Psychiatric Patients (n = 47)	M	2.47	2.17	3.29	1.61	9.50
Age: 39; Education: 11 years; Female: 66%	SD	1.95	1.87	2.14	1.70	6.53
Psychiatric Day Hospital Patients (n = 22)	M	2.89	.86	3.23	.99	7.99
Age: 40; Education: 14 years; Female: 78%	SD	2.19	1.70	1.31	1.72	5.13
Hospitalized Psychiatry Patients (n = 201)	M	1.37	.72	1.47	.83	4.37
Age: 40; Education: 13 years; Female: 51%	SD	1.65	1.05	1.21	1.48	4.88
Sample Using Cards 7 BM, 10, and 13 MF		**SD**	**SO**	**SS**	**SR**	**Total**
Undergraduate Students (n = 120)	M	4.44	3.45	6.48	2.78	17.16
Age: 20; Education: 14 years; Female: 58%	SD	1.66	2.17	3.60	2.08	7.22

Generalizability

PPSS-R means and standard deviations are available for the following adult samples: college students, community residents, jail inmates, psychology department affiliated clinic clients, seriously impaired community mental health center clients, and psychiatric day treatment clients. Because analyses reveal no gender differences, means and standard deviations are not broken down by gender (Table 10.2).

Reliability

Interrater Reliability

Developing an objective means for scoring narratives demands clear scoring criteria: If independent raters cannot obtain similar results when scoring the same protocol, the scoring criteria are too ambiguous. Procedures for estimating interrater reliability range from correlating raters' scores (Nunnally, 1970) to computing intraclass correlations (Shavelson & Webb, 1991). Table 10.3 presents the citations, samples used, number of

TABLE 10.3 Sample of Published Interrater Reliability Estimates

Citation	Participants	*n*	Agreement
Ronan, Colavito, & Hammontree (1993)			
Study 1	Undergraduates	87	.83
Study 2	Undergraduates	56	.86, .89
Ronan, Date, & Weisbrod, 1995			
Study 1	Undergraduates	59	.90
Study 2	Undergraduates	44	.92
Ronan et al., 1996			
Study 1	Psychiatric	46	.83
Study 2	Psychiatric and Community	94	.88

TAT protocols (three stories per protocol) scored, and reliability estimates for six different studies. Interrater reliability estimates using TAT cards 1, 2, and 4 range from .83 to .92. Several studies under review have found similar levels of interrater reliability.

Raters for the aforementioned studies were advanced clinical psychology doctoral students who were well trained in problem-solving models of psychopatho logy; therefore, their interrater reliability estimates probably represent upper limits. To assess whether people with little prior exposure to the TAT and models of personal problem solving could learn to use the system reliably, college students enrolled in Introduction to Psychology courses were used as raters. Forty randomly selected freshman undergraduates received approximately 20 minutes of training in one of the four components of the scoring system ($n = 10$ per component). Participants subsequently scored a TAT story to card 4 from each of the following samples: a depressed community resident, a jail inmate, and a college student. Table 10.4 presents the variance attributable to raters and stories as well as the intraclass correlation for the 10 raters.

TABLE 10.4 Intraclass Correlations (ICC) and Variance Attributable to Design Facets and Minimally Trained Raters

PPSS-R Component Scores	ICC	Rater Variance	Story Variance
Story Design	.68	.09	.50
Story Orientation	.72	.03	.59
Story Solutions	.78	.14	.47
Story Resolutions	.75	.13	.44

TABLE 10.5 Principle Component Analysis Using College Students

Variables	I	II	III	IV
Story Design	.78	.55	.28	.01
Story Orientation	.88	–.37	.16	.24
Story Solutions	.84	.15	–.51	.04
Story Resolution	.91	–.25	.07	–.29
Eigen Values	2.93	.53	.38	.15
Variance Explained	.73	.13	.10	.04

Data presented in Tables 10.3 and 10.4 are encouraging. Although sophisticated raters obtained significantly higher levels of agreement than minimally trained raters, both groups obtained generally acceptable levels of agreement. We recently completed a study that used different TAT cards (cards 7BM, 10, and 13MF), and a similar estimate of interrater reliability was obtained ($r = .88$); the results have yet to be published (Ronan, 2002).

Internal Consistency

Although problem-solving performance can be reduced to component skills, components are typically viewed as somewhat interdependent. For instance, if a problem is poorly specified, the generated story solutions are unlikely to result in problem resolution. Personal problem solving is generally conceptualized as including several different skills that load on a single, underlying dimension. This predicted structure of the PPSS-R was initially tested using 87 undergraduate students (Ronan et al., 1993), and the results are presented in Table 10.5. Component scores loaded on a single dimension that accounted for 73% of the variance. Very similar results have been found for a clinic sample from a psychology department training clinic, a mixed group of psychiatric patients and nonpsychiatric community residents, and a mixed sample of community residents and patients enrolled in a day treatment program. We interpret these data as supporting our conceptualization that PPSS-R component scores load on a single, underlying dimension.

Temporal Stability

Personal problem-solving skills are expected to be relatively stable—a measure of personal problem-solving skills should show significant test–retest reliability. Ronan et al. (1993) administered three TAT cards to 56 undergraduate students who were readministered the same cards an average of 45 days later. On both occasions, participants also completed the PSI (Heppner, 1988). As previously discussed, the PSI is a 32-item self-report measure of problem solving behaviors and attitudes. A Pearson product–moment correlation between the first and second administrations revealed acceptable levels of reliability for both the PPSS-R ($r = .83$) and the PSI ($r = .81$). Table 10.6 lists the test–retest coefficients for the PPSS-R. To summarize, the test–retest reliability of the PPSS-R total score equaled that of the most frequently used self-report measure of personal problem solving: the PSI.

TABLE 10.6 Test–Retest Reliability Estimates for a 45-Day Interval

Components	Pearson r
Story Design	.65
Story Orientation	.64
Story Solutions	.78
Story Resolution	.71
PPSS Total	.83

☐ Case Illustrations

The use of narratives in therapy represents psychotherapy as a storytelling process. The client has a story, and the therapist seeks, through storytelling of his or her own, to modify the narrative. Costantino, Malgady, and Rogler (1996) developed, in fact, a specific narrative therapy that teaches cultural values and adaptive behavior to troubled Puerto Rican youth through reading and highlighting aspects of traditional folktales. *Reframing* (Watzlawick, Weakland, & Fisch, 1974) has become a catchword for therapists of all stripes, and *restorying* is a variation of that principle (Eron & Lund, 1993). According to Eron and Lund, "people have multiple stories that define who they are; some are preferred and some are not. When new events are construed in a way that contradicts peoples' preferred narrative accounts, problems 'evolve.' Problems 'dissolve' when people begin to see others seeing them in line with their preferred ways of being and acting.... The 'strategy' is ... to provide alternative explanations that change the negative and unsettling ways in which people have come to see each other" (p. 308).

The following examples explicate how the PPSS-R can enhance the process of assessment and psychotherapy. The focus of these cases shifts from the four broad scoring categories to differences in responses to individual cards. Take the following response (story A) to card 1.

> I see a very confused little boy. He's afraid. He has a violin before him and he wants to be able to play it but he's afraid to pick it up. He's afraid of doing something wrong. He's afraid that he can't play it. His eyes show hurt, pain, and not being understood. His heart is sad and grieved. He doesn't know what he's going to do. He wants to do right, but maybe he has been told he can't do right. So he's afraid to pick it up. He's afraid to even try. He needs his mother and his father and to be loved and understood. He doesn't have that though. No one's telling him to pick it up and play it. You can do it. It may not sound right but you can still pick it up and play with it until you learn to do it right. I see a child that wishes he was never born. I don't know what the outcome will be.

Scoring this story provided a low total score, and the total score for the participant's other two stories was low. Three very low scores is unusual for an individual in a community sample. Though any clinician would identify psychopathology in this story without the PPSS-R scoring, using the system shows how central problem solving is for the client. Here is a person who is clearly telling us, "Because I was never encouraged to tackle problems, I am afraid of doing something wrong and cannot confront the issues in my life." Although a psychodynamic therapist might focus on loss and damaged object relations, this story alerts us to the importance of encouragement and training in problem solving as a mechanism to improve this person's functioning.

In addition to identifying general problem-solving deficiencies, the PPSS-R allows us to compare the individual's scores within each of the four coding categories and to determine which areas of problem solving need remediation. As an example, take the following response (story B) to card 1:

> I was so happy when mom got me this violin for my birthday. My best friend, Susan, and I are going to take violin lessons this summer and join the orchestra in the fall. But then I found out that there are no teachers of violin in my neighborhood. That is, none except old Mr. Fredrik, and he scares me. He chases all the kids off the lawn whenever we pass his house. Now I am not sure whether to take lessons or not. Tomorrow Susan and I are going to decide what to do. I really want to learn how to play this. I wish a new instructor would move in. Gosh, I hate it when things don't go my way.

Without the use of the PPSS-R system, a rapid reading of this story would give a positive impression of emotional health to a clinician, with the possible exception of the last sentence. Looking at the scoring categories, however, we see that where this individual does well is in story design. The story encompasses a past, present, and future (i.e., to play in the orchestra); has a clearly laid-out problem with clear specification of the problem's cause; shows no distorted beliefs; and is well integrated and detailed. A look at the story orientation component reveals that the person is not coping so well. The problem is not perceived as a challenge, is distressing, and is not approached with confidence. Only one story solution is generated (i.e., decide with Susan), and there is no story resolution. If this pattern is continued throughout the other stories, then this individual seems like an excellent candidate for problem-solving therapy, focused on generation of solutions and problem-solving confidence. The individual's ability to formulate problems well is a positive prognostic sign. Practice at generating solutions and looking at possible outcomes of solutions would increase this person's problem-solving confidence and ability to confront problems. Compare the story with the following response (story C) to card 1:

> This boy doesn't know how to play the violin. It looks like he is sad and maybe angry because of it. He could take lessons to learn or ask someone to teach him to play if he knows anyone that plays. And if his parents couldn't pay for the lessons, he could find a job and save to pay for the lessons himself.

The overall score for story B and story C is about the same, but notice how the score is obtained in different categories. This person is excellent at generating solutions and demonstrates a confident approach to the problem. However, here the story design does not encompass past or future, does not indicate cause of the problem, and shows little detail or integration. There is no story resolution, and this may be due to the lack of detail in the formulation of the problem. That is, if the story indicated more about the boy's circumstances it would be easier to determine whether any of the proposed solutions could be effective. This individual would benefit from a therapeutic focus on problem formulation.

As noted in the previous section, it is important to look at the type of solutions scored within story solutions. Note the following response (story D) to card 1:

> The boy is having problems playing the violin. The notes just aren't coming out right. He's taking a break to talk himself into playing it right. He's concentrating very hard, and when he is done, he will play that violin like it was born attached to his hands.

This story has a positive outcome, and a good total score, although story design is a little low. Compare the story solutions with those generated for story C. Whereas the solutions in story C are external and overt, the story solutions in story D are internal and covert, with the exception of *taking a break*. Covert solutions are not inferior to overt ones, but they show a different orientation to problem solving. More introverted types of people, in the Jungian sense, may be more likely to use covert solutions, whereas extroverted types may be more likely to employ external solutions. Just as Carl Jung recommended a balance between introversion and extroversion, individuals who rely on covert solutions may need to be encouraged to take a more external perspective, and individuals who never use covert solutions may benefit from focusing on the role played by their thoughts and feelings.

Another dimension to look at in story solutions is to what extent the individual uses social support systems. Covert solutions tend not to involve other characters, but overt solutions do not always involve social support either. The following story (story E) to card 1 is a good example of one using social support:

> He looks really worried about his violin. He looks like he's discouraged with his lesson, and he's thinking about something not associated with the violin. I don't think he likes violin lessons. I think he needs to talk to his mother and tell her he doesn't like violin lessons. Then maybe she'll talk to his teacher, and they can figure out how to make lessons interesting. If they both understand his problem and work together it will work out.

The effectiveness of problem solutions should always be noted. Story resolution within the PPSS-R scoring system rates the narrator's view of the effectiveness of the solution, not the test administrator's view. The administrator should, when looking at story solutions, also decide whether in his or her view the solution is likely to be effective. For example, if the subject plans to solve his interpersonal problems through murder or her financial problems through gambling, regardless of the story resolution, the clinician will question the subject's problem-solving expertise. In cases like these, therapy should be focused on helping the client anticipate outcomes.

As a general principle of interpretation, it is important to note large differences in the scores obtained for particular cards. Although a sample of three cards is small, in many cases other TAT cards are available and interpretive hypotheses can be checked out with more information. A client who shows dramatic differences in the scores obtained for different cards may be indicating areas of strength and weakness. The following two stories were told by the same 34-year-old woman.

> Card 2. This girl in the front wants to have a better life for herself, to go to school, be independent, and live in the city and not on the farm. She's happy and optimistic. The other woman is content and looks pregnant or fat. She is happy to be where she is, and life's simple and good. The guy is just a worker. The woman will have a healthy baby, and the girl will go to school to be a doctor in the city. The fat woman will remain in the country.

> Card 4. The ever-avoidant male personality and the dependent girl. She loves him and wants him to marry her. He wants to have fun. He'll go to 50 other girls just like her, and she'll learn what life is really about.

In these two stories, note the differences that would be obtained on scoring categories for positive motivation and problem-solving confidence, and on all the story resolution elements. One can hypothesize that this client has no difficulty tackling achievement areas of her life but that problems in relationships with men are less well understood and resolved. Checking the other stories, we see a similar pattern, with poor resolution to problems indicated on stories involving male relationships. The following story is a good example:

> Card 6GF. She's startled and annoyed. She's ready to go out to dinner, and her husband just announced that he'd rather stay home. He's got his smoking jacket on and has no intention of leaving. She'll do what he wants but resents him.

The facts about this participant indicate that she is a woman with an IQ only in the average range who is succeeding in a master's program, while her marriage has recently ended. One might argue that these facts reveal all that needs to be known without the PPSS-R scoring. The scoring system, however, alerts to some of the reasons why this woman may have difficulties solving her relationship difficulties with men. For one thing, the stories reveal the woman's lack of understanding of causes of the problem. The situation in card 2 is presented not as a problem at all—the girl wants to leave the farm, and she simply does. In card 4, the problem in the relationship is due to stable personal attributions, even less likely to be changeable because they are gender stereotypes. In addition, notice the difficulty in generating problem solutions, especially in card 4. Also, the male character in card 2 is not a part of the story, and the three characters are not integrated, leading to a low score on integration and detail. It may be that the client's difficulties with men are part of a general difficulty in object relations or in understanding relationships.

This client could benefit from therapy focused on improving her understanding of her own and others'—especially men's—behaviors and motivations, either from a cognitive-behavioral or dynamic perspective. A problem-solving approach seems especially well suited to her difficulty in framing problems and generating solutions. Her general optimism and approach to, rather than avoidance of problems—other than those with men—suggest a positive prognosis.

The clinician can examine the individual stories to assess differences in many other areas as well as work versus interpersonal problems. For instance, the clinician can be alert to problem-solving ability with structured versus abstract problems or when social support is available versus when social support is not available, and so forth. In most cases when such differences in functioning are noted, it is helpful to form hypotheses and to test them with the aid of the client. Awareness of differential coping across different spheres should structure the focus of treatment.

Summary

Because problem solving, broadly conceived as coping or functioning, is central to all theories of psychotherapy, the information provided through the PPSS-R is relevant to every clinician. As an example, the TAT and the PPSS-R can be valuable to a family therapist, since TAT stories, by their interpersonal nature, provide a picture of interpersonal systems. It is perhaps not coincidental that Haley (1987) calls his family systems approach Problem-Solving Therapy, with the focus not on the problem of the individual but on the problem of the system. Haley asked the question, "How does the client's symptom solve a problem for a family or other system?" Although the PPSS-R focuses on the impact of the story resolution for the hero, it is an easy matter also to look at the outcome for the TAT characters other than the hero, and in so doing we may find the answer to Haley's question.

The use of the PPSS-R will enhance clinical assessment by showing general difficulties in problem solving or coping (total score), the particular aspects of problem solving or coping that need to be addressed (subscale scores and specific elements), and the particular areas of life in which the individual is having problem-solving or coping difficulties (specific cards). Information is also gained by looking at qualitative information such as the type of story solutions generated and the impact on characters other than the hero.

TAT stories can also be used directly in the therapy as examples of the client's preferred narrative accounts. For instance, a client could be asked to contrast her or his stories about work and achievement with those about relationships. Therapy could address what makes situations different and how the client's story about herself or himself as achiever could be retold in a relationship format. Using the principle in narrative therapy of finding one story that is an exception to the symptoms the client is showing, the clinician could look for situations in which the client best solves problems and could use those situations to produce new learning and generalizations.

☐ Future Research

Several methodological considerations emerge when using the PPSS-R to score TAT responses. First, research has not evaluated the specificity of PPSS-R scores derived from scoring responses to different TAT cards. Although we have data indicating that subjects are likely to generate a certain domains of problems to specific TAT cards, we have not empirically tested whether PPSS-R scores for specific TAT cards differentially predict coping with similar real-life problems. Indeed, the domain specificity of PPSS-R scores generated to TAT cards has yet to be tested; therefore, we urge caution when differentially attributing levels of problem-solving ability to real-life problems similar to those identified in a specific TAT card. Second, virtually all of the available research on the PPSS-R has been garnered using nomothetic research designs. Most clinical applications involve the intensive study of an individual case. Findings employing single subject research designs are necessary prior to having confidence in the clinical application of the PPSS-R. Finally, some researchers have found a relationship between scores obtained on traditional TAT scoring systems and the length of the scored response. Although we have not found a significant relationship between story length (e.g., number of words used) and the magnitude of obtained scores, reliability estimates, or validity estimates (e.g., Ronan et al., 1993, 1995, 1996), additional research is needed prior to developing firm conclusions.

The PPSS-R is a relatively new scoring system, and a major goal for writing this chapter was to stimulate additional basic research on what we believe to be a promising system for scoring narratives. Indeed, we presented considerable unpublished findings to demonstrate the types of projects completed and to encourage additional research. This system does not enjoy enough empirical support to warrant routine clinical applications, and additional peer-reviewed findings are necessary across all areas covered. Nonetheless, there are some specific areas in need of immediate attention. Research is needed on cultural factors that influence PPSS-R scores and the resulting interpretations. Preliminary data we collected comparing adolescents in Brazil and the United Sates suggested that several story design elements might be particularly sensitive to cultural factors. Difficulties emerged when we attempted to decipher whether these interpretative challenges were a function of language (e.g., Portuguese) or other sociocultural factors (e.g., beliefs resulting from living with an economy experiencing rapid economic inflation). Cross-cultural research can help to provide a better understanding of emic and etic components of the PPSS-R.

Research on the clinical utility of the PPSS-R is sparse. We do not know whether PPSS-R scores add significantly to the accuracy of clinical judgments based on interview data or whether PPSS-R scores add incremental validity to clinical decisions made during routine clinical work. Research on clinical utility and incremental validity is required prior to disseminating the procedure in clinical settings. Similarly, research suggests a relationship between affective states and performance on measures of social problem solving (e.g., Ronan, Nezu, & Gibbs, 1986). Unfortunately, the current version of the PPSS-R devotes little attention to assessing affective states. Preliminary data collected in our lab suggest that coding the affective connotation of words used when responding to TAT cards can discriminate between those with high versus low negative affect. Research on using narratives to assess affective states is in its infancy and this research would help spur the development of a more robust PPSS-R scoring system.

Finally, basic research is needed on the cognitive components that underlie the process of social problem solving measured via the PPSS-R. Further research in this area would help to identify the basic cognitive components related to PPSS-R scores and perhaps would result in a measure that could have some applicability within rehabilitation settings where decisions about levels of everyday problem-solving ability are often made based on limited assessment data.

References

Allen, M. J., & Yen, W. M. (1979). *Introduction to measurement theory.* Monterey, CA: Brooks/Cole.

Alvardo, N. (1994). Empirical validity of the Thematic Apperception Test. *Journal of Personality Assessment, 63,* 59–79.

Atkinson, J. W. (Ed.). (1958). *Motives in fantasy, action, and society.* New Jersey: Van Nostrand.

Atkinson, J. W. (1992). Motivational determinants of thematic apperception. In C. P. Smith (Ed.), *Motivation and personality: Handbook of thematic content analysis* (pp. 21–86). New York: Cambridge University Press.

Barends, A., Westen, D., Leigh, J., Silbert, D., & Byers, S. (1990). Assessing affect–tone of relationship paradigms from TAT and interview data. *Psychological Assessment, 2,* 329–332.

Beck, A. T., Ward, C. H., Mendelsohn, M., Moch, J., & Erbaugh, J. (1961). An inventory for measuring depression. *Archives of General Psychiatry, 9,* 324–333.

Bellack, A. S., Sayers, M., Mueser, K. T., & Benett, M. (1994). Evaluation of social problem solving in schizophrenia. *Journal of Abnormal Psychology, 103,* 371–378.

Bellak, L. (1973). *A guide to the interpretation of the Thematic Apperception Test.* New York: Psychological Corporation.

Brickman, P., Rabinowitz, V. C., Karuza, J., Coates, D., Cohn, E., & Kidder, L. (1982). Models of helping and coping. *American Psychologist, 37,* 368–384.

Butler, L., & Meichenbaum, D. (1981). The assessment of interpersonal problem-solving skills. In P. C. Kendall & S. D. Hollon (Eds.), *Assessment strategies for cognitive-behavioral interventions* (pp. 197–225). New York: Academic.

Campus, N. (1976). A measure of needs to assess the stimulus characteristics of TAT cards. *Journal of Personality Assessment, 40,* 248–258.

Cantor, N., & Harlow, R. E. (1994). Personality, strategic behavior, and daily-life problem solving. *Current Direction in Psychological Science, 3,* 169–172.

Clum, G. A., & Febbraro, G. A. R. (1994). Stress, social support, and problem-solving appraisal/skills: Prediction of suicide severity within a college sample. *Journal of Psychopathology and Behavioral Assessment, 16,* 69–83.

Costa, P. T., & McCrae, R. R. (1992). *Revised NEO Personality Inventory (NEO-PI-R) and NEO Five Factor Inventory (NEO-FF) professional manual.* Odessa, FL: Psychological Assessment Resources.

Costantino, G., Malgady, R., & Rogler, J. (1986). Cuento therapy: Folktales as a culturally sensitive psychotherapy for Puerto Rican children. *Journal of Consulting and Clinical Psychology, 54,* 639–645.

Cramer, P. (1996). *Storytelling, narrative, and the Thematic Apperception Test.* New York: Guilford.

Dana, R. H. (1955). Clinical diagnosis and objective *TAT* scoring. *Journal of Abnormal and Social Psychology, 50,* 19–24.

DeCharms, R. (1992). Personal causation and the origin concept. In C. P. Smith (Ed.), *Motivation and personality: Handbook of thematic content analysis* (pp. 325–333). New York: Cambridge University Press.

Derogatis, L. R. (1983). *SCL 90-R administration, scoring, and procedures manual - II.* Townson, MD: Clinical Psychometrics Research.

Dobson, K. S., & Block, L. (1988). Historical and philosophical basis of the cognitive-behavioral therapies. In K. S. Dobson (Ed.), *Handbook of cognitive-behavioral therapies* (pp. 3–38). New York: Guilford.

Dreer, L. E. (2002). *Social problem solving and college drinking behavior: The utility of self-report versus performance based measures.* Unpublished doctoral dissertation, Central Michigan University.

Dugas, M. J., Letarte, H., Rheaume, J., & Freeston, M. (1995). Worry and problem solving: Evidence of a specific relationship. *Cognitive Therapy and Research, 19,* 109–120.

D'Zurilla, T. J. (1988). Problem-solving therapies. In K. S. Dobson (Ed.), *Handbook of cognitive-behavioral therapies* (pp. 85–135). New York: Guilford.

D'Zurilla, T. J., & Goldfried, M. R. (1971). Problem solving and behavior modification. *Journal of Abnormal Psychology, 78,* 107–126.

D'Zurilla, T. J., & Maydeu-Olivares, A. (1995). Conceptual and methodological issues in social problem solving assessment. *Behavior Therapy, 26,* 393–408.

D'Zurilla, T. J., & Nezu, A. M. (1980). A study of the generation of alternatives process in social problem solving. *Cognitive Therapy and Research, 4,* 67–72.

D'Zurilla, T. J., & Nezu, A. M. (1982). Social problem solving in adults. In P. C. Kendall (Ed.), *Advances in cognitive-behavioral research and therapy* (Vol. 1) (pp. 201–274). New York: Academic.

D'Zurilla, T. J., & Nezu, A. M. (1990). Development and preliminary evaluation of the Social Problem Solving Inventory. *Psychological Assessment, 2,* 156–163.

D'Zurilla, T. J., & Sheedy, C. F. (1991). Relation between social problem-solving ability and subsequent level of psychological stress in college students. *Journal of Personality and Social Psychology, 61,* 841–846.

Ellis, A. (1962). *Reason and emotion in psychotherapy.* New York: Lyle Stuart.

Epley, D., & Ricks, D. (1963). Foresight and hindsight in the TAT. *Journal of Projective Techniques, 27,* 51–59.

Eron, L. D. (1965). A normative study of the Thematic Apperception Test. In B. I. Murstein (Ed.), *Handbook of projective techniques* (pp. 469–507). New York: Basic.

Eron, J. B., & Lund, T. W. (1993). How problems evolve and dissolve: Integrating narrative and strategic concepts. *Family Process, 32,* 291–309.

Fine, R. (1955). Manual for a scoring scheme for verbal projective techniques (TAT, MAPS, stories and the like). *Journal of Projective Techniques, 19,* 310–316.

Fiske, D. W. (1971). *Measuring the concepts of personality.* Chicago, IL: Aldine.

Freeman, A., Pretzer, J., Fleming, B., & Simon, K. M. (1990). *Clinical application of cognitive therapy.* New York: Plenum.

Freud, A. (1946). *The ego and the mechanisms of defense.* New York: International Universities.

Galotti, K. M. (1995). Memories of a "decision-map": Recall of a real-life decision. *Applied Cognitive Psychology, 9,* 307–319.

Garner, H. (1970). *Psychotherapy: Confrontational problem solving technique.* St. Louis, MO: W. H. Green.

Gibbs, M. S., Ronan, G. F., Nezu, A. M., Cariedo, C., & Grossman, B. (1985, March). *The TAT as a measure of social problem solving.* Paper presented at the 56th Annual Meeting of the Eastern Psychological Association, Boston, MA.

Goddard, P., & McFall, R. M. (1992). Decision-making skills and heterosocial competence in college women: An information processing analysis. *Journal of Social and Clinical Psychology, 11,* 401–425.

Goodman, S. H., Gravitt, G. W., & Kaslow, N. J. (1995). Social problem solving: A moderator of the relation between negative life stress and depression symptoms in children. *Journal of Abnormal Child Psychology, 23,* 473–485.

Haley, J. (1987). *Problem-solving therapy* (2nd ed.). San Francisco: Jossey-Bass.

Harman, H. H. (1976). *Modern factor analysis.* Chicago: University of Chicago Press.

Hartman, A. A. (1970). A basic TAT set. *Journal of Projective Techniques and Personality Assessment, 34,* 391–396.

Hartmann, H., & Loewenstein, R. (1962). Notes on the superego. *The psychoanalytic study of the child,* 17, 42–81.

Heppner, P. P. (1978). A review of the problem solving literature and its relationship to the counseling process. *Journal of Counseling Psychology, 25,* 366–375.

Heppner, P. P. (1988). *Manual for the Personal Problem-Solving Inventory.* Palo Alto, CA: Consulting Psychologist Press.

Heppner, P. P., & Anderson, W. P. (1985). The relationship between problem-solving self-appraisals and psychological adjustment. *Cognitive Therapy and Research, 9,* 415–427.

Heppner, P. P., Hibel, J. H., Neal, G. W., Weinstein, C. L., & Rabinowitz, F. E. (1982). Personal problem solving: A descriptive study of individual differences. *Journal of Counseling Psychology, 29,* 580–590.

Heppner, P. P., & Petersen, C. H. (1982). The development and implications of a personal problem-solving inventory. *Journal of Counseling Psychology, 29,* 66–75.

Heppner, P. P., Reeder, B. L., & Larson, L. M. (1983). Cognitive variables associated with personal problem-solving appraisal: Implications for counseling. *Journal of Counseling Psychology, 30,* 537–545.

Heyns, R. W., Veroff, J., & Atkinson, J. W. (1957). A scoring manual for the affiliation motive. In J. W. Atkinson (Ed.), *Motives in fantasy, action and society* (pp. 205–218). New York: Van Nostrand.

Hiroto, D. S., & Seligman, M. E. P. (1975). Generality of learned helplessness in man. *Journal of Personality and Social Psychology, 31,* 122–128.

Holt, R. R. (1978). *Methods in clinical psychology.* New York: Plenum Press.

Husain, O., Rossel, F., & Merceron, C. (1988). "Or" responses on the Rorschach and the T.A.T.: The logic of alternative and its psychopathological aspects. *British Journal of Projective Psychology, 33,* 18–30.

Jacobson, E. (1964). *The self and the object world.* New York: International Universities.

Janis, I. L., & Mann, L. (1977). *Decision-making: A psychological analysis of conflict, choice, and commitment.* New York: Free Press.

Johnson, J. L. (1994). The Thematic Apperception Test and Alzheimer's disease. *Journal of Personality Assessment, 62,* 314–319.

Karon, B. P. (1981). The Thematic Apperception Test (TAT). In A. I. Rabin (Ed.), *Assessment with projective techniques* (pp. 85–121). New York: Springer.

Katz, J. (1985). The sociopolitical nature of counseling. *Counseling Psychologist, 13,* 615–624.

Kelly, G. (1955). *The psychology of personal constructs.* New York: Norton.

Kluckhohn, C. (1951). Values and value orientations. In T. Parsons and E. Shils (Eds.), *Towards a general theory of action* (pp. 388–433). Cambridge, MA: Harvard University Press.

LaFromboise, T. T., & Rowe, W. (1983). Skills training for bicultural competence: Rationale and application. *Journal of Counseling Psychology, 30,* 589–595.

Lazarus, R. S., & Folkman, S. (1984). *Stress, appraisal, and coping.* New York: Springer.

Leigh, J., Westen, D., Barends, A., & Mandel, M. J. (1992). The assessment of complexity of representations of people using the TAT and interview data. *Journal of Personality, 60,* 809–837.

Lewinsohn, S., & Mano, H. (1993). Multi-attribute choice and affect: The influence of naturally occurring and manipulated moods on choice processes. *Journal of Behavioral Decision Making, 6,* 33–51.

Levine, B., Dawson, D., Schwartz, M. L., Boutet, I., & Stuss, D. T. (2000). Assessment of strategic self-regulation in traumatic brain injury: Its relationship to injury severity and psychosocial outcome. *Neuropsychology, 14,* 491–500.

Loehlin, J. C. (1992). *Latent variable models: An introduction to factor, path, and structural analysis.* Hillsdale, NJ: Lawrence Erlbaum.

Loevinger, J., & Wessler, R. (1970). *Measuring ego development* (Vol. 1). San Francisco: Jossey-Bass.

Lubin, B., Larsen, R. M., & Matarazo, J. D. (1984). Patterns of psychological test usage in the United States: 1935–1982. *American Psychologist, 39,* 451–454.

Lyubormirsky, S., & Nolen-Hoeksema, S. (1995). Effects of self-focused rumination on negative thinking and problem solving. *Journal of Personality and Social Psychology, 69,* 176–190.

Malgady, R. G., Costantino, G., & Rogler, L. H. (l984). Development of a Thematic Apperception Test (TEMAS) for urban Hispanic children. *Journal of Consulting and Clinical Psychology, 52,* 986–996.

Marx, E. M., Williams, J. M., & Claridge, G. C. (1992). Depression and social problem solving. *Journal of Abnormal Psychology, 101,* 78–86.

Maydeu-Olivares, A., & DiZurilla, T. J. (1996). A factor-analytic study of the Social Problem Solving Inventory: An integration of theory and data. *Cognitive Therapy and Research, 20,* 115–133.

McClelland, D. C., Atkinson, J. W., Clark, R. A., & Lowell, E. L. (1958). A scoring manual for the achievement motive. In J. W. Atkinson (Ed.), *Motives in fantasy, action, and society* (pp. 179–204). Princeton, NJ: Van Nostrand.

Metcalfe, J. (1986). Feelings of knowing in memory and problem solving. *Journal of Experimental Psychology: Learning Memory, and Cognition, 12,* 288–294.

Miller, D. (2002). *Problem solving as a predictor of symptomatic relapse and hospital readmission in psychiatric patients.* Unpublished doctoral dissertation, Central Michigan University.

Miller, W. R., & Seligman, M. E. P. (1975). Depression and learned helplessness in man. *Journal of Abnormal Psychology, 84,* 228–238.

Mischel, W. (1977). On the future of personality assessment. *American Psychologist, 32,* 246–254.

Mitchell (1998). *Personal problem-solving scoring of TAT responses: Validation with Rorschach protocols.* Unpublished thesis, University of Alaska–Anchorage.

Monk, G., Winslade, J., Crocket, K., & Epston, D. (Eds.) (1997). *Narrative therapy in practice: The archaeology of hope.* San Francisco: Jossey-Bass.

Morgan, C. D., & Murray, H. A. (1935). A method for investigating phantasies: The Thematic Apperception Test. *Archives of Neurological Psychiatry, 34,* 289–306.

Murray, H. A. (1943). *Thematic Apperception Test Manual.* Cambridge, MA: Harvard University Press.

Neimeyer, R. A. (1993). An appraisal of constructivist psychotherapies. *Journal of Consulting and Clinical Psychology, 61,* 221–234.

Nezu, A. M. (1987). A problem solving formulation of depression: A literature review and proposal for a pluralistic model. *Clinical Psychology Review, 7,* 121–144.

Nezu, A. M., & D'Zurilla, T. J. (1979). An evaluation of the decision making process in social problem solving. *Cognitive Therapy and Research, 3,* 268–277.

Nezu, A. M., Kalmar, K., Ronan, G. F., & Clavijio, A. (1986). Attributional correlates of depression: An interactive model including problem solving. *Behavior Therapy, 17,* 50–56.

Nezu, A. M., Nezu, C. M., & Perri, M. G. (1989). *Problem solving therapy for depression: Theory, research, and clinical guidelines.* New York: Wiley.

Nezu, A. M., & Ronan, G. F. (1985). Life stress, current problems, problem solving, and depressive symptoms: An integrative model. *Journal of Consulting and Clinical Psychology, 53,* 693–697.

Nezu, A. M., & Ronan, G. F. (1987). Social problem solving and depression: Deficits in generating alternatives and decision making. *The Southern Psychologist, 3,* 29–34.

Nezu, A. M., & Ronan, G. F. (1988). Social problem solving as a moderator of stress-related depressive symptoms: A prospective analysis. *Journal of Counseling Psychology, 5,*134–138.

Nisbett, R. E., & Wilson, T. P. (1977). Telling more than we can know: Verbal reports on mental processes. *Psychological Review, 84,* 231–259.

Nunnally, J. C. (1970). *Introduction to psychological measurement.* New York, NY: McGraw-Hill.

Ornduff, S. R., Freedenfeld, R. N., Kelsey, R. M., & Critelli, J. W. (1994). Object relations of sexually abused female subjects: A TAT analysis. *Journal of Personality Assessment, 63,* 223–238.

Ornduff, S. R., & Kelsey, R. M. (1996). Object relations of sexually abused and physically abused female children: A TAT analysis. *Journal of Personality Assessment, 66,* 91–105.

Osborne, A. F. (1963). *Applied imagination: Principles and procedures for creative problem solving.* New York: Scribners.

Perls, F. S. (1970). Four lectures. In J. Fagan, and I. L. Shepherd (Eds.), *Gestalt therapy now* (pp. 14–38). New York: Harper & Row.

Peterson, C., & Ulrey, L. M. (1994). Can explanatory style be scored from TAT protocols? *Personality and Social Psychology Bulletin, 20,* 102–106.

Piotrowski, C., & Keller, J. W. (1984). Psychodiagnostic testing in APA-approved clinical psychology programs. *Professional Psychology: Research and Practice, 3,* 450–456.

Piotrowski, C., & Zalewski, C. (1993). Training in psychodiagnostic testing APA-approved Psy.D. and Ph.D. clinical psychology programs. *Journal of Personality Assessment, 61,* 394–405.

Pistole, D. R, & Ornduff, S. R. (1994). TAT assessment of sexually abused girls: An analysis of manifest content. *Journal of Personality Assessment, 63,* 211–222.

Polyson, J., Norris, D., & Ott, E. (1985). The recent decline in TAT research. *Professional Psychology: Research and Practice, 16,* 26–28.

Platt, J. J., & Husband, S. D. (1993). An overview of problem solving and social skills approaches in substance abuse treatment. *Psychotherapy, 30,* 276–283.

Platt, J. J., & Spivack, G. (1972). Problem solving thinking of psychiatric patients. *Journal of Consulting and Clinical Psychology, 39,* 148–151.

Rath, J. F., Hennessy, J. J., & Keitel, M. A. (August, 2000). *Social problem solving and community integration in adults with traumatic brain injury.* Paper presented at the 108th Annual Convention of the American Psychological Association, Washington, DC.

Reece, J. (2001). *Evaluation of the PPSS TAT scoring system in a partial hospitalization sample.* Unpublished doctoral dissertation, Central Michigan University.

Riggs, D. S., & Foa, E. B. (1993). Obsessive compulsive disorder. In D. Barlow (Ed.), *Clinical Handbook of Psychological Disorders, Second Edition* (pp.189–239). New York: Guilford.

Ridings, W. J., & Mvlver, S. B. (1997). *Rating the presidents.* Secaucus, NJ: Carol Publishing Group.

Ritzler, B. A., Sharkey, K. J., & Chudy, J. F. (1980). A comprehensive projective alternative to the TAT. *Journal of Personality Assessment, 44,* 358–362.

Rogers, C. R. (1969). *Freedom to learn.* Columbus, OH: Merrill, 1969.

Ronan, G. F., Colavito, V., & Hammontree, S. (1993). Personal problem-solving scoring of TAT responses: Preliminary reliability and validity data. *Journal of Personality Assessment, 61,* 28–40.

Ronan, G. F., Date, A. L., & Weisbrod, M. (1995). Personal problem-solving scoring of the TAT: Sensitivity to training. *Journal of Personality Assessment, 64,* 118–127.

Ronan, G. F., Jaffa, M., Dollard, K., & Forsche, W. (2000, March). *Using PPSS scoring of presidential inaugural addresses to predict ratings of presidential greatness.* Paper presented at the annual meeting of the Society for Personality Assessment, Albuquerque, NM.

Ronan, G., Nezu, A., & Gibbs, M. S. (1985, April). *On the relationship between perceived social problem-solving competence and actual performance.* Paper presented at the Annual Convention of the Eastern Psychological Association, Baltimore, MD.

Ronan, G. F., Nezu, A. M., & Gibbs, M. S. (1986, April). *On the relationship between mood and social problem solving.* Paper presented at the 57th annual meeting of the Eastern Psychological Association, New York, NY.

Ronan, G. F., Senn, J., Date, A. L., Maurer, L., House, K., Carrroll, J., et al. (1996). Personal problem-solving scoring of TAT responses: Known-groups validation. *Journal of Personality Assessment, 67,* 641–653.

Rotter, J. B. (1946). Thematic Apperception Test: suggestions for administration and interpretation. *Journal of Personality, 15,* 70–92.

Sacco, W. P., & Hokanson, J. E. (1978). Expectancies of success and anagram performance of depressives in public and private settings. *Journal of Abnormal Psychology, 87,* 122–130.

Sarason, I. G., Johnson, J. H., & Siegal, J. M. (1978). Assessing the impact of life change: Development of the Life Experiences Survey. *Journal of Consulting and Clinical Psychology, 46,* 932–946.

Schafer, R. (l948). *The clinical application of psychological tests: Diagnostic summaries and case studies.* New York: International Universities Press.

Scheier, M. F., & Carver, C. S. (1992). Effects of optimism on psychological and physical well-being: Theoretical overview and empirical update. *Cognitive Therapy and Research, 16,* 201–228.

Semenoff, B. (1976). *Projective techniques.* New York: Wiley.

Shapiro, J., Gilborn, L., & Grolnic, J. (Eds.) (1991). *A guide to the data resources at the Henry A. Murray Research Center.* Cambridge, MA: Henry A. Murray Research Center at Radcliffe College.

Shavelson, R. J., & Webb, N. M. (1991). *Generalizability theory: A primer.* Newbury Park, CA: Sage Publications.

Shneidman, E. S. (1951). *Thematic test analysis.* New York: Grune & Straton.

Shon, S. P., & Ya, D. Y. (1982). Asian families. In M. McGoldrick, J. K. Pearce, & J. Giordano (Eds.), *Ethnicity and family therapy* (pp. 208–228). New York: Guilford.

Sifneos, P. E. (1969). Short-term anxiety provoking psychotherapy: An emotional problem solving technique. *Seminars in Psychiatry, 1,* 389–398.

Singer, M. T., & Wynne, L. C. (1966). Principles of scoring communication defects and deviances in parents of schizophrenics: Rorschach and TAT scoring manuals. *Psychiatry, 29,* 260–288.

Silverton, L. (1991). *Problem Experiences Checklist.* Los Angeles: Western Psychological Services.

Sitkin, S. B., & Weingart, L. R. (1995). Determinants of risky decision-making behavior: A test of the mediating role of risk perception and propensity. *Academy of Management Journal, 38,* 1573–1592.

Shneidman, E. S. (1951). *Thematic test analysis.* New York: Grune and Stratton.

Sobel, H. J. (1981). Projective methods of cognitive analysis. In T. V. Merluzzi, C. R. Glass, & M. Genest (Eds.), *Cognitive Assessment* (pp. 127–148). New York: Guilford.

Spangler, W. D. (l992). Validity of questionnaire and TAT measures of need for achievement: Two meta-analyses. *Psychological Bulletin, 112,* 140–154.

Spliberger, C. D. (1883). *Manual for the State-Trait Anxiety Inventory.* Palo Alto, CA: Consulting Psychologist Press.

Spivack, G., & Platt, J. J. (1975). *Manual for the Means-Ends Problem-Solving Procedure (MEPS): A measure of interpersonal cognitive problem-solving.* Philadelphia: Hahnemann Community Mental Health/Mental Retardation Center.

Spivack, G., Platt, J., & Shure, M. (1976). *The problem solving approach to adjustment.* San Francisco, CA: Jossey-Bass.

Stein, M. I. (1955). *The Thematic Apperception Test: An introductory manual for clinical use with adults.* Cambridge, MA: Addison-Wesley.

Suedfeld, P., Tetlock, P. E., & Streufert, S. (1992). Conceptual/integrative complexity. In C. P. Smith (Ed.), *Motivation and personality: Handbook of thematic content analysis* (pp. 393–400). New York: Cambridge University Press.

Thomas, A. D., & Dudeck, S. Z. (1985). Interpersonal affect in Thematic Apperception Test responses. *Journal of Personality Assessment, 49,* 30–36.

Tomkins, S. S. (1947). *The Thematic Apperception Test: The theory and technique of interpretation.* New York: Grune & Straton.

Tubbs, M. E., & Dahl, J. G. (1992). An examination of an individual's information processing in the formation of goal commitment judgments. *Journal of Psychology, 126,* 181–188.

Veroff, J. (1992). A scoring manual for power motive. In C. P. Smith (Ed.), *Motivation and personality: Handbook of thematic content analysis* (pp. 286–300). New York: Cambridge University Press.

Veroff, J., Douvan, E., & Kulka, A. (1981). *The inner American*. New York: Basic Books.

Viney, L. L. (1996). *Personal construct therapy: A handbook*. Norwood, NJ: Ablex Publishing.

Watzlawick, P., Weakland, J., & Fisch, R. (1974). *Change: Principles of problem formation and problem resolution*. New York: W. W. Norton.

Wechsler, D. (1981). *Wechsler Adult Intelligence Scale-Revised*. New York: The Psychological Corporation.

Westen, D., Lohr, N., Silk, K., Gold, L, & Kerber, K. (1990). Object relations and social cognition in borderlines, major depressives, and normals: A Thematic Apperception Test analysis. *Psychological Assessment, 2*, 355–364.

Westen, D., Lohr, N., Silk, K., Kerber, K., & Goodrich, R. (1985). *Object relations and social cognition TAT scoring manual*. Ann Arbor: University of Michigan.

Willis, M. H., & Blaney, P. H. (1978). Three tests of the learned helplessness model of depression. *Journal of Abnormal Psychology, 87*, 131–136.

Winter, D. G. (1973). *The power motive*. New York: Free Press.

Yerkes, R. M., & Dodson, J. D. (1908). The relation of strength of stimulus to rapidity of habit formation. *Journal of Comparative Neurology and Psychology, 18*, 459–482.

Ziegler, R. (2002). *The efficacy of neuropsychological measures in the prediction of social problem solving: Self-report versus performance*. Unpublished master's thesis, Central Michigan University.

11

CHAPTER

Scoring Manual for Personal Problem-Solving System—Revised

George F. Ronan and Margaret S. Gibbs

Abstract

The Personal Problem-Solving System-Revised (PPSS-R) consists of four components: story design (four elements); story orientation (four elements); story solution; and story resolution (four elements). The typical format is to administer and score three Thematic Apperception Test (TAT) cards. The PPSS-R consists of 13 elements. Twelve elements are rated to describe each story using a five-point scale, and one element is based on the counting of story solutions. Information on administering the TAT cards, scoring criteria, methodological considerations, and practice stories are presented in this chapter.

Administration

Format

Either standard or Personal Problem-Solving System-Revised (PPSS-R) instructions can be employed. Standard instructions are listed in the original Thematic Apperception Test (TAT) Manual (Murray, 1943, p. 3). Unpublished data from our lab revealed that altering the instructional set did not influence PPSS-R scores but did result in TAT responses that were rated as easier to score. The suggested PPSS-R instructions are listed as follows:

> This is a problem-solving task. I have some pictures I am going to show you. For each picture identify the main character and describe what his or her problem might be. Develop a story around this problem. Be sure to note how the problem developed, what is happening

TABLE 11.1 Typical Problems Elicited for Six TAT Cards

Card	Problem Themes
1	Interplay between desires and obligations
2	Coping with difficult family relationships or environmental constraints
4	Resolving heterosocial conflicts
7 BM	Interacting with a male authority
10	Displaying affect in a supportive relationship
13 MF	Managing intimate heterosexual relationships

> now, how the problem will be resolved, and what the outcome might be. Say what the main character and the other people in the story are thinking and feeling. The type of problem you develop is up to you.

TAT cards are most often individually administered, with the verbal responses recorded and subsequently coded. Some of our research has used group administration of the TAT cards. That is, TAT cards were administered to small groups of participants using a slide projector and a standard white screen. Participants were typically allowed about 10 minutes to compose a written response to each card. Both group and individual administrations have resulted in similar scores.

Stimuli

Though not all TAT cards are equally likely to elicit an interpersonally oriented response (cf. card 2 vs. card 19), many do seem to tap this domain (Alvarado, 1994; Barends, Westen, Leigh, Silbert, & Byers, 1990; Leigh, Westen, Barends, & Mendel, 1992; Thomas & Duceck, 1985; Veroff, Douvan, & Kulka, 1981). Results both from previous research (e.g., Campus, 1976; Holt, 1978) and from data collected in our labs were used to develop the typical problem situations generated in response to the six frequently administered TAT cards that have normative data available (Table 11.1).

□ Scoring Process

The first task is to identify the main character and the main story problem. The main character typically plays the biggest role in the story. Counting the number of words associated with each character can help to reduce uncertainty. When identifying the main problem, it is important to separate historical background from the problem itself. The main problem typically reflects the current concern of the main character. Answering the following questions can help to clarify the main problem: (1) Who has the main problem? (2) When/where is it a problem? (3) What is the main problem? (4) Why is it a problem? Counting the number of words used to describe each problem can help to identify the main problem when multiple, unrelated problems are present.

TABLE 11.2 PPSS Scoring Sheet

Date: ____________ **Participant Number:** __________ **Card Number:** __________

Main Character: ____

Problem: ____

Story Solutions: ____

Story Resolution: ____

I. Story Design

1._______ **2.**________ **3.**________ **4.**_______ **SD (1 + 2 + 3 + 4 / 4)**_______

II. Story Orientation

1._______ **2.**________ **3.**________ **4.**_______ **SO (1 + 2 + 3 + 4 / 4)**_______

III. Story Solution

_______________ **SS** ___________________

IV. Story Resolution

1._______ **2.**________ **3.**________ **4.**_______ **SR (1 + 2 + 3 + 4 / 4)**_______

V. PPSS TAT Card Total

Total (SD + SO + SS + SR) ___________

The scoring criteria are applied using the main character and the main problem situation. Though whole numbers are used to designate response options (–1, 0, 1, 2, 3), the use of a mid point (e.g., 1.5) is acceptable. Table 11.2 presents a data sheet for recording scores, and the specific scoring criteria are presented in the next section.

Scoring Criteria

Story Design

(1) *Does the story problem contain a past, present, and future?* This element assesses the degree to which participants formulated a story with a past, present, and future. "John was sad yesterday when he found out he had been drafted into the military, but now he is angry. John will feel better tonight when he discusses these concerns with his wife." *John was sad yesterday when he found out he had been drafted into the military* would be scored for past. *John is now angry* would be scored for present. *John will feel better tonight when he discusses these concerns with his wife* is scored as future. Thinking about the past or future counts as a past or future.

–1 Present state of affairs only: The description of the story problem only contains a present; there is no other time specified. (The girl is thinking about her father working in the field.)

0 Past and present state of affairs only: The story problem includes a past and present. (Her parents spent their life working hard to keep the farm productive, and, as a result, they have a nice farm.)

1 Present and future state of affairs only: The story includes what is going on currently and what will happen in the future. (The girl is wondering whether to work on the farm or go to school; she goes to school.)

2 Past, present, and future state of affairs: The story contains all three types of statements. (She is upset about having to work on the farm yesterday and is wondering what her teacher will say after she tells her that she did not study for the exam.)

3 Past state of affairs longer than one day, present state of affairs, and a detailed future greater than one week. (Two days ago he found out his mother is once again pregnant; he is upset, and this motivates him to graduate and become a family planning counselor.)

(2) *What is presented as the cause of the story problem or trouble?* The goal is to assess the degree to which the story problem derives from a reasonable interpretation of the story components. If there is more than one problem, then choose the problem most emphasized. The one most emphasized can be determined by rereading the story or counting the number of words used to describe each problem. Personal deficiencies result from making internal and stable attributions for a problem: "He can't learn to play the violin because he is not talented enough." Concerns that result from personal deficiencies cannot be easily remedied. Personal obstacles result from making internal and unstable causal ascriptions for a problem. That is, the person could alter or change the problem: "He wants to play the violin well, but he needs more lessons." Environmental obstacles and deficiencies are scored when the reasons for a problem relate to a suboptimal environment: "The family was too poor to send him to violin lessons." Personal and environmental obstacles are scored when the problem is attributed to both personal variables and environmental factors.

–1 Personal deficiency: The problem results from an unchangeable personal deficiency. (She cannot finish school because she is not smart enough.)

0 Not specified: No causal ascription is presented.

1 Personal obstacle: The problem results from a personal obstacle that can be overcome. (She was worried that she would not find a job because she lacked computer skills, so she decided to take classes.)

2 Environmental obstacle or deficiency: The problem deals with an environmental concern. (The family was starving due to the drought and the resulting crop failure.)

3 Personal and environmental concerns: The problem stems from both personal and environmental obstacles. (She had difficulty at school because her parents made her work on the farm and she did not study enough.)

(3) *Indicate the level of distorted beliefs, appraisals, and assumptions about the story problem.* The goal is to assess the degree to which the story problem derives from a reasonable interpretation of the story components. Illogical connections between elements of the story or the lack of connection between behaviors and consequences

are scored as distorted. Descriptions of feelings are not typically rated. For example, if feelings attributed to the main character are irrational (e.g., "He was so angry he felt like killing him") and the main character acts rationally (e.g., discusses his anger with the person), then the irrational feelings should not be scored as a faulty appraisal.

–1 - - - - - - - - - -	0 - - - - - - - - - -	1 - - - - - - - - - -	2 - - - - - - - - - -	3
Poor	Can't Score	Fair	Typical	Exceptional

- Unpredictable reactions typically reflect distorted beliefs, appraisals, or assumptions.
- Impulsive behaviors frequently stem from faulty problem appraisals. (The woman in this story is trying to talk him out of going off to fight the terrorists so he kills her.)
- Overly pessimistic or punitive conceptualizations often stem from distorted thinking.
- Loss of distance (e.g., use of personal pronouns) often involves distorted appraisals or assumptions.
- If nothing can be done to make the problem better (lots of hopelessness or helplessness), it is probably a faulty appraisal.
- If the proposed solutions do not match the problem, it is scored as distorted.
- If the behavior and the results of the behavior do not match, it is scored as distorted.

(4) *Indicate how well the story problem is integrated and detailed.* Integration involves forming a connection among the story characters, whereas detailed responding requires the use of all card elements (e.g., environment, facial expressions, pictures on the wall). An exceptionally well-detailed and integrated story problem uses all the characters, contains depth, and coherently flows from beginning to end. Typical stories are reasonably detailed and integrated, but often a story character or a part of the problem is not addressed. Serious card misperception or story distortions typically result in poor integration and details. Well-integrated and detailed stories have organizational complexity (i.e., all the story characters interacting) and cognitive complexity (i.e., sensitivity to each character's perspective).

–1 - - - - - - - - - -	0 - - - - - - - - - -	1 - - - - - - - - - -	2 - - - - - - - - - -	3
Poor	Can't Score	Fair	Typical	Exceptional

- Incoherent stories are not well integrated. (The problem is that he doesn't like his niece, so she has to go to school.)
- Pollyannish stories have positive endings but lack details that would connect the beginning with the ending. (The girl was feeling sad about the few opportunities she will have in life. The story ends with her becoming wealthy.)
- Poorly integrated and detailed responses are often just card descriptions.

Story Orientation

(1) *How positively motivating is the problem situation?* This question is answered by focusing on the reaction to the problem. Although the problem situation may be dreadful, it is the reaction to the problem that is the focus. For example, if the main character loses his or her job, he or she may view the situation as insurmountable and wallow in despair (scored as not positively motivating) or view it as a way to explore career options and develop a plan to find another job (very motivating). If positive steps are taken toward dealing with the problem, it should be scored as positively motivating. Immoral reactions should not be scored as positively motivating.

–1 Not at all positively motivating: The main character reacts in a negative manner or does nothing to solve the problem. (Because they could not agree on who would get custody of the dog, he decided to shoot it.)

0 Not specified: Motivation cannot be determined.

1 Slightly motivating: The main character tries to do something to solve the problem. (Because they were having so many problems in their relationship, she decided to get away for the weekend.)

2 Moderately motivating: The main character addresses a significant component of the problem. (He decided to tell her how he felt about their relationship and to work with her to resolve their concerns.)

3 Very motivating: The main character addresses the entire problem and views the situation as an opportunity to explore new options. (They both realized they were not devoting enough attention to each other so they decided to reorganize their work and leisure schedules to place each other first.)

(2) *How likely is it that there will be an attempt to exert control over the problem?* Personal control is the willingness to do something about a situation. It does not necessarily relate to the effectiveness of the behavior. Even if the behavior seems wrongheaded or out of control, it is the fact that something is being done to change the situation that counts. If personal control is exerted but the problem still is not resolved, the score should reflect that personal control occurred. If the main character generates ideas about how the problem can be solved, but no future is presented, the generation of these ideas would count as personal control being exerted. If the main character opts to do nothing, then personal control was not exerted. (He decided he would wait and see what happens.)

–1 Not at all likely: The main character sees the situation as uncontrollable and nothing can be done. (Her life will always be the same and there is nothing she can do about it.)

0 Not specified: Personal control cannot be determined.

1 Somewhat likely: Story solutions are listed, but no outcome is presented; it is assumed the solutions would be implemented.

2 Moderately likely: Personal control is exerted, but the situation is not improved.

3 Extremely likely: Personal control is exerted, and the situation is improved.

(3) *How much confidence is demonstrated for dealing with the problem situation?* This element assesses the degree to which the main character believes in his or her ability to solve the problem. Statements such as, "He would ... but he doesn't think it will work ..." indicate a low level of confidence. Conversely, statements indicative of positive expectations convey a high degree of confidence: "She feels capable of dealing with ..." Story solutions that lead to a desired outcome imply a high degree of confidence.

–1 Not at all confident: Statements such as "He doesn't think he can handle it," or "She is certain that things won't get better."

0 Not specified: Level of confidence cannot be determined.

1 Slightly confident: Statements such as "He doesn't know if it'll work, but he'll try."

2 Moderately confident: Statements such as "She's pretty sure she can do it."

3 Extremely confident: Positive statements about being able to resolve the problem or if the problem is resolved.

(4) *Record the level of emotional distress.* The goal is to rate the degree to which emotional distress is hindering the resolution of the story problem. (She was so depressed that all she could do was cry.) Raters should not rely on the general tone of the story: If feelings are not mentioned, then this element should be scored 0. If the main character uses an emotional reaction to facilitate problem resolution, then a score of 3 should be assigned. (He thought about how sad he was at the thought of not seeing her for two weeks, and this helped him decide that he does love her.)

–1 High: A level of emotional distress wherein the main character is overwhelmed, making it unlikely that any action will be implemented.

0 Can't score: Emotions are not specified.

1 Medium: The main character appears upset, and there is only a slight chance the problem will be addressed.

2 Low: The main character is upset but still acts on the problem.

3 None: The main character demonstrates an emotional reaction and uses this to help solve the problem.

Story Solutions

Story solutions can address either the main problem or the main character's reaction to the main problem. Because the goal is to evaluate the person's ability to generate alternative story solutions, potential solutions generated by any story characters should be counted. Complex story solutions should be decomposed into discrete strategies. The goal is to count the number of story solutions generated regardless of whether they are effective or even implemented. Story solutions can be overt or covert. A score of 0 could result when the person does not specify any problem situation or the person develops a problem but fails to engage in any instrumental acts. (He feels depressed and there is nothing he can do.)

- Avoidance strategies are scored as story solutions. (He decided to avoid his friends.)
- Emotional symptoms are not story solutions. (He just felt depressed about the whole thing.)
- Deciding to go to someone for help is counted as an overt story solution. (John decided to talk with his best friend about the problem.)

Overt story solutions are action strategies for dealing with the problem. These instrumental acts alter the problem or the main character's reaction to the problem. Others easily observe overt story solutions. Story solutions of dubious value should still be counted. (He decided to pay his bills by winning money gambling at the local casino.) Actively avoiding the situation can be an overt story solution. (She went to the meeting so she would not have to deal with his complaining about plowing the fields.).

Covert story solutions are within person responses and, therefore, not readily observable by others. Covert solutions often alter perceptions of the problem rather than the problem itself. Thinking about the problem is scored as a covert story solution. "She did not know what to do, so she thought about it over breakfast" would be scored for thinking about the problem. Covert solutions often reframe the problem as less distressing. (She was upset that her boyfriend left her, but she feels better after deciding he was not such a great boyfriend after all.) Deciding to put up with the problem should be scored as a covert story solution. Contemplated action often involves both overt and covert solutions. "He thought about the problem and decided he could do three things. First ..." would be scored as one covert solution (thinking) and possibly three overt solutions (one point for each of the overt solutions).

Story Resolution

(1) *Rate the degree to which the story solutions minimize personal distress.* The focus is on story solutions. If no story solutions are implemented, then evaluate the best solution or set of solutions generated. The goal is to evaluate the degree to which the proposed story solutions decrease distress. "The boy decides to tell his parents that he does not like playing the violin and they respect his decision" is an example where personal distress is minimized. "The boy busted the strings to the violin so his parents get angry and use his allowance to buy new strings" is an example where personal distress is not minimized.

–1 Not at all: Personal distress is not reduced. (She knows all her dreams will never come true and she will never be able to do the things she wants.)

0 Not specified: The story does not mention personal distress or no story solutions are presented.

1 Somewhat: The story solution results in a temporary reduction of personal distress, but distress is likely to increase to presolution levels in the near future.

2 Moderately: There is a reduction in personal distress, but some less-than-presolution level of personal distress is likely to remain.

3 Extremely: Personal distress is eradicated, and there is no indication of future distress. (The girl decided to tell her parents that she does not want to live on the farm, and they respect her decision.)

(2) *Rate the degree to which the positive consequences for the main character outweigh the negative consequences.* Scoring is based on the generated story solutions. This element requires a cost–benefit analysis. A stated solution might resolve the problem, but the cost (e.g., impact on time, money, family, and environmental factors) may be greater than the potential benefit. If story solutions were not implemented, choose the best story solutions and estimate how much effort would be required to implement the solutions and solve the problem. If no solutions are generated the score would be *not specified.*

–1 Not at all: The costs (e.g., time, financial, emotional outlay) outweigh the possible benefits.

0 Not specified: No story solutions are specified.

1 Somewhat: The costs (e.g., time, financial, emotional outlay) for the main character equal the benefits.

2 Moderately: The positive consequences for the main character are a little better than the costs (e.g., time, financial, emotional outlay).

3 Extremely: The problem is resolved, and the positive consequences for the main character clearly outweigh the costs (e.g., time, financial, emotional outlay).

(3) *Rate the degree to which the story solutions deal with both short- and long-term goals.* Scoring is based on the generated story solutions. Typically, the implemented solutions are evaluated. If no story solutions are implemented, then evaluate the best solution or set of solutions generated.

–1 No goals are dealt with.

0 Only short-term goals are dealt with. (The boy busts the strings to the violin so his parents get angry and use his allowance to buy new strings.)

1 Short-term goals are more adequately addressed than long-term goals.

2 Long-term goals are more adequately addressed than short-term goals.

3 Both short- and long-term goals are adequately addressed.

(4) *Rate the degree to which the concerns are ameliorated.* This element requires an overall determination about whether the problem-solving goals were attained. This question taps the overall level of success in resolving the problem. It is analogous to answering the question, "Was there success in bringing about problem resolution?" If no outcome is specified score *not specified.*

–1 Not at all: The problem remains the same.

0 Not specified: No outcome is specified.

1 Somewhat: The problem is partially resolved (less than half resolved).

2 Moderately: The problem is mostly resolved (more than 50% and less than 100% resolved).

3 Extremely: The problem is completely resolved.

Calculating Scores

Four component scores and a total per-card score are obtained for each TAT card. Three of the component scores—story orientation, story design, and story resolution—are derived by summing the scores for each of the elements associated with that component and dividing by four. The story solutions score is derived from adding the number of story solutions generated. Per-card scores are obtained by adding the four component scores. Per-card component scores are added to obtain aggregate component scores. Aggregated component scores are added to obtain a total PPSS-R score.

Which scores—component, per-card, aggregate, or total—should be interpreted? Aggregate component scores are useful for assessing specific problem-solving skills in clinical settings. For instance, some individuals may evince deficits in orienting to problems, generating solutions, and so on. Aggregate scores can be used to determine what types of interventions may be most helpful. Several published studies provide support for aggregating component scores across three TAT cards. We expect, however, that for research purposes the PPSS-R will most often be used to assess general levels of personal problem-solving skills; therefore, the total PPSS-R score is likely to be most often used.

☐ Practice Stories

Although considerable effort has been devoted to ensuring the clarity of the PPSS-R scoring criteria, practice with the scoring system is needed to obtain consistent interrater agreement. There are likely to be considerable individual differences in the amount of time required to achieve high levels of agreement; however, the typical format is to (1) have raters read the manual; (2) jointly discuss the scoring of 12 stories; (3) independently score 12 stories; (4) discuss discrepancies in scoring; and (5) independently score an additional 12 stories. There are various strategies for selecting scored examples. The most popular approach is to select only stories that reflect prototypical scoring dilemmas.

Unfortunately, the use of prototypical stories often results in the presentation of atypical protocols that do not readily generalize to the types of stories normally encountered. This section contains stories to TAT cards 1, 2, 4, 7BM, 10, and 13MF. One subject was randomly selected from each of five different databases. Their responses to TAT cards 1, 2, and 4 are presented here. Responses from two participants, each from a different database, were used to provide practice stories for TAT cards 7BM, 10, and 13MF. Each practice story also identifies the main story character, the main problem, the story solutions, and the story resolution. Familiarity with deconstructing a story in this manner is crucial to the successful application of the specific scoring criteria. Scoring the stories presented should help to promote mastery of the scoring system.

(1) Card 1: Student. His parents forced the boy to take violin lessons. Right now he feels tired and bored of the violin; he wants to be outside playing like his friends. This boy is angry with his parents for making him practice so much and not being able to do things that are more fun. He feels he needs to let his parents know that he doesn't want to play the violin anymore, but doesn't know how. I believe that he'll let his parents know he wants to quit, and they'll understand.

Main Character: Boy

Story Problem: Does not want to play the violin, but parents want him to

Story Solution: Thinks about telling his parents, lets his parents know he wants to quit

Story Resolution: They'll understand

(2) Card 1: Participant. This is a picture of a little boy who seems to be distraught over the task of practicing the violin. From the look on his face it appears that he doesn't want to, yet he must. Hopefully he can express to his parent or teacher what he is feeling and perhaps come to the compromise of time for practice and time for play.

Main Character: Boy

Story Problem: Distraught over violin playing

Story Solution: Express his feelings to his parents, express feelings to teacher

(3) Card 1: Client. He is feeling upset. It looks like something just happened to his violin and that he's upset about that. He looks like something happened to his violin. He looks like he'll probably get it fixed. He's thinking about what happened to his violin. Somehow he'll get it fixed. He's feeling frustrated. He looks like he's thinking about what to do.

Main Character: Boy

Story Problem: Violin is broken

Story Solution: Thinking about the problem

Story Resolution: He'll get it fixed

(4) Card 1: CMHC. It's a little boy looking at a violin, and he's wondering if he can play it. He looks like he thinks it's too hard for him. He looks like he's feeling kind of down. He's going to have to pick it up and try to play it. It almost looks like he got hit. There's a spot of something by his mouth. Maybe someone hit him. I think if he tries to play, it will work. I don't know though.

Main Character: Boy

Story Problem: Insecurity about playing the violin

Story Solution: Think about playing it, try to play it

Story Resolution: It works

(5) Card 1: Inmate. He has been told that he has to take violin lessons, and he does not want to. He is thinking about what his friends are doing right now.

Main Character: Boy

Story Problem: Doesn't want to take violin lessons

Story Solution: Thinks about what his friends are doing

Story Resolution: None

(6) Card 2: Student. The girl with the books is picturing how her future could be. She fantasizes that she'll have a hard working husband and a beautiful farm. She wants to have many children to love and take care of. For now she just wants to get finished with her schooling and get into the real world.

Main Character: Girl with the books

Story Problem: Deciding what she will do with her future

Story Solution: Fantasize

Story Resolution: Finish school and get into the real world

(7) Card 2: Participant. An unusual circumstance, this picture shows a scene from the past. Fields are being plowed manually. What is unusual is the woman up front holding the books. She is being educated. It may be her parents' wishes that she be educated in hopes that she'll have a better future. The woman seems to portray a look of guilt because she's unable to help with the farming chores and sees how tired her mother is. However, the man in the picture appears to have a strong back. She shouldn't worry; he's there to help with the farming.

Main Character: Woman holding books

Story Problem: Feels guilt because she is unable to help on the farm

Story Solution: Man helps with the farming

Story Resolution: She shouldn't worry

(8) Card 2: Client. The girl looks lonely. Looks like this guy just took off on her with his horse. Looks like his mother is just standing there watching everything. She (girl) looks lost. Thinking she might not see him again and feeling sad. He's leaving. Mother looks like she is proud of whatever happened. The way she's standing, she's proud of whatever happened. The guy just blew the girl off. Might have been a fight or something. I don't think she said a word.

Main Character: Girl

Story Problem: They had a fight

Story Solution: Guy took off, thinking that she might not see him again

Story Resolution: She feels sad

(9) Card 2: CMHC. It looks like a young girl going to school. They are working the fields. She looks like she is wondering if she should go to school or stay at home and work. She's deep in thought wondering what to do. I don't know how she decided, but it looks like she made up her mind because she's got her books. In those days they often had to stay home and work and only go to school in the winter. She's feeling kind of sad because she can't do both.

Main Character: Girl

Story Problem: She's torn between going to school and working in the fields

Story Solution: Thinks deeply, makes up her mind

Story Resolution: She is sad because she can't do both

(10) Card 2: Inmate. The girl is worried about her folks. They do not understand that she wants to go to school to learn more. She wants to go so that she can have a better life then what they had.

Main Character: Girl

Story Problem: Worried about her folks

Story Solution: Thinks about problem

Story Resolution: None

(11) Card 4: Student. These people are sitting at home just talking about things. They both are single. She doesn't want it that way, but he does. The closer she tries to get to him, the farther he backs away. He doesn't want to give a commitment, he's just

not ready. This man loves her, but only at his convenience. When he wants to see her or talk to her, he does; other times he won't do either for weeks. She wants him to ask her to marry him but realizes that this will never happen. She breaks up with him and ends up marrying someone else a year later.

Main Character: Woman

Story Problem: She wants a commitment and he does not want to make one

Story Solution: Talking about things, she tries to get closer, she breaks up with him, he relates to her at his convenience

Story Resolution: She marries someone else a year later

(12) Card 4: Participant. An angry man being held by a woman. My guess is that he's out for revenge and she's trying to prevent him from getting into any trouble. He's trying not to be influenced by avoiding her gaze. Her eyes look soft and sincerely concerned. Perhaps by speaking calmly and softly, she can prevent him from leaving.

Main Character: Woman

Story Problem: He wants to get revenge, but she doesn't want him to leave

Story Solution: She holds him, he avoids her gaze, she speaks calmly and softly

Story Resolution: She can prevent him from leaving

(13) Card 4: Client. Looks like the girl is trying to keep the guy from going out. He's not paying any attention. They got into an arguement [*sic*] of some kind—must have been the girl's fault. Looks like she's trying to apologize somehow and get him to stay, but he's not listening. He just wants to leave and not hear any more about it. She's not feeling good about what happened; he probably won't come back now. He'll walk away and won't come back. She'll be upset for awhile and then live her life.

Main Character: Woman

Story Problem: Argument

Story Solution: Trying to keep guy from going out, apologizes, he just wants to leave, he'll walk away and not come back

Story Resolution: She'll be upset for awhile then live her life

(14) Card 4: CMHC. It must be a husband and a wife. It looks like he is angry. It looks like she is trying to get him to not be angry. It looks like he is going to hit somebody. He's really angry. I don't know about what—maybe at his kids or something. He looks really angry. She looks like she is trying to talk to him out of being angry. I don't think she'll succeed because he's too mad. He's going to take it out on somebody.

Main Character: Couple

Story Problem: Coping with his anger

Story Solution: Tries to talk to him

Story Resolution: She fails, and he takes it out on someone

(15) Card 4: Inmate. The man is an alcoholic and has drunk his life away. The lady is his wife or sister and wants nothing more than to help him. At this point he is not listening. She is patient, and in time he will listen.

Main Character: Man

Story Problem: Drinking his life away

Story Solution: Lady tries to help him

Story Resolution: In time he will listen

(16) Card 7BM: Student. The boy and his father are at the funeral of the boy's best friend. We will call the boy Tom. Tom doesn't want to cry because he thinks he will appear not to be a man. His father explains to him that you must cry to release your feelings. His father tells him of a time when he was young. He was a football player, and they lost the championship game. He and some other players cried, and some other players laughed at them. Then when they looked at the coach, he too was crying. His father tells Tom that someday he will die and he hopes Tom will be man enough to cry or else he will never be able to deal with it. Tom fights the tears, but then he begins to cry. He realizes that if his friend could see him crying he would feel good to know that Tom cared that much about him to cry in front of everyone. Tom feels better about himself and hopes that when he dies someone will cry for him.

Main Character: Tom

Story Problem: Coping with grief

Story Solution: Father explains he must cry to release his feelings, father tells him a story, Tom begins to cry, he realizes that it shows how much he cared

Story Resolution: Tom feels better about himself

(17) Card 7BM: Client. Two guys are talking about the problems they have at work. They have to learn to do their job more efficiently, more competitively. Another company came to town, and there's a little competition. So there's a new kid on the block, so to speak. The older gray-haired gentleman tells the younger one that he has to come up with new ideas to make their company more efficient. He trusts him and reassures him. He tells him that he can do this and wishes him well. He wants to hear new ideas from him as soon as possible. The younger person is glad that his boss

gives him the challenge. He is happy that this boss thinks he's responsible enough to make the necessary changes to get good results.

Main Character: Younger guy

Story Problem: Dealing with job demands

Story Solution: Boss is reassuring, boss asks for new ideas

Story Resolution: Happy that boss thinks he can do it

(18) Card 10: Student. This man is embracing his new wife because he loves her and she needs his strength right now. She has gone through a traumatic experience and broke down and told her new husband what happened to her when she was a young girl. Someone hurt her very bad, and she could never trust anyone to tell them. But she trusts her husband and feels that to get over it she must tell him, and he can help her. He is very understanding and comforting. He is warm and sensitive as she cries her heart out. He tells her that no one can ever hurt her again because he will protect her always. She trusts him, but she is still afraid and torn up inside. She has taken the first step in overcoming her fears. He kisses her on the forehead and holds her until morning comes.

Main Character: Wife

Story Problem: Coping with past trauma

Story Solution: She tells what happened to her, he is understanding and comforting, he is warm and sensitive, she cries her heart out, he kisses her on the forehead, he holds her till morning

Story Resolution: She has taken the first step but is still torn up inside

(19) Card 10: Client. This elderly couple is just going to sleep. Their children or grandchildren visited them earlier that evening, and they're just talking to themselves about what a fine family they had and how healthy their children and grandchildren are. They're patting each other on the back for raising such a wonderful family. This woman will call up the daughter or daughter-in-law, whichever the case might be, and tell her how much she enjoyed the visit. She wishes them to visit again as soon as possible. Then they will go to bed and fall asleep.

Main Character: Elderly couple

Story Problem: Want family to visit again

Story Solution: Tell them how much they enjoyed visit

Story Resolution: Go to bed and fall asleep

(20) Card 13MF: Student. The man comes to his girlfriend's room only to find her unconscious and the victim of a sick man's sexual pleasures. She has lost a lot of blood as a result of a blow to her skull. This is probably why she is unconscious. He cannot tell how long she has been lying there, but he guesses the incident happened early in the evening and it is now the next morning. He covers her body and turns his back because he cannot look at his beautiful maiden. He cannot believe what this evil person has put her through. He calls for an ambulance and waits for it to arrive. He holds her and caresses her hair, telling her how pleasant and safe he wants to make her life. He promises her he will take care of her forever if she will only survive. He speaks through his tears as if she can hear him, and he prays to God to help her. He tells her justice will be taken onto whomever did this to her.

Main Character: Man

Story Problem: Girlfriend was assaulted

Story Solution: Covers her body, calls for an ambulance, holds her and caresses her hair, tells her how pleasant and safe he'll make her, promises he'll take care of her, prays to God, tells her justice will be taken

Story Resolution: None

(21) Card 13MF: Client. Looks like this man is just getting up to go to work. His wife is still in the bed. He's going off to work. He'll go, have a good day of work, and come back home in the evening. He might wish that his wife got up with him to walk him to the door. But he understands that she has a family and a lot of things to do. So, it's not a big deal that she gets more sleep.

Main Character: Man

Story Problem: Wishes his wife would get up with him in the morning

Story Solution: He understands

Story Resolution: She continues to sleep in the morning

☐ Expert Scoring

Table 11.3 provides PPSS-R element scores for each story listed in the previous section. These scores were generated by the first author. Several of his graduate students served as coraters.

Table 11.3 Sample Story Scores

#	Card	Subject	Element Score												
			SD1	SD2	SD3	SD4	SO1	SO2	SO3	SO4	SS	SR1	SR2	SR3	SR4
1	1	Student	2	3	2	2	2	3	2	2	2	3	3	3	3
2	1	Participant	1	3	3	2	3	3	3	2	2	3	3	3	3
3	1	Client	2	2	1	1	1	3	2	2	1	3	3	1	2.5
4	1	CMHC	2	1	1	1	1	2.5	1	2	2	2	2	1	2
5	1	Inmate	0	3	3	–1	1	1	0	1	1	1	1	0	0
6	2	Student	1	1	1	1	1	2	1	2	1	1	1	2	1
7	2	Participant	0	3	1	2	1	0	0	1	1	1.5	1	2	1
8	2	Client	0	1	1	1	–1	1	0	–1	2	1	–1	–1	1
9	2	CMHC	1	3	2	1	1	2	1	1	2	1	1	1	1
10	2	Inmate	2	3	2	1	1	1	0	1	1	1	1.5	0	0
11	4	Student	3	3	1	2	2	3	3	2	4	2	2	2	2
12	4	Participant	1	3	2	2	2	3	2	2	3	2	2	1	2
13	4	Client	2	1	1	2	–1	2	1	–1	4	–1	–1	–1	–1
14	4	CMHC	2	3	1	2	1	2	–1	–1	1	–1	–1	0	–1
15	4	Inmate	2	3	2	1	1	1	0	1	1	1	1.5	0	0
16	7BM	Student	2	3	2	2.5	3	3	3	3	4	3	3	3	3
17	7BM	Client	2	2	2	1	0	0	2	3	2	1	1	1	1
18	10	Student	0	1	1	2.5	2	2	1	2	6	1	2	1	1
19	10	Client	2	1	3	2	1	1	2	3	1	2	2	3	0
20	13MF	Student	0	2	2	2.5	2	1	1	2	7	1	2	3	0
21	13MF	Client	2	3	2	1	1	2	1	2	1	1	1	1	1

References

Alvardo, N. (1994). Empirical validity of the Thematic Apperception Test. *Journal of Personality Assessment, 63,* 59–79.

Barends, A., Westen, D., Leigh, J., Silbert, D., & Byers, S. (1990). Assessing affect–tone of relationship paradigms from TAT and interview data. *Psychological Assessment, 2,* 329–332.

Leigh, J., Westen, D., Barends, A., & Mandel, M. J. (1992). The assessment of complexity of representations of people using the TAT and interview data. *Journal of Personality, 60,* 809–837.

Murray, H. A. (1943). *Thematic Apperception Test Manual.* Cambridge, MA: Harvard University Press.

Thomas, A. D., & Dudeck, S. Z. (1985). Interpersonal affect in Thematic Apperception Test responses. *Journal of Personality Assessment, 49,* 30–36.

Veroff, J., Douvan, E., & Kulka, A. (1981). *The Inner American.* New York: Basic Books.

12

CHAPTER

The Picture Projection Test

Barry Ritzler

Abstract

The Picture Projection Test (PPT) was developed as an alternative to the Thematic Apperception Test (TAT) to provide more contemporary picture stimuli with more characters depicted and more positive emotional content. Early studies indicated that the new method yielded a wider range of scores and better discrimination in depressed–nondepressed and psychotic–nonpsychotic comparisons. A coding system, practical for clinicians, was used for the early studies and was further tested by a dissertation comparing the TAT and the Rorschach Comprehensive System (RCS) and a recent study comparing the PPT with the RCS in which the PPT yielded higher correlations than the TAT study. This chapter includes a description of a recent revision of the PPT with nine painted pictures and a more extensive scoring system.

Description of System

Conceptual Framework

The TAT (Murray, 1938), the most popular apperception test for personality assessment, was developed to provide "a method of revealing to the trained interpreter some of the dominant drives, emotions, sentiments, complexes and conflicts of a personality" (Murray, 1943, p. 1). It was originally conceptualized as a projective technique "to expose the underlying inhibited tendencies which the subject, or patient, is not willing to admit, or can not admit because he is unconscious of them" (ibid.). Murray initially intended the method "as a preface to a series of psychotherapeutic interviews or to a short psychoanalysis" (ibid.), but he also suggested that it could be very effectively combined with the Rorschach.

Murray's (1943, p. 1) rationale for developing an apperception test was that "[such] stories ... often reveal significant components of personality [because of] two psychological tendencies: the tendency of people to interpret an ambiguous human situation in conformity with their past experiences and present wants [and to] draw on the fund of their experiences and express their sentiments and needs, whether conscious or unconscious."

Unfortunately, the TAT has become the poor stepsister of personality assessment. In the clinical arena, its more empirically glamorous siblings—the Rorschach and the Minnesota Multiphasic Personality Inventory (MMPI)—get much more attention and are widely recognized as very effective for use with clients. However, the TAT has a notable number of interested suitors who see potential in the method for obtaining information about personality characteristics and functioning not directly obtainable from the Rorschach or MMPI. Nevertheless, lacking the trappings of a clinically feasible scoring system and extensive norms, the TAT essentially has been relegated to a sort of scullery maid's role in personality assessment.

Perhaps because it has gone so long without these trappings, the TAT has become somewhat dingy and out of date. Many of the stimulus pictures depict clothing and hairstyles from the late 1930s and early 1940s (the period when the pictures were selected by Murray) and lack vibrancy and activity. For instance, there are no smiles on the faces of the figures in the 29 TAT pictures (card 16 is blank). Furthermore, the postures of the people in the pictures and the lighting effects are low key and gloomy. It would seem that the TAT would benefit from a fairy godmother makeover to give it more vitality and brightness to provide a more balanced set of pictures potentially covering a wider range of human situations and relationships.

The Tell-Me-A-Story (TEMAS) (Costantino, Malgady, & Rogler, 1986) is an example of a newer apperception test that involves more active and vibrant scenes. However, the TEMAS is primarily designed for use with children and adolescents and differs so much from the TAT in its colorful, cartoon-like art that it may have lost some of the coverage of important adult issues that arise in stories elicited by the TAT cards.

PPT Stimuli

A number of years ago, an attempt was made to develop an apperception method as an alternative to the TAT that provided a wider range of pictures (i.e., more smiles, more vibrant activity, and more depicted characters) while maintaining a focus on adult issues. Ritzler, Sharkey, and Chudy (1980) selected pictures from the Metropolitan Museum of Art's Family of Man collection (1955) to make a 20-card alternative apperception method. This initial set of pictures was referred to as the Southern Mississippi Thematic Apperception Test (SM-TAT) because of the setting in which it was developed—the University of Southern Mississippi.

Encouraged by the empirical results from initial research on the SM-TAT (see section on research evidence), I attempted to obtain permission from copyright holders to use the selected Family of Man pictures to make a set of pictures that might be distributed for clinical and research use. For nearly every photograph, the permission was refused or the costs of obtaining the rights to reproduce the pictures were prohibitive. Consequently, Ritzler and Alter (1987) solicited photographs from amateur photographers with the incentive of a more reasonable fee for permission to reproduce. In response to ads placed in local shoppers' guides, the author received more than 1,000 photographs. They selected 20 of these for an experimental set of pictures and renamed the method the Picture Projection Test (PPT). The initial studies conducted on the SM-TAT were replicated with the PPT with similar encouraging results (see following).

For many years, the PPT lay dormant. Lately, however, the method has been dusted off and a new study was conducted comparing TAT measures with Rorschach Comprehensive System variables as criteria. Initially, the renewed interest in the PPT was stirred by a dissertation comparing the TAT with the Rorschach Comprehensive System that yielded modestly significant correlations between the TAT and the Rorschach (Silberman, 1998). This dissertation is presented in this chapter, followed by a study comparing the PPT with the same Rorschach variables that obtained more favorable results.

During the study comparing the 20 PPT photographs with the Rorschach, it became apparent that some problems remained with the method. For one, 20 pictures made for a very long testing period—one that would not be very feasible for clinical settings and time constraints. For another, the black-and-white photographs still lacked some of the ambiguity and vibrancy thought desirable for an ideal apperception test. Consequently, a new set of nine paintings based on the most promising of the 20 photographs has been made by a graduate student in clinical psychology who had been a professional artist before becoming a graduate student.[1] A copyright was obtained for the nine paintings, and they have been installed on an experimental Web site that allows researchers to present the paintings via computer and to record the stories in a scorable file for each participant.

Scoring Categories for the PPT

As it currently stands, the PPT method has nine coding categories designed for convenient —and hopefully valid—assessment. Some of the categories—form quality, affect modulation, emotional stress, emotional tone, and aggression—were taken directly from the studies conducted with previous versions of the method. A computer coding method was added for productivity and complexity. Table 12.1 summarizes the nine categories with brief descriptions. For more complete descriptions, consult chapter 13 on the PPT scoring manual. Two new categories were devised by the authors for investigation with the revised PPT: benevolent–malevolent and degree of relationship.

□ Research Evidence

Validity

The first validity study with the alternative apperception test method was conducted when Ritzler et al. (1980) compared the performances of nonpatient, undergraduate participants with the SM-TAT and the TAT. As hypothesized, the SM-TAT yielded significantly higher standard deviation scores than the TAT for the following variables: emotional tone (Eron, Terry, & Callahan, 1952), word count, form quality (i.e., how well

TABLE 12.1 Current Variable Categories for the Picture Projection Test

Category Brief	Definition
Form Quality	A rating of how well the content of the story matches the picture.
Affect Modulation	The overall affective modulation of the story is coded: low key (1); dramatic (2); highly unmodulated (3) if no affect is articulated in the story, no rating is made.
Emotional Stress	Coded for the presence or absence of four types of emotional stress: Helplessness (HLP), Suppression of Affect (SUP), Self-Dissatisfaction (SD), and Loss (LOSS). High scores indicate high levels of stress.
Productivity	A count of the words used in a story provided automatically by the computer.
Complexity	A computer-provided count of words of more than two syllables (Kincaid, Fishburne, Rogers, & Chissom, 1975).
Benevolent-Malevolent	Categorical ratings for general tone of the main character's involvement in the story; Benevolent (B), Malevolent (M); or a combination (C).
Aggression	Coded according to a method developed by Hafner and Kaplan (1960):
Degree of Relationship	Rated on a 4-point Likert scale from 1 (first-time encounters) to 4 (nuclear family and other very close relationships).
Emotional Tone	Rated on a 4-point Likert scale developed by Eron, Terry, and Callahan (1952) for assessing the overall emotional tone of a story. A high score indicates a positive emotional tone.

the story matched the picture), and benevolence–malevolence of story themes. The latter two measures were specially designed for the study by the authors.

In a second study of the SM-TAT compared with the TAT, Sharkey and Ritzler (1985) found that the new method was more effective at differentiating between depressed and nondepressed patients and between psychotic and nonpsychotic individuals.

After the SM-TAT was converted to the PPT by exchanging solicited amateur photographs for the family of man pictures, Ritzler and Alter (1987) replicated the two earlier studies and once again found that the more modern, vibrant set of pictures (i.e., the PPT) yielded a wider ranger of scores and did a better job than the TAT in differentiating between contrasting diagnostic groups.

The study that renewed my interest in the PPT was a dissertation that compared the TAT with the Rorschach Comprehensive System using several TAT variables similar to the PPT variables. The dissertation was conducted by Silverman (1998) with help from her committee members, myself, Sidney Ornduff, and Jill Howard. Archival data from three sources were used for this study: patients at an outpatient university psychology clinic ($n = 38$); volunteers tested by clinical psychology doctoral students to fulfill class requirements ($n = 40$); and patients (both inpatients and outpatients) tested by senior clinicians in their private practices ($n = 19$).

Participants ranged in age from 18 to 53, were residents of a large metropolitan area, and were almost equally divided between male ($n = 50$) and female ($n = 47$) gender. They ranged from high-functioning individuals who had achieved a considerably high level of vocational or educational success with no obvious psychopathology to individuals who showed mild to severe psychological problems. There were no diagnosed psychotic individuals in the sample.

Each Rorschach protocol was administered and coded according to the Rorschach Comprehensive System by a well-trained doctoral-level graduate student. I rescored each protocol; I was directly trained by John Exner, Jr. in Comprehensive System coding.

The following Rorschach Comprehensive System (Exner, 2003) variables were used in this study:

(1) Conventional form quality ($X+\%$), the proportion of perceptually accurate and conventional responses given by at least 2% of the normative sample

(2) Unusual form quality ($Xu\%$), the proportion of responses that fit the contours of the blots but were given by less than 2% of the normative sample

(3) Distorted form quality ($X-\%$), the proportion of responses that were perceptually inaccurate

(4) Weighted sum of chromatic color responses (*WSumC*), the weighted sum of chromatic color responses calculated by the formula ($.5FC + CF + 1.5C$)

(5) Aggressive movement (*AG*), movement responses in which the action is clearly aggressive

(6) The depression index (*DEPI*), an index of several variables which indicates emotional difficulties, usually diagnosable depression

(7) Diffuse shading (*Y*), responses in which the shading features of the blot are used in a nonspecific, general manner

(8) Achromatic color (*C′*), responses that use the black, gray, or white color as characteristics of the response

(9) Vista (*V*), responses using the shading features of the blot to give a three-dimensional quality to the response

(10) Texture (*T*), responses in which shading characteristics of the blot are used to represent a tactual stimulus

(11) Experience stimulation, the sum of all occurrences of shading determinants

(12) Lambda (*L*), the proportion of responses with only form as a determinant

The TAT was administered according to standard administration procedures delineated in the Thematic Apperception Test Manual (Murray, 1938). Eight cards were used for each participant. Since the data were archival, there was no control of the specific cards selected by the examiner. A total of 776 stories were scored—eight stories for each of the 97 participants).

The construction of the TAT scoring manual occurred in several steps. A review of the literature yielded an extensive list of existing TAT nonquantified interpretative constructs and a small list of constructs that included methods for deriving numerical scores. Those constructs that on initial investigation appeared to be operationalizable, as well as those constructs for which the variables were already operationalized, were examined more closely. Highly complicated scoring schemes for single variables were eliminated, as were interpretative constructs that were not defined clearly enough to yield simple scoring criteria. The remaining constructs were given preliminary operationalized criteria for scoring. A panel of scorers tried the first draft of the criteria. [2]Results were compared, and discussions were held concerning the scoring difficulties encountered. After three revisions of the manual, the final version was used for the study and the reliability assessment. Most of the variables from this manual were incorporated for use with the PPT. Table 12.2 summarizes the TAT variables used in the dissertation and the Rorschach Comprehensive System variables hypothesized to be correlated with the TAT results.

Generally, it was hypothesized that the TAT variables would be significantly correlated with the corresponding Rorschach Comprehensive System variables. TAT word count was correlated with Rorschach Lambda on the reasoning that simpler psychological functioning would yield less extensive stories. A final analysis compared the sum of emotional stress indicators on the Rorschach (*Y, C′, V, T*) with the corresponding sum on the TAT. Table 12.2 also summarizes the hypothesized correlations between the TAT and the Rorschach Comprehensive System. Table 12.3 summarizes the results of the study.

The results for form quality yielded a fair amount of confirmation of the hypothesized relationships. There was support for the notion that the Rorschach and the TAT are both sensitive to conventionality. Conventional form quality on the TAT correlated significantly with Rorschach *X*+%. However, the variables assumed to measure eccentricity (Rorschach *Xu*% and unusual form on the TAT) did not correspond. Furthermore, unusual form on the TAT did not correspond to any Rorschach variable in this study. Variables hypothesized to be measuring distorted form (*X*–% on the Rorschach and distorted form on the TAT) showed a significant correlation of .21. Not surprisingly, distorted form on the TAT was negatively correlated with *X*+% on the Rorschach. In addition, distorted form on the TAT was correlated with Lambda on the Rorschach, suggesting that more complex individuals told less distorted or unusual stories on the TAT.

One of the highest correlations was between the measures of affective modulation and several Rorschach variables. Specifically, the degree of affective modulation on the TAT correlated positively with a number of other Rorschach variables, including *X*+%, *DEPI*, texture, sum shading, and Lambda.

Surprisingly, given the high reliability of the involved variables, aggression on the Rorschach (*AG*) had no correspondence with aggressive content on the TAT. However, aggression on the TAT correlated significantly with the Rorschach variables of *DEPI* and sum shading suggesting that aggression in TAT stories has a different interpretive significance than aggression on the Rorschach.

TABLE 12.2 TAT Variables and Their Corresponding Rorschach Comprehensive System Variables

TAT Variable	Definition	Rorschach Variable
Conventional Form	Given to a story in which the common theme was prominent	*X*+%
Unusual Form	Given to a story that fit the TAT picture but did not emphasize the common theme	*Xu*%
Distorted Form	Given to a story that had no correspondence to the picture or contained a clearly distorted perception	*X*–%
Affect Modulation		*WSumC*
1.	Given for low-key expression of affect	*FC*
2.	Given for dramatic expression of affect	*CF*
3.	Given for highly charged, unmodulated affect	*C*
Helplessness	Story content emphasizing helplessness	*Y*
Suppression of Affect	Story content indicating that affect is suppressed	*C′*
Self-Dissatisfaction	Story content indicating dissatisfaction with self	*V*
Loss or Loneliness	Story content indicating loss or loneliness	*T*
Productivity	The actual number of words used in the story	(*L*)[3] Lambda
Emotional Tone	A five-point Likert estimate of depression–elation	*DEPI*
Aggression	A three-point Likert scale measure of aggression	*AG*

[3]A better Comprehensive System variable to contrast with TAT Word Count may have been the number of responses (R), since Word Count may be a better indicator of productivity (R) rather than complexity (Lambda).

Consistent with expectations, emotional tone on the TAT yielded significant negative correlations with *DEPI*, vista, and sum shading. This may occur because depressed individuals are more likely to tell gloomy stories.

For the indicators of emotional stress, a hypothesized correlation was significant only for loneliness or loss (Rorschach *T* and TAT loneliness or loss). However, there was no significant correspondence between the paired measures of helplessness (Rorschach *Y* and TAT helplessness), suppression of affect (Rorschach *C′* and TAT affect suppression) or self-dissatisfaction (Rorschach *V* and TAT self-dissatisfaction). TAT helplessness, however, correlated positively with *SumC* on the Rorschach. Affect suppression on the TAT also correlated positively with *SumC* and texture on the Rorschach and showed a very high negative correlation with Lambda. Loss or loneliness on the TAT correlated most often with Rorschach variables in addition to texture. In addition, the total of overall stress on the TAT showed the hypothesized correlation with sum shading on the Rorschach but also was correlated positively with *DEPI*, texture, and Lambda.

Finally, TAT word count did not show the predicted correlation with Rorschach Lambda but was significantly correlated with vista, texture, and sum shading while being

TABLE 12.3 Hypothesized and Significant Correlations Between TAT and Rorschach Variables

	Rorschach Variables											
TAT Variables	X+%	Xu%	X–%	WSumC	AG	DEPI	Y	C′	V	T	Shading	Lambda
Conventional Form	.17*											
Unusual Form		.09n.s.										
Distorted Form	–.23*		.21*									.17*
Affect Modulation	.22*			.22*		.24**				.18*	.22*	.20*
Aggression					–.03n.s.	.21*				.19*	.18*	
Emotional Tone						–.19*		–.21*	–.23*	–.28**	–.28**	
Helplessness				.19*		–.17*	–.06n.s.		.21*	–.18*		
Affect Suppression				.21*				.10n.s.		.17*		–.31**
Self Dissatisfaction									.08n.s.			
Loss or Loneliness						.28**		.24**	.18*	.21*	.29**	
Overall Stress						.18*				.22*	.19*	.23*
Word Count				–.18*					.18*	.19*	.23*	–.10n.s.

Note: Hypothesized correlations are underlined.
$*p < .05$; $**p < .01$

negatively correlated with *SumC*. Lambda on the Rorschach is an indicator of psychological complexity, whereas TAT word count may be a simpler indicator of productivity. Consequently, a more appropriate comparison may have been between TAT word count and Rorschach productivity (i.e., the number of responses).

Most of the hypothesized relationships between TAT and Rorschach variables examined in this study proved to be statistically significant—albeit with modest effect sizes. Thus, there appears to be a meaningful correspondence between the TAT and the Rorschach Comprehensive System. However, the findings also indicate that several hypothesized relationships between parallel constructs were not significant. Thus, while there was notable overlap between the TAT and the Rorschach Comprehensive System, there were enough differences and modest enough correlations to suggest that the two methods also provide different information about personality functioning.

Form quality showed varied results that can be understood by noting the contrast between the operational definitions of common themes and conventional form quality on the TAT. Conventional form quality on the TAT correlated positively with *X+%* on the Rorschach. In other words, participants who told stories on the TAT that were mainly conventional and perceptually accurate tended to give Rorschach responses that used the form features of the card in a commonplace, reality-oriented manner. Consequently, this result gives indication that conventionality and perceptual accuracy can be assessed on the TAT in a fashion similar to the assessment of the same constructs using the Rorschach.

In contrast to results for conventional form, the correspondence between TAT unusual form and Rorschach *Xu%* was not significant. It is likely that the lack of statistical significance has to do with the restriction on the TAT that conventional form quality could not be scored if the story did not have a common theme in the first half. It may be that too many conventional stories were scored as unusual on the TAT because the common theme appeared in the second half. As further evidence that this may be the case, the pattern of TAT form quality scores showed more unusual form than conventional form (50% and 40%, respectively), whereas the Rorschach form quality pattern showed more *X+%* than *Xu%* (60 to 30%, respectively). Perhaps the scoring criteria for TAT conventional and unusual form should be modified.

Distorted form on the TAT correlated positively with *X–%* on the Rorschach indicating that participants who either told TAT stories in which the plot and action did not correspond to the picture or obviously distorted the identity of something in the picture tended to give Rorschach responses that disregarded the contours of the blot. Also, distorted form on the TAT correlated negatively with *X+%* on the Rorschach, indicating that distorted thinking can be assessed by the TAT. Furthermore, the positive correlation between distorted form on the TAT and Rorschach Lambda suggests that individuals of less psychological complexity (i.e., high Lambda) are likely to show more distortion in activities such as storytelling.

Affect modulation on the TAT was significantly and positively correlated with its counterpart, *SumC* on the Rorschach. That is, participants who were affectively oriented on the Rorschach tended to tell TAT stories that were more emotionally expressive. Also, participants who told more emotionally expressive stories on the TAT had higher *X+%*, *DEPI*, texture, sum shading, and Lambda scores on the Rorschach. Apparently, the TAT is quite sensitive to strong emotional characteristics of the storytellers—at least in a negative emotional sense—and may be a good method for assessing emotionality.

There was no correspondence between the TAT and Rorschach on measures of aggression. Other investigators who have examined the relationship between aggression on the TAT and Rorschach have obtained similar results. Davids (1973) found no relationship between direct measures of aggression using the two methods, and Hafner and Kaplan (1960) obtained similar nonsignificant results with a more complex weighted system of scores for overt and covert hostility on the TAT (used in this study). Hafner and Kaplan speculated that the lack of correspondence might have been due to the broader range of content on the Rorschach. They suggested that the structural elements of the TAT cards may have pulled for aggression more often, whereas the Rorschach allowed for a more projective display of aggressive tendencies. However, since aggression is not included in all participants' TAT stories to cards with a strong pull for aggression, aggressive content on the TAT may be easily dismissed by a reference to card pull.

Although it is risky to explain nonsignificant correlations, a possible alternative reason for the lack of correspondence between measures of aggression may be that the appearance of aggressive content on the Rorschach requires a degree of integration of aggression into the basic personality style that then becomes manifest in the projection of aggression onto the Rorschach stimuli. With the TAT, aggression may be a more direct response to situational cues by individuals who have poorly sublimated aggressive behavior. Gacono and Meloy (1994) found that very antisocial psychopathic individuals gave few aggressive movement (*AG*) responses on the Rorschach even though their behavior in the test situation often was clearly hostile and oppositional. Although there were no obvious psychopaths in the current study, aggression in the TAT stories may have occurred because individuals were responding to cues in the pictures that were more directly associated with aggression than the more ambiguous Rorschach cards. Gacono and Meloy (1994) found that by coding aggressive content in Rorschach responses (e.g., guns, monsters, tigers) they were able to identify individuals who have a predisposition to aggressive behavior even though the aggression was not integrated in more socially appropriate ways (i.e., psychopaths). In contrast, individuals who gave aggressive movement responses showed more sublimated aggressive behavior in the Gacono and Meloy studies.

Further evidence of the need for more study of aggression on the Rorschach and TAT is that the Rorschach *AG* variable is the only Rorschach variable in this study that did not correlate significantly with at least one TAT variable. This suggests a unique interpretive meaning for the Rorschach *AG* variable that may be different than "… the notion that elevations in AG signify an increased likelihood for aggressive behaviors, either verbal or nonverbal, and that they also indicate attitudes towards others that are more negative and/or hostile than is customary" (Exner, 1986, p. 405).

The low interrater reliability for emotional tone on the TAT (r = .59) casts doubt on the findings regarding this variable. However, it did correlate significantly with the depression index on the Rorschach. It is no surprise that depressed people tell gloomy stories, but the low reliability of the emotional tone measure may not allow more extensive conclusions to be drawn. Another problem for the TAT emotional tone variable is that the low-key, rather gloomy nature of the pictures restricts the range of stories. In other words, it is unusual for a very positive, energetic story to be told to the pictures selected by Murray (1938). This restricted range limits the possibility of finding significant correlation with other variables.

Turning from the statistically limited emotional tone variable to the relationships between the Rorschach variable, the depression index, and more reliable TAT variables, it is apparent that TAT aggression, loss or loneliness, and overall stress correlate with *DEPI*. Consequently, it seems that depressed individuals tell stories about psychological pain and misfortune, and the TAT, therefore, has potential to identify depression and other negative affective experiences.

The results of this study give an even closer look at the TAT's potential for identifying emotional problems. For instance, there were no significant correlations between corresponding Rorschach and TAT variables indicating helplessness, Suppression of affect and self-dissatisfaction and a modestly significant positive correlation between the Rorschach and TAT measures of loss or loneliness. These results suggest that the TAT is somewhat sensitive to issues of loneliness or loss but may not be a good method for assessing helplessness, emotional suppression, or self-dissatisfaction. However, the lack of correspondence on the helplessness variables may result primarily from content validity problems in operationalizing the TAT equivalent of the Rorschach diffuse shading variable (*Y*). For this study, helplessness was chosen as the defining construct for the TAT equivalent of *Y*, but this definition does not take into account two aspects of Rorschach *Y*: diffuse anxiety and situational stress. Since most stressful TAT stories tell of ongoing events, the generalized anxiety on the TAT lacks the specificity needed for reliable scoring as a sense of helplessness. Consequently, the TAT helplessness variable in this study may not be an accurate representation of the construct behind *Y* on the Rorschach.

Affect suppression on the TAT and *C'* on the Rorschach did not correlate in this study. A possible reason for this lack of correspondence may be that the Rorschach is sensitive to all attempts at suppression of emotion, both successful and unsuccessful, whereas TAT affect suppression may be indicative of only successful suppression. Consequently, a better Rorschach variable for assessing the relationship between TAT and Rorschach affect suppression might be the ratio of *C'/SumC*, used on the Rorschach to identify successful suppression.

Continuing with the emotional stress variables, it is apparent that the Rorschach *V* and *C'* variables are correlated with gloomy emotional tone and stories of loneliness and loss on the TAT; furthermore, Rorschach *V* is significantly correlated with TAT helplessness, and Rorschach *T* is correlated with TAT aggression. Obviously, the helplessness, affect suppression, and self-dissatisfaction variables on the TAT lack the specificity the authors were hoping for when they developed the TAT scoring manual. *T* on the Rorschach, on the other hand, seems more specifically related to its TAT counterpart, loss or loneliness. The correlation between Rorschach *T* and TAT aggression would seem to suggest that individuals experiencing loneliness or pain of loss tend to include aggression—anger?—in their TAT stories, perhaps as a reaction to a sense of abandonment or rejection.

The Rorschach Lambda variable is an indication of psychological involvement and complexity. Consequently, the positive correlations between Rorschach Lambda and TAT distorted form, affect modulation, and overall stress suggest that less psychologically involved and complex individuals tell more unusual and more emotional TAT stories with greater mention of stress. Since it seems that the Rorschach Lambda score is consistent with the degree of creativity in TAT stories, the study appears to have added to the construct validity of Lambda.

In general, the results of the Silberman (1998) dissertation indicate that there are some similarities between the TAT and Rorschach as well as differences in what they assess about personality, supporting the use of both methods as corroborating and complementary sources of information for personality assessment. Also, the results of this study suggest that the TAT has a strong emotional component and is sensitive to individual differences in affective expression. It also seems evident that the TAT yields specific information about social problems and their accompanying stress levels. The results of this study show that emotional stress takes the form of stories about troubled relationships and suggest that the TAT can be useful in determining how an individual plays

TABLE 12.4 Hypothesized and Significant Correlations Between PPT and Rorschach Variables

	Rorschach Variables														
PPT Variables	*P*	*X*+%	*Xu*%	*X*–%	*SumC*	*AG*	Space	*MOR*	*DEPI*	*Y*	*C′*	*V*	*T*	Shading	Lambda
Conventional Form	.21*	.17*													
Unusual Form			.14												
Distorted Form	–.23	–.20*		.22*											
Affect Modulation					.24**				.25**					.19*	.20*
Aggression						.05	.10	.18*	.18*				.18*	.19*	
Emotional Tone								.07	–.15			–.25**		–.20*	
Helplessness					.18*				–.20*	–.01					
Affect Suppression					.19*						.03				–.35**
Self-Dissatisfaction					.19*							.19			
Loss or Loneliness							.22*	.26**	.28**			.25**	.20*	.31**	
Overall Stress								.18*	.18*				.24**	.18*	.23*
Word Count										.18*				.23*	.10

Notes: Hypothesized correlations are underlined. $*p < .05$; $**p < .01$.

out psychological stress in social contexts. Nevertheless, the obtained correlations were modest at best and several hypothesized relationships between TAT and Rorschach variables were not confirmed.

An additional source of error variance might be the heterogeneity of the TAT cards used. Card pull might have at least a small influence on some of the scores, especially affective modulation and emotional stress.

Enter the PPT

After the Silberman (1998) dissertation, the same study was conducted replacing the TAT with the PPT. A sample of 100 participants was obtained from three sources: (1) volunteers tested by advanced graduate students in their second semester of doctoral-level assessment training (n = 35); (2) clients tested by graduate students at a university psychology clinic (n = 24); and (3) outpatient clients tested by doctoral-level psychologists (n = 41). Each participant was administered the Rorschach according to the procedures of the Comprehensive System (Exner, 2003). Also, the participants told stories to eight PPT cards selected by the examiners from the original set of 20 photographs.

The Rorschachs were coded by the examiners and the current author according to the Comprehensive System coding criteria (Exner, 2003). The PPT stories were coded by the current author and a graduate student research assistant using the same coding criteria used with the TAT in the Silberman (1998) dissertation. Table 12.4 summarizes the initial correlation results. Inspection of the table reveals almost identical patterns of correlations. It is apparent that the TAT and PPT relate in a very similar way to the Rorschach variables.

In an additional analysis of the PPT data, a procedure was followed as suggested by Meyer, Reithmiller, Brooks, Benoit, and Handler (2000) for comparing the Rorschach and MMPI-2. That is, "open" records were identified for both methods—PPT and Rorschach—and a new pattern of correlations was analyzed. The reasoning is that some test results are the product of defensive or limited functioning and that the ensuing constricted results may represent less complete information regarding the participant's personality. When the analyses are restricted to open records, true correlations are more likely to emerge.

For the purpose of the PPT study, open Rorschachs were defined as those with Lambda scores less than 1.00, and open PPT protocols were defined as those containing stories that averaged more than 50 words. When these criteria were applied to the 100 cases in the PPT study, 57 were identified as having open protocols for both the Rorschach and PPT. Table 12.5 presents the correlations for the PPT and Rorschach variables on the 57 open protocols. It is apparent from the table that although the correlation pattern remains essentially the same, the size of the correlations has been increased. Form quality emerges with strong consistency across the methods. The affect modulation and emotional tone results support the earlier contention that apperception tests have a strong emotional component. Aggression on the PPT clearly relates to depression on the Rorschach, but not Rorschach aggression. Of the emotional stress constructs, only loss or loneliness has a consistent impact on the relationship between the PPT and the Rorschach. Finally, word count from the PPT has little relationship to Rorschach phenomena with only a slight positive correlation with Lambda even when defensive or constricted protocols are eliminated from the analysis.

TABLE 12.5: Hypothesized and Significant Correlations Between PPT and Rorschach Variables for "Open" Protocols (n = 57)

	Rorschach Variables											
PPT Variables	X+%	*Xu*%	X−%	WSumC	AG	DEPI	Y	C′	V	T	Shading	Lambda
Conventional Form	.26**	.18*										
Unusual Form	.20*	.26*										
Distorted Form	−.40***		.31**									.24**
Affect Modulation				.35***		.20*					.35***	
Aggression					.11n.s.	.24**				.20*	.18*	
Emotional Tone						−.30**			−.20*			
Helplessness				.20*			−.06n.s.			.21*		−.25*
Affect Suppression				.21*				.10n.s.		.19*		−.39***
Self-Dissatisfaction									.15n.s.			
Loss or Loneliness						.35***		.19*		.26**	.25*	
Word Count												.19*

Note: Hypothesized correlations are underlined.
*p <.05; **p <.01; ***p <.001

TABLE 12.6 Reliability Results for Previous Picture Projection Test (or SM-TAT) Studies

Study	Identity of Coders	Reliability Results
Ritzler, Sharkey, and Chudy (1980)	2 graduate students and 1 senior clinician (Ritzler)	Pearson correlations ranging from .79 to .92 for all categories except emotional tone (r = .62)
Sharkey and Ritzler (1985)	1 dissertation student and 1 senior clinician (Ritzler)	Pearson correlations ranging from .75 to .95 (emotional tone = .75)
Ritzler (1987)	3 graduate students and 1 senior clinician (Ritzler)	Pearson correlations from .73 to .89 except for emotional tone (r = .59)
Silberman (1998)	1 dissertation student, 3 graduate students and 1 senior clinician (Ritzler)	Category of affect modulation added with reliability at r = .83. emotional tone still low.

Note: All reliability estimates were made on at least 20% of the sample. In the Silberman dissertation, the reliability sample was 50% of the total.

Generalizability

We know very little about the generalizability of the PPT. Since it compares favorably with the TAT and Rorschach Comprehensive System, we can hope that it shares much of the substantiated generalizability of those methods. The earlier versions of the PPT yielded significantly better discriminations than the TAT with patient samples that were geographically different, but the method has not been studied for important generalizability across age, ethnic, and gender differences. Consequently, it is hoped that the revised form will be implemented in future diversity studies.

Reliability

Although reliability has not been assessed for the newest version of the PPT scoring categories, several previous versions have yielded impressive results. Table 12.6 summarizes the previous reliability data for the PPT. The reliability of the simple measures used with the PPT and TAT were in a satisfactory range except for emotional tone, which consistently failed to show good reliability. Consequently, conclusions drawn from correlations with emotional tone should be evaluated with caution.

□ An Early Report on a PPT-R Normative Study

Participants

The goal of the normative study for the PPT-R is 300 participants. To date, 175 have been tested. All participants were well-adjusted individuals who had not had treatment for serious psychological problems.

TABLE 12.7 Means, Standard Deviations, and Ranges for Preliminary Picture Projection Test Normative Sample (n = 175)

Variable	Mean	Standard Deviation	Range
Words	85.46	43.73	12–326
Percentage of Complex Words[a]	6.66	4.02	0–44
Form Quality	1.52	.55	0–2
Affect Modulation	1.75	1.04	0–4
Hostility	1.10	1.23	0–2
Free-Floating Anxiety	.25	.43	0–1
Suppression of Affect	.07	.26	0–1
Self Dissatisfaction	.11	.32	0–1
Loss	.17	.38	0–1
Benevolent–Malevolent[b]	3.11	1.73	0–6
Relationships[c]	2.54	1.41	0–5

[a] A complex word is one with more than two syllables.
[b] 0 = most benevolent; 6 = most malevolent.
[c] 0 = most distant; 5 = closest.

The results of the normative study indicate that the variables in the coding system can be reliably coded with Cohen's kappa estimates ranging between .85 and .90 (Cohen, 1968). Also, all variables yield results that appear to fall in an average or high-functioning range. Table 12.7 provides a summary of the nine coding variables for the 175-participant normative sample.

Future Research

The immediate future of the PPT lies in the development of the PPT-R (Ritzler & Ben-Zvi, 2004). Instead of a series of 20 photographs, the new version consists of nine oil paintings based on the nine most productive photographs from previous PPT studies. The paintings are in full color and add a degree of ambiguity that is designed to increase the projective quality of the method. The nine paintings preserve the more active, more positively toned quality of the original PPT along with the greater number of characters per card compared to the TAT. The stimulus pictures are available through a secured Web site currently open only to authorized researchers.

In addition to providing a more vibrant and varied set of stimuli compared to the TAT, the new PPT is designed to be more efficient for clinical use. The pictures can be presented on a computer screen and the participant's stories can be typed under each picture into the computer. The coding manual provides simple criteria for coding variables associated with constructs that may be useful to clinicians in understanding their clients. The ultimate goal of this work is to provide an empirical base for use of the new apperception method similar to the quantitative foundations that now exist for the Rorschach and MMPI-2. Obviously, that goal lies in the distant future, but the new version of the test promises to be a more manageable and, hopefully, more valid tool for personality assessment.

References

Cohen, J. (1968). Weighted kappa: Nominal scale agreement with provision for scaled disagreements or partial credit. *Educational Psychological Measurement, 20,* 37–46.

Costantino, G., Malgady, R., & Rogler, L. (1986). *Standardization and validation of TEMAS, a pluralistic Thematic Apperception Test.* New York: Fordham University, Hispanic Research Center.

Davids, A. (1973). Aggression in thought and action of emotionally disturbed boys. *Journal of Consulting and Clinical Psychology, 40,* 322–327.

Exner, J. (2003). *The Rorschach: A comprehensive system. Volume 1: Basic foundations (4th ed.).* New York: Wiley.

Gacono, C., & Meloy, R. (1994). *The Rorschach assessment of aggressive and psychopathic personalities.* Hillsdale, NJ: Lawrence Erlbaum Associates.

Kincaid, J., Fishburne, R., Rogers, R., & Chissom, B. (1975). *Derivation of new readability formulas (Automated Readability Index, Fog Count and Flesch Reading Ease Formula) for Navy enlisted personnel.* Research Branch Report 8-75, Millington, TN: Naval Technical Training, U.S. Naval Air Station, Memphis TN.

Meyer, G., Reithmiller, R., Brooks, R., Benoit, W., & Handler, L. (2000). A replication of Rorschach and MMPI-2 convergent validity. *Journal of Personality Assessment, 74,* 175–215.

Murray, H. (1938). *Explorations in personality.* New York: Oxford University Press.

Murray, H. (1943). *The Thematic Apperception Test manual.* Cambridge, MA: Harvard University Press.

Museum of Modern Art (1955). *The family of Man.* New York: Museum of Modern Art.

Ritzler, B., & Ben-Zvi, A. (March, 2004). The Picture Projection Test Revised. Paper presented at the Society for Personality Assessment Midwinter Meeting, Miami, FL.

Notes

1. The nine photographs used for models for the nine paintings were selected because they tended to yield the highest correlations with the Rorschach Comprehensive System variables in the previously mentioned study. The artist is Anat Ben-Zvi, a graduate student in the clinical psychology Ph.D. program at Long Island University.
2. The panel of scorers consisted of Anna Smith, Stuart Ebner, and Shahal Rosenblatt, psychology graduate students.

13

CHAPTER

Scoring Manual for the Picture Projection Test

Barry Ritzler

Introduction

The main purpose of this manual is to provide personality assessment information from the Picture Projection Test-Revised (PPT-R) in a quantified form that can be used effectively and efficiently by clinicians. A second goal is to provide variables for personality assessment research—both for empirical validation of the PPT and, eventually, for the use of the PPT as a criterion method.

To achieve these goals, the criteria for PPT coding must be clear and comprehensive enough to enable adequately trained assessment psychologists to reliably code the variables in each category. Also, to facilitate clinical application, the coding must be efficient enough to yield data without overly long coding procedures.

The current PPT manual was developed over a series of studies using early forms of the procedure (Ritzler & Alter, 1987; Ritzler, Sharkey, & Chudy, 1980; Sharkey & Ritzler, 1985; Silberman, 1998). Also, several computer-generated story length and complexity measures have been added.

Although the specific criteria for coding each category are presented here, the coding seems to be most effectively conducted with a basic approach to the stories. That is, the coder should read the entire story before focusing on each coding category. This gives the coder an overall sense of the story that will aid in coding the individual categories. Each category should be completed immediately following the first reading of the story. The categories have been designed to be scored in less than 30 minutes for most protocols by a well-trained coder—that is, about three to five minutes per category.

□ Administration

Format

The PPT consists of nine pictures that are administered to an individual client through the use of a computer program. Each picture is presented on the computer screen with a box underneath for recording the story. The story is typed into the box by the examiner as the client tells the story. Care should be taken to type the story in exact verbatim fashion. The initial instructions are as follows: "I will show you nine pictures on the computer screen, one at a time. For each picture, I want you to tell a story. Tell me what is happening in the picture, what led up to the picture (that is, what happened before), what the people in the story are thinking and feeling, and how the story ends. Do you have any questions?"

Any questions should be answered as directly as possible. It may be necessary to say that the question will be answered after the procedure is over so as to not interfere with the process, but most questions probably can be answered immediately.

After the client completes his or her story, the examiner should review it to determine if each requested element has been included. If something has been left out, the examiner should ask for it (e.g., "What are the people thinking?"). Any such inquires should be noted in parentheses in the story box. No other inquiry is to be conducted.

Clients are not allowed to reject a picture. If they say they cannot think of a story, say, "We need a story for each picture" and do not go on to the next picture until a story has been told.

Stimuli

The current PPT stimuli are nine paintings based on previously used photographs. The paintings are in color and are presented on a computer screen. A brief description of each picture follows.

(1) Five adults are seated, apparently in an audience. One of the three women has her fingers crossed and is smiling.

(2) A young woman appears to be running with her arms in front of her. Her expression is a smile or a grimace.

(3) Three people are conferring—two young people (boy and girl) and an older man with a peace symbol on his collar. The boy, at least, is smiling.

(4) Four adolescents (two boys and two girls) dressed in bathing suits are standing in a pose in a wooded area. A bicycle lies on the ground.

(5) An elderly woman sits at a table with her hand on her chin.

(6) A young boy is in the grasp of a man whose face is not seen. The boy is laughing (as if he is being tickled) or is in distress. He has a pine cone in his hand.

(7) Two middle-aged women, dressed for winter, have a look of distress or surprise.

(8) A young boy with long hair is playing a violin in front of a music stand with a sheet of music on it.

(9) A young adult male dressed in white shorts and a T-shirt is entering a room where another man is seated at a table with a drink in his hand. Gladiolas are on the table, and a vacuum cleaner sits against a wall.

☐ Scoring Process

Scoring Category Criteria

Form Quality

Ordinary (FQo) should be scored when the story predominantly reflects the common themes (see following list) in the first half of the story. Some elaboration and additions of minor thematic material may exist in an FQo story, but the major emphasis must not deviate significantly from the common themes. However, inclusion of a common theme will not always be scored FQo even though the common theme may be embedded in the first half of the story because it may be combined with much unique elaboration or addition of unusual themes. A useful guideline might be that a story should sound essentially ordinary and commonplace to be scored FQo.

Unusual (FQu) should be scored when the story has a clearly unique quality with significant elaborations. The common theme may appear, but only in the second half of the story. Also, to be scored FQu a story must have no misperceptions or misinterpretations (see following for FQ–). In other words, if a story is not scored FQo and has no misperceptions or misinterpretations, it should be scored FQu: for instance, on card 1, "It's a child who has gained a deep appreciation for fine art. He loves art and music and classical literature and has a deep respect for the amount of work and dedication necessary to become an artist. He often imagines himself as an artist—in this case a violinist." Note how late the mention of the boy's contemplation of the violin enters the story. Also, the story is an unusual, but not inaccurate, response to the picture.

Distorted (FQ–) should be scored when one or both of the following conditions are apparent:

(1) The story does not seem to be referring to much of the scene in the picture. In other words, does it have a gross thematic distortion?—for instance, on card 8, "It's a boy about to enter the Olympics as a sprinter. He has been preparing for years to compete against the world's best and is confident that he will succeed." Note that this story does not misrepresent or distort anything in the picture; it simply does not show much regard for the stimulus.

(2) The story contains an obvious misperception of a clearly depicted element in the picture—for instance, on card 8, "A boy is practicing a saxophone," or "A woman is playing a violin." Note that the elements of the picture have not been disregarded but

have been distorted or misperceived. Note that if a story qualifies for FQo but has a clear misperception or thematic distortion, it should be scored FQ–. In other words, FQ– overrides FQo.

A suggested method for scoring form quality is to first read the story to form a general impression and then to follow these steps:

(1) Does the story have a clear misperception or thematic distortion? If so, score FQ–.

(2) If the story is not FQ–, it is a candidate for FQo (do not score yet).

(3) If the story is a candidate for FQo, is it predominantly a common theme story (score FQo), or does it have significant elaborations and additions that go beyond the common themes (score FQu)?

(4) If a story does not include a common theme in the first half and has no misperceptions or misinterpretations, score FQu.

Common Themes

The preliminary normative study (see chapter 12, this volume) enabled the investigators to identify common themes by the frequency of their occurrence in the normative sample.

- Card 1: A group of adults constitute an audience either at a performance or a church service.
- Card 2: A young woman is running in positive anticipation or distress.
- Card 3: Two young adults and an older man are engaged in a friendly conversation.
- Card 4: A group of adolescents is posing audaciously at a swimming hole.
- Card 5: An elderly woman is contemplating her current life circumstances or her past.
- Card 6: A boy with a pine cone is being handled roughly or is being tickled by a man.
- Card 7: Two women are surprised or in distressed.
- Card 8: A boy is concerned about playing the violin.
- Card 9: The two men are roommates or in some form of intimate relationship.

Modulation of Affect

This variable measures modulation of affect. To score, read the entire story to get an overall, general sense of affect modulation. Do not identify and average separate instances of modulation. The following categories should be considered:

- AL: Low-key expression of affect
- AD: Dramatic, but still somewhat contained, expression of affect
- A+: Highly charged, unmodulated expression of affect
- O: No affect expressed

There may be stories in which characters' internal experience of affect is not well modulated, but their behavior serves to contain or reduce affect—for instance, "The woman was very angry, but she just ignored the man and didn't say a word." In cases like this, where the emphasis is on the overt modulation, consideration should be given to raising the modulation score one level (e.g., A+ to AD; AD to AL). When the emphasis is on the internal lack of modulation (e.g., "The woman was extremely angry, she was as mad as she ever had been and could hardly contain herself, but she decided to say nothing"), the modulation score should not be modified by the overt containing behavior, and the modulation score should not be raised.

If the affective expression is mentioned in the past tense (e.g., "The boy was very angry when he heard the news—now he's trying to decide what to do"), it should be given less emphasis than affective expression in the present tense.

Explosive or otherwise highly charged physical events that do not include human emotion should also be considered as projections of affective modulation—for instance, "The river surged down the canyon, smashing through the dam and destroying everything in sight" (score A+), or "The river was running rapidly at a high level" (score AD), or "The water dripped annoyingly" (score AL). Finally, impulsive behavior should not be considered as poor modulation unless it is clearly and specifically driven by emotion. For example, "The boy fired the gun without thinking" should not be scored for affect modulation; "The boy was so frightened he fired without thinking" should be scored.

Emotional Stress

This variable is scored when there is specific mention of the following:

- FFA: Anxiety with no clear reference to its cause ("free-floating anxiety") or some distress about the storytelling task itself (e.g., "This is very upsetting—I can't think of a story") or feelings of helplessness in the story itself (i.e., not displayed by storyteller).
- SUP: Emotion being held back, covered up, or denied.
- GLT: Extreme dissatisfaction with self (i.e., self-loathing), guilt, or shame.
- LOSS: A sense of loss or loneliness.

The emotions and situations expressed in the story must be those that commonly are experienced as painful by regular, nonneurotic individuals. A minor discomfiture or social awkwardness should not be scored. Any clear instance of emotional stress should be scored. If more than one instance of the same stress occurs in a story, the stress category should be scored only once. If a later part of the story resolves, lessens, or disqualifies the stress, the stress category should be scored anyway. For instance, if a couple separates because of an argument (LOSS) but later are reconciled in the story, LOSS should be scored.

Productivity

For productivity, or amount of effort expended in telling the story, any computer provides a simple count of the number of words. Every word is counted, even if it is an aside comment by the subject—for example, "This is a pretty picture," or "It's hard to make up a story." Each word in a contraction is counted as a separate word. Each word in a hyphenated word also is counted separately.

Complexity

The computer also provides a measure of the mean number of complex words used in the nine stories (Kincaid, Fishburne, Rogers, & Chissom, 1975). A complex word is defined as a word with more than two syllables.

Benevolent–Malevolent Dimension

This category refers to the character's style of relating to others as well as his or her perceptions of other story characters. Coding is based on the following category criteria:

- B: Either the behavior of the story characters or the environment is relatively benign.
- B+: Either the behavior of the story characters or the environment is clearly nurturing (more than just benign).
- M: Either the behavior of the story characters or the environment is unresponsive, nonempathic, or mildly threatening.
- M+: Either the behavior of the story characters or the environment is cruel and clearly malevolent.
- C: Either the behavior of the story characters or the environment reflects a combination of positive and negative attributes as described already. For example, a man might show love for a woman or appear to have positive feelings for her while at the same time he is impatient or angry with her.
- C+: Either the behavior of the story character or the environment reflects an extreme combination of positive and negative characteristics as, for example, the Mafia criminal with a strong sense of loyalty to friends or family.
- NU: Either the behavior of the story characters or the environment is neutral or it is unclear whether the descriptive characteristics reflect a benign or malevolent orientation.

Aggression

This variable, taken from Hafner and Kaplan (1960), measures the degree of hostility expressed in the story. The hostility must be taking place in the story; reference to past or future hostility should not be scored. *Hostility* is defined as feelings, thoughts, or actions that involve destruction, aggression, enmity, derogation, criticality, anger, guilt, negativism, and physical deformities, illness, and death. Each PPT story is scored on a 0- to 2-point scale according to the degree of hostility involved, with 2 being the most hostile and 0 being indicative of no hostility in the story. If more than one level of hostility exists in the same story, the highest level should be scored.

- 2 = Themes involving direct physical hostile acts between people or toward the self; themes involving hate; thoughts, feelings, dreams, or threats of direct physical hostile acts between people or toward the self; themes involving punishment, permanent debilitating injury, or death.
- 1 = Themes involving verbal hostility; derogatory descriptions of people; antisocial acts; people forced by others to do things; hostile or negative emotionality; rejections; illness and accidents involving injury; destruction of inanimate objects; predatory animals; destructive forces; weapons; themes involving emotional deprivation; guilt feelings; escaped misfortune; death symbols; broken objects.
- 0 = Themes without hostile content.

Degree of Relationships

(1) First-time encounters with no previous contact

(2) Relationships that are neither first-time encounters nor close relationships nor nuclear family or very close relationships

(3) Extended family and other moderately close relationships (e.g., grandparents, aunts, uncles, cousins, friends who are not "best," mentors, coworkers, teammates)

(4) Nuclear family and other very close relationships (e.g., parents, siblings, children, lovers, best friends).

When a subject increases the intimacy of a relationship, add a .5 to the rating. When a subject decreases the intimacy of a relationship, subtract .5. The former would include a grandparent who is living with a character; the latter might be a grandparent he or she scarcely knows. Relationships with animals are also scored for degree of intimacy. Pets that are the objects of strong feelings are scored 4. Animals that are more casually mentioned are scored according to the aforementioned criteria.

Emotional Tone

Again, the overall story should be coded. Individual circumstances within the story should be combined to rate the overall emotional tone.

- 0: A neutral emotional tone or no emotional component at all
- 1: A highly positive emotional tone
- 2: A mildly positive emotional tone

- 3: A mildly negative emotional tone
- 4: A highly negative emotional tone

Emotional tone is coded according to the criteria presented by Eron, Terry, and Callahan (1952). For PPT, emotional tone is coded for the entire story; and, unlike in Eron's study, the emotional tone for outcome is not coded separately.

Calculating Scores

Form Quality

X+% = FQo stories divided by number of stories told (usually 9). This is a measure of conventionality.

XA% = FQo + FQu divided by number of stories told. This is a measure of reality testing.

Modulation of Affect

AL + 2AD + 3(A+) divided by number of stories told. This is a general measure of degree of affect modulation.

Relationships

Add all the relationship scores together, and divide by the number of relationships mentioned across all stories.

Emotional Tone

Add all outcome scores together, and divide by the number of stories told.

□ Practice Stories

(1) Card 3: This old man just finished playing the harmonica on the street and these two teenagers came over and started talking to him. He told them his life story and they enjoyed talking to him. He was a funny, kooky old man, and wise. The kids have to continue on their way to go to school so they say, "Goodbye, nice talking to you, keep playing. The teenage boy is thinking, "I really like this old man, he's cool, I love meeting new people. She's thinking, "This is cool, but I'm ready to leave." The old man's thinking that it was good to talk to them and that he loves his music. The young boy's feeling admiration for the old man and the young girl is ambivalent, just

hanging out with her friend and the old man. The old man looks a little crazy—just good and happy, and he will keep playing his harmonica.

(2) Card 9: This looks like two roommates or brothers or roommates who are living together. They look about the same age. Maybe one has a girlfriend or a wife because of the flowers and chandelier, which has more of a woman's touch. It's a family house because of the dog bowl and the water bowl for a pet dog. My guess it's somewhere in Europe because the man is wearing slippers and one is joining the other and they are both doing work or reading magazines and keeping each other company. The guy at the table is a photographer because he is looking at professional-type photographs. They are going to do work together. It seems very lazy.

(3) Card 4: Looks like these are kids going down to swim in a waterhole. It's a sunny afternoon. They are giddy, happy, goofing around. They all look wet. Look like they've been swimming. They rode down on their bicycles and went swimming in a pond. They look like they are happy and content with what they are doing. The two girls look giddy and goofy. Definitely look like they are posing for a picture. Their attention is on the photographer. The girls are trying to be silly. Looks like the two guys in the back don't like pictures taken. The main emotion is with the person taking the picture. They're just concentrating on getting their picture taken. They are ready to go home.

Coding for Practice Stories

Card 3

- Form quality: o (common theme appears early in story)
- Affect modulation: AL (characters mostly think about feelings)
- No emotional stress
- Productivity: 154 words
- Complexity: .39
- Benevolent–malevolent: B
- Hostility: none
- Relationships: 2 (acquaintances only)
- Emotional tone: 1

Card 4

- Form quality: o (common theme comes early in story)
- Affective modulation: AD

- No emotional stress
- Productivity: 121 words
- Complexity: .74
- Benevolent–malevolent: B
- Hostility: none
- Relationships: 2
- Emotional Tone: 1

Card 9

- Form quality: o
- Affective modulation: AL (*lazy*)
- No emotional stress
- Productivity: 116 words
- Complexity: .78
- Benevolent–malevolent: NU
- Hostility: none
- Relationships: 4 (nuclear family and girlfriend)
- Emotional tone: 0

References

Eron, L., Terry, D., & Callahan, R. (1952). The use of rating scales for emotional tone of TAT stories. *Journal of Counseling Psychology, 14,* 473–478.

Hafner, J., & Kaplan, A. (1960). Hostility content analysis of the Rorschach and TAT. *Journal of Projective Techniques, 24,* 137–143.

Kincaid, J., Fishburne, R., Rogers, R., & Chissom, B. (1975). *Derivation of new readability formulas (Automated Readability Index. Fog Count and Flesch Reading Ease Formula) for Navy enlisted personnel.* Research Branch Report 8-75, Millington, TN: Naval Technical Training, U.S. Naval Air Station, Memphis, TN.

Ritzler, B., & Alter, B. (March, 1987). The Picture Projection Test: A comprehensive alternative to the TAT. Paper presented at the Society for Personality Assessment Midwinter Meeting, San Francisco, CA.

Ritzler, B., Sharkey, K., & Chudy, J. (1980). A comprehensive projective alternative to the TAT. *Journal of Personality Assessment, 44,* 358–362.

Sharkey, K., & Ritzler, B. (1985). Comparing diagnostic validity of the TAT and a new Picture Projective Test. *Journal of Personality Assessment, 49,* 406–412.

Silberman, N. (1998). *Comparisons between a new coding method for the Thematic Apperception Test and scores from the Rorschach Comprehensive System.* Unpublished doctoral dissertation, Long Island University.

III

SECTION

Psychodynamic Systems

14

CHAPTER

Reuben Fine's Scoring Scheme for the TAT and Other Verbal Projective Techniques

Sidney Ornduff

Abstract

The Scoring Scheme for the Thematic Apperception Test (TAT) and Other Verbal Projective Techniques (Fine, 1955a) is a system for codifying the manifest content of projective material. Considered a shorthand method for extracting potentially useful clinical information, this chapter focuses on the application of this system to TAT (Murray, 1943) stimuli. According to this system, content is scored with respect to feelings, outcomes, and interpersonal relationships. Each TAT story is considered to be a unit, and the use of a psychogram, or analogous summary sheet, is recommended to facilitate scoring. After the stories are scored, grand totals are calculated and provide "a sort of qualitative 'summing up' of the results" (Fine, 1951, p. 64). Although relatively few references for the system can be found in the literature, this scoring scheme has been shown to be a reliable, straightforward, and efficient method for yielding clinically important information. Relevant studies are reviewed herein, and scoring criteria and examples are provided.

Description of System

The Scoring Scheme for the Thematic Apperception Test (TAT) and Other Verbal Projective Techniques is a content-based coding system for projective material. This system can be applied to verbal material provided to pictorial stimuli (e.g., TAT, Make-A-Picture-Story [MAPS]) or to that presented in the therapy setting (e.g., free association, clinical interviews). With few exceptions, only manifest content is scored. Scoring categories include feelings, outcomes, and interpersonal relationships. The selection of these three domains appears to be guided by Reuben Fine's psychoanalytic training and the sentiment that the manifest content of dreams may yield valuable clinical information when looked at from these perspectives.

Although Fine's (1955a, p. 308) scoring scheme emphasizes analysis at the manifest level, he notes that it "... never tells the whole story, nor can it be expected to. Rather, it is to be looked upon first as a means of highlighting important information, and second as a framework for more detailed analysis." The advantages of this scoring system include the ease with which it can be learned, the timeliness with which clinical data are yielded, and the foundation it provides for subsequent protocol analysis.

Conceptual Framework

Influenced by the writings of Freud (1938), Balken and Massermann (1940), and Bellak (1944), Fine's system emphasizes the inherent richness of the manifest content of verbal productions to projective stimuli. By focusing on what is explicitly stated in response to storytelling cards, clinically useful information can be gleaned about an individual's present concerns as well as salient aspects of one's history that influence current perceptions of the pictorial stimuli. This point of view is consistent with psychoanalytic theory as it relates to personality development and the structure of the psyche. Moreover, psychoanalytic theory recognizes the utility of projective methods and other imaginative creations in revealing rich clinical data, the significance of which the respondent may be unaware. For example, in our work with sexually abused girls (Pistole & Ornduff, 1994) and with children exposed to domestic violence (Ornduff & Monahan, 1999), we found numerous references to sexuality and parental violence, respectively, in the verbal productions of these children. The first study used the TAT as the primary source of data and the second study relied on transcripts from therapy sessions. These findings are relevant in the present context because such children are often reluctant to reveal information about these personally sensitive issues on direct questioning. In response to projective stimuli or in the safety of a therapeutic setting, such disclosures become permissible as the participant engages in the clinical process. In this way, access to the individual's private world—that is, the individual's way of organizing and imposing meaning on her or his personal reality—is achieved.

Scoring Categories

The Manual for a Scoring Scheme for Verbal Projective Techniques (Fine, 1955b) includes the following major scoring categories: (1) feelings; (2) outcome; and (3) interpersonal relationships. Thirty-six categories of feelings that reflect those "most frequently encountered on the TAT" (Fine 1955a, p. 306) are tallied as present (versus absent) if they are expressed by any character in a story. Repetition is ignored; thus, a feeling is scored as present regardless of the number of times it is articulated in a given story. Analogously, no attention is given to which characters express the feeling. To ensure that no affects are omitted, a special states category is included to allow for any feelings not incorporated elsewhere in the system. Outcome is categorized as favorable, unfavorable, or indeterminate, and each story is summarized by a single outcome based on its conclusion from the point of view of the hero. Interpersonal relationships are classified according to type of interpersonal combination and primary type of interaction. With respect to the former, 16 dyadic groupings are listed; the latter are organized under the broad headings of moving toward, moving against, and moving away from (see Table 14.1).

TABLE 14.1 Scoring Categories for the Scoring Scheme for the TAT and Other Verbal Projective Techniques

Feelings

In this system, *feeling* is broadly defined and refers to any affectively tinged state.

1. Affection
    - 1a. Physical
    - 1b. Verbal
2. Anger
3. Anxiety
4. Compulsion
5. Conflict
6. Crime
7. Depression
8. Drink
9. Effort
10. Escape
11. Excitement
12. Frustration
13. Guilt
14. Hostility
    - 14a. Verbal
    - 14b. Physical
    - 14c. Death
15. Inferiority
16. Loneliness
17. Orality
18. Pain
19. Pathological Indicators
    - 19a. Tabooed Activity
        - 1) Homosexuality
    - 19b. Bizarre Verbalization
    - 19c. Rejection of Card
    - 19d. Other
20. Pleasure
21. Possessiveness
22. Sexuality
23. Special States
24. Suicide

(*Continued*)

TABLE 14.1 Scoring Categories for the Scoring Scheme for the TAT and Other Verbal Projective Techniques (Continued)

25. Superiority
26. Wishful Thinking

Outcome

This section has three categories:

1. Favorable
2. Unfavorable
3. Indeterminate

Interpersonal Relationships

This section lists 16 varieties of interpersonal interactions and 3 main types of interaction. The interpersonal interactions are:

1. Mother-child (M-C)
2. Child-mother (C-M)
3. Father-child (F-C)
4. Child-father (C-F)
5. Mother-father (M-F)
6. Father-mother (F-M)
7. Sibling-Sibling (Sib-Sib)
8. Man-man (M-M)
9. Man-woman (M-W)
10. Woman-man (W-M)
11. Woman-woman (W-W)
12. Authority-subject (A-S)
13. Subject-authority (S-A)
14. Friend-friend (F-F)
15. Stranger-strange (S-S)
16. Other

The three main types of interaction are:

1. Moving toward
2. Moving against
3. Moving away from

(Continued)

TABLE 14.1 Scoring Categories for the Scoring Scheme for the TAT and Other Verbal Projective Techniques (Continued)

Moving toward has the following subcategories:

1a. Affection
    1. Verbal
    2. Physical
1b. Acceptance
1c. Dominance
1d. Submission

Moving against has the following subcategories:

2a. Verbal
2b. Physical
2c. Death

Moving away from has the following subcategories:

3a. Separation
3b. Rejection

Research Evidence

Validity

The first reference to the Scoring Scheme for the TAT and Other Verbal Projective Techniques is Fine's (1948) doctoral dissertation, the findings of which are summarized in a later publication (Fine, 1955a). Fine used his scoring scheme to compare asthmatic children with their siblings. Using 15 TAT cards—1, 2, 3BM, 4, 8BM, 9GF, 11, 13MF, 15, 16, 17BM, 18BM, 18GF, 12M, and 14—he found that the manifest content of children with asthma contained significantly more references of sadness, orality, wishful thinking, and various types of hostile feelings as compared with their physically healthy brothers and sisters. A number of relational concerns also distinguished the groups, with the asthmatic children having significantly more references involving parents, particularly mothers, and feelings of hostility than their siblings. Fine reported similar findings in an application of this scoring system with these children with MAPS (Shneidman, 1947). Theoretical implications of the findings are not delineated, as the purpose of Fine's article and the accompanying scoring manual is the introduction of the scoring method.

In 1951, Fine used his scoring system to devise a diagnostic formulation of John Doe based on responses to 11 TAT cards—1, 3, 4, 6BM, 7BM, 11, 12M, 13MF, 13B, 14, and 16. This book chapter is especially informative as the author guides the reader through his detailed analysis of the patient's TAT record. Beginning with the psychogram, Fine reviewed the three major scoring categories of the scoring scheme and developed a tentative diagnostic picture of John Doe. He then provided a card-by-card analysis of the record. Drawing on his personal experience with the TAT, he compared the patient's responses with his own internal norms and used this information to supplement his clinical impressions of John Doe. He also commented on four additional variables that are not included in the formal scoring system but provide useful information: story length, story cohesiveness, story plot, and vocabulary. Finally, he offered an interpretation of the TAT based on an amalgam of these data and arrived at a diagnosis of the patient. This chapter continues with an analysis of the patient's MAPS, and points of convergence and divergence with the TAT are discussed.

Using 20 TAT cards (not enumerated in print) recommended for adult males, Davison (1953) employed Fine's (1948) version of the scoring scheme to differentiate among groups of hospitalized World War II veterans. The sample included 10 patients in each of the following diagnostic categories: anxiety reactives, conversion reactives, depressive reactives, catatonic schizophrenics, hebephrenic schizophrenics, and paranoid schizophrenics. Results were most notable for the depressive reactive group, whose TAT records included significantly more references to hostility (i.e., verbal, physical, death), conflict, frustration, and doubt than any other clinical group. A trend of more references to guilt was also observed. These patients also produced a significantly higher number of unfavorable outcomes and interpersonal relationships as compared with their counterparts. With respect to the latter, patients in the depressive reactive group had significantly higher frequencies of relationships involving both moving toward and moving against on the parts of the characters in the stories. Together, these findings were thought to be supportive of dynamic formulations regarding the nature of depressive reactions. Differences were also noted in comparisons of the schizophrenic patients to the three groups of neurotic patients. Specifically, patients with schizophrenia had significantly higher frequencies of bizarre verbalizations and other pathological indices, as well as no relationships, than did patients with various neuroses.

Pistole and Ornduff (1994) used Fine's (1955b) scoring scheme to distinguish 30 sexually abused girls from a demographically similar clinical comparison group of 30 nonabused but distressed girls. Responses to four TAT cards—1, 2, 3BM, and 4—were scored with respect to feelings and outcomes. Both raters were blind with respect to the group status of the respondent. Results revealed significant differences between the groups, with sexually abused girls having higher frequencies of stated sexual preoccupation and guilt than nonabused girls. No significant group differences were observed with respect to other specific negative feelings or negative outcomes. The salience of themes of sexuality and associated guilt in the TAT stories of the maltreated girls in this sample is consistent with clinical and research accounts of the predominance of such concerns in the feelings, thoughts, and real-world experience of sexually abused children.

Three other published references to the scoring scheme were found by this author. In each of these studies, the scoring system or the manner in which it was applied were modified for the purposes of the study; thus, the generalizability of the results of these investigations is limited when compared to with the aforementioned reports. The first study, conducted by Lessa and Spiegelman (1954) and summarized by Fine (1955a), applied the scoring scheme to TAT protocols of the people of Ulithi. This study involved a blind analysis of the data by a psychologist, whose results were compared with those of an ethnographer. Details regarding, for example, rater training, mode of administration, TAT cards, and sample size are not included here. However, the researchers report that "the close agreement between the psychological and ethnographic interpretations is considerably greater than that expected by either of the investigators" (Fine, 1955a, p. 308). Interestingly, the interpersonal relationships categories had to be revised for this sample because those based on relational patterns in the United States did not occur frequently enough for scoring to be meaningful. Substituting inferiority, kinship, and superiority for the three relationship categories of the scoring system, the researchers found the results to be satisfactory. Thus, it appears that although the particular categories may vary, the principles of this scoring system remain valid.

The second study used a variation of Fine's (1955b) scoring system to evaluate possible gender bias of the TAT (Worchel, Aaron, & Yates, 1990). Undergraduates—30 male and 30 female—were randomly assigned to one of two card conditions (male cards: 3BM, 6BM, 7BM, 8BM, 9BM, 12M, 13B, 17BM, 18BM; female cards: 3GF, 6GF, 7GF, 8GF, 9GF, 12F, 13G, 17GF, 18GF). Participants were given 30 minutes to generate verbal stories to nine TAT cards. Stories were transcribed and scored by three raters who were blind to the experimental condition of the respondents. Interrater reliability data are not reported. Data were factor analyzed and then subjected to multivariate analysis of variance (MANOVA), with gender and type of card as the independent variables and the seven derived TAT factors and the three outcomes categories as the dependent variables. Results revealed a significant effect for type of card on one of the derived TAT factors: general concerns. This factor contained the following content categories: conflict, effort, escape, verbal hostility, sexuality, ambivalence, fear, acceptance, and separation. Subjects responded more frequently to this category when the female TAT cards were administered. Moreover, women verbalized material categorized on the derived interpersonal relations factor more often than men. No gender differences were observed for the aggression factor, and no differences were found on the outcome variables. According to the authors, these findings provide support for a nonspecific sex bias across the two sets of cards.

Finally, eight unspecified TAT cards and the Apperceptive Personality Test (APT) (Karp, Condrell, Holstrom, & Silber, 1989) were administered in counterbalanced order to 53 female and 51 male undergraduates (Condrell, Karp, Holmstrom, & Silber, 1998). The purpose of the study was to investigate the relation between the Fine (1955a) system for scoring aggressive story content and objective measures of aggressive feelings and aggressive actions derived from the APT.

Developed for both clinical and research purposes, the APT is composed of eight storytelling stimulus cards of moderate ambiguity that portray recognizable figures (e.g., male versus female, old versus young) in commonplace situations. Designed for use with adolescents and adults, the cards are presented in fixed order of increasingly demanding material. Respondents are instructed to write an imaginative story for each of the eight cards, after which the APT questionnaire is administered. The questionnaire provides objective scoring of the APT by asking the subject to answer a series of six questions about the two key characters of each story. Subjects' answers to the questions are coded with the use of a scoring manual and then are submitted to a computer program for final scoring of the basic 21 variables for the entire protocol (see Holmstrom, Silber, & Karp, 1990, for preliminary findings of the method).

Correlations of the judge's TAT ratings with APT scores were .13 for hostile feelings and .41 ($p < .01$) for hostile actions. Thus, the APT questionnaire scores for hostile feelings of the characters are independent from content reflecting aggressive feelings on the TAT, whereas APT questionnaire scores for hostile actions of the characters are moderately similar to content reflecting aggressive activities contained in TAT narratives. Based on these results, the authors suggest that, with respect to hostility, APT questionnaire ratings supplement, rather than repeat, information obtained from the TAT.

Generalizability

With respect to stimuli, the studies reviewed include a range of TAT cards. Whereas Fine (1955a) recommended using 20 cards, Pistole & Ornduff (1994) distinguished sexually abused and nonabused girls with four cards. Other investigations have used various numbers of cards (e.g., 8, 9, 11, 15, 20). There is no indication from any of these studies that certain cards are more effective than others in eliciting specific contents. This is another advantage of this scoring system, as the number and selection of cards can be tailored to the sample under study. Since no particular probing beyond that recommended by Bellak (1993) is required, this scoring scheme can be applied to archival as well as newly acquired data. Additionally, the system has been used successfully in studies of outpatient children, inpatient adults, and college undergraduates in the United States and in a sample of Pacific Islanders. Obviously, respondents must be willing and able to comply with the storytelling instructions; otherwise, this system can be broadly applied to a variety of subject samples.

Reliability

As with any scoring system, emphasis must be given to rater training and reliability. Raters from the previously reviewed studies included advanced undergraduate students, graduate students in clinical psychology, and experienced professionals. The amount of time to achieve acceptable levels of interrater reliability is addressed only by Fine (1955a, p. 307), who indicated that he and his team of raters required "minimal instruction" to attain interrater rs ranging from .84 to .91 across the various scoring categories.

Fine (1955a) detailed the means by which he established interrater reliability for his method using a team of five graduate students in clinical psychology. Fine's scoring was used as the standard, and the rater's results were compared with his. Following two relatively brief training and practice sessions, high levels of interrater agreement were achieved (empirical *rs* = .91, .81, .89, .88, .85, respectively). On this basis, Fine determined that other comparable groups of raters could reach acceptable levels of reliability with minimal instruction. Davison's (1953) stories were coded by three independent, highly reliable raters (percent agreement = .84 for the entire scoring scheme). The raters, one of whom was Davison, were all experienced with the TAT. In Pistole and Ornduff (1944) two independent raters (one graduate student in psychology and one senior psychology major) with high levels of interrater reliability (overall r for feelings = .93; overall r for outcomes = .85) scored the stories. With respect to Condrell et al. (1998), interrater agreement for the TAT was accomplished by two independent raters who scored a sample of the stories; correlations between the judge's ratings ranged from .47 to .80. A single judge then rated all of the TAT stories to test the study hypotheses with respect to aggressive feelings and aggressive activities. Decisions of the judge were guided by the scoring criteria provided by Fine (1955a), as well as the number of times a subject selected a feeling or action from the APT questionnaire that involved hostility or aggression (e.g., hates, kills, harms, dislikes).

Based on personal experience with this scoring system, I estimate that a dedicated team of two or three raters that adheres to the scoring instructions could achieve acceptable levels of interrater reliability with three or four group practice sessions and an additional 10 hours of individual scoring. Given the system's focus on manifest content, raters do not need to have an extensive background in clinical psychology, psychopathology, or personality assessment. More important, they need to appreciate research methods and design and the importance of reliability as it relates to the validity of a proposed study.

□ Future Research Needed

Although few in number, these studies provide empirical support for the use of Fine's (1955a, 1955b) scoring scheme for manifest content. This is not surprising given the importance of verbal productions in interpersonal situations, including personality assessment with unambiguously social projective methods. The strengths of this system include its simplicity and straightforward nature with respect to rater training and scoring and its applicability to any number of samples of interest. I agree with Fine's initial assessment of his theory-based method as a springboard for further hypothesis development and testing. The clinical utility of analogous scoring approaches (e.g., computer-based dictionary programs; Rosenberg, Blatt, Oxman, McHugo, & Ford, 1994) is a testament to the value of coding systems that focus on the manifest content of verbal productions.

□ References

Balken, E., & Massermann, J. (1940). The language of fantasy: III. The language of the fantasies of patients with conversion hysteria, anxiety state, and obsessive-compulsive neurosis. *Journal of Psychology, 10,* 75–86.

Bellak, L. (1944). The concept of projection: An experimental investigation and study of the concept. *Psychiatry, 7,* 353–370.

Bellak, L. (1993). *The T.A.T., C.A.T., and S.A.T. in clinical use* (5th ed.). Boston: Allyn and Bacon.

Condrell, C., Karp, S., Holmstrom, R., & Silber, D. (1998). Measures of aggression in questionnaire ratings and stories from the Apperceptive Personality Test. *Perceptual and Motor Skills, 86,* 1187–1191.

Davison, A. H. (1953). Comparison of the fantasy productions of the TAT of sixty hospitalized psychoneurotic and psychotic patients. *Journal of Projective Techniques, 17,* 20–33.

Fine, R. (1948). *A quantitative study of personality factors related to bronchial asthma in children*. Unpublished doctoral dissertation, University of Southern California.

Fine, R. (1951). Blind analysis of "John Doe's" tests. In E. Shneidman (Ed.), *Thematic Test Ayalysis* (pp. 64–82). New York: Grune & Stratton.

Fine, R. (1955a). A scoring scheme for the TAT and other verbal projective techniques. *Journal of Projective Techniques, 19,* 306–309.

Fine, R. (1955b). Manual for a scoring scheme for verbal projective techniques (TAT, MAPS, stories and the like). *Journal of Projective Techniques, 19,* 310–316.

Freud, S. (1938). *The interpretation of dreams*. New York: Random House.

Holmstrom, R., Silber, D., & Karp, S. (1990). Development of the Apperceptive Personality Test. *Journal of Personality Assessment, 54,* 252–264.

Karp, S., Condrell, C., Holstrom, R., & Silber, D. (1989). *Apperceptive Personality Test stimulus plates.* Worthington, OH: IDS Publishing Corp.

Lessa, W. A., & Spiegelman, M. (1954). Ulithian personality as seen through ethnological materials and thematic test analysis. *University of California Publications in Culture & Society,* 2, 243–301.

Murray, H. (1943). *Thematic Apperception Test manual.* Cambridge, MA: Harvard University Press.

Ornduff, S., & Monahan, K. (1999). Children's understanding of parental violence. *Child & Youth Care Forum, 28,* 351–364.

Pistole, D., & Ornduff, S. (1994). TAT assessment of sexually abused girls: An analysis of manifest content. *Journal of Personality Assessment, 63,* 211–222.

Rosenberg, S., Blatt, S., Oxman, T., McHugo, G., & Ford, R. (1994). Assessment of object relatedness through a lexical content analysis of the TAT. *Journal of Personality Assessment, 64,* 345–362.

Shneidman, E. (1947). The Make-A-Picture-Story (MAPS) projective personality test: A preliminary report. *Journal of Consulting Psychology, 11,* 315–325.

Worchel, F., Aaron, L., & Yates, D., (1990). Gender bias on the Thematic Apperception Test. *Journal of Personality Assessment, 55,* 593–602.

□ Note

This chapter is dedicated to the memory of Reuben Fine.

15

CHAPTER

Scoring Manual for Reuben Fine's Scoring Scheme for the TAT and Other Verbal Projective Techniques

Sidney Orndoff

Introduction

The Scoring Scheme for the Thematic Apperception Test (TAT) and Other Verbal Projective Techniques is a content-based coding system for projective material. The focus of this chapter is the application of the scoring system to verbal material provided to TAT cards. With few exceptions, only manifest content is scored. Major scoring categories include feelings, outcome, and interpersonal relationships. Scoring instructions and examples are presented here.

Administration

Format and Stimuli

Published reports of this scoring system have used subsets of cards from the original Thematic Apperception Test (TAT) (Murray, 1943). When mentioned, TAT administration is consistent with that recommended by Bellak (1993), with probes limited to story antecedents and outcomes and to characters' thoughts and feelings. Because of this, the scoring scheme can be applied to archival as well as newly acquired data. Studies using this system have included a range of TAT cards (4–20), with variable numbers of characters portrayed (1–3). There is no indication from any of the reviewed studies that certain cards are more effective than others in eliciting specific contents. This is an advantage of this scoring system, as the number and selection of cards can be tailored to the sample under study. The system has been used with outpatient children, inpatient adults, and college undergraduates in the United States and with a sample of Pacific Islanders. Data have been acquired from both individual and group settings and in both oral and written formats. The only requirement of the system is that respondents comply with the storytelling instructions; thus, it can be broadly applied to a variety of subject samples.

Scoring Process

With few exceptions, only the manifest content of TAT responses is scored. Major scoring categories include feelings, outcome, and interpersonal relationships. Each TAT story is considered to be a unit, and the use of a psychogram or similar summary sheet is recommended to facilitate scoring. After the stories are scored, grand totals are calculated to provide an overall summary of the respondent's record.

Following are the basic scoring instructions for the Scoring Scheme for Verbal Projective Techniques.

(1) Under feelings and outcome, number the columns for the cards used in the evaluation.

(2) Place a checkmark in the appropriate column to indicate the presence of any feeling expressed in the story.

(3) Check one outcome. This is scored from the point of view of the hero of the story.

(4) Under interpersonal relationships, enter the number of the story (i.e., TAT card) in the appropriate column. Note that interactions between any two people are recorded; thus, more than one interpersonal relationship may be coded for a given card.

(5) Repetitions of any feelings and interpersonal relationships within a story are disregarded.

(6) Score only what is explicitly stated. Exceptions to this scoring rule are permitted only to the extent that it is necessary for categorization.

(7) Design the psychogram or scoring sheet so that each TAT card has its own column under feelings and outcome (Table 15.1). For interpersonal relationships, the psychogram should include a row for each relational category and subcategory and columns for the 16 dyadic scenarios (Table 15.2).

(8) After all the stories are scored, enter the totals in the appropriate columns.

TABLE 15.1 Scoring Sheet for Verbal Projective Techniques-TAT: Feelings and Outcome

Feelings	Card 1	Card 2	Card 3BM	Card 4	Total
Affection, verbal					
Affection, physical					
Anger					
Anxiety					
Compulsion					
Conflict					
Crime					
Depression					
Drink					
Effort					
Escape					
Excitement					
Frustration					
Guilt					
Hostility:					
a. Verbal					
b. Physical					
c. Death					
Management of:					
a. Externalized					
b. Internalized					
c. Repressed					
d. Displaced					
e. Punished					
f. Other					
Inferiority					
Loneliness					
Orality					
Pain					
Pathological Indicators:					
a. Taboo Activity					
b. Bizarre Verbalization					
c. Rejection of Card					
d. Other					

(*Continued*)

TABLE 15.1 Scoring Sheet for Verbal Projective Techniques-TAT: Feelings and Outcome (Continued)

Feelings	Card 1	Card 2	Card 3BM	Card 4	Total
Pleasure					
Possessiveness					
Sexuality					
Special States					
Suicide					
Superiority					
Wishful Thinking					
Outcome	**Card 1**	**Card 2**	**Card 3BM**	**Card 4**	**Total**
Favorable					
Unfavorable					
Indeterminate					

Scoring Category Criteria

The following examples are based on Fine (1955b, pp. 311–316).

Feelings

(1) With the exception of hostility, frustration, and certain pathological indicators, only feelings explicitly described in the protocol are scored. No interpretation is permitted.

(2) If a feeling is described as occurring in the future or conditional (e.g., "He's going to feel excited," or "He might feel excited"), it is scored unless the context of the story makes it explicitly clear that the feeling in question will not be expressed. Fine (1955b, p. 311) gave the following examples: "He's going to be angry and she's going to be sad" is scored for feelings of anger and depression. Conversely, "He'll be angry but she won't be sad" is scored for anger but not depression.

(3) Common synonyms for the various feelings and additional scoring rules are as follows:

(a) Affection: like, love, or some affectionate action. Physical affection is scored if there is physical contact (e.g., "She hugged him," or "She patted the boy on the head"). Verbal affection is scored if there is no physical contact and the action is explicitly expressed.

(b) Anger: mad, sore, angry. Context is important, as *mad* may indicate craziness, or *sore* could refer to pain. The example, "She is mad at him" is scored for both hostility and anger. "She is mad" is only scored for anger.

TABLE 15.2 Scoring Sheet for Verbal Projective Techniques-TAT: Interpersonal Relationships

Interpersonal Relationships	Mother–Child	Child–Mother	Father–Child	Child–Father	Mother–Father	Father–Mother	Sibling–Sibling	Man–Man	Man–Woman	Woman–Man	Woman–Woman	Acquaintance–Stranger	Stranger–Acquaintance	Friend–Friend	Stranger–Stranger	Other	Total
MOVING TOWARDS																	
Affection																	
a. Verbal																	
b. Physical																	
Acceptance																	
Dominance																	
Submission																	
MOVING AGAINST																	
Verbal																	
Physical																	
Death																	
MOVING AWAY FROM																	
Separation																	
Indifference																	
Rejection																	
NO RELATIONSHIP																	
Total																	

(c) Anxiety: anxious, afraid, worried, insecure, fearful

(d) Compulsion: compelled to, forced to, made to

(e) Conflict: cannot make up one's mind; does not know what to do. Note that a conflict on the part of the examinee is not scored; rather, the conflict must be expressed by a character in the story. In the example, "I don't know whether this is a boy or girl. I guess it's a girl," conflict is not scored. For the response, "This is a boy and he can't decide whether to go outside and play or stay inside and practice his violin," conflict is scored.

(f) Crime: any crime committed by any character in a story

(g) Depression: sad, unhappy, depressed

(h) Drink: drinking of alcoholic beverages by any character in a story

(i) Effort: tries, tries hard, works, works hard, persists, perseveres. Note that the effort must involve something beyond the ordinary. For example, "She works as a teacher" is not scored for effort. However, "She has to work hard to be a good teacher" is scored for effort.

(j) Escape: runs away, flees, escapes, hides

(k) Excitement: gets excited, screams, shouts

(l) Frustration: failure, any situation considered to be a serious frustration by a character in a story. For example, frustration is scored in the following example: "This is a man whose wife has just left him. He gets really depressed and can't cope anymore." In this example, however, frustration is not scored: "This man's girlfriend just left, and he says to hell with her. I never cared about her anyway."

(m) Guilt: sorry, regretful, guilty, feel bad

(n) Hostility: any aggressive or unfriendly action, intention, or statement. Verbal hostility is scored when there is no indication of physical violence or death: "She hates his guts." Physical hostility is scored for any expression of aggressive contact: "She kicked him in the stomach." Death hostility is scored when the hostility results in death. Note that death is always scored as hostility even if the cause of death is not specified or when it is attributed to natural causes.

(o) Inferiority: weak, poor, inadequate

(p) Loneliness: lonely, lonesome

(q) Orality: any oral activity such as eating, drinking, smoking

(r) Pain: hurt, tired, sick, in pain

(s) Pathological indicators: tabooed activity refers to any socially tabooed activity, such as intercourse in public or murder without mitigating circumstances. Homosexuality refers to expressions of overt homosexual activity. Bizarre verbalization includes a response such as, "An electric bulb hath the darkness. Figureless the street activity hath little trace of humans. It was a busy night for the weather and few sounds were heard to indicate a pattern of common knowledge" to card 20 (Fine, 1955b, p. 315). Rejection of card is rare for individuals of average or above-average intelligence, although exceptions may occur for cards 11 and 16. Rejection of a card is often associated with severe psychopathology. Other is scored for any other activity or thought that is bizarre (e.g., ideas of reference).

(t) Pleasure: pleased, contentment, satisfaction, happy, joyful

(u) Possessiveness: possessive, stingy, stubborn

(v) Sexuality: sexual intercourse

(w) Special States: Place a check in the appropriate box for feelings not included elsewhere. Note the feeling on the scoring sheet.

(x) Suicide: killed oneself, committed suicide

(y) Superiority: superior, successful, rich, prestige

(z) Wishful thinking: indications of a desire that has special significance to the character and that she or he has been unable to achieve it for the time being. For example, "The boy wants to go outside and play" is not scored for wishful thinking, but, "The boy is sitting there and dreaming about how nice it would be if he could outside and play" is.

Outcome

The three subcategories are favorable, unfavorable, and indeterminate. These are scored from the point of view of the hero of the story; thus, some judgment on the part of the rater is required.

Interpersonal Relationships

These are scored for actions specifically described in the stories, not for interactions that are inferred. This domain stresses the direction of any interaction between two people and allows for interaction in one direction with omission of activity in another (i.e., non-mutual interaction). For example, "The mother hugged her daughter" is scored as M-C (mother-child) physical affection; there is no score for C-M (child-mother). Fine's (1955b, p. 316) example, "The boy hates music," is scored only for the feeling (verbal hostility) because there is no other person involved. Parents must be identified as such; *folks* and *parents* are checked for both mother and father. For example, "His parents bought him a book" is scored for M-C acceptance and F-C (father-child) acceptance. *Mother* is synonymous with wife, as is *father* for husband, *boy* with son and brother, *girl* with daughter and sister. The 16 listed relationship categories are those most often encountered in TAT stories. Other significant relationships expressed by the respondent (e.g., grandmother–grandson) should be recorded in the column titled "Other."

For any two people, each interaction must be categorized as one of the following: moving toward, moving against, moving away from.

Moving toward includes:

(1) Affection: any action or statement expressing love, fondness, or affection. Affection is further classified as verbal or physical depending on the presence or absence of physical contact.

(2) Acceptance: refers to favorable actions short of affection, the difference being primarily one of degree

(3) Dominance: all commands and authoritative actions that are not hostile in nature. For example, dominance is scored for, "The sergeant ordered his men to march." However, "The sergeant decided to punish his soldier and ordered him to clean the latrines" is scored for hostility (moving against).

(4) Submission: all actions or statements indicating submission or subservience. Obedience is automatically scored as submission.

Moving against includes the subclassifications of verbal, physical, and death. These are identical to those defined under the feeling of hostility; however, to score an interpersonal relationship as hostile, both persons involved must be explicitly mentioned. In the example, "The mother whipped her son," physical hostility is scored and entered under both the feeling and interpersonal relationship categories. "The boy hates the violin" is scored only under the feeling of verbal hostility since no other person is involved.

Moving away from includes (1) separation, all interruption of interpersonal contact in which separation, but not overt rejection, is expressed; and (2) rejection, instances of acts of thoughts of rejection. In this example, "Joe and his friend were talking. It got late so he left to go home," acceptance (*talking*) and separation (*he left to go home*) would be scored. For the response, "Joe and his friend were talking. They had a fight and he left angrily," acceptance (*talking*), verbal hostility (*fight*), and rejection (*he left angrily*) would be scored.

As with hostility, both the feeling and interpersonal relationship are scored if the two persons involved are specified. If only one person is identified, only the feeling is scored. Fine (1955b, p. 316) gave the following example: "He becomes frightened and runs away" is scored only for feelings (escape); "When he saw the cops he got scared and ran away" is scored under both feelings and interpersonal relationships.

A fantasied relationship (i.e., a relationship that is wished for by a character in a story) is indicated by circling the number of the TAT card to which it is expressed on the scoring sheet. Fine (1955b, p. 311) gave the following example: "He thought that when he got home he would kiss his mother." If this response was given to card 10, it would be scored as C-M (fantasy) physical affection and the number 10 would be circled in the appropriate column on the psychogram.

Scoring Sheet and Calculating Scores

Tables 15.1 and 15.2 present a score sheet similar to that used by Pistole and Ornduff (1994) in their comparison of sexually abused and nonabused outpatient girls. The scoring sheet contains columns for the four TAT cards used by these investigators for each of the feelings and outcome categories. A "Total" column is included to provide a quick tally of the most frequently expressed feelings and outcomes for the respondent's record. Similarly, the Interpersonal Relationships component of the scoring sheet contains a "Total" column that allows for rapid examination of the nature and quality of interpersonal themes contained in the storyteller's productions.

☐ Practice Stories

The following stories are a subsample of those included in Pistole and Ornduff (1994). Use the scoring sheet in Table 15.1 to tally the feelings and outcome for each story. Ignore repetitions of feelings expressed in a story, and score a single outcome for each narrative. Focus on what is explicitly stated by the storyteller when scoring content. In some instances, interpretation of a feeling is required depending on the context of the statement or the overall tone of the story.

(1) Card 1: Once upon a time there was a little boy that had an instrument. I don't know what the name of it is. He went home after school to go to practice his instrument. Then he sat down in his room and was thinking about what to play. So he sat down and thought and thought about it. (**Query** – happens next) The next morning he went to school and they were going to have a program. He took his instrument with him but forgot he didn't know what to play. So he went up in front of the audience and just stood there. (**Query** – feeling) Very sad. (**Query** – thinking) That he felt just like a dummy just standing there. Everybody in the audience was just making fun of him 'cause he was just standing there.

(2) Card 1: I don't know how to make a story. I don't know ... just a little boy playing an instrument and it broke. He needed money to replace it. That's all. And he didn't have no one to give money so he was mad. (**Query** – end) He finally got someone to help him pay for it and they've been real good friends. The end.

(3) Card 1: Looks like he just got a violin, can't play it yet. He's depressed because he can't play it. (**Query** – happens next) Probably gave up.

(4) Card 2: A girl that's going away and she's looking at something. She's carrying some books and she doesn't look very good. Her father looks like he's planting the yard or something, and they're all mad at her. Her mommy and daddy. Maybe they don't want her. She's walking away and feeling sad or funny or something. (**Query**) A sad day, a very lonely day.

(5) Card 2: There was once a girl who lived with her parents on a farm. She had no neighbors and no friends. She had been the only child for a long time. Then she found out that her mother was pregnant and she felt like she wouldn't get all the attention anymore. She felt that she wouldn't be loved because a new child was coming into the family. She talked to her mother and her mother explained that she would always be the first child that she ever loved. Then she felt needed again.

(6) Card 2: Once there was a family who lived on a farm and got up every morning to do their chores. They had a little girl who went to school while her dad would plow the fields and her mother would rest. One day she woke up not feeling good, but her mother didn't believe her and thought she didn't want to go to school. At school she got real sick and had to go to the doctors. Her mother said she was sorry and would always listen to her.

(7) Card 3BM: Sad person. She is sad, wearing a dress. She can't come out of her room 'cause mom and dad are talking about something they don't want her to hear. Probably about how good or bad she is doing at school (**Query** – happened before) They wanted her out of the room. (**Query** – happened after) Holler for her to get out of her room. (**Query** – girl thinking) She wants out of her room. (**Query** – girl feeling) Sad.

(8) Card 3BM: I hate this kind of picture. Somebody's sad and tired and sort of feeling bad. It's a girl. She's feeling bad because someone hurt her feelings at school by saying, "Ooh, you look ugly," and by calling her names because they're mean. (**Query** – story end) They get in trouble for making her feel bad and she told the teacher.

(9) Card 3BM: Don't be surprised if this one's not very long. (Nervous laughter). Somebody took all her money. They took everything. They broke into her apartment. She told the cops but they didn't believe her. They said she sold her stuff. She got so depressed that she killed herself.

(10) Card 4: There was this lady that had problems with her husband because he drank. So she tried to comfort him and he turned her away. And she became angry for what he was doing and tried to work things out. So all in all they lived happily ever after.

(11) Card 4: Lady and man very much in love a long time ago. He went away for a long time to do something with his work. When he came back they got into an argument and now thinking about getting a divorce. (**Query** – work) Taking cows somewhere. (**Query** – argue about) He didn't leave her enough money when he left. (**Query** – man thinking) Upset, but he knows he can do without her. (**Query** – woman thinking) Shocked he's not really wanting to stay with her. (**Query** – end) Getting a divorce … separating. Realize they really love each other and get back together.

(12) Card 4: There's this lady talking to this man. This man does nothing but ignore this beautiful lady. He doesn't listen to her. She says she wants a kiss, but he turns and looks at another woman. She said she loved him, but he does nothing. Finally she says "Fine," and gets up and walks away. (**Query** – feeling) Like strangers.

The following stories were provided by Worchel, Aaron, and Yates (1990); TAT cards are not indicated.

(13) She's all excited because he asked her to go out and he hasn't asked her to do something in a long time because they've so busy working and so she decides to go out and they had a really good time and she was real happy.

(14) So they got in this big fight and started wrestling around and stuff and she started screaming things at him and all of a sudden he swung and hit her in the face.

(15) He is climbing, he's got a firm grip on the rope and so he is showing his determination during the performance.

☐ Expert Scoring

The TAT stories in Pistole and Ornduff (1994) were scored with respect to feelings and outcome. Scoring of these stories is provided following. Note that repetitions of feelings expressed by any of the characters in a story are ignored—that is, each feeling is scored only once. Analogously, a single outcome from the perspective of the hero is scored for each story.

- Story 1: Scored for depression, inferiority, unfavorable outcome
- Story 2: Scored for anger, favorable outcome
- Story 3: Scored for depression, indeterminate outcome
- Story 4: Scored for anger, anxiety, depression, loneliness, unfavorable outcome. Given the context, *funny* is interpreted as an anxiety state, analogous to feelings of insecurity.
- Story 5: Scored for inferiority, pleasure, favorable outcome
- Story 6: Scored for guilt, pain, favorable outcome
- Story 7: Scored for depression, verbal hostility, unfavorable outcome
- Story 8: Scored for depression, indeterminate outcome
- Story 9: Scored for depression, suicide, unfavorable outcome
- Story 10: Scored for anger, frustration, orality, favorable outcome. Effort is not scored as the woman's attempts to work things out with her husband are not expressed as extraordinary.
- Story 11: Scored for anger, affection, verbal hostility, favorable outcome. In this context, both *upset* and *shocked* are judged to be synonymous with anger.
- Story 12: Scored for verbal affection, anger, frustration, inferiority, unfavorable outcome

The following scoring is provided by Worchel et al. (1990, p. 597) based on Fine (1955a, 1955b).

- Story 13: Scored for excitement, acceptance, pleasure
- Story 14: Scored for conflict, verbal hostility, physical hostility, moving against-verbal, moving against-physical
- Story 15: Scored for effort

References

Bellak, L. (1993). *The T.A.T., C.A.T., and S.A.T. in clinical use* (5th ed.). Boston: Allyn and Bacon.

Fine, R. (1955a). A scoring scheme for the TAT and other verbal projective techniques. *Journal of Projective Techniques, 19,* 306–309.

Fine, R. (1955b). Manual for a scoring scheme for verbal projective techniques (TAT, MAPS, stories and the like). *Journal of Projective Techniques, 19,* 310–316.

Murray, H. (1943). *Thematic Apperception Test manual.* Cambridge, MA: Harvard University Press.

Pistole, D., & Ornduff, S. (1994). TAT assessment of sexually abused girls: An analysis of manifest content. *Journal of Personality Assessment, 63,* 211–222.

Worchel, F., Aaron, L., & Yates, D., (1990). Gender bias on the Thematic Apperception Test. *Journal of Personality Assessment, 55,* 593–602.

Note

This chapter is dedicated to the memory of Reuben Fine.

16

CHAPTER

Primary Process Scoring for the TAT

Robert R. Holt

Abstract

The scoring scheme began as a direct translation of Sigmund Freud's writings about primary process thinking into a method of identifying it in Rorschach responses, later adapted for the Thematic Apperception Test (TAT) and expanded into measuring adaptive versus maladaptive regression in thought–products. Though conceived as a way of operationalizing Freud's conceptualization of the disordered cognitive-affective processes generating dreams, pathological and creative thinking, the scored variables—especially the forms of controlling and defending against drive-laden and deviant thinking to make it adaptive—have turned out to be more broadly useful measures of key aspects of personality.

Description of System

Conceptual Framework

Unlike many scoring schemes that were designed with just the Thematic Apperception Test (TAT) in mind, mine began as an attempt to apply psychoanalytic theory to the understanding of Rorschach responding. In the early and mid-1950s, I found it quite feasible to translate Sigmund Freud's clinical descriptions of how primary processing works into specific rules for scoring Rorschach responses. The most important advance began when I grasped the practical significance of the distinction between pathological emergence of primary process thinking and its appearance in playful, humorous, and creative thought. Shortening Kris's (1952) term *regression in the service of the ego* to adaptive (versus maladaptive) regression, I was able to find scorable indications of controlling and defensive operations that made the difference.

To compare the ways primary process thinking emerged in Rorschach, TAT stories, and dreams, a doctoral student of mine adapted the scoring scheme in her dissertation (Eagle, 1964). Since then, I have worked it over further myself, and as I write, a book is in press (Holt, 2008) containing both the Rorschach version and the more general adaptation, which has been used with story-like material of various kinds and less constrained types of text such as free associations. The condensed version presented here omits the minor modifications that are needed in scoring dreams.

The scheme began as a way of measuring key concepts in the psychoanalytic theory of thinking: the primary process and adaptive versus maladaptive regression. Despite the fact that most psychoanalytic sources asserted that the odd formal features of primary process thinking arise because of defenses against the crude drives that motivate it, the scheme takes no position on the point. Empirically, it happens that the motivational—here called *content*—aspects of primary process are only moderately correlated with its formal aspects; therefore, they are scored separately.

In the complete book-length manual (Holt, 2008), the first volume is devoted mainly to a detailed historical exegesis of the concept of primary process. Briefly, though Freud emphasized his anachronistic and now useless metapsychological formulation of his theory of thinking, it is susceptible of being reformulated in terms that are consistent with contemporary knowledge about cognitive neuropsychology. Even though the status of primary process—and even more so, of secondary process—as systems in the sense of modern systems theory is uncertain, there is enough empirical justification for continuing to treat them as such for clinical and many research purposes. The convergent evidence of several independent factor analyses demonstrates their coherence in data (Holt, 2008, volume 2, chapter 12).

The scoring of Content* focuses on distinguishable varieties of Libidinal and Aggressive themes, viewed as expressions of wishes. Though I was guided by Freud's psychosexual developmental stages in distinguishing the libidinal categories, the specific scores I ended up with were dictated as much by the way the data fell as by theory. And though I experimented for a while with scoring other types of motives, I abandoned them for just Libidinal and Aggressive categories. I am by no means a convinced advocate of the dual-instinct theory; it was simply that the goal was to produce a tool for the quantitative study of Freudian hypotheses. The nature of the Rorschach happens to make the rich variety of motives that may be scored in TAT stories less apparent. And there are plenty of other systems for measuring the full motivational gamut.

The second large group of scoring categories delineates the types of Formal Aspects of primary process that may be seen in stories. Here, many of the specific category names are taken directly from Freud (e.g., Condensation, Displacement, Symbolization, Contradiction), though others are more empirically derived. They are particularly useful in measuring schizophrenic thought disorder, in conjunction with indications of pathological defenses.

The third group of categories, Control and Defense, includes a number of the classical defenses described by S. Freud and A. Freud, but many others from a variety of nontheoretical sources, notably the Remoteness scores directly derived from Silvan Tomkins's (1947) TAT book. All three classes of categories are presented in Table 16.1.

*Capitals indicate groupings of scores; symbols of the scores are italicized.

Table 16.1 Primary Process Content Scoring Categories

Content
Libidinal
L 1 O (oral)
L 1 A (anal)
L 1 S (sexual)
L 1 E-V (exhibitionistic/voyeuristic)
L 1 H (homosexual)
L 1 M (miscellaneous libidinal)
L 2 O (oral)
L 2 A (anal)
L 2 S (sexual)
L 2 E-V (exhibitionistic/voyeuristic)
L 2 H (homosexual)
L 2 M (miscellaneous)
Aggressive
Ag 1 A (aggressor)
Ag 1 O (oral aggression)
Ag 1 V (victim)
Ag 1 R (results)
Ag 2 A (aggressor)
Ag 2 O (oral aggression)
Ag 2 V (victim)
Ag 2 R (results)
Formal Variables
Condensation
C-ctm 1 (contamination)
C-ctgn 1 (contagion)
C-int 1 (interpenetration)
C c-i 1 (collective image)
C-co 1 (composition)
C-co 2 (conventional compositions)
Displacement
D-chain 1 (chain association)
D-dist 1 (distant association)

(*Continued*)

Table 16.1 Primary Process Content Scoring Categories (Continued)

D-clang 1 (clang association)
D-clang 2 (puns, etc.)
D-sub 1 (substitution)
D-sub 2 (substitution, mild)
D-time 1 (distorted time)
D-time 2 (anachronism)
D-a-t 1 (arbitrary turn of events)
D-a-t 2 (arbitrary turn)
D-acc 2 (displaced accent)
D-fig 2 (figures of speech)
D S 2 (slips of tongue)

Symbolism
Sym-C 2 (conventional color symbolism)
Sym-I 1 (image symbols)
Sym-I 2 (conventional image symbols)

Contradiction
Ctr A 1 (affective)
Ctr L 1 (logical)
Ctr R 1 (of reality)
Ctr R 2 (lies)

Distortions (miscellaneous)
Au Lg 1 (autistic logic)
Au Lg 2 (reasoning from detail)
Intr 1 (intrusions)
B C 1 (break in continuity)
B C 2 (break in continuity, mild)
Un Rel 1 (unrealistic relationship)
Trans 1 (fluid transformation)
Trans 2 (transformation of percept)
P D 1 (perceptual distortion)
P D 2 (perceptual distortion, mild)
S-R 1 (self-reference)
M C 1 (magical causation)
M C 2 (religious miracles)
F-msc 1/2 (other)

(*Continued*)

Table 16.1 Primary Process Content Scoring Categories (Continued)

Verbalizations
V I 1 (incoherence)
V C 1 (condensation)
V Q 1 (queerness)
V P 2 (peculiarity)
Controls and Defenses
Remoteness
R-min (minimal)
R-eth (ethnic)
R-an (animals, most)
R-(an) (animals, ego-alien)
R-pl (plants)
R-ia (inanimate)
R-dep+ (depictions)
R-geo+ (geographic)
R-time+ (in time)
R-time (less appropriate)
R-char (character)
R-fic s+ (fictional, specific, appropriate)
R-fic s, s– (fictional, indifferent/bad)
R-fic n+ (nonspecific, good)
R-fic n, n– (nonspecific, indifferent/bad)
R-rel+ (religious, good)
R-rel, – (indifferent or bad)
R-fan+ (fantasy, good)
R-fan, – (indifferent or bad)
R-fig+ (figurative, good)
R-fig, – (figurative, indifferent or bad)
R-spch (speech)
R-cond (conditional)
R-pers (non-hero)
R-pers-H (other→hero)
R-pers-O (other→other)
Contexts
Cx C+ (cultural, good)
Cx C, – (cultural, indifferent, unsuccessful)
Cx E+ (esthetic, successful)

(*Continued*)

Table 16.1 Primary Process Content Scoring Categories (Continued)

- Cx E, – (esthetic, indifferent or unsuccessful)
- Cx I+ (intellectual, successful)
- Cx I (intellectual, indifferent)
- Cx I– (intellectual, unsuccessful)
- Cx H+ (humorous, successful)
- Cx H, – (humor, indifferent or unsuccessful)

Other Controls

- Refl+ (reflection, good)
- Refl (reflection, less successful)
- Mod+,– (adaptive modification)
- Del (delay)
- Neg+ (negation, successful)
- Neg– (lack of gratification)
- Inh (inhibition)
- Ratn+ (rationalization, successful)
- Ratn (rationalization, less good)
- Minz (minimization)
- Eu (euphemism)
- Vulg– (vulgarity)
- Impl (implication)
- Discl (disclaimed responsibility)

Defenses (pathological)

- Repr (repression)
- Blkg– (blocking)
- Cphb– (counterphobic)
- Va– (vagueness)
- Self-D– (self-deprecation)
- Rep– (repudiation)
- Fake– (phoniness)
- Gram– (disrupted grammar)
- Prj– (projection)
- Obs– (obsessiveness)
- Iso– (isolation)
- Eva– (evasiveness)
- Imp– (impotence)

(*Continued*)

Table 16.1 Primary Process Content Scoring Categories (Continued)

Overtness
- O-beh (behavioral)
- O-vbl (verbal)
- O-exp (experiential)
- O-pot (potential)

Miscellaneous
- C/D msc (other; specify)

Research Evidence

Validity

The bibliography of the pripro system—to fall back on my neologistic abbreviation for *primary process*—includes several hundred items, though only half a dozen have as yet used the modification for the TAT. Nevertheless, there is abundant evidence from the Rorschach research for the construct validity of the pripro system's measures of adaptive and maladaptive regression, and many other replicated findings relating other indices and scores to important aspects of personality and psychopathology, enough to encourage their use in personality assessment even when there is no particular focus on psychoanalytic constructs. (For a detailed summary of the construct validity of the system, see Holt, 2007, volume 2, pp. 475–763.)

In addition, the original version of the TAT rating scale for Adequacy of Hero, which was developed by Holt and Luborsky (1958), showed promise as a measure of the sense of adequacy. My average ratings of it over stories to 11 cards, which had a judge reliability of .78 against another rater, were correlated ($r = .31$) with the overall competence of a group of 53 psychiatric residents as rated by their supervisors, and ($r = .28$) with competence in ward administration (Holt & Luborsky, 1958).

Generalizability

Unhappily, too little work has been done with my method using the TAT for me to be able to cite data on its population generalizability. It does happen, however, that there is some relevant information about its big brother, the pripro scoring of the Rorschach, because of the almost unique initiative of Douglas H. Heath. He developed an original conception of personal maturity and a series of innovative assessment techniques to measure it, including among them the application of pripro scoring to Rorschachs. Some of his early data provided striking evidence of the latter's construct validity. Not content with his extensive efforts to cross-validate these and other findings in four different classes of undergraduate males at Haverford College (Heath, 1965), he decided to explore the cross-cultural applicability of his theoretical scheme and methods of measuring its constructs. The ambitious undertaking (Heath, 1977) involved translating many instruments into Italian and Turkish, recruiting collaborators to assess samples of college students in both modernized and more traditional areas of Italy and Turkey, analyzing the data (again including pripro scoring of the Rorschachs), and integrating the resulting enormous mass of findings.

Not surprisingly, there was a great deal of cross-validational shrinkage. On the whole, however, there were enough mutually supportive trends in the four new samples and the original ones for him to conclude that his conception of maturity has a modest but sturdy modicum of validity for male college students in the contemporary world. Similarly, encouraging findings on a number of pripro indices emerged despite many disappointments. It seems safe to say that in a number of respects, much of what has been cross-validated on well-educated American males is probably specific to that population, but some may be cautiously generalizable to others. If one can make the further assumption, so far not empirically established, that what holds for the Rorschach may be asserted for the TAT also, there is some similar hope for the utility of the pripro method when applied to narrative data.

Reliability

The pripro system has been used with TAT stories, and similar data, by graduate students for the most part. It does not require extensive clinical experience or theoretical sophistication, granted the scorer is an intelligent person who is willing to devote a number of days to mastering it. Positive findings in distinguishing normal from schizophrenic and from suicidal patients have been obtained, in addition, from an Italian translation of Eagle's (1964) original manual by several graduate students under the supervision of Caprara (Caprara et al., 1977), though they do not report scorer reliabilities.

Data on scorer reliabilities of principal indices were reported in two dissertations (Eagle, 1964; Levin, 1973); the results are presented in Table 16.2 along with reliabilities for the scoring of dreams from the same manual and Rorschach responses from the original manual.* Eagle's reliabilities for the pripro scoring of TAT stories are, on the whole, adequate and somewhat better than most of her figures for the Rorschach—except for an idiosyncratic measure, the proportion of formal responses that are condensations, needed for one of her hypotheses. Levin's, being based on such a small sample, fluctuate more widely but at least show that good results can be obtained working solely from the original adaptation.

Goodman (1965) reported a pioneering piece of research on measuring primary process thinking in children's stories, using his own adaptation of the Rorschach manual (draft 9). For 10 stories obtained from each of 20 boys, he and another scorer—neither of whom had been trained by Carol Eagle or me—obtained an r of .99 for total drive-related ideation—apparently the sum of content scores, levels 1 and 2 combined.

Wiseman and Reyher (1973) hypnotized 13 highly susceptible undergraduates and obtained dreams about two Rorschach cards from each of them. Two raters, scoring the dreams, obtained the following coefficients of agreement (rho): % Pripro, .99; % Content, .97; % Formal, .79; % Level 1, .54; % Level 2, .98; % Libidinal, .98; % Aggressive, .89;

*These happen to be among the lowest of many reliabilities for the Rorschach application (Holt, 2007, volume 2, chapter 11).

TABLE 16.2 Judge Reliability of Pripro Indices in Rorschach, TAT, and Dreams

	Rorschach				TAT				Dreams			
	Eagle		Levin		Eagle		Levin		Eagle		Levin	
Types of Score	r	N	r	N	r	N	r	N	r	N	r	N
Total Pripro	.93	33	34	5	.93	30	.69	8	.90	28	.39	8
Σ Level 1/Σ Pripro	.93	33	.13	6	.90	30	1.00	8	.85	28	.78	8
Σ Formal/Σ Pripro	.89	16			.95	30			.83	28		
Σ Condens/Σ Formal	.85	16			.73	30			.82	28		
Mean DE	.46	33	.76	5	.84	30	.59	8	.65	24	.81	8
Mean DD			.34	5			1.00	8			1.00	8
Mean FL			.82	5			.17	8			.87	8
ARI			.14	5								

mean DD, .91; and mean DE, .61. The poor showing of mean DE is not surprising, since the present rules for scoring it from dreams were not then available.

Future Research Needed

Little work has been done to extend Eagle's (1964) original comparison of pripro measures from TAT and Rorschach, which shared much variance but diverged in ways not yet fully understood. My 2008 monograph contains dozens of specified directions for following up many promising research leads as well as gaps in needed knowledge. It also lists many replicated findings based on Rorschach pripro scores, which should be tested using the TAT version. Chapter 11 of its second volume describes needed explorations of the several types of reliability.

In the usually more attractive realm of validity, one particularly promising possibility is looking further into the several types of TAT Controls and Defenses as indices of healthy and adaptive functioning. Another is to expand the Content realm to include the various types of attachment, an area of great contemporary interest where one might make advances by relating behavioral observations to TAT themes of anxious and avoidant attachment plus accompanying indications of Controls and Defenses. In addition, the first 13 pages of chapter 18 (Holt, 2008, volume 2) detail needed types of instrument-focused and external problem-focused research. A good many others are scattered through the pages of volume 2, awaiting a new generation of investigators.

References

Caprara, G. V. e altri (1977). *Studi sulla personalità: Quattro richerche con il metodo di R. Holt* [*Studies in personality: Four researches with the method of R. Holt*]. Torino: Boringhiere.

Eagle, C. (1964). *An investigation of individual consistencies in the manifestations of primary process.* Unpublished doctoral dissertation, New York University.

Goodman, J. T. (1965). *Primary process thinking in children.* Unpublished doctoral dissertation, Michigan State University.

Heath, D. H. (1965). *Explorations of maturity.* New York: Appleton Century Crofts.

Heath, D. H. (1977). *Maturity and competence, a transcultural view.* New York: Gardner Press.

Holt, R. R., & Luborsky, L. (1958). *Personality patterns of psychiatrists* (2 vols.). New York: Basic Books.

Holt, R. R. (2008). *Primary process thinking: Theory, measurement, and research.* Vols. 1 & 2, Lanham, MD: Rowman & Littlefield. *Psychological Issues,* Monograph 69/70.

Kris, E. (1952). *Psychoanalytic explorations in art.* Madison, CT: International Universities Press.

Levin, L. A. (1973). *Hypnosis and regression-in-the-service-of-the-ego.* Unpublished doctoral dissertation, Boston University. *Dissertation Abstracts International, 33* (12-B), 6083.

Tomkins, S. S. (1947). *The Thematic Apperception Test: The theory and technique of interpretation.* New York: Grune & Stratton.

Wiseman, R. J., & Reyher, J. (1973). Hypnotically induced dreams using the Rorschach inkblots as stimuli: A test of Freud's theory of dreams. *Journal of Personality & Social Psychology, 27,* 329–336.

17

CHAPTER

Primary Process Scoring Manual

Robert R. Holt

Introduction

The pripro, or primary process, scoring system, as it is informally known, was originally developed to provide an operational measure of Sigmund Freud's concept of primary process thinking and its control. After several decades of clinical and research use, mostly with the Rorschach test—for which it was originally devised—it has become a means of assessing a limited number of important motivational variables as well as a person's inner (defensive or controlling) reaction to experiencing and communicating about them; an assessment of disordered thinking; a way to measure a person's capacity for adaptive regression or regression in the service of the ego, an important aspect of creativity; and measures of a variety of defensive and coping strategies. It is thus useful for, but by no means limited to, research or clinical practice with a psychoanalytic orientation.

Administration

Format and Stimuli

The method is flexible enough to be used to score stories told about any of the usual thematic apperceptive technique (TAT) cards or thematic test stimuli of various other sorts (e.g., other pictures, verbal cues, blank colored cards), narratives of many kinds (e.g., dreams, autobiographies, folktales), and free verbal texts like recorded free associations or therapeutic sessions.

Nevertheless, the scoring is most easily—and probably most validly—used if the Thematic Apperception Test (TAT) is administered as follows. The first and most important point is that there should be a complete, verbatim protocol of everything the subject says. There is no point in trying to apply the pripro scoring to a record taken down in telegraphic style; it will be impossible to gauge accurately the deviancy of the verbalizations, for example. The patient or other subject may make some initial remarks before the first card is presented, indicating fantasies of being on the point of being tortured or sexually exposed. Such comments and others between cards are not only scorable but are clinically revealing, even though usually not recorded. Thus, if the subject's comments to the experimenter have sexual or hostile meaning, the relevant content category should be scored thus: "You're writing too slow; why don't you learn shorthand?" (*Ag 2 A wk*); "You're too pretty to be a psychologist" (*L 2 S wk*). Less indirect hostility or seductiveness would receive full scores.

It is generally considered advisable to use some variant of Murray's (1938) instructions, such as, "I'm going to show you a series of pictures, which might be used to illustrate stories. For each, I want you to make up a story, telling what is going on in the picture, what led up to the scene, what the characters are thinking and feeling, and how it all turns out. It doesn't have to be an elaborate literary story, just a basic plot with a beginning, middle, and end, with something about the people in it and how they think and feel. OK? Try this one."

After the subject seems finished, I have found it helpful to say, "All right, good; you told me a story about the picture, with a beginning leading up to the scene, the characters' thoughts and feelings, and an ending." Except, of course, if any of these specified elements was missing, the experimenter should say: "except you didn't include ..." covering the omissions one at a time. After that, the experimenter might remark, "All right, now we have a complete story. Your job is to do the same thing each time I give you a new picture." After the second story, inquire into missing parts simply and directly: "How did she feel about it?" or "How does the story end?"

It is valuable to include an affect inquiry in the training of examiners who administer the TAT when it is to be scored for pripro. All that is necessary is for the experimenter to explain, after other inquiry following the first story, "I'm also interested in your feelings, too, while you were telling the story. Please try to recall how you felt when you saw the picture and any changes in your emotions as you told your story." Thereafter, a brief reminder usually suffices: "And what were your feelings during the telling of the story?" Such inquiry not only helps the scoring of Defensive Effectiveness but often yields clinically valuable information as well.

☐ Scoring Process

First, each story is divided into scoring units, roughly equivalent to sentences. Then each unit must be examined for motivational content and for formal manifestations of primary process. Only Libidinal (six subtypes) and Aggressive (four subtypes) motives are scored, each further split into level 1 (more extreme, blatant, or primitive) and level 2 (more civilized and socially acceptable). Likewise, many of the 28 varieties of Formal Deviations from logical, coherent, straightforward thinking are similarly subdivided for a total of 44 possible scores. If any one of these 64 categories is scored, you must also score relevant Controls and Defenses. A rating of Demand for Defense is recorded for each of these scorable bits of pripro, also.

After each unit of a story is scored, the narrative as a whole is considered in an overall rating process ending up with a rating of the Defensive Effectiveness with which the teller has coped with the challenges implicit in the material he or she has produced.

The simplest way to begin explaining the scoring is to exemplify it by going, step by step, over its application to a sample TAT story. The following story was told by a young male college student about card 4, 30 years or so ago when the actors mentioned were popular. ("Sentences" have been numbered.)

> (1) The people resemble Clark Gable and Gene Tierney. (2) The curtains give the impression this takes place in a house, but the pin-up picture in the back seems to negate this, so I conclude that it's in a bar or a roadside stand or someplace like that, (3) and this waitress is trying to prevent this truck driver from leaving. (4) He's not too well-liked by the other drivers on the route so one of them started a rumor that his girl friend here was cheating on him. (5) The eyes of the girl make it clear that she'll convince him of the falseness of the rumors. (How does he feel?) (6) He has a tinge of doubt, but he believes him ... her, basically, but he had doubt. (7) The doubt makes him have a not very convincing fit of anger but then they forget it.

Scoring Category Criteria

Scorable Units

The first step in scoring is to identify and number the pripro-scorable units. It is essential to begin the training of scorers by focusing on identifying scorable units, though that cannot be done apart from the context of learning the scoring as a whole. The basic unit used is the sentence: a complete thought with subject and object (including verb). To some degree, however, the unit of scoring is determined by the applicable pripro scores: You must know, for example, autistic logic (Au Lg) when you see it and identify as one unit no less than the smallest bit of text in which you can see it or any content or formal score; but one unit may contain several bits of pripro-scorable material.

No special scoring sheets are necessary, but it is helpful to prepare some pieces of lined paper divided into columns, as in Table 17.1.

Content

Considering sentence (1), we have to ask first if it contains any scorable Content?* As we look down the list of Libidinal categories in Table 16.1, the only kind of theme that seems relevant is exhibitionistic–voyeuristic (E-V), since there is a reference to movie actors. No such wish is attributed, even implicitly, to either of the characters in the picture, however, so it is not scorable. For some purposes, however, you may find it useful to take note of even such subtle hints as this one, as a tendency to the milder, more socially acceptable form of the motive, abbreviated L 2 E-V tend.

---

* For fuller descriptions of scoring categories, see next section.

TABLE 17.1 Scoring of Sample TAT Story (Card 4)

Units	Content and Formal	(DD)	Controls and Defenses	DD*
1. Clark Gable	L 2 E-V tend			
Gene Tierney	L 2 E-V tend			
2. Curtains give impression that...	Au Lg 2 tend			
pin-up picture	L 2 E-V	(2)	R-dep, Cx C+, O-pot	2
seems to negate...	Au Lg 2 wk	(2)	X	
a bar roadside stand	L 2 O	(1)	R-ia, Cx C+, O-pot	
	L 2 O	(1)	R-ia, Cx C+, O-pot	
3. waitress trying to	L 2 0	(1)	R-pers, Cx C+, O-pot	1
prevent	Ag 2 V wk	(1)	R-pers-H, O-beh	
4. not...well liked...				
one started rumor	Ag 2 V wk	(1)	R-pers-H, O-exp, Eu tend	2
his girl friend was	Ag 2 V wk	(1)	R-pers-H, O-vbl	
cheating on him	L 2 S	(1)	R-pers, O-pot	
	L 2 S, Ag 2 V wk	(2)	R-pers-H, Del, R-fan+, O-beh	
5. The girl's eyes make	L 2 E-V	(1)	R-pers	3
it clear that...	Au Lg 2	(3)	X	
falseness of the	Ctr R 2	(1)	X	
rumor	Ag 2 V wk	(1)	R-pers-H, O-vbl	
6. him...her	D S 2	(2)	Mod+	2
	L 2 H wk	(1)	R-min, Del	
7. fit of anger	Ag 2 A	(2)	R-min, Del, Fake–, O-vbl	2

*Rating based on entire unit, considering DDs for each pripro score.

Computation of DE

Story #	FL	Starting DE	Affect	Structure	C & D	Adequacy of Hero	Final DE
4	Fo	+1.5	–.5	(1,1,1,1, 1 = 5) = 0	0	–.5	+.5

* Mean DD = 1.7 (or 2, if first sentence is omitted). DD × DE = + .85 or +1.

Formal Categories

Second, we consider the Formal categories to see if any of them might apply. None of them does in this sentence, but see following.

Control

Third, every manifestation of pripro is given one or more Control scores (if only *X*, for no defense). Tendencies are presumed so minimal as not to require any control or defense, as is the case here. The Defensive Demand (DD) of the whole unit must finally be rated (see following).

Motivation

We move on then, to sentence (2), looking first for motivational stuff. The explicit mention of the pin-up picture (even though it is present on the card) earns a full L 2 E-V. The number 2 in that score indicates that the wishful material is of the socially mentionable sort. Actual peeping or exhibiting oneself earns L 1 E-V; posting a girlie picture on the wall seems a bit crude in some circles but is generally considered more socially acceptable so it is over the arbitrary line between the two levels. The parenthetical numbers in the middle column are ratings of the implicit demand the pripro material makes to be controlled or defended against, called DD. The ratings for individual scores are given in the manual. The muted signs of oral wishes make about as little demand to be coped with as one finds, so DD is 1, minimal. The voyeuristic wish implied by the girlie picture poses a slightly stronger demand, 2 on the six-point scale.

Any Formal scores? Notice that the subject starts in with an attempt to figure out the story from the picture, reasoning from details in classic fashion. This approach to storytelling is familiar to clinicians who have worked on closed wards, for paranoid patients often proceed in this inappropriate application of inference, which in pripro lingo is autistic logic. The inference he makes here is reasonably straightforward, however: The curtains are indeed of the kind to be expected in an ordinary dwelling house, so the first sign of Au Lg is not only of the level 2 variety but is only a tend. Yet, sounding too much like a lawyer, he reasons from the pinup that it cannot be a house and continues with enough of an attempt at logical deduction to warrant the weak Au Lg 2, which poses a DD of 2.

Since there is fully scorable pripro, some Control (C) and Defense (D) scoring is required. First, the pinup: The exhibitionism–voyeurism is controlled by being expressed in a picture (Remoteness–Depiction), which is culturally accepted (Context: Cultural +), and its Overtness is only potential. Likewise, the orality implied by *bar or roadside stand* is at a safe distance (Remoteness–Inanimate), enjoys the same Cultural Context, and is Potential. None of these scores apply to the forced reasoning, however; that gets an *X* (lack of C or D).

Notice, also, in the right-most column of Table 17.1, that the response's total DD must be rated on the same scale; despite the cumulation of small individual scores, the overall impact amounts to only a 2 on the DD scale.

In sentence (3), the subject's over-long sentence was split here, since after the *and* follows a new, complete thought. The L 2 O is for *waitress,* a role of oral provider; and her physically restraining him puts him (barely) in the role of victim: Ag 2 V weak. Again, each of these Content scores is worth the lowest DD rating. There is nothing scorable in a Formal category, so we consider C & D. Now that motivated behavior is attributed to a person, we have to consider Remoteness in terms of the classical hero assumption that the teller identifies with the figure in the story he most resembles: the man. The woman is the implicit nurturer here, so the orality is at some remoteness in person (R-pers). He is the victim of her very mild aggression, however, so the R-pers-H indicates that the action is directed toward him. (Compare the next sentence.)

Incidentally, it is interesting to note that the libidinal wishes or gratifications in this story are in no case allowed to the hero, and he is the object of all but the final expression of aggression, as he is here in her restraining him, physically (hence, O-beh).

Arguably, the fourth sentence could have been split into its two clauses, but they were considered linked by the *so.* The hero's being rejected by his peers, expressed with a hint of Euphemism, is another Ag 2 V wk, this time given the minimal Overtness of being Experiential (only their feelings are described). Starting a rumor is clearly a hostile act, albeit still a muted one (Ag 2 V wk), now given Verbal Overtness. Like the previous bit of Aggression, it is attributed to another person, directed toward the hero (R-pers-H). A girlfriend is clearly a sexual object (L 2 S, R-pers). The idea of her cheating on him clearly implies an act of betrayal—hence, Ag 2 Ob wk again, done by sexual acting out (L 2 S). Notice that it is the only Content in the sentence that rises to a DD level of 2. Of course, such cheating often implies fully sexual behavior (O-beh), which would be scored L 1 S with a DD of 4, but the pripro system deliberately makes conservative assumptions. All this takes place, moreover, on a plane of unreality—in a rumor—hence, it has the distance of R-fan+, and its Overtness is Verbal. Here, too, the several slight motivational expressions add up to no more than a DD of 2.

In sentence (5), since the eyes are mentioned only in an implicitly physiognomical context, the E-V theme is entirely Potential. Again, the reasoning from detail is without controls (*X*) and this time is far-fetched enough for a full Au Lg 2 with a DD of 3. The issue of the rumor's falseness is a bit tricky. A false rumor is a lie, a Contradiction of Reality; hence, it qualifies for Ctr R 2. It still remains an expression of hostility toward the hero (R-pers-H) expressed in words (O-vbl). The Aggression is not undone by the fact of its falseness, so there is no Negation (Neg). Notice that the overall DD is 3; it is never lower than the highest DD given a particular score.

In sentence (6), the repeated theme of doubt, though clinically interesting, is not scored in the pripro system. The slip (i.e., saying *him* for *her* [D S 2]) occurs during inquiry. Usually, what is said after being questioned is scored Delay (Del), but the manual has a rule that slips are never considered to have been held back and only released under questioning. By the same token, the implied feminine identification (scored L 2 H wk) does not receive a Del, being an intrinsic part of the slip, and because it is implicit and inferential. The subject did correct himself spontaneously, earning Adaptive Modification (Mod+).

In sentence (7), the Ag 2 A, however, is a pure example of the usual kind of Del. It is scored O-vbl because that seems the most likely way in which it would have been expressed; anger can be purely experiential but then is not called a *fit*. Further, a fit of anger may mean purely behavioral rampaging, breaking things, and so forth, but that seems out of character for this mild, passive hero. *Not very convincing* qualifies it for the rather unusual Defense, Fake–. Calling the rumor *false* did not qualify, since in that context the word clearly means simply *untrue*.

Compared with most TAT scoring systems, this one involves intensive, fine-grained scrutiny. It is sensitive to nuance and to subclinical manifestations of neurotic trends, like the passivity betrayed in this story, with a possible masochistic and paranoid flavor (the massed Ag 2 V and Au Lg 2 scores). The teller seems not to be in good touch with his own true feelings (the distancing Remoteness scores until the very end and the Fake–).

There remains one more important part to the scoring—Defensive Effectiveness (DE), which can provide critical information on how adaptively or maladaptively the teller copes with his or her primary process material. Before we can consider this story further, it is necessary to take a detour through several aspects of the system.

The most important component of DE scoring, for a Rorschach response, is its perceptual adequacy, an estimate of the accuracy with which the blot was perceived and matched to a remembered, definitive form. The picture plays a much less prominent part when one evaluates a TAT story, yet one has nevertheless an opportunity to evaluate the quality of a person's perception of his or her world. We start, then, with a perceptual adequacy rating for each story taken as a whole. In any clinical data, evidences of affect should be present in the text, especially if there was an affect inquiry. Consider the affects of the narrative's characters only when they are the only emotional data available. Of course, the Control and Defense scores given must always be considered. Two final considerations are the story's structure (or coherence and organization), and the Adequacy of the Hero. Let us now consider each of these aspects in more detail.

Perceptual adequacy is evaluated using a scale developed by Martin Mayman (Mayman 1970; Mayman & Holt, 2007) for the Rorschach, based on Rapaport's (Rapaport, Gill, & Schafer 1946) work. Most normal subjects perceive the scenes depicted in TAT cards adequately, and it is not easy to distinguish the ordinary, acceptable (Fo) level from sharply accurate (F+) perceiving. Consequently, no attempt is made to separate them unless the perceptual acuity of the subject is really noteworthy, when you may give an F+. Otherwise, handle ordinary acceptable perception as if it is all Fo. Slightly substandard but not really bad perceiving is called weak (Fw). When an object with a more or less definitive shape is described in nondefinitive terms, score it as vague (Fv). Noticeable perceptual distortions are scored F–. Finally, when the perceptual adequacy is good enough for Fo but there is a glaring lapse with respect to one item, score as spoiled (Fs).

Thus, seeing the *gun* in card 3BM as a similarly shaped object such as *cigarettes spilling out of a pack* is scored Fo; saying it was *scissors* or a *knife* earns Fw; describing it as *some kind of object, sort of long in shape* gets an Fv; but something quite inappropriate to the form such as a *box* or *toy truck* deserves F–. Yet if the rest of the picture is more or less adequately seen and described, but there is a misperception of just this item, score Fs. By and large, distortions scored (under formal aspects) P D 2 are Fw; those scored P D 1 are F– (see Holt, 1978, chapter 3, for data on the frequency of these and other types of perceptual distortions, such as misrecognitions of sex.)

Table 17.2 presents trial DE ratings or starting points for the various levels of perceptual adequacy. The form-level rating is strongly influenced by the worst-perceived detail in the picture, but try to consider the total perceptual adequacy. In addition to Fs, it occasionally happens that the subject grossly misperceives one detail while functioning at an F+ level, noticing and correctly describing often overlooked things. Such a rare

TABLE 17.2 Tentative Ratings for Starting the Assessment of DE for TAT Stories From Levels of Perceptual Adequacy

Perceptual Adequacy	Starting DE
F+	+1.5
Fo	+1
Fw	0
Fv	–0.5
Fs	–1
F–	–1

phenomenon, which may indicate paranoid symptoms, should be noted thus: F+/F–, with a starting point of 0.

Affect

Give greatest weight to direct observations of the subject's emotional state in the experimenter's notes (e.g., sighs, tears, laughter, frowning). Then consider the general affective tone of the story in relation to picture pull (again, for normative data, see Holt, 1978).

- If there is genuine and appropriate pleasure and enjoyment, add +1 to +2.
- If apparent positive affect is inappropriate (e.g., with Ag 1), lower by –1.
- If no affect, make no change in DE.
- If anxiety, defensiveness, or discomfort are present, lower DE by –1 to –3.

Control and Defense Scores

Consider the entire range of scores for the story, paying particular attention to plus and minus signs, and raise or lower DE by no more than 1 point.

Structure

Score the following five subscales for stories to all TAT cards except 16 (the blank card). They measure compliance with standard instructions.

Beginning ("Events leading up ..."—may be given in flashbacks)

0: No beginning; the subject starts with the scene in the picture ("The boy is practicing his violin, and then ...").

1: Minimal compliance; the subject starts just before the pictured scene or gives no more than one brief sentence of introductory material ("The boy's mother made him practice the violin, and he has just stopped....").

2: Full compliance; the subject starts well back in time, giving at least one substantial statement about events before the pictured scene ("When this boy was four or five, his parents gave him a violin and lessons. Here we see him during one of his practice sessions.").

Middle ("What's going on in the picture")

0: No mention of the pictured scene; implied or bypassed.

1: Minimal compliance; the subject refers to the scene but does not develop it.

2: Full compliance; the subject gives a reasonable amount of description or development of the scene in the picture.

End ("The outcome")

0: No outcome; story left up in the air, or an overt refusal to end it.

1: Minimal compliance; the subject states outcome briefly without enough development to be convincing, or merely very short. If there is no change of scene or time between the situation as given and the outcome, ordinarily code it 1. Score also for inappropriate endings.

2: Full compliance; the subject gives a reasonable and appropriate amount of outcome, the story comfortably ended—for the reader, not necessarily for the hero. Ideally, a satisfactory ending will both extend into time beyond the day of the scene pictured and will amount to at least one full sentence of denouement.

Thoughts ("What the characters are thinking")

0: No thoughts mentioned, none directly implied.

1: Minimal compliance; thoughts implied or briefly alluded to.

2: Full compliance; at least one character's thoughts are clearly stated.

Feelings ("... and how they feel")

0: No feelings mentioned.

1: Minimal compliance; judgments, affects combined with thoughts, attitudes, or the like ("He wants to get out of there as soon as he can"), or, a very brief statement of minimal affect ("She feels good").

2: Full compliance; a reasonable amount of emotion or feeling is described for the hero (or at least one other character).

In any of the aforementioned subscales, treat overcompliance as full compliance, but if it is obnoxious, take that into account in your clinical judgment.

Next, sum the scores on these subscales, and also count the number of zeroes; then enter them into Table 17.3. In addition, a point may be taken off for disruption of the structure of the story when it jumps about in the normal sequence and goes off on tangents. It is evident from Table 17.3 that a person might comply fully with every aspect but one and may earn a zero for that (e.g., excellent story without an ending). The contribution to DE would then be the sum of +1 (for a sum of 8) and –.5 (for one zero), or +.5.

It should be noted that regarding the structure ratings, in an unpublished doctoral dissertation, Rock (1975) used the sum of these ratings, with TAT stories, in a research project on self-confrontation. He found that two judges, both trained at The Research Center for Mental Health, achieved a reliability of .93 in a sample of 20 undergraduate female subjects. This score was correlated –.51 with the experimenter's independent clinical ratings of defensiveness after observing each subject during the experiment, .60 with cooperativeness (indicating that it does indeed measure compliance with instructions), and .49 with interest in the experiment.

TABLE 17.3 Contributions to DE Based on the Sum of Sub-scale Ratings and Number of Zero Ratings of TAT Stories

Sum of Ratings	Contribution of DE
10	+2
9	+1.5
8	+1
7	+0.5
6 or less	0
Number of zeroes	
None	0
1	–0.5
2	–1
3	–1.5
4 or more	–2

Adequacy of Hero

We assume that a positive feeling about oneself and one's place in the world gives rise to two aspects of stories: (1) heroes who are capable, actively striving people who take charge of their fates and do not give up when they encounter opposition or obstacles; and (2) happy endings, reflecting a sense that things will turn out okay despite temporary setbacks. The first issue is one of activity versus passivity; the second issue is the security or optimism that gives rise to fantasies and expectations of happy endings. We have to assess both of these qualities of stories, therefore, and their interaction, as in Table 17.4.

Do not treat these guidelines mechanically, but keep in mind the general meaning of the DE scale: positive ratings imply good enough control to contribute to the final assessment of adaptive regression, and negative ones imply pathological loss of control or

TABLE 17.4 Contributions of DE From Conjunction of Happiness of Ending of a TAT Story and Ability of Hero to Exert Effort

	Hero's Ability to Exert Active Effort		
Ending	Good	Not Specified	Bad
Happy, positive, appropriate	+1	0	–0.5
Unclear, ambiguous, or none	+0.5	0	–0.5
Unhappy, tragic	+0.5(0)	–0.5	–1

defensiveness. If the procedure of following the guidelines seems off, you may correct it by as much as a full point. If more than a point's adjustment seems called for, reexamine your scoring; it may be that what you are responding to clinically should have been picked up earlier in the process.

Now we can return to the sample story and complete its scoring by computing its DE score:

- Perceptual adequacy: *F*+ = +1.5, for the better-than-average description of characters and mention of curtains and pin-up.
- Affect: None is explicit (no examiner's notes), but there is a vaguely negative undertone, and affects in the story are both negative and not genuine or forthright. So, lower starting level to +1.
- Control and defense scores: Generally adequate; the negative ones bear on affect and have been taken into account previously. They are consistent with +1; no need to lower or raise.
- Structure: All subscales are rated barely adequate. The sum then is 5, with no zeroes, so no change in DE, even though +1 may seem a trifle generous for minimal compliance, with a need for inquiry to extract feelings and outcome.
- Adequacy of hero: –.5, because the ending is not clearly happy (things are smoothed over as the hero repressed his doubts) and the hero is almost wholly passive, even his anger ineffectual. So lower rating to the final +.5; 0 would also be defensible.

There follows a brief summary of the scoring manual. For full details, rules for a giving a category a full, weak (wk), or tend score (or none), and examples of each, see Holt (2007, vol. 2, ch. 10).

□ Content Scoring

L 1. Libidinal Content, Level 1 (Crude, Direct, Primitive)

L 1 O. ORAL: Images and themes from the early, oral-sucking/oral-receptive period of life, but also crude oral material that has no further qualitative specification. Distinguish carefully from Ag 1 O, however.

DD:3 Breasts, nipples. Score when seen in isolation or unclothed. Famine, drought, starving; nausea, vomit (score also Neg).

DD:2 Sucking, nursing; mouth, lips, tongue.

L 1 A. ANAL: Includes both anal-retentive and anal-expulsive themes.

DD:4 Excretory organs or functions; defecation; feces. Includes exclamations ("Shit!"; "You asshole!").

DD:3 Buttocks; hemorrhoids.

L 1 S. SEXUAL: Phallic or genital content.

DD:4 Mention of genitalia, sexual acts, orgasm, ejaculation.

DD:3 Prostitution, adultery, intercourse.

L 1 E-V. EXHIBITIONISTIC-VOYEURISTIC content.

DD:3 Explicit voyeurism or exhibitionism; peeping Tom, flasher; mention of pornography; nudity.

L 1 H. HOMOSEXUAL content; SEXUAL AMBIGUITY.

DD:5 Overt homosexual acts.

DD:4 Less blatant homosexual acts (e.g., kissing); character a hermaphrodite.

L 1 M. MISCELLANEOUS LIBIDINAL content: A residual category.

DD:4 Menstruation (simply mentioned: DD:3).

DD:3 Urination; childbirth or contraception as events in story.

L 2. Level 2 (Indirect, Controlled, Socialized Libidinal Content)

L 2 O. ORAL content of the receptive (or nonspecific) kind, milder than L 1 O.

DD:3 Reference to breasts, not explicitly bare.

DD:2 Kissing; strong attraction to mouth, lips, etc.; gorging, excessive drinking; extreme hunger or thirst.

DD:1 Mouth, lips, tongue, throat; stomach, belly when explicitly mentioned or emphasized; eating, drinking, smoking, doing drugs; utensils or equipment for such activities; cooking or serving food or drink, or settings for it; (ordinary) hunger, thirst; persons or animals associated with eating or drinking.

L 2 A. ANAL content.

DD:3 Explicit mention of buttocks, abnormal bowel function (e.g., constipation, diarrhea).

DD:2 Indirect mention ("kicked his ass"; "fell on her behind"); references to toilets (e.g., latrine, loo, the john) sewer, cesspool, privy; intestines; suppository.

DD:1 Score these weak: Bad smell; disgust; mud, dirt, smear, filth, snot; animal's tail (if emphasized).

L 2 S. SEXUAL content.

DD:3 Breasts when scorable for L 1 O or L 2 O; vague or abstract references to sex ("I can put in some sex to make it more interesting").

DD:2 Kissing (score also L 2 O); necking, petting.

DD:1 Love, marriage, romance, dating, hugging; going steady; engaged; valentine; cupid; sexually attractive person ("He thinks she has nice legs"); also, virginity; sex education; abstract references. Not: married couple.

L 2 E-V. EXHIBITIONISTIC-VOYEURISTIC content.

DD:2 Embarrassing or shaming exposure; disturbing notoriety.

DD:1 Receiving applause, fame, public acclaim.

DD:2 Underwear, partial nudity.

DD:1 Peering, peeking, peeping, leering; discovery; staring; looking when strongly emphasized (e.g., repeated); emphasis on eyes of a figure; actors, actresses, stage, theater, movie house. Score also Neg: blind person, mask, hiding, something concealed.

L 2 H. HOMOSEXUAL content, or SEXUAL AMBIGUITY of a more socially acceptable kind than L 1 H. Note: Do not score misrecognition of sex of pictured figures.

DD:2 Transvestism (but not "She's wearing slacks or her pants suit").

DD:1 Latent or sublimated homosexual acts ("men holding hands"); slips of tongue mixing gender.

L 2 M. MISCELLANEOUS LIBIDINAL content.

DD:3 References to internal sexual anatomy; embryo, fetus.

DD:2 Mentions of the bladder, urethra, urinary tract, concept of urination; childbirth, pregnancy.

DD:1 Narcissistic self-admiration and other descriptions of self-love.

Ag 1. Level 1 (More Primary) Aggression

Level 1 categories are to be used conservatively. They are meant to include only the most blatant, uncontrolled kinds of violence. The dividing line between level 1 and level 2 Ag is that lethal violence is scored as Ag 1.

It is critical to identify the hero and to score from his or her point of view. Thus, a scene in which one person ambushes and wounds another would have quite a different meaning—and a different score—if the hero is the aggressor or the victim.

Ag 1 A. ATTACK: SADISTIC AGGRESSION.

DD:5 Castration, torture, sadism, and other vivid sadistic fantasies. Primitive annihilation of persons or animals may get DD:5 if "He tore his enemy into pieces," but 4 for "He gouged the man's eyes out."

DD:3 Murder not sadistically elaborated.

Ag 1 O. PRIMITIVE ORAL AGGRESSION. Material that Freudians call drive-derivatives from the late, oral-biting stage. The work of Lavoie (see Holt, 2003, ch. 15) suggests that poorly controlled oral aggression is strongly associated with schizophrenia and schizotypy.

DD:4 Cannibalism; eating of human beings (if done by animals, score wk and R-an). Sadistic biting ("He bit off the other man's ear in the fight").

DD:3 Reference to parasitic animals (tapeworm).

Ag 1 V. VICTIM OF EXTREME (MASOCHISTIC) AGGRESSION (formerly Ag 1 Ob).

DD:5 Castrating or explicitly sexual masochism (also score L 1 S).

DD:4 Being tortured; extreme victimization of other kinds.

DD:3 Suicide, explicitly stated; nightmarish helplessness.

Ag 1 *R*. RESULTS OF EXTREME AGGRESSION.

DD:5,4 Aftermaths of sadistic, lethal action; decayed or putrefied flesh.

DD:4 Mutilated persons or animals.

DD:3 After effects of ferocious, sadistic violence to plant or objects.

Ag 2. Level 2 (More Secondary) Aggression

Ag 2 A. ATTACK of a more socially accepted kind.

DD:3 Explosions, erupting volcano, bombs bursting; hot action in war; house burning.

DD:2 Fighting, physical conflict between people or animals; hitting, beating, physical violence against someone, abortion. Ghosts, witches, giants, dragons, monsters, skeleton, skull: any of the frightening creatures of children's fairy tales, TV, Nintendo or other video games, etc. Devil, Satan, Mephistopheles; frightening or potentially dangerous people (criminals) or animals except those that bite (Ag 2 O). Also, weapons and other dangerous objects; anger, hatred, and related affects.

DD:3–1 Hero is subjected to ridicule, shaming, loss of reputation, notoriety, or other painful effects of the attention or regard of others.

DD:2 Stealing, robbing, holdup, (nonviolent or unspecified) crime.

DD:2 Power over others (nonbenevolent); forcible restraint.

DD:1 Cops, police officers; soldier, those in the service (with Cx C+).

DD:1 Score weak if one character *dupes* another, *tricks, cheats,* or *lies* to him; and if one character rejects another, socially excludes him, or acts in an unfriendly way.

Ag 2 O. ORAL AGGRESSION. Scored regardless if done by hero or other.

DD:3 Poison: poisonous foods and plants, poisonous snakes or spiders.

DD:2 Big, biting animals: shark, alligator, crocodile, tiger, lion; also vampire bat.

DD:2 Acts of biting less serious than Ag 1 O, more noticeable than biting off a piece of something to eat, unless emphasized. Also, mention of teeth, jaws, beak if emphasized. Verbal aggression (e.g., arguing, cursing, bawling out, tirade); spitting on or at someone.

DD:1 Prey taking by animals other than those specified already.

Ag 2 V. VICTIMS OF AGGRESSION.

DD:3 Victims of any of the kinds of attack in Ag 2 A and most of Ag 2 O; hero is subject to the malevolent power of another.

DD:2 Victims of verbal aggression.

DD:2 Illness, suffering, pain when serious enough to be incapacitating, including mental illnesses; expressed feelings of endangerment, impotent rage, persecution.

DD:2 People or animals frightened, threatened, or forcibly restrained.

DD:1 Convicts in prison, prisoners (with Cx C+).

DD:1 Defensive activities or objects (e.g., building a fort; shield).

DD:1 Hopelessness, which implies victimization.

Ag 2 R. RESULTS OF (MODERATE) AGGRESSION.

DD:3 Injured or dead persons or animals (less gory or distressing than Ag 1 R).

DD:3 Deformed persons or animals, monsters in the medical sense.

DD:2 Death with no suffering or foul play ("When his father died, he went ..."); grave; tomb; funeral. But for card 15, DD:1 because of card pull.

DD:2 Injuries, blood, cuts, etc., no pain involved (e.g., dissection, transfusion).

DD:2 Decayed or rotten plants or objects; aftermath of fire or other destruction.

DD:1 Dead, injured, or broken plant or object.

☐ Formal Aspects

The formal deviations or aspects of pripro are familiar to clinicians as the devices of the dream work or of thought disorder.

C. Condensations

In the form of more or less fused separate images, most commonly seen in Rorschach responses, these are rare in the TAT so will be merely listed.

C-ctm 1. FUSION OF TWO SEPARATE PERCEPTS (contamination) (DD 5 or 4).

C-ctgn 1. CONTAGION: Loss of boundary between self and percept (DD 4) "The man looks sad. I feel like crying when I see that—please take it away".

C-int 1. INTERPENETRATION: Partial fusion of two separate percepts (DD 3).

C c-i 1. CONDENSATION: COLLECTIVE IMAGE: Familiar in dreams is the occurrence of characters who look like one person but the dreamer knows that it is really someone else (DD 3).

C-co. COMPOSITION (COMPOSITE IMAGE): Freud's term for an image that is a composite of parts that do not actually belong together in nature.

C-co 1. COMPOSITION, LEVEL 1: If the teller tries to produce a dream, science-fiction story or fairy tale, a character may be such a composite. (DD 4 for impossible fusions, e.g. across species; DD 3 for improbable fusions: e.g., person with three legs, Cyclopean eye).

C-co 2. COMPOSITION, LEVEL 2: Composite beings that exist in mythology, art, folklore, TV, etc. (Score Cx C or Cx E, usually +) (DD 2) 'Dragon'; 'centaur'; 'Cookie monster.'

D. Displacement

D-chain 1. CHAIN ASSOCIATION: Fluid associative thinking, going from one idea to another without overall guidance. It is the principal defining feature of manic thought disorder. Score only when there is more than one associative jump, with no—or only very belated—return to the original theme, and give the score for each such discontinuity in the train of thought (DD 4).

D-dist 1. DISTANT ASSOCIATION: Sometimes, this takes the form of nonsense, or inappropriate elaboration (DD 4). Score when the subject loosely strays off the point, though it may be more or less possible to follow the train of thoughts (DD 3).

D-clang 1. CLANG ASSOCIATION: Just the sound of a word leads to an inappropriate one (DD 3).

D-clang 2. PUNS AND MALAPROPISMS: The substitution of one word by another of similar sound, or by a homonym, often used with humorous intent (DD 3 or 2).

D-sub 1 or 2. SUBSTITUTION: An expected person, object, etc. is replaced by an unexpected or inappropriate one; scored on Level 1 if the substitution would be impossible in reality (DD 3, 2, or 1).

D-time 1 or 2. DISTORTION OF TIME: Unrealistic reversal or anachronism (DD 3, 2).

D a-t 1 or 2. ARBITRARY TURN OF EVENTS: A sudden or unexplained shift in a narrative, sometimes in an attempt to shock the tester (DD 4 or 3).

D-acc 2. DISPLACEMENT OF ACCENT: A small or incidental feature, not necessary to the story, obtrudes itself and gets particular emphasis; or something that is usually innocuous seems uncanny, horrible, etc. (DD 2).

D-fig 2. FIGURES OF SPEECH: Score when figures are unusual enough to attract notice, not clichés or faded metaphors (DD 3 for metaphors, 2 for hyperbole or inappropriate similes).

D S 2. VERBAL SLIPS. Score slips in which one word is substituted for an unintended one (DD 1). If corrected, also score Mod +.

Sym. Explicit Symbolism (Visual Representation of the Abstract)

Score when the subject explicitly attempts to represent an abstract idea, an activity, or an object that she or he feels cannot easily be represented directly.

Sym-C 2. CONVENTIONAL COLOR OR SHADING SYMBOLISM. Rarely encountered except with the blank card, where the white may be interpreted as *purity* or some other such concept. Occasionally the dark shading of other cards gives rise to explicit symbolism (DD 1). Idiosyncratic symbolism may be scored Sym-C 1 (DD 3).

Sym-I 1 or 2. IDIOSYNCRATIC OR CONVENTIONAL IMAGE SYMBOLISM: Interpreting some part of the picture symbolically. "This mixed-up mess down by his leg symbolizes his confused state of mind" (card 3BM; Sym-I 1) (DD 3). "She is carrying a handkerchief as a symbol of her grief" (Sym-I 2) (DD 2).

Ctr. Contradictions

Ctr A 1. AFFECTIVE CONTRADICTION: S starts out stating or clearly implying one affect and without ever clearly changing this interpretation ends up taking a patently opposed, contradictory affective position. The emotion may be personal, attributed to a character or directed toward the tester (DD 4*).

Ctr L 1. LOGICAL CONTRADICTION: One statement made by S is logically incompatible with another that he or she maintains simultaneously (DD 4).

Ctr R 1. CONTRADICTION OF REALITY: The assertion of something factually impossible, at least at the time the narrative was produced, or quite unlikely (DD 4, 3, or 2, depending on degree of impossibility or implausibility).

Ctr R 2. CONTRADICTION OF REALITY: Lying by a character in the story. "This old country doctor has been telling people for years that he has invented a formula for bringing dead people back to life." Score Ctr R 2, DD = 1 for the lie, but Ctr R 1, DD = 4 for the claimed miracle.

Miscellaneous Distortions of Thought and Perception

Au Lg 1. AUTISTIC LOGIC, Level 1: The failure of thinking to follow a logical course is ordinarily considered one of the hallmarks of the primary process. There must be, at least implicitly, an attempt at reasoning, which is not only fallacious but implausible (DD 4 or even 5).

Au Lg 2. AUTISTIC LOGIC, Level 2: Attempting to deduce the story from details in the picture (DD 3).

Intr 1. INTRUSION OF IRRELEVANCY: A remark from left field, not relevant to the story. Or, after being asked a question, the subject responds with puzzling irrelevance or unresponsiveness (DD 3).

B C 1 or 2. BREAK IN CONTINUITY: Unexpected material, suddenly introduced, is part of the narrative; if it is an interpolation of something else, score Intr 1. Score level 1 or 2 depending on the irrelevancy and inappropriateness of the introduced material that breaks up the continuity of the story's theme (DD 4, 3).

---

* As with most scores, a weak form may be scored with DD lowered by one point.

Un Rel 1. UNREALISTIC RELATIONSHIP: Carrying over a character or story-line from one card to another (DD 3).

Trans 1. FLUID TRANSFORMATION OF THE PICTURE: A report that, as the subject looks at it, the picture visibly changes (DD 3).

Trans 2. TRANSFORMATION OF PERCEPT: Correcting initial misperception. Card 11: "There's a strange form that appears to be going in two directions. [P D 2, Ctr R 1] One to cross a bridge and ... another direction to return by the path.... As I look closely the scale changes, I see two or three small persons there ... whereas before, it seemed like two bison-like animals" (DD 2).

P D 1 or 2. PERCEPTUAL DISTORTIONS: Misperception of the picture. Card 1: "This child is sick in bed. He has been given sheet music to study, but instead of the music, he has come across a novel that interests him more than the music" (DD 4).

S-R 1. SELF-REFERENCE of a magically unrealistic kind (DD 3).

M C 1. MAGICAL CAUSATION: Explicit or implicit magic, witchcraft, sorcery, etc. (DD 4 or 3); and superstition come true (DD 2). "After he broke the mirror, he had a series of misfortunes" (DD = 2); "I was then somehow transported through the solid walls into the spaceship" (DD = 4).

M C 2. MAGICAL CAUSATION: RELIGIOUS. "This old man is a religious fanatic who believes that by praying long and hard enough he can bring his wife back to life" (DD 2). Also score *R-rel.*

F-msc 1 or 2 MISCELLANEOUS OTHER FORMAL DEVIATIONS. Unexpected, unlisted (because rare) formal signs of pripro. Notable among them is physiognomic responsiveness, most often to the heavy blackness of several cards. Distinguish carefully from Sym C, which must be explicit.

V. Verbalization Scores

V I 1. VERBAL INCOHERENCE: Unintelligible language (DD 5).

V C 1. VERBAL CONDENSATIONS: Portmanteau words or neologisms (DD 4).

V Q 1. QUEER VERBALIZATIONS: Psychotic distortions of linguistic usage, predominantly found in schizophrenia (e.g., highly stilted or idiosyncratic, or autistic, use of words) (DD 4).

V P 2. PECULIAR VERBALIZATIONS: Language that is autistic enough to sound odd, bringing the auditor up short even though he or she may quickly understand the meaning (DD 3).

☐ Control and Defense Scores (C&D)

These categories need be scored only in conjunction with responses that have received scores on either Content or Formal variables, but every unit that gets a Content or Formal score must get some Control or Defense, if only its failure or absence (*X*).

R. Remoteness

This group of categories was borrowed from Tomkins (1947, pp. 78–82) but was expanded. An R-score is to be given to every response for which a Content score has been recorded and may also control many Formal scores when the remoteness has any relevance to the formal quality scored. R-min is never to be scored for Formal deviations, and Remoteness in Person almost never, except for R-dep. It should be noted that usually, the strategy will put the potentially hot motivational material at a safer distance, in which case score +. Occasionally, however, it may fail, and the plus is omitted.

R-min MINIMAL REMOTENESS: Do not score if any other remoteness score can be given. Characters or objects inhabit here-and-now reality (assumed unless stated otherwise).

Remoteness in Person

R-eth. REMOTENESS—ETHNIC: Score when actors are different from the subject in ethnic group.

R-an. REMOTENESS—ANIMAL (of an ego-syntonic kind): Mammals.

R-(an) REMOTENESS—ANIMAL (ego-alien): Bugs, worms, fish, dragons, but also bats.

R-pl. REMOTENESS—PLANT: When a plant gets a Content score for being dangerous, edible, etc.

R-ia. REMOTENESS—INANIMATE: Content-scorable things (*wine glass, explosion, mud, knife*).

R-dep+. REMOTENESS—DEPICTION: The motivational focus is seen as graphically depicted in a painting, drawing, statue, cartoon, etc.

R-geo+. REMOTENESS—GEOGRAPHIC: usually but not always explicit.

R-time. REMOTENESS IN TIME, past or future in relation to timeline of the story. Regard something as long ago enough if it seems to have occurred before the events of the story's beginning. And any reference to a possible future beyond the point when the story ends is scorable. A plus sign may be added when the implied remoteness seems to make the implicit threat significantly recede.

Remoteness in Level of Reality

R-char+. CHARACTER IS A SPECIFIC, REAL (famous) PERSON.

R-fic s+. REFERENCE TO (use of) A SPECIFIC FICTIONAL PERSON, ANIMAL, OR OBJECT: Score also for material that appears as a story within the subject's story. "This boy is Hans Brinker; he wanted skates for his birthday but his parents gave him this violin, which he hates."

R-fic n+. REMOTENESS, FICTIONAL—NONSPECIFIC: Character is a nonspecific fictional, mythological, supernatural or similar person or animal.

R-rel+. RELIGIOUS CHARACTER OR CONTEXT: Includes gods, devils, hells of current world religions.

R-fan+. CHARACTERS OR CONTEXT ARE FROM DREAM OR EXPLICIT FANTASY: Score for dreams that occur within a TAT story, but when scoring actual dreams, do not use R-fan except for the rare dream within a dream or for pripro that occurs only in dream characters' thoughts.

R-fig+. FIGURATIVE (linguistic or poetic) REMOTENESS: Use of figures of speech (especially simile, hyperbole, and metaphor).

R-spch. REMOTENESS: CONTENT ATTRIBUTED IN SPEECH: One way in which the issue of to whom wishes and fears belong gets fuzzed up is unique to narratives. In a speech, directly or indirectly quoted, one character (hero or other) can attribute something to the hero or to another. It can get terribly complex and involuted: "He said, 'You [hero] made him think I hate you, but ...'" This is simplified by giving this score to all content in a speech, regardless of its source.

R-cond+. REMOTENESS—CONDITIONAL: Teller refuses to commit self about an event, thus: "I don't know how it ends. If he decides he loves her, he will come back, but I can't tell if he will." (also score Discl.). Or pripro is introduced conditionally only to be withdrawn: "He could have killed him, but suddenly ..." (score also Neg and O-exp.).

R-pers. REMOTENESS IN PERSON: Scorable material may be expressed in a story or dream through the actions or feelings of other characters, not the hero.

R-pers-H. REMOTENESS IN PERSON, DIRECTED TOWARD HERO. "She set out to seduce him" (the hero).

R-pers-O. REMOTENESS IN PERSON, DIRECTED TOWARD OTHER: "He began to beat the child, while James [hero] looked on in horror."

Cx. Contexts

Score if the context-giving material occurs in the same sentence. About the use (or not) of +, see the first paragraph of the Remoteness section.

Cx C+. CULTURAL CONTEXT: Reference to a ritual, custom, mythology, folklore, occupational role or other social reality (including historical actuality).

Cx E+. ESTHETIC CONTEXT: Any of the fine arts. Score references to mass media only when it is clear that S considers the particular one mentioned a work of art.

Cx I+. INTELLECTUAL CONTEXT: Decontaminating themes by putting them in a scientific, technological or professional context.

Cx H+. HUMOROUS CONTEXT: Score only when a joke, bit of wit, or clowning is the medium for introducing the pripro. Use this score also for pathos.

Other Controls

Refl+. REFLECTION: Attaining a kind of detachment from a story by standing back from it in an attitude of self-observation or criticism of self or the production.

Mod+. ADAPTIVE MODIFICATION OF RESPONSE: Converting pripro material into more secondary form, wording that tends to tone down the demand for defense.

Del. DELAY: Score for material that appears only in response to inquiry.

Neg+. NEGATION (appropriate): Terminating: bringing to an end some kind of scorable action; explicit rejection or condemnation of an undesirable act or outcome.

Neg. NEGATION: Score for deprivation, absence, loss, or failure of gratification.

Inh. INHIBITION: The inhibitory defense expressed thematically in the response.

Ratn. RATIONALIZATION: Without doing away with the pripro theme or object.

Minz. MINIMIZATION: Trying to cope by making it just a little one, in effect.

Eu. EUPHEMISM: Substituting a genteel or roundabout word for a direct one.

Vulg–.VULGARITY OF VERBALIZATION: The use of crude, shocking slang when neutral terms are standard and technical ones are often used.

Impl. IMPLICATION: Closely related to euphemism is the use of wording that implies the taboo topic without actually mentioning it. Do not score if Eu is scored.

Discl. DISCLAIMER: Evading responsibility of the self or a character.

Implicitly Pathological Defenses

Repr. REPRESSION: Indications that the subject forgets something he or she intended to communicate or other clear signs that the process of repressing is going on.

Blkg–. BLOCKING: Inability to get going on a story for two minutes or more, followed by scorable pripro. Also, score if the subject seems to want to continue speaking but is unable to do so after touching on pripro material.

Cphb–. COUNTERPHOBIC DEFENSE: For example, doing daring things in the situations where one is most afraid.

Va–. VAGUENESS: Pripro material reported in cloudy, indistinct terms.

Self-D–. SELF-DEPRECATION: Inappropriate self-criticism, in conjunction with phrasing containing pripro.

Rep–. REPUDIATION OR DISAVOWAL OF A RESPONSE: In inquiry, denying that the subject said something, or "He then killed her—no, no, don't write that down."

Fake–. FALSE, UNGENUINE BEHAVIOR by a character.

Gram–. DISRUPTION OF GRAMMAR and other linguistic aspects: Do not confuse with formal verbalization scores.

Prj–. PROJECTION: Projection of responsibility for the pripro material ("You made me say that"), or extreme rejection of response, test, or the experimenter ("I refuse to look at any more of your filthy pictures").

Obs–. OBSESSIONAL DEFENSE: In a relatively decompensated, maladaptive form.

Iso–. ISOLATION: Affective deadness or frozenness, or careful segregation of ideas or themes that naturally belong together (but would be scorable if so).

Eva–. EVASIVENESS AND AVOIDANCE.

Imp–. IMPOTENCE: Inability to answer a simple question.

Overtness

O-beh. OVERTNESS—BEHAVIORAL: Whenever sexual or aggressive wishes are acted out by the dramatis personae.

O-vbl. OVERTNESS—VERBAL: Scorable material expressed in the speeches of characters in a story.

O-exp. OVERTNESS—EXPERIENTIAL: A character is described as having thoughts or feelings related to desires or fears or is a passive receiver of something unprovoked (mainly with Ag 2 V).

O-pot. OVERTNESS—POTENTIAL: The motive (libidinal or aggressive) is expressed only as a potentiality.

C/D msc. MISCELLANEOUS: Specify other, nonlisted control or defense if necessary.

Calculation of Indices

Once all the stories for a given the subject have been scored, next comes reducing their profusion to a manageable set of indices (summarizing or combining scores). The first step is the rather tedious one of tallying scores on the Primary Process Summary Sheet. Notice that on its first page, you make a stroke or tick for each score: Content, Formal, and C&D. That concludes in the first column of the second page, plus the tally of DD, but the rest of the entries there come from the DE scoring where the unit is the story.

Because of considerable differences in card pull (Holt, 1978, vol. 1, ch. 3), it is often desirable to compute indices for each story separately, especially when one is comparing data from different sets of cards. Within a single study, or within a given clinical setting where the same set is used for all subjects, most users prefer to compute means across all cards. The unit for many indices is, as stated already, the sentence (or complete clause); averaging across the total number of units (ΣU) provides a generally satisfactory compensation for individual differences in verbal productivity. For more precision, one may use sums but correct for fluency and talkativeness by covarying mean word count of all sentences *not* scored for pripro (see Kalter & Marsden, 1970). Research is needed to find out which of these two procedures yields better results in terms of construct validity.

In the larger literature on pripro scoring of the Rorschach, perhaps the most frequently presented index is *%Total Pripro*, though on simple empirical grounds it is the least useful. It is obtained by counting the number of units with any pripro scores (called *PPU*) and dividing it by the ΣU. If you want a measure of primary process thinking to test some theoretical hypothesis, compute the sums of Level 1 scores (both Content and Formal) and of Formal scores (both Level 1 and Level 2), dividing each by the number of units to yield a percent and either averaging those despite their overlap or entering them separately in a multivariate analysis.

□ Complete Scoring of an Entire TAT

The following 11-card TAT was administered to a 25-year-old male subject ("Doe") and was tape recorded for research purposes (Holt, 1951; Shneidman, 1951). Each story is divided into scoring units and is followed by scoring and commentary on it. Finally, the process is completed by tallying and computation of indices, plus some interpretive guidance and a brief clinical summary.

Card 1

(1) This child is sick in bed. (2) He has been given sheet music to study, (3) but instead of the music, he has come across a novel that interests him more than the music. (4) It is probably an adventure story. (5) He evidently does not fear the chance that his parents will find him thusly occupied as he seems quite at ease. (6) He seems to be quite a studious type, and perhaps regrets missing school, (7) but he seems quite occupied with the adventure in the story. (8) Adventure has something to do with ocean or water. (9) He is not too happy, though not too sad. (10) His eyes are somewhat blank—coincidence of reading a book without any eyes (11) or knowing what is in the book without reading it. (12) He disregards the music and falls asleep reading the book.

Commentary

- Sentence (1): The scoring of content and its control is straightforward, but the surprising misperception of the picture calls for a PD 1, which—as is usual for this distortion—is uncontrolled (*X*). The bizarreness of *sick in bed* contrasts strongly with the sharpness of perception implied by the next unit (not scorable).

- Sentence (3): How can a child who is sick in bed come across a novel? Anyone who was not disregarding reality would have explained. Seeing the violin as a book is a very rare perceptual distortion.

- Sentence (5): The next scorable material is his somewhat far-fetched reasoning (*evidently … as*) based on his seeing the boy as at ease. The negated fear, it is clearly enough implied, is that his parents would punish him if they knew—hence, the Ag 2 V. Thusly occupied is stilted to the point of being slightly peculiar in this context.

- Sentence (8): Where in the world did this notion come from? If you had that reaction, it indicates a distant association. It is again oddly worded, but notice how important it is that the session was tape recorded. Too many testers take notes in a telegraphic fashion that ends up looking like this and cannot be sure whether that's what the subject said or not.

- Sentence (9): The words are not quite contradictory, but they also seem out of keeping with his former statement, quite at ease. Even in schizophrenia full-blown Ctr A 1 is rare, however, and a sniff of it may be diagnostically helpful.

- Sentence (10): The weird reasoning and language of this sentence bring the diagnostic hypothesis front and center, however. Note the implication that the somewhat blank appearance of the eyes means that, despite all he has said, the subject now decides that the boy is blind (also a negated L 2 E-V and Ag 2 R)—surely an arbitrary turn of the story, undoing much of what has been said. The loading of so much pripro on one unit sends its DD up to 5.

- Sentence (11): And it is pretty weak to account for *knowing what is in the book without reading it*—a realistic impossibility (Ctr R 1) suggesting delusional ideas—as a *coincidence.*

- Sentence (12): The final attempt to return to the original story is one more lurch, here scored a break in continuity.

TABLE 17.5 Scoring of Doe's TAT Story (Card 1)

Units	Content & Formal	(DD)	Controls & Defenses	DD
1. sick in bed	Ag 2 V	(2)	R-min	4
	P D 1	(4)	X	
2. given sheet music				
3. has come across a novel	Ctr R 1 wk	(3)	X	4
	P D 1	(4)	X	
4. an adventure story				
5. doesn't fear parents . . . thusly occupied	Ag 2 V wk	(1)	R-min, Neg, O-exp	3
	Au Lg 2, V P 2 wk	(3, 2)	X	
6. studious, regrets missing				
7. quite occupied				
8. to do with ocean, water	D-dist 1, V P 2 wk	(4)	X	4
9. not too happy. . . sad	Ctr A tend			
10. eyes blank. . . no eyes coincidence of reading	Ag 2 R, L 2 E-V	(3)	R-min, Neg	5
	V Q 1, Au Lg 1 wk	(4, 3)	X	
	Ctr R 1	(4)	X	
11. knowing (not) reading	Ctr R 1	(3)	X	3
12. disregards, falls asleep	B C 2 wk	(2)	X	2

Computation of DE

DD & FL	Starting DE	Affect	Structure	C & D	Adequacy of Hero	Final DE	Final DD×DE
5 –F	–1	–.5	(1,2,1,2,2 = 7) = +1	0	0	–.5	–2.5

DE Scoring

Overall DD is 5. The accumulation of perceptual distortion earns an F– for form level so the starting point is –1. The apparent blandness with which Doe produced such psychotic-sounding material, together with the hint of affective inappropriateness, subtract another half-point. In terms of the conventions of story structure, he did not do badly; one could argue to raise the total a point. Neither the consideration of controls nor the adequacy of hero push the decision one way or another, which means it adds up to a DE of –.5. Now we must see whether our clinical judgment of his capacity to cope with an apparently psychotic level of preoccupations and disordered thinking is worse than that. I decided not, on the basis of his ability to grasp the task and carry it out as well as he did despite the emergence of some unmistakably schizophrenic thinking, not really losing his composure. In retrospect, after scoring the rest of the stories, I feel justified (see following). This man's defenses are intact enough so that he is able to keep pripro at bay a good deal of the time, repeatedly recovering after momentary regressions. That is sometimes scored as sequence change (not used here).

Card 3BM

(1) This girl is in a cell and she has been jailed because she was found guilty of prostitution. (2) She is in this position in the picture because she is very ashamed, not because of being arrested, (3) because she is quite familiar with the police (4) but because of the fact that her picture and a newspaper write-up was being sensationally spread across the country. (5) She knew that her sister, who was a nun, would suffer from it, (6) and it makes her feel very badly because she, at one time, had a chance and an opportunity to follow her elder sister's example, (7) but it was too late now. (8) She grabs a concealed knife from under her blouse and stabs herself.

TABLE 17.6 Scoring of Doe's Story, Card 3BM

Card 3BM	Content & Formal	(DD)	Controls & Defenses	DD
1. jailed, guilty	Ag 2 V	(2)	R-min, Cx C+, O-beh	3
of prostitution	L 1 S	(3)	R-min, Cx C+, O-pot	
2. in this position because	Au Lg 2 tend	(2)	R-min, Cx C+, O-exp	2
ashamed, not of arrest	Ag 2 V			
3. familiar with police	Ag 2 A	(1)	R-pers, Cx C+, O-pot	1
4. sensationally spread	Ag 2 V, L 2 E-V	(3)	R-min, O-vbl	3
5. sister a nun	L 2 S	(1)	R-pers, Cx C+, Neg+, O-pot	2
would suffer	Ag 2 V	(2)	R-pers, R-cond, O-exp	
6. had chance to follow her example	L 2 S	(1)	R-min, Cx C+, Neg+, Impl, O-pot	1
7. too late now				
8. takes out a concealed	L 2 E-V wk	(1)	R-min, Neg	3
knife, and	Ag 2 A, P D 2 wk	(2)	R-ia	
stabs herself	Ag 1 V	(3)	R-min, O-beh	

Computation of DE

DD & FL	Starting DE	Affect	Structure	C & D	Adequacy of Hero	Final DE	Final DD×DE
3 Fw	0	0	(2,2,1,2,2 = 9) = + 1.5	+1	–.5	+1	+3

Commentary

- Sentence (1): Quite a straightforward beginning, with no hint of formal pripro. Note the reappearance of Ag 2 V, the theme of victimization that will crop up in almost every story, but here within safe, culturally accepted bounds. R-min: different sex does not count.

- Sentence (2): One way of maintaining control over fantasy, which the test's instructions imply one should draw on, is to maintain the position of inferring major aspects of the story—here, the figure's emotions—from the picture. He seems to reverse the usual procedure, so Au Lg is not scorable and it is easy to miss the hint of it here. Notice that the Ag 2 V is scored for the repeated mention of the arrest, not for the shame. Plausible attribution of emotion is not considered pripro.

- Sentence (3): Here, the controlled violence of the police is scored as it is because it is attributed to another character (*R-pers*) and is potential as well as conventional.

- Sentence (4): The E-V theme makes another of its many appearances, now as a form of Ag 2 V. Notice that as presented here, the issue of attracting attention is felt as enough of an assault to warrant a DD of 3.

- Sentence (5): The only thing scorable here is suffering (again Ag 2 V) of the hero's sister and the concept of nun, of which chastity is a central part—hence, the negated sexual score, highly defended. Note the R-cond for the statement that the sister would suffer and the R-pers for the fact that both kinds of content refer to someone other than the hero.

- Sentence (6): Closely related is the scoring here for the clear implication in following her example that the hero could have been a nun. Implying something without plainly stating it is a control you have to remember to look for. Notice how this does not violate the rule against scoring by interpretation (which might be, for example, incorrectly scoring an oral wish when a character longs to be taken care of).

- Sentence (8): Three content scores here: L 2 E-V wk for *concealed,* Ag 2 A for the knife, and Ag 1 V for the suicide. Calling the ambiguous object a knife is unusual enough to call for a weak perceptual distortion 2.

DE Scoring

The PD pulled the form level down to Fw, so the starting point is 0. The affect is not positive but appropriate, and the structural aspects, except for the very brief ending, show full compliance, so the DE gets raised to +1.5. Controls and defenses are consistent with that. The ending is clearly unhappy, and though the hero did exert effort to end her own misery, she brought that on by apparent drifting, so the result is a lowering by half a point to +1. With an overall DD of 3, the contribution to the ARI is +3—not a big creative achievement, but a striking recovery from the previous story.

Card 4

(1) The girl in the picture is half-caste. (2) She is in love with the man who is going to leave her and return to his wife. (3) They have spent quite some time together in intimacy. (4) She is pleading with him to stay with her (5) or help figure some way to plan for the coming of the child she is going to bear. (6) She is in poor circumstances financially (7) and he tells her she should make arrangements to conclude the birth and thus everything would iron out (8) because he is definitely determined to leave as the affair in his mind is at an end. (9) She is very broken up by it. (10) She pleads for him to spend one more night, which he agrees to, (11) and in the middle of the night she sets fire to the house, (12) thus solving the problem of all concerned.

Commentary

- Sentence (2): Notice that R-ethn should be scored for content pertaining to the woman even though it comes from the first (unscored) sentence. One has to read the whole

TABLE 17.7 Scoring of Doe's Story, Card 4

	Content & Formal	(DD)	Controls & Defenses	DD
1. girl is half-caste				
2. in love with the man	L 2 S	(1)	R-eth, Cx C+, O-exp	1
going to leave her	Ag 2 A	(1)	R-pers, Cx C+, O-pot	
3. spent time in intimacy	L 1 S	(4)	R-eth, Eu, O-beh	4
4. she pleads, stay	Ag 2V tend			
5. child she is to bear	L 2 M	(3)	R-eth, R-time+, O-pot	3
6. she is poor	Ag 2V tend			
7. he says, conclude the birth	V P 2 Ag 2 A, L 2 M	(3)	X; R-pers-H, R-time+, R-spch, Eu, O-pot	3
8. He will leave the affair	Ag 2 A, L 1 S	(4)	R-pers-H, R-time+, Eu, O-pot	4
9. she is very broken up	Ag 2 R	(2)	R-eth, R-fig+, O-exp	2
10. pleads, spend 1 night	L 1 S	(4)	R-eth, R-spch, Impl, O-pot	4
11. she sets fire to house	Ag 1 A, Ag 1 V, Ag 2 A	(4)	R-eth, R-ia, Impl, O-beh	4
12. solving the problem	Ctr A 1 wk	(3)	Cphb-	3

Computation of DE

Card	DD & FL	Starting DE	Affect	Structure	C & D	Adequacy of Hero	Final DE	Final DD×DE
4	4 Fo	+1	–.5	(2,2,1,2,2 = 9) = +1.5	0	–.5	0	0

story first to be sure who the hero is (here, the woman), but that should become apparent during the division into units. This is also a good example of using O-exp for the report of an experience that is not like a feeling or perception; being in love is as it were an existential state. The Ag score is another instance in which the hurt inflicted on the woman does not need psychoanalytic interpretation to be apparent, but might be missed because it is implicit.

- Sentence (5): The L 2 M is scored for the potential future (R-time) childbirth. In a sense, of course, O-pot always implies a possible future event, but here it is clearly expected.

- Sentence (7): The birth needs only to be mentioned to be scored again. Though I am personally strongly pro-choice, I do not see that there are political implications to scoring an abortion Ag 2 A any more than any other operation. The awkward Eu *conclude the birth* is obviously a peculiar way to put it. Now, how do we handle the fact that both the birth and its prevention do not exist except in what he says? With R-spch, not O-vbl; the latter is for talking aggressively, not talking about an aggressive act—which has not happened, making its overtness potential.

- Sentence (10): Again, this man brings up sex only implicitly. Notice that if it were not for his opening statement of her somewhat alien ethnicity, the content in this and the next unit would require R-min.

- Sentence (11): Fire earns the Ag 2 A (R-ia), but her act is, the subject implies, both murder (Ag 1 A) and suicide (Ag 1 V).

- Sentence (12): A tragedy? Oh, no, a neat bit of problem solving. We experience that final comment as jarringly unexpected, an ironic effect to which you may be so used that you merely shrug. To do so is to miss the teller's intent of shocking by affective incongruity (Ctr A 1), though it is weak enough to be overlooked as a counterphobic strategy of warding off negative emotion.

Computation of DE

The final affective contradiction drags the starting +1 down half a point for affect. The rather good structure of the story brings it back up to 1.5, which is reduced again a half point for the bad ending and a relatively hapless hero. I exercised my clinical-judgmental right to lower the resulting +1 to zero, on the grounds that the final cynical flourish spoils what might otherwise be plausible as a creative use of heavy pripro in a tragedy. So it ends up making no net contribution to an ARI.

Card 6BM

(1) This is a scene in a play. (2) The two characters are on the stage, (3) one is a famous elderly actress, who has a son about the age of the young man appearing opposite her. (4) The dialogue in the play has suddenly taken a new meaning for her. (5) She now sees that the play, which was written by her son, has an entirely different meaning, in this scene in

the picture. (6) The boy is telling the mother that he has just committed a murder. (7) She understands now that this was her son's way of conveying to her the terrifying facts that this is actually what had happened. (8) In the play, as her son had written it, the climax comes when the mother calls the police. (9) But the famous actress decides to put her own climax into action after the play is over. (10) She calls her son and says, "The climax of your play will have to be changed." (11) She says, "I think the audience will prefer this one," (12) so here she draws a revolver and shoots him. (What kind of murder was it?) (13) Oh, a girl. Motive primarily to do with sexual. (14) She had been unfaithful.

TABLE 17.8 Scoring of Doe's Story, Card 6BM

	Content & Formal	(DD)	Controls & Defenses	DD
1. scene in a play	L 2 E-V	(1)	R-fic n+, Cx E+, O-pot	1
2. characters on stage	L 2 E-V	(1)	R-fic n+, Cx E+, O-beh	1
3. famous actress	L 2 E-V	(2)	R-min, Cx E+, O-beh	2
young man playing opp.	L 2 E-V	(1)	R-pers, Cx E+, O-beh	
4. dialogue, new meaning	D-a-t 2 tend			
5. Play has diff. meaning	L 2 E-V	(1)	R-fic n+, Cx E+, O-pot	1
6. telling about murder	Ag 1 A	(4)	R-fic n+, R-pers, R-spch, Cx E+, O-beh	4
7. terrifying fact	Ag 2 V	(3)	R-fic n+, Cx E+, Impl, O-vbl	3
8. she calls the police	Ag 2 A	(1)	R-fic n+, R-pers, Cx E+, Cx C+, O-pot	1
9. famous actress, play	L 2 E-V	(2)	R-min, Cx E, O-pot	2
10. calls son, change play	L 2 E-V	(1)	R-fic n+, R-spch, Cx E+, O-vbl	1
11. audience will prefer	L 2 E-V	(1)	R-pers, R-spch, R-time Cx E+, O-pot	1
12. draws revolver, shoots him	Ag 2 A, Ag 1 A C-ctm 1 wk, D-a-t 1	(4) (4, 4)	R-ia, O-beh X	5
13. motive primarily to do with sexual	L 2 S	(2)	R-pers-O, Del, Gram–, O-exp	2
14. she was unfaithful	L 1 S, Ag 2 A tend	(4)	R-pers-O, Del, R-time tend, 0-ben	4

Computation of DE

Card #	DD & FL	Starting DE	Affect	Structure	C & D	Adequacy of Hero	Final DE	Final DD×DE
6BM	5 Fo	+1	–.5	(1,2,1,2,1 = 7) = +.5	–5	+.5	0	0

Commentary

- Sentence (1): Again, a preliminary framing remark, establishing distance scored throughout, but a kind that itself is scorable. The next two units essentially repeat it, just changing the overtness from potential to behavioral. Hereafter, any scorable content that occurs in the play with the story gets R-fic n+ (nonspecific because it is not the performance of a known play) and Cx E+ because a stage play is considered a work of art, not just a cultural artifact.

- Sentences (4) and (5): The theme of sudden new meaning hints at paranoid insight, often expressed as an arbitrary turn of events, but not quite at a scorable level. After all, ordinary storytellers often use the same device to spark interest.

- Sentence (6): Notice that, since the mother figure is clearly the hero (TAT jargon, nonsexist), the murder is not only fictional but committed by one secondary character against another. Overtness scoring here is tricky: A murder is a behavioral act, but it is only being spoken about, which gives it additional safe distance (R-spch).

- Sentence (7): Oddly, because of the way it is worded, the only pripro scorable here is the word *terrifying*: The news is a kind of implicit verbal assault, putting her in the role of victim. Remoteness is tricky here: It is a transition between fictional and real, but since she is still on stage and in character, R-fic n+ and Cx E+ still hold, here and in unit 8.

- Sentence (9): Here, though *famous actress* and *play* are scored as before with Cx E+, the play is over so R-fic n+ drops out.

- Sentence (10): Again, only the word *play* is scored as before and in 11 only *audience.* Since the audience she refers to is a future one and exists only in her lines, R-time+ and R-spch are scored.

- Sentence (12): By now we should be ready for a shocking last act, an unexpected (D-a-t 1) filicide (Ag 1 A); the weapon gets scored too (Ag 2 A, R-ia). Are you surprised by the formal score, C-ctm 1 wk? It is easy to overlook the fact that two different situations are here described simultaneously: The heroine is *calling* her son (on the phone, I assume) to tell him about the new climax she wants him to write in, and she describes it by actually shooting him (over the telephone!). If we could be sure that the subject meant it as much as the patient did who described a red detail on card X as "the bloody island where they had all those revolutions," it would be a full-blown contamination. His first story convinces me that he is capable of that much looseness of thinking, but the score is cautiously weak. The accumulation of all this strong content and formal pripro earns a DD of 5 again.

- Sentences (13) and (14): The inquiry invokes the rule that material produced by questioning gets a delay control. Though my first reaction was that it was unnecessary, it did provoke some odd wording, which lacks the specific flavor of the peculiar but seems rather the disruption of normal verbal functioning (Gram–). Another infidelity also appeared, a theme we are learning is important to him. In terms of pripro, however, the scoring is straightforward.

DE Scoring

Again he shows us that his perceptual accuracy is usually ordinarily adequate, but his affect a bit off key. This time the structural scoring is a little misleading, not taking into account the confusion and condensation at the end. Likewise, when Table 17.6 tells us to add another positive half point, something seems wrong. The presence of a negatively signed defense subtracts a half point, and I believe that we too readily accepted his unusual gambit of seeming to identify himself with the mother figure. On second glance, it may be a device to conceal his own feelings of inadequacy while portraying heartless moral punitiveness when he would have normally longed for understanding and nurturance. That press is strikingly absent throughout, as we shall see. In sum, then, I compromise on another zero for DE and, accordingly, for this story's contribution to the adaptive regression index (ADI).

Card 7BM

> (1) This would be a man and his son. (2) The son is very depressed over his health. (3) The father is telling him that as a young man he too had the same illness (4) and that it can be cured if the son has the will to cure it. (5) The father tells the young man that he himself alone can cure it. (6) The son believes that there is no hope (7) but replies that he will go away for a little while and think it over. (8) The father replies, "You are not doing a favor to me by saying that. (9) I am thinking about your getting well for the simple reason that you have a wife and children to support, (10) and in the event of your being bed-ridden, the responsibility for your family will be put entirely on your mother and I." (11) The young man finally concludes that he will take his wife and family with him and try to make things go better in a healthier climate. (12) (What kind of disease does he have?) T.B. (13) (Did he get better?) No, I don't think he does. After a few years he dies, (14) and the children are old enough to support mother or perhaps he left insurance. (15) Never contacted father again. No correspondence. (16) After not having heard from each other for a long time, the old man dies and leaves the children a large estate. (17) This is his way of having repented.

Commentary

- Sentence (1): Which is to be the hero? At first, I went by the rule that the hero is the one about whom the story seems mainly to be told, the one to whose thoughts we are given access—the father. But I reconsidered, in favor of the prior rule that other things more or less equal, it is the character who most resembles the S in sex and age—the son.
- Sentence (2): The DD goes up to 3 because of being depressed over being ill.
- Sentence (3): The same illness and content score but different controls: it was the father's (R-pers) and well before the story's beginning (R-time). It also enters only via a telling (R-spch).
- Sentences (4) and (5): These are good examples of clinically significant themes that are outside the purview of pripro scoring. It is not intended as an all-purpose system.
- Sentence (6): Having an illness you believe hopeless is surely victimization.
- Sentence (10): By now, the father's long speech quite clearly implies not only a cold lack of nurturance but also a punishing accusation of making him a victim—all distanced somewhat by R-spch.

TABLE 17.9 Scoring of Doe's Story Card 7BM

Units	Content & Formal	(DD)	Controls & Defenses	DD
1. man and son				
2. son depressed re health	Ag 2 V	(3)	R-min, O-exp	3
3. he had same illness	Ag 2 V	(2)	R-pers, R-time, R-spch, O-exp	2
4. can be cured by will				
5. you alone can cure it				
6. son believes, no hope	Ag 2 V	(2)	R-min, O-exp	2
7. will go think it over				
8. F: doing me no favor	Ag 2 A tend			
9. you have wife & kids				
10. if you're bed-ridden responsibility falls on me	Ag 2 V Ag 2 V wk, Ag 2 A wk	(3) (1)	R-pers, R-spch, R-cond, O-exp	3
11. will go away, try to make things better				
12. son has TB	Ag 2 V	(3)	R-min, Del, O-exp	3
13. he dies	Ag 2 R	(3)	R-min, Del	3
14. Children old enough..				
15. never contacted fath.	Ag 2 A wk	(1)	R-min, Del, Impl	1
16. Father dies	Ag 2 R	(3)	R-pers, Del	3
17. his way of repenting	Ag 2 V tend			

Computation of DE

Card #	DD & FL	Starting DE	Affect	Structure	C & D	Adequacy of Hero	Final DE	Final DD×DE
7BM	3 Fo	+1	−.5	(1,2,1,2,1 = 7) = +.5	0	−.5?	0	0

The remaining meager scores should be self-explanatory. Repentance (in 17) is a difficult matter. It can be thought of as a self-reproach, but it is portrayed here as a kind of final attempt at redemption, a last act of giving to try to undo his prior coldness. In the end I compromised on a tend.

DE Scoring

If we follow the rules mechanically, we end up with a +.5. Then comes the difficult part, for reliable scoring: the exercise of clinical judgment. The basic question to be faced is whether the subject seems to have enough useful control over his threatening motives (and deviant cognitive structuring, which here is not in evidence) to be able to make any constructive use of them. He appears preoccupied again with a sense of being the victim of parental coldness, and pretty gloomy about it. Again it is not easy to say that he has clearly identified himself with either character, but neither is particularly effective and the original ending is inconclusive—the son makes a feeble effort, which on inquiry turns out to be a failure. So I decided to erase the remaining +.5 and leave DE again in the limbo of zero, neither clearly adaptive nor maladaptive.

Card 11

(1) This is a fantasy. (2) This highway cuts over an arched bridge. (3) The people on the road are black and wearing capes. (4) There are perhaps two pack animals carrying supplies. (5) About the middle of the picture there is a prehistoric animal with just his serpentine neck showing and a web foot. (6) He has been waiting for these travelers until they came into sight, (7) and then, when he saw them, he started rolling huge boulders across their path. (8) However, they must have been predestined to reach their goal, (9) because the boulders have fallen short of the highway. (10) They are evidently the first travelers to get this far because it is presumed that the black area to the right of the beast is a pit full of lost human souls. (11) However, the beast looks as though he will race ahead of them and in some future spot along the road send them to whatever fate has for them in the future. (Fate?) (12) Looks like wicked people trying to escape or something, and this seems to be going deeper into more of a dark place than from where they came from.

Commentary

- Sentence (1): Again a preliminary distancing remark, situating the following material in the realm of fantasy, a magic blanket, as it were, covering all implausibilities. He proceeds cautiously with three more unscorable units of description.

- Sentence (5): At last, the *prehistoric animal* with three appropriate remoteness scores. We disregard the fact that the period of prehistory when there were such critters long preceded human beings, because the subject cannot be presumed to have known that. (It was, anyway, the painter Böchlin who put what appears to be a water-dwelling dinosaur in this rocky setting with people, so no Ctr R should be scored.) The composition score is thus level 2 rather than 1, Cx I+ wk is scored for the correct use of *serpentine neck,* and all the controls are good.

- Sentence (7): Most of the controls are presumed to carry over to control what is a less terrible attack than might have been expected. Easy to overlook is the implausibility that a dinosaur would roll boulders—almost tool-using—rather than attack directly (Ctr R 1 but with a DD of only 2).

- Sentences (8)–(10): Here's a nice instance of magical causation: predestination. In sentence (9), again his tendency to want to deduce things from details in the picture shows itself faintly, as it does also in the *evidently* and *looks as though* of the next two units, amounting to enough to be scorable. In sentence (10), the Cx I– wk is given for *it is presumed that,* which one might be tempted to call a bit peculiar, but it is more likely somewhat pretentious intellectualizing in the service of disclaiming personal responsibility.

- Sentence (11): He continues to speak as if the picture itself contains the idea he next produces, which does not quite reach the threshold for an additional Au Lg 2. Without warning, he has reversed the earlier predestination and now has consigned the travelers to fate: a failure to maintain a set, scored B C 2. Notice that throughout this story, but especially here, he avoids using words that express the feared attack directly but cloaks everything in indirection or, as here, Eu.

- Sentence (12): After a mild probe, he turns it into a morality tale: Victimization is the wages of sin. *Wicked people* are treated as aggressors (Ag 2 A) who are also punished (Ag 2 V)—somehow, but just how is cloaked in vague wording.

TABLE 17.10 Scoring of Doe's Story, Card 11

Units	Content & Formal	(DD)	Controls & Defenses	DD
1. This is a Fantasy				
2. highway...bridge				
3. people in black, capes				
4. two pack animals				
5. prehistoric animal	Ag 2 A, C ≢2	(2)	R-fan+, R-time+, CxI + wk R-(an), O-pot	2
6. waiting for travelers				
7. rolling boulders	Ag 2 A, Ctr R 1	(2)	R-fan+, R-(an), O-beh	2
8. predestined to reach	M C 1	(3)	R-fan+	3
9. boulders fell short	Au Lg 1 tend			
10. evidently...presumed pit of lost souls	Au Lg 2 wk Ag 2 R	(2) (3)	Cx I- wk, Discl R-fan+	3
11. looks as though will send them to fate	Au Lg 2 tend, B C 2 Ag 2 A	(2) (2)	R-fan+, R(an), R-time, Eu, O-beh	2
12. wicked people	Ag 2 A, Ag 2 V	(2)	R-fan+, Del, Va-, O-pot	3

Computation of DE

Card #	DD & FL	Starting DE	Affect	Structure	C & D	Adequacy of Hero	Final DE	Final DD×DE
11	3 F+	+1.5	0	(1,2,1,1,0 = 5) = –.5	–.5	–.5	0	0

DE Scoring

This is an unusually sharp and accurate interpretation of an ambiguous picture, which gives many people much trouble; hence, F+ and a starting level of +1.5. Nevertheless, there are a couple of hints that he is somewhat vulnerable to the dark colors. Nothing in the realm of affect to change DE, except that the failure to say anything about the characters' feelings makes the structural contribution slightly negative. C&D: Despite a good start, and what looks like many pluses, they amount to only the single mention of fantasy at the start, and another singular invocation of R-time+. As the story progresses, the subject has more difficulty telling a scary fantasy story: Stilted wording is followed by two negatively signed defenses. So this sequence suggests another slight lowering of DE. The unhappy ending and inability of the wicked to avoid their fate, which they are not described as making actual effort to do, cause another minimal lowering to zero. DDxDE is therefore zero: Even though he spontaneously took advantage of an opportunity to let some pripro out under safe cover, he could not really do it.

Card 12M

(1) This is a young artist in Paris who is badly off financially; so badly in fact that, because he hadn't sold a painting in over a month, he is prostrate from starvation. (2) But the painting he had sold for a loaf of bread had somehow gotten into the home of a wealthy patron of the arts who had seen great magnificence in it (3) and had turned it over to the director of an art institute. (4) The picture was sold for a large sum. (5) The director, after great pains, had finally located the artist and was standing over him now trying to get some response, (6) trying to tell him that he was to be commissioned to paint for the wealthy woman for a large retaining fee. (7) But, however, it was too late. (8) The picture that had brought the director to his bedside had had too great an effect on the artist. (9) It was a picture of a loaf of bread.

Commentary

- Sentence (1): Sets the scene remotely again, but the R-geo+ is not repeated because it has little or no relevance to pripro in the remainder of the story. Note that his strongest expression of an oral wish so far comes out negated. The Cx C+ is given for the fact that the starving artist is a cultural cliché.

- Sentence (2): Notice how, in this story too, there is a good deal of interesting content that is not scorable for pripro—here, only the oral theme.

- Sentence (5): Only the figure of speech *after great pains* is scorable.

- Sentence (7): The words *it was too late* clearly imply that he was dead. By contrast, *passed away* would have been a euphemism.

- Sentence (8): Now, between the lines, Doe tells us that he died, not from starvation but from the effect of the picture. That is both an arbitrary turn of events, deliberately used for its shock value, and an instance of magical causation. Again, the subject seems to have lost track of his own story: He had traded the picture for a loaf of bread, on which

TABLE 17.11 Scoring of Doe's Story, Card 12M

Units	Content & Formal	(DD)	Controls & Defenses	DD
1. Artist...Starvation	L 1 O, Ag 2 V	(3)	R-geo+, Cx E+, Neg, O-exp	3
2. painting sold for bread	L 2 O	(1)	R-min, O-pot	1
3. to director, art institute				
4. sold for large sum				
5. after great pains	Ag 2 V, D-fig 2	(2)	R-pers, R-fig+, O-exp	2
6. to paint for large fee				
7. it was too late	Ag 2 R	(3)	R-min, Impl	3
8. picture, too great effect	Ag 2 V	(2)	R-min	3
	D a-t 2, M C 1 wk	(3)	X	
9. picture of loaf bread	L 2 O	(1)	R-dep+, Cx E+, O-pot	1

Computation of DE

Card #	DD & FL	Starting DE	Affect	Structure	C & D	Adequacy of Hero	Final DE	Final DD×DE
12M	3 Fo	+1	0	(2,2,1,2,1 = 8) = +1	0	−.5	+.5	+1.5

he had presumably lived for a month, so it becomes wholly implausible that it was the effect of the picture of bread (R-dep+) that had done him in, even when we learn in the last sentence what it depicted.

DE Scoring

I considered giving another −.5 for the slightly phony, exaggerated emotional tone of this story, but decided I might be overreacting. Though the starting level was +1 and the contribution of the story's structure is also given as +1, notice that you do not simply add them. If the starting level is lower or higher than the structural component, the latter may raise it or lower it; here it merely confirms the first approximation. The ending is certainly intended to be tragic, but the adequacy of the hero is ambiguous: unable to fend for himself well enough to survive, yet a genius hidden until too late. So, it is treated the same as unspecified, and the DE is brought down barely over the border of adequacy.

Card 13MF

(1) These two people have come to a strange city and taken lodging in a middle-class hotel. (2) They both met while riding on a bus. (3) The girl approached him first by saying she was a stranger and had no place to stay. (4) The man too was a stranger and welcomed the opportunity because she did not appear to be just a common pickup. (5) They registered as

TABLE 17.12 Scoring of Doe's Story, Card 13MF

Units	Content & Formal	(DD)	Controls & Defenses	DD
1. two people in a hotel				
2. met on a bus				
3. She: no place to stay				
4. not like a pickup	L 2 S	(3)	R-pers-H, Neg, Eu tend, O-pot	3
5. registered man & wife	L 2 S	(1)	R-min, Impl, O-pot	1
6. in light saw her 1st time	L 2 E-V wk	(1)	R-min, O-exp	1
7. saw in her things...	L 2 E-V tend			
8. like one he cd not have	L 2 S, L 2 E-V tend	(2)	R-min, Neg, O-pot, Eu tend	2
9. girl at home died	Ag 2 R	(2)	R-pers	2
10. they had relations	L 1 S, L 2 E-V tend	(4)	R-min, Eu, O-beh	4
11. with lights, shame	L 2 E-V	(2)	R-min, O-exp	2
12. this girl morally diff.	L 2 S	(2)	R-pers, Imp, O-pot	2
13.could never get other	L 2 S	(2)	R-min, Neg, O-pot, Eu tend	2

Computation of DE

Card #	DD & FL	Starting DE	Affect	Structure	C & D	Adequacy of Hero	Final DE	Final DD×DE
13MF	4 Fo	+1	–.5	(2,1,1,2,2 = 8) = +1	–.5	–.5	–.5	–2

man and wife and retired to their room, (6) where the man in the glaring bright light of the room saw the girl for the first time. (7) He saw in her the very thing he had come to this town to get away from. (8) She was the same in proportion, in color, and even in manner as the girl he could not have at home, (9) because the girl at home had died. (10) Overcoming this feeling by turning off the light, they had relations, (11) and now with the lights on again, a feeling of shame has come over him and he leaves. (12) This girl was morally a different girl from the one that had died. (13) He could never get the other girl.

Commentary

- Sentence (4): From the slow beginning, it seems apparent he is aware of the pull of this card for a sex story. *Common pickup* is scored like *prostitute* but is negated.
- Sentence (5): The sexual implication of registering as married should be evident.
- Sentence (6): The special importance to Doe of looking and being seen is suggested here, foreshadowed by his prior concern with her appearance, shortly to be repeated.
- Sentences (8) and (9): More deprivation, now sexual (but discreetly worded)

- Sentences (10) and (11): Note the special importance of light and seeing, closely related to sex. Here the DD of 4, unusual for him, may seem exaggerated, especially because of his Eu, but one must remember the date when this story was told (1947), before the sexual revolution of the sixties.

- Sentences (12) and (13): Once again, he changes his story as he goes along. At first, he could not have her because she died; now he never could get her because of her morals. Not scorable, but if you like you could note D-a-t 1 tend.

DE Scoring

The slight negative contribution of affect is given partly because he thinks feelings turn off and on with the light switch, partly because of the low mood of the whole story. Structure brings it back up to +1, but when we examine the C&D scores, it is evident that even though there are no minus signs, he relied heavily on negation, implication, and euphemism, indicating that he is not at all comfortable with sexual themes. Then, the ending is clearly unhappy and the hero is rather powerless to find real gratification, so a slight negative contribution seems clinically warranted. I saw no reason to alter the final DE = –.5, and the DDxDE = –2 seems about right.

Card 13B

(1) This doesn't say much to me. (2) This scene is of a very poor farmhouse in an isolated part of the country. (3) The little boy has just been told that he is going to have a little brother. (4) However, he can't quite figure it out. (5) He has been told to stay out of the way, (6) and some other small children have told him that they have had little brothers too, (7) and since they arrived the mother has not had so much time for them. (8) The little boy in the picture is thinking all this over, (9) and since he cannot get much affection from his father who is too busy working in the fields to even be kind to him, (10) the boy, in his small mind, has come to the conclusion that it's a hopeless case. (11) He looks behind him into the black room, which only accentuates the fact that his case looks black also. (12) He decides to leave home, (13) and just then his mother calls him; (14) the baby is going to arrive and he must rush over to get Mrs. Smith, the nearest neighbor. (15) The mother tells him that she thanks God that she has a son like him to help her now, (16) which makes him feel very elated (17) and he decides he will never leave home. (18) He had really done more than his father had in doing this.

Commentary

- Sentence (1): This preliminary remark is a warning: What follows is not likely to have conscious meaningfulness but may have some important unconscious significance to the subject. In either event, it is not scorable for pripro, little of which appears in the story.

- Sentence (3): This theme of childbirth, implying future sibling rivalry and loss of some of mother's love and nurturance (see unit 7) is not suggested in the picture and may have personal meaning. We are familiar with the theme lack of parental nurturance (as Henry Murray might have put it) from several stories; see also unit 9.

TABLE 17.13 Scoring of Doe's Story, Card 13B

Units	Content & Formal	(DD)	Controls & Defenses	DD
1. this doesn't say much				
2. very poor farmhouse				
3. boy will have brother	L 2 M	(1)	R-pers, R-time, Impl, O-pot	1
4. can't figure it out	L 2 E-V tend			
5. told to stay out of way				
6. others have brothers				
7. mothers have no time				
8. boy is thinking				
9. no affection from F				
10. boy . . . hopeless	Ag 2 V	(2)	R-min, O-exp	2
11. black room: his case	Ag 2 V, F-msc	(1)	R-min	3
look black	2 tend, F-msc 1	(3)	Cx I+ tend, X	
12. decides to leave home				
13. mother calls				
14. baby will arrive	L 2 M	(1)	R-pers, O-pot	1
15. she praises him				
16. he is elated				
17. decides, won't leave				
18. has excelled father	F-msc 2		X	3

Computation of DE

Card #	DD & FL	Starting DE	Affect	Structure	C & D	Adequacy of Hero	Final DE	Final DD×DE
13B	3 Fo	+1	0	(1,2,2,2,2 = 9) = +1.5	0	+1	+1	+3

- Sentence (4): The emphasis on the hero's bafflement suggests a feeling that something is hidden—another version of Doe's E-V preoccupation.

- Sentence (10): Hopelessness is an interesting form of Ag 2 V, feeling like a victim of that invulnerable aggressor, fate. A good deal of research has shown that it and its twin, helplessness, have malign prognostic implications.

- Sentence (11): The emergence of this physiognomic responsiveness (a form of F-msc 1) to the black color betrays the depth of his hopeless feeling, doomed by lack of love. Notice that he never explicitly says that the blackness symbolizes or means hopelessness, required for the less diagnostically ominous score of color symbolism. There is a hint of an attempt at intellectual control in his use of a vocabulary that implies higher education (*accentuates*), not previously noted but present throughout and an asset worthy of attention. It is a little difficult to assign DD here, because the schizophrenic flavor of the unit (4?) is not apparent to clinically untrained persons (2?). The 3 is thus a compromise.

- Sentence (18): Doe regained control, however, until the very end. In his almost manic reversal of gloom into elation, the hero indulges in a fantasy of oedipal triumph quite unjustified by the child's small accomplishment. Again, however, the manual provides only a residual score, F-msc, for the implicit grandiosity of this bit of wishful thinking, here considered level 2 because in real life if verbalized it would have been thought cute rather than alarming. Another possible way to handle it would be Au Lg 1 wk, on the grounds that the reasoning in this self-evaluation is faulty.

DE Scoring

Here the affect is basically appropriate if rather extreme (from utter blackness to elation); the 0 is conservative. Doe came closer to meeting the structural requirements than anywhere else, raising the tentative DE to 1.5. Though the C&D scores seem hardly consistent with that level, there is nothing really bad about them. And the ending is unambiguously happy, with an active, adequate hero who feels good about himself. We cannot deny Doe Table 17.2's +1, which would put DE at the maximum—except for clinical judgment. It has to be conceded that the ability to allow himself a conscious wish-fulfilling fantasy is a plus, despite the fact that signs of psychotic thinking did peek through it, along with a hint of a capacity to look normal through manic denial (mood swings)—all of which adds up to a warrant for full exercise of clinical judgment to lower the rating by one point to +1.

Card 14

(1) This is a photograph that the man has taken while exploring a deserted house. (2) Directly after taking this picture he had turned his flashlight to the floor and discovered a mutilated human body. (3) This was the only possible suspect, the figure in the picture. (4) He could, with imagination, almost put together characteristics of the figure shown in the picture. (5) As this man lived in a small town not frequented often by visitors, he knew who this figure was seen leaving the window, (6) but he being a minister, was not sure he should divulge the identity (7) because between the time that the murder was committed and the time that the police discovered it, the suspect had confided in the minister what had occurred. (8) The man in the picture had told the minister that it was in self-defense, (9) that he had been startled by an intruder who had suddenly sprung upon him. (10) However, the minister believed that it was the other way around and did notify the police, (11) who found out actually what had happened. (12) The man in the picture was hiding because earlier he had robbed a jewelry store (13) and been followed by the victim.

Commentary

- Sentence (1): The E-V theme of this story, secrets and discovery, begins as a hint (the photograph) and became full-fledged as discovery.

- Sentence (2): Surprisingly, level 1 aggression appears more strongly than before (mutilation trumps simple murder, so DD is 4, not 3), perhaps, I speculate, because of the

TABLE 17.14 Scoring of Doe's Story, Card 14

Units	Content & Formal	(DD)	Controls & Defenses	DD
1. photo...exploring	L 2 E-V	(1)	R-pers-O, O-beh	1
2. light...discovered multilated body	L 2 E-V Ag 1 R	(1) (4)	R-pers-O, O-beh	4
3. suspect, figure in pic.	Ag 2 A	(3)	R- pers, R- cond, R-dep+, O-beh	3
4. could imagine character	Au Lg 1 tend			
5. knew who, had seen	L 2 E-V tend			
6. shd divulge identity?	L 2 E-v tend			
7. betw. murder & discovery confided what had happ.	Ag 1 A, L 2 E-V D-time 1 tend	(3)	R-min, O-beh	4
8. told, it was self-defense	Ag 1 A, Ag 2 V	(3)	R-pers-O, R-spch, Cx C+, O-beh	4
9. startled ...attacked	L 2 E-V, Ag 2 V	(2)	R-pers-O, R-spch, O-beh	2
10. (untrue) told police	Ag 2 A wk, Ag 2 A	(1)	R-pers-H, R-pers, Cx C+, O-pot	1
11. found out what happ.	L 2 E-V	(1)	R-pers, O-beh	2
12. hiding, had robbed	L 2 E-V, Ag 2 A	(2)	R-pers, Neg, O-beh	2
13. followed by victim	Ag 2 V	(2)	R-pers	2

Computation of DE

Card #	DD & FL	Starting DE	Affect	Structure	C & D	Adequacy of Hero	Final DE	Final DD×DE
14	4 Fo	+1	0	(1,1,2,2,0 = 6) = −.5	0	0	0	0

impact of the intense blackness. In keeping with the voyeuristic theme, the hero is primarily a spectator throughout the story.

- Sentence (3): *Suspect* implies the R-cond—he may be the murderer, but we are not yet sure. The R-dep is justified because the perpetrator is twice depicted: the picture (unit 14) depicts a photograph taken by the hero. With three R's, the gory crime is held at considerable distance.

- Sentences (4) and (5): A hint of contradiction here: Unit 5 says, matter-of-factly, he recognized the suspect, immediately after 4 has invoked "imagination, almost put together characteristics ..." It is almost a confession of paranoid thinking: If I can imagine something on the basis of a few perceptual cues, I know it. This is, however, somewhat speculative interpretation not recommended in scoring. So only a couple of tends are noted.

- Sentence (6): *Divulge* means undoing a secret, revealing truth: more hints of L 2 E-V.
- Sentence (7): The content is easily scored here, but the formal scoring is tricky. What exactly was the sequence of events? We do not yet know that the police discovered the murder or just when the confiding took place. After careful reconstruction, I figured that the events could have happened in the claimed sequence so gave only a D-time 1 tend. At best, however, we may judge this man capable of convoluted thinking about the discovery of secret crimes.
- Sentences (8) and (9): A nice example of R-spch, even though it is an indirect quotation: The scored actions take place within the realm of hearsay. It may seem a lot to give the one word *self-defense* two Ag scores, but it literally means striking out at someone who has attacked you. And since self-defense is culturally accepted as a legitimate form of aggression, we score Cx C+. Unit 9 merely makes the attack explicit and adds the element of surprise, another implication of L 2 E-V, all taking place between third parties (R-pers-O).
- Sentence (10): Though not directly stated, this story was a lie, which earns the first of two Ag 2 A, the second for *police.*
- Sentence (11): *Finding out* is another bit of L 2 E-V. The final two units summarize the events leading up, put appropriately last in the style of a detective story. The Neg is for the fact that hiding cancels out seeing or being seen.

DE Scoring

Again, unremarkable perceptual adequacy, and no indication that Doe displayed any emotion. It is most striking that the hero's emotional response to the vivid events of the story is never given. Under Structure, the Beginning gets only a 1 because it was never explained why the minister was exploring a deserted house. The second element is minimal, though for picture 14 this degree of elaboration is not unusual. The minus score for Structure pulls down the initial +1 a half point. The controls are unremarkable, just adequate to keep the impact of implied DD at bay, and the final zero was earned—if perhaps a bit harsh—because the story's ending was neither unhappy nor explicitly happy, with the hero passive through most of it. The final DE = 0 is justified by the clinical judgment that Doe's controls and defenses served only to stave off any threats from pripro without allowing enjoyable or effectively creative use of it.

Card 16

(1) This is a great plain where there used to be a settlement not so long ago. (2) It is very hot and dry on the plain, (3) and the people who had been inhabitants had suffered a great

deal from the heat, lack of water, and even outside influences. (4) They were entirely reliant upon themselves, and no one was reliant upon them. (5) Because of the reason that they were alone was also the reason that they came to their doom. (6) If they had had one line of contact, one way of conversing, even a telepathic touch with the outside world, they could have perhaps been saved. (7) Now nothing is left except ruins and destruction of something that had once been evident as at least having been here. (8) We know that it must have been there because of the ruins, (9) and yet no one is sure because no proof is offered in either having had contact or having seen. (10) It could be all imagination.

Commentary

- Sentences (1) and (2): A scene of desolation and deprivation, not quite verbalized to a scoring level, but coming fast in sentence (3). Note that the normal expectation is for images of gratification, so the Neg is for the implied thirst. And note particularly the ominously paranoid sound of *outside influences,* not explained and unfortunately not inquired into. Perhaps that association prevented me at first from seeing that he probably meant *lack of outside influences,* though that last word still has an odd ring if he meant *help.*

TABLE 17.15 Scoring of Doe's Story, Card 16

Units	Content & Formal	(DD)	Controls & Defenses	DD
1. a plain, once settled				
2. very hot & dry	L 2 O tend			
3. suffered, lack of water even outside influences	Ag 2 V, L 2 O M C 1 tend	(3)	R-min, Neg, Impl, O-exp	3
4. entirely self-reliant				
5. came to their doom	Ag 2 V	(3)	R-min, Gram– wk	3
6. could have been saved even telepathic touch	Ag 2 V wk M C 1	(1) (4)	R-cond, O-beh X	4
7. ruins, destruction	Ag 2 R	(3)	R-ia	3
8. we know bec. of ruins	Ag 2 R	(3)	R-ia	3
9. no proof. . having seen	L 2 E-V tend, V P 2, Au Lg 1 wk	 (3, 3)	X	4
10. It could be all imagination.				

Computation of DE

Card #	DD & FL	Starting DE	Affect	Structure	C & D	Adequacy of Hero	Final DE	Final DD×DE
16	4 Fo	0	–.5	(2,0,1,1,1 = 5) = –.5	0	–1	–1.5	–6

- Sentence (4): Though not scorable for pripro, the theme of utter self-reliance remarkably echoes the father's harsh advice in 7BM.

- Sentence (5): "Because of the reason ... was also the reason" is a reasonably normal verbal mix-up, worth only a Gram– weak. Only the now-familiar concept of doom is scored.

- Sentence (6): It is hard to tell if the pathos here was a deliberate effect (perhaps a covert appeal to the tester) or simply a breakthrough of genuine feeling. The reference to *telepathic touch* reinforces the magical implication found in unit 3. Because of the oddity that Freudian drive theory had no room for non-oral longing for help and care, the only Content scorable in this unit is the victimized aspect of the implied fantasy of abandonment.

- Sentences (7) and (8): Now the image of total devastation, for which the stated DD of 3 seems perhaps too mild. It strongly suggests the classical schizophrenic fantasy of world destruction.

- Sentence (9): Surely a strangely worded statement about an odd notion: that the presence of ruins is not enough to conclude that anyone was ever there; a lapse in logical reasoning as well as verbalization.

- Sentence (10): Finally, a belated gesture that does not quite work. Instead of saying that the whole idea was a product of the imagination, he implies that a person in such a blasted scene might doubt its reality. Nothing to score as pripro, but it does not take a great leap of clinical intuition to conclude that this man has at best a tenuous hold on reality and is not always capable of securely distinguishing it from fantasy.

DE Scoring

As in scoring dreams, spontaneous stories and others stimulated nonpictorially, we have no assessment of perceptual acuity with which to begin. The best substitute seems to be compliance with the instructions, here called structure (of the story) for short. There is quite an adequate account of events leading up to the scene. But then we have to say that there either is no middle or no end. It seems that Doe took the blankness of the card as indicating the end (of everything?), so I gave the zero to middle. He complied with every other stipulation only minimally, with a total of 5 and one zero for a first take on DE of –.5. Next we consider the affect. Here, as so often before, there is a contrast between the dysphoric tone of the story and a lack of any statement about feeling other than suffering. Again, we give it –.5. The controls and defenses contain nothing obviously pathological but nothing associated with constructive aspects of the imagination either; a zero contribution seems generous. The sum so far is –1, but there is more bad news. The ending was totally unhappy and the hero figures wholly unable to help themselves. There is an interesting implied contradiction between their stoutly asserted total independence and their perishing for lack of help from someone else. So much for your moralistic advice, dad, he seems to be saying; that great virtue you prescribe is worth nothing. Since nothing is said about any efforts the people made to save themselves, we have to give a full –1. This time, I feel that the simple total, –2, is too harsh even for such a bleak story, but –1.5 feels right. With the large defensive demand, the contribution to ARI becomes –6.

Tallying and Calculating Indices

Once all the stories for a given the subject have been scored, next comes reducing their profusion to a manageable set of indices: summarizing or combining scores. The first step is the rather tedious one of tallying scores on the Primary Process Summary Sheet (Table 17.16). Feel free to photocopy both pages of it, enlarging if possible, for your regular use. Notice that on its first page, you make a stroke or tick for each score: content, formal, and C&D. Instead of a line for each possible wk score, there is a space in which you may enter them as needed. That concludes in the first column of the second page, plus the tally of DD, but many of other entries there come from the DE scoring where the unit is the story. Entries in the 4 × 4 box derive from counts of units.

Because of considerable differences in card pull (Holt, 1978, vol. 1, ch. 3), it is sometimes desirable to compute indices for each story separately, especially when one is comparing data from different sets of cards. Within a single study, or within a given clinical setting where the same set is used for all subjects, most users prefer to compute means across all cards. Dividing sums by the total number of units (ΣU) provides a generally satisfactory compensation for individual differences in verbal productivity. For more precision, one may use sums but correct for fluency and talkativeness by covarying mean word count of all units not scored for pripro (see Kalter & Marsden, 1970). Research is needed to find out which of these two procedures yields better results in terms of construct validity.

At this point, I urge the reader to make a copy of the summary sheet and try your hand at tallying the scores in Tables 17.5 through 17.15 and then to compare yours with mine in Table 17.16. Do not be discouraged; it is trickier than it seems, and it is easy to lose your place when the phone rings or someone pops in. I find it helpful to make a mark on the scoring sheets being tallied as I enter the strokes on the summary sheet, but even then I sometimes find I have to go back and recheck. It is probably easier to go down the columns on the scoring sheets, doing the content first, then the formal, and so forth; you may lose your place less often.

After you have tallied everything, count up your strokes and enter the number for each non-zero category. That goes faster if you have made the strokes in groups of five. Weak scores count as one half each; tendencies do not contribute to the total, but I usually note the number of them for each category, as you will see. Then enter the totals for the various subgroupings (e.g., Σ Ag, Σ D) of content and formal scores. The only such totals for C&D are the total of all categories with plus signs (e.g., R-geo+, Cx E+) listed on page 2 of the summary sheet as Σ+, and likewise for the negatively signed ones.

Most of the rest of the second page leans on the DE scoring box at the bottom of each scoring sheet. Under form level, make a stroke for each instance in the T column, making sure that they add up to the number of stories told to cards with pictures (notice that there was no FL for card 16). Enter the product of the total for each FL used times its weight in the fourth column, add those, and enter the mean where indicated. The process for DD is very much the same; but remember that these are the DDs for whole stories—not the ones given to units. Procedure for DE is also much the same, with the extra twist that you also enter the $DD \times DE$ for each story in a list over at the right side of the page. This is the only column not aligned meaningfully with what is to its left; coincidentally, numbers of DE scores here are same as of number of stories. Then enter the means where called for and the counts of stories, units, units with pripro scores (not counting tends): PPU, and units with *X* scores.

TABLE 17.16 Primary Process Summary Sheet

S:____________________ Tallied by: _______________Date:_______________

Content	Formal Aspects		Controls Defenses	
L 1 O	C-ctm 1	Ctr A 1	R-min	Cx C+
L 1 A	C-ctgn 1	Ctr L 1	R-eth	Cx C
L 1 S	C-int 1	Ctr R 1	R-an	Cx E+
L 1 E-V	C c-i 1	Ctr R 2	R-(an)	Cx E
L 1 H	C-co 1	Σ Ctr =	R-pl	Cx I+
L 1 M	C-co 2	Au Lg 1	R-ia	Cx I
L 2 O	Σ C =	Au Lg 2	R-dep+	Cx I–
L 2 A	D-chain 1	Intr 1	R-geo+	Cx H+
L 2 S	D-dist 1	B C 1	R-time+	Cx H
L 2 E-V	D-dist 2	B C 2	R-time	
L 2 H	D-clang 1	Un Rel 1	R-char	Refl+
L 2 M	D-clang 2	Trans 1	R-fic s+	Refl
Σ L =	D-sub 1	Trans 2	R-fic s	Mod+
	D-sub 2	P D 1 2	R-fic n+	Mod–
	D-time 1	P D 2	R-fic n	Del
Ag 1 A	D-time 2	S-R 1	R-rel+	Neg+
Ag 1 O	D-a-t 1	M C 1	R-rel	Neg
Ag 1 V	D-a-t 2	M C 2	R-rel–	Inh
Ag 1 R	D-acc 2	F-msc 1	R-fan+	Ratn+
Ag 2 A	D-fig 2	F-msc 2	R-fan	Ratn
Ag 2 O	D S 2	Σ Distortn =	R-fig+	Minz
Ag 2 V	Σ D =		R-fig	Eu
Ag 2 R		V I 1	R-spch	Vulg–
Σ Ag =	Sym-C 2	V C 1	R-cond	Impl
Σ Cont =	Sym-I 1	V Q 1	R-pers	Discl
	Sym-I 2	V P 2	R-pers-H	Repr
Σ Formal =	Σ Sym =	Σ V =	R-pers-O	Msc

(*Continued*)

TABLE 17.16 Primary Process Summary Sheet (Continued)

C & D	Form Level				Defensive Effectiveness			
Self-D–	wt FL	T*	Txwt		DE	T*	DExT	DDxDE
Rep–	6 F+			Σ[Txwt] =	+2			
Va–	5 Fo			weighted mean	+1.5			
Prj–	4 Fw			FL =	+1			
Obs–	2F+/F–				+.5			
Iso–	3 Fv				0			
Eva–	1 Fs				–.5			
Imp–	1 F–				–1			
Blkg–		*Demand for Defense*			–1.5			
Cphb–		DD	T	DdxT	–2			
Fake–		1			–2.5			
Gram–		2			–3			
		3			Σ =			
O-beh		4						
O-vbl		5			Σ DExT/N*		Σ DDxDE/N	
O-exp		6			=		=	
O-pot					(Mean DE)		(ARI)	
		Σ DDxT =						
Σ + =		Mean DD =						
Σ – =		*T is the tally for each score; N is number of stories =						

a. Σ Content + Σ Formal scores =

#units =	Level 1	Level 2	Levels 1 + 2
Content	14 10%	75 54%	80 58%
Formal	13 9%	12 8%	21 15%
(any) Pripro	25 18%	76 55%	87 63%

b. Σ PPU = Density: a./b. = 1.36 #Units with X (Ux) =14 Σ U_x/PPU =16%

When you have done all the simple arithmetic, what remains are the empty nine boxes at the end. Following the Rorschach tradition, we count here not scores but the number of units containing various scores. Thus, in the intersect of level 1 and content, put the count of units that contain any L 1 or Ag 1 scores—regardless of how many such scores a unit may contain—all the way from a single L I S wk to a gaggle of honking L 1s and snarling Ag 1s in a single unit. We actually get both kinds of information, since both have their uses. Because of the fact that a single unit may contain any combination of formal and content scores on both levels, the totals either down the columns or across the rows may not add up: You have to make a separate count for each of the nine boxes. Sorry about all the trouble. Enter totals and percentages in the boxes; the base for percents is the total number of units.

Now that you have filled out the summary sheet and have compared yours with mine, in Table 17.16, try to figure out why we differ by rereading.

At last, what does it all mean? Let us start at the end of the tallying and work backward. The box scores are not particularly unusual, at least in terms of experience with

TABLE 17.17 Primary Process Summary Sheet for Doe

S:_______Doe______________ Tallied by: ____RRH______ Date:_____7/10/07_________

Content		Formal Aspects				Controls & Defenses			
L 1 O	1	C-ctm 1	.5	Ctr A 1	.5 +1t	R-min	31	Cx C+	11
L 1 A		C-ctgn 1		Ctr L 1		R-eth	6	Cx C	
L 1 S	5	C-int 1		Ctr R 1	3.5	R-an		Cx E+	12
L 1 E-V		C c-i 1		Ctr R 2		R-(an)	3	Cx E	1
L 1 H		C-co 1		Σ Ctr =	4 +1t	R-pl		Cx I+	.5 +1t
L 1 M		C-co 2		Au Lg 1	1 + 2t	R-ia	5	Cx I	
L 2 O	3 +1t	Σ C =	.5	Au Lg 2	1.5 +2t	R-dep+	2	Cx I–	.5
L 2 A		D-chain 1		Intr 1		R-geo+	1	Cx H+	
L 2 S	9	D-dist 1	1	B C 1		R-time+	4	Cx H	
L 2 E-V	18 +7t	D-dist 2		B C 2	1.5	R-time	4+1t		
L 2 H		D-clang 1		Un Rel 1		R-char		Refl+	
L 2 M	4	D-clang 2		Trans 1		R-fic s+		Refl	
Σ L =	40 + 8t	D-sub 1		Trans 2		R-fic s		Mod+	
		D-sub 2		P D 1	2	R-fic n+	7	Mod-	
		D-time 1	1t	P D 2	.5	R-fic n		Del	7
Ag 1 A	5	D-time 2		S-R 1		R-rel+		Neg+	2
Ag 1 O		D-a-t 1	1	M C 1	2.5 + 1t	R-rel		Neg	9
Ag 1 V	2	D-a-t 2	1 + 1t	M C 2		R-rel–		Inh	
Ag 1 R	1	D-acc 2		F-msc 1	1	R-fan+	6	Ratn+	
Ag 2 A	16.5 + 2t	D-fig 2	1	F-msc 2	1 +1t	R-fan		Ratn	
Ag 2 O		D S 2		Σ Distortn =	11+6t	R-fig+	2	Minz	
Ag 2 V	21.5 + 3t	Σ D =	4.5 + 2t			R-fig		Eu	5+3t
Ag 2 R	10			V I 1		R-spch	9	Vulg–	
Σ Ag =	55.5	Sym-C 2		V C 1		R-cond	4	Impl	10
Σ Cont =	95.5	Sym-I 1		V Q 1	1	R-pers	21	Discl	1
		Sym-I 2		V P 2	2 + 2t	R-pers-H	4	Repr	
Σ Formal = 22.5		Σ Sym = 0		Σ V =	3 + 2t	R-pers-O	6	Msc	

(*Continued*)

TABLE 17.17 Primary Process Summary Sheet for Doe (Continued)

C & D		Form Level					Defensive Effectiveness			
Self-D–		wt FL	T*	Txwt			DE	T*	DExT	DDxDE
Rep–		6 F+	1	6	Σ[Txwt] = 46		+2			–2.5
Va–	1	5 Fo	7	35	weighted mean		+1.5			3
Prj–		4 Fw	1	4	FL = 4.6		+1	2	2	0
Obs–		2F+/F–					+.5	1	.5	0
Iso–		3 Fv					0	5	0	0
Eva–		1 Fs					–.5	2	–1	0
Imp–		1 F–	1	1			–1			1.5
Blkg–				*Demand for Defense*			–1.5	1	–1.5	–2
Cphb–	1			DD	T	DdxT	–2			3
Fake–				1			–2.5			0
Gram–	1.5			2			–3			–6
				3	5	15	Σ =	11	0	–3
O-beh	21			4	4	16				
O-vbl	3			5	2	10	Σ DExT/N*		Σ DDxDE/N	
O-exp	17			6			= .00		= –.27	
O-pot	26						(Mean DE)		(ARI)	
				Σ DDxT = 41						
Σ +	42.5			Mean DD = 3.73						
Σ – =	4			*T is the tally for each score; N is number of stories = 11						

a. Σ Content + Σ Formal scores =118

#units = 138	Level 1	Level 2	Levels 1 + 2
Content	14 10%	75 54%	80 58%
Formal	13 9%	12 8%	21 15%
(any) Pripro	25 18%	76 55%	87 63%

b. Σ PPU = 87 Density: a./b. = 1.36 #Units with X (Ux) = 14 Σ U_x/PPU = 16%

Rorschach pripro scoring. The subject could be almost any unmarried male in his twenties of that time, normal or with several kinds of psychopathology. But the ARS, being slightly on the minus side, is an immediate sign of some pathology. Yet it also assures us that the person is reasonably well compensated, just as his fairly low % Level 1 does, likewise the range of DE scores, only from +1 to –1.5: not an obvious madman. Of course, the tone of most of the stories told us that, but I am trying to see what can be extracted from the final summary.

The Mean DD is not very high, but the total lack of stories with DD of 1 or 2 (not to say, zero) indicates that as soon as he lets down his defenses at all, fairly strong stuff starts coming out, challenging his coping and defending devices, which as we shall see comprise not a terribly good set. The Form Level scores show us that although he is capable of quite sharp perception and testing reality, there are occasional serious gaps—though still not more than might be found in a neurotic outpatient. Though his Level 1 Formal scores are not so numerous as to suggest outright psychosis, the fact that so many are undefended (X) is troubling. By and large, creative, humorous, or playful people are often so comfortable with primary process thinking that they can allow a good deal to emerge without taking any special pains to domesticate it, but that is in the context of safely positive DE scores.

Turning to the first page of the summary sheet, let us look first at content. The most striking negative finding is the dearth of usually expected images of oral gratification, plenty of L 2 O—the comfort food of the pripro table. Moreover, every one of his four oral scores carried a Neg, meaning that they indicated images of deprivation, not of a benign and nurturing kind. Thus, even though the pripro system does not score Murray's (1938) *n* or *p* Nur as such, the message of their lack comes through. What is here in unusual abundance is L 2 E-V. He seems both to want the notice and attention of others, even if he has to shock to get it, and to be vulnerable to paranoid ideas of reference. There is a fair amount of material bearing on sex and love (L 1 S, L 2 S), but it too was mostly about frustrated longing for love, and occasional sex without real gratification or an extended relationship. Mark his discomfort with these themes, too: heavily defended by Eu and indirection (Impl).

Notice how helpful it is to keep in mind not just the total amount of any given content score but also the C&D accompanying it. That context makes it clear that our man may be somewhat preoccupied with sexual matters, but not like a bon vivant or happy hunter. The scores accompanying his libidinous themes speak for his conflict and inability to establish a satisfying, security-giving relationship to a woman. The C&D with the E-V scores indicates that he has some capacity to use this kind of motivation adaptively, in study or curious seeking, but enough of it has to do with concealment and shame to suggest strong ambivalence about being seen by others both literally and figuratively, whereas the sheer frequency of concern with seeing and being seen (the six tendencies indicating that even more of such interest was present) indicates the likelihood that it takes symptomatic form, as in distressing preoccupation with what people think of him or even delusions of reference. If his interest took the form of voyeurism, getting pleasure from pornography for example, one would have expected to see some L 1 E-V.

The balance of his content scores is strongly toward the aggressive, a sign of maladjustment, especially because he racked up eight Ag 1 scores, That and the highly unusual predominance of Ag 2 V, with even some Ag 1 V, speaks for a man with a strong sense of victimization, of living uncomfortably in a hostile world where much of the aggression is directed at him. Together with the already noted profusion of E-V themes, these scores point toward at least a paranoid outlook, probably outright paranoid symptoms.

Let us look next at the formal scores to check on the possibility of a schizophrenic process. Plenty of confirmation here—there are ominous, occasional breakthroughs of disordered thinking (C-ctm 1, D-dist 1, Ctr A 1, Au Lg 1, P D 1, M C 1, F-msc 1, V Q 1), sometimes accompanied by momentary loss of secure contact with reality (F–) or the emergence of pathological defenses (Va–, Cphb–). Other Formal scores are softer signs of psychosis (V P 2, B C 2, and most of the other formal deviations, especially when accompanied by substandard FL and negative affect).

Putting the pieces together, we see a man who is struggling against the onset of a psychosis, probably paranoid schizophrenia. If it were not for the glimpse of a burnt-out future in story 16, I would say that he was on the brink of a florid acute break, but it seems more likely, with as much Ag R as he presents and his failure to notice and try to compensate for such psychotic lapses as occurred in the first story, that he has had an acute break and is in a somewhat patched-together state of partial remission. Clearly he can function pretty well much of the time, possibly well enough to get along out of a hospital, and may conceal his psychosis from people who do not spend much time with him. The prognosis without expert therapeutic help looks poor, despite his evident good intelligence and resources. Some evidence of the latter may be seen in the many positively signed controls and in the general impression of creativeness in his stories. In the Rorschach scoring manual, there is a scale for rating creativity (Cr), but I have not tried to develop one for TAT stories.

I cannot present the aforementioned brief analysis as blind, because though I did once publish a blind analysis of this TAT some years before I began the development of the pripro system (Holt, 1951, reprinted in Holt, 1978), I then learned the clinical facts, which I have not completely forgotten in the intervening years. Nevertheless, I wrote the previous summary before rereading the clinical vignette supplied by Shneidman (1951), which is summarized briefly following.

John Doe's Clinical History

After serving in the navy during World War II, he began having insomnia, somatic signs of anxiety, difficulty in concentration, and feelings of inadequacy and sensitivity about being looked at. Unable to hold a job, he sought admission to a VA neuropsychiatric hospital, with several somatic complaints. His father had died of tuberculosis when Doe was 12, after several years in which he was forbidden to have close contact with the father because of the danger of infection. He has two older brothers, one an alcoholic. The patient lives with his mother, an emotional and demonstrative woman. As a child, he had many fears, some obsessive-compulsive traits, and a couple of traumatic experiences, but he did well in school. His social relations have always been marred by his fear of having people look at him. He has had one girlfriend, from whom he believes he contracted syphilis, and in the navy he experienced several sexual contacts with women without gratification.

The diagnosis on admission was acute and severe psychoneurosis; schizophrenia and anxiety hysteria were considered, but obsessive-compulsive features were more prominent. In the hospital, after he had some episodes of confusion and upset, he was considered an incipient schizophrenic and had a course of six insulin coma treatments. He took the TAT along with several other diagnostic tests shortly afterward; the tester concluded that he was "attempting to adjust on an obsessive-compulsive level in order to prevent a schizophrenic break."

After a month of psychotherapy, he felt well enough to be discharged and continue treatment as an outpatient. After eight sessions over two months, his therapist's final report contains interesting confirmation of the personal relevance of many themes in the TAT stories. She and the supervising psychiatrist agreed that he was a paranoid schizophrenic struggling with aggressive and suicidal thoughts but able to maintain precarious control.

Rather than reprint the full six-page clinical summary, I strongly urge the reader to peruse it and notice the ways in which the subject's life experiences and conflicts are transformed in his stories. I might just add that the main way in which I feel the diagnostic picture was not reflected in the pripro scores is that the latter is not sensitive to obsessive-compulsive material. The one directly relevant defense score, Obs–, picks up only rather decompensated obsessing and vacillation. I also seem to have relied too much on the ominous similarity of the last story to classically described world destruction fantasies and their conventional interpretation as indications that an acute break had occurred. In retrospect, it seems that the story is intelligible in terms of the man's inner sense of desolation after years of struggle with so little gratification, overlooking the fact that it was not really so many years—he was just 25. I underestimated his capacity to hold himself together, however grimly, and to keep trying.

A final word: My published analysis of Doe's TAT plainly contains in germ a good deal of what I have spelled out here. For, to a considerable extent, the scoring system is an attempt to crystallize in the form of rules the somewhat intuitive but theoretically based approach to diagnostic psychological testing that I learned from David Rapaport.

References

Holt, R. R. (1951). An analysis of TAT and MAPS test. In E. Shneidman, W. Joel, and K. B. Little (Eds.), *Thematic test analysis* (pp. 101–118). New York: Grune & Stratton.

Holt, R. R. (1978). *Methods in clinical psychology: Vol. 1. Projective assessment.* New York: Plenum.

Kafka, H. (1967). *The use of color in projective tests and dreams in relation to the theory of ego autonomy.* Unpublished doctoral dissertation, New York University.

Kalter, N., & Marsden, G. (1970). Response productivity in Rorschach research: A caution on method. *Journal of Projective Techniques and Personality Assessment, 34,* 10–15.

Mayman, M. (1970). Reality contact, defense effectiveness, and psychopathology in Rorschach Form-Level scores. In B. Klopfer, M. M. Meyer, F. B. Brawer, & W. G. Klopfer (Eds.), *Developments in the Rorschach technique. Vol. 3. Aspects of personality structure* (pp. 11–46). New York: Harcourt Brace Jovanovich.

Mayman, M., & Holt, R. R. (2007). Form Level Scoring Manual. In R. R. Holt (Ed.), *Primary process thinking: Theory, measurement, and research* (vol. 2) (pp. 235–284). *Psychological Issues,* Monograph 69/70.

Murray, H. A. (1938). *Explorations in personality.* New York: Oxford University Press.

Rapaport, D., Gill, M. M., & Schafer, R. (1945-46). *Diagnostic psychological testing* (2 vols.). Chicago: Yearbook Publishers. (Revised edition, R. R. Holt, ed., Madison, CT: International Universities Press, 1968.)

Rock, M. (1975). *Self-reflection and ego development.* Unpublished doctoral dissertation, New York University.

Shneidman, E. S. (with W. Joel and K. B. Little) (Eds.) (1951). *Thematic test analysis.* New York: Grune & Stratton.

Note

1 Incidentally to her research on color in dreams, Kafka (1967) tried adding two colored blank cards to the TAT (one all red, one all blue), asking for stories in the usual way. She found that the number of color words subjects used in responding to these cards was correlated with the % Formal (.54) and with Mean DE (–.57). Reacting with color responses rather than with stories was correlated with the same two indices (.54 and –.71), more strongly with DE. Corresponding correlations from the same subjects' Rorschachs were insignificant and trivial. These striking findings warrant further exploratory use of colored blank cards with the TAT.

18 CHAPTER

Pathogenesis Index

Bertram P. Karon

Abstract

The Pathogenesis Index for the Thematic Apperception Test (TAT) was originally derived to investigate the controversies about whether there were unconscious psychological defenses used by some parents that made the development of schizophrenic symptoms in their children more likely. Although no simple hurtful behaviors consistently differentiate parents of persons with schizophrenia from parents of normals, the masked evaluation of this unconscious defense led to striking and consistent findings in a series of studies. It has also been used to study child abusive parents, parents of delinquents, helpful and unhelpful psychotherapists, and the effects of helpful and unhelpful parental defenses on nonpsychotic teenagers. In each application, masked evaluations of pathogenesis led to large predictive validities.

Description of the Pathogenesis Index

Conceptual Framework

Pathogenesis is defined as the degree to which, when the needs of someone who depends on you conflict with your own needs, you do or do not take their conflicting needs into account (without awareness of its impact). Since it is understood to be an unconscious defense, not merely conscious malevolence, it was necessary to use a measurement technique capable of measuring unconscious processes. The Thematic Apperception Test (TAT) was an obvious choice (Karon, 1981; Murray, 1943). The Pathogenesis Index has been used to study the differences between parents of schizophrenics and parents of normals and to study helpful versus unhelpful therapists, child-abusive parents, parents of delinquents, and problematic parenting in general. It has been useful in research, and the hope is that it may be useful in clinical work in predicting problematic parenting, in studying reparative treatments, and possibly in selecting potentially problematic parents so that reparative treatments might be used before their children develop serious problems.

The *schizophrenogenic mother* (or parent) concept was originally postulated by Fromm-Reichmann (1959, pp. 163–164) on the basis of her clinical experience—intensive psychoanalytic therapy of persons with schizophrenia—that there seemed to be some parents whose relationship to their children was such as to make their children vulnerable to schizophrenia. However, the schizophrenogenic parent concept had never been clearly operationally defined and measured until the Pathogenesis Index was developed.

Understandably, parents of schizophrenics find the concept of a schizophrenogenic parent offensive. Parents do not want to believe that they could have caused, even inadvertently, such terrible suffering in someone they love. One of the reasons parents join organizations like the National Association for the Mentally Ill, which is financially supported by the pharmaceutical manufacturers, is that they will be told that schizophrenia is a purely biological disease, for which there are adequate treatments consisting only of medication and that parents have no role in either causing symptoms or in making them worse. Even though the accepted biological models presented by biologically oriented professionals and espoused by that organization are inconsistent with each other (e.g., 70% of the variance is accounted for by genetics, and 70% of the variance is accounted for by a virus)—both facts are presented as true in Torrey, Bowler, Taylor, and Gottesman, 1995—the inconsistencies of the biological models are never dealt with. Both that organization and the parents are happy as long as it is pronounced that a purely biological theory is known to be true and that parents have played no role in the development or exacerbation of symptoms. For a careful critique of current biological models, see Colbert (1997).

The schizophrenogenic parent concept has been attacked on the political grounds not only that it makes families feel bad but also that purely biological theories of causation—as opposed to interactional or vulnerability or stress-diathesis models—make any consideration of parental involvement superfluous and that observations of specific behaviors or questionnaire studies of consciously reported attitudes have not led to consistent findings.

My clinical observations (Karon, 1960; Karon & Rosberg, 1958; Karon & VandenBos, 1981) made it clear that the typical parent of a schizophrenic was not a consciously destructive person, although experiences of obvious child abuse are more frequent among schizophrenic patients than in normals or other patients (cf. Read, Perry, Moskowitz, & Connally, 2001; Read & Ross, 2003). Indeed, the parents of schizophrenics who are seen in private practice are usually decent people who are consciously highly motivated to make considerable sacrifices to give their children an adequate opportunity for a normal life. They are often admirable people with respect to their actions that are under conscious control. Problems in parenting, however, usually have unconscious bases and are better understood as symptoms or coping devices developed to come to terms with the parents' own childhood (Karon, 1960; Karon & Rosberg, 1958).

Other clinicians and researchers have expanded the schizophrenogenic concept to include the family system. Lidz (1973), on the basis of his family studies, described two types of schizophrenia-producing families: the skewed and the schismatic. The skewed family was organized about the unrealistic views and needs of one person, usually the mother, whereas the schismatic family was organized around the unrealistic views and needs of both parents, which were inconsistent with each other, and the child was not able to accept either view. According to Lidz, the patient in a skewed family tended to be a boy, and the patient in a schismatic family tended to be a girl.

Leff and Vaughn (1985) and other British investigators found that families characterized by what they term *expressed emotion* tend to have schizophrenic patients who relapse. The name, which seems to imply that any emotion is dangerous, may be an attempt to be tactful, because it is misleading. The family characteristics to which it refers are more accurately described as intrusive hostility—indeed, Julian Leff (personal communication) stated that positive affect expressed by their family has a benign effect on schizophrenic patients.

Wynne and Singer (1963) described an aspect of family functioning in families of schizophrenics that they termed *communication deviance.* Roughly, it may be described as not being clear about concepts and distinctions that may be anxiety provoking. Singer and Wynne (1966) developed scoring keys for the Rorschach and for the TAT as well as for evaluating direct family observation, all of which seem to differentiate families of schizophrenics from normal families. In Wynne, Singer, and Touhey (1976), Margaret Singer was able to pick out the masked Rorschachs of adopted parents whose adopted children became schizophrenic from those whose adopted children were normal, using data from Wender, Rosenthal, Zahn, and Kety's (1971) Danish adoption study. Her masked evaluations of the intermingled Rorschachs were astounding: There were no mistakes—no false positives and no false negatives. Indeed, Wender et al., whose purpose was to bolster a genetic theory, did not publish her findings, although they had sent her the data and knew the findings. Instead, they published only what their research assistants had found; with an arbitrarily altered scoring system for communication deviance their research assistants had not differentiated the two groups of adoptive parents on the Rorschach or anything else. Wender, Rosenthal, and Kety (1976) later acknowledged the real Rorschach findings when they were confronted in print (Karon, 1975) but characterized them as of no importance since there were no findings for the Minnesota Multiphasic Personality Inventory (MMPI), the Word Association Test, or the TAT when scored by their research assistants—they did not send the TAT data to Singer.

Tienari (1992) and Tienari et al. (1985), whose Finnish adoptive study is far more rigorous than the Danish studies, found that communication deviance scored from the interactions of the adoptive parents without the child being present—so that it could not be a reaction to a disturbed child—was the best predictor of whether an adopted child became schizophrenic. Adopted children whose biological mothers were schizophrenic did not themselves become schizophrenic if their adoptive parents were low in communication deviance. Most recently, Pekka Tienari has referred to this finding in terms of low communication deviance being a protective factor rather than high communication deviance being a pathogenic factor.

Finally, Doane, West, Goldstein, Rodnick, and Jones (1981) studied the families of disturbed adolescents, none of whom were psychotic. If the families were characterized by high communication deviance—both family interactions and TATs were studied—and high so-called expressed emotion, all of the adolescents were psychotic or borderline five years later. If the families were characterized by low levels of both variables, none of the adolescents were psychotic or borderline five years later.

Despite these important and promising studies, it should be noted that the Pathogenesis Index was slightly better than communication deviance scores in differentiating the TATs of parents of schizophrenics from parents of normals when Wynne and Singer made available the TATs from their National Institute of Mental Health (NIMH) sample to Mitchell (1974) as described herein.

To repeat, the rationale for the Pathogenesis Index, based on observations during the psychoanalytic psychotherapy of patients with schizophrenia and the psychotherapy of parents of patients with schizophrenia, was that although there was no general consistency between families of person with schizophrenia in specific overt parental behaviors, there usually did seem to be a difference in the unconscious defenses activated in the relationship of parents with their children and manifested in different overt behaviors in different families.

To test this, a Pathogenesis Index was operationally defined from the TAT (Meyer & Karon, 1967). Stories were scored pathogenic if there was an interaction between a dominant and a dependent character with potentially conflicting needs, and the dominant character did not take the dependent person's needs into account. An easily scored pathogenic story is, "One person murders another." Clearly, the dominant person is not taking the dependent person's needs into account. A story is scored benign if the dominant person takes the potentially conflicting need of the dependent person into account. An easily scored benign story is, "Parents force a child to do something; the child is unhappy; the parents change." Stories are scored unscorable if it is not possible to tell whether it is pathogenic or benign, or if there is no interaction. The Pathogenesis Index is the number of pathogenic stories divided by the total number of stories scored either pathogenic or benign—that is, $P/(P + B)$, where P is the number of stories scored pathogenic and B is the number of stories scored benign; in other words, it is the percentage of the total number of scorable stories that were scored pathogenic. It is important to use this ratio; attempts to correlate raw number of pathogenic stories or raw number of benign stories with criteria did not work in studies where the ratio did. The ratio assumes that the unscorable stories have an unknown number of stories that would be scorable if we understood them, or if the subjects had elaborated them, and so the stories we can score give us an estimate of what the ratio might be if we had been able to score more of the stories. This thus corrects both for length of stories and for number of scorable stories.

In a series of studies the Pathogenesis Index differentiated mothers of schizophrenics from normals and fathers of schizophrenics from normals (Meyer & Karon, 1967; Mitchell, 1968, 1969, 1974; Nichols, 1970). There have been no negative findings. It has been used to study child-abusive parents, and they too are elevated in pathogenesis, as expected (Evans, 1977; Melnick & Hurley, 1969). Psychotherapy, like parenting, is a situation where two people interact; one person (the therapist) dominates the relationship that is intended for the benefit of the dependent person (the patient). Pathogenesis of the therapist might well be expected to interfere with the therapist's helpfulness, and that is the general finding (MacDonald, 1980; Miller, 1982; Robbins, 1980; VandenBos & Karon, 1971). Parents of male delinquents from intact families have been studied, and the finding is that the fathers are elevated in pathogenesis but not the mothers (Mitchell, 1974). Finally, mothers and fathers of normal early adolescent girls have been studied, and the pathogenesis scores of both mothers and fathers are negatively related to school functioning and Rorschach indices of ego functioning; the average pathogenesis scores of the two parents was the best predictor (Leigh, 1987).

Scoring Categories

Each story is scored pathogenic, benign, or unscorable. Each story is given only one score. Final score for each subject is $P/(P + B)$—that is, the ratio of the number of pathogenic stories to the number scored either pathogenic or benign, or, stated equivalently, ratio of the number of pathogenic to the total number of scorable stories. Following is a fairly complete list of easily scorable themes, although more detailed guidelines for difficult-to-score stories are presented in the chapter on scoring.

Pathogenic Themes

(1) Murder

(2) Rape

(3) Physical assault

(4) Suicide attempt to frighten someone

(5) Going to cemetery to scare people

(6) Parents make boy study or practice when he does not want to

(7) Losing interest in playing the violin (It is assumed that card 1 reveals relations with parents even if the parent is not mentioned. The child playing the violin against his will is assumed to imply coercion.)

(8) Mother supposedly kind but does not meet expressed needs of child

(9) Mother showing particularity for one daughter or son over another

(10) Any kind of talking to as punishment

(11) Mother warning child on things that can harm him in growing up

(12) Mother telling child he has not worked up to ability

(13) Mother reading to child from Bible to teach her a lesson (This assumes no further clarification. A lesson emphasizing forgiveness might be benign; a lesson implying, as is most likely, "You are wrong, defective, should be guilty or ashamed, or will be punished" would be obviously pathogenic.)

(14) Mother feels what she has said to daughter has done little good

(15) Mother does not like something about daughter or son (e.g., looks, makeup, attitude) even though daughter or son likes it

(16) Mother checking up on son or daughter (e.g., study)

(17) Woman harming child by punishment (In general, punishment is to be scored as pathogenic, reflecting the need of the parent rather than the child, even though it is usually rationalized by the parent, and sometimes the child, as good for the child.)

(18) Husband or father jealous or forbidding

(19) Family- ruled or -dominated

(20) Husband gives wife news he is leaving town (or her)

(21) Man telling wife something to hurt her (e.g., took secretary to dinner)

(22) Husband interrupts something wife is interested in

(23) Man pulling out of an extramarital affair and woman does not want to

(24) Refusal of marriage bid; one is interested, one is not

(25) Spying on girlfriend (or being stood up)

(26) Boss driving workers hard

(27) Being fired from a job

(28) Trying to find a job and cannot (implies the hero has been turned down)

(29) Nasty remarks to a subordinate, making him or her unhappy

(30) King or leader leading a nation to ruin

(31) Destructive witch themes

(32) Happy old witch and pretty young woman

(33) Woman and evil conscience (e.g., devil behind her)

(34) Monster ready to attack child or smaller animal

(35) Accidental injuries due to human error (e.g., accidentally shooting someone, automobile accidents)

(36) Unsuccessful rescues

Unscorable Themes

(1) No interaction between two people, though somewhat conflicting needs

(2) One person enjoying himself

(3) No people or living things

(4) Two people, but no indication of interaction

(5) Conflict with person's own needs, not other people's

(6) Thinking about a mother who was kind to her—it is assumed that this indicates the existence of such a fantasy, but it is at least as likely to be defensive as it is to be reflective of reality.

(7) Wanting to join a dead person—an intrapsychic problem

(8) Nothing in the story speaks to a shared bond, conflicting needs, or interaction; nothing to indicate that the people know each other—applies to all cards, including card 1 (In card 1 we assume the presence of a parental figure.)

(9) No evidence of pathogenic or benign behavior

Benign Themes

(1) Parents force child to do something; he is unhappy; they change.

(2) Parent interrupts punishment of a child by the other parent.

(3) Stopping children from activity in which they would likely get hurt

(4) Son or daughter interested in advice from parents (or stories)

(5) Woman working hard for the benefit of her children

(6) Mother thinking about children and being happy (Of course, if what she is happy about is described and it is pathogenic, that would obviously change the scoring to pathogenic.)

(7) Mother admiring work of children or making something they like

(8) Mother enlightening child about the birds and the bees

(9) Mother caring for the child.

(10) Father and daughter consoling each other after death of mother

(11) Teacher consoling a problem child; helping a gifted child

(12) Woman trying to console a man in trouble

(13) Helping people at a disaster

(14) Guides leading animals across, for example, a difficult area

(15) Reunion of two people, both pleased

(16) Person springing a pleasant surprise on another

(17) Accepted protestations of love, or mutual love

(18) Man heeds woman's wish not to leave

(19) Any attempt to help or console with no ulterior motive

(20) Prevention of disaster (e.g., suicide, murder)

(21) On card 11, hero slaying a bad dragon (because implies successful rescue)

(22) Two people being happy together

☐ Research Evidence

Validity

Parents of Schizophrenics

Meyer and Karon (1967) tested six mothers of schizophrenic boys and six mothers of normal boys the same age and social class, using 40 TAT cards. The TAT stories were intermixed and were scored blindly by Karon, and a theoretically generated scoring key was transcribed during the initial scoring (using themes from the sample of 480 stories as specific instances of the scoring categories). When the protocols were reassembled, there was practically no overlap: Mothers of schizophrenics varied from 65 to 89% pathogenic, and the control mothers varied from 23 to 69% pathogenic; the findings were clearly statistically significant ($p = .003$) even with this small number of cases. In the same study, Kevin Mitchell, using this scoring key, was able to score blindly the intermixed stories, and his scoring again discriminated between the samples, so it was a useable scoring key ($p < .02$).

Mitchell (1968) then administered standard 20-card TATs to new samples of 20 mothers in each group—mothers of schizophrenics and mothers of normals—and replicated Meyer and Karon's (1967) findings. He found that, again, masked scoring, on the average, differentiated mothers of schizophrenics from mothers of normals using this unconscious variable. Mothers of normal children, as in the previous study, had average pathogenesis scores of about 35%. No one is perfect, but children do not require perfect mothers. If the TAT is representative, mothers of normals ignore the conflicting needs of their children about one third of the time. Mothers of schizophrenics, as in the previous study, had average pathogenesis scores of about 75%; the mothers of schizophrenics do not always ignore the conflicting needs of their children, but the more consistent problem makes children vulnerable.

Margaret Singer made available to Mitchell (1974) the TAT data from the Wynne and Singer (1963) and Singer and Wynne (1966) NIMH studies of parents of male schizophrenics, male delinquents, and male normals—five pairs of parents in each group—which Wynne and Singer had used to validate their TAT scoring for communication deviance. Mitchell again replicated the finding for pathogenesis. For the first time, fathers of schizophrenics were examined with the pathogenesis scale, and they were more pathogenic than fathers of normals, although they seemed a little less pathogenic than the mothers—however, that difference was not statistically significant. Interestingly enough, the masked scored Pathogenesis Index differentiated the parents of schizophrenics from the parents of normals in that study slightly better than Wynne and Singer's (1963) own communication deviance TAT scale, although the communication deviance scale also differentiated parents of schizophrenics from parents of normals in masked evaluations.

Clinical experience suggests that schizophrenics usually have two parents who are not helpful enough—unless they do not have two parents. As described in Karon and VandenBos (1981), usually there are two pathogenic parents or one parent who is pathogenic and one parent who is physically absent or emotionally so weak as not to serve as an effective alternative. The TAT of one such emotionally weak parent (father) scored high on pathogenesis: His apparent parental weakness seemed to be expressing pathogenesis by proxy; the other parent's hurtfulness expressed this parent's hurtful needs without his having to actively acknowledge them. Of course, withdrawing rather than facing a conflict with a spouse over the treatment of a child is solving one's own need for marital harmony at the expense of the child's needs. The parental solid front advocated by many child-care experts is overvalued. Frequently, schizophrenic patients recount incidents where it would have been helpful if the other parent had intervened or at least overtly said that he or she disagreed with the parent who was being hurtful.

Nichols (1970) found that the TAT Pathogenesis Index scores of 30 mothers of adult white male hospitalized schizophrenics correlated significantly with the severity of the thought disorder of their sons as measured by the Becker Rorschach Genetic Level Scale. Pathogenesis Index scores of the mothers were also correlated significantly with the length of hospitalization of the sons. The Rorschach thought disorder measure itself was not significantly correlated with length of hospitalization. Neither the Becker Rorschach Genetic Level scale scores of the patients nor the Pathogenesis Index scores of the mothers were correlated with the premorbid social competence of the schizophrenic sons as measured by the Phillips Social Competence Scale. The Pathogenesis Index scores of the mothers were not correlated with the social class of the mothers or with their age.

To attempt to deal with the issue of whether pathogenesis was a learned trait that resulted from the inordinate demands of a sick child—so that the parent learned in self-defense not to respond—Beavers (1975) investigated the TATs of mothers of mentally retarded children and found no increase in pathogenesis over mothers of normal children. Thus, it does not seem that a child with unusual needs teaches a parent to be pathogenic but that pathogenic defenses on the part of the parent make the child vulnerable, as seems to be consistent with clinical observations reported by therapists.

Parents of Male Delinquents

Using Wynne and Singer's (1963) and Singer and Wynne's (1966) data, Mitchell (1974) also studied the parents of male delinquents. The pathogenesis scores of the mothers were not clearly different from the mothers of normals, but the fathers were about as pathogenic as fathers of schizophrenics, suggesting that the healthier relationship with the mother permitted the development of a sense of self but that the problematic relationship with the father interfered with the development of a stable set of socially acceptable standards. Kenneth Howard (personal communication, 1983) said that one of his graduate students at Northwestern University had found similarly elevated Pathogenesis Index scores for fathers of male delinquents. Unfortunately, since that time Howard passed away, and it has not been possible to locate any published reference to that data.

Psychotherapists

Since therapy, like parenthood, involves an interaction between a dominant and a dependent person for the dependent person's good, a pathogenic therapist would not be expected to be very helpful. VandenBos and Karon (1971) administered the TAT to

10 student therapists—five graduate students in clinical psychology and five psychiatric residents—before the Michigan State Schizophrenia Psychotherapy Research Project began and found that Pathogenesis Index scores of student therapists correlated negatively with patient gain scores in the first six months of treatment on measures of thought disorder (Drasgow-Feldman Visual Verbal Test, $r = .73$; Wechsler Adult Intelligence Scale, $r = -.71$; Porteus Mazes, $r = -.64$) and on a measure of overall functioning (i.e., Clinical Status Interview Ratings, $r = -.69$): that is, the more pathogenic the therapist the less improvement. Patient gain scores were regressed scores holding initial scores constant. For the Visual–Verbal Test the gain score was a decrease in errors; for the Wechsler, Porteus Mazes, and Clinical Status Interview Rating it was an increase in score achieved. The Clinical Status Interview Ratings were based on careful clinical status interviews conducted by an experienced psychoanalytic psychiatrist who was familiar with psychotic patients but not connected with or aware of the specific treatment, aside from spontaneous remarks by the patient during the interview. The interview was conducted with the aim of eliciting information with respect to ability to take care of self, ability to work, sexual adjustment, social adjustment, absence of hallucinations and delusions, degree of freedom from anxiety and depression, amount of affect, variety and spontaneity of affect, satisfaction with life and self, achievement of capabilities, and benign versus malignant effect on others. The interviews were recorded on audiotape—with any giveaways to type of treatment being deleted by a secretary—and then masked ratings were made for emotional health by two graduate students in clinical psychology. Their ratings were quantified by a scaling technique, and the two ratings were averaged. Pathogenesis scores of therapists also correlated with length of hospitalization of their patients during the first six months of treatment ($r = .48$)—that is, the patients of less pathogenic therapists tended to spend less time in the hospital.

There have been three other studies relating the pathogenesis scores of therapists to their effectiveness, with lesser findings, although in the predicted direction. MacDonald (1978) correlated Pathogenesis Index scores of 14 beginning graduate students with patient gain scores of neurotic patients after the initial 15 sessions of psychodynamic therapy, once or twice per week. The therapists were administered the TAT before the therapies were begun. There were no statistically significant findings, although the Pathogenesis Index of therapists correlated –.45 with improvement in subjective distress, the measure most centrally related to neurotic problems, which was still short of statistical significance. Patient gain scores on other variables showed no clear pattern.

MacDonald (1978) discovered after collecting her data that there was a point-biserial correlation of .90 between pathogenesis scores and whether the students had sought out and were receiving personal dynamic psychotherapy (a mean of 260 hours). According to MacDonald, the fact that the student therapists most in need of psychotherapy (high pathogenesis) were also the ones most likely to obtain it may have tended to obscure the relationship between pathogenesis and change in their patients.

The second was Robbins (1979). Pathogenesis Index scores rated from TATs of 53 psychiatric residents given before the beginning of training at a prestigious psychoanalytic psychiatric residency correlated only –.13 with supervisors' ratings of overall competence as therapists at the end of the three-year residency. However, the most incompetent therapists were removed from the sample on which data was available (restricting the range, which would lower any correlation); the time lag was three years, during which most of the residents were undergoing psychoanalysis which would be expected to possibly change pathogenesis; and the criterion was supervisors' ratings rather than actual patient change scores. Examination of the relationship of Pathogenesis Index scores at the beginning of the residency and competency ratings at the end of the residency showed that psychiatric residents low in pathogenesis were uniformly rated as competent but that those high in pathogenesis might be rated anywhere from high to low in competence, which is consistent with the possibility that some of the pathogenic residents changed as a result of their training experiences and personal psychoanalyses.

Miller (1982) studied 20 beginning counselors. They were administered 10 TAT cards, which were scored for the Pathogenesis Index. After 10 weeks of a counseling technique course, they were subjected to a standardized "client" interview. The "client" rated the counselors on the Barrett-Lennard Relationship Inventory, which was the criterion measure. High (n = 6) and low (n = 5) Pathogenesis Index counselors were significantly different according to t-tests on the regard and empathy subscales, just short of significance for congruence, and significantly different on total score (p = .005, .01, .07, and .02, respectively). The correlation coefficients using the total sample fell short of significance (–.38, –.43, –.42, and –.40, respectively).

There has been one study attempting to relate the Pathogenesis Index of therapists to patient gain where there was no finding (A. Frank, personal communication, July 22, 2003); hence, it was not reported in the study publications. The McLean study (Gunderson, Frank, Katz, Vannicelli, Frosch, & Knapp, 1984), which compared expressive and supportive psychotherapies for persons with schizophrenia, scored therapist TATs for pathogenesis and found no relationship with outcome. However, only 28 out of 81 therapists took the TAT, and all of these therapists scored relatively low on pathogenesis (mean = .38), so there was very little variance among tested therapists. The most striking finding of the project was that two thirds of the patients in both groups dropped out of treatment and that one fourth of those who completed treatment would not allow themselves to be evaluated (Karon, 1984). This dropout rate may be related to the fact that all patients in both groups were required to take their medication (by the research design, therapists were not permitted to reduce medication). However, for those patients who were assessed, therapeutic alliance measures were reported to predict gain, the supportive therapy was a little better at getting patients back to work, and the expressive therapy was better at improving ego functions and reducing negative symptoms. There was no untreated group or medication-only group in that study.

Child-Abusive Parents

Melnick and Hurley (1969) studied 10 child-abusive mothers and compared them with 10 control mothers matched for age, social class, and education. Evans (1976) replicated this study using 20 child-abusive mothers who were receiving Aid to Families with Dependent Children as compared to 20 control mothers also on Aid to Families with Dependent Children. As might be expected, in both studies the child-abusive mothers were significantly elevated on pathogenesis. But their scores tended not to be as high as those of the parents of schizophrenics. The meaning of this is that the child-abusive parent, when he or she is being child abusive, is more gruesome than the typical parent of a schizophrenic, but the child-abusive parent is not so consistently insensitive to the conflicting needs of the child. The pressures that lead to schizophrenia tend to be subtler, not so obvious to the parent or the child, but definitely more consistent.

There are two somewhat confusing studies. Selfridge (1985) found that 19 self-identified child-abusive mothers had higher average Pathogenesis Index scores than 19 system-identified child-abusive mothers (.70 vs. .61), although both were high.

Selfridge suggested that perhaps system-identified cases were consciously trying to suppress any story that might make them look bad, since they knew they were under scrutiny and that their case workers considered them suspect, and this may have affected their Pathogenesis Index scores. Amberg (1976) studied incarcerated criminals who were diagnosed with Psychopathic Personality Disorders. Three groups were compared: (1) incarcerated psychopaths who spontaneously had mentioned in group therapy that they had abused a child; (2) psychopaths who had not described in group therapy having abused a child; and (3) normal control fathers. There were 15 subjects in each group. The average TAT Pathogenesis Index scores of both groups of psychopaths were more Pathogenic than that of normal control fathers. Surprisingly, the average Pathogenesis Index scores of those psychopaths who had spontaneously mentioned in group therapy that they had abused a child was less than the average Pathogenesis Index score of those who did not mention ever having abused a child. Possibly, mentioning committing child abuse as a problem during therapy might be a sign of a lesser commitment to hurtfulness in a psychopathic patient than an index of being more hurtful, as the investigator originally thought.

Paraprofessionals and Residential Treatment Home Staff

There are two surprising studies. Small (1976) and Small and Hurley (1978) studied paraprofessionals at an inpatient treatment facility for disturbed children and adolescents. Paraprofessionals in that setting were bachelor's-level staff in the residence who supervised the patients, developed relationships with them, recorded daily progress, and carried out the recommendations of the therapist—in other words, all staff other than therapists or teachers. Small found a small nonsignificant relationship of patient liking ($r = .28$) for paraprofessionals with higher Pathogenesis Index scores (the opposite of what one would expect), whereas their coworkers found the more pathogenic paraprofessionals less likable. Patient change was not measured. Similarly, Bengt-Ake Armelius (personal communication, 1995) found a relationship between higher Pathogenesis Index scores of staff and being liked by schizophrenic patients in a residential treatment center in Sweden. The center was not particularly effective for schizophrenic patients. It may be that pathogenic people are more like the patients' parents and consequently seem more likable to patients with schizophrenia.

Parents of Nonclinical 12-Year-Old Girls

Leigh (1987) determined the Pathogenesis Index scores of mothers and fathers of 20 12-year-old seventh-grade girls, who were within the normal range—that is, attending school and neither in treatment nor diagnosed with a mental disorder. There were no adopted children or single-parent families in the study. The Pathogenesis Index scores of both fathers and mothers were each negatively correlated with ego functioning as measured by Rorschach indices and with teacher ratings of the student's success in meeting the student's objectives, both in terms of academic achievement and school adjustment. The academic achievement was rated in terms of the student's objectives so that it was not just a reflection of level of achievement. Rather the teacher in each class would set objectives for each student for that term based on previous levels achieved and what the student needed to learn next. The student was graded on the degree to which the student had achieved this term's objectives. The average of seven teachers' ratings was used. The best predictor was the average pathogenesis score of both parents.

Changing Pathogenesis

There has only been one investigation of whether pathogenesis changes with psychotherapy. In the Michigan State Schizophrenia Psychotherapy Research Project (Karon & VandenBos, 1981), Borofsky (Borofsky, Karon, & VandenBos, 1970) found no statistically significant change in masked pathogenesis ratings of the 23 patients who received an average of 70 sessions of psychotherapy—with or without adjunctive medication. However, most of these patients did not have children; therefore, the pathogenic effect on children was not an issue in their treatment. Seventy sessions for schizophrenia has to be considered brief treatment, in which only urgent issues get adequate attention. The patients who did have children, however, tended to show large changes in pathogenesis. It was suggested that for pathogenesis to change, the following must occur:

(1) The patient's relationship with one or more dependent persons (e.g., their children) becomes important in the patient's life.

(2) The patient makes a conscious choice between a benign or pathogenic approach toward the dependent person or persons; that is, the patient makes a decision to help or not help, attack or not attack, the dependent person.

(3) The patient experiences gratification as a result of the decision or action.

Mayne (1990) studied whether courses for college students intended to make them better parents change their Pathogenesis Index scores. There were three groups: (1) a control group that was tested and retested to examine the effects of time (10 weeks) and was retested without any special intervention; (2) those taking a course in parenting skills based on Thomas Gordon's (1988) Parent Effectiveness Training, which was characterized as cognitive-behavioral; and (3) those taking Gershen Kaufman's Psychology of Health and Self-Esteem, which is designed to increase affect tolerance, to decrease shame, and to increase healthy self-esteem and spontaneity among college students (Kaufman, 1985; Kaufman & Rafael, 1983), which was characterized as psychodynamic. Pathogenesis Index scores did not change in the control group, but they did decrease significantly with the parent effectiveness training and decreased even more with the Kaufman course on affect tolerance and self-esteem. A three-group analysis of variance of change scores was statistically significant, but the only group difference that was statistically significant, using Scheffe's test, was the largest difference: that between the control group and the Kaufman group. Thus, this relatively inexpensive group intervention did change (lessen) pathogenesis as well as causing improvement in other traits related to healthy functioning.

Generalizability

The theory of the Pathogenesis Index was derived from Karon's (1960; Karon & Rosberg, 1958) clinical observations of parents of schizophrenics, and the specific scoring criteria were dictated by Karon during masked scoring of the TAT's of mothers of schizophrenic and normal boys using Meyer's (1964; Meyer & Karon, 1967) data. It was cross-validated on other samples of parents of schizophrenics by Mitchell (1968,1974) and by Nichols (1970) as described previously. It has been used with therapists, child-abusive parents, parents of delinquents, and parents of normal teenagers.

The Pathogenesis Index has been used with subjects of different socioeconomic statuses, differing educations, both genders, pathology from normal to schizophrenic, and with both White and African American subjects. It has not been used with children, mentally defective individuals (although it has been used with their mothers), or individuals outside the United States. One of the therapists in the Karon & VandenBos (1981) study was an Iranian doing his psychiatric residency at Detroit Psychiatric Institute. His English was very good, and his TAT pathogenesis score seemed to reflect accurately his therapeutic effectiveness. It was also used with residential staff in Umea, Sweden, but there were no major findings in that study.

There have not been any statistically significant findings of relationships with any of the demographic variables so far. Mitchell (1969) found no main effect for social class but did find a statistically significant interaction between social class and whether or not the child was schizophrenic. Using Hollingshead and Redlich's (1958) five socioeconomic class categories, mothers from class 1 (1 subject) and class 2 were termed *upper class* (13 subjects); mothers from class 3 were termed *middle class* (26 subjects); and mothers from class 4 were termed *working class* (11 subjects). There were no mothers from class 5. There was a slight trend—not statistically significant—in both groups of mothers for middle-class mothers to score lower on pathogenesis than working-class mothers, but the statistically significant interaction effect was due to the upper-class mothers. Surprisingly, the upper-class mothers of normals (n = 8, average pathogenesis score = .57) were significantly more pathogenic than the middle-class mothers of normals (n = 13, average pathogenesis score = .42), whereas among mothers of schizophrenics the upper-class mothers were the least pathogenic (n = 6, average pathogenesis score +.68) although still higher than the average pathogenesis score of upper-class mothers of normals and not significantly different from middle-class and working-class mothers of schizophrenics. It may be that upper-class mothers are more likely to arrange for other people to do more of the care of their children so that their own pathogenesis might not have as much of an impact as that of middle-class and working-class mothers, although that has not been demonstrated. Nichols (1970) found no correlation of the Pathogenesis Index of mothers of schizophrenics with their social class, and Leigh (1986) found no correlation of the Pathogenesis Index with social class among mothers and fathers of normal 12-year-old girls. Subjects have been from Michigan, California, and Kansas. There is no reason to doubt its general applicability in the United States. Likely limitations on suitability have not been determined, although a usable sample of scorable stories is required. Length of story is not in itself an issue, because even brief stories may be scorable.

Reliability

Scorers have been primarily graduate students in clinical psychology, although fully trained clinical psychologists and undergraduate students also have been used. There is no consistent finding among the groups other than that the ratings of the originator, Dr. Karon, seem to be slightly more valid than alternative raters. It seems relatively easy to learn, with raters spending anywhere from a minimum of 1 hour to a maximum of 10 hours to learn it.

Meyer and Karon (1967) reported interjudge reliability (correlation) to be .89. Mitchell (1974) reported the interjudge reliability to be .79. Melnick (1968) reported the interjudge reliability to be .94. Robbins reported the three reliability correlations among three judges to be .79, .82, and .86. Evans (1976) reported that the correlations among each of three judges were greater than .81. All reliability coefficients and other correlations are between Pathogenesis Index scores based on the whole protocols. Mitchell (1965, 1968) determined split-half reliabilities within each of two judges and found correlations of .81 and .76.

It is an axiom of psychometric mental test theory (Gulliksen, 1950; Karon, 1966) that low reliability cannot account for positive findings, unless the experiment is not masked, but only for a lack of findings. On this basis, the validity findings are good evidence of its reliability as well.

☐ Future Research Needed

(1) Does pathogenesis of therapists generalize to other therapies besides psychodynamic therapy? How intensively do the therapist and patient have to be involved with each other? If the type of therapy is not particularly effective would pathogenesis of the therapist still make a difference?

(2) There are families where one or more children are schizophrenic and one or more are not. How does pathogenesis occur in such families? Clinically, it has been noted that parents do not treat all children equally. Bruno Bettelheim (personal communication, 1955) said that the favorite child in the family of schizophrenics is usually the sickest, because that is the child who meets the parents' unconscious but hurtful needs. Karon has observed that, in families where one child is schizophrenic and the other is not, the mother has been kinder to the less sick child than to the schizophrenic child, but in many such cases the mother says, and believes, that she has been kinder to the schizophrenic child. In other cases parents will reveal in private, and with guilt, that they never could relate to the more disturbed child the way they related to their other children. It is important to note that pathogenesis is not evil; it is an unconscious defense that does not deserve blame but does deserve help, because it causes so much pain to both child and parent. One stringent test of the theory, which has not yet been carried out, would be to find a sample of families where there is at least one schizophrenic child and at least one child without serious pathology. If all of the boys in the family, or all of the girls, are schizophrenic, and all of the nonschizophrenics are of the opposite gender, then it should be possible to score two Pathogenic Indices from the parents' TAT: one derived from stories where the dependent person is male and the other from stories where the dependent person is female. One would predict that the Pathogenesis Index for the gender of the schizophrenic child should be higher than for the gender of the less disturbed child, if parental pathogenesis is a major causal factor.

(3) More research is needed on ways to change pathogenesis. This might be important for future therapists and even more for future parents.

(4) The ideal utility of the Pathogenesis Index would be to screen parents or prospective parents and to tell those high in pathogenesis that their children might be at risk for

psychological problems and that we would like to make available counseling, therapy, or a course (such as Kaufman's Affect and Self-Esteem Course), which would reduce that risk. The research needs to be done as to whether that would actually reduce the risk of severe problems.

(5) Teaching clients the scoring system (cf. McClelland & Winter, 1969) would be a bad intervention, because it would make it impossible to assess pathogenesis accurately, if the individual did not wish to be assessed accurately. As Tomkins (1949) pointed out, anything of which the subject is fully aware and which they do not wish to disclose can be kept out of the TAT. Knowledge of the scoring system would allow individuals to fake stories that would score low on pathogenesis. At the present time the scoring rationale is not widely known among patients or therapists and therefore yields valid scores.

(6) It would be useful to see if it generalizes to other cultures and languages. Even in the United States, it would be useful to verify that Spanish-speaking individuals yield protocols that may be validly scored. Of course, it will be important to be careful to correct only differences in scoring due to oddities of a language or culture that are not related to pathogenesis. There may be real differences between cultures in pathogenesis, in the sense of parents using hurtful defenses, which one would not want to eliminate from study, as might be found by anthropologists comparing cultures like Yap (where parents are unusually kind by Western standards) and Dobu (where parents are unusually mean by Western standards).

(7) Gary VandenBos (personal communication, 1980) reported clinical observations from one community mental health center that when the Pathogenesis Index has been gathered along with other measures in custody evaluations, and the final custody decision placed the child with the parent with the higher Pathogenesis Index, the placement has not worked out well for the child. It would be worthwhile determining whether the Pathogenesis Index would be a useful tool for child placement and custody decisions by carrying out research where the placement is not made on the basis of the Pathogenesis Index although it is measured and evaluating whether it would predict how well the child does.

☐ References

Amberg, E. (1976). *Fathers who abuse their children.* Unpublished doctoral dissertation, Michigan State University.

Beavers, W. J. (1976). A study of the mothers of retarded children and the concept of pathogenesis utilizing the Thematic Apperception Test (Doctoral dissertation, University of Georgia, 1975). *Dissertation Abstracts International, 36,* 6369B. University Microfilms 76-13, 989.

Borofsky, G. L., Karon, B. P., & VandenBos, G. R. (1970). *Changes in the "Pathogenesis" of schizophrenic patients resulting from psychoanalytic treatment.* Unpublished manuscript, Michigan State University Psychotherapy Research Project 12.

Colbert, T. (1997). *The four false pillars of biopsychiatry.* Tustin, CA: Kevco Publishing.

Doane, J. A., West, K. L., Goldstein, M. J., Rodnick, E. H., & Jones, J. E. (1981). Parental communication deviance and affective style. Predictors of subsequent schizophrenic spectrum disorders in vulnerable adolescents. *Archives of General Psychiatry, 38,* 679–685.

Evans, A. L. (1976). *Personality characteristics of child-abusing mothers.* Unpublished doctoral dissertation, Michigan State University.

Fromm-Reichmann, F. (1959). *Psychoanalysis and psychotherapy: Selected writings of Frieda Fromm-Reichmann* (D. Bullard, Sr., Ed.) Chicago: University of Chicago Press.

Gordon, T. (1988). *P. E. T. in action.* New York: Bantam Books.

Gulliksen, H. (1950). *The theory of mental tests.* New York: Wiley.

Gunderson, J. G., Frank, A. F., Katz, H. M., Vannicelli, M. L., Frosch, J. P., & Knapp, P. H. (1984). Effects of psychotherapy in schizophrenia: II. Comparative outcomes of two forms of treatment. *Schizophrenia Bulletin, 10,* 564–598.

Hollingshead, A. B., & Redlich, F. C. (1958). *Social class and mental illness.* New York: Wiley.

Karon, B. P. (1960). A clinical note on the significance of an "oral" trauma. *Journal of Abnormal and Social Psychology, 61,* 480–481.

Karon, B. P. (1966). Reliability: Paradigm or paradox, with especial reference to personality tests. *Journal of Projective Techniques & Personality Assessment, 30,* 223–227.

Karon, B. P. (1975). All in the family. [Review of the book, T. Lidz, *The origin and treatment of schizophrenic disorders*]. *Contemporary Psychology, 20,* 473–475.

Karon, B. P. (1981). The Thematic Apperception Test. In A. I. Rabin (Ed.), *Assessment with projective techniques* (pp. 85–120). New York: Springer.

Karon, B. P. (1984). The fear of reducing medication, and where have all the patients gone? *Schizophrenia Bulletin, 10,* 613–616.

Karon, B. P., & Rosberg, J. (1958). Study of the mother–child relationship in a case of paranoid schizophrenia. *American Journal of Psychotherapy, 12,* 522–533.

Karon, B. P., & VandenBos, G. R. (1981). *Psychotherapy of schizophrenia: The treatment of choice.* New York: Aronson.

Kaufman, G. (1985). *Shame: The power of caring.* Cambridge, MA: Schenkman.

Kaufman, G., & Raphael, L. (1983). *The dynamics of power: Building a competent self.* Cambridge, MA: Schenkman.

Leff, J., & Vaughn, C. E. (1985). *Expressed emotion in families: Its significance for mental illness.* New York: Guilford.

Leigh, L. D. (1987). The relation between "Pathogenesis" in parents and Rorschach indices of ego functioning in preadolescent daughters (Doctoral dissertation, Michigan State University, 1986). *Dissertation Abstracts International, 48*(12), 3684B.

Lidz, T. (1973). *The origin and treatment of schizophrenic disorders.* New York: Basic Books.

MacDonald, B. L. (1978). *An investigation of therapist pathogenesis.* Unpublished doctoral dissertation, University of Detroit.

Mayne, B. L. (1990). *Lessening pathogenesis: Preventive interventions.* Unpublished master's thesis, Michigan State University.

McClelland, D. C., & Winter, D. G. (1969). *Motivating economic achievement.* New York: Free Press.

Melnick, B., & Hurley, J. R. (1969). Distinctive personality attributes of child-abusing mothers. *Journal of Consulting and Clinical Psychology, 33,* 746–749.

Meyer, R. G. (1964). *A study of the schizophrenogenic mother concept by means of the TAT.* Unpublished master's thesis, Michigan State University.

Meyer, R. G., & Karon, B. P. (1967). The schizophrenogenic mother concept and the TAT. *Psychiatry, 30,* 173–179.

Miller, Catherine R. (1982). The evaluation of beginning therapist effectiveness using Karon's Thematic Apperception Test Pathogenesis Index: A psychological approach. (Doctoral dissertation, Western Michigan University, 1981). *Dissertation Abstracts International, 42* (8-A), 3516–3517.

Mitchell, K. M. (1965). *An elaboration of a study of the schizophrenogenic mother concept by means of the Thematic Apperception Test.* Unpublished doctoral dissertation, Michigan State University.

Mitchell, K. M. (1968). An analysis of the schizophrenogenic mother concept by means of the Thematic Apperception Test. *Journal of Abnormal Psychology, 73*(6), 571–574.

Mitchell, K. M. (1969). Social class and the schizophrenogenic mother concept. *Psychological Reports, 24,* 463–469.

Mitchell, K. M. (1974). Relationship between differential levels of parental "pathogenesis" and male children's diagnosis. *Journal of Clinical Psychology, 30*(1), 49–50.

Murray, H. A. (1943). *Thematic apperception test manual.* Cambridge, MA: Harvard University.

Nichols, N. (1970). The relationship between degree of maternal pathogenicity and severity of ego impairment in schizophrenic offspring. (Doctoral dissertation, University of Michigan, 1970). *Dissertation Abstracts International, 31,* 5003B.

Read, J., Perry, B. D., Moskowitz, A., & Connally, J. (2001). The contribution of early traumatic events to schizophrenia in some patients: A traumatogenic neurodevelopmental model. *Psychiatry, 64,* 319–345.

Read, J., & Ross, C. A. (2003). Psychological trauma and psychosis: Diagnosed schizophrenics must be offered psychological therapies. *Journal of the American Academy of Psychoanalysis and Dynamic Psychiatry, 31,* 247–268.

Robbins, D. (1979). *The pathogenesis index and the prediction of personality and performance of psychiatric residents.* Unpublished doctoral dissertation, United States International University.

Selfridge, E. B. (1985). A comparative study of self-identified abusive mothers and system-identified abusive mothers. (Doctoral dissertation, United States International University, 1978). *Dissertation Abstracts International, 46*(4-B), 1346.

Singer, M. T., & Wynne, L. C. (1966). Principles for scoring communication defects and deviances in parents of schizophrenics: Rorschach and TAT scoring manuals. *Psychiatry, 29,* 260–288.

Small, D. J. (1976). *Job effectiveness and personal attributes of mental health paraprofessionals.* Unpublished doctoral dissertation, Michigan State University.

Small, D. J., & Hurley, J. R. (1978). Work effectiveness and personal attributes of mental health paraprofessionals. In K. B. Nash (Ed.), *The paraprofessional: Selected readings* (pp. 286–301). New Haven, CT: Advocate Press.

Tienari, P. (1992). Interaction between genetic vulnerability and rearing environment. In A. Werbart and J. Cullberg (Eds.), *Psychotherapy of schizophrenia: Facilitating and obstructive factors* (pp. 154–172). Oslo, Norway: Scandinavian Universities Press.

Tienari, P., Sorri, A., Lahti, I., Naarala, M., Wahlberg, K., Ronkko, T., et al. (1985). The Finnish adoptive study of schizophrenia. *Yale Journal of Biology and Medicine, 58,* 227–237.

Tomkins, S. S. (1949). The present status of the Thematic Apperception Test. *American Journal of Orthopsychiatry, 19,* 358–362.

Torrey, E. F., Bowler, A. E., Taylor, E. H., & Gottesman, I. I. (1995). *Schizophrenia and manic-depressive disorder: The biological roots of mental illness as revealed by the landmark study of identical twins.* New York: Basic Books.

VandenBos, G. R., & Karon, B. P. (1971). Pathogenesis: a new therapist dimension related to therapeutic effectiveness. *Journal of Personality Assessment, 35,* 252–260.

Wender, P. H., Rosenthal, D., & Kety, S. S. (1976). Wender et al. reply. *Contemporary Psychology, 21,* 74.

Wender, P. H., Rosenthal, D., Zahn, T., and Kety, S. (1971). The psychiatric adjustment of the adopting parents of schizophrenics. *Archives of General Psychiatry 127,* 1013–1018.

Wynne, L. C., & Singer, M. (1963). Thought disorder and family relations of schizophrenics. II. A classification of forms of thinking. *Archives of General Psychiatry, 9,* 199–206.

Wynne, L. C., Singer, M. T., & Toohey. M. L. (1976). Communication of the adoptive parents of schizophrenics. In J. Jorstad and E. Ugelstad (Eds.), *Schizophrenia 75; Psychotherapy, family studies, research* (pp. 413–450). Oslo, Norway; Universitetsforlaget.

19 CHAPTER

Scoring Manual for the Pathogenesis Index

Bertram P. Karon

Introduction

Pathogenesisis is defined as the degree to which, when the needs of someone who depends on you conflict with your own needs, you do or do not take their conflicting needs into account (without awareness of its impact). Since, as described in chapter 18, it is understood to be an unconscious defense, not merely conscious malevolence, it is necessary to use a measurement technique capable of measuring unconscious processes. The Thematic Apperception Test (TAT) was an obvious choice. The Pathogenesis Index was an attempt to operationally measure this concept that was based on clinical observations in psychoanalytic therapy of patients with schizophrenia and their parents, plus observations outside of therapy of patients with schizophrenia and their parents, and the clinical and research literature available at that time.

Although, for each schizophrenic patient, there usually had been a pattern of interactions between parents and children that made the children vulnerable, the specific overt hurtful behaviors varied widely, and no single simple behavior occurred frequently enough among different parents to be likely to lead to statistically significant findings (Karon, 2003; Karon & VandenBos 1981). Nor, in the families seen in psychotherapy, were the hurtful interactions the result of conscious malevolence on the part of the parents. This has led to the conclusion from behavioral and questionnaire studies that parents of schizophrenics are not different from other parents. Only recently have there been consistent findings that physical and sexual child abuse are more frequent, but not universal, in the case histories of patients with schizophrenia than in patients with other diagnoses, or normals (e.g., Read & Ross, 2003). But the Pathogenesis Index has led to consistent findings. The Pathogenesis Index has been used to study not only the differences between parents of schizophrenics and parents of normals but also helpful versus unhelpful therapists, child-abusive parents, parents of delinquents, and problematic parenting in general.

For each TAT story, the scorer must decide whether there is an interaction between a dominant and a dependent person with potentially conflicting needs. If not, the story is unscorable. If there is such an interaction, does the dominant person take the dependent person's potentially conflicting needs into account? If the dominant person does, the story is scored as benign. If the dominant person does not, the story is scored as pathogenic. If after careful thought, it is still not clear, the story is scored as unscorable.

☐ Administration

Format

The Pathogenesis Index has been used with TATs individually administered with the tester recording the response on a tape recorder or writing the response. It has been used in group administrations with the subject writing his or her response. Although my preference is for untimed, limited responses, time limits have been used, and the resulting protocols still seem valid. The standard Murray (1943) instructions may be used, but I prefer, "I'm going to show you a set of pictures, one at a time. I want you to tell me what is going on, what the characters might be feeling and thinking, what led up to it, and what the outcome might be. In other words, tell me a good story" (Karon 1981).

The examiner should be interested in the story as story. If individually administered, the subject should be praised for what is good about the story—thus, at the end of the first story, "Okay, that was pretty good. Now let's see what you can do with this one." If individually administered, I recommend asking for the requested elements that are missing in the first story but after that accepting what the subject gives you. If you use 20 stories, it is probably a good idea to do it in two sessions or at least to take a short break after 10 as Murray (1943) originally suggested. However, the specific instructions and method of administration are not critical as long as you obtain scorable stories.

Stimuli

Most of the research has used the standard Murray cards. The original research by Meyer and Karon (1967) used additional cards taken from Symonds (1949) as well. Since scoring requires a number of cards that can be thought of as samples of the individual's fantasy life, the specific cards are not critical. The critical issue would be to get a number of varied stories—the more the better. The recommendation is to use 20 cards, but the minimum should be 10. Tomkins (1947) suggested that people really do not have more than 20 stories to tell but recombine elements of other stories if asked for more than 20.

Mitchell (1965), who did not use card 16, reported that cards 2, 7BM, 9GF, 12M, 17GF, 18BM, and 18GF had the greatest differential (significantly differentiating the samples on that single card by itself) and that cards 1, 3BM, 3GF, 4, 6BM, 7BM, 7GF, 8BM, 8GF, 11, 12M, 12F, 13G, 13MF, 14, 15, 17BM, 19, and 20 were all useful, increasing the differentiation. Cards 5, 6GF, and 10 did not work well in his study (small difference in the wrong direction or no difference); 12BG and 13B were equivocal (in the right direction for one rater and the wrong direction for the other).

Stories told to other stimuli should be just as scorable as those to the Murray cards. The card is not important; it is the story which is scored. At this point there are no explicit criteria for the adequacy of a protocol other than whether it includes scorable stories. What is the minimum number of scorable stories to be able to use the index has not been determined.

☐ Scoring Process

Scoring Category Criteria

Each story is scored pathogenic, benign, unscorable, or not clear. There is only one score per story.

The sequence of decisions is as follows:

(1) Does the story include an interaction between a dominant and a dependent person with potentially conflicting needs? If there is not, the story is unscorable.

(2) If it is scorable, does the dominant person take the potentially conflicting needs of the dependent person into account? If the dominant person does not, it is scored pathogenic. If the dominant person does take the potentially conflicting needs of the dependent person into account, it is scored benign.

(3) If the answer to questions (1) or (2) is not clear, defer a decision. On the first run-through, score stories that are clearly pathogenic, benign, or unscorable, and put the remainder in a group that are not clear. On the second run-through of only the not clear stories, it will usually be easier to score them. But on each run-through, score the stories as pathogenic, benign, unscorable, or not clear. Do as many run-throughs as necessary. The final set of somewhat arbitrary judgments will involve very few stories.

Read the scoring criteria before you begin scoring. It is best to score a number of stories at one time. Masked, or blind, evaluations are best and are absolutely necessary for research purposes.

If you interrupt your scoring, it is best to read the scoring criteria again before starting again. In fact, before each run-through of the not clear stories, it is usually helpful to reread the scoring criteria. The criteria include clarifications by Kevin Mitchell, Gary R. VandenBos, and Daniel Robbins.

Pathogenic Themes

(1) Murder

(2) Rape

(3) Physical assault

(4) Suicide attempt to frighten someone

(5) Going to cemetery to scare people

(6) Parents make boy study or practice when he does not want to

(7) Losing interest in playing the violin (It is assumed that card 1 reveals relations with parents even if the parent is not mentioned. The child playing the violin against his will is assumed to imply coercion.)

(8) Mother supposedly kind but does not meet expressed needs of child

(9) Mother showing particularity for one daughter or son over another

(10) Any kind of talking to as punishment

(11) Mother warning child on things that can harm him in growing up

(12) Mother telling child he has not worked up to ability

(13) Mother reading to child from Bible to teach her a lesson (This assumes no further clarification. A lesson emphasizing forgiveness might be benign; a lesson implying, as is most likely, "You are wrong, defective, should be guilty or ashamed, or will be punished" would be obviously pathogenic.)

(14) Mother feels what she has said to daughter has done little good

(15) Mother does not like something about daughter or son (e.g., looks, makeup, attitude) even though daughter or son likes it

(16) Mother checking up on son or daughter (e.g., study)

(17) Woman harming child by punishment (In general, punishment is to be scored as pathogenic, reflecting the need of the parent rather than the child, even though it is usually rationalized by the parent, and sometimes the child, as good for the child.)

(18) Husband or father jealous or forbidding

(19) Family- ruled or -dominated

(20) Husband gives wife news he is leaving town (or her)

(21) Man telling wife something to hurt her (e.g., took secretary to dinner)

(22) Husband interrupts something wife is interested in

(23) Man pulling out of an extramarital affair and woman does not want to

(24) Refusal of marriage bid; one is interested, one is not

(25) Spying on girlfriend (or being stood up)

(26) Boss driving workers hard

(27) Being fired from a job

(28) Trying to find a job and cannot (implies the hero has been turned down)

(29) Nasty remarks to a subordinate, making him or her unhappy

(30) King or leader leading a nation to ruin

(31) Destructive witch themes

(32) Happy old witch and pretty young woman

(33) Woman and evil conscience (e.g., devil behind her)

(34) Monster ready to attack child or smaller animal

(35) Accidental injuries due to human error (e.g., accidentally shooting someone, automobile accidents)

(36) Unsuccessful rescues

Unscorable Themes

(1) No interaction between two people, though somewhat conflicting needs

(2) One person enjoying himself

(3) No people or living things

(4) Two people, but no indication of interaction

(5) Conflict with person's own needs, not other people's

(6) Thinking about a mother who was kind to her—it is assumed that this indicates the existence of such a fantasy, but it is at least as likely to be defensive as it is to be reflective of reality.

(7) Wanting to join a dead person—an intrapsychic problem

(8) Nothing in the story speaks to a shared bond, conflicting needs, or interaction; nothing to indicate that the people know each other—applies to all cards, including card 1 (In card 1 we assume the presence of a parental figure.)

(9) No evidence of pathogenic or benign behavior

Benign Themes

(1) Parents force child to do something; he is unhappy; they change.

(2) Parent interrupts punishment of a child by the other parent.

(3) Stopping children from activity in which they would likely get hurt

(4) Son or daughter interested in advice from parents (or stories)

(5) Woman working hard for the benefit of her children

(6) Mother thinking about children and being happy (Of course, if what she is happy about is described and it is pathogenic, that would obviously change the scoring to pathogenic.)

(7) Mother admiring work of children or making something they like

(8) Mother enlightening child about the birds and the bees

(9) Mother caring for the child.

(10) Father and daughter consoling each other after death of mother

(11) Teacher consoling a problem child; helping a gifted child

(12) Woman trying to console a man in trouble

(13) Helping people at a disaster

(14) Guides leading animals across, for example, a difficult area

(15) Reunion of two people, both pleased

(16) Person springing a pleasant surprise on another

(17) Accepted protestations of love, or mutual love

(18) Man heeds woman's wish not to leave

(19) Any attempt to help or console with no ulterior motive

(20) Prevention of disaster (e.g., suicide, murder)

(21) On card 11, hero slaying a bad dragon (because implies successful rescue)

(22) Two people being happy together

Additional Rules for Complicated, Confusing, or Sparse Stories

General Issues

(1) Parent–child interactions take precedence over equals interacting in the same story.

(2) The emphasis is on behavior in the story, not intentions or thoughts of the characters. The pathogenic or benign interaction has to be acted on. Particularly taking the other person's needs into account (benign) has to be done actively.

(3) If a helping relationship does not help, it is scored pathogenic.

(4) It is the total package of behaviors in the story that is important, not just how it ends.

(5) A pathogenic situation followed by hope is still scored pathogenic. Just a wish or hope is not sufficient; there must be concrete evidence in the story that the possibilities are based on some reality—that they really are likely to occur.

(6) Recasting a pathogenic childhood event into positive terms in memory later in life is seen as a rationalization and is not scored benign. The pathogenic childhood event is scored pathogenic unless there is evidence in the story that the victim handles things differently (benignly) toward others as an adult or parent.

(7) Interaction need not be the central focus of the story as long as the interaction alluded to is pathogenic or benign.

(8) In complex stories where there is a story within a story, score primarily the events in the main story, and score the stories within only if the main story is unscorable or to help understand the meaning of the main story.

(9) It does not have to be clear that there is an unequal status relationship or who is the dominant person. We can assume that a friendship or peer relationship may have mutual dependency. If the story can be scored as pathogenic or benign, whichever person is dominant, it is not important to know who is dominant.

(10) Conflict of needs does not have to be evident for the story to be scored benign.

(11) Card characteristics are irrelevant; it is the story that is scored. There are two exceptions. On card 1 (the boy and the violin), as is usual with the TAT, one can assume the relationship with a parent is being described, for example, when the boy is practicing and does not want to, even if the parent is not explicitly mentioned. On card 11, describing the monster or dangerous animal is almost unavoidable as an element because of the stimulus. That is not enough to score the story as pathogenic, unless it is a small animal or a human child that is being threatened. A story about a large animal attacking a small one is assumed to represent human beings, that is, an adult attacking a child, and so would be scored pathogenic. In general, including card 11, it is the relationship between the human beings in the story that will determine the scoring, unless no relationship between people is described.

(12) It is possible to give a story on card 1 that describes an internal struggle and is thus unscorable.

Parents, Children, and Families

(13) A child trying to please parents by something he or she does not really want to do is scored pathogenic. A child not saying something out of fear of hurting parent's feelings is pathogenic—the parent is assumed to be dominant.

(14) If a parent wants a child to do or not do something, and the child does not want to, then score (a) pathogenic, usually; (b) benign, if there is a real and clear danger; or (c) even if what the parent wants is unreasonable, but the parent includes the basis of the request, the story is not scored pathogenic. It may be scored benign, depending on the whole story.

(15) A son or daughter leaving an older parent is not pathogenic. It is the role of a parent to help a son or daughter grow up and separate. If the parent does not do that, it is pathogenic. If the parent expresses concern and feelings but allows child to separate in spite of fears, it is scored benign. If the parent says, "Don't go," and tries to talk the child out of going, whether or not the child goes, it is scored pathogenic.

(16) When members of a family are silently unhappy together and do not interact to attempt to resolve it, it is scored pathogenic.

Love Triangles and Prostitution

(17) Triangle love affairs are basically pathogenic. However, the scorer can consider whether anything in the story indicates that the people are benignly handling it. Almost always the answer is no.

(18) Prostitution in itself is scored pathogenic. Of course, there may be benign stories in which a prostitute, client, or other is helped.

Suicide

(19) Suicide is usually scored pathogenic, because suicide is interpreted as an unconscious or conscious expression of anger or the wish to hurt someone else. An exception, for example, would be a story that a terminally ill man unplugged his life-support system because of the emotional and financial burdens on his family (scored benign).

Successful Effort

(20) Stories in which persons succeed, or are benign to themselves, or take care of their own needs are scored as

Benign if (a) someone was encouraging and helpful; or (b) person overcame odds and there is an indication of logical assumption of some support

Pathogenic if (a) this person is able to help himself or herself and no one else will (it is obviously pathogenic if the person is unable to help himself or herself and no one else will); or (b) no one else notices person struggling, and other people are in a position to notice; or (c) someone else could have helped and chose not to

Unscorable if it is ambiguous whether or not someone else will help, because it is not stated

Punishment, Guilt, Worry, and Pseudo-Helpful Comments

(21) Dungeon, jail, and locking people up (even criminals) is scored pathogenic. Arresting themes are usually pathogenic, but arresting is not pathogenic if the arresting person says explicitly it is so the person will not commit a crime again. Arresting someone to explicitly save another person would be scored benign.

(22) Guilt production is not benign. It may be pathogenic or unscorable. Scoring is to be inferred from the statements about guilt. Concern about someone, even if accompanied by guilt, leading to appropriate behavior, however, is not pathogenic. It may be benign or unscorable depending on the whole story.

(23) Someone worried about but not acting is not benign. It may be pathogenic.

(24) Pseudo-helpful comments meant to taunt are pathogenic.

Cruel World, Boredom, and Startle

(25) *Cruel world* is scored pathogenic if there is nothing more immediate and specific to score. The word *world* has to be used. Having a good relationship as a solution to a cruel world is scored benign.

(26) Boredom is scored as pathogenic if people are bored with something someone else is doing, and the boring one continues to do it without regard for the other's feelings. If it is a temporary situation and not an ongoing one, it is not pathogenic. The issue is whether one person takes the other person's needs into account.

(27) A startle reaction is not scored pathogenic. It is not scorable in itself and can only be scored on the basis of other content in the story.

Sparse Stories

(28) Arbitrary rules for use in sparse stories are as follows:

   (a) Sometimes consequences of the story for other people not described in the story have to be considered.

(b) Overt actions are more important than expectations. Score impact-effect, not intent-hope.

(c) Expectation based on earlier experience has greater weight than expectation based on hope.

Calculating Scores

Each story is scored as pathogenic, benign, or unscorable. The number of pathogenic stories, divided by the total number of stories scored pathogenic or scored benign, is the Pathogenesis Index—that is, the proportion of all scorable stories that are pathogenic, leaving out the unscorable stories. Expressed as a formula this is $P/(P + B)$, where P is the number of pathogenic stories and B is the number of benign stories. This corrects for story length and stories that are not possible to score. Attempts to use the number of pathogenic stories or the number of benign stories alone, rather than the ratio, have found no meaningful results in studies where the ratio differentiated the groups of subjects as predicted.

Practice Stories

These two TAT protocols may be used for practice. They were given by two graduate students in clinical psychology in their 20s. Both have their M.A. and are working on their Ph.D. Both have equivalent training in psychotherapy, both have done well academically, and both are rated highly by previous psychotherapy supervisors. Both are psychotherapists, and their case load includes schizophrenics as well as other patients. An expert scorer's scores follow, with comments about difficult issues. The stories are numbered consecutively, followed by the Murray (1943) numbers in parentheses.

Therapist A, Female

(1) Card 1: This little boy is sitting, contemplating a violin on which he has been practicing. He plays the violin very well and has been considered a child prodigy by many. He is dreaming of a career as a concert violinist and of a concerto, which he will be playing soon in a recital. Soon he will leave his daydreams and return to his practicing.

(2) Card 2: This is the picture of a young woman who is about to leave her farm home to go to school. She's thinking about the life she would have if she remained at home. As depicted in the background it would involve hard, manual labor working the land. Also she thinks that had she not chosen a career she would probably now be married and pregnant. Though she has some regrets now about the choice she has made, she will go on to school and find her career more satisfying than she expected. She will also find that the things she had left behind are possible for her to achieve in this somewhat different life.

(3) Card 3GF: This young woman has just left the room where her grandmother has died peacefully in her sleep. She is feeling very depressed and sad at the death of her grandmother and feels some regrets that she had not spent more time with her or showed more directly how much she cared for her. She will come to realize, however, that her grandmother had led a full, rich life and will feel some thanksgiving that she had died without considerable pain.

(4) Card 4: This young couple has just had an argument over some trivial matter. Though initially it seemed unimportant each has become more and more angry, and finally she said something to him which she immediately realized was unnecessarily cruel. She is now trying to make amends and apologize to him, but he is hurt and pulling away. The hurt will eventually be soothed, and with greater calmness and perspective they will come to some agreement on the matter they were discussing.

(5) Card 5: This woman has just come downstairs to the living room to find much to her surprise that her son who has been away for several years has come home for a visit. He has been out of the country working and without forewarning his parents has arrived at home. Though extremely happy she is at this moment somewhat startled to find him there. They will spend the next few days in happily recounting all that he has accomplished and remembering the happy times before he left.

(6) Card 6GF: This young couple has just spent a happy evening with friends. The husband is returning from the door where he has said goodbye to some of the guests. They have not been married long, and the couple who just left were friends of his before they were married. As he comes into the room, his wife turns to gaze at him and listen to what he is telling her. He is commenting that the couple had said they had a very nice evening and enjoyed his wife's company very much. His wife is very pleased and will tell him that she too had enjoyed the evening and hopes to see this couple again very soon.

(7) Card 7GF: This is the happy story hour before bedtime. As is usual, mother and daughter spend some time together before the girl goes to bed when they talk about the day, and mother frequently reads her a story as she is doing now. She's reading a delightful adventure story, and as she reads the girl looks dreamily off into space trying to imagine the scenes the mother is describing. The story hour is almost over, and soon the girl will go upstairs to bed.

(8) Card 8GF: This young woman has just taken a break from her daily routine to sit down and rest. She is looking dreamily off into space and thinking about her first baby due in a few months. She's wondering what kind of child it will be and is thinking how wonderful it is that this long-awaited child is now almost here. Soon she will return to the work she has been doing—preparing a nursery for the baby, a task which is more a labor of love than work.

(9) Card 9GF: These are two high school girls who have been friends for a number of years. The girl in the foreground was taking a walk toward the beach on her way home from school when she happened upon her friend and her boyfriend on the beach together. They appeared to be having an argument, though she could not hear what they were saying. She paused for a moment debating whether to go on or not. As she waits her

friend becomes more upset and runs away. She is most unhappy to see this and plans to visit her friend later in the day to see if she can help console her.

(10) Card 10: This is an elderly couple who have just received the news that their son has become quite ill and is in the hospital. The woman is very upset, as is her husband, and they are holding each other very close, comforting each other. Soon they will regain some composure and get ready to go to the hospital to see their son. His wife and children will be there too and will come home with the parents to stay until the son is better.

(11) Card 11: This is like a scene from a science fiction movie. Two anthropologists were in a remote part of the world looking for a primitive tribe whom they hoped to study in some depth. Suddenly there was an earthquake, which caused a break in the mountain wall and a prehistoric creature like a dinosaur broke loose. They are both very frightened. The younger of the two is already running away. The other man is collecting some things from their pack horses and will soon be running away too.

(12) Card 12M: This is a scene from the pioneer days. This young man, lying on a table in the crude log cabin, has just died unexpectedly. It is a relatively small community, and the family has just called in the local preacher to bless the boy and say prayers over him as he is doing now. Soon the community will gather round and hold a wake for him throughout the night. The next day he will be buried in the family cemetery near by.

(13) Card 12F: These two women live in an impoverished European country and have just come to a local welfare station to receive their weekly food rations. Though they are not related, they live near each other, and the younger woman has tried to be as helpful as possible to the older woman. She is much stronger and more healthy than the older woman who has in the past been very ill. As is her usual practice, the younger woman will be giving her part of the food ration she is going to receive.

(14) Card 13MF: The man has just returned home from a long business meeting that lasted until after midnight. He is extremely tired and is now getting ready to go to bed. He has entered the room very quietly so as not to disturb his wife who is asleep. She had planned to wait up for him but became so drowsy that she finally went to bed. Her sleep has been light, however, because her husband was not yet home. She will awaken, and they will talk for a few minutes about the events of the day.

(15) Card 14: This young man is standing in his bedroom window gazing out at the stars and full moon, which have made the night so bright. He is a student and has been studying until late at night. He is thinking now of the day ahead and takes this moment to relax before going to bed. He is dreaming too of the career he will have when he is through school and hopes he will be successful.

(16) Card 15: This rather quaint, troubled looking man, who is dressed in the frock coat of years ago, is standing in a cemetery gazing at the headstones marking his wife's grave. He frequently goes to the cemetery like this when his sleep is troubled and fitful. His family has just become aware of this and are beginning to notice how severely disturbed he is. They have been making plans for his hospitalization.

This will be discussed with him the following day; he will agree to their plans and in time will be much improved.

(17) Card 17GF: This is a scene in a small seaport town just as the sun is breaking through the storm clouds. The boats have just come in and are being unloaded after a long and arduous journey. The young woman on the bridge has been waiting there for her husband's return and is looking down toward his boat, which is just coming into the harbor. She is extremely happy to see him returning safely home and will soon run down to the docks to greet him.

(18) Card 18GF: This is a very tragic scene. The woman in the background has just rushed to the foot of the stairs to find that her daughter who has been very ill has fallen down the stairs. She's holding the limp body in her arms grasping her tightly and praying that she is not dead. Her husband who has heard the noise too is on the telephone calling an ambulance. They will rush her to the hospital and find that fortunately her injuries were not serious—that she will be all right.

(19) Card 19: This is a cabin in the far north country. A storm raging outside, but in the cabin there is a roaring fire and the family is warm and cozy sitting there making popcorn and talking gaily. They have lived here for some time and are not at all troubled by the blustery storms so typical of the winters here. Spring is not far off, and the beauty of that time of year makes the winter even more tolerable.

(20) Card 20: This man is standing under a lamppost in a very deserted part of the city waiting for a bus to come along. He is an older man who retired some years ago but found that he really preferred to be working. He's taken a job as a night watchman in a small factory and, now that his work is finished, is waiting to go home. Off in the distance, the lights are beginning to come on in the various city apartments. It is almost dawn, and as his day is ending, the rest of the city is just coming awake. He's thinking as he waits that he will ask for a day-time job so that he can spend more time in the evenings with his family and friends.

Therapist B, Male

(21) Card 1: That's a boy looking at a violin; he's supposed to practice, but he doesn't want to so he's just staring at it. I guess he's mad at it or mad at his mother for making him practice. He doesn't want to practice. After a while he starts practicing again and his mother comes in and tells him to practice.

(22) Card 2: Oh, that's a farm. The girl in the front looks sort of mad because she's going off to school. That must be her father at the horse and her mother—her mother looks pregnant. Maybe the girl has to do a lot of work around the house and the mother just seems to be standing there and she's probably mad at the mother for making her do more.

(23) Card 3BM: This boy is crying ... sobbing. He doesn't look very happy. I guess somebody got mad at him. Looks like a toy gun or something down on the floor. Maybe

he pretended to shoot his mother or scare her or he got mad and now he feels guilty and is crying.

(24) Card 4: Looks like the man wants to get away. His wife or somebody is trying to talk him into staying. Maybe they had a fight. He looks like he wants to get out of there. I don't really know what they fought over. Maybe she was nagging. She looks like the type that sort of nags and then wants to make up and be sweet again, and he doesn't want to have anything to do with it.

(25) Card 5: Looks like a nosy woman, looking in the room. Maybe she heard some noise or something—looking to see what's there. Probably nothing there, but she was pretty curious to see what's going on. She doesn't look very happy.

(26) Card 6BM: That's a man and his mother ... or somebody. Looks like he's trying to get something from her—apologize to her—and she's thinking about what he said and he's hoping that she'll agree with him and forgive him. I don't know what they were talking about. But it looks like he's trying to get her approval. He isn't sure whether he's going to get it.

(27) Card 7BM: That's a father and uncle and a young man. The young man looks sort of mad, where the older man looks much friendlier. I don't know, maybe the young man's mad at him; I don't know why, or maybe the older man is trying to stop him from doing something, but the younger man doesn't want to be under his control but yet feels the older man is sort of nice and doesn't know how to go about getting out from under his control.

(28) Card 8BM: Oh, there ... looks like two doctors are operating on a guy or going to operate on him, and the younger fellow over there looks sort of phony—looks like he just got out of church or something. A—a gun over there ... maybe he shot him—don't look like the type that shoot him but you never know and the guy who's being operated on, looks like he isn't looking forward to them cutting into him. The other guy looks pretty self-righteous. I don't know—I don't like the other guy.

(29) Card 9BM: This looks like some—oh some men are working on a road and are taking time off for lunch and just sort of laying down resting, getting in some of the sun (asleep). Maybe their boss is going to come back and get mad at them for it—laying around instead of working. They sort of look like they're out of it.

(30) Card 10: This is a man trying to comfort a woman—could be his wife. She may have been upset about something. He's trying to make it easier on her. Looks like he's trying to be good to her.

(31) Card 11: This is a weird one. Looks like some serpent is coming down and—the road with rocks on the side and looks like man or another man trying to push something off on the cliff. Looks like the serpent is going to push them off. Don't know really but looks like they're going to get it. No, I guess they're not going off the cliff. It's sort of confusing. Looks like there's a bridge there and maybe trying to get across the bridge. I don't know where they're going, but the serpent over there looks like he's going after them.

(32) Card 12M: This guy is sleeping on the bed. Another guy looks like he's trying to wake him up or hypnotize him or something. I don't know why he would want to do that. Looks like the guy in bed is sleeping pretty well and seems pretty comfortable. I guess he's going to wake up the fellow on the bed.

(33) Card 13MF: I was going to say at first it looks like the guy—they were fucking or something, and he got up and the light was too bright for him—it's pretty hard to fuck with your pants on. A—it must be something else. It looks like something's bothering the fellow. The woman looks like she's sleeping and seems to be pretty happy. Looks like he's upset about something. It bothered him that they were fucking and he got his pants on—I don't know. Maybe he's got to go to work.

(34) Card 14: It's a guy looking out the window from a dark room. He sort of likes the sun out there. He'd like to go out and sleep in the sun. I'm surprised he hasn't turned on the light in the room. He'll probably go outside and see what it's like.

(35) Card 15: This is a weird one—something that should go along with an Edgar Allen Poe story. Looks like some sort of nut is there in the cemetery trying to talk to the graves, maybe trying to get the spirits to come back and help him. He looks sort of upset. I don't know, maybe he's just praying there, but something seems to bother him and he's trying to ask for it—supernatural or unhuman help to help him solve his own problems.

(36) Card 16: This is the blank card. What do I see here. Oh, you know the other night I listened to that song, "The Leaves Are Turning Gray in California Ballad." The other card? There is a guy looking out the window in the sun and there isn't any sun now. I guess I was thinking to myself lying on the beach in Santa Monica or someplace and just sort of reading and watching the waves and not having to worry about school and classes and stuff, and I sort of had a fantasy that life would be beachcombing for a while. You might get bored at it, but it would be a fun thing to get bored at.

(37) Card 17BM: Man either going up or down a rope. Seems like he sees something over on the side there. Maybe a girl caught his eye or something and he's pretty interested in her and they go down and try to see her and introduce themselves. I don't know—it looks like he's looking at something else other than climbing the rope.

(38) Card 18BM: Looks like a man fainted from drinking too much, and another guy is trying to hold him up. Guy's pretty fat. Must have been drinking a lot of beer or something. Guess he's pretty unhappy and tries to drown out his problems in booze, but he'll be pretty unhappy when he wakes up in the morning. Don't know who the other guy is, looks sort of funny—looks like another hand there on the side—two hands in back and his arms. Maybe they were throwing him in the back of another guy, I don't know. Sort of funny card. Looks like he's got dandruff, too. He sort of looks out of it.

(39) Card 19: Oh, this is sort of pretty like something you see in a child's book. Looks like there's some type of ocean scene with some people living in a little house or at the bottom of the sea with a smokestack. Some little fish up above looking around and

thinking that maybe they'll let them in and give them something to eat and they'll go around front and see if they'll take care of them.

(40) Card 20: A guy standing under a lamp. It's probably cold out, and he's waiting for his wife or somebody to come pick him up, and can't see his face, but maybe he's sort of mad that he has to wait out there and they haven't come sooner, but he doesn't have much choice in the matter. Or he may be starting to walk back and maybe he'll see her along the way. Looks like a lot of fog.

□ Expert (B. Karon) Scoring

Therapist A, Female

(1) Card 1: *B*. This is a difficult story to score. Most of the story is intrapsychic, concerned with the boy's thoughts without any mention of an interaction, and would be scored *U*. However, the casual mention of *He has been considered a child prodigy by many* is sufficient under principle 20a for difficult to score stories for the story to be scored *B*.

(2) Card 2: *U*. The story concerns the young woman's thoughts, with no explicit mention of interaction.

(3) Card 3GF: *U*. This again is a difficult story to score. One could argue that her regrets over not having spent more time or showing her grandmother more directly how much she cared indicates a *P* relationship, but it does not have that flavor. The story seems more like feelings and thoughts intrapsychically that do not necessarily reflect a bad relationship—if anything they suggest a good relationship.

(4) Card 4: *B*. At last an easy story to score. One person hurts another, changes, and there is a good outcome.

(5) Card 5: *B*. Either the mother or the son could have acted in a way that would make the other unhappy, but neither did.

(6) Card 6GF: *B*. This is a situation that has many possibilities of bad outcomes, none of which occur. The husband, the wife, and even the guests all have their needs met by other people.

(7) Card 7GF: *B*.

(8) Card 8GF: *B*. Most of the story is about thoughts and would be *U*. But at the end of the story she takes action for the benefit of the prospective baby.

(9) Card 9GF: *B*. The boyfriend seems to be treating the girlfriend in a hurtful way; that might be scored *P*. But the main story seems to be about the heroine, who clearly is going to act to be helpful.

(10) Card 10: *B*. Both are trying to help each other and their son's family.

(11) Card 11: *P.* The younger man is saving himself without regard for the older man.

(12) Card 12M: *U.* It is not clear that there are potentially conflicting needs in the story. One could argue that the preacher and the community holding the wake are meeting the family's needs (which might be scored *B*), or, as seems more likely, that they all are simply doing what they always do when someone dies (which is scored *U*).

(13) Card 12F: *B.* An easy story to score.

(14) Card 13MF: *B.* He tries not to wake her up. When she wakes, they talk, meeting both their needs.

(15) Card 14: *U.* This seems just thoughts without an interaction.

(16) Card 15: *B.* Though some of us may have qualms that psychiatric hospitalizations by family are not always helpful, in the context of this story it is clear that it is helpful.

(17) Card 17GF: *B.* It is not clear whether the husband or the wife is the dominant one, but in any case, within the story each is meeting the other's need.

(18) Card 18GF: *B.* Here someone helps, and it does help.

(19) Card 19: *B.* The family members are meeting each other's needs. Although there is no mention of conflicting needs, we know such potential exists in any family.

(20) Card 20: *B.* A difficult story to score, that arguably only concerns the man's thoughts (i.e., scored *U*). The benign elements are that he has taken a part-time job when he wanted it (implying someone hiring him when he wanted it, but that probably would not be enough for scoring if it were the only benign element) and that he will try to change to a day-time job to spend more time with family and friends, suggesting that he is meeting their needs as well as his own. The probable implication is that a part-time job met his needs to be back at work, but not the needs of those who would like to spend time with him. Obviously, if being with them in itself met his needs, he would have stayed retired.

If your scoring agreed with this, there would be 15 benign stories, 4 unscorable stories, and only 1 pathogenic story. The subject's Pathogenesis Index would be 1/(1+15) or 1/16 or .06. Even if your scoring only approximated this, you would still conclude that the subject was likely to be a very helpful therapist.

Therapist B, Male

(21) Card 1: *P.* This is easy to score. Since one can usually infer the nature of the relation with the parent from this card (Karon, 1981), it would be enough to be able to score if the subject had simply said the boy had to practice and did not want to. But the subject goes on and makes it clear that it is the mother making him practice against his will.

(22) Card 2: *P.* Again, easy to score—the girl is mad because the mother is making her do more (work).

(23) Card 3BM: *P.* He is unhappy because *Somebody got mad at him.* "Maybe he ... scare her" also suggests a pathogenic relationship.

(24) Card 4: *P.* It is not clear which of the couple is the dominant person, but neither of them is meeting the needs of the other. Whether the man or the woman is the dominant person, it would still be a pathogenic relationship.

(25) Card 5: *U.* There is no relationship with another person described.

(26) Card 6BM: *P.* This is a questionable scoring. It sounds like the mother is the dominant person. Although she does not give him what he wants (forgiveness and maybe something else), she also does not refuse it. However, the story ends with the son still left hanging in uncertainty. Since that is the story, it ends with him uncomfortable and her still in charge, justifying a score of *P.* A different, less probable, reading of the story is that he is trying to manipulate her to get something from her, in which case he is the dominant person, but the relationship would still be *P.*

(27) Card 7BM: *P.* The younger man is under control, does not like it, and does not know how to not be under control. The statement that the older man looks nice does not change the scoring. There is nothing in the story that indicates that the older man's advice would save the younger man from real danger.

(28) Card 8BM: *P.* The shooter is described as unlikable, a phony, self-righteous, and the victim is not looking forward to them cutting on him.

(29) Card 9GF: *P.* The boss getting mad at them is enough to score the story.

(30) Card 10: *B.* At last a story where the dominant person—the husband—is meeting the other person's needs.

(31) Card 11: *U.* The evil monster is an almost unavoidable part of the stimulus card, so calling it a monster or dangerous animal is not enough to score the story. If it were threatening a small animal (so that the animals are really people) or a child or children, the story would be scored *P.* If the people either helped each other or hurt each other, the story would be scored on that basis. In this story there is no indication of the people helping or hurting each other.

(32) Card 12M: *P.* The sleeper wants to sleep, but the other man wakes him: *I don't know why.*

(33) Card 13MF: *P.* This is very difficult story to score. It is not clear, but the man is unhappy. *The light is too bright for him* suggests—but not clearly—that someone else is responsible for it being too bright. The woman is happy. *It bothers him that they were fucking and he got his pants on* implies either that he had sex with his pants on against

his wishes or that he has had to get up. *Maybe he's got to go to work* suggests someone else is making him go to work and he does not want to.

(34) Card 14: *U.* This is a description of thoughts and feelings without mentioning a relationship.

(35) Card 15: *P.* A difficult story to score. The phrase *Edgar Allen Poe story* suggests something *P* may be going on. The fact that he is asking *for supernatural or unhuman help to solve his own problems* suggests that human help is not available to him.

(36) Card 16: *U.* Again, this is a description of thoughts and feelings without mentioning a relationship.

(37) Card 17BM: *U.* There is just not enough detail about the relationship with the girl to make any judgment about it.

(38) Card 18BM: *B.* Although it is not clear, sounds more like the other men are trying to help the drunk man.

(39) Card 19: *U.* There is just no clear indication of whether the people in the house do or do not meet the wishes of the little fish.

(40) Card 20: *P.* The man is mad because he has been kept waiting.

If your scoring agreed with this, there would be 12 pathogenic stories, 6 unscorable stories, and only 2 benign stories. The subject's Pathogenesis Index would be 12/(12+2) or 12/14 or .86. Even if your scoring only approximated this, you would still conclude that the subject was not likely to be a very helpful therapist.

These predictions that therapist A with a Pathogenesis Index of .06 should be a very helpful therapist and that therapist B with a Pathogenesis Index of .86 is not likely to be a helpful therapist were borne out by the actual measured progress on a variety of symptoms of the patients they treated.

It was puzzling that therapist B, whose Pathogenesis Index was high and whose patients did not seem to do very well, should have been evaluated as very competent by previous psychotherapy supervisors. However, another graduate student later mentioned—after both students were no longer working in the same setting—having been surprised when therapist B had said to him, "Why do you tell the truth in supervision? You know what he wants to hear. Why don't you just tell him that?" Of course, glossing over difficulties in treatment to make a good impression on a supervisor was in itself pathogenic, since it made it impossible to learn from the supervisor how to cope with these difficulties and to help the patient.

☐ References

Karon, B. P. (1981). The Thematic Apperception Test. In A. I. Rabin (Ed.), *Assessment with projective techniques* (pp. 85–120). New York: Springer.

Karon, B. P. (2003). The tragedy of schizophrenia without psychotherapy. *The Journal of the American Academy of Psychoanalysis and Dynamic Psychiatry, 31*, 89–115.

Karon, B. P., & VandenBos, G. R. (1981). *Psychotherapy of schizophrenia: The treatment of choice.* New York: Aronson.

Meyer, R. G., & Karon, B. P. (1967). The schizophrenogenic mother concept and the TAT. *Psychiatry, 30,* 173–179.

Mitchell, K. M. (1965). An elaboration of a study of the schizophrenogenic mother concept by means of the Thematic Apperception Test. Unpublished doctoral dissertation, Michigan State University.

Murray, H. A. (1943). *Thematic Apperception Test manual.* Cambridge: Harvard University.

Read, J., & Ross, C. A. (2003). Psychological trauma and psychosis: Another reason why people diagnosed schizophrenic must be offered psychological therapies. *Journal of the American Academy of Psychoanalysis and Dynamic Psychiatry, 31,* 247–268.

Symonds, P. M. (1949). *Adolescent fantasy.* New York: Columbia University.

Tomkins, S. S. (1947). *The Thematic Apperception Test.* New York: Grune & Stratton.

20

CHAPTER

TAT Oral Dependency Scale

Steven K. Huprich

Abstract

This chapter describes the development of the Thematic Apperception Test of Oral Dependency (TOD) as created by Masling, Rabie, and Blondheim (1967). Research on the development of the TOD is discussed, as is the history of assessing dependency with the TAT with other scoring systems. To evaluate further the validity and utility of the TOD, some methodological revisions were made to Masling et al.'s original study, and a group of 82 undergraduate students were evaluated with the newly revised TOD. Although the TOD has promise for further utility, substantial research is needed with the instrument to demonstrate its reliability and validity, as well as refining the method by which it is administered and scored. Six major areas of research are suggested to assist in this endeavor.

Description of System

Conceptual Framework

The assessment of oral dependency has its origins in psychoanalytic theory. Here, it is believed that overgratification or excessive frustration in this earliest stage of psychosexual development leads to the development of high levels of dependency on others for nurturance, guidance, and support. Likewise, it is believed that certain behaviors will develop in adulthood that are related to activities of the mouth, such as smoking or excessive eating. To assess oral dependency, both a Rorschach and Thematic Apperceptive Test (TAT)-based measure have been created: the Rorschach Oral Dependency Scale (ROD) and the TOD (Masling, Rabie, & Blondheim, 1967).

Since its development, the ROD has been used extensively. Results of many past studies have been consistent with what was theoretically predicted. For example, Shilkret and Masling (1981) found that ROD scores predict help-seeking behavior of participants in a research project. High ROD scores also are positively and significantly correlated with the Interpersonal Dependency Inventory (IDI) (Hirschfeld, Klerman, Gough, Barrett, Korchin, & Chodoff, 1977), cooperation and compliance with authority figures (Bornstein & Masling, 1985; Masling, O'Neill, & Jayne, 1981), self-reported levels of insecure attachment (Duberstein & Talbot, 1993), eating disorders (Bornstein & Greenberg, 1991) and behavioral difficulties in terminating inpatient psychiatric treatment (Greenberg & Bornstein, 1989). Summarizing 28 years of research with the ROD, Bornstein (1996) concluded that the ROD has construct validity and is a good measure of overt dependent behavior.

History of Oral Dependency Assessment with the TAT

Although the ROD has been well researched and validated as a measure of oral dependency, substantially less research has assessed oral dependency with the TAT. Along with the Rorschach, Masling et al. (1967) assessed oral dependency with the TAT by quantifying oral dependent content from psychological testing material. What follows is a brief description of their study and how oral dependency was assessed.

Masling et al. (1967) obtained a sample of 18 obese and 20 control participants outpatients at a local hospital in Jerusalem. They hypothesized that obese subjects would have higher levels of oral-dependent content on projective test data than controls, given that obese individuals had historically been characterized as dependent (Bruch, 1961, Schopbach & Matthews, 1945), immature (Bruch, 1961; Shovron & Richardson, 1949), passive (Nicholson, 1946; Schopbach & Matthews, 1945), and helpless (Bruch, 1961, 1964). To assess oral dependency, participants were given the Rorschach and the TAT.

Masling et al. (1967) found that the obese participants gave a significantly greater number of oral-dependent responses than controls ($X^2 = 6.08$, $p = .02$). On inspecting the types of themes provided by both groups, a pronounced difference was observed in passive-dependent themes, good luck and optimism themes, and themes emphasizing helplessness, loneliness, and depression. The Pearson correlation between individuals' number of ROD responses and TAT oral-dependent themes was .58 ($p < .01$). Masling et al. concluded that oral dependency can be assessed on both TAT and Rorschach data and that, as expected, obese individuals provided significantly more oral-dependent content than controls. However, this study was limited by several factors. First, this study was conducted in Jerusalem, thereby limiting the generalizability of the findings. Masling et al. noted that the "Jewish family (is) said to be traditionally matriarchal" (p. 238), which may inadvertently reinforce dependency. Second, some of the participants may have been exposed to extreme food deprivation either in concentration camps during World War II or during the 1948 War of Independence, which could have impacted their oral dependency score. Third, this study was conducted with a relatively small sample, selected from one outpatient treatment program, which further limited the generalizability of the results. Fourth, the sample was predominantly female (16/18 controls and 18/20 obese participants). Accordingly, it is questionable as to the extent to which these results are generalizable to any other population except Jewish females. Fifth, participants' body mass index (BMI) was not computed, which may serve as a better indicator of obesity severity.

Other Measures of Dependency on the TAT

Several other studies have been conducted in which dependency has been assessed with the TAT. However, there have been numerous methods of scoring dependency. Most of these studies have led to published findings. The results of these studies will be summarized.

Two studies have used the TAT dependency scoring system provided by Kagan and Mussen (1956). They proposed a scoring system based on two of Murray's (1943) scoring system of psychological needs: succourance (*D*) and nurturance (*d*). In the former, stories are scored positively if a story depicts an individual as either seeking help from another person in solving a problem or feeling disturbed over the loss of a source of love and support. In the latter, stories also are scored positively if a story depicts an individual being given some help or a gift that was not requested. In a study of 27 male undergraduates, Kagan and Mussen used cards 1, 3BM, 6BM, 7BM, 12M, 13B, 14, and 18BM to assess dependency themes. Participants wrote stories to the aforementioned cards and then underwent an Asch-like conformity activity. Two raters independently scored the stories for both themes. Agreement for *D* themes was 93%, and agreement for *d* themes was 95%. Kagan and Mussen found that individuals high in *D* themes had higher rates of yielding on the conformity activity than did those low in *D*. They concluded that succourance needs, as assessed on the TAT, were positively associated with conformity to group opinion.

Weiss and Emmerich (1962) conducted the identical experimental procedure with ulcer, psychosomatic, and nonulcer, nonpsychosomatic medical patients. They predicted that ulcer patients would have higher levels of dependency, as it was believed that their chronically frustrated dependency needs would be converted to gastric stimulation and ulceration. Weiss and Emmerich found that succourance themes were significantly greater in ulcer and psychosomatic patients than in medical patients but that the ulcer and psychosomatic groups did not differ significantly. Furthermore, they found that ulcer patients yielded in the conformity task more often than the psychosomatic and medical patients and concluded that, although dependency themes are common in ulcer and psychosomatic patients, they are only expressed in ulcer patients.

Melnick (1968) created a scoring system for several of Murray's (1943) needs, including dependency, in an unpublished master's thesis. In his system, scales were created for nurturance, dependence, and dependence frustration. These scales were scored along with a Pathogenic Index (PI) scale, which reflected either an inability of characters to empathize with others or a character's lack of trust in the environment. Using this scale, Melnick and Hurley (1969) compared characteristics of physically abusive mothers to a control group of mothers. Women in the study were given two measures of personality traits: (1) the Manifest Rejection Scale (Hurley, 1965), which measures overt punitive behavior of parents toward children; and (2) the TAT. Melnick and Hurley found that abusive and control mothers did not differ on dependency needs but that abusive mothers had significantly higher levels of dependence frustration than control mothers. They also found that the PI scale was negatively correlated with nurturance needs ($r = -.62$) and with the Manifest Rejection Scale ($r = -.40$). Melnick and Hurley concluded that abusive mothers had greater frustration of their dependency needs and speculated that, because these needs are not met, abusive mothers may not be able to form a healthy attachment to their children, thereby limiting their ability to regulate their own aggressive impulses. Although the findings are interesting, Melnick and Hurley did not report which TAT cards were used, nor did they report interrater reliability statistics.

In a study of dependency in male fraternity members, Fitzgerald (1958) obtained 80 participants' peer ratings of dependency, interview data for each participant, and TAT responses on cards 3BM, 4, 6BM, 7BM, 8BM, 10, 12M, 13MF, 15, 17BM, 18BM, and 20. Fitzgerald created scoring manuals to code the TAT and interview for dependent behavior—dependency needs and freedom of movement for dependency satisfaction—based, in part, on Murray's (1943) descriptions of such needs. Having been trained for more than 30 hours in coding, raters obtained interrater reliability correlations between .45 and .75. Fitzgerald found that TAT ratings did not correlate with peer ratings or interview ratings of dependency. To assess the magnitude of an individual's conflict over dependency, Fitzgerald subtracted the number of dependency needs' ratings from the number of freedom of movement needs ratings. He found a high degree of correspondence between dependency needs and the magnitude of the dependency conflict. Fitzgerald concluded that TAT ratings are not related to interview or peer ratings of dependency but that TAT dependency ratings are associated with the importance of dependency conflict.

Stewart (1982, 1992) developed a TAT scoring system that provides a rating for an individual's life stance, which is an individual's level of receptivity to environmental stimuli that falls into one of four stances: receptive, autonomous, assertive, and integrated. These stances reflect Sigmund Freud's oral, anal, phallic, and genital stages of psychosexual development and also parallel Erik Erikson's four earliest stages of psychosocial development. Thus, the earliest stance is reflective of a psychological orientation in which individuals are preoccupied with dependency or receptivity to environmental stimulation. Stewart (1982) proposed that when individuals encounters a life change, such as a move, they will revert to an earlier life stance as an adaptation to the change but later will return to their characteristic stance.

Ratings on each of these stances are made by an independent rater (i.e., the stance is present or absent) across four dimensions on each TAT card—attitude toward authority, relations with others, feelings, and orientation to action—thus providing 16 different ratings. Although there are alternative ways of tabulating these ratings, Stewart and colleagues used the modal life stance score across the TAT stories as an individual's score. In five cross-sectional studies of children and adults undergoing a life change, Stewart, Sokol, Healy, Chester, and Weinstock-Savoy (1982) rated life stances. They found a linear increase in modal mean scores (1.50, 2.73, and 3.65) for children transitioning from kindergarten, first grade, and second grade, respectively. They also found that, when assessed in the fall semester, freshmen had significantly lower modal scores than sophomores (2.30 vs. 2.80). Interestingly, recently married women had a lower mean modal score than engaged women (2.20 vs. 3.23), and new mothers had significantly lower mean modal scores than expectant mothers (2.05 vs. 2.75). Stewart et al. concluded that, across all ages, individuals earlier in the change process are more likely to be concerned with issues of dependency than those who are later in the change process.

In a longitudinal study, Stewart, Sokol, Healy, and Chester (1986) found that individuals' life stance increased over time after initially completing an event requiring adaptation. Life stance mean modal scores significantly increased over the course of 1 or 2 years for children beginning middle school, adolescents transitioning from junior high to high school, males transitioning into college, and young adults beginning marriage. Scores at time 1 ranged between 1.95 and 2.59, and scores at time 2 ranged between 2.35 and 3.15. In sum, these results suggest that, when undergoing a significant life change, individuals tend to move toward an earlier life stance, in which themes of dependency and passivity increase.

Some studies have evaluated dependency on the TAT in a dichotomous or categorical format with a measure that appears to have been created and used only for that study. Ehrenreich (1990a, 1990b) asked raters to evaluate the relationship of the characters in a given TAT story for cards 1, 2, 3BM, 12M, and 13MF as falling into one of four categories: dependent, interdependent, autonomous, or noninteractive. In one study, individuals in a working-class socioeconomic group had more dependency ratings than those in a middle-class socioeconomic group. Interrater reliability was reported to be in the .80s (Ehrenreich, 1990a). In another study, TAT dependency ratings were not correlated with the IDI total score or any of its related scales (Hirschfeld et al., 1977). Unfortunately, no interrater reliability statistics are reported, nor is there any reference to a scoring manual.

Huang (1998) evaluated the object relations of adult women who reported an incestuous relationship with their father during childhood. Raters evaluated five dimensions of object relations on TAT cards 1, 2, 3BM, 5, 13MF, and 18MF, which consisted of yes–no questions about the nature of the dimension of interest. One of the object relations dimensions was described as dependency and need fulfillment. Raters were asked to answer yes or no to each of the following questions after reading all of an individuals' TAT stories:

- Are parental figures described as ineffective, unreliable, unprotective, and unavailable?
- Do characters feel helpless and unable to influence others and situations?
- Are characters having to care for others?
- Do characters seem dependent, needy, and childlike?
- Are there parental substitutes in the stories?

Huang found that women reporting an incestuous relationship with their father had significantly higher levels of dependency and need fulfillment (i.e., lower quality of object relations) than did a group of women not reporting a paternal incestuous relationship.

Three studies that used measures of TAT dependency have provided some interesting findings about trait-like dependency and dependent behavior. To assess dependency, Zuckerman and Grosz (1958) rated participants' stories with Murray's (1943) scoring system. They found an association between suggestibility and dependency. Specifically, they found that student nurses who scored high on the Sway test (Furneaux, 1946)—thus being classified as highly suggestible—had significantly higher scores on succourance ratings on the TAT than low suggestible participants.

Heilbrun (1977) evaluated the relationship between defensive style (i.e., repression, projection) and dependency in a sample of 34 undergraduate students. He hypothesized that those who use projection would have higher levels of dependency than those who use repression. To assess projection, Heilbrun measured the frequency with which individuals denied negative information about themselves and attributed it to someone else during an experimental task. To assess repression, he measured the amount of information forgotten during the task. And to assess dependency, he selected cards 6BM, 8BM, and 8GF, because they were believed to elicit themes that included dependency. A score of +2 represented strong dependency needs, and a score of –2 represented strong independence needs. Individuals were classified as projectors, nonprojectors, repressors, and nonrepressors. He found that dependency was positively correlated with projective defenses ($r = .65$) and with nonrepression ($r = .59$). Dependency ratings were made by graduate students, who had perfect agreement on 55% of the ratings and differed by a score of 1 on 31% of the ratings.

In one of few studies with children, Stamler and Palmer (1971) evaluated the relationship between dependency and repetitive visits to the school nurse. To assess dependency, all 20 TAT cards were selected, and children were given four choices of descriptions that best characterized the picture. All stories included one that involved dependency themes. For example, the dependent description for card 1 was, "He doesn't know how to play the violin. He is waiting for his first lesson." To assess the reliability and validity of the dependency descriptions, three licensed psychologists read each description and decided which one had the dependent theme for each story. Stamler and Palmer reported that the psychologists had complete agreement on the dependent statement for each card. Stories were then read to the children, who subsequently selected the most descriptive statement. After their parents gave consent, 34 children participated. Of the participants, 17 boys were classified as repeaters if they had four or more visits to the nurse, whereas 17 girls were classified as repeaters if they had three or more visits. Stamler and Palmer found that the mean number of dependency descriptions selected for the repeaters was 5.11, which was significantly higher than the mean of 3.88 for nonrepeaters. They also found that repeater girls had significantly higher scores than repeater boys. This gender difference was not observed in the nonrepeaters.

In summary, it appears that there are multiple systems by which interpersonal dependency has been assessed. Many of these systems are appealing, given their ecological validity (e.g., changes in dependency when facing a new life situation, gastric stimulation being associated with frustrated oral dependency needs, visits to a school nurse associated with higher levels of dependency). Such systems are promising, as implicit measures of dependency and their association with real-world behaviors provide impressive support for the utility and incremental validity of implicit measures (Bornstein, 1998, 1999). Despite such promising findings, many of these systems have received very little empirical attention. Furthermore, information about scoring each system is scant, as is documentation of reliability data. For implicit assessment tools such as these to be better understood by scientists, additional research is needed to extend the psychometric properties and advantages of such measures.

Given that the ROD scale has had such high promise, it appears that Masling et al.'s (1967) TAT measure of oral dependency is worth further investigation for several reasons. First, given that the content of the TOD is similar to its Rorschach sibling, there is reason to believe that a TAT-based measure developed in the same way would share similar psychometric properties. Second, Masling et al. found that measures of oral-dependent themes were correlated positively with ROD scores ($r = .58$), thus providing preliminary support for the validity of a TAT-based measure of oral dependency. Accordingly, it is possible that this relationship may be found in larger, more representative samples. Third, mastery of TAT administration is substantially easier than the Rorschach, thus providing an advantage to weary users of the Rorschach to detect oral dependency without compromising the implicit nature of the assessment technique (McClelland, Koestner, & Weinberger, 1989). Finally, Masling et al. codified oral-dependent themes, thereby laying a template by which to evaluate other kinds of material (e.g., interview data, early memories).

TABLE 20.1 TAT Oral Dependence Themes with Examples

	Oral Dependence
TAT Theme	**Example**
(1) Passive Dependence	(Card 13 B) "This little boy is waiting for his mother to come pick him up from school."
(2) Asking for or Receiving Help	(Card 7BM) "The younger man wants to get advice about moving to a new job."
(3) Presence of Parental Figures or Nurturers	(Card 7GF) "This mother is reading a story to her daughter."
(4) Food Sources	(Card 9BM) "These men are thinking about going to Charley's for a drink after a long day of work."
(5) Food Providers or Food Objects	(Card 2) "Here's a farmer who is planting his corn crop on a hot day."
(6) Belief in Luck or Magic	(Card 12M) "This man went to a spiritual healer who is praying over him now."
(7) Optimistic Story Endings	(Card 13MF) "This man's wife just died. He's very sad, but somehow, he knows that he'll find another woman to love and that he'll be happy again."
(8) Helplessness, Loneliness, or Depression	(Card 1) "Johnny has been looking at his violin for an hour. He cannot figure out how to play it and is sad because he thinks he will never learn how."
(9) Mouth Behavior	(Card 7BM) "Uncle Joe is telling his nephew about the good old days."

Scoring Categories

The original TOD scoring system reported by Masling et al. (1967) is as follows. Participants are asked to write stories to TAT cards 2, 7GF, 13B, and 18GF. The stories are then scored for oral-dependent content, which consists of the following: passive dependency, asking for help or receiving help, the presence of parental figures or nurturers, food sources, food organs, food providers or food objects, belief in good luck, magic, or optimistic story endings, helplessness, loneliness, or depression, and mouth behavior. A list of these items with examples is provided in Table 20.1.

□ Research Evidence

Validity

It appears that only one other study has assessed dependency on the TAT with the criteria described by Masling et al. (1967). Ballner (1975) assessed anxiety and dependency within samples of heroin addicts, alcoholics, and matched controls. Based on past theory, he predicted that heroin addicts and alcoholics would have higher levels of dependency than controls and that, when stressed, heroin addicts and alcoholics would have higher levels of anxiety and dependency than the controls. Participants were African American patients admitted to a local hospital for treatment of their heroin addiction or alcoholism. Controls were selected from hospital and federal government employees. Participants were assessed for anxiety and dependency on the Holtzman Inkblot Test and TAT, using systems devised by Elizur (1949) and Masling et al. (1967), respectively. To assess dependency, Ballner also employed a modification suggested by Holt (1970). In this modification, each dependent response was scored for degree of dependency on a scale of 1 to 2, with 2 representing extreme levels of dependency.

Ballner (1975) administered cards 1, 3BM, 4, 6BM, 6GF, 11, 13B, 14, 15, and 17GF to participants to assess anxiety and dependency before an experimentally manipulated stress task (a modified Stroop activity), which was believed to evoke anxiety and dependency feelings. After this task, participants were assessed with cards 3GF, 5, 8BM, 9GF, 10, 12M, 13MF, 18BM, 18GF, and 20. He found that heroin addicts were significantly more anxious and dependent than alcoholics and controls. Interestingly, anxiety and dependency did not increase after the stress manipulation.

More recently, I conducted a pilot study on the assessment of oral dependency with Masling et al.'s (1967) TAT Oral Dependency Scale. At a private, southern university, 82 undergraduates were administered the TAT, the ROD, and IDI. Students completed all measures in a standardized small group format. The ROD was administered first, using the standardized administration procedure described by Bornstein (1996). After that, students were presented with TAT cards 1, 2, 3BM, 7GF, 12M, 13B, 13MF, and 18GF one at a time. They were given the following instructions: "Please write a story in which you describe what is currently happening in this picture. Make sure you describe what led up to this picture, what is going on in the picture, and what the outcome will be. Also describe what the characters are thinking and feeling." Following that, participants completed the IDI and then were measured for height and weight by a research assistant so that BMI could be computed. TOD scores were computed and compared with ROD scores and the IDI.

In their original study, Masling et al. (1967) hypothesized that TOD scores would be higher in obese patients compared with nonobese patients. Their results supported their hypotheses. In the current study, however, BMI was calculated, as it provided a more quantifiable method by which to assess the oral dependency and obesity relationship. Further, the sample size of this study was expanded beyond past studies and included an even representation of males and females.

The final sample consisted of 41 males and 41 females, and the overwhelming majority was Caucasian and unmarried. Their mean age was 20.18 (SD = 1.72) years. Their mean height was 67.85 (SD = 3.62) inches, and the mean weight was 168.56 (SD = 41.96) pounds, which yielded a mean BMI of 2.48 (SD = .58) pounds per inch.

The mean ROD score was .08 (.07), which is comparable to other studies (Bornstein, 1995). Mean IDI scores were as follows: Total IDI = 44.78 (15.24); IDI Emotional Reliance on Others = 42.43 (8.65); IDI Assertion of Autonomy = 28.54 (6.35); and IDI-Lack of Confidence = 30.25 (6.25). Mean scores for the total of each TOD content area, total TOD score for each TAT card, and total TOD are presented in Table 20.2.

In general, each card averaged one TOD response, although cards 2 and 7GF tended to average more TOD responses than the other cards. Also, the distribution of TOD scores per card and per scoring category tended to be positively skewed. The percentages of individuals providing responses to each TOD category by card are presented in Table 20.3.

TABLE 20.2 Means, Standard Deviations, and Ranges of TAT Oral Dependency Scores in Undergraduate Sample

Scale	Mean	Std. Deviation	Range
Passive Dependence	.44	1.13	0–9
Ask/Receive Help	1.34	1.06	0–4
Parental Figures/Nurturers	3.34	1.63	0–7
Food Sources	.59	.75	0–3
Food Objects	.30	.60	0–2
Belief in Luck or Magic	.16	.37	0–1
Optimistic Story Endings	.16	.46	0–3
Helplessness, Loneliness, Depression	2.84	1.43	0–7
Mouth Behavior	2.90	1.64	0–8
Card 1	1.18	.88	0–3
Card 2	1.83	1.06	0–4
Card 3BM	1.46	.89	0–4
Card 7GF	1.99	.95	0–4
Card 12M	1.52	1.03	0–5
Card 13B	1.44	1.05	0–4
Card 13MF	1.01	.95	0–5
Card 18GF	1.57	1.10	0–5
Mean TOD per Card	1.50	.99	—
TAT Oral Dependency	12.07	3.72	0–22

In general, parent figures/nurturers, helplessness/loneliness/depression, and mouth behavior were the most commonly observed TOD categories produced across all cards. The only time in which the belief in luck or magic category was observed was on card 12M.

Intercorrelations of TOD total score per card, TOD category per card, and the total TOD score are presented in Table 20.4. The number of significant correlations between and within cards and categories was generally low; however, significant correlations were obtained for parental figures/nurturers, asking/receiving help, and mouth behavior across most cards.

Correlations were computed with the mean of each TOD content area, total TOD score for each TAT card, and total TOD, ROD, the IDI and its subscales. Card 3BM TOD score and total TOD scores were positively and significantly correlated with ROD scores ($rs = .22, .21, p < .05$, respectively). Emotional Reliance on Others was positively correlated with belief in luck or magic ($r = .25, p < .05$) and optimistic story endings ($r = .25, p < .05$) and was negatively correlated with parental figures/nurturers ($r = -.22, p < .05$). Lack of Self-Confidence was negatively correlated with passive dependence TOD category ($r = -.22, p < .05$), and BMI was negatively correlated with asking/receiving help ($r = -.22, p < .01$).

The results of this study provide some preliminary support for the validity of the TOD. Total TOD scores were significantly and positively correlated with ROD scores.

TABLE 20.3 Percentage of Individuals Providing TAT Oral Dependency Scores to Each Card Listed by Category

				TAT Card				
Category	**1**	**2**	**3BM**	**7GF**	**12M**	**13B**	**13MF**	**18GF**
Passive Dependence	0	6	4	0	4	11	4	2
Ask/Receive Help	2	13	8	31	38	2	7	32
Parent Figures/Nurturers	46	60	17	82	34	50	10	35
Food Sources	0	40	2	1	0	10	1	4
Food Objects	2	7	5	2	1	10	2	0
Belief in Luck or Magic	0	0	0	0	16	0	0	0
Optimistic Story Endings	1	0	1	0	6	2	1	2
Helplessness/Loneliness/ Depression	37	31	76	12	21	33	40	35
Mouth Behavior	29	26	33	71	32	26	35	44

The Emotional Reliance sub-Scale of the IDI was also positively correlated with the belief in luck or magic and optimistic story endings TOD categories and was negatively correlated with the parental figures/nurturers category. These correlational findings appear to capture one element of dependency—that is, that by placing one's emotional well-being in the hands of others, the dependent individual forfeits his or her own reason and sense of self-efficacy to that of another who assumes a caretaking role.

Somewhat surprisingly, there were no significant correlations between any TOD category and BMI. Given that Masling et al.'s (1967) sample consisted of patients being

TABLE 20.4 Correlations of TAT Oral Dependency Category Totals by Card

	1	**2**	**3BM**	**7GF**	**12M**	**13B**	**13MF**	**18GF**
Passive Dependence	.03	–.06	.00	–.11	–.03	.16	.14	.17
Asking/Receiving Help	–.07	.18	.08	.37	.28	.08	.22	.39
Parental Figures/Nurturers	.39	.40	.39	.27	.41	.42	.14	.23
Food Sources	–.07	.30	.35	.04	–.02	.22	.04	–.10
Food Objects	.13	.10	–.06	.09	.00	.35	.12	.24
Belief in Luck or Magic	–.01	–.15	.00	.25	.33	–.02	–.08	.05
Optimistic Story Ending	.24	–.27	–.15	–.05	.37	.08	.00	.04
Helplessness/Loneliness/ Depression	.01	.28	.24	.10	.10	.16	.38	.06
Mouth Behavior	.17	.36	.35	.27	.31	.31	.38	.32
TAT Oral Dependency Total	.28	.53	.50	.42	.52	.57	.42	.45

Notes: Underline indicates $p < .05$. All correlations are reported as two-tailed.

treated for obesity, it may be that BMI scores do not have the same meaning or relation to dependency in the range covering nonclinical populations. Alternatively, TOD as measured here may not be a valid means by which to assess interpersonal dependency as related to obesity in modern American society, which is a health problem related to diet and lack of exercise (in contrast to Israeli culture in the 1950s).

Interestingly, there was a significant negative correlation between the parental figure/nurturer category and the Emotional Reliance subscale. Since this sample consisted of undergraduates who were in the process of separating from parents and establishing their own sense of independence, it could be that dependency needs were expressed through a somewhat magical expectation that someone other than their parents could satisfactorily meet their needs.

Generalizability

The three studies conducted on the TOD to date have included primarily obese and non-obese female participants from an Israeli hospital during the 1960s, individuals with heroin and alcohol abuse, and undergraduates. All three studies reported some degree of support for the TOD, two of which demonstrated that oral dependency is associated with clinically significant impairment (e.g., obesity and substance abuse). Moreover, TOD scores were significantly correlated with ROD scores, as well as various subscales of a self-report measure of interpersonal dependency. However, given the relatively small sample size of these studies and the limited support for the validity of the TOD, the generalizability of these findings to other clinical and nonclinical populations is meaningfully limited. Optimism for the use of this scale remains warranted, though, as significant findings have traversed gender, cultural, and the patient status dimensions.

Reliability

As noted already, three studies have been conducted on the TOD, all of which reported reliability data. Masling et al. (1967) computed Pearson's r between the number of oral dependent responses scored by raters. In this case, the interrater agreement was .83 ($p < .01$). Ballner (1975) also assessed reliability by computing Pearson correlations between two raters. Combining scoring for the presence of anxiety or dependency content, Pearson's r was .83. Disagreement between raters was resolved by discussion.

In the previously mentioned pilot study, an undergraduate and graduate student met with the author to learn about the TOD system. They then were asked to read the TOD categories and to practice scoring on three stories. Subsequently, they exchanged stories, provided blind ratings for the new stories, and then compared each other's ratings across stories. Questions about scoring a given category were directed to the author, a licensed clinical psychologist with expertise in personality assessment and projective testing. This process took approximately 1.5 to 2 hours. After this first practice session, the two raters agreed on 91% of the ratings. After that, five cards were scored by each rater. Raters exchanged cards, scored TOD content blindly again, and then compared answers. A 97.5% agreement was obtained at this stage of training. Subsequently, each rater rated TOD content for the entire sample. Twenty cards were randomly selected from the sample, and interrater reliability was calculated. In this case, raters agreed on 96.8% of the TOD responses.[2] There was little correlation among TOD ratings per card or per TOD category, suggesting that TOD as currently assessed does not yield high levels of internal consistency.

□ Future Research Needed

Since the TOD has not been researched much since its development, substantial work is needed to continue to demonstrate the measure's psychometric properties. There are at least six major areas in which ongoing research is needed with this instrument. First, the validity of the TOD received modest support. However, the link between weight and oral dependency was not supported in this study, which contradicts the utility of the scale for the purposes for which it was created.

Second, the pilot research presented here assessed 82 nonpatients, who were mostly traditional undergraduates in their first or second year of higher education at a private, religiously affiliated university. Most of those evaluated were unmarried and Caucasian. Thus, a greater diversity within sociocultural factors is needed in future samples.

Third, the issue of stimulus pull of the cards needs to be evaluated. In one sense, it was not surprising that some cards had greater stimulus pull. Several TOD categories were reported on card 2, with the predominant categories being parental figurers/nurturers and food sources. Not surprisingly, three characters are in this picture, often described as a mother, father, and daughter. Likewise, this card depicts a farm scene. As another example, card 3BM often had themes of helpless/loneliness/depression and mouth behavior. This card depicts an individual who is kneeling with his or her head placed into his or her arms.

The issue of stimulus pull is of tremendous importance for the TOD. Although the TOD is not a self-report measure, which is usually associated with greater face validity, it seems in these preliminary findings that certain cards almost always are associated with an oral dependent response, given their content. Although such is the case on the Rorschach (e.g., card V, popular responses), an important issue for the development of the TOD will be the extent to which the TAT cards pull for dependent content. To the extent that this is true, the TOD may act less as a projective measure and more as a measure of consensual perception of social situations.

A fourth area of research has to do with the scoring categories themselves. Some scoring categories were rarely detected, such as belief in luck or magic and food objects. As the TOD's sibling, the ROD, has categories that are not frequently observed, it may be the case that the TOD's current categories are satisfactory in detecting dependency. Alternatively, it may be that these categories are not needed, should reliability and validity studies of the TOD without these categories be as strong as those studies that include them.

Fifth, other TAT cards should be evaluated for inclusion in the TOD system. The current study selected cards based on Masling et al.'s (1967) original study, along with TAT cards commonly used in other studies of dependency. Other cards may pull better for dependency themes than the ones selected here. Unlike the Rorschach, the TAT allows examiners to select which cards he or she will use. The TOD cannot be used in a standardized format until the card selection is fixed. Related to this, though the Rorschach has been found to generate reliable and valid findings with 10 cards, the TOD as presently proposed only uses 8 TAT cards. It may be that this is just not a sufficient number of cards to produce viable results. Similarly, more cards may be needed to expand the range of TOD scores, as any restrictions in range would certainly affect the measurement of oral dependency.

Finally, the scoring system of the TOD should be critically evaluated. With nine TOD categories and eight TAT cards, it is theoretically possible to obtain a score of 72 on the

TOD. However, the sample mean was 12.07, and the highest observed TOD score was 22. Further research on the use of TOD percentages, along with the scales with which the TOD is measured, would be helpful, especially if the scoring system as it currently exists is restricting the range of scores unnecessarily.

Notes

Special thanks are extended to Derrick Carter, Oscar Espinoza, Rebecca Helfand, Elizabeth Hutton Teal Kozel, Christina Miller, Kathryn Mullin, Carisa Jones, Lacey Rhoades, and Alyssa Seeber for their contributions in data collection, TAT scoring, and feedback about the scoring instructions. At the time of publication, ongoing research is being conducted with a clinical sample.

Because up to nine oral-dependent responses theoretically could be scored per story, it is not appropriate to compute coefficient alpha (Streiner, 2003a, 2003b).

References

Ballner, W. G. (1975). *The effects of emotional stress upon levels of anxiety and oral dependence as measured in the Holtzman Inkblot Test and TAT protocols of matched groups of heroin addicts, alcoholics, and controls.* Unpublished doctoral dissertation, Catholic University of America, Washington, DC.

Bornstein, R. F. (1996). Construct validity of the Rorschach Oral Dependency Scale: 1967–1995. *Psychological Assessment, 8,* 200–205.

Bornstein, R. F. (1998). Implicit and self-attributed dependency strivings: Differential relationships to laboratory and field measures of help seeking. *Journal of Personality and Social Psychology, 75,* 778–787.

Bornstein, R. F. (1999). Criterion validity of objective and projective dependency tests: A meta-analytic assessment of behavioral prediction. *Psychological Assessment, 11,* 48–57.

Bornstein, R. F., & Greenberg, R. P. (1991). Dependency and eating disorders in female psychiatric inpatients. *Journal of Nervous and Mental Disease, 179,* 148–152.

Bornstein, R. F., & Masling, J. M. (1985). Oral and latency of volunteering to serve as experimental subjects: A replication. *Journal of Personality Assessment, 49,* 306–310.

Bruch, H. (1961). Transformation of oral impulses in eating disorders: A conceptual approach. *Psychiatric Quarterly, 35,* 458–481.

Bruch, H. (1964). Psychological aspects of overeating and obesity. *Psychosomatics, 5,* 269–274.

Duberstein, P. R., & Talbot, N. L. (1993). Rorschach oral imagery, attachment style, and interpersonal relatedness. *Journal of Personality Assessment, 61,* 294-310.

Ehrenreich, J. H. (1990a). Effect of social class of subjects on normative responses to TAT cards. *Journal of Consulting Psychology, 46,* 467–471.

Ehrenreich, J. H. (1990b). Comparison of self-report and projective measures of dependency. *Psychological Reports, 66,* 845–846.

Elizur, A. (1949). A content analysis of the Rorschach for anxiety and hostility. *Rorschach Research Exchange, 13,* 247–284.

Fitzgerald, B. J. (1958). Some relationships among projective test, interview, and sociometric measures of dependent behavior. *Journal of Abnormal and Social Psychology, 56,* 199–203.

Fitzgerald, B. J., Pasewark, R. A., & Fleisher, S. (1974). Responses of an aged population on the Gerontological and Thematic Apperception Tests. *Journal of Personality Assessment, 38,* 234–235.

Furneaux, W. D. (1946). The prediction of susceptibility to hypnosis. *Journal of Personality, 14,* 281–294.

Greenberg, R. P., & Bornstein, R. F. (1989). Length of hospitalization and oral dependency. *Journal of Personality Disorders, 3,* 199–204.

Heilbrun, A. B. (1977). The influence of defensive styles upon the predictive validity of the Thematic Apperception Test. *Journal of Personality Assessment, 41,* 486–491.

Hirschfeld, R. M. A., Klerman, G. L., Gough, H. G., Barrett, J., Korchin, S. J., & Chodoff, P. (1977). A measure of interpersonal dependency. *Journal of Personality Assessment, 41,* 610–618.

Holt, R. R. (1970). *Manual for the scoring of primary process manifestations in Rorschach responses.* New York: Research Center for Mental Health.

Hurley, J. R. (1965). Parent acceptance–rejection and children's intelligence. *Merrill-Palmer Quarterly, 11,* 19–32.

Huang, A. (1998). *Father-daughter incest: Daughters' object relations and perceptions of maternal response to disclosure.* Unpublished doctoral dissertation, California School of Professional Psychology at Alameda.

Kagan, J., & Mussen, P. H. (1956). Dependency themes on the TAT and group conformity. *Journal of Consulting Psychology, 20,* 29–32.

Masling, J. M., Rabie, L., & Blondheim, S. H. (1967). Obesity, level of aspiration, and Rorschach and TAT measures of oral dependence. *Journal of Consulting Psychology, 31,* 233–239.

Masling, J. M., O'Neill, R. M., & Jayne, C. (1981). Orality and latency of volunteering to serve as experimental subjects. *Journal of Personality Assessment, 45,* 20–22.

McClelland, D. C., Koestener, R., & Weinberger, J. (1989). How do self-attributed and implicit motives differ? *Psychological Review, 96,* 690–702.

Melnick, B. (1968). *Distinctive personality attributes of child-abusing mothers.* Unpublished master's thesis, Michigan State University.

Melnick, B., & Hurley, J. R. (1969). Distinctive personality attributes of child-abusing mothers. *Journal of Consulting and Clinical Psychology, 33,* 746–749.

Murray, H. A. (1943). *Thematic Apperception Test.* Cambridge, MA: Harvard University.

Nicholson, W. M. (1946). Emotional factors in obesity. *American Journal of Medical Science, 211,* 443–447.

Schopbach, R. R., & Matthews, R. A. (1945). The psychological problems in obesity. *Archives of Neurology and Psychiatry, 54,* 157.

Shilkret, C. J., & Masling, J. M. (1981). Oral dependence and dependent behavior. *Journal of Personality Assessment, 45,* 125–129.

Shorvon, J. H., & Richardson, J. S. (1949). Sudden obesity and psychological trauma. *British Medical Journal, 2,* 951–956.

Stamler, C., & Palmer, J. O. (1971). Dependency and repetitive visits to the nurse's office in elementary school children. *Nursing Research, 20,* 254–255.

Stewart, A. J. (1992). Scoring manual for psychological stances toward the environment. In C. P. Smith (Ed.), *Motivation and personality: Handbook of thematic content analysis* (pp. 457–480). New York: Cambridge University Press.

Stewart, A. J. (1982). The course of individual adaptation to life changes. *Journal of Personality and Social Psychology, 42,* 1100–1103.

Stewart, A. J., Sokol, M., Healey, J. M., & Chester, N. L. (1986). Longitudinal studies of psychological consequences of life changes in children and adults. *Journal of Personality and Social Psychology, 50,* 143–151.

Stewart, A. J., Sokol, M., Healey, J. M., Chester, N. L., & Weinstock-Savoy, D. (1982). Adaptation to life changes in children and adults: Cross-sectional studies. *Journal of Personality and Social Psychology, 43,* 1270–1281.

Streiner, D. L. (2003a). Starting at the beginning: An introduction to coefficient alpha and internal consistency. *Journal of Personality Assessment, 80,* 99–103.

Streiner, D. L. (2003). Being inconsistent about consistency: When coefficient alpha does and doesn't matter. *Journal of Personality Assessment, 80,* 217–222.

Weiss, P., & Emmerich, W. (1962). Dependency fantasy and group conformity in ulcer patients. *Journal of Consulting Psychology, 26,* 61–64.

Zuckerman, M., & Grosz, H. J. (1958). Suggestibility and dependency. *Journal of Consulting Psychology, 22,* 328.

21

CHAPTER

Scoring Manual for Oral Dependency

Steven K. Huprich

Introduction

The TAT Oral Dependency Scale (TOD) is a theoretically and empirically derived measure of oral dependency. This construct is based on a psychoanalytic theory of dependency, in which overgratification or frustration in the earliest stages of development lead to adulthood manifestations, such as a high need to be nurtured and excessive reliance upon other people (Schafer, 1954). The TOD initially was developed by Masling, Rabie, and Blondheim (1967), who described oral dependency scoring systems for Rorschach and Thematic Apperception Test (TAT) data. Both systems involve the scoring of Rorschach and TAT content for all oral dependency themes that fall into one of several categories. In the case of the Rorschach, content falls into one of 16 categories, compared with 9 categories for the TAT. In both systems, oral dependent content is scored and a raw score is obtained.

Administration

Format

Examinees are presented the cards one at a time, in the sequential order just described, and are given the following instructions: "We would like you to tell a story about this picture. Please describe what is currently happening in the picture, what events led up to this story, and what the outcome of the story is. Also, please describe the thoughts and feelings of the characters." Examinees are asked to write each story on a separate piece of paper, although stories may be told individually to an examiner, who writes down the stories. For ease of administration in the research process, it is preferred that individuals write their own stories. Whether a clinician or researcher, the examiner must review the first two or three stories to determine that all elements of the story are included. If not, the examiner should prompt the examinee to add those elements to the story that are missing. Of course, this is not typically done when administration occurs in a group format, although some guidelines for this procedure have been reported by Smith, Feld, and Franz (1992).

Because this system has received very little empirical attention, there have been no studies to determine whether TOD differences exist in written versus spoken TAT stories. Likewise, there is no normative data on the TOD scores for different cards—except those reported here—or for total TOD scores across given combinations of cards. As such, it is recommended that a written procedure with the aforementioned cards be used for now, until the measure has been studied in more depth.

Stimuli

Similar to Murray's (1943) administration procedures, the TOD is assessed from stories provided by examinees to the following TAT cards: 1, 2, 3BM, 7GF, 12M, 13B, 13MF, and 18GF. Four of these cards (2, 7GF, 13B, and 18GF) were included in Masling et al.'s (1967) initial study on assessing oral dependency. The remaining cards were added for the following reasons:

(1) Several past studies that assessed dependency themes on the TAT have included these cards (see Huprich, 2003, and chapter 20, this volume).

(2) By doubling the number of cards, there would be a greater likelihood of obtaining oral dependent responses without making the task overwhelming for examinees.

(3) It was believed that cards 1 and 12M would pull for dependency themes.

(4) This compilation of these cards presented a satisfactory combination of single characters versus multiple characters (3 vs. 5), and male characters versus female characters (6 vs. 5).[1,2]

Other cards may be used for scoring TOD content; however, the use of a standard set of cards would improve the methodological strength of empirical studies of the TOD system.

☐ Scoring Process

Scoring Category Criteria

In the TOD system, there are nine different dependency theme categories:

(1) Passive dependence

(2) Asking for or receiving help

(3) Presence of parental figures or nurturers

(4) Food sources

(5) Food providers or food objects

(6) Belief in luck or magic

(7) Optimistic story endings

(8) Helplessness, loneliness, or depression

(9) Mouth behavior.

Each of these categories is described in more depth in the following sections (Table 21.1).

Passive Dependence

This involves any situation in which one person is waiting or wanting to receive help, nurturance, assistance, or care from another person. In these situations, it must be clear that the individual seeking help is not actively taking steps toward getting his

TABLE 21.1 TAT Oral Dependence Themes With Examples

TAT Theme	Example
(1) Passive Dependence	(Card 13 B) "This little boy is waiting to be picked up from school."
(2) Asking for or Receiving Help	(Card 7BM) "The younger man wants to get advice about moving to a new job."
(3) Presence of Parental Figures or Nurturers	(Card 7GF) "This mother is reading a story to her daughter."
(4) Food Sources	(Card 9BM) "These men are thinking about going to Charley's for a drink after a long day of work."
(5) Food Providers or Food Objects	(Card 2) "Here's a farmer who is planting his corn crop on a hot day."
(6) Belief in Luck or Magic	(Card 12M) "This man went to a psychic healer who is praying over him now."
(7) Optimistic Story Endings	(Card 13MF) "This man's wife just died. He's very sad, but he'll meet his soul mate, and they will be happy for many years."
(8) Helplessness, Loneliness, or Depression	(Card 1) "Johnny has been looking at his violin for an hour. He cannot figure out how to play it and is sad because he thinks he will never learn how."
(9) Mouth Behavior	(Card 7BM) "Uncle Joe is telling his nephew about the good old days."

or her needs or goals met on his or her own. For example, on card 1, an individual writes, "The little boy has finished his violin lesson and wants to go home, but is waiting for his mother to pick him up from the teacher's house." Here, the individual cannot reach his or her goal (i.e., getting home) and is waiting for the mother to help him reach that goal. Another example would be on card 2, in which the following portion of a story is provided: "The young woman wants to attend college, but she cannot go unless she knows her father gives his approval." Here, the young woman is seeking approval and support from her father and desires to advance her education, yet she is dependent on the father to provide approval prior to her leaving. Note that in this story, passive dependence is scored because the storyteller does not provide any indication that the young woman will ask for her father's approval or that she does not attend school because of a lack of his approval. If the story had stated the young woman attended college without his approval, this would not be classified or scored as passive dependence.

Asking for or Receiving Help

This theme is fairly straightforward to score. These situations occur when an individual clearly is getting some form of assistance from another person. Some examples of these are as follows. On card 13B, an individual writes, "The young boy wants to build a sand castle, so he decides to ask his big brother how to do it." Likewise, on card 18GF, the following description is told: "The woman passed out from heat exhaustion, and when her older sister came home, she picked her up and looked to make sure she was still breathing."

Presence of Parental Figures or Nurturers

This category is scored whenever a parental figure or nurturer is reported. Even if there is no parental figure or nurturer in the picture and one is reported, this category is scored. Thus, as described in the previous section in card 1, if the boy is waiting for his mother to pick him up, one point is scored in this category. Perhaps the most difficult aspect in determining whether a response meets this category is the concept of *nurturer.* There are many cases in which an individual likely assumes a nurturing role: teacher, physician, preacher, rabbi, spiritual healer, and God. In most cases, these individuals will be considered nurturers. There will also be situations in which a nonparental figure is acting in a nurturing way (e.g., "The man is wiping his tired eyes, because he has sat by the bed of his sick wife all night"). However, the context of the story must be read very carefully to determine if the individual is functioning in a nurturing way. For example, on card 2, the following portion of a story is told: "Allison came by Jack's farm to see him. She had been in love with him, but learned that he got married when she went off to college. She just saw Jack, who also saw her. They cannot look at each other because it is too painful." Although the storyteller writes about former lovers and about their feelings toward each other, there is not a nurturing component to this aspect of their experience. Thus, it is not scored. However, consider this slight modification to the story: "... She had been in love with him, but could not look at him now. She was reminded too much of how nice it was to be with him and how he encouraged her to go to college. Allison had followed his advice, but now was pretty lonely and longed for the days of being together again." In this case, Jack is a nurturer, and it is clear from the story that a nurturance theme is being elicited.

Food Sources

This category as a dependency theme may have different manifestations. To be scored in this category, there must be a reference to an item or place that functions as a source of food. Examples of these include grocery store, restaurant, Coke machine, refrigerator, references to going hunting for food, a bar or tavern, or apple tree. This category, however, should be differentiated from the next category.

Food Providers or Food Objects

This category includes items such as waiter, cook, farmer, apple, can of Coke, spoon, or cup. In some cases, an individual may articulate both thematic areas together. For instance, one might say, "The boy was really thirsty, so he went to the drug store, opened up the cooler, and bought himself a soda." Here, both a food source (i.e., cooler) and food object (i.e., soda) are mentioned and should be scored in two different categories. If, however, the boy bought a soda and a candy bar, the food object theme would only be scored one time.

Belief in Luck or Magic

This category is perhaps one of the most difficult thematic areas to score. In part, this is due to the fact that cultural or religious characteristics of the examinee must be considered. For instance, an individual states on card 12M, "... The boy gets well through the power of Jesus Christ." Here, it would be important to know something about the background of the examinee as well as to understand the context in which the story was told. Suppose the examinee is devoutly religious, and the story on card 12M was prefaced with the following: "The boy has been very ill. He has been treated by many physicians, and they do not think there is much hope. The family's pastor comes to the boy's side, prays for his healing, and the boy gets well...." In this case, it does not appear as if the examinee is blindly anticipating luck or magic to account for the boy's healing; rather, it would appear that the individual has the reasonable expectation that spiritual healing could occur. In contrast, suppose the same individual tells the following story: "The boy is on his death bed. He is very ill, but his family knows that God will heal him. So, the pastor comes and prays over him. The pastor claims God's promises in his prayer, and the boy is miraculously healed. The physicians are baffled, but the family knew all along that God would do this." In this case, though the individual does appear to have the expectation that spiritual healing could occur, notice that the storyteller's description of the story excludes reliance on modern medicine and has a tone of expectation of the supernatural, despite the fact the boy is described as being on his *death bed*. Indeed, the tone is almost hostile toward modern medicine and harbors the expectation that something miraculous would occur.

There are also times when the individual's cultural experiences may produce a response that appears as if luck or magic accounts for the results when this is not the case. An examinee who is Native American may believe that the ill individual on card 12M will be well when she or he has found harmony and accord with the natural world. For those of the Euro-American culture, such a belief may appear somewhat mystical, yet such a belief would not be incongruent with Native American culture. Thus, the response would not necessarily be a belief in luck or magic.

Although these examples may appear somewhat clear-cut, there are other times when it may be more difficult to ascertain the individual's religious or cultural expectations or when the story itself may not be specific enough to make a determination. In these cases, the best judgment possible should be used to make the rating. However, the rule of thumb in scoring these ambiguous scenarios is this: When in doubt, do not score.

Optimistic Story Endings

This is again a difficult theme to score. Perhaps the best way to make a scoring decision here is to consider the logical chain of events that lead up to the ending and the specificity and likelihood with which such an ending could occur. A well-reasoned, realistic series of events that lead to positive outcomes for the characters is typically considered an adaptive response in TAT stories. This is not what is to be rated. Rather, stories that have a gullible, almost childlike, ending should be scored. It is as if the story ends with the childlike expectation, "And they lived happily ever after." Likewise, when a negative or ambiguous situation has been described in a story and an optimistic tone is put on the outcome, then this theme should be scored. Consider two examples, using card 13MF:

(1) This man's wife just died. He's very sad, but somehow he will find another woman to marry and be happy with the rest of his life.

(2) This man is sad because his wife has just died. He loved her very much and knows he will not be able to spend the rest of his life with her, as they had planned. After the funeral, he goes through a period of grieving and begins to feel hope again. His friends are supportive and introduce him to other women when he is ready to date. A few years later, he finally meets someone who he loves, and they decide to marry.

Clearly, both examples produce optimistic endings, but the chain of events in the second story involves a man who takes intentional steps toward seeking solace, comfort, and ultimately love, whereas the first involves a wish for happiness that seems to be fulfilled with no effort on the part of the main character. In other words, the storyteller assumes a happy ending without demonstrating any efforts or means by which she or he will solve the problem and will obtain an optimistic result.

Helplessness, Loneliness, and Depression

This theme is more readily discernible than some of the previous themes. Stories with these themes involve characters who are in need of assistance, encouragement, support, or comfort from others. In other words, these characters' states place them into a situation in which they are easily dependent on others. Common phrases used to describe these characters include sadness, desperation, isolation, and darkness.

In some cases, the adjective upset will be used to depict this theme within an individual. However, this phrase does not automatically require a score in this category. For example, an individual who is upset may be angry, physically ill, or anxious. Thus, the context is very important. Consider portions of two stories as exemplars:

(1) The boy was upset that he could not play the violin. He so much wanted to be outside with his friends and found tears welling up inside him.

(2) Johnny was upset. He played and played his violin and could not make the sounds he wanted to. He considered smashing the violin against a wall, but decided not to because his mother would not be happy.

Here, the first example is a clear representation of depression and helplessness, whereas the second example depicts frustration and aggression. Obviously, the upset boy in example 2 is not eliciting nurturance from others. Rather, he is angry and wants to discharge his frustration. Once again, examiners must read the context of the story very carefully when scoring this category.

The same is true for other phrases. A character who decides he's not good enough or feels inadequate must be read in context to determine whether helplessness, loneliness, or depression occurs. For example, the boy on card 1 who "decides he's not good enough to play the violin and gives it up to pursue his interests in the trumpet" does not appear to have feelings of helplessness, loneliness, or depression. However, if he "decides he's not good enough and feels sad," then he does appear to be depressed, and hence the item would be scored.

The issue of transient conditions also poses a challenge for scoring this category. Stories that describe temporary feelings of experiencing helplessness, loneliness, and depression likely will be scored in this category, as all of these states readily evoke dependency feelings. However, the context of the phrase must be considered. For instance, in card 2, the story may read, "... Earlier that day, the man had pulled a muscle in his shoulder while working in the fields and could not continue to lift the equipment." Here, it is implied that he was helpless (i.e., could not continue with his work), and the category should be scored. However, if the story read, "... Earlier that day, the man had pulled a muscle in his shoulder while working in the fields and could not continue to lift the equipment. Now, he's better and looking at the work he has to do," then it would appear that the helpless state was somewhat parenthetical to the focus of the story.

Mouth Behavior

This final category includes any form of mouth behavior that is occurring, has occurred, or will occur. Several examples include speaking, humming, chewing, arguing, singing, yawning, tightening one's lips, kissing, sucking, gritting one's teeth, telling a story, and calling someone. Past tense words also should be included (e.g., talked, spoken). Interestingly, the description of being hungry seems to be highly suggestive of oral dependency, yet there is no category for which this is scored.

Other Content Areas

These can be identified that are suggestive of oral dependency yet do not have a category in the TOD. For instance, consider the description of pregnancy or a reference to breasts. Both of these are scored in the ROD as oral-dependent content. In written communications with the creator of the ROD and TAT scales (Masling et al., 1967), Joseph Masling noted that this seems to be an oversight on the part of the TOD. For now, hunger items will not be scored to be consistent with the initial TOD scale. However, further refinement and development of the TOD may wish to include these categories or a category for other oral dependent themes that do not qualify for membership in preexisting categories.

Technical Notes

Multiple categories may be scored on each card; however, having multiple examples of one category per card does not merit scoring that category twice. A question that is likely to arise is whether one should score the same words twice for different categories. In essence, certain phrases or words assume more weight in the scoring process than others. Ideally, one would not want to overrate the same material because of the artificial inflation of the examinee's score. However, it is my opinion that such inflations are appropriate for certain content. For example, consider an individual who tells many stories that have children asking parents for help. Examinees such as this one are clearly revealing the extent to which seeking guidance or help (category 2, Table 21.1) from a parental figure (category 3, Table 21.1) is prominent in their mental life. Such content in the inner world of such individuals is the hallmark of dependency. Thus, in cases such as these, where specific content has multiple dependency themes, it seems appropriate to account for the prominence of the dependency in the scoring. Perhaps future research could evaluate content such as this to determine its relationship to the degree of dependency within the individual.

Calculating Scores

Each story is read and evaluated for nine different oral dependency themes. The rater then decides which, if any, of the themes are present in a given story. One point is assigned to each dependency category per story, and a total TOD score is obtained by summing across stories. Thus, it is possible to have multiple dependency themes in one story. In some cases, one story might involve two examples of a given theme; however, the latter scenario is only scored one point for that category. For example, on card 7GF, the following portion of a story is told: "… After talking to the mother, the little girl picks up the baby, tells her, 'I love you,' and gives the baby a kiss." In this example, three mouth behaviors are provided: talking to the mother, the little girl talking to the baby, and the little girl giving the baby a kiss. When multiple examples of a given theme occur in one story, that theme is only scored once. Thus, only one point would be assigned to the mouth behavior dependency theme despite multiple examples of it in the story. In theory, the maximum number of points that could be obtained is 72 (9 categories × 8 cards). The mean score obtained in our initial sample was 4.40 (2.20).

☐ Practice Stories

Listed here are 10 sample stories with which to practice scoring TOD themes. Then answers are provided along with the rationale for the scoring decisions.

(1) Card 1: The boy in the picture is tired or practicing. He is meditating, thinking of a relaxing place he has been before. His break, however, is only temporary, as he knows he will have to practice this chore once his relaxation period is over. He dislikes practicing the violin but loves the music.

(2) Card 1: The boy is upset because he cannot get a song right on his violin. His parents want him to be first chair in his band, and he just can't seem to get it. In a while, his parents will come in after they notice that the playing has stopped, and they will either scold him or talk him into trying again until it is right. They will be annoyed but not yet upset.

(3) Card 12M: Dr. Mesmer is hypnotizing Peter in order to help him vent his pent up feelings about his childhood sexual abuse experience. Peter is unemotional and seems resistant to talk about hurtful things.

(4) Card 13B: The boy is sad because he is hungry and there is no food to eat. His mother tried to explain to him that they were broke, but he doesn't understand, so he is pouting outside their old, run-down house.

(5) Card 3BM: A boy is crying because his mother forgot to pick him up from school again because she was at a luncheon with her friends. She does not come until later on when she sees the time. She is apologetic and says it will never happen again, even though he knows it will. He feels sad and then becomes disdainful and gets rides home with friends. He says it doesn't matter, so she doesn't feel bad. Life goes on.

(6) Card 13MF: The man has just come home to find his wife dead. She has been attacked and killed by someone after her husband left for work. He will call the police. The man is thinking about how horrific and strange this all is and feeling confused, scared, sad, and shocked.

(7) Card 18GF: The evil step mom is trying to suffocate one of the stepkids. The girl said something really mean to the lady. Dad will walk in and stop everything. The girl's thinking, "This lady's psycho and needs to be locked down," and the stepmom is thinking, "That'll teach her to stop messing with me."

(8) Card 12M: Sean is lying on his back sick from a sudden illness he picked up overseas. He has been put in a room far away until they know what is wrong. The family's pastor has come over and has asked to see Sean. The pastor has faith that he will be healed. The pastor prays over him and by the power of the Holy Sprit, Sean is well.

(9) Card 2: A girl has come home from school and before she got there, her parents brought in extra help for the farm. It will help knowing the crop will get done faster and also help to know some money will come as well. The girl is a little doubtful of the new help, but the mother feels sure it will benefit them all. They are all happy people, though a little stressed, and eventually they will turn out great.

(10) Card 7GF: The mother is trying to teach her incredulous child. The child thinks of adventure and fun while the mother preaches learning and working. The mother will lose her daughter after the daughter reaches maturity. The daughter will become pregnant and be rejected by the mother and family, leading to her emotional demise.

Expert Ratings

Story 1

There are no TOD themes in this story.

Story 2

There are two TOD themes in this story. One is the presence of parental figures and the other is the parents scolding or talking to him (i.e., mouth behavior). Although upset may represent unhappiness, loneliness, or depression, it is too ambiguous from this story to classify. Thus, it is not scored.

Story 3

There are three TOD themes in this story. The first is passive dependence. This is scored because Peter is being hypnotized by Dr. Mesmer. In essence, Peter is in a passive, helpless state and is anticipating that the doctor can assist him. The second theme is asking or receiving help. This is clearly stated in the context of the story. The third theme is mouth behavior. This is scored in reference to Peter's resistance to talking. Even though it is mentioned as resistance and Peter is not actually talking, it is scored because the content was mentioned.

Story 4

There are three TOD themes in this story. The first of these is under the category of food provider or food object. Specifically, food is directly mentioned and hence is scored. The second TOD theme is scored for the presence of the maternal figure in the story. The third TOD theme is scored under helplessness/loneliness/depression. This is scored for the fact that the family is described as financially destitute and the boy is pouting.

Story 5

This story provides five good examples of TOD oral dependency themes and should be scored accordingly. The first score is assigned for the presence of the mother. The second TOD theme is passive dependence and is scored for the fact that the boy is waiting on the mother to pick him up from school. The third theme is scored for the content, "She is apologetic and says it will never happen again," as the reference is to mouth behavior of the mother. Fourth, a score is given to the helplessness/loneliness/depression category for the fact that the boy is described as sad. Finally, luncheon is scored as a food source.

Story 6

Two TOD dependency themes are present in this story: helplessness/loneliness/depression and mouth behavior. The former is obvious from the description of the male character. The second is not quite so obvious. Here, it is stated that the man will call the police. Again, though this is written in a future tense and is a reference to a behavior—placing a telephone call—mouth behavior is subsumed in the fact that one is making a call. That is, it is difficult to assume in this story that the man would call the police and not speak.

Story 7

This story is scored in three categories: parental figures, asking/receiving help, and mouth behavior. The first two are fairly evident: A mother and father are reported, and the father is helping the children. The latter is scored for suffocating. Being suffocated is a behavior that involves the mouth and should be scored accordingly.

Story 8

This is an interesting story. Three categories are readily identifiable and scorable: helplessness/loneliness/depression, asking/receiving help, and parental figure/nurturer. A person lying on his back sick is clearly an example of helplessness. The presence of a pastor is indicative of nurturance, which is made all the more clear by the fact that he is providing help. The story ends somewhat quickly and abruptly, with a prayer followed by healing from a divine source. What is interesting is that the pastor is described as having faith that the boy can be healed by divine intervention. Two potential scores could be assigned here: optimistic ending and luck or magic. Let us address these sequentially.

First, the story clearly ends on a positive note. How the examinee describes this ending is crucial to deciding how to score this. As noted previously, stories that have a gullible, childlike quality to them without a clear sequence of cause and effect are to be scored as optimistic. In this case, the story tells of a pastor who comes to see the sick boy. The next sentence describes the faith of the pastor. Interestingly, the boy is not described as terminally ill. Rather, he is isolated until they know what is wrong. Then, the pastor arrives, and, without consulting the medical community or waiting for a diagnosis and prescribed treatment, the pastor prays for healing. The story ends, "... and by the power of the Holy Spirit, Sean is well." It could be argued that this individual's story reflects religious beliefs that are consistent with his or her culture—this individual is an undergraduate student at a large, Southern Baptist university. However, given the childlike quality of the ending, along with the exclamatory declaration of Sean's healing, the story has an immature quality to it. Consider the difference if the examinee stated that the pastor consults with the family, learns of the medical condition, and then decides to say a prayer with the boy. Then, the story ends with a statement that the healing was a result of both physical and spiritual influence. In this case, there is a more mature, well-reasoned approach to the story. As such, it would probably not be appropriate to score the story as optimistic within the context of TOD.

The issue of scoring luck or magic is another conundrum. However, it would appear that the decision is mediated by the previous decision. Since the story was rated as optimistic, the rater must decide whether luck or magic accounted for this ending. In this case, the examinee attributed the results to a divine force, namely, the Holy Spirit. This force is commonly accepted throughout the Christian community. This being the case, then, scoring luck or magic is likely not appropriate.

Story 9

This story is scored for three TOD themes: asking/receiving help, parental figures/nurturers, and food sources. All of these scores are relatively straightforward. One might think that describing the family as a little stressed qualifies for the helpless/loneliness/depression category. However, being a little stressed is not specific enough to qualify for depression. Furthermore, stress is typically associated with anxiety and not depression.

Story 10

There are three TOD themes here. The first is parental figures/nurturers and is readily scored because of the presence of a mother. The second theme and third themes are scored based on the content in the first sentence, while the mother is trying to teach her child. In the next sentence, the mother is described as preach[ing] learning and working. These phrases warrant scores in the asking/receiving help and mouth behavior categories. Regarding the former, teaching and preaching may be considered forms of providing help. Regarding the latter, teaching and preaching are forms of verbal activity.

References

Bornstein, R. F. (1996). Construct validity of the Rorschach Oral Dependency Scale: *Psychological Assessment, 8*, 200–205.

Masling, J. M., Rabie, L., & Blondheim, S. H. (1967). Obesity, level of aspiration, and the Rorschach and TAT measures of oral dependence. *Journal of Consulting Psychology, 31*, 233–239.

Murray, H. A. (1943). *Thematic Apperception Test*. Cambridge, MA: Harvard University.

Schafer, R. (1954). *Psychoanalytic interpretation in Rorschach testing*. Orlando: Grune & Stratton.

Smith, C. P., Feld, S. C., & Franz, C. E. (1992). Methodological considerations: Steps in research employing content analysis systems. In C. P. Smith (Ed.), *Motivation and personality: Handbook of thematic content analysis* (pp. 515–536). New York: Cambridge University Press.

Notes

The characters in cards 3BM and 18GF were not included in this count, because it was decided a priori that there was not enough stimulus pull from these characters to state with certainty the gender of the characters.

Special thanks are extended to Dr. Joseph Masling for his helpful comments in the preparation of this manuscript (Communicated in an electronic message with Masling, November 2002).

22

CHAPTER

Symbiosis

Frank Summers

Abstract

Lack of differentiation between self and other is an important concept in the understanding of severe psychopathology. The current instrument is a way of administering and scoring the Thematic Apperception Test (TAT) that measures the degree of differentiation in the subject's relationships with others. Dyads in TAT stories are scored for the presence or absence of several constructs, each of which is a component of symbiotic attachment. In this way, the investigator can determine the specific way in which the subject is not differentiated. Scores can be interpreted at the level of the dyad or as a total score. Each dyad is defined by a gender–generation combination, so that the researcher obtains scores on the following dyads: older woman–younger woman, older woman–younger man, older man–younger woman, older man–younger man, and older man–older woman. These scores are then added to arrive at a total symbiosis score. This chapter describes the conceptual foundations of the scoring system, definitions of the variables, research evidence of reliability and validity, and uses of the system.

Description of System

Conceptual Framework

Lack of differentiation between self and other, often called *symbiosis,* has gained an important place in the understanding and treatment of psychopathology (e.g., Mahler, 1952, 1958, 1967, 1968; Mahler, Pine, & Bergmann, 1975; Winnicott, 1965, pp. 37–55). Margaret Mahler and her colleagues view symbiosis as a normal phase of early development which, if not overcome, results in a fixation at the inability to differentiate self from other. The result, according to these theorists, is a lack of boundaries between self and other, setting the stage for borderline or psychotic outcomes in later life. Although the concept of a normal symbiotic phase is disputed by developmental researchers such as Stern (1985), lack of differentiation between parent and child has frequently been reported in backgrounds of patients suffering from severe character pathology, and a tendency toward fusion of boundaries between self and other has been widely noted as a characteristic of severely disturbed patients (e.g., Fairbairn, 1952; Gedo & Goldberg, 1972; Giovacchini, 1972; Guntrip, 1969; Kernberg, 1976, 1984; Lidz, Fleck, & Cornelison, 1966; Mahler, 1958, 1971; Searles, 1965; Summers, 1988; Winnicott, 1975, pp. 145–156, 255–261). For example, D.W. Winnicott and many others have noted that borderline patients, when they form affective connections, tend to merge their sense of self with the other. The widespread clinical observation that severely disturbed patients suffer from blurring of self and other boundaries suggests the need for an objective measure of this slippery notion. The present report describes a manual for coding symbiosis on certain cards of the TAT and the Make-A-Picture-Story (MAPS).

Undifferentiation, or symbiosis, may be said to obtain in a dyadic relationship to the degree that either party has some difficulty perceiving himself or herself as a separate, distinct individual. In the extreme this may mean experiencing the other as a part of oneself, but lack of differentiation may manifest itself in various forms and to different degrees. For example, some narcissistic patients tend to expect, or even assume, that the other shares their deeply held values or viewpoint, suggesting a degree of undifferentiation, but they are able to separate from the other without extreme anxiety (Kohut, 1971). More deeply undifferentiated patients are unable to be apart from the other without a threat of annihilation (ibid.). The degree to which a relationship is differentiated is the extent to which the subjective states of both parties are recognized and respected, whether they are similar or different. Complete differentiation would be expressed in the ability to recognize the other's differences and to cherish them, a state Benjamin (1995) called *mutuality.* The present instrument is designed to assess the degree to which each of the various components of differentiation has been achieved.

This instrument can be used to assess the degree of undifferentiation in the ways of relating to others in individual patients, irrespective of family studies. As noted, many current conceptualizations of borderline and other severe character disorders emphasize the blurring of self–other boundaries in these relationships. Indeed, many clinicians view this variable as pathognomonic of borderline and schizoid psychopathology (e.g., Fairbairn, 1952; Guntrip, 1969; Kernberg, 1975, 1984; Winnicott, 1975, pp. 145–156). The suitability for different types of treatment is often based heavily on this factor. Due to the importance of assessing self–other differentiation, Kernberg (1984) proposed an elaborate interview system to determine the extent of fusion in patients' relationships. The present projective testing system has the potential to ascertain the extent of undifferentiation in a reliable, valid way.

An additional benefit of this system is its capacity for measuring separate components of undifferentiation. The division of symbiosis into six component variables allows for the assessment of the specific way an individual may lack differentiation in her or his relationships. Thus, the clinician or researcher can refine the way in which the patient's relationships lack differentiation as opposed to a simplistic classification into symbiotic or not symbiotic, or differentiated versus undifferentiated. The researcher or clinician can assess a relationship according to the ways it may lack differentiation. These component variables have been shown to be distinct parts of symbiotic bonding and have proven useful in assessing relationships between mothers and schizophrenic patients (Summers & Walsh, 1977).

It must be emphasized that this definition is based on the perceptions of the parties to the relationship, not behavioral interaction. Two individuals who do not perceive themselves as separate are, by definition, engaged in a symbiotic relationship.

Scoring Categories

Symbiosis, the broadest concept, denotes the tendency to fuse self with others. However, the concept of a symbiotic, or undifferentiated, relationship is used clinically to refer to a variety of different phenomena, each of which reflects an aspect of undifferentiation. In its most extreme form, most typically used in reference to borderline and severe pathologies, symbiosis is used to mean the equation of one's thoughts and feelings with the mental states of others. However, somewhat less extreme forms of this tendency are often manifested clinically in behavior that, although less overtly fused, carries the implication that the other either does or should feel the same as the subject. The most common forms of this behavior are intruding on others, difficulty separating, negative reactions to the other's relationships, dependency on the other, and injunctions for the other to perform in a given manner. These five tendencies are commonly seen in clinical practice with patients who have some difficulty accepting boundaries between self and other. Because all these behaviors reflect blurring of the self–other distinction, symbiosis can be broken down into six component variables (Table 22.1).

(1) Undifferentiation is the difficulty in distinguishing one's own thoughts or feelings from those of the other. It is most frequently indicated by the assumption that the other feels or believes the same as oneself or failure to recognize any mental state of

TABLE 22.1 Scoring Categories for Symbiosis

Category	Description
(1) Undifferentiation	Merger of thoughts and feelings
(2) Behavioral Intrusiveness	Active effort to impose on other
(3) Nonbehavioral Intrusiveness	Lack of recognition of other's boundaries without active effort to interfere
(4) Separation Difficulty for Other	Negative reactions to separation or loss focused on concern for well-being of other
(5) Separation Difficulty for Self	Negative reactions to separation or loss focused on well-being of self
(6) Disapproval of Other Relationships	Negative reactions to third-party relationships
(7) Dependency	Reliance on the other
(8) Injunctions	Expectations for other to behave in a certain way
(9) Injunctions Fulfilled	Behavior that conforms to other's injunctions

the other different from one's own but may also be shown by resistance to perceiving the other as different.

(2) Intrusiveness is the failure to recognize the other's boundaries by imposing one's own ideas on the other. It includes active unsolicited efforts to change the other's behavior or seeing the other as in need of oneself.

Behavioral refers to violating the other's boundaries in overt behavior, such as active interference or imposing one's will on the other.

Nonbehavioral is shown by the lack of recognition of the other's boundaries without active violation, such as by making the assumption that the other cannot function or make decisions without the subject.

(3) Separation difficulty is indicated by intense negative reactions, such as anxiety or depression, to movement apart or indications of possible movement apart.

For other refers to a reaction that is negative out of concern for the well-being of the other.

For self is a negative separation reaction that consists of a threat to the self.

(4) Disapproval of other relationships involves resistance or negative reactions, such as anxiety or depression, to the other's formation of relationships independent of the self or active interference with the formation of such relationships.

(5) Dependency is the need for the other to do or be something for oneself; it may be shown by direct request for help, advice or comfort, threats to the other's independence, or inability to function without the other or anxiety in having to act without reliance on the other.

(6) Injunctions are expectations of the other to act in a given manner or efforts to guide the other's behavior via directives for the other to behave as one wishes she or he should.

(7) Injunctions fulfilled are injunctions that result in the other's compliance.

As separation difficulty and intrusiveness are divided into two component variables, there are a total of nine component symbiosis scores.

The TAT and MAPS stories are scored by coding separately each dyadic relationship portrayed in the story. For each such dyad, the coder scores each variable as either 1 for present or 0 for absent. The scores are then summed in a variety of ways in addition to a total symbiosis score. All scores for each gender–generation combination are combined for each component variable to reach a total score for the gender–generation dyad on each variable. For example, all scores for older male–younger female dyads are added to produce a father–daughter score on each variable. Scores for component variables may also be summed separately.

This scoring system is a way to assess the type and degree of differentiation achieved in relating to others, a key variable in the diagnosis and understanding of personality disorders. This instrument may be used in lieu of or in conjunction with the interview process. By providing an empirical measure of differentiation, this TAT scoring system offers the clinician a measure with demonstrated reliability and validity to be used along with interview data and against which such less structured data can be judged.

This system can be used to measure both vectors of a dyadic relationship from the viewpoint of each party. For example, a researcher investigating a mother–son relationship could obtain (1) the mother's score for both her degree of enmeshment with the child and her perception of the child's attachment to her; and (2) the child's score for his perception of the mothers' symbiotic attachment to him, and the degree of his own differentiation with his mother. Thus, there are four possible perceptions measurable in any dyadic relationship under investigation. This capability renders the scoring system adaptable to the needs of family studies, many of which have investigated undifferentiation without a reliable means for measuring the concept (Lidz, Fleck, & Cornelison, 1966; Lu, 1969).

☐ Research Evidence

Validity

The validity of the scoring system has been supported by the results of the family study already alluded to (Summers & Walsh, 1977; Summers, 1978). The study subjects were 31 hospitalized young adult patients and their families, 17 diagnosed with schizophrenia, and 14 with other diagnoses. Another 15 families with at least one young adult member with no diagnosable emotional disorder composed the comparison group, yielding a total of 46 young adults and their families. The young adults were between 18 and 26 years of age. That investigation demonstrated that the total symbiosis scores and the scores on each component variable from both the mother–child and father–child dyads distinguished the three groups of patients and their mothers. That is, schizophrenic patients scored higher on each component of symbiosis and the total score than nonschizophrenic hospitalized patients, who, in turn, scored higher than young adults with no psychiatric disorder. Further, mothers of schizophrenic patients scored higher than mothers of hospitalized nonschizophrenic patients, who had significantly higher scores than mothers of young adults with no known psychiatric disorder. This study showed that the instrument can be used to find differences among not only patients but also mothers of patients. However, it must also be noted that n for each group is between 14 and 17, so the results, though promising, must be interpreted with caution until larger samples can be tested.

Generalizability

This scoring system, although promising in the results achieved in the family study, has not been tested on other populations, and even within the family study, the number of protocols is not large. Consequently, the breadth of applicability is not clear. More broad-ranging studies will have to be done to determine the usefulness of the instrument beyond its demonstrated utility in differentiating young adult schizophrenic patients from other young adults and mothers of these patients.

Reliability

This instrument has proven reliability and validity on the small sample of subjects to whom it was administered. Reliability was tested on a sample of 14 protocols, 10% of the 138 subjects used in a study of families of schizophrenic patients, hospitalized non-schizophrenic psychiatric patients, and ambulatory young adults (Summers, 1978). The estimate was based on the interrater method. Two experienced clinicians made independent blind ratings of the sample protocols. Ratings were scored 1 or 0 on each variable, and the reliability estimate was the percentage of agreement between the two raters. The same method was later used on a second sample of 28 protocols drawn from an enlarged pool of the same sample and an additional 24 protocols from siblings of the index subjects in the original study (Summers, 1978). In the original sample, 91% agreement was reached with rates on individual variables ranging from 80.2% to 100%. These results indicate that the raters tested achieved a remarkable level of agreement in scoring each of the component variables of undifferentiation. For this sample, the instrument was reliably rated between the trained raters. Nonetheless, the total of 42 protocols is not a large sample, and the preliminary nature of the reliability estimate must be acknowledged.

To warrant the treatment of the component variables as separate measures of symbiosis, they must be correlated, but not highly. The correlations of the nine component measures varied from .04 to .47, and three fourths (12 of 16) were between .21 and .39. These results show sufficiently low correlations to justify the treatment of the component scores as separate variables, and the correlations indicate that the variables are related to each other.

☐ Further Research Needed

The results of the reliability and validity studies are promising, but the number of research subjects is too small to be convincing. Consequently, the first need for subsequent research is to do further reliability and validity studies with larger sample sizes. If this work confirms the preliminary testing of reliability and validity, the instrument would be a proven method of measuring symbiosis and, indeed, the first such measure possessed by the field. The study of symbiosis would then become possible for the investigation of psychopathology.

The most important arena for further study would be the investigation of the degree to which the inability to differentiate self from others is characteristic of a variety of types of psychopathology. This is an especially important area of study because the blurring of self–other boundaries has been suggested as an important factor in a variety of different pathologies. It would be helpful to the clinician to know the degree to which the lack of differentiation is characteristic of the spectrum of pathologies from neurotic disorders to character pathology to psychosis. This measure of symbiosis, with confirmed reliability and validity, would be an established device for the assessment of the tendency to blur self–other boundaries, and, therefore, the importance of this variable in the spectrum of psychopathology.

☐ References

Benjamin, J. (1995). *Like subjects, love objects,* New Haven, CT: Yale University Press.

Fairbairn, W. D. R. F. (1952). *Psychoanalytic studies of the personality.* London: Tavistock.

Gedo. J., & Goldberg, A. (1972). *Models of the mind.* Chicago: University of Chicago Press.

Giovacchini, P. (1972). The symbiotic phase. In P. Giovacchini (Ed.), *Tactics and techniques of psychoanalytic therapy* (pp. 137–169). New York: Science House.

Guntrip, H. (1969). *Schizoid phenomena, object relations, and the self.* New York: International Universities Press.

Kernberg, O. (1975). *Borderline conditions and pathological narcissism.* New York: Jason Aronson.

Kernberg, O. (1984). *Severe personality disorders.* New Haven, CT: Yale University Press.

Kohut, H. (1971). *The analysis of the self.* Monograph Series of the Psychoanalytic Study of the Child, 4. New York: International Universities Press.

Lidz, T., Fleck, S., & Cornelison, A. (1966). *Schizophrenia and the family.* New York: International Universities Press.

Lu, Y. (1969) Mother–child role relations in schizophrenia. *Psychiatry, 24,* 133–137.

Murray, H. (1943). *Thematic Apperception Test.* The Psychological Corporation.

Mahler, M. (1952). On child psychosis and schizophrenia: Autistic and symbiotic infantile psychoses. *Psychoanalytic Study of the Child, 7,* 286–305.

Mahler, M. (1958). Autism and symbiosis: two extreme disturbances of identity. *International Journal of Psychoanalysis, 39,* 77–83.

Mahler, M. (1967). On human symbiosis and the vicissitudes of individuation. *Journal of the American Psychoanalytic Association, 15,* 740–763.

Mahler, M. (1968). *On human symbiosis and the vicissitudes of individuation.* New York: International Universities Press.

Mahler, M. (1971). A study of the separation–individuation process. *Psychoanalytic Study of the Child, 26,* 403–424.

Mahler, M., Pine, F., & Bergmann, A. (1975). *The psychological birth of the human infant.* New York: Basic Books.

Searles, H. (1965). *Collected papers on schizophrenia and related subjects.* New York: International Universities Press.

Stern, D. (1985). *The interpersonal world of the infant.* New York: Basic Books.

Summers, F. (1975). *Symbiosis and confirmation in the families of schizophrenics.* Unpublished doctoral dissertation, University of Chicago.

Summers, F. (1978). Manual for the measurement of symbiosis in human relationships. *Psychological Reports, 43,* 663–670.

Summers, F. (1988). Psychoanalytic therapy of the borderline patient: Treating the fusion–separation contradiction. *Psychoanalytic. Psychology, 5,* 339–355.

Summers, F., & Walsh, F. (1977). The nature of the symbiotic bond between mother and schizophrenic. *American Journal of Orthopsychiatry, 47,* 484–494.

Summers, F., & Walsh, F. (1979). Symbiosis and confirmation between father and schizophrenic. *American Journal of Orthopsychiatry, 49,* 136–148.

Winnicott, D. (1975). *Through pediatrics to psychoanalysis.* New York: Basic Books.

Winnicott, D. (1965). *Maturational processes and the facilitating environment.* New York: International Universities Press.

23

CHAPTER

Scoring Manual for Symbiosis

Frank Summers

Introduction

Symbiosis is lack of differentiation between self and other. The scoring system identifies for each dyad in a story the presence or absence of several components of symbiotic attachment. The scorer must determine in each Thematic Apperception Test (TAT) and Make-A-Picture-Story (MAPS) story what dyads are being described and then for each one whether there is sufficient evidence to warrant a positive score. There is no spectrum or scale; the scorer decides if the variable is present or absent. For example, is there sufficient evidence to say that a given figure does not differentiate his or her feelings or thoughts from the other? If so, a score is given; if not, that vector of the dyad for that variable is scored as not present, or 0.

Administration

Format

The administrator of the test gives standard Murray (1943) instructions for each of the six stimuli. After the subject gives his or her story, the administrator asks the thoughts and feelings of each character toward every other in the card, whether or not the subject has mentioned every figure in the story. If feelings and thoughts of one character toward another have been given in the story, the administrator asks for elaboration. The typical questions are "What more can you tell me about how this character feels toward this other character? What other thoughts might this character have about the second character?"

If the subject does not respond or says, "I don't know," the administrator asks for imagination— for example, "What can you imagine this character could possibly be feeling? What would be a possible feeling?" The administrator makes every effort to elicit a response for each character toward every other. If the subject introduces a character, the administrator asks for that character's thoughts and feelings toward each figure in the picture and vice versa. That is, any introduced figure is treated like any figure in the picture.

Stimuli

The stimuli used were TAT cards 2, 6BM, 7GF, 7BM, and 10 and a scene from the MAPS constructed for this instrument. The MAPS scene was composed of a backdrop of a living room with an open door and three figures standing in front: a brash young man gesturing furtively outside stands between an older man with his hands in his pockets and an older woman with one hand to her face. Thus, the MAPS scene consisted of three dyads with two sides each so that there are six scorable dyadic units: older man–woman, woman–older man, younger man–woman, woman–younger man, younger man–older man, and older man–younger man. Card 2 of the TAT also has three figures, resulting in six scorable dyads: man–woman, woman–man, man–girl, girl–man, woman–girl, and girl–woman. Cards 6BM, 7GF, 7BM, and 10, having only two figures each, consist of two scorable units each as follows:

- 6BM: Man–woman, woman–man
- 7GF: Woman–girl, girl–woman
- 7BM: Older man–younger man, younger man–older man
- 10: Man–woman, woman–man

In all, there are a minimum of 20 scorable dyads for each subject, each of which is scored on each symbiosis component variable. As there are nine variables, each protocol has at least 180 possible scores, each of which is marked 1 for present or 0 for absent. There can be more than 20 scoreable dyads if the subject introduces dyads into the story, such as including a male figure on card 7GF or a woman on card 7BM. If such dyads are introduced, they are scored like any other dyad.

□ Scoring Process

The scorer reads each story and then organizes them into dyadic vectors. That is, all statements referring to one character's perception of another are grouped together. Then, the scorer reads these statements to determine whether any of the component variables of symbiosis are present. If so, a 1 is scored on the scoring sheet. The construct definitions and descriptions described following are read and referred to as the criteria for making this decision.

To arrive at the determination of present (coded 1) or absent (coded 0) the scorer uses the following scoring manual.

Scoring Category Criteria

Undifferentiation (Undiff)

This is difficulty in distinguishing own desires, perceptions, opinions, or interests from those of another. It may be shown by failure to perceive other as different, or the presumption that what is true of oneself is true of the other. It does not include simple agreement of viewpoint: It requires either a presumption (unstated by character) of sameness or failure to recognize a difference.

> Example: "He doesn't ask her because he feels that she always agrees with him anyway. He feels that he always knows just how she feels."

- He to she: 1
- She to he: 0

> Example: "The parents both believe in the farm life. They assume she'll spend the rest of her life on the farm like them."

- Older man to older woman: 0
- Older woman to older man: 0
- Older woman to younger woman: 1
- Older man to younger woman: 1

Intrusiveness—Behavioral (Int-Be)

This encompasses any action taken to interfere with or prohibit the other's autonomous action. It is shown by any indication of taking over other's activities, taking responsibility for other, attempting to solve other's problems, or interfering with activities that belong to other.

> Example: "... His father tells him that he's messed things up, that he's got to do things differently from now on.... He just tells him what to do, you know. How not to get into this kind of thing anymore. He sets up a new business for him...."

- Father to son: 1
- Son to father: 0

Intrusiveness—Nonbehavioral (Int-Nobe)

This is feeling that other is in need of one to function, without overt interference. It is shown by feelings of concern about other's ability to function independently, such as by worries or fear.

Example: "He doesn't really think that he knows what he is doing.... He doesn't think he's old enough, but he doesn't try hard to stop him.... He figures the kid will learn the hard way."

- First man to second man: 1
- Second man to first man: 0

Separation Difficulty—for Self (SepFS)

This includes problems for oneself as a result of separation either anticipated or actual. It is shown by suggestions of depression, unhappiness, anxiety, worry, or fear for one's functioning or well-being in response to separation of whatever type. The loss must be explicitly stated and the affective reaction clearly indicated as a response to the loss.

Example: "The mother will get sent off to a nursing home. He will visit now and then, but it won't be enough. She will be lonely."

- Mother to son: 1
- Son to mother: 0

Separation Difficulty—Concern for Other (SepFO)

This is concern for the well-being of other on separation. It is shown by any expression of concern for how other will get along or feel during or after separation, such as by worry for other's safety and security.

Example: "She's afraid something's going to happen to him. I guess she doesn't think he's old enough to handle it (leaving)."

- Father to daughter: 1
- Daughter to father: 0

Disapproval of Other Relationships (DisOR)

This is one character's resistance to or discomfort with another character's relationships. It is shown by negative emotional reactions to relationships with third parties, such as anxiety, depression or unhappiness; or by active efforts to sabotage such relationships.

Example: "This man is mad because he does not want his daughter to go out with this guy. The daughter gets mad. She does not see why her father won't let her."

- Father to daughter: 1
- Daughter to father: 0

Dependency (Dep)

This is the need for other to be or to do for one. It may be shown directly by request for help, advice, or comfort or indirectly by negative reaction to lack of the same.

> Example: "... He is not sure about a business deal. He's going to his dad for help. Want advice. He will probably give it to him."

- Son to father: 1
- Father to son: 0

Injunctions (Inj)

This is the expectation that other should be or act in a given manner. It is shown by expressed desire for other to behave in some way, whether by proscription or prescription.

> Example: "The older guy tells the other guy what he's got to do to get out of this mess.... He tells him he better sell the whole business now if he knows what's good for him."

- Older man to younger man: 1
- Younger man to older man: 0

Fulfilled Injunctions (InjFul)

This involves carrying out other's injunction. It is shown by any action that conforms with other's injunction.

> Example: "... So the younger man sells the business like the guy told him to.... He doesn't know what else to do."

- Younger man to older man: 1
- Older man to younger man: 0

Calculating Scores

The number of positive scores can then be calculated in various ways. The total score for each variable can be summed for each type of dyad—for example, man–woman, woman–man, woman–girl, Thus, the researcher can find a symbiosis component score, such as intrusiveness, for each such dyad. All scores can be totaled to yield the total symbiosis score.

Practice Stories

Card 2

Seems to be some farm workers, maybe a family. Three different people in three different situations. One girl's chosen education, it appears. She's going to school or studying. The man has chosen working on the farm. The woman has chosen to be a housewife, just the stage of their lives.

Interviewer: What thoughts and feelings might the characters have?

Subject: The girl holding the books seems to be thinking, far off, thinking of the future, where she's going to go, what she's going to do, she's thinking about things far from the farm. From her face, she seems to be a worrier, worrying about the future: will she be able to make it on her own? She's afraid she can't, that she can't do it, that she'll fail, that she can't live without the others, that she'll have to come back, she doesn't want to, but she's afraid she'll have to—that she'll be too unhappy without her family. But, the other woman is stuck on the farm, it's the choice she made, but she's not sure.... She's worried about the other woman leaving, the younger one, she's afraid she's going to lose her, she might be her daughter or her sister, she's afraid she'll be lonely.

Interviewer: What about the man?

Subject: He's not thinking; he's doing his job.

Interviewer: Can you imagine what he might be thinking or feeling about the others?

Subject: He's thinking they worry too much—they should get to work; he doesn't care—he has too much to do.

TABLE 23.1 Card 2 Scoring

Dyad	Undiff	Int-Be	Int-Nobe	SepFS	SepFO	DisOR	Dep	Inj	InjFul
Man–Woman	0	0	0	0	0	0	0	0	0
Woman–Man	0	0	0	0	0	0	0	0	0
Man–Girl	0	0	0	0	0	0	0	0	0
Girl–Man	0	0	0	1	0	0	1	0	0
Woman–Girl	0	0	0	1	0	0	1	0	0
Girl–Woman	0	0	0	1	0	0	1	0	0

Card 6BM

Seems like it might be a mother and her son, or something. They both have—well, he has a very serious expression on his face ... seems like he's worried, very worried about something. She seems sort of surprised or shocked about something. That expression on her eyes ...

Interviewer: What might it be?

Subject: Maybe trouble with her family, if this were her son—maybe her husband just died or maybe he's dying—doesn't look like he's dead yet, and she's shocked, and she needs her son—and he feels the need, too. He knows she needs him and he needs her too—this is getting confusing, they need each other—they're both worried about her husband, his father—he worries just like her, he's got the same worry ...

Interviewer: What does she feel toward him?

Subject: She wants to tell him to stay, that she needs him—that he can't leave her, not like this—she's thinking she should tell him that.

Interviewer: What does he feel toward her?

Subject: He knows she needs him. She doesn't have to say anything—he's in a bind—he knows she needs him, and he needs her, too, but at the same time, he wants to go at some point, but he's not sure.

TABLE 23.2 Card 6BM Scoring

Dyad	Undiff	Int-Be	Int-Nobe	SepFS	SepFO	DisOR	Dep	Inj	InjFul
She to He	1	0	1	1	0	0	1	0	0
He to She	1	0	0	0	0	0	1	0	0

Card 7GF

Mother and daughter ... I guess she's reading from a book ... The girl is dreaming about the story her mother is reading to her. It's some sort of fairy tale, a fantasy and the girl is dreaming about it.

Interviewer: And the mother?

Subject: She's doing her job as mother, she's enjoying what she's doing, well not enjoying, but it isn't bothering her to read the story. What's bothering her is she's thinking the daughter is far off in dreamland somewhere, thinking of her future. The mother knows the girl will leave her someday, and she's not happy about it. Her husband may already be dead or left her, and the daughter is all she's got, and she's going to lose her, too. She's not happy—she's doesn't know what she's going to do when the daughter isn't with her anymore. She's thinking her daughter will get married someday and forget about her; she'll lose her to her husband, and the mother will be all alone.

Interviewer: What are the daughter's thoughts and feelings toward the mother?

Subject: She's not aware of what her mother is worried about, thinking about—she's oblivious, she's far off in fantasyland, not thinking about the mother.

Card 7BM

Father and son ... They're conferring about some important matter—say business or something. Maybe in this situation it seems that the older man is wiser and yet the son has to

TABLE 23.3 Card 7GF Scoring

Dyad	Undiff	Int-Be	Int-Nobe	SepFS	SepFO	DisOR	Dep	Inj	InjFul
Mother to Daughter	0	0	0	1	0	1	1	0	0
Daughter to Mother	0	0	0	0	0	0	0	0	0

make the decision, and he's looking towards the son because maybe he's maybe he's old enough to have a family, and he's ... in this situation, and the father's not sure he's going to make the right choice and he's going to screw up life for the family, so the father's telling him, trying to get his attention so he can tell him where he's going wrong, what he's not thinking about, but the son doesn't seem interested; he's got his own ideas and he's not listening, and the father tells him what course of action he needs to pursue, where his thoughts are going wrong, but the son is not going to listen. It could be a disaster.

Interviewer: Father's thoughts and feelings?
Subject: Frustrated because the son won't listen to him; he feels helpless; he can't do anything.
Interviewer: Son's thoughts and feelings?
Subject: He's on his own course—he's not really paying attention to the father. He's a little bullheaded.

TABLE 23.4 Card 7BM Scoring

Dyad	Undiff	Int-Be	Int-Nobe	SepFS	SepFO	DisOR	Dep	Inj	InjFul
Father to Son	0	1	1	0	0	0	0	1	0
Son to Father	0	0	0	0	0	0	0	0	0

Card 10

I guess that's a couple. They look like they're about 45 or so.... I've got to put this into a situation. I'll make one up.... It looks like they're older and maybe their kid is getting married or something, and even though they're very happy, they're distressed.... Their baby's growing up. They're happy because they lived together for so long; finally their kid's growing up.

Interviewer: Thoughts and feelings of the woman?
Subject: They're both thinking they don't have their child anymore—their baby's leaving them, and they're happy, but they're distressed, sad, upset ...
Interviewer: The man?

TABLE 23.5 Card 10 Scoring

Dyad	Undiff	Int-Be	Int-Nobe	SepFS	SepFO	DisOR	Dep	Inj	InjFul
Man to Woman	1	0	0	0	0	0	1	0	0
Woman to Man	1	0	0	0	0	0	1	0	0
Man to Daughter	0	0	0	1	0	0	1	0	0
Daughter to Man	0	0	0	0	0	0	0	0	0
Woman to Daughter	0	0	0	1	0	0	1	0	0
Daughter to Woman	0	0	0	0	0	0	0	0	0

Subject: Same thing—distressed, his baby's growing up, they don't have her at home anymore. The kid gets married, and they're left alone with each other—it's a different stage of their life, they live it out.

Interviewer: How does the daughter feel, think?

Subject: She's thinking about her husband-to-be and her life in the future; she's not thinking about her parents. She knows they're upset, but she's focused on her husband and her new life—they're left alone.

MAPS

The door's open, and this is a mother and father, I guess, and their son and he's leaving, and uh ... The car is out in front. He's going someplace, and he's dressed up, so ... maybe he's going to church tomorrow. Anyhow, he talks about what he's going to be doing, telling his parents. They're listening; he's independent, judging from the way he's gesturing—from his parents. Yet judging from the expression on his parents' face, they're not angry with what he's saying.... His independence, whatever he's going to do. Do I have to get more specific—where he's going?

Interviewer: If you could, please—where he's going, what he going to do, what he might be saying ...

Subject: He's going to take a trip or something, a vacation. His parents aren't in favor of the idea—they don't want him to be so independent. The father is telling him not to do it, that he's not ready.... But he thinks he's old enough and he's going to make the right decision, and the parents are going to accept it. They have no choice. He'll go on the trip, and he'll be fine.

Interviewer: Thoughts and feelings of the son?

TABLE 23.6 MAPS Scoring

Dyad	Undiff	Int-Be	Int-Nobe	SepFS	SepFO	DisOR	Dep	Inj	InjFul
Father to Son	0	1	1	0	1	0	0	1	0
Son to Father	0	0	0	0	0	0	0	0	0
Mother to Son	0	0	1	0	1	0	0	0	0
Son to Mother	0	0	0	0	0	0	0	0	0
Father to Mother	1	0	0	0	0	0	1	0	0
Mother to Father	1	0	0	0	0	0	0	0	0

Subject: He's thinking—he's a college student—he's thinking, "I've earned my own money, and it's my own car, and I feel I'm old enough to make the decision to go to California with my friend. My parents don't agree with me, but I'm going."

Interviewer: Thoughts and feelings of the father?

Subject: He thinks the son is being too rash, trying to be too independent—he's afraid for him, he's afraid he's not old enough to take care of himself, that he could be in danger.... He's worried.

Interviewer: Thoughts and feeling of the mother?

Subject: Just like the father—he's too young, too rash, he could get into trouble, not old enough for what he's trying to do.

Interviewer: Thoughts and feelings of the mother and father toward each other?

Subject: They agree with each other. They're glad they're thinking the same way.

☐ Reference

Murray, H. A. (1943). *Thematic Apperception Test.* Cambridge, MA: Harvard University.

24

CHAPTER

The TAT Ambitious-Narcissistic Style Scale

David W. Harder and Deborah F. Greenwald

Abstract

This chapter describes the conceptual background and development of the Harder Thematic Apperception Test (TAT) Ambitious-Narcissistic Character Style Scale, which was constructed to assess ambitious-narcissism—an interrelated set of personality dispositions involving highly ambitious, assertive, self-confident, vigorous, and dominant behavior. Based upon clinical writings and observations, five components of the ambitious-narcissistic style were articulated, including Intrusiveness/Thrusting, Exhibitionistic/Voyeuristic, Urethral Excitation, Mastery/Competence/Power, and Self-Potency. Criteria were written for scoring these components and two allied, but conceptually different, TAT story themes, Oedipal and Autonomy. Only one published study (N = 40, all males) reports use of the scale, which showed promising relationships with analogous scales developed for an early memories test and the Rorschach. In addition, the TAT measure correlated significantly with an interview measure of ambitious-narcissism.

Description of System

Conceptual Framework

The Thematic Apperception Test (TAT) instrument described here was designed to measure a broad, yet relatively specific, type of character structure or personality style, a characteristic way of experiencing and presenting the self, termed *ambitious-narcissism.* This style has many characteristics that, in extreme form, merit a DSM-IV (American Psychiatric Association, 1994) diagnosis of narcissistic personality disorder but can also occur in much milder form. Because this narcissistic style involves so much ambitious striving, it seems to propel its possessors toward positions of prominence and thus often appears in well-known figures. In some cases, however, these tendencies can be problematic, either for the individual or those around him or her. A more systematic means of assessing ambitious-narcissistic tendencies can aid in understanding the origin and maintenance of the style and its components and in the prevention of ill-advised choices that might result from them.

The concept of character or personality style is derived from ego-psychological and psychodynamic theory, referring to habitual modes of perceiving, understanding, and reacting to the world (Green, 1967; Johnson, 1994; Josephs, 1992; Mayman, 1968; Reich, 1933). As such, it is a typical mode of overall ego operation, a relatively stable generalized pattern of functioning across numerous situations and internal psychic states. It implies a readiness or disposition to perceive and respond to the environment, to relate to others, and to behave cross-situationally. Thus, character style refers to a dynamic interrelationship of personality elements, including important motivational needs, characteristic coping and defensive patterns, usual perceptual and cognitive tendencies, typical emotional experiences, and preferred interaction patterns—that, in psychodynamic terms, also reflect internalized object relations (Krohn, 1973; Mayman & Faris, 1960). This dynamic organization of aspects of personality helps the individual to interpret ongoing experience in an anxiety-reducing, self-perpetuating manner that provides consistency in behavior and self-experience, such that adaptive paths toward goals are provided, positive self-esteem is maintained, and dysphoric affect levels are kept manageable. Here the terms *character style* and *personality style* are used interchangeably.

The notion of ambitious-narcissistic style has been derived from the reports of psychodynamic clinicians, chiefly Reich (1933), who described some male patients as exhibiting a particular, interrelated set of character traits. These individuals appeared as highly ambitious, assertive, self-confident, vigorous, dominant, and egocentric, with strong motivations to emphasize mastery, potency, and physical attractiveness. Reich named this style the *phallic-narcissistic* character, for its presumed psychogenic origins in the phallic psychosexual stage of development. Although Reich did not specifically exclude women from exhibiting this style, he described it only in males.

Other psychodynamic clinicians have also observed configurations of personality elements that seem to be aspects of the style. Fenichel (1945) and Murray (1955) emphasized the role of urethral excitation fantasy themes in persons with strong ambitions and wishes to be admired. Bibring (1953) linked aspirations toward competitive dominance with wishes to be admired and repeated attempts to demonstrate prowess. Mayman (1968) pointed out that interpersonal intrusiveness and preferences for rapid locomotion through the environment were often associated with competitiveness and bodily exhibitionism.

In the construction of the TAT scale described here the term *ambitious-narcissistic* style was used in place of Reich's *phallic-exhibitionistic* style. The first term is more descriptive of the observable elements of the personality pattern, which could be separated from theoretical speculations about the developmental origins of the style and could be applied more readily to both males and females. Although the style has generally been described as occurring only in men (Fenichel, 1945; Murray, 1955; Reich, 1933), it is assumed here that it might well appear in women also, particularly in cultures that allow, or even encourage, occupational success and autonomy in women as well as men. Certainly, empirical research (Butcher, 1998; Rhodewalt & Eddings, 2002; Simmonds, 2001; Wallace & Baumeister, 2002) has reported similar elements in narcissistic attitudes and self-descriptions in both sexes, some of which would seem to reflect this particular variant of narcissistic style, although some research (e.g., Rathvon & Holmstrom, 1996) suggests that it should appear more prominently in males.

This character style can arise in healthy as well as pathological individuals, with its intensity and centrality constituting the determining factors in its pathognomonic significance. In fact, strong elements of such a style can often be an advantage in the attainment of personally important and socially prominent achievements (Campbell, 2001; Harder, 1975; Reich, 1933). However, an extreme prominence of this character style can produce a lack of intimate relationships, alienation from broader social networks, and avoidance of real achievement to protect self-esteem (Bursten, 1973; Reich, 1933). Adler (1924) described another example of this defensive phenomenon, which he called *masculine protest* for both male and female patients, who exhibited exaggerated, stereotypically masculine styles: highly competitive, hard driving, interpersonally dominant, and aggressive.

Ambitious-narcissism could be thought of as one subtype among several narcissistic personality styles, all of which include traits of egocentricity, inflated self-importance (often with a sense of entitlement and expectations of excessive admiration from others), and, frequently, devaluation or disdain of others (Bursten, 1973; Morf & Rhodewalt, 2001; Pulver, 1970; Rothstein, 1979). In its most extreme forms such styles would manifest the pathological characteristics detailed by Reich (1960), Kohut (1971), Kernberg (1970, 1974), and others and would merit a modern-day DSM-IV diagnosis of narcissistic personality disorder. In less extreme forms such character patterns would be distinctive but not at pathological levels. Empirical studies have supported clinical notions that self-enhancement (e.g., Raskin, Novacek, & Hogan, 1991; Simmonds, 2001; Wallace & Baumeister, 2002) or protection of vulnerable self-esteem (e.g., Raskin et al., 1991; Rhodewalt & Eddings, 2002; Smalley & Stake, 1996) are core motivations that underlie narcissistic styles. Research has also reported strong correlations between narcissism and anger or blame directed at others (Butcher, 1998; Rathvon & Holmstrom, 1996), consistent with the observed tendencies of narcissists to devalue and disdain others. In addition, the distinctive characteristics of the ambitious subtype of narcissism would be the emphases on competitiveness and demonstration of potency, prowess, or bodily beauty.

Because a projective test such as the TAT is presumed to reflect the typical personality tendencies of the person providing the protocol, and there is ample empirical evidence to support this presumption (e.g., Koff, 1999; Peterson & Ulrey, 1994; Westen, Lohr, Silk, Gold, & Kerber, 1990), it was expected that the TAT responses would prove to be an excellent indicator of ambitious-narcissistic style. Such a coding scheme could be useful in understanding the personality dynamics of many people in prominent and leadership positions, for example, in business, the military, athletics, or politics (Reich, 1933), as well as in other walks of life.

Scoring Categories

The various aspects of ambitious-narcissistic style just described were organized into five major components (Harder, 1979) that could be expected to appear as TAT story themes: (1) intrusive/thrusting themes, reflective of aggressive, vigorous assertion; (2) exhibitionism/voyeurism, reflecting pleasure in being admired for bodily beauty; (3) urethral excitation, symbolized by gushing liquids; (4) mastery/competence/power (i.e., pleasure in prowess, achievement, competitive victory, dominance, and striving); and

TABLE 24.1 Scoring Categories for the Harder TAT Ambitious-Narcissistic Style Scale

Category	Description
	Main Categories
Intrusiveness/Thrusting	Aggressive, vigorous assertiveness
Exhibitionism/Voyeurism	Being admired for bodily beauty
Urethral Excitation	Indicated by gushing liquids
Mastery/Competence/Power	Pleasure in prowess, achievement, competitive victory, dominance, and striving
Self-Potency	Admiration or exposure of a phallus or a blatant symbolic substitute
	Ancillary Categories
Oedipal (Oed)	Oedipal themes without explicitly ambitious-narcissistic or "phallic" content
Autonomy (Aut)	Autonomy concerns; distinguished from ambitious-narcissism
0 (Zero)	Ambitious-narcissism is absent, or such themes are so muted or mixed in with other content that no score is justified

(5) self-potency pleasure, symbolized by admiration of, or exposure of, a phallus or of relatively blatant symbolic substitutes.

A subscale for each of the five components was created (Table 24.1). Examples of positively and negatively toned TAT stories that reflected each of these components were written to serve as anchor points for the coding done independently by clinical raters. Examples from pilot participants and clinical case records are included in chapter 25 in this volume and contain each of the five components, at three intensity levels. Definitions were also included for the classification of TAT stories showing Oedipal issues (Oed) without ambitious-narcissistic/phallic characteristics, autonomy (Aut) concerns separate from ambitious-narcissism, and the absence of ambitious-narcissistic themes (0) (Table 24.1). The Oedipal and autonomy story criteria were included to help users of the scale distinguish between such story themes and the sometimes similar-sounding ambitious-narcissistic stories. Stories that include Oedipal or autonomy themes, which may have some similarities to ambitious-narcissism themes, are seen as reflecting essentially distinct personality dispositions. In the case of Oedipal themes, the focus of the respondent is on winning a competitive struggle to attain a prize, such as the affection of a love object. Similarly, autonomy themes reflect the need to assert the ability of the self to do things one's own way rather than to demonstrate their special qualities or to win power, admiration, or envy.

Raters were instructed to judge the subject's psychological investment in the ambitious-narcissistic content and the mode represented by the story as a whole. Each TAT story was to receive a primary code for one of the ambitious-narcissistic (AN) components or an Oed, Aut, or 0 rating. If an AN code seemed justified, the rater was then expected to assign an intensity rating from +1 to +3, with +3 representing a particularly striking ambitious-narcissistic story. If more than one AN component was present, the rater decided which theme appeared primary, based on the intensity of the theme, and scored that on a 1-to-3 basis. The secondary theme would then automatically be given an intensity of level 1.

Stories with a clear protagonist that ended badly or expressed a general negative tone were given a minus (–) rating and not counted in the total score representing ambitious-narcissism, because it was believed that such stories indicate generally unsuccessful attempts or rejected temptations to use the character style. For example, a failure, such as in the tale of Icarus, may indicate that the storyteller is creating a cautionary moral tale, suggesting that ambitious-narcissism leads to difficulties. Though such stories may indicate attempted or tempting ambitious-narcissism, it is likely that this failed variant would show sufficient behavioral differences to warrant a distinct category.

If a TAT story had no clear protagonist and the outcome indicated that one character's ambitious-narcissism was successful whereas another's was not, then the story should be coded for both positive and negative AN components. The clinical raters would then decide whether the positive AN intensity outweighed the negative. If so, the story could still be given an overall rating of +1 or +2.

After first rating the stories independently, the raters resolved disagreements by discussion. Consensus scores for each component were calculated by summing all positively toned intensity ratings in that category across the 10 TAT cards administered to each participant, and a total ambitious-narcissism score was created by summing across all five components.

☐ Research Evidence

Validity

All validity and reliability data for the TAT Ambitious-Narcissism Scale derive from the original study ($N = 40$) conducted by Harder (1979). As described by Harder (1979), the TAT Ambitious-Narcissism variable correlated significantly with comparable measures of ambitious-narcissism developed for two other projective tests, the Rorschach ($r = .39, p < .05$) and Mayman's (1974) Early Memories Test ($r = .38, p < .05$). In addition, the TAT scale successfully differentiated ($p < .01$) a group of men rated as ambitious-narcissistic in style from a group rated as nonambitious by three clinically trained raters—one working directly from interview interaction and the other two from verbatim participant self-description.

This TAT measure is a potentially useful tool for the assessment of ambitious-narcissistic personality style, even for groups other than the white, upper-middle-class males investigated so far. Its main advantage is the ability to assess a personality style for which there is currently no other measure. Because this style is not limited to pathological cases, the instrument has much research promise for studies of other correlates of the ambitious-narcissistic character style as they occur across the general population. However, the scale is clearly in need of further use by other investigators with other samples to verify fully the instrument's reliability and validity.

Generalizability

The main limitations of the scale are two. First, there exists only one reliability and validity study so far, and that study did not include women. Second, the scoring system is complex and requires practice by raters not already clinically familiar with the psychodynamically inspired constructs reflected in the scale components. These observations probably make the scale more readily useful for research as compared with clinical purposes, but for someone familiar with it, clinical usage is a distinct possibility.

Reliability

The sample consisted of generally well-functioning males who were juniors and seniors (between 20 and 22 years old) at a prestigious Midwestern state university. All volunteers were Caucasian, from predominantly upper-middle-class homes, with a grade-point average slightly above the university mean. None reported being in personal counseling during the previous year. They volunteered in response to campus advertisements for paid participation in a research study of self-concept. The first 40 from the initial pool of 105 volunteers who showed medium to high self-esteem were included. This sample supplied ample variance for a first examination of the ambitious style variable. Ten TAT cards (1, 4, 8BM, 9BM, 14, 17BM, 13MF, 7BM, 15, and 12M) were used. Although scoring manual examples included stories drawn from other cards as well, the 10 chosen for the study included those commonly used with men in many clinical administrations of the TAT. Two cards, 17BM and 8BM, were expected to have special potential to draw ambitious-narcissistic themes from men.

The three raters in the original study were all advanced doctoral students in a psychodynamically oriented clinical psychology program who had had at least four years of half- to full-time clinical experience. Pearson product–moment interrater reliability coefficients were calculated for each of the five component subscales of the TAT Ambitious-Narcissism instrument and for the overall total scale score. The total score and four of the five subscales exhibited acceptable interrater coefficients above .70 (ranging from .74 to .94). Only the self-potency subscale showed a disappointingly low correlation ($r = .50$) among the raters, probably, at least in part, because this subscale was used very infrequently. The most frequently used components (totaling 94% of the non-zero consensus ratings) were mastery/competence/power (40%), intrusiveness/thrusting (37%), and exhibitionism/voyeurism (17%). Percentage of exact agreements for all TAT subscale ratings between pairs of clinician judges reached 60%, with agreements on the use of zero (absence of an AN subscale theme) at 75% and acceptable agreements (that is, within one intensity scale point) at 74%.

☐ Future Research Needed

The first study (Harder, 1979) of the scale found acceptable levels of interrater reliability. However, since ambitious-narcissistic style is assumed to be an enduring trait, test–retest reliability studies are necessary. An additional obvious area for future research is the investigation of the extent to which the scale can be usefully employed with groups other than young male college students with high career ambitions. Among males the scale still requires validation with individuals of other ages and demographic groups. A major question in this connection is how the scale might be adapted for use with women, among whom ambitious-narcissistic traits are also expected to appear in a normally distributed pattern. It may be that women will show different themes than those found in males, and the relative importance of the five scale components may differ by gender. TAT cards other than the male-oriented set employed by Harder (1979) might eventually be verified as more useful with women. Even in male samples, modified card sets might prove more effective. For example, a post hoc examination of pilot subject examples in the scoring manual suggested that card 11 has particular promise for the assessment of AN among men. Another important gender question is the relative prominence of ambitious-narcissism in men and women.

Further validational work could include studies of clinically diagnosed narcissistic personality disorders and other individuals high in narcissism—assessed, for example, with instruments such as the Narcissistic Personality Inventory (Raskin & Hall, 1979, 1981) or the Butcher (1998) Treatment Planning Inventory—compared with decidedly nonnarcissistic persons. Although narcissism as a general trait would be broader than the specific ambitious-narcissism variant discussed here, it could reasonably be predicted that narcissistic groups should show more ambitious-narcissism than low-narcissism groups. Similar predictions could be tested for those in professions involving the limelight (e.g., politicians, performers, athletes) versus those in other careers (e.g., teachers, accountants, engineers, nurses). Studies might also test behavioral predictions, such as whether high levels of ambitious-narcissism would be associated with other relevant personality variables or behaviors (e.g., the willingness to perform in front of a group or the amount of speaking time a person would demand in group interaction settings). Another empirically uninvestigated aspect of the TAT scale to this point is the meaning of negative AN codes—that is, whether they are truly reflective of unsuccessful attempts at maintaining an ambitious-narcissistic style, as clinical observation suggests, or whether they reflect the style as effectively as the positively scored codes.

Finally, cross-cultural research could test the hypothesis that ambitious-narcissism would appear more prominently in individualistic societies compared with societies that emphasize a more collective identity.

☐ References

Adler, A. (1924). *The practice and theory of individual psychology.* Translated by P. Radin. New York: Harcourt, Brace.

American Psychiatric Association (1994). *Diagnostic and Statistical Manual of Mental Disorders—fourth edition (DSM-IV).* Washington, DC: APA.

Bibring, E. (1953). The mechanisms of depression. In P. Greenacre (Ed.), *Affective disorders* (pp. 13–48). New York: International Universities Press.

Bursten, B. (1973). Some narcissistic personality types. *International Journal of Psychoanalysis, 54,* 287–299.

Butcher, J. N. (1998). *Butcher Treatment Planning Inventory (BTPI): Manual.* San Antonio: Psychological Corporation.

Campbell, W. K. (2001). Is narcissism really so bad? *Psychological Inquiry, 12,* 214–216.

Fenichel, O. (1945). *The psychoanalytic theory of neurosis.* New York: International Universities Press.

Green, B. A. (1967). Character structure and its functions. *Psychoanalytic Review, 54,* 329–354.

Harder, D. W. (1979). The assessment of ambitious-narcissistic character style with three projective tests: The Early Memories, TAT, and Rorschach. *Journal of Personality Assessment, 43,* 23–32.

Johnson, S. M. (1994). *Character styles.* New York: W. W. Norton.

Josephs, L. (1992). *Character structure and the organization of the self.* New York: Columbia University Press.

Kernberg, O. (1970). Factors in the psychoanalytic treatment of narcissistic personalities. *Journal of the American Psychoanalytic Association, 18,* 51–85.

Kernberg, O. (1974). Further contributions to the treatment of narcissistic personalities. *International Journal of Psychoanalysis, 55,* 215–247.

Koff, E. R. (1999). Object relations and defense mechanisms: Related structural personality variables. *Dissertation Abstracts International: Section B: The Sciences & Engineering, 59 (7-B)*: 3754.

Kohut, H. (1971). *The analysis of the self.* New York: International Universities Press.

Krohn, A. D. (1973). Level of object representation in the manifest dream and projective tests—a construct validation study. *Dissertation Abstracts International, 33,* 5520B.

Mayman, M. (1968). Early memories and character structure. *Journal of Projective Techniques and Personality Assessment, 31,* 303–316.

Mayman, M. (1974). *Early memories test manual.* Unpublished manuscript. (Available from Psychological Clinic, 1027 E. Huron St., Ann Arbor, MI 48104).

Mayman, M., & Faris, M. (1960). Early memories as expressions of relationship paradigms. *American Journal of Orthopsychiatry, 30,* 507–520.

Morf, C. C., & Rhodewalt, F. (2001). Unraveling the paradoxes of narcissism: A dynamic self-regulatory processing model. *Psychological Inquiry, 12,* 177–196.

Murray, H. A. (1955). American Icarus. In A. Burton & R. E. Harris (Eds.), *Clinical studies of personality,* (vol. 2) (pp. 615–641). New York: Harper and Row.

Peterson, C., & Ulrey, L. M. (1994). Can explanatory style be scored from TAT protocols? *Personality & Social Psychology Bulletin, 20,* 102–106.

Pulver, S. (1970). Narcissism: The term and the concept. *Journal of the American Psychoanalytic Association, 18,* 309–341.

Raskin, R. N., & Hall, C. S. (1979). A narcissistic personality inventory. *Psychological Reports, 45,* 590.

Raskin, R. N., & Hall, C. S. (1981). The Narcissistic Personality Inventory: Alternate form reliability and further evidence of construct validity. *Journal of Personality Assessment, 45,* 159–162.

Raskin, R., Novacek, J., & Hogan, R. (1991). Narcissism, self-esteem, and defensive self-enhancement.*Journal of Personality, 59,* 19–38.

Reich, A. (1960). Pathologic forms of self-esteem regulation. *Psychoanalytic Study of the Child, 15,* 215–232.

Rathvon, N., & Holmstrom, R.W. (1996). An MMPI-2 portrait of narcissism. *Journal of Personality Assessment, 66,* 1–19.

Reich, W. (1933). *Character analysis.* London: Vision Press.

Rhodewalt, F., & Eddings, S.K. (2002). Narcissus reflects: Memory distortion in response to ego-relevant feedback among high- and low-narcissistic men. *Journal of Research in Personality, 36,* 97–116.

Rothstein, A. (1979). An exploration of the diagnostic term narcissistic personality disorder. *Journal of the American Psychoanalytic Association, 27,* 893–912.

Simmonds, J. E. (2001). Gender comparisons on the expression of narcissistic traits, dominance/submission and shame. *Dissertation Abstracts International: Section B: The Sciences and Engineering, 61 (12-B):* 6721.

Smalley, R. L., & Stake, J. E. (1996). Evaluating sources of ego-threatening feedback: Self-esteem and narcissism effects. *Journal of Research in Personality, 30,* 483–495.

Wallace, H. M., & Baumeister, R. F. (2002). The performance of narcissists rises and falls with the perceived opportunity for glory. *Journal of Personality and Social Psychology, 82,* 819–834.

Westen, D., Lohr, N., Silk, K. R., Gold, L., & Kerber, K. (1990). Object relations and social cognitions in borderlines, major depressives, and normals: A Thematic Apperception Test analysis. *Journal of Consulting and Clinical Psychology, 58,* 355–364.

25

CHAPTER

Scoring Manual for the TAT Ambitious-Narcissistic Style Scale

David W. Harder and Deborah F. Greenwald

Introduction

This chapter provides criteria and examples for scoring the Thematic Apperception Test (TAT) for the ambitious-narcissistic character style, an interrelated set of personality tendencies that typically result in highly ambitious, assertive, self-confident, vigorous, and dominant behavior (Harder, 1979). This construct was derived from earlier descriptions of psychodynamic clinicians, chiefly Reich (1933), who described male patients as exhibiting this set of character traits, which he termed *phallic-narcissistic,* for its presumed psychogenic origins in the phallic psychosexual stage of development. *Ambitious-narcissistic style* was used in place of Reich's term in the construction of the TAT scale, because it was more descriptive of the observable elements of the personality pattern, which could be separated from theoretical speculations about the developmental origins of the style. Further, consistent with clinical observations, it was expected that women as well as men would demonstrate this style.

Criteria are presented for the five components of ambitious-narcissistic (AN) content—intrusiveness/thrusting (ANi/t), exhibitionism/voyeurism (ANev), urethral excitation (ANue), mastery/competence/power (ANm), and self-potency (ANsp)—and two themes, Oedipal (Oed) and autonomy (Aut), which are not scored for ambitious-narcissism.

Administration

Format and Stimuli

The standard TAT administration (Newmark, 1996) is used. The examiner asks, "What is happening in the picture? What is (are) the character(s) thinking and feeling? What led up to this? What will the outcome be?" There is no specific additional questioning procedure or follow-up associated with this scoring system, other than that typically used to obtain a complete story. Each story is recorded verbatim, and the transcripts are scored by trained clinical raters. Thus, this scoring system can be applied to any TAT story collected with standard instructions or to other narrative material.

Scoring Process

In coding TAT stories for ambitious-narcissistic style, each story should be viewed as a metaphorical molar unit that is read and interpreted intuitively and psychodynamically. The characteristic relational paradigms and self-representations of the participant should be considered empathically to arrive at a judgment about the extent to which the story content is ambitious-narcissistic. Content thema or story elements that are probably ambitious-narcissistic are not, in and of themselves, indications that the story should be given an ambitious-narcissistic main code. The participant's psychological investment in the ambitious-narcissistic content must be assessed and the mode represented by the story as a whole.

If there is a clear protagonist in the story, the respondent's psychological investment is assumed to be most identifiable by the ambitious-narcissistic elements enacted or experienced by that character. Stories with a clear protagonist that end badly or embody a general negative tone are to be given a minus (–) rating, because it is assumed that such stories indicate generally unsuccessful attempts or rejected temptations to use the character style.

However, if a story has no clear protagonist and the outcome indicates that one important character's ambitious-narcissism was successful whereas another's was not, then the story should be coded for both positive and negative AN components.

First, assign a main code to each story. If there is a psychologically invested ambitious-narcissistic theme (as defined following), assign one of the five ambitious-narcissistic content codes, and, if the story outcome is positive, determine the intensity rating of +1, +2, or +3 according to the following schedule: +1, probably an ambitious-narcissistic story, but not certain; +2, definitely an ambitious-narcissistic story, or a +3 that is said to occur in a dream or daydream; or +3, a particularly striking ambitious-narcissistic story.

If a story that is positive in tone and would ordinarily garner a +1, +2, or +3 AN score also includes a negative aspect, the story's score should be lowered one point.

If the story outcome is negative for the protagonist, the theme is given a negative rating (–) with no score for intensity. In stories with no clear protagonist and central characters who show both positive and negative elements, then the decision must be made as to whether the positive intensity outweighs the negative, in which case the story might merit a +1 or +2 score (but never a +3). If there is no ambitious-narcissistic content to the story, determine if there is content that warrants an Oed or an Aut score or if it should only receive a zero for no ambitious-narcissistic, Oed, or Aut main theme. Finally, in stories that merit a positive AN component score, if some other AN component also seems noticeably present, add this component as a secondary code with a +1 intensity.

Scoring Summary

When any of the five ambitious-narcissistic themes are present, code them according to content and assign an intensity rating of +1, +2, or +3, if the story has a positive outcome, or – if the story has a negative outcome for the protagonist. A story may be scored for more than one positively toned AN component, with secondary components receiving +1 ratings. After all stories are scored for AN, the intensity ratings of all positively coded stories are summed, for each subcategory and for total ambitious-narcissism to create five subcategory scores and one overall score. Negatively toned stories, scored –, are not subtracted from the positive ambitious-narcissism totals.

Scoring Categories

Intrusiveness/Thrusting (ANi/t)

- Use of phallic-locomotor conveyance, powerful vehicles
- Exploration of new territory; yearning for adventure; pioneer in his or her field
- Vigorous physical activity or movement, especially of a propulsive, forward-moving sort; emphasis on speed through space
- Mischievous baiting, aggressive teasing, especially as to taunt, challenge, or disparage, and to force a response from another character
- Giving of symbolic sexualized gifts to partner
- Sexualized relationships, if aggressiveness or active pursuit of the partner is emphasized or strongly implied
- Negative (minus score) stories: Any of the thema just noted, if they result in physical injury, narcissistic insult (e.g., embarrassment, shame), or physical punishment; failed sexual aggressiveness

Scoring Examples

Card 9BM: This is a group of racers—motorcyclists. They had a helluva intense race an hour or two before, but now that the competition is all over, they've been drinking and having a good time, telling all their stories about how I passed Jim on that curve or how I messed up Mark with all that mud I sprayed on the far turn. They're just resting now after all the drinking and joshing each other.

Score: ANi/t +3

Card 11: Cool! It's a quest, that's what it is. A swordsman, a sage, a midget magician, and a slave are on a quest for maybe a cup or a tea kettle, something that's needed to gain the love of the maiden, to get her heart, so maybe it's a rose in a cup. And it's a long, arduous quest with many dangers. And one obstacle is they're going down the road and see this horrible monster. It will attack them but they are well equipped to deal with it, will kill it and continue on their quest.

Score: ANi/t +3

Card 17GF: She's looking down at the boatmen, dreaming of sailing off to foreign lands. This young girl is brave and plucky, and she'll travel widely. One day, she'll become a well-known anthropologist.

Score: ANi/t +2

Card 17BM: He's climbing up, slowly but surely, his strength and determination taking him up the rope to the top. He's racing to be the first up, and he'll win even though he's not certain he can, because he's the strongest man there.

Score: ANi/t +1

Card 6GF: The young maiden was surprised by the voice—a strong man's voice, and she turned and noticed the unfamiliar face. It was a party, and as a single woman she hoped to meet some handsome young men. "But *not* this old guy," she murmured, looking disdainfully at the older man.

Score: ANi/t –

Exhibitionism/Voyeurism (ANev)

- Pleasure or pride in bodily display, including dancing, singing, or performing before an audience of potential admirers; showing off such that the self is admired or desired
- Sexually tinged curiosity; description of the physical attractiveness of a character's body; exhibitionism or showing off of one's body (but not intentional exposure of sexual organs or intentional voyeurism, which should be scored under ANsp)
- Seductiveness, sexual provocativeness, by being attractive, sexually appealing, or endearing. The emphasis here should be on attracting a sexual object rather than on aggressively pursuing one, as it would be for ANi/t
- Negative (minus score) stories
    - Any of the activities or behaviors just described that result in physical injury, narcissistic insult, or physical pain; attempts to be sexually attractive that result in rejection or humiliation

Scoring Examples

Card 4: Looks like a scene from a bad movie, or actually a modern parody of an old movie.... He's a rough and rugged hero type. Actually he has an ironic sense of humor to him, and maybe he's a war hero or has the reputation of being one ... and here's a woman in the background who's partially undressed. He's supposedly wounded, but not really, and for some reason the only hospital nearby was a woman's hospital. And he's being treated there and, because of his good looks, and because it's a woman's hospital they don't care too much about, you know, their underwear or whatever. And they haven't changed things 'cause this guy is there. And the nurse is making advances at this guy, which he's happy for.

Score: ANev+3

Card 2: There's a serious, studious woman, who's attracted to this muscular, macho man, who knows she's attracted to him. She knows she can't have him, and she wants to educate him. His wife has found out that he's been visited by the woman. She's feeling guilty and realizes that she has to stop. The wife has everything under control. Keeps an eye on her husband 24 hours a day. Man pretends not to care.

Score: ANev +1 (score would be ANev +2, except that outcome is almost negative)

Card 13MF: This man was going on the train at Penn Station and was attracted to this woman he saw looking at him at the newspaper shop. She started giving him the eye, kind of a come-hither look, so he went after her, even though he should have been going home. She fawns on him and draws him on and even though he's suspicious, he gets a hotel room with her. And they have sex, and she really just finds him attractive and is sexually free, but then she has a heart attack and dies; and now he's real sorry he ever got into this mess.

Score: ANev –

Urethral Excitation (ANue)

- Exciting themes of fires, great heat, firefighters, setting fires, fire fighting, or fire-setting materials
- Excitement over floods, waterfalls, gushing liquids, dams, or other structures holding back rushing liquids; use of phallic-urethral objects (e.g., water hose)
- Negative (minus score) stories: Any of these themes resulting in destruction or injury; ineffective structures against destructive floods or rushing liquids, such as dams that break, flooded levees.

Scoring Examples

Card 17BM: This is a firefighter, and he's going up a rope to get to the top of a burning building, so his other firemen helpers can throw him a hose, so that he will blast the fire with water and put it out.

Score: ANue +3

Card 5: This is a mother who is looking for her little girl, who is supposed to be doing homework in this room. But, instead, the girl has slipped outside and right now is having a wonderful time watering the flowers with the garden hose.

Score: ANue +2

Card 16: This is what it looks like when the gusher at Yellowstone overdoes it. (Laughs) Tourists going up to the Big Geyser, and it doesn't go off, even though it's supposed to be regular. They wait and wait, edge closer and closer, and are just about to give up when the thing blows, and they're surrounded by all this water and foam. And they get worried at first that they'll get burned by the steam, but it doesn't feel that way at all. Just can't see anything.

Score: ANue +1

Card 11: There are people escaping a flood that knocked out a dam in the valley. And this is in medieval times when people didn't travel far from their villages, so they're pretty scared to come up the mountains and see what kind of creatures live up there. And, wow, there are some real weird animals and monsters up there. The waters are rising in the valley, so they have no choice but to go on, but they're trapped—eaten if they go on, drowned if they go back.

Score: ANue –

Mastery/Competence/Power (ANm)

- This category involves success in a struggle, either with competitors or impediments that are overcome or mastered: competitive struggles; battles or struggles with a sense of victory highlighted (if the emphasis is on defeated party, score ANm–); characters who assert dominance over others or conquer impersonal obstacles; success in proving oneself as good as or better than someone else; standing up for one's honor

- The presence of a powerful figure, one worthy of admiration because of skills or behavior

- Masterful, powerful, or successful handling of a new or difficult situation; heroic actions

- A novice, younger person, or apprentice living up to the standards or achievements of a model

- Negative (minus score) stories: Primary identification figure in the story is defeated, dominated, injured, physically or narcissistically, in a competitive struggle, or battle; a new or difficult situation is handled badly or unsuccessfully; attempted emulation of a highly valued model ends badly

Scoring Examples

Card 11: Several people are trying to escape the wrath of the dragon and cross the bridge to safety. They are very scared but very brave, because they have risked their lives to save a prisoner trying to escape captivity. The dragon slipped and fell on the rocks below while exiting the cave, allowing the men enough time to reach safety.

Score: ANm +3

Card 8BM: "How I want to be like Dr. Bertrand!" the young Chinese student activist was dreaming. "The Red Army needs me," he continued to dream, as he just got the acceptance by the medical school of St. John's College, the best school in the country. The thought got him all excited. He could almost see the legendary doctor tirelessly working in the tents.

Score: ANm +3

Card 1: This is a young boy who likes to play the violin. He wasn't that good, but he always studied his music. One day he wanted to play the violin like a master, and he wanted to do all the classical music, and he does and gets rich.

Score: ANm +2

Card 8BM: Well, this is a young boy and it's a representation of his thoughts or his past.... And he recalls the presence.... The man with the knife is his father, and the man standing next to his father is his brother or uncle. He comes from a medical family, and he thinks that the highest calling always was to be a doctor or a surgeon. And the patient is just a patient having surgery, and he's seeing a representation of surgery and medicine, which is good and purity, and the rifle is, I'm not sure, so I'll have to invent that, maybe the way the patient got hurt. He sees himself as not going in the way of the goodness of his past, but taking on an aggressiveness, so maybe he became a corporate banker or like a lawyer, and ... less compassion but a lot of success anyway.

Score: ANm +2 (the negative tone reduces this story from a +3 to a +2)

Card 13B: Sitting under the hot afternoon sun of the West, the little boy is waiting, after school, for his dad, a cowboy to come home. Through the dust he sees the shadow of his strong father. "Will I grow up to become just like him?" he pondered. Eager to grow up.

Score: ANm +1

Card 7BM: "Do you see the man in the dark three-piece suit?" the boss said to his private aid, who was always ready for action. "I want you to follow him and note down who he talks to in this cocktail party. He is an agent from the opposition," he whispered, without showing expression on his face. "Espionage is his intent, and we will do our best to foil his plans."

Score: ANm +1 (because the outcome is uncertain, the score is not +2 or +3)

Card 17BM: In gym class Rod was always picked last for sports. He wondered why. He knew that he wasn't very athletic but felt it was more because he had no friends and was always the new kid on the block. He had moved 13 times. He had no allies. In high school, he looked at his chubby exterior and decided to change that in order to get a better personal life. When he changed that, he found that he was still picked last. In a spur of anger, Rod went to climb the rope and yelled at the other students. "Look what I can do but you pick me last." They were astonished, and he finally started to get picked earlier.

Score: ANm +1 (The negative tone here, despite the positive ending, leads to a low rating)

Card 8GF: A young woman is thinking about what to wear on an interview for a managerial position. She wants to make a good impression but doesn't want to look too old-fashioned or too flashy. She picks out a dress suit but is indecisive. Should she wear the double-breasted blue suit or her red dress, which makes a powerful statement, a controlling and in-charge statement? She goes with the red dress.

Score: ANm +1

Card 11: This is Middle Earth, and the man is a hobbit. He's looking over the edge of a cliff, and it's real dark at the bottom. He needs to find away to get into the dragon's lair. He's scared because of the dragon and the height, and he's also excited because of the riches that the dragon guards. He enters the dragon's chamber by running up the dragon's tail. The dragon sees him and burns him.

Score: ANm –

Self-Potency (ANsp)

- Explicit, intentional sexual exhibitionism or voyeurism
- Admiration or envy of others' sexual attributes or objects, actual or symbolic
- Size or strength comparisons of characters that reflect favorably on the primary identification figure
- Negative (minus score) stories
  - Intentional sexual exhibitionism or voyeurism that ends in injury, humiliation, or feelings of inadequacy on the part of the primary identification figure; comparisons of size or strength that reflect unfavorably on the primary identification figure
  - Blatant castration themes

Scoring Examples

13MF: They've had great sex, and it's a hot day. Just a one-night stand. He picked her up in a bar, had a good time, no regrets.

Score: ANsp +3

Card 17BM: "I am still strong," the Vietnam War veteran well in his middle age proudly proclaimed, holding onto the rope. "We SEALS are trained to endure." Well-built and carefully maintained, he managed to climb up 20 feet in less than five minutes. No one can deprive him of his pride and satisfaction.

Score: ANsp +2, ANm +1 (secondary code)

Card 2: The woman leaning against the tree—she's looking very pleased with herself. She has a strong, capable husband, a healthy daughter, and most of all, she's pleased with her swelling belly, with her baby growing inside her, a sign of her continued fertility.

Score: ANsp +2

Card 1: The little boy is gazing at his father's violin. He is despairing; he just knows he'll never be able to play like his dad. Even his hands will always be too small for the job.

Score: ANsp –

Card 13MF: Bad sex trip! This man met this woman in a bar, and she was very sexually attractive and she immediately turned him on so he wanted to get invited back to her apartment. She does that, and he goes into the bathroom while she gets into the bed. And when he comes out, he can't see her eyes but she's naked on top. When he pulled the cover off, he discovered that her whole torso was gone, as if someone had cut her in half and left just the top there. And he was horrified ... the horror and guilt of his arousal and wondering how he can complete the act.

Score: ANsp –

When Oedipal or Autonomy Themes Are Most Prominent

(1) Oedipal: Oedipal triangle themes where the primary identification figure wins the struggle against his or her rival.

Negative (minus score) stories: Oedipal triangle themes where the primary identification figure loses the struggle against his or her rival or gets injured or humiliated

Scoring example: (Card 2) There's this girl who's in love with that guy in the field, but his wife is also pregnant, so the girl doesn't want to hurt the family. But she's really in love with the guy and doesn't know what to do.... The outcome is, I guess, that she'll go off to school and try to concentrate on her studies, but knows she won't really forget the guy. (Score: Oed)

(2) Autonomy (Aut): Themes highlighting autonomy or independence from others without any clear ambitious-narcissistic derivatives involved.

Negative (minus score) form: Failed attempts at autonomy, or autonomy stories that result in negative outcomes or humiliation

Scoring example: (Card 4) The man is trying to leave because he is no longer in love with the woman, but she's having a hard time letting go and tries to make the relationship work. She is asking him to think about it before making any hasty decisions, but he is not ready for a commitment with her and leaves. She probably was a bit too pushy. (Score: Aut)

When Ambitious-Narcissistic, Oed, and Aut Themes Are Absent

The score is a 0. There is no ambitious-narcissistic message to the story. It is not a representation of an ambitious-narcissistic mode or modes, nor does the story exhibit prominent Oedipal or autonomy characteristics. TAT stories that simply describe the card, without providing a story line, do not usually receive anything but 0 scores, because there is not enough fantasy present to show personality tendencies.

Scoring Examples

Card 9BM: Here are a bunch of farm laborers, tired after a long day of work just resting on each other. After a while when it's not so hot, one will wake up and that will wake up the rest of them and they'll just go back to work.

Card 13MF: Okay, it's early morning.... The man and the woman are married. The man is getting ready for work, and the wife is still asleep. They're sleeping on the couch in the living room because they don't have bedroom furniture yet. The man is sleepy still and not wanting to go to work, and the lady's just out of it, just asleep. But, alas, the man goes to work. He's tired, kind of apprehensive about work. The lady's too asleep to feel anything.

Card 4: The man and woman are in the movies—I'd say a heartbreaking scene. The man needs to leave back to South America. The woman doesn't want him to leave because she may never see him again. He's confused. He doesn't want to go, but he has to because the war needs him. She is heartbroken. He leaves and returns, and she's no longer waiting for him. She found someone else when he was gone.

Card 2: This is a young girl living on a farm with her parents. She's having to make a decision to stay home and work or go away to school. She ends up leaving and going. The farm survives without her, and she gets the education she wants. But her father and mother aren't pleased.

Card 3BM: Looks like a guy who went out drinking—drank too much at a friend's house. He's in the hallway too drunk to do anything—can't drive himself home. Probably ends up sleeping there the rest of the night and hopes somebody takes the keys.

Card 1: Looks like he is doing his practice and is not real happy with it. The boy is feeling depressed. His mother has told him to practice, and that is what he is doing. He's feeling pressure. He's going to practice until his mother says it's enough. That's it.

References

Harder, D. W. (1979). The assessment of ambitious-narcissistic character style with three projective tests: The Early Memories, TAT, and Rorschach. *Journal of Personality Assessment, 43,* 23–32.

Newmark, C. S. (1996). *Major psychological assessment instruments* (2nd ed.). Needham Heights, MA: Allyn & Bacon.

Reich, W. (1933). *Character analysis.* London: Vision Press.

SECTION IV

Social-Emotional Systems

26

CHAPTER

Singer and Wynne's Communication Deviance Scoring System

Benjamin P. Chapman

Abstract

This chapter describes the development and use of the communication deviance (CD) scoring system for the Thematic Apperception Test (TAT), first proposed by Singer and Wynne (1966) and later developed by Jones (1973, 1977) and Jones and Doane (1979). The CD construct refers to confused, distorted communication patterns that prevent speakers from sharing a common focus of attention. The scoring system involves 29 scoring categories grouped into four general problem areas: (1) closure problems (e.g., word fragments, integration problems); (2) disruptive behavior (e.g., tangential verbalizations, interruptions of examiner); (3) peculiar perceptions and verbalizations (e.g., odd word usage, peculiar reasoning); and (4) other formal characteristics (e.g., reaction time, story length average). Validity research has focused mainly on the association between parental CD and schizophrenic-spectrum disorders in offspring. Reliability for the scoring system has been fair to good, but reliable scoring may require special training from researchers experienced in its use, such as those who were associated with the University of California–Los Angeles Family High Risk Project.

Description of the System

Conceptual Framework

Disturbed and disordered communication has been known to characterize the families of schizophrenics for some time (Bateson, Jackson, Weakland, & Haley, 1956). The construct of communication deviance (CD) was first articulated by Singer and Wynne (1965a,

1965b; Wynne & Singer, 1963) to describe confused, distorted, and inconsistent communication arising from an inability to negotiate a shared focus of attention in the families of schizophrenic patients. Singer and Wynne (1965a) hypothesized that because children's development occurs in a transactional family context, exposure to chronically abnormal communication patterns may impede the development of organized and meaningful thought. They believed that when exacerbated by the trials of adolescence and by adult stressors, and when combined with a genetic vulnerability to schizophrenia, parental communication would play a significant etiological role in the development of subsequent schizophrenic spectrum—which they broadly defined to include schizoid, schizotypal, and borderline personality disorders, in addition to various forms of schizophrenia.

Parental CD was indeed reliably linked to offspring schizophrenic-spectrum disorders in early (Goldstein, Gould, Alkire, Rodnick, & Judd, 1970; Singer & Wynne, 1963, 1965a, 1965b; Wynne & Singer, 1963; see also Stabenau, Tupin, Werner, & Pollin, 1965; Werner, Stabenau, & Pollin, 1970) and subsequent (e.g., Goldstein, 1987; Jones, 1977) research (see Doane, 1985 for a review of classic research). However, later studies suggested that CD was present in the parents of offspring with other diagnoses (see Miklowitz & Stackman, 1992, for a review). The etiologic pathway proposed by Singer and Wynne has been partially substantiated by longitudinal evidence suggesting that parental CD predicts onset of schizophrenia-spectrum disorders 5 (Doane, West, Goldstein, Jones, & Rodnick, 1981) and 15 (Goldstein, 1987a, 1987b) years later. In general, though, researchers have also questioned whether parental CD may not be a result of living with a schizophrenic child, an indicator of subclinical schizophrenic symptomatology in parents themselves, or a reflection of shared genetic vulnerability to schizophrenic-spectrum disorders. Miklowitz and Stackman (1992) found little support for the first two possibilities in a comprehensive review, but recent studies on CD and deficits in attention provide some evidence for underlying information processing difficulties with a possible genetic substrate (Nuechterlein, Goldstein, Ventura, Dawson, & Doane, 1989; Velligan, Mahurin, Eckert, Hazleton, & Miller, 1997; Wagener, Hogarty, Goldstein, Asarnow, & Browne, 1986).

CD research has employed many different methods of assessing deviant communication. Early investigations used conversation elicited from the Object Sorting Task (Stabenau et al., 1965; Wild, Singer, Rosman, Ricci, & Lidz, 1965), the Revealed Differences Test (Stabenau et al., 1965), and segments of family therapy sessions (Morris & Wynne, 1965). These early efforts focused on a variety of transactional dimensions, including drifting attention and aberrant affective expression, and derived quantitative measures of conversational markers such as the number of interruptions or pauses occurring over a temporal unit of analysis. Such methods produced evidence that specific transactional abnormalities might characterize the parents of schizophrenics more so than other diagnostic groups.

Wynne and Singer (1965b) first used the TAT to tap an *amorphous* style of CD characterized by blurred perception, unclear referents, and indefinite meanings and a *fragmentation* style defined by instances in which ideas begin clearly but the speaker's communication subsequently breaks down because of attentional drift or other disruptions. The former was associated with parents of schizophrenic offspring who were more severely impaired. A year later, they elaborated on the amorphous–fragmentation typology with a detailed typology of CD operationalized in scoring manuals for the Rorschach and TAT (Singer & Wynne, 1966). After this, Singer and Wynne relied slightly more on the Rorschach or consensus Rorschach than the TAT in their research over the next decade (Doane, 1985), which culminated in a major replication study (Wynne, Singer, Bartko, &

Toohey, 1977), and the Rorschach CD system remains in active use (e.g., Wahlberg et al., 1997, 2000). The TAT, on the other hand, was used heavily in the University of California–Los Angeles (UCLA) Family High Risk Project (e.g., Goldstein, 1987a, 1987b; Jones, 1977). CD has also been scored from various interactional tasks (Jones, Rodnick, Goldstein, McPherson, & West 1977; Rund, 1986), the most recent of which is the interactional communication deviance (ICD) task (e.g., Velligan et al., 1990), but the focus of this chapter is on the TAT scoring system.

Singer and Wynne's initial (1966) TAT CD scoring system was based on their theory of abnormal ego development in schizophrenic patients[1] (see, e.g., Wynne & Singer, 1963) and on extensive prior studies of schizophrenics and their families at the National Institute of Mental Health (NIMH) (see, e.g., Singer & Wynne, 1963, 1965a, 1965b). Thus, the initial system was both theoretically and empirically derived. They described three general classes of CD: (1) closure problems; (2) disruptive behavior; and (3) peculiar language and logic. These three classes were the same for both the Rorschach and TAT, and though the scoring categories for each test overlapped somewhat, substantive differences in the nature of the tests also led to a number of unique scoring categories and procedures for each.

In developing the individual scoring categories, Singer and Wynne (1966) emphasized the formal or structural elements of CD. Verbalizations may be difficult to comprehend because grammar is grossly distorted or fragmented, incompatible ideas and images are mingled, conversational points are initiated and then dropped without conclusion, or odd words impede listeners' ability to follow. These are formal elements that characterize deviant communication, independent of the content in a message. Singer and Wynne considered the form–content distinction particularly important for the TAT (as opposed to the Rorschach), because traditional TAT scoring systems often code content.

Eight different scoring categories were initially included under closure problems to reflect these formal deficiencies: (1) failure to create a story; (2) fragments of words, phrases, or ideas; (3) unintelligible passages; (4) a part of the story given as a question; (5) the story left hanging; (6) no mention of the violin (only card 1 was administered under their system); (7) uncertainty about whether the violin is a violin; and (8) contradictions or inconsistencies within the story. These scoring categories assessed an inability to relay a complete story in a clear manner, usually due to an inability to sustain attention or commit to firm interpretations of percepts. Under disruptive behavior, Singer and Wynne (1966) proposed two scoring categories: (1) interruptions of task; and (2) disruptions of set. Task interruptions involve examinee digressions and utterances that impinge either on the examinee's own speech or the examiner's, whereas set disruptions involve reconstruing or misconstruing the task of the TAT (e.g., writing the story down instead of telling it). The final class of CD, peculiar perceptions or verbalizations, contained seven different scoring categories: (1) misperception of the card; (2) assignment of idiosyncratic meaning to a card; (3) regarding the picture as a dream; (4) odd phrasing or word usage; (5) slips of the tongue; (6) peculiar reasoning; and (7) repetitiveness of words or phrases.

Singer and Wynne (1966) noted the preliminary nature of these categories and called for further development and elaboration of the scoring system. A revised version of the scoring system appeared in an unpublished scoring manual in 1973 by James Jones, then a researcher with the UCLA Family High Risk Project, who had been trained by Singer in the original scoring system.[2] The Jones (1973) scoring manual was an elaboration of the Singer and Wynne (1966) original; all but two Singer-Wynne scoring categories were retained—the scores "no story is created" and "regarding the card as a dream" were dropped.

Rather than administering only card 1, a broader set was also developed: 1, 2, 3GF, 6BM, 7BM, 8BM, and 13MF. The rationale seems to have been that this collection of particular cards would provide broader and more diverse stimuli that could sample all—or more—categories of parental communication behavior. A single or more limited subset of cards might not permit the emergence of certain categories (e.g., the misperception score might be more likely on some cards than others). In addition to expanding the card set, Jones (1973) made several substantive changes to scoring categories. First, two scoring categories were borrowed from the Singer and Wynne (1966) Rorschach scoring system: (1) responses in negative form; and (2) responses in subjunctive form. Second, eight new content codes were developed (see following section). Third, a reaction time average and story length index—important formal elements—were added to the 27 verbal scoring categories for a total of 29 different categories. Jones formally revised the manual again in 1979 with Jeri Doane (Jones & Doane, 1979). The revisions consisted of elaborated descriptions of scoring categories, extensive examples, and an indicator of rater certainty about whether a code was applicable or not (see following section). Almost all subsequent TAT CD research has used the Jones and Doane (1979) scoring system, with the exception of Sass, Gunderson, Singer, and Wynne (1984), who seem to have used a hybrid of the original Singer and Wynne (1966) system and the Jones (1977) system as it appeared in Jones's doctoral dissertation, which predated the Jones and Doane (1979) manual and was probably very close to the Jones (1973) manual. Substantive differences between the Sass et al. scoring methods and others studies relying on Jones and Doane appear minimal.

In summary, the CD construct represents a failure to develop a shared focus of attention, first observed in the families of schizophrenics and found by early and later research to reliably characterize the transactions of parents of schizophrenic-spectrum patients. A CD scoring system was operationalized by Singer and Wynne (1966) for the TAT and involves three general problem areas: closure problems, disruptive behavior, and peculiar language. Jones (1973, 1977) and Jones and Doane (1979) refined the scoring system, and it now contains 29 individual scoring categories. Published research has relied on the Jones and Doane (1979) manual.

Scoring Categories

We now turn to descriptions of the currently used individual scoring categories as they appear in the Jones (1973) and the Jones and Doane (1979) manuals. The categories are arranged by class of problem (e.g., closure problems, disruptive behavior), and brief descriptions are provided, which are not sufficient for actual scoring purposes. Full descriptions and examples are found in the actual Jones and Doane (1979) manual. Following descriptions, the ways in which the 29 scoring categories have been used to derive index variables of CD (primarily six factor scores and total CD scores) are briefly reviewed. Table 26.1 summarizes the categories, their problem area, and the principal factor and loading for each code that emerged in Jones's (1977) factor analysis, which are discussed here.

Closure Problems

This class involves difficulties completing or integrating stories.

TABLE 26.1 CD Scoring Categories by Problem Area and Factor

Problem Area	Coding Category	Factor and Loading	Description and Content
Closure Problems	(1) Fragments of words, phrases, and ideas	1 (.57)[a]	Fragmentary speech
	(2) Passages unintelligible	1 (.44)[b]	Ideas not articulated well, points unclear
	(3) Parts given as question, listener called on to supply meaning	6 (–.29)[c]	Speaker unsure or will not commit to story or percept
	(4) Story left hanging	4 (.46)[d]	Unfinished thoughts, no endings provided, trailing off
	(5) No spontaneous mention of major perceptual element	6 (.61)	Leaving out central percept, such as violin on card 1
	(6) Grossly uncertain about major perceptual element	4 (–.29)	Unsure what obvious things are (e.g., if a figure is male or female)
	(7) Contradictions or inconsistencies	1 (.36)	Any statement contradicting a previous utterance
	(8) Negative responses	1 (.57)	Describing something in terms of what it is not
	(9) Subjunctive responses	1 (.50)	Statements offered in conditional
	(10) No integration of elements	6 (.35)	Failure to bring all important aspects of a card into story
	(11) Card 2 figure left out	3 (–.49)	No mention of a figure
	(12) Attributions of intention to cards	1 (.54)	Response framed in terms of what the artist was trying to portray, or what the examiner expects
	(13) *I hope* endings	4 (.49)	Endings offered without commitment, but in the form of something hoped for
	(14) *I don't know* endings	6 (.50)	Speaker abdicates responsibility for providing an ending

(*Continued*)

TABLE 26.1 CD Scoring Categories by Problem Area and Factor (Continued)

Problem Area	Coding Category	Factor and Loading	Description and Content
	(15) Other closure problems	4 (.34)	Other failures to complete the story
Disruptive Behavior	(16) Interruptions of the task	5 (.46)	Interrupting self or examiner during story
	(17) Peculiar set toward task	5 (.83)	Operating on own or unknown directions (e.g., writing a story instead of telling, connecting all stories together)
	(18) Questions about task after story begun	3 (.41)	Seeking examiner reassurance or direction after initial instructions
	(19) Associations with self not part of story	4 (.34)	Reminiscences or turning back toward own experience
	(20) Tangential replies to examiner questions	2 (.40)	Irrelevant remarks (e.g., discussing current events)
Peculiar Perceptions and Verbalizations	(21) Card is misperceived	2 (.73)	Some element of the card is not seen correctly (e.g., card 1 violin is a gun)
	(22) Idiosyncratic meaning assigned to details	1 (.49)	Some detail is infused with bizarre meaning evident to individual only
	(23) Odd phrasing and word usages	1 (.52)	Malapropisms, strange use of words or phrases
	(24) Slips of the tongue	1 (.30)	Uncorrected slips of the tongue
	(25) Peculiar reasoning of any kind	1 (.41)	Unusual or alogical reasoning about events or percepts
	(26) Repetitiveness of words, phrases, or ideas	1 (.33)	Perseverating on some element of speech or concept
	(27) Incorrect abstract word usage	5 (.56)	Using words to mean different things than they actually do, or using them with gross lack of clarity

(*Continued*)

TABLE 26.1 CD Scoring Categories by Problem Area and Factor (Continued)

Problem Area	Coding Category	Factor and Loading	Description and Content
Additional Formal Characteristics	(28) Reaction time average[e]	3 (–.55)	Time to begin story after being handed card
	(29) Story length index[e]	1 (.57)	Either line count or word count

Source: Jones (1973) and Jones and Doane (1979) unpublished scoring manual.

Notes: Factor loadings from Jones (1977). Factor 1, odd language; factor 2, misperceptions; factor 3, flighty anxiousness; factor 4, overpersonalized closure problems; factor 5, faulty intellectualization; factor 6, failure to integrate closure problems. Category descriptions are insufficient for actual scoring. Readers wishing to score protocols are referred to Jones and Doane's (1979) scoring manual.

[a] This code also loaded .56 on factor 3, flighty anxiousness.
[b] This code also loaded .44 on factor 5, faulty overintellectualization.
[c] This code also loaded .28 on factor 2, misperceptions.
[d] This code also loaded .44 on factor 4, overpersonalized closure problems.
[e] Category added by Jones (1973) not present in Singer and Wynne's (1966) original manual.

(1) Fragments of words, phrases, and ideas appear in the story: This category captures piecemeal verbalizations that are not well connected. Here, the subject has not committed his or her full attention to ideas but has stated them nonetheless.

(2) Passages of the story are unintelligible: This is scored whenever it is not clear what the speaker is saying about portions of the story. It may also be scored under the category of peculiar perceptions and verbalizations, because such peculiarities may be contributing to the lack of clarity in the speaker's narrative.

(3) Part of the story is given as a question, or the listener is called on to supply meaning: Here, the speaker escapes from committing to any particular ideas or narrative course and abdicates responsibility for the task, leaving the listener unsure about the speaker's actual perceptions. If an examinee seems to be musing aloud and is not clearly directing a question at the examiner, this category is not scored.

(4) The story is left hanging: This category is scorable when completion failures of any sort are present. It is also scored if two alternative endings are provided without one being noted as more important. No score is given when a speaker gives two alternative interpretations or uses words like *maybe, possibly,* and *probably.* Two particular types of ending are also scored under (13) and (14).

(5) Spontaneous mention of a major perceptual element is not made: This category captures instances when a speaker has completely omitted an obvious portion of the card that is usually considered central to the story. Failing to mention the violin in card 1 is an example, although the specific response, "He is looking at the instrument,"

is not scored. For the other cards the category is scored if the spontaneous mention of the following percepts is not made: 3GF, female figure; 2, the three persons; 6BM, the woman and man; 7BM, the two men; 13MF, the man and woman; 8BM, the boy and three figures in the background.

(6) The subject is grossly uncertain about a major perceptual element: This is scored if the speaker mentions some central element of the card but is unsure what it is; for instance, an examinee might not be able to identify the violin in card 1. However, the category is not scored for uncertainty about what characters are thinking, feeling, and so forth but only for major percepts.

(7) Contradictions and inconsistencies are present: Any internal contradictions in a narrative are scored here. Singer and Wynne (1966) provided the example of a subject telling a card 1 story about a boy breaking the violin and then concluding that the boy did not break the violin. Essentially, this category taps a speaker's tendency to jar the listener by committing to one conception of reality and then suddenly reversing it. Indefinite pronoun usage is also scored.

(8) Responses in negative form: This is scored by describing a portion of the card or story in terms of what it is not. For example, describing the violin in card 1 as, "It's not a banjo, it's not a piano, it's not a ..." would qualify for this score. By referring to things in an exclusionary way, the speaker communicates in a nonspecific and obscure way leaving listeners uncertain about his or her precise meaning. Negative descriptions paired with positive descriptions of the same story element are not scored.

(9) Responses in subjunctive form: This is scored when the subject frames things in a conditional sense, qualifying a piece of the story with *if.* Here, the speaker again escapes responsibility for making a clear commitment to a story, idea, or percept by making them contingent on some other circumstance.

(10) No integration of picture elements: This is scored only when the subject explicitly says he or she cannot relate the card's figures to each other. This is considered an attempt to oversimplify the task, but it is one that confuses the listener because major elements of the stimulus material are excluded from the story. This score is more likely on cards 2 and 8BM, which tend to present more elements to be integrated.

(11) A card 2 figure is left out of the story: Here, the speaker simply does not mention one of the card 2 figures. This is a specific example of (5), but *the parents* is not a scorable response because the figures are mentioned collectively rather than referred to individually. (5) is also scored automatically.

(12) Attribution of intention to the cards: This category is scorable if an examinee references the intentions of the card artist, how the examiner intends for the subject to respond, any notions that the cards themselves have intentions for the speaker's response, and so forth. Such responses abdicate responsibility for providing interpretation. (17), peculiar set, is scored automatically with this.

(13) *I hope* endings: This category is a more specific version of (4), where the examinee concludes a narrative by indicating that she or he *hopes* it ends in a certain way. The subject refuses to take responsibility for the story, effectively imbuing the characters with agency instead. The category is not scored if an ending for the I hope statement or scenario is later provided, however.

(14) *I don't know* endings: This is scored only if the subject specifically indicates that an ending cannot be provided because he or she does not *know.* (4) is scored automatically with this.

(15) Other closure problems: This category is rather vague and includes difficulties finishing the story that are not covered in other categories previously outlined. Sudden mutism, refusals to finish a narrative (e.g., *I won't*), and similar failures to provide the ending elicited by standard TAT instructions are scorable.

Disruptive Behavior

This class of categories refers to examinee verbalizations that interrupt the examiner, the task, or the speaker's own narrative.

(16) Interruptions of the task: This category covers verbal intrusions into the subject's own or examiner's speech. Mildly positive or affectively neutral comments are not scored, but platitudes or morals of life inserted into narratives, as well as negative comments interjected, are scored. Two specific instances of this are also scorable under (18) and (19).

(17) Peculiar set toward the task: A peculiar set constitutes a strange interpretation of the rules or requirements of the TAT. Gross misinterpretations of the task, such as thinking the examinee must write a story or thinking he or she must connect all the cards to one another are scored. Another common response scored here involves speakers thinking they must comment on the symbolism depicted in the cards, and (12), attribution of intent to cards, is also often scorable along with peculiar sets.

(18) Questions about the task instructions after the story is begun: This category covers verbalizations designed to seek further clarification, reassurance, or information subsequent to the initial instructions. Questions immediately after the examiner's instructions are not scored.

(19) Associations about self that are not part of the story: This category is scored when subjects associate or include personal history, feelings, or other personal experiences in the narrative when such associations are only tangential to the story and not part of the narrative proper. These behaviors represent a tendency to personalize and digress when confronted with a narrative task. It is not double scored with (16).

(20) Tangential replies to examiner questions: This category covers irrelevant remarks in response to examiner questions.

Peculiar Perceptions and Verbalizations

This problem area involves bizarre, unusual, and distorted perceptions and speech.

(21) The card is misperceived: This category is scorable when a subject "mis-sees" the card or some element in it, thinking that a clearly depicted object or person is something else entirely. Examples include perceiving the boy in card 1 as a girl or the violin as some other object such as a gun or machine, although the response *guitar* is permissible.

(22) Idiosyncratic meaning is assigned to details: Here, the speaker invests some detail of the card with a meaning that is not significant to anyone else. This may include paranoid overinterpretations of details that assign special meaning to something inconsequential. Mere description of obscure details is not scored. Responses that score here may also score for peculiar reasoning.

(23) Odd phrasing and word usage are present: The item is not scored merely for incorrect grammar; rather, words must be used in a way that significantly obscures meaning or with such vagueness that it is totally unclear how the speaker is using the word. (23) and (27), incorrect abstract word usage, are not scored together. In individuals with English as a second language, the category should be applied very cautiously.

(24) Slips of the tongue occur: This category covers everyday slips of the tongue. Originally, Singer and Wynne (1966, p. 286) scored both corrected and uncorrected slips of the tongue. Jones and Doane (1979) revised this to score only uncorrected slips of the tongue. In this instance, the speaker accidentally miscommunicates but then is not aware enough or concerned enough to correct any misperceptions likely to ensue.

(25) Peculiar reasoning of any kind is present: Any reasoning that is unusual, illogical, or involves non sequiturs scores in this category. Idiosyncratic logic, or reasoning based on a system that has meaning only to the speaker, also scores.

(26) Repetitiveness of words, phrases, or ideas occurs: This category covers perseverative responses, suggesting a speaker is unable to move his or her attention on from a particular word or idea. It is not scored if the subject uses the same word in different ways and is applied with caution to nonnative English speakers.

(27) Incorrect abstract word usage: This includes common words used inappropriately as well. The effect is to obfuscate meaning, leaving listeners unsure what the speaker is trying to say. The category cannot be scored simultaneously with category (23).

Additional Formal Characteristics

These are elements of the TAT task that are not scored directly from the examinee's speech but that nonetheless are informative.

(28) Reaction time average: This is the time taken to begin a story after being handed the card. It is averaged over the cards.

(29) Story length average: This can be taken either as a word count or line count and provides a measure of the subject's productivity.

Administration and Scoring Procedures

CD studies employ standard administration procedures for the TAT but require detailed information gathering for accurate scoring, as is evident from the scoring category descriptions. Usually, TAT sessions are video- or audiotaped, and protocols are scored based on these recordings. The vast majority of studies have used the full set of seven cards for which the Jones (1973) and Jones and Doane (1979) scoring manuals were written (i.e., 1, 2, 3GF, 6BM, 7BM, 8BM, and 13MF). It is important to note here that the Jones and Doane manual stipulates that a category may be scored only once per story. Also, each score assigned is given a double plus (++) if the rater is certain about the occurrence of a category. In situations where the rater thinks the category is applicable but has some questions, a single plus (+) is given. The single plus is coded for "weak or mild (borderline) instances" or "equivocal occurrences" of a code (p. 3). This is relevant especially in instances in which examiners have provided inadequate instructions or probes, and such potentially CD eliciting behavior on the part of the examiner is to be taken into account in assigning scores. Many individual codes in the manual contain specific rules for assigning singe or double plusses.

Most studies have calculated six factor scores or a total score as predictor variables or as variables with which to create high–intermediate–low CD groups. Factors were derived by Jones (1977) in a sample of 141 parents, high-risk adolescents, and siblings (a total of 44 intact families) from the UCLA Family High Risk Project. These families were recruited through the UCLA Psychology Department Clinic after presenting for help with adolescents displaying various problems from moodiness to delinquency; few were formally diagnosed at the beginning of the study. The procedure Jones used involved comparing several different principal axis orthogonal factor solutions with a group of four clinically meaningful clusters of CD categories. The category clusters were derived by dichotomizing category scores, selecting four primary categories to serve as anchor variables and by statistically cross-tabulating these anchors with the remaining categories with an eye for theoretical consistency. Thus, clusters were both conceptually and empirically coherent. The clusters then served as a guide with which to compare several mathematically equivalent principal axis factor solutions. The factor solution that most closely approximated the clusters resulted in six factors: (1) contorted, peculiar language; (2) misperceptions; (3) flighty anxiousness; (4) overpersonalized closure problems; (5) faulty overintellectualization; and (6) failure-to-integrate closure problems.

Jones (1977) is not precise on the method by which factor scores were computed, although such fine distinctions are rarely provided by researchers. Since it was done with a 1970s version of the Statistical Package for Social Sciences (SPSS), it seems likely that the regression method, which involves unit weightings,[3] was used—although other methods, such as Bartlett's, may have been available on SPSS at the time. Most other researchers seem to have used this method. For instance, Velligan, Goldstein, Nuechterlein, Miklowitz, and Ranlett (1990) and Doane et al. (1989) report that they relied on the unit weighting based on Jones's factor solution to calculate factor scores.

Miklowitz, Velligan, Goldstein, Nuechterlein, and Gitlin (1991) referenced a computer program that was used to calculate factor scores based on Jones (1977) loadings, again suggesting a unit-weighted method. The number of codes Miklowitz et al. (1991, p. 166) list as defining each factor is at first sight difficult to reconcile with the pattern matrix in Jones's (table 3, p. 330) (e.g., in Jones, only two codes load over .4 on the misperception factor with other categories all loading equally low, but Miklowitz et al. stated that seven codes compose the factor). What seems likely is that Miklowitz et al.'s report of the number of scores composing factors is based on the initial Jones factor loading matrix, which, before rotation to simple structure, may have had many more higher loadings on each factor; by contrast, Jones appears to have reported the rotated pattern matrix. It also seems likely that Miklowitz et al. referenced the loading matrix because it, rather than the pattern matrix, is used to produce the factor score coefficient matrix (see note 3).

One other method to calculate factor scores appears to be have been used. Velligan et al. (1997) computed factor scores by taking the mean *z* score of items loading .4 on each factor in the Jones (1977) pattern matrix. Although this is a common convention considered adequate for most research purposes (Tabachnik & Fidell, 1996) it should be noted that seven categories (6, 7, 10, 14, 15, 19, 24, and 26) did not load over .4 on any factor in the Jones solution. Thus, although these categories contributed minimally to factor scores in other studies calculated by the unit-weighting methods, they did not contribute at all to factor scores in Velligan et al.

The way overall CD scores have been calculated has also varied a bit. Most studies convert raw scores for each scoring category to *z* scores on the basis of the Jones (1977) distributions, which are not printed in the article. An overall or total CD score is usually then computed by averaging the *z* score of all categories. Most recently, Velligan et al. (1997) computed a mean CD *z* score by averaging the factor *z*'s; in this case, categories failing to load on any factor were not included in total CD scores. Scores for each CD category are also often adjusted to reflect a CD category per card ratio. For instance, Miklowitz et al. (1991) divided the total raw score for each category by the number of cards administered (seven) and then converted the results to *z* scores on the basis of Jones's distribution. This method has been adopted by quite a few others (Doane & Mintz, 1987; Doane et al., 1989; Miklowitz et al., 1991; Velligan et al., 1990). Nutger, Dingemans, Linzen, Van der Does, and Gersons (1997) derived another type of CD per-unit score by summing the total (evidently raw) scores for the 27 coding categories and dividing by the number of lines of speech, providing an index of the amount or density of CD within a discrete unit of speech. This procedure has been used by a few others (Doane & Mintz, 1987; Doane et al., 1989) to combat criticism that total scores not adjusted in this way may simply reflect more CD as an artifact of verbosity. The variety of methods with which scores have been calculated is an important point because it makes comparisons across studies more difficult (a problem that characterizes CD methodology in general; cf. Doane, 1985).

☐ Research Evidence

Validity

This section reviews available validity evidence for the scoring system. Basic criterion validity has been assessed by the extent to which CD is more characteristic of the parents of schizophrenic-spectrum patients compared with the parents of patients with other psychiatric diagnoses and behavior problems such as delinquency (e.g., Jones, 1977). Some efforts have also focused on TAT CD's utility for differentiating between the parents of different diagnostic groups (Asarnow, Goldstein, and Ben-Meir, 1988; Miklowitz et al., 1991). Longitudinal predictive validity has been assessed in a 15-year prospective study (Doane & Mintz, 1987; Goldstein, 1987a, 1987b). A number of studies have also investigated the convergence of TAT CD scores with related measures, such as ICD (Velligan et al., 1990), the communication conflict situation (Rund, 1986), and other theoretically related constructs such as attention deficits (e.g., Velligan et al., 1997). Discriminant validity has been assessed by the extent to which CD is uncorrelated with theoretically different family interaction constructs (e.g., Affective Style, in Miklowitz et al., 1990). Two cross-cultural studies (Doane et al., 1989; Rund, 1986) dealing with discriminant validity are discussed in the section on generalizability. Table 26.2 summarizes the findings of empirical studies reviewed in these sections.

Criterion Validity (Concurrent)

The original Singer and Wynne (1966) scoring system had demonstrated criterion validity by the fact that CD characterized the parents of schizophrenics and was much lower in the parents of nonschizophrenic controls (see Singer & Wynne, 1965a). Based on this, Jones (1977) assessed his revised system's usefulness in differentiating parents of offspring differing in diagnostic severity—operationalized along a six-point continuum from normal (1) to chronic schizophrenia (6), with adjustment and behavioral disorders closer to normal, followed by increasingly severe schizophrenic-spectrum disorders—in family data from the UCLA High Risk Project. He supplemented the UCLA data with family data from Singer and Wynne's original NIMH sample (see, e.g., Singer & Wynne, 1966). Both samples consisted of families with offspring characterized by a variety of problems, from delinquency to severe psychopathology. The offspring in the UCLA sample were adolescents considered at risk for the development of later psychopathology, including broad schizophrenic-spectrum disorders. The offspring in the NIMH sample were young adults, but the samples were fairly similar with respect to parent's education and family socioeconomic states (SES)—although parents in the NIMH sample were 47 years old, on average, compared with 43 in the UCLA sample (see Jones, 1977 for further details).

From the combined UCLA and NIMH data, Jones formed two subsamples. The first subsample (A) was composed of TAT protocols common to both the UCLA and NIMH groups and thus was most related to the revised scoring system because he derived the factor structure in the UCLA data. The second subsample (B) consisted of protocols based on cards only in the NIMH data and constituted a cross-validation sample independent of the sample in which the scoring system's factor structure had been derived.

In both subsamples combined, parents' overall CD scores and individual factor scores were uncorrelated with the continuum of offspring diagnosis. However, T scores on factor 2 (misperception) in the mothers of subsample A were strongly correlated with schizophrenic-spectrum diagnosis, operationalized continuously—that is, by numerical increments of diagnostic severity ($r = .60$). Factor 6, failure to integrate closure problems, in fathers was moderately correlated in subsample B with spectrum diagnosis ($r = .44$). In the sample as a whole, factors 2 and 6 were elevated ($T > 60$) only in the parents of schizophrenic offspring who had been hospitalized. Likewise, offspring had schizophrenic-spectrum diagnoses in all cases where both parents had at least one factor T score of 60 or greater. In addition, mothers with any factor T score over 60 were more likely ($r = .50$) to have a child with a schizophrenic-spectrum diagnosis. When parents

TABLE 26.2 Summary of Validity Evidence for TAT CD Scoring System

Study	Finding
Velligan, Mahurin, Eckert, Hazleton, and Miller (1997)	Specific types of CD related to specific types of attention problems in schizophrenic patients
Nutger, Dingemans, Linzen, Van der Does, and Gersons (1997)	Individual and family interventions ineffective at reducing parental CD in Dutch sample
Miklowitz, Velligan, Goldstein, Nuechterlein, and Gitlin (1991)	CD high in parents of both schizophrenic and bipolar patients; modest convergence between TAT and ICD
Velligan, Goldstein, Nuechterlein, Miklowitz, and Ranlett (1990)	TAT and ICD converge modestly and may tap different aspects of CD
Doane et al. (1989)	CD high in parents of both Anglo-American and low acculturation Mexican American schizophrenics
Nuechterlein, Goldstein, Dawson, and Doane (1989)	Factors 1 and 2 associated with poor visual discriminatory attention
Asarnow, Goldstein, and Ben-Meir (1988)	Parental CD higher in schizophrenic spectrum than depressive-spectrum children
Doane and Mintz (1987)	CD increases from adolescence to young adulthood, regardless of diagnosis; aspects of CD stable only in women over 15 years
Goldstein (1987a)	Parental CD not linked to parental history of psychopathology; parental history psychopathology + high CD = 86% offspring schizophrenic-spectrum diagnosis (UCLA High-Risk sample)
Goldstein (1987b)	Combination of high parental CD and negative Affective Style predicted diagnosis of UCLA High-Risk Project patients and of siblings at 15-year follow-up
Wagener, Hogarty, Goldstein, Asarnow, and Browne (1986)	Among schizophrenic mothers, CD associated with poor attention; mothers factor 2 associated with offspring CPT commission errors
Rund (1986)	High CD parents more characteristic of schizophrenic patients than normals; TAT CD only modestly associated with CCS
Miklowitz et al. (1986)	High expressed emotion (EE) families higher in CD; only weak correlation between CD and EE
Sass, Gunderson, Singer, and Wynne (1984)	CD highest in parents of schizophrenics with severe thought disorder, CD in parents of low-thought-disordered schizophrenics similar to normals
Lewis, Rodnick, and Goldstein (1981)	High CD families less able to focus on topic, share feelings, more affectively constricted than low CD families

(*Continued*)

TABLE 26.2 Summary of Validity Evidence for TAT CD Scoring System (Continued)

Study	Finding
Doane, West, Goldstein, Rodnick, and Jones (1981)	CD alone does not predict development of schizophrenic-spectrum disorder at five-year follow up but does when combined with affective style
Jones, Rodnick, Goldstein, McPherson, and West (1977)	High CD families show slightly more pathology on a problem-solving task; CD and interactive pathology only weakly correlated
Jones (1977)	High scores on factors 2 and 6 distinguish parents of schizophrenics from parents of normals; elevated CD in both parents also discriminates

were considered together and either had a *T* score on any factor over 60, this correlation increased to .56. On the basis of these findings, Jones (1977) proposed that parents be categorized as high CD if either had a *T* score higher than 60 on factors 2 or 6 or if both had one or more factor scores higher than 60; parents were considered intermediate level if either had a factor *T* score (other than factors 2 or 6) over 60; and parents were considered low CD if neither had a factor *T* score over 60.

Lewis, Rodnick, and Goldstein (1981) used this classificatory system to examine the extent to which a sample of high, intermediate, and low CD families from the UCLA Family High Risk Project varied in their ability to maintain a focus of discussion. Lewis et al. also examined the relative role dominance of either father or mother, and the type of affect in family interactions. High CD families were unable to focus in their discussion, to share feelings appropriately, showed nonverbal attitudes of avoidance and rigidity, and were characterized more by mothers who were active—either alone or in combination with the father. None of the offspring in this study were diagnosed schizophrenic but instead consisted of adolescents with a range of problems, including externalizing–antisocial behavior and social withdrawal. Although levels of CD were not reported across symptom groups, 43% of the sample's parents were classified as high CD, and 32% were classified as intermediate CD, suggesting that CD may characterize parents of dysfunctional nonpsychotic and nonthought disordered youth—although it is important to note that the sample was considered at risk for the development of later psychopathology, including schizophrenic-spectrum disorders, on the basis of guidelines that at the time were considered to be associated with later spectrum diagnosis (e.g., social withdrawal).

Sass et al. (1984) directly assessed the relationship between parental CD and offspring thought disorder in a sample of schizophrenics. They found that parents of high thought-disordered schizophrenics had significantly higher TAT CD scores than parents of non-thought-disordered schizophrenics and parents of another non-thought-disordered group with various diagnoses such as adjustment disorder and depressive neurosis. They derived indices of disorganization and focus problems, which were highly correlated ($r = .85$), and found that both were higher in the parents of severely thought disordered schizophrenics than of moderately thought-disordered schizophrenics, who in turn scored higher on disorganization and focus problems than the parents of non-thought-disordered schizophrenics and psychiatric controls. Although the number of patients, and consequently parents, in each category was relatively small (only five patients in the severe thought-disordered group), the fact that these differences still emerged as significant probably reflects the robustness of the relationship between parental CD and severity of thought disorder in offspring. Rund found a similar pattern in a Norwegian sample (see following), and both studies found that parents of non-thought-disordered, paranoid patients showed levels of CD similar to the parents of nonpatients.

Later, Asarnow et al. (1988) returned to high–intermediate–low classification (modified to high–low groups) and assessed CD's usefulness for differentiating between parents of 7- to 13-year-old children with different diagnoses. Twenty-five children met DSM-III criteria for either schizophrenia or schizotypal personality disorders, and 25 met criteria for either major depressive or dysthymic disorders. They found significantly more high CD parents among the schizophrenia-spectrum children than among the depressive-spectrum children. The effect was slightly more pronounced when only mothers' CD was considered. They also calculated the sensitivity (i.e., true positives) and specificity (i.e., true negatives) of parental CD, achieving a sensitivity of 84%, a specificity of 48%, and 66% overall correct classification. When the mother's CD alone was considered, sensitivity dropped to 72%, but specificity and overall correct classification improved to 68% and 70%, respectively. Finally, they found that schizophrenia-spectrum disorders were associated with relatively more (i.e., two vs. one or none) high CD parents (*tau c* = –.42). It is important to note that CD was not entirely absent in some parents of depressed children, although high CD discriminated well between parents of differentially diagnosed offspring.

Miklowitz et al. (1991) were interested in a similar issue: whether CD scores differentiated between two different diagnostic categories, both of which featured thought disorder. They found that TAT CD did not discriminate between the parents of 39 schizophrenic and 16 bipolar adults (mean ages 22 and 21, respectively). The mean *z* score of the 27 CD categories did not differ significantly across groups, and only scores on factor 1—odd and peculiar language—served to differentiate the groups, with parents of manic patients scoring significantly higher. Miklowitz et al. qualitatively noted that the parents of manic patients tended to try to talk faster and fit too many ideas into discreet speech units, which probably produced higher scores on factor 1. They concluded that high CD characterizes the parents of both schizophrenic and bipolar patients and suggested that parental CD might be connected to disordered thinking in general rather than to schizophrenic-spectrum diagnoses in particular.

Another interesting line of evidence for the construct validity of the TAT CD scoring system comes from studies linking CD to specific attention deficits (Asarnow et al., 1988; Nuechterlein, Goldstein, Dawson, and Doane, 1989; Velligan et al., 1997; Wagener et al., 1986). These investigations were sparked both by evidence that schizophrenics display various attention difficulties, and Singer and Wynne's theorizing (e.g., 1965a) about the role of attention in CD. Specifically, they believed that in the family interactions of schizophrenics, interlocutors' attention lapsed prior to developing a shared focus. In the families of neurotics, by contrast, attention lapsed only after speakers had achieved this shared focus.

Wagener et al. (1986) provided some initial support for this by demonstrating in a sample of 25 mothers of DSM-III schizophrenic patients that the mothers' TAT CD factors 2 (misperceptions) and 4 (failure to integrate closure problems) correlated modestly with mothers' total errors (*rs* of .47 and .34, respectively) and errors of omission (*rs* of .45 and .39, respectively) on the Continuous Performance Test (CPT), a measure of many aspects of attention. Mothers' factor 2 also correlated with commission errors (r = .33). Together, mothers' factors 2, 3, and 4 accounted for 50% of the variance in mothers' total CPT scores. Maternal CD did not show significant zero-order correlations with offspring CPT performance, but in a stepwise regression with patients' CPT commission error scores regressed on maternal CD and CPT scores, mothers' factor 2 accounted for 50% of the variance in offspring CPT commission errors. This latter result is consistent with Asarnow et al.'s (1988) observation that the worst impairment in the distractibility–attention factor of the Wechsler Intelligence Scale for Children Revised (WISC-R) was in schizophrenic-spectrum children from high CD parents. However, high CD mothers' (T > 60 on factors 2 or 6) and their offsprings' CPT performance did not differ significantly from other that of other families in Wagener et al.'s study.

Nuechterlein et al. (1989) extended Wagener et al.'s (1986) results to a group of 40 recent onset schizophrenics and their mothers. In their study, mothers' factors 1 (peculiar language) and 2 (misperceptions) were significantly related to offsprings' performance on a visual signal discrimination factor (i.e., differentiating a target stimulus from irrelevant stimuli) derived from multiple indices of attention (r = –.40, and –.34, respectively; more CD reflecting poorer discriminatory attention). These results suggest that particular parental disturbances in communication-—particularly the gross misperceptions tapped by factor 2—are tied to various difficulties in sustaining attention.

Velligan et al. (1997) examined the relationship between CD and attention in 27 DSM-IV schizophrenics themselves. They found moderate associations between CD indices and attentional performance: total CD scores correlated modestly (*rho* = .37) with errors on the Stroop Color-Word Test (a measure of sustained attention, discrimination, and executive functioning) and negatively with visual discrimination ability on the CPT (*rho* = –.34, that is, greater CD related to worse performance). Various factor scores also correlated moderately to strongly with other indices of visual and auditory attention. The strongest relationship was observed between the misperception factor (2) and visual discrimination (*rho* = –.51) and between the faulty intellectualization factor (5) and auditory sustained attention errors (*rho* = .50) on the CPT. Velligan et al. concluded that relatively specific attention deficits are associated with particular forms of deviant communication in schizophrenic patients and that if cognitive deficits underlie both poor attention and communication skills, these deficits are relatively discrete and differentiated, rather than generalized. Again, factor 2 appeared quite important, consistent with Jones's (1977) original findings that it was most strongly associated with schizophrenic-spectrum diagnoses.

In sum, concurrent validity evidence suggests that CD scores correlate modestly with severity of offspring diagnosis when it is considered along a schizophrenic spectrum, with expected negative family interaction styles, and is higher in families where patients are more severely thought-disordered. However, CD to some extent characterized the families of depressed children and appears to be just as prevalent in the families of manic as well as of schizophrenic patients. CD tends to be associated with poor attentional functioning as well, consistent with Singer and Wynne's (e.g., 1965a) conceptualizations of the construct.

Predictive Validity

In addition to these studies, the UCLA Family High Risk Project study has produced some longitudinal data speaking to the predictive validity of parental CD scores. Doane et al. (1981) found at a five-year follow-up of the UCLA High Risk sample that a TAT CD index composed of the six factor scores was higher in adolescents who subsequently developed schizophrenic-spectrum disorders as young adults. Predictions were better, however, when CD was considered in conjunction with a measure of Affective Style.

In a 15-year follow-up of this same sample, Goldstein (1987a, 1987b) found that Jones's (1977) parental high–intermediate–low CD profiles and a measure of Affective Style each significantly and independently predicted offspring's subsequent extended DSM-III schizophrenic-spectrum diagnosis (i.e., schizophrenia, schizotypal, paranoid, schizoid, or borderline personality disorder) in a log-linear analysis. Furthermore, using chi-square tests to examine submatrices of the classification matrix on which the log-linear analysis was performed, Goldstein found that CD and Affective style in combination resulted in maximum separation of the broad schizophrenic-spectrum group from groups composed of (1) all other diagnoses and (2) no diagnoses. Thus, the two variables provided considerable specificity of in their prediction of broad schizophrenic-spectrum diagnosis. When CD and Affective Style were used together in a discriminant function analysis, both were significant, and together they properly classified 71.4% of the broad schizophrenic-spectrum cases. When siblings with schizophrenic-spectrum diagnoses were included in these analyses, CD's association with subsequent spectrum diagnosis was even stronger.

In a further analysis of the UCLA data (Goldstein, 1987a), two other important findings emerged. First, although CD was independently predictive of offspring schizophrenic-spectrum diagnosis at follow-up, it was not associated with family history of severe mental disorder; high CD was equally present in families with and without a history of severe mental disorder. This provides some evidence that CD is not a function of parent mental disorder itself. Second, for families who had a history of severe psychopathology and high CD, 86% of the offspring received a subsequent broad schizophrenic-spectrum diagnosis, whereas only 20% of high CD families with no history of major psychopathology had an offspring with subsequent spectrum diagnosis. Goldstein suggested that this provided some evidence for a diathesis-stress conceptualization, in which family history of mental disorder constituted a risk factor exacerbated by CD. Goldstein also reported that families classified as high CD on the basis of only one parent scoring high on factors 2 or 6 (i.e., the single-parent criterion) were more likely both to have a family history of major psychopathology and to produce broad and narrow schizophrenic-spectrum offspring, compared with families classified as high CD because both parents scored high on some factor other than 2 or 6 (i.e., the dual-parent criterion). However, numbers were too small to permit tests of statistical significance, so this finding should be interpreted with caution, although it does provide some tentative support for the notion that factors 2 and 6 are particularly related to offspring schizophrenic-spectrum disorders.

Also of relevance, Doane and Mintz (1987) found that in the UCLA High Risk Project patients themselves, low CD factor scores and low CD per line of speech were associated with an absence of diagnoses over the course of the 15-year follow-up period. Thus, there is evidence of the predictive validity of CD scores for patients themselves, with respect to subsequent psychopathology. In sum, the UCLA High Risk Project has provided a wealth of information about family risk factors in general and the predictive validity of the CD scoring system in particular. The latter does seem to be associated with broad schizophrenic-spectrum diagnoses in offspring, at least over a 15-year period. Naturally, replication of these results will strengthen evidence of the scoring system's predictive validity.

Convergent and Discriminant Validity

Finally, some studies have investigated the convergent validity between CD indices and between TAT CD and separate family constructs. Scores between the TAT and other interactive measures of CD initially correlated fairly weakly. Jones, Rodnick, Goldstein, McPherson, and West (1977) found a correlation of .26 between TAT CD and CD measured from a family problem-solving interaction task. Similarly, Rund (1986; see also following) found only a .26 correlation between TAT CD scores and deviant verbalizations in an interactive measure called the communication conflict situation in a Norwegian sample. More recently, two studies examined the relationship between the TAT and the ICD task. These two methods tend to converge somewhat more but still at very modest levels. Velligan et al. (1990) reported correlations between the TAT mean and ICD overall scores of .44. Miklowitz et al. (1991) found that mean TAT CD z scores correlated moderately ($r = .41$) with total ICD scores.

Both Miklowitz et al. (1991) and Velligan et al. (1990) concluded that the TAT does appear to tap a slightly different variety of the CD construct from ICD scores. Velligan et al. concluded that CD elicited from a semistructured projective task is dictated to some extent by the stimulus materials. Therefore, the variety and type of deviant perceptions and verbalizations assessed may be method-specific. CD elicited in an interactional context not involving test materials may reflect a more generalizable form of CD. Singer and Wynne's (1965a) original notion that projective tests simulate between the parent and examiner the same deviant transactional styles present within family units may be partially true, but the ICD task may represent a closer picture of how communication deviance actually transpires (Velligan et al., 1990).

There appears to be some support for the discriminant validity of TAT CD scores, however. Velligan et al.'s (1990) monotrait–multimethod correlation for CD was higher than heterotrait–monomethod correlations, and Miklowitz et al. (1991) reported higher correlations across methods for CD scoring categories meant to measure the same dimension than between categories measuring different dimensions of CD. TAT CD correlates only weakly with other family–distress constructs. Doane et al. (1981) noted that TAT CD scores were essentially independent from a measure of affective style, with almost no overlap in the variance each captured in later outcome variables. Miklowitz et al. (1986) found a point biserial correlation of .27 between TAT CD and expressed emotion (EE), although high EE parents also had significantly more CD across three samples. So, although convergent validity between the TAT and other measures of CD tends to be somewhat weak, existing evidence suggests that CD measured by the TAT is distinct from other measures of problematic family functioning.

Generalizability

The generalizability of the TAT scoring system should be considered somewhat limited as yet due to the homogeneity of samples used in most research (there are a few exceptions, discussed below). Specifically, most TAT-related CD research has been conducted on predominantly Anglo-American middle-aged adults who are low-middle to low SES on the Hollingshead Index and typically have two or fewer years of college (e.g., Doane & Mintz, 1987; Miklowitz et al., 1991; Nutger et al., 1997; Velligan et al., 1997).

Studies have tended to focus on the demographics of identified patients rather than parents, and parental age in particular is rarely reported. Available evidence suggests that most parents are in their 40s, 50s, or 60s. Sass et al. (1984) excluded parents over 66, and fathers in subsamples of the UCLA Family High Risk Project have reported ages of 47.4 (Lewis et al., 1981) and 47.8 (Jones, 1977), with mothers from this sample 43.3 (Jones, 1977; Lewis et al., 1981). Wagener et al.'s (1986) mothers averaged age 51.2. All studies except Asarnow et al.'s (1988) used parents of adult schizophrenics, but since Asarnow et al.'s identified patients were children, parents might have been slightly younger. Exceptions to the Anglo-American low to middle-low SES norm include the sample of Velligan et al. (1990), which used middle-income parents, and Velligan et al.'s (1997) sample, which was 43% Caucasian and 44% Hispanic.

There has been no discussion in the literature of how subcultural vernacular has been scored for minority clients. Jones and Doane (1979) did provide cautionary notes at times about scoring certain categories for speakers for whom English is a second language. This specific issue is revisited later in this chapter. In general, however, Miklowitz and Stackman's (1992) review of general CD literature concluded that CD does not seem to vary according to ethnicity or SES, but they noted the tentative nature of this conclusion and recommended caution extending CD scoring to nonnative English speakers, who have been excluded from published studies for obvious reasons.

With respect to the TAT, three specific studies have examined the cross-cultural validity of TAT CD scores. In a Norwegian sample, Rund (1986) assessed the classificatory usefulness of TAT CD and the Communication Conflict Situation (CCS), an interactional task used by Norwegian researchers to assess communication patterns. Two Norwegian graduate psychology students were trained in TAT CD scoring procedures. Over 100 TAT protocols, the scorers obtained an overall kappa of .72, consulting closely with Doane herself throughout the process. Because the nuances that constitute CD in Finnish might be lost in translation to English, assessing interrater reliability with an American criterion rater was not deemed feasible.

Rund (1986) reported that no differences existed among the parents of a group of schizophrenic patients, a group of nonpatient controls, and a group of psychiatric patient controls on total CD scores. When families were classified as high CD (one standard deviation or higher on total CD), however, 19% of the schizophrenic group had high CD parents, 5% of the nonpatients had high CD parents, and none in the psychiatric patient control group had high CD parents, a statistically significant difference. Scoring categories (14) (*I don't know* endings), (22) (idiosyncratic meaning), (12) (attribution of intent to cards), and (27) (incorrect abstract word usage) were the most robust predictors of group membership, resulting in a correct classification rate of 73.8% when used together in a discriminant function analysis on the schizophrenic and nonpatient groups. However, only the Jones (1977) factor 2 successfully differentiated the parents of schizophrenics from nonpatients, and the egocentricity index of the CCS proved to be a more powerful tool for discriminating group membership. Most interesting, and similar to the Sass et al. (1984) findings with an American sample, CD in parents of paranoids was similar to that in parents of nonpatients. Rund concluded that the TAT and CCS may tap different but complementary aspects of CD, similar to American researchers' conclusions with respect to the TAT and the ICD (Miklowitz et al., 1991; Velligan et al., 1990).

In a second cross-cultural study, a team of researchers lead by Doane et al. (1989) assessed the generalizability of CD scores to a low-acculturation, non-English speaking sample of Mexican American parents of schizophrenics. Doane served as the criterion rater and trained a Spanish-speaking psychologist, Roberto Flores de Apodaca, in the CD scoring system, eventually obtaining an average kappa of .77 across scoring categories, based on agreements both on the presence and absence of CD codes from English-language protocols (kappas for individual scores ranged from .27 for peculiar reasoning to .93 for card 2 figure omitted). Apodaca then translated the CD scoring manual into Spanish and scored the Spanish TAT protocols of the parents of 32 Mexican American schizophrenics. The parents of 32 Anglo-American schizophrenics served as a comparison sample, matched on various demographics such as age, sex, number of offspring hospitalizations, and SES. The results revealed no significant difference between groups in overall levels of CD or factor scores. Anglo-American fathers scored higher only on the overpersonalized closure factor, but when fathers' and mothers' data were considered together, no differences were evident between the groups.

A final study, Nutger et al. (1997), involved assessing the effects of a family or individual intervention on levels of parental CD in a Netherlands sample; however, because it was primarily an assessment of the stability of CD, it will be discussed in detail following. Nutger et al.'s article did indicate that CD can be scored reliably in Dutch but provided no details about whether the manual was actually translated or a bilingual rater used an English manual. In general, however, these studies indicate that CD can be scored reliably in Norwegian, Spanish, and Dutch, although in the cases of Rund (1986) and Nutger et al. it is not clear if there was a formal translation of the CD scoring manual or whether the scorers were bilingual and simply used English CD scoring criteria to score TAT protocols in Norwegian and Dutch. Although there are no data in the literature on interrater reliability of CD within Spanish, the bilingual psychologist who translated the manual did achieve good agreement across language with an English-speaking criterion rater. In Rund (1986) and Doane et al. (1989), results were consistent with previous research, suggesting some cross-cultural criterion validity (e.g., more parental CD for schizophrenics than nonpatients, high parental CD for both English- and Spanish-speaking schizophrenics).

However, caution is recommended applying the scoring system to individuals who do not speak Norwegian, Spanish, or standard American English. Aside from the Velligan et al. (1997) sample in which Anglo-Americans and Hispanics were represented equally, the CD scoring system has been used on Anglo-American populations that would be expected to conform to the grammatical rules and speaking conventions of standard American English. Jones and Doane (1979) also provided a few specific cautions about scoring certain categories in examinees who are not native English speakers. But a more nuanced concern is how to handle subcultural vernacular within the English language.

Many subcultures have speech patterns, grammatical structures, and colloquialisms that range from marginally to substantially different from standard American English. Oppressed groups have also traditionally developed unique modes of communication, in part to veil the meaning of their messages from members of the majority culture. Such discrepancies may not reflect pathogenic markers for offspring thought disorder, an inability to develop a shared focus of attention, or underlying processing or attention deficits at all. Rather, they may simply reflect terminology, phrasing, and speaking styles that others within the subculture understand perfectly well. Thus, great caution should be exercised in application of the TAT CD scoring system to members of subcultures that implement different dialects or strains of English.

Reliability

Researchers do not appear to have systematically explored scorer education levels below which CD scoring becomes unreliable, but nearly all scoring seems to have been done by the study authors themselves, who have generally been associated at one point with the UCLA Family High Risk Project or the NIMH work of Singer and Wynne (1966) (see also Werner et al., 1970). Jones (see Jones 1973, 1977; Jones & Doane, 1979) developed the contemporary scoring system for use in the UCLA project and reported that he was trained by Singer. Jones (1977) in turn trained a graduate student in clinical psychology using five protocols, after which a satisfactory interrater reliability was obtained on another 11. Rund (1986) also trained two graduate students to score CD, but they were closely supervised by Doane. Doane also served as the criterion rater in the Spanish translation project (Doane et al., 1989) and published studies suggest that new raters have typically been trained by a criterion rater associated with the UCLA group.

Interrater reliability calculated based on agreement about the occurrences of CD categories has ranged from .69 (Miklowitz et al., 1991) to .80 (Velligan et al., 1990). Sass et al. (1984) obtained higher agreement for their three indexes of focus, evasiveness, and disorganization. Some studies, such as those of Goldstein (1987a, 1987b), have been follow-up analyses based on the UCLA protocols originally scored by Jones (1977) and thus did not report reliability again. Others, such as Nuechterlein et al. (1989), did not report reliability but simply stated that protocols were scored according to Jones (1977) or Jones and Doane (1979). Table 26.3 displays the average scoring reliability across all CD categories in each published study that reported it. With respect to interrater agreement for factors scores, one study reported intraclass correlations between .55 and .99, with a mean of .79 (Miklowitz et al., 1991). Miklowitz et al. (1991) also had a rater rescore a set of protocols seven years after initially scoring them to assess potential drift. Intraclass correlations between old and recent scores ranged from .82 to .98 for the six factors, and were .99 for overall CD scores. Also of note, Jones (1977) reported a score–rescore correlation of .88 over a three-month interval.

Considerations of test–retest reliability are complicated by the fact that CD may not be a stable trait, despite the initial contentions of Singer and Wynne (e.g., 1965a). The most definitive study of stability was a 15-year longitudinal follow-up of 29 UCLA sample patients (Doane & Mintz, 1987). Patients' mean CD scores as adolescents correlated .40 with their mean scores as adults, and factor 1 (peculiar language) scores were stable at .41 across time. However, a different pattern of results emerged when genders were examined separately. Factors 4 (overpersonalized closure problems), 5 (faulty overintellectualization), and 6 (failure to integrate closure problems) correlated .51, .51, and .45 across time for women—although the last was not significant. But no scores, including mean CD, correlated significantly for men at the two time points, although factor 2 approached significance at $r = .45$. CD per line, and scores on factors 4 and 6, were also significantly higher in adulthood for men and women, independent of their psychiatric diagnosis (9 had no diagnosis in adulthood; the diagnoses of the remaining 20 varied widely, but no particular diagnosis was linked to these mean increases in CD). The authors attributed overall mean CD increases to greater reliance on verbal defenses and perhaps increased perceptions of threat in the TAT task with age. This study assessed CD stability in offspring, however. Nutger et al. (1997) attempted to decrease CD in the parents of schizophrenic-spectrum patients with individual and family treatment for one year and found that neither intervention significantly reduced

TABLE 26.3 Summary of Scoring Reliability for TAT CD Scoring System

Study	Scoring Reliability	Type of Reliability Coefficient and Sample
Nutger, Dingemans, Linzen, Van der Does, and Gersons (1997)	.80	Kappa; Dutch sample
Miklowitz et al. (1991)	.69	Kappa; based on agreement of code occurrence only; from developmental processes in outcome longitudinal study sample (see Miklowitz et al., 1988)
Velligan et al. (1990)	.80	Kappa; based on agreement of code occurrence only; from developmental processes in schizophrenic disorders longitudinal study sample (see Nuechterlein, Edell, Norris, & Dawson, 1986)
Doane et al. (1989)	.77	Kappa; based on agreement of presence or absence of code; based Anglo-Americans sample protocols drawn from broader Miklowitz et al. (1986) sample
Asarnow et al. (1988)	.77	Kappa; based on agreement of presence of codes only; based on a sample from the UCLA Neuropsychiatric Institute
Doane and Mintz (1987)	.77	Kappa; based on agreement of code occurrence only; based on UCLA sample patient initial protocols and protocols at 15-year follow-up
Wagener et al. (1986)	.78	Kappa; based on sample of mothers only from Western Psychiatric Institute
Rund (1986)	.72	Pearson *r* between two raters' codes over 100 transcripts; Norwegian sample
Miklowitz et al. (1986)	.77	Kappa; based on agreement of code occurrence only; based on protocols from Pittsburgh and Los Angeles/Camarillo California (not UCLA High Risk sample) and London sites
Sass et al. (1984)	.84–.90	Pearson *r* between two raters' codes; location and recruitment of sample not given
Jones (1977)	.86	Pearson *r* between two scorers for total CD scores; based on UCLA High-Risk Project protocols

Notes: Doane and Mintz (1987) patient protocols from University of California–Los Angeles High Risk Project; Doane et al. (1989) Anglo-American protocols drawn from Miklowitz et al. (1986) sample.

CD. Families high in CD at pretest were also high in CD at posttest, though correlations are not reported.

Based on their findings, Doane and Mintz (1987) questioned the viability of trait-like notions of CD. However, Nutger et al.'s (1997) data indicate that CD does remain stable over a short period, even in the face of interventions designed to decrease it. One possibility consistent with both studies is that CD is somewhat malleable from adolescence to adulthood but that once CD stabilizes in adulthood, it remains relatively consistent, even in the face of intervention. Another possibility is that CD may be less stable in a mixed population of at-risk adolescents with a variety of diagnoses but may be more trait-like specifically within parents of schizophrenic-spectrum parents. Yet a third possibility is that certain types of CD are stable in men but not in women (consistent with Doane & Mintz, 1987). Clearly these three explanations are not mutually exclusive, and they may interact in various ways, producing a complex pattern of stability and change in CD for different people at different ages.

Since the stability of CD itself is open to question, it would be premature to interpret these studies with respect to the test–retest reliability of the TAT CD scoring system. If CD is not stable or is stable only in certain populations or across certain portions of the lifespan, one would not expect the scoring system to produce similar scores across time. Conclusions about test–retest reliability must await the results of multimethod longitudinal investigation of CD, which will establish whether the construct itself should be expected to remain stable or fluctuate.

Future Research Needed

A research agenda for the TAT scoring system is related to, but necessarily more limited than, a research agenda for CD in general. For a review of the latter that is dated only in some respects, see Miklowitz and Stackman (1992). For the TAT scoring system in particular, five general areas require further elucidation: (1) whether method variance might be responsible for low correlations between TAT CD and other measures of CD, or whether the measures actually tap different constructs; (2) the degree of stability in TAT scores across situations and time periods; (3) a confirmation of the Jones (1977) factor structure in a larger sample; (4) further explorations (with taxometric analysis) of whether the high–intermediate–low CD grouping scheme is supported, or whether CD is better considered a continuously distributed variable; (5) and the validity of the TAT in assessing CD across other non-English speaking cultures and English-speaking subcultures that employ a nonstandard English idiom.

With respect to the first area, it is unclear whether the low correlations observed between the TAT and, for instance, the ICD (e.g., Velligan et al., 1990) are due to qualitative differences in the underlying constructs tapped or due more to variance attributable to assessment method. Correlations attenuated primarily by method variance might provide greater evidence that there is a common underlying CD construct, different elements of which are perhaps tapped by different measurement devices. Low correlations not resulting from method variance might suggest distinct constructs. A multitrait multimethod matrix (MTMM) (Campbell & Fiske, 1959) would be the most obvious way to assess this and should initially employ the most commonly used assessments of CD: the TAT, the Rorschach, and the ICD. Structural equation modeling techniques specific to

MTMM data can be used to model method factors, providing fairly precise estimates of variance due to method, construct, and error (see, e.g., Marsh & Grayson, 1995).

Further work is also need on the stability of TAT CD across situations and time. Situational fluctuations seem inherently confounded with method variance in CD research, because one method is often an individual projective and the other an interactional or problem-solving task with the whole family. Therefore, the persons present covary with assessment method. One way to disentangle situational from method variance would be to develop a consensus TAT like the consensus Rorschach and to compare this with interactional tasks among the same unit of family members. More important, however, may be the temporal stability of TAT CD scores, which requires further elaboration. As noted before, assessments of test–retest reliability must await some sort of consensus among CD researchers about whether CD is temporally stable or changes over time.

In addition, the Jones (1977) factor structure should be replicated. It has served as the basis of score calculation in numerous studies, but its robustness across samples is unknown. Because of the difficulties inherent in recruiting very large clinical populations, Jones's factor analysis was limited to 144 people for 29 variables, a proportion about half the optimal 10 subjects per variable recommended for exploratory factor analysis (e.g., Gorsuch, 1983). Jones also included the patients, parents, and siblings to derive a factor structure applied primarily to parents themselves; the extent to which the factors derived would characterize the data of only parents is open to question. However, the heterogeneous sample used by Jones probably decreased the likelihood of range restriction that could have occurred by using parents only. Also, a different factor structure itself would not affect mean levels of CD: parents of schizophrenic-spectrum patients would still score higher than parents of non-schizophrenic-spectrum patients on any derived factors whether patients and siblings were included in the factor analysis or not.

However, if one wanted to replicate the factor structure in a sample of parents only, the Doane et al. (1986) sample might be a good candidate because it was quite large ($N = 205$), included only the parents of schizophrenics, and studied three different subsamples, one of which was from England. Although the subsamples would be too small for subjects-to-free parameters ratios (e.g., minimally 5:1) recommended for multisample confirmatory factor analysis (CFA), a single confirmatory factor analysis across a homogenous sample would also provide evidence of a robust factor structure. Again, however, one might encounter range restriction in a homogenous sample, which would attenuate variable covariances (relevant for case of CFA) and therefore correlations (relevant for exploratory factor analysis EFA) and might make it more difficult to cross-validate the factor structure.

Another area in need of systematic investigation is actually contingent on the factor structure itself. Many researchers have found that Jones's (1977) high–intermediate–low CD classification scheme works fairly well in predicting hypothesized outcomes (Asarnow et al., 1988; Goldstein, 1987; Nuechterlein et al., 1989). However, it is unclear whether high CD families are qualitatively different from intermediate or low CD families. Whether this classification depicts distinct taxons could be investigated through taxometric analysis. Essentially, this technique assesses the degree to which data supported a categorical or a continuous conceptualization of some construct (Meehl, 1995). Failure to support a distinct high–intermediate–low taxonomy may mean that CD scores in continuous form will have more robust predictive validity. Also relevant here, research could develop standardized cut points on CD scores that will reliably classify offspring as schizophrenic spectrum or bipolar—the diagnoses so far associated with high parental CD).

Finally, more research is needed into the cross-cultural validity of TAT CD scores. This must involve not only nonnative English speaking cultures, after the efforts of Doane et al. (1989) and Rund (1986), but also subcultures within America, the dialects of which do not conform to standard American English. Jones and Doane (1979) also offered occasional cautions about scoring categories in speakers for whom English is a second language; however, the reliability of scoring among scorers of a given language or subcultural dialect should be a central concern. Reliability between a scorer operating within a given language or dialect and a standard English scorer would also be of theoretical interest. It may be that the elements comprising CD are translatable into English from some languages but not others. Similarly, interrater reliability between a standard English speaker and a scorer fluent in a subdialect of English, such as Ebonics, would be an interesting illumination not just of the reliability of TAT CD scoring but also of nuanced linguistic variations in general.

If reliability of scoring can be established within other languages or dialects, research can proceed to examine the extent to which parental CD is associated with offspring diagnosis and distress in other populations. If high CD in other cultures is not particularly linked to offspring dysfunction, this would vitiate claims that it is an etiological factor in or the result of psychopathology, as well as hypotheses that there is a shared genetic basis for parental CD and offspring pathology. On the other hand, cross-cultural replication of links between parental CD and offspring diagnosis would not necessarily strengthen the hypothesis that there is some genetic substrate underlying this relationship, only that the causal elements responsible for both are generalizable across language and culture. In any event, the causal role of parental CD in subsequent offspring psychopathology remains difficult to deduce.

☐ References

Asarnow, J. R., Goldstein, M. J., & Ben-Meir, S. (1988). Parental communication deviance in childhood onset schizophrenia spectrum and depressive disorders. *Journal of Child Psychology and Psychiatry, 29,* 825–838.

Bateson, G., Jackson, D., Haley, J., & Weakland, J. (1956). Toward a theory of schizophrenia. *Behavioral Sciences, 1,* 251–264.

Campbell, D.T., & Fiske, J.C. (1959). Convergent and discriminant validation by the multitrait–multimethod matrix. *Psychological Bulletin, 56,* 81–105.

Doane, J. (1985). Parental communication deviance and offspring psychopathology. In L. L'Abate (Ed.), *Handbook of Family Psychology and Therapy, 2,* 937–958.

Doane, J., & Mintz, J. (1987). Communication deviance in adolescence and adulthood: A longitudinal study. *Psychiatry: Journal for the Study of Interpersonal Processes, 50,* 5–13.

Doane, J., Miklowitz, D. J., Oranchack, E., Flores de Apodaca, R., Karno, M., Strachan, A. M., et al. (1989). Parental communication deviance and schizophrenia: A cross-cultural comparison of Mexican and Anglo-Americans. *Journal of Abnormal Psychology, 98,* 487–490.

Doane, J. A., West, K. L., Goldstein, M. J., Rodnick, E. H., & Jones, J. E. (1981). Parental communication deviance and affective style: Predictors of subsequent schizophrenia-spectrum disorders in vulnerable adolescents. *Archives of General Psychiatry, 38,* 679–685.

Goldstein, M. J. (1987a). Family interaction patterns that antedate the onset of schizophrenia and related disorders: A further analysis of data from a longitudinal prospective study. In K. Hawlweg & M. J. Goldstein (Eds.), *Understanding major mental disorder: The contribution of family interaction research* (pp. 11–32). New York: Family Process Press.

Goldstein, M. J. (1987b). The UCLA High-Risk Project. *Schizophrenia Bulletin, 13,* 505–514.

Goldstein, M. J., Gould, E., Alkire, A., Rodnick, E. H., & Judd, L. L. (1970). Interpersonal themes in the Thematic Apperception Test stories of families of disturbed adolescents. *Journal of Nervous and Mental Disease, 150,* 354–365.

Gorsuch, R. L. (1983). *Factor analysis.* Hillsdale, NJ: Erlbaum.

Jones, J. E. (1973). *Communication deviance scoring manual.* Unpublished manuscript.

Jones, J. E. (1977). Patterns of transactional style deviance in the TATs of parents of schizophrenics. *Family Process, 16,* 327–337.

Jones, J. E., & Doane, J. A. (1979). *Communication deviance scoring manual.* Unpublished manuscript. University of Rochester School of Medicine and Dentistry.

Jones, J. E., Rodnick, E. H., Goldstein, M. J., McPherson, S. R., & West, K. L. (1977). Parental transactional style deviance as a possible indicator of risk for schizophrenia. *Archives of General Psychiatry, 34,* 71–74.

Lewis J. M., Rodnick, E. H., & Goldstein, M. J. (1981). Intrafamilial interactive behavior, parental communication deviance, and risk for schizophrenia. *Journal of Abnormal Psychology, 90,* 448–457.

Marsh, H. W., & Grayson, D. G. (1995). Latent variable models of multitrait–multimethod data. In R. H. Hoyle (Ed.), *Structural equation modeling: Concepts, issues, and applications* (pp. 177–198). Thousand Oaks, CA, Sage Publications.

Meehl, P. (1995). Bootstrap taxometrics: Solving the classification problem in psychopathology. *American Psychologist, 50,* 266–275.

Miklowitz, D. J. (1994). Family risk indicators in schizophrenia. *Schizophrenia Bulletin, 20,* 137–149.

Miklowitz, D. J., Goldstein, M. J., Nuechterlein, K. H., Snyder, K. S., & Mintz, J. (1988). Family factors and the course of bipolar affective disorder. *Archives of General Psychiatry, 45,* 225–231.

Miklowitz, D. J., Strachman, A. M., Goldstein, M. J., Doane, J. A., Snyder, K. S., Hogarty, G. E., et al. (1986). Expressed emotion and communication deviance in the families of schizophrenics. *Journal of Abnormal Psychology, 95,* 60–66.

Miklowitz, D. J., & Stackman, D. (1992). Communication deviance in families of schizophrenic and other psychiatric patients: Current state of the construct. In E. F. Walker, E. H. Dworking, & B. A. Kornblatt (Eds.), *Progress in Experimental Personality Research,* (vol. 15) (pp. 1–46). New York: Springer Publishing Company.

Miklowitz, D. J., Velligan, D. I., Goldstein, M. J., Nuechterlein, K. H., & Gitlin, M. J. (1991). Communication deviance in the families of schizophrenic and manic patients. *Journal of Abnormal Psychology, 100,* 163–173.

Morris, G. O., & Wynne, L. C. (1965). Schizophrenic offspring and parental styles of communication: A predictive study using excerpts of family therapy recordings. *Psychiatry, 28,* 19–44.

Nuechterlein, K. H., Edell, W. S., Norris, M., & Dawson, M. E. (1986). Attentional vulnerability indicators, thought disorder, and negative symptoms. *Schizophrenia Bulletin 12,* 408–426.

Nuechterlein, K. H., Goldstein, M. J., Dawson, M. E., & Doane, J. A. (1989). Patient–environment relationships in schizophrenia: Information processing, communication deviance, autonomic arousal, and stressful life events. *British Journal of Psychiatry, 155 (Suppl. 5),* 84–89.

Nutger, M. A., Dingemans, P. M. A. J., Linzen, D. H., Van der Does, A. J. W., & Gersons, B. P. R. (1997). Parental communication deviance: Its stability and the effect of family treatment in recent-onset schizophrenia. *Acta Pyschiatrica Scandinavia, 95,* 199–204.

Rund, B. R. (1986). Communication deviances in parents of schizophrenics. *Family Process, 25,* 133–147.

Sass, L. A., Gunderson, J. G., Singer, M. T., & Wynne, L. C. (1984). Parental communication deviance and forms of thinking in male schizophrenic offspring. *Journal of Nervous and Mental Disease, 172,* 513–520.

Singer, M. T., & Wynne, L. C. (1965a). Thought disorder and family relations of schizophrenics: III. Methodology using projective techniques. *Archives of General Psychiatry, 12,* 187–200.

Singer, M. T., & Wynne, L. C. (1965b). Thought disorder and family relations of schizophrenics: IV. Results and implications. *Archives of General Psychiatry, 12,* 201–212.

Singer, M., & Wynne, L. C. (1966). Principles for scoring communication defects and deviances in parents of schizophrenics: Rorschach and TAT scoring manuals. *Psychiatry, 29,* 260–288.

Stabenau, J. R., Tupin, J., Werner, M., & Pollin, W. (1965). A comparative study of families of schizophrenics, delinquents, and normals. *Psychiatry, 1965,* 45–49.

Velligan, D. I., Goldstein, M. J., Nuechterlein, K. H., Miklowitz, D. J., & Ranlett, G. (1990). Can communication deviance be measured in a family problem-solving interaction? *Family Process, 29,* 213–226.

Velligan, D. I., Mahurin, R. K., Eckert, S. L., Hazleton, B. C., & Miller, A. (1997). Relationship between specific types of communication deviance and affective performance in patients with schizophrenia. *Psychiatry Research, 70,* 9–20.

Wagener, D. K., Hogarty, G. E., Goldstein, M. J., Asarnow, R. F., & Browne, A. (1986). Information processing and communication deviance in schizophrenic patients and their mothers. *Psychiatry Research, 18,* 365–377.

Wahlberg, K. E., Wynne, L. C., Oja, H., Keskitalo, P., Anais-Tanner, H., Koistinen, P., et al. (2000). Thought disorder index of Finnish adoptees and communication deviance of their adoptive parents. *Psychological Medicine, 30,* 127–136.

Wahlberg, K. E., Wynne, L. C., Oja, H., Keskitalo, P., Pykalainen, L., Lahti, I., et al. (1997) Gene-environment interaction in vulnerability to schizophrenia: Findings from the Finnish adoptive family study of schizophrenia. *American Journal of Psychiatry, 154,* 355–363.

Werner, M., Stabenau, J. R., & Polling, W. (1970). Thematic Apperception Test method for the differentiation of families of schizophrenics, delinquents, and "normals." *Journal of Abnormal Psychology, 75,* 139–145.

Wild, C., Singer, M., Rosman, B., Ricci, J., & Lidz, T. (1965). Measuring disordered styles of thinking: Using the Object Sorting Test on parents of schizophrenic patients. *Archives of General Psychiatry, 13,* 471–476.

Wynne, L. C., & Singer, M. T. (1963). Thought disorder and family relations of schizophrenics: I. A research strategy. *Archives of General Psychiatry, 9,* 191–198.

Wynne, L. C., Singer, M., Bartko, J., & Toohey, M. (1977). Schizophrenics and their families: Recent research on parental communication. In J. M. Tanner (Ed.), *Developments in psychiatric research* (pp. 254–284). London: Hodder & Stoughton.

□ Notes

[1]Briefly, Singer and Wynne (1966, p. 261) believed that normal personality development is disrupted in schizophrenics when environmental characteristics do not accommodate a child's maturational needs: "This means that certain transactional conditions are necessary as a framework for children to learn culturally appropriate skills, such as 'reality testing,' a sense of self and self-boundaries, an interest and ability in establishing interpersonal relationships, and an interest and ability in establishing directionality and goal-directedness in his [sic] life."

[2]Jones subsequently went to the University of Rochester, where he was when he published the major introduction to the contemporary CD scoring system (Jones, 1977).

[3]The so-called regression method is the current default for factor score computation in SPSS. Factor score computation in this manner involves standardizing variables and weighting them by a factor score coefficient matrix, which is produced by multiplying the inverse of the variable correlation matrix with the factor loading matrix. Using the resulting factor score coefficient matrix, a variable's score is computed by summing its standardized score weighted by each factor–score coefficient in the row. Tabachnik and Fidell (1996, pp. 649–650) provided a readable summary of this procedure.

27

CHAPTER

TAT Affective Scale

Antoinette D. Thomas

Abstract

Affect toward parental, spousal, and nonspousal figures in Thematic Apperception Test (TAT) responses was evaluated in two studies. Higher positive spousal than parental and nonspousal affect was hypothesized to associate with marital adjustment. In study 1, positive and negative scores ranging from +2 to −2 were assigned to each story. Scoring guides were based on frequent responses, stimulus pull, and quality of responses. Test–retest reliability over two weeks rendered r = .88 similarity in affect and 86% agreement in interpersonal categories. Interscorer agreements on affective scores ranged from r = .93 to .97 and interpersonal categories ranged from 96 to 98% agreement. Interviewees were 30 married Caucasian middle-class couples. Cards 1, 2, 4, 6GF, 13MF, and 16, as well as the Dyadic Adjustment Scale (Spanier, 1976), were administered. Results, significant at the .001 level, were discussed in terms of development in interpersonal choices. Study 2 focused on couples as a unit of analysis. Qualitative analysis on the couple level was based on quantitative affective scores obtained by each spouse within each couple in study 1. Four conjugal profiles were identified: spousal primacy, affective imbalance, underlying difficulties, and apparent difficulties. These profiles present positions on a developmental continuum of interpersonal choices ranging from highest to lowest positive affect within spousal projected interactions as opposed to parental and nonspousal affect.

Description of System

In an early qualitative study of adjusted married couples (Thomas, 1966), it was noticed that Thematic Apperception Test (TAT) stories evolved around one dominant interpersonal relationship. Subjects talked about a main figure interacting with one TAT figure perceived as a spouse, a parent, or a friend more than they did about the other figures. The affective content could be positive or negative. This result was elaborated in a quantitative system to evaluate the two affective polarities. The relationship that obtained the highest net (positive minus negative) total score was considered the dominant interpersonal relationship. Comparisons were made among three relationships: spousal, parental, and nonspousal. It was hypothesited that interpersonal affect attributed to TAT figures interpreted as spousal, parental, and nonspousal figures would reflect the quality of affect directed toward spouse and parents in the married partners' lives. This scoring system for interpersonal affect demonstrated its effectiveness with a group of married couples (Thomas, 1979; Thomas & Dudek, 1985). An "Other" category, such as brother–sister, included relations apart from spousal, parental, and nonspousal, but these relationships were not studied separately. An important subcategory, nonattributed affect, within the Other category, which reflects internal affect and a general affective disposition in the absence of an interpersonal relationship, was added (Thomas, 1994). The TAT Interpersonal Affective Scale became the TAT Affective Scale. The present work is a revision and expansion of the scale.

Conceptual Framework

The theoretical orientation to interpersonal affect as an index of emotional maturity was influenced by the writings of Freud (1961a, 1961b, 1961c), Erikson (1963), Sullivan (1953), and in particular by the object relations theory of Fairbairn (1946). Focusing study this was chosen on marital adjustment, the TAT such as the ideal instrument to serve purposes. Several interpretive methods have emphasized interpersonal relations (Bellak, 1975; Fine, 1951 cited in Bellak, 1975; Goldstein, Gould, Alkine, Rodrick, & Judd, 1970). However, they were not suited to our purpose. It was it necessary to elaborate a scoring system that would reflect the quality and direction of interpersonal affect and that was simple, direct, and quantitatively scorable.

The scoring system and its rationale are similar to Holt's (1951) and to Bellak's (1975) inspection technique, in aiming at a condensed interpretation. Holt's method tends to condense clinical hypotheses in the course of analyzing the stories and integrates them in a summary. Bellak's technique underlines any significant or special statements in the stories. These significant statements usually fall into a meaningful whole. These methods, however, do not allow research comparisons. The present technique resembles other traditional expansive methods in making use of a fixed framework of categories (Bellak, 1975). The problem with expansive methods is that a protocol becomes much larger, but the present system transfers stories into just a few numerical values and locates them within three main interpersonal categories.

Subjects have perceived in the TAT ambiguous human situations according to their past experiences and emotions (Murray, 1943). "The strength of this projective technique lies in its ability to elicit the content and dynamics of interpersonal relationships" (Bellak, 1975, pp. 66–67). Our work was described as "carefully reasoned, well researched and the scoring system should be very useful" (Bellak, personal communication, May 13, 1985). This is particularly relevant in understanding married couples and comparable dyads. For example, in a construct validation study, based on a large national sample in the United States, Richardson and Partridge (1982) asserted that the choice of imagery and themes within apperception stories was not a haphazard process. The apperception data reflected the salience of marriage and the family.

Affect is mostly directed toward parents in childhood. Adolescents usually give their peers this position, whereas in adulthood a stable lover becomes the primary recipient of one's affect. A host of theoretical and empirical material has supported this developmental progression. The studies of Floyd and South (1972) and of Walshe, Ferrell, and Tolone (1976) showed that significant or orientation others gradually proceed from parents to peers during adolescence, whereas Levinson, Darrow, Klein, Levinson, and McKee (1978) reported that early adult transition necessitates separation from parents as well as giving up adolescent groups.

On a less conscious level, unsolved parent–child emotional problems, which preclude detachment from parents, can be a source of future marital discord (e.g., Blood, 1969; Dicks, 1971; Kubie, 1956; Stewart, Peters, Marsh, & Melinda, 1975) whereas parents are unrealistically idealized (Fairbairn, 1952). Negative aspects, internalized from the early parent–child relationship, are projected onto the present heterosexual partner (Bouvet, 1959). In other words, a spouse may employ with the marriage partner the negative affect learned in childhood. To avoid admitting childhood conflicts, one may idealize parents, whereas on a less conscious level, elicited by TAT cards, adult respondents may convey old feelings toward their parents.

Many researchers have pointed out that strong attachments to parents underlie some types of marital problems (Ackerman, 1958; Blood, 1969; Bouvet, 1973; Dicks, 1971; Kubie, 1956; Stewart et al., 1975). Unconscious demands are often made by a spouse to solve an old conflict with a parent of the opposite (or same) sex, by expecting the spouse to play the anticipated parental role (Ackerman, 1958; Kubie, 1956). The anger and disappointment centered on the original important objects—the parents—are projected onto the now important and available person, the wife or husband (Borzormenyi-Nagy & Spark, 1973).

In addition, the adult who still lives in the parent–child relation unrealistically tends to idealize the parents that continue to be psychologically needed (Fairbairn, 1952), and the spouse suffers by comparison. The internalized negative feelings are projected onto the love object (Bouvet, 1959), and the unconscious nature of this projection makes resolution of the problem difficult. Empirical findings have supported an inverse relationship between closeness to extended family and friends versus spouse (Bott, 1957; Burgess, Locke, & Thomas, 1963; Farber, 1966; Wimberly, 1973).

By comparison, in institutional marriages the extended family organization implies precedence of the parent–child over the husband–wife relationship. Extended family solidarity is more important than the desires for individual expression of nuclear family members (Burgess et al., 1963). Weaker ties with one's own family are associated with more husband–wife closeness (Goodrich, Ryder, & Ransh, 1968).

The scoring guidelines were prepared after lengthy discussion with several consultants; this study is a part of a larger one (Thomas, 1979), which included other tests. Findings from the initial study are consistent with the classical notion in psychoanalytic literature that emotional detachment from parental ties is found where there is a stable attachment in adulthood to one person of the opposite sex (Freud, 1961a, 1961b, 1961c). Such detachment is based on predominantly gratifying parent–child relationships in childhood. An easy transition to spouse or stable lover takes place in adulthood. In addition, normal adults deal with their parents on an adult–adult level. Therefore, they may not deny some negative feelings toward them. In the initial study, the overall affect in the parent category was an almost split in half, with a slight tendency toward positive feelings. On the contrary, those who had predominantly troublesome relationships with their parents in childhood may tend to idealize their parents and direct negative feelings

TABLE 27.1 Scoring Categories for Affect

	Emotional Quality of Transaction?				
	Negative Feelings			Positive Feelings	
With Whom?	Strong	Weak	Not in Story	Weak	Strong
Spouse	– 2	–1	0	+ 1	+ 2
Parent	– 2	–1	0	+ 1	+ 2
Nonspouse	– 2	–1	0	+ 1	+ 2
Other	– 2	–1	0	+ 1	+ 2
Nonattributed Affect	– 2	–1	0	+ 1	+ 2

toward their spouses (Ackerman, 1958; Borzormenyi-Nagy & Spark, 1973; Bouvet, 1959; Dicks, 1971). This notion has been generally accepted. The first study to test this developmental concept in a nonpathological group using the TAT was Thomas (1979) and Thomas and Dudek (1985).

Scoring Categories

The scoring technique was devised to assess the manifest content. The central questions are as follows: With whom does the hero carry out the personal interaction—that is, spouse, parent, nonspouse (friend), or child? What is the emotional quality of the transaction? The quality of the affect is evaluated in each story and is placed within an interpersonal category. The four basic interpersonal categories are spouse, parent, nonspouse (i.e., same generation, either sex), and other (e.g., brother–sister). Nonspousal themes may refer to life or imagined persons. Nonattributed affect (i.e., internal feelings not involving another figure) is also a scored category (see Table 27.1).

☐ Research Evidence

Validity

In comparison with the typically reported predominantly negative emotions projected on the TAT cards (Bellak, 1975; Morval, 1977; Murstein, 1965) participants in this study scored somewhat on the positive side. The mean affective net scores (positive minus negative) were as follows: spouse = 1.7; parent = .1, nonspouse = .7; and all categories = .37. Thus, this group had relatively more positive interpersonal emotionality than other groups reported in TAT literature, especially affect toward spousal figures. Positive affect predominated over negative affect consistently for the group, χ^2 (1, N = 238) = 45.4,

$p < .001$. This may reflect the fact that we dealt with a nonpathological group. Most couples projected both positive and negative affect in their total record as would be expected in any close relationship (correlation between presence of positive and negative in the same record was .22, $p < .05$).

The findings supported our initial hypothesis that married partners who project evidence in the TAT of greater detachment from their parents by associating TAT figures described in spousal terms—as opposed to parental terms—with positive as opposed to negative affect show evidence of better adjustment as measured by the Dyadic Adjustment Scale (DAS), χ^2 (2, n = 60) = 17.40, 19.58, respectively, $p < .001$. Higher overall affect directed to spouse than to either parent or nonspouse on the TAT was associated significantly with marital adjustment on the Dyadic Adjustment Scale. The sample was divided into two groups based on marital adjustment scores; the higher group obtained more than the whole sample's average score. Both the higher and the lower groups gave higher mean spouse scores than parent and nonspouse mean scores. For the higher maritally adjusted group, the mean overall affective score for spouse was 8.0, whereas the mean score for parent was 5.56 and for nonspouse was 5.41, a significant difference, F (2, 57) = 10.62, $p < .001$. Similar though less dramatic results were obtained for the lower adjusted group.

Our group scores on the DAS (mean [M] = 114.8, standard deviation [SD] = 17.8) was compatible with Spanier's normative married group (M = 113.9, SD = 14.0). Our group (N = 60) was largely homogeneous to avoid intervening variables reported in literature. They were Caucasian Canadians, equally Catholics and Protestants, had school-age children (6–18 years), had high school education or above, had no psychiatric hospitalization or marriage counseling, were on their first marriage, and had dual-family income. This contributed to criterion validity of the scale.

The inverse relation between affect toward spouse versus parents was shown in two TAT correlation coefficients: (1) negative parent scores with positive spouse scores (r = .32, $p < .01$); and (2) positive parent scores with negative spouse scores (r = .21, p = .05). These results are consistent with other empirical findings on the inverse relation in married couples between closeness to spouse versus extended family. The net affective scores on the TAT attributed to the three interpersonal categories of spouse, parent, and nonspouse were independent of sex as well as demographic variables such as religious affiliation, age, number of years married, number of children, education or occupation.

Generalizability

Although there is little formal research evidence published, it appears that this scoring system is also useful with children, other dyads, and for cross-cultural comparisons (see chapter 28, this volume).

Reliability

Interscorer reliability was computed between two scorers and the first investigator (Thomas, 1979; Thomas & Dudek, 1985). Scorers were experienced psychologists who were familiar with the scoring system. Each had independently scored 20 protocols chosen from the studied group protocols by means of random numbers tables. Pearson product–moment correlations of the agreement on affective scores were .97, .93, and .93. Percentages of agreement between scorers were 93%, 89%, and 87%. Agreements on orientational others categories were 98%, 98%, and 96%.

Test–retest reliability was done on an independent group (4 couples and 12 married persons) who met the selection criteria (Thomas, 1979; Thomas & Dudek, 1985). The two administrations were two weeks apart. The Pearson product–moment correlation coefficient was .88 for the affective scores. The congruence between the two test results was 88% for affective scores and 86% for the orientational others categories.

□ Case Illustration

The following is a couple profile fitting the spousal primacy profile from the couple level in study 2. The stories—some have been condensed—scores, and qualitative analysis for a husband and wife are presented here and may be used for practice to begin learning the system. Similar materials for the other three profiles appear in the scoring manual as additional materials to practice scoring.

A couple profile can be created using the scoring scheet provided in the scoring manual chapter. A set of small red circles for the wife's scores and small blue triangles for husband's give a visual layout of the couple's respective positions on the scored categories. It also displays the pattern of positive and negative scores.

Husband TAT

Card 1: My impression is that he doesn't want to play the fiddle. His mother wants him to. He'll do it anyway because his mother wants.

Card 2: The girl is turning her back to the rural way of life, wondering whether she should or shouldn't (Q) possibly a relationship between her and him, mother and son I guess, it could be husband and wife, no, mother, son and daughter (Q: girl–mother) good relationship.

Card 4: A bar room scene, she's trying to restrain him from making trouble, he isn't willing to be restrained (Q) possibly lovers, she doesn't want him to be in trouble.

Card 6GF: She's apprehensive to the guy with the pipe in his mouth, probably know each other but not too well yet (Q) nothing, honorable intention (Q), social function, no personal relation as love or marriage.

Card 10: Trust and affection based on a long relationship, either probably been married for a while or getting married, whatever.

Card 13MF: This picture conveys sexual relationship without love or having lasting relationship. Neither feels good about each other, the man feels guilty; the woman doesn't care.

Card 16: Card 10 keeps coming back; it's bringing the same story I said, the trust and love in a meaningful relationship between a man and a woman.

- Categories and scores: Card 1, parent −1; card 2, parent +1; card 4, nonspouse +2; card 6GF, nonspouse −1; card 10, spouse +2; card 13MF, nonspouse −1; card 16, spouse +2.
- Net TAT scores: Spouse = 4; parent (+1, −1) = 0; nonspouse (+2, −2) = 0.

Wife TAT

Card 1: A little boy, I have to relate it to (son's name) he was attracted then found it was difficult, he's wondering what he wants.

Card 2: A girl going to school, she comes from a farm. She's trying to study, she thinks about the farm a lot. Her mother is looking at her father. Her father is a strong farmer. She's divided, leaving it behind to study.

Card 4: A man and a woman, it seems that the woman tries to hold to him. He has a pin-up woman, maybe a playboy. She wants to hold to him and he's trying to go, not interested (Q) must be lovers, don't think they are married.

Card 6GF: She looks a bit weary, conscious. He's quite interested in her. What relationship I don't know, could be daughter and father, he seems to be the stronger one, makes a point. An old-fashioned picture.

Card 10: Two lovers—I don't know whether husband and wife or not. They seem to be happy together, enjoy holding each other. In the two other pictures, there is a feeling of staying away from each other, this one no (Q) either married or not.

Card 13MF: He's upset about something. She's lying there. She could be dead for all I know. She's gone to bed ready for him. He can't face it, his mistress. He has a wife, a single bed.

Card 16: A happy family, my family, my husband, our two children and me (showed photo).

- Categories and scores: Card 1, other 1, nonattributed affect +1; card 2, parent +1; card 4, nonspouse −1; card 6GF, parent +1; card 10, spouse +2, nonspouse +2; card 13MF, nonspouse −1; card 16, spouse +2, other 2, self–offspring +2.
- Net TAT scores: Spouse = +4; parent = +2; nonspouse (+2, −2) = 0; other 1, nonattributed affect = +1; other 2, self–offspring = +2.
- Couple summary scores:
  - Husband TAT: Spouse = 4; parent = 0; nonspouse = 0; DAS = 116
  - Wife TAT: Spouse = 4; parent = 2; nonspouse = 0; other 1, nonattributed affect = 1; other 2, self–offspring = 2; DAS = 124

Comments

This couple presented a stable, smooth affective tone. The spousal relationship was explicitly described as meaningful and lasting, characterized by trust, love, and happiness.

No negative affect was employed in spousal themes—though not categorically true for this subgroup. For both partners, overall affect toward spousal figures was more positive than that directed toward parental and nonspousal figures. The wife reflected respect for children's autonomy as well as happiness. Both spouses chose a happy couple or nuclear family in response to the blank card (16), a revealing card for couple-interaction profiles. On the marital adjustment scale, both scored above normative and study averages.

☐ Couple Level, Study 2: Conjugal TAT Affective Profiles

In study 1, the TAT Interpersonal Affective Scale provided quantitative assessment of affect projected on TAT figures perceived as spouse, parent, and nonspouse (Thomas, 1979; Thomas & Dudek, 1985). In study 2 (Thomas, 1993, 1996), a second level of analysis was employed on data collected for the previous study. Qualitative analysis on the couple level, based on quantitative affective scores obtained by each spouse within each couple, rendered four conjugal profiles: (1) spousal primacy; (2) affective imbalance; (3) underlying difficulties; and (4) apparent difficulties. These profiles present couples' dual positions on a developmental continuum of interpersonal choices ranging from highest to lowest positive affect within the spousal projected interaction as compared with parental and nonspousal affect. The profiles were supported by perceived marital adjustment on the DAS (Spanier, 1976). Nonattributed affect scores (Thomas, 1994) were reported to complement the general display of each profile. This subcategory deals with affect that is not directed toward a person. It includes general affect, such as a character's happiness or sadness.

In this within-subject design using subject attributes, three research questions were posed: What kind of conjugal interaction occurred when (1) both married partners obtained higher spousal than parental and nonspousal scores; (2) both married partners obtained lower spousal than parental and nonspousal scores; and (3) one partner obtained higher whereas the other obtained lower spousal than parental and nonspousal scores.

Couples were located on a continuum of interpersonal choices. The continuum proceeded from higher to lower spousal than parental and nonspousal scores. Five subgroups emerged. To answer the research questions, conjugal interactions were examined in three subgroups: (1) In the spousal primacy profile, both married partners obtained higher spousal than parental and nonspousal scores (13 couples, 43%; see case illustration, this chapter); (2) both married partners obtained lower spousal than parental and nonspousal scores (2 couples, 7%), as illustrated in the underlying difficulties and apparent difficulties profiles; and (3) one partner obtained higher whereas the other obtained lower spousal than parental and nonspousal scores (2 couples, 7%), portrayed in the affective imbalance profile. TAT stories, affective scores, and categories of the three previous profiles are displayed in chapter 28 in this volume as further training practice.

The two other (4, 5) subgroups (13 couples, 43%), which had subsequent positions to the first subgroup, were beyond the scope of this study. These results are not surprising in view of the selection criteria that were geared toward a homogenous adjusted married group.

Profiles identified in this maritally adjusted group may be theoretically and clinically significant as a hypothetical expansion in the opposite direction from distressed couples typologies (e.g., Falls-Stewart, Birchler, Schafer, & Lucente, 1994) in spite of methodological differences.

Future Research

Research studies are needed on larger married samples as well as other adjusted and maladjusted dyadic groups. Constructing similar scales for other TAT cards is recommended. Using our guidelines for adapting the TAT Affective Scale in research for use with children and adolescents is equally required. Some suggested topics for future studies are problems and affect toward siblings versus peers, parents versus teachers or other adults, and nonattributed affect or anticipated spousal affect compared to spousal affect, in a longitudinal study, are interesting. Investigating frequent negative nonattributed affect, which reflects a general affective disposition and nonsocial affect, in groups of antisocial subjects and those who have difficulties expressing their feelings in words, would be interesting. Adding all positive versus all negative score for all relationships may give a picture of general positive versus negative affectivity.

References

Ackerman, N. (1958). *Psychodynamics of family life.* New York: Basic Books.

Bellak, L. (1975). *The TAT, CAT and SAT in clinical use* (3rd ed.). New York: Grune & Stratton.

Blishen, B. (1971). A socio-economic index for occupations in Canada. In B. Blishen, F. Jones, K. Naegell, & J. Porter (Eds.), *Canadian society: Sociological perspectives* (pp. 741–755). Toronto: Macmillan.

Blood, R. O., Jr. (1969). *Marriage.* New York: Free Press.

Boszormenyi-Nagy, I., & Spark, G. M. (1973). *Invisible loyalties, reciprocity in intergenerational family therapy.* New York: Harper & Row.

Bott, E. (1957). *Family and social network.* London: Tavistock.

Bouvet, M. (1959). Clinical analysis. In S. Nacht (Ed.), *Psychoanalysis of today* (pp. 13–70). New York: Grune & Stratton.

Burgess, E. W., Locke, J. H., & Thomas, M. (1963). *The family from institution to companionship.* New York: American Book.

Chusmir, L. H. (1983). Male-oriented versus balanced-as-to-sex Thematic Apperception Tests. *Journal of Personality Assessment, 47,* 29–35.

Dicks, H. V. (1971). Experiences with marital tensions seen in the psychological clinic. In J. G. Howells (Ed.), *Theory and practice of family psychiatry* (pp. 267–287). New York: Brunner & Mazel.

Erikson, E. H. (1963). *Childhood and society.* New York: Norton.

Eron, L. D. (1959). The Thematic Apperception Test: Review. In O. K. Buros (Ed.), *The fifth mental measurement yearbook* (vol. 1) (pp. 306–310). Oxford, England Gryphon Press.

Eron, L. D. (1962). The Thematic Apperception Test: Review. In O. K. Buros (Ed.), *The seventh mental measurement yearbook* (vol. 1) (pp. 460–462). Oxford, England Gryphon Press.

Fairbairn, W. R. D. (1946). Object-relationships and dynamic structure. *International Journal of Psychoanalysis, 27,* 30–36.

Fairbairn, W. R. D. (1952). *Psychoanalytic studies of the personality.* London: Tavistock.

Fals-Stewart, W., Birchles, G., Schafer, J., & Lucente, S. (1994). The personality of marital distress: An empirical typology. *Journal of Personality Assessment, 62,* 223–241.

Farber, B. (1966). *Kinship and family organization.* New York: Wiley.

Floyd, H. H., Jr., & South, D. R. (1972). Dilemma of youth: The choice of parents or peers as a frame of reference for behaviour. *Journal of Marriage and the Family, 34,* 627–634.

Freud, S. (1961a). Family romances. In J. Strachey (Ed. and Trans.), *The standard edition of the complete psychological works of Sigmund Freud* (vol. 9) (pp. 237–243). London: Hogarth Press.

Freud, S. (1961b). The development of the libido and the sexual organization. In J. Strachey (Ed. and Trans.), *The standard edition of the complete psychological works of Sigmund Freud* (vol. 16) (pp. 320–338). London: Hogarth Press.

Freud, S. (1961c). The dissolution of the Oedipus complex. In J. Strachey (Ed. and Trans.), *The standard edition of the complete psychological works of Sigmund Freud* (vol. 19) (pp. 173–179). London: Hogarth Press.

Goldstein, M. J., Gould, E., Alkire, A., Rodrick, E. H., & Judd, L. L. (1970). Interpersonal themes in the TAT stories of families of disturbed adolescents. *Journal of Nervous and Mental Disorders, 1550,* 334–365.

Goodrich, D. W., Ryder, R., & Rausch, H. (1968). Patterns of newly wed marriage. *Journal of Marriage and the Family, 30,* 383–391.

Holt, R. R. (1951). The Thematic Apperception Test. In H. H. Anderson (Ed.), *An introduction to projective techniques* (pp. 181–229). New York: Prentice-Hall.

Kahn, M. (1984). The usefulness of the TAT blank card in clinical practice. *Psychotherapy in Private Practice, 2,* 43–50.

Kalliopuska, M. (1982). Empathy measured by Rorschach and TAT. *British Journal of Projective Psychology & Personality Study, 27,* 5–11.

Karon, B. P., & O'Grady, P. (1970). Quantified judgments of mental health from the Rorschach, TAT, and Clinical Status Interview by means of a scaling technique. *Journal of Consulting and Clinical Psychology, 34,* 229–235.

Kubie, L. S. (1956). Psychoanalysis and marriage: Practical and theoretical issues. In V. W. Eisenstein (Ed.), *Neurotic interaction in marriage* (pp. 10–43). New York: Basic Books.

Levinson, D., Darrow, C. N., Klein, E. B., Levinson, M. H., & Mckee, B. (1978). *The seasons of a man's life.* New York: Knopf.

Lundy, A. (1988). Instructional set and Thematic Apperception Test validity. *Journal of Personality Assessment, 52,* 309–320.

McClelland, D. C., Atkinson, J. W., Clark, R. A. & Lowell, E. L. (1953). *The achievement motive.* New York: Appleton-Century Crofts.

Mitchell, K. M. (1974). Relationship between different levels of parental "pathogenesis" and male children's diagnosis. *Journal of Clinical Psychology, 30,* 49–50.

Morval, M. V. G. (1977). *Le TAT et les fonctions du moi* [The TAT and the functions of the ego]. Montreal: Les Presses de l'Université de Montréal.

Murray, H. A. (1943). *Manual for the Thematic Apperception Test.* Cambridge, MA: Harvard University Press.

Murstein, B. I. (1963). *Theory and research in projective techniques: Emphasizing the TAT.* New York: Wiley.

Murstein, B. I. (1965). The stimulus. In B. I. Murstein (Ed.), *Handbook of projective techniques* (pp. 509–546). New York: Basic Books.

Peterson, C. A., & Schilling, K. H. (1983). Card pull in projective testing. *Journal of Personality Assessment, 47,* 265–275.

Piotrowski, C., & Zalewski, C. (1993). Training in psycho-diagnostic testing in APA-approved PsyD and PhD clinical psychology programs. *Journal of Personality Assessment, 61,* 394–405.

Richardson, V., & Partridge, S. (1982). Construct validation of imaginative assessment of family orientation and status perception: Theoretical and methodological implications for the Thematic Apperception Test. *Educational and Psychological Measurement, 42,* 1243–1251.

Rosenwald, G. G. (1968). The Thematic Apperception Test. In A. I. Rabin (Ed.), *Projective techniques in personality assessment* (pp. 172–221). New York: Springer.

Spanier, G. B. (1976). Measuring dyadic adjustment: New scales for assessing the quality of marriage and similar dyads. *Journal of Marriage and the Family, 38,* 15–27.

Stewart, R. H., Peters, T. C., Marsh, S., & Melinda, J. (1975). An object-relations approach to psychotherapy with marital couples, families and children. *Family Process, 14,* 161–178.

Sullivan, H. S. (1953). *The interpersonal theory of psychiatry.* New York: Norton.

Thomas, A. D. (1966). *Dynamics of marital adjustment.* Unpublished master's thesis, Ain Shams University, Cairo, Egypt.

Thomas, A. D. (1979). *The relationship between a couple's pattern of financial management and the dominant "orientation other" of each spouse.* Unpublished doctoral dissertation, Université de Montréal, Montreal, Quebec, Canada.

Thomas, A. D. (1993, August). *Patterns in marital interpersonal affect and quantitative TAT affective scores.* Poster session presented at the annual meeting of the American Psychological Association, Toronto, ON, Canada. (ERIC Document Reproduction Service No. 377 411).

Thomas, A. D. (1994). The TAT Affective Scale: Scoring norms. Washington DC: Copyright Office Records, TXu 621 856.

Thomas, A. D. (1996, July). *Conjugal TAT affective profiles.* Paper presented at the meeting of the International Congress of Rorschach and Projective Methods, Boston, MA.

Thomas, A. D., & Dudek, S. Z. (1985). Interpersonal affect in Thematic Apperception Test responses: A scoring system. *Journal of Personality Assessment, 49,* 30–36.

Vane, J. R. (1981). The Thematic Apperception Test: A review. *Clinical Psychology Review, 1,* 319–336.

Vestiwig, R. E., & Paradise, C. A. (1977). Multidimensional scaling of the TAT and the measurement of achievement motivation. *Journal of Personality Assessment, 41,* 595–603.

Walshe, R. H., Ferrell, M. S., & Tolone, W. L. (1976). Selection of reference groups, perceived reference group permissiveness and attitudes and behavior: A study of two consecutive panels (1967–1971; 1970–1974). *Journal of Marriage and the Family, 38,* 495–507.

Wimberley, H. (1973). Conjugal-role organization and social networks in Japan and England. *Journal of Marriage and the Family, 35,* 125–130.

28

CHAPTER

TAT Affective Scale Manual

Antoinette D. Thomas

Introduction

The Thematic Apperception Test (TAT) Affective Scale (Thomas, 1994; Thomas & Dudek, 1987) quantifies affective expressions in stories given to seven TAT cards. Each theme is weighed to qualify for a score within a range of +2 to –2, for either positive or negative affect. Degrees of positive and negative affect are evaluated within certain categories. The scale initially included three main interpersonal relationships categories: spouse, parent, non-spouse or peer (and other, e.g., brother–sister and self–offspring), to study a group of married participants. Nonattributed affect was added to other. It deals with internal feeling and generalized affect in the absence of a relationship. Administration instructions, rationale, and scoring guide may be adapted for other cards. Adaptation for children and adolescents is included. Respondents determine by and large the number of themes, scoring categories, and quality of affect. Stimulus pull and frequent responses cited in TAT literature, as well as the emotional content projected on cards, served as guidelines for specific numerical values attributed to themes. The stimulus pull of each card and frequent responses imply certain positive or negative responses, which was taken in consideration. However, the nature of subjects' own interpersonal relationships and affective disposition actively contribute to the affective quality of their TAT stories.

Administration

Administration instructions included in forms A and B in Murray's (1943) manual (1943) were modified. The following elements were excluded: (1) reference to imagination as a form of intelligence; (2) asking for dramatic stories; (3) the task as a storytelling test; (4) the position of the interviewer behind the respondent; (5) time limits; and (6) length of stories.

Instructions are systematically observed after each story, not at the end of all stories. For example, if a subject refers to the woman in card 4 as *she*, ask, "What is the kind of relationship between them?" Additional responses are added to the protocol. Several short stories are accepted, not discouraged.

Instructions for card 16 were also modified. Subjects are not asked for a full description of the imagined picture before being asked for a story. They are simply asked, "As you see, there is nothing on this card. Choose any picture or scene and tell me a story about it. Remember all the points I asked you for in the previous cards."

The instructions basically elicit past and present events, characters' feelings, thoughts, and explanation of how the story ends. The instructions draw explicit attention to affect, be it one character's feelings or those expressed between two or more characters. This is an additional feature to the classical instructions to facilitate the evaluation of affect.

The interviewer would say, "I am going to show you some pictures, one at a time; you will use your imagination to make up a story for each. There are no right or wrong stories. Describe what is happening at the moment, what had led up to the event shown in the picture, and what the characters are feeling and thinking of. Then give the outcome—how the story ends. When your story includes more than one person, tell me whether they are related to each other or not—for example, are they strangers, family members, friends, enemies or anything else? You can make up any kind of story; tell your thoughts as they come to your mind." Encourage responses if the subject only describes the cards; repeat instructions but do not push. Accept rejected cards.

In addition, subjects are not merely reminded of missing responses to instructions after the first story, as stated in Murray's (1943) manual, without giving them a chance to do so beyond the first story. Rather, restricted inquiries follow a given story only if basic elements in the instructions were missing, such as how the story ends and characters' thoughts and feelings. For example, if the child in card 1 *has to practice*, do not ask, "Who makes him practice?" The answer would invariably be *a parent*. The introduction of a parent in this card should be spontaneous. Consequently, a story that does not include a parent is not scored under the parent category; the child's affect is scored under other, nonattributed affect.

All the cards are given in one instead of two sessions. They are equally administered to men and women. The interviewer records subjects' responses verbatim. This could be in writing or by using an electrical device after receiving prior subjects' consent.

Stimuli

The seven cards used for adults were 1, 2, 4, 6GF, 13MF, 10, and 16, applicable to male and female respondents. For boys use cards 1, 2, 3 BM, 6BM, 7BM, 8BM, and 16. For girls administer cards 1, 2, 3GF, 6GF, 7GF, 8GF and 16. Card 4 is added for adolescent boys and girls. The quantitative affective values and rationale used in this manual are applicable to children and adolescents' TAT stories.

Most adults' cards (i.e., 1, 2, 4, 10, and 13MF) are among the most valuable 10 cards as judged by 90 experts (Hartman, 1970). The same cards plus card 16 were still among the most used cards in a subsequent review of literature (Keiser & Prather, 1990). Three cards (2, 4, and 13MF) have been used in a shortened version of the TAT set for family and heterosexual situations in clinical practice (Jacquemin, 1981). Three cards

(1, 2, and 4) were among the four richest TAT cards in content (Bellak, 1975). The blank card (16) was considered valuable for family imagery (Anzieu, 1960; Kahn, 1984; Shentoub & Shentoub, 1958, cited in Morval, 1977). Interpersonal themes were elicited in two thirds of the stories given to this card in the studies reported in chapter 27 in this volume.

☐ Scoring Process

This scoring system deals with the manifest, not the latent, level of content analysis. Defense mechanisms are not considered. The focus is on affect, be it within interpersonal relationships or nonattributed affect. The question posed is, "With whom does the main character deal, and what is the quality of this dealing?" In the case of one character, the quality of the character's affect is evaluated. If the subject introduces one or more persons, the affect of the transaction is evaluated.

Scoring and Category Criteria

First, classify a story under one or more of the following categories, and then assign affective scores. Researchers may create other categories depending on participants' stories and the nature of the research. The following categories are not exclusive. Other categories may be created using the scale's rational and guidelines.

(1) Spouse: The TAT theme revolves around married partners.

(2) Parent: One or both parents interact with a TAT character. Other categories may include family, father, mother, grandparents, or stepfather–stepson or stepdaughter. Parental figures, such as grandparents, are scored separately. They may be combined to parent category after obtaining a written note containing the employed logic.

(3) Nonspouse or peer: A TAT character interacts with a same-generation figure of either sex, such as a lover, a friend, a casual acquaintance, or a business associate. Research showed two clusters of stories—romantic as distinct from sexual relationships. Create different categories—nonspouse–romantic and nonspouse–sexual.

(4) Other: Subcategories may include self–offspring, brother–sister, and nonattributed affect. The last subcategory is meant to encompass internal feelings such as joy or sadness. It reflects a general affective disposition and nonsocial affect in the absence of a relationship. This category is often found in stories for cards 1 and 16.

It should be noted that the parent category differs from self–offspring in the direction of respondents' identification. For example, in card 6GF, a story that focuses on a woman's reactions to her father is a parent response, whereas another describing a father's talk with his daughter is a self–offspring story. It is rare but possible that responses include both directions. Thus, both are scored. Use discretion.

General Affective Point Scale

The following general affective four-point scale is applicable to all cards: +2, a strong positive theme; +1, a lukewarm positive theme, or mere presence of a category; 0, no relevant theme, no score; −1, a mild negative theme, or ambivalence, a mild negative element mixed with a positive one; and −2, a strong negative theme. Card description (Murray, 1943), frequent responses (Bellak, 1989; Morval, 1977), guidelines, and examples for each card are detailed in this section.

Themes are scored positively or negatively according to their affective content. All kinds of affect are weighed for each score under each category. In case a respondent rejects a story, do not score it. There are only two degrees of intensity in each direction to facilitate accuracy. Specific weights attributed to themes are determined by two guiding principles: (1) stimulus pull and frequent responses; and (2) the emotional content of the story or stories given to a card.

Interacting TAT figures may be present in cards. Additional figures with whom a TAT character deals may be introduced to the card (e.g., *parents*, card 1). Figures may also be distorted, such as the woman in card 10 who may be perceived as a man or a child.

Each theme is scored under the appropriate category. Respondents determine the number of themes. When subjects change their stories and explicitly ask to discard the first versions, only the last versions are scored. However, rejected themes provide clinical value. In cases where respondents cannot decide on the nature of the relation between figures, the theme is scored under both categories (e.g., "She is his wife or girlfriend").

The TAT Affective Scale With Children

This scale can easily lend itself to other groups. The author often uses it in psychotherapy with children and adolescents. Stories indicate categories. The following are commonly used categories.

(1) For stories that deal with both parents, use the parent category. However, some children give stories about each parent. Therefore, add father and mother categories. Also, add parental unit in stories about the parental relationship.

(2) Use siblings or brother and sister categories, according to the wording in stories.

(3) Peers–same sex and peers–opposite sex.

(4) Usually adolescents give stories about married couples or lovers, though they have no life love relationship. Anticipated spouse and anticipated nonspouse categories may be added.

(5) Other, nonattributed affect—one's feelings, such as joy or sadness, is often used for cards 1 and 16.

"A girl is happy having fun on a beach" (card 16): +2.

"He was tired, fell asleep on a couch, now feels better" (card 3BM): +1.

"A boy upset can't play the violin, tried several times, gave up" (card 1): –1.

"She hates her life on the farm" (card 2): –2.

Stimulus Pull and Frequent Responses

TAT card description as well as frequent responses reported in TAT literature determines, in part, the role of each card's stimulus pull in shaping responses. Remember that the TAT predominantly taps negative emotions—for example, "a young woman's head against a man's shoulder" (card 10) (Murray, 1943); by virtue of the structure of the picture, the stimulus pull is to elicit some kind of positive closeness between the two figures. Therefore, a response that negates this closeness, such as, "They had a disagreement, the relationship is threatened, he is making up to her," acquires a negative affective score of –1. On the other hand, the distance between figures in card 13MF, "a young man is standing with downcast head buried in his arm. Behind him is a figure of a woman lying in bed" (Murray, 1943), and the half-naked woman with her arm falling down impose predominantly negative content. Therefore, negative themes in the latter are much more tolerated than in the former, and scores follow suit. For example, "She is sick, and he is sad" gets a score of +1, since *sick* and *sad* are relatively positive responses for this card.

Emotional Content

TAT themes usually depict interpersonal relations. The quality of the relationships and expressed feelings contribute to the affective scores. That is, only the quality of the relationship is evaluated. For example, whether the farm in card 2 is prosperous or not is not taken into consideration. The man's anger in card 4 attains a positive value if caused by an outer source such as difficult working conditions, whereas the woman is trying to calm him. That is, the source of the anger is outside their relationship. Such anger acquires a negative value if triggered by the nature of the relationship between the two characters. For example, "This is a seven-year itch; he wants to move to greener pastures, but he'll listen to reason and remain with his wife" gets a –1 under spouse, whereas "He is leaving her" obtains a –2 under the appropriate category—spouse, nonspouse, or both. As long as you are scoring a relationship do not score under nonattributed affect, which is meant to evaluate affect in the absence of a relation.

What about changed affect within a story? All affect is weighed, unless the storyteller asks to delete a part. Each story should be considered separately; do not use words out of context. For example, if for card 1, "boy hates violin initially, parents forced him, he becomes successful and is glad they made him do it," then because of *hating the violin* and *parents forced practice,* the score is parent –2. But *being glad* (an affect) *about parents' forcing him* reduces the score to parent –1. Success or fame is not affect and therefore does not count by itself here. Success without practice does not count either. Remember that only mild negative affect mixed with mild positive acquires –1.

Most of the cards may elicit varied relationships: Use card 2 as an example:

"A man and wife, content and happy with their life" (spouse +2)

"A girl—she is appreciative of her parents hard work to send her to school" (parent +2)

> "This girl is in love with the man" (nonspouse +2)
>
> "Strangers—the girl will become a rural teacher; she is happy with her life" (other, nonattributed affect +2).

A theme is not scored at all if it does not include animate figures or no affect is expressed:

> Card 2: "Unrelated country people, each going his own way"
>
> Card 16: "Old farm, old houses, no animals, no people"

Clinical value, however, can be derived from these themes, such as avoidance of explicit emotional expression. The symbolic value of clouds, pounding sea, or sunshine can serve as additional clinical cues.

Actions and Affect

Daydreams in stories reflect hopes. Thoughts are a step further. Decisions are stronger. Actions are more powerful. All are accounted for in evaluating affect. Affect is more readily derived from decisions and actions than from daydreams and thoughts.

Civil Status Versus Story Characters

There may be a discrepancy between life events and characters in stories. A person who was never married may give spousal themes, so score under spouse. The emotional impact may correspond with a previous life experience, a hoped-for relationship, or mere disposition. Such links may be found on investigation.

Death, Suicide, and Murder

The differences in stimulus pull between cards 10 and 13MF led to corresponding affective weights of stories, as mentioned previously. Only normal death of the woman in card 13MF along with the man's sadness is scored as –1. Death of one of the two characters in card 10 is not tolerated; it is systematically scored –2. Death of a third introduced person such as their son, along with mutual comfort, is scored +1. Suicide, rape, and murder, being actions reflecting strong negative affect, in responses to all cards are scored –2. Nevertheless, nuances exist in the following responses to card 13MF:

(1) "Someone else killed her; he loved her and is in pain."

(2) "Someone killed her; he is furious."

(3) "He found her murdered; the smell is disgusting."

(4) "He killed her" or "She committed suicide."

Negative affect relatively increases from (1) to (4) under spouse or nonspouse. This could have corresponded to one eighth or one quarter. Getting into psychometric mazes was avoided, which would have departed from the Affective Scale simplicity. What is crucial is the absence of a third person, blood, knife in the woman's body, or a nearby weapon.

That is, the stimulus pull does not justify murder by a third person, by the man, or by the woman herself. The negative weight is by and large within the –2 score for all examples. Similarly, in the stories' outcome, *finding the killer to kill him* is relatively less negative than *killing anybody out there.* Such revenge affect is scored –2 under other, nonattributed affect.

Words Within Context

The Affective Scale does not lend itself to mechanical weighing of scores. Words are weighed within stories' context, such as the response, "She is sick, and he is sad" to card 13MF. The term *sad,* though denoting a negative affect, acquires a +1 score. Consider a response such as, "The girl fed the chicken…then sat down to dream about being a famous actress in a fancy city" for card 2: She did not dislike or hate rural life and performed her role. Her daydream seemed to give her some entertainment; she did not intend to fulfill it. Thus, this is scored as nonattributed affect, +1.

Foreground Versus Background

In general, focus on affect between characters in cards. Usually, other persons and events in the story help in weighing such relationships. They serve as background and are not scored. Consider the following example responses to card 4:

(1) "He is sad because his grandmother is dead; she is comforting him—their strength will keep life going." The man's relationship with his grandmother is not scored being background to his interaction with the woman.

(2) "She is pleading with him; he is leaving her to return to his wife and children." The man's relationships to his wife and to his children are not scored. This is a background. The story did not include any other statements about the wife and the children to warrant additional interpersonal relationships.

(3) "He cannot stay with her anymore; his wife and children need him. He has a loving wife and children; the only thing he needs is his family—he returned to them." Here are two stories. The first one is a nonspouse –2, and the second is spouse +1. His guilt and lack of strong affect at the end does not make the spousal affect a +2. The spousal relationship is scored on account of the action, having a loving wife and children, and the declaration of his need for his wife and children to the girlfriend. Also scored is other, self–offspring +1.

☐ Card Descriptions, Frequent Responses, and Scoring Guides

Card 1

Description: "A young boy is contemplating a violin which rests on a table in front of him" (Murray, 1943).

Frequent Responses

This is the single most valuable picture. It usually brings out the relationship toward the parental figures: whether they are perceived as aggressive, domineering, helpful, understanding or protective. Frequently, we get themes on the conflict between autonomy and compliance with authority. It also brings out parents' ambitions if the boy resists practicing. The boy may practice or not, out of pressure or self-will. He may think of future success or feels discouraged. It also allows introspection (Bellak, 1986; Morval, 1977).

It should be noted that one or both parents should be explicitly mentioned in the story to be scored under the parent category. A teacher category may be created. If the story does not include a relation with another person, such as "He has to practice," score under other, nonattributed affect.

Parent Scoring Guide

+2: Happy parent–child relationship; no parental pressure, no resentment on child's part

Example: Got violin from father, valuable, happy; he is given a lot of encouragement by parents

+1: Parents want child to learn; child has a choice

Example: Parents want him to learn the violin; he is wondering if he wants to play it or not

–1: Parents want child to learn; child in conflict or ambivalence between child's desire not to play and his wish to please parents

Example: Parents told him to practice; he wants to play outside; he does not want to play it (see example in "Emotional Content")

–2: Parents punish child; parents force or push child, child dislikes task; child damages father's violin

Example: Parents pushing him to practice; he does not like it; the violin is a present from parents gave him; he wants to smash it; he damaged father's violin

Other, Nonattributed Affect Scoring Guide

+2: The task may be difficult, but the child chooses to practice; he enjoys learning, likes music, willing to practice, and anticipates success. (In all, child makes the decision)

Example: He is having a break will be glad to practice; he loves music, will practice and becomes a good musician

+1: Child weighs alternatives, play outside or practice, and has a choice.

Example: He was attracted to it, then found it was difficult. He is wondering what he wants; a boy given a problem, interested in what he is doing; child disliked it at first but came to enjoy it

–1: Child sad, frustrated, annoyed or does not want to practice; child is distracted due to life problems; someone broke the violin; he gave it to his father to repair it, can play but does not enjoy it

Example: A depressed boy, he seems lonely; he does not know how to play, frustrated; he is sad, sitting in a solitary room, he does not want to take violin lessons

–2: Child hates himself, music, or violin, wants to break it or actually did; very frustrated, miserable; forced to practice (no mention by whom)

Example: He is looking at it like it is broken; he damaged it to get rid of violin lessons; he wants to smash violin, very frustrated

Note that future fame may be an illusion and magical thinking in the absence of practice; therefore, it would not score +2. Having the choice to practice or not, being able and willing to practice, and enjoyment qualify for +2.

Card 2

Description. "Country scene in the foreground is a young woman with books in her hand, in the background a man is working in the fields and an older woman is looking out" (Murray, 1943).

Frequent Responses

It offers excellent indications of the subject's family relations whether harmonious or conflictive. Even males usually identify with the figure of the young girl. Varying themes of autonomy from the family versus compliance with the conservative background existence are extremely frequent. The way the relationship of the two women to the man is discussed adds a good deal of information about the role of the sexes. It elicits the opposition between the two women: rural–urban, manual–intellectual, or single–married. The girl may want to leave farm to live in the city or go to school (Bellak, 1986; Morval, 1977).

Spouse Scoring Guide

+2: A positive description of couple's life style or relation

Example: Content and happy with their life; a man very hard at work to provide for wife

+1: A man and wife

Example: The woman is the man's wife the girl is passing by; she is watching her husband while leaning on a tree

–1: Discontent with their rural life

Example: Woman dreaming her child will not experience what she and her husband had to

–2: Distance or conflict

Example: She (older woman) is watching to prevent any relation between the girl and her husband; she does not trust him; man has two women in his life—wife and mistress; different interests, backs to each other

Nonspouse or Peer

Scoring guidelines are comparable to spouse category.

Example, + 2: The girl and the man are happy lovers

Example, + 1: The man and the girl like each other; they are testing their relationship

Example, –1: The girl loves the man but wants to move to the city; he wants to stay

Example, –2: The man will break up with the girl; they cannot agree on important issues; he will end the relationship; the girl cannot confront her parents with their love

Parent Scoring Guide

+2: Parents do not object to girl's education or move to city; girl is thankful for parents' financial help; girl loves parents

Example: She thinks how hard her parents worked to send her to university; she loves her parents, but she wants to go to city; girl leaving parents to go to the city; nobody is unhappy; they accept it

+1: The conflict between rural and urban lives exists in the girl's mind, not between her and her parents

Example: She has a mental conflict between staying and leaving her parents (not just the farm)

–1: Parents object to girl's move to the city; the girl does not like her parents' lifestyle

Example: Girl does not like what goes on around her; walking away, not what parents have planned; parents want her to stay, she wants to go to the city

–2: Breaking away from parents; emotional distance between girl and parents

Example: On the outs with her parents; mother is the boss; girl wondering why she is there; parents force the girl to live on the farm

Other: Nonattributed Affect Scoring Guide

+2: Positive affect for farm or farm and city; people's work is praised

Example: Time of the social revolution; people are glorified with hard work and learning everything will be all right; this girl is becoming a teacher in her community; she is happy to keep her habitual life and participate in educating her people

+1: The girl has conflict between rural and urban lives (not with parents)

Example: She is attracted to a life of ideas; she has this conflict of wanting a more exciting life

–1: Girl does not like rural life

Example: She used to like her life on the farm; now she does not

–2: Girl hates her rural life; miserable

Example: She hates life on the farm, wishes she was born in the city

Card 4

Description. "A woman is clutching the shoulders of a man whose face and body are averted as if he were trying to pull away from her" (Murray, 1943).

Frequent Responses

It elicits a great variety of needs and sentiments in regard to male–female relationships. Themes of infidelity are often found. The female may seek to prevent the man from leaving her. She may be a protector who tries to keep him from rushing into something poorly thought out or one who tries to hold onto him for evil purposes. Similarly, a woman's attitude toward men as persons who may have been aggressive toward her becomes apparent. They may be seen as having a conflict between them or that their happiness is threatened by an outer force. The picture of the seminude in the background may lead to themes of triangular jealousy (Bellak, 1986; Morval, 1977).

Spouse and Nonspouse or Peer Scoring Guide

Scoring guidelines are applicable to both categories, with reversal of relevant importance attributed to wife and girlfriend.

+2: Direct expression of love or interest between the two foreground figures, no negative feelings; conflict is not between the man and the woman, but connected with an external source, woman tries to help man

Example: Wife loves husband; husband ripped off his job, wife very affectionate; wife loves and encourages husband, he has work problems (Work situation explains his gesture and gives background for wife's expressed love; do not score man's anger separately under other, nonattributed affect)

+1: Discussion, partial agreement, woman tries to have full agreement

Example: Wife is talking husband into something

–1: Man wants to break up; woman wants to keep him against his will; man divided between two women, ambivalent

Example: Affectionate wife, husband not returning the affection

–2: Irrevocable break; one of them cheated on the other

Example: Husband not wanting to get along with wife, the other woman is his mistress (background); husband will go away, difference in their nature; she told her husband she had an affair with his brother or friend, he is in tremendous pain

Nonspouse or Peer Examples

+2: He received bad news she is very sympathetic; both passionate; she is holding him from getting in trouble

+1: He is not in total agreement; she is trying to convince him

–1: She is pleading with him to stay, he wants to go; a man cannot make up his mind, he loves her, and has a wife

–2: He is leaving her; he loves another woman

Card 6GF

Description. "A young woman sitting on the edge of a sofa, looks back over her shoulder at an older man with a pipe in his mouth who seems to be addressing her" (Murray, 1943).

Frequent Responses

This card was meant to reflect the relationship of females to the father. However, the man is usually seen as a contemporary, who may thereupon be invested with any number of qualities from those of an aggressor, a seducer, to someone who proposes marriage. It may elicit suspicion, quarrel, or pressure, occasionally jealousy from a third person (Bellak, 1986; Morval, 1977).

Spouse and Nonspouse or Peer Scoring Guide

+2: Attached to each other; emotional bond, dealing with a matter in their life or man giving woman a pleasant surprise

Example: Husband suggesting to go to the movies, wife did not expect it, pleased; loving married couple, she has to decide about something he asked her

+1: Having a discussion

Example: Husband and wife having a discussion; dependable husband masculine wisdom versus wife feminine need protection

–1: Having a temporary quarrel or argument; he shocked her, she is disinterested

Example: She is startled at his appearance, could be quarrelling

–2: Emotional distance; distrust; accusation

Example: Husband is accusing her of spending much money or something else; she has been cheating on him, husband asks why.

Nonspouse or Peer Examples

+2: Both attracted to each other; intense relation, telling her good news, she was not expecting to see him; lovers, he is telling her something nice, fond of each other

+1: Social acquaintances, she is surprised; a messenger brought her a surprise; two friends, he is talking, she is surprised

–1: She is shocked about what he said; she refuses his offer to go out; he is making initial approach, she is not interested

–2: He asks her to go to bed with him she turns him down

Parent and Other, Self–Offspring Scoring Guide

For both male and female respondents, identification with the female figure is scored under parent, whereas identification with male figure is scored self–offspring. The direction is judged by the wording of the story, whose words are directed to whom (see "Scoring and Category Criteria").

+2: Positive attitude between the two figures, daughter surprised

Example: She is upset about something, her father is comforting her; she is surprised, father gives her advice, she is interested in what he says

+1: Daughter surprised (no negative emotions); talking

Example: Daughter startled by father, did not expect to see him; daughter and father contemplating on a TV program

–1: Temporary discord

Example: Daughter shocked or not too happy about father's advice; temporary conflict, quarrel or disagreement between daughter and father

–2: Emotional distance

Example: Daughter is planning an escapade, waits until father goes away

Other, Self–Offspring Examples

+2: A father and daughter, pleasant, wise understanding, he came into the room, she is upset about something, he is trying to console her

+1: This woman I get nothing from, the old man is sympathetic, he is complementing, she is surprised, father and daughter; could be father giving advice, she is arguing with him a bit but not angry, he is paternal, probably a problem with boyfriend, you better think it over, he does not say do not go out with him

–1: A man and his daughter, he said something that annoyed her in some way, he wants to help her, she wants to mind her business, she is drawing away from him; a father and daughter, quarrelling scene, they will get back together, the quarrel is not permanent

–2: A father image, his position indicates authority; he is confronting her with something she is about to deny

Card 10

Description. "A young woman's head is against a man's shoulder" (Murray, 1943).

Frequent Responses

This card will bring about the relation of man to woman. They may embrace as an expression of happiness or be one of parting or reunion. If it is interpreted as an embrace between males by a male subject, it is a strong clue to latent [or manifest] homosexuality or friendship (Bellak, 1986; Morval, 1977).

All Categories Scoring Guide

+2: A positive relation clearly expressed, no negative element

Example: Man and wife, in a loving moment; trust and affection in a long happy marriage

+1: Mere presence, no emotions; flat interaction; a positive relation between the two figures within a negative context, such as death, illness, sadness, unhappiness in another relationship or comfort

Example: They are comforting each other, their son died in war

−1: A mild negative element within the relationship; mixed positive and negative elements (e.g., anger and kissing)

Example: They had a disagreement; husband caused it, emotional relation threatened, making it up

−2: A strong negative element or emotional distance between the two figures; one against the other; one or both dead

Example: Fed up with illness the old married couple committed suicide together

Nonspouse or Peer

+2: Two men, homosexuals having a great deal of caring; two lovers, tenderness

+1: Two men talking in a political meeting; two friends, comforting each other

−1: An embrace after a fight

−2: One trying to betray the other; a pickpocket and his victim; he pressed his hand on her mouth, she cannot move or whisper

Parent Examples

+2: Mother and son dance, very intimate dance; parent–child closeness and need dependence

+1: Mother and child comforting each other

−1: Son repenting, mother comforting him

−2: His mother is dying, he is thinking about his inheritance

Other, Brother–Sister Examples

+2: Brother and sister, obvious affection and shared concern, love, normal affection in a particular circumstance

+1: No sadness parting of brother and sister

−1: A moment of peace within usual arguments

−2: Incest between brother and sister

Card 13MF

Description. "A young man is standing with downcast head buried in his arm. Behind him is a figure of a woman lying in bed" (Murray, 1943).

Frequent Responses

This is an excellent picture of disclosing sexual conflicts in both men and women. In females, it may elicit fears of being raped, attacked, or otherwise abused by men. In males, it will often bring out guilt feelings about sexual activity. The woman may be ill, dead, or murdered or may have committed suicide. Social conflicts or absence of conflicts may be elicited such as an accident, childbirth, going to work, or economic problems (Bellak, 1986; Morval, 1977).

All Categories Scoring Guide

+2: Positive relatedness, no negative element between man and woman or story events related to them

+1: Woman sick, no negative element between them

–1: Normal death of woman, man's grief; man impotent, he harmed woman or is guilty; man in conflict resulting in a distance between them; voyeurism (brother–sister category)

–2: Woman's suicide; he or someone else killed her; rape or incest; one of them cheated on the other

Spouse Examples

+2: She is resting, they made love, and he is between resting and going back to his books

+1: She is sick; he is sad

–1: She died, he is expressing grief; he failed to please his wife; he came late, in trouble with his wife; his wife is alcoholic, would not take his advice

–2: Husband killed his wife, guilty; someone killed his wife; wife ran away with another

Nonspouse or Peer

+2: Lovers, made love, he is going out of her room

+1: His girlfriend is sick; he cannot do anything about it

–1: He found her dead, very sad; he cannot make love to her, because he is married; she is dead, he is horrified; he had neglected her when sick, she is dead

–2: He killed her; she committed suicide, because he did not marry her

Other, Brother–Sister Examples

+2: He cares a lot about his sister, he found her sick, will take her to a doctor

+1: His sister is sick, he is sorry for her

–1: A boy in his teens going to his sister's room, you are not supposed to see your sister in this position, covering his face symbolic of repentance

–2: An affair between an older brother and his sister; he raped his sister

Card 16

Description. "A blank card" (Murray, 1943).

Frequent Responses

This card may reflect self-image or contemporary family or professional life (Bellak, 1986; Morval, 1977).

All Categories Scoring Guide

+2: Explicit positive feelings, no negative element

+1: Presence of characters

–1: Conflict

–2: Separation between characters; negative affect or harmful actions that lead to separation

Spouse Examples

+2: Our family, me my husband (wife) and children on a dinner table, joking and having a good time; (also score under other, self–offspring); quite romantic, music, candles, husband and wife having a nice time; my husband and I, after children went to bed, listening to music, enjoying each other

+1: Our family picture, the four of us (also score under other, self–offspring)

–1: A woman in conflict does not know whether to stay in marriage or split

–2: A man walking away from his house, done with his wife

Nonspouse or Peer Examples

+2: Me years ago, with my pretty beloved girlfriend

+1: A man and his boat with a friend

–1: Lovers, they often fight and get on each other's nerves

–2: Lovers who lived together, now each is going his own way

Parent Examples

+2: Me as a child, loved by my parents, we were happy
+1: My home, a section for my parents
–1: My parents who always want me to do more work

–2: My parents often punish or shout at me

Other, Self–Offspring Examples

+2: My daughter's graduation, a happy day in my life, I tell her how much we love her and are proud of her

+1: Interesting picture, the graduation time for my son who is finishing his education as a musician and being enrolled in the country's band

–1: My daughter receiving her degree, I feel envious, her time is better than mine

–2: My son breaking up with me

Other, Nonattributed Affect

+2: Children coming out of school, happy as they went to the fields, everything is new to them; white, bright, happy future

+1: First day of school, a teacher misses the holidays only for a few hours, and then he is happy with his work

–1: The calmness of Labor Day, stillness before the storm, the tension of the worry of a school year begins

–2: A hopeless person, sick of life

☐ Calculating Scores

A set of red small circles for the wife's scores and blue small triangles for the husband's will give a visual layout of the couple's respective positions on the scored categories. It will also display the pattern of positive and negative scores. Place your score for every story by circling the appropriate affective weight under one or more categories on the scoring sheet (Table 28.1). The nature of the scored story in the category other should be specified on the scoring sheet. In case 2 others are included in the protocol; they

TABLE 28.1 The TAT Affective Scale Scoring Sheet

Name: ______________________ Date: ______________________

Parent			Spouse			Nonspouse			Other		
Card #	Score (circle one)		Card #	Score (circle one)		Card #	Score (circle one)		Card #	Score (circle one)	
1	+2+1	−1−2	1	+2+1	−1−2	1	+2+1	−1−2	1	+2+1	−1−2
2	+2+1	−1−2	2	+2+1	−1−2	2	+2+1	−1−2	2	+2+1	−1−2
4	+2+1	−1−2	4	+2+1	−1−2	4	+2+1	−1−2	4	+2+1	−1−2
6GF	+2+1	−1−2	6GF	+2+1	−1−2	6GF	+2+1	−1−2	6GF	+2+1	−1−2
10	+2+1	−1−2	10	+2+1	−1−2	10	+2+1	−1−2	10	+2+1	−1−2
13MF	+2+1	−1−2	13MF	+2+1	−1−2	13MF	+2+1	−1−2	13MF	+2+1	−1−2
16	+2+1	−1−2	16	+2+1	−1−2	16	+2+1	−1−2	16	+2+1	−1−2
Total (+): ________			Total (+): ________			Total (+): ________			Total (+): ________		
Total (–): ________			Total (–): ________			Total (–): ________			Total (–): ________		
Net:________			Net:________			Net:________			Net:________		
(subtract total [–] from total ([+])			(subtract total [–] from total ([+])			(subtract total [–] from total ([+])			(subtract total [–] from total ([+])		

Note: Dominant relationship: Parent, spouse, nonspouse, other (circle the one with the highest net score).

should be numbered as well as designated. Within each category, add positive scores, place in (Total +)—likewise with negative scores. Subtract the lower value from higher one; keep the mathematical sign of the higher value, and place in "Net." Compare net scores in all four categories; circle the highest positive value in "Dominant Interpersonal Relation."

When the scale is used with children and adolescents, modify this scoring sheet. Replace the categories on the sheet with those used by your subjects.

☐ Practice Scoring

You may want to practice scoring the 56 TAT responses beginning with the spousal primacy stories in chapter 27 of this volume. Identify the scoring categories; then weigh the affective content. Compare your scores with those made by the author. You should not be alarmed if you tend to be too stingy or too generous, as long as you are consistent. The ratios between the scoring categories are the most important consideration. Eventually, when checking your scores against guidelines and training levels, you will maintain accurate scoring.

Couple Level, Study 2: Three More Profiles to Practice Scoring

The TAT Interpersonal Affect Scale (Thomas, 1997; Thomas & Dudek, 1985) and the TAT Affective Scale (Thomas, 1994) provide quantitative assessment of affect projected on TAT figures and perceived as spouse, parent and nonspouse. Subsequent qualitative investigation (Thomas, 1993, 1996) was based on couples' dual positions on the developmental line of interpersonal choices and supported by perceived marital adjustment on the Dyadic Adjustment Scale (DAS) (Spanier, 1976). Three of the four identified couple profiles—affective imbalance, underlying difficulties, and apparent difficulties, for which protocols and expert scoring follow—can be used to practice scoring. The spousal primacy profile, for which comparable material appears under "Case Illustration," is in chapter 27.

Affective Imbalance

Husband TAT

Card 1: Me, as a child playing the violin, looking inside to see if there is enough strings, kind of happy and warm feelings, wondering if the violin I got of my father is a valuable instrument, someday I'll sell it for a lot of money, a sunny day.

Card 2: A young woman that is leaving, on the outs with her parents, is out to university leaving the land, father in the field, mother with child again. She's having conflict whether staying or leaving for school (Q) parents resigned with what they have.

Card 4: A man who wants to do something, to take action of some sort, his girl friend pleading with him to be more rational, about to charge off and vindicate, and she's trying to moderate his thought, no wedding ring.

Card 6GF: A woman who is in her 30s surprised by her father, she's been doing something, suddenly surprised by her father, reading something she's not supposed to be reading.

Card 10: Two women, one comforting the other, she's not brave but there was a loss, a separation, the one on the right distressed and her neighbor, her husband or son left or died (Q) she's old enough, her husband.

Card 13MF: A harder one, he's committed murder, she's dead, he is upset she suddenly passed away (Q) husband and wife, I can't know why she's died of something rather than murdering her, he feels guilty, responsible.

Card 16: A tranquil, no people, sunny day on a beach, my favorite pastoral scene, cool old barn, old houses, no people, no animals.

Categories and scores:

Card 1, parent +2

Card 2, parent –2

Card 4, nonspouse +2

Card 6GF, parent –1

Card 10, nonspouse +1

Card 13MF, spouse –2

Card 16, no score

Net TAT scores:

Spouse –2

Parent (+2, –3) –1

Nonspouse 3

Wife TAT

Card 1: An English schoolboy was given a problem. Interested in what he's doing. I can't make out what it is, a violin. He likes it. A well cared for child.

Card 2: Family sequence, may or may not be related, a girl, a pregnant woman, a farmer and a horse. None of them belongs to the other, except the woman is related to the man. It isn't likely she'd look at a man when she's tired if not his wife. The girl I can't tell whether she's the daughter, she sprang from this milieu, no antagonism, each going his own way.

Card 4: A young woman and a man. She's trying to get him to do something or not do something. A woman in semi negligee seems to be a poster. Close relationship between the two, she likes him, she's persuading him (Q) lovers, not wearing a ring, time to themselves, no children.

Card 6GF: She's been doing something, he tells her something else. Surprised, she's interested. May or may not related, old enough to be her father don't think they're married. (Q) Friendly gesture, she's been caught at a funny pose, she's surprised no hate on her face.

Card 10: Comforting one another, probably man and wife. Older, resemblance in eyebrows, comfort love not sexual love, but it could be. (Q) Probably married certainly living together and mutually dependent.

Card 13MF: A woman undressed, he is dressed. He's been asleep, I don't know, one hand is for guilt or fatigue, the other hand not. Maybe he made love to her and sorry, she's relaxed not paying any attention to him, not married.

Card 16: Those weren't stimulating, trees, forest, abstract.

Categories and scores:

Card 1, other, nonattributed affect +2

Card 2, spouse +1

Card 4, nonspouse +2

Card 6GF, parent +1 (the respondent ruled out *not related* and *married,* leaving *father* as the most plausible relation)

Card 10, spouse +1

Card 13MF, nonspouse –1

Card 16, no score

Net TAT scores:

Spouse 2

Parent 1, nonspouse (+ 2, – 1) 1

Other, nonattributed affect 2

Couple summary scores:

Husband TAT: Spouse – 2; parent –1; Nonspouse 3; DAS 99

Wife TAT: Spouse 2; parent 1; nonspouse 1; other, nonattributed affect 2; DAS 127

Comments

The two measurements rendered consistent results. The husband gave only one negative spousal score; the affect was that of murder by the male TAT figure, whereas the wife's spousal themes were only positive, reflecting mutual dependence and love. On the DAS, the couple's scores were about two standard deviations apart, in opposite directions from the mean. His somewhat discontent with marriage attains more significance in view of the unilateral positive nonspousal themes. The couple's responses to card 16 were similar, consisting of scenery without people or affection. This mutual preference seemed to be a sustaining element in their marriage, both being prominent professionals.

Underlying Difficulties

Husband TAT

Card 1: A boy looking at a violin, if he's come back from a violin lesson, disappointing time, he reached crossroads obviously looking at his own talents and efforts he puts in it, not a broken violin?

Card 2: The girl obviously comes from a rural background, in a moment of decision, whether or not she would lose a great deal in turning her back to the life she has had, whether or not it would be the right thing to do, she wants something better, she'll turn her back and it will be final, (Q) I can tell husband and wife the other two, the woman is pregnant (Q) she's the sister of the girl.

Card 4: A guy who's tired of the women he's with, trying to free himself, seek his chances elsewhere, disagreeing about something (Q) lovers, husband and wife in actuality. Wait, the picture in the background, maybe a seven-year itch, he wants to move to greener pastures, she looks so strangely, maybe they're married, he doesn't look so distraught, certainly uses an argument (Q) he wouldn't go, a guy has to have a more turnover, but if you're married you have a lively interaction, temporary thing in his life, his life can't be idealistic, going to listen to reason.

Card 6GF: Two very related emotionally, I suppose husband and wife could be brother and sister. He looks as if he said something a bit surprising; he made a suggestion she finds disagreeable, he showed a side of himself she didn't think is there. They'll go to watch TV (Q) she ignored it and they carried on, pretended it had not happened (Q) he didn't like her mother.

Card 10: They're husband and wife or man and woman, had disagreement. The man who may have been the main cause, is talking round his wife trying to set things right by making promises it wouldn't come about (Q). It will be my own experience, anything can upset a woman, problem with their marriage. The man has to do this when he feels his wife thinks their emotional relation is threatened.

Card 13MF: Two situations: (1) it could be a young boy, in his teens, gone to his sister's room and found her in this situation, 30 years ago you're not supposed to see your sister in this situation. He's covering his face symbolic of repentance, (2) a young guy who's been to bed with her. He found himself inadequate probably feels sorry with the whole thing. After a sex act he feels they ought to be ashamed, remorse.

Card 16: Not easy, a boy looking up into the sky, he sees airplanes, German and British. He is 12 or 13, realizes there is a great deal that depends on the outcome. Watching, not qualified to participate and help.

Categories and scores:

Card 1, other 1, nonattributed affect –1

Card 2, spouse +1; other 1, nonattributed affect +1

Card 4, spouse –1

Card 6GF, spouse –1

Card 10, spouse –1

Card 13MF, other 2, brother–sister –1; nonspouse –1

Card 16, other 1, nonattributed affect –1

Net TAT scores:

Spouse (+1, –3) –2

Nonspouse –1

Other 1, nonattributed affect (+1, –2) –1

Other 2, brother–sister –1

Wife TAT

Card 1: A little boy who the violin belongs to his father, who could play it very well. His father died and his mother sent him to learn it. He didn't have the same talent he is looking at it regretfully and he wishes he had it.

Card 2: A girl who was born of poor parents in the land, very clever, got the opportunity to go to college. Unfortunately she had to go back to marry there, she's wondering whether the education was worthwhile (Q) A girl, a father and a mother. She is not married yet, she's just thinking of the fact that she has to marry someone from the farm someday.

Card 4: Someone who has got involved with this beautiful prostitute didn't intend to love her, but he did and she too. But he has got to go back to his family.

Card 6GF: Husband and wife having a discussion, look perfectly respectful

Card 10: Two homosexuals making love to each other, two men

Card 13MF: A father, who came, found his daughter had an overdose of sleeping pills, found her pregnant and dead

Card 16: My father with his three grandchildren whom he had not seen. He loved children, used to write children stories

Categories and scores:

Card 1, parent +1; other, nonattributed affect –1

Card 2, parent +1; spouse –1

Card 4, nonspouse –1

Card 6FG, spouse +1

Card 10, nonspouse +2

Card 13MF, parent –2 (In this card the story cannot be said from the dead daughter's perspective but she is the one who inflicted pain on the father, so it is parent or father if you have this category –2.)

Card 16, parent +1 (In this card the subject is in fact talking about herself, making a link between her father and her children. So it is from her perspective. The deceased father had no way of expressing his own perspective, so it is parent or father +1.)

Net TAT scores:

Spouse (+1, −1), 0

Parent (+3, −2), 1

Nonspouse (+2, −1), 1

Other, nonattributed affect, −1

Couple Summary Scores

Husband TAT: Spouse −2; nonspouse −1; other 1, nonattributed affect −1; other 2, brother–sister −1; DAS 101

Wife TAT: Spouse 0; parents 1; nonspouse 1; other, nonattributed affect −1; DAS 110

Comments

The husband's scores indicated the poor quality of all interpersonal relations, with the spousal affect being the most negative. Feelings of inadequacy and disappointment added to the more explicit feelings of remorse and guilt associated with extramarital attractions and inappropriate incestuous curiosity. Throughout, the husband seemed to be more concerned with self than others. However, he felt more bad than good about himself. A rational superficial layer of courtesy seemed to keep up a facade in the spousal imagery. The main figure in the wife's fantasy was her deceased father. She spoke passionately and consciously about him in two cards. Her response to card 13MF was the only one in the 60 cases that dealt with father and daughter figures, though dramatic and quite negative in content (suicide). As a couple, spousal themes were more negative than other interpersonal categories. Neither gave a loving response in a spousal interaction. His superficial courtesy was matched with her sterile respectfulness. The husband's DAS was about one standard deviation below the normative and the study groups. The wife's DAS was slightly below these averages. The TAT responses revealed an underlying relation at a distance (Bouvet, 1959).

Apparent Difficulties

Husband TAT

Card 1: A boy 13 or 14 years old, thinking deeply. He seems to be in trouble, sad looking at his violin as a source of inspiration, he loves music. He seems lonely and lost.

Card 2: The daughter coming back from school, her mother eagerly waiting for her. The brother is working hard on the farm. Misery evident on her face, the mother seems to be in mourning, sad (Q) the father died.

Card 4: The lady in the picture seems to be in love with the man, who's trying to hide his own feelings, for one reason or the other, the picture of the lady in the background seems to be the same lady (Q) lovers.

Card 6GF: Oh! The husband arriving late at home, to find his charming wife eagerly waiting for his arrival, when he screamed and yelled, "Why are you still awake? Are you checking on me?"

Card 10: Difficult, is it a son or a husband? I have to assume he's the son, who was lost, is back to his mother. The sign of sympathy is on her face and of repentance on his.

Card 13MF: Tiring, a lady lying on a bed. Most probably sexually assaulted, a man standing. Probably her husband, who has been frightened to see his wife in such an unpleasant situation and a dead body. It's horrible (Q)—not him who killed her.

Card 16: White, virgin, bright future, happy landing of a peaceful house.

Categories and scores:

Card 1, other, nonattributed affect –1

Card 2, parent +1; other, nonattributed affect –2 (Do not score other for the brother, because there is no expressed affect or even a thought between the heroine and the brother. It is just a description of the figure in the background. *Working hard* is not feeling)

Card 4, nonspouse –1

Card 6GF, spouse –2

Card 10, parent –1

Card 13MF, spouse –2

Card 16, other, nonattributed affect +2

Net TAT scores:

Spouse –4

Parent (+1, –1) 0

Nonspouse –1

Other, nonattributed affect (–1, –2, +2) –1

Wife TAT

Card 1: He looks miserable, he doesn't know how to compose, very frustrated.

Card 2: A student in love with the man in the background. Can't tell what is the relationship with the woman.

Card 4: He's angry she tries to talk to him. He wouldn't listen, a naked woman in the background? A nice looking man, they must be married, if they were in love he would not have acted this way (Q) I think it's a picture.

Card 6GF: Not married, maybe an old type of lovers, she said "is that so?" What is this? I think a table. He's talking and she's surprised, maybe 2 friends.

Card 10: That is love! He's kissing her on her forehead. May be his daughter or lover, he's closing his eyes and really loving.

Card 13MF: He killed her? How can she have her breast that way? Are they married? He's dressed and she's sleeping. There is a chair he slept while sitting. He killed her in anger. They're married he killed her and he's guilty.

Card 16: A nice family, a man, wife and two children sitting in peace

Categories and scores:

Card 1, other 1, nonattributed affect –2

Card 2, nonspouse +2

Card 4, spouse –1

Card 6GF, nonspouse +1

Card 10, parent +2; nonspouse +2

Card 13MF, spouse –2

Card 16, spouse +1; other 2, self–offspring +1

Net TAT scores:

Spouse (+1, –3) –2

Parent 2

Nonspouse 5

Other 1, nonattributed affect –2

Other 2, self–offspring +1

Couple Summary Scores

Husband TAT: Spouse –4; parent 0; nonspouse –1; other, nonattributed affect –1; DAS 97

Wife TAT: Spouse – 2; parents 2; nonspouse 5; other 1, nonattributed affect –2; other 2, self–offspring 1; DAS 85.

Comments

Within spousal themes, affect was predominantly negative for both partners and much lower than other interpersonal categories. The husband gave an unreasonably harsh response to card 6GF, which linked well with the wife's fruitless attempts to communicate in response to card 4. The husband reflected a stormy temperament in his themes, whereas the wife's stories reflected helplessness. Such TAT spousal exchange seemed to betray a sadomasochistic relationship. No wonder both of them wished for peace in card 16.

Both spouses projected attachment to the parent of the opposite sex, which added to, or provided the foundation for, marital tension. Card 10 (frequently elicited spousal themes) was perceived as parental interaction: mother–son by the husband and father–daughter by the wife. Clinically, the husband's response *son or husband ... he's the son* portrayed the son's wish to replace his father. *The deceased father* in card 2 reinforces this interpretation. The son's repentance was an appropriate affect in card 10. On the DAS, the couple's scores were below the normative and the study means (–1 SD for the husband; about –2 SD for the wife).

Interesting Couple's TAT Stories: More Scoring Practice

The following are examples of interesting TAT stories. They have qualitative values in spite of the limited information about research subjects. Some themes directly reflected subjects' life events and related feelings. Others show the unique value of card 16 in studies with couples. Comparisons between husband and wife shed light on the couples' interpersonal dynamics. Notice that husbands were given odd numbers and their wives the following even numbers. Some stories are not easy to score. Compare your scores with mine, found at the end of this section.

TAT Themes and Life Events

Case 19

> Card 2: A painting, I suppose it is representative of hard work as far as the man is concerned. If I take them to be man and wife, there is a difference in background. He has a love for the land and she for academics. A mother symbol, she resents, if the girl is her daughter, going away from life on the land to something abstract. Their backs to each other, were married when young before she was mature enough to know what she wants, sadness in her eyes because they can't follow the same interest, she might be a school teacher.
>
> Card 16: My son is going to university; he's very enthusiastic. It takes me back to my age. I was younger and doing the same thing, rather envious being middle aged, that's normal.

Case 57

> Card 10: An elderly man and woman, they had some kind of quarrel and making it up. Sorry they had been sharp or ill tempered, both ill tempered. When you know one well enough, you can be ill tempered because you know you can make it up, no real damage.

Case 58

> Card 4: Probably husband and wife, they had an argument he's been angry with her for some reason, she feels he has every reason to be angry. She's feeling guilty and asking him to forgive her, saying I am sorry.

Categories and Scores

- Case 19: Card 2, spouse –1, other, self–offspring –1; card 16, other, self–offspring –1
- Case 57: Card 10, spouse –1
- Case 58: Card 4, spouse –1

Comments: Case 19

The husband had an early retirement from a career that required a high school certificate, whereas his wife had recently obtained a master's degree and held a part-time academic position. The importance he gave to different levels of education as a source of distance and negative feelings in card 2 reappeared in a similar response to card 16—notice *doing the same thing* as his son reflected his wish to have gone to university, which he never did. His as well as his wife's perceptions of marital adjustment were below average (husband DAS 106, below average; wife DAS 95, –1 SD).

Comments: Cases 57, 58

Both stories have a negative element mixed with a positive one: quarrel or argument and making it up or apology. The husband justified his ill temper and attributed it to both of them, whereas his wife unfairly blamed herself, gave him reason for being angry, and apologized for the discord. These balanced dispositions seem to serve their perception of their marital adjustment. The husband's evaluation of marital adjustment was above average (DAS 124, very close to +1 SD). The wife's was almost average (DAS 111). This interplay, if common in their life, would support the marriage, as you will see in their responses to card 16 in the following section. They gave almost identical themes and concerns reflecting family happiness.

The Special Value of Card 16 in Couples Studies

Elicited themes to this card seem to reflect the couple's main interaction patterns and concerns.

> Case 57: The family, mother, father and children sitting around the table on Thanksgiving or Christmas, have a good conversation, fun, laughter, something good to eat.

> Case 58: My family around the table, having Christmas or Thanksgiving meal, talking and joking, all have a great time, the most beautiful picture.

> Case 51: A father who has been younger with his children. He'd spend more time with his children, a father who would have not lost his touch with his teenaged sons and daughters.

Case 52: Table of all little ones probably grandchildren celebrating. They look so happy, but what is the occasion? This man is coming in and it must be their grandfather and they are so excited just as if they have seen Santa Claus. That's what would happen with my husband.

Case 23: I am in a high field overlooking green fields, a very warm piece; I have books, wine, and a naked 16-year-old girl.

Case 24: Conflict, distance, closeness, being pulled in two directions. A woman being stretched in several directions, husband, lover-friend, children. If I were to live only three years, I'd go away, have a simple apartment.

Categories and Scores

- Cases 57 and 58 have the same scores: Spouse +2; other, self–offspring +2
- Cases 51 and 52 both have the same score: Other, self–offspring +2
- Case 23: Nonspouse –2
- Case 24: Spouse, nonspouse, other, self–offspring, other, nonattributed affect—each of these categories –1

Comments: Cases 51, 52

This couple was 12 years apart in age. The husband's wish to spend more time with his children gives the response the high positive score. Though the wife did not mention herself, you can feel her happiness with her family and the age difference. The two partners seem to focus on one of them: the husband. The partners' evaluation of marital adjustment was very high (husband DAS 130; wife DAS 131; +1 SD for both).

Comments: Cases 23, 24

This couple had problems, though they were still together. The husband, a middle-aged person, had at least promiscuous fantasy. The score considered the degraded female who was perceived as merely an added object to his belongings. No wonder the wife faced conflicts in her roles as wife and mother (husband DAS 96, –1 SD; wife DAS 107, below average).

☐ Difficult Scoring

Fine-tune your skills with the following more-difficult-to-score stories. Challenging scorings are discussed in the Appendix.

Card 1, story 1: This boy is taking violin lessons. He looks like he does not care whether he takes them or not. He is looking at it; it looks like it is broken.

Card 1, story 2: A boy with his violin. He's thinking, "My son had to give up his violin." His parents make him take it. He doesn't like it. He is bored.

Card 1, story 3: Do I have to practice? I wish I didn't have to. He does not seem to enjoy it. I can be out playing.

Card 1, story 4: A boy who is daydreaming that one day he'll be a success, giving a performance in Carnegie Hall. A very thoughtful boy—he is given a lot of encouragement. He is a little tired, having a rest. The violin was a present.

Card 2, story 1: A family, the man is tilling in the field, the woman is pregnant, and the daughter is turning her back to this type of life. She does not identify at all with them.

Card 2, story 2: This is a mother, a father and a daughter. The laborious pregnant mother is watching her husband. The daughter is getting a better education. Her look could be sadness for her mother. She is thinking, "Hopefully I wouldn't have this type of life with education."

Card 4, story 1: They are not communicating very well. He's not telling her what she wants to know (Q); Husband and wife or lovers; I'd say husband and wife. (Q) He's keeping something away from her.

Card 4, story 2: They are arguing. He's sort of trying to go somewhere; she is trying to stop him. He wants to go after someone; she is trying to stop him, when you see the picture in the background. (Q) They seem married, in a house.

Card 6GF, story 1: What is this? (The table in the card). This man has surprised her, but he is a gentleman. He'd be more gentle than she would be. I do not see anything there. (Q) Could be father and daughter or husband and wife, if so she's younger than he is. (Q) She's not very pleased or happy, sort of saying, "What do you want?" as if he's bothering her. (Q) Most likely man and wife. (Q) He's very kind, more than she is. It disturbed what she was doing even if he'd come up saying he loved her, he's telling her something positive, but she feels interrupted; she's cold.

Card 13MF, story 1: He looks very sorry about something. She looks sick. He's come home found her sick or passed out. (Q) A small bed, it doesn't look he lives there; they are lovers.

Card 13MF, story 2: A young couple—he is ashamed. Maybe there is rape. The room is not unorganized; maybe she is sick. (Q) I don't think there was make-love scene, he's dressed, and there are books, young students, not rich, not married.

Card 16, story 1: Children coming out of school, happy as they went to the fields, everything is new to them.

Card 16, story 2: A whole lot of friends, all of us together, (wife's name) and me, and all our friends in a field, loving and sharing.

Categories and Scores

- Card 1, story 1: Other, nonattributed affect –2. The strong negative element is on account of *broken* violin and lack of an attempt to repair it.
- Card 1, story 2: Parent –2. Though the child is *thinking,* he has no choice; he does not like it and is bored.

- Card 1, story 3: Other, nonattributed affect –1. The child *has to practice* but parents are not mentioned (no parent score). He does not enjoy it, but there are no negative feelings; therefore, the score is –1 not –2.

- Card 1, story 4: Other, nonattributed affect +2. *Lot of encouragement* could be from a teacher; therefore, the score is not under parent.

- Card 2, story 1: Parent –2. The man and the woman are mentioned in their role as parents, so a spouse category is not present. The emotional distance between the girl and her parents *does not identify with them at all* renders the –2 score for parent. It is not a mere dislike to the rural life.

- Card 2, story 2: Spouse 1; parent 2. The conjugal relationship between the man and the woman is described as *the laborious pregnant mother is watching her husband.* Therefore, a spouse category is present and obtains a +1 not +2 because there is no explicit very positive affect. The sympathy for the mother *sadness for her mother* acquires a score of parent +2. The girl wishes for a better life without a condescending remark, such as *turns her back* in the previous example.

- Card 4, story 1: Spouse –1. The man–woman relationship is still present. There is a negative element, *keeping something from her,* so the score is –1, not –2.

- Card 4, story 2: Spouse –1. In many stories the woman *tries to stop the man from going after someone,* like fighting with another man. This story includes such a statement. But *the picture in the background,* which is linked to *he wants to go after someone,* points to the man's relationship with another woman. This changes the score from (+) to (–).

- Card 6GF, story 1: Spouse –1. She is *not very pleased or happy,* and she is *cold.* He is *bothering her* and *disrupting what she was doing.* He is *gentle, very kind, telling her something positive,* and *even if saying he loved her.* The discrepancy between their respective feelings makes the score negative. It is not just being surprised, which would have scored positive.

- Card 13MF, story 1: Nonspouse +1. *Very sorry about something* may lead you to think he did something wrong to her. The rest of the story shows he did not. She became sick or passed out in his absence. He could be sorry about her illness.

- Card 13MF, story 2: Nonspouse –1. The theme changes from a possible rape to her being sick. That is, if it were rape the score would have been –2. Then negating *making love* does not allow for any positive element between the characters. The –1 score is on account of his feeling *ashamed.* The initial response could provide clinical value.

- Card 16, story 1: Nonattributed affect 2. There are humans and affect *happy,* so it does not score 0.

- Card 16, story 2: Spouse 2; nonspouse 2. The relationship with *friends* is emphasized three times in the short response. Therefore, *loving and sharing* is also scored for nonspouse. This category here is of a general nature.

Appendix: Challenging Scoring

The TAT Affective Scale was used in several research studies directed by Sharon Rae Jenkins. The researchers are Linda Chlipala, Lindsay Londenberg, Mike McFarland, Rachel White, and Lizzie Woodruff. The TAT was administered in a group setting. Inquiry was omitted. The researchers posed questions pertaining to difficult-to-score stories. Questions, and example stories, are displayed. Attempt to score each story; then compare yours with mine, as cited with answers and logic at the end of this chapter. Please note that all stories are given verbatim.

Card 1

Q: Do we score parent as a +1 if included in the story, but basically only mentioned, as in 156 and 234?

156: It happened when I was in fifth grade, and I had not had any sleep, due to the tornado that hit my house. I didn't sleep the whole night. I kept thinking of my mother and father, as well as the room that I use to sleep in until that tornado hit it. I had nothing left; at all I had was my school supplies, which were in my backpack, which I grabbed when the tornado came, as well as my lucky violin. We had stayed at my uncle's house last night. I woke up feeling depressed.

234: As the little boy daydreamed about the toy store, he sat and thought about what he was going to get at the store. He starts to look back at when he went to the toy store last. He then realizes how fun it was. The boy wants a new toy truck to ride around the block in. So his parents come tell him that it's time to go, and he's on his way to get his new truck.

Q: How do we score the employer when no specific emotional interaction is mentioned?

165: Little Mickey is tired and hungry. He has been working all day for Mr. Hanson. Now he is daydreaming about a big steak and potatoes. But he knows it's not going to come true. Dinner will be the same cold grits he's accustomed to. Suddenly he hears his name and turns to see Ms. Hanson behind him. He is given orders to scrub the floor of the basement. Even though he did it last week, the Hansons want every nook and cranny in their home sparkling. Tired and hopeless Mikey makes. ...

Q: If the boy breaks the instrument—not because his parents are forcing him to play (although he is being forced to play by his parents) but because he is frustrated about his playing level—would this be scored a nonattributed affect –2 or a parent –2 or both?

216: The boy is crying because he broke his guitar out of frustration of not being able to play it. He was punished by his parents and now has to look at it in disgust. His parents are forcing him to think about what he did. And all he is thinking is that he wishes he wouldn't have smashed it so he could try to play it again instead of having to stare at it and have it stare back.

Q: When the bulk of a story has a negative theme, but the last sentence ends with a positive outcome in the future, do we score the final positive theme, or blend the scores, as in 228 and 229?

228: A little boy seems to be upset, because he cannot play his musical instrument as well as he would like. He has heard other people play this instrument, and it has sounded great but just cannot make it work like he wants to. The boy is very unhappy right now, but he is going to continue to practice, and he eventually becomes good at it.

229: This boy seems to not want to go for violin lessons, even though in the long run he knows it would be good for him. The boy is very depressed because his parents force him to learn the violin; his parents were trying to help him. He seems lonely now. As he gets old, he will learn this instrument and be very good at it. He will thank his parents for sending him for the lessons.

Q: For 208, we scored a nonattributed affect of –1. Our question is whether we score a parent relationship of –1 or –2 and/or a spouse relationship of –2?

208: The 10-year-old boy is upset because he saw his father violently hit his mother before coming to school. He can't concentrate on what the teacher is teaching because the incident is on his mind. He feels like he is stuck in the middle. He knows that it is wrong, but he feels powerless. He doesn't know whether to tell his teacher about it or just forget it.

Q: How should a teacher or parent be scored when he or she is only mentioned, as in 208 above, 213, and 248?

213: The young man is discouraged about playing his musical instrument. He practices but doesn't seem to get any better. This is hard for him, because he wants to make his parents and teachers proud. He loves to play music and have fun, but also he knows he is nothing spectacular at this moment.

248: A young boy has been taking violin lessons for a few years now. He has a major concert coming up and for the first time is not enjoying practice. The doubt he is newly feeling is holding him back from doing as well as he knows he can. For the first time it is not something he wants to do; now it is something he must do. He doesn't want to let his teacher or his parents down for all of the effort, time, and money they have invested in his talent. He blames himself for not being able to get past this block he is having, and he wishes that he could go back to just doing it (performing) for the love of it.

Q: Do we score 172 to 2801 under parent or nonattributed affect?
A: It helps to ask about the child's feelings, not only thoughts.

172: I would say this is a story about education. Umm... This child is attempting to do his homework, but he's a latchkey child and he's feeling very sad and frustrated. And is about to... um... lose his confidence in his intelligence. And the article is to encourage parents to get their kids into after-school programs that can help them with after school programs. (Q—story end?) I guess that was my ending—the beginning of the article being there are latchkey kids, middle—end. Being to get their kids into these programs. (Q—boy's thinking) That he doesn't understand why school creates bad feelings inside of him.

204: He looks as if he's been practicing for a while and has grown a little bit tired of practicing. Or he could be a little bit reluctant to start practicing. I'm having a little bit of trouble deciding on one particular theme. He looks somewhat fatigued or despondent—not that enthusiastic about practicing. As far as the situation leading up to this, I'm sort of imagining a typical grade-school kid who was pressured or encouraged in a slightly coercive way to take up the violin. (Q—outcome?) Probably, I would guess that a majority of kids who play an orchestral instrument at a really young age don't stick with it. (Q—thinking?) He looks as if his mind is wandering somewhat. He's looking sleepy, or he doesn't look like he's very concentrated. He looks as if he's thinking about how he generally doesn't enjoy practicing. Maybe he's dwelling on feeling a little frustrated about what's expected of him. (Q—what he did to bring this about?) He agreed to play in his elementary school orchestra, or he allowed himself to be, he allows everybody to choose that for him. (Q—others' react?) They would be approving. (Q—how he treats himself afterward?) He probably tried to distract himself from having to practice. Maybe he went outside and rode his bike. Maybe he watched TV or played with his cat.

2303: This looks like it's mid-afternoon, and this boy looks tired. He's probably being forced to practice. He'll probably start practicing again after he rests for a few minutes. (Thinking?) That he's frustrated and doesn't want to play anymore. He'd rather be outside.

2401: Okay, this is a little boy sitting in front of a violin. From the look on his face and the way his hands are placed on his face and temple, and his eyes look kind of droopy, he either is unhappy, or he may have vision problems, either unhappy or doesn't know what's in front of him. His mouth is not smiling or frowning, maybe resignation. Before, someone asked him to sit down and presented him with a violin and possibly is giving him verbal instruction. After I think, after he is probably going to be allowed to put his hands on the instrument with instructions of how to do that properly. And I think this is probably an introduction so I'm not sure that he will be happy or feel anyway different after than he does now. But I would say that if it continued he might learn to enjoy it.

Q: What does it take to score +1 versus +2 for nonattributed affect; how do we evaluate fame, skill, being able to play, and enjoyment?

A: In general, fame is an illusion when there is no work. Enjoyment is positive, as we are dealing with affect. Being able to play, willing to practice, and enjoyment qualify for +2.

194: He's told he has to take violin lessons, and he doesn't want to. But eventually he winds up being very famous for being very good at the electric violin. (Q—feelings) He really doesn't want to learn how to play it; he really prefers electric instruments.

121: This little boy is going to have to practice the violin, and he's not too happy about it. He's not too thrilled. He does it even though he doesn't like and becomes a famous violinist.

2801: (excerpted; a long story). He's contemplating whether to play this thing or not. He's studying it, and he doesn't look very happy. So his mother ... I don't want to say she's forcing him, but she's strongly encouraging him.... So, he's going to do it.... He doesn't like it at first because he feels like he's being forced.... His mother is forcing him.... As he continues to play, he starts to enjoy it and realizes that later in life ... if his mother hadn't forced him, he wouldn't have learned how ... to express himself.

Q: The following three stories puzzle us. Could you score and explain?

132: This boy's bored. He's been pushed off into a back room of the house where he lives and told he has to practice his violin. And so he did that for a few minutes—maybe as long as half an hour. And then he became so utterly disinterested with this thing that he just put it down. He's staring at it right now trying to figure out whether he should tell his parents he utterly hates this thing or if he should try and get rid of it somehow. Maybe if there were a clever way to sabotage it then he wouldn't have to play it anymore. And his parents, of course, are out of the picture. The truth is they just gave him the violin to keep him occupied, so they're just as happy whether he plays it or just sits and stares at it. So really this boy's dilemma is no dilemma at all.

131: I think that his mom is probably making him sit down and do his violin lessons or maybe the teacher. He sitting there contemplating whether or not he is wanting to practice and he's sitting there thinking—he's thinking of what he's gonna do to start practice because he's not motivated at all. Looks like he's not feeling too well. He's bored. The outcome I think is that he's probably gonna pick up the violin and practice but probably won't do to well because he's not motivated. He put in his 30 minutes, and now he gets to go outside and play—watching that clock.

1105: Well, young Yohan stared despondently at his violin. He'd been practicing for days and still can't play it. It wasn't like playing ball that he picked up right away. It wasn't like going fishing; he took to that right off. But this was confounding. Finally, he decided to see if it would float, so he took it to the lake, put a sail on it, and finally learned to enjoy his violin. The end.

☐ Card 2

Q1: Do we score parents as a +1 if included in the story but basically just mentioned?

Q2: How do we interpret *family* when not explicit; perhaps we need a family category?

229: This is a story of a girl who had great ambitions. She came from a poor family background. Her father was a farmer, her mother a housewife. Even though she was from this poor background, she had the determination to study and achieve something, even through her hard difficulties in life.

169: Rosa, who had just arrived from church, was walking home as she saw her husband working the crops. Although she wanted Juan to go with her, she knew it wasn't possible because if he didn't work in field, they would not eat. Rosa and her husband were very young, but they loved each other very much. She enjoyed living at the farm because she was close to her family.

227: Anastasia began to ponder: "I have so much studying to do, but my family needs help with the farm. Maybe I can find time later to study and do my chores now. I have to do better on my history test, than last week. It is such a beautiful day outside; maybe if I have time, I will ride Thunderbolt, the family horse, down the vast meadow countryside. Look at Tommy doing his chores right on time; I wish I could manage my time better like he can. He gets so much work done, in so little time, and he does a good job. I could learn a lot from him."

Q: How is spousal relationship defined?

168: Dave and Jan were high school sweethearts. Their love was stronger than any has seen. You could see the nervousness in their eyes as the draft was approaching. They both feared that Dave would be called to duty. As his birthday was announced Jan sobbed, and Dave was very sad but proud to serve his country. On the day of his departure Jan walked him to the train station. As he got ready to board the train Dave gripped her and slid a shiny ring on her finger. Jan said yes, hugged him tightly, and waited for her prince to return to her.

203: It is 1932, and Jane has just left school and is on her way home. On her journey Jane begins to cross over an old cornfield being plowed by her future husband, Bob. As Jane looks out into the distance she realizes that Bob is not who she really wants. Although her parents and his have arranged everything she still feels unsatisfied. To call it off now would be like telling her parents that all the years they have saved every penny just for her special day was for nothing. Jane had no idea what to do. Bob was great to her and treated her like a queen; what will he say? As Jane dazed off Bob turns to her and waves, and her thoughts are lost.

Q: We were not clear about scoring nonattributed affect when there are relationships in the story—for example, when there is strong negative affect that seems to be attributed to circumstances or society rather than the relationship and strong positive for relationship. Do we score nonattributed affect in addition to the relationship scores or bundle it with the relationship?

150: Caroline is a sophomore in high school in Wattsville, Ohio. Caroline wants so badly to graduate from high school and move away from home to New York. Jimmy is a farmer just like Caroline's father. He is much older than Caroline. Jimmy wants to stay in Ohio forever and be the best farmer that he can. Caroline is madly in love with Jimmy but can't hide her passion for the big city with wonderful new things, ideas, and people. Caroline wants to go to college but struggles with her father and Jimmy wanting her to stay in Ohio.

Q: How do we determine whose perspective to score when there are multiple perspectives? Do we choose one person's and ignore the rest or score from multiple perspectives?

332: The teacher at the school came to Bob's house because Bob does not show up for school as often as he should. Bob is the son of a farmer, and during the harvest season he is expected to stay home and help with the work. The teacher at school knows Bob is very talented so she is taking him some schoolbooks that she bought so he can continue his studies. However, Bob's mom won't let the teacher give the books to Bob. The mom says that Bob is stupid and he would just be wasting his time trying to learn. The real reason, however, is that mom is afraid Bob will get an education and leave the farm. Bob is going out working in the fields when the teacher comes and never even knows because his mom sent the teacher away and never told him.

223: The young girl is on her way to school. She is in love with the young man. Her parents forbid her to see him because they don't consider him to be in the higher class of society. She sneaks to see him on her way to school. She is sad that she will have to leave him, and she feels something not right. The young man is in deep thought. He is getting tired of their sneaking around. He doesn't understand why she just doesn't tell her family what she really wants. He's thinking of ending their relationship. He knows he is a hardworking man and has goals for his future. He then looks on to the day's work he has ahead of him so he can make his money and fulfill his goals.

Q: We have trouble when there is clearly positive affect in an inappropriate relationship, such as a girl and a married man. Does it score positive, since there is clearly positive affect and no negative affect expressed, or negative, because the relationship is inappropriate?

143: Walking to school, on a hot summer day, I saw Mr. Porter plowing his field. I've always had a crush on him, but he doesn't know that I like him. Anyway, his wife is pregnant, but I don't think it is his. She's the town whore. He is way too good for her. The way she looks down on everyone and the way she treats him—it's just not fair. Don't worry; I'll get him and he'll be happy with me.

208: The young 14-year-old girl has a huge crush on the 25-year-old man working in the field. She wants to talk to him, but his pregnant wife just walked up. So she tries to pretend she wasn't looking at him. She is planning on returning when his wife is not around so she can seduce him.

Q: When scoring a fantasy or daydream, do we score the fantasy versus reality (as in wishing for a better life), or do we score the fantasy as reality (and score the relationships in the fantasy)?

167: Every day as Emily would get up and tend to her chores of feeding the chickens, milking the cows, and gathering the eggs, she would daydream. She pictured herself in a faraway country, like France, making a living by being an actress. She would wear long beautiful dresses, as she would walk through the town square. And everyone would turn their heads to stare at her. Everyone knew who she was, and little children would swarm around her as she would sit on the fountain and tell them of the wonderful story of a farm girl moving to France becoming a famous movie star.

Q: We would like clarification; do we score the relationship with a person who is dead or gone? Do we score affect for father in 314?

314: The young girl is walking home from school, and she sees the man and his wife in their fields. The husband is plowing, and his wife is watching him. The young girl is taken back to when she used to come home from school and see her mother watching her father working in the fields. She is sad and is missing her father because he passed away a few months ago. She wants to have him back and so does her mother. She goes home feeling lost and depressed. She finds her mother, and the two of them go plan and run around the fields that her father used to work in. It makes them both feel better, and they go on living one day at a time.

Q1: When a group of people are referred to in general, such as slaves, workers, women, or men in general rather than a specific person or specific people, should we score the affect as nonattributed affect?

Q2: How do we score a story that has both positive and negative elements for the same story for the same person or that starts negative and ends positive or vice versa?

113: A memory in an older woman's mind. Her mother was widowed by her father just a few years before. Her mother took over the land and home. She and her sisters were sent off to school every morning to become educated. There were many male servants on the land to till and work it. The young woman was in love with one of the workers. But her mom, still resenting her husband for leaving her, would not allow an educated woman to conspire with a male laborer. Today the girl is an older woman married to a businessman. They are rich and unhappy. She wishes she could follow her labor love to be with him.

115: The girl lives on the family farm that is struggling during hard economic times. She had been attending college throughout this time. She continues to go to college while the rest of her family tends to the farm to keep the bank from taking away their home. This causes her to feel guilty. Her family insisted though that she continue her education despite their troubles. She was the first and only family member to ever go to college, and they were very proud of her, especially since she is doing well. This, however, does not make her feel any better.

215: Sara is going to school, the first day of the new school year. As she is leaving the farm, she notices that her brothers are all working. Her dad needs them to help with the farm so they can't go to school. She thinks back to the beginning of our country when it was the exact opposite: Boys were the only ones who went to school while the girls stayed home with their mothers. This makes her both happy and sad: happy for herself, because she is getting a higher education, but sad for her brothers, because they don't get the same opportunity.

☐ Card 3BM

Q: How do we score illness, assault, death, and suicide?

A: The general guidelines are as follows: Assault, death, and suicide are usually scored as –2. If death is a result of illness and the main character perceives it as moving to a better life free from pain, then it is treated differently (i.e., not a –2). Using the gun on the floor is expected. In normal administration, you would ask, "What is this?" in inquiry if it is not perceived.

Q: For 109, would you have scored the baby?

109: This is a story about a woman named Gloria who was beaten by her boyfriend because she told him that she was pregnant. Gloria is just 17 years old. Her parents threw her out of the house, and she has no place to go but her boyfriend's house. Gloria is so confused that she wanted to commit suicide. She always wanted a baby, but she can't afford it, and she has no place to go to for help. In conclusion, Gloria decided to get an abortion for the sake of her boyfriend so she can keep him happy and so she can have a place to live instead of being homeless.

Q: We often had trouble deciding who to score and who is background and does not score.

120: Mary came home from a hard day's work at the office. The first thing she did was listen to her messages. One was from her daughter, and the other was from her mother. Her mother had bad news about her father. He had a heart attack and passed away. Mary loved her father very much, and all she could do was fall to the floor and weep. Mary thought she could not go on so she had scissors in her hand, but they rolled out when she fell. She ended up not killing herself because she had family to stay strong for.

228: There is a middle-aged lady that is very upset. She is in a hospital grief room where the doctor has just told her that both her husband and only child have died in an automobile accident. The lady is very upset because has no other family and she has just lost the two most important things to her. After the doctor left she found some scissors and is thinking of killing herself.

244: This woman is sad because she has just lost her husband in the war. Feeling as though she has lost everything, she sits sobbing on the floor while contemplating death. She feels as though she has lost everything. She had gone against her parents to marry this man, and he was the only thing she had left. Her family disapproved of the marriage, because they felt as if she had rushed into it without thinking logically. Now her last truly concrete relationship is gone, and she is left with thoughts of joining her one true love.

277: Kristin was a smart, pretty girl who got caught up with a bad crowd. Her friends did bad drugs and drank and stole from even old people. Kristin didn't care. She met a strange young man named Latham, who promised to give her a wonderful life. He took her away and bought her a car and diamond necklace. Latham was strange. Kristin, after some time, decided he must be a homosexual but was too afraid to come out of the closet. She questioned him about it, and he got mad and threw her into a wall and broke her arm. She told her old set of friends, and they beat him up for hurting her. The he went to counseling and became happy with the real him.

293: A woman is crying because her husband is dying soon. He tried to help their child from a car accident. And then the child was rescued but he was heavily injured. She wanted him to come over.

409: It was a horrible thing to happen to a young lady. Ana had been pregnant with her first child for about a month. She and her husband, William, were so excited about the baby to come. They had names picked out for if it was a boy or a girl. Then, the unthinkable happened. Ana wasn't feeling well so William took her to the hospital. There, she had a miscarriage. The doctor said there was nothing any of them could have done. Ana asked to be alone and cried with her head down on a bench in the room.

331: A woman is sad. She doesn't know how to express her emotions. She is just sitting on the floor with her head on the couch and her arms near her head. She could either be upset, sad, or tired—which it is we don't know but can only think what we want. If she were sad or upset it could be because of relationship problems, family problems, or possibly work problems. If she were tired it could be from a long of work or stressful event. Maybe even a bad day. She's a casual woman as she wears a knee por slightly above the knee-length skirt, a blouse, and shoes to go with this outfit. She is sitting thinking in her mind what went wrong to make her feel this way and will she ever make it through—come back in one piece.

Q: We have trouble deciding what to do with stories that are negative but end with a positive statement (or in some cases a happy ending).

341: This is a girl who has a lot of problems; I can tell that she is depressed, scared, and lonely. As a young girl she grew up as popular but was mistreated by many guys. She has struggled all her life to overcome her past, but she has not succeeded. She has turned to alcohol for comfort. She has just come home from a wild night out with her friends. She is drunk. All the men were hitting on her and buying her drinks. It was fun. But as she got home she was alone. She sat down by the bed as she began to weep. She doesn't know what to do. She is so lonely and scared. She is sad. She decided that she is going to win this battle.

407: A young girl gets into a fight with her parents, or someone else of meaning to her. It is a fiery argument with lots of regretful words and actions. The other person slaps the girl across the face leaving her sobbing and slung over the couch. The girl will persevere though. She is the tragic hero and must suffer before able to overcome adversity and show the world her true virtue. She wants nothing more than to please others, though she will find that some are not worth pleasing and will live a glorious life.

Card 4

Q: For 133, we are unable to decide whether we should score the spouse relationship, nonattributed affect (since she is talking about her own past), or both?

133: The four devils crept through their relationship: lust, hate, envy, and temperament. They loved each other like no other. I once wished for this same type of love. It was a basket of fruit, and I was the supplier when I first met and then it was love at first sight. This transcended into years of a hopeful marriage and family. Yet it was not to be true or meaningful.

Q: This story and the next ones present multiple versions of what could be happening in the picture without deciding on any of them. Do we score all the possibilities or, if not, how do we decide which to score?

138: This appears to be a couple with a troubling relationship. He can't even look her in the eyes. There could be two possible reasons for this scene that pop out in my mind: either he is having an affair and he won't acknowledge it to his wife, or she is having an affair and seeks his forgiveness. He might even be married, and she could just be a girl-friend he met through work. He works a lot so he sees her all the time—even more than his wife and kids. So he falls for temptation and has an affair with her. She heard about his marriage and kids, and she begs him to tell her it's not so. Or she's having an affair and he can't even bear to look at her. But in a way he's glad. Now he can be free to seek another relationship, which he desired all along.

226: Mary Beth and Kevin are happily married. Or shall I say were happily married. Mary Beth just told Kevin she was having an affair, an affair with his brother. Kevin's world is shattered into a million unamendable pieces. Mary Beth says that she loves Kevin and that his brother means nothing to her. Kevin does not know what to do. He tries to walk away from the pain, but Mary Beth's grasp on his shirt and love keeps him at bay.

229: This is a story of a man who had a nice wife and a good job. He worked hard every day and made money. He loved his wife very much, but he was tempted to go with another woman. He began seeing this other woman and started seeing her day to day. His wife came to know of this and was devastated. She asked and pleaded with her husband why he had done this. He had no reply and was embarrassed. She cared for him but later had nothing to do with him.

240: The young woman seeks comfort and love in the man. He doesn't care for her though his heart is somewhere else. She longs for him and thinks about him constantly. She wonders what is so wrong with her that he doesn't love her. All he can think about is another woman. She tries to hold onto him, but he breaks free never to be seen again.

Q: In these two stories (274 and 284), children are listed when referring to family, (i.e., wife and kids). Since they are specifically mentioned, would we score a self–offspring relationship or just include them in the relationship with the spouse?

274: "No," he screamed. "I can't do this anymore. I have a loving wife and children at home. I can't have them anymore. I don't love you; I just need someone else, and I realized that the only thing I need is my family. We had problems before and that's why I cheated. So we can't do this anymore. I gotta go." "You can't go! I love you! Please don't leave me! Leave your wife, I'll make you happy!" She screamed as he walked away. He returned to his wife and children, and they never knew about the other woman, but he was guilt-ridden but eventually forgot about it.

284: "Rick, please don't leave yet," Margie pleaded. "I have to go," Rick said, gently pushing her away. The days before, Rick had been called to service by the U.S. Navy. He had to go to war; it was his duty as a citizen of America. But Margie, his lover, couldn't bear to let him go. He had already said his good-byes to his wife and kids and now he was trying to say good-bye to Margie. She was heartbroken. She had so many plans for her and Rick. She wanted him to leave his family and marry her and move to a farm in New England. Now, she might never see him again and her heart was torn apart.

☐ Card 10

Q: How much can we infer in scoring 175, when it is not explicit just what happened?

175: As J sat there, I couldn't move; I couldn't utter a whisper. This person was supposed to be a friend of the family's. What is he doing: I was asleep, and the next thing I know I was awakened by R.E.M song playing and the pressure of a hand over my mouth. Now the person has brought me to their chest and is simply holding me. When suddenly, a hand … hand …

Q: We seem to be having trouble differentiating when a relationship discussed in the story is scored and when it is considered just background information and is not scored.

216: This is a father whose son is crying because his mother and his father's wife just died of a horrible disease. She died in her own bed, and both her husband and son watched her take her last breath of life. Now they have stood up and are comforting each other for this loss is painful for both.

117: Harley holds Sara close to him after another tear fall downs his cheek. Losing his grandmother was a trying experience and has left him with a sense of loneliness. Now, as he embraces Sara, he remembers all the good times he and his grandmother shared together: the hugs and kisses she use to give, along with her sweet embraces. As he longs for this day to be over, he knows that through thick and thin, Sara will always be by his side. With his strength and her courage they will only survive together.

128: This is a couple that the divorced woman sees looking through her window after her husband leaves. This couple just found out that they will be having a baby. They want comfort from each other. Later they go to the hospital and find out that the woman is having a baby girl.

149: The two people are sad because they have just lost a loved one. They are embracing each other at a reception following the funeral. The two are showing that they will be there for each other. The person that died was a close loved one—someone in their family. It was a slow death of a disease such as cancer. The family knew that the person was going to die. They were prepared for the death, but it still is upsetting. They will struggle for a little while but will get back on their feet because that is what the deceased person wanted. They will be happy again.

114: Mildred and Gertrude are the best of friends. They are telling each other good-bye with a feeling of discontent. Mildred has to leave and is going to get married to Earl. Gertrude knows she wants the best for Mildred so all she can do is wish her friend luck for the future and hope things will turn out alright. She knows they will, because their friendship has seen it through. They've had their ups and downs, but it's been a great friendship. They both want to stay in the same country but Earl is stationed in England so Mildred is leaving U.S. to go to England so they feel far away. They will both call each other and make the best of the new situation. Gertrude will soon find her own husband and start a new life too.

Q: We have some suicides that seem to be somewhat mixed positive and negative, good relationship but bad context. How do we decide?

121: Sleep is good. Grandma and Grandpa look so tranquil lying together holding each other in their arms. The old man had been suffering from memory laps, and the old woman had been suffering from rheumatoid arthritis. They could barely take care of each other anymore, and they felt that they had lived a long and happy life together. I was shocked to come into their small home of 50 years together to find them both dead laying next to each other. They had taken poison together and wanted to die together. I felt very sad, but at the same time I knew that is the way they would have wanted it.

226: It should never had turned out this way. He was supposed to live forever, but he died. Why now; why today? Today was June's birthday; it was her day to celebrate, but now she mourns for her one true love. She is constantly being comforted but to no prevail she is left feeling desperate and alone. She hates being alone because only misery awaits her now.

247: Time is short. They took the pills just an hour ago. How do you sum up a lifetime together in 20 minutes? How do you show the love that exists in your heart? How can a word, two words, a sentence describe the emotion you feel? How can you go on living just to watch the one you love slowly move on? How can you not want to stop the problems and begin the solutions? How can you be external? Death takes us all away like actors in a passion play.

249: The two guys love each other but won't tell anyone. They feel they will be persecuted if they do. They feel their families will disown them, especially their fathers. This is tearing them up inside. They hate having to hide their love. They need a way out. They think of Romeo and Juliet and consider the option they took. Finally they decide that the only way to be together is in the afterlife. So together they commit suicide, and finally they can be happy and together. They leave a note for their families explaining the whole thing.

Q: We find parent child relationships challenging when other relationships are present along with negative events.

268: This involves a daughter coming to the last person in the world who will help her: her father. She has been divorced twice by two abusive husbands and wants to feel pure, clean, and young again. Although her father has not agreed with her lifestyle of late, he cannot help but feel the natural bond and love to his only daughter.

283: A son is caught in a difficult situation, where he should either do the right thing or not. He is alone and confuse. The mother saw him in his despair and approached him. She hugs him and gives him advice. She uses her wise words, and somehow everything seems lighter. She always knows what to say to make everything feels better. The son wakes up from his dream and knows what decision to make now.

288: A father is consoling his wife after the loss of their unborn child. This is a bittersweet loss for them because they knew that they were not ready financially or emotionally to care for a child, but they had come to love the baby anyway. Part of their feelings is relief, but most of them are of grief and sadness. They love each other and know that this has happened for a reason and they will eventually move on.

299: Mr. and Mrs. Smith had just buried their youngest daughter, Carrie, in Mansfield cemetery. Mr. Smith hugged his wife tightly as she quivered with grief. "Shhh," he said, trying to soothe her. "She's in a better place now." Carrie Smith had been born severely retarded seven years ago. She required 24-hour attention and was always ill. It was always known Carrie would live a full lifespan, but the loss was still devastating to her parents. "I know you're right, Phil," Mrs. Smith said quietly. "But I loved her so." Mrs. Smith buried her face in her husband's chest and sobbed.

417: A mother and daughter are embracing one another. The daughter is having problems with her own family and goes to her mother for comfort. The mother is protective over her family, and the daughter knows she will make everything alright. The daughter will stay with the mother for a few days visit and then will journey back home and try to make everything right.

238: This is about two guys fighting the adversities of the world. They are struggling to come out of the closet together. They are afraid of what their parents are going to say but want to be openly gay. Shown here embraced in each other's arms they are consoling each other after a hard long day of being in a world against them. It is becoming more liberal now-a-days, but the fear is always with them.

208: Jack and Colin just broke the news to their family that they were gay. Both families rejected them, so they are consoling one another. They decided to run away together and live with one another to start a new life and in two years go back to try to reunite with their families.

Q: We were not sure what category to use for the Janet–Ginger relationship. We were not sure what *no sister* means.

420: This is Bob (formally known as Steadmund) and Janet. They have just left the country to go to Rome. They hug one another. They are relieved to be away from Ginger. They laugh and sip champagne together. They talk about how they pulled a fast one on Ginger. Back at home Ginger realizes that she had no sister Janet. She also realizes that all her furniture and all her valuables are missing. Damn that Janet and Bob.

☐ Card 13MF

Q: How do we define these relationships?

205: Steve is an attorney. He is married to Jill, who is a D.A. Jill has a daughter from a previous marriage, Marlene. Marlene has always suspected that something was wrong with Steve when one night he came in her room while she was sleeping. He tried to rape her and beat her. But just when he thought that he had seriously injured her she sprung out of the bed and kicked him in the crotch. As he was sprawled on the floor in pain Marlene grabbed a robe and went and told her mother. They went to the police, and Steve had his male parts cut off and lived in a home for sex offenders for the rest of his life. Marlene became a renounced author of women's literature.

411: Mathew had to look at the clock, for he had lost all sense of time. Mary had been fast asleep for hours but could not pull himself away from her side. It had been so long since she could talk to him without crying that he had to take advantage of all the time she would give him. They lost their first and only child four months before. Mary had not been able to function in real life. All she could do was lay in bed or get up for an occasional meal. She could not have any more children, and they could not afford to adopt. Mathew was upset, but Mary felt she could not go on. Life would never be the same.

415: The man has come home from work to find the woman naked in bed. Maybe she wants sex and he is having some kind of problem. Maybe he found out that she's been cheating on him. The woman is probably now feeling neglected for whatever reason and the man doesn't know what to do. Maybe he came in from work late and is in trouble with the wife. Or maybe that's his mistress and he's feeling guilty and confused because he now has to go back to his wife. The man will have to fix the situation accordingly.

Q: Should we score affect for the killer?

123: There was once a man by the name of Tom. He was about 35 and worked at a law firm. He was driving home one night from work when his cell phone rang. When he said hello he got no reply. When he reached his house he noticed the front door's glass was busted. He immediately ran upstairs to find his wife in bed naked. Someone had broken into their house and raped and killed his wife. Tom didn't know what to do. All he could do was cry. He had just lost the most precious thing in his life. Somehow he was going to find whoever did that to her. From that moment he dedicated his life to tracking them down.

151: A man walks into the bedroom of his wife and finds her lying in bed. He walks up to her and realizes that she is not breathing. He realizes that she has been murdered at night and rises up quickly and begins to scream and cover his eyes so that he does not see her. He is horrified by what he sees. The young wife lies there helplessly, and the man does not know what to do. After a short period of time he becomes full of rage and is determined to find the killer and kill him.

Q: We are not sure how to handle the man's suicide in the next three stories.

100: Edgar suffered from blackouts. He could wake up anywhere and anytime. He was born wealthy so he had no job. His wife left him at some point in the marriage, and that is when the blackouts began to occur. Once he had awakened with a cat that he had stabbed thousands of times in his hands over his kitchen sink. He awoke one morning laying next to a horror who had a needle jammed in her vein. Edgar looked at her naked body with disgust and hate. What had he become? He called the police to clean it up, and he left. He went home and got his gun and then went to the park. He watch the children play. When he stood up, it looked as if he was to go, but he did something else instead. He stuck the gun in his mouth and pulled the trigger. Little pieces of brain landed on a little girl, and she was scared for life.

158: Muder of a Protetute: (1) Setting 19th century Hotel Braffol. Man + a protetute. (2) Drinking absenthe + folandering for days. (3) Man felt elation then during a hallucination do to the absenthe + days without sleep he strangles the protetute. The women first playful becomes terrified + withers after trying to fend off the attack. (4) Man will hurriedly leave. Magistrate will investigate murder briefly .... + ... The man's card. Man in his fear of losing face commits suicide.

202: The stench was overwhelming. The smell of rotting flesh permeated the room. The pungent aroma made his eyes water, and he gagged. He never should have left her alone here with the disease spreading. Her arm lay limp over the edge of the bed, and her eyes were open, turned away from him and towards the wall. He slumped down to the floor and began to weep. "It's all my fault; it's all my fault," repeated to himself. Pulling a gun from the bedside table, he placed it in his mouth and pulled the trigger.

Q: How do we distinguish spouse and nonspouse?

117: This is a very disturbing picture. Okay, let me start over—a married man looking for some outside attention. Uh, finds it in his secretary and she has him over one night late, they end up fooling around and he sleeps with her that night. In the middle of the night he wakes up and can't believe what he's done. So he, instead of taking it out on himself blames the secretary in his mind and decides to strangle her while she's sleeping. After he strangles her and kills her he is in extreme disbelief as to what he has done. So he cries and covers his face and then goes over to kill himself. She, okay, the husband feeling restless at home, feeling a bit adventurous; he feels good about the attention he's getting from the secretary and he feels attractive by the young secretary and afterwards feels remorseful to the point of suicide. Remorseful using regretful, is that correct? I want to make sure I understand that word.

122: This guy looks like he's a kind of tired, may be a little bit remorseful or sad, relatively young woman on the bed, naked. She appears she's dead. I wonder this guy kills her, but there is no sign of great struggle—maybe she's passed away at a young age and he is pretty upset. Looks to me he is sitting awhile with her. May be she is ill, there are books on the table, maybe he is awhile with her. He is to leave and cannot do anything for her. It's unusual. Her breasts are exposed; I try to figure why she's in the position. Maybe he wants to take a last look at her before he is left. I think this is wife. It's not a ... I think it is not a family member. It's a woman who he knows. He seems to be upset.

136: This looks different. It looks like a ... Kinda reminds me of a scene from A Hard Times? A man named Steven Blarpoole with his wife in a small apartment. She's been drinking. He's tried to get her to stop drinking and she hasn't taken heed. So he's kind of unsure what his obligations are what's morally correct. Because he's tried to get her to stop drinking before and she won't listen. The man seems really upset 'cause he cares about her as a human being but doesn't like her as a person. He has to support her. If he knew how, he would make her a better person. She seems to be unconscious and selfish, kind of. She doesn't mean to cause her husband pain, but her addiction just kind of takes control of her life. The man's not sure what to do. He tired from working all day doesn't want to deal with it now he's too worried to sleep. It ends up he goes to bed; next morning she runs off with the butler and his life gains stability and happiness.

190: (Sighs) Married couple—he woke to discover his wife died in her sleep not knowing the cause, feeling guilt, anger, and pain, I don't know whatever feeling they have. He's in total shock and doesn't know what to do. (Q—What does he do?) He goes totally insane and goes on a murder rampage and kills a whole bunch of people and gets put in jail for life.

□ Answers and Expert Scoring

Card 1

156: Yes, parent +1. There is no problem with parents. Mere mention of a relationship acquires this score, as indicated in the manual. You also score nonattributed affect –2. It is not a violin practice problem; the main character lost everything to the tornado.

234: It is a chosen gift from parents; the main character is happy in anticipation of own choice, so it is parent +2.

165: There is a lot of felt oppression: poor meals, hard work, frustrated boy and miserable, hopeless. What more do you need for emotions? It is –2. The category could be other, employee–employer as well as nonattributed affect.

216: It is both. The relationship with the parents is clear. His parents forced him to practice; his resentment and frustration reached the point of damaging the violin; they punished him for damaging it. So it is parents –2 as well as nonattributed affect –2. He is frustrated, crying, and regrets damaging it. He is evaluating his action. All these words are feelings.

General comment on stories 228-121 and 1105: Magical thinking is common in stories to card 1. For this card, there should be practice, going to lessons (i.e., investing effort) for the nonattributed affect score to be positive. But if the story magically moves from inability to play to being famous it would not be considered positive.

228: It is nonattributed affect +1. Yes, we generally weigh all emotions. Though he was very unhappy due to inability to produce like what he heard *sounded great,* he will practice and be good at it. He has made this decision, had the choice. If the strong negative emotion *very unhappy* was not there—only the task was difficult—then he will practice and succeed it would have been +2. If the story were about having the *choice* to drop violin but succeed in school or another hobby and being happy it would have been positive. The degree (+1 or +2) would depend on the included feelings.

229: Notice that the child's depression is caused by parents forcing him not because of the child's own judgment of his capacity to achieve. Up until this sentence it would have been parent –2. Then there are *parents trying to help* and *thanking them,* which relatively modifies the negative feeling within the relationship, so parents becomes –1. Nonattributed affect: Child does not want now to attend lessons; he will learn and be good at it—so it is +1.

208: This has nothing to do with a relationship with a teacher. It is focused around the child's pain and helplessness in a family tragedy. Telling the teacher or not is only an expression of *keeping it in or asking for advice*—which deals with the child's confusion, not his relationship to the teacher. So, as he is distracted, stuck, powerless; it is nonattributed affect –1, as you did. Certainly, there is no spouse relationship. You score the character's affect toward others. The category parent is not scored either. The boy did not say he is angry with his father, for example. The content can be clinically useful.

213: It is nonattributed affect +1. The boy is thinking about his limitations as well as his aspirations. Parents and teachers are his world; they are a background—not scored.

248: This is another nonattributed affect +1. The boy is examining his own situation. He has enjoyed playing before. Now that it is not for mere enjoyment he has a blockage or stage fear. He wants to please all involved in his past achievement. They did not push him; he did not resent years of practice.

172: Nonattributed affect –2, on account of *very sad and frustrated.* The background is *about to lose confidence in his intelligence* and *school creates bad feelings.* All statements about what parents should do are not scored, but they contribute to putting the blame on parents; thus, the child does not take the main responsibility. Parent category is not scored because there is no direct affect between the child and his parents.

204: There is no mention of parents; *was pressured, encouraged* could be by a teacher: *He allowed everybody to choose that for him.* No score under parent. It is nonattributed affect –1 on account of *He generally doesn't enjoy practice* and *feeling a little frustrated.*

2303: Nonattributed affect +1: *Start practicing again after he rests for a few minutes.* That is, now he wants to play for a few minutes, so he did not drop practice. Parents are not clearly who is forcing him.

2401: There are a lot of hesitant statements and refusal to choose between two affects such as *smiling* and *frowning.* Someone *asked,* there is no mention of parents, so no score under parent. *Asked him* allows a choice for the child, in connection to how we evaluate nonattributed affect. The story leans toward possible enjoyment, though not specific, in addition to *choice.* Therefore, one cannot score negatively; it is nonattributed affect +1.

194: No parent score. It is nonattributed affect –1. *He has to* implies no choice for the child. *He doesn't want to* adds to this negative direction. There is the child's interest in using an electric violin and *becoming famous*. So, not wanting to play and preferring an easier instrument led to a negative score. Great success without any mention to practice constitutes magical solution of problems (see note at beginning of this section).

121: Nonattributed affect –1: *He has to practice, not too happy or thrilled* and *He does it ... he doesn't like it;* thus, the affect is negative. There is no mention of positive feelings even when he becomes famous. Fame here does not count.

2801: Mother or parent –1. After hesitation *mother is forcing him*. It would have been a –2 if the story stopped here. But in view of the following statements, in particular the child's enjoyment and self-expression, the score becomes –1.

132: The parents are avoiding interaction with the child. They are detached. Otherwise they would have been in the same place as he is and encouraged or praised him. The phrase *just as happy* does not express real happiness. Consider *he's been pushed off into a back room,* far from the parents. And *he has to practice* leaves no choice for him. *This thing* shows a condescending feeling added to *bored, disinterested*. Then, more negative statements follow: *utterly hates, get rid of it,* and *sabotage,* as well as underhandedness *a clever way*. All are –2. The last sentence is far from being a happy ending: parents –2.

131: Score under mother and teacher. There could have been an inquiry question about the two persons. *Making* him do violin lesson is more negative than wanting him to. *Putting in the 30 minutes* and *not motivated at all* and *bored* are more negative than dislike. The score is moved from –2 to –1, on account of an invested effort.

1105: Sarcastic end of story, which is not real enjoyment. It is nonattributed affect –2 on account of destroying the violin. The previous negative statements about nonreadiness to invest effort would have scored –1. Only days of practice are not sufficient to play it.

Card 2

229: Re: Q1: Yes, the story is about the main character and her parents, as indicated in the manual. Re: Q2: You may have a family category in this case.

169: We need to know what *her family* means. If it is her extended family you score family +2. In the event that it meant her nuclear family and there are no children it would remain as spouse. Add spouse +2.

227: Here, family is not defined as parents. Tommy is most likely her brother. Yes, you create a new category for family.

168: Though most of the story evolves around a lover's relationship, it ends with an engagement and a continued relationship. You create a category for engaged; it is +2.

203: There are two themes in this story: first parents, though they saved money for her there is an underlying lack of openness and understanding. The parents are preparing things without realizing that she does not want Bob. So it is parents –1 (mild positive along with mild negative). The second is engaged –1 (same guideline). As a guideline, there could be a category for a long-term same- and opposite-sex relationships, if there is evidence in the story. To score under spouse there should be explicit mention (e.g., wife–husband, married). That is why inquiry is important.

150: There is no nonattributed affect here. What turns in Caroline's head is her conflicts regarding her relationships with her father and with Jimmy. It is parent –1 and nonspouse –1: They cannot agree about rural versus urban residence, in addition to all the examples you gave. Please do not bundle anywhere. Usually nonattributed affect is found in stories about one person (card 1) or in response to the blank card 16. Negative circumstances are usually background to characters' relationships. Nonattributed affect is scored separately from relationships.

332: There is one story. What you consider different perspectives revolve around the mother's relation with her son. It is other, self–offspring –2 (i.e., unfair conflict of interest to the son unexpected from a mother). The teacher's account sheds light on the mother–son relationship. Some responses include two themes, such as the girl's conflict about life in the country versus the city, nonattributed affect +1. The second theme is the man and the woman being a separate couple, spouse +1.

223: This is a nonspouse relationship to be scored as –1. The parents' attitude has to do with the girl's life forces that she has to account for in her relationship with the man.

143: The girl has a positive feeling toward the man. She thinks he will be happy with her, as if she is sure of herself. Then there is the negative, *ignorance of the man*. So you have a positive mixed with a negative, nonspouse –1. If the man loved her in spite of having a family it would have been a +1.

208: It is nonspouse –1, on account of the man's unknown feelings or indifference. It is a one-sided affect.

167: Fantasy and reality are to be considered in TAT stories. Fantasy in a story reflects hopes, plans, or just wishful thinking. Decisions are stronger than mere ideas. Actions are even more powerful. This is an important point. You do not give subjects a story followed by questions as done in experimental psychology. Subjects make theirs. This is nonattributed affect +2. The girl does not hate her farm life; she wishes for success in a city, which is quite positive. She does not have a conflict either concerning a decision to stay on farm or move to a city.

314: Re: Q1: It depends. It is scored under this category if the story does not include a relationship. Re: Q2: Yes, feelings about the deceased father are as good as a live one. This is one story, not two. The man and woman in the card only serve as reminder of the girl's parents. It is parent –1 (*sad, lost and depressed* as strong negative –2 added to *feeling better* +1).

113: You account for all emotions. But if the story changed direction at the end you account for the last affect. For this story, parent –1 (daughter indirectly blamed mother for her unhappiness; mother imposed her opinion on daughter); spouse –2 (she is unhappily married; dreams about an earlier lover). Nonspouse is not scored, as we know only about one person.

115: It is parent or family +2. The girl's guilt is not to be considered as a negative affect. Her feelings are not against her family. They are about the circumstances that make her family continue to pay for her education. Such feelings are an expression of care and sensitivity to her family's positive feelings and behavior. I do not see any conflicting affect in both stories

215: Here is what appears to be positive and negative affect attributed to the main character. Yet her sadness is not to be considered as negative toward her brothers or father's decision. She is sorry for her brothers, which is a positive feeling toward them. We do not use a machine to weigh words. The evaluation of affects focuses on relationships or own feelings when nonattributed. It is nonattributed affect +2.

Card 3BM

109: Q: We scored parent –2, nonspouse –2. We did not score affect for the baby, but we weren't confident in this decision. What do you think? Did we make the right call? A: the category and score are right. Self–offspring would also be –2. Nonattributed affect is also –2, as she is willing to abort, is almost desperate, did not care about herself in the first place to prevent pregnancy, thought of suicide, took her boyfriend's abuse, and did not think of going to a shelter. All were negative attitudes about self.

120: Q: We ended up with parent +1, self–offspring +1, nonattributed affect –1. A: All categories and scores are correct. As the story included statements and direct feelings toward father, nuclear family, and eventually thoughts and action concerning self, all can be scored.

228: Q: We scored spouse +1, self–offspring +1, nonattributed affect –1. A: We discussed whether or not the parent and self–offspring relationship might be considered background and receive no score. A: I doubt and disagree about the positive scores. Subjects bring forth death of characters. She did not mention love for her husband and child. I would be inclined to score spouse –1 (death along with importance) and self–offspring –1. Nonattributed affect –1 is correct considering that killing herself is a thought, not a decision.

244: Q: We scored spouse +1 (death of spouse with positive relationship), parent –2, but we were not sure how to handle this one. A: The spouse +1 is right, but on account of very strong positive feelings about him combined with death. If such strong feelings were absent, it would have been –1 (positive mixed with negative). Parent only –1: They did not disown her, just disapproved. They did not hate the man, only that she *rushed … not logical.* In a previous story the parents threw out the daughter. Nonattributed affect would be –1 as it is only thoughts, not decision.

277: Q: We scored nonspouse –2 (for Latham). We were not sure what to do with the rest of the story. A: This story has no real end. It would have helped if there were inquiry. I would consider her friends as a background to her self-esteem. She is said to be intelligent but associated with those who stole from old people. The subject uses bad people to fight another bad person to save the main character. That is, the main character has no backbone. She is unable to get out of an abusive relationship on her own. She lived with a stranger and seemed enticed with money. She then talks about the abusive man getting into counseling and becoming happy, which is inconsistent with having him beaten up as well as herself being abused. Nonspouse –2 would be –1 to leave room for a –2 for killing and on account of the silly last sentence about making him happy. I would score nonattributed affect –1.

293: Q: We agreed spouse +1 (positive relationship with a death) but could not decide if we should score the self–offspring. A: The guideline about a positive mixed with a negative is –1, when the context is mild positive and negative. It is spouse +1 as you scored it, but on account of her wish for him to live. If the story included a strong positive feeling for the husband or he came through, it would have been +2. This story includes a heroic act on behalf of the father. I would score self–offspring, saving the child on account of sacrificing self is +2, which describes the man's love for his child.

409: Q: We scored spouse +1. Were we correct not to score the unborn child in this case? A: Yes, that is right.

331: Q: We scored nonattributed affect –1. A: Yes, this is correct. If in the last sentence she came up with a solution it would have been a +1. But *will she ever make it* shows uncertainty.

341: Q: We scored nonattributed affect –1. A: The happy ending is accounted for, not this one. The last sentence is magical thinking. There is no real solution. There is no change in lifestyle. So there is no positive anywhere. The score is right.

407: Q: We scored parent –2, nonattributed affect +2, but we did not know what category to put *or someone else of meaning to her* in. A: There is no relation with anybody, since it was not specified. You consider it background as she is explaining issues within herself. The *fiery arguments ... regretful words and actions* come from both parties, since it is not said that *others* only were mean to her. In addition, if the other person *slaps her across the face* it implies a response to something negative she did. That is to support the category as only nonattributed affect. You cannot give her a +2. First, these sentences imply negative actions, words on her behalf. She does not see where she went wrong to change it. She makes a hero of herself. The last words *live a glorious life* are a clichéd, magical solution too. She also reveals what she really feels about some others as being not worth her pleasing them. Therefore, a +1 is as high as it can get.

Card 4

133: A most unusual story for this card. It is spouse. You have the term *marriage and family.* The kind of relationship the subject wanted had both love and hate among other negative elements, which is clinically useful. But the only statement you can evaluate as affect is her disappointment in a marriage that was not *true or meaningful.* So, it is spouse –1. Do not worry about the subject's past or present. You cannot make any category out of the four devils. There is not nonattributed affect.

138: There are no spouse themes in 138. There are two versions of the same nonspouse –1. The mention of a wife or the other lover just gives you reason to judge the *affair* as nonsatisfactory.

Q: All of these stories (226, 229, 240) contain a love triangle. We have scored the initial relationship that was broken (spouse –1 for 226; spouse –2 for 229; nonspouse –2 for 240), but do we score the other lover if they are only mentioned to state that someone cheated on their spouse with them?

226: Spouse –2. Though there is no murder and he ends up staying, the tremendous pain Kevin has regarding the cruel affair that his wife has with his brother accounts for the –2 score.

229: Another spouse –2. He was unfaithful. Loving her very much does not balance his action. The story ends in a split. It seems that some of your subjects use the word *love* loosely.

240: Nonspouse –2. The relationship is over. As you see, a third person may give quality to the initial relationship the subject is dealing with. That is, this person becomes a background and is not scored. You focus on the two persons in the card: Is it spouse or nonspouse? Other persons or the picture in the background only shed light on the kind of relationship between the main persons. But if the subject focuses on and expresses feelings toward the third person as an introduced figure, then the relationship is scored.

274: Here you have two stories. The first one is a nonspouse –2. The second is spouse +1 due to his guilt and lack of strong affect at the end, which does not make the spousal affect a +2. The spousal relationship is scored on account of the action, declaration of his need for his wife, and children to the girlfriend. Also score self–offspring +1.

284: Though he is leaving on duty not on his accord he did not make a promise to keep the relationship: nonspouse –2, on account of the termination of the relationship. The wife and children are casually mentioned within the emphasis on the relationship with Margie. Unlike the previous story spouse and self–offspring are not scored. You score self–offspring when relevant. In 274 he had a *loving wife and children, he only needed his family.* The man goes back to the wife and children. There are a couple of sentences after about the family. On the other hand, in 284, the wife and children are mentioned as a lump to describe the relationship with Margie as being an adventure or affair.

Card 10

175: Q: We discussed this one quite a bit. If we score just the words we gave it a –1 because it does not explicitly say anything more happened than *a hand over my mouth* and *simply holding.* However, a betrayal is implied in *supposed to be a friend,* and we could infer a molestation of some sort, which we would score a –2. So do we score just the words, or do we make the inference? A: You have enough material that you do not need inferences. You have a paralyzing sensation *(couldn't move)* and *pressure of hand on mouth,* which are sufficient to score nonspouse –2. We agreed that actions imply affect. Your comment on betrayal is correct. As a rule, words alone are not enough. Mere words differ in significance from one story to another.

216: Q: We scored the father–son (self–offspring +1) interaction and the husband–wife (spouse +1) and the son–mother (self–offspring +1) for being with her when she died. But we wondered if we were correct to score all of these interactions. A: There is only one interaction: other, self–offspring +1. There are a lot of details around one story.

117: Q: Were we correct to score the affect for dead grandparent? A: No, the interaction is between a man and a woman within a sad event; it is nonspouse +1.

128: Q: We scored spouse +1 for *couple having a baby … comfort.* We gave no score for the spousal relationship *divorced woman after her husband leaves.* Were we correct not to score the divorced woman–husband relationship? A: Yes, we do not know about the affect between the woman and her divorced husband or a present husband. The present tense indicates that he lives with her. There is no expressed affect toward the couple either to warrant including the woman in the interaction. In such cases the relationship would be scored. Though a mere presence of a man and wife is scored in card 2, when a story is said only about the girl, I cannot figure out a clear relationship and an interaction. The spouse score is correct.

149: Q1: Regarding the category, from the story we could tell that this couple is in the same family, but we do not know the specific relationship or category so we put it under nonspouse. Q2: In this card, we had a lot of grandparents. We usually put them in the parent category—and made note of them so we could find them later if we needed to change them. We also considered putting them in the other category. What do you think? A: Re: Q1: Your question is valid, yet it is the new category family +1 rather than nonspouse. Re: Q2: Grandparents should not be put in parent category; make an other, grandparent–grandchildren category.

114: Q: We scored nonspouse +1 (for Mildred–Gertrude relationship) and spouse +1, but we questioned whether we were correct to score the spouses; Mildred is going to get married, and Gertrude will find her own husband? A: There is no spouse here. The relation is between two girlfriends. As one or the other's future husband is talked about, you only evaluate the main relationship between the two girls. Husbands are only side topics that contributed to the girls' separation, but they will continue to be friends.

121: Q: We scored spouse +1 for grandparents' positive spousal relationship in negative context such as illness and parent +1 for narrator's positive affect for grandparents (parent?) in a negative context such as death. We wondered if we should have scored it negatively since the story is about the grandparent's suicide and in other card set examples suicide receives a negative score? A: Other, grandparents–grandchildren –2. This is the only category to score. The story is told from the grandchild's perspective. It is not an old couple's suicide, which would have been spouse –2: Suicide is much stronger in a negative direction than any love between the figures. Death is negative suicide is even more negative. The closeness in this card between the two figures makes negative content more so than in card 13MF as is explained in the manual. Similarly, the narrator's love for the grandparents is greatly overweighed by their suicide. Remember, the subject who is the narrator made the figures commit suicide.

226: Q: We scored nonspouse +1 for the someone who is *constantly* comforting her regarding death, and nonattributed affect –2 for *feeling desperate and alone* and *hates being alone ... only misery awaits*. We did not score *one true love* because he's dead; no interaction between them is described. A: Nonspouse –2. I understand that she lost her lover (not in card) and is being comforted by an unidentified person in the card. She is not accepting comfort, which we see in most stories when the two persons in the card are doing so, or that she is holding the deceased lover. On account of the last sentence, nonattributed affect is also –2.

247: Q: We scored this suicide –1 (not –2 as in other stories) because it seemed to be in the context of a loving relationship and seemed somewhat positive and therefore mixed + and – elements. A: Nonspouse –2. The subject makes the story; why in the world should one or both characters die, even more induce such death? It is absolutely very negative.

249: Q: Suicide again with a mixed positive and negative. We scored parent –2, nonspouse –1. A: Nonspouse –2. Parents are a background for the main characters relationship. But the last sentence would be scored parent –2, as their suicide would grieve them and cause them to feel guilty.

268: Q: We scored spouse –2, parent +1. Were we correct to score the spousal relationship? A: Parent +1. You have nothing to do with the daughter's life. You are only evaluating father–daughter affect. She could have been unhappy due to any reason. Her father comforted her.

283: Q: Since this was just a dream, we were not sure what to do with it. We scored parent +1. A: Yes, since the described relationship is with a parent, be it in real life or a dream. Besides, the dream is based on a quality life relationship in the story. It is scored +1 as you did on account of the son's despair and so forth.

288: Q: We scored spouse +1, self–offspring +1. We scored the affect for the lost unborn child or baby since the story deals with affect for the unborn baby (i.e., *they had come to* *love the baby*), but we wondered if we were correct to do this? A: Spouse +1. As a couple of sentences describe what they felt about the unborn baby, self–offspring would be –1 love mixed with sadness and grief.

299: Q: We scored spouse +1, self–offspring +1, but we wondered if we were correct to score self–offspring. The child is dead, but a large portion of the story deals with the child. A: Spouse +1, self–offspring –1 since the daughter died in the story.

417: Q: We scored parent +1, self–offspring –1. We did not know whether to put the daughter's family in the category of self–offspring or spouse or both. A: It is only a parent +1 relationship. The daughter's own problems are not scored, as there is no direct statement of affect there.

238: Q: We scored nonspouse +1. We did not score the parents, but should we have scored the parents? A: Nonspouse +1. You are right: Only this relation is scored, not parents, whose mention is within the context of this relationship.

208: We understand the nonspouse +1 (for the gay couple), but we do not understand why their families do not score. They *broke the news to their families* and their *families rejected them*, and later they go back and *try to reunite with their families*, which seemed like an interaction to us. A: I responded above to 238. These two stories demonstrate how they differ, though apparently they are similar. In 238 the only mention of parents was *afraid what their parents will say*. This fits with the several sentences about the world's position. There is no actual emotion or action from the family. On the other hand, in 208 there is *both families rejected them*. This is a clear statement about the family and the action and emotion are clear. Then, there is the other statement about the men's intention or wish to resume the relationship with their families, allowing time to be on their side. In the previous story there is nothing of this. That is, in 208 the relation with the parents was given in two clear sentences; there is actual rejection and a plan to *reunite*. In 238 the parents are in the background, not scored. In 208 it is parent –1 for the negative rejection plus a positive thought of an attempt.

420: Q: We scored nonspouse +1 for the Bob–Janet relationship and nonspouse –2 for the Janet–Ginger relationship. A: This is a difficult one. The last sentence gives the impression that the subject identifies with Ginger. Therefore, we do not score the Bob–Janet relationship. Ginger realized that her sister Janet had fled with her man Bob. Nonspouse –2 for Ginger and Bob (he ran away with her sister and robbed her); other, sister–sister –2.

Card 13MF

205: Q: This is stepfather–daughter, so we wondered whether self–offspring or other, step-? A: It is other, stepfather–stepdaughter –2.

411: Q: We were not sure if her depression should rate –2 or –1, but we settled on –2. A: You are right. It is nonattributed affect –2 on account of the baby's death as well as all the depression in the story. Though the story starts with the man, all the negative affect is the woman's.

415: Q: We were not sure what to do with this one. It is confusing. A: This is an example of subjects' indecisive choice of a category. This could occur even on inquiry. Both categories are scored. It is nonspouse –1, spouse –1.

123: Q: Should we score the *someone* who killed the wife? A: You do not score the *someone.* In a detective story you may sympathize with the husband. The subject got the wife to be killed. It is spouse –2.

151: Q: We did not score the killer because the interaction (i.e., *he is determined to find killer and kill him*) is in the future and has not happened yet. A: You are psychologists, not police officers. The future is scored as a decision. It conveys the subject's affect. It is spouse –2. You also score nonattributed affect –2 for the husband's strong revenge feelings. He could have otherwise intended to report to the police, for example. In 123, which is very similar, the husband planned only to track the murderer.

100: Q: The man's suicide does not seem to fit cleanly with spouse relationship, nonspouse (whore) relationship, or nonspouse (child) relationship. We considered other, nonattributed affect –2, nonspouse –2. A: This is an extremely sick subject who needs immediate referral to psychiatry. The blackouts seem to be part of the subject's own experience. Please do him and me a favor. I did not correct language errors. This subject's inner life is extremely morbid and aggressive. I see the subject as an extreme example of sadomasochism. Such emotions are directed toward same-generation women, female children, and animals. The scores clinically exceed –2. You score nonspouse –2, nonattributed affect –2 (suicide), other 1, self–female child –2, and other 2, self–animals –2. There is no nonspouse category for children.

158: These are not four stories; they are phases of one story. The writer is in (1) and (4), nonspouse –2, and nonattributed affect –2. I did not correct spelling.

202: Another sick subject, on account of the morbid details, but much less so than 100. The subject would also benefit from psychiatric help. Nonspouse –2, nonattributed affect –2.

117: Q: We scored spouse –2, nonspouse –2, and nonattributed affect –1. Were we correct to score the spousal relationship, or is this background? A: You do not score spouse at all. It is only a background. Nonspouse –2 is right. Nonattributed affect is also –2, as he decided to commit suicide. A side point: Clinically the subject feels insecure or inadequate by asking those side questions and repeating himself.

122: Q: We scored spouse –1 and nonspouse –1. We could not decide if he ruled out the wife or not? A: You just score one interpersonal relationship. The subject keeps changing his or her mind. The themes get milder as far as aggression is concerned. The last identification of the woman is a nonspouse, and the last state is illness, so it is nonspouse –1. In the guidelines he has to be sad due to her illness to score +1, but here he is upset. He ruled out wife in *it is not a family member, a woman he knows.*

136: Q: We scored spouse –2, nonattributed affect +2. Were we correct to score *his life gains stability and happiness* as nonattributed affect +2? A: You are right: spouse –2 for running away with the butler, Nonattributed affect +2.

190: Q: We scored spouse –1, nonattributed affect –2. We questioned whether *kills a whole bunch of people* is nonattributed affect –2 or nonspouse –2? A: Spouse –1—due to her death, his guilt and anger—is correct. I agree about nonattributed affect –2 for the very strong aggressive feelings, which are unjustified, and for the life sentence. I would be also inclined to add other, unknown crowd –2, as it is not one person.

References

Bellak, L. (1986). *The T.A.T., C.A.T. and S.A.T. in clinical use* (4th ed.). New York: Grune & Stratton.

Bellak, L. (1975). *The Thematic Apperception Test, the Children's Apperception Test and the Senior Apperception Test in clinical use.* New York: Grune & Stratton.

Bouvet, M. (1959). Clinical analysis. In S. Nacht (Ed.), *Psychoanalysis of today* (pp. 13–70). New York: Grune & Stratton.

Hartman, A. A. (1970). A basic TAT set. *Journal of Projective Techniques & Personality Assessment, 34,* 391–369.

Jacquemin, A. (1981). L'Echelle d'Aperception Thematique (TAT) dans la pratique clinique [The Thematic Apperception Test (TAT) in clinical practice]. *Bulletin de Psychologie Scolaire et d'Orientation, 30,* 25–31.

Keiser, R. E., & Prather, E. N. (1990). What is the TAT? A review of ten years of research. *Journal of Personality Assessment, 55,* 800–803.

Morval, M. V. G. (1977). *Le TAT et les fonctions du moi* [The TAT and the functions of the ego]. Montreal: Les Presses de l'Université de Montréal.

Murray, H. A. (1943). *Manual for the Thematic Apperception Test.* Cambridge, MA: Harvard University Press.

Spanier, G. B. (1976). Measuring dyadic adjustment: New scales for assessing the quality of marriage and similar dyads. *Journal of Marriage and the Family, 38,* 15–27.

Thomas, A. D. (1994). *The TAT Affective Scale: Scoring norms.* Washington D C: Copyright Office Records, TXu 621 856.

Thomas, A. D., & Dudek, S. Z. (1987). *The Thematic Apperception Test: Scoring norms.* Washington D.C: Copyright Office Records, TXu 307 129.

29

CHAPTER

Tell-Me-A-Story (TEMAS)

Giuseppe Costantino and Robert G. Malgady

Abstract

This chapter details the development of Tell-Me-A-Story (TEMAS) as a multicultural projective/narrative test and its problem-solving scoring system. Early cross-cultural and multicultural research using the Thematic Apperception Test (TAT) indicated the need to develop and use culturally specific projective stimuli. The significant work of Henry (1955) and Thompson (1949), however, was not continued by subsequent psychologists. Approximately four decades later, the TEMAS test was developed as the multicultural offspring of the TAT. There are parallel minority and nonminority versions of TEMAS stimuli (Costantino, 1987) embodying the following features: structured stimuli and diminished ambiguity to pull for specific personality functions; chromatically attractive, ethnic/racially relevant and contemporary/familiar stimuli to pull for diagnostic meaningful stories; representation of both negative and positive interpersonal and intrapersonal functioning in the form of conflicts or problems that require a solution; and an objective scoring system of both narrative structure and content.

Description of System

Conceptual Framework

From the inception of cross-cultural investigations using projective/narrative tests in the 1940s, it was observed that the Thematic Apperception Test (TAT) (Murray, 1943) stimuli had questionable relevance to individuals of different cultures; hence, culturally sensitive TAT stimuli were developed to study such groups as Mexican Indians, Ojibwa Indians, Southwest Africans, and South Pacific Micronesians (Henry, 1955). However, such early efforts to provide a culture-specific and sensitive interpretive TAT framework have not been eagerly pursued by psychometricians (Dana, 1986a). More recently, the work of Monopoli (1984, cited in Dana, 1986a) indicated that culture-specific stimuli were necessary for personality assessment of unacculturated Hopi and Zuni Indians, but the Murray TAT was more useful with acculturated individuals. Avila-Espada (1986) found that, following the development of an objective scoring system and norms, the standard TAT can be a clinically useful instrument for personality assessment of European Spaniards.

Traditionally, projective tests have fared well in clinical settings but have presented a host of problems with respect to psychometric rigor (Murstein, 1963). Since the 1980s, however, there has been increasing interest in clinically useful projective/narrative techniques satisfying psychometric standards (Avila-Espada, 1986; Dana, 1986b; Sobel, 1981). There is a need to develop psychological tests for reliable and valid diagnosis and personality assessment of minority children (Costantino & Malgady, 2000; Dana, 1998; Padilla, 1979) and to create culture-specific or multicultural norms for projective/narrative tests (Costanting Dana, & Malgady, 2007; Dana, 1986a, 2000; Exner & Weiner, 1982).

Based on these considerations, the Tell-Me-A-Story (TEMAS) TAT was developed with stimuli relevant to multicultural children and adolescents. The TEMAS was designed for use with minority and nonminority children and adolescents aged 5 to 18; it has two parallel versions: (1) minority for Blacks and Hispanics/Latinos; and (2) nonminority for Whites (Costantino, 1978, 1987). A third Asian American version is in the process of being validated (Yang, Kuo, & Costantino, 2004). Each version is composed of a short form of nine cards, which can be completed within 40 to 50 minutes and is usually administered in clinical practice, and the long form of 23 cards, which is more comprehensive and suitable for research purposes.

Development of TEMAS

Developing a consensual formal scoring for the TAT has challenged psychologists for more than a half a century. At this time, there seem to be two productive approaches to developing an objective scoring system. The first would be to expand the initial work of Murstein (1972) by focusing the scoring on those cards that have medium ambiguity and using the remaining cards as clinical tools. The second approach, suggested by Dana (1998), would be to redraw several TAT cards to reflect the emic validity of the various cultural groups, to collect a large library of protocols on different groups, and subsequently to develop a consensual formal scoring system. Problem-solving scoring could be best developed by using redesigned TAT cards with medium ambiguity depicting multicultural characters.

The rationale for developing TEMAS by departing from the traditional features of the thematic apperception techniques by such modifications as the use of color, reduced ambiguity, and an objective scoring is based on empirical research conducted with the TAT (e.g., Dana, 2000; Murstein, 1963, 1972). Since this test was developed as part of the family of the projective/narrative techniques, the TEMAS appropriately deserves the appellation of the multicultural offspring of the TAT.

The TEMAS scoring system presents a systematic and a psychometrically reliable and valid system to score the complexity of personal narratives. Its clinical utility is based on the design of structured pictures, which depict characters that promote identification between the storyteller and the stimuli and on the development of a scoring system that closely captures the most salient aspects of the projected narratives. Thus, the test was developed with attention to both emic and etic validity (Cardalda, Costantino, Malgady, & Maron, 1998; Carnabuci, 2000; Costantino, Dana, & Malgady, 2007; Costantino & Malgady 1996, 1999; Costantino, Malgady, Casullo, & Castillo, 1991; Dana, 1996; Sardi, 2000; Summo, 2000).

The TEMAS is best described as an empirically derived projective/narrative test (Costantino, 1978, 1987; Costantino, Dana, & Malgady 2007; Costantino & Malgady, 1996; Costantino, Malgady, & Rogler, 1988). As an offspring of the TAT (Costantino & Malgady, 1999), the TEMAS was developed as part of the family of the traditional projective/narrative techniques. However, this test presents several features that are at variance with the traditional TAT technique (Murray 1943; Thompson, 1949). There are six basic variations from the TAT:

(1) The TEMAS is the first test to be developed exclusively for both minority and nonminority children and adolescents (Ritzler, 1996).

(2) The cards are all chromatic and depict minority and nonminority characters in urban settings, which are culturally relevant to the normative groups.

(3) The cards have diminished ambiguity, but the scenes present antithetical events or psychological problems that require a solution.

(4) The TEMAS stories are scored in an objective manner.

(5) The TEMAS is the first projective/narrative test normed for Puerto Rican, other Hispanic, Black, and White children ages 5 to 13 (Dana, 1998).

(6) There are parallel minority and nonminority versions of TEMAS stimuli (Costantino, 1987).

The rationale for these and other departures from traditional projective/narrative techniques (e.g., reduced ambiguity, color) is based on empirical research conducted with the TAT (Murstein, 1963). Culturally relevant and familiar projective test stimuli were originally presented in Thompson's (1949) TAT for African Americans, based on the assumption that similarity between stimulus and examinee facilitates identification with the characters in the pictures and therefore promotes greater verbal fluency and self-disclosure. Projective stimuli traditionally have been ambiguous to bypass ego defenses and to allow genotype motivated psychological conflicts (Atkinson, 1981) to be more freely expressed; however, TEMAS was conceived following the notion that diminished ambiguity and increased structure facilitates verbal fluency and enables a more focused understanding of the examinee's personality functioning (Epstein, 1966; Sobel, 1981). If projective stimuli are more structured, a more reliable and valid clinical interpretation of the thematic content may be achieved.

Both clinicians and researchers alike acknowledge that color has an impact on the perception of projective stimuli (Murstein, 1963) and that integration of color and form is considered a sign of emotional maturity and cognitive organization (Siipola, 1950). During the 1950s several studies documented that chromatic TAT stimuli enhanced verbal fluency and more accurately discriminated between clinical and normal examinees (e.g., Brackbill, 1951). Murstein (1963) suggested that color facilitates such differentiation of clinical and normal examinees because achromaticity reinforces sadness as an affective response to TAT stimuli.

Thus, based on this evidence and reasoning, the TEMAS stimuli were developed in color. The representation of psychological conflicts/problems in TEMAS stimuli was based on the methodology of Kohlberg (1976), who developed stories portraying moral dilemmas to assess the moral development of children. Similarly, the TEMAS stimuli portray a split scene showing psychological dilemmas; the examinee must resolve the antithetical situations portrayed, and the examining clinician evaluates the adaptiveness of the resolution of conflict/problem. For example, one TEMAS card depicts a scene in which children are helping an elderly woman carrying her groceries versus an antithetical scene in which children are stealing groceries from a second elderly woman.

The conflicts/problems depicted in TEMAS stimuli were designed to evoke disclosure of specific personality functions that are prominent in personality theory and also are key diagnostic indicators of psychopathology (Bellak, Hurvich, & Gediman, 1973).

TEMAS Pictures

The TEMAS pictures were created by a beginning artist, Phil Jacobs, who worked closely with the test author (Costantino, 1978) in an attempt to depict a variety of psychosocial situations. The stimuli embody a wide variety of problematic life situations and experiences in inner-city impoverished environments, such as familial scenes within the home, solitary dreamlike and fantasy states, street scenes involving peers and adults, sports activities, and situations occurring in school settings. The antithetical nature of the situations portrayed in the pictures enables positive or negative feelings to be projected in thematic content and manifested as adaptive or maladaptive resolutions of the underlying genotype motivation. These situations pull themes expressive of varying degrees of psychopathology, ranging from severe pathology (e.g., morbidity, suicidal ideation, depression, impulsivity, isolation, delusion) to highly adaptive functioning.

The TEMAS pictures were designed to capture 18 cognitive functions, 9 personality functions, and 7 affective functions (Table 29.1). With respect to personality functions, each card was designed and psychometrically tested to pull for a minimum of two to a maximum of four personality functions; however, pictures 10B (Boy) and 10G (Girl) and 20 pull for only one personality function. Specific picture functions for each card are denoted by a triangle in the scoring boxes of the personality functions; for complete explanations of all the scorable indices read the TEMAS manual. The pulls for each card were originally generated clinically (Costantino, 1987); however, following a strong disagreement on the merit of a clinical versus statistical determination of the pulled functions between the two main TEMAS collaborators, the statistical method prevailed; hence, functions were empirically assessed (Costantino et al., 1988).

An early study (Costantino et al., 1988) assessed the degree of interjudge agreement about card pulls in a sample of school ($N = 8$) and clinical psychologists ($N = 6$), assessing the nine personality functions pulled by each TEMAS card. Six of the psychologists were Ph.D.s, and eight had their M.A.; their ages ranged from 24 to 54 (Mean [M] = 36.67, standard deviation [SD] = 7.53). The participant psychologists had a mean of 7.79 years (SD = 5.36) of professional experience with psychological testing and with mental health assessment and treatment of culturally and linguistically diverse children, adolescents and adults; they had also a mean of 8.64 years (SD = 6.53) experience in personality assessment, including projective techniques. With respect to race and ethnicity, seven

TABLE 29.1 Cognitive, Personality, and Affective Functions of the TEMAS Scoring System

Cognitive Functions	Personality Functions	Affective Functions
Reaction Time (RT)	Interpersonal Relations (IR)	Happy (HAP)
Total Time (TT)	Aggression (AGG)	Sad (SAD)
Fluency (Fl)	Anxiety/Depression (A/D)	Angry (ANG)
Total Omissions (OM)	Achievement Motivation (AM)	Fearful (FEAR)
Omissions of:	Delay of Gratification (DG)	Neutral (NEUT)
Main Character (MCO)	Self-Concept (SC)	Ambivalent (AMB)
Secondary Character (SCO)	Sexual Identity (SEX)	Inappropriate Affect (IA)
Event (EO)	Moral Judgment (MJ)	
Setting (SO)	Reality Testing (REAL)	
Total Transformations (TRANS)		
Transformation of:		
Main Character (MCT)		
Secondary Character (SCT)		
Event (ET)		
Setting (ST)		
Conflict (CON)		
Sequencing (SEQ)		
Imagination (IMAG)		
Relationships (REL)		
Inquiries (INQ)		

were White, one was Black, and six were Latino. Their theoretical and clinical orientations were eclectic, cognitive/behavioral, psychoanalytic, and ego psychological.

In this study, the participating psychologists were given in random order the 23 TEMAS pictures and were individually instructed to check at least two and no more than four of the nine functions pulled by each card, in accordance with their theoretical orientation and the definition of the nine personality functions from the TEMAS Manual. The percentage of agreement among the 14 clinicians ranged from 100% on card 1B and 1G for interpersonal relations to 71% on card 15 for achievement motivation.

TEMAS Administration

The TEMAS administration is a reformulation of both the traditional TAT administration (Murray, 1943) and the Rorschach Comprehensive System administration (Exner, 1993). To reduce the examiner's bias, the test should be administered in the child's dominant language by an examiner fully familiar with the child's cultural background and proficient in the standardized administration of the test (Dana, 1998). Individual administration is important because the normative data were obtained by this method. Unlike the TAT and Rorschach, the TEMAS cards are administered in a random order, except for card 1, which is administered first because of its nonthreatening content. Recent studies have explored group administration in a classroom setting, with the student writing instead of telling a story (Cardalda et al., 2007; Flanagan, Losapio, Costantino, Greenfeld, & Hernandez, 2004). The test is administered face to face, and the examiner should make sure that the child is as comfortable as possible and is experiencing a minimum of test anxiety.

After establishing rapport with the examinee, the examiner introduces the TEMAS cards with the following instructions: "I have several interesting pictures that I am going to show you. Look at the persons and places in the pictures and tell me a complete story about each picture, one that has a beginning and end. The story should answer three questions: What is happening in the picture now? What has happened before? And what will happen in the future?" Subsequently, the examiner hands the card to the student, records the story verbatim, and notes the reaction time, the spontaneous time, and the total storytelling time. The maximum time for a story typically is three to five minutes. Examinees are given the opportunity to tell a complete story in a spontaneous manner without structured inquiries. A story is complete if it relates (1) the identities of and relationships among the characters, (2) identification of the setting, (3) what the characters are doing and saying, (4) what the characters did before, (5) what the characters will be doing in the future, and (6) what the main character is thinking and feeling upon resolution of the story's conflict/problem. The prompting is conducted only for indices not present in the story and only after it is apparent that the child's spontaneous story telling is complete (a 15- to 30-second pause).

Categories for Problem Solving Scoring System

The TEMAS scoring system was developed as an objective, problem-solving system (Costantino, 1987; Flanagan, 2000) involving scoring by consensus (Dana, 1998). The TEMAS scoring system is composed of 9 personality functions, 18 cognitive functions, and 7 affective functions. Functions are scored in numbers of seconds and minutes for reaction time, spontaneous time, and total time. Other cognitive functions are scored dichotomously (1, missing; blank, not missing) when the specific function is missing from the story versus when it is recognized in the story for conflict (problem solution), sequencing, imagination, relationships, inquiries, omissions and transformations. The affective functions are scored as 1 when they are present in the stories and blank when they are not mentioned. Table 29.1 shows cognitive, personality and affective functions; for detailed information consult the TEMAS Manual. The 9 personality functions represented by the TEMAS pictures are as follows:

(1) Interpersonal relations

(2) Control/aggression

(3) Coping/anxiety/depression

(4) Achievement motivation

(5) Self-concept

(6) Delay of gratification

(7) Sexual identity

(8) Moral judgment

(9) Reality testing

These are scored on a scale from 1 (highly maladaptive) to 4 (highly adaptive) when these functions are present in the stories, whereas designed personality functions that are not present in the narratives are scored as N (the function not pulled) in a marked triangle on the scoring sheet. Some specific examples of the scoring system are provided in the next section.

A Score of 1 for any Personality Function Indicates the Presence of a Highly Maladaptive Action or Resolution for a Particular TEMAS Card

For example, inclusions of murder, rape, assault, or physical fighting with the intent to harm in TEMAS stories are always scored 1 for interpersonal relations (IR), aggression (AGG), and moral judgment (MJ). Suicide or feeling hopelessly anxious or depressed is scored 1 for anxiety/depression (A/D). The anticipation of complete failure and a concomitant refusal to attempt a given task results in a score of 1 for self-concept of competence (SCC). Failure to study because school is not important at all gets a score of 1 in achievement motivation (AM). Spending one's meager savings in edible goods now instead of saving to buy a larger reward because no one knows what will happen tomorrow is scored 1 for delayed gratification (DG). A character that strongly identifies with the opposite sex or who rejects his or her gender earns a 1 in sexual identity. In summary, a score of 1 in IR and AGG with parental figures reflects a total disregard for parental command, total lack of respect for parental authority, and harmful threats against parents; 1 in IR and AGG with peers reflects a total disregard for socialized interaction with intent to cause death or serious harm; 1 in MJ reflects a total lack of regard for the consequences of antisocial behaviors. Severely impaired RT is scored only for the most bizarre and impossible resolutions (e.g., inanimate objects come to life; a child causes events to occur by a strange power of the mind).

A Score of 2 for any Personality Function Reflects a Maladaptive Response or Resolution

Example of responses scored as a 2 are as follows:

- IT: Children fail to obey their parents.
- MJ: Children fail to admit wrongdoing, without feeling guilty, and get away with it.
- AGG (Control of): Conflicts are resolved by fighting.
- DG: Money is spent to achieve immediate gratification (e.g., buying an ice cream rather than saved to buy a bike at a later date).

- AM: Homework is avoided in favor of play.
- A/D: A child is extremely frightened by a nightmare about a monster; a child runs away from home and never returns or is thinking about jumping off a bridge.
- SCC: A youngster is not so confident that he or she will get a passing grade even if she or he studies.
- RT: The monster in a dream is perceived as a real threat.
- SEX: A youngster is confused about his or her gender identity and unable to resolve the confusion in a gender-appropriate manner.

A Scoring of 3 Represents an Adaptive Resolution

Responses scored as 3 include the following examples:

- A child compromises between obeying a parental command and playing with his or her friends following compliance (IR, DG).
- Two siblings accept responsibility for wrongdoing instead of fighting (IR, AGG, RT).
- Money is saved for a time and then is spent to buy a larger reward (DG).
- Homework is completed for fear of punishment or failing in school (AM).
- A threatening monster in a nightmare is not perceived as a real threat and is neutralized by a benign monster (AGG, A/D, RT).
- A youngster who is confused about his or her sexual identity has clear perception about the feminine and masculine role consequences and resolves the confusion in a sexually adaptive manner (SEX, A/D, RT).

A Score of 4 Represents a Highly Adaptive Response or Resolution

The child must perceive the intended conflict and solve the problem in a mature, socially adaptive manner. A score of 4 includes the following types of responses:

- A child rejects the notion of cheating as being antithetical to learning and thinks only of wrongdoing (if depicted in the picture) but rejects it because is socially unacceptable.
- Conflicts are discussed and compromises reached; money earned by working is saved for the future.
- Homework is completed because good grades are instrumental for excelling in school and obtaining a higher degree.
- A child decides to talk to his or her parents rather than run away; dreams are never real.

An N-Score (N) is entered in the appropriate triangle on page 2 of the Record Booklet whenever an examinee fails to verbalize an expected theme that is pulled by the specific card. Conversely, if a specific personality function that was not designed to be pulled by a particular card is not present in the corresponding story, it is scored additionally in the appropriate box outside the triangle.

Standardization Sample

TEMAS was standardized on a sample of 642 children (281 males and 361 females) from public schools in the New York City area. These children ranged in age from 5 to 13 years, with a mean age of 8.9 years ($SD = 1.9$). The total sample represented four ethnic/racial groups: Puerto Ricans, other Hispanics, Blacks, and Whites. Data on the socioeconomic status (SES) of the standardization sample indicate that these youngsters were from predominately lower- and middle-income families.

Stratification of the Standardization Sample

In the standardization sample, significant correlations of low magnitude were found between age and many of the TEMAS functions. Correlations ranged from .01 to –.52 (Table 29.2). Although these correlations are small, it is believed that they reflect real developmental trends in the children's cognitive, affective, and personality development. While still retaining respectable sample sizes, age was collapsed into three age-range groups: 5-to-7-year-olds, 8-to-10-year-olds, and 11-to-13-year-olds. Therefore, for each of the 17 quantitative scales, three-way analyses of variance (ANOVAs) were computed by age, ethnic/racial background, and gender of the standardization sample. The three-way interaction terms were not significant for any of the quantitative functions. The two-way interactions between gender and age were also nonsignificant for these scales. However, the two-way interaction of sex and ethnic/racial backgrounds was significant for the following personality functions, aggression and sexual identity in the Hispanic, and anxiety/depression in the Black samples; and several other cognitive and affective functions. (Table 29.2). Given the number of hypotheses tested, this result may be attributable to chance. On the other hand this makes sense because different ethnic groups culturally organize gender roles and identities differently.

There were no significant main effects of gender for any of these functions. This result is consistent with the results of other studies that have investigated the effects of gender on TEMAS functions. (Table 29.2).

Short Form

Means and standard deviations for the short form were derived by extracting the scores of the 9 cards from the 23-card protocols of the standardization sample. The correlations between the 23-card long form of TEMAS and the 9-card short form for each function were computed separately for the total sample and for each ethnic/racial group (Table 29.3). The correlation between the long form and the short form was uniformly high across samples. The median correlation between forms was .81 for the total sample, .82 for Whites, .80 for Blacks, .80 for Puerto Ricans, and .81 for other Hispanics.

TABLE 29.2 Correlations of TEMAS Indices With Age

Cognitive Functions	Hispanic	Black
Reaction Time	.00	.22
Total time	.11	.01
Fluency	.18	.20
Total Omissions	–.23	–.11
Total Transformation	–.17	–.52*
Inquiries	–.13	–.25
Main Character Omissions	–.17	–.19
Main Character Transformations	–.14	–.35*
Secondary Character Omissions	–.01	–.24
Secondary Character Transformations	–.12	–.40*
Event Omissions	–.13	–.11
Event Transformations	–.05	—
Setting Omissions	–.31*	.00
Setting Transformations	–.19	–.37*
Conflict	–.21	–.18
Sequencing	–.11	–.38*
Imagination	–.14	–.31*
Relationships	–.20	–.39*
Personality Functions		
Interpersonal Relations	–.21	.17
Aggression	–.26*	.02
Anxiety/Depression	–.18	.34*
Achievement Motivation	.02	.23
Delay of Gratification	.07	.20
Self-Concept	–.05	.10
Sexual Identity	–.34*	.29
Moral Judgment	.05	.12
Reality Testing	–.10	.18
Affective Functions		
Happy	.16	–.12
Sad	–.28*	.08
Angry	.08	.13
Fearful	.12	.04
Neutral	.00	–.29
Ambivalent	.00	.12
Inappropriate Affect	–.09	–.05

* $p < .05$.

TABLE 29.3 Correlation Between TEMAS Long (23 Cards) and Short Forms (9 Cards)

	White Sample		Puerto Rican Sample		Other Hispanic Sample		Black Sample	
Function	N	r	N	r	N	r	N	r
Quantitative Scales								
Reaction Time	87	.95	117	.95	84	.94	113	.96
Total Time	124	.97	122	.98	84	.97	114	.99
Fluency	123	.98	125	.97	86	.97	113	.97
Total Omissions	172	.72	164	.70	93	.81	206	.74
Interpersonal Relations	143	.95	164	.87	45	.99	206	.91
Aggression	136	.92	164	.96	38	.99	206	.95
Anxiety/Depression	171	.90	151	.84	100	.83	206	.89
Achievement Motivation	172	.79	163	.79	100	.81	203	.88
Delay of Gratification	163	.89	161	.87	84	.82	203	.96
Self-Concept	166	.82	155	.70	98	.77	193	.82
Sexual Identity	145	.69	76	.86	86	.80	127	.90
Moral Judgment	158	.81	163	.78	90	.64	197	.73
Reality Testing	171	.75	125	.84	100	.66	206	.83
Happy	172	.87	163	.81	94	.96	206	.71
Sad	172	.82	163	.79	94	.94	206	.72
Angry	172	.77	163	.84	94	.87	206	.77
Fearful	171	.88	163	.83	94	.88	206	.80
Descriptive Indicators								
Neutral	171	.86	163	.86	94	.86	206	.91
Ambivalent	171	.72	163	.61	94	.79	206	.94
Inappropriate Affect	171	.77	163	.39	94	.86	206	.74
Conflict	172	.77	163	.80	100	.82	206	.91
Sequencing	172	.82	163	.57	100	.79	206	.57
Imagination	172	.82	163	.97	96	.84	206	.65
Relationships	172	.62	163	.76	94	.75	206	.59
Total Transformations	172	.76	164	.80	96	.72	206	.71
Inquiries	172	.87	162	.04	98	.66	206	.72
Main Character Omissions	172	.64	164	.82	95	.79	206	.95
Secondary Character Omissions	172	.78	164	.75	98	.78	206	.80
Setting Omissions	172	.69	164	.65	100	.60	206	.64
Event Omissions	172	.68	164	.66	100	.87	206	.63

(Continued)

TABLE 29.3 Correlation Between TEMAS Long (23 Cards) and Short Forms (9 Cards) (Continued)

	White Sample		Puerto Rican Sample		Other Hispanic Sample		Black Sample	
Function	N	r	N	r	N	r	N	r
Secondary Character								
Transformations	172	.60	164	.68	100	.65	206	.34
Setting Transformations	172	.66	164	.94	100	.76	206	.61
Event Transformations	172	.83	164	.73	100	.72	206	.70

Derivation of Standard Scores

To enable users to compare scores directly within a single protocol for the purpose of personality profiling or to profile a clinical client's psychological strengths and needs, raw scores of quantitative scales were converted to standardized unit normal *T* scores ($M = 50$, $SD = 10$). To minimize irregularities in the raw score distribution, an analytic smoothing technique was also used (Cureton & Tukey, 1951). Because it was inappropriate to transform raw scores of the qualitative indicators to standard scores, critical levels based on raw score distributions have been developed. Based on expert clinical evaluation, the qualitative indicators should be named clinical indicators.

□ Research Evidence

Reliability

Interrater Reliability

The protocols of 27 Hispanic and 26 Black children were drawn at random from a sample of 73 Hispanics and 42 Blacks participating in another research study. Each protocol was scored independently by two raters. These scores were then correlated to estimate the degree to which the two raters agreed in their scoring of a particular picture for a given TEMAS personality function.

Interrater reliabilities in scoring total omissions and transformations are generally moderate to high for both the Hispanic and the Black protocols (Table 29.4). Little difference is evident as a function of ethnic/racial group. Raters generally showed greater agreement in scoring omissions than transformations. Although illogical synthesis and integration of ideas regarding resolution of conflict, sequencing, imagination, and relationships generally occurred rarely in both samples, available estimates of correlations are suggestive of moderate to high interrater agreement.

For the affective functions, the pattern of correlation between raters is generally high, with no substantive differences between the Hispanic and Black samples. With respect to the personality functions, correlations are low to moderate for reality testing and sexual identity in the Hispanic sample and substantially higher for the remaining functions. The interrater reliabilities obtained for Hispanics are generally higher than for Black sample.

Interrater reliability was also estimated in a recent study of the nonminority version of the TEMAS short form (Costantino et al., 1991). Two experienced clinical psychologists—one with extensive training in scoring TEMAS and the other a newly trained scorer—independently rated 20 protocols. The results of this study indicated a high interrater agreement on the precise 1–5 rating in scoring protocols for personality functions, ranging from 75% to 95%. The mean level of interrater agreement was 81%, and in no cases were the two independent ratings different by more than one rating scale point. It is important to clarify that whereas the interrater agreement for personality functions in the first interrater reliability study ranged from 31% to 100%, in the recent study, the interrater agreement ranged from 75% to 95%. The explanation for this discrepancy is that during the first study, which was conducted in 1983, the TEMAS scoring system was still undergoing changes, whereas in the second study, which was conducted in 1987, the scoring system and the instructions were completely formulated.

Reliability of the TEMAS scales was high in a second study by Cardalda (1995). Two trained clinicians independently scored a random sample of 15 of 74 protocols. Interrater reliability based on correlations between the two clinicians' assessments is shown in Table 29.4. As is evident in the table, the adaptive functioning scales showed high interrater agreement, ranging from .74 to .84. Similarly, the cognitive scores were also rated consistently, with interrater correlations ranging from .73 to .87.

TABLE 29.4 Interrater Reliability of TEMAS Scales Reported by Cardalda (1995)

Scales	Reliability
Adaptive Personality Functioning	
Interpersonal Relations	.76
Control of Aggression	.80
Achievement Motivation	.74
Delay of Gratification	.84
Self Concept of Competence	.78
Cognitive Functioning	
Omissions	.87
Transformations	.73
Recognition of Conflict	.83
Narrative Imagination	.87

Internal Consistency

In this context, internal consistency refers to the degree to which individual TEMAS cards are interrelated in measuring particular functions. It should be noted that TEMAS cards are analogous to test items, and it is widely known that reliability is a function, in part, of test length. Therefore, functions pulled by relatively few cards (e.g., sexual identity, $N = 3$ cards) will tend to show low reliability for this reason alone.

Using the long form (23 cards), internal consistency reliabilities of the TEMAS functions were derived using a sample of 73 Hispanic and 42 Black children (Table 29.5). The internal consistency reliability coefficients for the Hispanic sample ranged from .41 for ambivalent, an affective function, to .98 for fluency, a cognitive function, and had a median value of .73. For the Black sample, coefficients ranged from .31 for setting transformations to .97 for fluency, with a median of .62.

TABLE 29.5 Interrater Reliabilities for Hispanic and Black Samples ($N = 27$) Across 23 TEMAS Cards

	Hispanic Sample		Black Sample	
Function	**Range *r***	**Median *r***	**Range *r***	**Median *r***
Cognitive				
Omissions	.54–1.00	.82	.33–1.00	.87
Transformations	.32–.95	.69	.37–1.00	.80
Congruence	.47–1.00	.80	.42–1.00	.69
Affective				
Happy	.70–1.00	.87	.70–1.00	.92
Sad	.70–1.00	.85	.65–1.00	.85
Angry	.55–1.00	.85	.46–1.00	.85
Fearful	.61–1.00	1.00	.40–1.00	.78
Neutral	.30–1.00	.84	.40–1.00	.75
Ambivalent	.55–1.00	.75	.68–1.00	.78
Personality				
Interpersonal Relations	.27–1.00	.63	.40–.88	.62
Aggression	.35–.81	.50	.54–.87	.73
Anxiety/Depression	.43–.73	.52	33–.85	.58
Achievement Motivation	.20–.65	.51	.41–.80	.59
Delay Gratification	.53–.58	.56	.40–.87	.54
Self-Concept	.59–.84	.65	.38–.73	.59
Sexual Identity	.32–.36	.34	.66–.87	.76
Moral Judgment	.44–1.00	.80	.31–1.00	.69
Reality Testing	.32–.60	.39	.74–.83	.75

Reaction time, fluency, and total time demonstrated high levels of internal consistency in both Hispanic and Black samples. However, in general, omissions and transformations of perceptual details—main character, secondary character, event, and setting—had lower magnitudes of internal consistency than other TEMAS functions in both samples. This may be attributable to the fact that these two functions, being clinical scales, tend to occur less frequently in nonclinical children (Costantino, Colon-Malgady, Malgady, & Perez, 1991). The internal consistency reliabilities for omissions and transformations were uniformly lower for Blacks than for Hispanics.

Conflict, imagination, and relationships demonstrated moderate to high internal consistency reliability in both ethnic/racial groups. The alpha coefficient for sequencing, a cognitive function, was moderately high in the Hispanic sample but low in the Black sample. With respect to affective functions, reliability estimates in the Hispanic sample were highest for happy, sad, angry, and fearful, whereas in the Black sample, the highest reliability was evident for sad, angry, neutral, and ambivalent.

With respect to personality, pictures pulling for IR, AGG, and MJ showed the highest levels of internal consistency in the Hispanic sample, whereas A/D, AM, DG, SC, SEX, and RT had a low to moderate reliability. For Blacks, alphas were again uniformly lower than for Hispanics, with the highest reliabilities associated with AGG and MJ. Low reliabilities for the personality functions may be due partially to the fact that personality function scores are based on relatively few TEMAS cards.

The coefficient alphas for the standardization sample, differentiated by ethnic/racial group membership for the long form, were, for the most part, in the moderate range, with a median alpha of .83 for the quantitative scales for the total sample. On these functions, the median reliability ranged from .80 for Black children to .69 for other Hispanic children. On the short form, alphas were generally lower, with a median reliability of .68 for the total sample on the quantitative scales. Reliability coefficients for ethnic/racial groups on these functions ranged from a median coefficient of .65 for the White sample to .54 for the Black sample. Reliability coefficients on the qualitative indicators were lower, due, in large part, to the nonmetric nature of the scoring system used with these scales.

Test–Retest Reliability (Short Form)

Test–retest stability of the TEMAS functions was computed for the short form (9 cards) by correlating the results of two administrations, separated by an 18-week interval. The sample used in this study consisted of 51 subjects chosen at random from the 210 Puerto Rican students screened for behavior problems. Results indicated that TEMAS functions exhibited low to moderate stability over an 18-week period (Table 29.6). The eight TEMAS functions with significant test–retest correlations were as follows:

(1) fluency

(2) event transformations

(3) conflict

(4) relationships

(5) happy

TABLE 29.6 Internal Consistency (Alpha) Reliability and Test–Retest (*R*) Reliability Over 18-Week Interval

N of Items	Hispanic	Black	*N*	*r*
Cognitive Function				
Reaction Time	.95	.92	50	.17
Total Time	.98	.97	50	.06
Fluency	.98	.97	50	.45*
Total Omissions	.80	.75	50	.13
Total Transformations	.64	.45	51	.05
Inquiries	.82	.59	51	.27
Main Character Omissions	.76	.59	51	.04
Main Character Transformations	.52	—	51	–.05
Secondary Character omissions	.65	.56	51	–.06
Secondary Character Transformations	.77	.36	51	–.07
Event Omissions	.74	.72	51	.27
Event Transformations	.48	—	51	.46*
Setting Omissions	.75	.60	51	.15
Setting Transformation	.55	.31	51	–.08
Conflict	.69	.83	51	.53*
Sequencing	.82	.46	51	–.01
Imagination	.98	.75	51	.11
Relationships	.75	.68	51	.39*
Personality Function				
Interpersonal Relations	.92	.62	50	.24
Aggression	.84	.78	50	.16
Anxiety/Depression	.50	.49	50	.45*
Achievement Motivation	.65	.52	48	.11
Delay of Gratification	.45	.45	50	.17
Self-Concept	.59	.45	45	–.07
Sexual Identity	.58	.63	33	.38*
Moral Judgment	.72	.70	49	.07
Reality Testing	.56	.44	49	.21
Affective Function				
Happy	.86	.67	51	.35*
Sad	.89	.79	51	.15
Angry	.76	.77	51	–.04

(*Continued*)

TABLE 29.6 Internal Consistency (Alpha) Reliability and Test–Retest (*R*) Reliability Over 18-Week Interval (Continued)

N of Items	Hispanic	Black	*N*	*r*
Fearful	.82	.50	51	.25
Neutral	.50	.84	51	–.03
Ambivalent	.41	.77	51	.45*
Inappropriate Affect	—	—	—	

*$p < .05$.

(6) ambivalent

(7) anxiety/depression

(8) sexual identity

Three explanations for the generally low level of test–retest reliability have been proposed. First, test–retest correlations may be lower-bounds estimates of reliability in this case because different raters were employed at pre- and posttesting. Therefore, they include error variance due to different raters. Second, the indicators of this instrument have limited range; hence, the correlation may be attenuated. Third, the test interval was over four months, a lengthy period for reliability estimation, especially with the younger the children, who are undergoing maturational changes (i.e., the trait itself may be changing developmentally over time).

Validity

Face Validity

TEMAS pictures were designed to pull for specific personality functions based on the nature of the psychological conflict represented in each picture. As previously described in the "Scoring" section, all TEMAS pictures are scored for at least two and not more than four personality functions. Face validity was established by a panel of bilingual/bicultural expert clinicians. The percentage of agreement among 14 clinicians on the likely pulls of each TEMAS card revealed very high agreement (71% to 100%) across the pictures, thus confirming the pulls scored for specific personality functions.

Criterion-Related Validity

A group of 210 Puerto Rican children screened for behavior problems were administered a number of measures along with the TEMAS, and their adaptive behavior in experimental role-playing situations was observed and rated by psychological examiners. The measures administered were as follows:

- The Sentence Completion Test of Ego Development (SCT) (Loevinger & Wessler, 1970) or its Spanish version (Brenes-Jette, 1987)
- The Trait Anxiety Scale of the State-Trait Anxiety Inventory for Children (STAIC) (Speilberger, Edwards, Lushene, Montouri, & Platzek, 1973) or its Spanish version, Inventario de Ansiedad Rasgo-Estado Para Ninos (Villamil, 1973)
- The Teacher Behavior Rating Scale (TBR) (Costantino, 1980)
- The parallel Mother Behavior Rating Scale (MBR) (Costantino, 1980) in both English and Spanish

Finally, the children participated in four experimental role-playing situations designed to elicit adaptive behavior.

Results of multiple regression analyses indicated that TEMAS profiles significantly predicted ego development (SCT), $R = .49$, $p < .05$; disruptive behavior (DIS), $R = .51$, $p < .05$; and aggressive behavior (AGG), $R = .32$, $p < .05$. However, the multiple correlations for predicting trait anxiety were not significant. TEMAS functions accounted for between 10% (for AGG) and 26% (for DIS) of the variability in scores on the criterion measures. Predictive validity was established using hierarchical multiple regression analysis to assess the utility of TEMAS profiles for predicting posttherapy scores ($N = 123$) on the criterion measures, independent of pretherapy scores. In the first step of the hierarchy, the pretherapy score on a given criterion measure was entered into the regression equation, followed in the second step by a complete TEMAS psychotherapy profile. Results of these analyses showed that pretherapy TEMAS profiles significantly predicted ($p < .05$) all therapeutic outcomes, ranging from 6% to 22% variance increments, except for observation of SCC. Variance explained in the outcome measures was as follows: SCT (14%); STAIC (22%); Conner's Behavior Rating Scale (6%); and observational tasks measuring delay gratification (20%), disruptive behavior (17%), and aggression (14%).

In her dissertation study, Cardalda (1995) explored the relationship of TEMAS assessment to school achievement and performance measures in reading and mathematics of Puerto Rican children in grades six to eight, ranging in age from 11- to 15-years old. Specifically, Cardalda correlated the TEMAS personality functions of IR, AGG, AM, DG, and SCC with reading and math scores and the TEMAS cognitive variables of fluency, omissions, conflict, imagination, and transformations with reading and math scores, and she examined the relationship between TEMAS adaptive personality function scores and cognitive scores as a function of grade level.

In this study, 74 Puerto Rican children (44 males, 30 females) were recruited from a public school in a low SES school district in New York City. Students were administered the nine-card minority version of the TEMAS, in their preferred language, and protocols were scored according to the standardized procedures in the manual.

As Table 29.7 shows, the correlations of TEMAS personality functioning and cognitive indices with school achievement and performance indicators were largely nonsignificant and relatively weak in magnitude. The notable exception to this pattern was a

TABLE 29.7 Partial Correlations of TEMAS Scales With Reading and Mathematics Achievement and School Performance ($N = 74$)

TEMAS Scale	Reading	Math	Reading
Interpersonal Relations	.11	.10	.17
Control of Aggression	.13	.00	.19
Achievement Motivation	.24*	.28*	.16
Delay of Gratification	.19	.29*	.16
Self-Concept of Competence	.04	.06	.11
Verbal Fluency	.11	.20	.16
Omissions	.01	–.07	.06
Recognition of Conflict	.09	.00	–.02
Narrative Imagination	–.04	–.06	–.13
Transformations	–.11	–.20	–.13

* $p < .05$

significant, low to moderate correlation of AM with reading and mathematics achievement, and a moderate correlation of DG with mathematics achievement. When cast simultaneously into multiple regression equations, TEMAS profiles were significant predictors of both reading and mathematics achievement. With respect to reading achievement, $r = .60$, $p < .01$, and with respect to mathematics achievement, $r = .64$, $p < .05$.

Cardalda (1995) further explored the relationship between TEMAS assessment as a predictor of school achievement and performance within grade levels. These results are shown in Table 29.8. The pattern of within grade level correlations of TEMAS scores with achievement and performance is more interesting than the total sample analysis. Despite the smaller within group sample size, more correlations were statistically significant within groups, and the magnitude of the correlations was uniformly higher. For sixth graders, Cardalda identified moderate correlations between IR and reading and mathematics achievement; between control of AGG and mathematics achievement; between AM and mathematics achievement; and between DG and reading and mathematics achievement.

For seventh graders, moderate correlations were found for control of AGG with reading achievement, AM with mathematics achievement and school performance, and DG with reading achievement and school performance. Finally, Cardalda (1995) introduced an interesting new index for scoring TEMAS protocols, the dysfluency score. The Dysfluency Index consists of a count of a number of dysfluent utterances, such as *um* and *eh*. Dysfluency scores for the combined sample ranged from 1 to 80 ($M = 12.44$, $SD = 15.59$) summed across TEMAS cards. The correlation between dysfluency and fluency scores was significant but moderate ($r = .39$, $p < .001$), indicating that there was a tendency for the more verbal respondents to also present more meaningless speech utterances. It is important to note that dysfluent utterances are not included in the standardized fluency word count. Dysfluency was not related to grade-level or bilingual language switching or to school achievement or performance indicators.

TABLE 29.8 Correlations of TEMAS Scales With Reading and Mathematics Achievement and School Performance Within Grade Levels

TEMAS Scales	Reading	Math	Performance
	Grades 6 (*N* = 25)		
Interpersonal Relations	.48*	.45*	.23
Control of Aggression	.28	.40*	–.25
Achievement Motivation	.53**	.43*	–.02
Delay of Gratification	.33	.52**	–.08
Self-Concept of Competence	.17	.16	.27
Verbal Fluency	.16	.13	.20
Omissions	.11	.16	.28
Recognition of Conflict	.21	.30	.33
Narrative Imagination	–.23	–.26	–.13
Transformations	–.05	–.11	–.20
	Grades 7 (*N* = 27)		
Interpersonal Relations	–.04	.14	.08
Control of Aggression	–.29	–.25	.34
Achievement Motivation	.15	.25	.46*
Delay of Gratification	.09	.32	.39*
Self-Concept of Competence	–.02	.10	.12
Verbal Fluency	.19	.36	–.01
Omissions	.03	–.16	.21
Recognition of Conflict	–.20	–.38	–.05
Narrative Imagination	.23	.25	–.30
Transformations	.07	–.25	.13
	Grades 8 (*N* = 22)		
Interpersonal Relations	.04	.07	.17
Control of Aggression	.34	–.19	.24
Achievement Motivation	.19	.47*	.51*
Delay of Gratification	.30	.24	.32
Self-Concept of Competence	.17	.09	.08
Verbal Fluency	–.17	.12	.35
Omissions	.04	–.01	.32
Recognition of Conflict	.02	.07	.15
Narrative Imagination	.11	–.24	.02
Transformations	.06	.06	–.04

* $p < .05$
** $p < .01$

Population Generalizability

The usefulness of TEMAS scores as a function of examinee level of impairment is limited primarily to normal children and adolescents, on which the test was standardized and researched. The first consideration in using the TEMAS test clinically is that it has been primarily researched with urban children and adolescents in the age range of 5- to 18-years old. Ethnically, the norm groups for standardization include Puerto Ricans, other Hispanics (i.e., Cubans, Dominicans, Central/South Americans, and Mexican Americans), African American Blacks, and non-Hispanic Whites. Although pilot work has been conducted with Asian Americans, using an Asian form of the test (i.e., with Asian-looking characters), insufficient research is currently available to justify reliable and valid clinical decision making with this version of the TEMAS test. Similarly, given that virtually all TEMAS research has been conducted in urban settings and that the stimuli depict inner-city environments, there is no evidence of generalizability to rural populations; moreover, the nature of the stimuli may be inappropriate for such settings.

These concerns not withstanding, clinical information provided by TEMAS profiling of personality, cognitive, and affective functioning is generalizable with a high degree of confidence to multiple ethnic groups in the 5- to 13-year-old range. Gender differences are relatively inconsequential based on statistical comparisons of differential reliability and validity as well as normative performance. Socioeconomic status is indeed a limitation of the test. The TEMAS test has been researched in school districts and clinical settings that sociodemographically correspond to low to medium SES catchment areas, according to U.S. Census reports and personal demographics collected on research participants. Attempts to generalize findings from TEMAS administration to examinees from upper-middle and higher SES should be viewed with extreme caution.

Language of TEMAS administration has been thoroughly researched in both English and Spanish. Although the test has been used on a pilot basis in other languages, including Italian, Portuguese, Cantonese, and Mandarin, insufficient data are available to confirm the psychometric properties of the instrument with these and other non-English languages.

Clinical status of examinees is another important consideration in the generalizability of TEMAS scores. For the most part, participants in TEMAS research have fallen into three categories: normal, borderline behavior problems, and ADHD clinical cases. No research has been conducted with children experiencing other specific DSM disorders of childhood and adolescence. More research in this area is warranted.

Cross-Cultural Validity

There are several studies assessing the cross-cultural validity of TEMAS. Herein we report four dissertation studies conducted at the University of Rome La Sapienza (Carnabuci, 2000; Sardi, 2000; Summo, 2000; Sulfaro, 2000). The literature shows that aggression and conduct disorder in American and European schools are very prevalent (Pellegrini & Long, 2002). Studies assessing aggression, moral judgment, other personality functions, and cognition in school children have primarily used behavioral observation or paper-and-pencil tests with parents and teachers as the respondents. School children have seldom been assessed in an objective manner with projective/narrative tests to reveal the underlying dynamics and make a valid comparison between the genotype motivations and phenotype traits.

The objective of these studies was to use TEMAS to assess the genotype motivation and the Child Behavior Checklist (CBCL) to assess the phenotype traits in 7- and 8-year-old children in Rome, Italy.

Following informed consent by their parents, 92 children (50 males, 42 females) participated in these studies. The children were administered the short version of TEMAS (9 cards) while their mothers completed the CBCL. Demographic data were collected with emphasis on the SES and occupation.

The Pearson correlation between aggression in TEMAS and aggressive behavior in CBCL was $r = -0.41$, $p < .001$. When gender was controlled for, correlations were stronger for males than females with $r = -0.54$, $p < .002$ and $r = -0.29$, $p < .05$, respectively. When socioeconomic status was controlled for, the correlation was stronger at lower SES level, $r = -0.51$, $p < .002$ than at a medium SES level, $r = -0.21$, $p < .089$. In addition, the secondary hypotheses predicting that a relation exists between an impulsive cognitive style (TEMAS) and adaptive aggression (TEMAS) and between adaptive aggression (TEMAS) and hyperactivity (CBCL) were statistically supported. There was a statistically significant correlation between an impulsive cognitive style and adaptive aggression ($r = -0.19$, $p < .05$) and between adaptive aggression and hyperactivity ($r = - 0.25$, $p < .02$). Moral judgment in TEMAS was positively correlated with adaptive aggression in TEMAS ($r = .74$, $p < .001$), whereas moral judgment in TEMAS was negatively correlated with aggressive behavior in the CBCL ($r = -0.29$, $p < .007$).

TEMAS moral judgment was highly adaptive among high SES students, whereas it was maladaptive among low SES students. Moreover, there was a positive relation between the interpersonal relations and adaptive aggression in TEMAS with a significant strong $r = 0.87$, $p < .001$, whereas the TEMAS IR correlated negatively with AGG in CBCL ($r = -0.33$, $p < .002$). Medium SES children showed a highly adaptive moral judgment. There was a significant adaptive moral judgment among high SES examinees, and feeling happy correlated with a number of omissions and transformations (selective attention) among low SES examinees.

The moderate correlations between a projective/narrative test (TEMAS) and a methodogically different index (e.g., paper and pencil, observational rating) (CBCL) showed that children's personality, cognitive, and affective functions can be validly assessed both at genotype level and phenotype level, thus giving a more complete picture of cognitive/personality functions in children. And SES seems to be a strong contributing variable in the significant relationship between aggression and moral judgment.

□ Future Research Needed

Cardalda's (1995) work represents perhaps the most comprehensive body of psychometric research conducted on the TEMAS test, independent of the TEMAS authors. Her work augments the reliability and validity studies reported in the TEMAS Manual (Costantino et al., 1988), and in their subsequent work. Based on her findings, Cardalda offered some insightful directions for further research on the TEMAS test.

A follow-up of archival data from student records would be useful to examine the issue of lower achievement in the junior high school. This would entail a longitudinal analysis of the sample, looking at this sample's sixth graders who are now seventh graders and seventh graders who are now eighth graders. The objective is to determine whether the sampled cohort of sixth graders was particularly high functioning or whether the students' achievement also declines in junior high school. Regarding the students who became eighth graders, the question is whether the pattern of underachievement is sustained as compared with the previous eighth graders.

The future research plan is to examine the achievement test records of the students that were previously sixth graders who then became seventh graders in the study (Cardalda, 1995). Looking at the ones who stayed in the system and are attending the junior high schools in the school district, are they functioning at the same high level or do their achievement scores lower in junior high school? Regarding the ones no longer in the school district, are they the high achievers? With respect to the seventh graders who became eighth graders in 1995, who stayed and who left, are they functioning at the same level or are there further decrements suggesting the possibility of a gradient in achievement? Another avenue for exploration is retrospective, comparing this study's seventh graders to when they were in sixth grade to examine whether they were doing better then. But still it would not be known why there is a drop in achievement; teaching could just be different in the junior high schools.

Cardalda's study has pointed out a significant phenomenon among Hispanic/Latino Junior High School students, namely, a lowering of achievement motivation, starting at the 6th grade, which coincides with the beginning of drop-out among Latino youngsters. Future TEMAS research should focus on a large study comparing, fourth, fifth, sixth, seventh, and eighth grade Latino students by examining variables, such as TEMAS achievement motivation among other scales, school achievement, psychosocial experiences in school, drop-out rates, and social changes in the family and their peer groups.

☐ References

Atkinson, J. W. (1981). Studying personality in the context of an advanced motivational psychology. *American Psychologist, 36,* 117–128.

Avila-Espada, A. (1986). *Manual Operativo para el Examen de Apercepcion Tematica.* Madrid: Ediciones Piramide, S.A.

Brackbill, G. A. (1951). Some effects of color on thematic fantasy. *Journal of Consulting Psychology, 15,* 412–418.

Brenes-Jette, C. (1987). *Mother's contribution to an early intervention program for Hispanic children.* Unpublished doctoral dissertation, New York University.

Bellak, L., Hurvich, M., & Gediman, H.K. (1973). *Ego functions in schizophrenics, neurotics, and normals.* New York: Wiley.

Cardalda, E. (1995). *Socio-cognitive correlates to school achievement using the TEMAS (Tell-Me-A-Story) culturally sensitive test with 6th, 7th, and 8th grades Puerto Rican students.* Unpublished doctoral dissertation, New School for Social Research, New York.

Cardalda, E., Costantino, G., Malgady, R. G., & Maron, N. (1998, August). *Multicultural achievement motivation as assessed by TEMAS.* Poster session presented at the 106th Annual American Psychological Association Convention, San Francisco, CA.

Cardalda, E. B., Costantino, G., Jiménez-Suárez, V., León-Velázquez, M., Martínez, J. V., & Perez, M. (2007). Cross-cultural comparisons with the TEMAS test using group versus individual methodology. In G. Costantino, R. H. Dana, & G. R. Malgady (Eds.), *TEMAS (Tell-Me-A-Story) assessment in multicultural societies* (pp. 255–271). Mahwah, NJ: Lawrence Erlbaum Associates, Publishers.

Cornabuci, C. (2000). *Relationship between aggression and interpersonal relations in 7 and 8 year old Italian children.* Unpublished doctoral dissertation, Universita di Roma La Sapienza, Rome, Italy.

Costantino, G. (1978, November). *TEMAS, a new thematic apperception test to measure ego functions and development in urban Black and Hispanic children.* Paper presented at the second annual conference on fantasy and the imaging process, Chicago, IL.

Costantino, G. (1980). *The use of folktales as a new therapy modality to effect change in Hispanic children and their families.*(National Institute of Mental Health Grant 1-RO1-MH33711. Rockville, MD: National Institute of Mental Health.

Costantino, G. (1987). *TEMAS (Tell-Me-A-Story) Pictures.* Los Angeles: Western Psychological Services.

Costantino, G., Malgady, R. G., & Rogler, L. H. (1988). *TEMAS (Tell-Me-A-Story) Test Manual.* Los Angeles: Western Psychological Services.

Costantino, G., Malgady, R. G., Rogler, L. H., & Tsui, E. (1988). Discriminant analysis of clinical outpatients and public school children by TEMAS: a thematic apperception test for Hispanics and Blacks. *Journal of Personality Assessment, 52,* 670–678.

Costantino, G., Malgady, R., Casullo, M. M., & Castillo, A., (1991). Cross cultural standardization of TEMAS in three Hispanic subcultures. *Hispanic Journal of Behavioral Sciences, 13,* 48–62.

Costantino, G., Colon-Malgady, G., Malgady, R. G., & Pérez, A. (1991). Assessment of attention deficit disorder using a thematic apperception technique. *Journal of Personality Assessment, 57,* 87–95.

Costantino, G., & Malgady, R. G. (1996). Development of TEMAS, A multicultural thematic apperception test: Psychometric properties and clinical utility. In G. R. Sodowsky & J. Impara (Eds.), *Multicultural Assessment in Counseling and Clinical Psychology* (pp. 85–136). Lincoln: University of Nebraska, Buros Institute of Mental Measurements.

Costantino, G., & Malgady, R. G. (1999). The Tell-Me-A-Story Test: A multicultural offspring of the Thematic Apperception Test. In L. Geiser & M. I. Stein (Eds.), *Evocative images: The Thematic Apperception Test and the art of projection* (pp. 191–206). Washington, DC: American Psychological Association.

Costantino, G., & Malgady, R. G. (2000). Multicultural and cross-cultural utility of the TEMAS (Tell-Me-A-Story) Test. In R. H. Dana (Ed.), *Handbook of Cross-Cultural/Multicultural Personality Assessment* (pp. 481–514). Mahwah, NJ: Lawrence Erlbaum Associates, Inc.

Costantino, G., Malgady, R. G., & Flanagan, R. M. (2001). Narrative assessment: TAT, CAT and TEMAS. In L. A. Suzuki, J. G. Ponterotto, and P. J. Meller (Eds.), *Handbook of multicultural assessment* (2nd ed.) (pp. 217–237). San Francisco: Jossey-Bass.

Costantino, G., Dana, R. H., & Malgady, G. R. (2007). *TEMAS (Tell-Me-A-Story) assessment in multicultural societies.* Mahwah, NJ: Lawrence Erlbaum Associates, Publishers.

Cureton, E. E., & Tukey, J. W. (1951). Smoothing frequency distribution, equating tests, and preparing norms. *American Psychologist, 6,* 404–410.

Dana, R. H. (1986a). Personality assessment and Native Americans. *Journal of Personality Assessment, 50,* 480–500.

Dana, R.H. (1996). Culturally competent assessment practice in the United States. *Journal of Personality Assessment, 66,* 472–487.

Dana, R. H. (1998). *Understanding cultural identity in intervention and assessment.* Thousand Oaks, CA: Sage.

Dana, R. H. (2000). Multicultural assessment of child and adolescent personality and psychopathology. In A. L. Comunian & U. Gielen (Eds.), *International perspectives on human development* (pp. 233–258). Lengerich, Germany: Pabst Science Publishers.

Epstein, S. (1966). Some considerations on the nature of ambiguity and the use of stimulus dimensions in projective techniques. *Journal of Consulting Psychology, 30,* 183–192.

Exner, J. (1993). The Rorschach: A comprehensive system (vol. 1, 3rd ed.). New York: John Wiley & Sons.

Exner J. E., & Weiner, I. B. (1982). *The Rorschach: A comprehensive system* (vol. 3). New York: Wiley.

Exner, J. E., & Weiner, I. B. (1994). *The Rorschach: A comprehensive system* (vol. 3): *Assessment of children and adolescents* (2nd ed.). New York: Wiley.

Flanagan, R. (1999). Objective and projective personality assessment: The TEMAS and the Behavior Assessment System for Children, self-report of personality. *Psychological Reports, 48,* 865–867.

Flanagan, R., & DiGiuseppe, R. (1999). A critical review of the TEMAS: A step within the development of thematic apperception instruments. *Psychology in the Schools, 36,* 21–30.

Flanagan, R., Losapio, G., Costantino, G., Greenfeld, R., & Hernandez, A. (2004, July). The use of narratives to assess children's social problem solving skills. Paper presented at the 13th Convention of the American Psychological Association, Honolulu, HI.

Henry, E. W. (1955). The Thematic Apperception Technique in the study of group and cultural problems. In H. H. Anderson & G. L. Anderson (Eds.), *An introduction to projective techniques and other devices for understanding the dynamics of human behavior* (pp. 230–278). New York: Prentice-Hall.

Kohlberg, L., (1976). Moral stages and moralization: The cognitive-developmental approach. In T. Lichona (Ed.), *Moral development and behavior: Theory, research, and social issues* (pp. 31–53). New York: Holt, Rinehart & Winston.

Loevinger, J., & Wessler, R. (1970). *Measuring ego development 1. Construction and use of a sentence completion test.* San Francisco: Jossey-Bass.

Monopoli, J. (1984). *A culture-specific interpretation of thematic test protocols for American Indians.* Unpublished master's thesis, University of Arkansas, Fayetteville.

Murray, H. A. (1943). *Thematic Apperception Test Manual.* Cambridge, MA: Harvard University Press.

Murstein, B. L. (1963). *Theory and research in projective techniques.* New York: Wiley.

Murstein, B. L. (1972). Normative written responses for a college sample. *Journal of Personality Assessment, 41,* 194–247.

Padilla, A. M. (1979). Critical factors in the testing of Hispanic Americans: A review and some suggestions for the future. In R. Tyler & S. White (Eds.), *Testing, teaching and learning: Report of a conference on testing* (pp. 219–233). Washington, DC: National Institute of Education.

Pellegrini, A. D., & Long, J. D. (2002). A longitudinal study of bullying, dominance, and victimization during the transition from primary school through middle school. *British Journal of Developmental Psychology, 20,* 259–280.

Ritzler, B. A. (1996). Projective methods for multicultural personality assessment: Rorschach, TEMAS, and Early Memory Procedures. In L. A. Suzuki, P. J. Meller, & J. G. Ponterotto (Eds.), *Handbook of Multicultural Assessment: Clinical. psychological and educational applications* (pp. 115–136). San Francisco: Jossey-Bass Publishers.

Sardi, G. M. (2000). *Relationship between aggression and cognitive functions in conflict resolution in 7 and 8 year old Italian children.* Unpublished doctoral dissertation, Universita di Roma La Sapienza, Rome, Italy.

Siipola, E. M. (1950). Influence of color reactions to inkblots. *Journal of Personality, 18,* 358–367.

Sobel, H. J. (1981). Projective methods of cognitive analysis. In T. Merluzzi, C. Glass, & M. Genest (Eds.), *Cognitive assessment* (pp. 127–148). New York: Guilford Press.

Spielberger, C. D., Edwards, C. D., Lushene, R. E., Montouri, J., & Plaztek, D. (1973). *Preliminary test manual for the State-Trait Anxiety Inventory for Children.* Palo Alto, CA: Consulting Psychologist Press.

Sulfaro, C. (2000). *Relationship between aggression and moral judgment.* Unpublished doctoral dissertation, Universita di Roma La Sapienza, Rome, Italy.

Summo, B. (2000). *Relationship between aggression and emotional functions in conflict resolution of 7 and 8 year old children.* Unpublished doctoral dissertation, Universita di Roma La Sapienza, Rome, Italy.

Thompson, C. E. (1949). The Thompson modification of the Thematic Apperception Test. *Journal of Projective Techniques, 15,* 469–478.

Villamil, B. (1973). *Desarollo del Inventario de Ansiedad Estado y Rasgo para ninos* [Development of the State-Trait Anxiety Inventory for Children]. Unpublished master's thesis, University of Puerto Rico.

Walton, J. R., Nuttall, R. L., & Vazquez-Nuttall, E. (1997). The impact of war on the mental health of children: A Salvadoran study. *Child Abuse & Neglect, 21,* 737–749.

Yang, C.-M., Kuo, L.-H., & Costantino, G., (2004, July). Validity of the Asian American TEMAS in Taiwanese children: Preliminary data. In G. Costantino (Chair), *Multicultural/cross-cultural validation of TEMAS: A projective/narrative test.* Symposium presented at 9th European Congress of Psychology, Vienna, Austria.

Notes

The authors would like to thank Elsa Cardalda, Ph.D., Director, Clinical Doctoral Program, Carlos Albizu University, San Juan, P.R., and her students for their important contribution to the cross-cultural validation of TEMAS. Parts of this chapter were adapted from Dr. Cardalda's studies and from the TEMAS Manual, published by Western Psychological Services, Los Angeles, CA.

30

CHAPTER

Empathy

Hedwig Teglasi, Constance Locraft, and Kelly Felgenhauer

☐ Abstract

Three procedures for coding Thematic Apperception Test (TAT) stories that are consistent with theory and research pertaining to empathy and to social-emotional adjustment were reliable across raters, consistent across cards, and differentiated between children classified as high and low in empathy on the basis of teacher ratings. The coded variables, described previously (Teglasi, 2001), were perceptual integration, affect source, and mutuality of autonomy. Regression analyses predicting each of the three TAT variables showed that empathy grouping accounted for substantial variance and that grade grouping (low = k–3; high = 4–6) made a unique but small contribution. Average number of words and number of inquiries per story did not add unique variance beyond that contributed by grade group. Scores on all seven TAT cards differentiated between empathy groups and most cards differentiated grade groups.

☐ Description of System

Conceptual Framework

The processes involved in the experience of empathy overlap conceptually and empirically with processes contributing to social and emotional adjustment. To the extent that empathy and socioemotional adjustment share common elements, units for coding Thematic Apperception Test (TAT) stories that are designated to assess empathy will also pertain to adjustment. The importance of the empathy construct derives from its linkage with prosocial behavior and positive adjustment (Bryant, 1987; Cohen & Strayer, 1996; Eisenberg, Zhou, & Koller, 2001; Roberts & Strayer, 1996). Although some evidence supports stable individual differences in prosocial responding from early childhood to adulthood (Eisenberg et al., 1999), there are many influences on the translation of empathy into prosocial behaviors.

The Empathy Construct

Cognitive and emotional processes converge in the definition of empathy as a vicarious emotional response elicited by and congruent with the recognition of another's emotional state or condition as distinct from that of the perceiver (Eisenberg & Fabes, 1998; Hoffman, 2000). The ability to take the perspective of the other is necessary to differentiate between one's own and another's distress and to accurately determine the nature of another's emotional reaction (Hoffman, 1982). However, the connection between empathy and altruistic behavior is complex and depends on several personality and situational variables.

Two considerations in the translation of empathy into prosocial acts are the individual's emotional response to the apprehension of another's condition and the perceived cost of action or inaction to the actor. When the experience of empathy is regulated, the emotion is called *sympathy,* defined as a feeling of concern for others, whereas an aversive feeling evoked by another's plight that leaves the individual emotionally overwhelmed is called *personal distress* (Batson, 1991). The former motivates altruistic actions, and the latter prompts self-focused behaviors to alleviate one's own negative emotional response. Nevertheless, even when experiencing sympathy, individuals may refrain from helping due to perceived cost to the self (Batson & Oleson, 1991).

Studies have shown that the "human capacity for altruism is limited to those for whom we feel empathy.... When empathy for the person in need is low, the pattern of helping suggests underlying egoistic motivation. It is not that we never help people for whom we feel little empathy; we often do—but, the research suggests, only when it is in our own best interest" (Batson & Oleson, 1991, p. 80). Although individuals who experience high levels of empathic concern may use various mechanisms to disengage their conduct from those concerns such as by focusing on larger purposes (Bandura, Barbaranelli, Caprara & Pastorelli, 1996), the greater the emotional bond to the person in need, the less likely that the altruistic impulse will be overridden by self concerns. In the presence of a strong bond, altruistic responding has been viewed as an expression of the interpersonal connection, or oneness with the other, and therefore as a manifestation of self-interest (Cialdini, Brown, Lewis, Luce, & Neuberg, 1997). Yet it is precisely the sense of connection with others (i.e., the attribute of empathy as shared affect and a balance in the focus between self and other) that makes the construct of empathy so appealing. In clinical practice, problems with empathy have been associated with psychopathology (Kovacs & Pollock, 1995) characterizing many disorders including autism, sociopathy, and dysfunctions in the brain (see Baron-Cohen, Tager-Flusberg, & Cohen, 1994; Blair, Jones, Clark, & Smith, 1997; Cohen & Volkmar, 1997; Gillberg, 1999; Sigman & Ruskin, 1999).

Empathy as the experience of emotional connections with and accurate cognitive understanding of others points to the self as part of a bigger picture where actions have impacts not only on the self and in the here and now but also on others and in the future. Without the big picture, the individual is captive of the moment, relying only on the cues in the surroundings and on the pull of immediate emotions without balancing between fleeting and durable emotions, and possibly without awareness of others' feelings that are not overtly expressed. The big picture emerges when cues in a given context are coordinated with relevant information from memory (Karniol, 1995). In day-to-day life, judgments about another's internal state (e.g., feelings, thought, intentions) are formed by coordinating the on-line processes to size up situational cues with the activation of stored mental representations that organize past relationships in memory and inform the current interaction (Anderson, 1990; Higgins, 1981; Teglasi, 1998). Cognitive complexity buffers the individual from experiences of stress (Linville, 1987). The more complex the mental structures, the more the individual is able to see alternatives (e.g., long- and short-term views) and temper emotional reactions (e.g., by understanding intent). However, only a handful of studies have used the TAT to examine the link between children's empathy and internal representations of relationships (e.g., Westen, Klepser, Ruffins, Silverman, & Boekamp, 1991; Locraft & Teglasi, 1997; Niec & Russ, 2002).

Schemas and Experience

The story is the language of experience connecting events with emotions, intentions, thoughts, actions, and anticipated outcomes (see Bruner, 1986). The overlap of the story form and experience leaves open the temptation to view TAT story content as representing actual events in the narrator's life. However, assuming any direct correspondence between story content and life circumstances is neither correct nor useful. Historical information is gathered more accurately and efficiently through other methods, and data derived from the TAT are of interest to the extent that they elucidate the narrator's view of how the parts of the story and, thus, the various dimensions of experience go together. The aim is to assess the schemas and the information processing strategies applied to meet the task demands to interpret the pictured cues and to compose the story (Teglasi, 1998). However, just as scores on an achievement test may be clarified by knowing the person's learning history, so the data gleaned from TAT stories may be put in perspective by information about the individual's current and prior experiences.

Traits and Schemas

Measures of traits and schemas offer contrasting perspectives on individual differences. The study of traits classifies attributes from the point of view of the observing other or the observing self, noting regularities across time and settings. The study of schemas focuses on the inner world of the actor to understand the mental structures that represent the individual's synthesis of experiential regularities in specific types of situations. As individuals with different temperamental predispositions repeatedly face situations, each becomes familiar with the cycle of happy feelings or of distressing emotions and their resolutions, noting the regularities in what actions do or do not bring about desired effects in specific situations (Teglasi & Epstein, 1998). Thus, schemas coordinate the outer and inner worlds by connecting situations, actions, and outcomes with the inner world of emotions and intentions. These emotion–intention–action–outcome linkages, in the context of specific situations, represent the individual's perceived efficacy to attain short- and long-term goals as well as beliefs about sources of happy or unhappy emotions.

Traits are typically measured with questionnaires and rating scales that produce scores on clusters of behaviors, thoughts, or feelings, whereas schemas are measured with more open-ended and less direct methods such as logs, narratives, dreams, associations, or transcriptions of therapy sessions. Schema measures yield information about how the individual connects thoughts, feelings, and behaviors and about how the individual encodes, interprets, and organizes intra- and interpersonal information. Rather than pitting traits and schemas and their associated methods against each other, it may be fruitful to focus on uncovering the linkages between them in the process of development (see Cervone & Williams, 1992; Teglasi & Epstein, 1998).

Empathy, as a trait, involves complex emotional processes to enable the individual to experience a multitude of emotions that accurately match the inner states and cognitive perspectives of others and to respond in a prosocial manner. The interplay of cognitive, affective, and behavioral processes in the expression of empathy is strikingly similar to the definition of social competence as the processes of coordinating behavioral, cognitive, and affective skills to meet the adaptive demands of diverse contexts (Sroufe, 1996). An emphasis on coordination implies the operation of mental structures or schemas that organize and regulate the cognitive, emotional, and behavioral dimensions of experience. In a comprehensive clinical assessment, disorganized mental structures would be further investigated to clarify possible mechanisms in the person–environment exchanges involved in their development and maintenance.

Trait formulations regard differences in situations and across time as error variance to be minimized (McCrae & Costa, 1989) whereas schema-driven social information processing is specific to the particular setting or psychological state. In designing interventions, it is precisely these situation-specific linkages among emotions, cognitions, intentions, actions, and expected outcomes that are the targets of change and not the traits that influenced their development. Nevertheless, to the extent that certain traits, such as the regulation of attention and emotion, continue to exert their influence on the maintenance of schema-driven information processing (see Teglasi & Epstein, 1998), they are important to assess.

(1) Attention: Chronic difficulty regulating attention and disorganized storage of information into memory limit the usefulness of internal representations to point to what is salient in the current situation. Children with attention deficit hyperactivity disorder (ADHD) were less accurate than their more attentive peers in identifying emotions from facial expressions shown in picture stimuli (Cadesky, Mota, & Schachar, 2000; Singh et al., 1998) and in encoding social cues from videotaped vignettes (Matthys, Duperus, & Van Engeland, 1999). Because problems with attention may be evident in some situations and not in others, the systematic accumulation of knowledge structures may be disrupted only in those domains that are problematic. For instance, individuals who tend to focus on isolated stimuli without considering the context may have most difficulty in complex situations where they need to select the target of attention and where organized schemas are most needed.

(2) Emotional self-regulation: Empathy is basically an emotional response to another person's experience that stems from the apprehension of that person's state. Problems occur when the emotions are too intense or not sufficient. Chronic difficulty in the regulation of negative emotionality limits the complexity and organization of children's self-regulatory schemas assessed with the TAT (Bassan-Diamond, Teglasi, & Schmitt, 1995). Individuals who are overwhelmed with intense emotions upon apprehending another's condition may focus on alleviating their own discomfort whereas those better able to manage their emotions have more resources to attend to other's needs (Eisenberg & Okun, 1996; Eisenberg, Fabes, Nyman, & Bernzweig, 1994; Eisenberg et al., 1996). However, poor emotional regulation may also stem from low reactivity, and lack of empathy (as characteristic of the sociopath) may be due to the absence of normal autonomic responses to the distress of others (Blair et al., 1997). Without this ability to respond to the suffering of others, the individual cannot

understand and learn about the state of others from his or her own affective experience. Children with extremely low self-reported anxiety were less accurate in their interpretation of the emotional tensions in TAT pictures than children who were high or average in anxiety (Michaels, 1999).

The expression of empathy as altruistic behavior involves the coordination of cognitive, affective, and behavioral processes as well as situational factors. Assessment of empathy with storytelling methods such as the TAT places emphasis on the individuals' schemas for coordinating the elements that pertain to prosocial responding.

Assumptions of Storytelling Methods

The TAT and other storytelling techniques are performance measures of personality that present the respondent with a task, the demands of which depend on the type of picture and instructions (Teglasi, 1998, 2001). The TAT cards generally depict intra- or interpersonal tensions, and the instructions (Murray, 1943) call for telling a story that coordinates the outer (i.e., what is happening, what happened before, and what will happen in the end) and inner (i.e., what do the persons think and feel) worlds. The narrator's task is to (1) identify the emotions in the pictured scenes and organize the cues to define a central dilemma that is congruent with the scene; (2) put the emotions into a context of relationships, time frame, causal sequences, justifying events, intentions, and cognitions; and (3) attribute to characters coping responses that are appropriately linked to the identified problem and to the outcomes. The narrator's schemas and social information processing styles are encapsulated in the structural organization of the various parts of the story content (i.e., events, feelings, actions, and outcomes) and in the logical organization of the unfolding story (i.e., accuracy, cohesiveness, complexity) (Teglasi, 1998, 2001).

Variables, consistent with theory and research pertinent to empathy and adjustment, were used to recode TAT protocols of children with high and low empathy who participated in a previous study (Locraft & Teglasi, 1997). The use of teacher ratings of prosocial behavior and concern for others as bases for assigning children to empathy groups sets the defining parameters of empathy. Among children between kindergarten and third grade, teacher-rated prosocial behaviors were more consistently related to children's observed empathy related responding than were parent and peer ratings (Holmgren, Eisenberg, & Fabes, 1998). In the current data set, given that the children were classified into empathy groups according to behaviors that were observable by teachers, the grouping included the sympathy component of empathy. The sympathy construct implies processes of self-regulation of affect and of attention, variables that also contribute to social competence and adjustment. Therefore, methods of coding TAT stories that differentiate the empathy groups are expected to be clinically useful as well.

Scoring Categories

The specific coding categories and procedures have been described previously (Teglasi, 2001) and are applicable to any stimulus that portrays an intra- or interpersonal tension, regardless of whether one or more individuals are pictured. The units emphasize formal aspects of story content including the structural organization of ideas in ways that

TABLE 30.1 Summary of Empathy Scoring Categories

Perceptual Integration—Four Levels
Discrepant
Literal
Imprecise
Accurate and Complex
Source of Affect
Unrecognized
Descriptive
External
Internal
Mutuality of Autonomy—Five Levels
Disorganized
Momentary
Functional
Reciprocal
Mutuality of Autonomy

minimize the role of verbal productivity and are applicable to a wide age range. These categories are summarized in Table 30.1 and are highlighted next.

Perceptual Integration

Empathic individuals are characterized by openness to affective experiences and by accuracy in identifying affective cues in self and other (Roberts & Strayer, 1996). Understanding others' emotions entails taking on the perspective of the other (Feshbach, 1978). Four ordinal levels of perceptual integration (PI) are defined by two dimensions: accuracy in sizing up the inter- or intrapersonal tensions in the stimulus and match between the emotions depicted and the context of the unfolding narrative (see Teglasi, 2001):

(1) Discrepant: Significant misperception of the emotions and relationships depicted in the scene or failure to recognize tensions.

(2) Literal: Feelings are correctly identified but the narrative fails to capture the implicit meaning of the stimulus in terms of the psychological processes (e.g., cause–effect, intentions). Thus, interpretation of feelings and relationships is not wrong but is limited by being simplified or superficial. Causal inferences are nonexistent, vague, or scripted, suggesting perceptual, not conceptual emphasis or inflexible cognitive sets.

Simplified: Story details are descriptively tied to the stimulus or are very simple associations to isolated parts of the picture. The narrator may identify various people or things in the picture without positing any—or making only minimal—connections between them. Simple emotions (e.g., sad, mad, happy) may be slightly off. Intentions are not durable but immediate reactions.

Superficial: Major elements of the scene are recognized (e.g., characters, basic emotions, relationships), but interpretation of the scene is hampered by poorly understood psychological processes (e.g., emotions or relationships are elaborated by associations to the scene that may be vague, scripted, or stereotypic). The unfolding story may be somewhat at odds with the picture as the narrator may not grasp all contextual cues, like facial expressions, and implications of background or clothing.

(3) Imprecise: The tension or problem set fits with the stimulus and the narrative conveys at least a rudimentary grasp of psychological process, but the developing story does not capture the subtle nuances of the scene or the unfolding story leaves gaps in understanding social causality.

(4) Accurate and complex: The central dilemma, identified through a nuanced interpretation of the stimulus configuration, is placed in a narrative context that precisely accounts for social causality and understanding of psychological processes.

Source of Affect

A focus on inner states rather than external characteristics has been tied to prosocial behavior (Bengtsson & Johnson, 1992) and empathy. Taking on the perspective of the other implies the coordination of stimuli from the inner and outer sources to understand the feeling in terms of the events in the moment (provoked by external stimuli) and in relation to the meaning of those events (intentions, values, principles). In the previous study, source of affect, although defined differently, distinguished between groups of children who were high, medium, and low in empathy (Locraft & Teglasi, 1997). Those with high empathy are assumed to be more inclined to incorporate the viewpoints of others (their inner states and intentions) rather than respond directly to their outward actions. The source of affect (SA) variable—viewed as ordinal but discrete rather than as continuous—captures the extent of coordination between the inner and outer perspectives on experiences.

(1) Unrecognized: Tension states are not acknowledged.

(2) Descriptive: Feelings stem directly from how the characters look in the stimulus.

(3) External: Feelings are evoked directly by external events, or, in other words, responses are reactive to events without benefit of internal organization of feelings.

(4) Internal: Feelings are embedded in a cognitive network that coordinates inner and outer sources of affect and are informed by understanding motives, values, or principles for setting priorities.

Mutuality of Autonomy

The construct of mutuality of autonomy (MA) is rooted in differentiation and coordination of the inner and outer worlds within and across individuals. The highest level of autonomy is defined as perceived ability to regulate one's feelings, thoughts, and behaviors to carry out purposeful, intentional actions that produce the anticipated outcomes for self and other, not only in the moment but in the long term (see Teglasi, 2001). In turn, mutuality of autonomy is the reciprocal valuing of the autonomy of different individuals (see Urist, 1977). Autonomy fosters prosocial behavior because persons who have a sense of control over their actions and expect their efforts to be beneficial are more likely to offer help to a distressed individual (Smith, 1992). Repeated experiences that connect intentional actions with outcomes become internally represented in schemas that guide expectations about the likely impact of one's actions in particular situations. As noted earlier, self-regulation of attention and emotion is essential to accurate processing of information in complex or unfamiliar settings, a prerequisite for building cohesive inner structures that organize experiences into schemas.

When inner structures are limited, awareness of self and other is dominated by simplistic distinctions within and among individuals, and the perceiver does not have the inner resources to focus attention beyond the here and now or beyond stereotyped understandings. The complexity of representations of people is a central concept in mutuality of autonomy. More complex representations foster more nuanced intra- and interpersonal distinctions and more cohesive integration of these distinctions. In turn, greater differentiation and integration of representations enable empathic responses to be more accurate. Accordingly, apprehending a friend's distress typically activates the perceiver's own distress memories as well as representations of the friend that put the current distress in a context. Greater familiarity with a person and more complex information processing are likely to produce a richer representation that permits the response to be more in tune with how the friend experiences the distress. However, it is important to note that individuals may compensate for limited representations through a variety of strategies, including reliance on normative rules for appropriate behaviors in that situation.

Differentiation and integration are two constructs underlying mutuality of autonomy. Differentiation of viewpoints and attributes within and across individuals involves insight into the various dimensions of the self and others (e.g., preferences or values vs. possessions or what one wants from another). Integration of feelings and perspectives within and across individuals refers to coordinating what is distinguished in ways that are beneficial to the long-term interest of a single individual, balance the needs of two or more characters, are in accord with understanding of social causality, and are appropriate to the story context. Whereas differentiation reveals what characteristics of self and others are important to notice, integration shows the relationships among the characteristics within a single individual or as individuals relate to each other. Thus, the constructs of differentiation and integration underlying mutuality of autonomy are applicable even when only one character is portrayed.

Mutuality of autonomy is coded into five levels (see Teglasi, 1993, 2001):

(1) Disorganized or detached experience of relatedness: Differentiation and integration, respectively, are simplified and highly disorganized. Restriction of autonomy is so

severe that characters are unable to formulate reasonable intentions or are helpless against more powerful forces.

(2) Momentary experience of relatedness: Autonomy or mutuality is rudimentary, limited by a self-serving orientation where actions and relationships are restricted to the concerns of the moment. Awareness is dominated by the immediate needs or moods of the perceiver and by dichotomous, one-sided (self-centered) processing of information that does not coordinate short- and long-term perspectives within or across individuals. Thus, characters are differentiated on the basis of momentary need without the sense that they are whole persons or that the relationship is enduring. The experience of relatedness requires the physical presence of the other because of inability to call on the internal representation.

(3) Functional experience of relatedness: Whether an individual's characteristics are salient depends on their perceived contribution to the functional exchanges or to meeting expectations rather than on the quality of the human connection. Individuals set goals to conform to expectations and maintain quid pro quo exchanges, but characteristics are discerned or valued only to the extent that they contribute to the continuous exchanges. The give and take of functional relatedness has a longer-term flavor and involves more complex differentiation and integration than momentary relatedness. Aspects of the individual that do not contribute to the functions served may not be noticed.

(4) Reciprocity and standards as bases for relatedness: Individuals are differentiated in terms of their goals, intentions, and actions, and these reflect investment in principles of fair play according to normative standards for prosocial behavior and for accomplishing tasks. Individuals' decisions and actions are implicitly constrained by internally organized principles, and these internalized standards and rules of conduct are sufficiently flexible to permit balancing intrapersonal conflicts and making appropriate compromises among characters through integration of perspectives. Violations of expectations are explained in terms of long-term purposes, larger principles, or duress.

(5) Relatedness through mutuality of autonomy: Differentiation within and coordination among individuals reflect both societal values and individual moral standards. Fine-tuned distinctions in the inner life and external circumstances of each character are seamlessly coordinated to balance the short- and long-term interests of all (self and other). Interactions are understood as occurring between individuals who are aware of each other's viewpoints and psychological processes, recognize short- and long-term disruptions in the relationship, modulate reactions in light of their understanding of others and of their circumstances, and entail goals that balance interests of all according to general principles of justice and social responsibility.

The concept of mutuality of autonomy may be assessed even if only one person is portrayed in a TAT picture. When telling a story about a single individual, the level of mutuality of autonomy is implicit in what is noted about individuality (i.e., intrapersonal distinctions) and how the person sets and pursues intentional actions (i.e., autonomy) in relation to internalized standards or moral values and concerns for the welfare of others (i.e., integration).

Research Evidence

Previous Research on Empathy With the TAT

The few studies that have used the TAT to assess empathy using earlier scoring systems share a common focus on internalized representations of relationships as the essence of empathy. An early study defined the term *empathy* as the "imaginative transposing of the self into the thinking, feeling, and acting of another and so structuring the world as he does" (Dymond, 1949, p. 127). The same author referred to empathy as an "ability" that depends on the "basic internalized self–other patterns which represent the subject's view of his interpersonal relations" (ibid., p. 232). This research regarded insight into the self as part of the empathic process because it requires the ability to view the self through the eyes of others by taking the other's perspective. Although the scoring criteria were not fully described, Dymond (1950) reported that TAT stories of those with high as compared with those with low empathy—defined as "insight"—indicated greater interest in people and relationships, higher expectation of warmth and support in relationships, and tendencies to set goals that are more focused on relationships and less on self-aggrandizement (e.g., rich and famous).

Kalliopuska (1982) coded TAT stories with the MA scale introduced by Urist (1977) to code human responses to the Rorschach. The participants (15 adolescent girls ranging in age from 13 to 17 years) were administered the TAT and the Rorschach, and both protocols were coded along the seven-point MA scale describing interactions among figures as follows:

(1) Conveying reciprocal acknowledgment of individuality

(2) Engaging in parallel activity

(3) Leaning on each other or needing support in some way

(4) One figure being a reflection or extension of the other

(5) One exerting malevolent control over another

(6) Depicting malicious imbalance of power or autonomy, a parasitic relationship where the existence of one diminishes the other

(7) Figures being swallowed up by forces beyond their control

Given the pattern of correlations among the scoring methods applied to the Rorschach and the TAT, Kalliopuska (1982) encouraged further application of the MA scale to the TAT to assess patterns of self–other representations pertinent to empathy.

Locraft and Teglasi (1997) used teacher ratings of socially competent behavior and empathic responding to designate groups of children (kindergarten to sixth grade) as high, medium, and low in empathy (40 in each group). They designated units for analysis that aimed to clarify internal processes associated with empathic behaviors with four coding categories, each of which was rated on a four-point scale: realistic expression of feelings, source of positive and negative feelings, mutuality in relationships, and inner cohesion. Each of these variables distinguished between the high, medium, and low empathy groups.

Niec and Russ (2002) used a modified version of the Social Cognition and Object Relations Scale (Westen, 1991, 1995 [SCORS-Q]) to investigate the relationships of children's internal representations assessed with the TAT, empathy ratings, and fantasy play. They coded each of the following five dimensions of object relations on five-point scales:

(1) Cognitive structure of representations including complexity (differentiation and integration)

(2) Affect tone of relationship schemas

(3) Emotional investment in relationships

(4) Emotional investment in moral values and standards

(5) Understanding of social causality

The authors found all dimensions of internal representations to be correlated with teacher, self, and peer-rated empathy in children ages 8 to 10 ($N = 86$). Children's internal representations accounted for a significant proportion of empathy (10%) beyond the contribution of verbal achievement, grade, or gender.

Validity of Present System

Construct validity was shown by the strong relationship between each of the TAT variables and empathy grouping in the reanalysis of the stories collected previously (Locraft & Teglasi, 1997). A repeated measures multivariate analysis of variance (MANOVA), conducted to compare empathy groups (high and low), grade groups (k–3 = low; 4–6 = high), and gender groups on the three TAT coded variables, showed significant main effects for all three grouping variables. Follow-up univariate analyses of variance showed that high empathy groups received significantly higher scores on all three TAT variables: PI $F(1,72) = 217.81$, $p < .01$; SA (internal is higher), $F(1,72) = 242.79$, $p < .01$; and MA $F(1,72) = 268.99$, $p < .01$. The grade level comparison revealed higher scores on all three TAT variables for the higher grade grouping: PI $F(1,72) = 30.69$, $p < .01$; SA $F(1,72) = 4.96$, $p < .05$; MA $F(1,72) = 13.35$, $p < 13.35$, $p < .01$. Despite significance at the multivariate level, none of the univariate tests comparing TAT variables across gender groups reached significance. The means and standard deviations of TAT variables are displayed in Table 30.2.

Two variables—average word count and average number of inquiries per story—were calculated to check their relationship with TAT scores. Table 30.3 shows the bivariate correlations among the TAT variables, grouping variables (i.e., empathy, gender, and grade), word count, and inquiry. All variables that were significantly correlated with TAT scores were entered into separate ordered regression analyses to assess the unique contribution of empathy grouping (Table 30.4). When entered last, empathy grouping contributed an additional 45% to 50% to the variation in TAT scores. Inspection of the

TABLE 30.2 Means and Standard Deviations of TAT Coding Dimensions

	Low Empathy		High Empathy	
Variable	Mean	SD	Mean	SD
Perceptual Integration	2.08	.43	3.38	.49
Lower Grades	1.84	.26	3.14	.54
Males	1.79	.28	3.20	.46
Females	1.90	.23	3.07	.62
Higher Grades	2.32	.43	3.64	.28
Males	2.21	.48	3.59	.26
Females	2.43	.36	3.69	.29
Source of Affect	.07	.19	.87	.27
Lower Grades	.02	.05	.80	.35
Males	.01	.05	.87	.31
Females	.03	.06	.74	.40
Higher Grades	.12	.25	.94	.14
Males	.20	.33	.91	.18
Females	.04	.10	.96	.10
Mutuality of Autonomy	1.95	.53	4.08	.69
Lower Grades	1.74	.34	3.82	.80
Males	1.64	.36	3.93	.70
Females	1.83	.32	3.70	.91
Higher Grades	2.16	.61	4.34	.44
Males	2.11	.81	4.24	.58
Females	2.20	.34	4.44	.22

Notes: Lower grades = K–3; higher grades = 4–6. PI range = 1–4. SA range = 0–1. MA range = 1–5.

standardized beta weights further indicates that empathy group membership contributes the lion's share of the variance to the TAT scores when considered together with grade level, word count, and inquiry. Grade level contributes significantly to the variance of all three TAT variables, but when grade level is controlled, word count and inquiry do not contribute further—with the exception of a small contribution of word count to SA. The finding that grade grouping correlates with TAT scores is consistent with the expectation of greater accuracy and complexity of schemas with development as a result of greater access to emotional experiences. However, by the time children enter kindergarten, they are able to identify basic emotions and to converse meaningfully about their own and other's emotional experiences (Denham, Zoller, & Couchoud, 1994). The relatively small contribution of grade grouping compared with empathy grouping in the prediction of TAT scores indicates that what is measured is not primarily a maturational phenomenon but a reflection of the empathy construct.

TABLE 30.3 Bivariate Correlations

	Gender	Empathy	Grade	Words	Inquiry	PI	Affect	Mutuality
Gender	—							
Empathy	ns	—						
Grade	ns	ns	—					
Words	ns	.326**	.500**	—				
Inquiry	ns	–.519**	–.344	–.670**	—			
PI	ns	.821*	.319**	.349**	–.551*	—		
Affect	ns	.866**	.127	.277*	–.523**	.848**	—	
Mutuality	ns	.869**	.202	.332**	–.542**	.948**	.885**	—

Notes: $*p < .05$; $**p < .01$. Spearman correlations were used for dichotomous variables (gender, affect source) and Pearson for the other variables.

Given that an equal number of boys and girls were assigned to the empathy groups, the absence here of the gender differences that are often reported in the literature may be an artifact of the methodology. One may conclude from these data that, regardless of gender, in comparison with their highly empathic peers, those classified with low empathy

TABLE 30.4 Hierarchical Regression Analyses

Variable Step	R2	R2change	Partial Correlation	*B*	Significance
Perceptual Integration					
1. Grade Group	.095	.095	.520	.329	.000
2. Word Count	.152	.057	–.190	–.129	.098
3. Inquiry	.325	.173	–.146	–.105	.207
4. Empathy	.778	.453	.819	.808	.000
Source of Affect					
1. Grade Group	.015	.015	.258	.144	.024
2. Word Count	.077	.061	–.226	–.154	.048
3. Inquiry	.284	.208	–.191	–.139	.096
4. Empathy	.778	.494	.831	.844	.000
Mutuality of Autonomy					
1. Grade Group	.037	.037	.369	.204	.001
2. Word Count	.113	.076	–.154	–.099	.180
3. Inquiry	.296	.182	–.140	–.096	.226
4. Empathy	.798	.502	.844	.851	.000

are characterized by less accurate, less internally organized, and less complex views of intra- and interpersonal relationships.

In coding the protocols, it was not necessary to correct for number of words or inquiries despite their correlation with the TAT variables for two reasons. First, after controlling for grade grouping, the influence of number of words and inquiries was not significant. Second, these variables were also correlated with the construct of empathy (as they differentiated the groups) and not just to TAT scores; therefore, procedures to control for these variables would undermine the purpose of delineating units that differentiate empathy groups. The number of words and inquiries may be linked to scores on the TAT through their common associations with the construct of empathy. For instance, MA assumes autonomy, which should be related to greater self-direction in narrating the story and less reliance on prompting by the examiner.

Convergent and Discriminant Validity

Each of the three coded TAT variables correlated with empathy, and, given that they are aspects of the empathy construct, their intercorrelations provide evidence of convergent validity. However, as noted earlier, empathy is related to social competence and general adjustment; therefore, TAT variables that assess empathy should also correlate with adjustment. Accordingly, the correlation of PI with emotional disability also provides convergent validity (Lohr, Teglasi, & French, 2004).

If viewed as a performance task (see Teglasi, 1998), correlations among the various TAT scores indicating empathy would be expected just as would the subtests on cognitive measures. If, as assumed, the competencies for managing the task of telling TAT stories differ from those needed to handle more structured cognitive tasks, then demonstration of discriminant validity should entail (1) low correlations between TAT coded variables and structured cognitive tasks and high correlations with tasks that require the application of schemas to organize information; and (2) high correlations with real-life tasks that make demands to interpret complex or unfamiliar information and low correlations with real-life tasks that require script-based responding to routine situations. Findings from a meta-analysis indicated that the TAT predicts spontaneous responses in situations that are chosen or where responses are not scripted or well rehearsed whereas responses to well-structured self-report measures predict behavior in situations with clear expectations (see Spangler, 1992).

Differences Among Cards

Multivariate repeated measures analyses of variance with seven cards and grouping variables of empathy, grade, and gender showed the following results for each variable:

- PI had a main effect for empathy, $F(7,66) = 34.04$, $p < .01$, and grade group, $F(7,66) = 4.97$, $p < .01$ but no effect for gender and no interaction effects
- SA had a main effect for empathy, $F(7, 66) = 38.01$, $p < .01$ and no other effects
- MA had a main effect for empathy group, $F(7, 66) = 42.43$, $p < .01$ and for grade group, $F(7, 66) = 2.49$, $p < .05$

TABLE 30.5A Multivariate Analysis of Variance by Card—Perceptual Integration

Source	F
Empathy	34.04**
Grade Group	4.97**
Sex	.83
Empathy × Grade Group	1.02
Empathy × Sex	.65
Empathy × Grade Group × Sex	.57

Notes: *$p < .05$; **$p < .01$. df = 7.66.

TABLE 30.5B Univariate Analysis of Variance Perceptual Integration

			Empathy	Grade Group	Sex
Source	Mean	SD	F	F	F
Card 1[a]	2.88	.92	60.65**	19.38**	.46
Card 2	2.80	.92	101.40**	18.15**	.15
Card 3BM	2.75	.94	110.25**	6.89*	.14
Card 4[a]	2.55	1.07	65.64**	8.37**	2.09
Card 5	2.85	.97	120.00**	3.33	.53
Card 7GF	2.75	1.00	24.99**	8.38**	3.39
Card 8BM[a]	2.56	1.00	91.67**	14.93**	.25

Notes: *$p < .05$; **$p < .01$. PI range = 1–4. df = 1.72. Overall mean for PI was 2.73.
[a] Mean for card as contrasted to the average for PI was significant at .05 level according to a dependent samples t-test.

Follow-up univariate tests (Tables 30.5, 30.6, 30.7) showed that all cards differentiated the empathy groups on all three TAT variables and that some cards differentiated grade groups on each TAT variable. No analysis involving gender reached significance.

Generalizability

Reliability across raters and construct validity of the PI variable has been shown in two studies with different populations (Blankman, Teglasi, & Lawser, 2002; Lohr et al., 2004) as well as with the current data. In contrast, data for SA and MA variables are available only for this population of children attending a private school, from lower-middle to

TABLE 30.6A Multivariate Analysis of Variance by Card—Source of Affect

Source	F
Empathy	38.01**
Grade Group	1.79
Sex	1.89
Empathy × Grade Group	.71
Empathy × Sex	.47
Empathy × Grade Group × Sex	1.29

Notes: *$p < .05$; **$p < .01$. df = 7.66.

TABLE 30.6B Univariate Analysis of Variance Source of Affect

			Empathy	Grade Group	Sex
Source	Mean	SD	F	F	F
Card 1[a]	.53	.50	144.00**	2.25	2.25
Card 2	.49	.50	268.90**	5.49*	1.98
Card 3BM	.44	.50	129.09**	3.36	3.36
Card 4	.44	.50	118.48**	.12	.12
Card 5	.46	.50	118.48**	1.11	1.11
Card 7GF	.47	.50	103.85**	7.39**	.46
Card 8BM	.47	.50	226.17**	7.04**	3.13

Notes: *$p < .05$; **$p < .01$. SA range = 0–1. df = 1.72. Overall mean for SA was .47.
[a] Mean for card as contrasted to the average for SA was significant at .05 level according to a dependent samples t-test.

TABLE 30.7A Multivariate Analysis of Variance by Card—Mutuality of Autonomy

Source	F
Empathy	42.43**
Grade Group	2.49*
Sex	.85
Empathy × Grade Group	.84
Empathy × Sex	1.24
Empathy × Grade Group × Sex	1.04

Notes: *$p < .05$; **$p < .01$. df = 7.66.

TABLE 30.7B Univariate Analysis of Variance Mutuality of Autonomy

			Empathy	Grade Group	Sex
Source	Mean	SD	F	F	F
Card 1[a]	3.15	1.29	160.36**	5.82*	.000
Card 2	3.10	1.29	192.38**	6.66*	.42
Card 3BM	2.93	1.31	116.13**	3.56	.07
Card 4[a]	2.84	1.43	171.08**	5.72*	2.39
Card 5	3.04	1.34	108.35**	2.79	.02
Card 7GF	3.12	1.37	90.96**	13.46**	.24
Card 8BM	2.91	1.45	191.12**	15.44**	.53

Notes: $*p < .05$; $**p < .01$. MA range = 1–5. df = 1.72. Overall mean for MA was 3.01.
[a] Mean for card as contrasted to the average for MA was significant at .05 level according to a dependent samples t-test.

upper-middle class backgrounds, ranging in grade from kindergarten to sixth grade with at least average cognitive scores (with no differences between groups) and with ethnic backgrounds of 78% European American, 15% African American, 6.7% Hispanic American, and 2.5% Asian American. Although the correlation of SA and of MA with PI suggests that these variables may generalize to other populations, generalizability has yet to be demonstrated.

Reliability

Two earlier studies provide support for interrater reliability and construct validity of PI. With second- and third-grade children, exact agreement on the four levels was 62.5% (100% agreement within one point), and the intraclass reliability coefficient was .94 (Blankman, et al., 2002). Higher levels of PI were associated with higher comprehension scores on listening and reading tests among average to superior listeners. As hypothesized, the schemas applied to infer the problem presented in TAT pictures also operate when children listen to or read stories. Among children diagnosed with emotional disability (ED) and their nondiagnosed brothers, PI was also reliably coded, with intraclass correlation of .90 (Lohr et al., 2004). PI was substantially related to temperamental negative emotional reactivity and identification with ED (a consensual committee determination within the school system, in accordance with federal guidelines of the Individuals with Disabilities Education Act, 1997).

The three coding categories used to recode TAT protocols, previously collected (Locraft & Teglasi, 1997), showed acceptable rater reliabilities (between the present first and third authors) as follows:

(1) Intraclass reliability for PI was .83 (based on 196 stories).

(2) SA was condensed from four categories into two because failure to recognize tension occurred infrequently (likely because children were not clinically referred) and the

card description category is conceptually an external source of affect. Cohen's kappa coefficient was .80 (based on 160 stories).

(3) Intraclass reliability of MA was .92 (based on 160 stories).

☐ Clinical Case Illustrations

Protocols of two children referred primarily because of poor academic performance are discussed in terms of the empathy related variables previously detailed. The intent is not to present a comprehensive clinical picture but to show the contribution of the selected variables to understanding differences in the two children's social and emotional functioning. For each story, scores on the coding categories are discussed and an import is formulated. As introduced by Arnold (1962), the import encapsulates the moral of the story from the perspective of the narrator and not of the story characters.

Both children had similar patterns of scores on the Wechsler Intelligence Scales for Children (WISC). However, distinct TAT protocols explain their discrepant behavioral adjustment, and common features in their TAT protocols relate to their academic difficulties. Paul, a third grader, aged 10.0 with a WISC Full Scale IQ score of 78 (performance IQ 82; verbal IQ 78), was referred for evaluation because he was performing below grade level in nearly all subjects and was having attendance problems, missing about two days per week. In addition, the teacher noted problems with attention in the classroom such as frequently being distracted during seat work and often talking to peers rather than completing his work. Reggie, a fourth grader, aged 10.5 with WISC Full Scale IQ score of 78 (performance IQ 81; verbal IQ 79), was also referred because of below-grade-level performance and distractibility in the classroom. However, teachers were also concerned about increasingly escalating behavior problems including fighting with classmates and disrespect to teachers.[1]

Paul

Card 1

> It looks like he's sitting at the table and he's sad because he don't know how to play the instrument and he thinks everybody else knows how to play the instrument but him. I think it might be his first time playing an instrument. He think he need practice to know how to play the instrument. I think he should practice to know how to play the instrument and he'll get better and better and better.

- PI = 3; tension is appropriate to the scene and incorporated into a plausible narrative but the coordination of the various narrative elements is not precise. The proposed resolution of just needing to practice does not seem realistic given that the boy has never played the instrument before and others already know how.

- SA = internal; at first affect source seems external (boy wants to play to be like everyone else) but the character takes internal responsibility for the learning process (getting better and better) not just the outcome.

- MA = 3; the boy wants to meet expectations to play like everyone else (functional) and, although he takes responsibility for the learning process, he is restricted in his autonomy by not grasping the reasons (cause–effect) for his predicament (being behind his peers)
- Import: A boy is sad because he is the only one who cannot play an instrument because he never played before, but if he merely practices he will know how and he will get better and better.

Card 2

She look like she's just coming home from school because she got books in her hand. That's why she look like she's just coming home from school and she looking at people training the horses and stuff and that thing looks like a barn. It's like she looking at animals or something 'cause she's staring over there. Like she's looking at an animal or a person or something or somebody that she knows from school. And it looks like she got a uniform on like us, but like old time uniform that she got on. (thinking? [T]) She thinking about going over there to touch it or something (Turn Out? [TO]) She falls when she's about to walk over there and the man helps her and then they start going out and being friends and stuff and then at the end he gonna ask her can she marry him and that's the end.

- PI = 2; difficulty inferring a unifying theme or intention (thinking to go touch something).
- SA = descriptive/external.
- MA = 2; it is worth noting that the immediate offer of help is extended to a more long term relationship, albeit with a naive, stereotyped quality. Thus, Paul seems to value interpersonal connection but is restricted in autonomy (forming clear, long-term intentions and realistically carrying them out, even in a stereotypical fashion) and hence in mutuality when cues are complex as they are in some of the TAT cards.
- Import: You need to look carefully around you to figure out what is going on, but when you try, you stumble and that is how you get help and a friend for life (married).

Card 3BM

It looks like the lady crying like it looks like somebody hit her or something or she's sad about her child or something. That looks like scissors on floor. It look like she don't know how to do good art. It look like she's crying on the bed or something. It looks like in the nurse cubbyhole, the little bed looks like the nurse got. It might be like her son he got hurt or something and she might call. (TO?) Her son go to the hospital and that's where she like to stay there with her son but people won't let her in because they don't know if that's his mother and then the little boy woke up and he said that it's his mother and then they let her in and she slept with son every night until he got better.

- PI = 2; suggesting several situations to match the character's feelings but without understanding the psychological process
- SA = internal; feelings are tied to events but the mother wants to stay with her son and does eventually comfort her son indicating a basic coordination between inner and outer experience

- MA = 3; the mother and the son help each other to meet each other's needs
- Import: Things appear complicated (a scene can look like many things; people are sometimes confused—they do not know if that is his mother), but eventually, things get sorted out and people help each other

Card 4

It looks like she hugging the man and the man look like he don't like her 'cause he's staring and not touching her and she trying to hug him but he look like he don't like her. He looking at like a car or people or like a fire or something or looking at somebody like the police chasing somebody or something, I think. (feeling?) The lady really happy but the man feeling like he don't like her. (TO?) The man went to a place and there liked another lady so then the lady like him but then the man keep on going for the other lady and he said that was the lady that he wanted and then he said he went for another woman he said he met this lady and this is the lady he want but then lady didn't like him because she already had a man and then the man started crying and then the man killed himself because he liked that lady and everybody went to his funeral and that was the end everybody went home. That story was long.

- PI = 2; a tension is posited that is somewhat related to the scene (the woman does not look happy and she does not experience happy events in the story) but there is no grasp of the psychological process (beyond liking and not liking)
- SA = external; whether someone likes you or not
- MA = 1; the narrator cannot find a solution other than killing off the man following a rejection, indicating severe imbalance of mutuality
- Import: When a situation is complex, you focus on one aspect at a time and cannot put all the parts together, and will impulsively get out of the situation (you kill off your character)

Card 5

Looks like the lady walking in the house and she see like robbers in her house taking something 'cause she opening the door and she like or she might be surprised by a party or something or she might see her son cooking or the house on fire. She look happy 'cause she walking in the door. She should have felt the door if she heard a noise she should have felt the doorknob first to see if it was hot 'cause that's what my father told me to feel the door to see if it's hot if people see fire in the building you supposed to feel the doors and see if it's hot. When you're little you're supposed to feel doors first before you walk in the door. (T?) She thinking about going inside to throw something. It's like this about to fall over and she like about to go in and grab it and she might not grab it 'cause it might fall. (TO?) That she caught the plant and she was happy and slept with the plant all night and she kept the plant in her room and that's the end of story when she got the plant and she always looking at this one plant and watering it.

- PI = 1; the narrator gives many associations to this card without accounting for the woman's feelings as depicted in the picture (*look happy 'cause she's walking in the door*).

- SA = internal; although there is much here that is concrete and external, the care given to the plant (though naive and excessive) suggests inner sources of satisfaction.

- MA = 2; in the midst of a fire, the character focuses on a very concrete action that is unlikely to contribute to resolving the larger problem. Paul may be unable to act constructively on his caring impulse unless the situation is highly structured and expectations are clear. His autonomy and mutuality are restricted by schemas that are not sufficiently accurate, complex, or organized to size up ambiguous stimuli or to anticipate reactions of others. Even his reliance on scripted knowledge (*feel the doorknob*) is ineffective because he cannot use the information in an organized fashion.

- Import: When you cannot figure out what is going on, you find some small way that you can be helpful.

Card 6BM

Looks like the man about to go to jail or something 'cause he did something bad. No, it's like his son might go to jail because his son did something bad and then the lady looking out the window 'cause she's probably mad at that man for not watching his son. Then the man looking at somebody like they did something bad and why they do it. (TO?) That his son did something bad so his son thought he was gonna be in jail for a long time but his friend's mother paid for him to get out of jail and his father told him not to do something bad.

- PI = 3

- SA = internal; feeling relates to doing something bad, not the consequence of going to jail

- MA = 3; people approve or disapprove but do not set and pursue autonomous goals; they do expect to be punished for misdeeds, help each other, and have prosocial expectations of one another

- Import: A father is held responsible for his son's misdeed and though the son is bailed out of jail, he reminds the son not to do anything bad

Card 7GF

What's that a baby? It look like the girl holding a baby but if she hold the baby like that it look like the baby gonna fall 'cause she looking at somebody else she holding the baby down by knees and the baby could fall, but this lady is looking at the baby and like smiling at the baby kind of like smiling at the baby and the little girl looking at her friends and what they doing and stuff. She think it's like she looking at somebody thinking they doing bad stuff or something. This is #7. I got two more to go though. (TO?) That she went out there and told her friends to stop then she went and told the police and the police stopped the little kids and they ran and then the police try to follow them but they was already gone and the little girl saw them where they went she already know everywhere they go but she didn't tell on them.

- PI = 2.

- SA = internal; concern for baby, helping the police without being disloyal to friends.

- MA = 2; again, the narrator's prosocial intentions are evident in detailing how the baby was being held and in helping the police but protecting her friends. Yet, given Paul's problems with coordinating what comes to awareness (integration and differentiation), he would have difficulty carrying out well-intended actions proactively unless the situation were highly scripted or structured.

- Import: Although you have difficulty understanding the scene, you can see that someone needs help, but your response is not organized.

Card 8BM

Looks like the people saying that the little boy can't look 'cause that might be his father like they cutting his father open and the little boy is probably mad because wanted to see his father 'cause the people are cutting him open. He probably got shot with something or something flew in him or something. (TO?) Like the little boy by the time the little boy turned around his father was dead and he was crying and crying then the people stopped and then they told the boy to get out because his father was dead and then the little boy grew up then he met friends he then his friends said where's his father and he said that his dad died a long time ago and then his friends said sorry for him and that's the end and then they started hanging out.

- PI = 3; despite the concrete view of the stimulus (boy not allowed to look), Paul implicitly attributes to others the intent to spare the boy from the horror of seeing his dad cut open (also a literal response to the stimulus) and eventually dead. The simplistic/imprecise understanding of the psychological process speaks to a score that is a high 2 or low 3.

- SA = external; it is worth noting that he is not a passive recipient of help but makes friends.

- MA = 3; the expectation is that people respond to one another's needs without much differentiation–integration of their attributes.

- Import: A difficult situation may end badly but, in time, others will help you get over your troubles and become your friends.

Card 13B

The little boy looks like he doesn't have a house because he doesn't have no shoes on and he looks like he's locked out of that door and this looks like a barn it's like looking at something his mother is doing or his father is doing. And it looks like it's hot outside 'cause it look like the sun is shining on the wood. And then he got older and then his father let him help them every time that his father work and help pick stuff up and then he grew up to a grown man and then he became a worker. (feeling?) I think he's feeling sad kind of like sad 'cause he can't help his father.

- PI = 3; after detailing the scene, the narrator jumps ahead in time (as in the previous story) rather than deal with the dilemma at hand. Paul has difficulty formulating the tension in a way that is conducive to autonomous action and his character must wait for others to allow him to be helpful and reach his goal of becoming a worker.

- SA = internal, wanting to be helpful; the theme of looking to the future for things to get better is repeated in several cards suggesting difficulty meeting the demands at hand and relying on the passage of time and the help of others. The characters do not have the resources to work their way out of their dilemmas or even ask for help. However, the assumption of assistance to attain long-term well-being and acknowledgement of some reciprocity speak to MA at level 3.

Summary of Paul's Protocol

(1) PI: In defining the dilemma in the pictured scenes, Paul has difficulty grasping the motives and psychological processes unless he can draw on personal experience (familiarity) or is presented with stimuli that are less complex (single figures, cards 1 and 3).

(2) SA: With the exception of the more complex stimuli (cards 2, 4, 8), Paul's narratives suggest that affect stems from internal sources. He pursues his intentions but given that his theory of mind is not well developed, he is vulnerable to abandoning purpose-driven behavior when he does not understand the cues in the situation. On cards 3 and 5, much content is driven by the stimulus, and though coded as internal, the external flavor of the narratives underscore Paul's difficulty with directing his behavior internally.

(3) MA: The level of Paul's interpersonal relatedness varies from disorganized to functional depending on the circumstance. When he is not overwhelmed he can relate in a reciprocal manner with a focus on relatively enduring give- and-take relationships among individuals. However, when there are discrepant cues, his reaction may be responsive to part of the information because he cannot put the pieces together. He is at his best during structured situations where he can act on his understanding of reciprocity based on functional exchanges. The thought processes reflected in Paul's narratives are generally in tune with social expectations and are to the best of his understanding, Paul's behavior is responsive to others, motivated by interpersonal connections and prosocial intentions. In situations that do not present clear expectations, Paul has difficulty generating and following plans for self-directed actions. He enjoys being helpful and would benefit from being allowed to do so whenever possible. He may need to be shown how to act in accord with what is expected, as he may have difficulty inferring this on his own. Likewise, to facilitate academic learning, Paul may need guidance to draw proper inferences by explicit instructions and support for practice that reinforces his learning.

Reggie

Card 1

The boy is feeling sad because his violin is broken and he got his hand on his face and he got his eyes closed 'cause it looks like he just doesn't want to look at it because it's all broken up and there's pieces missing to it. I think he gonna wrap up in the paper and throw it in the trash so nobody can see it like his parents.

- PI = 2; lacking enduring intentions or understanding of psychological process.
- SA = external; the feeling emanates from the object being broken and anticipated parental reaction.
- MA = 2; momentary relatedness is implied in the boy's strategy of deceiving his parents. There is no concern with the attributes of the characters in relation to the broken violin or to one another.
- Import: If a boy's violin is broken, he will pay lip service to feeling sad and dispose of the instrument in a way that makes sure his parents do not see it.

Card 2

It looks like she is holding books to take it to somebody's house and the lady on the side, somebody cut her and she's just standing up with her eyes closed and feeling down and the man is pulling the horse with his arm out and looking at something that's on the left side and he's walking down this garden here and it looks like he's going to the house like he's going home. (T?) It looks like she's thinking about if she going home it looks like she thinking "I don't want to go home I want to stay outside" because she's coming home from school. (TO?) She looks like she might want to go home now and started walking.

- PI = 1; cannot pull the various parts of the scene into a common framework that relates foreground with the background
- SA = descriptive/external; story is pegged to how things look in the stimulus without attributing any durable intentions
- MA = 1; there is no connection to a guiding principle or to relationships—the girl is carrying books to someone's house (not reading them), the woman described as cut by someone continues to stand as she is portrayed in the picture (detached from her own experience), and the central issue of deciding whether to stay outside or go home is devoid of context or intention that would guide the decision
- Import: As she is walking home from school, a girl is carrying books to someone's house and thinking that she will go home when she has had enough of being outside

Card 3BM

It looks like she's dead and she looks like she somebody stabbed her with her own keys or it looks like she's sleeping with her hand over her face and she's sitting down and her keys on side just beside her. That's all I can think of this. (T?) (pause) She thinking about whoever killed her or did something to her. She might get back on them and how it ended she might have got back on them and then she probably did something to scare him and his family and stuff like that.

- PI = 1; given that there is no psychological process, the best possible score would be a 2. A score of 1 was assigned because the figure's posture is not a good fit with being dead.
- SA = external; no intention but reaction to provocation (revenge) or how the stimulus looks (sleeping).

- MA = 1; problems with reasoning (she's dead but gets revenge) and highly simplistic differentiation of people as hurting each other for no apparent reason or taking revenge.

- Import: If someone stabs you to death with your own keys, you will get revenge.

Card 4

It looks like he's about to kill somebody and she is telling him not to go, it looks like he thinking it looks like there's blood on his shirt and the person who stabbed him he's going to go get and she's telling him not to go because she don't want him to get killed. She's holding him back. (feeling?) She don't want him to get killed and he want to get back on that person who stabbed him or shot him. (TO?) By her pulling him back, he not gonna go. He's like forget it so he can get his shirt cleaned off.

- PI = 2; he identifies a tension in the scene but does not understand the psychological process as the man who is so enraged that he wants to kill the man who just stabbed him, just forgets about it, and gets his shirt cleaned off. The character takes no constructive action (e.g., calling the police) but reacts to an external restraint.

- SA = external; the man does not rethink his action—just loses any inner purpose when restrained by the woman.

- MA = 2; the woman successfully restrains the man and this score indicates momentary relatedness where the man responds to the immediate external constraints. Again, detachment from one's own emotions is evident in the man's abandonment of his rage as he concerns himself with getting his shirt cleaned off.

- Import: If a man wants to kill a man who has just stabbed him but a woman holds him back for his own safety, he just forgets about the other man and gets his shirt cleaned off.

Card 5

It looks like the lady is scared because probably her house got burned down and she just woke up from taking a nap and it look like her house got set on fire and it look like she's thinking that somebody's in house still and they looking for her so they can kill her and she's like she ain't ready to die yet. (TO?) She ... nobody was in the house and it wasn't a fire just lots of lights on.

- PI = 1; the scene of a woman opening the door is not a good fit with being scared that someone in the house has set it on fire and is still trying to kill her

- SA = external; no understanding of intentions or causes for events

- MA = 1; the woman jumps to the conclusion that someone is trying to kill her but when it turns out that she was mistaken, she does not question her judgment

- Import: A woman is scared because her house has been set on fire and she thinks that someone who wants to kill her is lurking, but everything turns out fine because she mistook the lights for a fire

Card 6BM

She's the old lady looking out the window and that's probably the man's mother or grandmother and they probably got done having a funeral of his aunt or grandmother or something and then it looks like he's feeling real sad and she ... (pause). It looks like he's forgetting about it and his grandmother is in a better place.

- PI = 2
- SA = external
- MA = 2; after a funeral, there is momentary sadness but the grief is quickly forgotten with a stereotyped reference to the individual being in a better place (no one misses the person, no one honors the person's memory, and no one offers each other comfort)
- Import: After someone dies, family members forget their grief right after the funeral because the person is in a better place

Card 7GF

She's looking at something and her maid is telling her not to go do something and it looks like she's gonna do it anyway 'cause it looks like she's a bad little girl and it looks like she thinking she's good and the story ends when the maid went to clean up and she just sat right there until the maid went all the way to the kitchen and she left out of the house to go do something really bad.

- PI = 2; recognition of tension state between the two people but not enduring psychological processes.
- SA = external; the desire to do something bad without an internally organized purpose.
- MA = 2; individuals are distinguished only on the basis of vague intentions, and the maid is viewed only as an obstacle to the girl. As in card 1, the protagonist hides his or her actions from the person in authority.
- Import: A girl who wants to do something bad will do it just as soon as she can get away with it (there is momentary response to external restraint).

Card 8BM

It looks like this the little boy's father and they doing surgery on him and the boy is looking out window and he's feeling bad and they are cutting his intestines or something these two doctors and the man is still alive while they cutting him, no, the man is dead with his eyeballs sticking out. (pause) And how it ended the two doctors really killed him and they took his eyes out first and they were stabbing him and cutting him up and they took his intestines out and they got lights everywhere.

- PI = 1; the scene is interpreted in two discrete parts: (1) a boy is looking out the window while his father is undergoing surgery and feeling bad; and (2) two doctors kill his father, take out his eyes, stab him, cut him up, and remove his intestines. The first part would be coded a 2 in PI because the scene is plausibly described but without understanding psychological processes (e.g., what is the boy doing there, why looking out the window). The second part, a series of gruesome associations to the scene is out of tune with the stimulus (and with social conventionality) and undermines the first part.

- MA = 1; the narrator has no aversion to the gruesome content where individuals destroy others without apparent motive and ends the story with *they got lights everywhere* (there were lights in card 5 as well).

- Import: A boy looks out the window as two doctors kill his father (or even people whose job it is to help will end up murdering you).

In his response to this card and to others, Reggie appears to have difficulty setting limits on associative thought processes that are fueled by assumptions of ill intent—or no concern with intent—but are not constrained by interpersonal connections or prosocial values. In contrast, Paul also has difficulty organizing his thought processes, but his responses are based on an implicit assumption of good intent and are bound within social conventionality and a sense of interpersonal connection.

Card 13B

> The boy just sitting down looking at something like in a scary movie or something and he's thinking like somebody killed my parents because the parents didn't come back for him and the parents left him and he couldn't find his parents so he ain't got no shoes or nothing and he's like wondering when are they gonna come back for me and the story ended how his parents came back for him and they was worried so much about him. (feeling?) Sad and feeling down because his parents left him and he was all by hisself in a dark room.

- PI = 2; at best this would be scored a 2 as there is no sense of the psychological process involved in the interpretation of the scene (e.g., to understand where parents are, to anticipate when they would return).

- SA = external.

- MA = 2; when telling a story about a boy who is sitting alone (e.g., rustic scene, no shoes on), Reggie assumes the worst—that the boy's parents are killed. The boy has no resources but to wait and hope for parents to return without understanding why his parents left him or why they were gone so long. Description of parents as being *worried so much* is not cohesive with the rest of the story (understanding intentions or social causality in ways that are consistent with parental worry); therefore, the narrator is not credited with understanding psychological processes involved (words that pay lip service to certain emotions or intentions but are not cohesive with the narrative context are not viewed as reflecting understanding of psychological process). The structural organization of the content of this story resembles that of card 5: the protagonist assumes the worst but turns out to be mistaken.

- Import: When a boy is alone and scared, he assumes that his parents have been killed but the parents came back for him and they were so worried.

Comparison of Reggie's and Paul's Protocols

To facilitate the comparison, the codes are displayed here.

Perceptual Integration

Narrator 1 2 3BM 4 56BM7GF8BM13B

Paul 3 2 2 2 1 3 2 3 3

Reggie 2 2 1 2 1 2 2 1 2

Mutuality of Autonomy

Narrator 1 2 3BM 4 56BM7GF8BM13B

Paul 3 2 3 1 2 3 2 3 3

Reggie 1 1 1 1 1 2 2 1 2

Source of Affect

Narrator 1 2 3BM 4 5 6BM 7GF 8BM13B

Paul I D/E I E I I I E I

Reggie E E E E E E E E E

Perceptual Integration

The modal PI score for Paul is a 2 or 3, whereas the modal score for Reggie is 2. Reggie's difficulty with processing motives and intentions is more pervasive and, in ambiguous situations, he assumes that individuals have ill intentions. When hostile cues are more explicit (cards 3 and 8), Reggie gets carried away with associations that are not constrained by logic or social conventionality.

Source of Affect

The modal SA score for Paul is internal (except on the most complex stimuli), whereas the modal score for Reggie is external. Paul's narratives incorporate awareness of intentionality, but his theory of mind is not well developed, and he needs clear expectations to act constructively on his intentions. Consistent with his external orientation, Reggie's narratives do not incorporate concern with intentions or long-term purposes but focus on the immediate external event and the feeling or action that it provokes. In Reggie's stories, the sources of tensions and impetus for behaviors are externalized as shown by characters blaming others for provoking reactions (vengeance) or relying on others for restraint (woman in card 4 physically holds the man back, not reasoning with him). Actions taken by characters in Reggie's stories are not governed by purpose-driven intentions or by prosocial principles or interpersonal connections, long-term goals and only minimally by fear of consequences. Even when characters worry or are sad these emotions are not integrated with actions (e.g., parents worry but leave their child feeling abandoned; grief is momentary). Characters abandon their initial view of a situation (e.g., the story ends when they discover that they have misinterpreted the situation) or detach themselves from intense feelings and intentions (card 4, after being restrained from killing someone the man wants to get his shirt cleaned off, ignoring his rage and the relationship with the woman who has just restrained him and focusing on something external).

Mutuality of Autonomy

The modal MA scores for Reggie and Paul are 1 and 3, respectively. Paul's scores fall below his mode when the card presents an unfamiliar situation or requires sizing up complex cues (as in cards, 2, 4, 7GF). In contrast, Reggie's schemas do not provide him with adequate resources to control his behavior even when he knows what is expected of him. His thoughts and behaviors are reactive to immediate provocations, and when he feels provoked his tendency is to assume ill intent, to blame others, and to counterattack. He is not motivated by others' approval and requires external structures to maintain appropriate behaviors. When characters in Reggie's stories act in a purposeful, deliberate way, it is to deceive others and to sidestep consequences. Reggie will need clear road maps and consequences to help him govern his behavior and external sources of motivation to guide his academic learning. He may benefit from interventions that help him see the bigger picture and to increase the complexity of his schemas.

In sum, numerous difficulties with integrating ideas and understanding social causality are evident in both protocols, and these difficulties are also reflected in their below-average IQ scores and academic problems. Paul's reasoning, however, is constrained by interpersonal connections and prosocial values, whereas Reggie's reasoning and thought processes are not governed by conventional standards or enduring attachments.

☐ Future Research Needs

The story form lends itself to the study of mental structures or schemas for integrating various dimensions of the human experience—emotion, cognition, and behavior—to meet adaptive demands of social situations and to organize and to pursue intra- and interpersonal goals. The schemas inherent to the narratives told to picture stimuli coordinate experiences in the inner and outer worlds. The many systems for interpreting the TAT highlight the flexibility with which the stories may be coded. However, progress in the field depends not only on careful documentation of the reliability and validity of the coded units to assess clear constructs but also on the organization of these constructs according to various processes involved in real life functioning. Storytelling may be viewed as a performance task (Teglasi, 1998), and responses may be viewed in terms of levels that pertain to functioning in situations that make similar demands. The empathy coding system used theoretically pertinent units that assessed processing of social information according to levels of functioning but the usefulness of the proposed system for assessing empathy needs to be investigated further with children of varying ages, cultures, and ethnic groups.

The clinical utility of the empathy scoring system does not rest with its contribution to making categorical diagnoses (such as listed in the DSM) but in assessing (1) the wide range of variability in the level of functioning within any diagnosable disorder and (2) individualistic styles of organizing intra and interpersonal information. More research is needed to demonstrate the usefulness of schema qualities—organization, accuracy, and complexity—in assessing the level of impairment or competency within diagnostic rubrics and in making decisions about interventions. It is premature to embark on extensive efforts to establish norms for specific coding procedures until they have been shown to be useful and reliably coded. Various types of units of narrative analysis (i.e., content analysis, structural organization of the narrative content, and narrative process) should be identified and related to one another and to external variables. Since the pictures given to elicit the story influence both the content and the difficulty of the task, it would be useful to investigate various dimensions of pictures such as complexity or ambiguity as well as the types of relationships and number of persons portrayed. In an ideal set of pictures, the emotions and relationships portrayed (psychological issues) would be universal, and contextual cues or features of specific individuals would be adjusted in keeping with culture and ethnicity. Again, it would be premature to agree on a common set of pictures until the properties of various stimuli are systematically researched.

☐ Note

[1]Thanks to Suzanne Chwirut for contributing these cases.

☐ References

Anderson, J. R. (1990). *Cognitive psychology and its implications.* New York: Freeman.

Arnold, M. B. (1962). *Story sequence analysis: A new method for measuring motivation and predicting achievement.* New York: Columbia University Press.

Bandura, A. (1991). Social cognitive theory and moral thought in action. In W. M. Kurtines, & J. L. Gewirtz (Eds.), *Handbook of moral behavior and development* (vol. A) (pp. 45–103). Hillsdale, NJ: Erlbaum.

Bandura, A., Barbaranelli, C., Caprara, G. V., & Pastorelli, C. (1996). Multifaceted impact of self-efficacy beliefs on academic functioning. *Child Development, 67,* 1206–1222.

Baron-Cohen, S., Tager-Flusberg, H., & Cohen, D. J. (1994). *Understanding other minds: Perspectives from autism.* New York: Oxford University Press.

Bassan-Diamond, L., Teglasi, H., & Schmitt, P. (1995). Temperament and a story telling measure of self-regulation. *Journal of Research in Personality, 29,* 109–120.

Batson, C.D. (1991). *The altruism question: Toward a social-psychological answer.* Hillsdale, NJ: Erlbaum.

Batson, C. D., & Oleson, K. C. (1991). Current status of the empathy–altruism hypothesis. In M. S. Clark (Ed.), *Review of Personality and Social Psychology* (pp. 62–85). Newbury Park, CA: Sage.

Bengtsson, H., & Johnson, L. (1992). Perspective taking, empathy, and prosocial behavior in late childhood. *Child Study Journal, 22,* 11–22.

Blair, R. J. R., Jones, L., Clark, F., & Smith, M. (1997). The psychopathic individual: A lack of responsiveness to cues? *Psychophysiology, 34,* 192–198.

Blankman, C., Teglasi, H., & Lawser, M. (2002). Thematic apperception, narrative schemas, and literacy. *Journal of Psychoeducational Assessment, 20,* 268–289.

Bruner, J. (1986). *Actual minds, possible worlds.* Cambridge, MA: Harvard University Press.

Bryant, B. K. (1987). Critique of comparable questionnaire methods in use to assess empathy in children and adults. In N. Eisenberg & J. Strayer (Eds.), *Empathy and its development* (pp. 361–373). New York: Cambridge University Press.

Cadesky, E. B., Mota, V. L., & Schachar, R. J. (2000). Beyond words: How do children with ADHD and/or conduct problems process nonverbal information about affect? *Journal of the American Academy of Child and Adolescent Psychiatry, 39,* 1160–1167.

Cervone, D., & Williams, S. L. (1992). Social cognitive theory and personality. In G. Caprara & G. L. Van Heck (Eds.), *Modern personality psychology: Critical reviews and new directions* (pp. 200–252). New York: Harvester-Wheatsheaf.

Cialdini, R., Brown, S., Lewis, B., Luce, C., & Neuberg, S. (1997). Reinterpreting the empathy–altruism relationship: When one into one equals oneness. *Journal of Personality and Social Psychology, 73,* 481–494.

Cobb, C. D., & Mayer, J. D. (2000). Emotional intelligence: What the research says. *Educational Leadership, 58,* no. 3, 14–18.

Cohen, D., & Strayer, J. (1996). Empathy in conduct-disordered and comparison youth. *Developmental Psychology, 32,* 988–998.

Cohen, D., & Volkmar, F. (1997). *Handbook of autism and pervasive developmental disorders* (2nd ed.). New York: John Wiley.

Dana, R. H. (1959). Proposal for objective scoring of the TAT. *Perceptual and Motor Skills, 9,* 27–43.

Denham, S. A., Zoller, D., & Couchoud, E. A. (1994). Socialization of preschoolers' emotion understanding. *Developmental Psychology, 30,* no. 6, 928–937.

Dymond, R. F. (1948). A preliminary investigation of the relation of insight and empathy. *Journal of Consulting Psychology, 12,* 228–233.

Dymond, R. F. (1949). A scale for the measurement of empathic ability. *Journal of Consulting Psychology, 13,* 127–133.

Dymond, R. F. (1950). Personality and empathy. *Journal of Consulting Psychology, 14,* 343–350.

Eisenberg, N., & Fabes, R. A. (1998). Prosocial development. In W. Damon & N. Eisenberg (Eds.), *Handbook of child psychology* (pp. 701–778). New York: Wiley and Sons.

Eisenberg, N., Fabes, R. A, Murphy, B., Karbon, M., Smith, M., & Maszk, P. (1996). The relations of children's dispositional empathy-related responding to their emotionality, regulation, and social functioning. *Developmental Psychology, 32,* 195–209.

Eisenberg, N., Fabes, R. A, Nyman, M., & Bernzweig, J. (1994). The relations of emotionality and regulation to children's anger-related reactions. *Child Development, 65,* no. 1, 109–128.

Eisenberg, N., Guthrie, I. K., Murphy, B. C., Shepard, S. A., Cumberland, A., & Carlo, G. (1999). Consistency and development of prosocial dispositions: A longitudinal study. *Child Development, 70,* 1360–1372.

Eisenberg, N., & Okun, M. A. (1996). The relations of dispositional regulation and emotionality to elders' empathy-related responding and affect while volunteering. *Journal of Personality 64,* 157–183.

Eisenberg, N., Zhou, Q., & Koller, S. (2001). Brazilian adolescent's prosocial moral judgment and behavior: Relations to sympathy, perspective taking, gender-role orientation, and demographic characteristics. *Child Development, 72,* 518–535.

Eisenberg-Berg, N. (1979). The development of children's prosocial moral judgment. *Developmental Psychology, 15,* 128–137.

Feshbach, N. D. (1978). Studies of empathic behavior in children. In B. A. Maher (Ed.), *Progress in experimental personality research.* (vol. 8) (pp. 1–47). New York: Academic Press.

Gillberg, C. (1999). Neurodevelopmental processes and psychological functioning in autism. *Development & Psychopathology, 11,* 567–587.

Higgins, E. T. (1981). Role taking and social judgment: Alternative developmental processes and perspectives. In J. H. Flavell and L. Ross (Eds.), *Social cognitive development: Frontiers and possible futures* (pp. 119–153). Cambridge, Emgland: Cambridge University Press.

Hoffman, M. L. (1982). Development of prosocial motivation: Empathy and guilt. In N. Eisenberg (Ed.), *The development of prosocial behavior* (pp. 281–313). New York: Academic.

Hoffman, M. L. (2000). Toward a comprehensive empathy-based theory of prosocial moral development. In A. C. Bohart & D. J. Stipek (Eds.), *Constructive and destructive behavior: Implications for family, school and society* (pp. 61–83). Washington, D.C: American Psychological Association.

Holmgren, R. A., Eisenberg, N., & Fabes, R. A. (1998). The relations of children's situational empathy-related emotions to dispositional prosocial behaviour. *International Journal of Behavioral Development, 22,* no. 1, 169–193.

Kalliopuska, M. (1982). Empathy measured by Rorschach and TAT. *British Journal of Projective Psychology & Personality Study, 27,* no. 2, 5–11.

Karniol, R. (1995). The implications of the transformation rule model for predicting each other's psychological experiences in close relationships. In S. Shulman (Ed.), *Human development, vol. 7: Close relationships and socioemotional development* (pp. 203–217). Norwood, NJ: Ablex Publishing Corp.

Kovacs, M., & Pollock, M. (1995). Bipolar disorder and comorbid conduct disorder in childhood and adolescence. *Journal of the American Academy of Child and Adolescent Psychiatry, 34,* no. 6, 715–723.

Linville, P. W. (1987). Self-complexity as a cognitive buffer against stress-related illness and depression. *Journal of Personality and Social Psychology, 52,* 663–676.

Locraft, C., & Teglasi, H. (1997). Teacher rated empathic behaviors and children's T.A.T. stories. *Journal of School Psychology, 35,* 217–237.

Lohr, L. B., Teglasi, H., & French, M. (2004). Schemas and temperament as risk factors for emotional disability. *Personality and Individual Differences, 36,* 1637–1654.

Matthys, W., Cuperus, J. M., & Van Engeland, H. (1999). Deficient social problem-solving in boys with ODD/CD, with ADHD, and with both disorders. *Journal of the American Academy of Child & Adolescent Psychiatry, 38,* no. 3, 311–321.

McCrae, R. R., & Costa, P. T. (1989). Reinterpreting the Myers-Briggs Type Indicator from the perspective of the five-factor model of personality. *Journal of Personality, 57,* no. 1, 17–40.

Murray, H. A. (1943). *Thematic Apperception Test manual.* Cambridge, MA: Harvard University Press.

Niec, L. N., & Russ, S. W. (2002). Children's internal representations, empathy, and fantasy play: A validity study of the SCORS–Q. *Psychological Assessment, 14,* 331–338.

Roberts, W., & Strayer, J. (1996). Empathy, emotional expressiveness, and prosocial behavior. *Child Development, 67,* 449–470.

Sigman, M., & Ruskin, E. (1999). Continuity and change in the social competence of children with autism, Down syndrome, and developmental delays. *Monographs of the Society for Research in Child Development, 64,* no. 1, 114.

Singh, S. D., Ellis, C. R., Winton, A. W., Singh, N. N., Leung, J. P. & Oswald, D. P. (1998). Recognition of facial expressions of emotion by children with attention-deficit-hyperactivity disorder. *Behavior Modification, 22,* 128–142.

Smith, K. D. (1992) Trait sympathy and perceived control as predictors of entering sympathy-arousing situations. *Personality and Social Psychology Bulletin 18,* 207–216.

Spangler, W. D. (1992). Validity of questionnaire and TAT measures of need for achievement. *Psychological Bulletin, 112,* 140–154.

Sroufe, L. A. (1996). *Emotional development: The organization of emotional life in the early years.* New York: Cambridge University Press.

Locraft, C., & Teglasi, H. (1997). Teacher rated empathic behaviors and children's T.A.T. stories. *Journal of School Psychology, 35,* 217–237.

Teglasi, H. (1993). *Clinical use of storytelling.* Boston: Allyn and Bacon.

Teglasi, H. (1998). Assessment of schema and problem-solving strategies with projective techniques. In M. Hersen & A. Bellack (Series Eds.), *Comprehensive clinical psychology, vol. 4 assessment* (pp. 459–499). New York: Elsevier Science Press.

Teglasi, H. (1998). Temperament constructs and measures. *School Psychology Review, 27,* no. 4, 562–583.

Teglasi, H. (2001). *Essentials of TAT and other storytelling instruments assessment.* New York: Wiley.

Teglasi, H. & Epstein, S. (1998). Temperament and personality theory: The perspective of cognitive-experiential self-theory. *School Psychology Review, 27,* 534–550.

Urist, J. (1977). The Rorschach test and the assessment of object relations. *Journal of Personality Assessment, 41,* 3–9.

Westen, D. (1991). Clinical assessment of object relations using the TAT. *Journal of Personality Assessment, 56,* 56–74.

Westen, D. (1995). *Psychology: Mind, brain and culture* New York: Wiley.

Westen, D., Klepser, J., Ruffins, S. A., Silverman, M., & Boekamp, J. (1991). Object relations in childhood and adolescence: The development of working representations. *Journal of Consulting and Clinical Psychology, 9,* 400–409.

31

CHAPTER

Scoring Manual for Empathy

Hedwig Teglasi, Constance Locraft, and Kelly Felgenhauer

☐ Introduction

This chapter provides practice protocols and specific guidelines for scoring Thematic Apperception Test (TAT) stories on the following variables that are theoretically and empirically linked to empathy: (1) perceptual integration (PI) (four levels); (2) source of affect (SA) (external/descriptive or internal); and (3) mutuality of autonomy (MA) (five levels) (Teglasi, 1993, 2001; also see chapter 30 in this volume). The stories presented for practice were told by children who participated in a study of empathy (Locraft & Teglasi, 1997), and, as detailed in chapter 30, the scoring was reliable and distinguished between the groups. The TAT scores were more clearly associated with empathy than with grade level, which ranged from kindergarten through sixth grade.

☐ Administration

Formats

Standard individual administration procedures were used (Murray, 1943) with standard encouragement and prompts (see Teglasi, 1993, 2001). There was one query for each of the four elements:

(1) What is happening in the picture?

(2) What happened before?

(3) What is the person thinking, and how is the person feeling?

(4) How does the story turn out at the end?

Stories were audiotaped, and transcriptions included the examiner's queries.

Stimuli

The stimuli administered (TAT cards 1, 2, 3BM, 4, 5, 7GF, and 8BM) varied in the number of persons portrayed (from one to three), complexity (foreground and background, seemingly discrepant emotions) and ambiguity (clarity of cues), but all included an implied dilemma to be resolved.

☐ Scoring Process

The scoring procedures described are applicable to any stimulus that portrays intra- or interpersonal tensions, regardless of whether one or more individuals are pictured.

Scoring Categories

Perceptual Integration

The manner in which the narrator uses the stimulus to construct the story has not received sufficient attention. Dana's (1959) concept of perceptual range, scored according to adherence to norms for mentioning designated stimulus and story elements (available for male and female versions of cards 2, 3, 4, 6, and 7), did not emphasize the relationships among the characters and activities or the degree of accuracy in identifying emotions or relationships. Perceptual integration (Teglasi, 1993, 2001) has two underlying dimensions: (1) degree of congruence between the stimulus configuration and identified emotions/tensions and relationships (identification); and (2) the match between the identified emotions/relationships and the unfolding narrative (understanding). These two dimensions are organized into four levels—discrepant, literal, imprecise, and accurate—that have a linear relationship with listening comprehension in early elementary school (Blankman, Teglasi, & Lawser, 2002), with adjustment (Lohr, Teglasi, and French, 2004) and with empathy (see chapter 30 in this volume).

Discrepant

A PI score of 1 is assigned when the central dilemma of the story is not appropriate to the stimulus configuration due to any of the following:

- Disregard or misperception of basic emotions or relationships portrayed in the scene (e.g., misreading facial expression or posture or ages of the people)

- Poor fit with the stimulus configuration (e.g., problem identified is related tangentially to the stimulus; characters with clearly different postures or facial expressions are identified as feeling the same way)

- A major character is omitted from the story

- Emphasis is on minor, irrelevant details (e.g., eyebrow) without perceiving the gestalt

The following story told about card 4 by a third-grade boy with low empathy is scored 1 because it does not identify a tension state:

> They are in love a lot. They're walking along, they met, and fell in love. They get married. They have 8 children and they get a house and added a lot to it. (Feel?) Happy that they had the children. (Think?) That they wish they had six children or less.

The following story told about the same card by a second-grade boy with low empathy does posit a tension but does not incorporate the differences in the pictured emotions of the man and the woman and thus also is scored 1.

> The wife is hugging the husband. (Before?) The wife walked up to the man. Before that the wife entered through the door. (Feeling?) Sad because they're having—the mother and father are going to get divorced. (Think?) That they are going to get divorced. (End?) They get divorced.

The following story told about card 2 by a second-grade boy low in empathy is scored 1 because it takes an unsystematic approach to accounting for the stimulus cues, as shown by listing a girl, a mom and dad, and a horse as people working on a farm:

> One day some people were working on the farm—a girl, a mom and dad, and a horse. A girl went off to school. Later, a car came and went right past, missed her by an inch and her dog went splat. She studies arithmetic and stuff; then she goes home. (Feel?) Sad because her dog died. (Think?) That she will go home.

Literal

A PI score of 2 is assigned when the narrator identifies the emotions and tensions of each character as portrayed in the scene but does not coordinate the various cues into a cohesive interpretation of the stimulus configuration that suggests awareness of psychological processes as indicated by any of the following:

- Recognition of different characters' emotions but without relating those emotions to psychological processes of the individuals in the pictured scene

- Emphasis on perception rather than conception (interpretation of emotion within the context of the pictured scene or with ties to relevant psychological processes) results in superficial, concrete, descriptive use of the stimulus, without meaningful links among the various elements of the pictured scene, and without sufficient connection of external cues with psychological (inner) processes such as intentions, purposes, long-term plans. Thus, emotions are evoked simplistically by external sources, and actions are triggered by emotions without being regulated by inner processes.

- Sequence of events does not transcend the moment captured in the stimulus as suggested by positing simplistic connection between emotions or tensions and story events (concrete, scripted/stereotypic or composed of associations to various aspects of the stimulus with no apparent tie to story events).

The response about card 5 by the same second-grade boy who told the story regarding card 4 in the previous section illustrates this level:

> A lady is scolding her child. He broke the kitchen window with a baseball while playing. He batted it too far and too low. The boy gets put to bed without supper. The end. (Feel?) The boy is mad because he did not get supper. (Think?) He was thinking, "I want to leave. I can't wait to leave this house." He runs away.

Although not discrepant from the pictured scene, the tension does not incorporate a psychological process to separate the intent from the impact of an action or to coordinate transient emotions with more enduring considerations. Feelings and actions are reactive to the immediate provocation (on the part of both characters) and are not moderated by a longer-term view or alternative perspective.

The following story, told about card 1 by the same second-grade boy with low empathy illustrates a simplistic connection between emotion and events:

> Once there was a boy who was doing some music lessons. Before, he was doing his math and he didn't want to go to music class. The teacher made him go to music class. He got an "F" for not doing what he was told. He's in 2nd grade. (Feel?) Glum, sad. He was thinking, "I want to finish my arithmetic." He didn't like music; he likes math. (End?) Every day after that he went to music. He never likes music class.

Imprecise

A PI of 3 is assigned when the narrative integrates inner and outer sources of tension in ways that suggest awareness of psychological processes and when the story premise is in accord with the stimulus configuration. However, the fit between the stimulus configuration and the story is not precise due to either of the following:

- Emotions and relationships are not in accord with subtle contextual cues in the stimulus or a major stimulus element (but not the central tension) is ignored or misperceived.

- Understanding of social causality suggested by depiction of psychological processes or sequences of events is slightly amiss or vague.

An example of this level is seen in the story told about card 2 by a fifth-grade girl with high empathy:

> A girl has these books in her hand; the other woman is looking at the guy with the horse. I think she's (the one with the books) jealous of the other one (by the tree) because she doesn't have to do work and just watches. She probably asks the other one what she's doing and she'll probably do her work later and watch and they get to know each other and she's not jealous anymore because they're friends now.

The nature of the relationships among the characters as the context for the feelings (*jealous*) is not clear. Although the message of the story—things are not what they seem at first glance—may be sophisticated, the coordination of the stimulus with the unfolding narrative is not precise.

Accurate

A PI score of 4 is assigned when the story conveys a precise understanding of social causality and of psychological processes suggested when the following is true:

- The story is consistent with all cues and subtleties of the stimulus configuration (despite possible omission of a minor stimulus element)
- The narrative conveys a clear and realistic understanding of causes and their effects and of psychological process such as intentions

An example of this level is seen in the story told about card 3BM by the same fifth-grade girl as in the previous section:

> Looks like someone hurt his feelings so he's just there until he stops crying. Someone called him names. He ignores the people who called him names and goes with another crowd who are his friends. He plays with his friends, not the ones calling him names. He thinks about what he should do to prevent them from calling him names. He will probably have to think about it for a while before he finds a solution.

This story gives a meaningful and realistic accounting of the scene. Although the gun (sometimes seen as another object such as keys) is not included, it is considered here as a minor stimulus element and does not influence the PI score. On card 8BM, the foreground and background are on different planes and to receive a PI score of 4, the relationship between them needs to be explained. In card 4, it is not necessary to attend to the background scene to receive a score of 4.

Source of Affect

Four categories have been described in relation to source of affect: unrecognized, descriptive, external, and internal (Teglasi, 2001). Among children participating in the empathy study, unrecognized affect was rare, and source of affect was dichotomously classified as internal or external. Affect that simply describes the pictured stimulus was considered as external since no inner process is invoked. Children classified as high in empathy more often attributed affect to internal sources than did children with low empathy (see chapter 30 in this volume).

Responses are coded external (E) if the following occur:

- The feeling is triggered exclusively by an external concern, situation or provocation (including the way someone looks in the picture, without attributing inner qualities)
- The actions stem from desire for external rewards with no inner purpose or genuine concerns
- There is rudimentary or stereotyped awareness of the inner world
- There is concern about external event, outcome, or possessions

Responses are coded internal (I) if the following occur:

- The internal and external sources of affect are coordinated and cohesive (emotions are tied to a network of inner concerns such as intentions, plans, prior experience, and external considerations such as circumstances or consequences)
- The actions stem from inner purpose
- The intentions for decisions or actions are considered important
- There is concern about a principle, standards, process, or valuing the common good (e.g., the relationship, or the feelings, intentions, or goals of others)

To check the coding decision, consider the following:

- What makes this individual happy? External sources of happiness include material goods, fun activities, fame, winning, approval, and becoming a hero, whereas internal source of happiness include meeting standards, following principles that may include commitment to the autonomy and self-direction of others, meeting an intrinsic goal, and interpersonal connection such as sharing enjoyment or pride in accomplishment.
- How does the individual justify actions or emotions? Are emotions or actions discussed in terms of individual's inner world or in terms of external triggers? What is the nature of schemas that mediate between the immediate emotion or action and longer-term meaning, concerns, or goals (distinction between the immediate emotional impact and the intent or longer-term implication)? Does the individual anticipate events that are associated with emotions (hence relying on anticipatory schemas for problem solving), or is he or she taken by surprise by events, reactions, or consequences (and hence responds to these external outcomes)?
- How does this individual resolve tensions? Emotions that are exclusively rooted in the external world (reactive) are likely to be similarly resolved (change in external world elicits a different emotion without any responsibility taken for the emotion or for changing the event).

Mutuality of Autonomy

As a mode of relatedness, mutuality of autonomy is the capacity to notice, appreciate, and value qualities of others independently of one's own feelings or self-interest. In other words, others' individuality is appreciated on its own merit apart from the perceiver's feelings, needs or preoccupations. Accordingly, others are perceived and respected for who they really are and are not judged in terms of how the perceiver wants or needs them to be. The definition of mutuality of autonomy as the reciprocal valuing of the autonomy of different individuals is also central to the scoring system with the same name proposed by Urist (1977) for the Rorschach. To study empathy, Kalliopuska (1982) coded TAT stories and Rorschach protocols with the seven-point Mutuality of Autonomy scale introduced by Urist (1977) to code human responses to the Rorschach. Urist's seven levels, from highest to lowest mutuality of autonomy, depend on the nature of the interacting figures as follows:

(1) Conveying reciprocal acknowledgment of individuality

(2 Engaging in parallel activity

(3) Leaning on each other or needing support in some way

(4) One figure being a reflection or extension of the other

(5) One exerting malevolent control over another

(6) Depicting malicious imbalance of power or autonomy, a parasitic relationship where the existence of one diminishes the other

(7) Figures being swallowed up by forces beyond their control

Level of mutuality of autonomy in the current system is predicated on two basic processes: the capacity to discern individuality apart from personal preoccupations and the integration of what is perceived into a cohesive understanding of intra- and interpersonal processes. These respective processes of differentiation and integration briefly described following contribute to five levels of MA.

(1) Differentiation: The attributes of self and others that are characteristically noticed are the bases for differentiation, and these attributes may be examined in terms of the number of distinctions that are made, what is distinguished (outward attributes vs. inner concerns) and the clarity or specificity of these distinctions (fine-tuned vs. vague). Individual variations in distinguishing qualities within and across persons as seen in TAT stories may be ordered approximately from least to most differentiated:

Viewpoints of different characters remain fuzzy as needs and perspectives within a single character are vague and virtually no distinction is made among different characters (i.e., individuality within or across characters is not recognized in the basic dimensions of experience: intentions, goals, feelings, actions, thoughts, or outcomes)

Distinctions between characters are based on superficial, outward attributes (appearance, wealth, how they look in the stimulus)

Characters are distinguished in terms that are too global (diffuse negative affect, pervasive sense of upset)

Distinctions are based on simple event–feeling connections or vague intention without grasping the psychological process (e.g., feels good because she got out of her punishment)

Distinctions are dichotomous (good vs. bad, weak vs. strong, threatening vs. safe, special vs. ordinary)

Distinctions are based on stereotypes or duty such as carrying out one's obligations as friend, spouse, parent

Attributes of individuals are seen only in relations to another's preoccupations, needs or desires (emotions are misperceived; reasoning about interpersonal events is based on wishes, fears, preoccupations or associations of the perceiver rather than on realistic understanding of social causality)

Characters differ in their needs, feelings, views, actions, and outcomes, and these are seen as legitimate in a mutually respectful relationship

Distinctions are based on elaboration of characters' values, goals, principles, long-term investment

(2) Integration: Individual differences in coordinating the attributes that are discerned are also evident in TAT stories. The following story characteristics reflect integration:

Feelings, tensions, and conflicts are incorporated into a meaningful context that coordinates perspectives within individuals (prosocial connections among one individual's intentions, actions, and outcomes) and across individuals (coordination of intentions, actions, and outcomes across the parties involved in the interaction)

Continuity of relatedness is evident in the reconciliation of characters' negative and positive attributes or genuine connections (rather than isolated traits or interactions)

Continuity of time perspective is evident by coordinating past, present, and future interests of interacting parties so that resolutions of tensions are realistic and no character is left to wallow in misery

Coordination of perspectives is seen when characters communicate ideas or engage in constructive actions motivated by purpose, principles, mutual respect, and understanding

Levels of Mutuality of Autonomy

Styles of differentiation and integration of intra and interpersonal attributes just described are ordered according to five levels of relatedness with the highest being mutuality of autonomy. The highest score characterizing each story is assigned.

(1) Disorganized or detached level of relatedness: At this level, disorganized or highly simplified cognitive processing (poor reality testing) may disrupt the differentiation and integration of various perspectives (mutuality) and interferes with the sense of self-cohesion (autonomy). Impaired social reasoning may stem from problems coordinating affect, intention, and thought within or across individuals, from problems differentiating wishes from realistic considerations, and from problems with understanding social causality. This level is evident in TAT stories characterized by any of the following:

A severe imbalance of autonomy with helplessness in the face of the whims of controlling and powerful others

A character's evaluation of persons as obstacles or hindrances without considering any other attributes

Severe restrictions on a character's autonomy

Individuality is not perceived—characters feel the same way despite postures or facial expressions that are clearly different or boundaries are unclear between the inner (self) and outer worlds (others)

Severe limitations in autonomy and disparity of power are evident in characters who exploit, malign, or overpower others or feel similarly victimized

Absence of remorse for hurtful actions

Characters make unreasonable or unrealistic demands on one another

(2) Momentary experience of relatedness: A rudimentary sense of autonomy or limited mutuality coincides with a self-absorbed and self-serving mode of relatedness that pertains to the moment. Individuals are differentiated on the basis of momentary need or immediate gain without the sense that they are whole persons. Characteristics of others are noticed only if they pertain to the observer's immediate need states so that perceptions of self and others shift according to circumstances without insight or reflection. This level is shown in TAT stories that are characterized by any of the following:

Emotions are tied to immediate external considerations, and remorse is linked to immediate consequences

Inner attributes are ill defined (diffuse negative affect) or based on stereotypes (unconvincing verbalization about duty or blind obligation) without a sense that the personality as a continuous, cohesive whole

Significant imbalance in mutuality of autonomy where one character may be competent, heroic or intrusive whereas others are incompetent, helpless, or ignored (also when a person in the scene is left out of the story)

Characters experience relatedness only if another person is physically present, and when single characters are portrayed, they are unable to cope with their misery but no one is introduced to help

Concerns of characters are basic, revolving around safety, survival, or protection

The relationship per se is neither important nor durable, and others who meet needs are interchangeable

Characters take no responsibility for their feelings or actions (fantasy may replace actual relationships—characters are actors or characters easily abandon their intentions, convictions, or intense feelings)

(3) Functional experience of relatedness: At this level, individuals notice attributes that pertain to reciprocity in the form of rigid quid pro quo exchanges where the emphasis is on duty or function served rather than on the human connection. Responsibilities

are not internally rooted or valued as ends (matter of principle) but constitute give-and-take responses in relationships that are valued for mutual exchanges. Approval or disapproval, as well as rewards and consequences, may be salient in these exchanges. Individuals anticipate punishment for wrong doing and express genuine remorse for transgressions. However, they do not set their own standards but strive to conform to expectations. Attributes of others that are noted and appreciated are those that contribute to their expected functions. At this level, what is salient in others is no longer dependent on the perceivers' immediate needs and feelings but on a longer-term view of the functional exchanges with recognition of reciprocity. The following can be said of characters in TAT stories:

They are differentiated in terms of what they can provide and relate in terms of what they do for or want from one another without recognition of one another's autonomy

They respond with a short-term view to situations without consideration of prior history, personal conviction, or investment

They fail to act or act without deliberate intention

They take turns as givers and takers, although in a rigid or stereotypic manner

(4) Reciprocity and standards as basic to relatedness: Autonomy and relatedness are governed by a sense of fair play or prosocial standards that promote continuity and consistency in relationships with others and within the self (commitment to standards, pursuit of self-directed purposeful action). Reciprocity is not perceived as quid pro quo but as a natural mode of relating among individuals who care about each other. Thus, the range of attributes of others that are salient and appreciated is wider and more independent of the perceiver's needs or preoccupations. Individuals accord one another the freedom to have their own views and to pursue self-directed and purposeful activities. TAT stories portray characters that are as follows:

Clearly differentiated in terms of internalized standards and rules of conduct that are sufficiently flexible to permit appropriate compromise

Autonomous, having a sense of goals or principles, and able to take self-determined actions that are prosocial; if only a single character is included, the autonomy implies appreciation of the other's individuality

Balanced in their respective sense of autonomy (intentions, actions, outcomes are distinct but coordinated), and characters' initiative, purpose, conviction, and deliberate pursuit of goal-directed activities do not diminish others

(5) Relatedness through mutuality of autonomy: Autonomy is well balanced with appreciation of uniqueness and individuality of self and others, apart from needs or requirements of social exchange or conventional morality. The narrative conveys a fine-tuned understanding of multiply interacting dimensions of experience through awareness of both transient and enduring psychological experiences and of complex motives in self and others by any of the following:

Inner lives and concerns of all characters are portrayed in line with their depictions in the stimulus and entail mutual respect for individualistic styles together with appreciation of subtle intra and interpersonal nuance

Characters value societal conventions and obligations in the context of mutual care and commitment to moral standards and have the flexibility to compromise in ways that enhance the autonomy of all parties

Interpersonal ties are strong enough to transcend the threat of consequences or disapproval

The narrative coordinates the concerns of characters in ways that balance short- and long-term considerations and their respective autonomy.

It is important to note that the TAT assesses the level of the schemas that are available without assuming that the individual will use these schemas at all times and in all relationships. Participants in a carpool may indeed value the quid pro quo aspect of the relationship. However, given the basic ingredients of empathy and the capacity to discern intra- and interpersonal attributes accurately and to coordinate them cohesively, other carpool participants are still viewed as whole persons. When gripped by intense emotions or in the context of specific relationships (e.g., authority figures, past history), individuals may not function according to their characteristic levels. Under stress, individuals tend to be more self-focused and more likely to notice qualities in others that pertain to their immediate needs. Different situations and relationships may call to mind different schemas, and examiners should note variations in scores when stories are told to cards that differ in complexity of the emotions depicted and when the story content differs in types of relationships (e.g., family members, strangers) and in types of contexts (e.g., achievement, routine encounter, adverse circumstance).

Calculating Scores

Each story is assigned a score for each of the three coding categories previously described, and these scores carry descriptive information about the examinee's style or level of functioning. Averaging scores across cards for each dimension may be suitable for research but may obscure some clinically relevant information. Characteristics of the stimuli such as intensity of the emotions or interpersonal conflict portrayed or degree of complexity or ambiguity may influence the reasoning process of the narrator. For instance, an individual may receive high PI scores on all but two cards that depict the most intense negative emotions because of a tendency to avoid dealing with conflict, and this pattern would not be evident from an average score. Thus, it is helpful to take stock of variation across cards. Because two stories may be assigned the same numerical score for different reasons, for clinical purposes it is important for examiners to systematically evaluate the responses within each level. Assigning a numerical score is a starting point for systematically coordinating information from the TAT protocol with data from other sources.

Practice Stories

Protocol 75

Card 1: He's sad because he doesn't know how to play a violin. He asks his mother if he can get a teacher and she says ok. He gets a teacher and he practices and he learns and he finally knows how to play the violin.

Card 2: There's a girl and she's walking from school and she's carrying a book. She sees people, a woman looking at the trees and a man walking a horse. She thinks about school and feels happy because of what she learned. And she thinks about what they are going to do tomorrow. She goes home.

Card 3BM: He's sad because he fell off the chair. He tries to get up. His mother helps him get up. (Think?) He thinks how to get up, he's stuck. (Turn Out?) He sits on the chair and thinks what to do. He hears kids outside, and he goes out to ride bikes with them.

Card 4: She's hugging her husband 'cause she loves him. Right now, they're in a doctor place because he is sick because he got a cold. He looks at something—at the window, some people talking and the other people are laughing when a person is talking—telling jokes. They go home from the doctor and he is still sick. (End?) He gets better and they are happy.

Card 5: There's a woman opening the door. And she is in a room and she sees something, a light. And she sees a person in the room. The person is looking at a book. She goes inside the room and she tells the person it's time for dinner. (Feel?) Happy because they ate dinner. At the table they talk about what they did today. (Think?) They think about what they are going to do tomorrow. Maybe the person goes to school, the woman, she stays home and she sits down and looks at a book.

Card 7GF: I think there's a little girl and she's holding a cat. And the other has another cat, and she is sitting in a chair looking at the cat. (End?) They play with the cats and they're happy. (Think?) Maybe they are thinking that they could have another cat.

Card 8BM: People, maybe they're giving the man an operation. And the other man is going out of the room. The man went to another room where there's a big window and the man is looking inside. He feels sad for that man. The operation gets over and the two men go to where the other man is and they talk about the man what was operated on. (End?) He's gotta rest a lot and he gets better. (Think?) He's thinking about what he's going to do tomorrow.

Protocol #90

Card 1: He's just being still, staring at the toy. (Think?) He's thinking about getting a new toy—he likes that one but is thinking about getting a new one. (Feel?) Sad because he's thinking of something like getting a new toy. (End?) He just thinks if his father can get a new toy. His mother and father say he can get a new one tomorrow and the little boy still stares at the violin.

Card 2: A man, a horse, a lady. They're farmers. That's a statue (woman on the right). The lady's holding the books; the man is seeing the world. They're going to grow flowers. Then they go home and eat dinner and go to bed. The next day they make some more flowers. The girl can make food for the man. (Feel?) They feel happy because they are making some flowers and they like to. (Think?) They think they can have chickens and farm animals.

Card 3BM: This girl, she's on the floor crying because they punished her because she did something bad. Maybe she said, "Yucky soup" and just wants to eat some candy. She was punished because she plays and doesn't eat the soup. They make her eat the soup. She feels unhappy because they treat her like a baby.

Card 4: Maybe they got married and the man came home from work and the lady wants to give him a kiss. She kisses him. He says, "I think we better go on a trip." When they finish dinner, they go out. (Feel?) They feel so happy.

Card 5: This—she's a grandma. She comes home from work and saw her, her husband sleeping, snoring. She was going to eat something and he ate all the food and he became fat. (Feel?) She feels so mad and so sad. Then she goes to the grocery store to buy some food. She tiptoes in, walking carefully, and puts the food away. Her husband peeked and went to bed again because his wife was going to see him. She tiptoes back to work and then she feeds the animals. Her husband was in the living room and he ate all the food again. He became more fat than ever. His wife came home and wanted to eat some food and she opened the refrigerator and there was nothing but an apple and juice and she ate the apple and drank the juice. She was mad and went again to the grocery store. She said, "If my husband eats the food again, I'll call the police." She tiptoes again and he comes in and eats the cake and milk. She tells her husband to stand up and see how fat he is. She calls the police and said, "He ate all my food." They took him to jail and talk to him. She eats the food.

Card 7GF: Her friend is looking at her. The little girl has something in her hand. They play. The next day a boy came to her home too. He punches her friend. He said, "No girls are allowed to be here." He said, "I'm going to punch her in the face." He punches her. She calls their mother and she punishes him. (Feel?) Her brother punches her in her face. The brother feels so happy because he's glad he punched her. (Think?) He thinks about he could be a monster and eat her. She said, "I'm telling my mom."

Card 8BM: This is going to be a hard one. Four boys and one is real bad that—two was bad. One was dead and they were putting a knife in—killing that man because they were fighting with them. The boy is staring at him. Those three were bad because they want to kill Rosa's father. (Feel?) She was crying because they were killing her father. She just went home and she thought a handsome man could be her father. Now she has another father. They live happily ever after.

Protocol 53

Card 1: Once upon a time there was a boy who just started school and he wanted to play music and he didn't know how to play the violin. Then he felt sad that other kids next to him knew how to do it. Then he starts studying how to play it and he learns how to play it. Then he started playing the flute and he learned how to play that because his father taught him. He said he liked to play the flute better. That made his father happy that he liked the flute better and now they can play music together.

Card 2: Once upon a time there lived a girl whose name was Sally. She went to school and she had straight A's and she lived on a farm and one day her father and mother was planting some corn. Then she thinked to herself, could I do this? Then the next day she tried it.

Then she planted a apple tree. Then her mother and father were glad. Then she helped her mother and father plant other things. Sally felt happy and the mother and father felt happy too.

Card 3BM: There was this girl named Kathy. She was down because she couldn't go to a party with her friends. She had to wash dishes and clean her room, so she was crying on her bed. And then, when she was finished crying, she finished all her work and went to the party because she did all her work. Then she came back and told her mother and father about the fun she had and then she went to sleep.

Card 4: There was this man named Bob. He liked to work in the garden. Then one time this woman named Michelle invited him to her house. Then one man tried to fight Bob. Bob wanted to fight him back but Michelle said, "No." So Bob says he doesn't want to fight and the man goes away. Bob feeled sad and Michelle was sad and mad too that the man tried to fight Bob.

Card 5: Once upon a time there lived this woman. Her name was Barbara. One time she heard something upstairs so she ran upstairs and opened the door. There was a robber trying to steal her purse. Then she called the police. Then the robber was gone and the police didn't believe her. She, then she just went back to her husband named Frank. One day he came back and Frank heard it this time and then he called the police and then Barbara tied him up and the police came and arrested him and he went to jail. Then they were happy because they didn't have a robber in the house.

Card 7GF. Once upon a time there lived this girl who was spoiled. Her name was Esther. One time, her mother told her to clean her room, but she didn't. She used to have her way all the time; she was really spoiled. One time, she asked if she could drink her medicine. Her mother told her not to drink it but she drinked it anyway. And then she got sick and her mother was sad and they took her to the doctor. The doctors said they could do something with her and they did. She had to stay in the hospital for two months and when she got out she started to listen to her mother and started to be a good girl like the rest of the kids and then they were all happy.

Card 8BM: Once upon a time there was a boy named Tom and his father was named George. One day George got very sick and these doctors are trying to save him. Tom was sad, his mother was sad, and his brother and sister were sad that George was so sick. The doctors give George medicine and operate on him and he lives. Then they were all happy.

Protocol 114

Card 1: He's thinking of playing the violin. He wants to play the violin and he does play the violin. (Feel?) Happy that he saw the violin. (End?) He plays the violin.

Card 2: The man's fixin' the garden. The lady's watching him fix the garden. This one just finished reading a book. She starts to think what page she's on. The man's going to start to pull the horse on the garden. (Feel?) Happy that they make crops and get their own food. (Think?) They're thinking about making the crops grow. (End?) The girl finishes reading the book.

Card 3BM: This guy's laying down. This is a toy. The guy dropped the toy. (Feel?) Sleepy—not sleepy but tired. (Think?) He's thinking that one day he's have a rest and there would be peace and quiet. (End?) He wakes up, picks up a toy, and goes anywhere he wants.

Card 4: A guy is trying to get away from the lady because he's looking at something. He gets away from her and turns his face around. (Feel?) She feels she didn't know why he's turning around and not looking at her. He walked away from her but he doesn't know why he left her.

Card 5: A lady's opening the door. She's trying to come in the room. I think she sees something. (Q. A lamp?) She's thinking about turning the lamp on. (Feel?) She feels like she doesn't know why she's going to turn the lamp on. (End?) She turned off the lamp, closed the door, and went back downstairs.

Card 7GF: A girl is holding the baby. The mother is looking at her and she wonders what she's doing. She's thinking about training the baby so she'll grow up and be a young lady. (Feel?) Happy because she has a baby and because she'll become a young lady. (End?) She put the baby down.

Card 8BM: What is this, a body? It's a body all right. This boy is thinking of something—to become a killer. He became a ... had a knife and cut the person because he wanted proof—a piece of the man's skin because he wanted everyone in the town to know he was the one that captured him. (Feel?) He feels glad that the killer is dead. (Before?) He tried to kill the person who captured him but he set a trap for him.

Protocol 85

Card 1: Once there was a boy who was doing some music lessons. Before, he was doing his math and he didn't want to go to music class. The teacher made him go to music class. He got an "F" for not doing what he was told. He's in second grade. (Feel?) Glum, sad. He was thinking, "I want to finish my arithmetic." He didn't like music, he likes math. (End?) Every day after that he went to music. He never likes music class.

Card 2: One day some people were working on the farm—a girl, a mom and dad, and a horse. A girl went off to school. Later, a car came and went right past, missed her by an inch and her dog went splat. She studies arithmetic and stuff, then she goes home. (Feel?) Sad because her dog died. (Think?) That she will go home.

Card 3BM: A person banged his head on the ceiling and he went out cold. The boy one hour later woke up. He was in the cellar. (Feel?) Down in the dumps. (Think?) A tornado had come and hit their house. (End?) The tornado came and ripped off the roof of the house.

Card 4: The wife is hugging the husband. (Before?) The wife walked up to the man. Before that the wife entered through the door. (Feel?) Sad because they're having—the mother and father are going to get divorced. (Think?) That they are going to get divorced. (End?) They get divorced.

Card 5: A lady is scolding her child. He broke the kitchen window with a baseball while playing. He batted it too far and too low. The boy gets put to bed without supper. The end. (Feel?) The boy is mad because he didn't get supper. (Think?) He was thinking, "I want to leave. I can't wait to leave this house." He runs away.

Card 7GF: The girl's grandmother—the girl is looking out the window. She's waiting for her grandson. The girl just turned 12 and she is celebrating her birthday by bringing one of her cousins over. (Feel?) Grateful. (Who?) The grandma ... because her grandson came over.

(Think?) That the grandson will never show up. (End?) They celebrate her birthday and she gets lots of presents.

Card 8BM: They're operating on a boy for his own good. If they don't, his appendix will burst. The other boy is just turning away because he doesn't want to see blood. (Feel?) Sad. (Who?) The boy who is getting his appendix out. (Think?) The doctors think, "If we don't get that appendix out the boy's gonna die." (End?) They get the appendix out and the boy lives.

Protocol 111

Card 1: He's sad because he's too young to play the violin. He had bought a violin and the music teacher said he wasn't old enough to play it. (Think?) He's thinking that he can play the violin. (End?) The music teacher teaches him and he's able to play the violin.

Card 2: A man's plowing the fields and a woman is standing under the tree to get some shade and a woman is going to school. They feel happy because they have a whole bunch of seeds to plant. (Before?) They were poor. He had a lot of horses and sold all but one and then they bought a farm and they lived happily ever after.

Card 3BM: A girl is crying because she has to go to her room because she didn't listen to her mother and she's feeling sad. She's thinking her mother is the meanest person in the world. (End?) She gets to come down from her room and watch TV and go out and play.

Card 4: The man—someone busted into his house and now he's mad because they took some of his gold and precious jewels. He's going to go get the person who did it and his wife is trying to hold him back. Then she calms him down and he gets over it within two days. (Think?) He had totally forgot about it and doesn't think about it at all.

Card 5: A lady, she heard a gunshot and she walked over and opened the door and she sees her son on the floor and she starts walking toward him and a man jumps out from behind the door and puts a gun in her back and says, "Don't move or I'll shoot you." The man says, "Give me all your gold and jewels or I'll shoot." She gives him all the gold and jewels and he runs out and gets in a car and drives away. When her husband comes home he felt real mad because the man had taken his jewels. (Think?) He was thinking that he'd go find the man and kill him. (End?) The man goes out and finds the man and shoots him and he goes to jail for the rest of his life (the husband goes to jail).

Card 7GF: She's her mother and she's talking to her daughter because her daughter wants to get a job babysitting and everybody thought she wasn't experienced enough. Her mother says, "It's alright if you don't get a job at first." (Feel?) Her mother feels sad that she didn't get one and her daughter is feeling mad. (Think?) Her mother thinks that she's going to get a job before she's 14 and she'll be 14 in two weeks. The 13-year-old thinks she's not going to get one because everyone says she's inexperienced. (End?) She gets a job.

Card 8BM: They were driving to the country one day and they had an accident and the son was wearing seat belts and he did not get hurt. The man got hurt because he went through the windshield and they had to go to the hospital and the doctors had to operate on him and the son was feeling bad. (Think?) He's thinking his father is going to die, but the doctors keep telling them he's going to be all right. His father gets all right and they go on another trip and have a nice trip. (Why did the son feel bad when he thought his father might die?) Well, he thought he might not have any more trips.

Protocol 32

Card 1: He's looking at a violin, probably studying it. He's probably in the school band and got interested in the violin. He probably joins the band and plays along. He probably thinks his parents are proud of him for being a musician. And he wants to keep playing because he wants his parents to feel proud. He didn't like the violin and he quits and he's thinking about what to do, what else so his parents will be proud. He'll try another instrument that he likes to play and then he'll be happy and they will be happy too.

Card 2: A girl has these books in her hand. The other woman is looking at the guy with the horse. I think she's (the one with books) jealous of the other one (by the tree) because she doesn't have to do work and just watches. She probably asks the other one what she's doing and she'll probably do her work later and watch and they get to know each other and she's not jealous anymore because they're friends now.

Card 3BM: Looks like someone hurt his feelings so he's just there until he stops crying. Someone called him names. He ignores the people who called him names and goes with another crowd who are his friends. He plays with his friends, not the ones calling him names. He thinks about what he should do to prevent them from calling him names. He will probably have to think about it for a while before he finds a solution.

Card 4: The guy and lady—probably the guy was going out with his girlfriend and she came in and she was surprised because she saw him with this other girl. Then he probably has to break up with both of them because they'll both be mad at him. The girl feels that he likes the other better. They probably both find other guys and he'll find a different girl. This time he has just one girlfriend so this won't happen again.

Card 5: A lady comes in to look around, probably came in to check on something like her sons. So, when she checked in they weren't there, so she checked the other rooms. They're outside and probably didn't do their chores and that's why she's looking for them. When she finds them they get punished for not doing their chores. Now they have to stay inside until they do their chores. The boys feel dumb that they went outside and forgot their chores because they had got excited because all their friends were outside and they wanted to join the fun. The woman thought the boys were ignoring the chores because they wanted her to do them. They tell her why they went outside and what happened and their mother understands and lets them go back outside when they're finished the chores.

Card 7GF: This is probably the mother reading a story to her while she's sitting there. The girl was distracted from her mother reading—probably got distracted by a noise in the house. Her mother noticed the noise also while she was reading so they went on and tried to find what the noise was. The noise was the father coming home from work. He opened the door while the mother was reading. Before they were scared because they didn't know what the noise was; then they felt relieved that it was father. They said to the father not to just drop in like that because it scared them and if he said hello when he comes in then they wouldn't be scared. The father said he didn't want to interrupt the story but now he understands how they got scared and so the next time he says, "Hello, I'm home," when he comes in.

Card 8BM: The boy in the picture probably is worried about the man getting operated on. It's probably his grandfather and he's getting operated on just from old age. The boy feels worried because he might not survive. The grandfather also feels worried that he might die. I guess the boy's parents would be worried also because it would be the mom's dad. He survived the operation. After the operation, he was relieved.

Protocol 26

Card 1: Before, he was learning how to play a violin and kept practicing and practicing and still couldn't figure out how to get it right. And he's sad 'cause he couldn't do it. Later on he asks his teacher what he's doing wrong and his teacher tell him that he was reading some of the notes wrong and shows him how to do it. He plays it better after that and feels happier. (Think?) He was puzzled 'cause he couldn't figure out how to play it right.

Card 2: A girl lives on a farm and is going to school. She tries to read well 'cause her mother and father are working real hard to put her through school. She feels happy that her parents are doing that for her but she also feels bad that they have to work so hard. (Before?) The girl wasn't doing very well in school and her parents got angry 'cause she wasn't doing well 'cause they thought she wasn't trying. She tells them that she was trying. After they talk for a while she says she'll try to do better. (Turn Out?) When the girl finishes school she gets a good job 'cause she's good at some things and she does do better in school. With some of the money she earns she gives some to her parents and they don't have to work so hard on the farm.

Card 3BM: It's a girl and she had a fight with her mother and she's sad and crying. She got into a fight 'cause she wanted to go out and her mother wouldn't let her. She thought her mother was being mean and she thinks she should be able to go. The mother and daughter have a talk and the mother lets her go out. The daughter realizes that her mother was not being mean but she was concerned about her going out too much. The daughter thinks she'll do something special for the mother because she was so understanding.

Card 4: This man is mad at somebody and the girl is trying to hold him back from hitting somebody. He's very angry, but she stops him and he decides not to hurt the person, but to talk things out. (Before?) The guy the person's mad at stole some money and even though he came back and gave him the money, the guy was still angry with him. The guy who took the money felt guilty so he brought the money back. He took it because he didn't have enough money to feed his family because he was out of work. After they talk, the man in the picture helps the guy find a job and everyone feels relieved.

Card 5: This is a mother and she told her daughter to go in the living room to do her homework. And when she went in she saw that her daughter was watching TV. She was mad and she yelled at the girl; then she felt sad because she found out that the girl had already finished her work. The girl was not mad at her mother because she understood it looked like she wasn't doing her work. (Think?) The girl was thinking her mother shouldn't have said all that stuff, but she understood.

Card 7GF: The girl just got a new doll and she was showing it to her friends. Now she's talking to her mother and about the doll and what her friends said about the doll and they both feel happy. (Think?) That the doll is really pretty. The mother had two other daughters and she liked the doll so well she got two for her other daughters. Then they all play with the dolls together and have fun.

Card 8BM: Okay, this is the boy's father and he is being operated on. The boy is scared 'cause he thinks his father is going to die. The man is happy 'cause he thinks that operation is going to help him. At the end, the disease is cured and both are happy. (Before?) The boy's mother had the same disease and she died and he was worried that might happen again. The doctors feel good 'cause they were able to cure the disease.

Protocol 87

Card 1: He's wondering if he has to practice the violin. He does not want to play it. It gets boring. (Before?) He was wondering if he has to do it. (Feel?) Unhappy ... that he has to practice every day for three hours. He wishes he didn't have to do it. (End?) He didn't play it.

Card 2: She is feeling good because she doesn't like to do the work. She is feeling good because she doesn't have to do the work. Sometimes she feels sorry for the slaves for doing the work ... and thinks sometimes that she should help. (Before?) She was walking home from school and going past the fields. (End?) She decides to help them. She does work that they think is very hard and she thinks it is easy.

Card 3BM: He is crying because he broke something of his brother's. He was playing with it very rough and he dropped it. His brother finds out and says, "It's alright; I can find a way to put it back together again." He felt better and he helped his brother put it back together with Krazy Glue. (Feel?) Happy and not so good (?) About breaking his brother's airplane. He was happy when his brother said it was alright and started to help. (Think?) It's a little alright if you break something if you admit you broke it.

Card 4: They are in love a lot. They're walking along, they met, they fell in love. They get married, they have eight children and they get a house and added a lot to it. (Feel?) Happy that they had the children. (Think?) That they wish they had six children or less.

Card 5: She's peeking in a room that has flowers, a lamp, a dresser, a table. She's wondering where the person who sleeps in there is ... drinking beer and all. He goes to this bar and she knows where it is and she goes there and she has a mean look on her face. She gets the boy who sleeps there and carries him all the way home. She puts him in bed and he sleeps like a baby and he never goes there again—ever. (Feel?) She was feeling very mad, because she loves him a lot and didn't want him involved in beer and all. (Think?) Where he could be, and when she remembers it she goes to the Cecil B. Bar.

Card 7GF: The woman is looking at her daughter. The daughter took some money from her mother's purse. She didn't know until she opened the purse and saw she was short of money. (Feel?) The woman is very mad but she is keeping her anger in. The daughter is feeling mad at herself for taking her mother's money because she has to go to her room for four weeks. The daughter starts to feel good because her mother let her go before the time was up. She never steals money again from her mother in her whole life.

Card 8BM: A guy got shot and they're trying to get the bullet out. The guy who did it felt sad because he's going to die and he just wanted to shoot him, not kill him. (Before?) The guy was trying to kill him and he had to defend himself and he had to shoot him in the stomach. They were fighting because one got mad at his brother and killed him and he's very mad at the guy who killed his brother. (End?) He lives and the guy still feels sad and mad because someone killed his brother. The guy who got shot and the guy become friends and fight crimes together.

Protocol 67

Card 1: Looks like this kid he plays the violin and really doesn't like it but he has to. He's going to go to a strings concert the next day. He'll be in the first row. After the first song, he'll have to do a solo. His parents are going to be there and his school. Looks like he doesn't know how to play. He's going to tape someone else playing the song and pretend he's playing. The night comes, he goes up to do his song, he starts the tape recorder and it's a cello playing. The conductor gets really mad. He talks to the guy after and says, "You're in detention." He wants to quit but his mom won't let him. He's trying to figure out the notes and he can't because the conductor quits and his mom hires someone else. Now he has lessons every afternoon and every morning. His mom is really mad because he's not learning and the person she hired is real discouraged. At the end, he breaks his violin so he can't play anymore.

Card 2: There's a lady about 20 and she went to elementary school and her husband worked in the fields while her mother watched him. He has this horse and the girl likes to ride it a lot. She really hates school and wants to ride the horse. Then they sell the horse to a glue factory. Then she goes out to buy white Elmer's Glue and starts to cry in the store. So they go out and buy another white horse. But they don't like it. So she buys the horse back from the glue company and she doesn't go back to school.

Card 3BM: This is the person in the army. They're laying on the bench because he's so tired from hauling stuff. He just parachuted out of an airplane into this camp and he forgot his keys so he can't get into his tent. He's sad because he can't get in so he takes a knife and cuts the side so he can get in. There was a sniper attack and they shoot his arm and he has to keep it on a bench. He shoots the sniper. Now he's sleeping. He goes into the operating room and something goes wrong and he dies.

Card 4: This looks like a movie where this one guy who's a detective. He's working for this lady and he's trying to catch this one guy but the lady is hanging on to him. She really doesn't want him to go and get shot. He goes and tackles the guy. The other guy gets sent to the jail. Then the lady fires him 'cause he's being a real jerk and she didn't want him to do it. Then he gets hired to find someone else's wife. He goes to the movies and sees her (the wife) on the screen. He goes to Hollywood and tracks her down and tells her husband. The guy comes to Hollywood and they live there from then on. The detective goes to New York and gets hired by other people.

Card 5: This looks like a nurse that's at home. She's coming in to check on the guy that's sick. The guy that's sick is a millionaire. She sees the respirator is off, so she turns it back on but it's too late because the guy's dead already. In the will the guy left equal parts of the money to his servants and she goes tracking the other guys who got it and robs them of their money. Then someone finds out and goes over to the guy's house and shoots her. They hire a detective and he goes to hospitals and checks bullet wounds in people. She goes to jail and stays there the rest of her life for stealing so much money. She felt real bad because she wanted all the money and when she goes to jail she feels bad because she was pushed around and she tries to pay the fee but she doesn't have any money. Then she's bullied around for the rest of her life.

Card 7GF: This looks like a lady and she's trying to teach the little girl and she won't listen because she's playing with her little monkey. The lady gets real mad and tells the little girl's mom. The mom is real mad because she wants her to learn so she sends her to boarding school. The girl doesn't want to go so she hides in her room. Her parents move and they don't know she's there. The people who own the house now don't know who she is. Finally, one kid went into the room and she didn't know her name anymore so they started to call her the little girl and then she starts to teach their kids math and spelling and stuff. (Think?) Probably she's thinking what her parents are thinking and why if they would make her go to boarding school.

Card 8BM: This is this guy cleaning his musket and the powder blew a hole in his side and a doctor looked at the wound and could see the guy's stomach. They fed him food and his stomach would move. When they gave him alcohol and pepper his stomach would turn red. When the doctor saw he was happy his stomach wouldn't do anything. When sad—there was too much acid and it would turn red. So doctors all over the world learned that emotions and different foods affect the stomach. He went around the world training people. The one in the front is the patient.

☐ Expert Scoring

Protocol 75, First-Grade Boy, High Empathy

Card 1: Internal, sad about not knowing how to play violin and takes responsibility for learning; PI = 4; MA = 5.

Card 2: Internal, feeling happy about having learned; PI = 3; MA = 4, girl engaged in purposeful activity, walking home from school, cares about the people she passes and about what she has learned.

Card 3BM: Internal, takes responsibility for feelings, thinks what to do before mother helps; PI = 3; MA = 4, tries to get up before being helped and initiates appropriate activity (autonomy).

Card 4: Internal; PI = 1, the narrator does not account for the intense emotions on the man's face and minimizes the tension but does attempt to explain the difference between the emotions of the man and the woman and this is reflected in the MA code; MA = 4, characters are differentiated and care about each other.

Card 5: Internal; PI = 3, good match with the stimulus and shows awareness of psychological process but coordination of the stimulus with the unfolding story is not precise; MA = 4, not a functional exchange, they talk at the dinner table and the woman who made dinner also reads books.

Card 7GF: External; PI = 1; MA = 2, individuality and relatedness pertain to the moment.

Card 8BM: Internal; PI = 3, foreground and background are distinct (figure in the front is in the observation room) but the relationship of the characters to one another is not clear; MA = 4, concern for the man's welfare and constructive action.

Protocol 90, First-Grade Girl, Low Empathy

Card 1: External, the concern is with getting a new toy; PI = 2, tension does not involve the boy and the violin and a related psychological process; MA = 2, no initiative or autonomy as the story begins and ends with the boy sitting and staring at the violin.

Card 2: External; PI = 1, use of stimulus suggests problems organizing the scene (narrator lists the man, a horse and a lady as farmers and identifies the woman on the right as a statue). The response is a series of associations to the scene that is not cohesively organized. The farmer schema includes a horse along with humans, and, of course, farmers plant. This card requires the narrator to explain the character's individuality and relate them in some way; MA = 2, a man, horse, lady, and statue seem interchangeable as the narrator describes the stimulus without making these distinctions, no individual purposes or viewpoints.

Card 3BM: External, trivial behaviors are punished without considering intentions and resolution depends on external change; PI = 2; MA = 2, people are obstacles, disparity in mutuality and limited autonomy.

Card 4: External, not dealing with inner tensions portrayed and happiness comes from external source, going on a trip; PI = 1; MA = 2.

Card 5: External, series of actions and counteractions on the same theme without a strategy for resolving the conflict other than reliance on external authority; PI = 2; MA = 2, a coercive interaction but not extreme helplessness.

Card 7GF: External, emotion provoked by being hit, no purpose, need for external restraint; PI = 1, neither the tension nor age difference is recognized; MA = 1.

Card 8M: External; PI = 1; MA = 1.

Protocol 53, Second-Grade Girl, High Empathy

Card 1: Internal, PI = 3; MA = 5.

Card 2: Internal, PI = 4; MA = 5.

Card 3BM: Internal; PI = 4; MA = 5.

Card 4: Internal; PI = 4; MA = 5, Bob took initiative in saying he did not want to fight and was not merely restrained by Michelle. Therefore, he made his own decision rather than merely comply (autonomy).

Card 5: Internal, the woman stuck to her belief and in time others saw her point; PI = 3, explain; MA = 5, patience, constructive action and support from others (husband and authorities) eventually overcomes external obstacles and concern about not being believed.

Card 7GF: Internal, lesson learned by a spoiled girl; PI = 3, tension recognized but not a precise match to the scene; MA = 5, a near tragedy leads a child to realize that parental rules have reasons and if rules are followed everyone is happy. The child wants to be autonomous and tests limits but does what is right after becoming convinced.

Card 8BM: Internal; PI = 3, explanation of the scene is not precise in terms of foreground and background; MA = 4, family members share the concern of the boy in the foreground. Indeed, the spontaneous introduction of family members indicates a network of relatedness that may warrant an MA score of 5.

Protocol 114, Second-Grade Boy, Low Empathy

Card 1: External, happy that he saw the violin but no indication of inner purpose; PI = 1, narrator merely follows the storytelling directions and does not recognize the tension in the task implied by the scene; MA = 2.

Card 2: External, everyone acts in accord with their depiction in the stimulus with no inner life; PI = 2; MA = 3, though characters are distinguished on the basis of how they look in the stimulus, without inner attributes (ordinarily a 2), there is also a sentence about them growing their own food, suggesting some autonomy.

Card 3BM: External, PI = 2, no specific feeling is identified, except a physical state of being tired, and there is no rationale; MA = 2.

Card 4: External, describes what is in the picture in physical terms; PI = 1, does not recognize emotion, just physical act of looking at something; MA = 2.

Card 5: External, nothing beyond cues from picture; PI = 2, no emotion is attributed to the woman who is described by physical actions; MA = 2.

Card 7GF: External; PI = 1, basic tension not recognized, holding the baby and looking; MA = 2, no autonomy is recognized as the baby will grow up to be a "young lady" with no individual characteristics.

Card 8BM: External, narrative is reactive to cues, purpose of the action is to become a hero—an external outcome; PI = 1; MA = 1, imbalance of autonomy as one is killed and the other is a hero.

Protocol 85, Second-Grade Boy, Low Empathy

Card 1: External, reacts to outside pressure; PI = 2; MA = 2, coerced by others, the boy has no autonomous resources.

Card 2: External; PI = 1, although the narrator refers to a family in the background related to the girl in the foreground (typically a 2), there is a disorganized, haphazard accounting of the stimulus (listing the horse among people on the farm); MA = 1, disorganized, detached, her dog dies but the girl continues on her way to school.

Card 3BM: External; PI = 2; MA = 2.

Card 4: External, very concrete sequence; PI = 1; MA = 2, no recognition of individuality.

Card 5: External; PI = 2; MA = 2.

Card 7GF: External; PI = 2; MA = 2, what people want from each other.

Card 8BM: External; PI = 2, piecemeal treatment of the scene, no explanation for the presence of the boy in the front—it is the patient and not the onlooker who is sad; MA = 2.

Protocol 111, Fifth-Grade Boy, Low Empathy

Card 1: External, authority decides if he is old enough to play; PI = 3; MA = 3.

Card 2: External, stereotypic; PI = 2, psychological process of the various characters is not considered; MA = 2.

Card 3BM: External; PI = 3; MA = 2, waits out her punishment without concern for the relationship.

Card 4: External; PI = 3, MA = 2, held back by his wife, the man forgets about his intense feelings and does not take legitimate action such as calling the police.

Card 5: External, concern with stolen jewels, the son who has been shot is not mentioned again; PI = 2, woman reactive to gunshot, rushes to open the door without caution or other intervening thought process; MA = 1, lack of concern for the son, disorganized and detached.

Card 7GF: External, the concern with having a job is akin to acquiring a possession as there is no understanding that lack of experience may cause harm; PI = 2; MA = 2, an interpersonal responsibility is treated as a possession (having a job).

Card 8BM: External, basic concern is about trips; PI = 3; MA = 2.

Protocol 32, Fifth-Grade Boy, High Empathy

Card 1: Internal, coordinates what his parents want with what he wants; PI = 4; MA = 5, he is not coerced but wants his parents to feel proud—so mutuality of autonomy.

Card 2: Internal, concern with the relationship and overcoming jealous feelings—message is things are not what they seem outside; PI = 3, how the characters are related to each other is not clear; MA = 4.

Card 3BM: Internal, takes responsibility for the feeling, even in the first sentence, he's just there until he stops crying; PI = 4; MA = 5 because of the high level of autonomy.

Card 4: Internal, takes responsibility for the relationship; PI = 4; MA = 5, trust in a relationship is important and it takes time to learn one's lesson.

Card 5: Internal, motives and intentions behind actions are important to both parties; PI = 4; MA = 5.

Card 7GF: Internal, intentions are salient and well developed; PI = 4; MA = 5.

Card 8BM: Internal, worried about another's welfare; PI = 3, relation of foreground and background not explained; MA = 5, combine many perspectives of individuals who shared the worry.

Protocol 26, Fifth-Grade Girl, High Empathy

Card 1: Internal; PI = 4; MA = 5.

Card 2: Internal, intent is salient, communication around emotion, acceptance of limitations and strengths, taking responsibility for helping others; PI = 4; MA = 5.

Card 3BM: Internal, intent is important, wants to reciprocate for mother's understanding; PI = 4; MA = 5, characters value each other's perspectives.

Card 4: Internal, intentions are salient, the thief has a good reason and feels guilty; PI = 4; MA = 5.

Card 5: Internal; PI = 4; MA = 5.

Card 7GF: External; PI = 1; MA = 3, characters are happy talking to each other about the doll.

Card 8BM: Internal; PI = 3; MA = 4, characters' views are well differentiated, the boy's worry is explained in terms of his prior experience.

Protocol 87, Third-Grade Boy, Low Empathy

Card 1: External; PI = 2, does not recognize purpose for playing the violin, simply bored and doesn't want to play; MA = 2, relationship of boy to the expectation of playing the violin is simply not to play. Others' expectations are coercive (not reciprocal) and intentions are not considered.

Card 2: External, good feelings come from avoidance of work or from doing easy work that others think is hard; PI = 2, naive psychological process; MA = 2, giving help aggrandizes the giver and seems to demean the recipient.

Card 3BM: External, though concerned with having broken his brother's toy, he only feels better when his brother says it is all right and it is the brother who initiates gluing the toy together; PI = 4; MA = 3.

Card 4: External; PI = 1; MA = 2.

Card 5: External, compliance is due to external pressure and intentions are stereotyped, lacking insight; PI = 3; MA = 2.

Card 7GF: External, actions are regretted after being punished, intentions are not relevant (Message: if you can't get away with something, you won't do it); PI = 2; MA = 2, response to coercion.

Card 8BM: External, feelings and actions are provoked, not internally organized; PI = 2, difficulty with psychological process (intentions are stated, and concern is expressed for the patient but these are highly simplistic and stereotyped); MA = 2, people seem to be interchangeable as neither character answers to society for shooting/killing someone and the man who killed the protagonist's brother joins him in fighting crime.

Protocol 67, Sixth-Grade Boy, Low Empathy

Card 1: External, note external resolution of breaking his violin; PI = 2; MA = 2.

Card 2: External, characters act and react to their immediate impulse or external circumstance, with no plan, or intent; PI = 1, the premise of the story is not compatible with the stimulus, the girl is identified as 20 years old who goes to elementary school (thus, the identified tension has an implausible relationship with the stimulus configuration); MA = 2.

Card 3BM: External; PI = 1; MA = 1.

Card 4: External; PI = 1; MA = 1.

Card 5: External; PI = 2, checking in on a guy who is sick is a good match with the stimulus but then the concern departs from this initial premise and turns to getting the guy's money. Thus, the translation of the scene is considered literal because the narrator is not able to develop the story in tune with the initial intent of the character; MA = 1 (character ends up helpless).

Card 7GF: External; PI = 2, the initial differentiation of the tension is a good fit but the remainder of the story is composed of immediate reactions that are not informed by psychological process; MA = 2, short-term relatedness, relationships are not enduring; understanding social causality is restricted by problems with logic and these limit autonomy and mutuality.

Card 8BM: External, a doctor takes advantage of an opportunity to become well known (external outcome) without considering the welfare of his patient (principle); PI = 1, the stimulus configuration is not a good fit (the surgery scene is defined in an unusual way, there is no hole evident in the man's stomach, as an afterthought, the boy in the front is referred to as the patient without otherwise explaining his presence in the scene); MA = 2, no concern for the patient who is at the mercy of the self-serving physician. Although the patient presumably survives (appears in the foreground of the pictured scene), much of the story deals with the physician's experimentation on the patient without considering his individuality.

☐ References

Blankman, C., Teglasi, H., & Lawser, M. (2002). Thematic apperception, narrative schemas, and literacy. *Journal of Psychoeducational Assessment, 20,* 268–289.

Dana, R. H. (1959). Proposal for objective scoring of the TAT. *Perceptual and Motor Skills, 9,* 27–43.

Locraft, C., & Teglasi, H. (1997). Teacher rated empathic behaviors and children's T.A.T. stories. *Journal of School Psychology, 35,* 217–237.

Kalliopuska, M. (1982). Empathy measured by Rorschach and TAT. *British Journal of Projective Psychology & Personality Study, 27,* no. 2, 5–11.

Lohr, L. B., Teglasi, H., & French, M. (2004). Schemas and temperament as risk factors for emotional disability. *Personality and Individual Differences, 36,* 1637–1654.

Murray, H. A. (1943). *Thematic Apperception Test manual.* Cambridge, MA: Harvard University Press.

Teglasi, H. (1993). *Clinical use of storytelling.* Boston: Allyn and Bacon.

Teglasi, H. (2001). *Essentials of TAT and other storytelling instruments assessment.* New York: Wiley.

Teglasi, H. (2001*). Essentials of TAT and other storytelling instruments assessm*ent. New York: Wiley.

Urist, J. (1977). The Rorschach test and the assessment of object relations. *Journal of Personality Assessment, 41,* 3–9.

32

CHAPTER

The Adult Attachment Projective

David Joubert

Abstract

This chapter reviews the development, validation, and use of the Adult Attachment Projective (AAP) (George, West, & Pettem, 1997). The AAP is a projective instrument designed to provide a valid assessment of adult attachment states of mind, as conceptualized by Bowlby (1969). The AAP consists of a set of eight pictures depicting situations that activate the attachment behavioral system, such as loss of an attachment figure or physical threat to the self. The individual is asked to make up a story based on the pictures, and specific probes are used to ensure that essential elements are included in the story. Research evidence to date provides strong support for the reliability and validity of the AAP. Results of studies looking at interrater reliability and construct validity have been especially impressive. The use of the AAP in psychological assessment is illustrated using an actual clinical case.

Description of the System

Conceptual Framework

Attachment theory (Bowlby, 1969, 1973, 1980) is concerned about the ways that early relationships with primary caregivers contribute to the development of one's personality, adaptation, and emotional well-being. Attachment is conceptualized as a biobehavioral system designed to promote proximity with the caregivers in times of stress, in such a way as to optimize emotional regulation (Sroufe, 1988). Research over the past three decades has provided strong support for Bowlby's original hypotheses. Attachment has been linked to a wide variety of outcomes and appears to influence functioning in many areas, including cognitive, social, and emotional development, in both adults and children (Main, 1995; Thompson, 1999). The link between internal representations of attachment figures and relationships and various forms of psychopathology in adults is well established (see review by Dozier, Stovall, & Albus, 1999). In addition, several papers have been published in recent years that describe clinical applications of attachment theory with a range of populations and problems (Eagle, 1997; Fonagy et al., 1996).

One area of interest for attachment-oriented researchers and clinicians concerns the assessment of individual differences relative to Bowlby's (1969, 1973) concept of internal working models of attachment relationships. Because caregivers respond differently to infant's expressed needs for proximity, attachment researchers have theorized that the caregiver's response patterns become integrated into the child's developing psyche as a representational template for predicting and interpreting parental behavior in response to this child's attachment needs. Bowlby (1973, 1988) proposed that this template would serve as an integral part of the individual's personality and would determine the person's typical response to stressful situations and relationships.

Ainsworth, Blehar, Waters, and Wall's (1978) seminal work with children using the strange situation procedure documents the presence of specific patterns of child attachment behavior and caregiver's response in mother–infant dyads. Secure children demonstrate a capacity to express needs for proximity with caregivers in a clear and modulated way. Upon reunion following separation with the attachment figure, the child is soothed and can return to exploration and play within a short period of time. Cross-sectional and longitudinal research has shown that secure children generally show higher levels of functioning or development compared with insecure children (Grossmann, Grossmann, & Waters, 2005; Sroufe, Egeland, Carlson, & Collins, 2005; Thompson, 1999). Their behavior in the strange situation is thought to reflect an internalization of caregivers as available and responsive (Sroufe & Fleeson, 1986).

Insecure children, on the other hand, exhibit behaviors that suggest defensive interference in attachment-related situations (Bretherton, 2005; George & West, 1999; Solomon, George, & De Jong, 1995). Insecure-avoidant children attempt to limit their interactions with the caregiver as a way to avoid experiencing distress related to the attachment figure's unwillingness or inability to respond to their signals for proximity. Insecure-ambivalent children, on the other hand, both desire and resist proximity and soothing from the attachment figure. Paradoxically, insecure-ambivalent children can express much distress during separation with the parent. It is the incapacity to be soothed or comforted by the caregiver that distinguishes this group.

Another attachment configuration in children, historically identified later by Main and Solomon (1990), is composed of children for whom organized attachment patterns (e.g., secure, avoidant, ambivalent) are undermined throughout the strange situation by behavioral disorganization, dysregulation, and conflict, such as freezing, approach/avoidant conflict behavior, withdrawal, failure to recognize the attachment figure, and trance-like states. These signs of attachment disorganization often appear especially during the moments of reunion following separation from the attachment figure. This attachment group is termed *disorganized*. The disorganized group has been found to be significantly at risk for negative outcomes in a variety of developmental areas, including cognitive, interpersonal, emotional, and physical. Not surprisingly, disorganized infants and children are overrepresented in clinical populations (see review by Lyons-Ruth & Jacobvitz, 1999).

Although research looking at attachment in children has been progressing steadily for several decades, interest for attachment-related processes in adults is relatively new by comparison. Bowlby (1969) and Ainsworth (Ainsworth et al., 1978) believed that an individual's attachment history is an important building block for personality development and therefore remains relevant from the cradle to the grave (Bowlby, 1969). According to attachment theorists, early interactions with caregivers become internalized as representations or models of relationships (internalized working models), which can then be used to predict and understand social interactions, especially those involving close emotional bonds or intimacy. Such representational models tend to remain stable over the person's life, although significant evidence exists that such models can and do change over time (Fonagy, 1999; Waters, Merrick, Treboux, Crowell, & Abersheim, 2000). A thorough assessment of attachment can be of considerable research or clinical interests because it provides the professional an empirically established conceptual lens to better understand the meaning of interpersonal behavior in terms of attachment processes (e.g., proximity seeking) related to the individual's past experiences with caregivers. One implication of attachment theory, consistent with other theoretical formulations (e.g., object-relations theory), is that such models will determine the individual's behavior in current relationships with significant others, thus accounting for existence of phenomena such as transference in therapeutic work or partner selection and processes in adult relationships.

Part of the challenge of examining internal models of attachment in adults for clinical or research purposes lies in selecting a form of assessment that is appropriate for the construct. A construct-appropriate assessment of attachment in adult and adolescent populations must consider the following points: (1) attachment in adults consists of a set of internal representations, which exist in a more or less integrated form in the individual's psyche; and (2) attachment-related internal processes (i.e., thoughts, fantasies, affects, defensive exclusion) are more likely to be accessible when the individual's attachment behavioral system is activated. Such considerations clearly make certain forms of assessment more relevant than others.

The search for a reliable and valid method for assessing attachment in adults has been the object of considerable attention in the literature for the past two decades. Work has focused primarily in two areas: (1) the assessment of attachment-related cognitions and self-reported perceptions using paper–pencil questionnaires; and (2) the assessment of representational models of attachment relationships using unstructured or semistructured methods.

The use of self-report questionnaires to assess attachment has stemmed from the work of social psychologists such as Hazan and Shaver (1987) and Bartholomew and Horowitz (1991) looking at the construct of romantic attachment. A large number of such questionnaires now exist in the literature, and recent evidence suggests that these self-report measures tap into similar romantic attachment constructs (see Crowell, Fraley, & Shaver, 1999). That is, scores obtained on those instruments appear to reflect conscious perceptions of self and others, relative experiences of anxiety in interpersonal relationships, and management of distress through behavioral avoidance. Unfortunately, self-report questionnaires tend to correlate better with other self-report data than with other outcomes (e.g., observations, peer or parent report, physiological markers), which makes their validity questionable for the purpose of assessing a construct such as adult attachment, whose foundations lie in the individual's internal representations of early relationships (Waters, Crowell, Elliott, Corcoran, & Treboux, 2002). Further, these measures were designed following Ainsworth, Blehar, Waters, and Wall, (1978) original infant attachment model, poorly assess disorganized attachment, and do not adequately integrate theory or research in attachment on adults (George & West, 1999; West & George, 1999).

A more fruitful approach to the assessment of adult attachment, as conceptualized by Bowlby (1969, 1973) and others, is represented through the use of narrative and semistructured techniques employed to access the individual's representational world. Among these techniques, the Adult Attachment Interview (AAI) George, Kaplan, & Main, 1985) is considered the gold standard for the assessment of attachment in adults. The AAI is a semistructured interview covering various aspects of the individual's relationships with his or her primary caregivers. The interview is designed to assess current representational structures and states of mind relative to attachment by eliciting autobiographical memories concerning attachment-related experiences. Information obtained during the interview is not considered factual; rather, the main focus of interest lies in the individual's capacity to use autobiographical memory to inform current representations of attachment relationships. The classification system focuses on coherence of discourse when the individual discusses attachment with attachment figures.

The AAI uses a classification system that is designed to assess conceptually categories as developed by Ainsworth (1978) and Main and Solomon (1990) in their research with infant–mother dyads. Secure-autonomous individuals are characterized by a coherent discourse and complex, well-integrated representations of attachment figures. This is illustrated, for example, by their capacity to present balanced, reality-based descriptions of primary caregivers and by the presence of metacognitive activity throughout their discourse. Individuals classified as dismissing tend to present with difficulties providing descriptions of attachment figures that are informed by autobiographical memory. They frequently report an incapacity to recall specific attachment-related events, tend to minimize the importance of early attachment relationships, or provide unrealistic, idealized descriptions of caregivers. Preoccupied individuals appear to be highly ambivalent about attachment relationships. Their descriptions of relationships with primary caregivers lack coherence and are poorly integrated. They may experience confusion or appear enmeshed with past relationships with caregivers. Last, individuals classified as unresolved with respect to loss or trauma show manifestations of behavioral, affective or cognitive dysregulation when discussing relationships with early attachment figures. Such manifestations might include, for example, disorientation or signs of dissociative process, discourse manifestations that are interpreted similarly to the interferences in attachment behavior observed in disorganized infants.

There has been abundant research using the AAI over the past 25 years, a full description of which goes beyond the scope of this chapter (see overview by Hesse, 1999). What is evident from using the AAI, however, is that it is costly to use in terms of time of administration and coding. This contributed to a search for alternative ways of measuring attachment, leading to the development of numerous self-report questionnaires, as described earlier. It is also evident that there are other important attachment-related constructs that the AAI does not measure. Evaluation of idealization or the inability to recall childhood experience, for example, does not provide specific information about the defensive exclusion processes that lead to idealized images of attachment figures or memory interferences. Carol George and Malcolm West have developed a method that identifies the same basic AAI attachment groups, preserves attachment theory's emphasis on representational structures and process-oriented analysis of discourse, examines attachment-derived operationally defined defensive processes, and is more user friendly than the AAI.

Projective methods have traditionally played an important role in the assessment of attachment in children. In 1972, Hansburg described the Separation Anxiety Test (SAT), which used pictures similar to the TAT to evaluate responses to separation in older children and adolescents. Subsequently, Klagsbrun and Bowlby (1976) modified the SAT for use with younger children. This tradition is still very much alive as researchers have continued to develop projective assessments, including further modifications of the SAT (e.g., Slough, Goyette, & Greenberg, 1988) and doll-play story-stem methods (e.g., Bretherton, Ridgeway, & Cassidy, 1990; Solomon, George, & De Jong, 1995) to evaluate individual differences in attachment representations in children. However, development of similar methods to evaluate attachment in adults or older adolescents has not been undertaken until recently.

Stimuli

George, West, and Pettem (1997) used their extensive knowledge of attachment theory and projective testing to build a coding system that addresses content, process, and linguistic aspects of narratives obtained from exposure to a set of cards visually depicting attachment-related situations. The Adult Attachment Projective (AAP) includes eight pictures that are presented to the individual in a predetermined sequence. The first picture is a neutral scenario depicting two children playing ball and is intended as a warm-up for the other cards. The remaining cards describe seven attachment scenes:

- "Child at Window" depicts a child with her back turned to the viewer, looking out of a window.
- "Departure" presents two characters, man and woman, facing each other with suitcases next to them.
- "Bench" depicts a person sitting alone on a bench.
- "Bed" shows a child lying in bed with his arms forward and an adult character sitting at the end of the bed.
- "Ambulance" depicts two characters, a child and an older woman, looking out of window at an ambulance outside.
- "Cemetery" shows a man standing in front of a grave.
- "Corner" illustrates a child standing in a corner, his head turned with an arm extended forward.

The AAP cards were specifically designed to elicit attachment-related states of mind, and for this purpose the level of detail in the background (i.e., the environment surrounding the characters) was kept to a minimum. In addition, facial features were omitted from the drawings to heighten the level of ambiguity and facilitate the expression of projective material. The administration sequence activated the attachment behavioral system in a way that is analogous to the separation from the caregiver and introduction of a stranger episodes during the strange situation. The visual themes that compose the AAP set relate to events that are known to elicit attachment, such as separation, threat, illness, or death.

Administration

The administration is similar to that of the apperceptive class of projective techniques in general, although there is a more structured component based on the presence of specific probes and instructions. Individuals are presented with the cards one at a time and are told to create a story based on their perception of what is happening in the picture, what led to the scene, what might happen next, and what the characters are thinking or feeling. The interviewer uses probes corresponding to these elements (present, past, future, character's internal states) to ensure that they are present in the narrative.

Scoring Categories

The evaluation of attachment states of mind using the AAP focuses on three primary dimensions: (1) content; (2) discourse; and (3) defensive processes. The content dimension refers to specific features of the narrative and the characters included in it. The discourse dimension has to do with the way that the individual constructs the narrative and attempts to build a coherent plot. The defensive processes dimension refers to the manner in which attachment-related information may be excluded from the person's consciousness. An overview of scoring categories is included in Table 32.1.

TABLE 32.1 Adult Attachment Projective Scoring Categories

Content	Discourse
Agency	Coherency
0 = No agency	0 = Not coherent
1 = Capacity to act	1 = Moderately coherent
2 = Internalized Secure Base or Haven of Safety	2 = Highly coherent
Synchrony	Personal Experience
0 = No relationship described	0 = Absent
	1 = Present
1 = Failed synchrony, functional relationship	Defensive Functioning
2 = Synchrony, reciprocity-based relationship	Ds = Deactivation
Connectedness	E = Cognitive Disconnection
1 = Own activity	S.S. = Segregated Systems
2 = Not connected	(Resolved, Unresolved)
3 = Connected	

Content

The way that content features are considered varies according to the nature of the situation depicted on the card. Pictures presenting a character alone are coded according to the level of agency attributed to the character. The concept of agency refers to the individual's capacity to negotiate the activation of the attachment behavioral system, through summoning internal cognitive resources, receiving help or comfort from an attachment figure, or taking action. Three levels of agency are thus possible: (1) internalized secure base (use of internal resources as illustrated through the use of expressions such as *think about*) or haven of safety (use of an attachment figure); (2) capacity to act (use of action); or (3) absence of agency.

In addition, pictures depicting characters alone are assessed for the degree of connectedness shown in the narrative. This term refers to the degree to which relationships are desired and established by the character. Stories are examined to determine if connectedness is present, blocked, or simply not described (i.e., not an element in the story).

By contrast, pictures describing characters dyads are scored according to the level of synchrony included in the narrative. The concept of synchrony relates to the extent to which dyadic relationships are reciprocal, goal-corrected, attachment-caregiving relationships, following Bowlby (1969). Three levels are possible: (1) synchrony (evidence of a reciprocal, goal-corrected partnership between the characters); (2) failed synchrony (evidence of a more functional relationship, not characterized by genuine reciprocity); and (3) absence of synchrony (lack of relationship described between characters).

Discourse

The evaluation of the characteristics of the individual's discourse is based on two variables. The first, coherency, involves an assessment of the degree to which each individual narrative is constructed in a logical, consistent, articulated, and intelligible way, following Main's (1995) reformulation of Grice's (1975) rules of conversational discourse to attachment interview material. This approach evaluates four criteria: (1) quality (how good, cohesive, or creative the plot is); (2) quantity (sufficient level of detail provided without being excessive); (3) relation (whether the elements included are relevant to the plot or not); and (4) manner (the way that the narrative is told). The evaluations of these specific four variables are used to generate an overall relative coherency code that designates a story as highly, moderate, or not coherent. In addition, each story is rated according to whether personal experience is present or not. This variable refers to the use of any element pertaining to one's own life or experience in the narrative construction process. Recent work on attachment has shown that the presence of such material can indicate problems in maintaining appropriate self–other boundaries (Solomon & George, 1999).

Defensive Processes

The assessment of defensive functioning has traditionally been a central element of projective personality testing (e.g., Schafer, 1954). The concept of defense in attachment theory refers to how people process attachment-related material while at the same time maintaining psychological equilibrium as well as preserving existing representational structures (Bowlby, 1980). The purpose of defenses is, therefore, to terminate or modulate activation of the attachment behavioral system to prevent potentially disequilibrating subjective experiences of distress or discomfort. Projective testing is an excellent way to observe defensive processes at work because the ambiguous nature of the stimuli constitutes an implicit threat to the self (Lerner, 1991). The AAP is designed to assess the ways that individuals process and exclude attachment-related thoughts, emotions, and needs.

Bowlby (1980) identified three primary attachment-related defensive processes: (1) deactivation; (2) cognitive disconnection; and (3) segregated systems. Solomon et al. (1995), and later George and West (2001), clarified and operationally defined these defensive exclusion processes based on attachment research in children using projective doll play stories and the AAP, respectively. Deactivation effectively takes the individual's attention away from all attachment-related information, focusing instead on exploration and mastery. In other words, deactivation implies a form of attachment shutdown that excludes certain aspects of distressing attachment information, events, and emotions before reaching a conscious level. On the AAP, an individual using deactivation as a defense will often provide stories devoid of themes involving distressing attachment-related material (e.g., avoid themes of needing help, sadness, anger). Deactivation is evidenced by themes of personal strength or power, achievement, peer relationships, or social status. Deactivation is also observed through attempts at minimizing or normalizing situations, stereotypical statements, or negative evaluations of characters.

Cognitive disconnection involves splitting attachment-related information from its source to attempt to terminate the activation of the attachment behavioral system and the discomfort associated with it. Such defensive process, in contrast with deactivation, usually fails to terminate the attachment behavioral system, as the actual source of the activation is maintained out of consciousness and, therefore, is never really addressed. Cognitive disconnection manifests as deep-seated uncertainty and ambivalence about attachment figures and their capacity or willingness to meet individual's needs (Solomon et al., 1995; George & Solomon, 1999). One example of this process is the evocation of anger and aggression as a way to retaliate against perceived insult or frustration by the attachment figure. Although angry behavior is likely to be experienced by the person as tension relieving, a potential solution to psychological discomfort, and a way to distance oneself from the source of the frustration (i.e., the other person), its function in attachment-related situations is to elicit caregiving behavior and to create proximity with the attachment figure (Bowlby, 1973). Bowlby used the term *functional* anger to describe appropriate, clearly directed angry signals to attachment figures in achieving proximity. He differentiated this from dysfunctional anger, the pervasive use of diffuse or augmented anger signals. Dysfunctional anger shifts the relationship from successful proximity to threatening to push the attachment figures away, implying a loss of autonomy vis-à-vis the attachment figure and, to some extent, a loss of self–other boundaries. This representational status does not allow for a resolution of the underlying issues (e.g., unavailability of the object). On the AAP, cognitive disconnection is manifested in narratives involving, for example, uncertainty, anger, ambivalence, radically opposite interpretations, or glossing over attachment distress.

Segregated systems most often refer to themes of danger or threat to the self. Issues of vulnerability, abandonment, physical threat or danger, abuse, disasters or catastrophic events, or a need to escape a situation (e.g., flee, become invisible, hide, run away) are considered segregated systems markers. Themes of emptiness or isolation also constitute markers for this type of defense. Any indication of odd, bizarre, or peculiar ideas is coded as segregated systems, along with manifestations of dissociative process, intrusive material, or extreme constriction. Segregated systems coded in the AAP to determine (1) their presence and (2) whether or not they are contained or resolved, a representational quality that suggests at least a minimal degree of integration within the individual's psyche.

Forms of resolution of segregated systems typically include the use of internal resources to manage attachment-related distress, assistance or care from others, use of action as a problem-solving strategy, or psychologically leaving the location of the dysregulating attachment material, as indicated by statements such as "... moving on with his life." Segregated systems markers that are not contained by these story features indicate that some traumatic material involving attachment relationships is left unintegrated and is blocked from consciousness—that is, segregated from the rest of the psyche. Bowlby (1980) stressed that such material may emerge from the unconscious if attachment is activated and contribute to behavioral, emotional, or cognitive disorganization, the expression of which may be subtle or readily observable in the individual's behavior.

Classification Process

Assessment of attachment states of mind using the AAP culminates in a classification process that evaluates the coding variable patterns of the individual's protocol according to four groups conceptually similar to the framework developed by Ainsworth (1978) and Main and Solomon (1990) for child and adult attachment, respectively.

The secure-autonomous (F) group is characterized by the capacity for internal representations of attachment to portray integrated agency; that is, the portrayal of attachment figures as providing an internalized secure base or external comfort is the primary mechanism for managing stress and conflict. Relationships with attachment figures are important and satisfactory, as portrayed by successful connectedness when attachment distress occurs in contexts when the individual is alone. Secure-autonomous people portray attachment relationships in dyadic relationships as synchronous—that is, as functioning in a goal-corrected partnership based on sharing and reciprocity. They are aware of interpersonal boundaries (no personal experience). Their AAP protocols are diverse in terms of patterns of defensive processes; there is a wide range of individual differences in how deactivation, cognitive disconnection, and segregated systems are evident in the narratives. Overall, secure individuals tend to show less evidence of defensive process than insecure individuals. Their stories tend to be more coherent than those of insecure individuals, although some secure-autonomous individuals are secure and incoherent. Coherency only evaluates story discourse, communicating the story to another in a conversational context. The sin qua non of security in the AAP is the individual's ability to portray flexibly integrated representational attachment mechanisms, as evidenced in agency, connectedness, and synchrony.

Dismissing (Ds) individuals tend to emphasize agency as a form of taking action that does not involve attachment figures as a primary way to manage internal conflict. This action also includes functional activity (synchrony), such as interactions or activities performed together (e.g., go on a vacation, have a meal) that circumvent emotions or events related to attachment distress. Although reciprocal in nature, functional synchrony does not portray comfort or mutual enjoyment as important to the attachment–caregiving relationship. Dismissing individuals may describe connectedness to others, but these story elements often involve peer relationships rather than attachment relationships as the primary way of meeting needs for social interactions and security. Their narratives also involve a blend of deactivation, cognitive disconnection, and segregated systems markers that are contained. Dismissing individuals are typically moderately coherent or incoherent. The defining feature of dismissing individuals is the effective use of deactivation to filter distress from attachment events and thoughts, a form of defensive exclusion that appears to be used as a substitute for flexible integration and internalized security.

Preoccupied (E) individuals generally show an absence of agency, functional synchrony with attachment figures, and lack of connectedness with others because they are alone or blocked from relationships. Their protocols are often restricted and include much uncertainty or contradictory statements. Although a range of defensive processes may be observed in their story narratives, the defining feature of individuals preoccupied with attachment experiences is the dependence on cognitive disconnection to manage attachment. Their narratives demonstrate the ability to evoke deactivation; however, these attempts are widely unsuccessful due to the continuous activation of the attachment system and their sensitivity to attachment distress. Preoccupied individuals tend to provide stories containing segregated systems markers. Minimal agency, inconsistent connectedness, functional synchrony, and representations of nonrelated individuals (e.g., strangers, neighbors) as comforting prevent attachment representations and the self from hyperarousal. Cognitive disconnection is the underlying representational mechanism related to their incapacity to create a coherent narrative, which in many ways parallels their failed attempts at terminating the attachment behavioral system.

The unresolved (U) group is defined by a state of vulnerability to dysregulation due to attachment-related trauma which has not been sufficiently integrated. All unresolved individuals also maintain organized representations of attachment and behavioral strategies (Main & Solomon, 1990). The expression of such dysregulation in the individual's functioning may depend in part on the primary organized attachment classification (F, Ds, or E). Consequently, there is no prototypical AAP protocol for U individuals, as they constitute a heterogeneous group. The defining feature of this group involves the presence of at least one narrative in which a segregated systems marker is not resolved. Other characteristics of the protocols are a function of their primary attachment configuration. For example, U individuals with F as a primary attachment configuration will be more likely to show some evidence of integrated agency, synchrony, or connectedness, albeit not in every story. For the time being, researchers and clinicians using the AAP refer to U individuals as a specific attachment profile (i.e., a group) in itself, although future research should be able to tell us whether other ways of considering this variable may be more helpful.

☐ Research Evidence

Although the AAP is still a relatively new method, recent research has provided some interesting data supporting its use with a variety of populations. The majority of studies to date have investigated the instrument's construct validity or test–retest reliability.

Validity

The original validation study performed by the original authors (George et al., 1997) intended to provide some basic data to support the validity and reliability of the AAP. Because the AAP was developed as a valid, cost-effective alternative to the AAI, the authors compared attachment classification on both instruments across various samples, including

25 at-risk mothers, 23 women participating in a large-scale study on depression, and 48 (42 women, 6 men) individuals recruited in community, university, and clinical settings. In this study, the authors were able to show strong convergence between AAP and blind-rated AAI classifications, as suggested by values of .92 ($\kappa = .75$, $p < .001$) and .85 ($\kappa = .84$, $p < .001$) for secure–insecure and four-group (F, Ds, E, U) classifications, respectively.

More recent data on construct validity, as well as discriminant validity (intellectual level and social desirability), are also available for a sample of 144 adult subjects (100 women, 44 men ranging from 18 to 65 years of age) recruited from college and community settings in California and Alberta, Canada. In this study, the authors (George & West, in press) essentially replicated their previous findings by obtaining a 97% ($\kappa = .88$, $p < .000$) agreement for secure–insecure and 90% ($\kappa = .84$, $p < .000$) agreement between four-group AAP and AAI classifications. Discriminant validity was documented by a lack of association between attachment status and verbal intelligence (as measured by the vocabulary and similarities of the Weschler Adult Intelligence Scale) and social desirability (Bindra Inventory of Desirable Responding).

Because attachment theory involves understanding the importance of qualities of parent–child relationships for the development of the child, establishing an empirical link between attachment states of mind in the caregiver and salient features of child functioning may provide support for the validity of the method used to assess adult attachment. In a series of studies, Béliveau, Cyr, and Moss (2002), Cyr, Béliveau, and Moss (2003), and Moss, Cyr, and Dubois-Comtois (2004) investigated such a link using the AAP as a measure of adult attachment. More specifically, they examined whether mothers' attachment states of mind were valid predictors of child development, as documented by strange situation separation–reunion behavior and behavior problems, in a normative sample recruited from various daycare centers in a large urban setting. The authors found that secure-autonomous mothers were more likely to raise children assessed as secure in the strange situation, whereas insecure (Ds, E, or U) mothers were more likely to have insecure children. They reported an overall match of 73% between mother and child attachment status. Moreover, children of dismissing and unresolved mothers appeared to be more at risk for presenting behavior problems, as compared with children of secure-autonomous mothers. In an interesting look at potential variables that may explain this association, these studies found that some factors related to the mother herself (e.g., stressful life events, feelings of helplessness), as well as factors related to her actual behavior in her relationships with her child (e.g., discourse, conversational patterns), contributed to the development of psychosocial vulnerabilities in the child. Data were also obtained pertinent to the discriminant validity of the AAP, as attachment classification in this sample was independent of socioeconomic level.

Similar results linking attachment states of mind and caregiving representations and behavior were obtained by Odipo (2002) with a sample of foster mothers. Foster mothers classified as secure on the AAP displayed more positive affect and capacity to develop coherent representations of the children under their care than mothers classified as insecure. Insecure mothers reported more negative affect, feelings of burden and subjective distress, and less ability to adopt the child's perspective.

Data supporting the construct validity of the AAP also come from its use with clinical or high-risk samples. In a study by the original authors (West & George, 2002), the AAP protocols of 24 women diagnosed with dysthymia were examined to determine the prevalence and to understand the attachment mechanisms that characterized this severe form of depression. The authors found that preoccupied attachment was overrepresented in this sample (58% for four-group and 75% for three-group classifications), suggesting that the inability to deactivate attachment distress and the confusion resulting from the inability to disconnect elements of attachment experiences contributed to this disorder.

Mezzich et al. (2006) used the AAP in their follow-up study designed to examine the role of attachment in substance abuse disorder and antisocial disorder in adolescent girls. Cross-sectional data using the AAP at age 24–28 during their longitudinal study focused on substance abuse disorder. They reported that substance abuse disorder was significantly related to insecure attachment and that this relationship was not mediated by antisocial disorder. They interpreted their findings to suggest that poor affect regulation as associated with insecure attachment may be a prominent mechanisms underlying substance abuse disorder.

A series of studies by Buchheim and colleagues (Buchheim et al., 2006a; 2006b) provided concurrent and predictive validity for using the AAP in non-English-speaking and clinical populations. Buchheim pioneered the use of the AAP to examine attachment activation in a neuroimaging environment, using functional magnetic resonance imaging (fMRI) technology. Buchheim administered the AAP in Germany to clinical patients (described more fully following) and established convergent validity for the AAP in both the German and English translation transcripts. Convergent validity for the AAP (coded by a reliable English-speaking AAP judge from English translations of German transcripts) was established using AAI classification as the criterion (determined from German transcripts by a reliable German AAI judge). Correspondence combined for Buchheim's studies were as follows: 84% for four classification groups ($\kappa = .71$, $p < .000$), 91% for secure–insecure ($\kappa = .70$, $p < .000$), and 88% for unresolved–resolved groups ($\kappa = .75$, $p < .000$) (George, personal communication, 2006).

The first study (Buchheim et al., 2006a) was designed to assess the capacity of the AAP to elicit activity in certain specific visual and semantic brain regions. The authors were interested in learning how lack of integration of traumatic events, as indicated by the unresolved status, was linked to brain activity in a normative sample (11 healthy female participants). They successfully demonstrated that the AAP task elicits activity in areas of the brain linked to visual and semantic processes, a theoretically expected finding. More specifically, the AAP card administration sequence (i.e., increasing activation of the attachment system) was associated with activation of the right inferior frontal cortex, a region of the limbic system responsible for affect regulation. The validity of AAP classifications based on fMRI administration was checked against AAI classifications based on interviews administered outside the fMRI environment. There was 100% convergence for the organized–unresolved groups.

An important piece of information uncovered by the authors is that in unresolved subjects, gradual exposure to more traumatic stimuli through the card sequence was linked with increased activation of medial temporal regions, including the amygdala and hippocampus. These structures are thought to be involved in the processing of negative emotions and the retrieval of autobiographical memory. These data are important in that they constitute strong evidence supporting the capacity of the AAP to elicit neural activity patterns that are consistent with activation of the attachment system. Activation of the attachment behavioral system is thought to be essential to the assessment of attachment in both adults and children and may require a form of stimulus that most commonly used self-report questionnaires cannot provide (George & West, 1999).

Extending this neuroimaging methodology, Buchheim et al. (2006b) investigated the neural correlates of attachment patterns in borderline personality disorder (BPD) patients compared with normal controls. Because of the high prevalence of unresolved attachment linked to experiences of abuse in childhood for individuals with BPD, the authors hypothesized that pictures including traumatic segregated systems marker material in the AAP narratives (e.g., abandonment, abuse) would be associated with different neural activation patterns in BPD subjects when compared with controls. BPD patients showed significantly more traumatic segregated systems language indicators in response to alone pictures than nonpatient controls. Alone picture fMRI response scans showed significantly greater anterior midcingulate cortex activation. Dyadic picture fMRI response scans showed greater right superior temporal sulcus activation and less right parahippocampal gyrus activation.

In addition to providing further evidence of the validity of the AAP for the purpose of eliciting attachment-related representations, Buchheim's work clearly illustrates difficulties experienced by individuals with BPD in inhibiting their internal states when exposed to conflictual attachment-related situations. Such a finding is quite consistent with the existing literature on BPD (e.g., Gunderson, 1996; Stone, 1990) and may contribute to a better understanding of this disorder from the standpoint of attachment theory.

Buchheim and George (2006) examined attachment status and traumatic AAP segregated systems markers in a larger adult patient population: 34 BPD (13 inpatients from the fMRI study and 21 outpatients), 20 anxiety patients, and 21 healthy controls. BPD (74%) and anxiety patients (80%) were largely unresolved; the majority of health controls were secure and dismissing (62%). These classification distribution patterns are consistent with the clinical attachment literature (Dozier et al., 1999). Borderline and anxiety patients showed significantly more trauma dysregulation markers in their narrative responses to alone pictures than controls. Traumatic segregrated systems appeared predominantly in personal experience material for the anxiety patients. The intrusion of attachment dysregulation directly related to self material during the AAP suggests important attachment related processes related to the blurring of self–other boundaries in anxiety patients. This pattern appears to be related to anxiety patients' unresolved loss, not abuse (the primary correlate of BPD traumatic dysregulation).

Recent studies have begun to use the AAP with adolescents. These studies are beginning to establish predictive validity for the AAP during the teen years, although more studies are needed to examine concurrent and psychometric validity of the AAP for teens. Theoretically expected associations were found between attachment status on the AAP and variables related to psychosocial adjustment in a sample of 13- to 14-year-old adolescents (Moss, Thibaudeau, Joubert, Beliveau, & Dubois-Comtois, 2006). Preoccupied adolescents were more likely to use substances and report more externalizing problems. In a sample of young mothers, Joubert, Mazzarello, Moss, Paquette, and Zoccolillo (2006) found that mothers in the preoccupied group were more likely to show a significant history of antisocial behavior and their children were more likely to have problems with aggression. Working with a sample of adolescents referred to an outpatient mental health clinic, Webster and Joubert (2006) reported associations between unresolved status and impairments in thought processes, self–other boundaries, reality testing and emotional constriction, as assessed using the Rorschach Inkblot Method.

Generalizability

Studies to date have demonstrated that the AAP can be used to measure attachment status in a diverse range of individuals. It has been validated for adults (age 18–65), predictive validity has been established for adolescents, and it has been used in normal and clinical populations. Studies described in this review have included samples originating from the United States, Canada (including narratives in French), and Germany. Because of the focus placed on language and narrative process in the AAP system, the use of this instrument across groups whose primary language is not English might be problematic. However, results obtained with French- and German-speaking samples suggest that the AAP assessment system can be used with non-English-speaking individuals. Studies using the AAP with populations in Italy, Russia, Japan, and Taiwan are in progress.

The AAP assessment process requires that an individual be able to construct narratives based on the visual depiction of certain attachment-related situations. Because preschool-age children typically demonstrate a capacity to construct coherent narratives based on visual stimuli, educational level requirements for the AAP are fairly low. This is indirectly supported by research showing no association between AAP classification and verbal intelligence (George & West, in press).

Reliability

Data aggregated from the original validation samples (George et al., 1997) show strong evidence of interrater reliability, as indicated by values of .93 ($\kappa = .73$, $p < .001$) for secure–insecure classification and .86 ($\kappa = .79$, $p < .001$) for the standard four-group classification.

George and West's (in press) replication study obtained similar results. Four-group interrater reliability was excellent, the values reported between two pairs of raters being 90% ($\kappa = .85$, $p < .000$) and 85% ($\kappa = .79$, $p < .000$), respectively. Interrater agreement values reported in various other studies using the AAP are generally in the .80 to .90 range.

Temporal stability was also investigated in this study, as attachment is presumed to be a fairly stable component of one's personality (Bowlby, 1969). The authors reported test–retest reliability estimates over a three-month period of 84% ($\kappa = .78$, $p < .000$) for the four-group classification. Stability estimates for specific attachment groups included 82% for secure-autonomous, 96% for dismissing, 62% for preoccupied, and 80% for unresolved.

It must be pointed out that the values reported here were obtained from research using reliable, certified coders. Use of the AAP requires that coders complete a training and reliability trial under the supervision of Carol George. It is recommended that potential coders have a graduate degree in the social sciences and be familiar with human development, particularly attachment theory as developed by John Bowlby, as well as with the fields of personality, cognition, emotion, and basic psychometrics.

☐ Case Illustration

This section presents an example pertaining to the use of AAP data in a clinical setting. For this purpose, the AAP protocol of a man referred for individual psychotherapy is reviewed, along with background information and psychological test data. The discussion focuses on the way that information obtained from the AAP protocol can enhance the clinician's understanding of the individual's dynamics and personality and can by extension inform decision making by adding attachment information.

Background Information

Mr. L is a 40-year-old, single, Caucasian man who was referred by his treating psychiatrist to an outpatient mental health clinic for individual psychotherapy. At the time of the assessment, Mr. L had been clinically depressed for the last six months following the loss of a relative. He was hospitalized for a brief period due to his reporting suicidal ideation. Mr. L was administered the Wechsler Adult Intelligence Scale-Revised (WAIS-R), Minnesota Multiphasic Personality Inventory-2 (MMPI-2), Early Memories Procedure, Rorschach, and AAP as part of his assessment.

Mr. L is the seventh in a family of 12 children, with 6 brothers and 5 sisters. He grew up on a farm in a rural area. He initially described his childhood as a "happy" period, without significant problems. Mr. L's father is described as a soft-spoken man who used to "hide feelings" and generally kept to himself. His mother is described as "special," "nice," and responsible for disciplining the children. Mr. L described himself as very close to his mother. He reported liking school at the time and got along well with teachers and peers. His relationship with his siblings was also described as "good," without any major conflicts.

According to Mr. L, adolescence was a difficult time for him. His father partially lost the use of his hands due to exposure to extreme cold. His father then became severely depressed and withdrew from family life, isolating himself in his room. This isolation was punctuated by several suicide attempts. The father finally committed suicide by hanging when Mr. L was 12. The client reported being traumatized by finding his father hanging from the ceiling of the barn. He reportedly started skipping school and avoiding friends following this incident. Mr. L can recall no involvement in romantic relationships during adolescence.

The client left the family home when he was 17 and moved to the city. He had several jobs for short periods of time but felt that he could not stay long in any one place. He started at that time to frequent gay bars, where he would meet older men who would promise him financial or material support to develop a romantic relationship with him. Such relationships were typically conflictual and short-lived. Mr. L eventually met a young woman with whom he started a relationship, which lasted seven years. However, this girlfriend was prone to episodes of depression and was often suicidal. Mr. L reported feeling confused at the time because his girlfriend, who was bisexual, would bring lesbian lovers to the apartment and requested that the client takes part in sexual activities with them. Mr. L eventually left the relationship. He resumed frequenting gay bars to find sexual partners.

Mr. L met an older man, a former law enforcement officer, with whom he established a friendship. The relationship had a sexual component, although Mr. L insists that sexual activities between them were only on an occasional basis. This man was married to a woman who was severely ill at the time, and most of his time was spent caring for her. He allowed Mr. L to stay at their house, where he had his own room. Mr. L would spend entire weeks at this friend's house and would only rarely spend time in his own apartment. Mr. L's friend experienced problems with depression and made several suicide attempts during the years of their relationship. Mr. L reported feeling very anxious at times because of this, even though he claims that this was a "good" period of his life.

Some time later, the client's mother was hospitalized due to a serious, terminal illness. Mr. L spent most of his time taking care of her at the hospital for the three months preceding her death. Following his mother's death, the client's younger brother, who had financial problems at the time, committed suicide by hanging. Mr. L reported feeling devastated by these losses, especially his younger brother's suicide. He became increasingly depressed and was spending all of his time at his friend's house watching TV. Approximately a year later, Mr. L's friend committed suicide by locking himself into his running car. Mr. L's depression worsened even further, and he was feeling burdened by the responsibility of taking care of his friend's wife, whose condition kept deteriorating. His friend's wife passed away shortly after, and Mr. L's depression became chronic. He was then unable to function and was reporting persistent suicidal ideation. He was admitted to a psychiatric unit for observation and stabilization. Mr. L reported that the medication used as well as the safe, structured environment in the hospital were helpful in making him feel better.

Upon discharge, Mr. L felt that he was able to provide himself with basic care, but his depression had not entirely remitted. He resumed a romantic relationship with a former lover who had just opened a small business. This man promised Mr. L material support as well as partnership in this business as soon as it became financially viable. Mr. L was hesitant to involve himself in the relationship, but his friend's promises eventually convinced him.

Mr. L claims that since these losses, things have changed for the worse and that he cannot get out of his depression. He reports chronic fatigue, lack of motivation or interest, persistent sadness, difficulties going to sleep, lack of appetite, and social withdrawal. He also reports drinking large quantities of alcohol on a regular basis. Mr. L cannot frequent public places such as shopping malls due to severe agoraphobia. Mr. L is currently romantically involved with his business partner but reports marked conflicts in the relationship, partly due to feeling disappointed and frustrated by his partner not keeping the promises made. This will be Mr. L's first experience in individual psychotherapy.

Summary of Psychological Test Data

A brief description and integration of psychological test data are presented here, as space limitations prevent us from discussing individual test results in more detail.

Mr. L's intellectual level is in the low–average range (FSIQ = 84), with a nonsignificant discrepancy between verbal (88) and nonverbal (80) functioning. His lowest scores were obtained on object assembly (3), similarities (5), picture completion (5), digit symbol (5), and comprehension (6). Significant difficulties were noted in the areas of visual concentration, nonverbal memory, perceptual organization, as well as abstract thinking.

Mr. L's Rorschach protocol, scored using the Comprehensive System (Exner, 1993), is notable for the high number of responses provided (R = 35), presence of shading as a determinant (C' = 3, T = 4, V = 2, Y = 3), low frequency of human movement (M = 2) or whole human percepts (H = 1), overemphasis on details (W = 3, D = 25, Dd = 7), moderately high level of distortions in thinking (*FABCOM* = 2, *ALOG* = 1), idiosyncratic or highly subjective interpretations of reality (*Xu%* = 52), low reactivity to emotional stimulation (*Afr* = 0.40), absence of cooperative movement or reciprocity (*COP* = 0), presence of food as content (*Fd* = 2), and chronic, pervasive deficits in coping skills (*CDI* = 5). Mr. L mentioned the content *fur* in nine different responses in his protocol. Other responses alternated between passive (*joined hands; small animals*) and more aggressive (*men pulling, blood, their chest torn apart; dragon's head*) percepts.

Mr. L produced a valid, interpretable MMPI-2 protocol with significant elevations on scales 2 (depression) and 4 (psychopathic deviate). An examination of supplementary scales revealed high score on repression and low scores on ego strength, dominance, and gender role–masculine. Content scales revealed that Mr. L's depression as reported on the MMPI-2 is characterized primarily by lack of drive and motivation.

Mr. L's Early Memories Procedure protocol (Bruhn, 1990) involved many episodes of accidents in early childhood. His first reported memory involved trying to ride his uncle's tractor by himself and barely escaping when the tractor tipped over. Interestingly, his second memory involved picking and eating strawberries with his mother in a special, secret place that no one knew about, where the strawberries were larger than anywhere else in the area. Subsequent memories involved Mr. L being either surprised or scared by unexpected events occurring in his life (e.g., his father wounding himself with an axe).

WAIS and Rorschach data suggests that Mr. L experiences problems accessing and using mental representations for adaptive purposes. In the absence of external support, he is likely to become overwhelmed by demands and becomes confused, frustrated, and powerless. This overreliance on external, rather than internal, adaptive mechanisms is compounded by his lack of capacity to use concepts, his stereotypical approach to situations, and his passivity. On the other hand, there is no evidence of formal thought disorder or major impairment in reality testing in his protocols.

Mr. L's personality dynamics as represented in the test data are characterized by passive-dependent traits and a tendency to rely on an idealized figure for preserving psychological integrity. Underlying his submissive and dependent stance lies an intense fear of rejection or abandonment by others. Mr. L expects the unexpected—that terrible consequences may stem from banal situations. Perceiving himself as unable to face challenges and problems, his only recourse as he sees it is to rely on others to rescue him. He is clearly more comfortable in relationships in which he can adopt such a passive and receptive role. Paradoxically, he does not anticipate positive interactions with others but perceives relationships as potential sources of rejection and abandonment. This conflict may manifest as chronic ambivalence and dissatisfaction with his social life.

Test data clearly indicate marked distress and dysphoria in Mr. L. Predominant mood states appear to be characterized by subjective distress, anxiety, frustration, apathy, and pessimism. Such affects are likely to predominate in the absence of external support. In the absence of such support, more regressed or less adaptive ways of managing emotional dysregulation may appear, such as substance use or compulsive activity.

In summary, test results as well as the client's history suggest a diagnosis of major depressive disorder as well as agoraphobia, with dependent personality traits.

Adult Attachment Projective Protocol

Narratives obtained from the administration of the AAP with Mr. L will now be discussed, along with their implications for clinical work with this client.

Picture 1: Neutral

This picture is used as a warm-up for the rest of the task and is therefore not coded.

Picture 2: Child at Window

> That's pretty weird.... Little girl, she's in the front room at her place. I don't know, the patio door there.... She's looking outside, she's waiting maybe her friend, her little girlfriend or boyfriend, I don't know.... Yeah ... I don't see ... / Or maybe she's sad, she's waiting her parents, I don't know. (What might happen next?) Well, next ... / Uh ... If it's a friend she's waiting for, maybe they'll go eat an ice cream somewhere ... hm-hm ... Or if she's still ... / if her parents ... / Maybe she's ready, she's waiting for them to go to the restaurant ... yeah ... yeah (What is she thinking or feeling ?) The little girl ... she's anxious, she's waiting impatiently, she's waiting impatiently for either her friend, her girlfriend, or her parents. She's anxious, she's just waiting. Yeah ... (Anything else comes to mind?) No, not really ... No.

This narrative is characterized by marked uncertainty about what is going on in the story and what the outcome will be. One gets the sense that thoughts are often interrupted and that the subject is hesitant to commit to one story line. In addition, the plot remains vague, and there is very little elaboration. There is too much interference in the development of the story for this narrative to be considered coherent (Score: incoherent). No reference to a personal experience is evoked. There are indications in the story of an attempt to terminate the attachment system through action (*going to eat an ice cream*) (Score: agency, capacity to act). The reader should note the reference to an oral theme, consistent with other test data, although this feature is not part of AAP coding. There are references to a desire for connectedness with others (peers, parents) throughout the story, although fulfillment of this need is only evoked in the context of a relationship with peers (Score: connected). Attachment figures are representationally absent; there is no mention of any interaction with parents actually taking place in the story. In terms of defensive functioning, the narrative is characterized by the presence of marked cognitive disconnection as evidenced by repeated uncertainty (e.g., *I don't know; waiting*) and entanglement (*anxious*).

Picture 3: Scene of Departure

> Oh, oye-oye-oye ... Well, I don't know.... Maybe the husband going on a business trip ... and his wife came to drop him at the airport. Here she's asking him when he's gonna be back. Yeah, yeah, yeah ... Hum, I don't .../ (What might happen next?) Uh, he could—he could leave—leave and not come back, I don't know.... Yeah ... hm (And what are they thinking or feeling?) Well if he leaves ... / Maybe he's got a lover somewhere, he's anxious to leave.... Yeah, anyways, if he told her that he's coming back, she's gonna wait—she's gonna wait, she's gonna learn the bad news later. Hm-mm. Yeah ... I ... / That's what I can see. (Anything else comes to mind?) No. No, there's no .../

This story is much like the first one in that Mr. L experiences difficulties developing a clear story line. Both the beginning and the conclusion of the narrative are unclear. There seems to be no logical connection for the transition between the themes of the business trip and the husband leaving the wife for a lover. The presence of repetitions, fillers, and interrupted thought processes make the narrative difficult to follow (Score: incoherent). There is no personal experience in the story. There is no indication of reciprocity in the relationship, the narrative emphasizing conflict and betrayal (Score: failed synchrony). As in the initial story, there is a marked presence of uncertainty (e.g., *I don't know; wait*) and unfinished sentences in the narrative, thus pointing to the importance of cognitive disconnection as a primary defense mechanism for this person.

Picture 4: Person Sitting on a Bench

> Oh!... Uh, it might be a little girl, she's sad, she's sitting on a park bench. She's sitting on a bench, she's sad, her boyfriend left her. Her boyfriend left her for ... / Hm ... So she's taking it all out, she's crying, she's wondering what she's—what's gonna happen. Hm ... Yeah. So what's going to happen next is, she's gonna quit crying, she's gonna go meet one of her friends. Yeah. (And what is she thinking or feeling?) Well, that's ... / She's wondering how she's gonna get through this. You know, she's—she's gonna have the idea to go see her friend. And she's gonna talk to her about it, she's ... Hm ... Yeah (Anything else comes to mind?) No, I think that's pretty much it for this one.

This narrative is much more coherent than the previous stories. There is a clear plot and sequential description of a narrative—boyfriend left girl; she is sad, upset; she decides to go see a friend and talk to her. The character's internal states are clearly identified and are consistent with the story line. Problems with completing sentences and thought processes are still noted in the narrative. Overall, this is a coherent narrative although significant interference with the process is still present (Score: moderately coherent). There is no personal experience in the story. The character is portrayed as using action (i.e., going to see a friend) to manage the internal conflict about the loss of the boyfriend (Score: agency, capacity to act). We see again the representation of peers for adaptive purposes (Score: connectedness). As in the Child at Window, attachment figures are representationally absent. Defensive functioning is characterized by uncertainty (e.g., *wondering*) and the inability to complete thoughts, both markers of cognitive disconnection. Note the inclusion of a third person in the story, a reference being made to the character's boyfriend potentially leaving her for someone else, but this thought process is quickly interrupted and is not integrated in the narrative. From this point, object-seeking behavior (with a friend) becomes the center of the narrative.

Picture 5: Child and Adult on a Bed

> Hm-mm ... No ... she's not coming to tuck him in, she's coming to wake him up. That's a mother who's coming to wake her—her son. Hm ... And there's—maybe he had a nightmare. She—she's coming to wake him up. Yeah, that's it, he had a nightmare. Hm-mm. And ... Yeah. I don't see ... / (And what might happen next?) Uh, she can ... / Uh ... she can bring him in the kitchen, give him a glass of milk or something, a cookie, I don't know. Yeah ... that's what I see (And, what are they thinking or feeling ?) Uh—maybe he's still in shock from his dream, he had a bad dream. I don't know what he might be thinking.... And her idea is that she's gonna comfort him.... Hm ... (Anything else comes to mind?) No.

A general plot is easily discerned in this narrative, and the theme evoked is appropriate to what is described on the card. An illogical connection is observed early in the narrative, where the mother is coming to wake the son, who just had a nightmare (and is therefore awake), to comfort him. The son's internal states cannot be elaborated in relation to the internal conflict (sense of threat, fear). Although some difficulties were present at the beginning of the narrative, the story can be considered coherent as a whole (Score: moderately coherent). No personal experience is noted. The attachment figure is described as wanting to comfort the son; however, there is no mention of any action on her part to do so, except to give him food, a substitute for parental care and comfort in this case. The description of the mother's actions in the narrative is not consistent with attachment-attuned care and represents a functional type of interaction (Score: functional synchrony). Defensive functioning on this card is represented primarily by markers for cognitive disconnection, as illustrated by statements relating uncertainty (*I don't know*) and by an attempt by the attachment figure to take the child's attention away from the distress (giving milk and cookies). The theme of nightmare constitutes a segregated systems marker, which in this particular case is resolved by the parent's actions and care. Although not optimal from an attachment perspective because functional care never addresses the child's fear directly, functional care is sufficient to contain the traumatic material and to prevent dysregulation.

Picture 6: Child and Adult Looking at an Ambulance

> Eh ... Uh, an ambulance, it's—it's coming to pick up the little guy. The grandmother is gonna go with him, she's waiting for the ambulance. Yeah, I don't know what he did to hurt himself, but the ambulance is coming to pick him up. Ow! That's a weird one! Uh, and he's gonna go to the hospital in the ambulance. The ambulance is here! I don't know what happened. Maybe he fell down the stairs. Yeah (laughs). That's pretty crazy. (And what might happen next?) Uh, I don't know, he's gonna go to the hospital, he'll probably come back with his leg in a cast. I don't know. Yeah ... that's it. (So what are they thinking or feeling?) Uh the grandmother, she's really upset, her grandson is hurt. They're only thinking about getting better. If he hurt his ankle ... / Yeah ... that's it. (Anything else comes to mind?) No.

This narrative is characterized by difficulties in elaborating the plot. The discourse is significantly impeded by comments intended to distance self from the situation (e.g., *That's a weird one; That's pretty crazy*), statements of uncertainty and unfinished thoughts. There is only minimal elaboration of the circumstances leading to the current situation, as well as the outcome. There is also minimal description of the character's internal states. This narrative therefore does not meet the basic requirements for coherency (Score: not coherent). There is no mention of personal experience in the story. There is no clear description of the attachment figure attending to the child's distress, an unusual occurrence on this card (Score: failed synchrony). As with the previous cards, defensive functioning is characterized primarily by a strong presence of cognitive disconnection markers, including uncertainty (*I don't know; waiting*) and unfinished thoughts.

Picture 7: Man Standing in a Cemetery

> Well, he's at the cemetery, he's visiting ... a friend or his wife. It might be someone he lost in a car accident and ... he's ... / (So, what might happen next?) I don't know! He'll go back home, sad, just went to the cemetery to visit someone.... He's sad, he's gonna go back home and ... / I guess life goes on (laughs). Yeah ... I can't see ... / It's weird. (And—what—what is the character thinking or feeling?) I don't know. If it's someone close who—who died in an accident or ... / He must be really sad about it. He would like to see this person again. Hm ... yeah, that's about it.

Mr. L appears to elaborate a narrative only with difficulty on this card, which pulls for themes of loss or death of attachment figures. The identity of the person who passed away is never clearly established, and there is a sense of disconnection between different ideas or thought processes as the individual struggles to build a story. No clear outcome is elaborated, and Mr. L is again unsuccessfully trying to distance himself from the testing situation (*I can't see ... / It's weird; I don't know*). The narrative on this card clearly lacks coherency (Score: not coherent). No element related to personal experience is noted. The character is not described as using internal resources, relationships, or action to manage the activation of the attachment system on this card (Score: no agency). In spite of lacking elaboration, the story is replete with cognitive disconnection markers, including uncertainty (*I don't know*), unfinished thoughts, as well as a statement suggesting that the character is glossing over the issue (*life goes on*). In addition, a segregated systems marker is present in the narrative, as the character is described as *visiting* a dead relative. The narrative does not provide indications that this marker is contained. The story must therefore be coded as unresolved with respect to trauma.

Picture 8: Child in Corner

> Oh no!... Uh ... What's that?!! ... It might be a little guy who end up being punished and sent to the corner. Maybe a person—a person wants to beat him up, he's trying to protect himself. Yeah ... And he must be thinking, "I'd like to be somewhere else" (laughs). So what happened before ... He had a fight, he had a fight with either his little brother, little sister, so his mum or dad sent him to the corner ... Yeah ... Hmm ... And what he's thinking, I already told you, he would like to be somewhere else (laughs) (And what might happen next?) Uh? ... (What might happen next?) Well, he might be asked to apologize to his sister or brother, if he had a fight with them. Hm-mm ... yeah. That's it.

This narrative shows a clear plot with a specific beginning and end, although some elements are left vague (e.g., the identity of the sibling). Internal states are minimally elaborated. Yet the discourse itself shows less interference than what was observed on previous cards (Score: moderate coherency). No personal experience is present. There is a reference to an attempt by the character at protecting himself from a threat (Score: agency, capacity to act), thus resolving the segregated systems marker in the story (*beat him up*). The narrative shows cognitive disconnection markers such as anger (*had a fight*) and disconnection (*either brother or sister*). A deactivation marker is also present, represented by the theme of punishment occurring in the story.

Mr. L's AAP protocol as a whole shows the following characteristics: evidence of unresolved attachment-related material; generally low level of coherency; personal agency as evidenced by capacity to act; absence of evidence suggesting capacity to mentalize conflicts; desire for and capacity to relate to others, albeit only in the context of peer relationships; strong representation of cognitive disconnection markers in the narratives. On the basis of the segregated systems material that was left unintegrated in the "Cemetery" story, Mr. L's attachment status is unresolved with respect to trauma. The protocol also suggests that Mr. L is also preoccupied as his primary attachment configuration.

The data obtained from the AAP are consistent with the other information obtained on Mr. L. The presence of unresolved, unintegrated material related to loss and death of attachment figures certainly seems to match his history of sudden, traumatic losses throughout his life, and probably accounts for the presence of severe anxiety in certain contexts (crowds). Suicidal ideation has also been linked to unresolved/preoccupied attachment status (Adam, Sheldon-Keller, & West, 1996). His primary configuration of preoccupied is consistent with his history of depression, his passive-dependent interpersonal orientation, and his chronic ambivalence in the context of attachment relationships (West & George, 2002). Both unresolved/preoccupied attachment status as revealed through the AAP and the psychological test data (e.g., low comprehension score on the WAIS, high scale 4 score on the MMPI-2) suggest that unprocessed anger may underlie Mr. L's presentation. Some of his behaviors, such as recurrent episodes of drinking or compulsive sexual object seeking, may constitute ways to prevent becoming overwhelmed by traumatic material or internal conflicts stemming from past relationships with attachment figures. Quite likely, Mr. L's level of involvement and preoccupation with past experiences with attachment figures, as well as his tendency to become enmeshed in current relationships, do not allow for resolution of the trauma and integration of conflictual material. Mr. L is thus likely to repeat the same dysfunctional patterns in his current relationships in an attempt to resolve the original trauma, while at the same time making himself vulnerable to reexperiencing loss, rejection, and abandonment by others.

The data obtained from the AAP also include some positive findings. Though Mr. L's primary attachment configuration was determined to be preoccupied, his protocol showed evidence of agency, in the form of capacity to act, an unusual finding in individuals with this attachment profile. Although Mr. L is prone to experience episodes of helplessness and dysregulation when confronted with situations that trigger unconscious, segregated, traumatic material, it appears that he has the capacity to use action for adaptive purposes in his everyday life. This finding is in some ways consistent with other psychological test data, for example, the relatively high number of responses provided on the Rorschach. This statement is not meant to imply that such capacity to act is associated with healthy behaviors in the individual. Indeed, there is evidence that Mr. L uses compulsive activity as a way to manage internal conflicts and distress. The transition to healthier, more appropriate ways to use activity to promote well-being could constitute a therapeutic objective in itself. Given Mr. L's lack of capacity to mentalize internal conflicts, more structured, reality-oriented treatment focusing on building appropriate coping skills might prove to be more beneficial to him than insight-oriented, reconstructive therapy, at least initially.

A second positive finding lies with Mr. L's desire for connectedness with others, as shown on the AAP. This finding is also consistent with other test data (e.g., texture and food responses on the Rorschach, MMPI-2 Scale 0 within normal limits). The problem, from an attachment perspective, is that Mr. L's desire for connectedness is at the level of affiliative rather than attachment relationships. Affiliative or peer-based relationships serve different purposes than attachment relationships and cannot assuage attachment-related internal conflicts and distress. In this case, Mr. L's ambivalence, anger, and deep-seated insecurity about attachment figure's availability are not likely to be addressed through his current relationships. Furthermore, given Mr. L's level of preoccupation with relationships and his tendency to assume a dependent stance, individual psychotherapy should promote the development of appropriate autonomy and boundaries in the context of a stable relationship with an attachment figure (therapist). The therapist should probably expect some boundary- or limit-testing behavior, perhaps in a passive-aggressive way, as the therapy takes its course and an attachment to the therapist as a nurturing, stable object starts developing.

☐ Future Research

Although research available to date appears promising, it is obvious that much work needs to be done before the AAP can be considered a viable alternative to the AAI. Although the AAP has done well in construct validity studies using appropriate criteria (e.g., AAI classification) and interrater reliability has been excellent across studies, there is a need for more research using diverse populations in terms of age, ethnicity, language, socioeconomic background, gender, and risk/clinical status. For example, it is not known whether individuals showing limited intellectual or educational level can provide narratives with sufficient material so that formal coding is likely to be valid.

In short, there is a need to build a research base that addresses a broader range of adolescent and adult development as well as problem populations for the purpose of theory-building and practical applications. As an important step, new research groups or individuals need to become involved in research evaluating the psychometric properties of the AAP to replicate seminal findings and establish the instrument's reliability and validity in a more definitive manner. From a professional standpoint, research is needed to establish the usefulness of AAP data to inform decision making and to assess clinically relevant variables. Studies are currently under way in the United States, Canada, Japan, Italy, Germany, Russia, and Taiwan that should address many of the points described here in the years to come.

References

Ainsworth, M. D. S., Blehar, M. C., Waters, E., & Wall, S. (1978). *Patterns of attachment: A psychological study of the strange situation.* Hillsdale, NJ: Erlbaum.

Bartholomew, K., & Horowitz, L. (1991). Attachment styles among young adults: A test of a four-category model. *Journal of Personality and Social Psychology, 61,* 226–241.

Beliveau, M. J., Cyr, C., & Moss, E. (June, 2002). *Introduction to a projective measure of attachment.* Paper presented at the Annual Attachment Conference, Quebec City, Canada.

Bowlby, J. (1969). *Attachment and loss: Vol. 1. Attachment.* New York : Basic Books.

Bowlby, J. (1973). *Attachment and loss: Vol. 2. Separation.* New York : Basic Books.

Bretherton, I., Ridgeway, D., & Cassidy, J. (1990). Assessing internal working models of attachment relationships: An attachment story completion task for 3 year-olds. In M. T. Greenberg, D. Cichetti, & E. M. Cummings (Eds.), *Attachment in the preschool years: Theory, research and intervention* (pp. 273–308). Chicago: University of Chicago Press.

Buchheim, A., & George, C. (in press). The representational, neurobiological and emotional foundation of attachment disorganization in Borderline Personality Disorder and Anxiety Disorder. In J. Solomon & C. George (Eds.), *Disorganized Attachment and Caregiving.* New York: Guilford Publications.

Buchheim, A., Erk, S., George, C., Kächele, H., Ruschow, M., Spitzer, M., et al. (2006a). Measuring adult attachment representation in an fMRI environment: A pilot study. *Psychopathology. 39,* 136–143.

Buchheim, A., Erk., S., George, C., Kächele, H., Martius, P., Pokorny, D., et al. (2006b). *Neural correlates of attachment dysregulation in borderline personality disorder using functional magnetic resonance imaging.* unpublished data set.

Crowell, J. A., Fraley, R. C., & Shaver, P. R. (1999). Measures of individual differences in adolescent and adult attachment. In J. Cassidy & P. R. Shaver (Eds.), *Handbook of attachment: Theory, research and clinical applications* (pp. 334–365). New York: Guilford.

Cyr, C., Beliveau, M. J., & Moss, E. (March, 2003). *Maternal attachment representations: Link with child attachment and externalizing behavior problems.* Symposium conducted at the annual meeting of the Society for Personality Assessment, San Francisco, CA.

Dozier, M., Stovall, K. C., & Albus, K. E. (1999). Attachment and psychopathology in adulthood. In J. Cassidy and P. R. Shaver (Eds.), *Handbook of attachment: Theory, research and clinical applications* (pp. 497–519). New York: Guilford.

Eagle, M. (1997). Attachment and psychoanalysis. *British Journal of Medical Psychology, 70,* 217–229.

Exner, J. E., Jr. (1993). *The Rorschach: A comprehensive system. Vol. 1: Basic foundations* (3rd ed.). New York: Wiley.

Fonagy, P. (1999). Psychoanalytic theory from the viewpoint of attachment theory and research. In J. Cassidy & P. R. Shaver (Eds.), *Handbook of attachment: Theory, research and clinical applications* (pp. 595–624). New York: Guilford.

Fonagy, P., Leigh, T., Steele, M., Steele, H., Kennedy, R., Mattoon, G., et al. (1996). The relation of attachment status, psychiatric classification, and response to psychotherapy. *Journal of Consulting and Clinical Psychology, 64,* 22–31.

George, C., & West, M. (1999). Developmental vs. social personality models of adult attachment and mental ill health. *British Journal of Medical Psychology, 72,* 285–303.

George, C., & West, M. Psychometric properties of the Adult Attachment Projective. Unpublished data set.

George, C., Kaplan, N., & Main, M. (1985). *Adult Attachment Interview* (2nd ed.). Unpublished manuscript, University of California at Berkeley.

George, C., West, M., & Pettem, O. (1997). *Adult Attachment Projective protocol and classification scoring system*. Unpublished manuscript, Mills College.

Grice, P. (1975). Logic and conversation. In P. Cole & J. L. Moran (Eds.), *Syntax and semantics III: Speech acts,* (pp. 41–58). New York: Academic Press.

Gunderson, J. G. (1996). The borderline patient's intolerance of aloneness: Insecure attachments and therapist availability. *American Journal of Psychiatry, 153,* 752–758.

Hansburg, H. (1972). *Adolescent separation anxiety: A method for the study of adolescent separation problems*. Springfield, IL: C.C. Thomas.

Hazan, C., & Shaver, P. R. (1987). Romantic love conceptualized as an attachment process. *Journal of Personality and Social Psychology, 52,* 511–524.

Hesse, E. (1999). The Adult Attachment Interview: Historical and current perspectives. In J. Cassidy & P. R. Shaver (Eds.), *Handbook of attachment: Theory, research and clinical applications* (pp. 395–433). New York: Guilford.

Joubert, D., Mazzarello, T., Moss, E., Paquette, D., & Zoccolillo, M. (Manuscript in preparation). *Attachment and antisocial characteristics in adolescent mothers and their children.*

Klagsbrun, M., & Bowlby, J. (1976). Responses to separation from parents: A clinical test for young children. *British Journal of Projective Psychology, 21,* 7–27.

Lerner, P. (1991). *Psychoanalytic theory and the Rorschach*. Hillsdale, NJ.: Analytic Press.

Lyons-Ruth, K., & Jacobvitz, D. (1999). Attachment disorganization: Unresolved loss, relational violence and lapses in behavioral and attentional strategies. In J. Cassidy & P. R. Shaver (Eds.), *Handbook of attachment: Theory, research and clinical applications* (pp. 520–554). New York: Guilford.

Main, M. (1995). Recent studies in attachment. In S. Goldberg, R. Muir, & J. Kerr (Eds.), *Attachment theory: Social, developmental and clinical perspectives* (pp. 467–474). Hillsdale, NJ: Analytic Press.

Main, M., & Solomon, J. (1990). Procedures for identifying infants as disorganized/disoriented during the Ainsworth strange situation. In M. Greenberg, D. Cichetti, & E. M. Cummings (Eds.), *Attachment during the preschool years : Theory, research and intervention* (pp. 121–160). Chicago: University of Chicago Press.

Mezzich, A. C., Heliste, J. L., George, C., Kolar, A.,B., Swaney, M., Raspet, D., et al. (2006). *Adult attachment and substance use disorder in young women*. unpublished data set.

Moss, E., Cyr, C., & Dubois-Comtois, K. (August, 2004*). Maternal attachment representations and child attachment at preschool age: The role of mother-child discourse*. In A. Bernier (Chair), *A further look into the attachment transmission gap: New conceptual and methodological approaches.* Symposium conducted at biennial meeting of the International Society for the Study of Behavioral Development, Ghent, Belgium.

Moss, E., Thibaudeau, P., Joubert, D., Beliveau, M. J., & Dubois-Comtois, K. (Manuscript in preparation). *Attachment in adolescents and their mothers.*

Odipo, C. (2002). *Adult attachment classification and foster mother's perceptions of their relationship with their at-risk foster children*. Unpublished doctoral dissertation, University of the Pacific, Stockton CA.

Schafer, R. (1954*). Psychoanalytic interpretation in Rorschach testing: Theory and application*. New York: Grune & Stratton.

Slough, N. M., Goyette, M., & Greenberg, M. T. (1988). *Scoring indices for the Seattle version of the Separation Anxiety Test.* Seattle, WA: University of Washington.

Solomon, J., & George, C. (1999). The place of disorganization in attachment theory: Linking classic observations with contemporary findings. In J. Solomon & C. George (Eds.), *Attachment disorganization* (pp. 3–32). New York: Guilford Press.

Sroufe, L. A., & Fleeson, J. (1986). Attachment and the construction of relationships. In W. Hartup & Z. Rubin (Eds.), *The nature and development of relationships* (pp. 51–71). Hillsdale, NJ: Earlbaum.

Sroufe, L. A. (1988). The role of infant–caregiver attachment in development. In J. Belsky & T. Nezworski (Eds.), *Clinical implications of attachment* (pp. 18–38). Chicago: University of Chicago Press.

Stone, M. (1990). *The fate of borderlines.* New York: Guilford.

Thompson, R. A. (1999). Early attachment and later development. In J. Cassidy & P. R. Shaver (Eds.), *Handbook of attachment theory and research* (pp. 265–286). New York: Guilford.

Waters, E., Crowell, J., Elliott, M., Corcoran, D., & Treboux, D. (2002). Bowlby's secure base theory and the social/personality psychology of attachment styles: Work(s) in progress. *Attachment and Human Development, 4,* 223–229.

Waters, E., Merrick, S., Trebous, D., Crowell, J., & Abersheim, L. (2000). Attachment stability in infancy and early childhood. *Child Development, 71,* 684–689.

Webster, L., & Joubert, D. (March, 2006). *Rorschach correlates of unresolved attachment in adolescents placed in foster care.* Poster presented at the annual meeting of the Society for Personality Assessment, San Diego, CA.

West, M., & George, C. (1999). Violence in intimate adult relationships: An attachment theory perspective. *Attachment and Human Development, 1,* 137–156.

West, M., & George, C. (2002). Attachment and dysthymia: The contributions of preoccupied attachment and agency of self to depression in women. *Attachment and Human Development, 4,* 278–293.

Note

The author would like to thank Carol George, PhD., and Malcolm West, Ph.D., for their useful comments.

33
CHAPTER

The Contemporized-Themes Concerning Blacks Test (C-TCB)

Michelle Hoy-Watkins and Valata Jenkins-Monroe

Abstract

It is vitally important that we develop, out of the authentic experience of Black people in this country, an accurate workable theory of Black psychology. It is very difficult, if not impossible to understand the lifestyles of Black people using traditional theories developed by White psychologists to explain White people. Moreover, when these traditional theories are applied to the lives of Black folks many incorrect, weakness-dominated, and inferiority-oriented conclusions come about.

White (1972, P. 5)

This chapter presents an overview of the theoretical construct and scoring system for The Contemporized-Themes Concerning Blacks Test (C-TCB) (Hoy, 1997). The C-TCB is a thematic apperception test for African Americans that was developed based on an Africentric theoretical framework. The test consists of 27 chromatic projective cards with thematic content that represents current-day situations commonly experienced within the African American community. The scoring system identifies eight aspects of personality traits and nine affective states. Based on the normative data, various affective states were attributed to each card. At least one aspect of personality functioning was attributed to each of the 27 projective cards. Results revealed a high degree of interrater reliability on 14 of the 27 thematic cards. Sample scoring and implications for future research are discussed.

☐ Description of System

Conceptual Framework

For decades traditional projective tests have been used cross-culturally. It became evident that the clinical utility of such instruments was limited due to test bias. Specific to projective instruments, there was a lack of cultural congruency (e.g., racial features, contextual or cultural setting) between the images in the projective cards (e.g., Caucasian) and the test taker. The use of such instruments with African American or Black test takers often led to shorter story length and lack of cultural identification (Brunson, 1981; Dlepu, 1981; Duzant, 2005; Matthews-Evans, 1992; Squire, 1985; Thompson, 1949; Triplett, 1981; Weaver, 1978). It became evident that there was a profound need for the development of tests that examined specific cultural issues and other relevant factors (e.g., race, language, level of acculturation) (Dana, 1996). Several problems are attributed to the administration, scoring, and interpretation of psychological tests that are not culturally congruent with the test population. First, the tests' normative data should be congruent with the examinees' cultural background. According to the Ethical Principles of Psychologists and Code of Conduct (2002, p. 12), "psychologists use assessment instruments whose validity and reliability have been established for use with members of the population tested."

Perhaps one of the earliest attempts to address test bias commonly purported with the original Thematic Apperception Test (TAT) was the research conducted by Thompson (1949). He modified the TAT (Thompson TAT, or T-TAT) to examine the usefulness of the test with African Americans. He hypothesized that the similarity between the examinees and the test stimuli would elicit greater emotional feeling tone and verbal fluency. Ten of the cards were modified, changing (by shading) the faces of Anglo-Americans to African American. Neither the physical characteristics nor the card theme of the stimulus figures were modified. Thompson found that implementation of a culturally specific measurement increased story length and identification and was overall more beneficial with African Americans than the traditional TAT. Subsequent studies revealed that the T-TAT was not applicable to all African Americans (Bailey & Green, 1977; Cook, 1953; Light, 1955). Specifically, critics found no significant difference in the responses (e.g., need expression, themes,) produced by African Americans between the TAT and the T-TAT. Because of this criticism, the T-TAT was widely abandoned, and its usefulness with African Americans was discouraged.

Bailey and Green (1977) found that the integration of Black American racial characteristics had a positive influence (e.g., increase in subject response) on participant's responses. They found that the T-TAT modification did nothing more than include a black face to its projective cards. Instead, Bailey and Green developed an Experimental TAT (E-TAT), which integrated Black cultural features such as facial features, hairstyles, and hair texture. They compared the stories told among the original M-TAT, T-TAT, and E-TAT of 135 Black Southern males. The results revealed that adding racial features to the cards was advantageous in that it enhanced the story length and elicited positive ratings among participants.

Perhaps the first culturally specific projective instrument that reflected the daily experiences of African Americans, captured the unique physical characteristics of African Americans, and was normed on an African American population was the

Themes Concerning Blacks Test (TCB), developed by Robert Williams (1972). The TCB was constructed in part as a response to the TAT. Williams questioned the validity of assessing Black personality from an Anglo-American theoretical worldview. The TCB is an Africentric thematic apperception test designed to stimulate responses from Blacks in relation to their daily lifestyles and experiences based on African-centered beliefs, ideology, and practices.

The TCB consists of 20 achromatic charcoal drawings that depict aspects of African American lifestyles in both rural and urban areas. Williams administered the TCB to 64 African American children. The most common themes elicited from the preliminary research were academic motivation, athletic drive, socialization (need affiliation and interpersonal relations), achievement, autonomy (self-reliance), Black pride, identification, aggression, and self-confidence.

Subsequent studies (Brunson, 1981; Dlepu, 1981; Hawley & Williams, 1981; Matthew-Evans, 1992; Squire, 1985; Triplett, 1981; Weaver, 1978) compared the relevance and usefulness of the TCB and TAT with African Americans. Overall, results revealed increased story length, a higher degree of positive feeling tone, greater achievement orientation, and identification with the TCB.

White, Olivieira, Strube, and Meertens (1995) assessed the usefulness of the TCB across three cultures of African descent in their respective countries: African Americans (United States), African Dutch (Europe), and African Surinamers (South America). In the study, 13 projective cards were administered and read in the participant's native language. Results revealed cross-cultural identification, and no significant difference between groups with regard to feeling tone.

The application and relevance of the TCB today may be limited given the obvious multigenerational gap in the thematic card stimulus. The TCB was developed during the early 1970s during the epoch of segregation and civil rights, and the cards largely reflect a dated era. The characteristics (e.g., political themes, hairstyles, clothing) of the individuals in the cards are consistent with current times. Another limitation is that most of the preliminary research is based on normative data collected from children.

Other culturally congruent projective tests for African Americans include the Roberts Apperception Test (Roberts, 1982) and the Tell-Me-A-Story-Test (TEMAS) (Costantino, Malgady, & Rogler, 1988). The TEMAS is a thematic apperception test that was initially developed for use with Hispanic and African American children and adolescents. The TEMAS contains minority and nonminority versions of the test stimuli. Regarding cultural specificity for African Americans, the TEMAS contains chromatic pictures and "ethnically relevant and contemporary stimuli to elicit diagnostically meaningful stories" (Costantino, Malgady, Casullo, & Castillo, 1991, p. 49). The normative group also included 42 Black children. Its theoretical constructs are based on a dynamic cognitive approach, which evaluates aspects of personality development from a sociocultural perspective.

The Roberts Apperception Test also contains a set of stimulus cards for African Americans that are illustrative of the culture physical characteristics. Although the stimuli will likely increase verbal fluency and identification given the test-takers' ability to relate better to the content, the cards were not at all normed (Roberts, 1994).

The scoring systems for the TEMAS and the Roberts Apperception Test do not embody an Africentric theoretical framework. That is, with regard to personality functioning, the objective scoring systems do not embrace a scoring criterion that takes into account cultural values and practices.

Although the underlying principles and general usefulness of the existing cross-cultural thematic apperception tests may yield good data for some clinical situations with

African Americans, the Contemporized-Themes Concerning Blacks Test (C-TCB) (Hoy, 1997) was developed to address their specific limitations. The C-TCB was created as an attempt to modernize the TCB, such that it reflects the current and future psychosocial experiences of African Americans.

Like its predecessor, The Themes Concerning Blacks Test, the C-TCB was developed based on an Africentric theoretical perspective, which posits that the psychosocial experiences of African Americans should be examined in the context of their historical, cultural, and social experiences (Williams & Johnson, 1981). Recurring sociopolitical issues such as racism, economic hardship, and marginalized social status should be considered in understanding the daily experiences of African Americans. This framework includes traditional African values learned through family, spiritual practices, and societal experiences. The C-TCB embraces the importance of extended family, spirituality, communality, and cultural pride.

The C-TCB consists of 27 chromatic thematic cards that depict various common daily-life experiences of African Americans. The situations (i.e., intended thematic card content) depicted are as follows:

(1) Kinship and extended family

(2) Teenage pregnancy

(3) Single parenting

(4) Media portrayal of African Americans

(5) Institutionalized racism

(6) Substance abuse

(7) Implications of HIV/AIDS

By depicting thematic content commonly experienced within the African American community, responses are expected to elicit similar themes to those produced by the TCB, including individual motivation (academic and social) family unity, Black pride, autonomy, and political leadership. Given the diverse physical characteristics (e.g., skin tone, facial features, hairstyles, hair textures, physique, clothes style) among African Americans, the characters depicted in the C-TCB are illustrative of such diversity.

Scoring Categories

The scoring system for the C-TCB was adapted from the TCB (Williams, 1972) and TEMAS (Costantino et al., 1988). Each protocol is scored to assess personality and affective functioning. The personality and affective scoring systems were constructed based on an Africentric theoretical framework. Each story is scored on a five-point Likert scale for personality functioning and on a four-point Likert scale for affective functioning (Tables 33.1, 33.2). Eight scales assess personality functioning, and nine scales assess affective functioning.

TABLE 33.1 Description and Scoring for Personality Traits

Personality Traits	Brief Descriptions of Personality Traits
Goal Setting/Motivation	Aspirational goals or coping strategy to be implemented
Interpersonal Relationships	Degree of relatedness to others (e.g., family, friends, community affiliation)
Family Unity	Individual's identification of family solidarity
Group Needs	Identified needs of the community, religious systems, family members, and so forth
Autonomy	Ability to manage independently
Self-Concept	Self-perception of emotional and physical representation of African Americans
Black Pride	Cultural/racial dignity, values, beliefs, or identification associated with being Black or African American
Identity Confusion	The attribution of a lack of connectedness or uncertainty with ones cultural identity (e.g., physical characteristics, gender, sex or role in the family)
Rating	**Level of Functioning for Each Personality Trait**
1	Highly adaptive behavior, feelings, decision, or outcome
2	Moderately adaptive behavior, feeling, decision, outcome
3	Moderately maladaptive behavior, feeling, decision or outcome; attribution of a negative behavior to accomplish a goal
4	Highly maladaptive behavior, feeling, decision, or outcome
0	Personality functioning not attributed to the card

The personality functioning scoring system is conceptualized based on an Africentric theoretical model. It is important to define this model, as discussed by Williams and Johnson (1981), which posits that the daily functioning of African Americans should be understood in relation to their historical, cultural, and social experiences. In this system, African Americans internalize culturally specific values, beliefs, and practices derived and practiced from African traditions. These values and belief systems are learned through the traditions of family, extended family, church or religious system, and society. Such values are internalized and projected in testing situations. Given the cultural specificity of the C-TCB stimuli, as compared with nonculturally normed thematic tests, responses are expected to include longer stories, greater feeling tone, and identification compared to the T-TAT. Eight personality traits are measured by this system:

(1) Goal-setting/motivation

(2) Interpersonal relationships

(3) Family unity

TABLE 33.2 Description and Scoring for Affective States

Affective States	Brief Description of Affective States
Responsibility	Subjective feeling of obligation to help resolve situations
Happy	Subjective feelings of satisfaction or gratification
Trust	The ability to have faith or the belief in oneself and others or the attribution of a positive outcome
Sad	Feelings of sorrow or disappointment
Anger	Feelings of extreme dissatisfaction
Lonely	Feelings of isolation, lack of family closeness, or socialization
Aggression	Expression of the intent to cause verbal or physical harm to others or property
Fear	Feelings of apprehension about the present or future situations
Depression	Multiple symptoms suggestive of feeling down, including worthlessness, helplessness, being withdrawn, or crying
Rating	**Level of Functioning for Each Affective State**
1	Attribution of high levels of a specific affective or emotional tone
2	Attribution of moderate levels of affective functioning or emotional tone
3	Attribution of low levels of affective functioning or emotional tone
0	This score results when the test taker omits attribution of emotions to the test stimuli; no emotional tone is conveyed. Missing Data

(4) Group needs

(5) Autonomy

(6) Self-concept

(7) Black pride

(8) Identity confusion

Each of these personality traits should be rated on all stories to assess for common themes across cards.

The affective functioning scoring system measures the emotional feeling tone projected onto the projective stimuli. Affective characteristics were included to encompass a range of emotions that may be experienced based on the thematic card content. Teen pregnancy, single parenting, institutionalized racism, and academic achievement are just a few of the thematic card situations that may evoke emotional feeling tone, depending on the level of identification by the examinee. It is not uncommon that African Americans who are familiar with such life situations have experienced a variety of emotions in response to their daily experiences. Given the social, historical, and political nature of the situations in each card, test takers may experience any range of individual or mixed emotions. There are nine affective states:

(1) Responsibility

(2) Happy

(3) Trust

(4) Sad

(5) Anger

(6) Lonely

(7) Aggression

(8) Fear

(9) Depression

Each of the nine affective states should be rated on all stories to assess whether specific emotional themes are projected onto the cards.

Research Evidence

Validity

Content validity was determined to assess agreement between the intended thematic content and the identified card content as identified by raters. Raters consisted of 10 African American women: one clinical psychologist, six doctoral level students, and three master's-level students. All raters had successfully completed course work in objective personality assessment and had clinical training with objective psychological test measures. Each rater participated in either an individual or group training sessions on the scoring procedures for the C-TCB. The duration of the training session was two hours. During the trainings, the raters were provided with practice protocols that they were required to administer and score. Once the training was complete, the raters were each given 10 participant protocols to rate. Each rater was provided with a description of each affective and personality scoring criterion and blank scoring forms.

Figures 33.1 through 33.26 represent the raters' frequency of attribution for each card of the nine expected themes. In summary, there were three cards designed to evoke each theme. Again, the expected card content themes were as follows:

(1) Teenage pregnancy

(2) Political leadership/Black pride

(3) Extended family/unity

(4) Single parenting

(5) Media portrayal of Blacks

(6) Institutionalized racism

(7) Individual motivation/autonomy

(8) Academic motivation/achievement

(9) Safe sex and drug abuse (implications of HIV/AIDS).

Results revealed that only one of the three intended cards elicited the expected theme of teenage pregnancy, although pregnancy was the prominent theme. Of the three expected to evoke the theme of single parenting, only one did so. Institutionalized racism was attributed to one of the expected three cards. All three of the cards that were intended to measure extended family and unity did so, according to the raters. Results revealed that two of three cards designed for the expected theme of media portrayal of Blacks tapped that theme. Academic achievement/motivation was measured on all three of the intended cards. Two of the three cards expected to measure individual motivation and autonomy were seen that way. Political leadership/Black pride was attributed to all three of the intended cards. Implications of safe/unsafe sex and substance abuse were not attributed to any of the expected cards.

Raters also assessed the attribution of personality traits to cards (Table 33.3). Results revealed that 11 cards represented group needs; 10 cards, goal setting and motivation; 13 cards, interpersonal relationships; 8 cards, family unity; 3 cards, autonomy; 1 card, self-concept; 2 cards, political leadership/Black pride.

TABLE 33.3 Attribution of Personality Traits by Raters Across 27 Cards

Personality Trait	Card Number
Goal Setting/Motivation	1, 7, 8, 11, 17, 20, 22, 25, 26, 27
Interpersonal Relationships	3, 4, 10, 11, 13, 15, 18–23, 25
Family Unity	4, 11, 13, 15, 19, 20, 22, 26
Group Needs	4, 7, 9, 11, 13, 15, 16, 22, 25–27
Autonomy	8, 11, 17
Self-Concept	27
Black Pride	18, 27
Identity Confusion	—

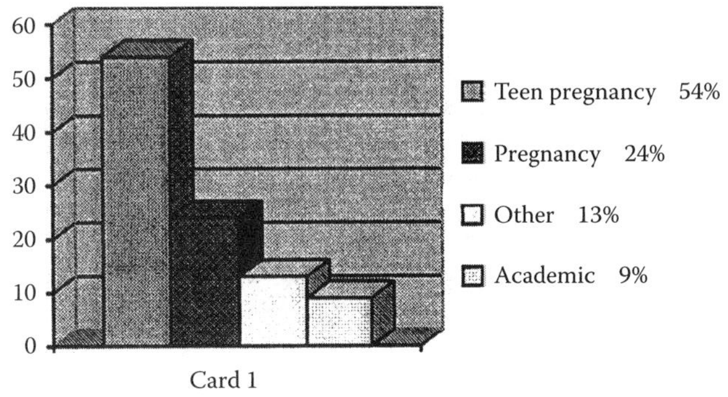

FIGURE 33.1 Card 1 Thematic Content Frequencies.

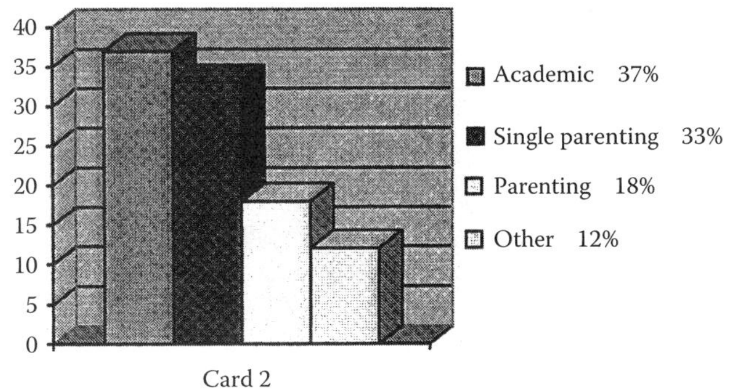

FIGURE 33.2 Card 2 Thematic Content Frequencies.

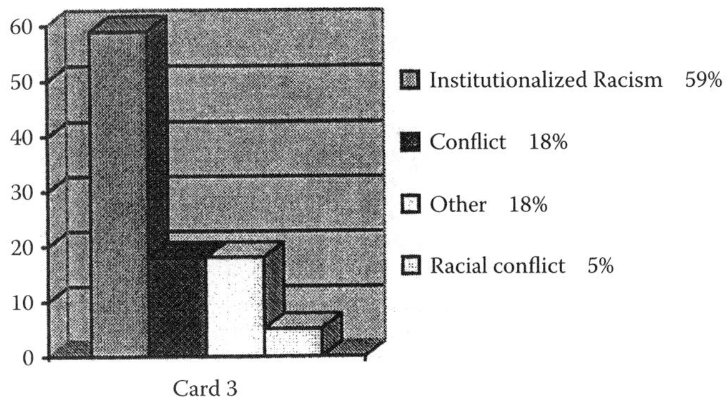

FIGURE 33.3 Card 3 Thematic Content Frequencies.

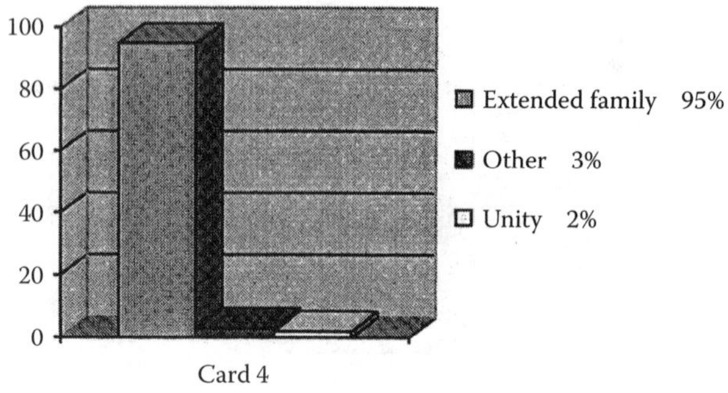

FIGURE 33.4 Card 4 Thematic Content Frequencies.

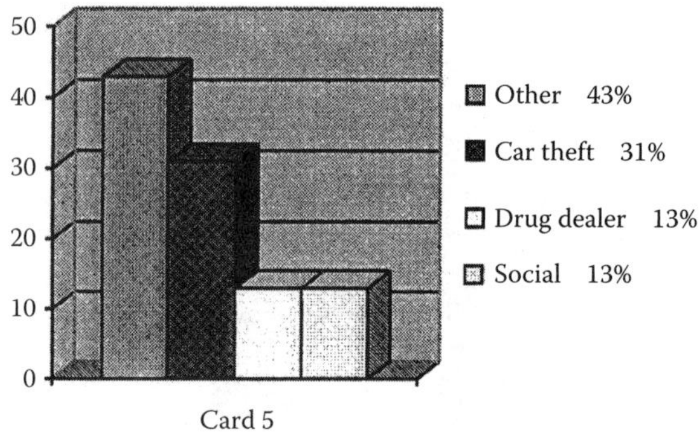

FIGURE 33.5 Card 5 Thematic Content Frequencies.

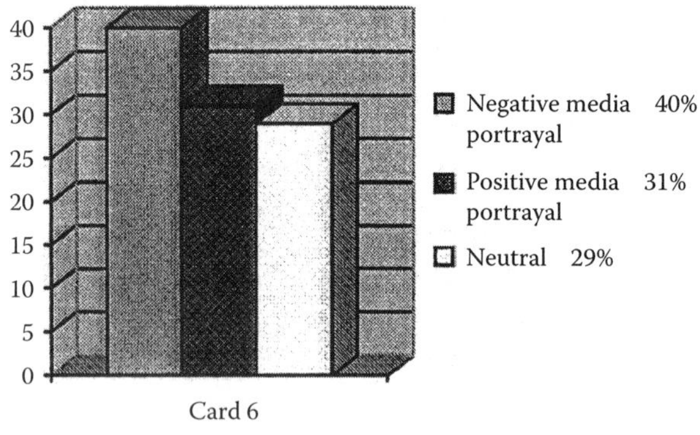

FIGURE 33.6 Card 6 Thematic Content Frequencies.

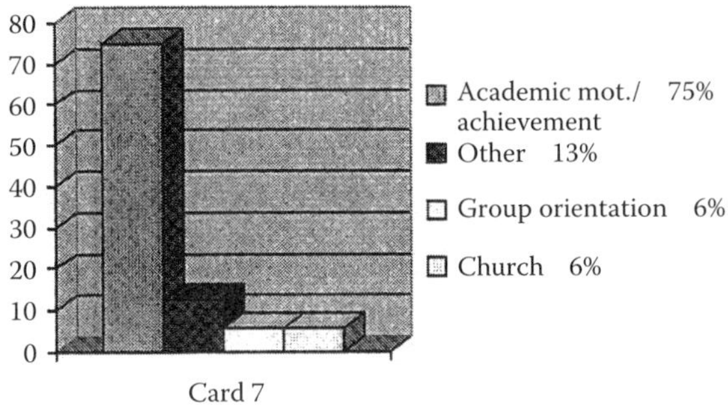

FIGURE 33.7 Card 7 Thematic Content Frequencies.

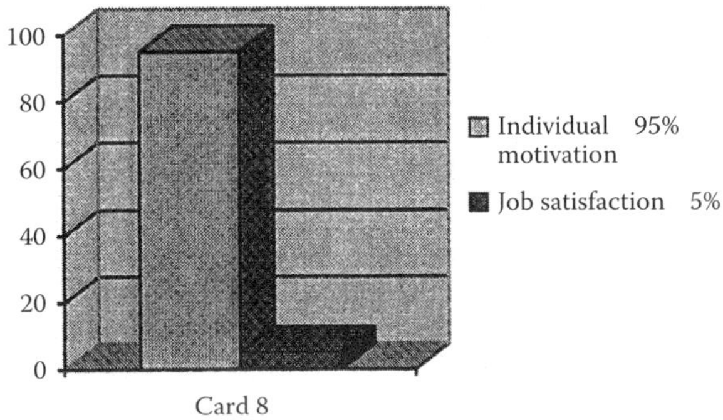

FIGURE 33.8 Card 8 Thematic Content Frequencies.

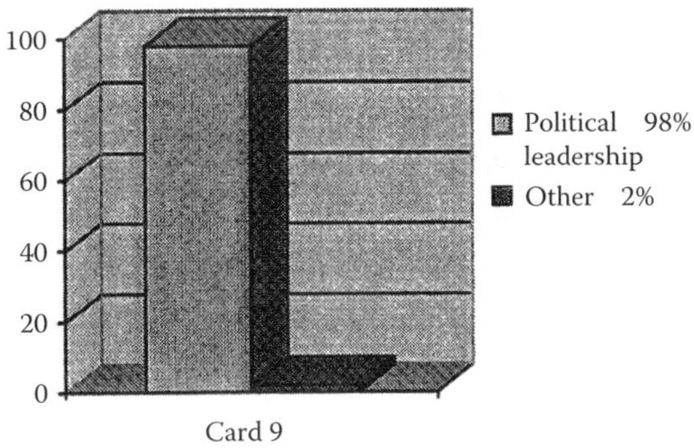

FIGURE 33.9 Card 9 Thematic Content Frequencies.

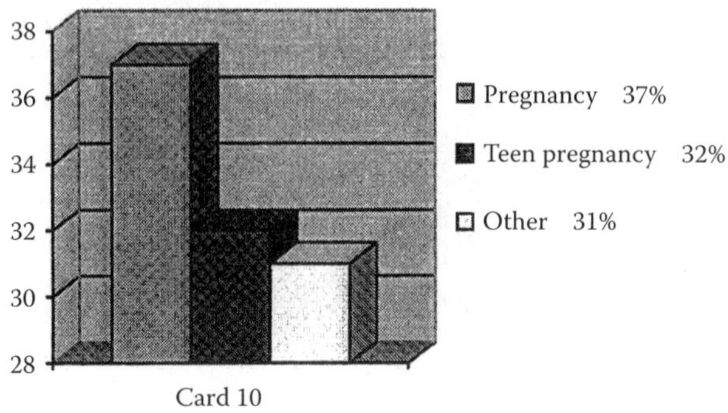

FIGURE 33.10 Card 10 Thematic Content Frequencies.

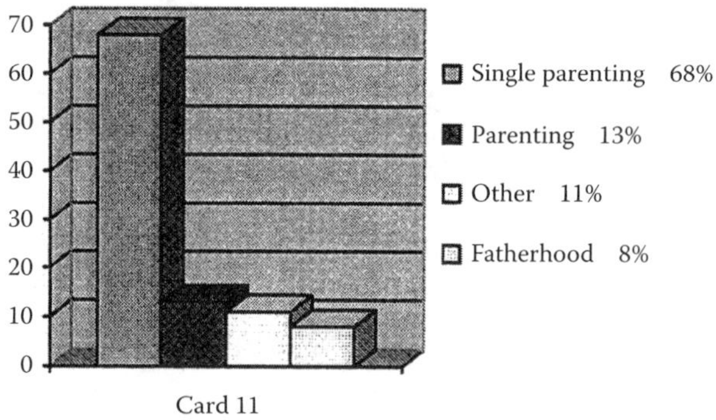

FIGURE 33.11 Card 11 Thematic Content Frequencies.

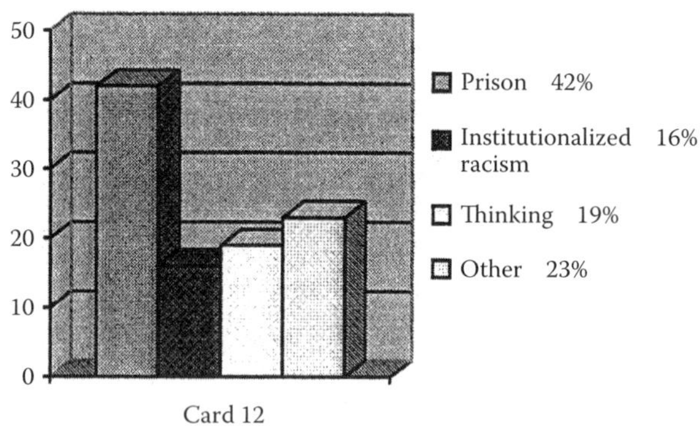

FIGURE 33.12 Card 12 Thematic Content Frequencies.

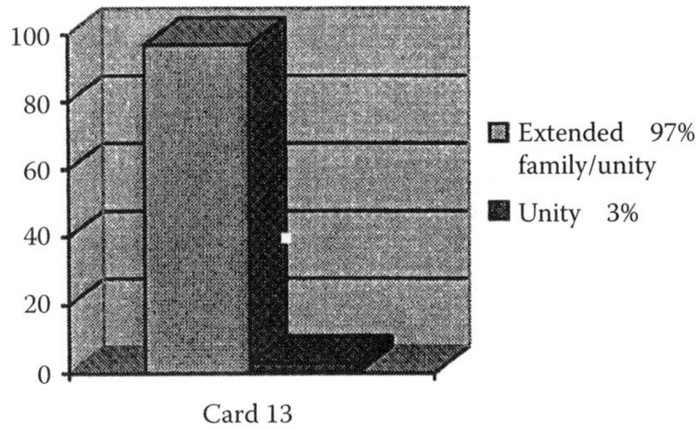

FIGURE 33.13 Card 13 Thematic Content Frequencies.

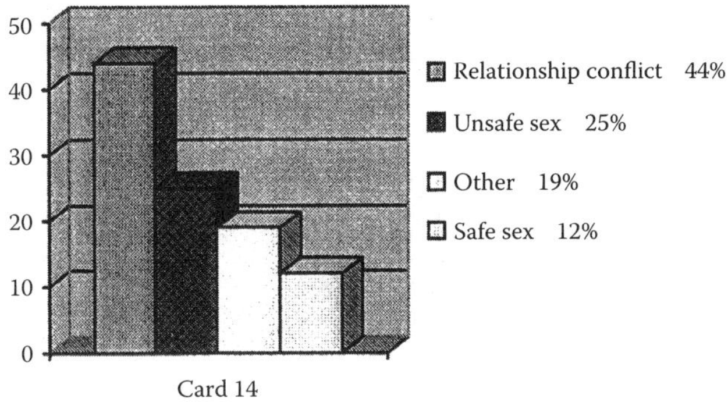

FIGURE 33.14 Card 14 Thematic Content Frequencies.

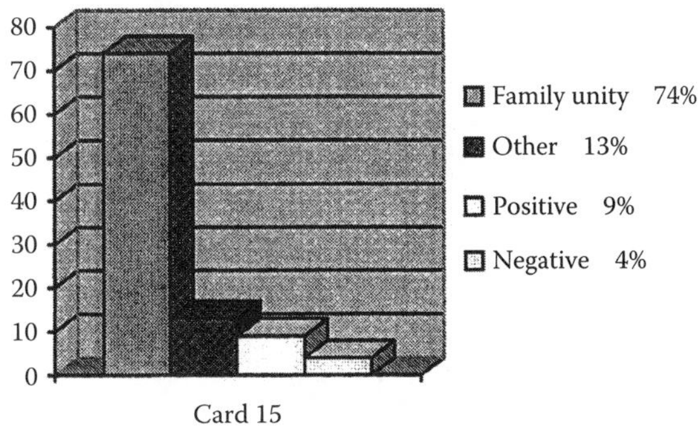

FIGURE 33.15 Card 15 Thematic Content Frequencies.

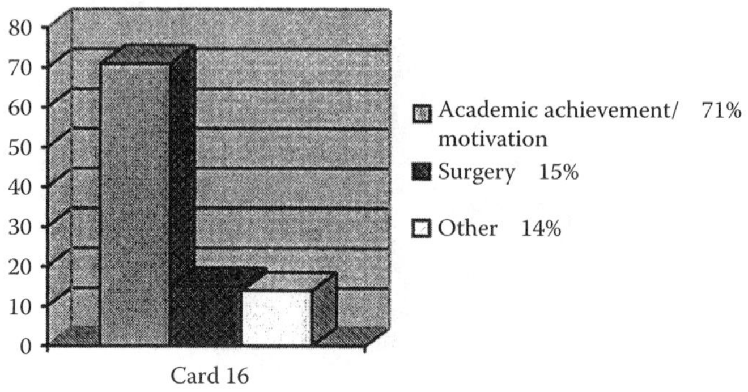

FIGURE 33.16 Card 16 Thematic Content Frequencies.

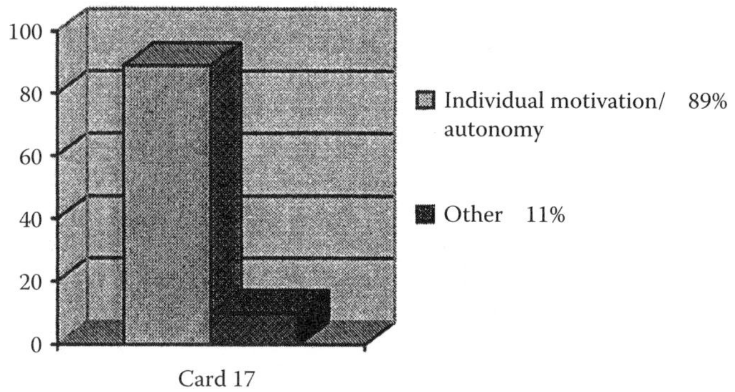

FIGURE 33.17 Card 17 Thematic Content Frequencies.

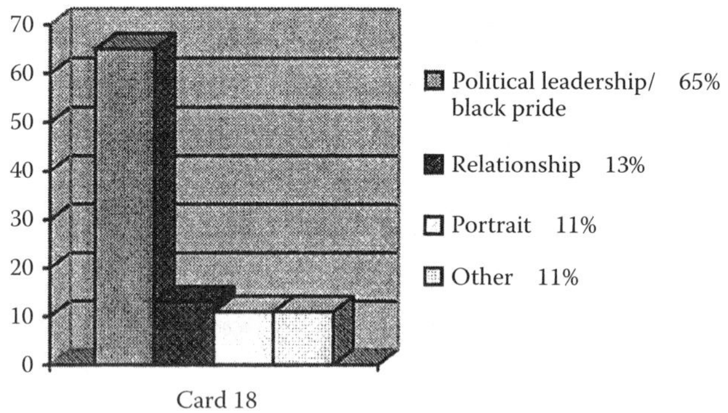

FIGURE 33.18 Card 18 Thematic Content Frequencies.

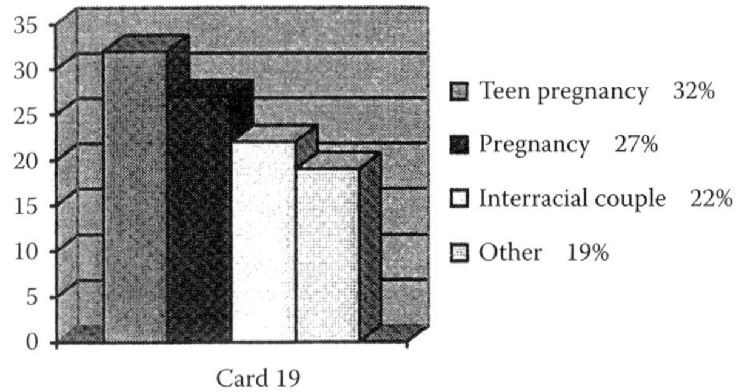

FIGURE 33.19 Card 19 Thematic Content Frequencies.

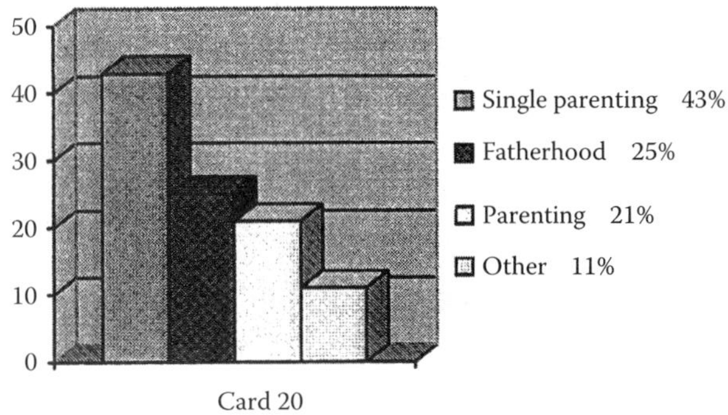

FIGURE 33.20 Card 20 Thematic Content Frequencies.

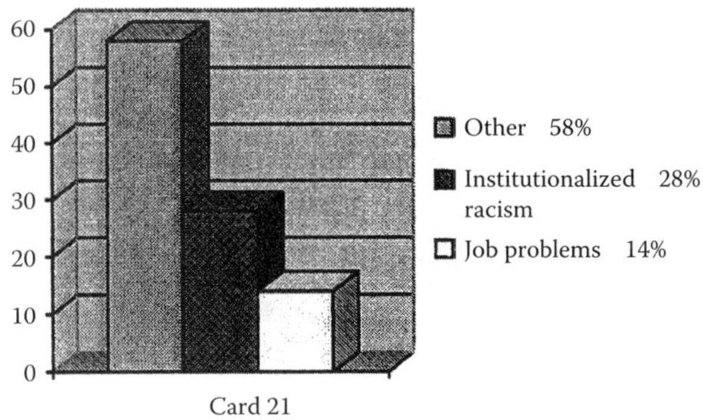

FIGURE 33.21 Card 21 Thematic Content Frequencies.

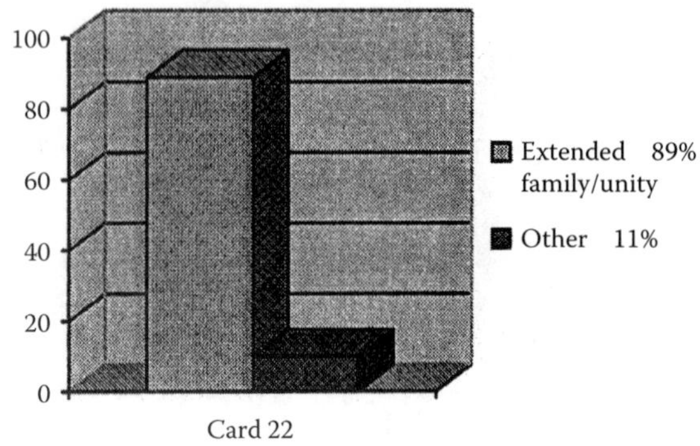

FIGURE 33.22 Card 22 Thematic Content Frequencies.

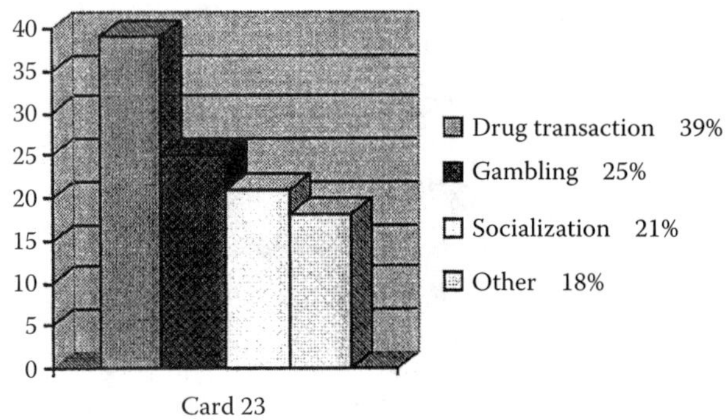

FIGURE 33.23 Card 23 Thematic Content Frequencies.

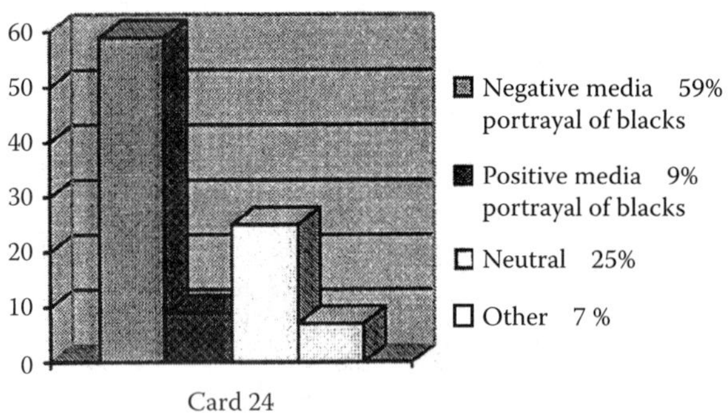

FIGURE 33.24 Card 24 Thematic Content Frequencies.

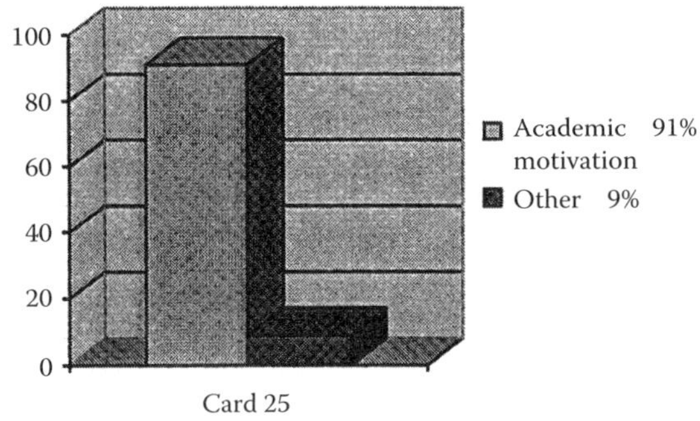

FIGURE 33.25 Card 25 Thematic Content Frequencies.

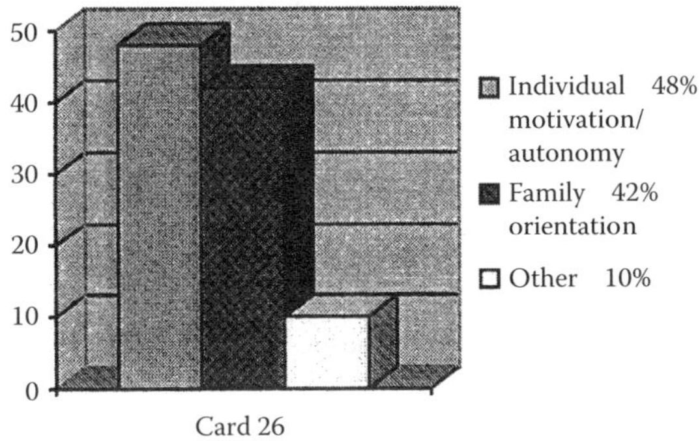

FIGURE 33.26 Card 26 Thematic Content Frequencies.

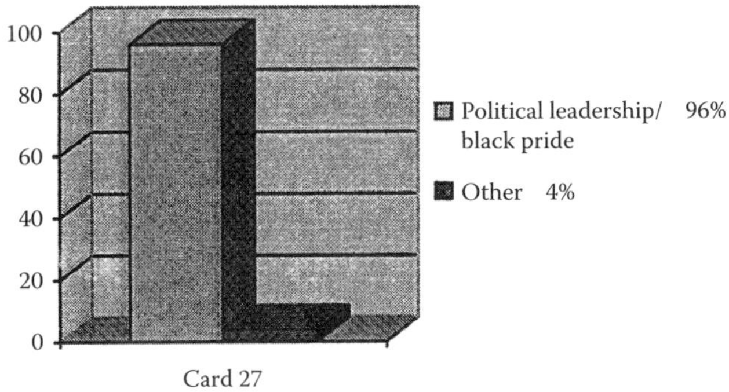

FIGURE 33.27 Card 27 Thematic Content Frequencies.

TABLE 33.4 Attribution of Affective States by Raters on the C-TCB Cards

Affective State	Moderate	High
Responsibility	1, 3, 7, 9, 10, 14–17, 19, 21, 22, 25	2, 8, 11, 13, 20, 26, 27
Happy	1, 7, 8, 10, 11, 13, 15, 16, 18, 19, 21, 22, 26	4, 9, 17, 20, 25, 27
Trust	1, 2, 4, 7–11, 13, 15–22, 25–27	—
Sad	12	—
Anger	14	—
Lonely	—	—
Aggression	—	—
Fear	—	—
Depression	—	—

The attribution of affective states attributed to each C-TCB card is illustrated in Table 33.4. As mentioned earlier, the raters measured nine affective states to assess the attribution of emotional feeling tone to the C-TCB cards by participants. Results revealed that the cards should elicit a high level of positive affective functioning from the average participant. A moderate level of trust was attributed to 20 cards; 7 cards were described as having high levels and 13 as having moderate levels of responsibility. Characters were described as having high levels of happiness in 6 cards and a moderate level of happiness in 13 cards. Sadness was attributed to one card (card 12), and anger was attributed to one card (card 14). Mean affective ratings for all 27 cards are indicated in Table 33.5.

Generalizability

Although the C-TCB has only been normed with African American males and females ages 18–32, it is thought that the general relevance of the thematic cards is applicable to the African American community at large. Given the cultural specificity of the C-TCB, the intended use of this instrument is to be administered to African Americans from childhood through late adulthood. The C-TCB is intended for use within community mental health centers, correctional settings, outpatient counseling settings, and college counseling centers (Hoy, 1997).

Reliability

Ten raters were trained during individual and small-group sessions with up to three raters. Each participated in a two-hour training session discussing the procedures and scoring criteria. During the training session, raters were given practice protocols to administer and score individually and with assistance from the researcher. On completion of training, each rater was given 10 participant protocols, which consisted of 27 stories to rate. Each story was rated based on each of the personality traits and affective states using the scales in Tables 33.1 and 33.2.

TABLE 33.5 Mean Ratings for Affective States Across 27 C-TCB Cards

Card	Trust	Loneliness	Responsibility	Happy	Sad	Anger	Fear	Aggression	Depression
1	1.08	.66	1.71	1.21	.98	.30	.47	.21	.46
2	1.26	.43	2.00	.88	.65	.20	.56	.30	.35
3	.65	.44	.71	.51	.42	.68	.83	.93	.31
4	1.15	.35	1.04	2.70	.33	.26	.22	.33	.22
5	.84	.33	.72	.90	.28	.48	.47	.35	.21
6	.74	.36	.396	.89	.50	.27	.32	.40	.25
7	1.50	.35	1.45	1.67	.37	.23	.26	.29	.22
8	1.62	.27	2.22	1.29	.39	.19	.25	.23	.29
9	1.99	.29	1.89	2.71	.39	.19	.22	.24	.20
10	1.20	.66	1.55	1.44	.99	.22	.45	.31	.41
11	1.73	.41	2.21	1.58	.60	.22	.46	.25	.27
12	.78	.93	.89	.64	1.37	.32	.45	.41	.78
13	1.67	.33	2.06	1.60	.46	.19	.21	.24	.25
14	.92	.51	1.13	.65	.69	.52	.65	1.39	.33
15	1.23	.35	1.22	1.95	.31	.28	.19	.29	.20
16	1.82	.29	1.81	1.02	.33	.21	.54	.16	.18
17	1.48	.32	1.35	2.38	.32	.21	.18	.20	.22
18	1.07	.37	.97	1.63	.38	.15	.20	.23	.21
19	1.35	.34	1.58	1.98	.52	.20	.44	.34	.22
20	1.61	.31	2.30	2.43	.65	.18	.19	.20	.20
21	1.00	.37	1.07	.83	.75	.28	.72	.61	.36
22	1.67	.34	1.66	1.97	.42	.21	.26	.35	.25
23	.68	.47	.58	1.59	.82	.36	.32	.65	.23
24	.71	.40	.82	.69	.28	.38	.29	.70	.41
25	1.82	.29	1.92	2.36	.46	.24	.30	.26	.20
26	1.66	.35	2.18	1.57	.28	.26	.28	.42	.29
27	1.80	.38	2.05	2.05	.46	.39	.25	.52	.25

Notes: 0–1 = neutral rating; 1–2 = low level; 2–3 = moderate level; 3 = high level.

Interrater reliability was established to measure the agreement between raters with regard to the presence or absence of the expected theme in the story (Table 33.6). As indicated in Table 33.6, there is high interrater agreement between .40 and 1.00 for 14 out of 26 cards. Results also revealed low to moderate levels of agreement on several of the C-TCB cards although not at a statistically significant level.

Kendall's tau coefficient was implemented to analyze the ratings for the personality traits and affective states (Tables 33.7, 33.8) to determine the strength of the association between two ranked variables. The numbers in Table 33.8 represent the mean scores attributed to each card for all raters.

TABLE 33.6 Interrater Reliability for Expected Theme (Kappa Coefficients) Across 27 Cards (N = 100 Participants)

Card	Expected Theme	Kappa Coefficient
1	Teenage Pregnancy	.57*
2	Single Parenting	.29
3	Institutionalized Racism	.50*
4	Extended Family/Unity	–.04
5	Substance Abuse	.83**
6	Media Portrayal of Blacks	.14
7	Academic Achievement	.71*
8	Individual Motivation	.23
9	Political Leadership/Black Pride	1.00**
10	Teenage Pregnancy	.27
11	Single Parenting	.33
12	Institutionalized Racism	.40*
13	Extended Family/Unity	.64*
14	Safe versus Unsafe Sex	.52*
15	Media Portrayal of Blacks	1.00**
16	Academic Achievement	.43*
17	Individual Motivation	–.08
18	Political Leadership/Black Pride	.30
19	Teenage Pregnancy	.39
20	Single Parenting	.50*
21	Institutionalized Racism	.70*
22	Extended Family/Unity	.64*
23	Substance Abuse	.26
24	Media Portrayal of Blacks	.20
25	Academic Achievement	.23
26	Individual Motivation	.03
27	Political Leadership/Black Pride	1.00**

Note: * = agreement, ** = excellent agreement.

☐ Case Illustration

Card 21 Participant 43: I see a man going to a job for an interview. He doesn't look confident that he'll get the job. He's in a big exec's office, has all his plaques about his Ph.D., his master's, all this other stuff. Now he's getting questions on whether or not he's capable of carrying out the job.

Researcher: What will happen next?

TABLE 33.7 Kendall's Tau for Personality Traits Across 27 Cards (N = 100 Participants)

Card	Self-Concept	Self-Concept Absent	Autonomy	Autonomy Absent	Goal Setting/ Motivation	Goal Setting/ Motivation Absent	Identity Confusion	Identity Confusion Absent
1	.45	17	—	19	—	18	—	24
2	–.33	21	1.00	23	—	18	—	25
3	–.50	22	—	25	—	25	—	25
4	—	23	—	24	—	24	—	24
5	—	25	—	23	—	24	—	23
6	.33	21	—	25	—	24	—	23
7	.57	21	—	19	1.00	21	—	25
8	.26	16	.52	7	—	13	—	25
9	—	15	—	16	—	14	—	25
10	.31	19	.25	18	.26	17	—	25
11	.61	20	—	15	–.14	14	—	24
12	.00	19	—	25	—	24	—	25
13	—	23	—	22	—	23	—	25
14	—	23	—	24	—	24	—	24

(Continued)

TABLE 33.7 Kendall's Tau for Personality Traits Across 27 Cards (N = 100 Participants) (Continued)

Card	Self-Concept	Self-Concept Absent	Autonomy	Autonomy Absent	Goal Setting/ Motivation	Goal Setting/ Motivation Absent	Identity Confusion	Identity Confusion Absent
15	—	22	—	25	—	24	—	25
16	—	23	—	16	—	18	—	25
17	—	16	–.14	14	—	13	—	25
18	—	18	—	24	—	24	—	25
19	—	21	—	24	.30	18	—	25
20	—	23	—	20	—	20	—	25
21	.00	17	–.38	18	—	17	—	24
22	—	23	—	23	—	22	—	24
23	—	23	—	25	.00	22	—	24
24	–.50	22	—	25	—	25	—	25
25	—	25	—	18	—	17	—	25
26	—	22	–.12	16	—	22	—	25
27	–.13	13	—	20	–.11	8	—	—

Card	Self-Concept	Self-Concept Absent	Autonomy	Autonomy Absent	Goal Setting/ Motivation	Goal Setting/ Motivation Absent	Identity Confusion	Identity Confusion Absent
1	.45	17	—	19	—	18	—	24
2	–.33	21	1.00	23	—	18	—	25
3	–.50	22	—	25	—	25	—	25
4	—	23	—	24	—	24	—	24
5	—	25	—	23	—	24	—	23
6	.33	21	—	25	—	24	—	23
7	.57	21	—	19	1.00	21	—	25
8	.26	16	.52	7	—	13	—	25
9	—	15	—	16	—	14	—	25
10	.31	19	.25	18	.26	17	—	25
11	.61	20	—	15	–.14	14	—	24
12	.00	19	—	25	—	24	—	25
13	—	23	—	22	—	23	—	25
14	—	23	—	24	—	24	—	24
15	—	22	—	25	—	24	—	25
16	—	23	—	16	—	18	—	25
17	—	16	–.14	14	—	13	—	25
18	—	18	—	24	—	24	—	25
19	—	20	—	25	.07	17	.32	8
20	—	23	—	25	.16	6	–.27	12
21	—	25	—	25	—	25	.58	16
22	–.11	11	—	25	–.10	3	.03	7
23	.00	21	—	25	—	25	.04	9
24	—	25	—	24	—	25	—	25
25	1.0	14	—	23	—	25	—	15
26	.37	10	—	25	.63	5	.35	7
27	–.07	4	—	6	—	25	.79	9

Note: The first column represents the Kendall's tau correlation for the mentioned theme. The column labeled missing represents the number of missing ratings due to the raters' agreement that it was not mentioned.

TABLE 33.8 Kendall's Tau for Affective Ratings Across 27 Cards (N = 100 Participants)

Card	Trust	Loneliness	Responsibility	Happy	Sad	Angry	Fear	Aggression	Depression
1	.35	—	.09	.68*	.73*	—	.42*	—	–.14
2	.22*	—	.07	.38*	.75*	.56*	—	—	—
3	—	—	–.13	—	—	.39*	.54*	.05	—
4	.15	.41*	—	.44*	—	.41*	—	—	—
5	—	—	-.09	.49*	—	—	—	–.10	—
6	.13	—	.16	.57*	.26*	.50*	—	–.07	—
7	.27*	.42*	.10	.59*	.27*	—	—	—	—
8	.40*	—	.14	.51*	—	.54*	.59*	—	—
9	.29*	—	.52*	.71*	–.08	—	.71*	—	—
10	.29*	.43*	.29*	.37*	.10	.30*	—	—	—
11	.63*	—	.25*	.70*	–.07		.52*	.50*	–.09
12	–.15	–.25	.45*	.19	.29*		—	—	.20*
13	.13	—	.18*	.49*	.54*	.39*	—	—	—
14	–.22	—	.44*	.16	.59*	.32*	.11	—	—
15	.21*	—	.23*	.59*	—	—	—	—	—
16	.26*	—	–.85	.28*	.31*	—	—	—	—
17	.19	—	.27*	.15	—	—	—	–.06	—
18	.18	—	–.02	.60*	.33*	—	—	—	—
19	.10	—	.20	.59*	.60*	—	.71*	—	–.06
20	.09	—	.33*	.43*	—	.59*	—	—	—
21	.03	—	–.22	.14	.40*	.47*	—	—	–.07
22	.04	—	–.01	.72*	—	.39*	—	—	—
23	—	.20*	–.20	.50*	.25*	.37*	—	.52*	—
24	.17	.45*	–.12	.37*	.27*	.78*	—	—	.40
25	.08	—	.17	.15	—	—	—	—	—
26	–.14	.45*	–.03	.22*	.50*	.45*	—	.35*	—
27	.03	—	–.07	.47*	–.06	.50*	—	–.14	—

Note: * denotes rater agreement.

Participant 43: He'll get hired due to the fact of Affirmative Action because it seems like this guy really doesn't care for Blacks as it is and the Black guy is going to turn out to be a workhorse doing, carrying a load for other people and he's going to realize that 90% of the jobs nowadays are due to affirmative action so he has to stick with it so he becomes more adept to get something about it.

Researcher: How are they feeling?

Participant 43: The White guy is—feels mad 'cause he could have gave the job to a White man but yet he had to deal with affirmative action and the Black man feels not wanted because that's the only way he got a job—because of his color, not just being a man.

Future Research Needed

All of the available research on the C-TCB is based on a normative sample of African American males and females from ages 18 to 35. These individuals represent a nonclinical college-level population. This test has not been normed on a clinical, school, or forensic populations. Likewise, this test should be normed with individuals across other age groups.

The cards of the C-TCB are chromatic. It is important to consider that the use of color may affect story length and emotional tone attribution. Although the average time for story telling was between 30 and 45 minutes, the time varied from 15 to 90 minutes for the administration of all 27 cards. Further research investigating the effect of the use of color on the C-TCB story length and emotional tone is needed.

Given that the initial goal of this research was test development, it was also a consideration to develop pictures that represented both male and female versions of each card to assess gender differences. Future research might include the development of gender-specific cards.

The C-TCB research was based on an Africentric theoretical model that conceptualizes the daily lifestyles of African Americans based on African values and traditions. African Americans with clinical training conducted the administration, scoring, and interpretation of the C-TCB. Given the Africentric theoretical framework of the test design, future research might compare the administration, scoring, and interpretation of cross-cultural groups. Based on the theoretical model, it is hypothesized that interpretation and scoring by individuals who do not conceptualize Black personality may lead to cross-cultural variations in scoring and misinterpretations of culturally based experiences. Likewise, it is of interest to compare the stories of other ethnic and racial groups to assess cross-cultural similarities and variations.

References

Bailey, B.E. & Green, J. (1977). Black thematic apperception test stimulus material. *Journal of Personality Assessment, 41,* 25–30.

Cook, R.A. (1953). Identification and ego defensiveness in the thematic apperception test. *Journal of Projective Techniques, 17,* 312–315.

Brunson, R.P. (1981). *A study of story length, racial attribution, and feeling tone of Black females ages five through eight to two thematic apperception tests: TAT and TCB.* Unpublished master's thesis, Washington University, St. Louis, Missouri.

Costantino, G., Malgady, R.G.., Casullo, M.M., Castillo, A. (1991). Cross-cultural standardization of TEMAS in three Hispanic subcultures. *Hispanic Journal of Behavioral Sciences, 13,* 48-62.

Costantino, G., Malgady, R.G.., & Rogler, L.H. (1988). *TEMAS (Tell-me-a-story).* Los Angeles: Western Psychological Association.

Dlepu, O.W. (1981). *The themes concerning Blacks culturally specific apperception test: normative data.* Unpublished master's thesis, Washington University, St. Louis, Missouri.

Duzant, R. (2005). *Differences of emotional tone and story length of African American respondents when administered the Contemporized Themes Concerning Blacks test versus the Thematic Apperception Test.* Unpublished doctoral dissertation, The Chicago School of Professional Psychology, Chicago.

Hawley, L. & Williams, R.L. (1981). Feeling tone and card references of Black college students for the TCB and TAT. *Journal of Non-White Concerns, 10,* 44–48.

Hoy, M.M. (1997). *Contemporizing of the themes concerning blacks test (c-tcb).* Unpublished doctoral dissertation, The California School of Professional Psychology, Alameda.

Light, B.H. (1955). A further test of the Thompson TAT rationale. *Journal of Abnormal Social Psychology, 51,* 148–150.

Matthews-Evans, D. (1992). *Psychological responses of Black Americans to the TCB and TAT projective techniques (culturally specific tests).* Unpublished doctoral dissertation. The George Washington University, St. Louis.

Roberts, G.E. (1994). *Interpretive handbook for the Roberts apperception test for children.* Los Angeles: Western Psychological Services.

Squire, L.H. (1985). *Race differences in responses to thematic apperception test stimuli material.* Unpublished doctoral dissertation. The California School of Professional Psychology, Berkeley/Alameda.

Thompson, C.E. (1949). The Thompson modification of the thematic apperception test. *Rorschach Research Exchange and Journal of Projective Techniques, 13,* 469–478.

Triplett, S. (1981). *A study of story length, racial attribution, and feeling tone of Black males, ages five through eight to two thematic apperception tests: TAT and TCB.* Unpublished doctoral dissertation. Washington University, St. Louis.

Weaver, V. (1978). *A study of the response of Black males ages 9-12 to two thematic apperception tests: TCB and TAT.* Unpublished master's thesis, University of Cincinnati.

Williams, R.L. (1972). *Themes concerning Blacks test and manual.* Saint Louis, Missouri. R.L. Williams & Associates.

Williams, R.L. & Johnson, R.C. (1981). Progress in developing afrocentric measuring instruments. *Journal of Non-White Concerns,* 3–18.

White, A.M., Olivieira, D.F., Strub, M.J., Meertens, R.H. (1995). The themes concerning blacks (TCB) projective techniques as a measure of racial identity: an exploratory cross-cultural study. *Journal of Black Psychology, 21,* (2), 104–123.

White, J. (1972). Toward a black psychology. In R. Jones (Ed.), *Black Psychology.* New York: Harper & Row.

34

CHAPTER

Manual for the Contemporized-Themes Concerning Blacks Test (C-TCB)

Michelle Hoy-Watkins

Introduction

The Contemporized-Themes Concerning Blacks Test (C-TCB) is a culturally specific projective measure that reflects social, intrapersonal, and interpersonal situations commonly experienced in the African-American community (Hoy, 1997). The test consists of 27 chromatic cards that depict several themes including single parenting, kinship and extended family, individual motivation/autonomy, teenage pregnancy, media portrayal of Blacks or African Americans, institutionalized racism, substance abuse, and implications of HIV/AIDS. The administrator selects the cards for administration. Thematic content of each card is assessed by rating eight personality traits and nine affective states. Each personality trait is rated based on a five-point scale, and the affective states are rated on a four-point scale.

Administration

Format

Administration of the C-TCB is fairly simple and easy to comprehend. The examiner should administer the test orally. The C-TCB should not be used in a group setting. Instead, it should be administered individually. Test responses should be recorded verbatim.

Prior to showing the test-taker the first card, the test administrator should read the following instructions verbatim: "I am going to show you a series of pictures. I would like you to tell me a story about each picture. Please look at the characters in each picture and tell me (a) What is happening in the picture now? (b) What happened before? (c) What will happen next? and (d) What is the character feeling or thinking?"

Once the instructions have been read, the test administrator should present the test taker each of the cards. The cards need not be administered in any particular order. Card selection should be specific to the general needs or referral question for each individual test taker. There is no limit for the administration of the C-TCB.

An inquiry is given if the test taker does not answer completely in response to the instructions for every card. An inquiry should include the following questions:

(1) What are the characters doing?

(2) What is the relationship between the characters?

(3) What is the character feeling or thinking?

(4) What does the character need most?

Stimuli

The following is a description of each projective stimulus card contained in the C-TCB. These cards are grouped according to their respective themes.

Teenage Pregnancy

Card 1: Pregnant teen standing in front of a high school with school books in her arms

Card 10: Teenage girls hanging out; one female looks as if she is pregnant; teenage female is playing with a baby (lifting her in the air); younger female sitting on stool observing

Card 19: Pregnant teen walking down the street with a male

Single Parenting

Card 2: Classroom setting; Teacher/parent conference. Mom with young child; one child (age 1 or 2) hanging on to her; mom appears to be talking to the teacher.

Card 11: Single father cooking a meal; standing over the stove; two children setting the table

Card 20: Young man pushing baby in stroller with baby bag over his shoulder

Institutionalized Racism

Card 3: A group of Black male youth walking down one side of the street and a group of White males across the street walking in the same direction. A police car is driving down the middle of the street.

Card 12: Young female sitting down; appears to be looking out of a window or behind bars

Card 21: Black male standing in front of desk with hand in his pocket; Caucasian male sitting behind his desk; plaques and diplomas appear on the wall

Extended Family/Kinship/Family Unity

Card 4: Family gathering of all ages. Backyard barbecue setting; people are sitting on grass and lawn chairs; children playing off to the side, adults standing around talking; others placing food on the table; man standing over the pit/grill.

Card 13: Older couple (grandparents) watching television with two young children (age 10–12): one boy and one girl. Girl is sitting on the floor on a pillow in between older woman's legs. The older woman is braiding the young girl's hair. Young boy sleep in man's lap; he appears to be asleep.

Card 22: Multigenerational family scene. The men appear to be working on a car in front of house; young girl and mother passing glasses of water; older woman sitting on the porch fanning herself.

Substance Abuse/Unsafe Sex/HIV and AIDS Implications

Card 5: Black man in expensive-looking car with someone (male or female) leaning in the car talking to him

Card 14: Man and woman sitting on bed with back toward one another; appears to be a small package on the bed

Card 23: Four or five males or females standing on the corner; some shooting dice; others standing around

Media Portrayal of Blacks

Card 6: Caucasian male news anchor reporting the news; picture of a man of African descent that appears to be the focus of the news story

Card 15: Family watching television; Image on the screen of Black people

Card 24: Middle-aged woman reading the newspaper with a surprised or shocking look on her face; perhaps showing some part of the headline with "African American" on it

Academic Motivation/Achievement (Individual Motivation)

Card 7: Adult group in class; lecturer at front of the room; some hands are raised; some individuals look bored or uninterested

Card 16: African American surgeon appears to be performing surgery; medical students standing around taking notes or looking through a window

Card 25: A racially mixed audience with a group of Black youth standing on a podium as if anticipating getting an honor or award

Autonomy/Individual Motivation

Card 8: Girl on a bike throwing newspapers (self-employment)

Card 17: Child involved in a task or chore with an image that shows a future scene that she or he is imagining as an adult

Card 26: Three children (ages 10–15) shopping at the grocery store pushing a shopping cart

Political Leadership/Black Pride

Card 9: Middle-aged woman standing at a podium who appears to be giving a speech before a large group of rallying people; people in audience have signs; appear to be excited and enthusiastic; other people on stage dressed in business attire

Card 18: Black woman and Black man dressed in African garb; no identified facial expressions

Card 27: People dressed in African garb and Kente' cloth who appear to be marching or participating in a rally; no identified facial expressions; some fists raised in the air

□ Scoring Process

Once the participants' responses have been recorded verbatim, the examiner can begin the scoring process. Each of the following personality traits and affective states should be assessed and rated to determine if common themes are elicited or projected on to the cards.

Scoring Category Criteria

Description of Personality Traits

The personality traits assessed by the C-TCB are as follows:

(1) Group needs (GN) refer to the identified needs of the community, church or religious system, or family members in the picture.

(2) Interpersonal relations (IR) refer to the degree of connectedness or relatedness to parental figures, family, extended family, community affiliation, authority, siblings, friends, and peers presented in the C-TCB.

(3) Black pride (BP) refers to the degree of dignity or cultural/racial identification associated with being Black or African American. Black pride also refers to the attribution of cultural identification with Black, African, or Pan African heritage, values, or practices.

(4) Family unity (FU) refers to individual's identification of solidarity among family members represented in the cards.

(5) Self-concept (SC) refers to the self-perception of emotional and physical representations of African Americans and the ability to control their environment.

(6) Autonomy (Au) refers to independence and the ability to handle the situation without the help of others.

(7) Goal setting/motivation (GS/M) refers to the identified aspiration or coping strategy to be implemented.

(8) Identity confusion (IC) refers to the identification of characters as uncertain about their identity as pertaining to skin tone, hair texture, or other physical characteristics, gender, sex, or role in the family.

Description of Affective States

Affective states represent the individuals' emotional state in response to the projective stimuli. The examinee identifies attributes, specific feelings, or emotions for the characters in each card. The nine affective states to be assessed by the C-TCB are as follows:

(1) Loneliness (L) refers to identified subjective feelings of isolation, lack of family closeness, peer relations, or societal involvement.

(2) Happy (H) refers to subjective feelings of satisfaction or gratification.

(3) Sad (S) refers to feelings of sorrow or disappointment.

(4) Anger (Ang) refers to subjective feelings of extreme dissatisfaction.

(5) Fear (F) refers to feelings of apprehension or fright about the present or outcome of a situation.

(6) Aggression (Ag) refers to the expression of the intent to cause verbal or physical harm to individuals, oneself, or property.

(7) Depression (D) refers to worries about present or future situations. The individual is identified as having somatic complaints, poor appetite, feelings of unhappiness, feelings of worthlessness, loneliness, helplessness, or being withdrawn or crying.

(8) Responsibility (R) refers to subjective feelings of obligation to help resolve the situation identified in the picture.

(9) Trust (T) refers to character's ability to have belief or faith in oneself, family members, peers, authority figures, or positive outcomes of situations.

Rating Scale—Personality Traits

The following is an overview of the scoring system for the C-TCB. Separate rating scales are provided for the assessment of personality traits and affective states. An example of each rating is provided and also a scoring sheet for each (Tables 34.1 and 34.2).

TABLE 34.1 Sample Scoring Sheet for Personality Traits

	GN	IR	BP	FU	SC	Au	GS/M	IC
1								
2								
3								
4								
5								
6								
7								
8								
9								
10								
11								
12								
13								
14								
15								
16								
17								
18								
19								
20								
21								
22								
23								
24								
25								
26								
27								

Highly Adaptive = 1

A rating of 1 represents a highly adaptive action, feeling, or resolution as represented by test stimuli. Highly adaptive behavior might include, for example, "The person feels good or is optimistic about oneself or an outcome of a situation." A highly adaptive trust might include, for example, "The character has strong faith in oneself, family members, and others." A rating of 1 for responsibility means that the characters are described as highly responsible or perhaps as attempting to resolve the situation identified in the picture.

TABLE 34.2 Sample Scoring Sheet for Affective Functioning

	T	L	R	H	S	An	F	A	D
1									
2									
3									
4									
5									
6									
7									
8									
9									
10									
11									
12									
13									
14									
15									
16									
17									
18									
19									
20									
21									
22									
23									
24									
25									
26									
27									

Inclusions or illustrations of hope, pride, self-gratification, family unity, high aspirations or a set goal, autonomy, self-concept, and self-control should be scored as 1. A rating of 1 for identity confusion means the main character is certain of identity.

Moderately Adaptive = 2

A rating of 2 represents a moderately adaptive action, feeling, or resolution attributed to the main character. For example, the family struggles yet maintains unity, responsibility, or trust, there are losses when someone achieves or sets a goal, or the individual is anguished but maintains motivation and self-control.

Moderately Maladaptive = 3

A rating of 3 signals a partially negative or maladaptive action or resolution. For example, a person must steal to provide for the family, or the main character cheats to gain success, is apprehensive about belief or faith in oneself or others (trust), or neglects responsibility for self, family members, or obligations.

Highly Maladaptive = 4

A rating of 4 indicates a highly maladaptive action, feeling, or resolution. Acts of suicide, homicide, or the attempt thereof are indicative of highly maladaptive personality functioning. Family discord without resolution, mistrusting others, pessimism or inability to resolve a conflict, impulsivity, identity confusion, and poor self-concept all represent a score of 4.

Neutral = 0

A rating of 0 is given when there are missing data. That is, no personality trait is rated for that particular card.

Rating Scale—Affective States

High Levels

A score of 1 stands for high levels of affective functioning or emotional tone. A rating of 1 for loneliness means the character is described as feeling very lonely and isolated. A character described as having high feelings of satisfaction or gratification would receive a 1 for the happy affective functioning. A character described as having great feelings of sorrow or disappointment (sad), extreme feelings of dissatisfaction characterized by destructive behaviors (anger), and persistent feelings of apprehension or fright about the present or outcome of a situation that leads to ineffective living (fear) would be given a score of 1.

Moderate Levels

A score of 2 is assigned to moderate levels of affective functioning. The following describes the level of functioning for each affective category: little family closeness, or peer relations characterized by isolation (loneliness); character described as not very satisfied (happy); character is somewhat disappointed and sorrowful (sad); extreme dissatisfaction that does not precipitate destructive behaviors (anger); and feelings of apprehension that do not interfere with interaction with others (fear).

Low Levels

A score of 3 is given to low levels of affective functioning. The following describes low levels of affective functioning: The character is described as not having feelings of loneliness

(loneliness); feelings of unhappiness (happy) are present; the character is described as having no feelings of sorrow or disappointment (sad); the character is not described as extremely dissatisfied (angry); and the character is not described as apprehensive or frightened of threatening situations (fear).

Neutral

A score of 0 is attributed to responses that do not mention any affective functioning.

Calculating Scores

Scoring based on the preliminary research does not provide a composite score. Instead, personality trait and affective state are individually rated and assigned to each card. The scores can be used to generate hypotheses about the most common themes—emotional tone/affective states and personality traits—elicited or projected onto each card. For example, if the test-taker's stories generated high ratings of sadness across the majority of cards, this information could be useful clinically.

☐ Practice Stories

Participant 22, Card 1

Okay, I see there is a young lady. I would say a teenager in high school and she's pregnant now. She's a child. She went ahead and completed her education and she's happy with herself and her decision that she completed her education and she's gonna have a child.

Participant 23, Card 12

Well, I see a woman that's locked up in jail. She's on lockdown. (What happened before?) Something ... can't say specifically but something unfathomable just like, "How did I get myself in this position. Why me? What's going on? How could this happen to me? So many things you know, going on in my life. This wasn't supposed to happen to me. Where did I go wrong? Why did they do this?" In the future, she's probably gonna do her time. She looks thoughtful in her own person. She's just sitting there—just thinking or whatever. I think she'll probably just serve her time. Good behavior, probably a model prisoner. (How's she feeling?) She's reflective, melancholy. You know, basically just really reflective.

Participant 23, Card 17

This is a little kid filling up buckets of full water. Happy-go-lucky kid. (What happened before?) Oh some kind of thought processes took place where he says, "If I fill three buckets of water maybe x, y, z will happen," or something like that. So he's really waiting to see what's going to happen if he fills these buckets of water. (What happens in the future?) That's a tough one. He's got his boots on and some type of little suit, and maybe he's playing fireman or something like that. Maybe he'll pretend that there is a fire someplace and just picks up the buckets and just throw the water or something like that. Like he's dousing flames. Happy kid, happy-go-lucky. He's a dreamer like all kids do.

Participant 24, Card 10:

Oh my goodness. Yeah, I remember this picture. All so familiar. Oh so familiar. Wait a minute—whose baby is it though? (It's your story?) See this picture can be taken two ways. It could be the one in the purple's baby. Okay if that is the case, I've been through that. I've been the young lady in the red holding the new baby while the other baby's watching and she's pregnant with the third one. And it's not anything to be ... I mean it's sad because you don't want to be ... when a child is born you suppose to be happy. Okay so it's hard.... It's hard to show being positive about her baby being born in a situation like this. So it takes a while to get use to. But to me it doesn't look like anybody is really happy. I mean everybody's jus numb. Yeah, that's the way to put it. (What happened before?) It looks like they might've had some words about this. I don't want to say words but some type of conversation came about concerning these kids or their no-good daddy or whatever. Something concerning the situation that's in this picture that's what I believe. (And what'll happen after that?) I think that ... I don't know, it's hard to say, 'cause it's so much that can happen. It really is so much that could happen. And hopefully she's as smart as my friend and that'll be the last one. It's jus hard to say but this woman's pregnant so more than likely she's gonna go to the bathroom or get something to eat after this. Or like my friend did, beg the one in red to get some ice cream. That's probably what's gonna happen. Sic a kid on her.

☐ Expert Scoring

Participant 22, Card 1

The rater scored the story as having a high level of trust in her ability to achieve her educational goal. Likewise, the character was described as happy with her life and decision to complete her education in light of having a child. Therefore, she was rated as having a high level (score of 1) of happiness and responsibility. No negative affect was attributed, therefore a score of 0 was assigned for loneliness, sadness, anger, and fear. Regarding attribution of personality functioning, the participant was identified as having highly adaptive levels of self-concept, autonomy, and goal setting/motivation. The story revealed no evidence of identify confusion; therefore, a score of 0 was assigned.

Participant 23, Card 12

Regarding affective functioning, this story was rated as having a low level of trust (score of 3) due to incarceration and the impending legal situation. The character was described as feeling *melancholy* and was assigned a score of 1 for sadness. The character was described as a reflective and thoughtful individual who will accept the punishment for her actions. Therefore, a rating of 2 (moderate level) for responsibility was given. Likewise, a moderate level of anger was identified. The story was rated as having high levels of sadness, as the character was described as regretful and in a state of disbelief. A high level of loneliness was rated. This participant attributed several of the personality traits to the characters. The character was described as being future oriented and hopeful; thus, a score of 2 was assigned for goal setting/motivation. Although disappointed with her actions, she will be a *model prisoner* and will overcome the setback of detainment. Therefore, a moderate level (score of 2) was assigned for self-concept, autonomy, and identity confusion.

Participant 23, Card 17

The character was described as feeling happy, gratified, and seemingly responsible. Thus, a score of 1 (high level) was assigned. Given that the character was not described as feeling lonely, sad, angry, or fearful a low level (score of 3) of affective functioning was given. The following personality traits were scored as highly adaptive. The character was described as having aspirations of being a firefighter, thus suggesting goal setting/motivation. He was content and appeared to enjoy individual/autonomous playtime. There was no indication of poor self-concept or identity confusion. Group needs, Black pride, family unity, and interpersonal relations were not present—so these traits were rated as 0.

Participant 24, Card 10

The participant expressed a high level of identification with the thematic card content. The character was described as feeling *numb,* which suggests an inability to experience emotions and feelings. The story was rated as having low levels of happiness. A moderate level of trust was attributed to the character. The characters were seemingly responsible, as each was described as being the primary caregiver. The rater assigned a score of 2 for fear of possible failure or future unwanted pregnancies.

Reference

Hoy, M.M. (1997). *Contemporizing of the Themes Concerning Blacks Test (C-TCB).* Unpublished doctoral dissertation, California School of Professional Psychology, Alameda.

V

SECTION

Needs and Concerns Focused Systems

35

CHAPTER

The Need-Threat Analysis
A Scoring System for the Children's Apperception Test

Louis A. Chandler

Abstract

The Need-Threat Analysis (NTA) is a scoring system developed for the Children's Apperception Test (CAT), which addresses concerns of reliability and validity while providing clinically relevant information on sources of perceived stress in a child's life. It is proposed as a method of systematically evaluating children's emotional status when conducting a comprehensive psychological evaluation of a child. The NTA is not meant to replace the more traditional content analysis of CAT stories but to supplement the information gathered with a reliable method of identifying the needs and threats that are most meaningful to the child whose life is the subject of clinical study.

Description of the System

Conceptual Framework

Over the years thematic projective techniques, like the Children's Apperception Test (CAT), have been found to be rich sources of clinical insight, and they have proven to be especially useful in the clinical assessment of children (Chandler & Johnson, 1991). Yet some issues of validity, and especially reliability, remain to be resolved if we are to go beyond ideographic, descriptive interpretations to fully exploit such useful techniques.

The Need-Threat Analysis (NTA) is a scoring system developed for the CAT that addresses concerns of reliability and validity while providing clinically relevant information on sources of perceived stress in a child's life. The NTA is not meant to replace a comprehensive content analysis of CAT stories but to supplement the more traditional interpretation with a reliable method of identifying the needs and threats that are most meaningful to the child who is the subject of clinical study.

To be effective, any clinical assessment—either implicitly or explicitly—must assume an underlying context. The NTA was developed within the context of a life-stress assessment for children (Chandler, 1985).

The analysis of stress lends an important dimension to clinical assessment. If stress is defined as a state of emotional tension arising from unmet needs or environmental demands or threats, then it can be seen as a stimulus impelling the child to adopt various responses in an effort to cope (Chandler, 1985). Some of these attempts may be seen as effective coping behaviors; others may be seen as ineffective, maladaptive, and extreme. When extreme maladaptive efforts to cope call attention to themselves and interfere with the child's effective functioning at home, in school, or with family or friends or impairs his or her physical health, such reactions are likely to be labeled as emotional adjustment problems or behavior disorders. For such children an analysis of their experience with stress can be the first step toward better understanding and more effective intervention.

Viewing children's behavior disorders from this perspective calls for an assessment of a child's life-stress experience. Such an assessment must be concerned with, among other things, the child's perception of potentially stressful events and situations, since the relative stressfulness of any given event is strongly influenced by the subjective perception of the event. Within this context, what is needed is a method for understanding the child's perceptions of needs and threats. The Needs-Threat Analysis is a scoring system for the CAT that provides such an entrée into the child's world.

The Children's Apperception Test traces its lineage to the seminal work of Henry Murray and his associates at the Harvard Psychology Clinic in the 1930s. Murray (1938) believed that motivation provided the key to the study of personality. The remarkable technique he developed for exploring personality, the Thematic Apperception Test (TAT), relied on the familiar tendency of people to express their inner needs in spontaneous, creative productions such as stories. This tendency, which became known as the *projective hypothesis*, has often been commented on in the study of lives of artists, authors, and composers.

Murray believed that motives could be assessed by the analysis of a set of stories created by a subject viewing a series of pictures. He advocated the analysis of the stories in terms of the needs of the main character and the environmental forces to which he or she was exposed. At one point he had identified some 40 needs and 30 or more presses that could be applied to each story (Murray, 1943). It was Murray who first suggested that any interpretation of TAT stories should include consideration of unusually high or low frequencies of motives in any given set of stories.

Murray's suggestions for scoring TAT stories proved to be cumbersome and time consuming and were never widely adopted by clinicians. Yet as the popularity of the TAT grew a number of other approaches were suggested for scoring the TAT that built on Murray's original ideas. One of the more promising approaches was proposed by Cox and Sargent (1950), who developed a scoring method that, in addition to needs and threats, analyzed the cards in terms of feelings, heroes, action, and outcomes—in all six broad scoring categories, with a number of possible variables in each.

Bellak and Bellak (1949), in response to the need for an instrument more suited for the expression of the needs, emotions, and drives of children, developed the CAT. Like the

TABLE 35.1 The Need-Threat Binaries

Binary	Description
Independence–Domination	Need for freedom and autonomy; desire to resist domination
Affiliation–Rejection	Need for forming relationships; threat of being isolated
Security–Insecurity	Need for physical necessities; danger in the environment
Achievement–Failure	Need for accomplishment, competence; fear of failure
Aggression–Punishment	Need to express hostility; fear of punishment

TAT, this technique consists of a set of pictures about which the subject is asked to tell stories. For interpretation, the authors suggest that 10 aspects of the protocol be examined: main theme, hero, needs of hero, concept of the environment, parental figures, significant conflicts, nature of anxieties, main defenses, severity of superego, and integration of ego.

Scoring Categories

The Need-Threat Analysis is a modification of the Cox and Sargent (1950) scoring system and is for use with the CAT. Because of its intended use within a stress assessment context, the original six broad categories were reduced to two: needs and threats. Experience with earlier versions of the scoring system suggested that forcing motivations into a dichotomy of either needs or threats was both impractical and unnecessary. Rather needs and threats might be viewed as polarities, with motives composed of some proportion of each. With these considerations in mind, selected needs and threats from the Cox and Sargent list were paired to form a set of five need-threat combinations or binaries: independence–domination, affiliation–rejection, security–insecurity, achievement–failure, and aggression–punishment. When used as scoring categories a sixth category, other, is added. Table 35.1 describes the five need-threat binaries.

The scoring protocol requires that each story be examined for the presence of each binary (a single story may hold multiple binaries), and the binaries are counted across all 10 stories so that the relative importance of the binary can be determined by the prevalence of the binary over the entire CAT protocol (see Table 35.1).

□ Research Evidence

Validity

Insofar as one accepts the projective hypothesis, techniques designed to tap into that tendency must be allowed some measure of credibility.

Beyond that, it has often been suggested that the individual cards used in thematic techniques tend to evoke certain themes (Holt, 1978). Bellak's (1980) contention that the

CAT cards are reflective of selected issues of childhood supports this view. To determine if specific CAT cards typically evoke specific binaries (i.e., need-threat combinations), a series of exploratory studies was conducted.

First, demographic variables were examined. In a study of the thematic productions of clinic-referred children, Johnson (1984) found no significant differences between the binary scores of boys and girls, suggesting that sex may not be a factor affecting binary scores. In a subsequent study Atherley (1986) confirmed the findings that the child's sex was not an important factor in discriminating between binary scores. The child's age was subsequently ruled out as an important variable affecting binary scores of children within the 5- to 9-year-old age group (Chandler & Pingel, 1986).

As a result of these studies it seemed feasible to group the scores of children who had been given the CAT and then to tally their responses to the individual cards so as to identify the binaries that are most closely associated with each card. This tabulation involved the NTA scores of 67 children (45 males and 22 females) between the ages of 5 and 9 years who had been referred to a university-based psychoeducational clinic because of school functioning and related problems. That tabulation found that the security–insecurity binary is the most popular scoring category used, typically found most commonly in thematic productions elicited by cards 1, 3, 4, 5, 6, and 9 (Chandler, 1983). The next most popular scoring category, aggression–punishment, is likely to be found on cards 3, 7, and 10, whereas affiliation–rejection is popular for cards 6 and 8 and achievement–failure for card 2. This response pattern suggests the typical pull of each card when conducting a need-threat analysis.

As yet another aspect of validity, a series of studies was conducted to explore possible relationships between children's NTA patterns and their behavior. For example, Johnson (1984) found that, as a group, clinic-referred children had a significantly greater prevalence of the security–insecurity binary in their CAT protocols than did nonreferred children. Although the relationship between CAT stories and overt behavior was shown to be a complex and often mediated one (Vercruysse, 1988), evidence was also found to suggest that children who show passive-aggressive behavior patterns had a significantly greater prevalence of the aggression–punishment binary in their CAT protocols when compared with clinically referred children who tended to show other types of behavior adjustment problems in stressful situations (Rosenberg, 1987).

Generalizability

It is widely recommended that the CAT be used with children between 5 < 9 years of age, (Chandler & Johnson, 1991), and the NTA seems appropriate for scoring the protocols of that age group. Of course, the CAT may not be appropriate for use with children with significant language impairment, and the same restrictions would obviously apply to the scoring system.

Reliability

Although validity rests fundamentally on the projective hypothesis, reliability, the most essential quality for any assessment technique, is quite another matter. Therefore, a number of studies have been conducted to establish the reliability of the NTA as a method of scoring the CAT.

To test the reliability of the initial version of the need-threat scoring system, a study was conducted using four judges who were asked to score 10 CAT protocols (Hughes, 1983). The judges were all advanced doctoral students in a school psychology program who had completed course work in psychological assessment and a clinical internship in school psychology. After a brief training session of less than an hour, the judges were asked to score the protocols using the need-threat analysis. After a four-week interval they were asked to rescore the same 10 CAT protocols.

Interjudge reliability for the first scoring of the 10 protocols was calculated by Spearman rank order correlations among the four judges. This technique was chosen because of its relevance to the intended clinical use of the scoring system. Specifically since in its clinical use the identification of the more dominant binaries is important, an analytic procedure that addresses the relative importance of the binaries in the opinion of each judge would seem to be most appropriated.

The mean correlation among the pairs of four judges was .69. Intrajudge correlations were calculated between the scores on the first and second scoring sessions for each judge. A mean correlation of .76 was found for the four intrajudge pairs. In addition, the judges were found to generally agree as to the presence or absence of a specific binary, and they tended to agree as to the primary (i.e., most frequently occurring) and secondary need-threat binaries on the various protocols.

A replication study using the current version of the need-threat scoring system found further evidence of the reliability of the system consistent with that just reported (Chandler, Shermis, & Lempert, 1989; Lempert, 1986). In this study, four judges with similar credentials were employed, although they were not given the brief training periods; rather, they were simply provided with the Need-Threat Scoring System Manual (Chandler, 1983) and were asked to score a set of 10 CAT protocols. Interjudge correlations were again computed for each CAT protocol, and the mean correlation among each pair of judges was calculated. The mean interjudge reliability coefficient was .68, whereas the mean intrajudge reliability coefficient was found to be .85 for the four intrajudge pairs.

To examine another aspect of reliability, Batterman (1993) investigated the use of a lexicon of common CAT terms—that is, a list words and phrases from stories, keyed to their most frequently cited binaries. It was hypothesized the NTA scoring of CAT protocols could be improved by using the lexicon. She found that although average interjudge agreement on the classifications of the words in the context of stories was reasonably good (61%), it improved with the use of the lexicon (67%).

Schachter (1996) further investigated the use of content analysis to increase reliability in scoring by developing and testing a computer-assisted scoring system. She reviewed some 200 CAT protocols to identify 1,912 words, phrases, and word stems to develop a content analysis dictionary that could be used by a computer program (TEXTPACK). Ten CAT protocols were then scored using both hand scoring and the computer-assisted scoring procedures. A correlation of .71 was found between the two procedures.

As a follow-up study Schachter (1998) extended the Need-Threat Dictionary to some 2,700 terms. The computer program then used this expanded dictionary to score 10 CAT protocols. Next, a panel of five school psychologists were given the NTA manual and were asked to score 2 CAT protocols (20 stories)—with and without computer-assistance. Since the rankings of binaries are clinically more important than raw scores, the most clinically relevant question was, "Did the two methods agree on the relative order of the binaries identified in each protocol?" Schachter found that the scoring of a panel of school psychologists became significantly more reliable when using the computer-assisted scoring, with an interjudge Spearman rank order correlation of .95 being reported.

In summary, when viewed in terms of the relative importance of various binaries, as reflected in the frequency with which they occur in CAT protocols, judges have been found to show considerable consistency with each other, and with themselves, over time.

The NTA therefore, has been shown to be a consistent, reliable way of identifying the current needs and threats in a child's life.

Future Research

Some directions that might be considered for future research include the following:

(1) Further validate the current concerns as identified by the NTA by associating them with the actual life events and situations that provide the context for the individual child's life-stress experience. Such a line of research would have considerable implications for consulting with parents and teachers in helping children to cope.

(2) Extend the work on computer-assisted scoring to increase reliability by using the computer in content analysis applications. Such a line of research might lead to more extensive use of the computer in scoring CAT protocols.

References

Atherley, E. A. (1986). *A study of the discriminant validity of the need-threat scoring system for the Children's Apperception Test.* Unpublished master's thesis, University of Pittsburgh.

Batterman, J. N. (1993). *The use of a lexicon in scoring the Children's Apperception Test.* Unpublished research project, University of Pittsburgh.

Bellak, L., & Bellak, S. S. (1949). *A manual for the Children's Apperception Test.* Larchmont, NY: CPS, Inc.

Bellak, L. (1980). *The TAT and CAT in clinical use* (2nd ed.). New York: Grune and Stratton.

Chandler, L. A. (1982). *Children under stress: Understanding emotional adjustment reactions.* Springfield, IL: Charles Thomas Co.

Chandler, L. A. (1983). *The use of a need-threat analysis for scoring the Children's Apperception Test.* Pittsburgh: The Psychoeducational Clinic, University of Pittsburgh.

Chandler, L. A. (1985). *Assessing stress in children.* New York: Praeger.

Chandler, L. A. (1990). The projective hypothesis and the development of projective techniques for children. In C. R. Reynolds & R. W. Kamphaus (Eds.), *Handbook of psychological and educational assessment of children* (pp. 51–65). New York: Guilford.

Chandler, L. A., & Johnson, V. J. (1991). *Using projective techniques with children.* Springfield, IL: Charles Thomas Co.

Chandler, L. A., & Pingel, L. A. (1986). *The effects of age on the NTA scores of children given the CAT.* Unpublished paper, University of Pittsburgh.

Chandler, L. A., Shermis, M. D., & Lempert, M. E. (1989). The Need-Threat Analysis: A scoring system for the Children's Apperception Test. *Psychology in the Schools, 26,* 47–54.

Cox, B., & Sargent, H. (1950). Brief reports, TAT responses of emotionally disturbed and emotionally stable children: Clinical judgments versus normative data. *Journal of Projective Techniques, 14,* 60–74.

Holt, R. R. (1978). *Methods in clinical psychology* (vol 1.). New York: Plenum Press.

Hughes, C. A. (1983). *Reliability of a need-threat scoring system for projective material.* Unpublished master's thesis, University of Pittsburgh.

Johnson, V. (1984). *The use of a needs-threat analysis of the Children's Apperception Test to discriminate between clinic-referred and non-referred children.* Unpublished master's thesis, University of Pittsburgh.

Lempert, M. E. (1986). *The need-threat scoring system: A study of reliability and agreement.* Unpublished research project, University of Pittsburgh.

Mundy, J. (1972). The use of projective techniques with children. In B. B. Wolman (Ed.), *Manual of child psychopathology* (pp. 134–147). New York: McGraw Hill Co.

Murray, H. A. (1938). *Explorations in personality.* New York: Oxford University Press.

Murray, H. A. (1943). *Thematic Apperception Test manual.* Cambridge, MA: Harvard University Press.

Rosenberg, L. (1987). *The association of children's thematic products and their behavior.* Unpublished master's project, University of Pittsburgh, Pittsburgh.

Schachter, L. S. (1996). *Developing a computer-assisted scoring procedures for the Children's Apperception Test.* Unpublished research project, University of Pittsburgh.

Schachter, L. S. (1998). *Developing and testing a computer-assisted scoring method for the Children's Apperception Test.* Unpublished doctoral dissertation, University of Pittsburgh.

Symonds, P.M. (1948). *A manual for the Symonds Picture-Story Test.* New York: Columbia University.

Vercruysse, N. (1988). *Relationships between Children's Apperception Test productions and overt behavior in a sample of clinic-referred children.* Unpublished research project, University of Pittsburgh.

36

CHAPTER

Scoring Manual for the Need-Threat Analysis

Louis A. Chandler

Introduction

The Need-Threat Analysis (NTA) is a system for use with the Children's Apperception Test (CAT) used to identify the needs and threats that are most meaningful to the child. With the NTA, needs and threats are viewed as polarities, with motives composed of some proportion of each. Selected needs and threats commonly found in children's lives were paired to form a set of five need-threat combinations or binaries: independence–domination, affiliation–rejection, security–insecurity, achievement–failure, and aggression–punishment. When used as scoring categories a sixth category, other, is added.

Administration

Format and Stimuli

It is assumed that all 10 cards of the Children's Apperception Test will be administered according to the instructions in the accompanying manual (Bellak & Bellak, 1949). The resulting CAT protocol is a verbatim transcript of the stories the child composes as each card is presented.

It is recommended that the CAT be used as part of the assessment process for children aged 5 to 9 years, inclusive, who have been referred for clinical assessment. Within this context, the CAT may provide valuable information as to the child's current emotional status.

☐ Scoring Process

In scoring the CAT protocol, the examiner does the following:

(1) Examines the child's responses to each card in terms of the six scoring categories

(2) Records the presence of a binary by checking the appropriate category on the Need-Threat Scoring Sheet. Although each card may be seen to elicit one major story, for some cards more than one scoring category may apply.

Need-Threat Scoring Sheet

(for the Children's Apperception Test)

Child's Name	
Age	**Sex**
Grade	
School/Clinic	
ID#	

CAT Card Number

	1	2	3	4	5	6	7	8	9	10	SUM	%R
Need-Threat Binary												
Independence–Domination												
Affiliation–Rejection												
Security–Insecurity												
Achievement–Failure												
Aggression–Punishment												
Other												
Total												**100**

(3) Adds the total number of checks for each scoring category and enters that incidence number opposite the category under the "SUM" column

(4) Adds the number of checks to obtain the total number of responses

(5) Calculates the percentage of each category score by dividing each category by the total number of responses and entering the percentage opposite the category in the "%R" column. This is the relative frequency of that binary in the child's protocol.

Scoring Categories

(1) Independence–domination: Need for freedom and autonomy; desire to resist domination, coercion; drive to rebel against authorities; desire for self-assertion. Feels coercion from others; loss of independence through domination by others, fear of losing freedom or being dominated. Common examples of thematic content include being allowed or being restricted, being told what to do, seeking permission, obeying or disobeying parents, going out of the house, running away from home.

(2) Affiliation–rejection: Need for forming relationships. Desire for friendship, love, sexual relations, acceptance, nurturance. Threat of being repulsed, ostracized, isolated, or rebuffed; deprived or denied affiliation (love, sexual relationships, friendships, acceptance by parents). Common examples of thematic content include being ignored or singled out for embarrassment or ridicule, returning to home, seeking family and friends for advice, assistance, social visits.

(3) Security–insecurity: Need for physical necessities (e.g., food, shelter); personal safety; protection from harm; fear of illness, death, catastrophe. Danger in the environment; physical harm. Common examples of thematic content include being hungry, thirsty, needing shelter, protection, nurturance, being easily upset, fearful, worried.

(4) Achievement–failure: Need for prestige, accomplishment, competence. Desire for success, recognition, respect, honor, power. Fear of inability to perform, failure, inadequacy, inferior status, lack of talent, prowess. Jealousy of the achievement of others. Fear of competition, rivalry. Common examples of thematic content include being seen as capable, able, winning or losing, attempting challenges.

(5) Aggression–punishment: Need to express hostility. Aggression directed toward peers or authority. Fears of punishment, violence from persons in the environment, being aggressed against. Common examples of thematic content include attacking or being attacked, being mad or angry, fighting, breaking or destroying property, being threatened, chased or punished.

(6) Other: Unique or idiosyncratic themes; enumeration of stimulus features.

Binaries that occur with the greatest frequency might be assumed to be especially meaningful for that child. This approach is consistent with the position taken by a number of writers who contend that elements that occur frequently in thematic protocols may be seen as having special significance for the subject (Munday, 1972; Murray, 1938; Symonds, 1948).

To assist in scoring the protocol, a lexicon of common CAT terms has been developed (see the Appendix). This list of words and phrases was constructed by reviewing 20 CAT protocols of children referred for clinical assessment. The list is arranged alphabetically by key words followed by variations. To the right of each word cluster is the recommended need-threat binary that should be given primary consideration in scoring the protocol. The final judgment as to the presence of a binary should be made only after reviewing the word or phrase in context.

TABLE 36.1 Need-Threat Binaries With Associated Life Events and Situations

Binary	Events and Situations[a]
Independence–Domination	Family rules, responsibilities; performing assigned chores; reacting to adult authority (e.g., parents, teachers, principals, law officers)
Affiliation–Rejection	Family moves and relocations; changing schools; birth of a sibling; mother beginning work
Security–Insecurity	Hospitalization of child; serious accident, injury, or illness; marital separation and divorce; death in family; hospitalization of parent; speech, hearing, or vision problems; loss of job by parent
Achievement–Failure	Academic failure; poor grades; learning problems; retention; special education
Aggression–Punishment	Discipline (including physical punishment); fights with peers or family members; arguments with parents; child abuse

[a] Items selected from the *Children's Life Events Inventory* (Chandler, 1985).

Interpretation

The Need-Threat Analysis yields scores that may be interpreted idiographically—that is, within the context of the pattern of binary scores for that particular child. Used in this way, the preferred scores are the higher binary scores since these reflect the strongest need-threat concerns for that individual. By examining the relative percentages of each binary the clinician can identify the dominant binary for that child. This may be seen as reflecting the types of needs and threats that, alone or in combination, are likely to make life events and situations particularly meaningful to—and hence stressful for—the individual child. For example, for the child for whom achievement and failure are especially important, taking an achievement test at school may prove to be an especially stressful experience. Actual events and situations may be linked to the underlying needs and threats as shown in Table 36.1.

□ Practice Stories

These examples were taken from the records of a set of clinically referred children, ages 5 to 9 years. In the following protocols, key words that led to the scoring decision are in italics. Each child's analysis summary is followed by an interpretive section that might appear in that child's psychological report, preceding the usual content analysis.

Alex, 5-Year-Old Male, Kindergarten

CAT Protocol

(1) Three baby bears and that's all I know. They're eating breakfast until their *mom tells them* it's work time.

(2) Three bears were playing tug-of-war and the rope *broke* and they came tumbling down the mountain. They're gonna rip that. I guess *they'll win* or else the rope will rip 'cause he's stronger than two bears, except two bears are heavier than one bear.

(3) One day the king of the beasts was bored so he sat down and think what to do. And a mouse creeped out to see if it was *safe,* but the king of the lions thought *to kill a mouse.*

(4) Once two kangaroos were going to the store, the mommy and the baby, and baby rode on the bike, and the *mommy jumped, and the bike broke down,* and so they had to go to the city. (Q) Beats me.

(5) A bear and there people in there—yes. Well once a mother, a father, and a baby were living in a forest and a bear came in, *ate the baby,* and the *mother and father* peeked and *hid* under the covers.

(6) Once a man got tired so they went to *sleep* but in the cave. He was peeking—"look see."

(7) Well once a tiger was snarling 'cause he wanted to eat something and so he ranned to get a monkey and the monkey climbed up and he *bite the tiger's tail* and so the *tiger ate him.*

(8) Once a stupid old monkey family was in a house and some people were spying and they *took the monkeys out of their house.* (Q) Feels stupid. Stupidy looking.

(9) Once there was a place,—a *house that was robbed.* Mommy and daddy were robbed and the baby was robbed. They put little baby bunny in the baby's bed. (Q) Beats me.

(10) Once some doggies were having a family, and one wanted to drink out of a pool and the other wanted to study.

Expert Scoring for Alex

(1) Independence–domination

(2) Security–insecurity; achievement–failure

(3) Security–insecurity; aggression–punishment

(4) Security–insecurity

(5) Aggression–punishment; security–insecurity

(6) Security–insecurity

(7) Aggression–punishment

(8) Affiliation–rejection

(9) Security–insecurity

(10) Other

NT Analysis Summary

- Independence–domination (1, 8%)
- Affiliation–rejection (1, 8%)
- Security–insecurity (6, 46%)
- Achievement–failure (1, 8%)
- Aggression–punishment (3, 23%)
- Other (1, 8%)

Interpretation for the Psychological Report

To identify those experiences that might be particularly stressful for Alex, he was administered the Children's Apperception Test. A need-threat analysis of the results suggests that, for Alex, the most important experiences are those events and situations where the need for security or the threat of insecurity is involved. Content analysis further indicates that ...

Hope, 7-Year-Old Female, First Grade

CAT Protocol

(1) The hen is watching the birds eat their supper and the hen is going to feed them supper so they can eat it.... (Q) They all feel happy but the hen ... (Q) feels sad because they *can't eat everything on their dishes....* (Q) All of a sudden they all start to eat.

(2) Momma bear, baby bear and daddy bear are playing tug-of-war and momma bear and baby bear are losing and they want to win but poppa bear thinks he is going to win.... (Q) They feel happy and he feels sad.... (Q) *He thinks he is going to lose;* (Q) *they win and he doesn't.*

(3) The lion wants to have his supper but the squirrel or whatever it is *won't let him....* The lion is very sad that he doesn't have any supper but the squirrel does and the lion is very, very sad and the squirrel and his *friends are laughing* 'cause they have food and he doesn't.

(4) A kangaroo is pulling a baby kangaroo and the other kangaroo is in mother's pouch and they are going out ... (Q) to a party *where their friends are....* (Q) They all feel good

because they have presents to take.... It is a birthday party at a friends home.... (Q) They *all have a good time* at the party.

(5) The baby bears are trying to sleep but they can't so they try to keep quiet 'cause they *are afraid*.... (Q) If they wake their mommy and daddy up they will *get yelled at*. They feel sad 'cause they can't sleep; then the morning comes and they fall asleep but mother and father *make them get up* and then they are sad again.

(6) The mother and father bear are awake, and little baby bear can't sleep, and mother and father *yell at him* to sleep because they have to go out tomorrow.... (Q) He is sad 'cause they make him go out and go to sleep.... (Q) Now mother and father bear are sleeping and baby bear *still can't sleep*.

(7) A tiger has found a monkey and is *trying to get* the monkey ... (Q) *to eat*, but the monkey doesn't want to get eaten by the tiger but the tiger is hungry and wants to eat him. The monkey is sad now cause the tiger wants to eat him.... (Q) The monkey keeps running and running and the tiger stops bothering him.

(8) The monkey family is having a party and the baby monkey feels sick and the *mother is mad* now.... (Q) She *wants him to go* upstairs and go to sleep now. *Friends are* talking and *ignoring* the baby too. The mother is *telling him* to go upstairs ... (Q) feels sad because *he wants to stay at the party*.... (Q) Baby start to cry and all the friends go home.

(9) A baby rabbit is not asleep, and he is so tired but is afraid to sleep because he is *afraid of the dark*. Then *mother* comes in and *yells at him* to do something.... (Q) He is sad because he wants to go to sleep but now he can't because has to do something. (Q) He is in bed looking at the door.

(10) Mother puppy is *trying to make baby* puppy clean up but baby puppy *doesn't want to go* and clean up so now he is trying to get away from her. (Q) He feels happy because he is laughing and he thinks he can get away from her.... (Q) *She is really mad* because he won't do it (Q) go and clean it up (Q) clean himself.... He gets away but she chases him.... (Q) No, and *she gets mad* but she can't do anything now.

Expert Scoring for Hope

(1) Security–insecurity

(2) Achievement–failure

(3) Independence–domination; affiliation–rejection

(4) Affiliation–rejection

(5) Independence–domination

(6) Independence–domination; security–insecurity

(7) Aggression–punishment

(8) Affiliation–rejection; independence–domination

(9) Security–insecurity; independence–domination

(10) Independence–domination

NT Analysis Summary

- Independence–domination (6, 40%)
- Affiliation–rejection (3, 20%)
- Security–insecurity (4, 27%)
- Achievement–failure (1, 7%)
- Aggression–punishment (1, 7%)
- Other (0, 0%)

Interpretation for the Psychological Report

To identify those experiences that might be particularly stressful for Hope, she was administered the Children's Apperception Test. A need-threat analysis of the results suggests that, for Hope, the most important experiences are those events and situations where the need for independence or the threat of domination is involved. Issues of security and insecurity will also like cause considerable concern. Content analysis further indicates that ...

William, 7-Year-Old Male, Second Grade

CAT Protocol

(1) Baby chickens eating dinner but *mother said* it was too hot. (Q) They started *eating it anyway* and *mother got very mad* and spanked them. (Q) So they waited until it cooled off and then they ate it.

(2) Three bears playing tug of war, and the rope broke and they all fell in the mud. (Q) *They all ended up* being muddy and then went home and all took a bath.

(3) The mouse was afraid of Mr. Lion because he thought he would eat him up. One day he went up to the lion and woke him up and *asked him to be his friend.* The lion said okay. (Q) So the mouse went home to tell his family.

(4) Baby kangaroo couldn't jump very well so his mother got him a bicycle. One day the mother had to go to her aunt's and baby came with her and peddled his bicycle and felt a little sad that he *couldn't jump good.*

(5) One day two baby bears went to bed. (Q) *One couldn't sleep* but the other one could. (Q) So the one that couldn't just went outside for a walk and then he came in and fell asleep too.

(6) Baby bear didn't want to hibernate through the winter so he watched the other animals outside the door. (Q) His mother and father *wanted him* to sleep but he didn't want to. (Q) He finally did.

(7) One day a monkey was jumping along and a *tiger jumped* out at him. (Q) The tiger ran after him but the monkey went to another vine where the tiger couldn't go. (Q) The monkey felt good because he got away.

(8) Monkeys were at a party drinking *tea and baby monkey was bad and went to bed.* (Q) *Feels kind of sad.... Mother wouldn't take him to bed* and just *ordered him* to go and do it.

(9) A bunny rabbit in bed with the door barely open so that a little light could get in.... (Q) Just so he would know when morning is here. (Q) So it will be time to get up for cartoons.

(10) The big dog *told his little dog* three times to just stop barking, but the little dog didn't and the *mother caught him* and gave him a spanking. (Q) The puppy felt sad. (Q) 'Cause he just got spanked.

Expert Scoring for William

(1) Independence–domination; aggression–punishment

(2) Affiliation–rejection

(3) Affiliation–rejection

(4) Achievement–failure

(5) Security–insecurity

(6) Independence–domination

(7) Aggression–punishment

(8) Affiliation–rejection; independence–domination

(9) Other

(10) Independence–domination; aggression–punishment

NT Analysis Summary

- Independence–Domination (4, 33%)
- Affiliation–rejection (2, 17%)
- Security–insecurity (1, 8%)
- Achievement–failure (1, 8%)
- Aggression–punishment (3, 25%)
- Other (1, 8%)

Interpretation for the Psychological Report

To identify those experiences that might be particularly stressful for William, he was administered the Children's Apperception Test. A need-threat analysis of the results suggests that, for William, the most important experiences are those events and situations where the need for independence or the threat of domination is involved. Issues of aggression and punishment will also like cause considerable concern. Content analysis further indicates that ...

Kerrie, 8-Year-Old Female, Third Grade

CAT Protocol

(1) These are little chicks having breakfast, and their mother is watching. (Q) Chicks *were hungry.* (Q) They'll be *full.*

(2) I see three bears—they're playing tug-of-war. Papa on one side and Mama is with the little baby bear, and they're having fun. (Q) They're happy, they look happy, when they finish they will have splinters because of the rope. (Q) They're excited because they want to win.

(3) The king, the lion is sitting in his chair and waiting for the mouse to come out. He has his pipe in his hand and his cane on the side of the chair. He looks bored; he has nothing to do. (Q) He wants to have supper. (Q) The mouse is supper. (Q) *Lion is hungry and mouse might be frightened.* (Q) Lion gets the mouse.

(4) There's two deer. Are those kangaroos? Oh, a joey. They're going on a picnic. Little joey is in Mama's pouch holding a balloon, and the other one is riding a tricycle. The mama wants to get home, and Mama's got a real flowered hat on. (Q) *The little kids are hungry.* (Q) I gotta get my kids home to feed them. (Q) The one on the tricycle is tired because he pedaled all that way.

(5) There is Mama and Papa in bed hiding their heads and two cubs in the crib cuddled up and going to sleep. It's real dark outside. It looks like it's snowing; it does. They think they're *lucky to be in a warm house.* (Q) They might be *frightened.* (Q) Of the snow.

(6) There is a Mama and Papa bear asleep in the cave with their cub. The cub is awake 'cause he can't get to sleep and the little bear might be thinking of Christmas 'cause it's winter out there. Papa is *hungry* and the *little one is trying to cuddle in the leaves.* (Q) Little one can't sleep because he's thinking of Christmas and all the kids having fun. (Q) Mom is probably *worried* about her little cub not sleeping and thinking about the winter.

(7) There's a tiger chasing a monkey 'cause the tiger's hungry and wants something to eat and the monkey's going to be it. And all the other animals are trying to hide from him and the monkey is climbing a tree so the tiger won't get him. And the tiger looks like it wants something; he wants that monkey. And the tiger's got *real sharp teeth* to chew monkey up. And the monkey just missed the rope. And after that I think *the tiger does get the monkey.*

(8) Well, there's mother and father and they're having tea and little baby is looking up at big sister because he's looking at her funny-looking earrings, and the *big sister's telling little baby what grandmother's* like 'cause he's never seen grandma before. And mother is telling Dad that the sister is telling baby something that's not true. (Q) 'Cause their grandmother died. (Q) The mother's mother. (Q) And the father is saying ... "Ah, just remember her the way she was."

(9) There's an open door and somebody is coming into the little bunny's room. The little bunny is *very frightened and someone's coming in* without knocking. Wind blows the curtains and gives him chills. And his lamp is going to fall over as soon as the rabbit hunter gets there. And it's real dark and he can't see who's coming. There's a book at the bottom of the bed on the cover. (Q) Lamp falling will scare hunter and he'll go away.

(10) The mother spanks the baby puppy 'cause he did something bad she didn't like, he was playing in the water and got all wet. Mother dog is not happy for what her child has done. He got the bathroom all wet and she has to dry it all up. She's spanking even harder 'cause he left water on and she told him to always turn it off. (Q) And the little puppy will never do it again.

Expert Scoring for Kerrie

(1) Security–insecurity

(2) Other

(3) Security–insecurity; aggression–punishment

(4) Security–insecurity

(5) Security–insecurity

(6) Security–insecurity

(7) Aggression–punishment

(8) Affiliation–rejection

(9) Security–insecurity

(10) Independence–domination; aggression–punishment

NT Analysis Summary

- Independence–domination (1, 8%)
- Affiliation–rejection (1, 8%)
- Security–insecurity (6, 50%)
- Achievement–failure (0, 0%)
- Aggression–punishment (3, 25%)
- Other (1, 8%)

Interpretation for the Psychological Report

To identify those experiences that might be particularly stressful for Kerrie, she was administered the Children's Apperception Test. A need-threat analysis of the results suggests that, for Kerrie, the most important experiences are those events and situations where the need for security or the threat of insecurity is involved. Issues of aggression and punishment will also like cause considerable concern. Content analysis further indicates that ...

Jason, 5-Year-Old Male, Kindergarten

CAT Protocol

(1) The mama chicken is feeding little chickens. (Q) They're *going to eat something.* (Q) They went to get food.

(2) They are doing a tug-of-war, *fighting.* (Q) There's more bears on this side so they're going to win. (Q) They thought of doing this because they saw the rope.

(3) Look at the little mouse. The lion is going to try to get the mouse. (Q) The lion thinks there's a mouse there. (Q) He's *going to eat the mouse.*

(4) The mother kangaroo is going to take two baby kangaroos. Going to go to the house back there. (Q) Play and have a picnic. (Q) It's a nice day.

(5) Baby bears are going to sleep. (Q) He's going to go to sleep and wake up. (Q) The other kids are hiding in the bed or they put pillows under the bed to *fool their Mom.*

(6) The bears are going to sleep in a cave. There's a light at the end of the cave. I think it's a way to get out of the tunnel. (Q) The Mom and Dad bear *tucked him in* the leaves. (Q) They're going to wake up.

(7) The tiger is trying to get the monkey because he is hungry. (Q) He is going to get him. (Q) He is going to get him. (Q) He *will eat him.* (Q) He found the monkey.

(8) Daddy bear is telling the baby monkey to be good. (Q) He is *not going to listen.* (Q) He was *being bad* and fighting with his sister and brother.

(9) The rabbit is going to bed. He's *going to go to sleep.* (Q) He *went to his Mom* and brushed his teeth and went to bed.

(10) The doggy's petting the other doggy. (Q) He was good. (Q) He's going downstairs and watch TV. (Q) He went to the bathroom.

Expert Scoring for Jason

(1) Security–insecurity

(2) Aggression–punishment

(3) Aggression–punishment

(4) Other

(5) Independence–domination

(6) Security–insecurity

(7) Aggression–punishment

(8) Independence–domination

(9) Security–insecurity

(10) Other

NT Analysis Summary

- Independence–domination (2, 20%)
- Affiliation–rejection (0, 0%)
- Security–insecurity (3, 30%)
- Achievement–failure (0, 0%)

- Aggression–punishment (3, 30%)
- Other (2, 20%)

Interpretation for the Psychological Report

To identify those experiences that might be particularly stressful for Jason, he was administered the Children's Apperception Test. A need-threat analysis of the results suggests that Jason shows many of the typical needs and fears of a child his age, with no particular issues dominating. Content analysis further indicates that ...

Marcus, 9-Year-Old Male, Fourth Grade

CAT Protocol

(1) One day three little chickens went to eat dinner. There was *no food* in their bowls. The only food that was there was their dad's food. "Where's my food?" said the first chick. *"I need my food,"* said the second chick. "Where's my food?" said the third chick. The little chicks went to bet with no food. They got up in the morning and they were *still hungry.* Still there was only the dad's food. They decided that they would eat their dad's food. He came in and saw them. *He yelled* and said that they should go out and eat their own food. They left.

(2) One day three little bears decided to play tug-of-war. Papa Bear wanted to show off and win all the days. He had a hard time with baby and Mama Bear. After three days the mama and baby *won the championship. Papa got mad* and wouldn't talk to them or play with them.

(3) One day the King Lion sat in his chair. He was rich and he had a lot but he *really wanted a friend.* Then one day he got married. His wife had a baby. His child had *a lot of friends* and the king got to know about being happy.

(4) Every morning the baby and the mother kangaroo go out to pick strawberries. One day they went and *there wasn't any.* The next day there wasn't any again. Father went to look for some and when he couldn't find any *so he got mad.* The family moved to another house. Then they had lots of cherries.

(5) Two little bears went to bed. They weren't tired and they had nothing to do. "I'm bored," said the little bears. They went to the kitchen and got *something to eat.* They played all night long. The next day they did terrible in school 'cause they were tired. They got home and *got a spanking.*

(6) One day three bears went to hibernate. All the mom and dad bears want to do is sleep. The baby bear didn't want to; he wasn't sleepy. He got up and *met up with his friends.* They played all the time. They had a great time.

(7) One day a monkey lived in the forest. A big tiger tried to get him. The monkey jumped into a tree but he started sliding. Coconuts fell and *hit him in the head.*

The monkey threw coconuts at the tiger. The tiger ran away. The monkey hated that forest. He moved away and never came back.

(8) Father and mother had a party. Mother told the little monkey that he *had to be good.* All the monkeys *were mean.* Little monkey had to go out to play. He hated that. He *hates it when* there are always people in your house and *you have to go outside* and play.

(9) The little bunny woke up to go to school. He doesn't have anything to do. He hates everything in his house. All he wants to do is *eat and go to bed.* (Q) He is unhappy at his house. (Q) He got up and went to school.

(10) The big dog *told* his little dog three times to just stop barking. But the little dog didn't. And their mother caught him and *gave him a spanking.* (Q) The puppy felt sad, 'cause he just got a spanking.

Expert Scoring for Marcus

(1) Security–insecurity; independence–domination

(2) Achievement–failure; aggression–punishment

(3) Affiliation–rejection

(4) Security–insecurity; aggression–punishment

(5) Security–insecurity; achievement–failure; aggression–punishment

(6) Affiliation–rejection

(7) Aggression–punishment

(8) Independence–domination; affiliation–rejection; aggression–punishment

(9) Security–insecurity

(10) Independence–domination; aggression–punishment

NT Analysis Summary

- Independence–domination (3, 17%)
- Affiliation–rejection (3, 17%)
- Security–insecurity (4, 22%)
- Achievement–failure (2, 11%)
- Aggression–punishment (6, 33%)
- Other (0, 0%)

Interpretation for the Psychological Report

To identify those experiences that might be particularly stressful for Marcus, he was administered the Children's Apperception Test. A need-threat analysis of the results suggests that, for Marcus, the most important experiences are those events and situations where aggression and punishment may be involved. Issues of rejection and resisting domination will also like cause considerable concern. Content analysis further indicates that ...

References

Bellak, L., & Bellak, S.S. (1949). *A manual for the Children's Apperception Test.* Larchmont, NY: CPS, Inc.

Chandler, L. A. (1985). *Assessing stress in children.* New York: Praeger.

Mundy, J. (1972). The use of projective techniques with children. In B. B. Wolman (Ed.), *Manual of child psychopathology* (pp. 134–147). New York: McGraw Hill Co.

Murray, H. A. (1938). *Explorations in personality.* New York: Oxford University Press.

Symonds, P. M. (1948). *A manual for the Symonds Picture-Story Test.* New York: Columbia University.

Appendix: A Lexicon of Common CAT Terms

Able, not being able	**Achievement–Failure**
Allowing, being allowed, not being allowed	**Independence–Domination**
Attacking, being attacked	**Aggression–Punishment**
Angry, being mad	**Aggression–Punishment**
Beating, (physical), being beaten	**Aggression–Punishment**
Beating, (winning), being beaten	**Achievement–Failure**
Breaking, being broken	**Aggression–Punishment**
Chasing, being chased, running after	**Aggression–Punishment**
Drinking, being given a drink	**Security–Insecurity**
Eating, being fed, not being fed, being hungry	**Security–Insecurity**
Embarrassing, being embarrassed	**Affiliation–Rejection**
Fearful, being afraid	**Security–Insecurity**
Fixing	**Achievement–Failure**
Going out, going away	**Independence–Domination**
Going home	**Affiliation–Rejection**
Grabbing (aggressive)	**Achievement–Failure**
Grabbing (acquisitive)	**Security–Insecurity**
Helping, not helping	**Affiliation–Rejection**
Hugging, being hugged	**Affiliation–Rejection**
Ignoring, being ignored	**Affiliation–Rejection**
Killing, being killed	**Aggression–Punishment**

Laughing, (at ridiculing)	Affiliation–Rejection
Laughing, (with enjoying)	Affiliation–Rejection
Leaving	Affiliation–Rejection
Listening (to, obeying)	Independence–Domination
Losing, not winning	Achievement–Failure
Marrying, getting married	Affiliation–Rejection
Protecting, being protected	Security–Insecurity
Ridiculing, making fun of	Affiliation–Rejection
Scaring, being scared	Security–Insecurity
Scolding, being scolded	Aggression–Punishment
Sleeping	Security–Insecurity
Spanking, being spanked	Aggression–Punishment
Starving, being hungry	Security–Insecurity
Staying	Affiliation–Rejection
Talking (with)	Affiliation–Rejection
Telling (ordering), being told	Independence–Domination
Telling (Informing, helpful assistance)	Affiliation–Rejection
Throwing out (rejecting)	Affiliation–Rejection
Trying	Achievement–Failure
Visiting, not visiting	Affiliation–Rejection
Watching, being watched (dominated)	Independence–Domination
Winning, not winning, losing	Affiliation–Rejection

37

CHAPTER

Psychocultural System

David Ephraim

☐ Abstract

This chapter presents a TAT scoring system for clinical practice and research that integrates features from a comprehensive psychocultural TAT scoring system developed by George A. De Vos within the field of psychological anthropology and concepts from contemporary theories of human motivation and interpersonal behavior developed within the fields of personality and clinical psychology. After examining the conceptual framework and the nature and background of the scoring categories, the chapter focuses on the system's advantages from clinical assessment, including relevance for multicultural/cross-cultural assessment purposes, amenability for the development of local norms, and usefulness for clinical training. Research evidence is presented regarding normative and comparative studies, comparisons of psychocultural data with other psychological measures, and interscorer reliability. The final section presents suggestions for future research.

☐ Description of the System

Many systems have been proposed over the years to score Thematic Apperception Test (TAT) narratives, but none of them has achieved widespread usage (Aronow, Weiss, & Reznikoff, 2001; Dana, 1985; Vane, 1981). Some of the systems intend to be comprehensive whereas others focus on specific variables. Comprehensive systems raise concerns about theoretical and cultural issues and are often described as cumbersome and time consuming. Conversely, TAT systems focused on single variables are considered more appropriate for research than for clinical practice. The system proposed in this chapter integrates features from a comprehensive psychocultural TAT scoring system developed by George A. De Vos within the field of psychological anthropology and concepts from contemporary theories of human motivation and interpersonal behavior developed within the fields of personality and clinical psychology. This system aims to overcome common objections to TAT scoring systems by combining comprehensiveness and practicality.

Conceptual Framework

The Psychocultural System for scoring TAT narratives was developed by De Vos with the purpose of identifying and comparing, in qualitative and quantitative terms, thematic concerns displayed in narratives by different ethnocultural groups (see De Vos & De Vos, 2004, for the most recent and complete presentation of the system). De Vos presented the Psychocultural System as a combined etic–emic tool. The scoring categories were described as universals or culture-general (etic) themes/concerns that appear in every social group; however, "cultures differ as to how these concerns are relatively emphasized, interrelated, or blended with one another in molecular patterns that may be quite culture-specific [emic]" (De Vos & Suárez-Orozco, 1990, p. 35).

The Psychocultural System analyzes TAT narratives from an experiential or subjective point of view in contrast to a structural or objective point of view. It focuses on the individual's internal, self perspective and not on the personality perspective, as externally observed.

Some of the themes coded by the De Vos system were part of Murray's (1943) original list of needs, which De Vos considered too extensive and without a unifying framework. De Vos also took into account David C. McClelland, John W. Atkinson, and their associates' extensive research regarding themes of achievement, power, affiliation, and intimacy (see Smith, 1992, for a thorough presentation of this approach). Although De Vos shared these authors' empirical approach and their focus on an objective scoring procedure, he did not share their atomistic methodology, which proceeds by isolating a few motives. Conversely, the TAT psychocultural approach sought to identify the relative saliency of those motives or themes as well as any others by classifying all the story material in a complex fashion (De Vos & Kim, 1993).

As stated by De Vos (1992), most of the research data on the Psychocultural System is normative and not clinical. However, the Psychocultural System's sensitivity to contextual issues makes it highly relevant for clinical psychologists under the assumption that historical, social, cultural, educational, or other contextual factors are unavoidable when assessing motives through the interpretation of narrative materials. According to Dana (1998, p. 13), "at present the system is invaluable for detailed personality studies and as an exemplar of etic-emic methodology in which the study of the cultural self can be addressed."

The scoring system presented in this chapter modifies De Vos's original system to increase its practicality and consistency with research and clinical practice in the fields of personality and clinical psychology. For example, an all-embracing conceptual distinction between agency and communion motives, initially proposed by Bakan (1966), has been incorporated into the scoring system. In Bakan's view, agency and communion constitute two fundamental modes regarding the individual's existence as separate from others (agency) versus participating in units larger than the self (communion).

The distinction between agency and communion has been presented as one of the most influential ideas in the contemporary psychology of personality (McAdams, 1993; McAdams, Hoffman, Mansfield, & Day, 1996). As described by McAdams, a variety of theories advanced by psychologists pose two general tendencies in human motivation: (1) a tendency that includes strivings for agency, such as power, autonomy, independence, achievement, or mastery; and (2) a tendency representative of strivings for communion, such as love, care, intimacy, union, or interdependence. According to Wiggins (2003), Bakan's concepts of agency and communion help to identify metaphors and philosophical-political assumptions from a variety of disciplines in the humanities and social sciences; Wiggins (1991, p. 106) illustrated how the concepts of agency and communion capture many fundamental aspects of social existence, such as "our worldviews, our understanding of persons, our language that describes social relations, and our view of the relations between men and women."

Inspired in part by the TAT-based literature on motivation that McClelland initiated, McAdams et al. (1996) developed a set of thematic categories to study motivational themes of agency and communion as expressed in narratives of significant autobiographical scenes. Some of McAdams's subcategories partially overlap with the subcategories proposed by De Vos and with those that are part of the modified scoring system presented in this chapter.

Among other modifications of De Vos's original format, the scoring system presented in this chapter incorporates a circumplex representation. Such representation allows visualizing similarities and differences between interpersonal concerns included in the Psychocultural System in a way that is consistent with models used to represent the interpersonal aspects of personality (Plutchik & Conte, 1997). In his landmark publication on organizing interpersonal phenomena in a circular manner, Leary (1957) presented a complete interpersonal diagnostic system, which included a private perception level to be assessed through TAT narratives. Circumplex models share two basic assumptions, which are also applicable to the interpersonal concerns of the TAT Psychocultural System:

(1) Interpersonal manifestations organized along a circular continuum vary in their degree of similarity to one another (manifestations that are closer on the continuum are hypothesized as being more similar conceptually and empirically than those that are farther apart)

(2) The various interpersonal manifestations are best represented as expressions of two basic dimensions: a vertical axis of dominance versus submissiveness and a horizontal axis of love versus hostility.

The broad scoring categories regarding agency and communion themes presented in the next section allow the identification of plot structures, but often those broad categories need to be further specified or subcategorized according to the particular experiential patterns expressed in the story. Such an open-ended and inductive process shares the openly dialogical nature of a hermeneutic inquiry as the scorer returns repeatedly to the story searching each time for an increased understanding that would allow for a more complete interpretation (Packer, 1985). The nature of the scoring procedure is also similar to a narrative approach, as described by Polkinghorne (1988), in that the uniqueness of a specific group's narratives, or of a particular narrative within a group, is as important as the features shared with other stories.

Scoring Categories

The scoring system analyzes contents of TAT narratives according to a framework of 10 major thematic concerns classified as related to agency or communion. The agency themes/concerns are (1) mastery, (2) achievement, (3) power, (4) competition, and (5) responsibility. The communion themes/concerns are (6) esteem, (7) nurturance, (8) affiliation, (9) harmony, and (10) solidarity.

De Vos's psychocultural scoring system included all the previous themes or concerns as well as other scoring categories and classified them as primarily instrumental or expressive. The difference between instrumental and expressive themes refers to Parsons and Bales's (1955) description of the gender-based division of labor in traditional families—for example, accomplishing tasks in the external world (instrumental) compared with maintaining harmony within the family (expressive). A distinction between the task leader and the emotional-social leader when coding small-group interactions was also proposed by Bales (1958). As described in the previous section, the modified version for psychological assessment proposed in this chapter substitutes De Vos's instrumental–expressive dichotomy by Bakan's partially overlapping distinction between agency and communion themes.

De Vos made a basic distinction between vertical and horizontal relations in those concerns that are primarily interpersonal. For example, power and nurturance themes refer to human relations of unequal level or status, whereas competition, solidarity/cooperation, and affiliation themes refer to peer, equal-level relationships. A parallel distinction was made by Bateson (1958) between symmetrical and complementary interaction patterns. As described by Watzlawick, Beavin, and Jackson (1967, p. 70), "all communication interchanges are either symmetrical or complementary, depending on whether they are based on equality or difference."

Complementary interactions, such as those scored under power (agency) or nurturance (communion) in the Psychocultural System, imply two different positions: a superior, or one-up position; and an inferior, or one-down position. Such positions interlock or reciprocate, as "dissimilar but fitted behaviors evoke each other" (Watzlawick et al., 1967, p. 69). Conversely, during symmetrical interactions the partners tend to mirror each other, as in affiliative, cooperative, or competitive interpersonal behaviors. According to Watzlawick et al., the concepts of symmetrical or complementary interactions are useful as long as they are not equated with judgments such as good or bad or strong or weak, since equality or difference can have any of those connotations. The current literature on interpersonal behavior deals with similar issues; however, the term *complementary* is used in a different way to indicate that each interpersonal behavior invites a particular class of reactions: "Complementary reactions are assumed to be the same with respect to affiliation and reciprocal with respect to dominance" (Horowitz, Dryer, & Krasnoperova, 1997, p. 89).

The Psychocultural System codes thematic concerns as positive, negative, or unresolved based on their outcome (Table 37.1). De Vos additionally proposed that the stories were coded as active or passive. Such distinctions, as well as De Vos's additional scoring categories (pleasure, inanimate objects/impersonal themes, and destiny/fate) are not included here to make the system more practical for clinical assessment research and practice.

A circumplex model is helpful to represent similarities and differences between concerns that primarily involve interpersonal issues (i.e., power, competition, esteem,

TABLE 37.1 Scoring Categories for the Psychocultural Scoring System

Themes/Concerns	Positive	Negative	Unresolved
AGENCY			
1. MASTERY (M - MAST)			
2. ACHIEVEMENT (A - ACHV)			
3. POWER (P - POWR)			
4. COMPETITION (C - COMP)			
5. RESPONSIBILITY (R - RESP)			
COMMUNION			
6. ESTEEM (E - ESTM)			
7. NURTURANCE (N- NURT)			
8. AFFILIATION (F - AFFL)			
9. HARMONY (H - HAR)			
10. SOLIDARITY (S - SLDR)			

nurturance, affiliation, harmony, and solidarity). The circumplex representation helps scorers to visualize the following important features of the scoring system:

(1) No concern is more fundamental than any other.

(2) The various concerns constitute polarities.

(3) They vary in degree of similarity to one another.

The order appears to be correct although the units around the continuum may not be as equidistant as the figure suggests (Figure 37.1).

By placing power concerns as the vertical axis and affiliation concerns as the horizontal axis, the interpersonal themes appear as combinations of the two factors often reported in the interpersonal literature: dominance–submission and love–hate. Esteem–disapproval (give–deny status) themes are difference based (vertical) as dominance–submission but also involve love–hate connotations regarding acceptance or condemnation by others or society. Love–hate connotations are comparatively more dominant when considering the neighboring category of nurturance–deprivation. This category does not focus on giving or denying status but on giving or denying love/affection, as its neighboring category affiliation–isolation, but it differs from the latter by distinguishing between a dominant and a subordinate position. Next to affiliation–isolation, harmony–discord concerns have also love–hate connotations that may be expressed interpersonally as well as in larger social units. Lastly, solidarity–cooperation and competition–rivalry are less expressive and more instrumental than harmony–discord. They both are also equality-based in contrast with their neighboring category of dominance-submission.

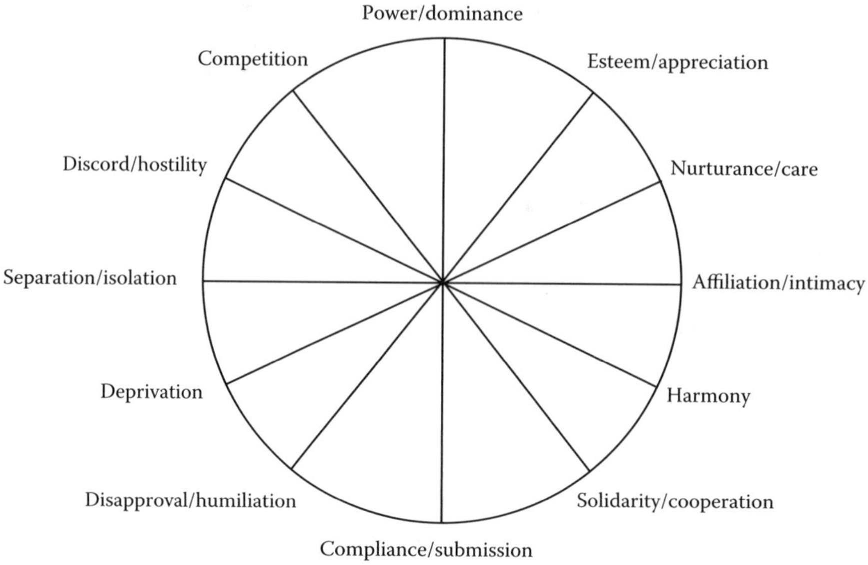

FIGURE 37.1 Circumplex Representation of Interpersonal Themes.

To represent other noninterpersonal, self, and task-related agency themes (achievement and mastery), a three-dimensional diagram may be used (Figure 37.2). Winter (1996) suggested that because power, affiliation, and achievement motives are usually independent or uncorrelated with each other, we could think of them as defining a three-dimensional space with power as the vertical up–down dimension, affiliation as the sideways horizontal dimension, and achievement as the forward–backward dimension. In any case, the independence of the three previous motives should not be assumed to be universal across cultures.

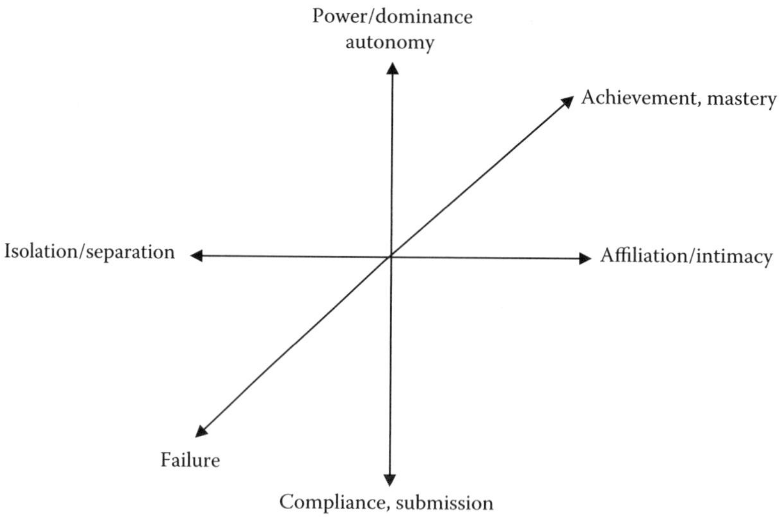

FIGURE 37.2 Three-Dimensional Representation of Achievement/Mastery, Power and Affiliation.

Advantages and Limitations of the Scoring System for Clinical Assessment

Three specific advantages of the scoring system for clinical assessment are considered in this section:

(1) Relevance for multicultural/cross-cultural assessment purposes

(2) Amenability for the development of local norms

(3) Usefulness for clinical training

Thematic contents in apperception methods have been described as "infinitely affected" by sociocultural factors (Bellak, 1993, p. 40). Bellak stated as an example that narratives from "New Yorkers of second generation Irish, Italian or Jewish background will differ markedly from each other, not to mention Midwesterners or Southerners" (ibid.). To be able to formulate valid and useful interpretations, clinical practitioners and researchers using picture-story methods need to be aware of the pervasive impact on narratives of cultural and other contextual variables.

According to Dana (1993), picture-story methods intended for cross-cultural assessment should meet various requirements, such as culturally relevant stimuli, scoring categories that reflect culturally important variables, availability of normative data, contextual grounding of interpretations, and culturally relevant personality theory. As a set of culturally sensitive scoring categories, the Psychocultural System may be used to address the previous requirements.

The Psychocultural System pays particular attention to thought and motivational patterns related to oppression as some categories are defined more in psychosocial than purely psychological terms. For example, De Vos and Vaughn (1992) defined achievement as a concern with accomplishment that guides behavior according to the value system of a particular society. Consequently, the opposite of achievement would not be failure but alienation, occurring when "there is a loss of a need to attain some success within established value patterns viewed positively by society" (p. 128).

The issue of norms for picture-story methods remains controversial. For example, Bellak (1993) considered the normative methodology hardly useful because of its atomistic emphasis. Certainly, the exceptional sensitivity of picture-story methods for a rich variety of individual or situational factors, including major changes across the life cycle (McAdams, 1993), conspires against the possibility of collecting meaningful normative data. Even within the field of multicultural assessment, researchers have cautioned against the utility of special norms for testing minorities, given their heterogeneity and the continually changing sociocultural contexts (Jones & Thorne, 1987).

Despite the previous caveats, a practical need remains regarding the availability of comparative data in order to identify the typical or unique character of TAT contents in individual stories. The Psychocultural Scoring System, in its attention to the narratives' distinctive nuances, may be used to collect normative data without sacrificing the richness of stories.

Based on the Psychocultural Scoring System, practitioners may develop local norms for a specific set of cards to be used for specific practical purposes. In general terms, individuals assessed in health, school, or work settings may be better understood if their TAT narratives are analyzed against the background of the normative motivations and concerns expressed by their reference group. Regarding multicultural assessment, norms based on acculturation status may be obtained for minority groups. The TAT narratives themselves could provide indirect and spontaneously generated data about the individual's cultural orientation, when compared with data collected from both minority and mainstream samples.

A particular advantage of the scoring system for clinical psychology involves clinical training. The scoring categories are comprehensive enough to heighten the student's awareness of individual and group differences in TAT narratives. Regarding multicultural/cross-cultural clinical training, sets of TAT stories could be used to encourage awareness of the cultural self, as proposed by Dana (1997) (see Ephraim, 2000, pp. 431–441, for a collection of stories to Murray card 1 by individuals from different ethnocultural and social-class backgrounds). TAT narratives scored through the Psychocultural System teach students to avoid stereotyped images of culturally different people by revealing not only differences between groups but also significant variations within each group.

Practitioners should be aware of the specific nature as well as strengths and weaknesses of the Psychocultural System for clinical assessment. As described already, the system focuses on thematic contents from an experiential perspective. Due to such focus, it is more appropriate for assessing motivational issues from an experiential, cognitive, or psychodynamic perspective than for assessing structural personality features associated with specific psychopathological conditions. Competent practitioners rely on interpretations based on all assessment data, whether thematic, structural, or behavioral. Consequently, the Psychocultural System's findings regarding TAT thematic contents should be supplemented for practical purposes with data generated from other perspectives that focus on the narratives' structural features, such as cognition/thought processes or defense mechanisms.

☐ Research Evidence

Validity and Generalizability

Normative and Comparative Research

De Vos's system has been used to analyze and compare TAT narratives from various populations, minorities, or class segments in different countries around the world, such as Brazil, Ireland, Japan, Mexico, United States, and Venezuela (De Vos, 1983, 1996; De Vos & Caudill, 1973; De Vos & Kim, 1993; De Vos & Vaughn, 1992; Ephraim, 2000; Ephraim, Söchting, & Marcia, 1997; Scheper-Hughes, 1979; Suárez-Orozco, 1989; Suárez-Orozco & Suárez-Orozco, 1995). These studies found common themes, differences in normative responses, and culture-specific nuances when comparing TAT narratives from different nations or sociocultural groups.

The results of a comparative study by Ephraim et al. (1997) are reported here to illustrate the kind of local normative data generated through the Psychocultural System.

The study focused on the normative concerns expressed in narratives to TAT card 6BM by a group of 54 undergraduate students from Anglo-Canadian backgrounds (male and female; mean age of 22) attending a West Coast Canadian university.

Murray card 6BM depicts an elderly woman standing parallel to a window. Behind her is a younger man with his head down, holding onto his hat. The most frequent concerns expressed by the Anglo-Canadian students involved the following themes: emotional distance/disengagement, son nurtures/supports older parent, and severity of the mother as an authority figure. Interestingly, the most frequent general category (46% of the narratives) referred to unresolved or negative affiliation or nurturance issues regarding mother–son relationship (e.g., "They are not connecting; the scene ends without any emotional interaction that has substance"). Clinicians interpreting such responses would greatly benefit from knowing that they involve typical developmental issues for this particular age group and population.

The study also reported concerns expressed to the same TAT card by a younger sample of senior high school Latin American students from Venezuela (male and female; mean age of 17). Although the stories of both groups involved the same general topics of bad news, separation, and wrongdoing, their narratives revealed clearly distinctive culture-specific issues and nuances. For example, within the Latin American group no themes related to negative mother–son affiliation were found. Also, wrongdoing stories, which were much more frequent in the Latin American group, often involved forgiveness from a benevolent maternal figure, in dramatic contrast with the strict disciplinarian mother figure displayed in the few Anglo-Canadian stories that focused on control or responsibility issues. The Latin American stories displayed a long-term reciprocal dependency between the mother and son characters, which was consistent with findings reported in the cross-cultural and cultural psychology literature. The previous results and those from other comparative studies in the field of psychological anthropology suggest that TAT data scored through the Psychocultural System are both culturally sensitive and cross-culturally comparable.

Criterion-Related Validity

Validity studies aim to establish to what extent scores from a particular measure relate to other criteria in a predicted manner. There is a need for studies that examine psychocultural data in relation to both real-life behaviors and other psychological measures.

The comparative study reflecting cross-cultural differences reported in the previous section (Ephraim et al., 1997) additionally explored the relationship between individual differences in the TAT normative concerns and individual differences in the level of care-based morality (Gilligan, 1982), assessed through the Ethic of Care Interview (ECI). This part of the study only involved the students from Anglo-Canadian backgrounds. The ECI presents a series of moral dilemmas allowing a distinction among three levels of care and responsibility in relationships: self-oriented (level 1); other oriented (level 2); and self–other oriented (level 3).

Results of the study confirmed the interest of a multimethod strategy in psychological practice and research (Koestner, Weinberger, & McClelland, 1991; Westen, Feit,& Zittel, 1999). For example, the study concluded that there was complete congruency between both types of data for the level-1 participants, as people who gave egocentric and self-serving solutions to the moral dilemmas consistently revealed negative concerns regarding agency or communion issues on the TAT measure.

Regarding the subjects described as caring exclusively for others (level 2), approximately one half of these presumed morally conventional young adults provided positive nurturance stories indicating an accessibility of care representations that was entirely absent in the stories of the level-1 participants. A subgroup of mostly female level-2 participants showed strong unresolved or negative relationship issues in their TAT stories; the authors described this subgroup as functioning according to a society's prescribed selfless role for women, which was accompanied in their case by significant emotional pain and distress ("Doing good and feeling bad").

Reliability

There is a study in progress regarding interscorer reliability (Jenkins, Howe-Martin & Mason, 2007).

Future Research Needed

The stimulus pull of specific picture-story cards should not be assumed but carefully researched. Clinicians performing comprehensive clinical assessment with a particular population or within specific settings may develop local norms regarding a selected set of cards. Researchers interested in studying specific agency or communion issues may explore with a variety of cards to establish their stimulus value for their particular purpose.

The issue of racially or culturally congruent stimuli has been raised regarding multicultural/cross-cultural validity for picture-story methods. According to Teglasi (1993), research findings have revealed that these adaptations do not necessarily elicit richer stories than the traditional TAT cards. There has been a parallel assumption in the TAT literature, which argues that a different set of cards must be used based on gender, as presumably individuals identify more with stimulus characteristics of the same sex as themselves. A research study conducted to examine this assumption did not recommend the use of different sets of cards for each gender (Katz, Russ, & Overholser, 1993). In any case, questions about the stimulus pull of specific picture-story cards according to culture or gender can only be answered empirically.

Research is needed to relate the Psychocultural Scoring System's data with real-life behaviors and other psychological measures to explore the system's validity for particular purposes. An ongoing research project is being conducted relating the concerns of undergraduate university students expressed indirectly through their TAT narratives with their responses to a variety of self-report relationship measures, involving variables such as social network, perceived mutuality, depressive experiences and symptoms, and interpersonal problems.

As proposed in a previous publication (Ephraim, 2000) a limited set of TAT cards could be researched extensively to reach saturation through collaborative efforts by clinical researchers and practitioners worldwide as well as within particular societies and specific assessment settings. Since the Psychocultural Scoring System is an open-ended methodology, such efforts would enrich its categories and may provide an extensive database for further studies.

References

Aronow, E., Weiss, K. M., & Reznikoff, M. (2001). *A practical guide to the Thematic Apperception Test.* Philadelphia: Brunner-Routledge.

Bakan, D. (1966). *The duality of human existence: Isolation and communion in Western man.* Boston: Beacon.

Bales, R. F. (1958). Task roles and social roles in problem-solving groups. In E. E. Maccoby, T. M. Neucomb, & E. L. Hartley (Eds.), *Readings in social psychology* (pp. 437–447). New York: Holt, Rinehart & Winston.

Bateson (1958). *Naven: A survey of the problems suggested by a composite picture of the culture of a New Guinea tribe drawn from three points of view.* Stanford: Stanford University Press.

Bellak, L. (1993). *The Thematic Apperception Test, the Children's Apperception Test, and the Senior Apperception Technique in clinical use* (5th ed.). Boston: Allyn and Bacon.

Dana, R. H. (1985). The Thematic Apperception Test. In C. S. Newmark (Ed.), *Major psychological assessment instruments* (2nd ed.) (pp. 166–205). Boston: Allyn and Bacon.

Dana, R. H. (1993). *Multicultural assessment perspectives for professional psychology.* Boston: Allyn and Bacon.

Dana R. H. (1997). Personality assessment and the cultural self: Emic and etic contexts as learning resources. In L. Handler & M. Hilsenroth (Eds.), *Teaching and learning personality assessment* (pp. 325–346). Thousand Oaks, CA: Sage.

Dana, R. H. (1998, March). *Using the TAT in cross-cultural/multicultural assessment.* Paper presented at the midwinter meeting of the Society for Personality Assessment, Boston, MA.

De Vos, G. A. (1983). Achievement motivation and intra-family attitudes in immigrant Koreans. *Journal of Psychoanalytic Anthropology, 6,* no. 1, 25–71.

De Vos, G. A. (1992). *Social cohesion and alienation: Minorities in the United States and Japan.* Boulder, CO: Westview Press.

De Vos, G. A. (1993). Psychological anthropology: A professional odyssey. In L. B. Boyer, R. M. Boyer, & H. Stein (Eds.), *The psychoanalytic study of society* (vol. 18) (pp. 23–88). Hillsdale, NJ: Analytic Press.

De Vos, G. A. (1996). Internalized achievement or external authority: Some cultural comparisons of responses to TAT Card 1. *Rorschachiana: Yearbook of the International Rorschach Society, 21,* 91–126.

De Vos, G. A., & Caudill, W. G. (1973). Achievement, culture and personality. In G. A. De Vos, *Socialization for achievement: Essays on the cultural psychology of the Japanese* (pp. 220–247). Berkeley: University of California Press.

De Vos, G. A., & De Vos, E. S. (2004). *Basic dimensions in conscious thought: the self and socialization of human concerns.* Lanham, MD: Rowman & Littlefield.

De Vos, G. A., & Kim, E.-Y. (1993). Koreans in Japan and the United States: Attitudes toward achievement and authority. In I. Light & P. Bhachu (Eds.), *Immigration and entrepreneurship: Culture, capital and ethnic networks* (pp. 205–241). New Brunswick, NJ: Transaction Publishers.

De Vos, G. A., & Suárez-Orozco, M. (1990). *Status inequality: The self in culture.* Newbury Park, CA: Sage.

De Vos, G. A., & Vaughn, C. A. (1992). The interpersonal self: A level of psychocultural analysis. In L. B. Boyer & R. M. Boyer (Eds.), *The psychoanalytic study of society* (vol. 17) (pp. 95–142). Hillsdale, NJ: Analytic Press.

Ephraim, D., Söchting, I., & Marcia, J. (1997). Cultural norms for TAT narratives in psychological practice and research: Illustrative studies. *Rorschachiana: Yearbook of the International Rorschach Society, 22,* 13–37.

Ephraim, D. (2000). Psychocultural approach to TAT scoring and interpretation. In R. H. Dana (Ed.), *Handbook of cross-cultural and multicultural personality assessment* (pp. 427–445). Hillsdale, NJ: Erlbaum.

Gilligan, C. (1982). *In a different voice: Psychological theory and human development.* Cambridge, MA: Harvard University Press.

Horowitz, L. M., Dryer, D. C., & Krasnoperova, E. N. (1997). The Circumplex Structure of Interpersonal Problems. In R. Plutchik, & H. R. Conte (Eds), *Circumplex models of personality and emotions.* Washington, DC: American Psychological Association.

Jenkins, S. R., Howe-Martin, L., & Mason, S. (2007). Calculating interscorer reliability for the Psychocultural TAT scoring system. Unpublished data analyses, University of North Texas.

Jones, E. E., & Thorne, A. (1987). Rediscovery of the subject: Intercultural approaches to clinical assessment. *Journal of Consulting and Clinical Psychology, 55,* 488–495.

Katz, H. E., Russ, S. W., & Overholser, J. C. (1993). Sex differences, sex roles, and projection on the TAT: Matching stimulus to examinee gender. *Journal of Personality Assessment, 60,* 186–191.

Koestner, R., Weinberger, J., & McClelland, D. C. (1991). Task-intrinsic and social-extrinsic sources of arousal for motives assessed in fantasy and self-report. *Journal of Personality, 54,* 57–82.

Leary, T. (1957). *Interpersonal diagnosis of personality: A functional theory and methodology for personality evaluation.* New York: Ronald Press Co.

McAdams, D. P. (1993). *Stories we live by: Personal myths and the making of the self.* New York: William Morrow & Company.

McAdams, D. P., Hoffman, B. J., Mansfield, E. D., & Day, R. (1996). Themes of agency and communion in significant autobiographical scenes. *Journal of Personality, 64,* no. 2, 339–377.

Murray, H. A. (1943). *Thematic Apperception Test manual.* Cambridge, MA: Harvard University Press.

Packer M. J. (1985). Hermeneutic inquiry in the study of human conduct. *American Psychologist, 40,* no. 10, 1081–1093.

Parsons, T., & Bales, R. (1955). *Family socialization and interaction process.* Glencoe, MN: Free Press.

Plutchik, R., & Conte, H. R. (Eds.) (1997). *Circumplex models of personality and emotions.* Washington, DC: American Psychological Association.

Polkinghorne, D. (1988). *Narrative knowing and human sciences.* Albany: State University of New York Press.

Scheper-Hughes, N. (1979). *Saints, scholars and schizophrenics.* Berkeley: University of California Press.

Scheper-Hughes, N. (1992). *Death without weeping: The violence of everyday life in Brazil.* Berkeley: University of California Press.

Smith, C. P. (Ed.). (1992). *Motivation and personality: Handbook of thematic content analysis.* New York: Cambridge University Press.

Suárez-Orozco, M. (1989). *Central-American refugees and U.S. high-schools: A psychosocial study of motivations and achievement.* Stanford: Stanford University Press.

Suárez-Orozco, C., & Suárez-Orozco, M. (1995): *Transformations: Immigration, family life and achievement motivation among Latino adolescents.* Stanford: Stanford University Press.

Teglasi, H. (1993). *Clinical use of story telling: Emphasizing the TAT with children and adolescents.* Boston: Allyn and Bacon.

Vane, J. R. (1981). The Thematic Apperception Test: A review. *Clinical Psychology Review, 1,* 319–336.

Watzlawick, P., Beavin, J.H., & Jackson, D.D. (1967). *Pragmatics of human communication: A study of interactional patterns, pathologies, and paradoxes.* New York: Norton.

Westen, D. (1991). Clinical assessment of object relations using the TAT. *Journal of Personality Assessment. 56,* 56–74.

Westen, D., Feit, A., & Zittel, C. (1999). Methodological issues in research using projective techniques. In P. C. Kendall, J. N. Butcher, & G. Holmbeck (Eds.), *Handbook of research methods in clinical psychology* (2nd ed.) (pp. 224–240). New York: Wiley.

Wiggins, J. S. (1991). Agency and communion as conceptual coordinates for the understanding of interpersonal behavior. In W. M. Grove & D. Cicchetti, *Thinking clearly about psychology* (vol. 2) (pp. 89–113). Minneapolis: University of Minnesota Press.

Wiggins, J. S. (2003). *Paradigms of personality assessment.* New York: Guilford.

Winter, D. G. (1996). *Personality: Analysis and interpretation of lives.* New York: McGraw-Hill.

☐ Notes

I thank George A. De Vos for sharing his knowledge and passion for the TAT method during the time I had the privilege to work with him in Berkeley under a Fulbright Scholar Grant. José Miguel Salazar, Irving B. Weiner, and Richard H. Dana have been generous mentors and friends throughout the years I have been involved with projectives. James E. Marcia provided financial support through research grants for some of my research work with the TAT. I particularly thank Sharon Rae Jenkins for her comments regarding the Psychocultural Scoring System and the preparation of this chapter; she also gave me the opportunity to work with her enthusiastic scoring team, whose questions, doubts, and comments were helpful in refining the scoring categories.

38

CHAPTER

Psychocultural System Manual

David Ephraim

Introduction

This manual presents a Thematic Apperception Test (TAT) scoring system for clinical practice and research that integrates features from a psychocultural scoring system developed by George A. De Vos (De Vos & De Vos, 2004) within the field of psychological anthropology and approaches from contemporary theories of human motivation and interpersonal behavior developed within the fields of personality and clinical psychology. The scoring system analyzes TAT narratives within a framework of ten thematic concerns broadly classified as related to agency or communion (Bakan, 1966; McAdams, 1996). The agency-related themes are mastery, achievement, power, competition, and responsibility. The communion-related themes are esteem, nurturance, affiliation, harmony, and solidarity.

Administration

Format

Picture-story protocols to be scored through this system may be recorded using TAT standard instructions in an individual or group setting through a variety of formats, such as examiners recording the stories, subjects recording their own stories, or machine recording.

Stimuli

This manual focuses on the use of the system to score picture-story narratives in the clinical field, although it can be used in other fields or for a variety of verbal materials, such as interview data, observation protocols, fiction, artwork, dreams, and folklore. Although TAT cards have been used in most of the studies, the system can be applied to narratives collected to any set of picture or verbal cues. Research studies with the psychocultural system have often focused on a few TAT cards, such as cards 1, 2, 6BM, and 7BM. Cards 3BM, 4, 5, 7GF, 8BM, 13 MF, and 17BM have also been or are currently being used in research studies.

The stimulus characteristics (i.e., stimulus pull) of any card to be scored through this system should not be assumed but carefully researched. Scores are strongly determined by the particular card being used. Consequently, it is not possible to directly compare data obtained through different cards.

Any particular TAT card stimulates a variety of themes (see the practice stories), but some are clearly dominant. For example, card 1 tends to generate more agency than communion themes, whereas the opposite happens with card 6BM; however, this may change across social classes, cultures, or educational levels. The author's experience scoring with the Psychocultural System both TAT and picture-story cards used in the David C. McClelland and John W. Atkinson tradition (Smith, 1992) confirmed the strength of the TAT set for clinical assessment, apparently based on its higher level of ambiguity. The stimulus configuration of the cards used in the McClelland and Atkinson tradition tended to generate more constrained and stereotyped narratives when scored with the Psychocultural System.

Clinicians using the Psychocultural System could rely on a smaller set of TAT cards than traditionally recommended. Not only are there practical reasons for this regarding time constraints when using the test as part of a battery (Aronow, Weis, & Reznikoff, 2001); also, clinicians would be better prepared to interpret those cards they are thoroughly familiar with regarding the cards' stimulus pull for specific populations. I suggest routine use of a set of approximately six cards administered in the same sequence.

Scoring Process

The coding routine proceeds by identifying the thematic concerns as they unfold in the narratives. They are coded sequentially in order of appearance. The unit of analysis is the scorable word or phrase; the same phrase may contain elements related to two or more categories, all of which should be scored. In some stories, one or more concerns are clearly dominant whereas others appear secondary. Secondary concerns are scored for independent issues that are only mentioned but not developed within the current story. The scorer acknowledges such distinction by using different values for dominant and secondary concerns when calculating scores, such as assigning half points for secondary concerns.

Some examples of single and double scoring to TAT card 1 follow to introduce the reasoning that underlies the scoring procedure. A narrative such as, "The child wants to become a famous violinist," involves an agency, task-oriented concern with achievement, whereas a story such as, "The child feels lonely," involves a communion, relationship-oriented concern with affiliation. The following narrative includes both agency and communion types of concerns: "He's looking at the violin which is a memento from his grandfather. He is having tender thoughts about his grandfather. He will practice and will succeed greatly as a violinist." The reference to the child's long-term goal would be coded as achievement (agency), whereas the reference to his tender thoughts about his grandfather would be coded as affiliation (communion). The following narrative is also double-scored, as it contains agency concerns in the context of communion goals: "The boy thinks a great deal about his family. His parents are fighting a lot and the family might just fall apart. The child dreams that if he were able to play well it would help to reconcile his parents." This narrative involves a communion concern with harmony, regarding parent's fights/reconciliation, and an agency concern with mastery.

Stories are also scored regarding their positive or negative outcomes, elaborations, or affective tone. The conclusion of the story must be studied to score whether it is successful or unsuccessful, happy or unhappy, and in such cases it is coded as positive (+) or negative (–). Another alternative is to code the story as unresolved (u) when the narrator does not give an outcome or gives conditional (i.e., *if*) or alternative outcomes involving both positive and negative outcomes or emotions.

Narratives that do not include outcomes or that only include them after the subject has been prompted create a frequent problem for scoring. In some instances, it might reflect the narrator's sense of uncertainty regarding the concerns involved, in which case it might be appropriate to score the narrative as unresolved; in other instances, recalling the instructions seems to be the only issue at hand. Sometimes the additional material is particularly rich in elaborations. The scorer must exercise his or her judgment and use it consistently when scoring such stories as unresolved or not. Examples of positive, negative, and unresolved outcomes for each scoring category are given in the section that follows.

The outcome must be coded from the narrator's perspective. Such perspective is sometimes unequivocally stated. In some instances it must be inferred from particular events that take place in the narrative. For example, "He became a drug addict" would be coded as negative based on the latter.

In some cases there may be discrepancies between the narrator's perspective and the scorer/clinician's perspective about the outcome of a story. For example, the narrator presents a character who expresses a strong sense of confidence that leads him or her to overcome a very difficult obstacle, but the scorer considers the extremely positive ending as expressing an inflated and unrealistic self-confidence. In cases where the inappropriateness of the ending is obvious, the outcome may be coded as unresolved, and the discrepancy should be analyzed during the interpretation process.

Stories that include humor are difficult to code regarding their outcome. Scorers may find helpful a distinction made by Vaillant (1993) between positive mature humor and negative or unresolved humor manifestations such as practical jokes, clowning, caricature, parody, irony, or other passive-aggressive elaborations. According to Vaillant, mature humor "permits the overt expression of feelings without individual discomfort or unpleasant effect on others" (p. 73).

The overall outcome usually subsumes the different concerns expressed in the narrative, but different concerns may have different outcomes or positive or negative connotations and should be scored accordingly. For example, "The boy comes from a family of very accomplished musicians (achievement +). He has a good teacher (mastery +) who likes him (affiliation +), but he will not approve the admission exams for the music academy (mastery –)."

A narrative may display abrupt changes in its emotional tone or outcome regarding a particular concern. For example, a particular story line may finally turn out positive but only after extensive negative or unresolved elaborations. In such cases an arrow (→) is used between the different outcomes (see, e.g., practice story 4).

A story may include the same general kind of concerns regarding two or more characters or independent issues—for example, "Laura loves him immensely, but he is married. As he and Laura walk out of the door, his wife walks out of the store across the street. Laura grabs him and says, 'Let her go!' He loses both women because of his indecisiveness" (card 4). The previous narrative includes affiliation concerns regarding two independent fragments: Laura's love (Affiliation +) and the indecisiveness of the male character (Affiliation U). Both scores should be included.

The general categories previously listed inform the analysis by allowing the identification of broad plot structures. However, assigning a general code may not capture the substance or distinctive nuance of a specific issue or concern. Therefore, after coding the more abstract general category the scorer should proceed to specify or subcategorize the issues involved. For example, a story focused on power issues may be further classified as, for example, parental control, obedience, autonomy, passive resistance, group pressure, or ineffective exercise of power. As with any scoring system that focuses on meaning structures, the scorers need to return as many times as necessary to the particular narrative searching each time to improve their understanding in an open-ended inductive process. It is worth mentioning that such open-ended scoring procedure may lead the researcher or clinician into uncharted territories. An unavoidable consequence of using hermeneutic, contextually sensitive assessment approaches is that, as described by Geertz (1995, p. 20) regarding ethnography, "everything is a matter of one thing leading to another, that to a third, and that to one hardly knows what." Scoring the narrative in the context of other stories from the individual's reference group is often very helpful in providing a context for interpretation.

Clinicians or researchers using the Psychocultural System to score TAT narratives should be attentive to cultural variations and nuances regarding the various scoring categories. For example, scorers should be familiar with culture-specific long-term goals or standards of excellence when coding achievement; when coding esteem issues, scorers must take into account that appreciation and self-respect themes vary widely across cultures.

The next two sections present in detail the agency and communion categories along with illustrations. A circumplex representation included in chapter 37 in this volume (Figure 37.2) may be useful to scorers for visualizing degrees of similarity and difference among those concerns involving interpersonal themes. The descriptions of most of the following scoring categories are based on De Vos's formulations. The reader would benefit from consulting his detailed presentation as well as discussion of the scoring categories from developmental, psychoanalytic, and anthropological perspectives (De Vos & De Vos, 1994).

Scoring Category Criteria for Agency

Bakan's (1966) concept of agency refers to "the individual's striving to separate from others, to master the environment, to assert, protect, and expand the self" (McAdams, 1993, p. 71). Included under this category are themes or concerns that express the individual's aim to become a competent, productive, achieved, strong, powerful, dominant, separate, autonomous, independent, or responsible agent. The category also includes attributes that are opposite or negatives of the previous themes, such as failure, incompetence, lack or loss of long-term aspirations and goals, powerlessness, abuse of authority, submissiveness, or irresponsible behavior.

Mastery (MAST)

Narratives that focus on the characters' sense of competence or self-confidence are scored under mastery. Its negative counterpart is a concern with failure. Some related notions in psychological theory are competence/effectance (White, 1959) and self-efficacy (Bandura, 1991), both of which refer to the person's belief in her or his ability to overcome obstacles.

Narratives about control over the environment or a problem-solving situation are scored under mastery, whereas concerns with dominance in the interpersonal sphere are scored under power. Although agency concerns regarding mastery or achievement are mostly self and task oriented, they may also include communion goals (e.g., a story about parents "raising better children" or about a couple "improving their marriage"), in which case the story is double scored. Concerns with status recognition, often scored under esteem/appreciation, may overlap with concerns about mastery, in which case the narrative should also be double scored. Concerns with mastery are sometimes difficult to distinguish from concerns with achievement. The latter imply a sense of accomplishment regarding a long-term goal, whereas mastery refers to a general sense of competence or to the ability to carry out everyday, routine, or specific tasks or performances. Mastery refers to *I can* statements, whereas achievement refers to *I will* statements (De Vos, 1992). The previous distinction between mastery and achievement appears to be easier to make and more relevant for scoring picture-story narratives than some other narrative materials, such as personal strivings (Emmons, 1986) or autobiographical scenes (McAdams, 1993, 1996).

MAST + is scored when characters express a sense of self-confidence or a belief in their capacity for agency regarding a specific task, a problem-solving situation, the acquisition of a skill or knowledge, or overcoming an immediate obstacle or challenge.

MAST – is scored in narratives depicting a character's failure in mastering a task or challenge, a problem-solving situation, or the acquisition of a skill or knowledge. It is also coded when a character is described as incompetent.

Severely traumatized individuals often experience a sense of being permanently damaged in terms of their instrumental capacities, self-efficacy, or ability for mastery. Stories referring to broken objects (e.g., *a broken violin* in card 1) may reflect such concerns. Stories where the characters are concerned about their instrumental capacities for successfully attaining long-term goals are scored under achievement (see next category).

MAST U is scored in narratives referring to difficulties, indecisiveness, worries, or anxiety in mastering a situation, solving a problem, or acquiring a skill or knowledge.

Examples of MAST are as follows:

(1) The boy is worried because he cannot quite grasp the violin lesson he has to study. (MAST U)

(1) He just finished his performance. He feels sad because he made many mistakes. (MAST –)

(6BM) This is a grandson and his grandmother. He is a very well-educated man, probably a doctor. His grandma is also very intelligent and wise. (MAST +)

(6BM) The man is the local sheriff. He has just arrived and told the older woman that her husband has had a serious car accident, not fatal. She is very concerned but will pull herself together, offer the sheriff a cup of tea, and hear the details of the accident. (MAST +)

Achievement (ACHV)

Achievement is defined as a concern with long-term aspirations or accomplishments. Identifying a long-term, self-imposed, or internalized goal is key in scoring for achievement in TAT narratives. Stories focusing on short-term goals, or doing better with a present task, are not coded as achievement but under the previous category of mastery, as in the following narratives:

The doctor and his student [regarding a medical operation] want to do a good job.

The student is worried about his two exams. He is wondering how he can ever manage to study sufficiently enough to be able to pass the exams.

The boy is diligently studying his course.

ACHV + is scored when the outcome concerning achievement is successful: The project or invention will work, the person will become what he or she aspires to be, or significant internal or external obstacles are overcome. Some narratives emphasize the efforts or persistence necessary to achieve the goal, whereas others refer to the inspiration or support given by significant others (double scored with nurturance).

ACHV – is assigned when the outcome of a story about achieving long-term goals is unsuccessful. Negative achievement is also scored when, according to De Vos and Vaughn's (1992, p. 128) psychosocial perspective, "there is a loss of a need to attain some success within established value patterns viewed positively by society." The loss of a need to accomplish may be indirectly expressed in narratives of individuals experiencing marginal social status, exploitation, or racism, currently or across previous generations. The following fragment of a narrative to card 1 from a Korean Japanese youth presented by De Vos and Kim (1993, pp. 223–224) illustrates this kind of concerns: "He is worrying if he will become a violinist. I wonder if he has a toothache." Similar concerns regarding the loss of any positive task-related future orientation may be expressed by individuals that have experienced severe trauma (e.g., child abuse or neglect, domestic violence, torture).

ACHV U is scored when the outcome of an achievement story line is unresolved or dubious—for example, characters are worried about their future goals and wonder whether they will ever succeed, or there is a possibility that the project might not be realized or the invention might not work. In the absence of a definitive action or commitment the story is also coded as unresolved, as when the character daydreams about future possibilities.

Examples of ACHV are as follows:

(1) The boy dreams about what he is going to accomplish with his violin. I think that some day he will become a famous violinist. (ACHV +)

(2) She is going to school now, but her deep aspiration is to raise well her own children. Maybe she will accomplish it. We don't know yet. (ACHV U)

(6BM) The son is visiting his mother. He has not been successful in his career plans. (ACHV –).

(6BM) He is determined to leave and to go to a faraway country to get a fortune and is now presenting his plans to his mother. He will work hard there for many years and will become rich. (ACHV +)

(7BM) The research they both are doing is going to be a real scientific advance. (ACHV +)

(7BM) These men are working on a new invention. They wonder if they will succeed. (ACHV U)

Power (POWR)

Power/control themes are primarily interpersonal and may be situated in family, work, or social contexts. Power themes are presented from either the superior or the subordinate position. Parental control is a power subtheme often found in TAT narratives (e.g., card 1: "He has been forced to practice the violin"). The level or status difference implied in stories involving power or control is questioned in narratives focusing on autonomy, which are also coded under power. Autonomy concerns are more common in Westerners' TAT narratives than in narratives from other cultures.

POWR + is scored when narratives given from the dominant perspective refer to "a benign, legitimate exercise of authority, persuasion, or guidance to achieve legitimate, socially approved individual and collective purposes" (De Vos & Suarez-Orozco, 1990, p. 53); power narratives given from the subordinate position are scored as positive when referring to themes such as proper compliance, justified resistance toward abusive or unsuitable authority, or appropriate exercise of autonomy.

POWR – is used to score themes such as abuse of legitimate power, autocratic behavior, incompetent exercise of authority, unjustifiable rebellion, oppositional-defiant behavior, or excessive submission.

POWR U is used for stories where a character displays indecision or ambivalent feelings toward authority figures or issues—for example, leading characters have difficulties in properly assuming their role, or subordinate characters are ambivalent or uncertain about the legitimacy of control or rebellion.

Examples of POWR are as follows:

(1) He has been forced to practice and does not want to concentrate. He will have to practice whether he likes it or not. He will never learn to play. (POWR –)

(1) He does not like to practice violin. He will convince his parents about joining a baseball team instead because that's what he wants to practice. His parents will agree. (POWR [autonomy] +)

(2) She could not stand the old-fashioned attitude toward women in her hometown. She got her diploma and left for another country. (POWR [autonomy]+)

(6BM) Looks like the grandfather has died and left the farm to his son. But the son wants to work in the city. The mother is sad. If he leaves they will lose the farm. He has to make a decision: stay on the farm or be a big shot in the city. But he is a good mamma's boy and he stays in the farm until the mother dies. Not that he wants her to die, but he is trapped. (POWR –)

Competition (COMP)

Characters may be involved in unregulated or regulated competition/rivalry in various contexts such as love, work, or sports. Concerns with competition are infrequent in narratives to the picture-story cards often used by clinicians.

COMP + is scored in stories where the character is winning or doing as well as someone else. Some of such narratives may be double scored with achievement.

COMP – is scored in stories referring to improper behavior in competing situations or to avoidance of the appropriate assertive behavior toward equals.

COMP U is coded in stories of unsettled rivalry.

Examples of COMP are as follows:

(1) He was challenged by another boy who thinks he is a better player, but this boy won because he was more persistent. (COMP +)

(2) The girl is in love with this guy. The older woman is her rival. She is his wife and works with him in the field. Who is going to get him? I don't know. Maybe the guy is going to choose the younger one, maybe not. (COMP U)

(2) "I don't want to go to school Papa," she whined while collecting her books. "Johnny doesn't have to go!" "Your brother Johnny is needed around here to help out," replied her mother. She felt the anger building up inside of her. "One day I'll prove my worth to them!" she thought to herself as she trudged to school imagining helping her family one day in the future. (COMP U)

(6BM) Her mother is ashamed of him. He won a contest but his mother knows that he cheated in order to win. (COMP –)

Responsibility (RESP)

Themes related to internalized rules or obligations are scored under responsibility. In narratives of responsibility, the approval or fear of punishment regarding proper behavior comes from within the individual, in contrast with the external authority portrayed in narratives scored under power/control (De Vos, 1992).

References to characters fulfilling or avoiding their responsibilities may refer to tasks or to other people. References to characters' responsibility for their own or others' performance in instrumental or task-related situations often involve agency issues. Narratives of taking or avoiding responsibility toward others may also involve communion themes, in which case the stories are double scored with nurturance/care.

Stories using the following words are often scored under responsibility: *duty, rules, obligations, guilt, remorse, delinquency, morality, conscience.* As described by Winter (1992), responsibility issues are associated with diverse topics, such as political leadership, moral judgment or actions, impulse control, and prosocial versus antisocial behavior. Winter's scoring system for responsibility includes some coding categories that overlap with those of the present system, such as references to internal obligations or moral-legal standards of conduct (expressed in dichotomies such as, e.g., morally good–morally bad, right–wrong, legal–illegal, honest–dishonest).

RESP + themes include carrying out everyday or extraordinary duties, or self-imposed responsibilities in instrumental or task-related or relationship contexts.

RESP – is coded in narratives where irresponsible, unscrupulous behavior, or violation of own obligations and duties takes place. Additional sets of issues that also fall under this category are excessive duties, guilt, or self-blaming (as with characters who judge themselves or others harshly).

RESP U is coded in stories that involve unresolved guilt, unresolved concern with duties or responsibilities, and internal conflict regarding moral dilemmas or role expectations.

Examples of RESP are as follows:

(1) A child is studying for a presentation. It is good that he is being so responsible with his homework. His presentation will turn out well. (RESP +)

(2) The girl feels that she is getting an education at the expense of her mother and father. She thinks that perhaps she ought to be working in the farm and helping her parents instead of studying. (RESP U)

(2) This story takes place in a very rural area. Emily is the oldest of seven children. Because she has so many brothers and sisters, Emily has a lot of responsibility although she is only 15 years old. She helps her mom cook and clean and take care of the kids. She really doesn't have an opportunity to be a kid herself. (RESP –)

(6BM) He disappointed his mother. When he goes and talks to her, she refuses to speak to him. He is trying to think of a way to make up for what he has done. (RESP U)

(7BM) He told his dad that he was going to another country to help fight against poverty. (RESP +)

(7BM) They are planning to do something wrong, to steal or something. The one in front doesn't want to do it. They will both go to jail. (RESP –)

Scoring Category Criteria for Communion

Bakan's (1966) concept of communion refers to "the individual's striving to lose his or her own individuality by merging with others, participating in something that is larger than the self, and relating to other selves in warm, close, intimate and loving ways" (McAdams, 1993, p. 71). The present scoring system includes under communion the following themes: esteem, nurturance, affiliation, harmony, solidarity, and their opposites or negatives, such as disapproval/denigration, deprivation, isolation/separation, discord/hostility, and lack of cooperation.

Esteem (ESTM)

Esteem/appreciation themes focus on how the self is considered, evaluated, or judged by other individuals, social groups, or society. Thematic concerns regarding giving or receiving status, approval, acceptance, recognition, or validation from others are scored under this category. Esteem issues are sometimes implied in references to a sense of belongingness, or with the use of words such as *shame/pride, honor, appearance,* or *sarcasm/teasing* in a relational or social context.

Esteem/appreciation is included in this system as a communion concern because individuals' sense of worth, self-esteem, or sense of belongingness develops in larger-than-self units, such as families, communities, and society at large. Narratives that refer to esteem/appreciation issues but focus exclusively on the self are not scored under this category. For example, the following narrative includes a word that suggests esteem issues but would only be scored under competence: "The child mastered his lesson and feels proud of himself" (Card 1).

ESTM + is scored in narratives referring to granting or receiving acceptance, respect, admiration, recognition, or validation in interpersonal, family, community, or social settings.

ESTM – is scored in narratives that refer to a sense of externally based personal, ethnic, or social disapproval, shame, lack of value, humiliation, denigration, or dishonor. External disapproval may also be expressed as contempt, disregard, or sarcasm.

ESTM U is scored in narratives where characters worry or have doubts about their social acceptability, recognition by peers, self-esteem, or appearance

Examples of ESTM are as follows:

(1) He spent hours and hours practicing. Then called his mom to listen to him. She was very impressed and proud that he evolved that much. (ESTM +)

(2) Her parents are working in the field. She will have to gain the respect at school from people that look down on poor farmers. (ESTM U)

(2) They consider that she does not belong to this place. That makes her unhappy. But maybe she will find her place in the big city. (ESTM U)

(6BM) They could be talking about the man's father. What the father did or said in the past. The son has just found out. He has to change the positive image he had of his father. (ESTM –).

Nurturance (NURT)

Characters in picture-story narratives may be portrayed within love/affection interpersonal relationships based on equality or difference. Communion themes involving love/affection, or its lack or loss in difference-based relationships (vertical, complementary) such as parent–children interactions, are coded under nurturance/care in contrast to love/affection themes in equality-based relationships (horizontal, symmetrical) such as partners or colleagues, which are scored under affiliation.

It is important to keep in mind that actions such as giving or receiving advice or help, as well as their negatives, may be more related to agency than to communion themes (e.g., references to supportive actions in contractual relationships focused on tasks rather than people).

NURT + is scored in narratives that describe positive relationships where one character supports, comforts, nurtures, cares for, helps, protects, rescues, aids, or consoles another. Inner states related to nurturance/care, such as pity, compassion or gratitude, are also coded under this category. Nurturance themes also include humanitarian actions, the protection of animals, or religious themes where a deity is perceived as compassionate, caring, or protective.

NURT – is scored in narratives of nurturance/care referring to a sense of deprivation or neglect. This category includes references to abusive parental behavior, attachment disruptions, or to a lack of emotional or material support (e.g., food, shelter). Concerns with culturally inappropriate dependency or clinginess are also scored under this category.

NURT U stories refer to uncertainty about emotional or material security, unresolved concerns with protection, or nostalgia.

Examples of NURT are as follows:

(1) The boy is filled up with gratitude, because his beloved father presented this violin to him with the words: "Dear son, this is for you." (NURT +)

(1) This is a sad boy. His parents did not care for him. (NURT –)

(1) He was a very poor kid and did not have money to buy a violin. (NURT –)

(2) She is very grateful for what her parents are doing for her. (NURT +)

(6BM) This is a son and his mother and they just found out that his dad died. Pretty soon the mother will start to cry and the son will come over and try to console and make her feel better. (NURT +)

(7BM) Father and son. Father is frustrated. He wants to reach his son and help him, but doesn't really know how to. (NURT U)

Affiliation (AFFL)

Communion concerns that involve equality-based, peer, horizontal relationships, such as friendship or love, are coded under affiliation, whereas those that portray difference-based, vertical relationships are coded under nurturance (see previous category). Affiliation concerns are often suggested by the use of terms that imply interpersonal closeness or intimacy (e.g., *sharing, union, fusion, sympathy,* or *understanding*) or emotional distance (e.g., *isolation, rejection, indifference, separation, loss, mistrust,* or *lack of understanding*). Purely instrumental association with another person or a group is not scored under affiliation (e.g., people getting together to cooperate on an impersonal task rather than to relate to each other).

AFFL + is scored in relatedness stories between equals partners involving affection/love or a positive emotional tone or outcome. The narrative may refer to emotional warmth/closeness, psychological and/or physical intimacy, or sympathetic understanding. Reestablishment of a relationship is also coded under this category.

AFFL – is scored in affiliation narratives that refer to negative relatedness issues such as separation, rejection, loneliness, isolation, loss of love, loss of friendship, inability to feel affection, betrayal, sense of distrust, jealousy, and fear of being replaced. Interpersonal overinvolvement, as within relationships portrayed by the narrator as enmeshed or symbiotic, would also be scored as negative affiliation.

AFFL U is scored for unresolved concerns regarding issues such as fear of rejection, nervousness or uncertainty about close relationships, fear of emotional commitment, separation imposed by circumstances, longing for someone or homesickness, fear of losing a significant relationship through death, or denial of affiliative needs.

Examples of AFFL are as follows:

(1) There was a boy called Jim who had problems at home. His parents were separating. (AFFL –)

(2) She fell in love with another student. (AFFL +)

(2) I don't see any connection between the girl and the other people. (AFFL –)

(6BM) Her son was killed in a car accident. The police officer came to inform her. There is a kind of empty space. He leaves and she stays by herself, alone with her loss. (AFFL –)

(6BM) Her son is leaving and she longs for having a family together again. He understands this and will return one day with his own family. (AFFL +)

(7BM) The older one betrayed the younger person's trust. He disclosed a secret he was supposed to keep to himself. They might become close again. I don't know. (AFFL U)

Harmony (HAR)

Communion concerns regarding interpersonal, family, community, or socially harmonious relationships, promotion of goodwill, reciprocal tolerance, or the avoidance of mutual injury are coded under harmony. This category also includes the opposites and negatives of the previous concerns, such as discord, hostility, conflict, or division themes.

According to De Vos (1992), projective materials from Asian Confucian communities often include harmony concerns reflecting the importance in those communities of behaving in accordance to role expectations of peaceful interaction in families and larger-than-kin units. Such concerns would not be equally important in the more individualistic Western societies. Discord, the negative of harmony, is an omnipresent theme in contemporary Western entertainment media.

HAR + is scored for references to peace, reconciliation, mutual respect and tolerance, and prevalence of justice in human affairs.

HAR – is scored for stories involving interpersonal, family, community, or social discord. Harmony narratives scored as negative may emphasize dissension, quarrel, hostility, conflict, division carried to the bitter end, violence as a result of injustice or institutional failure, or social paranoia.

HAR U is used to score unresolved concerns about harmonious relationships in interpersonal, family, community, or social settings, such as ambivalent feelings in family/social discord situations.

Examples of HAR are as follows:

(2) Looks like in the time of the pioneers. The good values. And certainly there is no tension. But things might explode any time sooner or later. (HAR U)

(6BM) A man wants to marry a woman that his mother doesn't like. He tries to convince her, but her mother says no. He is going to marry her anyway. After some time the mother will accept her son's decision and will try to establish some communication with her daughter-in-law.

She felt that the woman was going to steal his son from her. But she knows that if she doesn't overreact she still can keep her family together. (HAR +)

(7BM) The guy is saying to his dad, "I just crashed your car into your garage, and hit your Corvette, and it's now broken, and I am going to light the rest of your house on fire because I have not been taking my Risperidone (laughs), and now I'm going to shoot you and run off with your money." (HAR –)

Solidarity (SLDR)

This category includes concerns with issues such as cooperation, mutual support/help, peer interdependence, or a sense of community. Narratives of solidarity may be situated in family, small-group, organization, or community settings. Stories that do not involve communal goals in which people cooperate within strictly contractual obligations are not scored under this category. Solidarity themes are infrequent in narratives given to the picture-story cards often used by clinicians.

SLDR + is scored for narratives referring to acting or working together for a shared communion goal. Some examples would be acting or working together to protect less able members (nurturance/care), to promote friendship or mutual pleasure (affiliation), to stop hostility in the workplace (harmony), or to promote equality (esteem). Also stories about dedication, faithfulness, and loyalty to the group or organization are included under this category.

SLDR – is scored for references to lack of solidarity or to characters not fulfilling their part or sabotaging the attainment of communal goals.

SLDR U is used to score references to conflict, doubts, or lack of resolution or effort regarding participation in attaining communal goals. Unresolved concerns are also scored when characters dream or imagine instead of performing acts of solidarity.

Examples of SLDR are as follows:

(1) The boy will become a famous violinist. He will always be available to collaborate with the people from the poor neighborhood he came from. Like with fund-raising to collect money for poor children. (SLDR +)

(2) She is the daughter of a family of farmers. Although life is hard for the farmers, they support each other and work long hours to provide a better life for their daughter. (SLDR +)

(2) This is about one or two hundred years ago. They're farmers. A girl wants to go to school but her family members think that she should work as well as the others. She will study and read books, and at the same time, she will work and help family's works. (SLDR +)

(7BM) They are members of a union or a political party. The older man is scolding the younger one. "You only think of yourself. If all of us behave like you do we would lose all we have got over the years." He couldn't care less. (SLDR –)

Calculating Scores

Scores are assigned for each primary category + outcome pair by counting +1 each time it is scored. Secondary concerns are assigned half points. Also half instead of full points are assigned to stories that are scored with an arrow to represent more than one outcome, as when a story line ultimately results in a positive outcome after extensive negative or unresolved elaborations. The total number of scores regarding the 10 categories and the total number of outcomes (i.e., positive, negative, and unresolved) for all cards being used are also counted. A scoring sheet is used for each subject.

Scoring Sheet for the Psychocultural Scoring System

Themes/concerns **Cards**							**Sum**
Agency							
1. Mastery (M - MAST)							
Positive							
Negative							
Unresolved							
2. Achievement (A - ACHV)							
Positive							
Negative							
Unresolved							
3. Power (P - POWR)							
Positive							
Negative							
Unresolved							
4. Competition (C - COMP)							
Positive							
Negative							
Unresolved							
5. Responsibility (R - RESP)							
Positive							
Negative							
Unresolved							
Communion							
6. Esteem (E - ESTM)							
Positive							
Negative							
Unresolved							
7. Nurturance (N- NURT)							
Positive							
Negative							
Unresolved							
8. Affiliation (F - AFFL)							
Positive							
Negative							
Unresolved							
9. Harmony (H - HAR)							
Positive							
Negative							
Unresolved							
10. Solidarity (S - SLDR)							
Positive							
Negative							
Unresolued							
Total outcomes							
Positive							
Negative							
Unresolved							

☐ Practice Stories

TAT Card 1

This card depicts a young boy contemplating a violin that rests on a table in front of him.

(1) This is a picture of a boy who just finished practicing on his violin. He is daydreaming about his future when he will become a great violinist.

(2) He was playing outside. His mother called him to practice the violin. He would much rather be outside playing, but I guess that his mother would insist that he practices. He will comply, reluctantly of course. As he grows older, he will begin to appreciate the instrument and ultimately will be able to play it.

(3) He has probably been practicing on his violin. He failed and got frustrated. And he sat down and is looking at the violin in disgust, like he can't do anything right. (Future/outcome?) I don't know. Probably he will try again.

(4) He is worrying about a violin recital that is coming up the following week. He is feeling discouraged because he has been practicing but did not see much improvement. He's thinking about quitting the lessons, but the instructor is encouraging him to continue. The instructor's encouragement inspires him. He will practice very hard and will become a great violinist.

(5) His mom and dad want Jim to practice for his violin lessons. He doesn't like playing and often fights with his mom about it. He is going to talk with his dad about whether he really has to play the violin. He wants very much to join a football team and be with all his friends. His parents will finally agree about Jim switching from violin to football because they want him to be content.

(6) There was a poor boy that was very sad and unhappy. His father and mother had both died and he was left very poor. He decided that the only thing that remained was for him to go around playing his guitar and begging for money, and that is what he did.

(7) Troublesome. (Past and future for this boy?) In this day and age there is nothing special to say about the past or the present. Will he learn to play the violin? There is no future for him. That's it.

(8) This little boy is looking at his violin, but I am not sure. It's kind of broken. Maybe one of the strings broke or something. He wants to learn the instrument but because it is broken he can't.

(9) He doesn't want to play his violin because he is feeling sad. (Sad?) Maybe he is feeling sad because someone made fun of his fiddle. (What happened in the past?) They made fun of his violin and that is why he doesn't want to play it, because he thinks it's dumb. (Future/outcome?) He is going to get something, a new instrument, and play it a lot.

TAT Card 6BM

This card depicts an elderly woman standing parallel to a window. Behind her is a younger man with his head down, holding onto his hat.

(1) A scene involving a mother and a son. They are in the family home where they all grew up. The son has just told the mother that it is time to sell the house and that she should come and live with him. But there are so many memories. The mother is sad and melancholic. The son is also sad and they both know that the mother cannot survive on her own. She will come and live with him.

(2) The woman wanted him to study medicine and he said no, that he wanted sports. He does not know anymore how to deal with his mother. That makes him feel guilty and bad because she is very disappointed in him, but he will do what he wants.

(3) Looks like they are at a funeral or hospital. Both are trying to deal with something. Not talking to each other. They are both in their own world. A close relative has died, probably his father and her husband. They are wondering what life would be like without him. He looks concerned and in pain and worried about his mother. She looks more sad and as if she is not really there. They don't seem to be reaching out to one another. Maybe they will reach out later. Right now they just need to be alone.

(4) This is a mother and son relationship. Because she is looking away I think she is feeling upset with her son in some way. He is hanging his head and looking pretty gloomy. It may be because he is leaving the city they are in and she is upset, or that he is divorcing his wife, or he told his mom he is gay. She is pretty upset. They won't end up resolving it. This looks like the end of the conversation and he's getting ready to leave.

(5) Mother and son. The son went back to his mother to tell her that he failed in his business and lost everything. The mom knew it was going to happen.

(6) This is a son and his mother. It looks as if they are being told someone has died. They are both shocked. The doctor has come out of the room and told her that her husband, who has been sick, has died. But the son has just arrived, so he is feeling bad because he feels he should have arrived earlier, and should have been there. After the scene the mother, who is in shock, will start to cry, and the son will comfort her.

(7) Grandmother and grandson. She looks disappointed and he is ashamed he will do something against her wishes. He feels bad about it. It's a job or career—maybe the military. He's a patriotic person. She is a nonviolent person. He goes off to war and gets injured and has to come home. They both feel relieved that he is back. They are very happy to see each other.

(8) The son has to leave because he found work, not where he wanted but far from home. His quite old mother is inconsolable. There is always news that inflicts pain. She is widowed; he is father-orphaned. It was impossible for him to take his mom with

him or frequently stay in touch. His mom dies from sadness some months later. He knows the great pain that he is inflicting upon her, but he thinks that his mom has to understand he has to leave.

(9) She is scolding her son. He feels bad about what he did and asks for forgiveness: "You are old enough and you have to distinguish between good and bad, and I am not going to hound you all the time telling you what to do." They will talk and solve the problem.

(10) It was a clear crisp April day. A little handsome old lady with tears in her eyes walked down to her nephew's house. "What's wrong?" asked the nephew. "Your cousin three times removed died this morning." "What was his name?" The nephew asked. "Well, like most people in our family, he didn't have a name. You might remember that you met him two Christmas ago." The family, who was a close family, all piled into a sedan and drove to Idaho via Calgary. There, 33 people got together for the funeral and nobody had names. The nephew finally went up to his aunt and asked why nobody had names. This has plagued him since he was a little kid. "Well, it comes down to one thing," said the aunt. "Our family, as you may have noticed, has the worst posture in all of North America. Since it is such a shame we wanted to make sure that no one would ever find our name in a medical book."

TAT Card 4

(1) This woman has done or said something to upset this man. As he attempts to walk away from her, she grabs him trying to explain the situation and begging him to talk to her. He's not extremely upset, you can tell by his face, but he doesn't want to discuss the situation.

(2) Barbara told Butch, "Don't go or you'll lose me forever!" Butch didn't care about her. He had to let the babe go and continue his search around the world for Wayne McCousky. McCousky being his rival since he could remember. He was leaving on a midnight train to Paris.

(3) "Sweetie, it's okay! It happens to all men. You've been under a lot of stress lately, with work and the likes. It's all right; we can give a shot a little later. Okay?" "I'm just embarrassed; this type of thing has never happened. I'm a stallion, I'm a bull, I'm a man!" "Sweetie, I know you are. You're my little stallion, you don't have to try and convince me." "Damn it woman, get me a beer!" "Oh, sweetie, you're the cutest."

(4) For the past 10 months, Alice and Ben have been inseparable. Many people believed they were going to marry soon. All of a sudden Ben decided he needed to go find work somewhere else. Alice tries to convince him to stay there and find work, but his mind is made up. The only way that they could be together is for her to go with him, but she cannot. She feels obligated to stay where her family is, and feels she cannot leave them for anything or anyone. So Ben is about to get on the train and Alice is still trying her hardest to convince him to stay.

(5) A man who was happily married to his lovely wife went into a whore house. He was desperate for some attention that his wife was not giving him. To his surprise she was one of the girls working there. It all made sense to him now. That's why she was not interested in him; she was tired from days of work. He said some harsh words and was about to leave when she grabbed him and explained that they were both in the wrong. Why was he there in the first place? They decided that they needed to talk about this at a later time.

(6) This man and woman are married and in their bedroom trying to talk problems out and the kids and the dogs keep bothering them. They have money problems and have been arguing a lot lately. Finally, they are into a quiet, soft, good part of the conversation and someone knocks on the door. It is one of their kids saying that the dog bit him. They go out of the room, patch him up, go back into the bedroom, and talk some more. Eventually, they decide that they argue about stupid things and that their family is more important than money will ever be.

(7) "Sam, I love you." "And I love you, too." The curtain draws and the crowd cheers. It was the second performance and rolled perfectly. The curtain rose once again as the actors took their bow. A standing ovation! They had done it. They took a nothing of a play and turned it into the most sought-after show in all of the country. After the first production a year earlier, critics and fans raved for another. This was it and it was better than ever. The newspapers would surely have fantastic reviews. How often is a play given a standing ovation? Even intermission—nobody moved. They didn't want to miss the second act.

(8) The man and woman are engaged and the woman is adored in her community. There is another man who is in love with the woman and wants to win her love. This man is standing outside the house where the other two are. She is in love with the man she is with, but the man still feels as though he will lose her. He is very upset that this other man is trying to steal her away and wants to hurt him. He is very jealous. The woman is trying to tell him to stay with her and leave the man alone because there is nothing that could ever change the way she feels about him. After a while she finally convinces the man to stay with her but he is still mad.

(9) Sarah senses something is wrong. She can see it in Jimmy's eyes. "Tell me," she begs. "I can't," he declares. "I love you, whatever it is, it can't come between us," she urges. "If only that were true," Jimmy thought. How could he tell her he had been with another woman? Not only another woman but with Sarah's sister. Just that morning Jimmy received a call from Terry, Sarah's sister, that she was pregnant and it was his. He didn't love Terry, but a fit of passion has left him to pay the consequences. He wanted to marry Sarah but now she would hate him forever.

(10) "Oh Harry, I want you so much. Why do you have to go to war? Will I ever see you again? I always thought that our love would last through the ages until our death." "Oh Lorraine, will you marry me before I leave, even though there is a good chance that I will be killed in battle? Let us hurry now; my ship is set to sail in four hours." They got married. Loraine sobbed for hours after seeing her one true love sail off into the sunset.

☐ Expert Scoring

TAT Card 1

TAT card 1 often stimulates agency concerns about two different sets of thematic issues: (1) concerns with achievement or mastery issues; or (2) power/control issues, including concerns with autonomy. Stories from some cultural groups often combine achievement or mastery and care/nurturance concerns. Issues of psychological or material deprivation (NURT –) are common among poor or marginalized populations.

(1) ACHV +. The narrative is scored as positive achievement because it is clearly stated that the boy will become a great violinist even though he is currently daydreaming. Responsibility is not scored because there is no specific reference to duty or responsibility issues.

(2) POWR – [parental pressure and reluctant compliance]; MAST +. Mastery/competence is scored because the emphasis in the second part of the narrative is on being able to play the violin. Even though a task-related future orientation is mentioned, achievement is not scored because a self-imposed goal is not clearly stated.

(3) MAST –. Although there is also a reference to self-esteem issues in general (*He can't do anything right*), appreciation is not scored. Appreciation is an interpersonal category, and this narrative focuses solely on self issues.

(4) MAST U→+; NURT + [encouragement, inspiration]; ACHV +. Concerns with mastery/competence are elaborated in detail but are solved in the future. Using an arrow allows to score both aspects of the response.

(5) POWR AUT +; AFFL +; NURT +; ESTM +. Autonomy themes are scored under power/control. The narrative starts as vertical involving control issues between parents and child. The child's self-assertive behavior turns the narrative's focus from parental control to autonomy. The reference to playing with friends is scored under affiliation. The reference to parents wanting their child to be content is scored under care.

(6) NURT – [deprivation].

(7) The negative reference to the future is scored as ACHV –.

(8) Severely traumatized individuals like the person who made up this story sometimes describe the violin as broken, which appears to refer to their self-experience of having suffered an internal irreversible damage. Such damage may affect their sense of agency or communion. This particular narrative might be scored as MAST – based on the reference to the child wanting to but being unable to play the violin.

(9) ESTM –. Negative appreciation themes are involved in *Someone made fun of his fiddle* and *He thinks it is dumb.*

TAT Card 6BM

Card 6BM narratives generally refer to the following general topics: bad news, separation, and wrongdoing. Narratives of bad news often include communion concerns with affiliation and care/nurturance. Stories of wrongdoing often include agency issues regarding power/control or responsibility. Finally, narratives of separation may include agency issues regarding autonomy or communion issues of affiliation or care.

(1) Son's protective behavior is scored as NURT +. The separation and sense of loss (*There are so many memories; sad and melancholic*) are scored as AFFL –. There is also a score for an agency concern with mastery (*The mother can't survive on her own*).

(2) POWR AUT U; RESP –; ESTM –. The narrative focuses on power issues regarding autonomy. The outcome is scored as unresolved because of the guilt feelings, which involve negative concerns with responsibility. The mother's disappointment is scored as negative appreciation.

(3) Their sense of loss would be scored as AFFL U (*They are wondering what life would be without him*). There is a reference to emotional isolation between the characters, portrayed as unresolved or AFFL U (*They don't seem to be reaching out to one another; Maybe they will do it later*). Although portraying a mother and her son potentially involves a vertical concern (care/nurturance), this part of the narrative is not scored as such because it is about an equality-based relationship involving emotional closeness/isolation. Affiliation is scored two times because it refers to two clearly separate themes. NURT U should also be scored regarding the son worrying about his mother. What differentiates care from affiliation is not the age difference per se but rather the presence of a vertical, difference-based, communion concern. In this case, son worries involve a protective behavior toward his mother to be distinguished from emotional closeness. The concerns are unresolved because the outcome is left open (first two) or no action or outcome is mentioned (third).

(4) HAR –. Discord in mother–son relationship seems to be the main issue. Issues of power/control or affiliation might also be involved; however, these are not obvious.

(5) MAST – [failure].

(6) RESP –; NURT +.

(7) The most obvious concerns are ESTM – (*ashamed*) and AFFL + (*Very happy to see each other*). A concern with power/control and autonomy is implied by the character doing *something against his grandmother's wishes* (POWR AUT –); this concern is scored as negative because autonomous behavior results in injury. There is also a reference to discord regarding the mention of violence, war, and a character being injured (HAR –).

(8) ESTM –; AFFL –. This narrative of a conflict between agency and communion goals (*Son has to leave because he found work*) seems to focus on difference-based care concerns regarding deprivation and lack of support (*widowed* and *orphan*; a son not protecting his *quite old Mom* by taking her with him), and equality-based affiliation concerns with emotional distance (emotional pain; mother dies of sadness because of separation).

(9) POWR + [scolding]; RESP + (*Feels sorrow and ask for forgiveness*). They are scored positive based on the outcome (*They will talk and solve the problem*).

(10) This humorous narrative includes affiliation themes regarding emotional closeness–distance and appreciation themes regarding shame. Because the narrative is essentially a joke, such themes are scored as unresolved. According to the manual, stories where the narrator uses irony or joking are considered from the scorer's perspective as involving unresolved issues.

TAT Card 4

(1) HAR U.

(2) AFFL –; COMP U.

(3) Based on the female character's concerns, this narrative is scored as AFFL + (she is portrayed as loving and understanding) and ESTM + (*You're my little stallion … you're the cutest*). Based on the male character, the narrative is scored as MAST U and ESTM U (He is embarrassed at failing in bed).

(4) AFFL U; RESP +.

(5) AFFL U; RESP – (*They were both in the wrong*).

(6) HAR +; NURT +. A cluster of neighboring concerns appears to be involved in this narrative, such as affiliation, harmony, and cooperation. Nevertheless, only marital harmony versus discord issues are explicit enough to be scored (Have been arguing a lot about stupid things). Nurturance is scored because of the reference to parents taking care of their kids.

(7) MAST + (the performance *rolled perfectly*); ACHV + (turned a nothing of a play into the most sought after show; *better than ever*); ESTM + (*standing ovation*, critics and fans raved). The mutual love of the characters might be scored as secondary AFFL +. Even if the play's end is not the core of the narrative, it could have been portrayed differently, for example, as characters killing each other.

(8) Primary concerns are AFF + (*She is in love with the man she is with*); COMP U (another man *trying to steal her away*; *He is still mad*); and AFF U (regarding the male character's unresolved jealousy and fear of being replaced). Secondary concerns would be ESTM + (*woman is adored in her community*), and HAR – (*wants to hurt him*).

(9) RESP –; AFFL–. The male character's awareness of having been unfair/dishonest is scored as negative responsibility. Negative affiliation is scored regarding *betrayal* and *separation* issues (*she would hate him forever*; although the word *hate* is used, the core theme is the end of a relationship more than hostility per se).

(10) AFFL U. The narrative portrays the characters' great love for each other, but its outcome remains unresolved (she fears about her one true love being lost in battle). It

is important to keep in mind that their love and impending separation are closely connected as part of the same story line. If both aspects were also treated as separate, the story would be double scored as AFF + and AFF U.

References

Aronow, E., Weiss, K. M., & Reznikoff, M. (2001). *A practical guide to the Thematic Apperception Test.* Philadelphia: Brunner-Routledge.

Bandura, A. (1982). Self-efficacy mechanism in human agency. *American Psychologist, 37,* 122–147.

Bakan, D. (1966). *The duality of human existence: Isolation and communion in Western man.* Boston: Beacon.

De Vos, G. A., & Suarez-Orozco, M. (1990). *Status inequality: The self in culture.* Newbury Park, CA: Sage.

De Vos, G. A., & Vaughn, C. A. (1992). The interpersonal self: A level of psychocultural analysis. In L. B. Boyer & R. M. Boyer (Eds.), *The psychoanalytic study of society* (vol. 17) (pp. 95–142). Hillsdale, NJ: Analytic Press.

De Vos, G. A., & De Vos, E. S. (2004). *Basic dimensions in conscious thought: The self and socialization of human concerns.* Lanham, MD: Rowman & Littlefield.

De Vos, G. A., & Kim, E.-Y. (1993). Koreans in Japan and the United States: Attitudes toward achievement and authority. In I. Light & P. Bhachu (Eds.), *Immigration and entrepreneurship: Culture, capital and ethnic networks* (pp. 205–241). New Brunswick, NJ: Transaction Publishers.

De Vos, G. A., & Vaughn, C. A. (1992). The interpersonal self: A level of psychocultural analysis. In L. B. Boyer & R. M. Boyer (Eds.), *The psychoanalytic study of society* (vol. 17) (pp. 95–142). Hillsdale, NJ: Analytic Press.

Emmons, R. A. (1986). Personal strivings: An approach to personality and subjective well-being. *Journal of Personality and Social Psychology, 51,* 1058–1068.

Geertz, C. (1995). *After the fact: Two countries, four decades, one anthropologist.* Cambridge, MA: Harvard University Press.

McAdams, D. P. (1993). *Stories we live by: Personal myths and the making of the self.* New York: William Morrow & Company.

McAdams, D. P., Hoffman, B. J., Mansfield, E. D., & Day, R. (1996). Themes of agency and communion in significant autobiographical scenes. *Journal of Personality, 64,* no. 2, 339–377.

Parsons, T., & Bales, R. (1955). *Family socialization and interaction process.* Glencoe, MN: Free Press.

Smith, C. P. (Ed.). (1992). *Motivation and personality: Handbook of thematic content analysis.* New York: Cambridge University Press.

White, R. W. (1959). Motivation reconsidered: The concept of competence. *Psychological Review, 66,* 297–333.

Winter, D. G. (1992). Responsibility. In C. P. Smith (Ed.), *Motivation and personality: Handbook of thematic content analysis* (pp. 500–505). New York: Cambridge University Press.

Notes

Other than the acknowledgments mentioned in chapter 37 of this volume, I thank the members of Sharon Rae Jenkins' scoring team—Meryl Bazaman, Diane Brüger, Kirstine R. Carter, Michele Elefante, Steven D. Gomez, Tamara Hale, Raquel Hoersting, Stephanie Mason, Ashley Nicklas, Cara Santa Maria, Enedelia Sauceda, and Anita Varghese—for their questions and comments that were helpful in revision of this manual and refinement of the scoring categories. I also thank my Venezuelan colleagues Manuel Llorens, Pedro E. Rodriguez, Carolina Izquiel, and Juan Carlos Romero for their useful comments.

Author Biographies

Louis A. Chandler, PhD, is emeritus associate professor at the University of Pittsburgh where he taught for many years in the Department of Psychology in Education. Dr. Chandler has done extensive research in childhood stress and in psychological assessment. He was the former director of the university's psycho-educational clinic and has published numerous papers and articles on childhood stress. Dr. Chandler is the author of *Children Under Stress: Understanding Emotional Adjustment Reactions* (Charles Thomas, 1982) and *Assessing Stress in Children* (Praeger, 1985).

Benjamin Chapman, PhD, is a National Research Service Award postdoctoral fellow at the University of Rochester Medical School. His research interests involve personality, mood, health, and aging. His methodological interests include personality measurement and multivariate statistics. He is currently working on several projects related to the interface of personality and socioeconomic factors in health and aging. In his spare time, he enjoys writing and reading historical fiction, running and lifting weights, and spending time with friends.

Giuseppe Costantino, PhD, is director of training and new programs at Lutheran Medical Center Lutheran Family Health Centers. He is the originator of the Tell-Me-A-Story (TEMAS) test rationale and pictures. He is also the originator of Cuento Therapy. His work on culturally competent assessment and treatment was recognized by the surgeon general in 2001, the American Psychological Association (APA) in 2003, and the Society for Personality Assessment in 2003. He is an APA member and recipient of several major federal grants. He was consulting editor of *Journal of Personality Assessment, Hispanic Journal of Behavioral Sciences,* and *Buros Institute 8th and 9th Mental Measurements Yearbooks.* Dr. Costantino has written two books and more than 50 book chapters and articles on culturally competent assessment and treatment of culturally diverse groups.

Richard H. Dana, PhD, served as professor, Director of Clinical Training, departmental chair, and dean at various universities before retirement in 1988 as University Professor Emeritus at the University of Arkansas. As Research Professor for the Regional Research

Institute at Portland State University, he developed a research program on the Multicultural Assessment–Intervention Process model that was presented in 1993, 1998, 2000, 2005, and 2007 books, most recently Multicultural Assessment: Principles, Applications, and Examples (Erlbaum, 2005) and TEMAS (Tell-Me-A-Story) Assessment in Multicultural Societies with Giuseppe Costantino and Robert G. Malgady (Erlbaum, 2007). This process provides general, culture-specific, and step-by-step instrument-specific guidelines for application of the most commonly used clinical assessment tools with different cultural groups.

Lauren Dobbs received her BS in psychology from the University of North Texas in 2003. Her honors thesis examining interpersonal decentering and mutuality in a specific relationship segued to her role in editing Feffer's Interpersonal Decentering Scoring System and coauthoring a literature review. Following graduation she was a research assistant in the psychiatry department at the University of Texas Southwestern Medical Center at Dallas. Currently, she is a graduate student at Oregon Health Science University in the Department of Behavioral Neuroscience.

Laura E. Dreer received her PhD in clinical psychology from Central Michigan University. She is a clinical researcher in the Department of Ophthalmology at the University of Alabama at Birmingham with interests in adjustment to chronic health conditions, social problem solving, and issues related to competency evaluations in medical populations.

David Ephraim lives in Vancouver, Canada, where he works as clinical psychologist at the Maples Adolescent Treatment Centre and has an independent practice in psychotherapy and forensic trauma assessment of refugees, specializing in the clinical and cross-cultural use of the Rorschach and the TAT. Prior to that, he was Professor of Psychology at the Universidad Central de Venezuela (UCV), from which he earned his Doctoral Degree in Psychology. His graduate and post-graduate education included clinical training and/or research in the Department of Psychoanalysis, Université de París VIII, the Menninger Clinic, and the Department of Anthropology at the University of California-Berkeley.

Melvin Feffer (1924–2002) received his PhD at the University of Chicago in 1954. He was on staff at the Institute for Cognitive Studies and the psychology department at Rutgers University as professor emeritus. He was the author of *The Structure of Freudian Thought: The Problem of Immutability and Discontinuity in Developmental Theory* (International Universities Press, 1982), *Radical Constructionism: Rethinking the Dynamics of Development* (New York University Press, 1988), and *The Conflict of Equals: A Constructionist View of Personality Development* (Acta Universitatis Gothoburgensis, 1999).

Kelly Felgenhauer received her MA in school psychology in 2003 from the Department of Counseling and Personnel Services at the University of Maryland. She currently resides in London with her husband and two children.

Margaret Gibbs received her PhD in clinical psychology from Harvard University. She teaches in the School of Psychology at Fairleigh Dickinson University with interests in assessment, responses to trauma, and minority issues.

Deborah F. Greenwald completed her PhD in clinical psychology at the University of Michigan in 1977. She conducted research with high-risk families at the University of

Rochester School of Medicine and then joined the faculty of Northeastern University. Her research has centered on personality assessment, shame and its domains, and spirituality.

David W. Harder received his PhD in clinical psychology from the University of Michigan in 1975. He became instructor and then assistant professor of psychiatry (psychology) at the University of Rochester School of Medicine from 1975 to 1979. He was appointed assistant professor of psychology at Tufts University in 1979 and was promoted to full professor in 1993. Dr. Harder also joined the faculty of the Massachusetts School of Professional Psychology in 1990. His primary research areas have included life events stress, psychopathology outcome, shame and guilt, narcissism, and spirituality. He also has a part-time private practice in therapy and assessment.

Robert R. Holt received his PhD from Harvard in 1944 and was trained by David Rapaport in diagnostic testing and psychoanalytic theory at the Menninger Foundation, later becoming director of its psychological staff. In 1953 he went to New York University to direct, with George S. Klein, the Research Center for Mental Health. He was professor of clinical psychology (1958–1988) and held a Research Career Award from the National Institute of Mental Health (NIMH) from 1962 to 1988. He is a past president of the American Psychological Association's Division of Clinical Psychology, which gave him its award for Distinguished Contribution to Clinical Psychology in 1974. He has written or edited 16 books, including *Freud Reappraised* (Guilford, 1989) and three Psychological Issues monographs—*Motives and Thought* (International Universities Press, 1967) and *Psychoanalysis and the Philosophy of Science* (International Universities Press, 1997)—plus *Primary Process Thinking* (Jason Aronson Rowman & Littlefield, 2007).

Michelle Hoy-Watkins, PsyD, is Associate Professor in the Department of Forensic Psychology at the Chicago School of Professional Psychology. She maintains a private practice as a licensed clinical and forensic psychologist in Chicago, Illinois. Dr. Hoy-Watkins is the author of the Contemporized-Themes Concerning Blacks Test. Her clinical and research interests include cross-cultural assessment, evaluation and treatment of adult offenders, fitness for duty evaluations, and social security disability evaluations.

Steven K. Huprich, PhD is Associate Professor of Psychology at Eastern Michigan University. He is author of the edited text *Rorschach Assessment of the Personality Disorders* (Erlbaum, 2006) and has published more than 35 articles and book chapters. Dr. Huprich is on the editorial board of the *Journal of Personality Disorders* and currently is working on a textbook on psychodynamic psychotherapy.

Sharon Rae Jenkins received her PhD in Personality Psychology from Boston University and a postdoctoral certificate in Clinical Psychology from the California School of Professional Psychology, Berkeley/Alameda (CSPP-B/A). She was a National Institute of Mental Health postdoctoral fellow and assistant research psychologist at the University of California, Berkeley's Institute of Human Development. She has taught at the University of California, Santa Cruz and at CSPP-B/A. Currently she is a licensed clinical psychologist and Associate Professor at the University of North Texas, specializing in personality assessment in the context of culture. She has served on three journal editorial boards and is a Fellow of the Society for Personality Assessment and of the American Psychological Association Divisions 35 (Society for the Psychology of Women) and 12 (Clinical Psychology). Her website is http://www.psyc.unt.edu/~jenkinss/.

Valata Jenkins-Monroe, PhD, is a licensed clinical and forensic psychologist practicing in Oakland, California. She has extensive experience and expertise in multicultural assessment, both as a clinician and academician. Dr. Jenkins-Monroe is a professor at California School of Professional Psychology located at Alliant International University in San Francisco, California. She has conducted trainings and workshops focused on learning from cultural diversity in the classroom, and creating programs and services sensitive to the needs and concerns of ethnic minority populations.

David Joubert received his PhD in clinical and developmental psychology in 2006 from the Université du Québec à Montréal, Montréal, Canada. He is currently staff psychologist at Napa State Hospital in California, working with forensic populations. He has also been teaching in the School of Education at the University of the Pacific in Stockton, California. His clinical and research interests include attachment and object relations theory, forensic psychology, statistical techniques in clinical research, and personality assessment, with an emphasis on projective techniques.

Bertram P. Karon, PhD, is a professor of clinical psychology at Michigan State University. He has approximately 150 publications, including the chapter, "The Thematic Apperception Test (TAT)", in A.I. Rabin (Ed.), *Assessment with projective techniques* (Springer, 1981). He is a former president of the Division of Psychoanalysis of the American Psychological Association (APA) and 2003 recipient of their Distinguished Scientific Research Award, is an American Board of Professional Psychology (ABPP) diplomate in clinical psychology and in psychoanalysis, and is a fellow of the APA Divisions of Clinical Psychology, of Psychotherapy, and of Psychoanalysis.

Melissa Leeper received her BS in psychology from the University of North Texas. Her honors thesis focused on interpersonal decentering as related to interpersonal problems. After graduation, she was an English conversation teacher for the Nova Group of Japan in Kashihara, Nara, Japan for 18 months. Currently, she is a copyeditor for the Hearst Corporation.

Constance Locraft, PhD, a former student of Dr. Teglasi, is a nationally certified school psychologist employed by Fairfax County Public Schools in Virginia. Her research has centered on the development of empathy in children and its relationship to adjustment. She has presented her research at national and state association conferences and has published in the *Journal of School Psychology.*

Jennifer Lombardo received her PhD in clinical psychology from Central Michigan University. She is currently completing postdoctoral training at Ronan Psychological Associates, with an interest in adapting the application of clinical psychology to problems commonly experienced by Native Americans.

Robert G. Malgady, PhD, is professor of educational statistics at New York University and member of the advisory board of Albizu University in San Juan, Puerto Rico. He is a fellow of the American Psychological Association and the American Orthopsychiatric Association. Presently he is serving as the evaluation consultant to the New York State Department of Mental Retardation & Developmental Disabilities for research involving Prader Willi Syndrome. Dr. Malgady is the author and coauthor of more than 100 publications, including books, book chapters, and journal articles.

Sidney Ornduff, PhD, is an Associate Professor in the Department of Psychiatry at the University of Tennessee Health Science Center. She received her doctoral training in clinical psychology at the University of Louisville, and, following her internship, completed post-doctoral fellowships at the Institute of Living and SUNY-Stony Brook. Dr. Ornduff has published extensively in the areas of personality assessment, child maltreatment, and domestic violence. She is licensed in Tennessee and New York, and has held a number of clinical and academic appointments. She is also active in community crisis intervention, providing didactic training and crisis debriefings to first responders.

Luis E. Perez completed his BS with honors in psychology and a certificate in criminalistics from the University of North Texas. He has taken part in researching two TAT scoring systems under the supervision of Sharon Rae Jenkins. He was recognized as a Distinguished Honors Scholar by the Honors College and is a member of the Ronald E. McNair Postbaccalaureate Achievement Program, a research-intensive program for undergraduates wishing to pursue a Ph.D. Recently he has finished his honors thesis relating decentering and attachment in a clinical sample. He plans to attend graduate school soon.

Max Prola (1930–2004) graduated from Upsala College and received his master's degree from Columbia University and his doctorate from New York University. He taught at Columbia and at York College of the City University of New York and provided clinical services at Elmhurst Hospital, at the Steven's Institute of Technology, and in private practice.

Barry Ritzler is professor of psychology at Long Island University in New York City specializing in personality assessment. His PhD is from Wayne State University, and his postdoctoral fellowship was completed at Yale University. He was formerly director of clinical training at the University of Southern Mississippi and Fairleigh Dickinson University in New Jersey. Dr. Ritzler currently lectures and conducts workshops internationally on the Rorschach Ink Blot Test. He has published 10 book chapters and more than 75 articles in scientific peer-reviewed journals, and he has coauthored *The Quest for the Nazi Personality* (Erlbaum, 1995).

George F. Ronan received his PhD in clinical psychology from Fairleigh Dickinson University. He teaches in the Department of Psychology at Central Michigan University with interests in assessment, social problem solving, and interpersonal violence.

Cara L. Santa Maria earned a BS in psychology from the University of North Texas (UNT) in 2004. She received the Texas Psychological Association and Texas Psychology Foundation's Alexander Psychobiology/Psychophysiology Award for her undergraduate research regarding neuropsychological deficits among individuals with alcohol abuse or dependence in a visually impaired/blind population. In the clinical neuropsychological setting, in addition to diagnostics, she has aided in research and development of computer adapted guides for educational management of students with both visual impairment and neuropsychological dysfunction. She expects to complete her M.S. in biological science (with a neuroscience concentration) in late 2007 at UNT, where she teaches biology laboratory courses and performs electrophysiology research and neuronal cell culture duties at the Center for Network Neuroscience.

Frank Summers, PhD, ABPP, is a supervising and training analyst at the Chicago Institute for Psychoanalysis, Associate Professor at Northwestern University Medical School, and faculty member of several other psychoanalytic institutes. Author of *Object Relations Theories and Psychopathology: A Comprehensive Text* (Analytic Press, 1994), *Transcending the Self* (Analytic Press, 1999), and *Self Creation: Psychoanalytic Therapy and the Art of the Possible* (Analytic Press, 2005) , Dr. Summers maintains a private practice of psychoanalysis and psychoanalytic psychotherapy in Chicago, Illinois. His website is http://www.franksummersphd.com.

Hedwig Teglasi, PhD, ABPP, a professor in the School Psychology program at the University of Maryland, Department of Counseling and Personnel Services, is fellow of Division 16 of the American Psychological Association and of the Society for Personality Assessment and currently serves as president of the American Board of School Psychology. Her research has focused on personality processes including the role of temperament in the interpretation of life experiences. Consistent with her view of storytelling as a vehicle for assessing how individuals organize experiences, she has developed coding systems for the Thematic Apperception Test and has published journal articles, two books, and book chapters on the uses of storytelling. Dr. Teglasi has served as member of editorial boards of journals in the field of School Psychology and as guest editor and co-guest editor of special topics issues about temperament and personality assessment. She currently serves as an associate editor of *School Psychology Quarterly.*

Antoinette D. Thomas, PhD, accomplished her personal psychoanalysis with Dr. Clifford Scott and a three-year advanced theoretical and technical training in individual and group psychoanalytically oriented psychotherapy. She has four copyrighted works, and the TAT scale was presented in 14 workshops, publications, and papers, including Rorschach International, Society for Personality Assessment, American Psychological Association and Canadian Psychological Association. She has coedited two proceeding issues of the International Council of Psychologists and served nine years on its board, including a presidential term. She has held clinical and research positions at two hospitals and has taught at two universities, seven years each full and part time. Her website is http://antoinettedthomas.tripod.com/.

Edith Weisskopf (1910–1983) obtained her doctorate from the University of Vienna in 1937 and immigrated to the United States in 1939 to flee the Nazi occupation. She taught at Indiana University, Purdue University, Duke University, West Georgia College, and the University of Georgia. Her many publications included diverse topics such as picture perception, educational processes, logotherapy, brainstorming, and values. Her papers are archived at the University of West Georgia's Ingram Library Special Collections.

NAME INDEX

A

B

C

D

E

F

G

M

S

Y

Z

SUBJECT INDEX

D

E

N

O

P

Q

R

S

T

W